The African American Studies Reader

The African American Studies Reader

Edited by

Nathaniel Norment, Jr.

Carolina Academic Press
Durham, North Carolina

ISBN 0-89089-640-2
LCCN 2001091153

Carolina Academic Press
700 Kent Street
Durham, North Carolina 27701
Telephone (919) 489-7486
Fax (919) 493-5668
E-mail: cap@cap-press.com
www.cap-press.com

Printed in the United States of America.

Dedicated to

Our Gods,
Our Ancestors,
and
to my mother,
Noble Bell Alexander
(1924–1999)
and
to my granddaughter,
Assata Rose Norment

Contents

Section VIII — Curriculum Development

Preface

Thirty years ago, when I began working at the City College of New York at the beginning of the modern Black Studies Movement, many prominent black scholars, historians, literary artists and critics, political scientists, student and community activist organizations were located in and around New York City. At different times, my colleagues at CCNY included Addison Gayle, Jr., Barbara Christian, Charles V. Hamilton, Allen B. Ballard, Dennis Brutus, Toni Cade (Bambara), Wilfred Cartey, Jr., Leonard Jeffries, Audre Lorde, James Emmanuel, Michele Wallace, Eugene Redmond, David Henderson, June Jordan, Larry Neal, Raymond Patterson, Gwendolyn Brooks, Ishmael Reed, Ntozake Shange, Chinua Achebe, and a host of others who contributed to the development, direction, and destiny of African American/Black Studies on the East Coast. From exposure and interaction with them, along with the countless undergraduate and graduate students I have taught in African American Studies, literature and history courses, I began to see the need for this text.

This book has been organized around a sequence of interrelated perspectives and concepts of African American Studies. It seeks to provide a comprehensive account of the most important perspectives of African American Studies and to keep alive the intellectual, cultural, political, and above all, historical constructs of the discipline. If it advocates a "philosophy," it is the pursuit of academic excellence in the teaching of concepts and content areas of African American Studies, the reaffirmation of commitment to culture, responsibility to community, and to present knowledge about people of African descent in an accurate, critical, and challenging form if it is to play a significant and shaping role in both academia and society.

The African American Studies Reader introduces students to a unique discipline. It presents selections of the many scholars who have made substantial contributions in the development of African American Studies over the past thirty years. It encompasses a wide range of topics and includes every important issue discussed in African American Studies. An invaluable complement to basic books already in the discipline (i.e., *Introduction to Black Studies, All the Women are White, All the Blacks Are Men, But Some of Us Are Brave: Black Women's Studies, Africana Studies: A Survey of Africa and the African Diaspora; Dispatches from the Ivory Tower: Intellectuals Confront the African American Experience, Black Studies: Theory, Method, and Cultural Perspectives*), the reader can be used as an introductory text for both undergraduate and graduate courses. This outstanding collection of different perspectives in African American Studies will be of interest to those coming new to the field and to those who are already involved in research, teaching and other aspects of African American Studies. Each essay (appearing in its original form), represents—in its own way—theoretical, political, historical, etc. perspectives for African American Studies and promotes critical dialogue and debate about the discipline, which after thirty years is still emerging.

From the publication of Equiano's narrative in 1789 to the present moment, African American scholars have struggled mightily in an attempt to make sense of an unwanted black "question," "problem," or "presence" in America and how that very "presence" might thrive seemingly against the wishes of the masses of other "Americans." I remain steadfastly concerned now more than ever as we have ventured into the 21st century that not only is there a dire, critical need for African American Studies in American education and life, but that without the juxtaposition of the voices in this text to enable readers to hear old and new arguments simultaneously in an effort, finally, to solve the dilemma of exactly what constitutes "African American Studies" and what are the ways by which it can assist the liberation of the people, then we, all of us, will merely continue to "run the dangercourse."

Nathaniel Norment, Jr.
Philadelphia, PA
2001

Permissions

I would like to express my gratitude to all of the authors, journal editors and publishers who so kindly granted their permission to include the articles in this volume. The publisher is grateful for permission to reprint the following copyrighted material:

DeVere E. Pentony's "The Case for Black Studies" is reprinted by permission of the author.

Nathan Hare's "Questions and Answers about Black Studies" is reprinted from *The Massachusetts Review*, copyrighted 1970, The Massachusetts Review Inc.

John W. Blassingame's "Black Studies: An Intellectual Crisis" is reprinted by permission of the John W. Blassingame Estate, Tia Blassingame and John W. Blassingame, Jr.

Martin Kilson's "Reflection on Structure and Content in Black Studies" is reprinted by permission of Sage Publications, Inc., *The Journal of Black Studies* 1 (3): 297-313, 1973.

James B. Stewart's "The Field and Function of Black Studies" is reprinted by permission of The Monroe Trotter Institute, University of Massachusetts, Boston.

Philip T.K. Daniel's "Black Studies: Discipline or Field of Study?" is reprinted by permission of the *Western Journal of Black Studies*.

Darlene Clark Hine's "The Black Studies Movement: Afrocentric Traditionalist-Feminist Paradigms for the Next Stage" is reprinted by permission of *The Black Scholar*.

Nathan I. Huggins' "Afro-American Studies" is reprinted by permission of The Ford Foundation.

Carlos. A. Brossard's "Classifying Black Studies Programs" is reprinted by permission of *The Journal of Negro Education*.

Russell L. Adams's "African American Studies and the State of Art" is reprinted by permission of Carolina Academic Press.

LeRoi R. Ray, Jr.'s "Black Studies: A Discussion of Evaluation" is reprinted by permission of *The Journal of Negro Education*.

Charles P. Henry and Frances Smith Foster's "Black Women's Studies: Threat or Challenge?" is reprinted by permission of the *Western Journal of Black Studies*.

Beverly Guy-Sheftall's "Black Women's Studies: The Interface of Women's Studies and Black Studies" is reprinted by permission of the journal *Phylon*.

Molefi Kete Asante's "The Afrocentric Metatheory and Disciplinary Implications" is reprinted by permission of *The Journal of the National Council for Black Studies*.

Daudi Ajani ya Azibo's "Articulating the Distinction Between Black Studies and the Study of Blacks: The Fundamental Role of Culture and the African Centered Worldview" is reprinted by permission of *The Journal of the National Council for Black Studies*.

James B. Stewart's "Reaching for Higher Ground: Toward an Understanding of Black/Africana Studies" is reprinted by permission of *The Journal of The National Council for Black Studies*.

Mike Thelwell's "Black Studies" A Political Perspective" is reprinted from *The Massachusetts Review*, copyrighted 1970, The Massachusetts Review Inc.

J. Owens Smith's "The Political Nature of Black Studies Departments and Programs" is reprinted by permission of the *Western Journal of Black Studies*.

Delores P. Aldridge's "Toward a New Role and Function of Black Studies in White and Historically Black Institutions" is reprinted by permission of *The Journal of Negro Education*.

Nick Aaron Ford's "The Black College as Focus for Black Studies" is reprinted by permission of Dr. James P. Shenton.

William H. McClendon's "Black Studies: Education for Liberation" is reprinted by permission of *The Black Scholar*.

Robert L. Allen's "Politics of the Attack on Black Studies" is reprinted by permission of *The Black Scholar*.

St. Clair Drake's "Black Studies and Global Perspectives" is reprinted by permission of *The Journal of Negro Education*.

Alan K Colon's "Critical Issues in Black Studies: A Selective Analysis" is reprinted by permission of *The Journal of Negro Education*.

Ronald Walters' "Critical Issues on Black Studies" is reprinted by permission of the author.

Eugene D. Genovese's "Black Studies: Trouble Ahead" is reprinted by permission of the author.

Pat M. Ryan's "White Experts, Black Experts, and Black Studies" is reprinted by permission of Dr. S. Okechukwu Mezu, Black Academy Press, Inc.

Nick Aaron Ford's "White Colleges and the Future of Black Studies" is reprinted by permission of Dr. James P. Shenton.

Donald Henderson's "What Direction Black Studies?" is reprinted by permission of Dr. S. Okechukwu Mezu, Black Academy Press, Inc.

Floyd W. Hayes, III's "Taking Stock: African American Studies at the Edge or the 21st Century" is reprinted by permission of the *Western Journal of Black Studies*.

Gerald A. McWorter and Ronald Bailey's "Black Studies Curriculum Development in the 1980s: Its Patterns and History" is reprinted by permission of *The Black Scholar*.

William D. Smith's "Black Studies: A Survey of Models and Curricula" is reprinted by permission of Sage Publications, Inc. *The Journal of Black Studies* 10 (3): 269-277,1971.

Gloria I. Joseph's "Black Studies Consortia: A Proposal" is reprinted by permission of Gordon and Breach Publishers from *Women's Studies* 17 (12): 147153, copyright Overseas Publishers Association, 1988.

Karla J. Spurlock's "Toward the Evolution of a Unitary Discipline: Maximizing the Interdisciplinary Concept in African/Afro-American Studies" is reprinted by permission of the *Western Journal of Black Studies*.

William M. King's "The Importance of Black Studies for Science and Technology Policy" is reprinted by permission of the journal *Phylon*.

James A. Banks' "Teaching Black Studies for Social Change" is reprinted by permission of the author.

The Institute of the Black World's "Statement of Purpose and Program, Fall, 1969" is reprinted by permission of Dr. Vincent G. Harding, The Iliff School of Theology.

Erskine Peter's "Afrocentricity: Problems of Method and Nomenclature" is reprinted by permission of Carolina Academic Press.

Patricia Hill Collins' "The Social Construction of Black Feminist Thought" is reprinted by permission of the author and The University of Chicago Press from *SIGNS* 14, 745-773, copyright 1989.

William A. Little, Carolyn Leonard and Edward Crosby's "Black Studies and Africana Studies Curriculum Models in the United States" is reprinted by permission of *The Journal of The National Council for Black Studies*.

Melvin Hendrix, James H. Bracy, John A. Davis, and Waddell M. Herron's "Computers and Black Studies: Toward the Cognitive Revolution" is reprinted by permission of *The Journal of Negro Education*.

Carlene Young's "The Struggle and Dream of Black Studies" is reprinted by permission of *The Journal of Negro Education*.

Vivian V. Gordon's "The Coming of Age of Black Studies" is reprinted by permission of the *Western Journal of Black Studies*.

Robert L. Harris, Jr.'s "The Intellectual and Institutional Development of Africana Studies" is reprinted by permission of The Ford Foundation.

Tilden LeMelle's "The Status of Black Studies in the Second Decade: The Ideological Imperative" is reprinted by permission of the author.

Acknowledgments

I have long noted the need for a collection of readings that would address the issues surrounding the various courses that I taught and so began to amass a bibliography early on that could be used as a resource guide for myself and for my students. Over the years, students, friends, and colleagues have contributed names, articles, books and journals that I might use, as well as the readings that I have spent hours searching for in order to locate just the perfect addendum to a point of view or lesson construct. So it is with deep, deep gratitude that I attempt to acknowledge the many souls who helped to make this book a reality.

I thank especially Kipp White, Nina Camacho and Temple's Instruction Resource Center for scanning the hundreds of articles. Many, many thanks are due to five people. Dr. Daniel P. Black who gave me spiritual, emotional clarity and focus at times when I questioned the veracity of this entire project. Dr. Wilbert L. Jenkins, my colleague in the Department of History who provided direction and encouragement; Gloria Basmajian for her patience and her professionalism in completing the task of reading the original articles and the scanned copies and assembling the 1000-plus page manuscript. Jason B. Neuenschwander for sacrificing "a month of Sundays"—many mornings, afternoons, evenings, and nights—to help me to complete this project. To him I acknowledge my infinite gratitude and indebtedness. Finish your dissertation!!! And finally to Ernest P. Smith who helped in so many ways, but especially in reminding me that no thing or no person is perfect; the very best we can do is only try to be better.

I would also like to express my gratitude to all of the authors, journal editors and publishers who so kindly granted their permission to include the articles in the reader. I could not have found many of the articles had it not been for the help of librarians at Temple University, Fordham University, Hofstra University, Emory University, Howard University, New York University, The Schomburg Center for Research in Black Culture, Charles Blockson and Aslaku Berhanu of the Blockson Collection at Temple University.

Additionally, I would like to thank the many students of my AAS W051 (*Introduction to African American Studies*) and AAS 750 (*Teaching African American Studies*) classes at Temple University who provided commentary which was immensely helpful on the relevance and utility of a number of articles in the book. Finally, thanks to Kasia Krzysztoforska and Glenn T. Perkins, editors at Carolina Academic Press, for their tenacity, encouragement, professional expertise, and support of this project, and the throngs of people listed below (and those inadvertently omitted) for help offered and provided: Nina Camacho, Kipp White, Mariel Monroe, Ernest P. Smith, Jeann M. Bell, Tiffany Rankins, Gladys Smith, Patrick Spearman, David Norment, Michael Norment, Rosemarie Norment (Thank you for so much—especially for your prayers), Suzzette Spencer, Dr. Daniel Black, Dr. Greg E. Kimathi Carr, Dr. Gillian Johns, Dr. Jerome Brooks, Hofstra University, Schomburg Center for Research in Black Culture, Keith Mollison, Sara Cahill, Denise Mills (*Phylon*),

Brunilda Pabon, Brian Jones, Melvin Norment, Charlene Saunder (NCBS), Cheryl Jones, Dr. Philip Hart, Dr. Robert L. Allen (*Black Scholar*), Mary Loftus, Tanya Udin (SAGE Publications), Dr. Thomas James, Carol Feder, Erin Architzer, Dr. James P. Shenton, Dr. James A. Banks, Dr. Ronald Walters, Dr. Abdul Alkalimat, Beth Mullen, Pierre Steiner, John W. Blassingame, Jr., Tia Blassingame, Dr. Henry J. Richards, Perry Cartwright, Dr. E. Lincoln James, Dr. Eugene D. Genovese, Gretchen Voter, Nancy Grunewald (*Western Journal ofBlack Studies*), Dr. S. Okechukwu-Mezu (Black Academic Press), Sharon Howard, Andrew Rosa, Pam Austin, Catherine M. Meaney, Richard Lawless, Dr. Tilden J. LeMelle, Geraldine Bradner (*Journal of Negro Education*), my colleagues (present and former) in the Department of African American Studies at Temple University, Drs. Molefi K. Asante, Ella Forbes, Sonja Peterson-Lewis, Abu Abarry, Kariamu Welsh, James P. Garrett, Theophile Obenga, C. Tsheloane Keto, Ama Mazama, Alfred T. Moleah, Nilgun Okur, Terry Kershaw, Nancy Fitch, Daudi Ajani ya Azibo, Ayele Bekerie, Glendola (Rene) Mills, and Joyce A. Joyce, along with the countless undergraduate and graduate students I have had the fortune of both learning from and teaching over the past thirty-one years.

Introduction

"If we had something we could show you, if we had something we could show ourselves, you would respect us and we might respect ourselves. If we had even the names of our great men [and women]! If we could lay our hands on things we have made, monuments and towers and palaces, we might find our strength...."

—Henri Jean Christophe

The African American Studies Reader represents the largest and most comprehensive collection of essays available in the field. In that the discipline of African American Studies is relatively new as an "institutional" feature of higher education,[1] I have designed it in part to meet curricular needs created by the increased interests of students and researchers in African American Studies who are seeking, in the words of my colleague Russell Adams"(a) conceptual theory for thinking about how best to approach the black experience; (b) analytical theory or sets of ideas and concepts to study the black experience; and (c) strategical or social change[2] theories."[3] Until now, there has been no single, inclusive anthology of articles describing the discipline that students and teachers might use as a resource reference or as a textbook. This book should meet the needs of anyone involved in the serious study of the discipline; it is primarily useful for courses in African American Studies, but it will also serve the broader areas of Ethnic, Women, and Cultural Studies.[4] The volume has evolved from over 30 years of developing and teaching African American Studies and African American Literature courses—both graduate and undergraduate—at the City College of New York[5] and Temple University; and because of the need for a single volume to cover the history, development, and present status of the field. The contents reflect the diverse thinking of many scholars who have helped shape the discipline, and the articles provide readers with historical, theoretical, political, and philosophical perspectives of African American Studies scholars, perspectives that have evolved throughout the struggle of African people since the 1960s.[6]

To date, no textual guide existed which would instruct an emerging scholar of African American Studies as to how the discipline functions and what is supposed to be its scholarly and practical uses. In other words, the philosophical framework and theoretical underpinnings of the discipline have never been clearly delineated. This text offers one attempt to do so. In order for any discipline to thrive, students must be clear as to the academic validity of the enterprise and must know how the discipline was born and what are the empty spaces; it is then their job to fill. Further, arguments and debates which scholars such as Blassingame, Clarke, Drake, Ford, Hare and Kilson initiated some thirty years ago can now be resolved with the help of the text which juxtaposes voices and positions which now can be heard simultaneously. The subsequent discourse assures that contemporary scholars will accurately represent the ideologies of their forbearers as they utilize their academic legacy to transform both the people and intellectual institutions of America.

The design for this text was inspired by the intellectual architects who laid the foundation for and supervised the construction of African American Studies. Their voices were chosen in order for readers to know the original "blueprint" of Black Studies and to hear arguments made for its existence and place in the academy. I also chose these foundational essays in order for contemporary scholars to be able to trace the evolution of African American Studies and to evaluate the extent to which it has deviated from or held true to its original mission.

The perspectives of the book enhance the content areas, methodologies, philosophies, and concepts of African American Studies. African American Studies consists of research: knowledge production; interdisciplinary courses taught at high school, undergraduate, and graduate levels; and departments, programs, and institutes. African American Studies is the systematic study of descendants of Africans enslaved in America. The reader also provides useful scholarly information regarding definitions, scope, and relevance of the discipline. Its purpose is to show that African American Studies is a unique and significant field of study—one that intersects almost every academic discipline and cultural construct—and to show that the discipline has a noteworthy history,[7] a controversial present, and a challenging future. Thus, the reader is intended to represent a discipline committed to producing, coordinating, and disseminating knowledge about African Americans.

1. A Brief History of African American Studies

The development of African American Studies[8] has increased awareness of the contributions of African Americans to the civilizations of the world. The contents of this reader are an indication of the importance, scope, and relevance of the discipline; but the intellectual heritage of African American Studies precedes its emergence and institutionalization as an academic field on predominately white campuses in the late 1960s.[9] Scholars, within the academy and community, such as George Washington Williams, Carter G. Woodson, W. E. B. DuBois, Anna Julia Cooper, Arthur A. Schomburg, E. Franklin Frazier, Harold Cruse, John Henrik Clarke, John Hope Franklin, to name but a few, provided the foundational perspectives that helped shape African American Studies.[10] In the late 1960s, then, the efforts of Nathan Hare, Martin Kilson, Charles V. Hamilton, Ron (Maulana) Karenga, Jimmy Garrett, St. Clair Drake, Nick Aaron Ford, Sidney Walton, and John Blassingame, among others, forced predominately white universities to recognize African American Studies as a distinctive area of study.[11]

1900-1930 — The Intellectual Foundations

African American Studies originally appeared as an academic field of study in the early 1900s,[12] as a result of the pioneering efforts of W. E. B. DuBois, Arthur A. Schomburg, and Carter G. Woodson. Shortly after his arrival at Atlanta University, DuBois initiated an eleven volume monograph series (as an extension of his 1899 landmark study *The Philadelphia Negro*) which sought to present an accurate portrayal of post-Reconstruction life in communities of African descent in the South. Shortly after entering the United States in 1885, Schomburg, a Puerto Rican of African descent, began what would be a lifelong mission to "fill in the missing pages of world history."[13] As an extension of Schomburg's early efforts, Woodson founded the Association for the Study of Negro Life and History, with the express purpose and intent of ensuring that the history of African people would no longer be omitted from the world's historical record. Moreover, Woodson also established the first academic organ of African American Studies in 1916 with the inauguration of *The Journal of Negro History*.[14]

1930-1955 — Early Development on Black and White Campuses

As a direct result of the efforts of Woodson and the Association, in the mid-1930s a number of historically black colleges and universities (i.e., Howard, Wilberforce, Atlanta, Morgan State and Fisk Universities, Tuskegee Institute, etc.) began to offer courses which dealt with the history and culture of black people in America. At the same time, some predominantly white universities (i.e., Harvard, Stanford, The University of Chicago, and The University of Minnesota, etc.) offered courses in the study of "Negro life and culture."

It was reported that in the mid-thirties, black studies curricula were in place in many Southern Negro schools through courses in black history and culture. In addition, public high schools in New York, Philadelphia, Georgia, Texas, and Oklahoma taught course in Black history. It is worth noting that in the late 1930s and early 1940s a Pan-African perspective was taught at Lincoln University in Pennsylvania. Fisk University began an African Studies program in early 1940s and Lincoln University instituted its program in 1950.

1955-1970 — Social and Political Influences

Prior to the landmark 1954 Supreme Court decision in the case of *Brown v. Topeka Board of Education*, black students were routinely denied admission to most white colleges and universities in the North and all in the South. As a direct result of the sense of social responsibility that permeated the Civil Rights and Black Power movements, predominantly white institutions of higher education began to actively recruit and admit "qualified" African American students and faculty. Urban universities in predominately black communities were confronted with the additional responsibility of admitting students from the immediate vicinity who did not always meet admissions criteria. The presence of significant numbers of black students on newly integrated campuses led to their demands for courses that were relevant to their historical and contemporary experiences.

In its contemporary "institutionalized" form, the call for Black Studies arose out of the particular sense of discontent and dismay that the majority of first generation Black students[15] on predominately white college/university campuses felt both in and outside of the classroom. Their frustration, combined with the increased socio-political awareness taking place within the Black community in the form of Black Power and Black Consciousness movements,[16] galvanized Black Students, who began demanding more inclusive,[17] and sometimes separate courses, curricula, and programs representing the totality of African American history and culture, along with the hiring of Black faculty and mentors, and that universities open their facilities and provide institutional resources to/for the Black community. The first Black Studies program was established at San Francisco State in 1968.

1970-1985 — Questions, Crisis and Criticism

Beginning in the 1970s, Black Studies courses, programs, and departments faced intense, heightened criticism from a variety of fronts. Individuals such as Dr. Kenneth Clark, Dr. Martin Kilson,[18] Bayard Rustin, A. Philip Randolph, Professor Eugene Genovese, and Professor Arthur Schlesinger, Jr., were among those who questioned the validity of such an endeavor, arguing against the creation of an intellectually separate, autonomous field of study. Black Studies also suffered a decline in commitment and withdrawal of support from most predominantly white colleges and universities, as well as a backlash from historically black institutions on virtually every level.

Two divergent political-ideological perspectives helped shape the goals and direction of African American Studies. A politically moderate or liberal group was comprised of African American faculty members of "traditional" academic departments such as history, English, psychology, and sociology. These African American professionals, secure in their positions, taught courses treating the African American experience within the framework of their own academic discipline. A radical Black Nationalist group was comprised of African American student organizations, like the Student Non-Violent Coordinating Committee, or SNCC and faculty members, many of whom, upon arrival at predominantly white colleges and universities, were dissatisfied with the traditional disciplines' approaches to investigating and discussing the African American experiences. It was this dissatisfaction that fueled their struggle to create a new and invigorating approach to learning about the African American experience. The initial differences between these two schools in background and relationship to the university led to the debates concerning the goals and objectives of African American Studies. While the traditionalists, in many ways, accepted the status quo at the university, the radicals pushed for progressive changes in the arena of higher education.

The moderate or liberal perspective asserted that African American Studies should be relevant to both African Americans and the university by providing a distinctive and rigorous education that would effectively prepare students to become productive members of society. These scholars were opposed to the establishment of a completely autonomous department and advocated a departmental structure controlled by existing "traditional" disciplines. Martin Kilson, one scholar, who supported this approach, argued that "no interdisciplinary subject like black studies can evolve into a scholarly and intellectually viable field without the curricular control of an established discipline."[19] He further contended that students who majored in Black Studies should be tracked through an established discipline to ensure that the student would be prepared for graduate studies.

Radical scholars advocated that African American Studies should be relevant to both African American college students and African American communities. Radical students and faculty challenged the status quo and argued for a pedagogical approach that linked theory and practice in order to alleviate the social problems that existed within the black community. Similar to the approach instituted during the

1965-66 protests and demonstrators, many of these scholars advocated a race-specific ideology toward education.

During this formative period, the efforts of Toni Cade Bambara, Angela Davis, Beverly Guy-Sheftall, Gloria Joseph, Michelle Wallace, Vivian Gordon, Delores P. Aldridge, Gloria Hull, Barbara Smith, Patricia Bell Scott, June Jordan, Audre Lorde, Patricia Hill Collins, and bell hooks brought issues of race, sex, gender, and class which concerned the black women's movement[20] to the forefront of discussion in Black Studies. Later, the emergence of Black Women's Studies[21] as an academic discipline generated a dialogue within African American Studies that resulted in challenges to the existing epistemologies[22] that did not incorporate the significant presence and contributions of African American women to the field.

1985-2000 — Institutionalization

The 1980s marked a period of formal standardization and institutionalization of African American Studies, highlighted by the 1981 release of the National Council of Black Studies' Core Curriculum,[23] and the late Nathan I. Huggins' *Afro-American Studies: A Report to the Ford Foundation* in 1985.[24] In 1984, Harvard professor Nathan I. Huggins was commissioned by the Ford Foundation to conduct a research survey of the current status of African American Studies on American campuses in light of its early experience in the academy and future needs. He described the efforts to gain a place for Black Studies in the post-secondary curriculum as part of a broader movement to integrate Black students and faculty into a traditionally white educational system. He recommended that more sophisticated methodologies be brought to bear on the study of black issues and the expansion of Black Studies in conventional disciplines. Furthermore, he concluded that three basic concerns lay behind the demand for African American Studies: (1) the political need for turf and place; (2) the psychological need for identity; (3) the academic need for recognition. In 1988, Temple University developed and implemented the first doctoral program[25] in African American Studies. African American Women's Studies also began to assert itself simultaneously along with as well as outside of African American Studies. Research and writing which had been previously subjugated or neglected began to appear more frequently and prominently by black women.

Nathan Hare, chairman of the first African American Studies Department at San Francisco State College, asserted that the Black Studies curriculum could be divided into two basic phases: the expressive and the pragmatic-positivistic. The expressive phase would be therapeutic and focus on courses in the history and culture of African Americans. The pragmatic-positivistic phase would provide students with skills they needed to bring about change in their lives, and communities.

Although some radical scholars disagreed with Hare concerning the two distinct phases he outlined, others asserted that these two phases should be separated from the university's academic context. John Blassingame, for example, elaborating on the prospect of expressive and pragmatic-positivistic phases, suggested that "community action programs must be separated from academic programs and adequately funded, staffed, and truly related to community needs."[26] This disagreement has produced a dichotomy between the content, theory and pedagogy in African American Studies. Some scholars argued that many departments and programs 'missed the mark' in their emphasis on coverage of the history and culture of African Americans, and de-emphasis of the skills and techniques needed to combat oppression within African American communities.

In the nineties, along with the creation of four new doctoral programs at the University of Massachusetts at Amherst, the University of California at Berkeley, Harvard, and Yale Universities, there has been a resurgence in the debate about the content, scope, and most importantly, the direction African American Studies will take going into the twenty-first century.[27] Central to the contemporary questions facing African American Studies are issues surrounding academic excellence and community responsibility: that is, whether or not Black Studies will continue to take part in the "careerist culture" of the academy or reflect on its vision, retool its mission, and reshape its direction.

African American Studies has been, as we might expect, primarily involved in developing itself as an academic discipline, providing an historically accurate portrayal and interpretation of African American culture as well as enriching the "traditional" fields of study in American colleges and universities. But during its tenure as an academic discipline, African American Studies has had an important impact on the intellectual, political and cultural environment of higher education over the past thirty years.[28]

2. African American Studies Now: Some Challenges and Directions

Over the course of the past thirty years, the institutionalization of African American Studies has resulted in the disenfranchisement of African American people from the intellectual pursuits of those faculty and students in the African American Studies departments. This situation can be changed if we utilize the talents of African American intellectuals to fulfill the mission, scope and purpose of African American Studies. We must be concerned that several generations of young people have missed out on accessing the knowledge available through African American Studies. African American Studies must become an active agent and participant in educating, organizing and empowering children, families, and communities to improve their lives; African American Studies must (re)focus and (re)direct its efforts. Those of us in the discipline must ask ourselves some hard and true questions: What is the purpose of African American Studies? Why do we exist? What does it mean to be African-Centered or Afrocentric? What does it mean to be committed to the struggle?

What is African American Studies?

African American Studies is an academic discipline which seeks to investigate phenomena and interrogate issues of the world from an Afrocentric perspective. The resulting finds are then transposed into communally-digestible data which will ultimately liberate the African community and cause it to see its own worth once again.

Attempts to define a field of intellectual inquiry, such as African American Studies, allow for a wide variety of points of view. Nevertheless, there is need to define the limits of the discipline and to communicate the history, structure, function, content, philosophy, and method of the field of study. There is no definition on which the different schools of thought agree. In the widely used text, *Introduction to Black Studies*, Karenga defined Black Studies as "the systematic and critical study of the multi-dimensional aspects of Black thought and practice in their current and historical unfolding. It is systemic in that it is structured and coherent, critical in the sense of its focus on the search for meaning and concern with detail...; and multidimensional in its thrust to examine the many-sidedness of each issue, process or phenomenon."[29] Vivian Gordon viewed Black Studies as "an analysis of the factors and conditions which have affected the economic, psychological, legal, and moral status of the African in America as well as the African in the diaspora. Not only is Black Studies concerned with the culture of the Afro-American ethnic as historically and sociologically defined by the traditional literature, it is concerned with the development of new approaches to the study of the Black experience and with the development of social policies which will impact positively upon the lives of Black people."[30]

As evident in the previous examples, the primary objective and focus of Black Studies are African people. Philip T. K. Daniels argued his concept of Black Studies as being a "multidiscipline" that systematically focuses upon the experiences of Black people throughout the world. It is the study of Africa and the African diaspora... it simultaneously assesses the outer struggle of Blacks against oppression, discrimination, imperialism, racism and other pejorative forces, while also looking at their inner struggle to establish community, identity heritage, and a functional as well as practical and protective institutional infrastructure.[31]

Although one single definition of African American Studies may be useful, there has been — since its beginning — different nomenclatures for the discipline such as Negro Studies, Afro-American Studies, African American Studies, American Studies, Afro-American and African Studies, Black Studies, Africana Studies, Pan-African Studies and more recently Africology,[32] as suggested by Molefi Asante, William Nelson, Winston Van Horne and Maulana Karenga. William Nelson suggested that the building of a discipline of Africology is uniquely challenging because of the absence of a widely accepted paradigm. "An appropriate paradigm of Africology must also be an alternative and corrective to traditional scholarship. Such a paradigm must, [by] necessity, be Afrocentric in its basic orientation... it must be interdisciplinary in nature... must combine self-knowledge and self-realization with social action... it must prove beyond the borders of academia — to the broader community.... Finally, Africology must come to grips with the new methodologies and new technologies of the social sciences and the humanities."[33]

What is the Purpose of African American Studies?

The purpose of African American studies is to provide the academic world with a new lens through which to discover the beauty of all human beings and to acknowledge and celebrate — not simply tolerate — the gifts that all have to offer, regardless of cultural worldviews and resulting differences. Indeed, when black scholars and students first called for the Western academy to recognize and then to accept the place of Black Studies as a discipline, they were not simply reacting to white racist intellectual traditions; they were suggesting that the inclusion of all voices in the shaping of American education would assure that we ultimately create a society where everyone gets the chance to speak and to listen. The Afrocentric paradigm, a revisionist ideology, insists that we dismantle "the mask that grins and lies" as we search for a way of living and knowing which lifts all of humanity.

Since its institutional beginning, many perspectives as to the purpose and function of African American Studies have been presented. According to Nathan Hare, "The main motivation of Black Studies is to entice black students to greater involvement in the educational process. Black Studies is, above all, a pedagogical device."[34] Vivian Gordon wrote that "the curriculum of Black Studies must help the student develop his or her skills in the use of the tools which are important to both a critical analysis of interaction of the past and present and to the students' future participation in the analyses of factors which affect the life of black people in America."[35] Inez Reid suggested four purposes that assumed prominent roles in the debate over African American Studies: (1) Black Studies Programs can fulfill a need for scholarly correction of historical and cultural myths; (2) Black Studies can provide potential elementary and secondary school teachers, destined to serve in black communities, with much more knowledge about [African American children]; (3) Black Studies can fulfill a psychological need on the part of black students; and (4) Black Studies can fulfill the need to begin the process of resocialization and socialization of Americans destined to play roles in the United States [in the twenty-first century].[36] Harold Cruse viewed Black Studies to be an instrument of cultural nationalism specifically concerned with critiquing the integrationist ethic "and providing a counter-balance to the dominant Anglo-Saxon culture."[37] Some others argued further that Black Studies should be able to develop and to facilitate racial awareness and pride among black people. Many argued, in the late 1960s and 1970s that Black Studies must be communally based, community controlled, and committed to being a vehicle for social change. These arguments are still relevant to the purposes of African American Studies after more than three decades; there is an indisputable need for African American Studies.

As in any academic, social, political or intellectual endeavor, there is no single purpose that drives the field of African American Studies. However, its main purposes should be: (1) to analyze, produce, investigate, and disseminate knowledge about African people; (2) to involve and incorporate the content, ideologies and methodologies of African American Studies in all aspects of the community; (3) to prepare undergraduate and graduate students with knowledge, skills, and paradigms to analyze critically factors which affect African people in America; and (4) to identify issues and problems African Americans face and to provide leadership and solutions to resolve them. Furthermore, James Stewart has presented what five significant results and contributions of the discipline have been: (1) destruction of the myth of the passive acceptance of subjugation by blacks; peoples of African descent have always attempted to shape their own destinies; (2) documentation of the critical role of collective self-help in laying the foundations for black progress; (3) restoration of the record of accent and modern civilizations of blacks in developing high technology and establishing early civilizations in North and South America; (4) exploration of the contemporary implications of psychic duality, building on DuBois' classic formulation of the concept of Afrocentricity as a guiding principle; and (5) explication of the critical role played by black women in shaping the black experience.[38]

After examining over 50 Black Studies proposals and programs, Charles V. Hamilton summarized Black Studies as having six functions: (1) the gaps function—correcting the inadequacies of existing courses; (2) the functional theory—to educate black students for useful service in the black community; (3) the humanizing function—to help white students overcome racist attitudes by imparting new knowledge and new human values; (4) the reconciliation theory—to bring about a new spirit of cooperation between blacks and whites; (5) the psychological function—to instill a sense of pride in black students to develop a sense of identity; and (6) the ideological function—to serve as a means to develop new ideological, Third World orientations, to develop theories of revolution and nation-building.[39]

African American and African Diaspora Studies

Another item that must take priority in the African American Studies agenda is our connection and involvement with all people of the African Diaspora. The black power and black consciousness movements of the 1960s influenced social and political change in many countries, since as, England, France, Haiti, Nigeria, South Africa, and Zimbabwe and we must now become leaders in the global community. We need not abandon our commitment to African Americans, but what happens in these places is as critical to our uplift as what happens in Atlanta, Chicago, New York or Philadelphia.

Actually, to speak of African American Studies without first speaking of the 19th century Pan African movement is an historical misnomer. Scholars such as Henry Highland Garnett, Edward Blyden, and Henry McNeal Turner spoke of the viability of an "African Diaspora" long before the term was officially coined. They praised and wrote about their African heritage and urged for the study of its culture and history. So then, in truth, African American Studies is simply one component of the larger vision that is the reunification of African thought globally. Yet this global vision is not limited only to people of African descent; the belief simply is that the culmination of African voices will position African people sufficiently to then invite other voices of the world (Latinos, Native Americans, Asians, and even Europeans) to Martin Luther King, Jr.'s "table of brotherly love" as we figure out how to repair human relationships and to restore individual dignity which years of discrimination and abuse have destroyed.

The introduction of African and African American Studies into academia provides new possibilities and challenges for higher education and diaspora studies. The emergence of Asian American, Puerto Rican, Latin American, Chicano American, Women, and Gay and Lesbian studies can be attributed in part to the pioneering struggle black faculty and students fought in the late 1960s and 1970s. Martin and Young argued that "The gestation and birth of African and Afro-American Studies in the United States are as diametrically opposed as the experiences that shaped the colonizers and descendants of enslaved Africans. African Studies efforts were designed to provide knowledge to assist colonial interests, but Black Studies was the direct result of a liberation struggle by persons of African ancestry.[40] Nevertheless there is a need for African American Studies to incorporate African Diaspora Studies into its curricula, courses, research and ideological emphasis beyond that which is now to being done in a few programs. African American Studies should enhance the wisdom of Clarke, Drake, DuBois and their precursors.

St. Clair Drake noted that between 1915 and World War II, diaspora studies were an important component in the research, publication, and educational work of an influential complex of institutions founded and nurtured by... the Association for the Study of Negro Life and History under the direction of Dr. Carter G. Woodson. He further stated that... Black Studies programs constitute the single most important academic structure [in academics]... for initiating and consolidating cooperative relations with African, Latin American and [Asian] institutions interested in developing diaspora studies.[41]   African Diaspora Studies can enhance African American Studies by providing more inclusive cultural, political, economical and educational perspectives. It can provide a framework for correcting the misinterpretation and subordination of the African diaspora.

African American Women's Studies

The fact that a scholar such as Alice Walker felt the need to coin the term "womanism" is sign enough that the voices and needs of African American women have not been fully represented by our scholarship at large. Indeed, the absence of female voices seemed not to disturb most established black male activists and, in fact, when black women began to cry out for inclusion, some of their most fierce resistance came from within. Hence, my decision to create space and place for my sisters' voices is both an historical corrective as well as a pedagogical measure offered to make sure that gender does not cloud our vision of the future of the discipline.

African American women "...despite racist and sexist treatment in a variety of institutional contexts have...struggle[d] for equal access, fair treatment, and images of themselves within the academy. [African American women's studies] has transformed higher education by making it more responsive to the needs of black women, establishing black women's studies, and revamping both black studies and women's studies."[42]

The first Women's Studies class was taught in the 1960s and was based on the model set by African American Studies. Black women's studies emerged as a discipline in the late 1970s. Since it is a fundamental part of African American Studies, the lack of adequate scholarly treatment of black women in both African American Studies and the academy as a whole led to increased efforts by black women to create and sustain space for teaching and research with an alternative vision.

In "The Politics of Black Women's Studies," Barbara Smith and Gloria Hull posited four issues pertaining to African American Women's Studies: (1) the general political situation of Afro-American women and the bearing this has had upon the implementation of black women's studies; (2) the relationship of black women's studies to black feminist politics and the black feminist movement; (3) the necessity for black women's studies to be feminist, radical, and analytical; and (4) the need for teachers of black women's studies to be aware of our problematic political positions in the academy and of the potentially antagonistic conditions under which we must work. They further suggested that black women's studies will not be dependent on women's studies, Black Studies or "straight disciplinary departments for its existence, but will be an autonomous academic entity making coalitions with all three."[43]

Academic Excellence and Validity in African American Studies

For years, many scholars (black and white) have questioned the worthiness of the contributions of Africans and African Americans to civilization and to knowledge. Because African American Studies challenged the "traditional" disciplines, faculty in those fields took (and some continue to maintain) the position that it had no intellectual value in the academy and that it constituted an attack on established scholarly discipline and was geared more to politics than rigorous scholarship. These faculty members viewed Black Studies as being more concerned with separate social activities, community action programs, and courses that stressed black self-concept and black nationalism than with academic learning.

These critics questioned the academic abilities and training of the faculty involved in teaching and administering Black Studies. Kilson noted that Black Studies would be more desirable intellectually and academically if scholars who taught in Black Studies were represented in the established departments like classics, philosophy, history and economics and if university facilities adopted the policy of joint academic appointments.[44] Even today, there is debate about the quality of curricula, faculty, students, and administrators of some African American Studies programs and departments at various colleges and universities because academic reputation ranges from excellent and average to mediocre. Nevertheless, there is continued support of African American Studies as exhibited through the increase in majors—undergraduate and graduate programs—and the creation of Ph.D. granting programs at Harvard and Yale. Essays in sections one, seven and eight discuss topics related to the nature, content and structure of the discipline.

Theories and Paradigms of Traditional Disciplines

The major intellectual and scholarly contributions to the body of knowledge in African American Studies have come from academicians who received their training in "traditional disciplines." This is also true for the African American women scholars who have contributed to the development of African American Women's Studies and Feminist thought. From the early 1900s to the present, these scholars include W. E. B. DuBois, trained in history and sociology; Carter G. Woodson, John Hope Franklin, Vincent Harding, Nathan Huggins, Rayford Logan, Darlene Clark Hine, Paula Giddings, Gerda Lerner, Sterling Stuckey, Benjamin Quarles and Lerone Bennett, Jr. trained in history; St. Clair Drake and Allison W. Davis trained in anthropology; E. Franklin Frazier, Oliver C. Cox, Patricia Hill-Collins, Vivian Gordon and Nathan Hare trained in sociology; Kenneth Clark, Wade Nobles and Charles Sumner trained in psychology; Henry L. Gates, Jr., Huston Baker, Jr., Barbara Christian, June Jordan, Audre Lorde, Toni Cade Bambara, Alice Walker, Beverly Guy-Sheftall, bell hooks, Michelle Wallace, Addison Gayle, Jr., Saunders J. Redding in literature; Ronald Walters, Ralph Bunche, and Charles V. Hamilton trained in political science; and Leonard Harris and Alain Locke trained in philosophy; Katie Cannon and Jacquelyn Grant trained in religion; Angela Davis and Flo Kennedy trained in law.

It is important to note that the above listing of scholars demonstrates the role of "traditional" disciplines in the intellectual training of the pioneers in African American Studies. It would also suggest that these scholars also brought the major theories, paradigms, and philosophies of those disciplines to the field of African American Studies. The various approaches to literary criticism, black feminist thought, Marxism, social change theories, and analytical perspectives have come from the traditional disciplines, but are all approaches with broad interdisciplinary application. Adams suggested that the philosophies of African American scholars in [traditional disciplines] appear to have been the result of their own socialization, their individual attitudes towards the canons of their disciplines, the major political and intellectual currents of their eras, and the particular topics, problems, or questions addressed by them.[45]

Imperative, however, is the need for African American Studies to avoid the pitfalls of becoming complacent and stagnant in its scope, relevance, and responsibilities. We need to clarify the differing roles of the discipline for our own sake and for the sake of our next generation of scholars, students, and colleagues who will need to work in the academy's multidisciplinary world. We need to avoid rejecting work coming from disciplinary or methodological bases other than those that deemed ideologically "correct."[46] African American Studies has primarily used ideology (not methodology or pedagogy) as a basis for staffing African American Studies departments and programs. The continuing debate over the relative merits or various approaches serves as a distraction from our efforts to function effectively within academia. Will we align ourselves with our research and direct it in ways beneficial to the community? In choosing to pursue careers in African American Studies, we are selecting a frame of reference, a window from which to view the world, if you will, that will have a fundamental effect on the questions we ask and the recommendations we make to improve/enhance the life opportunities of African American people.

Afrocentricity and the African World-View

Many scholars use the terms "afrocentric" and "African-centered" interchangeably. I argue that this is an error. "Afrocentric" is a term that usually seeks to describe an individual or a scholarly effort in terms of its inclusion of African cultural phenomena. "African-centered", on the other hand, is a paradigmatic term that seeks to position the philosophical place of the scholar under question and the resulting body of knowledge, creative production, and authorial intent. Put simply, an African-centered scholar is one who examines all phenomena — unapologetically — from the worldview or cosmological place of the African. But to some "afrocentricity" has come to represent the shallow question of things such as what one wears and the style of one's hair. However, I posit that "African-centered" is a term which will usher scholars into a place where both the African world and all other realities get to speak for themselves and have value — on their own terms.

Even though Afrocentricity has its critics inside and outside of the disciplines (D'Souza, Howe, Moses, Lefkowitz, Ravitch and Schlesinger), it could be argued that during the last two decades in African American Studies, no other conceptual framework or theoretical construct has contributed more to the discussion and debate inside and out of the academy than the theory of Afrocentricity as presented by Molefi K. Asante in his works — *Afrocentricity: The Theory of Social Change* (1980); *The Afrocentric Idea* (1987); and *Kemet, Afrocentricity and Knowledge* (1990). To varying degrees, Afrocentricity has influenced the scholarship of the discipline. The Afrocentric perspective has provided the basis for reexamining all aspects of the African experience. Many articles, books, and dissertations use the concept as rationale for their methodologies and research designs.

While there are several schools of thought of Afrocentricity — Nile Valley Afrocentrists, Continental Afrocentrists, Afrocentric Infusionists, and Social Afrocentrists — it can be defined as "a quality of thought and practice rooted in the cultural image and human interest of African people."[47] Asante, its leading exponent, described it as an enterprise framed by cosmological, epistemological, axiological, and aesthetic issues. He further explained that the Afrocentric method pursues a world [view] distinctly African-centered in relationship to external phenomena.... The Afrocentrist seeks to uncover and use codes, paradigms, symbols, motifs, and circles of discussion that reinforce the centrality of African ideals and values as a valid frame of reference for acquiring and examining data."[48] Out of this position evolves the concept of African centeredness and worldview, a perspective which has influenced many African American scholars and students' research, teaching, and instruction.

The African worldview provides for an African-centered model of culture and knowledge and articulates a systematic structure for dealing with all aspects of the African and African American experiences. The construction of Black Feminist Thought developed by Patricia Hill-Collins incorporates some of the perspectives of Afrocentricity. Afrocentricity, African-centeredness, Black Feminist Thought, and the African worldview see "African American Studies as a human science that is committed to discovering in human experience, historical and contemporary, all the ways African people have tried to make their physical, social, and cultural environments serve [humanity]."[49]

African American Studies and Its Social-Community Responsibility

The intellectual development is only part of the discipline's mission. The other component concerns how we transform our scholarship into a social ideology that redirects the lives of African American people. Said simply, Black Studies is never Black Studies if there is no communal component. It was never intended to be an endeavor that lent itself exclusively to the academic world. Hence, Black Studies issues will never get completely resolved in the classroom, for the very being of Black Studies insists that the voices of the rejected get heard and included in the construction of "where we go from here."

There is need for African American Studies to fulfill its mission to liberate African American people and to commit itself to the communities' needs. In this connection, African American Studies must once again become committed to addressing the consciousness, realities, and urgencies of African Americans' life situations. It must seek to make significant contributions to the education and liberation of all African men, women, and children not just students and professors.

Though some of the goals set by the early leaders and architects of the Civil Rights and Black Power movements have been reached, there remains an urgent need for African American Studies to provide directions to non-academic communities in order that they can confront existing socio-political and economic challenges African Americans are still faced with on a daily basis. Perhaps the central goal in the years ahead should be for African American Studies to have an impact on the quality of life for all African American people. This requires research refocused and recommitted to our communities. It demands involvement in all institutions that affect our daily lives (e.g. the court system, family, schools, churches, labor, and entertainment). Programs and activities must be planned and implemented to deal with the systemic problems and challenges black people face in America (and the world over).

Needed Research and Related Projects in African American Studies

Research is needed in all areas of the African American community. Scholars and students in the discipline must identify projects in areas of need and design concrete research proposals. Researchers should investigate the system of public education, the criminal justice system, health issues, male and female relations, solutions to drug addiction, and violence within our communities.

We need to establish consortia of African, African American, Chicano, Asian, Latino and Native American Studies departments that incorporates a mission and framework similar to that of the Institute of Black World. The discipline needs to welcome scholars from related disciplines to work to improve the life experiences of African Americans in all situations.

Liaisons and partnerships must be established with the Congressional Black Caucus, churches, the Urban League, NAACP, along with other organizations and institutions to work together to complete projects similar to the aforementioned of those initiated by DuBois at Atlanta University and later the Carnegie Corporation under the auspices of Gunnar Myrdal. We need complete comprehensive investigations of all areas that affect our people.

Undergraduate and graduate students' research projects, theses and dissertations should research discrete problems and issues that affect the African community. Those departments that offer Ph.D.s in African American Studies should form a consortium that would sponsor conferences, conduct research, create new knowledge, research the diaspora, create a publishing company, and continue to produce inter- and intra-disciplinary research. The discipline needs to support the scholarly journals and professional academic organizations and to create new ones.

African American Studies: Its Challenges and Future

After thirty years of presence in predominantly white universities, major questions still surround the intellectual integrity and level of scholarship of much of the work produced within Black Studies. In addition, there remains continued controversy with regards to the political nature and mission of African American Studies. As we look toward the future, the agenda for African American Studies is a challenging and complex one. African American Studies departments and programs are rather stable in white institutions, and they will continue to exist as long as the presence of African American students increases on college campuses. What should be of concern, however, is the relationships African American Studies departments and programs establish with communities outside universities.

In the last decade, African American Studies has produced the first generation of scholars receiving M.A.s and Ph.D.s in the discipline. Those scholars who have graduated from Temple's Ph.D. program—Daniel P. Black, Greg Carr, Jose Pimiento-Bey, James Conyers, Jr., Ella Forbes, Victor Okarfor, Mario Beatty, Rodney Patterson Shabazz, and Valethia Watkins-Beatty (in addition to those who have a connection to Temple's program, Eddie Glaude, Karen Lacy, Ingrid Banks, Suzette Spencer—are already making significant contributions to the discipline. Their scholarship and epistemological perspectives will be influenced by the theories, topics, methods, and ideologies of Afrocentricity and African centeredness.

For African American Studies to advance, its focal point must be the production and utilization of knowledge to develop solutions to the various social, political, economic, and cultural issues African Americans face at the end of the twentieth century. At the turn of the century, DuBois initiated and carried out his research both in Philadelphia and Atlanta with the expressed purpose and intent of documenting the life and culture, thereby improving the life and culture of African Americans. By following his lead and bringing rigorous academic analyses and description to the discipline, scholars will continue to create new models of inquiry, examination, and evaluation useful to all disciplines.

3. Contents of the Book

Readers are going to notice the seeming absence of women scholars' writing during the formative years of the Black Studies movement. This is not an authorial/editorial omission. Indeed, the proliferation of male inclusion here is simply a reflection of the presence and prominence of patriarchy—even in Black "liberal" or "revolutionary" spaces. Black women were writing then—just as they are now—about not only women's issues, but also about the direction and future of the discipline in general, yet their voices were not always solicited and heard to the extent of their male counterparts'; those whose voices were anthologized were even fewer. Hence, the disproportionately few number of women represented in this text is more a reflection of historical communal sexism in the 1960s rather than an oversight on the part of the editor.

One might also ask why such a seminal scholar as James Baldwin did not get invited into the discussion of the birth of Black Studies as a viable academic discipline. Certainly no other black writer rivaled his public presence during the 1960s movement. Yet, I offer that homophobic tendencies, reflected even among our best scholars, caused many not to heed certain voices. Actually, even now, the inclusion of discourse about black life in America, written by black gay and lesbian scholars, still gets little to no recognition and almost never becomes part of the general scholarship we reference as we shape the future of African American Studies.

If this book advocates a theory of knowledge, it is of academic excellence in teaching the purposes, concepts and contents of African American Studies. Over the years, my colleagues and students have suggested that a book of wide-ranging readings would be valuable. First, it would complement basic texts[50] used in introductory and advanced courses. Second, it would facilitate wider discussion of the different perspectives[51] of scholars who have contributed to the study of our African American culture. This volume is thus organized around eight subject areas representing important historical, political, theoretical and social perspectives. Several criteria governed selection of the articles: (1) whether the article is provocative and/or scholarly; (2) whether it presents a new idea, method, or strategy for the discipline; (3) and whether it makes a contribution to the literature relevant to the discipline and to related areas of studies. In most cases, I have chosen essays treating contemporary critical issues; yet, in many cases, I have also included many works of longstanding concerns in which interest is currently dormant. Occasionally, an article has been included because it originally sparked discussion about a particular subject within the discipline or served as a prototype for later research and/or discussion on the subject. Such an article might have been especially provocative, and its ideas are still essentially relevant.

Most of the selections, included herein, somehow advanced, challenged or guided the evolution of African American Studies as a discipline. Some selections concerning the development of African American Studies are not included in this anthology. Yet the ones included give the reader a comprehensive overview of the critical issues and perspectives of most black scholars and students who established Black Studies. This volume's 61 entries are organized into eight sections: I. The Discipline: Definition and Perspectives; II. African American Women's Studies; III. Historical Perspectives; IV. Philosophical Perspectives; V. Theoretical Foundations; VI. Political Perspectives; VII. Critical Issues and Perspectives; VIII. Curriculum Development and Program Models. Within each section, essays are arranged to provide a representation of the trends, theories and patterns that have impacted the development of African American Studies since 1968.

Each section details the development of a specific area relevant to the discipline. The sections shape and reflect the questions, purposes, arguments, and debates that occurred during the past three decades of African American Studies in higher education. Equally important, the sections speak of the communal issues that plagued African American scholars as they sought to utilize their scholarship in practical ways. In other words, each section presents how African American intellectuals and activists sought to integrate the needs of the community and the academic tradition into a unique project of social-political change that was beneficial to African people.

The first section, "The Discipline: Definition and Perspectives," is arranged to present an overview of the discipline from various perspectives, examining whether African American Studies is a discipline or different fields of study. Many scholars still have not yet agreed that African American Studies is a viable discipline in a Western academic institution. This section of the text is offered both as a counter argument to that position and as an intellectual roadmap whereby the birth of the discipline and the justification for its place in the academy can be traced. Indeed, the need for such justification stands as proof of the ongoing struggle for recognition and validation which blacks have had to endure since our arrival in America. Significant dimensions of African American Studies, including questions regarding the structure, content, classification and evaluation, are discussed in order to define the discipline. In this section articles are included that address this important issue.

While the first section provides a group of essays attempting to define and determine the nature of the discipline, in Section II, "African American Women's Studies," the articles focus on the development of this subject as a discipline or area of study within the academy. Far too often the voices of our mothers, sisters, and daughters have gone unheard. The inclusion of women's writings along with those of men assures a balanced historical presentation as we attempt to tell our stories with dignity and honesty. This part of the text celebrates the contention which Black women held concerning their place both in the discipline and in the new black community. During the editorial process, at times it seemed logical to integrate the entries in this section into Section I, but it quickly became evident that a separate section was needed for this reader that dealt with questions raised about the significance and contributions of African American women who have previously been underrepresented in African American Studies in general.

The third section, "Historical Perspectives," presents viewpoints that address the impact of the relationship between socio-political movements and academic activity on the development of the discipline throughout different historical periods. In addition, several articles represent efforts to reconceptualize the struggle and conflicts related to the advancement of African American Studies. African American Studies as a discipline in higher education had its origin at San Francisco State in 1968. Since then, African American Studies departments and programs have developed in academic institutions throughout American colleges and universities attempting to serve the needs of all students interested in the plight and achievements of Africans in the New World. Many institutions sought to attach African American Studies as an appendage to "traditional disciplines" worthy only as a complement to the traditional disciplines. Only in recent years have certain schools allowed African American Studies to have an intellectual space of its own. Schools such as Temple, Harvard, Yale, University of Massachusetts at Amherst, and University of California, Berkeley trusted the integrity and validity of the discipline such that they have created Ph.D. programs.

Section IV, "Philosophical Perspectives," offers contributions of influential figures in African American Studies. The problem of African American Studies as a discipline results from the position by many scholars that Africans have no philosophical history. Yet, not only is this untrue, but it is also reflective of Eurocentric scholarship's inability to recognize philosophical inquiry in cultural form other than its own. The philosophical, epistemological, and ideological dimensions are presented as imperatives in the development of the discipline. Shifting from problems of paradigm, optimal theory, and intellectual questions, the articles in this section explore various philosophical constructs of the discipline.

The fifth section, "Theoretical Foundations," includes articles concerning and analyzing theory building, Afrocentric metatheory, culture and African-centeredness. Before the appearance of such seminal texts as Molefi Asante's *Afrocentricity,* theorizing about African American Studies was absent. Now, however, Miramba Ani's *Yurugu* and Jerome Schiele's *Human Services in the Afrocentric Paradigm* evidence the fact that theoretical frameworks are being offered to undergird the existence of a strong African American Studies discourse. The essays in this section chronicle the emergence and integration of theoretical perspectives currently central to the discipline.

Section VI, "Political Perspective," focuses on political perspectives that have affected African American Studies. Articles in this section examine the reactions of various university factions as well as various organizations and individuals critical of the purposes, functions, quality, content, and direction of African American Studies. The political climate in America during the 1960s was turbulent and in fact dangerous for African Americans. Individuals such as Stokely Carmichael, Amiri Baraka, Sonia Sanchez, and others put their lives on the line not simply for Civil Rights, but also for the right to read, write, and research black life in the institutions of higher learning. People died not only that they might be able to vote, but also that we might be able to study ourselves and thus guarantee ourselves a place in the American historical narrative. Attention in this section is given to the political nature of the discipline as well as to the politics of the attacks on the discipline. At the end of this section, the article by St. Clair Drake explores various conflicts facing African American Studies from a global perspective.

Section VII, "Critical Issues and Perspectives," identifies a number of issues and conflicts that have been present for many years and still continue to be points of contention inside and outside of the discipline. Many cultural issues cloud the clarity of just how African American Studies will serve the larger American community. Indeed, whether or not African American Studies belongs only to African American people is an issue which is as yet unresolved. I contend that the aim of the discipline is to transform, primarily, the lives of African Americans, and in general, all of humanity. The recurring issue of what should be the scope and purpose of African American Studies and its responsibility to the larger African American community is debated here. Thus the question of "applied or functional"[52] African American Studies emerges (e.g., the responsibilities of African American intellectuals and the promise of African American Studies to improve the "life chances" of African American people in areas of education,[53] employment, and political and social institutions).

Since its nascent period, before any standard or core curriculum plan of African American Studies, nearly all historically black and a few predominantly white universities and colleges offered a course in "Negro culture" or "Negro life." During the 1940s, Lincoln and Fisk Universities instituted programs in "Pan-American Studies." It was not until the appearance of black students on white campuses (and more importantly their demands for a curriculum and courses relevant to and taught from a perspective which highlighted their historical and contemporary life experiences) in the 1960s that any organized, systematic effort to develop the discipline as we now know it began to take place. The final section in this volume, "Curriculum Development and Program Models," details the various curriculum models, programs, institutes and topic areas of computers, science and technology contributing to the advancement of the discipline. An overview of curriculum development in African American Studies during the 1980s begins this section, and an article dealing with Black Studies and Africana curriculum models in the United States closes the book.

It should be noted that two articles that have contributed to the intellectual development of African American Studies could not be included in this reader. Each of these influential and seminal essays appeared in *The Next Decade: Theoretical and Research Issues in Africana Studies*, edited by Dr. James Turner of Cornell University's Africana Studies and Research Center. And each spurred subsequent articles that are included in this reader. The articles are significant for their impact in the formation of the discipline and warrant special mention here. The venerable Dr. John Henrik Clarke's "Africana Studies: A Decade of Change, Challenge, and Conflict," states that [within African American Studies]: "Beyond the search for definition and direction is the search for an ideology. Africana Studies without an ideology is a recitation of days, places, personalities, and events. A people search their past in order to understand the present and reshape the future."[54] In "Africana Studies and Epistemology: A Discourse in the Sociology of Knowledge," Turner himself notes: "As a methodology, history in Black Studies, constitutes the foundation for theoretical construction as an analysis of the fundamental relationship between the political economy of societal developments and the racial divisions of labor and privilege, and the common patterns of life chances peculiar to the social conditions of black people. . . . Therefore, Black Studies is a 'reconstruction discipline,' as a synthesis of what its criticisms imply, convergence with theories reviewed, and the philosophical methods of its pedagogical emphasis."[55]

Also, unfortunately, the editor was not able to include key selections for publication from several of the more prominent figures involved in the formation and evolution of African American Women's Studies. A host of factors prevented excerpts from seminal works published by bell hooks (*Ain't I a Woman*), Audre Lorde (*Sister Outsider*), Angela Davis (*Women, Race, and Class*), and Michelle Wallace (*Black Macho and the Myth of the Superwoman*) from being part of this reader.

Conclusion

The discipline of African American Studies is currently at a crossroads. Black scholars today, unlike their predecessors, are not concerned so much about justifying the place of Black Studies in the academy—that work has already been done. Rather their aim is to determine how Afrocentric and African-centered scholarship can transform the lives of everyone—not only those in the academy. Indeed, current grassroots movements are commanding the attention of the young black dispossessed brothers on the streets with those who write about him.

Nineteen ninety-eight represented three decades of accomplishments, challenges, conflicts, and unachieved objectives in Black Studies. Yet during this period of thirty years, the discipline of African American Studies has literally changed the face of the American higher educational system, along with the ways in which research is conducted to deal with issues concerning African Americans. Moreover, it has offered countless numbers of black and white students and faculty the option to pursue answers to intellectual and social questions which they otherwise would have ignored. The simple fact that Black Studies is still in existence after the first thirty years[56] with problems, issues and conflicts is a sign that the discipline has exhibited tremendous tenacity and unlimited possibilities for the future.

Nevertheless, as an academic discipline, African American Studies must continue to examine and expand its theories, methodologies, and epistemologies and to impact on the academic terrain at the beginning of the twenty-first century. Ideally, it must appeal to all facets of the intellectual community. At this juncture, we need to seriously consider and evaluate the role(s) African American Studies has traditionally occupied: (1) politically, it has sought to strengthen and influence the activities and policies of African American leadership; (2) intellectually, it has created an arena and elevated the level of discourse so that the historical and contemporary life experiences of people of African descent are viewed as significant, instructive, and unique; (3) socially, it has provided a space in which students can be mentored, recognized and supported in their efforts to realize their full academic and individual potential; (4) and culturally, it has presented people of African descent with alternative ways of viewing the world and living out traditional African ideas, beliefs, values, and mores.

"Black Studies is an open-textured and open-ended project, interdisciplinary and receptive to diversity as expressed in its ability to include various subject areas and various intellectual perspectives. But more important, it reflects also the history and character of the discipline itself which came into being as an emancipatory project which seeks to be both an ongoing and profound critique and corrective, intellectually and socially. Thus, if it holds true to its academic and social mission, it is compelled to practice internally what it demands externally, i.e., self-criticism and self-correction...and an intellectual rigor and relevance which both disarms its severest critics and honors its original academic and social mission."[57]

Endnotes

1. See B. Cleveland, "Black Studies in Higher Education," *Phi Delta Kappan* LI (September 1969), 44-46.

2. See Harold Cruse, "Black Studies: Interpretation, Methodology, and the Relationship to Social Movements," *Afro-American Studies* 2:1 (June 1971): 15-51.

3. Russell L. Adams, "African American Studies and the State of the Art," in Mario Azavedo (ed.), *Africana Studies* (Durham, NC: Carolina Academic Press, 1993), 25-49.

4. The area of Ethnic/Cultural Studies also emerged in part as a result of the African American Studies movement. Many of the early programs and departments of Asian, Latin American, Chicano Studies, etc. were in fact connected with those of Black Studies (i.e., Hunter College, City College of New York). Women's Studies, Cultural Studies and Gay and Lesbian Studies owe their very existence in the academy to the space opened by the creation of Black Studies.

5. Prior to 1969, Black and Puerto Rican faculty, students, and staff from various departments and the SEEK (Search Enrich and Enhance Knowledge) Program at the college proposed the development of a fully functioning Black Studies Institute and Department. Addison Gayle, Jr., Wilfred Cartey, Barbara Christian, James Emanuel, Jerome Brooks, Allen Ballard, Olga Taylor, Raymond Patterson, Malcolm Robinson, Nathaniel Norment, Jr., Osborne Scott, Melvin Norment, James Smalls, Robert Young, Charles Powell, Leonard Jeffries, James De-Jongh, Moyibi Amoda, Barbara Wheeler, Frank Laraque, Edward Scobie, George McDonald, Eugenia Bains, Margarita Matias, Illona Henderson, and Sederico Aquino-Berumudez (the first chair) organized curricula, course listings, and the basic structure for a Black and Puerto Rican Studies Department.

6. Though African American Studies, in its contemporary form, has a rich and invaluable heritage dating back to the nineteenth century, it was the 1960s which proved to be the galvanizing force behind the widespread emergence of programs and departments across the country. See Donald B. Easum, "The Call for Black Studies," *Africa Report* 14 (May/June 1969): 16-22, and Charles V. Hamilton, "The Question of Black Studies," *Phi Delta Kappan* 57:7 (March 1970): 362-364.

7. Shortly after African American Studies began to occupy space within the academy, a number of conferences and symposiums were held to debate the viability and necessity for the field. See, especially, Armistead L. Robinson, Craig H. Foster, and Donald I. Ogilvie, *Black Studies in the University: A Symposium* (New York: Bantam Books, 1969), and John Blassingame, *New Perspectives on Black Studies* (Chicago: University of Illinois Press, 1973).

8. For the purposes of this reader, the editor has chosen to utilize the terms African American Studies and Black Studies interchangeably.

9. Although African American Studies is considered to be a relatively new field of study in the university, Black Studies has in fact a long and rich tradition in academia. The African American scholars in the late nineteenth and early twentieth century who began to conduct research about and study of "Negro life and culture" represent the foundation of the discipline. See, especially, W. E. B. DuBois, who organized the eleven volume Atlanta University Studies of the "Negro Problem," editing papers on all aspects of "Negro life."

10. Several white intellectuals have contributed to the field of Africana and African American Studies. Prominent among them is Melville Herskovits, who is considered by some to be the "Dean of Africana Studies." See his groundbreaking study *The Myth of the Negro Past* (1941; repr. Boston: Beacon Press, 1958). For additional early scholarship by Herskovits, see "Education and Cultural Dynamics," *American Journal of Sociology* 48 (1942), 737-749; "Problem, Method and Theory in Afro-American Studies," *Afro-American* 1 (1945): 5-24, also published in *Phylon* 7 (1946): 337-354; "The Contribution of Afro-American Studies to Africanist Research," *American Anthropology* 50 (1948): 1-10; and "The Present Status and Needs of Afro-American Research," *Journal of Negro History* 36 (1951): 123-147. Other well-known white scholars include Herbert J. Aptheker, a pioneer Marxist historian who contributed significantly to the documentation of African American history in general and to the preservation of the papers of DuBois. Robert E. Park, a sociologist at the University of

Chicago, taught in 1913 one of the first black studies courses "The Negro in America" and who also trained three African American sociologists Frazier, Johnson, Cayton. Franz Boas was a German-American immigrant anthropologist whom some consider to be the architect of anti-racist thought in the American academy. See Herbert Shapiro and Herbert Aptheker (eds.), *African American History and Radical Historiography: Essays in Honor of Herbert Aptheker* (Los Angeles: MEP Publications, 1998) and Vernon C. Williams, *Rethinking Race: Franz Boas and His Contemporaries* (Lexington, KY: University Press of Kentucky, 1996).

11. See, especially, Ernest Dunbar, "Cornell: The Black Studies Thing," *New York Times Magazine*, April 1969; Harry Edwards, *Black Students* (New York: Free Press, 1970); and H. Rosovsky, "Black Studies at Harvard: Personal Reflections Concerning Recent Events," *American Scholar* 38 (Autumn 1969): 562-572.

12. This reader includes articles and essays that are relevant to the development of African American Studies in higher education since 1968. However, the history of the field itself dates back to the mid-1800s. See Lawrence Crockett, "Early Black Studies Movements," *Journal of Black Studies* 2:2 (1971): 189-200.

13. See Des Virney Sinnette and Arthur A. Schomburg, "The Negro Digs Up His Past," Alain Locke, (ed.), *The New Negro: Voices of the Harlem Renaissance* (1926; New York: Simon and Schuster, 1997).

14. Though a number of weekly and monthly journals were in existence prior to the founding of ASLNH, most were either organs of religious, fraternal, and/or literary organizations, and many were designed and written with the intent of popular appeal. *The Journal of Negro History* continues to this day as one of the richest sources of available data for African American Studies and historical research.

15. See Harry Edwards, *Black Students* (New York: Free Press, 1970). Vincent Harding, "Black Students and the Impossible Revolution," *Ebony Magazine* (August 1969): 144-149; James McEvoy and Abraham Miller, *Black Power and Student Rebellion* (Belmont, CA: Wadsworth Publishing, 1969); J. Saunders Redding, "The Black Youth Movement," *American Scholar* 28 (Autumn 1969): 584-587; and "Student Strikes: 1968-1969," *Black Scholar* 1:2 (January/February 1970): 65-75.

16. See William L. VanDeBerg, *New Day in Babylon: The Black Power Movement and American Culture, 1965-75* (Chicago: University of Chicago Press, 1993).

17. See Gerald McWorter and Ronald Bailey, "Black Studies Curriculum Development in the 1980s: Its Pattern and History," *Black Scholar* 16:5 (March 1984); and Howard J. Miller, "MCD Process Model: A Systematic Approach to Curriculum Development in Black Studies," *Western Journal of Black Studies* 10:1 (Fall 1987): 19-27.

18. See Martin Kilson and Bayard Rustin (eds.), *Black Studies: Myths and Realities* (New York: A. Phillip Randolph Educational Fund, 1969).

19. Martin Kilson, "Reflections on the Structure and Content in Black Studies," *Journal of Black Studies* 3:3 (March 1973): 303-312.

20. The black women's movement was both an extension and an interdependent part of the Civil Rights, Black Power, and Women's movements; however, it must be stressed that it has evolved as a distinct area of inquiry and study. See, especially, John Henrik Clarke, "The Black Woman: A Figure in World History," *Essence Magazine* (June 1971); Paula Giddings, *When and Where I Enter: The Impact of Black Women on Race and Sex in America* (New York: William and Morrow, 1996); Linda J. M. LaRue, "Black Liberation and Women's Lib," *Transaction* 2:8 (November/December 1970): 59-64; Margaret C. Sims and Julianne Malveaux (eds.), *Slipping Through the Cracks: The Status of Black Women* (New Brunswick, NJ: Transaction Publishers, 1987).

21. See Johnella Butler and John C. Walters (eds.), *Transforming the Curriculum: Ethnic Studies and Women's Studies* (Albany, NY: State University of New York Press, 1991), Liza Fiol-Maata and Mariam K. Chamberlain (eds.), *Women of Color and the Multicultural Curriculum: Transforming the College Classroom* (New York: Feminist Press, 1994).

22. "Challenging male-centered interpretations of African and human reality and the relationships which such interpretations cultivated and sustained, black women scholars produced and insisted on alternative visions." Maulana Karenga, *Introduction to Black Studies* (Los Angeles: University of Sankore Press, 1993): 38.

23. In 1980, NCBS proposed adoption of the report of the Curriculum Standards Committee chaired by Dr. Perry Hall of Wayne State University. The document provided a general framework for the development of Black Studies courses in three basic areas: (1) Social Behavioral Studies; (2) Historical Studies; (3) Cultural Studies.

24. See Nathan I. Huggins, *A Report to the Ford Foundation on African American Studies* (New York: The Ford Foundation, 1985).

25. The recommendation to create the first operational doctoral program in African American Studies was proposed in Temple University's 1986 Academic Plan. This graduate program was to include the granting of both Master's and Doctoral degrees in African American Studies. Since its initiation, the department has graduated approximately 70 Ph.D.s.

26. John Blassingame, "Black Studies: An Intellectual Crisis," *The American Scholar* 38:4 (1969): 561-572.

27. In 1996, the University of Massachusetts, Amherst, approved a doctoral program in African American Studies. The university has an extensive history in the field, dating back to the early 1960s. See "Directions in Black Studies," *Massachusetts Review* (Autumn 1969). As a result of the initiative proposed by Ward Connerly and other members of the University of California Board of Regents, the approval of a doctoral program in African American Studies is currently pending at the University of California, Berkeley. The university currently offers a Ph.D. in Ethnic Studies. In the past five years, there has been a growing tendency both inside and outside African American Studies to question the theoretical and intellectual foundations of various strains of thought within the field, particularly Afrocentricity. See Stephen Howe, *Afrocentricity: Mythical Pasts and Imagined Homes* (New York: Verso Press, 1998); and Wilson J. Moses, *Afrotopia: The Roots of African American Popular History* (New York: Cambridge University Press, 1998).

28. See B. Cleveland, "Black Studies and Higher Education," *Phi Delta Kappan* LI (September 1969): 44-46, Flournoy Coles, "Black Studies in the College Curriculum," *Negro Education Review* 20:3 (October 1969): 106-113; Douglass B. Davidson, "Black Studies, White Studies, and Institutional Politics," *Journal of Black Studies* 15:3 (March 1985): 339-347; and Carlene Young, "An Assessment of Black Studies Programs in American Higher Education," *Journal of Negro Education* 53:3 (1984).

29. Maulana Karenga, *Introduction To Black Studies* (Los Angeles: University of Sankore Press, 1993), 504-5.

30. Vivian V. Gordon, "The Coming of Age of Black Studies," *The Western Journal of Black Studies* 5:3 (1981): 231-236.

31. Phillip T. K. Daniel, "Black Studies: Discipline or Field of Studies?" *The Western Journal of Black Studies* 4:3 (Fall 1980): 195-99.

32. Africology is defined as the Afrocentric study of phenomena, events, ideas, and personalities related to Africa. See Molefi K. Asante's *The Afrocentric Idea* (Philadelphia: Temple University Press, 1987) and *Afrocentricity: The Theory of Social Change* (Trenton: African World, 1980).

33. William E. Nelson, "Africology: Building an Academic Discipline" in James L. Conyers, Jr. (ed.), *Africana Studies: A Disciplinary Quest for Both Theory and Method* (North Carolina: McFarland and Company, Inc., 1997): 60-66.

34. Nathan Hare, "Questions and Answers about Black Studies," *The Massachusetts Review* (1969): 727-736.

35. See Gordon, note 30.

36. Inez Smith Reid, "An Analysis of Black Studies Programs," *Afro-American Studies* 1 (1970): 11-21.

37. See Cruse, note 2.

38. James B. Stewart, "Reaching for Higher Ground: Toward an Understanding of Black/Africana Studies," *The Afrocentric Scholar* 1:1 (1992): 1-69.

39. Charles V. Hamilton, "The Challenge of Black Studies," *Social Policy* 1:2 (1970): 16.

40. Guy Martin and Carlene Young, "The Paradox of Separate and Unequal: African Studies and Afro-American Studies," *The Journal of Negro Education* 53:3 (1984): 257-267.

41. St. Clair Drake, "The Black Studies Movement," in Joseph E. Harris (ed.), *Global Dimensions of the African Diaspora* (Washington, DC: Howard University Press, 1993): 491-495.

42. See Beverly Guy-Sheftall (ed.), *Words of Fire: An Anthology of African American Feminist Thought* (New York: The New Press, 1995): 451.

43. Gloria T. Hull, Patricia Bell Scott, Barbara Smith (eds.), *All the Women are White, All the Blacks are Men, But Some of Us are Brave* (New York: Feminist Press, 1982).

44. See Kilson note 19.

45. Russell L. Adams, "Intellectual Questions and Imperatives in the Development of Afro-American Studies," *Journal of Negro Education* 53:3 (1984): 201-225.

46. In recent years, the ideology of Afrocentricity as a theoretical perspective has become nearly synonymous with Black Studies as a discipline. African American Studies should be constructed as a set of theoretical perspectives, rather than a single theoretical perspective. See Tilden J. Lemelle, "The Status of Black Studies in the Second Decade: The Ideological Imperative," in James Turner (ed.), *The Next Decade: Research and Theoretical Issues in Africana Studies* (Ithaca, NY: Cornell University Center for Research in Africana Studies, 1984).

47. See Maulana Karenga, "Black Studies and the Problematic of Paradigm: The Philosophical Dimension," *Journal of Black Studies* 18:4 (1988): 395-414.

48. See Molefi K. Asante, "Afrocentricity and the Quest for Method," in James L. Conyers, Jr. (ed.), *African Studies* (North Carolina: McFarland and Company, Inc., 1997): 69-90.

49. See Asante, note 48.

50. While there are a number of texts that are utilized in African American Studies introductory courses, the overwhelming majority are authored by a single individual and do not represent the various perspectives of the history, development, and significance of African American Studies as an academic discipline. Moreover, the anthologies that are utilized are usually incorporated into courses that focus on history, literature, sociology, and psychology. See "Black Studies 101: Introductory Courses Reflect a Field Still Defining Itself," *The Chronicle of Higher Education* 46:37 (May 2000): A20-A21.

51. Contrary to the beliefs of many external observers and critics, there exist a wide variety of theoretical, philosophical, cultural, political, and pedagogical perspectives within the field of African American Studies. See Russell L. Adams, "Intellectual Questions and Impera-

tives in the Development of Afro-American Studies," *Journal of Negro Education* 53:3 (Summer 1984): 201-225.

52. See James Upton, "Applied Black Studies: Adult Education in the Black Community—A Case Study," *Journal of Negro Education* 53:3 (Summer 1984): 322-333.

53. See Shirley Webber, "Intellectual Imperatives and Necessity for Black Education," in James Turner (ed.), *The Next Decade: Theoretical and Research Issues in Africana Studies* (Ithaca, NY: Africana Studies and Research Center, Cornell University, 1984): 63-75.

54. John Henrik Clarke, "Africana Studies: A Decade of Change, Challenge, and Conflict," in James Turner (ed.), *The Next Decade: Theoretical and Research Issues in Africana Studies* (Ithaca, NY: Cornell University Center for Africana Studies and Research, 1984): 31-47.

55. James Turner, "Africana Studies and Epistemology: A Discourse in the Sociology of Knowledge," in Turner (1984), v-xxv.

56. See Floyd W. Hayes, III, "Taking Stock: African American Studies at the Edge of the Twenty-First Century," *Western Journal of Black Studies* 18:3 (June 1994): 153-163.

57. Maulana Karenga, *Introduction to Black Studies* (Los Angeles: University of Sankore Press, 1993): 504-505.

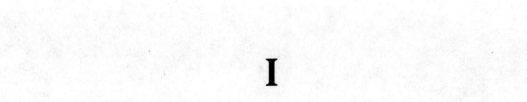

I

Section I

The Discipline: Definitions and Perspectives

Key Concepts and Major Terms

- Discipline
- Field of Study
- Area of Inquiry
- Interdisciplinary
- Multidisciplinary
- Black Intellectuals
- Program
- Black Studies
- White Studies
- Structural Issues
- White Universities

- Department
- Curriculum
- Paradigm
- Afrocentrism
- Nile Valley Afrocentrists
- Continental Afrocentrists
- Afrocentricity
- Ethnic Studies
- Research
- Epistemology
- Core Courses

- Marxist-Leninists
- Accommodationist
- Social Afrocentrists
- Afrocentric Infusionists
- Ideology
- Black Students Movement
- Traditional Disciplines
- Established Disciplines
- Quantitative Suggestion
- Qualitative Model
- Evaluation Model

Introduction

Since its inception, one of the major points of contention surrounding African American Studies has been whether it warrants scholarly recognition and functions as an individual, independent academic discipline, or merely as a subfield which is attendant to "traditional" areas in the social sciences. As the discipline has developed, we have still been confronted with some of the early questions that were posed as African American Studies became an integral part of higher education during the late 1960s and early 1970s. Thus, fundamental arguments about the nature of the discipline still exist: Is it an independent discipline? What nomenclature is most appropriate? Is it interdisciplinary or multidisciplinary? Should it focus solely on African Americans or include the experiences of the continent and rest of the diaspora? What ideology, methodology, and theoretical constructs should inform and dictate the content and structure of African American Studies? Has the original mandate of community responsibility and empowerment been followed and/or (effectively) maintained?

Each essay in this section describes a perspective from which to view African American Studies and argues its advantages over other perspectives. Yet, whether one looks at African American Studies as a discipline or as area studies, the contributions of African American scholars during the last thirty years have been significant. The academic discourse generated by it has provided historical, political and sociological data that have been at the center of debates surrounding higher education. However the field is defined and from whatever perspective, the strongest argument is for a disciplinary structure. DeVere Pentony's opening article can be seen as an attempt to provide a strong case for African American Studies in the academy. In "The Case for Black Studies," he describes the intellectual, social and moral importance of African American Studies, and he argues for the major focus of African American Studies to be on helping blacks discover their identity and to prepare leadership for the black community. With this position, Pentony supports Nathan Hare's responses to questions relevant to the development of the disciplines.

As chair of the first ever Black Studies department, Nathan Hare provided some of the earliest answers to questions regarding how the discipline would be constructed. In "Questions and Answers About Black Studies," Hare explains...that "A Black Studies Program may be divided into two phases—the expressive and the pragmatic. The expressive phase refers to the effort to build in black youth a sense of pride of self, of collective destiny, a sense of pastness...in the quest for a new and better future. It also refers to deracicize white students.... The pragmatic phase operates specifically to prepare black students to deal with their society."

John Blassingame contends that African American Studies creates a crisis for black intellectuals and white universities. In "Black Studies: An Intellectual Crisis," he notes, worriedly that "Black Studies is too serious an intellectual sphere, has too many exciting possibilities of finally liberating the racially shackled American mind, for intellectuals to shirk their responsibility to organize academically respectable programs. This possibility of curricular innovation must not be used to establish totally different programs, segregated entirely from traditional schemes."

The next three articles in this section take up the discussion of the content and structure of African American Studies. Martin Kilson's article presents the viewpoint that the discipline must establish and demand high criteria for students who select the area of study and that only qualified faculty be allowed to teach in the field. He also describes how programs should be structured and administered and the institutional role of the discipline, since he fears the politicization of departments and programs by militants. Similarly, James B. Stewart argues for a cadre of scholars to construct the discipline focusing on the contributions of scholars from traditional disciplines. He writes in "Field and Function of Black Studies" that "Many scholarly contributions to Black Studies have been produced under the auspices of traditional disciplines but have also provided data that undergird Black Studies as a disciplinary development.... If Black Studies is to become a truly self-perpetuating discipline, a cadre of scholars must be trained under the auspices of Black Studies. Darlene Clark Hine provides an overview of African American Studies and universities' administrators and faculty attitudes towards the discipline. She discusses various curriculum models, undergraduate and graduate degree programs and how Africana Studies has achieved legitimacy and has become institutionalized within higher education.

Philip Daniel's influential article discusses the need to formulate African American Studies as a discipline. In "Black Studies: Discipline or Field of Study," he asserts: "The fact that the other disciplines are not substitutable and that Black Studies may require a different set of constructs does not necessarily categorize Black Studies as a discipline. Neither does it mean that Black Studies is any less than other fields of study because it does not yet conform to all traditional discipline requirements."

The last four articles by Carlos A. Brossard, LeRoi Ray, Jr., Donald Henderson, and Russell L. Adams provide extended analyses which attempt to define African American Studies programs.

In "Classifying Black Studies Programs," Carlos A. Brossard states "Black Studies, since 1968, has rarely been permitted to be a single-task, highly goal-focused, exclusively academic enterprise. Consequently, no single behavioral definition of Black Studies prevails. Essentially, any definition of Black Studies emerges from pluralistic praxis, not grand theory."

Furthermore, LeRoi Ray, Jr., holds that the struggle for justice and freedom is central to an understanding of the role of Black Studies. However, every aspect of Black Studies, every effort in the instructional program is designed to accomplish certain basic objectives, which benefit black people, some of which are in direct confrontation with the interests of the white majority. Can a Black Studies program on a white university campus be successful...and if the answer is yes, then...who will assess and evaluate Black Studies at white universities?"

In "What Directions Black Studies," Donald Henderson observes that "In most cases Black Studies programs, however they are constructed, have their reasons for existence firmly based in political considerations and were only rarely introduced as academic undertakings in the host institutions...Black Studies, like any other legitimate intellectual endeavor, must be left free to become whatever its dedicated scholars are capable of making it. Anything less than that will prove intellectually dishonest and will ultimately work to the disadvantage of both black and non-black peoples...."

The last article in this section, Russell L. Adams' "African American Studies and the State of the Art," provides a comprehensive historical overview of the status of curriculum development, research, ideological position, political, theoretical, and paradigm constructs relevant to the discipline. The selections in Section I were chosen to illustrate the challenges involved during the last three decades in defining and developing African American Studies as a valid and intellectual academic discipline. They demonstrate the conscientious attempts of scholars to re-envision the boundaries of Black Studies to reinvigorate the material it addresses and to review its function for both its students and the university communities at large.

1.

The Case for Black Studies

DeVere E. Pentony

The history of the development of various American groups into an integrated culture is a complex story, but there is one simple fact that seems germane to the problems of black-white integration in the United States. This obvious fact is that almost every immigrant group with the major exception of the blacks came to these shores because they wanted to come. America was to be the land of opportunity, the land where the rigidities for social mobility would be relaxed, and the land where a man could be free. That these expectations were not quickly fulfilled is a cloudy part of the political and social history of the United States, but in retrospect the members of most of these groups — the Irish, the Germans, the Dutch, the Scotch, the Italians — now view the story of their ethnic past in the United States as a reasonably successful one.

No similar memories have been available to the black man and woman. Brought to this country in chains, torn from family and tribal past, physically and psychologically enslaved, taught by lash and example to be subservient, forced to suffer indignities to their basic humanity, and instantly categorized by the accident of color, black people have all too often found the American dream a nightmare. Instead of joining the dominant culture, many have learned to exist in the psychologically bewildering atmosphere neither slave nor free. That they have survived at all is tribute to their magnificent resiliency and basic toughness; but that some carry with them a heavy baggage of hate and rage is not surprising.

While many whites in America have congratulated themselves upon the progress toward freedom and equality that has recently been made, a number of black intellectuals are eloquently questioning whether, indeed, meaningful progress has been made. Perhaps blacks are all too familiar with the ability of white people to dash black hopes for freedom and dignity on rocks of intransigence and patience. Witness the rise and fall of hope in the story of black men in America in the aftermath of the Civil War they were told that they were freed from slavery only to find that they were not free — not free to be treated as individuals, not free to eat, or sleep, or live, or go to school, or drink from the same fountain, or ride the same conveyance, or enjoy the same political and economic privileges as people of "white" skin. And when in the twentieth century they had their hopes raised by long overdue court decisions and civil rights legislation finally demanding integration, these hopes were once again shattered as blacks found that significant segments of the white culture often lagged far behind the basic justice of these acts.

This has led some of the black community to question whether integration was not just another scheme to preserve the dominance of the whites, seducing blacks to give up their black identities and to copy the speech, manner, hair, dress, and style of the whites, and to accept the myths, heroes, and historical judgment of white America without reciprocity or without appreciation of, or respect for, black experience. Moreover, this estimate has been coupled with the hunch that in any significant way, only the "talented tenth" of the black community could really hope to overcome the monetary, social, and psychological barriers to true integration with whites. The remaining 90 percent would, therefore, be left in poverty and psychological degradation, doomed to an almost motiveless, hopeless existence, forever on the dole, forever caught in hate of self and of others. Thus has been posed a transcendent dilemma for the black man and woman: to succeed in the white world is to fail, to overcome the outrageous obstacles thrown in their way by white society seems partially to deny their black experience. Above all, to integrate on an individual basis in a society that makes this increasingly possible for the fortunate may well mean an exodus of the talented tenth from the black community, with the consequent decimation of the ranks of potential leaders whose commitment to the whole community could help set their people free.

Seen in this light, the demand for black studies is a call for black leadership. The argument is that if there is to be an exodus from the land of physical and psychological bondage, an informed and dedicated leadership is needed to help bring about individual and group pride and a sense of cohesive community. To accomplish this, black people, like all people, need to know that they are not alone. They need to know that their ancestors were not just slaves laboring under the white man's sun but that their lineage can be traced to important kingdoms and significant civilizations. They need to be familiar with the black man's contribution to the arts and sciences. They need to know of black heroes and of the noble deeds of black men. They need to know that black, too, is beautiful, and that under the African sky people are at proud ease with their blackness. In historical perspective they need to know the whole story of white oppression and of the struggles of some blacks, and some whites too, to overcome that oppression. They need to find sympathetic encouragement to move successfully into the socioeconomic arenas of American life.

To help fulfill all these needs, the contention is, a black studies effort must be launched. At the beginning, it must be staffed by black faculty, who must have the time and resources to prepare a solid curriculum for college students and to get the new knowledge and new perspectives into the community as quickly as possible. In a situation somewhat similar to the tremendous efforts at adult education in some of the less developed societies, the advocates of black studies press to get on with the urgent tasks.

It is in this context that a basic challenge is made to many of the traditional values of the college or university. Important critical questions arise: Will black studies be merely an exchange of old lies for new myths? Is it the work of the college to provide an ideological underpinning for social movement? Will the traditional search for the truth be subordinated to the goal of building a particular group identity? Is the ideal of the brotherhood of all men to be sacrificed to the brotherhood of some men and the hatred of others? Can the college teach group solidarity for some groups and not for others? Will the results of separatist studies be a heightening of group tensions and a reactive enlarging of the forces of racism? Will standards of excellence for students and faculty alike be cast aside in the interest of meeting student and community needs? Will anti-intellectualism run rampant? Will constitutional and other legal provisions be violated by this new version of "separate if not equal?"

A Remedy for White Studies

It seems clear that the advocates of a black studies program see it as a remedy for "white studies" programs that they have been subjected to all their lives and as a way to bring pride, dignity, and community to black people. They are questioning the relevance of the style and content of education designed to meet the needs and expectations of the dominant white culture, and some seem to be suggesting that the lifestyles and ways of perceiving the world in much of the black community are sufficiently different to justify a new, almost bicultural approach to educating the members of the community who are at once a part of, yet apart from, the general American culture. While they hope that this effort will range over the whole educational experience from childhood through adulthood, they seem to view the college or university as the place where talents can be gathered and resources mobilized to provide intellectual leadership and academic respectability to their efforts. The college is to be the place for the writing of books, the providing of information, and the training of students to help with the critical tasks. It is to be one of the testing grounds for the idea that black people need to have control of their own destiny.

But what of the outcome? There is obvious concern that efforts to focus on blackness as one of the answers to white racism will result in an equally virulent black racism. Black "nationalism," with its glorifying of the black in-group, may have powerful meaning only when it focuses on the hate object of whiteness. Indeed, it is painfully true that whites through their words and deeds over many generations have provided the black nationalists with all the bitter evidence they need for building a negative nationalism based mainly on hatred and rage. Thus we should expect that a significant ingredient in constructing black unity and group dignity would be an antiwhiteness.

Increasingly, the black intellectual is drawing a colonial analogy to the situation of the black community in the United States. Like people in the colonized lands of Asia, Africa, and Latin America, some black men look at their rather systematic exclusion from first-class citizenship in the United States as a close parallel to the exploitation and subjugation perpetrated by those who shouldered the "white man's burden" during the high tide of imperialism. Thus the focus on black culture and black history is to prepare the black community to be as free and proud as anyone in the newly emerging states. And the outcome of that may be the growth of the self-confidence and sense of personal dignity that pave the way for an easier integration into a common culture on the basis of feelings of real equality.

While it would be foolish to deny that ugly and self-defeating racism may be the fruits of the black studies movement, we should not forget that a sense of deep compassion and intense concern for all humanity has often shone through the rage and hate of such prophets of the movement as Malcolm X, Stokely Carmichael, and W.E.B. DuBois. Whether that hopeful strain of compassion and human concern will gain the upper hand in the days that lie ahead may well depend on the degree of understanding and tenderness with which the white community is able to react to these efforts.

There is the possibility that an emphasis on blackness, black dignity, black contributions, and black history will provide whites with new perspectives about the black man and woman. In turn, these new perspectives may indicate what clues of behavior and guides to proper responsiveness are necessary to enable whites to relate to blacks in something other than a patronizing or deprecating fashion. Through black studies there may be opportunities for whites to enrich their understanding of the black man and thus, perhaps, to help build more meaningful bridges of mutual respect and obligation. Moreover, if the truth can make blacks free and open, it may also free the whites from their ignorant stereotypes of the black man and his culture. Unfortunately, it may also be possible for those who teach black studies to reinforce those stereotypes by aping the worst features of the white society and becoming merely a mirror image of that aspect of white society that is insensitive and inhuman.

Standards and Scholarship

Will accepted standards and scholarship be maintained in the black studies program? When any new program is proposed, a question of this sort is certainly appropriate for members of the academic community. However, it is an extremely difficult one to answer for a black studies program or for any other new program. All that can be safely said is that the pressures for respectable scholarly performance and for recognized achievements will be at least as great for black studies as for any other new program.

In the performance and evaluation of students, we can probably expect the same ferment over learning, grading, and evaluating practices that perturbs the rest of the academic world. But academicians who are pushing the black studies idea give no indication that they will be content with a half-hearted, sloppy, shoddy intellectual effort on the part of themselves or their students. Indeed, one of the underlying assumptions of black studies seems to be that students who become involved in it will become highly motivated toward academic success not only in black studies but in the rest of the curriculum as well. Out of the black studies experience are to come black students, committed, socially aware, ambitious, devoted to the welfare of black people, and equipped for helping the black community assume its rightful place in American society. These are high ambitions which are not likely to be fulfilled immediately by a black studies program, but which deserve to be given the same benefit of doubt and the same opportunities for growth by trial and error that most new programs are given.

Will black studies scholars manipulate data, bias their studies, and create towering myths which bear little resemblance to the shifting realities of human existence? The answer is difficult to assess.

In one respect the quest for pristine outside objectivity may miss the point. A distinguished philosopher has argued that the search for intergroup accommodation must be based upon what he terms the discovery of the normative inner order—that is, the values, assumptions, and world views or images of various societies or cultures. It may be that one of the most important roles that the black scholar can play is to share in the discovery and articulation of this normative inner order of the black community, with the possible result of improving the chances for mutually beneficial black-white interaction.

In this process we should expect that there will be black professors who profess a certain "ideology" just as white professors do. We can even expect a case for racial superiority of blacks, but surely this is not a reason for opposing black studies. To do so on those grounds would be analogous to opposing the teaching of biology because a certain biologist has attempted to make a case for a black inferiority based on some of his genetic investigations, or of economics because certain economists continue to adhere to pre-Keynesian economic principles.

Moreover, the ideology argument may mean no more than that black scholars will attempt to emphasize common assumptions about American society from the perspective of the black experience. But this kind of "indoctrination" is not essentially different from what is found, for example, in many college textbooks in American government which rest on some value-laden assumptions about the American political system. A more serious charge would be that black professors may insist that their students follow some "party line" as they examine the various facets of the black situation. But students are not as gullible as we sometimes imagine and are generally quite capable of resisting efforts at indoctrination.

Closely allied to the questions of standards and scholarship are questions of curriculum. What is an appropriate beginning curriculum for a black studies effort? The unspoken consensus seems to be that an area studies program should dig as deeply as possible into the history, the culture, the language, the politics, the economics, the geography, the literature, the arts, the life-styles, and the world views of the people in the area concerned. How this is all put together in a way that students will understand and benefit from is a significant organizing problem for all area studies programs, including black studies. But it would be foolish to expect those problems to be creatively attacked before a working faculty is on the scene. The first efforts to establish a satisfactory curriculum in black studies will be experimental in many ways and as such subject to more rapid change than our established curricula.

Are Black Studies Legal and Proper?

The question of legality of a black studies program requires examination. Like the closely related area studies program, the curriculum would seem to face no legal questions from federal or state law. However, it is in the realm of staffing and student access that the most serious questions arise. For example, can tests of color be applied for hiring faculty members in the black studies program? Posed in this sharp way, the answer to the question is probably no. The equal protection of the laws section of the United States Constitution and various state legal requirements about nondiscrimination in employment could very likely be interpreted to preclude the hiring of faculty simply because they are black. However, if the qualifications for hiring are put on a broader experiential basis than color alone, then the questions and answers may change. Already factors of ethnic background and experience play a role in hiring at the colleges and universities in the United States. While this is particularly obvious in the hiring of teachers in foreign languages and literature — note, for example, the number of people teaching Chinese language and literature who are Chinese-ethnic background has often been considered in other aspects of area studies and other programs from the Peace Corps to social work.

The question of hiring black faculty is probably not a legal question at all. Rather the critical focal point for the black studies program would seem to be, on the one hand, whether the particular experiences gained from a black ethnic background tend to make the faculty member a better scholar and teacher or, on the other hand, whether the ethnic emotional involvement will permit a useful scholarly detachment in the evaluation and presentation of data. Completely satisfactory answers to this dilemma are not likely to be found. A short-run solution to the dilemma may rest on the ability of black studies programs to attract black faculty with a passion for the truth as well as an emotional identification with the subject of blackness, and on the certainty that nonblack scholars will continue to view, comment upon, and analyze the black experience in various parts of the academic community. Enough flexibility and openness should exist for students majoring in black studies to encounter the views of nonblack scholars. Similarly, the educational experiences of the rest of the academic community would undoubtedly be enriched by the participation of black studies faculty in the general intellectual life of the college. It would be tragic if the black studies faculty were to be prevented from commentary on the general questions of man in society by their own preoccupation with black studies. Few would argue that the infusion of all increasing number of black faculty into the academic community is not desirable. The black studies program would speed the process and provide the black community with incentives and opportunities for greater participation in the education of youth. The institutions of higher education cannot rely on narrow legal interpretation and conventional dogmas as trustworthy guidelines to hiring faculty in programs like black studies.

A second serious question about the legality of the black studies program is the question of student access to it. Can an academic institution worthy of the name deny access to any of its academic programs on the basis of color or ethnic background? The answer is no. Here the legal answer and the moral answer would seem to reinforce one another. If one of the purposes of the blacks studies program is to tell it as it really is, then the message should go out to students regardless of color even though it is likely to have a particular additional value to the black student. The college cannot be a place where knowledge is developed and subjects taught in semi-secret. Just as any college contracting to the government for secret research would be open to serious charge of violation of the traditional ethics of scholarship, so would any academic program that excluded students solely on the basis of ethnic background raise serious questions of propriety and legality.

However, even in this connection a dilemma remains. As anyone who has participated in an area program in a Peace Corps training effort knows, the things that can be easily said about one's own culture and about another culture tend to be modified when there are members of another culture in attendance. It seems to become more difficult to tell it "as it really is" or at least as it "really is perceived" when the outsiders are in. This is a significant problem that will have to be faced by the black studies program. The fortunate thing about many of those who are advocating black studies is that they want to tell it as it really is to anyone who will listen. They have been shielding their feelings, perceptions, and analyses so long that it will probably be refreshing for them to speak honestly with nonblack students as well as blacks. Nonetheless, they may feel that the first efforts to get their programs established will be so overrun by well-meaning whites anxious to gain new perspectives that black students will not have access to the courses.

In practice, the problem may not be so great, especially since courses about various ethnic communities will continue to be offered in the existing departments, with even the possibility of exchange of faculty on occasion. Nonetheless, the colleges must make every effort within the budgetary limitations imposed upon them to accommodate as many students as possible. No black student who enters the college should be denied an opportunity to take black studies courses; neither, of course, should he be forced to do so. In this connection, the attractiveness of the course offerings to whites as well as blacks may be important in the effort to sustain enrollments in a fledgling program, and thus help provide the necessary resources which are closely tied to the level of student demand for courses. So, the question of student access seems to be not so much a question of legality as of the availability of faculty and other resources.

A sometime country lawyer once said: "The dogmas of the quiet past are inadequate to the stormy present. The occasion is piled high with difficulty, and we must rise to the occasion. As our case is new, so we must think anew and act anew. We must disenthrall ourselves, and then we shall save the country" (Abraham Lincoln). The time is now for higher education to show that it can disenthrall itself and become relevant to the problems of social change highlighted by the call for black studies. If a black studies program serves only to awaken whites to the desperate need to change themselves, it will have been worth the effort.

2.

Questions and Answers About Black Studies

Nathan Hare

1. What would a sample curriculum or program of black studies look like?

A Black Studies Program may be divided into two phases — the expressive and the pragmatic. The expressive phase refers to the effort to build in black youth a sense of pride or self, of collective tiny, a sense of pastness as a springboard in the quest for a new and better future. It also refers to the effort to deracicize white students. It revolves around such courses as black history and black art and culture but hinges on applicability ("relevance") to the black community and its needs.

The pragmatic phase operates specifically to prepare black students to deal with their society. The student's ultimate use of his pragmatic skills can be directed toward overcoming (or, if need be, over-throwing) his handicaps in dealing with his society. The pragmatic phase, in either case, is highly functional: courses producing socio-economic skills (black politics, black economics, black science, black communications, and so forth), extensive field work and community involvement in collaboration with classroom activities.

For instance, students in a course even so abstract and non-functional (in the conventional view) as black history would have as a requirement some participation in panel discussions for younger children in church basements or elementary and junior high schools. A class project might be the establishment of a black history club. The possibilities are even greater, of course, for such subjects as black economics, black politics, black journalism and the like, where students additionally should do apprenticeships and field work in connection with classroom discussions. Thus the student gets a more "relevant" education, testing out theories learned (in the laboratory of life against experiences and observations and experimentation in his community). As education is made more relevant to the black community and its needs, the community is, so to speak, made more relevant to (or involved in) the educational process.

The mere presence of a black college student in the black slum, tutoring black youth and engaged in course-connected activities, would provide role models for youth who ordinarily would not come into intimate contact with college students and their orientation.

Here follows a sample black studies curriculum, already approved by the California State College Trustees and instituted at San Francisco State College. Bear in

13

mind that these courses and their descriptions are experimental and subject to change, as in the case of any new curriculum. Also, the curriculum was influenced heavily by the current necessity for approval by liberal-moderate administrators. And yet that is no real handicap here. In any case, a revolutionary program could be written but taught by a squad of Uncle Toms and we would still wind up with a "chitlin education." The key to success resides in the professors and, accordingly, in who has the power to hire and fire them.

A student receiving the bachelor's degree in black studies would be required to take the six core courses, to choose electives (24 units) in his area of concentration within the black studies program, and nine electives from throughout the college, on advisement from the black studies department. The rest of his units, some 76 or more in most colleges, would consist of general electives.

Core Courses:

101. Black History (3 units). African cultures from the Iron Age to the present; European colonization, contemporary nationalism; black cultural and scientific contributions, African and American. Political, economic, and social aspects of slavery and the contemporary black movement.

102. Black Math (3). Presentation of mathematics as a way of thinking, a means of communication and an instrument of problem solving, with special reference to the black community, using references from black experiences where possible for illustrative and reading-problem material. Deductive, inductive, and heuristic methods of mathematics are developed and used with special attention to application to the black community's needs.

193. Black Psychology (3). Introduction to the basic concepts of psychology with emphasis on their application to the life problems of black Americans. The scientific study of black behavior.

104. Black Science (3). Introduction to scientific development stressing the contributions of black scientists. Emphasis on the application of fundamental concepts and methods of science to the environment of black Americans.

105. Black Philosophy. The foundations of black philosophies as related to theories of knowledge and thought considered within the social and political context.

106. Black arts and Humanities (3). Introduction to, and exploration of, primary works by black artists and writers with special attention to values expressed in their works and values held by black students. Formation and development of black culture.

107. Literature of Blackness (3). A beginning course in the study of black literature, including methods of evaluation and analysis essential for understanding and appreciation.

108. Black Writers' Workshop (6). Advanced composition with special reference to the portrayal of the black experience. Group discussions as well as supervision of individual projects, apprenticeships, and class project.

109. Black Intellectuals (3). Major social and political thought within the black race from ancient Africa to the present. Analysis of the historical and cultural context with in-depth analysis of major black thinkers.

110. Black Fiction (3). Major contributions to black fiction, considered in relation to the development of poetic traditions and prose styles, with special reference to the history of black intellectuals. Examination of the style and techniques of representative black writers.

111. *Black Poetry* (3). Examination of structure, style, and techniques of representative black poets.

112. *The Painting of Blackness* (3). Fundamental concepts of the black aesthetic orientation and the black experience. Work with color, light, space, and motion in relation to major styles in black painting.

113. *The Music of Blackness* (3). Analysis of styles and techniques of major traditions in black music. Fundamentals of music reading and theory applied through development of basic skills in singing, conducting, and playing black music.

114. *Black Drama.* Introduction to the art of acting, including theory and technique with emphasis upon resources, methods, characterization, stage movement and business, using the social and art influences affecting black people as a frame of reference. Individual projects in selected aspects.

115. *Black Radio, Television, Film* (6). Special problems of radio, television, and/or film production in relation to black persons and the black community. Work on various programs with direct faculty supervision.

116. *Black Journalism* (6). The history, social role, function, and organization of the print and broadcast media in relation to black Americans. Field experience, apprenticeships, and supervised projects.

117. *Black Oratory* (6). Oratory as part of the black American political, social, and intellectual history; issues, ideas, spokesmen, and method of advocacy. Supervised study and experience.

118. *Black Classics* (3). Society, literature, thought, and art and their interrelationships in ancient and modern Africa, early and current America. Intensive humanistic study of black works in literature, the fine arts, history, philosophy, and the sciences of man.

119. *Sociology of Blackness* (6). Major features of black American society. Application of the principles and concepts of sociology and social change to analysis of movements for black parity.

120. *Black Politics* (6). The political values, structure and behavior of black Americans. Theories, problems, and issues relating to the political behavior of black Americans. Apprenticeships and supervised practicum.

121. *Economics of the Black Community* (6). Economic and social development of the black community from the slave trade to the present. Problems and growth of black economic enterprise, with field experience and supervised practicum.

122. *Geography of Blackness* (3). Location and geographic distribution of black people and black political and economic activities. Relationship of physical environment, population, and social-political factors of the black community. Special attention to the urban geography of blackness.

123. *Social Organization of Blackness* (6). Applications of the concepts of social organization to black institutions an interrelationships of black organizations. The social structure of the black community covering organizational patterns, leadership, cleavage and conflict, and planning and development of the black community, with field experience, apprenticeships, and practicum.

124. *Development of Black Leadership* (6). Analysis the black community power structure; changing patterns of the leadership, influence, and decision-making in the black community with supervised individual and group projects.

125. Black Counseling (6). The counseling process and counseling problems will be considered in relation to the black child as well as the dynamics of black-white relations; issues and legal aspects of counseling the black child. Clinical practicum and experience.

126. Demography of Blackness (3). Changes in quantity, composition, and distribution of black population throughout the world with special emphasis on the United States. The implications for the black race and its development will be stressed along application of theory and methods of population analysis to the black race.

127. Black Nationalism and the International Community (3). Analysis of the sources of black nationalism and its nature; major concepts, nomenclature, and symbols in relation to the rise of the black race in the international arena. The effect of international relations and its effect on international relations will be explored.

128. The Anthropology of Blackness (6). An examination of the peoples of Africa and blacks in other lands with emphasis upon the arts, customs, industries and social structure. Cultural origins and influences upon the western world, and the United States in particular, will be examined.

129. Black Consciousness (3). Analysis of the nature and trends of black consciousness through history. Intensive study of the psychology and sociology of the process and development of thinking black.

130. Black Statistics: Survey and Method (6). Analysis of the pitfalls and safeguards in statistical research on matters of race. Techniques of measuring, tabulating, analyzing, and interpreting statistical data, using examples and illustrative materials from the black community. Apprenticeships and supervised projects.

131. Black Economic Workshop (6). The structure, behavior and results of black economic enterprise and the policies appropriate to black social objectives. Apprenticeships and supervised projects.

132. Black Political Workshop (6). Direct investigation, analysis, and evaluation of political activities of black Americans. Current developments and issues concerning basic approaches to the acquisition of political power. Individual involvement in politics through group and organizational affiliations. Field work in local government offices and community services.

2. Should the aim of every Black Studies Program be to serve and transform the black community? If so, how is that aim best achieved: by, let us say, high-powered research institutes, "think-tank" centers, experimental and innovative programs that include extensive field work and relations with the black community, changing the usual degree or credential requirements, "beefing up" or ignoring traditional notions of academic soundness in black studies courses?

While we have no wish to appear disdainful of research in any form, it is our considered judgment that enough research has already been done to suit our current needs. There are studies on "Negroes and Potato Growing in South Georgia," "Negroes and the Consumption of Watermelons in Maine." And yet people still maintain their ignorance of what is wrong — or even that there is really something wrong — let alone about what we need to do about it. Four major white universities this year received $1 million from the Ford Foundation alone to study "the Negro." We believe that they have been studying the wrong man. We want $10 million from Ford to study the white man.

Actually, the problem is one of application of the knowledge we already have. The late great W.E.B.DuBois, who was the father of the modern scientific study of the black condition, eventually came to the realization that knowledge is not enough, that people know pretty much what needs to be done if they would only act. And so, he switched, in his own words, "from science to propaganda."

The notion that "academic soundness" would suffer is basically a racist apprehension, a feeling that any deviation on the part of blacks away from white norms and standards inevitably would dip downward. It also is based, perhaps, on the naive notion that traditional education is value-free and, because it is based on the ideology of the existing political forces, is blessed with "the end of ideology." That is, most emphatically, not the case. The whole need for black studies grows out of the current lack of true academic soundness in the educational system as we know it now. A key test of soundness for any structure is whether or not it works. Obviously our current educational system does not work for a growing number of black and oppressed "minorities" whose backgrounds and experiences have not coincided with those of white suburbia.

The matter of "qualifications" particularly is often farcical. The fact that even I.Q. tests, let alone achievement tests, too clearly fail to measure precisely what they purport to measure is now well known even among academicians. Besides, many persons eventually find success in a field outside their college field of studies. Even when they do achieve success within their own fields they are likely to be lifted out of that endeavor and made administrators over their inferiors who actually work in that field. Few public administrators are trained in public administration and few politicians or public officials have had more than the ordinary number of courses in political science. Most of what people learn in college is irrelevant to the actual performance of their specialty anyway. This observation was corroborated by the survey described in the book, *The Miseducation of American Teachers*, where a national cross-sample of teachers admitted that their courses even in the methodology of teaching had not prepared them for teaching, a skill they had to learn on the job.

Yet, despite the fact that most teachers report learning how to teach on the job, from tips culled from co-workers, most major school systems seldom honor more than five or six years of the teaching experience of teachers recruited from other cities. Recently, a black teacher from the District of Columbia applied to teach in San Francisco. Although she had been named by the Junior Chamber of Commerce previously as the Outstanding Young Educator for the District of Columbia, she was told by the personnel clerk that only persons of high quality are hired in San Francisco. She indicated that she had a master's degree plus thirty hours beyond and had taught for twelve years in such places as Chicago, the District of Columbia, Oklahoma and Virginia. She then was told she would have to pass the National Teachers Exam, whereupon she replied that she had passed that exam both in her special field and one other. She was informed that she would only be able to teach in San Francisco after she had taken five additional courses such as California history!

3. Should admission to Black Studies Programs be limited to black students? What then will likely be the effect of a recent HEW memorandum warning college officials they risk losing federal funds if they sanction such exclusion?

Admission to Black Studies in general should not be limited to black students; though, where there are not sufficient facilities to cover everybody, black students should receive priority because for them black studies are doubly therapeutic. However, a racist society cannot be healed merely by solving the problems of its black victims alone. The black condition does not exist in a vacuum; we cannot solve the problems of the black race without solving the problems of the society which produced and sustains the predicament of blacks. At the same time as we transform the black community, through course-related community activities, white students duplicating this work in their communities — predominantly — may operate to transform the white community and thus a racist American society.

White students also need educational relevance. For example, in place of foreign languages they seldom use, even when they learn them well enough, they might better be required to take courses in law along with their "civics" and English, algebra, geometry, trigonometry and the like. This would not put lawyers out of business anymore than algebra and trigonometry and French now put mathematicians and interpreters out of business. But it would seem to be more relevant to their lives as well as their performance in their various occupations. More particularly, an education which largely ignores the study of the black race and its problems, one of the gravest problems facing America, if not the entire world, is gravely irrelevant. No solution to the world's problems can come about without a solution to the problems of color conflict. White students frequently seem to know this intuitively, even if their learned elders pretend to be ignorant of this fact. They cry to get into black studies courses, not the least because they find their traditional courses typically so empty.

Understand me, black studies is based ideally on the ideology of revolutionary nationalism; it is not based on any form of racism, black or white, though it is dedicated, of course, to the destruction of white racism. Which may be why the establishment seems so determined (chiefly by way of its mass media) to confuse black students into a search for tangential, ultra-separatist goals such as separate dormitories, chitterlings in the cafeteria, and similar diversions having little to do with changing seriously the power relations of blacks and whites, let alone the nature of education. The media rush to play up such demands as "militant," leading black students who identify with militant blackness to seek divergent ends. Once students fall into this trap, the government (through HEW) rushes in with its "opposition" to such ultra-separatist goals. This sidetracks us onto insignificant battlefields.

This is no simple game; the quest for liberation cannot be based on absolutist notions, symbolic aspirations which enslave one's strategy, nor any other reaction-formation to the methods of white oppression. Black studies is nationalistic, not separatist. All separatists in a sense are nationalists but not all nationalists are separatists. Separatism or cultural nationalism may be a first stage of revolutionary nationalism, but it tends too often to be preoccupied with molding a cultural nexus and is therefore likely to get bogged down in that effort. Revolutionary nationalism by contrast seeks to transfer power, at least a portion thereof, to an oppressed group, and in that effort is more tolerant of white radicals.

4. Should black teachers for programs in white institutions be recruited from southern Negro colleges? What role can and should the Negro college play?

Black students do have a deep and abiding need for black professors as role models, particularly in black studies. Where these professors come from is not so important as what kind of professors they are. We hear much these days about a so-called "brain drain on Negro colleges." Just what brains they refer to I do not know. It is conceivable that these brains have been lying dormant all this time, but it is not likely in any case that they will suddenly come alive and function in an altogether different manner just because they migrate North to a white college. It is interesting to me that many of the same persons who once said that Negro colleges should not steal or pull away potentially token blacks from white colleges now wail that white colleges should not pull blacks from Negro colleges.

Ideally, Negro colleges should play the role of devising a new black ideology and a new black ethics (had we forgotten that academic "disciplines" teach ethics?). Negro colleges should be setting the pace and providing models of scholarly excellence and inquiry into the problems of color—the "problem of the twentieth century"—comprising laboratories for experimentation in the techniques and tactics of revolutionary change. But we do not believe in miracles. The Negro college is glued to the mores of its missionary origins. It is located invariably in the South, cemented to the prevailing cake of conservatism, and less free politically even than the typical white college there. Rather than address itself seriously to the solution of the problems of academia, the Negro college has been more inclined to ape and compound white trivia and miseducation.

We do not have any more time for dreams that already have been contaminated by the elements of nightmare. What happens to the Negro college ultimately is a matter for history to relate. Meanwhile, we cannot be anchored in excessive, time-consuming lamentation over decaying bodies. The Negro colleges, let us not forget, were established by the southern power structure. One doubts that the motivation was revolution for blacks in the South, let alone the North.

5. What, if any, may be the role of the white scholar in such programs (in such fields, say, as race relations, or Negro history and literature, where a person has made or continues to make important contributions; or in courses that require specialists the black community may not be able to supply; or courses that don't necessarily require a black experience as part of the person's qualification)?

There is going to be a need for some white scholars (who can qualify emotionally and ideologically) to help teach black education to white students. They would be more attuned to the white community and better able to arrange the relevant field work experiences there for white students in the white community.

The primary reluctance to admit white professors to the black studies program—aside from the present need for black role models on college faculties and the relative inability of white professors to operate within the framework of revolutionary-compensatory-black nationalism—is the tendency for whites, because of their recent socio-historical conditioning, to be inclined to take over whenever they take part in black enterprises.

Still, we need not be sidetracked into the refusal to hire a single white professor, resisting the government's policy of tokenism prematurely and unnecessarily. If the white race can perpetuate white racism by hiring a black now and then, we can fight racism and mold, compensatorily, our own nationalism by adhering to the policy of tokenism as well.

6. Where and how should control of the program be vested? Should there be complete autonomy within schools? Should there be specially appointed Trustees or overseers? How do state schools and private ones differ?

The control of black studies programs must, of course, be vested in the black community just as the control over white education indeed both Negro and white education—is presently vested in the white community. Special trustees or review boards may be established if necessary, but when revolutionary black nationalists call for a department of black studies they do not mean a separate department but a distinct or autonomous one. Nay more: self-determination or ultimate authority in determining their educational destiny.

Too often of course they are given black studies programs which merely represent black carbon copies of conventional education when they are given any autonomy at all. There must be complete autonomy at least, if not clear sovereignty. Autonomy gives the right to independence from one's oppressors and his institutions, the chance to establish one's own institutions alongside his, generally leaving political power and hence control over one's autonomous institutions in his hands. Sovereignty, or self-determination, implies supreme rank or authority. We must have sovereignty because, with mere autonomy, we would not be permitted to diverge too far from the norms and practices of existing white institutions without the probability of the sovereign axe of the oppressor falling upon our heads.

Yet the oppressor's institutional norms and practices were the source of the cry for black autonomy in the first place! It is not very reasonable, anyway, to assume that the same racist institutions (self-defined as such by the Kerner report) will suddenly reverse their present course and extend freedom where before they oppressed. It would be necessary first to reverse its norms and values, its regulations, even if it could.

This goes for private colleges as well. Their relative freedom, when it does exist, is only a matter of small degree. Many persons have advocated private schools as more realistic places to begin the implementation of black studies. But realism is a matter of definition and perception. What one perceives as reality not only may differ from person to person but neither may accord with objective reality. Why have private colleges not taken the lead? Notre Dame's president contrarily took a notoriously hard line in the other direction; the liberal University of Chicago has not stood out among recent responses to student demands; nor has Northwestern.

We can only conclude that a change has got to come within colleges as a whole; that any genuine and significant change will be resisted to the death by the powers that be; and that those of us concerned with the salvation of the black race and humanity have a lot of work to do.

3.

Black Studies: An Intellectual Crisis

John W. Blassingame

It is presumptuous of anyone to pretend to speak authoritatively on such a new development as black studies. At the end of a year fraught with the armed occupation of campus buildings and racial riots among students, I may rightfully be assigned to the camp of the foolhardy for attempting to speak on the rapidly escalating demands for increased attention to black people.

Black studies is such an emotionally loaded concept that most universities have had great difficulty in establishing programs. First of all, colleges started considered such programs at a time when the Negro community is furiously debating its place in American society. This in itself, is not new. Generally, however, this is the first time that whites have seriously considered the debate worth noting. Consequently, they are often overwhelmed by the force of the demands, confused by the rhetoric, and unsure of the legitimate intellectual response.

The first problem that one encounters in surveying black studies programs around the country is the confusion over objectives. In fact, most people who write these proposals never include objectives, goals or the justification for such programs. Instead, such ambiguous terms as "need," "demand," "relevance," or "such a program needs no justification" are used. It is inconceivable that any other kind of program could be established with so little thought being, given to long range goals. When I have asked college teachers around the country why they are establishing black studies, the usual answer has been that the black students demand them. When I ask black students what are the goals of Afro-American studies, I often get a blank stare. In one committee meeting, on black studies as a university in Washington, D.C., a Negro student demanded that thirty new courses be offered next year and a black studies department be created. When a faculty member asked what the objectives of the department would be, the student replied, "How, do you expect me, a freshman, to know?" and stormed out of the conference room.

There is often great confusion over objectives and contradictory patterns in the programs. Reacting to student demands for "relevance," a number of colleges have combined social service concepts with traditional academic pursuits. In spite of the fact that neither students nor faculty know what the students mean by "relevance," some effort is made to give students some contact with, or skills they can ostensibly carry back to, the black community. Few of them try to find out what the black community thinks is "relevant" to its needs. Then, too, such an objective clearly reveals other inconsistencies in goals. Although established at predominantly white universities apparently for all students, no consideration is given to the "relevance" of the programs to the white community. Of course, some blacks and whites argue that such programs are intended solely for Negro students.

Black students have demanded that black studies, above all else, should be "relevant" to their needs. As far as one can determine, the programs are supposed to give them pride, a sense of personal worth, and the tools for restructuring society. The attempts to fulfill the last objective are often the most confusing and contradictory aspects of the programs. Rarely is there much thought about what is needed to restructure society. Many students apparently forget that it is still true that the first requirement in any struggle is to know your enemy. What blacks need more than anything else is much more sophisticated knowledge about American society. It is not enough to know that "whitey" has been, and is, oppressing blacks; most Negroes do not have to go to college to learn that. Instead, Negroes must study business practices, high finance, labor law and practices, judicial procedures, consumer practices and the communications media.

Armed with this knowledge, blacks would know which of the interlocking corporations to boycott or buy stock in to bring about meaningful change in their economic position. Knowledge of labor unions may enable blacks to break down the almost invulnerable conspiracy to prevent blacks from earning a living that is based on the tripod of nepotism, political corruption, and prejudice. With serious study we may learn that injunctions, boycotts, campaigns for open shops in union states, government-operated apprenticeship programs, application of conspiracy laws, and other devices may force the unions to loosen their stranglehold on the black worker. While a study of the law may convince us that it is a device for oppression of the poor, we may find enough loopholes in it to afford some decree of protection to the weak. Investigation of law enforcement practices may permit Americans to regain civilian control over our quasi-military, autonomous police. A clearer understanding of the communications media may enable us not only to increase black representation in the publishing, radio, television and advertising fields, but to change white attitudes toward blacks and to create a more favorable image of blacks in the communications media. These are the things that are most "relevant" to the black community.

For many white colleges faced with the demand to lower admission standards to take in more black students, black studies represents a "soft" program that these students can pass. While I believe that it is criminal for any college to admit poorly prepared students without establishing academic support programs to help them, I do not think there is any predominantly white college that has the experience or the will to do this. If they are serious in their endeavors to establish academic support programs for poorly, prepared students, they will have to turn for advise to predominantly Negro colleges, which have had a great deal more experience in this area. Even so, a program that lacks academic respectability is of no use at all to black students and is certainly irrelevant to the black community.

The reasoning behind many of the black studies programs is more sinister than I have indicated. It is clear that in many cases predominantly white schools have deliberately organized ill-conceived programs because they are intended solely for Negro students. In short, a number of institutions are not seriously committed to Afro-American studies. Some professors at one of the leading universities in the country will approve, without question any proposal for black studies because they say "it's only for the niggers." At time when most traditional departments in state universities find it difficult to operate on a million dollar annual budget, black studies programs are established with a budget of less than a quarter of a million dollars to use for teaching, personnel *and* a plethora of community action programs. Many colleges are not seriously committed to black studies because they feel the demand will die out shortly. Consequently, rather than setting aside university funds to establish the programs, they turn to foundations for support. This, of course, is not conducive to long-term planning. As our experience with Latin American studies reveals, the cycle of foundation interest in such programs is, at most, ten years. The cycle of black studies, I predict, will be even shorter. The foundation money is likely to dry up very quickly when Mao Tse-tung perfects his intercontinental ballistic missile then, we will embark on Chinese studies.

The lack of commitment extends beyond inadequate financial support to far more serious realms. The most serious is the elimination of any required standards for teachers. While I accept many of the complaints against the traditional academic degrees, it is clear that Urban League officials and local black preachers are not, in very many cases, prepared to teach the college level courses in black studies that they have been assigned. Similarly, while I share the general arrogance of college teachers who feel they can teach anything in their general field, it is too late for most of us to retool quickly to teach topics we have ignored for twenty and thirty years. Yet, because of the lack of commitment and the urgent demand, many colleges are hiring all manner of people to teach black-oriented courses, especially if they are black. Social workers, graduate students who have just embarked on their graduate careers, high school teachers, principals, and practically anyone who looks black or has mentioned Negroes in an article, book or seminar paper are hired to teach Afro-American courses.

These poorly prepared teachers are hired in some cases to discredit the whole program. Given such teachers and in the face of such designs, black and white students are justified in running the teachers out of the classrooms as they have done in many cases.

Generally, Negro students have demanded that black instructors teach black-oriented courses. In many ways I sympathize with them. Having faced unprepared white teachers who have sometimes had to get their reading, lists from the black students and who have not learned that Negro is spelled with an "e" instead of an "i," the black students are skeptical. Besides, they reason, it was the white scholar who, by his writing, and teaching,, made the Negro the "Invisible man" of American scholarship. It is certainly asking a lot to expect one to accept cheerfully a man who has continuously embezzled from him his pride, culture, history and manhood for more than four hundred years.

In spite of these considerations, the black students often go too far. All White teachers are not racists. I submit that some of them have more "soul" than some blacks. "Blackness," in all its shades, represents no mystical guarantee of an "understanding" of the black man's problems, life or culture. Neither color nor earnestness but training, must be the test applied to any teacher. Since many black students suffer from contact earlier with poorly trained teachers, it is more of a disservice to them than to white students to add more ill-prepared instructors at the last stage of their education. Yet, in their favor find black teachers, Negro students ignore the possible crippling, effects of hiring, simply any black man. They have often suggested teachers whom no administrator, regardless of his designs, could accept. For example, a group of black students in one college suggested that a Negro graduate student who had not completed a year of graduate study be hired to teach a Negro history course. Upon investigation, it was discovered that the student in question had already flunked out of graduate school during the first semester.

The black students, however, must be applauded for forcing predominantly white colleges to come to grips with their discriminatory, hiring, practices. Still, the revolution in this area will fall short if Negro students only demand black teachers for black-oriented subjects. Instead, they must broaden their demands into other areas. How many blacks do we have teaching mathematics, biology, engineering, or law at predominantly, white schools? Faculty desegregation must expand into the areas if the black scholar is not to end up in an intellectual straitjacket where he is restricted to black-oriented subjects.

The threat to black intellectuals is real. Not only do the black students demand that the teachers in black studies programs be Negroes, they also want them to have the right shade of "blackness." In essence, this means that the black scholar must have the right ideological leanings. As some of us succumb to the persuasive arguments to hop on the treadmill and try to keep up with the mercurial changes in the black "party line," serious scholarship is likely to suffer. It is in this regard that the control of black studies programs by black students is most dangerous. Black scholars being considered for positions in these programs must not only gain the approval by the faculty of their academic credentials, they must also kowtow to the black students. On one occasion a friend of mine, after receiving faculty approval of his appointment at one college, was required to pay obeisance to the black students. Flamboyant by nature, he went home, donned flowing African robes, returned, wowed the students and received the appointment. The case of another black scholar was more tragic. After being approved by the faculty, he went before the black students to prove his ideological fitness. When he opened his remarks to them by pointing out that he had a white wife, the students rejected him. In spite of his qualifications he was not hired.

I do not mean to imply by the preceding remarks that I reject student involvement in decisions that affect their lives. On the contrary, I feel that we must do much more in this direction. In no case, however, should student control go so far as to restrict the intellectual freedom of the scholar. Even if one wants to push "black realism," this is not the way to do it. Black intellectuals have worked so long, and hard in their fight against the white intellectual establishment, often publishing their own books when white publishers rejected them because they were unorthodox, that they do not want manumission from their white masters only to be enslaved by black masters. In short, while we support student involvement, we reject it for black studies until the same degree of student control is extended to other areas.

Often, when the Negro scholar escapes the ideological snare of the black students, he faces the almost equally dangerous trap of being overworked by his white colleagues. Frequently, because he is one of few blacks on the faculty, presidents and deans use him as a flying troubleshooter to defang, militant students. Inevitably, he is appointed to every committee that is related in any way to Negroes (and the list of them seems limitless). Then, too, the Negro scholar is expected to serve as father-confessor, counselor, success model, substitute parent, general dispenser of pablum to overwrought black students, and all-around authority on the "Negro problem." Consequently, the Negro scholar finds himself more overworked than when he taught fifteen hours a week in a predominantly Negro school. The danger in all of this is that black scholars may find that they have almost no time for research and writing. Few students and administrators realize that by requiring an inordinate amount of work from black scholars they are seriously crippling them in their efforts to find out more about the black experience.

Few students seem to realize that their demands for black faculty are causing, raids of major proportions on the faculties of Negro colleges. Of course, some students have insisted that their schools raid only other white colleges. The impact of the current raiding practices (and they are likely to increase) on the Negro colleges is not clear. On the one hand, predominantly white colleges are finding that it is not easy to entice Negro faculty away from places they have been for several years. Many black professors, disdain the offers because they do not feel the predominantly white colleges will follow through later on promotions. Others argue that they were told to go and teach "their people" ten years ago and to hell with the white schools that have suddenly discovered them. Where were they ten years ago when they were really needed? Many black professors refuse the offers because they realize that their white colleagues will not respect their academic credentials.

In spite of all the hue and cry from black college administrators, the raids have had a salutary effect on the position of the black faculty member. Deans are suddenly discovering that they can add $5,000 to an instructor's salary at the same time that they cut his teaching load by six hours. Since he is now the rarest gem in the academic marketplace, the black teacher is rapidly approaching parity with his white colleagues in the perquisites of the profession. In many cases, black administrators have used the raiding, as a lever to pry more money out of reluctant state legislatures for teaching salaries.

The demands of black students for separate, autonomous black studies departments, separate social centers and dormitories have been a godsend to white racists engulfed by the liberal wave of the last ten years. Ivy League Ku Klux Klansmen applaud and vigorously support such demands. The immediate capitulation of white colleges to such demands is understandable: they support their traditional beliefs and practices. Take Harvard, for example. When a Negro graduate of Harvard, Roscoe Conkling Bruce, tried to reserve a room in the freshman dormitory for his son in 1923, President A. Lawrence Lowell refused the request. He wrote Bruce: "I am sorry to have to tell you that in the freshman halls we have felt from the beginning, the necessity of excluding Negroes. I am sure you understand why we have thought it impossible to compel the two races to live together." In April of the same year the Board of Overseers of Harvard voted unanimously that "men of the white and Negro races shall not be compelled to live together."

By endorsing the shibboleths of "self-determination," many white intellectuals are really supporting a recrudescence of "separate but equal" facilities. In this regard, black students can appreciably close the generation gap by asking their parents what separate facilities mean in practice. Few of them have forgotten that a separate railroad car meant uncomfortable, dilapidated, filthy, rarely cleaned cars where black women were insulted by drunken white hooligans. Separate residential areas meant, and still do mean, unventilated, rarely heated, overcrowded, unpainted apartments with high rents, few city services, consistent violation of housing codes by unfeeling, landlords who go unpunished by city officials, and black men and women dying of tuberculosis and in firetraps, and black babies dying, from rat bites.

When it has been possible for whites to give Negroes separate educational facilities, this has been done with enthusiasm. The result has always been disastrous. Separate facilities have never been equal. It is incomprehensible that black students can trust what they call the "white power structure" to provide separate but equal facilities at the same time that the current administration, as conservative as it is, has found that several Southern states are still offering separate but unequal education to blacks and whites. The evidence of this is overwhelming. A cursor check of state expenditures to black and white colleges supports the charge. How can blacks receive an equal education in Florida when the state expenditures for white colleges were twenty-seven times larger than appropriations for Negro colleges in 1963? For those who eschew research, an on-the-site investigation would be instructive. Who can compare the small cinderblock buildings of Southern University in New Orleans with the shiny, commodious brick buildings of Louisiana State University right down the street and believe that separate facilities can be equal?

Are predominantly white colleges any more justified in bowing to the demand of black students for separate social facilities and black roommates than they are for bowing to the same demands of white students? The answer is an unequivocal no. Instead, they must react the way Columbia University did in 1924 when a group of white students threatened to leave a dormitory because a Negro student was admitted. Dean Hawkes spoke for the faculty when he asserted: "If any student finds his surroundings uncongenial, there is no need for him to stay in Farnald Hall or anywhere else at the University."

I understand the very persuasive arguments of many black students that they need these separate facilities for emotional reinforcement. I sympathize with them but reject their argument. I have read too many autobiographies of black men who studied at white institutions when racism was much more violently overt and when they were much more deprived educationally and culturally than any of these students are, to accept their facile arguments. Often the lone student at Yale, Harvard, Oberlin, Iowa State and other colleges, these men succeeded in spite of the lack of organized programs of emotional reinforcement.

A number of predominantly white colleges have not only utilized black studies to set up separate social facilities for blacks, they have also organized all-black classes for their Negro students. When the black students at a California college complained that they were being used as resource persons in a "Racism in America" course, a separate all-black section was established with a black psychologist as the teacher. The reaction of the students to the course was mixed. One group told me that it was a great course because the teacher required no reading; allegedly, since all of the blacks understood white racism, they simply met and "rapped" with each other. The more astute students described the course as a "bull session" where everybody "got down on whitey."

While some California schools have retrograded further than most colleges, many of the others are not far behind. Even when these programs have been open to all students, the belligerent attitudes of the black students have often scared White students away. To the historian all of this is reminiscent of the treatment of black students when many white schools were first desegregated. Many contemporary black students are in these colleges because earlier black men were not even allowed in the classroom with their white classmates when they desegregated white colleges. Is it fair to the memory of men like this for black students to turn their college educations into "bull sessions" that they could have had without going to college?

Inadvertently, the white colleges are reinforcing the growth of apartheid in America, denying black and white students the opportunity to learn to understand all people, and approving the denial of social equality to Negroes. America's predominantly white colleges can follow one of two paths. The current separatist ideologies fostered by black studies plans can only lead to more Negro students feeling like one black Columbia University student who wrote in 1967: "I feel compelled to announce the fact that Columbia College will never be integrated. If half, or even three-quarters of the College population were black, there would still exist two separate and basically unrelated student communities..." Another student at Columbia indicated the other direction. He asserted that at Columbia, "Acutely aware of the white-problem-in America as I am, as prejudiced toward my own people as I am, I have still found individuals—not black—whom I can respect, admire, and even love."

I realize that any new program may initially encounter many problems. Those that I outlined above, however, can be avoided. The Negro community has too much at stake—its very existence—for the college community, again, to miss an opportunity to begin to end the centuries of neglect and repression of blacks in America. Black studies is too serious an intellectual sphere, has too many exciting possibilities of finally liberating the racially shackled American mind, for intellectuals to shirk their responsibility to organize academically respectable programs. This possibility of curricular innovation must not be used to establish totally different programs, segregated entirely from traditional schemes. Instead, we must take advantage of this opportunity to enrich the educational experiences of all students and teach them to think and to understand more clearly the problems of their age. While we may make our admissions procedures more logical in an effort to find more Negro students, they must be required, whether in black studies or in any other program, to meet the requirements that all other students must meet to graduate. The black community has suffered too much already from the "Negro degrees" given to us in the past by predominantly white colleges.

I do not mean to imply by the remarks made above that the growing maze of black studies programs has been developed only for sinister reasons. In all probability most of the individuals establishing and supporting them have been sincere. But goaded by the emotional demands of black students and pushed by a growing sense of guilt at having fiddled while America burned, many white intellectuals have organized instant programs of little worth. Characteristically, intellectuals, frustrated, by their inactive lives, often want to propose fuzzy plans for the immediate eradication of ills. In this instance they have been hamstrung by two things. On the one hand, the guilt they feel for having contributed to the perpetuation of racism in America causes them to clutch frantically at any straw that may atone for their sins. On the other, they are forced by the masterful rhetorical play on this guilt by black students to accept the most far-reaching, and often unworkable plans for a total restructuring, of American society. The key to the dilemma is the rhetoric of the black students.

Adopting the classic political technique of demanding more than one is willing to accept, black students discovered very quickly that white intellectuals actually believed that their demands were nonnegotiable. Consequently, white intellectuals have established programs that are, in many instances, practically closed to white students, are soothing to their consciences because they seek to provide services to the black community that only the state can provide, are organized and controlled by students, are contrary to the logical pattern of existing, programs, are based solely on emotional rather than intellectual needs, are designed to perpetuate the white myth that Negroes cannot compete on an equal basis, are suited to contemporary problems rather than equipping students to propose new solutions to the ever-changing nature of proscriptions against blacks in America, and permit Negroes to learn about themselves at the expense of knowledge about the larger American society with which they must battle. Such programs represent poor preparation indeed for black men who must survive in a white society.

The most serious effect of student rhetoric on black studies programs is undoubtedly the white acceptance of the demand for combining community action, academic and counseling programs. I agree with the students that the university cannot fulfill, its *raison d'etre* by ignoring community needs. Similarly, I feel that some students, in the best tradition of Rousseau, should have firsthand knowledge of the community in which they live. To provide this through community action programs is, of course, an enormous undertaking. A few years ago when Howard University officials adopted a community action program for the Washington census tract with the worst social problems, they found that the $400,000 they invested in the program made little impact. The problems encountered in our mini-war on poverty are also instructive in this regard. The poverty program with its well-meaning, paternalistic, relatively well-financed activities has not only in many cases been less than beneficial, but has often been positively destructive, to the black community. In light of the desire of blacks to "do their own thing," how are we to react to another series of paternalistic programs directed by people in the so-called "white power structure"?

Such programs can, of course, be highly successful. First, however, they must be much more carefully planned than most of those I have seen. One gets the vague impression upon reading, many of the proposals that a horde of idealistic black, and maybe white, students are going, to be let loose on the black community. Black men and women have played in this scene many times before. Nothing could be more self-defeating. A short time ago I watched a team of young, highly committed, but wholly undirected VISTA workers unintentionally insult blacks in their first public contact with them in a small rural Louisiana community. In light of the tensions in urban areas, community action programs must be well organized, carefully planned, and amply funded. They must, in addition, involve community leaders in the initial planning stages of the programs.

One question that apparently never arises in connection with this aspect of black studies proposals is how much community involvement students actually want. Are contemporary students *that* different from those of my own generation? Do they really have that much time after studying? In many cases investigation has shown that at the same time that students demand more community action programs they rarely participate in those that the colleges have already established.

While the lack of serious thought behind many of these programs can be hidden by skipping over objectives and using glittering generalities in regard to the community action arm, all of the confusion, guilt and sinister designs are revealed in the list of courses. All of the proposals begin by hiding the colleges' sins behind grandiose claims about the number of black- oriented or related courses they already offer. Many of these are often very tangentially related to blacks under the broadest conception possible. The revelations about the nature of the programs, however, are in the new courses, I realize the variations on a black theme may be endless, but I am frankly amazed as I read the list of some new courses. While it may be possible to teach a course on the "Afro-American on the Frontier." I have serious doubts about the course proposed for one black studies program entitled "The Sociology of Black Sports." And although we have done very little research on the Negro family, it may be possible to teach a course on the subject. But can we, as one college proposes, offer one course on "The Black Family in the Urban Environment" and another one on "The Black Family in the Rural Environment"? What in the world is the course proposed in a California state college entitled "Relevant Recreation in the Ghetto"? This same school must, have had a deeply disturbed home economist on its black studies committee, for it also proposed that one of the relevant courses for the Afro-American program should be "The Selection and Preparation of Soul Food."

That delectable tidbit indicates clearly the slim intellectual base of many programs. Even when the programs have not been this shallow, they have often been planned with little thought of what is going on in the American educational establishment. The contemporary revolution in public school textbooks, the burgeoning summer institutes, and rapid changes in public school offerings are bound to catch up with many college-level black studies programs in the next few years. The number of courses one takes is irrelevant if the reading list and general information are the same as that one received in high school. After all, the thrill of hearing Crispus Attucks praised in the first grade, rediscovered in the eighth, revived in the twelfth, and finally "evaluated" in college is just as deadening as our annual peregrinations with Columbus. Dry rot is already surfacing in some programs. Some students find that the "Introductory Seminar in Afro-American Studies" often exhausts the books and articles the teachers in their other courses are able to find. Strangely enough, the reading list for the "Sociology of Race Relations" is often identical to the one for "The Afro-American in American History." The toleration level of students for this kind of shallowness is understandably low.

While all of the problems I have indicated place black studies in serious jeopardy, they are not insurmountable. To overcome these obstacles we have to plot new courses for black studies. First, the programs should be rationally organized, fitted into the total pattern of university offerings, be directed to the needs of all students, amply funded, and as intellectually respectable as any other college program. The same qualifications should be required of teachers, the same work of students, and there should be clearly stated objectives, as there are in other academic programs. Community action programs must be separated from academic programs and adequately financed, staffed and truly related to community needs. Finally, if any of these programs is to succeed, we must break out of our airtight cage of guilt and emotionalism to the open arena where we can establish a meaningful dialogue on black studies.

4.

Reflections on Structure and Content in Black Studies[1]

Martin Kilson

Perhaps the first thing to note with regard to the nature of Black Studies is that those concerned with these studies today stand squarely on the shoulders of the precursors in the field of Black Studies. Nothing is more untrue than the notion of militant students and teachers involved in Black Studies thinking that what they began to call "Black Studies" several years ago was something they invented.

In truth, there is virtually no area, field, or subject related to the history, sociology, culture, politics, and anthropology of either Old World—Africa—or New World—America and other Western Hemisphere—black peoples that has not received major scholarly and intellectual attention between the late nineteenth century and the end of World War II. Numerous scholars of highest skill and sensitive humanity, both white and black scholars, contributed to the study of these facets of black peoples and societies during this period. Among the black American scholars who participated in this work, the following are notable:

(1) W.E.B. DuBois, the Harvard-trained sociologist and historian, whose brilliant book. *The Philadelphia Negro*, published in 1899, was one of the first urban sociological surveys in America and is a classic in the urban sociology of blacks;

(2) Carter G. Woodson, also a Harvard-trained historian, whose books were directed to scholars and laymen, who founded the Association for the Study of Negro Life and History in 1916 and established its organ, *The Journal of Negro History*, the oldest journal dedicated to the study of blacks;

(3) Horace Mann Bond, a Chicago-trained sociologist and educator, whose book, *The Education of the Negro in Alabama: A Study In Cotton and Steel*, published in 1937, is a classic in the sociology of education;

(4) Allison Davis, a Harvard and Chicago-trained social psychologist, whose book, *Deep South: A Social Anthropological Study of Caste and Class*, published in 1940, is a classic in the sociology of education;

(5) J. Saunders Redding, trained at Brown University in English and Literature, who produced a brilliant example of comparative analysis of Afro-American literature in his book, *To Make a Poet Black*, published in 1939;

(6) Rayford Logan, a Harvard-trained historian who succeeded Woodson as editor of *The Journal of Negro History*, wrote in 1954 a pioneering

31

study in the history of racist ideas, *The Negro in American Life and Thought: The Nadir 1877-1901;*

(7) St. Clair Drake, a Chicago-trained social anthropologist, whose book, *Black Metropolis: A Study of Negro Life in a Northern City*, published in 1945 is a classic analysis of the sociology of the black ghetto;

(8) John Hope Franklin, a Harvard-trained historian, whose book *The Militant South*, published in 1956, is the major work on the extremist ethos in Southern life and culture; and, finally,

(9) E. Franklin Frazier, a Chicago-trained sociologist, whose book, *Negro Youth at the Crossroads*, published in 1940, had partial collaboration with the white psychiatrist Harry Stack Sullivan and is a major study of the psychological forces that shape the personalities of black adolescents in cities.

The white precursors are equally numerous, but only several need mention here: *Robert Park*, the cofounder of the University of Chicago School of Sociology, not only studied Afro-Americans but was early in recruiting brilliant black students into sociology; among those who studied under Park were E. Franklin Frazier — perhaps the most seminal Afro-American social scientist whose book, *Black Bourgeoisie*, published in 1959, is a classic example of critical sociology; Charles Johnson, first director of urban research for the National Urban League in the early 1920s and a pioneer at institutionalizing research on the Afro-American, which he did at Fisk University; Horace Mann Bond, already mentioned for his classic study of the sociology of Afro-American education in the South; and St. Clair Drake, already mentioned for his brilliant study of blacks in Chicago in the 1940s. In addition to Park, *Thomas Woofter* deserves mention. He was an economist who spent his professional life studying the economic and social status of the urban Afro-American; his book, *Negro Programs in Cities*, published in 1928, is an early and major social survey of urban blacks. Finally, mention of Melville Herskovits is in order; he was an anthropologist who, in addition to having founded single-handedly the interdisciplinary field of African Studies in America, spent a lifetime studying black societies throughout the world — in Africa (Dahomey), in the American South and Chicago, in the West Indies (Trinidad), and in South America (Brazil). Indeed, Herskovits virtually conceived the field of Afro-American Studies, and his theoretical essays in this area are still among the most fertile writings available.

Structure in Black Studies

Who should administer them?

One notable feature of the black and white precursors of Black Studies mentioned above is that they were all well-trained scholars. They all pursued graduate studies and doctorates. None of these precursors was a charlatan or a dilettante. Nor was any of them an ideologue, or a politician sporting intellectual garb. They all were, to a man, either liberal or progressive, and a few were radical. But they knew that the scholarly study of blacks required special skills and a uniquely disciplined frame of mind — an outlook that enabled the scholar, white or black, to surmount his own prejudices and ideological proclivities in behalf of disciplined knowledge. One of these precursors, W. E. B DuBois, was indeed a very political man; yet he recognized the need to keep politics in its proper place when he sought the scholarly study of social and historical problems of Afro-Americans.

These attributes associated with the pioneers in the study of blacks must be the basis of the organization of Black Studies curricula today. Thus, only persons of tested scholarly abilities and training should be involved in the organization and administration of Black Studies curricula. This means, of course, that placing undergraduate students on the governing bodies, committees or departments, concerned with Black Studies curricula is out of order. A number of colleges and universities — including Harvard University — have allowed undergraduate executive roles in administering Black Studies curricula. Quite frankly, this is utter nonsense. With rare exceptions, no undergraduate is ready to exercise scholarly authority in any field - - he would not be a student if he were — and certainly not in as complex an interdisciplinary field as Black Studies.[2]

Indeed, granting students — and almost exclusively Negro students — positions on governing bodies in Black Studies represents a profound insult to blacks. Perpetrated by misguided militant black teachers — often themselves poorly qualified for roles in Black Studies departments, which probably explains their position on student participation, for students' militancy often got jobs for such teachers — and by guilt-ridden white faculty and administrators, the presence of students on governing bodies in Black Studies is disrespectful of the long-run educational needs of the black population. The calibre of Black Studies departments or programs is determined by the quality of the persons who make decisions and teach in these programs; clearly, undergraduates, whose scholarly and technical calibre is necessarily very low, do not aid the calibre of Black Studies programs. They have no tested scholarly and technical skills to impart to other students.

Unfortunately, however, what students can do as executive members of a Black Studies department or program is to turn it into a political affair, exploiting it for a lot of ideological and psychological purposes which are associated with the political style called black militancy. I am not myself opposed to black militancy — let me make this clear: it has its place in a racist society like ours, which has been cruel and vulgar in its social and political relationships with blacks; in this society, militant pressures are required to help change behavior and institutions in more progressive and humane directions. But once militancy has made its point, it should, so to speak, mind its business. What I am saying, in short, is that once militant students helped modify the limitations in college curricula with regard to the study of blacks, these militant students should return to being students. As students, they necessarily lack the trained skills and habits that enable a person to exercise scholarly authority — to teach, research, publish, and make decisions about curricula, and so on. They, therefore, simply have no role in governing Black Studies curricula, or any other curricula. At best, students might be given advisory roles, places on advisory committees in Black Studies — and other departments, for that matter, could conceivably be opened to students. The purpose would be to tap their feelings about trends in the curriculum and the like. But beyond this, students simply have no place in the administrative and governing structure of Black Studies curricula, and the numerous colleges and universities — both excellent ones and average-to-mediocre ones — who have succumbed to militant threats and allowed students to hold such positions must bring this practice to an end. Such Black Studies departments or programs will remain intellectually and scholarly of doubtful quality until this is done.

Role of established disciplines

Any of the major precursors of Black Studies that one can think of had his or her primary scholarly and intellectual training in an established discipline like comparative literature, anthropology, sociology, and so on. St. Clair Drake, for example, was trained in social anthropology at the University of Chicago; Ralph J. Bunche, a pioneer in the study of urban Afro-American politics in the 1920s to 1940s, was trained at Harvard University in political science; Harold Foote Gosnell, a white pioneer in the study of urban Afro-American politics in the same years, was trained at Chicago in political science; and Abraham Harris, a black pioneer in the study of the economic status of the Afro-American working class, taught at the University of Chicago most of his career and was trained in economics at Columbia University. The same holds for the current generation of black and white scholars who study the Afro-American and other black societies: e.g., James Gibbs, a black anthropologist at Stanford University who works on African traditional societies, was trained in anthropology at Harvard University in the 1950s; Andrew Brimmer, a black economist now on the Federal Reserve Board and studying economic problems of blacks, was trained in economics at Harvard in the 1950s; Elliot Skinner, a black anthropologist at Columbia University studying African tribal systems, was trained in anthropology at Columbia in the 1950s; and Nathan Huggins, a black historian at Columbia University who studies the social history of the Afro-American, was trained in social history at Harvard in the 1950s.

What I mean to suggest by the foregoing references to the type of academic training received by two generations of scholars involved in Black Studies is that the best approach to a field of such interdisciplinary complexity as Black Studies is through one of the established academic and technical disciplines like economics, anthropology, sociology, psychology, and so on. I would suggest that no interdisciplinary subject like Asian Studies, African Studies, Middle Eastern Studies, American Studies, and Black Studies (each of which intersects all major academic and technical disciplines) can evolve into a scholarly and intellectually viable field without the curricular control of an established discipline. Thus, if students are allowed to approach an intrinsically interdisciplinary subject like Black Studies without the curricular control of a discipline like economics, psychology, and so on, these students will be academically and technically diffuse and disoriented. They will be jack-of-all-disciplines, so to speak, but master of none. In a word, they will be dilettantes at best, and charlatans at worst.

Indeed, it would be tragic for the current generation of Afro-American students, nearly seventy-five percent of whom are now in white colleges, to have them become victims of academically and technically diffuse Black Studies curricula or programs. To allow students in Black Studies programs to pick, for example, in a hit-and-miss fashion among two black economic courses, two black sociology, two literature, one philosophy, one anthropology, two political science, two history, and so on, and then to graduate these students at the bachelor degree level as presumably qualified to apply social science analysis or to apply to graduate schools in history, economics, sociology, and the like is to perpetrate a cruel hoax on the black students. Unfortunately, this situation is now widespread in colleges with Black Studies curricula. But in view of the present small skill pool of professionally and technically trained Afro-Americans, the black community simply cannot afford this mode of organizing a Black Studies curriculum. Only at the rather low level of undergraduate training, as in training elementary teachers, could this kind of academically and technically diffuse Black Studies curriculum be acceptable. (Though I am told by colleagues in psychology and linguistics that, increasingly, elementary teachers will require more specialized undergraduate training, and they feel that this should already be the situation for teachers who will teach in ghetto elementary schools.) But I doubt that this academically diffuse curriculum would be satisfactory for teachers who intend to teach in secondary schools, for it is necessary in my view that most black secondary school teachers be trained in an academic or technical discipline in undergraduate school (like biology, chemistry, mathematics, or history) so that they can pursue at least some graduate studies both in a discipline and in teaching. Certainly this is the calibre of teacher that must be increasingly recruited into the secondary schools of the ghetto, for without them it will be nearly impossible to alter the currently low level of academic training in ghetto high schools.

Now let me be more concrete about how the interdisciplinary subject of Black Studies should be controlled by the established disciplines when shaping a curriculum. First, the principles underlying my view of the proper curriculum: The principle I employ is that of tracking; a student majoring in Black Studies should be "tracked" through an established discipline like, say, economics, in such a fashion that he would be in effect fulfilling two majors or concentrations. One major, dealing with the established discipline of economics, would require the student to meet at least the basic set of courses required of all economics majors—like economic doctrine, principles of macro-economics, principles of micro-economics, at least two primary courses in quantitative analysis (which, of course, would require the student to take the related mathematics courses in the math department), and several more applied analytical courses. The second major, dealing with Black Studies, would require the student to take courses which apply economic analysis to problems related to blacks—like welfare economics, labor economics, urban investment policies, economics of urban education, and related courses. Thus, with this mode of organizing a major in Black Studies, you can ensure against producing dilettantes and students ill-prepared for graduate studies; even if they do not pursue graduate studies, they would at least have a technical basis of some worth in a given discipline, rather than the diffuse set of "skills" provided by the catch-as-catch-can type of Black Studies curriculum I referred to above, which is far too prevalent today.

Of course, what is primary to the type of Black Studies curriculum I am proposing is that a student must decide first of all in favor of a particular discipline. He must be required to decide after his first year whether he wishes to be a sociologist, economist, political scientist, or whatever, and on the basis of this choice he has his curriculum in Black Studies "tracked" through an established discipline. To take another concrete example of tracking a student through a discipline within an overall Black Studies curriculum or program, let us say a student decides to be a sociologist. This student should first be required to fulfill at least the basic prerequisites required of sociology majors: thus, he should take statistics, social theory (e.g., Pareto, Parsons, Weber, Durkheim, Marx, Simmel, Merton, and so on), political sociology, social structure (e.g., kinship, formal organization, and the like), and demography. Solid grounding in these or other basic sociological subjects would be a prerequisite for the courses that apply sociology to the study of blacks. Once this is obtained—and some of these prerequisites could be taken simultaneously with courses specifically related to blacks—the student pursues a range of courses, available both in the Black Studies program or department and in other departments that relate to blacks. These courses might include demography of the ghetto, urbanization in the ghetto, Afro-American family structures, sociology of Afro-American health, deviant behavior among Afro-Americans, Afro-American leadership patterns, Afro-American voluntary organizations, and so on.

Another key feature of this model of Black Studies curricula is that a good number of the courses comprising the curriculum I suggest will be taught in the established disciplinary departments, while others would be offered explicitly by the Black Studies program or department. Of course, the average, American college that is concerned with Black Studies could hardly afford to acquire all the different social science skills required in a single Black Studies department. Even the elite and wealthier Institutions like Harvard, Yale, Chicago, and the University of California system will for the most part not be able to afford such a concentration of skills in the humanities and social sciences in a single, compact Black Studies department. Indeed, I consider it much more desirable intellectually and academically that the scholars who teach in the Black Studies curriculum be represented in all the established departments like classics, comparative literature, philosophy, and economics, and that to the extent there is a Black Studies department at all, it will be a composite body of those scholars who are in the established departments but teach a Black Studies curriculum. Perhaps the best way to realize this is to adopt the policy of joint academic appointments for scholars in the established departments who teach in the Black Studies curriculum. This is quite feasible at the wealthier colleges or universities, though again at the average college what is called the Black Studies department will be in effect a committee of scholars who teach in the established departments but also participate in the Black Studies curriculum.

But, of course, the important matter is not whether the Black Studies curriculum is housed in a department of its own, realized through coordination of existing departments and divisions or through some other means. The significant issue is to guarantee that students—especially those marked for graduate schools and professional schools—who pursue Black Studies are simultaneously grounded in an established academic and technical discipline. A Black Studies curriculum, like other interdisciplinary curricula. (American Studies, Asian Studies) cannot stand alone: it must, so to speak, be clothed in the tested scholarly and technical garment of an established discipline.

Who should major in Black Studies?

First of all, there should be no political or other extraneous qualification for majoring in Black Studies. Efforts by authoritarian and xenophobic militant black students to discourage white students from pursuing Black Studies—which occurs at some colleges—must be criticized and opposed. Although some black militants prefer the fantasy world on which their political style thrives, it is clear that blacks and whites in American society have a profound interconnection, and neither white racist nor black racist ideology can after this. Happily, this is already becoming more apparent to some militant black students at white colleges who several years ago shed associations with white peers, but today are restoring these relationships, which, of course, are fundamental to the black students' efforts to gain the optimum benefit from white colleges. This trend, however, is far from complete, and currently there are many black students who persist in imposing a separatist pattern upon their education at white colleges, and especially upon Black Studies departments or programs. But this must be openly and firmly opposed by all scholars who take the life of the mind seriously. Indeed, the only possible situation in which an all-black separatist educational pattern would be somewhat justified is under circumstances where black militants *formed and paid for* their own all-black college or Black Studies institute. Elements among other American ethnic or particularistic groups who were, like militant blacks today, obsessed with their ethnic particularism founded separatist educational arrangements. For example, some Catholics, obsessed with their

Catholicness, have done so; some Jews, obsessed with Jewishness, have done like-wise; *though, instructively enough, these are among the minority of these and other major American ethnic or particularistic groups; the majority, tuned in to reality, have sought their education in the pluralistic context of the elite American colleges like Yale, Princeton, Harvard, or of the great American state colleges and universi-ties.* Clearly, then, only in an all-black institution that is funded by blacks can those militants obsessed with their blackness justifiably pursue a policy of rejecting white participation in Black Studies; only in this situation can they justifiably indulge their special all-black educational and psychological life-style. *In the white colleges, both private and state, where now over seventy percent of all Afro-Americans in college are in attendance, the exclusion of whites from Black Studies is unjustified.*

Another aspect of who should take Black Studies is the issue of what proportion of black students in white colleges should major in this curriculum. Some militants among Negro students and teachers appear to support the majority of black students concentrating in Black Studies. This would be an enormous error, I think. We now have the majority of blacks in college attending white institutions, and this situation will persist. The opportunity this affords Afro-Americans at first-class institutions like Wayne State University, the University of Michigan, in the University of Califor-nia system, at the Massachusetts Institute of Technology, and elsewhere to major in the scientific and technological fields like chemistry, engineering, architecture, com-puter sciences, and biology should not be lost because of some ideological and psy-chological proclivity toward Black Studies. As Professor Arthur Lewis, perhaps among the top ten economists in the world and clearly the leading black economist, now at Princeton University, has pointed out in an article in the *New York Times Magazine* last year, the road to the top and middle jobs in American society is through the sciences and technologies, not through the humanities and social sci-ences, of which Black Studies is, of course, a part. Professor Lewis also noted that today Afro-Americans, while twelve percent of the American population, hold only two percent of the top or elite jobs in the society and only one percent of the middle-level jobs, but some sixty percent of the lower-level jobs. The black community can change this weak position in the structure of jobs (and thus of power) in American society only by entering in much larger numbers the technological and scientific fields. No amount of psychological, therapeutic, or symbolic dependence upon Black Studies should be permitted to prevent this development; if it does, the road to group suicide awaits us, for in the coming decades American society will be more, not less, dependent upon scientific and technological skills.

It is even doubtful that that large segment—perhaps the majority—of black stu-dents who become school teachers should major in Black Studies. *I am particularly concerned with high school teachers for the need in urban ghettos throughout the country is for high school teachers in mathematics, chemistry, physics, biology, me-chanical arts, and so opt.* It takes organized effort to get more black high school teachers trained in these crucial areas, whereas, in Black Studies, which is a part of the social sciences and humanities, there is a natural and easy proclivity among black students to enter this field. I would suggest, therefore, that it is actually necessary to discourage Afro-American students who intend to become high school teachers from entering Black Studies as a major field, and encourage them to choose a technical and scientific subject instead. There is certainly no need to encourage them to enter Black Studies.

Thus, one might ask me who, then, should major in Black Studies, since I have excluded a sizable chunk of Afro-American students from this major. My reply is that those special students, black and white, who have a serious appreciation of and good aptitude for the social sciences and the humanities are the ones who should major in Black Studies. This major, moreover, should be pursued simultaneously with a part-major in an established discipline; or, as I put it earlier, the Black Studies curriculum should be "tracked" through an established discipline. Major intellectual, scholarly, and practical problems remain to be solved by the bright student of the social sciences and humanities who has a special interest in Black Studies. The desire to help solve these problems is, to my mind, the only valid reason for a student to major in Black Studies.

Depoliticization of Black Studies

Perhaps the major obstacle to the realization of the type of Black Studies curriculum that I have in mind is the extensive politicization of Black Studies departments or programs in the past several years. Militant political action by black students, often involving both threats of violence and actual violence, was of course fundamental to the rapid spread of Black Studies in white colleges in the past several years. I believe this militancy went much too far; it became an end in itself, rewarding especially in psychological and therapeutic terms, but clearly divorced from the academic and technical issues of establishing Black Studies curricula that would be effective. *Militancy opened up the floodgates, so to speak; it allowed a wide variety of basically ill-trained persons—a kind of para-professional category—to enter Black Studies departments and programs as teachers of so-called black subjects, whereas in fact few of these persons were academically trained to the point where they could exercise scholarly authority in the academic and technical disciplines of anthropology, economics, sociology, comparative literature, and the like.* This situation has occurred, moreover, not only at average and mediocre colleges, but at elite institutions like Dartmouth, Harvard, the University of Michigan, and elsewhere.

Altering the political processes that allowed this situation to occur in Black Studies departments and programs throughout the country will not be easy. But alter it we must—that is, those of us who understand he necessity to place the training of students in Black Studies on academically and technically viable foundations. There are some forces, happily, working toward this alteration. First, a growing number of Negro students at white colleges—especially males—are slowly but surely retreating from the more stark, anti-white, separatistic black nationalist behavior they acquired several years ago. From Dartmouth to the University of Minnesota and beyond, more black students—males in particular—are restoring their ties with white peers; and some black males, even former leaders of the militant separatist nationalism of the past several years, are again dating white female students. All this suggests that the kind of psychological and therapeutic dependence that black students had with regard to Black Studies departments that excluded whites is fading. As this happens, it will be easier to redress the extensive politicization of Black Studies that occurred over the past several years.

Another factor facilitating the depoliticization of Black Studies is the growing evidence of disenchantment of the brighter black students—often middle-class students—with the poor quality of the Charlatans and the paraprofessional staff in Black Studies programs. Students who several years ago felt constrained, either personally or for reasons of pressure, from criticizing the quality of Black Studies programs, now do so. In some colleges where this situation has been observed, students do not attend courses by those on the staff they consider of poor quality. In other colleges, the students have requested that faculty of superior training and qualifications be added to the Black Studies program or to the departments that provide courses for the program. Happily, there is presently a major increase in black graduate students who pursue the doctorate, and this will certainly facilitate better-qualified faculty in Black Studies.

Yet despite these hopeful trends, the general situation with regard to the quality of Black Studies is not satisfactory. Perhaps the most disturbing thing in this unsatisfactory situation is the growing tendency among white faculty and administration—whether conservative, liberal, or radical—to apply double standards to the academic organization of Black Studies and to the appointment of black faculty. Although white faculty and administrators were in the first instance virtually coerced into having Black Studies programs, as the threats and violence from militant black students have abated, the white faculty and administrators have not made a serious effort to return to acceptable academic standards and procedures in Black Studies programs.

Indeed, at numerous colleges and universities white faculty and administrators have been far too ready to accept the most outrageous demands from militant black students and teachers with regard to Black Studies. This behavior by white faculty must be seen, in fact, as blatantly patronizing, comparable to one's tolerance of the antics of a child. What is equally disturbing, the black militant students and teachers in white colleges quickly accept the concessions granted by white faculty. Militant blacks at white institutions have, it seems, a pathetic dependence upon the psychologically satisfying but academically disastrous concessions they wrench from white faculty and administrators.

I would like to conclude with a warning, if I may. Unless this psychological immaturity, nearly endemic to the militants in the Black Studies movement, soon ceases, a large section of blacks who seek intellectual status will be relegated to the backwaters or the trash-heap of American academic and intellectual life. Perhaps, alas, this is the unconscious wish—a kind of death wish—of large segments of militant black students and intellectuals. Lacking the stamina and special stuff required of first-class students and scholars, these militant black students and teachers sport a fashionable and psychologically gratifying militant style in order to achieve a protected and segregated (but academically undemanding and inferior) educational niche called a Black Studies program.

References

Cartey, W. and M. Kilson [eds.] (1970) *The African Reader*. New York: Random House.

Emerson, R. and M. Kilson [eds.] (1965) *Political Awakening of Africa*. Englewood Cliffs, NJ: Prentice-Hall.

Hill, A.C. and M. Kilson [eds.] (1969) *Apropos of Africa: Sentiments of American Negro Leaders on Africa from the 1800's to 1950's*. London: Frank Cass.

Huggins, N., M. Kilson, and D. Fox [eds.] (1971) *Key Issues in the Afro-American Experience*. New York: Harcourt Brace Jovanovich.

Kilson, M. (1966) *Political Change in a West African State*. Cambridge, MA: Harvard Univ. Press.

——— (1964) "Grassroots politics in Africa." *Political Studies* (February).

——— (1963) "Authoritarian and single-party tendencies in African politics." *World Politics* (January).

Obichere, B.I. (1910) "The significance and challenge of Afro-American Studies." *Journal of Black Studies* (December).

Endnotes

1. Author's note: This essay is a revision of a lecture delivered at a symposium on Black Studies at Simmons College, Boston, Massachusetts, in March 1971.

2. To make a brief personal reference, I was valedictorian of my college graduating class in 1953 and, if I may be immodest, I was fairly smart—at least I thought so. But I was no more capable than the man in the moon of exercising scholarly authority on the governing body of a political science, sociology, or any other department. Even after five years of competitive and intensive graduate studies at Harvard, I was not at all certain about my ability to exercise scholarly authority. Surely it is nonsense for students, black and white, to hold authoritative positions on Black Studies departments or programs.

5.

The Field and Function of Black Studies[1]

James B. Stewart

> The university must become not simply a center of knowledge but a center of applied knowledge and guide of action. And this is all the more necessary now since we easily see that planned action especially in economic life is going to be the watchword of civilization.... [S]tarting with present conditions and using the facts and the knowledge of the present situation of American Negroes, the Negro university expands toward the possession and the conquest of all knowledge. It seeks from a beginning of the history of the Negro in America and in Africa to interpret all history; from a beginning of social development among slaves and freedmen in America and Negro tribes and kingdoms in Africa, to interpret and understand the social development of all mankind in all ages. It seeks to reach modern science of matter and life from the surroundings and habits and aptitudes of American Negroes and thus lead up to understanding of life and matter in the universe.
>
> — W.E.B. DuBois

This vision of the developmental objective of historically black "institutions of higher education articulated by W.E.B. DuBois in 1933 (1973, pp. 5-6) provides a historical context for the modern black studies movement and its development over the last two decades. Black studies on DuBois's mandate via its emphasis on: looking backward to understand the present; institutionalizing itself in centers of learning while maintaining strong ties active involvement in black communities; becoming a self-perpetuating enterprise; and looking forward in efforts to contribute to the development of viable public policies that can insure black progress into and during the twenty-first century.

This chapter reviews the progress made toward realizing each of these objectives.

The March of History

For black studies scholars looking backward has meant an emphasis on history and historical analysis. Karenga (1992) argues that black history is "indispensable to the introduction and development of all the other subject areas. Black history places them in perspective, establishes their origins and developments, and thus, aids in critical discussion and understanding of them" (p. 43).

In response to the combination of intellectual alienation created by the absence or distortion of the black experience in pre-existing curricula and cultural alienation generated by the unfamiliar and antagonistic milieu, the first wave of black students entering predominantly white colleges and universities in the mid-1960s offered black history as simply a starting point. It was inevitable that a broader call for a comprehensive interdisciplinary curriculum that used history as a foundation would be made. Historical support for this approach can also be found in the writings of DuBois (1905):

> [W]e can only understand the present by continually referring to and study-ing the past; when any one of the intricate phenomena of our daily life puz-zles us; when there arises religious problems, political problems, race prob-lems, we must always remember that while their solution lies in the present, their cause and their explanation lie in the past (p. 104).

Five of the most significant results of the historical search of black stud-ies have been: destruction of the myth of the passive acceptance of subjuga-tion by blacks; peoples of African descent have always attempted to shape their own destinies (Marable, 1981; People's College Press, 1977); docu-mentation of the critical role of collective self-help in laying the foundations for black progress (Davis, 1975; Morris, 1984); restoration of the record of ancient and modern contributions of blacks in developing high technology and establishing early civilizations in North and South America (Diop, 1974; Jackson, 1980; Van Sertima, 1976, 1982, 1983); exploration of the contem-porary implications of psychic duality (Cross, 1978a, 1978b; Semaj, 1981), building on DuBois's classic formulation of the concept of Afrocentricity (Asante, 1987) as a guiding principle; and explication of the critical role played by black women in shaping the black experience (Harley & Terborg-Penn, 1978; White, 1980).

Not all of these developments have emerged from within the enterprise of black studies itself. Many scholarly contributions to black studies have been produced under the auspices of traditional disciplines but have also provided data that under-gird black studies as a disciplinary development.

A Beachhead in Higher Education

DuBois's emphasis on building a permanent base in institutions of higher educa-tion has been put into operation by black studies professionals principally through the formation of a national professional organization, the National Council for Black Studies (NCBS), which represents both black studies scholar/activists and black stud-ies administrative units. NCBS initiatives include developing and disseminating posi-tion statements regarding the desirable organizational characteristics of black stud-ies units; establishing an accreditation mechanism and promoting curriculum standardization to insure coherency and quality standardizations in history, the so-cial and behavioral sciences, and the arts and humanities; and assessing the state of black studies through annual surveys.

The environment in which these initiatives have been pursued is dominated by continuing challenges to the legitimacy of black studies by its critics and the weak at-tachment of many scholars to the black studies movement and to black studies units even when the research of such scholars examines the black experience. But the extent to which black studies has established a beachhead in higher education can be seen from selected responses to the first annual NCBS survey (Stewart, 1985b):

88.5 percent reported that the number of full-time faculty members with appointments solely in black studies is stable or increasing;

91.4 percent reported that the number of full-time faculty members with appointments in black studies and another academic unit is either stable or improving;

70.2 percent indicated that the number of full-time faculty members who have appointments outside black studies but who are teaching courses included in the black studies curriculum is either stable or improving;

79.5 percent indicated that the overall budgetary situation was either stable or improving;

46.4 percent indicated that new faculty members had been hired during the 1984-85 academic year, and

45.3 percent reported that new courses were offered during the 1984-85 academic year.

Self-Perpetuation:
Challenges and Possibilities

For black studies the process of becoming a self-perpetuating enterprise has many dimensions. These include: research into the history and development of the black studies movement to guide current planning; ongoing assessment of the intellectual products of black studies; development of specialized black studies journals and other outlets for research; creation of black studies graduate programs; integration of black studies knowledge into the K-to-12 curriculum; and development of alliances with other organizations.

Research examining the history and development of black studies has been useful in correcting the misconceptions used by detractors to slander the discipline. For example, the misconception persists that in the late 1960s and early 1970s as many as 700 black studies units were established, only to be followed by a precipitous decline in the 1980s. Research by Daniel (1978) has clearly documented, however, that the number of units with an identifiable administrative structure never numbered more than approximately 300. The first NCBS annual survey (Stewart, 1985b) reveals that there are currently approximately 220 identifiable black studies units in institutions of higher education and that the vast majority of black studies units are responding creatively to new challenges in higher education, including the general education reform movement. At the same time, however, it is critical to recognize that black studies units remain in a state of flux; the results of the first NCBS annual survey reveal that 20.7 percent of respondents indicated that a change in the organizational format of the unit had occurred in the 1984-85 academic year, and 29.9 percent reported a change in unit leadership during the 1984-85 academic year. Currently, NCBS has approximately 100 institutional members and has established a

Council of Institutional Members to improve interunit cooperation and to better protect units under attack.

The implications of organizational flux and challenges to legitimacy have influenced intellectual developments in several ways. First, there has been a continuing search for a sustainable self-definition that coherently captures the essence and defines the scope of inquiry and related activities. At the highest level of abstraction, Turner (1984b) argues cogently that the term *Africana studies* best achieves this goal. However, for this term to become standard, it will be necessary to clearly articulate the distinction vis-à-vis traditional African studies (Young & Martin, 1984). At present a variety of terms are used to describe the enterprise, including *black studies, Afro-American studies*, and *African-American studies*. In general, these terms refer principally to the study of African-Americans in the United States, although studies of classical African civilization, postclassical Africa, and the African diaspora are also integral components of the database.

Aside from the issue of an overarching designation for the field of inquiry, the basic dilemma that continues to perplex black studies theorists was identified almost a decade ago by Allen (1974), who lumped into three general categories the various conceptions of the field that have been advanced:

> an academic conception whereby the mission of black studies is to research black history and illuminate the contributions of blacks;

> an ideological political conception whereby black studies is seen as an instrument of cultural nationalism; and

> an instrumental political conception whereby black studies is considered a vehicle for social change with a functional relationship to the black community.

Allen's second category masks the importance of ideologies other than cultural nationalism important in the continuing development of black studies. These include Marxism (People's College Press, 1917; Alkalimat & Associates, 1984) and the black women's studies movement (Hull, Scott, & Smith, 1982). As the third conception of black studies has "become increasingly submerged in search of credibility within academe, the Outreach Center at Ohio State University (Allen's first category) is one of the few examples of systematic institutional pursuit of stronger community ties (Upton, 1984).

The intellectual momentum of black studies that cuts across all of the distinct approaches identified above has been manifested in the establishment of a number of specialized black studies journals, such as *The Journal of Black Studies, The Western Journal of Black Studies, UMOJA*, and the *New England Journal of Black Studies*. A new national black studies journal, *Africanology*, appeared in 1988.

The volume of black studies research output has created the desire to rank units based primarily on published research and has resulted in greater participation of blacks on editorial review boards (McWorter, 1981). There have also been attempts to analyze factors contributing to variation in published research in periodicals (Brossard, 1984; Stewart, 1983). In addition, a special issue of the *Journal of Negro Education* has been devoted to examining the evolution and contemporary status of black studies (Young, 1984). *The Black Scholar* has also been a regular outlet for black studies materials. One of the most recent contributions to the continuing examination of the developmental profile of black studies has been provided in the volume edited by Turner (1984a). The publications that most clearly demonstrate the maturation of black studies as an area of inquiry are, however, the general introductory texts (Karenga, 1982; People's College Press, 1977; Alkalimat & Associates, 1984; Stewart, 1979).

Increased visibility of black studies has led to the funding of major projects examining black studies curriculum development (Institute of the Black World, 1981, 1982). More recently, Huggins (1985), under the auspices of the Ford Foundation, produced an assessment of black studies that has been roundly attacked by many in the field of black studies (Asante, 1986). Huggins's report envisions, in the long run, the submersion of black studies into a traditional discipline. This approach plays into the hands of the enemies of black studies, primarily those administrators who have sought ways to reduce the autonomy of black studies units. The emerging pattern of attacks involves one or more of the following strategies: downgrading units from departmental to program status; submerging black studies into larger administrative units, for example, ethnic studies; allowing only joint faculty appointments with traditional academic units; and appointing a new generation of administrators not originally part of the black studies movement who naively support administration policies.

The central issues in faculty and chair appointments are: To what academic unit will a faculty member/administrator develop principal allegiance? Will the approach to the study of the black experience pursued by a scholar reflect the emergent black studies paradigm or simply recast traditional disciplinary perspectives? Appointing persons endorsing Huggins's approach obviously works against one of the most critical dimensions of black studies: promoting self-perpetuation through the development of cognate graduate units. The most hopeful development in this area is the establishment of a doctoral program in African-American Studies at Temple University. If black studies is to become a truly self-perpetuating discipline, a cadre of scholars must be trained under the auspices of black studies; these scholars should be able to unite in ways that insure principal loyalty to black studies.

Even a free-standing academic unit with appropriately trained faculty is not a sufficient condition for the perpetuation of black studies. A necessary condition is a campus-based and non-campus-based constituency that serves as a watchdog against attacks. The current wave of attacks on black studies has been undertaken under the auspices of a broader retrenchment. Black studies departments and programs have been particularly vulnerable during this period because of the perception (and reality) of a declining commitment to black studies by African-Americans in the late 1970s and early 1980s as individual careerist initiatives flourished. The declining student support was observed by some administrators who leaped at the opportunity to move against black studies.

The erosion of black student support for black studies in part indicated the failure of the first wave of black studies advocates to achieve one of their principal goals. In the minds of the early black studies visionaries and in the original developmental profile of NCBS, the strategy of developing graduate programs to promote self-perpetuation was to be pursued simultaneously with efforts to introduce black studies knowledge into the K-to-12 public school curriculum. This was to lead to a continuing and growing base of student support in higher education. One of the factors working against success in this area has been the somewhat remarkable absence of black studies in colleges and schools of education. As a result, the preparation of teachers during the last decade did not include an introduction to black studies knowledge. As a consequence, the students of these teachers became the next generation of victims in what Woodson (1933) described as the "miseducation of the Negro."

In addition, black studies has not been able to effectively use either the popular media or community organizations to overcome its general exclusion from the public school curriculum. Thus, the image and nonimage of African-Americans reinforced their treatment in the primary and secondary curricula. However, the Reagan era appears to have pushed the latest wave of African-American students into a new realization of the continuing validity of DuBois's often- quoted declaration that the problem of the twentieth century is the problem of the color line. The new racism on college campuses is creating a new interest in and a black student support base for black studies.

This organic development is occurring simultaneously with the NCBS's pursuit of crucial alliances with critical organizations including the National Alliance of Black School Educators, the Assault on Illiteracy Program, the Black United Fund, the NAACP Legal Defense Fund, Occupational Industrialization Centers of America, the Association for the Study of Afro-American Life and History, and the African Heritage Studies Association. These initiatives will hopefully broaden the impact of black studies during this decade.

All Our Past Proclaims Our Future

Aside from the challenges posed by the continuing attacks from its detractors, black studies faces an even greater challenge in putting DuBois's vision into practice. In particular, DuBois spoke of the study of "modern science of matter and life" (1973). Black studies, as traditionally conceived, has encompassed the subject areas associated with the arts and humanities, the social and behavioral sciences, and, to a lesser extent, education. No systematic attempt has been made to integrate the subject matter of the natural and physical sciences and technology with black studies.

It is also important to note that, even within traditional subject matter, black studies analysts have tended to overemphasize the descriptive approach characteristic of traditional disciplines rather than focus on concrete application, policy development and analysis, or developing linkages to appropriate "helping professions," for example, social work, administration of justice, and so on. This pattern is only partially the result of inattention to these issues. Some black studies advocates have raised these issues sporadically (Anderson, 1974, Stewart, 1976). At the time the NCBS core curriculum was developed, there was some desire to include policy studies as a curriculum track. Unfortunately, that initiative failed, but this oversight may be corrected in the forthcoming revision to the core curriculum guide.

Another modern challenge to which black studies has begun to respond is the educational impact of microcomputers (Harvey, 1983; Hendrix, Bracy, Davis, & Herron, 1984). There are now first-generation black studies educational software packages (Harris, 1985; Stewart, 1985a). In addition, a major conference held at St. Cloud State University, hosted by Robert Johnson under the auspices of the Minority Studies Academic Program entitled "The Use of Computers in Minority Studies and Related Disciplines," has laid the groundwork for a subgroup of specialists to collaborate on additional projects in this area.

The various developments cited above can, if coordinated and nurtured, provide the foundations for the realization of DuBois's vision. What DuBois had in mind as the ultimate intellectual outcome of the systematic study of the black experience was a theory of history and social change in which scientific and technological developments are explained endogenously. Such a macrotheory could not only potentially reconcile the competing schools of thought within black studies but also provide a fully developed paradigm for black studies that would finally cut the rotting umbilical cord to traditional disciplines. Such a scientific revolution would also give new direction to contemporary educational and economic development initiatives designed to meet the challenges of high technology and economic transformation. In this way, the nightmares of the past and present may give way to a brighter future, where the problem of the twenty-first century will not be the problem of the color line.

References

Alkalimat, A., & Associates (1984). *Introduction to Afro-American studies: A peoples college primer* (5th ed.). Urbana, IL: University of Illinois at Urbana.

Allen, R.L. (1974, September). Politics of the attack on black studies. *Black Scholar,* 6 (1), 2-7.

Anderson, S.E. (1974, March). Science, technology and black liberation. *Black Scholar, 5* (6), 2-8.

Asante, M. (1986). A note on Nathan Huggins' report of the Ford Foundation on African-American studies. *Journal of Black Studies, 17,* 255-62.

Asante, M. (1987). *The Afrocentric idea* (rev. ed.). Philadelphia: Temple University Press.

Brossard, C. (1984). Classifying black studies programs. *The Journal of Negro Education, 53,* 278-95.

Cross, W.E. (1978a). Black families and black identity: A literature review. *The Western Journal of Black Studies, 2,* 111-24.

———— (1978b). The Thomas and Cross models on psychological nigrescence: A literature review. *Journal of Black Psychology, 4,* 13-3 1.

Daniel, T.K. (1978). A survey of black studies in midwestern colleges and universities. *The Western Journal of Black Studies, 2,* 296-303.

Davis, K. (1975). *Fundraising in the black community.* Metuchen, NJ: The Scarecrow Press.

Diop, C.A. (1974). *African origins of civilization, myth or reality.* (M. Cook, Ed. & Trans.). Westport, CT: Lawrence Hill.

DuBois, W.E.B. (1905). The beginnings of slavery. *Voice of the Negro, 2.*

———— (1973). The field and function of the Negro college. (Alumni Reunion Address, Fisk University, 1933). Reprinted in H. Aptheker (Ed.), *W.E.B. DuBois, The education of black people, ten critiques 1900-1960.* Amherst: University of Massachusetts Press.

Harley, S., & Terborg-Penn, R., (Eds.) (1978). *The Afro-American woman, struggles and images.* Port West, NY: National University.

Harris, N. (1985). *Blackfacts.* West Lafayette, IN: North Star Gateway. A computer-based black history educational exercise.

Harvey, W.B. (1983). Computer instruction and black student performance. *Issues in Higher Education, 9.*

Hendrix, M.K., Bracy, J.H., Davis, J.A., & Herron, W.M. (1984). Computers and black studies: Toward the cognitive revolution. *The Journal of Negro Education, 53,* 341-50.

Huggins, N. (1985). *Report to the Ford Foundation on Afro-American studies.* New York: Ford Foundation.

Hull, G., Scott, P.B., & Smith, B. (1982). *All the women are white. All the blacks are men. But some of us are brave: Black women's studies.* Old Westbury, NY: Feminist Press.

Institute of the Black World (1981). *Black studies curriculum development course evaluations.* Conference I. Atlanta: Institute of the Black World.

———— (1982). *Black studies curriculum development course evaluations.* Conference II. Atlanta: Institute of the Black World.

Jackson, J. (1980). *Introduction to African civilizations.* Secaucus, NJ: Citadel Press.

Karenga, M. (1982). *Introduction to Afro-American studies.* Los Angeles: Kawaida.

McWorter, G.A. (1981). *The professionalization of achievement in black studies* (Preliminary Report). Chicago: The Chicago Center for Afro-American Studies.

Marable, M. (1981). The modern miseducation of the Negro: Critiques of black history curricula. In *Institute of the black world, black studies curriculum development course evaluations.* Conference I (pp. C1-C28). Atlanta: Institute of Black World.

Morris, A.D. (1984). *The origins of the civil rights movement: Black communities organizing for change.* New York: Free Press.

People's College Press (1977). *Introduction to Afro-American studies* (4th ed., vols. 1 & 2). Chicago: Author.

Semaj, L.T. (1981). The black self, identity and models for a psychology of black liberation. *The Western Journal of Black Studies, 5,* 158-71.

Stewart, J.B. (1976). Black studies and black people in the future. *Black Books Bulletin, 4,* 21-25.

———— (1979). Introducing black studies: A critical examination of some textual materials. *UMOJA,* 111, 5-18.

———— (1983). Factors affecting variation in published black studies articles across institutions. *The New England Journal of Black Studies, 4,* 72-83.

———— (1985a). *Liberation 2000? The black experience in America.* [Computer program]. State College, PA: Dynastew Educational Software.

———— (1985b). *The state of black studies.* Final Report, National Conference of Black Studies Annual Survey.

Turner, J.E. (Ed.). (1984a). *The next decade: Theoretical and research issues in Africana studies.* Ithaca, NY: Africana Studies and Research Center.

Turner, J.E. (1984b). Africana studies and epistemology: A discourse in the sociology of knowledge. In J.E. Turner (Ed.), *The next decade: Theoretical and research issues in Africana studies* (pp. v-xxv). Ithaca, NY: Africana Studies and Research Center.

Upton, J.N. (1984). Applied black studies: Adult education in the black community — a case study. *The Journal of Negro Education, 53,* 322-33.

Van Sertima, I. (1976). *They came before Columbus: The African presence in ancient America.* New York: Random House.

———— (Ed.). (1982). *Egypt revisited.* Journal of African Civilizations, 4.

———— (Ed.). (1983). *Blacks in science ancient and modern.* New Brunswick, NJ: Transaction Books.

White, D.G. (1980). *Ain't I a woman: Female slaves in the plantation south.* New York: W. W. Norton.

Woodson, C.G. (1933). *The mis-education of the Negro*. Washington, DC: Associated.

Young, C. (1984). An assessment of black studies programs in American higher education. Special issue of *The Journal of Negro Education*, 53.

Young, C., & Martin, G. (1984). The paradox of separate and unequal: African studies and Afro-American studies. *The Journal of Negro Education*, 53, 257-67.

Endnote

1. Adaptation of the title of the Fisk Memorial Address delivered by W.E.B. DuBois in 1933 entitled *The field and function of the Negro college*.

6.

Black Studies: An Overview

Darlene Clark Hine

During the late 1960s and early 1970s, unique historical circumstances propelled the development of Afro-American and Africana studies in colleges and universities. Few of these early endeavors were the result of careful and deliberate planning and analysis. Typically, they were established in response to political exigencies rather than intellectual and academic imperatives. These and other factors contributed to ongoing structural and organizational diversity. Today it seems that no two black studies programs are alike. Their diversity is evidenced in faculty size and composition, relations with university administrators and more traditional departments, curriculum, degrees offered, budgets, spatial resources, range of special programs, and the nature of their community outreach.

An important objective of this investigation was to examine the present status of these programs: How well have they been supported by their institutions? To what degree have they been able to secure productive faculty? Have they provided their faculties with the requisite resources and nurturing that encourage the quality teaching, research, and service required for success in the academy?

The ongoing debate over nomenclature is a graphic illustration of residual problems growing out of the turbulent times in which these programs burst upon the academic scene. The term "black studies" has become a generic designation, vociferously opposed by some who view the phrase as less than illuminating. Critics argue that this designation suggests that only black students and black faculty should be interested in this area of intellectual inquiry. Most institutions appear to prefer the titles "Afro-American," "African and Afro-American," or "Africana" studies. On the one hand, those who insist on the term "Africana studies" maintain that "Afro-American studies" implies that the primary focus of teaching and research is the historical, cultural, and political development of Afro-Americans living within the boundaries of North America. Moreover, "African and Afro-American studies" neglect the Caribbean and other parts of the Americas. On the other hand, "Africana studies" encompasses a broader geographical, if not disciplinary, reach, spanning both North and South America, the Caribbean, and the African continent—in short, the African Diaspora. Of course, few of the current programs possess the requisite institutional resources, faculty positions, or budget lines to be truly "Africana." But the intent points in the right direction and therefore is certainly praiseworthy.

The attempt to identify and assess black studies endeavors accurately is further complicated by the differences in structure and mission between "departments," "programs," "centers," and "institutes." Black studies "departments" are best characterized as separate, autonomous units possessing an exclusive right and privilege to hire and grant tenure to their faculty, certify students, confer degrees, and administer a budget. Black studies "programs" may offer majors and minors but rarely confer degrees. And perhaps more importantly, all faculty appointments in programs are of the "joint," "adjunct," or "associate" variety. These professors are in the unenviable position of having to please two masters to secure appointment and tenure.

"Centers" and "institutes" defy easy categorization. As a rule, they tend to be administrative units more concerned with the production and dissemination of scholarship and with the professional development of teachers and scholars in the field than with undergraduate teaching. Unfortunately, considerable confusion surrounds the name "center." Many people view centers as merely cultural or social facilities designed to ease the adjustment of black students to predominantly white campus life. Thus, centers are often denigrated and dismissed as having little or no relevance to black studies, which is imagined to be purely an academic or intellectual endeavor, albeit with political-advocacy overtones. However, the good work being done at centers like those at the University of California at Los Angeles (UCLA) and the University of Michigan certainly should correct these misconceptions.

University Administrators

It was encouraging and refreshing to encounter so many white university administrators who sang the praises of their black studies departments, programs, centers, and institutes. In fact, there was scarcely a discordant note. From the perspectives of the more positively inclined administrators on predominantly white campuses, it appears that black studies not only has come of age but also has been making important contributions to the academy. Although it is heartening to witness this attitudinal transformation, given the initial vehement objections to the creation of black studies units, it is nonetheless necessary to probe beyond the surface to assess fully the contemporary status of black studies.

Twenty years ago, when black students first demanded the establishment of black studies departments, programs, and centers, few of the beleaguered white administrators would have predicted a long life for these enterprises. Many undoubtedly wished that black studies would go away; others tried to thwart growth and development. Most of those who opposed the creation of black studies units claimed that these units would lower academic standards because they believed such endeavors lacked intellectual substance.

It is not surprising that at some institutions black studies units offered little intellectual challenge. Undertrained people were brought in to head programs hastily contrived to preserve campus peace. Unfortunately, the early development and subsequent evolution of black studies were further tainted by the media's sensationalized cover age of the armed black students at Cornell University and the 1969 shoot-out at UCLA, which left two students dead. In the minds of many, black studies would forever remain nothing more than a new kind of academic ghetto. University administrators who valued "peace" and "campus rest" had little inclination, courage, or will to insist on quality. Thus, black studies units seldom were held to the traditional modes of evaluation and scrutiny observed elsewhere in the academy.

By 1987, however, the tide had turned. There has been a discernible shift among college administrators from amused contempt or indifference to enthusiastic support of black studies. Now administrators are eager to improve the quality of their programs and departments. One potent factor has been the availability of a larger pool of productive, well-trained black scholars willing, indeed anxious, to head and/or work in black studies. No longer do administrators have to rely on the local minister or community activist to oversee and teach black studies. If they are willing to put up the money, administrators can recruit productive black scholars.

Another motivation fueling the change in attitude toward black studies is institutional expediency. Faced with the specter of declining black student enrollments, university administrators are increasingly using strong black studies departments, programs, centers, and institutes as recruitment devices. Moreover, as is often the case, the only critical mass of black faculty working at many of these institutions is housed in black studies divisions. It is sad but true that without black studies, Chicano studies, women's studies, or Native American studies departments or programs, few colleges and universities could boast of having an integrated or pluralistic faculty.

Institutional expediency and a larger pool of black scholars not withstanding, one fact deserves underscoring. Black studies departments and their faculties have proven to be a continuing source of intellectual stimulation on many American campuses. Black studies has opened up vast and exciting new areas of scholarship, especially in American history and literature, and has spurred intellectual inquiry into diverse social problems affecting the lives of significant portions of the total population. Lectures, seminars, and conferences sponsored by black studies units provide a threefold benefit: Students introduced to authorities from outside of the academy are impressed with the fact that there are many ways of expressing and knowing. Faculty, black and white, have the opportunity to share their expertise, test assumptions, and receive immediate feedback on work in progress. Finally, black community residents are encouraged to perceive universities as more accessible and less foreign. As members of these communities begin to identify with universities, they develop a greater appreciation for learning, and a respect for the scholarship of black professors.

Black Studies Curriculum

Despite its contributions and successes over the past twenty years, black studies still has to contend with and resolve rampant confusion, conflict, and creative tensions. The issues being debated include nomenclature; curriculum; identity, mission, and structure; graduate programs; faculty recruitment, retention, and development; accreditation; and professionalization. There is an ongoing debate, with no signs of immediate resolution, over whether black studies is a field or a discipline. The problems surrounding curriculum are worthy of special attention. Even within the same departments, faculties often find it impossible to agree upon a standard or core for all sections of the same introductory course in Afro-American studies. It is regrettable that there is no special summer institute or training program where black studies administrators and faculty could discuss and perhaps map an appropriate and effective curriculum.

The curriculum—whether it is called black studies, Africana studies, or Afro-American and African studies—should reflect an ordered arrangement of courses progressing from the introductory through the intermediate to advanced levels. In terms of content, a sound black studies curriculum must include courses in Afro-American history and in Afro-American literature and literary criticism. There should be a complement of courses in sociology, political science, psychology, and economics. A cluster of courses in art, music, and language and/or linguistics should also be made available to students. Finally, depending on resources and the number of faculty, a well-rounded studies effort should offer courses on other geographical areas of the black Diaspora—the Caribbean and/or Africa. African and Afro-American and Africana studies programs and departments should, as their names imply, offer a variety of courses on black societies in the New World as well as on Africa.

Although deciding what to name a unit and developing a sound and coherent curriculum are challenging, a more daunting task is acquiring resources to recruit and retain an appropriate faculty, one that includes assistant, associate, and full professors. In the late 1960s and early 1970s, black studies units simply drew into their domain whoever happened to be available and willing to join them. Thus, little uniformity in curriculum could be achieved across the country. With the economic difficulties and retrenchment of the late 1970s, many black studies faculties declined in size, producing an even more fragmented curriculum. To ensure that existing courses were offered on a reasonable and routine basis, black studies administrators had to rely heavily on part-time, visiting, or temporary appointees. Most often those available to accept such positions were in the creative arts—musicians, dancers, poets, and fiction writers.

More recently, black studies departments have increasingly relied on cross-listing courses to augment curriculum. The cross-listing of courses is both reasonable and advantageous because it builds bridges between black studies and the more traditional departments within the university, thus decreasing somewhat tendencies toward isolation and marginality. To be sure, there are pitfalls, and cautious administrators must be ever vigilant. Adaptive "survival" measures may encourage some university administrators to reduce further the resources allocated to black studies. After all, if black studies is consistently able to "make do" with less, one could logically conclude that it needed fewer resources in the first place. This is a special concern for departments and programs with small numbers of majors and minors and with low course enrollments.

All of these factors—lack of a critical mass of well-trained faculty, excessive reliance on temporary hires, absence of a coherent curriculum and of content consensus for even introductory courses, and the increasing use of cross-listing of courses—bespeak the difficulties confronting and perhaps threatening the autonomy of many black studies departments. These are certainly among the concerns of the leadership of the National Council for Black Studies (NCBS). I suspect that the officers of NCBS will experience considerable frustration as the organization attempts to design a standardized curriculum. Although it is perhaps perverse to see anything positive in this disarray, the major strength of the black studies enterprise may well be its ever-changing and evolving nature. The rapid proliferation of knowledge in the field is a strong argument in support of institutional flexibility. Faculty in this area need to be free to develop new courses, to experiment with different methodologies, and to adopt nontraditional texts, just as quickly as new knowledge is produced.

Undergraduate and Graduate Degree Programs in Black Studies

One of the characteristics of a viable discipline is the authority to confer degrees and certificates to students who have mastered a particular body of knowledge. Black studies faculty and administrators have been quite concerned with this issue. The majority of the more autonomous departments of black studies do, in fact, award B.A. degrees. Programs in black studies vary. Some offer majors while most offer at least minors to students receiving a degree from the more traditional academic disciplines. In other words, the student may receive a B.A. degree in history, sociology, political science, or biology, chemistry, business administration, or education — with a concentration in Afro-American studies.

Few black studies units offer master's degrees. Of the half dozen or so that do, the departments at Cornell and UCLA and the program at Yale are the most visible and are highly respected. Most of the M.A. degree students at Cornell and Yale go on to pursue Ph.D. degrees in traditional disciplines at some of the better institutions in the country. Others enter the labor force, working in social service agencies, businesses, or state and local governments. Cornell's Master of Professional Studies degree is specially designed to prepare students to work in community settings.

As with many other issues in black studies, there is no consensus about the wisdom of developing graduate degree programs in Afro-American studies. Certainly, at this stage in the evolution of black studies, there is a need for a creditable Ph.D. degree program. As I traveled around the country, black studies scholars expressed enthusiasm about the prospects of making a Ph.D. degree program available to students.[1]

Black Scholars and the Modern Black Studies Movement

At present, there are a number of top-flight black scholars, more than at any time in history. They are producing first-rate, indeed award winning, books and articles in areas of black studies. By far the most exhilarating part of the entire project involved meeting these scholars and becoming familiar with their work. No assessment of the overall status and impact of black studies would be complete without noting the research activities of this latest generation of black professors and administrators. Because the absolute numbers of black professors is small and declining, it is easy to lose sight of the quality and breadth of their research and to minimize the impact that they have had on scholarship in all branches of knowledge.

The collective scholarship of black professors provides a sound foundation for the future development of black studies as a discipline. To a great extent, this scholarship will ensure the eventual institutionalization of black studies within the academy. As long as black scholars remain productive and competitive, and devote considerable attention to recruiting and training the next generation or scholars, black studies will enjoy a presence on America's campuses. It is, however, precisely the need to recruit, retain, and educate young black men and women in the humanistic and social science disciplines that casts a cloud over the joy and exuberance accompanying any serious examination of the quality of black scholarship in the last two decades. For a variety of reasons, fewer black students are entering graduate school with plans for academic careers. At every stop on my tour of black studies units, faculty members and administrators, black and white, broached the topic and admitted that this problem was of critical importance to the future of black studies.

The numerous monographs, articles, and manuscript editing projects produced by black scholars have fueled the movement to reclaim the forgotten or obscured dimensions of the Black past. Their new interpretations of past and present conditions affecting all aspects of black life have wrought a veritable revolution, albeit a still largely unheralded one, in the ways in which even traditional historians, literature theorists, sociologists, anthropologists, philosophers, psychologists, and political scientists approach their work whenever it touches upon the experience of black people.

There is reason to be excited and pleased with the record of intellectual accomplishment evident in scattered institutions around the country. Regrettably, most of these black scholars have little contact with each other. Nevertheless, because there are so many recognizably productive and accomplished scholars the future of black studies appears bright in spite of all of the structural complexities and creative tensions. In the remainder of this paper, I will address several factors concerning black scholars: the role of philanthropic foundations in their development, the perspectives reflected in some of their works, and the relationship between their scholarship and black studies as an organized unit within universities and colleges.

Any perusal of the acknowledgments and prefaces of some of the refreshingly original recent works of black scholars demonstrates the critical importance of the scholarships and fellowships made available by foundations and other organizations, including those specifically set aside for minority group scholars. Without these special fellow ships, I dare say the record of productivity in black studies would not be so impressive.

To illustrate this point, l shall discuss three recently published and widely praised (within black studies circles, that is) volumes authored by black women scholars, the most recent group to establish a viable presence in the academy. Gloria T. Hull, professor of English at the University of Delaware, co-editor of *All the Women Are White, All the Blacks Are Men, But Some or Us Are Brave: Black Women's Studies* (Old Westbury, N.Y.: The Feminist Press, 1982) and editor of *Give Us Each Day: The Diary of Alice Dunbar-Nelson* (New York: Norton, 1984), has recently published a provocative and icon-shattering book, *Color, Sex, and Poetry: Three Women Writers of the Harlem Renaissance* (Bloomington: Indiana University Press, 1987). No one who reads it will ever again be able to think of the Harlem Renaissance in quite the same way. Hull effectively unveils the rampant sexism and chauvinism of the black male leaders of the Renaissance. In her preface, Hull wrote that in addition to a faculty research grant from the University of Delaware and a summer stipend from the National Endowment for the Humanities, a Rockefeller Foundation fellowship enabled her "to do the requisite, remaining travel and research" (p. ix).

E. Frances White, MacArthur Professor of History and Black Studies at Hampshire College, Amherst, Mass., and author of *Sierra Leone's Settler Women Traders: Women on the Afro-European Frontier* (Ann Arbor: University of Michigan Press, 1987), observed in her preface: "I received funding from the African American Scholars Council, the Danforth Foundation (Kent Fellowship) and the Roothbert Fund to aid me in my initial research. An A. W. Mellon Faculty Development Grant and a Fulbright Senior Research Scholar Fellowship helped me to return to Sierra Leone to collect further material"[2] (p. x). White's brilliant study contributes a feminist perspective to the continuing debate over the impact of colonial rule on women in Africa.

I first learned of Sylvia Ardyn Boone's *Radiance From the Waters: Concepts or Feminine Beauty in Mende Art* (New Haven: Yale University Press, 1986) from black historian Nell Irvin Painter of the University of North Carolina. Painter commented, "It's a *wonderful* book that takes real black beauty, African beauty, seriously, in an academic not a commercial way." The volume is indeed dazzling. Boone noted in her acknowledgment, "The Foreign Area Fellowship Program of the Social Science Research Council funded the first part of my work in England and later in Sierra Leone. A Dissertation Year Fellowship from the American Association of University Women and a grant from the Ford Foundation National Fellowship Fund financed additional research and then the write-up" (p. ix). Boone is an associate professor of the history of art and African and Afro-American studies at Yale University.

I have highlighted these outstanding examples of black scholar ship because the study of black women is the current frontier in black studies. Combined with the historical studies of professors Jacqueline Jones of Wellesley College (*Song of Sorrow, Song of Love: Black Women, Work and the Family in Slavery and Freedom*, New York: Basic Books, 1985) and Deborah G. White at Rutgers University (*Ar'n't I a Woman: Female Slaves in the Plantation South*, New York: Norton, 1985), the novels of Toni Morrison, Alice Walker, and Paule Marshall, the literary criticism of Prof. Barbara Christian at the University of California, Berkeley (*Black Women Novelists: The Development of a Tradition*, Westport, Conn.: Greenwood,1980), and the black feminist theory of Prof. Bell Hooks of Yale University, the three examples of black scholarship mentioned above would make for a dynamic course. Because the curriculum in black studies is so flexible and fluid, unfettered by disciplinary constraints, such a course would be introduced and taught with elan. Moreover, it should be noted that quite a few of the directors and chairs of black studies—for example, at Cornell and at the University of Mississippi—have established working ties with women's studies.

In addition to fellowship support, foundations have provided major funding for a host of black editing projects. A few of the notable projects are: the Frederick Douglass Papers, John Blassingame, editor; the Booker T. Washington Papers, Louis Harlan, editor; and the Freedmen and Southern Society Project, Ira Berlin, editor. These projects have made accessible to scholars invaluable documents and primary sources. Their significance to black studies scholarship cannot be exaggerated.

The massive Black Periodical Literature Project edited by Prof. Henry Louis Gates, Jr., of Cornell University, who is also author of *Figures in Black: Words, Signs, and the "Racial" Self* (New York: Oxford University Press, 1987), is a particularly important venture. His monographs continue to break new ground in literary theory and are indeed changing the way theorists evaluate and interpret black literature. The fiction project, on the other hand, reclaims the literary efforts of past generations of black writers. Gates's efforts are well-funded and deservedly so.

An especially encouraging sign of the vitality of black studies is the rising number of black scholars who are contemplating and/or engaging in collaborative research projects. This progression from individual research to collaborative efforts involving many people from different disciplines is a natural one. A typical first book or major publication is usually a revised dissertation. Now that many black scholars are working on second and third books and, most importantly, have acquired tenure, they are eager to develop collaborative studies. This impulse should be encouraged, as it bodes well for the development of black studies as a discipline.

In the early years, black studies units justified their intellectual existence on the grounds that they shattered the confining and restrictive boundaries of traditional disciplines. Actually, as far as I have been able to discern, most of the individual scholars in these programs and departments have published works that are very much in keeping with the methodological canons of the disciplines in which they were formally trained. It was naive and unrealistic to expect the young historian or sociologist of the Afro-American experience to retool, master a new, still inadequately defined Afrocentric methodology, and then prepare publishable manuscripts and win tenure—all within a six-year period.

In sum, 1 am optimistic about the future of black studies because of the energy, creativity, industry, and achievements of black scholars. The dream that black studies can be in the forefront of interdisciplinary research and writing deserves all available nourishment. The contemporary black studies movement will be considerably enhanced and sustained by serious professional scholars engaged in research and writing of the black experience. The creative potential of black studies, however, will become a reality only to the extent that foundations and universities provide full support.

Endnotes

1. In 1988 Temple University established the first Ph.D. program in African American Studies.

2. Painter to Hine, June 22, 1987.

7.

Black Studies: Discipline or Field of Study?

Philip T.K. Daniel

This paper is an outgrowth of a heated debate that has been raging in the field of Black Studies since its inception. The question that has brought so much discussion affects everyone who studies Blacks on the continent or in the diaspora. Is Black Studies a discipline? More importantly, is the subject matter of Black Studies so different from other fields of study that it should be codified under some broader and more comprehensive rubric other than an academic discipline? The current study will seek to answer both these questions. Does one think of Black Studies in the same way that one thinks of history or geography? Is Black Studies perceived as being separate and distinct from other disciplines in the way that one differentiates the principles of sociology and psychology? Can Black Studies be studied in and of itself or must there be present some covariant attachment to another discipline? Is there a methodology within the field of Black Studies which is confined to disciplinary study, or are topics chosen for analysis according to fleeting interest to which there are no interconnecting facts, theories, or generalizations?

The fact that this discussion is even taking place is illustrative of the concern that many have for Black Studies. Most Black Studies professionals have been trained in some academic discipline other than Black Studies and have probably never questioned that discipline's authority to exist. Those trained in established traditional disciplines have instead gone straight into the substance and methodology of their subject without ever thinking about whether they should. The fact that Black Scholars are doing this in Black Studies has a great deal to do with how the subject originated and why no clear set of guidelines or concrete methodology was initially established.

Most researchers agree on the factors surrounding the most immediate rise of Black Studies. Separate courses and separate departments were demanded by Black students and faculty on campuses around the country after the death of Dr. Martin Luther King. These students and faculty demanded equal academic representation of a culture that was categorically different from the dominant Anglo-Saxon culture. In addition, unlike most other disciplines, Black Studies had within its core curriculum a component that involved the Black community. Black Studies, therefore, originated during a time of high spiritualism and idealism as well as a time when the need to solve community problems was great. The result of this set of phenomena was the establishment of several programs around the country that sought to illuminate the cultural contributions of Blacks in the diaspora and to counteract the pejorative forces imposing themselves on the Black community. Although most of these programs were in colleges and universities, little attempt was made to develop effective analytical tools and methodologies.

Some scholars in the field did recognize the need for theory and methodology, because such goals had to be achieved if Black Studies was to progress or at least become an established field of study. Nick Aaron Ford's *Black Studies: Threat or Challenge?*[1] helped to define the area of study which added to the knowledge of the kinds of programs in existence. Armstead Robinson, et al., in *Black Studies in the University*,[2] helped scholars realize that of all of the disciplines, Black Studies sought to project itself in the Black community, and on Black problem-solving techniques. Articles by Nathan Hare,[3] Charles Hamilton,[4] and Ronald Bailey[5] all represented initial steps in the establishment of Black Studies as a representative and permanent field of study. There are, of course, other important works that can be mentioned. Nevertheless, all of these treatises, however valuable they may have been as separate entities, did not and were not intended to result in a discipline. This circumstance is understandable for at that time there was no common core curriculum.

This writer is not alone in this assessment of Black Studies. James Stewart of the Pennsylvania State University espouses a similar point of view when he says that "no school of thought within the Black Studies movement has developed a [unique] basic framework of analysis...," and therefore has not met the minimum standards necessary for demarcating Black Studies from other fields of study.[6] Moreover, Turner and Eric W. Perkins of Cornell University comment that Black Studies theorists have done little in the way of espousing new theoretical concepts and constructs that separate it from "the obsolete ideological baggage" of traditional disciplines rooted in the Anglo-Saxon culture.[7]

Conflicting Views on Black Studies

The critical issue is that if there is no common disciplinary thread for Black Studies that has yet been brought to light, can Black Studies professionals borrow from other disciplines and apply their constructs to the Black Studies "intellectual enterprise?" This question has been answered by at least three scholars who have attempted to subsume Black Studies under the banner of one or more disciplines. One author thinks of Black Studies as being embodied in the methodology of sociology. He defines Black Studies as "the systematic study of Black people" in social rather than racial terms.[8] All resulting research in this area must therefore be based on the social" qualifier.

Another author views Black Studies as a component of the field of economics. He posits that Blacks should be studied in the field under two approaches: (1) men of ideas, inventors and innovators; and (2) the successes and failures of Blacks in their entrepreneurial history.[9] The qualifier in his analysis is that although Blacks may be innovators and men of ideas, they may nor perform the coordinating function of bringing together the "factors of production."[10]

Still another researcher writes that the best approach to the field of Black Studies is "through an established discipline like economics, anthropology, sociology, psychology, and so on."[11] In effect, he claims, "a Black Studies interdisciplinary curriculum cannot stand alone...and...must so to speak be clothed in the tested scholarly and technical garment of a discipline."[12]

Unfortunately for these scholars, but fortunately for Black Studies theorists, classifying Black Studies under an academic discipline is an impossible task. In sociology, seeing the Black experience in only social and not racial terms is ludicrous. One might review the criticisms of William J. Wilson's study, *The Declining Significance of Race*, to support this opinion.[13] In economics, the fact that Blacks are not seen as important actors in the field of production smacks of ethnocentrism and the pinnacle of Anglo-Saxon racist belief. To suggest that Black Studies cannot exist without the covariant presence of another discipline represents the worst of conjectural puerilism for it sees the Black experience as the recipient of an alien academic process rather than one which can produce forms and mechanisms of its own.

This is not to question the validity and the significance of sociology, economics, history and other traditional disciplines. For as separate entities they accomplish tasks for which no other disciplines are a substitute. Nevertheless, research and analysis in other disciplines do not entirely substitute for the job that the sphere of Black Studies would be required to perform.

The fact that the other disciplines, are not substitutable and that Black Studies may require a different set of constructs does not necessarily categorize Black Studies as a discipline. Neither does it mean that Black Studies is any less than other fields of study because it does not yet conform to all traditional disciplines requirements. In fact, Black Studies may be better off not to conform itself to such an esoteric rubric. In view of this presumption, it might be helpful to examine the meaning of *discipline* within the context of education in the United States.

Disciplines and the American Ethos

A discipline implies a set of formally interrelated facts, concepts, and generalizations. It also implies a set of standardized techniques and skills. The components are part and parcel of a body of theory, propositions, and a subject matter. The specific subject matter is normally what separates one discipline from another.

Most disciplines in the United States go far beyond the above definition in their search for efficiency, predictability, and, more importantly, specialization. Specialization as Apter[14] sees it has exaggerated differences between disciplines, so much so that there is a definite emphasis on training individuals only in their chosen area. Along the way these same individuals develop a bias toward other fields of study. This situation has even caused intradisciplinary fragmentation where persons in the same field develop processes that are meant to provide further distinctions between themselves and their fellow scholars.

This reality results from the fact that all knowledge and all learning flows out of the culture in which it is set. American culture tends to accentuate separatism by rewarding rugged individualism (and therefore extreme specialization). Consequently, a discipline in this culture is not only based on a subject matter, but a set of skills and techniques limited to the variations in one's special block of facts. Hence, one must be able to arrive at certain conclusions without dealing with material in another disciplinary domain.

Disciplines based in the Anglo-Saxon culture also tend to do other things. They either exclude or debase the experiences of African-Americans that seemingly fall into their purview. The subject matter within these disciplines emphasizes the imagined "pathology" and "deviance" of African-American culture, and, as said before, sees Black people as non-producers of goods and passive recipients of whatever knowledge is given to them. In effect, African-American scholars trained here are not expected to challenge any of the tenets of Anglo-Saxon disciplinary structures. Instead, as passive recipients they must continue to reproduce the same separationist type of studies which see Black society as disorganized, fragmented, and degenerative. The aforementioned examples in sociology and economics serve to buttress this statement.

Black Studies professionals should glean from the preceding discussions and examples that if those whose job it is to study and to teach the Black experience do not supply the necessary accoutrements for carrying on the field of study, someone else will. Black Studies theorists must therefore build on their own originality and take from other traditions that which is sufficiently useful and develop their own structures, paradigms, and typologies. This paper contends that a broader heading than the term "discipline" is more constructive for Black Studies, because of the way the term "discipline" is defined and, delineated in this society and because the experiences of Black people are too broad to be codified to one academic discipline.

Concretization of Black Studies

Black Studies specialists must create the kind of "multidisciplinary" structure and accompanying set of skills and techniques, which functions to further their research on the one hand, and which aids in community problem solving and social action on the other. A critical Black Studies multidiscipline must also "strengthen our intellectual work by making . . . scholarship the study of reality as it is and as it has been, not as it might have been or as we might have liked it to be."[15]

One approach to the establishment of this kind of study is through intervariates or systems. A system is "any set of variables, regardless of the degree of the interrelationships between them."[16] It is solely a matter of conceptual or theoretical convenience, meaning that a Black Studies theorist will use whatever tools are available, either self-created or borrowed from others, which aid in solving important questions and/or problems in the Black community. This also means that these sets of skills and techniques must aid Black Studies specialists in understanding the Black community in conjunction with other cultural and racial entities as well as the larger society without compromising or violating certain fundamental cultural principles.

A systems approach works best when there is a definite issue to be addressed. It is predicated on the idea that few if any human problems can be traced solely on the basis of knowledge possessed by a historian alone, an anthropologist alone, or a sociologist alone. While most of these specialists recognize their right to know more about these other fields, they do not or cannot because of the prejudicial confines of their discipline. Black Studies, as a multidiscipline, has the best opportunity to develop within itself the wherewithal to reverse this secular trend. This represents no quarrel with specialization, but only the frame of reference in which it is set. Problems in the Black community emanate from collective phenomena and can only be solved by techniques that are rooted in collective answers. Black Studies theorists must therefore be about the business of training people in terms of coping with problem areas rather than just disciplines. Black Studies professionals must train toward specialization, but the kind of specialization that sees a student as a master-craftsman, an Imhotep, who integrates all of the knowledge of the time. In other words, students must be trained to be simultaneously sociologist, historian, educator, political scientist, anthropologist, businessperson, and so on.

Now the effort will be hopeless if it is confined to an attempt to synthesize only the facts and opinions already reached by individuals in other fields as a result of their hitherto independent and unrelated studies. The Black Studies theorist who believes that he or she can greatly strengthen the subject merely by abrogating to it the generalizations and preconceptions of other disciplines is probably doomed to disappointment. Suggestive ideas he or she may well obtain. But unless he or she is ready to participate in the development of ideas and answers yet untouched by those disciplines he or she is likely to find his or her flirtations with these other areas largely a waste of time. To put it another way, the Black Studies professional can hardly hope to contribute much to the Black community if he or she does not go beyond the paths other disciplines have already trod. DuBois, quoted by Stewart in his analysis of the Black college, perhaps said it best: "the American (Black) college cannot begin with history and lead to (Black) history. It cannot start with sociology and lead to (Black) sociology."[17]

Ergo, greater progress toward the creation of a Black Studies multidiscipline must be begun by Black Studies practitioners themselves. These professionals and their students must carry the concept of Black Studies beyond its current confines. They must be just as concerned with the practical application of the subject matter and techniques as they are with their institutionalization.

Tentative Recommendations

This writer is under no illusions about his ability to help begin this process or settle definitively the issues raised above, particularly within the limits of this present paper. Nonetheless, some partial answers are attempted. What the writer shall do is to delineate some of what has already been said by stating certain propositions about the nature and scope of Black Studies. In setting these forth he does not mean to imply that they incorporate the final form of the subject. But the present forms of the field are far from satisfactory, and the next few years must bring the development of more imaginative classifications. The propositions about the field are phrased canonically, because there is not sufficient time or space to express all of the possible qualifications. For the same reason, some statements may still contain some ambiguity.[18]

1. Black Studies is a "multidiscipline" that systematically focuses upon the experiences of Black people throughout the world. More specifically, it is the study of Africa and the African diaspora, in general and specialized areas of inquiry in particular.

2. Black Studies is bifocal or dichotomous. It simultaneously assesses the *outer* struggle of Blacks against oppression, discrimination, imperialism, racism, and other pejorative forces, while also looking at their *inner* struggle to establish community, identity, heritage, and a functional as well as practical and protective institutional infrastructure.[19]

3. Black Studies does not exist in the particularistic milieu of physics; rather it deals with a unique set of peoples and their systematic study necessitates unique (non-traditional) forms.[20]

4. As a branch of learning, Black Studies consists of both a subject matter and a set of techniques and methods of analysis for dealing with new questions. The subject matter concerns anything that relates to Africa or the African diaspora. It also consists of whatever knowledge is available that can positively and culturally aid in solving both new and old prob-

lems of Black people. It includes both techniques and processes concerning theory and practice. In theory the techniques and methods of analysis include the logical devices for arriving at hypotheses and for testing, verifying, or rejecting them. In the case of practical questions they include the devices for revealing the issues involved, delineating objectives, focusing on the alternative courses of action and their consequences, and selecting the most desirable outcome or conclusion.

5. The distinguishing characteristic of Black Studies as a distinct multidiscipline is found in the nature of its domain. Black Studies is concerned with the questions that arise about Black culture,[21] or Black culture as it influences or is influenced by other cultures. This concern is the basis for all research and community participation.

6. The goal of Black Studies is not merely knowledge for its own sake, but knowledge for the purpose of pragmatic manipulation. In this sense, a Black studies analyst is simultaneously a theorist, historian, reformer, and pragmatic manipulator. His or her job is not only to provide studies in heritage, but also to attempt to improve the lot of all or a particular segment of the Black community. A Black Studies analyst is well trained in a multitude of disciplines and has the responsibility of researching these subjects past the limits of other researchers. The analyst's interest in these other subjects must be further distinguished through total interest in the Black community. In effect, the Black Studies practitioner must be an "Interested" scientist within the DuBoisian realm, as opposed to a "disinterested" scientist in the Einsteinian realm.

7. For the training of potential specialists in the field, Black Studies is both cultural and professional. As a cultural subject the aim should be to introduce students to the general field and the methods available for analyzing its problems. The subject of Black Studies has enormous cultural value both in teaching an analytical, reflective, critical African way of thinking, and in enabling a student to understand and come to grips with a very important part of human existence. As for professional training, Black Studies must employ a systems approach for analysis. This Systems or "integration" approach, if you will, must disregard the current parameters of all disciplines. Students of Black Studies must be taught to think reflectively and effectively about whole questions, issues, and problems, and not just about which secular disciplinary structures to apply to them. The advocacy of a systems approach to Black Studies does not limit the use of other forms of analysis. For example, a Marxist analysis might be instructive, if not appropriate, for scholars looking at such issues as ghettoization, the use of Black people as surplus and cheap labor, the relative underdevelopment of the African continent, and so on. However, no previously developed instrument, process, theory, or discipline should be looked upon as an umbrella under which Black Studies must fall.

The preceding, as indicated, represented an attempt to define Black Studies and to determine at least some of its elements. It is not enough merely to define Black Studies as a field of study or name its features; it must be studied and practiced as part of a coherent system that can be used to solve some of the Black community's most basic problems. This objective is the ultimate task of Black Studies.

Endnotes

1. Nick Aaron Ford, *Black Studies: Threat or Challenge?* (New York: Kennikat Press, 1973).

2. Armstead Robinson, et al., *Black Studies in the University* (New York: Bantam Books, 1969).

3. Nathan Hare, "What Should Be the Role of Afro-American Education in the Undergraduate Curriculum?" *Liberal Education*, 40, no. 1 (1969), pp. 42-50.

4. Charles Hamilton, "The Question of Black Studies," *Phi Delta Kappan*, 57, no. 7 (1970), pp. 362-363.

5. Ronald Bailey, "Why Black Studies?" *The Education Digest*, 35, no. 9 (1970), pp. 41-47.

6. James Stewart, "Introducing Black Studies: A Critical Examination of Some Textual Materials," *Umoja*, 3, no. 1 (1979), p. 8.

7. James Turner, and W. Eric Perkins, "Towards a Critique of Social Science," *The Black Scholar*, 7, no. 7 (1976), p. 7.

8. Maurice Jackson, "Towards a Sociology of Black Studies," *Journal of Black Studies*, 1, no. 2 (1970), p. 132.

9. Martin Ijere, "Whither Economics in a Black Studies Program?" *Journal of Black Studies*, 3, no. 2 (1972), p. 151.

10. *Ibid.*, p. 151.

11. Martin Kilson, "Reflections on Structure and Content in Black Studies," *Journal of Black Studies*, 3, no. 3 (1973), p. 303.

12. *Ibid.*, p. 307.

13. Joseph R. Washington, ed., *The Declining Significance of Race: A Dialogue among Black and White Social Scientists* (published proceedings of a symposium held at the University of Pennsylvania, March, 1979).

14. David E. Apter, *Introduction to Political Analysis* (Cambridge, MA: Winthrop Publishers, 1977), p. 28.

15. Turner and Perkins, *op. cit.*, p. 10.

16. David Easton, *A Systems Analysis of Political Life* (New York: John Wiley and Sons, Inc., 1965), p. 2.

17. Stewart, *op. cit.*, p. 15.

18. The author is very grateful to Professor Alphine Jefferson of Northern Illinois University for his aid in developing these propositions. They would not have been possible without his help.

19. *Ibid.*

20. *Ibid.*

21. The author is using the term culture here in the anthropological sense—as the total life experiences of a people.

8.

Classifying Black Studies Programs

Carlos A. Brossard

Practice and Definition

Contemporary Black Studies[1] programs incorporated the study and interpretation of the experience of Blacks of the United States, formally and organizationally, into the routinized institutional life of major universities. This incorporation coordinated and integrated disparate courses and prior selective emphasis on the meanings of the Black experience. It partially addressed prior exclusion, deliberate cursory treatments, or inferior status assignment to teaching, studying, and researching Afro-America. Reacting to institutional racism, this incorporation partially changed structural exclusion of the study and interpretation of Blacks of the United States in the everyday life of major universities. The emergence of contemporary Black Studies programs ended a period of studied indifference toward the inclusion of the Black experience in higher education offerings.

As an academic enterprise, contemporary Black Studies programs aimed to eliminate or neutralize the low intellectual valuation and gross distortions of the historical meanings and social roles, expressive virtues, and cultural strengths of involuntarily transplanted Africans and their descendants within the United States. However, its task structures were rarely tightly outfitted to meet this proclamation. In most instances, Black Studies programs combined and examined the experiences of United States Blacks with those of Africa or the Caribbean, or compared ethnicity in two or more domestic contexts, in the humanities or social sciences, alone or jointly.[2] In symbolic solidarity, Black Studies curricula rarely removed Blacks of the United States from their ancestral homeland.[3] To execute the functions of Black Studies, multi-task academic organizations grappled with varied teaching and research responsibilities. In addition, these units also experienced systematic calls for support services and campus conflict resolution, institutional social control, and involuntarily imposed social work.[4] Considered from its functional roles, Black Studies, since 1968, has rarely been permitted to be a single-task, highly goal-focused, exclusively academic enterprise.[5] Consequently, no single behavioral definition of Black Studies prevails. At best, a collection of organizational strategies, varied research goals, unsettled content domains, and multiple formats crossing and cutting humanities and social science permutations characterize Black Studies programs today. Essentially, any definition of Black Studies emerges from pluralistic praxis, not grand theory.[6]

In this vacuum, over the last five years, articles on administering Black Studies and unorthodox technical reports[7] provided empirical contentions on evaluating Black Studies. Presuming a plural definition of Black Studies, this discussion exam-

ines the growing body of demonstrations of performance, criticizes unattended measurement and conceptual confusions, and proposes clear research and demonstration
tasks to evaluate fairly and forcefully triumphs and tribulations, stunning creativity
and dismal disappointments. A second purpose is to force raw technical reports to
meet expected analytical and statistical adequacy.

Structural Issues in the Development of Black Studies

Philip Daniel and Asmasu Zike described the institutional development of Black
Studies in a 1983 survey report.[8] Clearly, three of every four contemporary Black
Studies programs with more than a decade of service began between 1968 and 1971.
Contrary to guesses about their actual size at formation, it is certain that 130 to 160
programs began in the blistering years 1968-1971.[9] At its zenith, the number of programs and departments reached no more than 300 formally organized units. (This is
the upper limit estimate from Daniel and Zike's data.) At no time measured did estimates show exponential growth or widespread diffusion into higher education.
Moreover, these departments or programs were formed primarily in the older American universities, i.e., those founded prior to 1928.[10] These institutions had long years
of experience at adapting to innovation and at initiating new subunits. In the vein of
the day, within a context of higher education expansion, Black Studies took hold as
an undergraduate teaching enterprise, not as a research training unit.[11] In turn, this
focus undermined proclaimed preferences and goals of the programs.

A majority of the programs preferred interdisciplinary tasks and displayed this preference by their names. Yet, neither interdisciplinary specialists nor long-term experience
with combining disparate content groupings prevailed. The young graduate students and
newly-minted doctorates who staffed the early departments had to resocialize themselves,
without strong attachment to exemplary university training programs, in interdisciplinary
work.[12] At the same time, they gained the experience of combining comparative ethnicity
or African and Afro-American studies, organizationally and institutionally, by trial and
error. This was the only available method, having been left alone without shared institutional guidance from established disciplines and their professional associations. Youthful
and energetic, but organizationally inexperienced and short on institutionally transferred
resources for building new intellectual enterprises, Black Studies faculty and administrators faced three strenuous, resource draining, and goal displacing requirements: (1) to
generate the interdisciplinary expertise by self-resocialization; (2) to experiment with
stand-alone Black Studies or combined studies of the African diaspora, and (3) to build
viable departments without clearly understood precedents for making and sustaining an
intellectual edifice.[13] They were to perform these tasks in a context where teaching automatically supplanted research in focus, effort, and energy.

This conflictual developmental path occurred not by accident. Gordon noticed
(but few others have systematically stressed) that established disciplines refused to
cooperate in the building of Black Studies departments.[14] The bedrock foundation for
the emergence of contemporary Black Studies was laid by Black urban, lower-class
students as they tried to get better Black Studies courses from traditional departments. These departments and their representatives, especially in sociology, refused
to extend manpower and built-up intellectual resources, forcing protesting Black students to insist on alternative structures for handling Black Studies. Consequently, al-

lied disciplines and professionals sparingly and grudgingly helped the organizational, curricular, and institutional-building tasks of the new academic specialization. Intellectual integration and effective and efficient organization could have resulted from cooperation with friendly disciplinary neighbors. Instead, unexpected and unanticipated Black Studies departments widened the social distance between allied disciplines and professionals.[15] New pioneers stood alone in resolving intellectual integration and discovering organizational building without shared support or prior role modeling of professional peers.[16]

Unexpected arrivals and poor cooperation were not the toughest bottlenecks, though. Finances were. Most Black Studies programs relied on "hard money," i.e., fixed institutional finances.[17] As a sudden event, Black Studies departments imposed new expenditures and, at the same time, blocked orderly rational expansions of allocations for competing university units. Tacitly, intra-organizational competition for available resources climaxed the commitment to establish programs. The staffing patterns of early programs, i.e., the cheaper labor of graduate students and new doctorates, resulted from the heavy, immediate crunch that establishment of new programs or departments imposed—especially when they were not self-financing by acquisition of research funds. Superior performances required well-financed scholars,[18] the highly valued professionals to the institution. This could not occur in the Black Studies departments unless research was the single-minded, highest priority, since it was in research that expanding funds were available. Reality displaced this emphasis.

Instead of starting where most disciplines begin—at the graduate level with preemptory emphasis on research skills and production—Black Studies programs began in undergraduate instruction. Next, the dominant clientele imposed immediate needs for compensatory education, since many poorly prepared inner-city students came to Black Studies departments.[19] *Ipso facto*, the mission of Black Studies departments had to include support services, i.e., academic social work and mediating embedded conflicts between students of poor backgrounds and their often hostile reception in the formerly segregated settings where Black Studies programs were formed. In very few places, a division of labor separated these tasks. Involuntarily, Black Studies became a multi-task operation with added compensatory education pressures extending the real domain of work.

The single-minded goal focus of improving and financing scholarly production was generally displaced by the countervailing pressures of meeting pressing, immediate student requirements of additive skill building. Compensatory education and social control competed with and undermined the ordinary insulated effort attached to making well-financed, scholarly production units (a task that in itself is more than a full-time job). Multi-task goals functionally fragmented organizational cohesion to drift off "hard money" by securing "soft money" which builds long-term research depth and its accompanying future self-financing. Drifting off institutional dependency on "hard money" would be difficult where pressing social control and social work erode effort and energy at substantial research execution.

Finances also harnessed the growth potential of Black Studies. About the time Black Studies programs began, higher education resources began to slip downward. Within universities, internal competition for dwindling resources rose. By the end of the 1974-75 recession, about three years after most Black Studies programs had begun, internal competition stiffened and modestly growing fiscal resources meant less in absolute terms. New claimants rose, in part from two Black Studies spin-offs, one from positive and the other from negative role modeling: women's studies and resurrected ethnicity such as stand-alone ethnic studies. At the same time, ordinary subspecialty expansions that had new claims on existing resources proliferated. What resulted was unexpected higher pressure on the dollar. The strife of increasing competition over a generally decreasing resource base firmly checked substantial fiscal growth for Black Studies as well as for all new claimants—unless, of course, they turned to outside funding. However, that source of support also had dipped downward. At best, uneven acquisitions of resources would meet the infant industry requirements for more and improved resources. Thus, increasing economic scarcity structured and limited the systematic growth potential of all new Black Studies departments.

After finances, curriculum and tenure took center stage in the development of Black Studies. In a recent review of Karenga's *An Introduction to Black Studies*, James Stewart summarized the state of affairs well,[20] pointing out that a guiding introductory text as a synthesis exemplar of the discipline still has not surfaced. All attempts at writing such a book have serious intellectual and analytical problems of omission or commission, faulty integration, or low explanatory power across disciplinary topics. Recombinations of subspecialities into a holistic description and demonstration have proved difficult to master. Stewart disclosed that most Black Studies professors work from their prior disciplinary backgrounds. The promised disciplinary synthesis in the vein of Thomas Aquinas, for Catholic medieval theology, or of Paul Tillich, for modern Protestant theology, has not come.

Again, this is not unusual. In the rise of sociology, between 1891 and 1929, the battle of introductory texts occurred among major sociologists.[21] The critical consensus work here, Park and Burgess's *Introduction to the Science of Society* (1921), was not widely used during its first decade in print. In the absence of a consensual work, Stewart calls the present phase of Black Studies the "pre-paradigmatic" stage. This label skirts around a central issue.

In the absence of a uniform introductory text, a plural context of theory construction and instructional variations are the norm. Although long-established historical, sociological, imaginative, and performing arts traditions of Black Studies must be consulted, they often prove insufficient and behind newer sophisticated analytical strategies in the social sciences. The debate over curriculum reduces itself to the question of what knowledge is worth having and how it should be approached with the best traditions of criticism and interpretations, scientific rigor, and contemporary advances. A measure of contemporary Black Studies excellence is the answer to that question in current practice. This issue will be resolved as greater institutional permanence permits the intentional institutionalization rather than the hurried costs of unexpected and unintended beginnings. The first decade searched for minimal formal content, adequate variants of that content across disciplinary lines, topic uniformity regardless of approach, and, more important, removed the charlatans and alchemists as well as the mechanical Marxists and romantic nationalists.[22] Of course, searching for and testing new curriculum ideas drained limited time and effort away from systematic research. The personal and professional costs of curriculum construction were rarely in the parent institution's master planning or organizational building schedules.

If curriculum development was troublesome, the tenuring of professors was even more so. Briefly, at the major research universities, performance evaluation, e.g., publish or perish, occurred as if ordinary conditions with settled routines applied. In fact, this state of affairs created what Merton called "true conformists or risk-taking rebellious"[23] faculty members. The conformist kept his nose on publication volume and relegated teaching to a secondary role. For the loyalist to a discipline of origin, reality dictated that organizational building run on automatic pilot. With expediency, he handled organizational crises on an ad hoc basis. The core function of the conformist was retention and promotion, since, rather accurately, he sensed that a double standard asked for institutional building and scholarly productivity as if they were compatible. The conformist traded off retention over organizational development.

On the other hand, the risk-taking rebellious person faced a real moral dilemma. To meet student demands, he sliced into research time to provide services. In turn, this stymied his career development. Sooner or later, the professor had to return to the careerist path. In the meantime, unrecoverable, valuable time and work went to low priority, service-oriented, or community-conflict resolution tasks that failed to count with the tenure review committee. Even where real organizational contributions, meritorious conflict resolution, or community consultant work were made systematically, risktakers usually gambled on doing research and other organizational work well. In reality, the activist side depleted the undivided attention needed for continuous research demands. Dividing attention virtually insured little promotional chances.

Yet, of all structural barriers, the hardest to address was the most unexpected in a period of proclaimed Black unity—the strong interpersonal warfare around ideological differences and national backgrounds of Blacks. On the first, the issues usually boiled down to "who was what," e.g., Marxists vs. nationalists, reformers vs. revolutionaries, accommodationist institutional role players vs. political activists on social change projects. The ideological differences were healthy in bringing out background variances and dispelling myths of uncritical racial unification. These differences also revealed differential aspirations as well as unshared identity, consciousness, and class aspirations. In effect, these differences advanced variant models of Black Studies for testing and challenge, as institutions considered adding Black Studies programs. However, they came with acrimony, which further fragmented organizational consensus. Polarization and alienation from within delayed the tunnel vision that went with well-defined rationalizations of institutional purposes.[24]

Another aspect of these interpersonal differences came across international boundaries. Many early programs with a Pan-Africanist bent rushed to include their "brothers and sisters," West Indian and African. Often the faculty in these programs had been trained overseas. Their concepts of university life differed from those of Black United States nationals. (Even younger anticipatory elites of the new nations who took their training in the U.S. showed such an orientation.) While most cross-cultural exchanges of the Black world were more than concordant, conflicts erupted in various ways and settings. For example, the mixed marriages of foreign nationals often met with disapproval by United States Blacks. Neither side examined customary practices and marital selection rules that differed by national backgrounds. Perhaps this problem was rivaled in intensity by attempted coup d'etat by foreign nationals against Afro-American leadership roles, styles, and tactics. Often, foreign nationals got along better with white faculty than with Afro-Americans, a situation that created more friction.

With students, these differences took another turn. Black American professors often showed more tolerance for class and cultural backgrounds of Black and poor students. The rigorous elitist push-out methods of the highly stratified educational backgrounds of foreign nationals, especially those who came from colonial educational systems with a British bent, were often internalized. To many Blacks of the United States, who had worked very hard against institutional odds, this elitism was intolerable. Before negotiated settlements and better understanding set in, emotional conflicts ran high and unexpected social distance trapped good intentions in unworkable interpersonal interactions.[25] When contractual obligations placed together professors with conflicting views for longer periods than they wished, the blending of effort, initiative, coordination, and consolidation that early institutional budding required was thwarted.

So far, most proposals for evaluating Black Studies systematically underplay or ignore these structural contexts, in general or in particular. This oversight clouds a clear understanding of how to appraise what happened and how to derive an explanation of intended or unintended outcomes. Yet, the well-advertised structural problems that exist must be understood for program evaluation to occur.

Proposals for Evaluation Measures

Two types of proposals for evaluation exist at present. One is a so-called quantitative approach that emerged from McWorter.[26] The other is a process/product approach that stresses the transactional context and its organizational processes. This approach is attributed to Ray.[27]

The Quantitative Suggestion

McWorter proposed that performance be assessed by ordinary norms, i.e., professional attainment by various status measures. His operational definition came to three measures: (1) institutional (*not* discrete individual) memberships on the boards of Black Studies journals; (2) publications in Black Studies Journals by institutional affiliations; and (3) institutional membership in leadership roles of professional associations of Black Studies.[28] Without norming these measures and by arraying ordered magnitudes without breaking ties (the customary statistical practice), he emerged with a set of rankings.[29]

At the outset, his population measures faltered. Although many articles on Black Studies appeared in mainstream journals, he counted only Black Studies journals. Similarly, he counted only domestic Black Studies journals. Yet, Caribbean, African, and other international journals routinely handled Black Studies materials. Thus, McWorter's list of journals failed to have the fullest accounting of the universe. In selecting a small subset of the true universe, McWorter rendered, at best, the easiest count, not the most complete or the best systematically sampled options. The possible Black presence on all boards that systematically and persistently published Black Studies should have been defined before such a limited subset was offered as the true universe.

Other universe characteristics are not classified well either. These include labeling journals by their disciplinary backgrounds, in the main and Black Studies streams, to segregate linkage effects. Moreover, journals have prestige rankings, formally and informally. Such weightings would count entries differently. (The weights are all the same for McWorter, a fact that ranked prestigious, older journals the same as new upstarts.) Before Black Studies journals can be weighted, the reputational surveys have to precede. These have not been done for McWorter's sample. This removed a critical backward linkage measure to proposed alternative, more powerful multivariate strategies of rating performances. Similarly, disaggregating the meaning of institutional affiliation cannot be done with the data as reported. Such disaggregations would look at department affiliation, professional age, continuity of well-established research by specific individuals, and differentially weighting new research endeavors as against exhausting long-term theory building from an aging or career project. Again, mere publication divorced from the rooted contexts of exponential appearance or glacial outputs rendered little substantive evaluation—other than a count.

If some reasonable, sufficient data were available on these matters, the pertinent correlational and regression analysis would make sense. Perhaps we could learn if economists, for example, published more than sociologists in Black Studies. If this is so, is it related to the higher quality of updated government-reported data as well as a higher standardization of mathematical normative reasoning in most economic modelings? Even within fields, differences may have a contextual basis. For example, would family sociologists be doing more than demographers because certain topics at present (e.g., the rapid spreading of single parenting across all class groupings) generate strong time series outputs tied to emerging policy debates? The contingent context of outputs requires some specifications. The real contexts of production should be specified more concretely, especially in settings where pay boosts come with added ink in journals.

Further, unnormed measures, i.e., only magnitudes by institutions without some reporting about individuals, defied the logic of ordinary measurement where, to get comparable units, standardization is employed.[30] In the same vein, magnitude was separated from its generative mechanism, i.e., organizational size, attributes, resources. In short, production inputs and the model of actual statistical test are never disclosed.[31] The use of decontextualized numbers, an unspecified model of a test of ranking, and the data, in unorthodox form, requires prior transformations or severe caution before they can be claimed as useful or adequate for the problem: ranking performances by a subset of journal board members, journal article representation, and particular professional association membership. These limitations could have been reduced, however, by exploratory data analysis on what is essentially a convenience sample.[32] This type of procedure would have provided a basis for subsequent confirmatory data gathering and analysis.

Exploratory findings, i.e., data-grounded findings, given the limitations of the data batch, and a conventional rearrangement of the data performed by the author went against McWorter's major claims.[33] Space does not permit reproduction of the statistical analyses performed. Interested readers may write to the author for these analyses. Suffice it to say here, neither journal board membership by institution nor output volume by institution fully captured professionalization in the McWorter study. That study gave a suggestive measure that was not properly explored, fully developed, or securely confirmed.

Organizational Mission and Outputs:
A Qualitative Model

Here, the example is Ray, who focused on Black Studies in predominantly white institutions, specifically Western Michigan University. Ray's argument is straightforward. Black Studies has educational functions because (1) Black students increasingly will be at predominantly white institutions and (2) the university's mission should be to generate and distribute new knowledge on Blacks. In performing its mission, Black Studies spearheads the attack against racism organizationally and in curriculum. Additionally, Black Studies has some content priority for students. This priority includes reinforcing a positive identity which prior education neither nurtured nor enhanced and giving support to students' aspirations for employment, power, and prestige acquisitions. In part, the instructional purposes of Black Studies are to clarify incorrect content domains throughout the university, to reduce the negative alienation of being Black in a white segregated setting, to tell the truth about the "American" myth of a just society, and to serve clients. In doing well its clarification of American values, it should replicate tomorrow's warriors for simple justice.

Ray pointed out that to evaluate Black Studies the first task is to see it within the mission of the university, i.e., generation and distribution of new knowledge. Accordingly, a measure of successful mission was the extent to which programs aided new conceptual frameworks as well as content clarification of American life and institutions to eliminate Black denigration to all-Black or white. This type of mission occurred across all traditional disciplinary boundaries. This is a production measure.

A consumption measure looked at client benefits. What were clients getting and for what? Clients need a counter-force to destruction or denial of their identity and self-esteem from prior educational settings and their continuation into higher education. Clients require ordinary support strategies for their first mission—enhancing achievement outcomes in college. At the same time, they should acquire defensive mechanisms to shield themselves from "offensive mechanisms," the systematic microaggression white youths have internalized as their birthright to gain competitive and comparative advantage over Blacks from schooling—cognitively and affectively. The best defense is to be on the offensive by giving Black students sharper academic and interactional weapons—cognitively and affectively. Together with content clarifications of "American" institutions, these support strategies should be concretely and explicitly backed by measurable goals and feedback strategies in five-year plans. Production and consumption units should be managed by these objectives.

Since community service is also expected in a university, Black community service should be, too. This should be explicitly linked to observable demands and legitimizing functions, the best defense against a hostile university setting to Black studies. Both a readiness to serve or to struggle should be expected.

Five-year planning and constituency advisory boards should be formed. The planning should resemble development programming of the developing countries, where five-year timetables, buttressed by annual emphasis of selective goals, motivate performance and explicitly chart institutional learning based upon what is learned from successes and failures, corrective paths, and promising events. The advisory councils integrate constituencies into planning and decision making, goal selection and monitoring progress. All of this resuscitates the vision of Black Studies as a school within a school, and culminates in a working (i.e., operational) definition of Black Studies:

> The present working definition of Black studies is a multi-disciplinary body of knowledge and experience about the struggle of people of African descent against racism and oppression and their relationship to White people, especially those of European descent. Black Studies...is for all students, Black, White and others. Its role is to research distortions in various disciplines, investigate the norms and values of the university, examine the disciplines and their omissions, bring the Black perspective to each discipline, monitor the offerings of each for racism, produce models of service of the Black community and Black students through direct action, test these models, disseminate information about Black culture, sponsor activities about Black culture, develop research skills in students, and provide additional student support systems.[34]

This model captures the multi-disciplinary view of Black Studies.[35] All of this, of course, presumed organizational capabilities, subunit specializations, and adequacy and, more or less, linear sequential progressions between aspirations and actualizations. The presumed organizational structure in manpower and tasks, coordination and control remained unspecified. For example, is undergraduate teaching, the dominant Black Studies, compatible with the goals at the research development levels? Often, the undergraduate Black Studies instructor provides courses in one area and conducts research in another. The linkage between teaching and current research is not present in most programs at the undergraduate level. The missing graduate settings and the organizational problems this creates rarely are addressed in the proclaimed models. The tendency to proclaim aspirations but failure to convert them into resource and organizational requirements is a gap in this model. What is required in an organization that harnesses effort and goals and allocates resources to me et intentional outcomes rarely is specified within prevailing limitations. Overloading meager resources and manpower literally follow from most small scale resource units of Black Studies today, when they follow this model without selection and priority of some goals. Operationally, the emphasis on the most pressing or preferred goals from this litany followed actual organizational capacity.

Moreover, subunit specialization is rare. One unit is the norm. Subunit specialization usually is one person who gets added tasks, blurring principal goals and displacing clear categorical goals.

Linear progression from goals to objectives to corrective feedbacks during execution of intended alms is also rare. In part, specialization and rewarded individual excellence created ordered anarchy, not planned coordination. In the conformist/rebellious conflict, discussed earlier, this model opted for the rebellious in settings that rewarded the conformists. This structural swing restrained the best collective coordination which interfered with strongly rewarded individual performances—and not around organizational building either. This also contributed to unstated warring aims—a Hobbesian state of war that virtually insured long-standing rule by early heads to keep continuity and regime interest intact—in ways that resembled individual interest, not collective interest. Especially when tenure density was high, conformist individualism persistently favored continued individual higher status (and income) attainments, not the explicit sacrifice structures of institutional building.[36] The "strongman," the head tradition in early "American" institutional sociology, with the blessing of the leading institutional center, has been replicated in Black Studies.[37] The highly developed, smoothly functioning and rationally divided bureaucracy projected by the multi-discipline model rarely is fact within today's restraints. Moreover, most leaders rarely plan or facilitate easy organizational succession. At this stage, the cult of the leader rather than the stand-alone, enduring features of routinized roles and tasks, still holds the organizational components together in many Black Studies departments. Internal cohesion and organizational integration have not yet set in. Without it, the multi-disciplinary model lacks teeth.

Ray's model, though, had another strength. It attended to the organizational process.[38] It moved closer to measuring and rationalizing a normal bureaucracy. But it clung to the multi-disciplinary goals and tasks of Black Studies in the face of a reality that precluded its possibility (under present organizational forms). The problem of splitting Black Studies by an avalanche of goals and persistent organizational fragmentations on a narrow resource base has not been faced. This occurs despite the fact that unexpected intruders—the social control and conflict resolution functions, the social welfare, and social work tasks and services that must be given to the wounded warriors of sustained microaggression—wear down the best organizational tunnel vision. The limits of a multi-disciplinary model have not been faced as yet.

Specifying the Evaluation Model: A Proposal

An evaluation model for Black Studies programs should consist of at least three interrelated tiers: (1) structural issues in the development of programs at particular institutional settings, (2) some external validation approaches (McWorter's bent), and (3) some organizational process data on actual organizational behaviors or an organizational process format (Ray's inclination). A mixed model, starting with concrete case studies, is required now, before reductionist proponents falsify these tiers. The case studies should provide access to actual intents or goals that are distinguished from proclaimed intents. Behaviorally, the prime focus of everyday activity, at the micro-ethnographic level of daily work routines, should be ascertained. Next, the real interactions between organizational capabilities and actual performances tagged to a goal structure — or the absence of one — should render what institutional feedbacks occurred between planning and execution from year-to-year. The crucial role of organizational learning in correcting preferred planning or restructuring preferred plans should illustrate how well goals and their continued presence or absence shaped what is or what is evolving. A structural etiology on contexts and their unique interactional patterns and Parsonian patterning should clarify the origin of this entity and how it came to be this way. The interaction between inception and corrective changes may tell us the difference between what we wanted and what we have.

The external validation issue is crucial. Despite the shortcomings in the Mc-Worter study, it pinpointed important issues for real analysis. Sooner or later, the real measures of performance across settings must be tackled. Retrenchment now will do it involuntarily. Exploring and confirming the suggestive issues in external validation offered a way to set external standards for emergent uniformity across settings. If nothing else, the backward linkage studies on mapping the actual publication universe, norming standardized output and prestige scales, doing the reputational studies and linking these to organizational traits in discipline and manpower characteristics, organizational development, and performance excellence are urgent pre-studies to sustain acceptable validation measures. It is crucial that hard core quantitative studies, explicitly refined by inescapable multivariate analysis and structural models, be pursued. Univariate measures alone will not suffice.

Ray is problematic but useful. His penchant to list all that ought to be done must cease. We can do only what our limitations permit. The multi-disciplinary preferences of Black Studies may have to be institutionally segmented across a division of labor before they are recombined in well-defined micro-replicas.[39] Some fragmentation and, recombinations derived from actual studies should tell us realistically how far the multi-discipline can go in today's specialized academic world. The inescapable multi-disciplinary demands are there and firmly preferred. These demands, though, need to be moved to actual demonstrations of well-balanced integration within limited capacity organizations. That challenge faces us now. Why?

Behaviorally, Black Studies developed case by case. It has had extremely varied forms: departments, programs, loosely connected research centers or institutes marginally connected to instruction, selectively focused disciplinary-based topics across departments without integration and coordination, junior college detachment from a longer term predictable college major, major Black university topical spreads at flagship institutions, single person programs, or curriculum coordinators on the periphery of higher education. Hence, no one model will cover all contexts, cases, and contingencies. What is needed initially is a stratified approach that matches evaluation with: (1) particular development contexts and resources; (2) discrete self-studies targeted to planned organizational changes and to replicating known successes; (3) selective research time series that link internal and external evaluation studies, external growth patterns of the specialization, and similar comparative contexts of differential successes and failures; and (4) developing strong external validation measures tied to: (a) known organizational strategies, (b) organizational growth and subunit differentiations, (c) institutional integration processes and patterns, (d) shared institutional collaborations or conflicts across departments and boundaries—in friendly competition or antagonistic competitive academic politics, within and across race, and (e) manageable social change measures and tasks that easily blend into routine work and that do not undermine the central educational production and consumption priorities.

The myth that Black Studies can do all well needs to be challenged. A multi-dimensional model—in organizational strategy and program content—with appropriate adjusted weights should begin to show context and performance, resource capability and organizational development, stratified structural limitations and easily transferred patterns of excellence. In a classical manner, the detailed case studies will have to precede. From there we get the face validity of issues and measures that must be brought under control. The start toward serious evaluation, within the context of developing evaluation research, has only just begun.

Endnotes

1. The phrase "Contemporary Black Studies" refers to the period after 1970, when formal programs or departments proliferated, partly in response to Dr. Martin Luther King, Jr.'s, death, and partly in response to the Black power mood and movement of the time. This phrase attempts to distinguish the birth of an era of institutional diffusion and incorporation into large-scale higher education.

2. The 1983 verifiable list of the National Council for Black Studies had 8 different groupings and 36 different organizational units that voluntarily identified themselves as Black Studies. The dominant focus was Black or Afro-American Studies, with Pan-Africanist Studies the next choice. These groupings duplicated ideological differences that existed when these departments or programs began between 1968 and 1972. See, "Afro-American Studies Chairpersons/Directors," (Bloomington, IN: National Council for Black Studies, Inc., January 1983), Mimeographed.

3. This is critical since state-sponsored interest, since 1957, propelled emergent African studies to meet foreign policy demands of the United States. No similar state-assisted thrust ever sustained or encouraged Black Studies development. At the central state level, the preference has been to cut connections between Africans and Afro-Americans except for the long-standing, approved Liberian linkages.

4. Detailed illustration of these tasks appears in W. L. Sims, *Black Studies: Pitfalls and Potential* (Washington, DC: University Press of America, 1978).

5. For early recognition of multiple contradictory aims and isolating research as the central mission and highest priority for institutional survival, see Elias Blake, Jr., and Henry Cobb,

Black Studies: Issues in *Their Institutional Survival* (Washington, DC: Institute for Services to Education, 1976). Blake accurately forecasted that research excellence would be undermined by mutually competing goals that were also incompatible.

6. See William D. Smith, "Black Studies: Recommendations for Organization and National Consideration," *Journal of Afro-American Issues*, I (Fall 1973), 350-375); William D. Smith and Albert C. Yates, "Editorial in Black Studies," *Journal of Black Studies*, 10 (March 1980), 269-277; Russell L. Adams, "Evaluating Professionalism in the Context of Afro-American Studies," *Western Journal of Black Studies*, 4 (Summer 1980) 140-148; Philip T.K. Daniel, "Black Studies: Discipline or Field of Study?" ibid., 4 (Fall 1980), 195-200; Sonja H. Stone, "Black Studies by Precept and Example: The Southeastern Black Press Institute," ibid., 201-207; Charles A. Frye, Black Studies: Definition and Administrative Model," ibid., I (June 1977), 93-97, Ewart Guinier, "The First Three Years of the Afro-American Studies Department: 1969-1972, Report to the Faculty of Arts and Sciences," (Cambridge, MA: Harvard University, October 16, 1972, Mimeographed); LeRoi R. Ray, Jr., "Black Studies: A Discussion of Evaluation," *Journal of Negro Education*, 45 (Fall 1976), 383-390.

7. Such as Gerald A. McWorter, "The Professionalization of Achievement in Black Studies: A Report on Ranking Black Studies in Universities and Colleges" (Technical Report, Afro-American Studies and Research Program, University of Illinois, Urbana-Champaign, 1981). This document has generated wide informal discussion about its content and intent.

8. Philip T.K. Daniel and Asmasu Zike, "Black Studies Four-Year College and University Survey" (Sample Survey Results, Center for Minority Studies, Northern Illinois University, May, 1983).

9. The straightforward binomial estimate from Daniel and Zike (see note 8 above) suggests this size after controlling for the sample size. An earlier sample, (David W. Smith, "Black Studies: A Survey of Models and Curricula," *Journal of Black Studies*, 1 [March 1971], 259-271) suggested that no more than .31 of two-year colleges and universities had Black Studies. The temptation to take the gap between the Smith and Daniel/Zike proportion of Black Studies and claim a decline should be resisted. Given the universe and the response rate, Smith runs a high likelihood of measurement error. Smith's results also differed significantly from those of Daniel and Zike since, with a 95 percent confidence interval, their upper boundary peaked at .29.

10. Peter M. Blau, The Organization of Academic Work (New York: John Wiley and Sons, 1973).

11. Kerr underlines the growing problems of undergraduate education during this period of neglect. Hence, Black Studies entered the worst attended unit of the emerging multiversity. See, Clark Kerr, *The Uses of the University* (New York: Oxford University Press, 1981).

12. Adams, "Evaluating Professionalism in the Context of Afro-American Studies." Adams stressed the isolated self-resocialization early actors underwent. Informally, though, at the University of Pittsburgh and elsewhere, early faculty raised the divided loyalty issue of interdisciplinary specialist: usually most were tied to the safe discipline of their origin and identified with its professional associations and cannons of acceptable performance. This was troublesome, especially since the combined probability that young Black Studies doctors were in another discipline (.18) or had a joint appointment (.14) exceeded those solely assigned to Black Studies (.14) by a factor of two. See, Daniel and Zike, "Black Studies Four-Year College and University Survey," for the data.

13. Critics within and outside of universities often played on this. If the University of Illinois and University of Pittsburgh are indicators, with the appointments of long-term heads chairpersons, early Black Studies stunningly paralleled the squabbles over the introduction of sociology in these two institutions. On Illinois, see the papers of the sociology department and the correspondence of the Dean of the Faculty of Arts and Science and Edward Carey Hayes

from 1906 to 1926 (Historical Archives, University of Illinois, Urbana-Champaign). On Pittsburgh, see Interview with Manual Conrad Elmer, founder and Chair, Department of Sociology, University of Pittsburgh, from 1926 to 1956 (transcript in the hands of Carlos A. Brossard from interviews of January 1978).

14. See Vivian V. Gordon, "The Coming of Age of Black Studies," *Western Journal of Black Studies*, 5 (Fall 1981), 231-236; and, Wilson Record, "Can Black Studies and Sociology Find Common Ground?" *Journal of Negro Education*, 44 (Winter 1975), 63-81.

15. Record, "Can Black Studies and Sociology Find Common Ground," is instructive of how even supporters were self-serving or managing tension reductions rather than concertedly building an organization.

16. Ordinarily, splinter movements within established disciplines, a standard way new departments form, benefited from prior institutional affiliations within a department and its interpersonal and professional strengths in buttressing work performances. This is not the case with Black Studies departments at Brandeis, Harvard, Carolina, Duke, and Pittsburgh, i.e., cases of direct participant observation.

17. Guinier, "The First Three Years of the Afro-American Studies Department," and, Blake and Cobb, *Black Studies: Issues in Their Institutional Survival*.

18. On this, Blake was blunt: The best people command good pay, which motivates them to secure even more resources to have well-stocked research funds. From another angle, Kerr noted that the better financed research academics climbed in power and prestige, developed power and prestige bases outside the university, and commanded better bargaining power in institutional conflict mediations. See Blake's terminal note in Blake and Cobb, *Black Studies: Issues in Their Institutional Survival*, and Kerr, *The Uses of the University*.

19. Adams sensitively discussed these realities in "Evaluating Professionalism in the Context of Afro-American Studies."

20. James Stewart, "Book Review of Maulana Karenga's *An Introduction to* Black Studies," *Western Journal of Black Studies*, 7 (Summer 1983), 113-117.

21. Specifically, Albion W. Small of Chicago, E. A. Ross of Wisconsin, Howard W. Odum of Carolina, Robert E. Park and Ernest Burgess of Chicago, Edward Carey Hayes of Illinois, Franklin H. Giddings of Columbia, and Lester Ward of Brown.

22. The curriculum quagmire is best exemplified by the horror stories that come from the few systematic attempts to collect reading list around course topics or disciplinary areas. They can be politely summarized as exhibiting extreme variability. Again, this should not be disconcerting since, if we use sociology again, a similar pattern of strong uneven development was experienced. On the passing of this variation, see Jesse Bernard, "A Brief History of American Sociology," G. Lichtenberger, *Trends in Sociology*.

23. For a clear definition of these categories, see Robert Merton, *Social Theory and Social Structure* (New York: Free Press, 1968).

24. These internal polarizations went along with institutional fights intended to destroy Black Studies. The struggles within and without merely aggravated the cost of internal polarizations. On destruction from institutional fights, see Ewart Guinier, "Black Studies: Training for Leadership," *Freedomways*, XV (1975), 196-198.

25. For the persistence of some of these problems between foreign national, and Afro-Americans, see "Black Students and Black Studies: An Update" (A Report of the Trinity College Meeting), *New England Journal of Black Studies*, (Black Women in Black and Women Studies Issue, 1981), 57-61.

26. McWorter, *"The Professionalization of Achievement in Black Studies."* (See note 7 above.)

27. Ray, "Black Studies: A Discussion of Evaluation." (See note 6 above.)

28. On the operational definition and its problems, see Hubert Blalock, *Social Statistics* (New York: McGraw-Hill 1972), pp. 11-25.

29. An example of a properly normed data set for ranking and large-scale institutional comparisons, see Maurice Eash, "Educational Research Productivity of Institutions of Higher Education," *American Educational Research Journal*, 20 (Spring 1983), 5-12.

30. For exploratory analysis, magnitudes were normed on a per capita distribution. This created a ratio of output to size where "size" equals publishing members at an institution. This was a way to look closely at what was in McWorter's data.

31. See Eric C. Hanushek and John E. Jackson, Statistical Methods for Social Scientists (New York: Academic Press, 1977), pp. 6-11 for the centrality of model specification in statistical tests.

32. See Seymour Sudman, *Applied Sampling* (New York: Academic Press, 1976) for a discussion of the worst offenders in selecting convenience samples.

33. See John Tuckey, *Exploratory Data Analysis* (New York: Addison-Wesley, 1977). I will provide upon request citations of the particular standardized routines used for both exploratory and categorical data analyses.

34. Ray, "Black Studies: A Discussion of Evaluation," pp. 393-394.

35. For a restatement of this view, see Daniel, "Black Studies: Discipline or Field of Study?"

36. Indeed, the problem of leadership succession in Black Studies today points to a common problem in the making of university departments in the beginning phases—coordination and cohesions are at low levels.

37. To get a feeling for the impact of the "strongman" tradition one has only to look at what happened at Illinois with the demise of Edward Carey Hayes in 1926. Sociology took sixteen years to get a replacement for him as department chairman.

38. See, Graham T. Allison, *The Essence of Decision-Making* (Boston: Little, Brown and Co., 1971); and, Barbara A. Sizemore, *The Ruptured Diamond* (Washington, DC: University Press of America, 1979).

39. An analog is changing writing in statistical texts. At present, we can go from unreadable texts to very well-written readable texts at the introductory and advanced levels. (An example of the readable, well-written variant is Donald Ary and Lucy Chester Jacobs, *Introduction to Statistics: Purposes and Procedures* [New York: Holt, Rinehart and Winston, 1976] at the intermediate level there is Elazar J. Pedhazur, *Multiple Regression in Behavioral Research* [New York: Holt, Rinehart and Winston, 1982]). The subject matter is the same. The levels of writing proficiency are extremely variable. Rewriting the same common materials has assisted fragmented and recombined discussions of the same topics in better ways in a long drive to make what once was in unreadable subject easily understood.

9.

Black Studies: A Discussion of Evaluation

LeRoi R. Ray, Jr.

Introduction

Black Studies is a contradiction in the white university; for the allegiance of the white university is to the values of the larger racist society and its corporate structure. One function of the university is to prepare people for their "rightful roles" in the social order. Racist teachers and administrators will not devote much attention to whether that place is the correct one or whether it will lift Black people out of poverty, crime, and apathy. The roles for the various members of the society are established by the leadership of the community in keeping with the accepted goals and values of the corporate structure and imposed upon the masses to maintain the status quo. Paul Harvey, George Wallace, Gerald Ford, and Henry Jackson have tremendous followings—they speak the language that millions of white supremacists want to hear.

The mission of the university should be the creation and expansion of knowledge. It should be the place where technology is used to improve the quality of life and to transform the world for that purpose. Instead, the university is set in a racist mold, funded by capitalists and guided by their captured "scholars" to preserve a tradition sanctioned by moral customs that permitted industrial growth to be developed by slavery, lynching, and massacre. As a result, the university is the bulwark of this society, biased by design, function, and values.

On the other hand, the mission of Black Studies is to provide Black students with the knowledge and skills necessary for the acquisition of power, status, and privilege. Ewart Guinier, who organized the first Afro-American Studies at Harvard University in 1969 and has led its development as Department Head and Professor, says the following about this mission:

> It is in Black Studies that our Black youth, especially those on white campuses, have been learning the great lessons needed to survive in a hostile environment: how to combine the training of the mind with struggles for justice, equality, and above all else for some measure of control over one's destiny.[1]

As a result, one function of a Black Studies' staff is to reveal the painful realities about the inadequacies of higher education for all people and, especially, for Black people. Ron Walters says that Black Studies is disciplined by the peculiarities of the centrality of racism in American life....

> ...this racism is so deep and pervasive that it has affected every aspect of the black existence such as to raise qualitative questions about many aspects of black existence compared to that of other non-black peoples. Because extant ordering principles have, in the main, failed to take into account the accumulative effect of racism on black people, it is necessary to construct frameworks for academic inquiry which proceed from the most correct assumptions of black life and, therefore, which are founded heavily on the assumption of racism.[2]

The answers to chronic problems in this area created by racism, sexism and elitism require careful study of the total environment. Black Studies must provide this direction.

The struggle for justice and freedom is central to an understanding of the role of Black Studies. However, every aspect of Black Studies, every effort in the instructional program is designed to accomplish certain basic objectives that benefit Black people, some of which are in direct confrontation with the interests of the white majority. Can a Black Studies program on a white university campus be successful and evaluated objectively with this inevitable confrontation as a key factor?

If the answer is yes, then the evaluation of Black Studies programs becomes a crucial issue complicated by critical factors as set forth in the following questions: Who will assess and evaluate Black Studies at white universities? How will the assessment and evaluation be handled? What criteria for assessment will be used? Where will the standard of reference for Black Studies originate? How are we going to define the role and meaning of Black Studies at white universities? The discussion that follows will entertain some thoughts and observations about these questions and pose some possible answers.

In answering the first question, determining the principal actors in the evaluation of Black Studies is important, for it is clear that the entire evaluation and assessment of Black Studies, and other disciplines, generally force scholars to make judgments about "good" or "bad" programs. "Good or bad" are relative terms frequently limited to a unique and subjective frame of reference. Who determines that a program is good or bad? What evidence is used to arrive at this conclusion? What definitions are presented? What are the measuring tools or standards? Who benefits from the findings? The technical problems and threatening issues concerning the relevancy of Black Studies and its place in the university need to be blackened because the educational evaluation process, to date, has been too biased against and too negative for Black people. Walters comments on this need as follows:

> ...We have begun to understand, therefore, that in order for black people to survive, the conditions under which we live must be radically changed in a myriad number of ways, and it is the function of Black Studies to assist Black people in the development of new values and new strategies for the kind of change which in some quarters must approach a complete revolution.[3]

More pointedly, until such change occurs, much of the evaluation will be conducted and interpreted by white men with the same biases toward white supremacy, male superiority, and affluent elitism.

Historically, institutions of higher education (and there is some question as to the meaning of "higher education") have been designed and operated to serve the sponsoring interest group, "the white majority." At Western Michigan University in 1975 there were no Black deans, vice-presidents, or persons in power positions. The role of Blacks in white universities must be closely analyzed regardless of their positions.

There is educational and political conflict because many Black activists do not agree upon whether or not accommodationist Blacks (Uncle Toms) in white universities do more harm than good to the Black community. The question is continually raised concerning the usefulness of these "colored" folk, trained (brainwashed) by the biased university system and their effectiveness for Black folks in the struggle for justice and freedom. Can "colored" folks who attend white universities and go through the racist processing leave with enough humanity and courage to build a just society? There is an abundance of evidence that many "colored" folks who have attended white universities are so accommodating, so co-opted into white western values, so brainwashed against their communities' needs that they become obstructionists, or ineffective, at best. Guinier describes the Harvard process in stark terms:

> ...Harvard pundits were deeply involved in the defense of alleged African inferiority during slavery, when it is recalled that Harvard professors played key roles in the defense of white supremacy in the aftermath of Reconstruction, and when it is noted that since slavery Harvard professors have felt a compulsion to advance theories of African genetic inferiority, it should not surprise that an academic lynching bee is surfacing at Harvard today.[4]

Guinier goes on to describe the activities of Blacks on Harvard's faculty who support these racist actions. Carter G. Woodson labeled this phenomenon the "Backdoor Syndrome." He said the following about it:

> The problem of holding the Negro down, therefore, is easily solved. When you control a man's thinking, you do not have to worry about his actions. You do not have to tell him not to stand here or go yonder. He will find his "proper place" and will stay in it. You do not need to send him to the back door. He will go without being told. In fact, if there is no back door, he will cut one for his special benefit His education makes it necessary.[5]

The perpetuation of this "Backdoor Syndrome" has been another mission of the university. Admitting that knowledge in and of itself does not solve problems, that a person needs to develop a praxis before meaningful and purposeful action can be initiated,[6] Black Studies will need to develop students who can overcome the cornerstones of the caste system, "the worthlessness of blackness," and "the fear of white reprisal."[7]

Assessment of Black Studies at White Universities

To avoid impossible options, several groups of people should be involved in the assessment of Black Studies at predominantly white universities. Surely, the students who take Black Studies courses and who live in the community need to participate. Resourceful black scholars who are dedicated to the search for new knowledge and who are committed to the struggle, should be included. Advisory Councils to Black Studies, made up of interested and knowledgeable groups of seriously committed persons who represent complementary factions of the community, should be established and should participate in the evaluation process. They should serve a political function, too; one that protects and supports the goals of Black Studies. The membership must include persons who are willing to strike a death blow to practices that place Black people in compromising positions. They must be willing to support the struggle of people who are taking the risks inside the racist institutions. Many dissolved or discontinued Black Studies departments did not have this kind of Advisory Councils or support from the outside. Far too many were closed down. The nature of this support will only be tested when attempts are made to eliminate or discredit those Black Studies departments with councils.

The evaluation of Black Studies must have a built-in "legitimate" link outside the university structure. Being totally accountable to racist white administrators or token "Uncle Toms" is risky and places the department in a precarious position. Guinier argues that the Afro-American Studies Department at Harvard is being destroyed from within, the most deadly threat being the refusal of the University to acknowledge that the Afro-American Department has needs which go beyond those of traditional departments.[8] An Advisory Council could neutralize this threat.

Since the Advisory Council should be made up of interested and knowledgeable, serious, and committed persons, a definition of a committed Black person may be in order. Some characteristics common in such persons follow. They are not listed in any order of importance or priority. A committed Black person:

— pays dues (money, time, talents) to Black organizations, Black caucuses and causes;

— attends community meetings, gives input and offers energy and support;

— attends the City Commission/Council meetings, representing his/her own position as well as the position of other Blacks;

— works with educators and politicians in analyzing problems of the community and in attempting to find solutions;

— supports community causes and special projects with time, energy, skills and money;

— invests a portion of his/her earnings in the community's financial projects, being willing to take risks with these projects;

— is available during crises providing, on short order, emotional, physical and financial assistance;

— confronts indifference and apathy, not "waiting for John to do it";

— makes purchases from businesses in the community and sees to it that the retailer or owner is complimented for fine services and is told about any shortcomings;

— writes letters to elected officials and registers his/her position on issues of special concern to the community;

— knows who the elected public officials are; votes and encourages other Blacks to register to vote;

— keeps abreast of current issues; studies those issues especially in political campaigns; reads the Black press, and informs other Blacks of the findings;

— takes it upon himself/herself to attend conferences bringing back information to be shared with others;

— has/uses a library of information in order to search for various kinds of information regarding economics, employment, housing, health, politics, law and justice and the actions of the local community;

— is in touch with Black activists and educational organizations locally and at the state, national and international levels;

— will not allow personality differences, even crucial ones, to interfere with working for the best interests of all Black people, always attempting to seek the truth and to work for the causes of the masses of the Black people.

These will be the criteria used for the selection of people to serve an the Advisory Council.

The procedure for handling the assessment and evaluation can be based on the DuBois Model used by Black Americana Studies (BAS) at Western Michigan University (WMU) in Kalamazoo, Michigan. Few scholars have demonstrated the "long distance runner" impact and influence on the problems and needs of Black people in America as well as DuBois. His works (which include writing, researching, planning, propagandizing, publishing and interpreting to the people) and his organizing efforts are shining *Black* examples of the search for truth and for meaningful education and scholarship. During his struggle of nearly a century, rarely a day occurred without conflict and confrontation. This is to be expected even today in the light of the contradictions inherent in a racist university education and the pressing, often conflicting, needs of Black people. Why select DuBois as the Model? One reason is because he has the longest track record of devotion to the struggle for liberation and justice — a century of fighting, from Great Barrington, Massachusetts, in 1868 to Accra, Ghana, in 1963. This is the consensus among Black scholars.

Never wavering nor faltering, never overcome with indecision, never in doubt of direction, with not a wince of dishonesty, he was, above all, always thorough, scientific and practical." ... With his books he had constructed an institution that would stand against the ravages of time, would inspire generations to come and help them to understand the task that lay ahead of them."[9]

DuBois collected data and presented it. He analyzed data, talked about it, made references to it. He sorted it, sought new strategies, implemented, organized, assessed and revised plans. And, he tried again and again. For a near century, this scholar, protagonist, activist, publisher, and, as Killens writes, "the Great Grand-Daddy of them all" produced knowledge and information about the condition of Black folks. No scholar of Black Sociology, Black History, Black Literature, Black Music, Black Dance or Black Art can avoid his works and comments.

The model for the study, evaluation and assessment of Black Studies is in DuBois.[10] His carefully designed studies provide a base and foundation for methodology. His predictions for reference and scheme, his ideas for creativity and spirit, his nobility for credibility, and his style for legitimacy, and give direction to appropriate research designs. He is everywhere in the Black movement. He commented on all topics and all communities including the international community. DuBois gives definitions, evaluative criteria, and style. His thoughts and values support the search for truth.

Black Americana Studies at WMU acknowledges that thorough, extensive investigations and research must be conducted around Black life and as Carter G. Woodson advised,[11] that data must be continuously collected, that proposals and select themes must realistically and efficiently be formulated and that plans must be implemented in the community for testing both short-term and long-term goals. Black scholars must test and retest, assess and reassess, continue trying, learning, never stopping, never for a moment being reluctant to push forward their central hypotheses about Black life. In order to paint the Black perspective, the need for approval by misguided white and "colored" scholars must be discarded. A willingness to accept confrontation, if present, is imperative, for the model of the "long distance runner" is confrontationist. The central and guiding question of the DuBois Model is, "What's in it for Black people?"

Keeping this thought in mind, the following points must be considered when establishing evaluative criteria for assessing academic disciplines: service to students, service to the community, course content, the question of Blackness, and identity and self-concept. Researchers, scholars, and staff who are chosen to design ways to apply these criteria must be certain that Black Studies is assessed in all of these areas.

Black Studies should provide services which recruit, maintain, and retain Black students. Extensive information for the definition and correction of political, educational and economic problems in the Black community should be examined so that poverty and deprivation can be eliminated. Tutors, counselors and professors in Black Studies should relate to Black youth on a personal basis from entry to graduation. Information about career opportunities should be known and disseminated by Black Studies staff to Black students. Research about technological advancements and information about the economy should be current and easily accessible to both students and professors. Cooperative processes and exchanges should be established between high schools and college students.

Special efforts should emanate from Black Studies to educate, inform and work with Black residents in the local community so that they benefit from the resources and facilities of the university. Surveys should be made to determine which, if any, university facilities are used most by Black residents. The nature of this usage should be determined also. An assessment of the mechanism for the exchange between the university and the Black community should be made to determine which techniques are effective and operating. The research of Black Studies should result in test models established in the Black community for the resolution of socioeconomic and socio-political problems.

Black Studies should create a new conceptual framework for the content of history, literature, drama, journalism, social science, music, art and the hard sciences. It is not enough to append Black History onto the racist history that now exists. A completely new history must emerge from the research. More emphasis must be placed on economics and political science in order to help Black students attain justice equal access to positions of power and influence. A thorough investigation should be made of Black institutions and organizations in order to be knowledgeable of the full resources in the Black community. Black Studies must improve the attitude of the entire university by providing new information to white students and professors assisting them in recognizing, isolating, attacking and solving problems such as racism.

Another quality which needs serious study is the spirit of unity, creativity and humanity which Black people often call "Soul." Black people have survived because of a certain "in" uniqueness. Some call it "Soul." Others refer to it as a kind of humanism; still others pen it as funk, or spirit, or negritude. There are qualities abounding in Black people that make them strong, hopeful and loving. Black Studies will not be void of this warm Black glow. Is there an appreciation for it? Can it be used to turn around the increasing rates of Black homicide and suicide? Do courses and activities reflect an awareness of the spirit of Blackness? Is there an awareness of the humor and laughter, the art of dealing with pain and suffering? Is planning in tune with the "two-ness" written of so eloquently by DuBois[12] that has made it possible for Black folks to Have in two different worlds with sanity? Has research addressed the potential of this fine quality of a hope beyond this earthly world?

Maybe America is still holding together because of "The Gift of Black Folk." Certainly Black people are part of every definition of this nation. Black Studies must strive to keep the "Soul of Black Folk" alive and protect the dwindling remnants of moral integrity. Programmatic efforts must reflect a serious analysis and investigation of this spirit and must seek ways to hold onto and pass on the positive features of this humanism. All of these must be assessed to determine the effectiveness of Black Studies.

Many Black educators have suggested that Black Studies should assist youth in their struggle for identity, since so much of what happens to them in schools tends to alter Black positive self-concept. There are numerous questions that must be posed and given serious consideration concerning identity and self-concept for Blacks and whites in this country. For example, does Black Studies help Blacks and other non-whites to know themselves better? Will Black Studies help present a basis for assisting in the determination or the individual and collective identity of all student? Equally as important is how most whites regard Black people. Chester M. Pierce says that the society is unrelenting in teaching its white youth how to maximize the advantages of being on the offense toward Blacks.[13] He further advances the notion that offensive mechanisms, "the small, continuous bombardments of micro-aggression by whites to blacks is the essential ingredient in race relations and race interactions."[14]

Black Studies must correct the beliefs which whites hold that Blacks race inferior and that whites are superior. Necessary to consider, also, is the fact that many Black people have been taught to behave that they are inferior to whites and have taught their children to behave in a prescribed manner which supports this belief. The evaluation of Black Studies must determine if and when Black people have accepted their physical features, and if they have positive attitudes towards themselves while under the pressure to dislike, degrade and hate their Black features. By the same token, a determination must be made about the feelings of whites regarding who they are in relation to Black people.

Black Studies must deal factually with how this nation came to be and why, in order to straighten out the deliberate distortions on which the present Black-white relationship has been based. Specific criteria must be developed to assess the effectiveness of Black Studies in teaching both Blacks and whites the accurate, true concept of self and identity without degrading either. The problem here, as Walters makes abundantly clear, is that no other people have succeeded in developing a completely objective history, thus raising the question of whether or not the creating of "a purely objective history would militate against the development of a story rich in its real and mythological content of past achievement and a subjective survival agenda for the future based on a conscious choice to preserve, elucidate and practice the black life style without apology." Walters continues, "to add to the destruction of black history and culture by practicing 'objectivism' is a type of black chauvinism we cannot afford."[15]

Walters shows that history, then, is the race's survival agenda. Consequently, whites will certainly resist any tampering with the history of this country in Black Studies' effort to deal factually with the creation and origination of the United States of America. In its effort to serve both the white and the black student, Black Studies finds itself in a dilemma of great proportions. Black Studies must build a positive self-concept and identity in both while at the same time try to paint the picture of this country's history so that neither is degraded.

There are a few other factors in evaluation which remain unmentioned here. A few would be similar to those used in other university disciplines. Some crucial ones,

however, are different, and it is here that the uniqueness of Black Studies is illustrated: what is the direction, philosophy, short-term and long-term goals of programs
struggling for the liberation of Black people? Careful attention must be given to the
fact that many traditional disciplines have not provided information, skills, identity,
and encouragement to Black and non-white students. Thus, the role of Black Studies
is to correct this situation. This being the case, confrontation with the university tradition and value structure is inevitable. DuBois' words issue this caveat: "When a
man faces evil, he does not call it good, nor evade it; he meets it breastforward, with
no whimper of regret nor fear of foe.[16] To be sure, there will be risks, and certain
sanctions may be used for coercion since institutional values are held in place by
force. But, then, that is the nature of struggle.

Standard of Reference

Without a doubt, the standards of reference for Black Studies must originate
from the people who are most directly affected by the negative, hostile conditions in
the various communities. These people are certainly in the best position to know
whether or not their problems are being solved. The Advisory Council to Black Studies will have an important role here, primarily that of long-term testing and revision.
Woodson, DuBois and Hare have provided generous documentation of the analyses
and recommendations of such a program.[17] These will be examined and tested in the
light of the serious problems, needs, and concerns of the Black community and the
Black students on campus. Specifically, attention will be given to the problems of student recruitment, training and re-training on the university campus, and the problems of employment upon leaving. The ripple-effect phenomenon of the department
an the university at large will be determined, keeping in mind that one of the major
objectives of Black Studies is to influence significant change in the structure, organization and operation of the university.

Role and Meaning of Black
Studies at White Universities

The role of Black Americana Studies at Western Michigan University is now
under study. The present working definition of Black Studies is a multi-disciplinary body of knowledge and experience about the struggle of people of African
descent against racism and oppression and their relationship to white people, especially those of European descent. Black Studies at WMU is for all students,
black, white, and others. Its role is to research distortions in the various disciplines, investigate the norms and values of the university, examine the disciplines
and their omissions, bring the Black perspective to each discipline, monitor the offerings of each for racism, produce models of service for the development of the
Black community and Black students through direct action, test these models, disseminate information about Black culture, sponsor activities about Black culture,
develop research skills in students, and provide additional student support systems. This role springs from the following objectives: (1) to assist students in de-

veloping a positive identity and self-concept; (2) to assist students in learning more about the status of Blacks in their environment; (3) to teach students how to research, study, analyze, and debate the critical issues for survival; (4) to provide all students with skills, information and the knowledge of the resources available for conducting effective services to the Black community; (5) to make the university a more just institution; and, (6) to create and expand knowledge for the improvement of the quality of life.

In implementing programs for accomplishing these objectives, a Five-Year Plan has been developed. It is based on three assumptions, each with a corollary. The first assumption is that the university has been chosen as a place to confront racism through the creation of new knowledge and the reconstruction of old knowledge. A corollary is that Black Americana Studies, therefore, has a legitimate reason to be in the university, to initiate and spearhead such activities. The second assumption is, that students will be using the university in the future to attain certain skills, information and credentials and possibly more and more Black students will be coming to the white university for such skills and information. The corollary to this assumption is that Black Americana Studies should assist in the development of these skills. The third assumption is that the university should serve to develop the Black community in the best interests of that community; the corollary is that Black Americana Studies should assist in this development.

The rationale for BAS at WMU is an attempt to create a more just institution out of the university with regard to answering the question, "What is the nature of man?" There is no answer to this question, but the various extant ideologies and philosophies assume that their conclusions applied to all men in all places at all times. In a democracy, man is regarded as rational and capable of fulfilling his own potential. He or she is regarded as best able to know his or her own needs and interests. He or she is most likely to know, even though through trial and error, what actions are necessary for attaining his or her objectives. The individual's efforts to improve the circumstances of his or her life can contribute to an improvement in the quality of life for the entire social order. But this will not just happen! Recent studies show that different experiences in colleges create two kinds of achievers—traditional and committed. The former are devotees of individual achievement and the latter are dedicated to the achievement of the group.[18] Consequently, in the university dominated by European values, Black Studies brings a different ideology to bear on these propositions.

Black Americana Studies at WMU

The Five-Year Plan in BAS at WMU is not the complete answer to all the many questions and issues raised above, but it does provide a beginning strategy for operating on the university campus with its unique circumstances. The ultimate goal of all Black Studies must be to see to it that people in the society are in the same position with respect to receiving goods and services. A second major goal of Black Studies is to assist in assuring that all people have equal access to positions of influence. All of these have to do with the struggle for justice for each and every citizen.

More immediately, there are certain pressing conditions of employment, education, health, and politics which are, in part, the result of the curriculum in the institutions of higher education. One of the first steps in dealing with these complex prob-

lems is to make an effort to correct the many factors that contribute to a miseducation of the student in the university. Whether this goal is practical and attainable
within the present structure and organization of the university is a major question;
however, no plan for Black Studies is universally applicable to all campuses. Each
campus has a set of unique elements that present variables unlike those common to
all campuses.

Each year, BAS at WMU activities have been designed and developed around a
general theme in conformity with the DuBois Model. This theme, based on the pressing needs of the Black community, is in keeping with the basic philosophy and definition of BAS. During the 1973 year, the general theme was *Black Survival*. The activities, guests and the course work reflected an appreciation for the question, "How
will Black Studies and how will Black people survive in a hostile environment?"
Through many efforts, deliberations and idea exchanges several basic themes
evolved. This led to *Black Music* for the 1974 theme.

Music has always played an important role in the lives of Black people. Many
people say that it has been a rallying point and a means of communication among
Black folks throughout the centuries of oppression. By directing efforts towards the
value of Black Music in the community, some of the activities that had significance in
determining the status of BAS were executed.

The theme during the 1975 year was *The Role of the Black Church*. The church
is the one institution in the Black community primarily controlled by Black people.
An effort was made to focus on the Kalamazoo Community Forum and the efforts of
the Black churches throughout the state of Michigan, presenting to this community
the highlights of their activities and contributions.

The central theme for 1976 is *Black Arts and the Performing Artists*. Art is a
great teacher. Artists are revolutionary risk-takers and creative explorers. Black Art
has had a guiding effect on the lives of Black people. Many Black artists have vision
and insight that have given hope and security to the community. The artists' methods, messages, and masterpieces bring philosophical input and teachings and must be
examined for their value in the overall struggle for justice. The 1977 theme will be
Black History and the Contributions of Black People, focusing particularly on the
immediate history of Kalamazoo residents, while not overlooking the history of
Black people throughout this country.

Summary

This paper is charged with questions, a model, and supporting references. But, it
is far from complete. It is not intended as a document to provide theoretical discussion of far-distant problems—these issues need attention now. The resolution of
these questions and issues rests in the minds, hands, and hearts of the dedicated and
committed Black people. Be aware of the fact that each and every proposal for Black
purposes will be taken out of context and misinterpreted in order to thwart efforts to
change the university by those with vested interests in the present inequitable
arrangement. Placing Black Studies on the campus agitates, to some degree, certain
areas of the university and the white community. But, if institutions were not designed to serve the needs of Black people, then every attempt must be made to alter
the philosophy and processes of those institutions. This alteration and change should

come from Black Studies. Any evaluation process should determine to what degree that change has occurred.

Endnotes

1. Ewart Guinier, "Black Studies: Training for Leadership," *Freedomways*, XV (1975), 196.

2. Ronald Walters, "The Discipline of Black Education," mimeograph, *Action Library*, Afram Associates, 1970, p. 1.

3. *Ibid.*, p. 2.

4. Guinier, *op. cit.*, p. 198.

5. Carter G. Woodson, *The Miseducation of the Negro* (Washington, DC: The Associated Publishers, 1933), p. xxxiii.

6. Paulo Freire, *The Pedagogy of the Oppressed* (N.Y.: Herder and Herder, 1970), p. 75.

7. Allison Davis, Buleigh & Mary Gardner, *Deep South* (Chicago: The University of Chicago Press, 1941).

8. *Ibid.*, p. 205.

9. John O. Killens, "Wanted: Some Black Long Distance Runners," *The Black Scholar*, (November 1973), p. 5.

10. See the works of W.E.B. DuBois. The following illustrate the model used in this paper. *The Philadelphia Negro: A Social Study* (Philadelphia, PA: The University of Pennsylvania, 1899); "The Morality Among Negroes in Cities" (1899); "Social and Physical Condition of Negroes in Cities" (1897); "Some Efforts of Negroes for their Own Social Betterment" (1898); "The Negro in Business" (1899); "The College Bred Negro" (1900); "The Negro Common School" (1901); "The Negro Artisan" (1902); "The Negro Church" (1903); "Some Notes on Negro Crime Particularly in Georgia" (1904); "A Selected Bibliography of the Negro American" (1905); "The Health and Physique of the Negro American" (1906); "Economic Cooperation Among Negro Americans" (1907); "The Negro American Family" (1908); and "Efforts for Social Betterment Among Negro Americans" (1909); *Atlanta University Publications Series* (*N.Y. Times*; New York: Arno Press, 1968-69).

11. Woodson, *op. cit.*, pp. 144-156.

12. W.E.B. DuBois, *The Souls of Black Folk* (Greenwich, CT: Fawcett Premier Books, Fawcett Publications, Inc., 1961), p. 17.

13. Chester M. Pierce, "Offensive Mechanisms," *The Black Seventies*, ed. Floyd Barbour (Boston: Porter Sargent Publishing Co., 1970). p. 269.

14. *Ibid.*, p. 282.

15. Walters, *op. cit.*, pp. 7-8.

16. W.E.B. DuBois, "The Revelation of Saint Orgne, the Damned," *The Education of Black People: W.E.B. DuBois*, ed. Herbert Aptheker (Amherst, MA: University of Massachusetts Press, 1973), p. 104.

17. See the editorials by Carter C. Woodson published in *The Negro History Bulletin* from 1915. See also Nathan Hare, *Black Studies Curriculum,* 1968 (San Francisco: 1600 Holloway, Spring 1968). Also see the works of W.E.B. DuBois listed in reference #10.

18. Patricia Gurin and Edgar G. Epps, *Black Consciousness, Identity, and Achievement: A Study of Students in Historically Black Colleges* (New York: John Wiley & Sons, Inc., 1975).

10.

What Direction Black Studies?

Donald Henderson

Introduction

Over the past several years a great many colleges and universities have undertaken a variety of efforts in response to the demands of black students and faculty members for improving the status of blacks on their campuses. A bewildering variety of structures, processes and practices have been established in the wake of these demands. They all tend to fall under the general rubric of black studies and include such diverse undertakings as: (1) recruitment programs for blacks and other minorities; (2) remedial, compensatory and tutorial programs; (3) the inclusion into the standard curriculum of courses designed more or less to deal with aspects of the black experience; (4) separate programs of courses dealing with the black experience for black students; (5) the establishment of Centers, Institutes, etc. that deal in some fashion with blacks; and (6) other activities such as recruitment and assistance of black graduate students. The situation is further confused by the fact that it is not unusual to find that all of these activities are being carried out simultaneously and independently at the same institution. Unless there is a structure clearly labeled as black studies, any or all of these activities may be perceived as the University's black studies program. For example, at one university, with which I am familiar, when black students requested a black studies program they were told by a representative of the Administration that the school had such a program and that it had been operative for two years. The administrator was making reference to a special recruitment and tutorial program for persons from minority groups while the students were requesting a substantive curricular effort. Further confusion often arises from the feeling that whatever effort is being carried out for black students it should address itself to all of their problems. While it is elementary, it seems necessary for many institutions to distinguish between recruitment and supportive programs for black students and programs of substantive academic effect aimed at teaching (and research) about the black experience. This alone, however, will not clear up the major sources of confusion. In the main it would seem that the most difficult problems to solve center around questions of the nature, content and structure of substantive efforts in the area of Black Studies. In the state of Illinois, in the fall of 1969, for example, sixty-four institutions offered a total of 548 courses that were labeled as black studies offerings. About half of these institutions indicate that they were in the process of expanding their offerings in this area. There seemed to be, with the exception of standard courses in Negro History and Race and Minority Relations, almost as many different course titles as there were courses. The courses were offered by traditional departments, such as history and sociology and by newly devised structures, such as departments of Black Studies and Afro-American Centers and Institutes. It is worth noting that most frequently these courses were offered by social science departments.

In short, in the area of black studies there is, at present, an enormous lack of coherence and coordination at all levels. The activities and structures that characterize black studies across the nation undoubtedly have resulted from the headlong rush of universities to offer something black. In this light it is worth questioning the sincerity of the institutions that movement such programs. There is reason to believe that most academicians do not believe that these programs have any real academic or intellectual validity. In the main, they are perceived as strategically useful ways of "cooling out militant black students." In most cases black studies programs, however they are construed, have their reasons for existence firmly based in political considerations and were only rarely introduced as academic undertakings in the host institutions.

There are a great many objections to black studies efforts. These objections range from academic considerations on the one hand to political considerations on the other. In the main, several arguments seem to predominate. (1) Black Studies programs are viewed of as chauvinistic attempts on the part of blacks to advocate black superiority and to glorify the history of blacks in the United States. (2) Black Studies programs are held to be efforts directed at circumventing the conventional and more difficult performance standards of higher education in order to enable ill-prepared and equally inept students to acquire the credentials of higher education. (3) Black Studies programs are the core efforts in the training of militant revolutionary agents to do battle with the white university community on a local level and the wider white community on a wider level. It is also argued that these efforts are directed toward developing separate educational structures for blacks and as such reflect "racism" in reverse. Perhaps, the most frequently used objection (which occurs usually with one or several of those noted above) is that black studies "by its very nature" lacks intellectual and academic validity — in short there is nothing worthwhile in the undertaking of such efforts. These arguments are used to deprecate black studies programs that are extant and to deny their legitimacy as a part of the offerings of universities. Most importantly they are the instrumentalities for withholding the resources that are necessary for their planning, implementation, growth and stability. The lack of resources, of course, dooms these efforts to failure from the outset.

On the other side of the issue those who argue for the development of black studies programs are by no means unified in their notions about what they should be, how they should be structured, where then, should be housed, what the content should be, etc. For example, some people argue that black studies should be geared toward developing and fostering racial awareness and racial pride among blacks. Others contend that such a program should not only foster racial pride but should also "teach black people how to be black" as an antidote to their present educational experiences that are designed to teach them to be white. Another school of thought contends that these efforts must actively undertake the political education and unification of the black community thus enhancing its position in the society. Another argument holds that the "true black studies program" must be community based and community controlled and aimed at the resolution of the myriad problems of the black community. These and a number of other arguments contribute to the confusion that characterizes the attempts to develop black studies programs around the corner. Obviously, closure on these issues will take time and many of the problems can only be worked out as attempts are made to establish and cultivate viable programs of this type. Nevertheless some thought must be given to notions that promise to structure, order and give coherence to black studies all over the country. Like any other limited undertaking black studies cannot be all things to all men — nor should it be.

Looking at the arguments of the dissenters and the aims of the supporters it is possible to see some legitimacy in them. It is conceivable that a move toward separation or a development of race pride for example may result from the operation of a black studies program. It is also conceivable that such programs can serve as an "antidote" to some present educational ills that devastate black youngsters. These occurrences in all probability will be spin-offs from black studies programs and as such should not be conceived of either individually or collectively, as the sum and substance of these efforts. My objection to all of these notions derives from a hidden implication in each of them that suggests that a black studies program cannot be an academically and/or intellectually legitimate undertaking for every college or university. The implication referred to above is related to one of the cardinal tenets of racism as I understand it — namely — there is nothing in the world black experience that is worthy of serious and extended intellectual activity or capable of contributing anything of value to our understanding of the universe or man's place in it. On the part of the detractors it smacks sharply of racism and on the part of the supporters, at very least, myopia and at worse an indirect subscription to the tenets of racism. Both are objectionable and cannot form the basis for a valid effort in the study of the world black experience.

At the same time one must not apologize for these spin-offs, if they in fact occur, nor can one attempt to design these programs to keep these things from happening. Sociology, for example, as far as I can tell was not designed in this fashion. It can be argued, as some do, that some of the notions of this discipline have contributed on the one hand to a number of "undesirable" social developments, particularly in the area of race relations, and on the other to some widespread challenges to traditional values. Black studies, like any legitimate intellectual endeavor, must be left free to become whatever its dedicated scholars are capable of making it. Anything less than that will prove intellectually dishonest and will ultimately work to the disadvantage of both black and non-black peoples.

Considering the widespread confusion that obtains with respect to black studies it is worth asking — what of the future of such programs? An honest answer suggests that their future as an integral component of university activities does not look promising. Two outstanding impediments loom as formidable roadblocks. One of these is centered in faculty hostility while the other concerns problems of financial support.

In many cases black studies programs, as noted above, were undertaken as a "temporary expedient" to preserve peace and order on campus. As such, rarely was there an attempt made to provide them with sound academic bases or full faculty sanction. A good many "courses," for example, were to be designed and taught by students. Moreover, the course content very often covered the whole academic landscape. Activities like these may be, in part, a function of the fact the field is new and the footing is uncertain; at the same time, however, it is possible that such activities were permitted to enable their results to discredit black studies efforts. It is worth noting that in a great many places, university faculties are requesting a thorough evaluation of black studies programs with the results often being a dissolution of the efforts. That is to say that the very circumstances that led to and surround the establishment of black studies programs are now being utilized to bring about their demise.

Black studies programs are also either facing or will be shortly faced by the growing shortage of funds that is afflicting universities all over the country. This is particularly critical for these programs because in most cases they have been established with little if any real financial support and little serious commitment to their permanency. This lack of commitment and of a firm base of support seems to portend a serious cut-back if not dissolution of many programs as universities begin to tighten their financial belts. Obviously, strategies must be devised (1) to broaden the support base for these programs and to enable their survival and necessarily growth; and, (2) to ensure their entree into the academic system of the university as full-fledged programs with their own particular body of knowledge and requisite skills and technologies. The next three sections of this paper attempt to address the latter of these two issues. Strategies that enable the accomplishment of this objective will go a long way toward establishing the bases for realization of a satisfactory resolution of the problem of funding.

A Proposal

As suggested above, there are presently a variety of notions as to what constitutes a bona-fide black studies effort. Accepting the risk of adding yet another I would like to submit my notions of what constitutes a legitimate black studies effort. I hasten to add that my principal interest here is in the intellectual and academic aspects of such an effort. It is not an attempt to suggest that the discipline, black studies has no social, personal or other action-oriented significance, for indeed it must. I must also confess a little discomfort with the need for calling what I wish to propose black studies because my proposal not only encompasses the universe of black studies but necessarily involves the study of whites albeit within a non-white framework. For want of a more appropriate rubric, however, I will use the designation black studies.

Let me begin by saying that black studies is as worthy and legitimate an intellectual and academic undertaking as any endeavor presently being carried out in the university. It is such in its own right and need not be propped, buttressed, or sold by any means other than its own historical and contemporary importance. It should not be viewed as a compensatory or remedial program for so-called high-risk disadvantaged students, although such students may certainly be enrolled. Their enrollment, however, should be unrelated to their "disadvantaged" status. Black studies should not be a program in rhetoric designed, as many seem presently to be, to teach black folks (or even Negroes) how to be black. In my opinion black people do not have to be taught to be what they already are and it is an affront for some blacks to presume that they can tell other blacks how they should define themselves or behave, value and aspire. This is what whites have been attempting to do to blacks for better than 300 years. The liberation of blacks from the ideological and attitudinal clutches of whites must not be at the cost of re-enslavement with misguided blacks pulling the strings. I do believe that black studies programs can contribute immeasurably to the true liberation of blacks.

Black studies programs should not be community action programs, although they can and should service black communities. In this regard, however, these programs should assess the nature of their resources and capabilities and on the basis of this assessment determine the types of services they can provide the community and then deliver on such services one hundred percent. Heads of these programs must realize from the outset that the programs cannot care for all the needs of the community. They must not make the mistake of promising to resolve all community ills as administrators of most urban colleges and universities have done in the past. Above all, the university-based black studies effort should be an educative effort and as such its primary obligation must be the educational fulfillment of its student and faculty membership. The important question is how this can best be done within the confines of the university system.

It seems that several types of efforts must be established in order to fulfill the promise of black studies. For the moment I wish to deal with the nature of these efforts on university campuses. Careful thought suggests that three major types of programs can be established to fulfill both the academic promise and the service capability of these undertakings, namely: (1) the Black Studies Department; (2) the School or College of Ethnic Studies and (3) the Black Studies Research Center. A brief formulation of each of these structures follows.

Department of African and Afro-American Studies

The primary goal of this department should be to provide the student with an encompassing knowledge of the history, culture, life-styles and futures of Africans and/or Afro-Americans. Such a department, unlike present substantive departments, would have to be truly interdisciplinary. Its membership would of necessity represent most of the established departments of the social sciences and the humanities. It is conceivable that geologists, biologists, geneticists and others from the natural sciences might be responsible for certain aspects of this department's program. The department would offer a broad concentration in African and Afro-American studies which would include, for example, surveys of art, literature, historic, philosophy, religion, biology, economics, etc. as these areas contribute to an understanding of the world black experience. A student would be able to specialize, for example, in African Studies or Afro-American Studies with emphasis on the black experience in Anglo-Saxon cultures, or Afro-American Studies with emphasis on the black experience in Latin cultures. The student thus majoring would concentrate his efforts, beyond certain required core courses, in the area of his specialty. For example, he would become familiar with the specific historic, art, economics, philosophy, religion, etc. of Afro-Americans of South America. He would of necessity study the linkages of that region to Africa and to North America and those unique features of the people themselves. In short, the student would become reasonably knowledgeable about the experiences of black people in a certain large geographical area and their relations to all other blacks in the world.

The department would most logically belong in the College of Liberal Arts and its students would of course be liberal arts majors. Upon graduation these young people would be able to acquire the types of positions that are usually available to liberal arts graduates. For those students wishing to continue their studies in one or more of these areas, graduate programs would be offered. The graduate programs would enable students to acquire an expert knowledge in one of the areas of study outlined above. For instance, a student may wish to specialize in Brazilian culture. He would of necessity then have to learn a good deal about Yoruba culture of Africa as many of the blacks in Brazil are descendants of this tribe. The lifeways of Brazilian blacks would be thoroughly examined through study of their religion, philosophy, art, music, family life, child-rearing practices, medicine, etc. The historical and contemporary similarities and dissimilarities between them and African Yoruba would be considered. The student would also be required to place the Brazilians into proper perspective vis-a-vis other blacks in the New World. This of necessity would require some knowledge about other New World peoples. At the same time, in order to place his work in world perspective he must learn, at least superficially, about the culture and lifeways, etc. of non-black people both in and out of the New World. His knowledge of cultural variety would be truly eclectic.

Ideally a good deal of time should be spent among the people being studied. The graduate student studying Brazilian blacks should be required to study in Brazil. It would be tremendously beneficial to this student if his "field work" in Brazil included, say, at least a year or two working and living as a Brazilian. He could, for example, teach in a Brazilian school and observe the scene as a Brazilian rather than anthropologize or do some other form of social sciencing during his "field work." His principal objective would be to understand Brazilian life from the point-of-view of the Brazilian. This might require the assumption of a perspective that at times would be decidedly non-objective.

As noted above, the structure of a department such as this must depart from what has been the norm for departments for most of the history of American universities. The Department of African and Afro-American Studies must be truly interdisciplinary and its members must be meta-disciplinarians. They must be academically and intellectually able to range across a variety of traditional areas with facility and sophistication. Obviously the selection of personnel will be a principal factor in the operation of such a department. The traditional and often arbitrary boundaries that divide sociology from history or philosophy from economics will not only be undesirable but dysfunctional in carrying out the mission of this department.

It seems reasonably clear that such a structure would be a desirable addition to the university complex. Not only would it provide exciting new areas for student and faculty attention but it would fill a void that has traditionally existed in the curricular structure of the American university. That void, of course, is a result of the almost total lack of attention to the world black experience or, what is worse, the abominable portrayals of that experience that resulted in the presentation of distorted versions of the history of both blacks and non-blacks. It would, of necessity, if only in the service courses it offered, begin to set the historical record straight for both blacks and whites.

School of Ethnic Studies

In thinking of the full scope of black studies in a university, setting it is necessary to consider how such an effort can be construed in a fashion substantially broader than a department. I can see the need and desirability of establishing a School or a College of Ethnic Studies. I suggest ethnic studies because it is a more inclusive notion than black studies and because I can also see the value of the serious study of other ethnic groups. In any case, such a structure would enable a student to pursue a degree in one of the traditional disciplines and at the same time concentrate his study on one or more ethnic groups. In this school, for example, a student would be able to major in sociology while concentrating substantively on some aspect of the experience of the black world. That is, the student would learn the concepts, theories and methods of a particular discipline with the lifeways, beliefs and institutions of the black world serving as the substance through which the concepts and theories are exemplified. If, for example, the student were an economics major the communal economics of the African world or ghetto economics of Afro-America could be the substance that would "put the meat on the theoretical or conceptual bones." I must hasten to suggest that this kind of academic undertaking is not equivalent to taking an established discipline like sociology and "coloring it black." What I am suggesting is a bona-fide attempt at developing an appropriate understanding within the discipline of the experiences of the non-white (perhaps it is more appropriate to say non-American) world. Such, I believe, is the thinking that underlies the call for the establishment of black psychology for example.

I find it difficult to understand the almost total lack of offerings in African philosophy among departments of philosophy in American universities. In my various inquiries about the lack of such offerings I invariably got an incredulous stare followed by "African philosophy! — What's that? Why there's no such thing!" It should be reasonably clear to any free-thinking intelligent person that such an entity must exist or must have existed at one time. Indeed, a sensitive examination of African thought reveals the presence of a very sophisticated and elegant body of philosophical notions. These notions are in a great many ways quite different from those that we in the Western world have been used to granting the status of philosophical concepts. The denial of the existence of African philosophy by Western scholars is the result of their very provincial notion of philosophy. The standard against which their judgments are made is the extent to which African thinking parallels western thought systems. We also seem to feel that our own thought systems are universal in time and space. Our explanations of the operation of the universe, for example, are arrogantly presumed to have exclusive validity. Therefore, when we are confronted by notions found in African thought that suggest the existence of some basic free-flowing power in the world that can be controlled and utilized by man through the selective use of the spoken word[1] we dismiss such notions as the primitive musings of savages. Such notions are not seen as elements in a complex thought-scheme for ordering the universe and explaining man's place in it. They are seen as primitive attempts to control the natural world through magic instead of science. These attempts at magic (which we understand to be wish-fulfilling rather than practical) are proof that such people have not yet evolved a systematic and logical way of thinking[2] and therefore could not have developed a system of philosophical thought in the grand sense of our philosophy. Hence — there is no such thing as African philosophy — it is at best "black magic."

I suggest that it is necessary to transcend such narrow notions. Although African notions of how the universe operates and the place of man in it may be entirely unfamiliar and alien to American philosophers they are nevertheless parts of a grand scheme that orders and structures the world in a fashion that is effective for those who subscribe to it. It has nothing to do with western philosophy nor does it need to be evaluated by western notions in order to assume the status of philosophy — it needs only to be seen as a philosophical system in its own right. The effort I am describing here would approach that study in just this way. A philosophy major would learn philosophy through concentrating on the understanding of African philosophical thought as a distinctively different system with its own history and dynamics.

It is obvious, however, that there is need for comparative work in such an undertaking. Our philosophy major would of necessity have to learn a good deal about non-African philosophy — but only because it will increase his knowledge of philosophy and as such is pedagogically sound; it should have no ideological, political or emotional motivating impetus. The work to be undertaken must be based on the meaningful education of the student who requires as full an educational experience as possible. This of necessity includes the examination of experiences of the non-black world.

The school of ethnic studies must obviously engage in graduate studies. It should be possible for a student to acquire any of the standard advanced degrees currently available. One should be able to acquire a master's or Ph.D. in one of the standard disciplines while concentrating his attention principally, on the substance of the black world. Obviously, one could also become involved in an elaboration of the under-graduate experience through increased involvement in research and teaching at this level. There is a desperate need for authentic and sensitive research in the many aspects of the black experience. Graduate students and their senior colleagues (professors) would be required to undertake such research.

Research in Connection with Black Studies

It seems important to complement the Department of African and Afro-American Studies and the School of Ethnic Studies with research capability. In addition there is much that can be contributed through applied research to the resolution of some of the problems that presently beset the black community. This two-fold mission characterizes the purpose of the Center for Research in the World Black Experience. The Center would provide for both basic and applied research activities.

As noted earlier there is great need for serious effort to reconstruct the world black experience in an accurate way. Much of the work of contemporary African writers is seriously challenging the formulations put forth by Western students. Continued and expanded research influenced by African formulations promises to be of immense value in realizing the accurate reconstruction of the African historical experience. Reformulation of traditional explanations of African life and thought stands as a major area for research effort. Jack Mendelsohn suggests that such areas are "the great unexplored subject(s) for research in Africa today."[3] Indeed, Mendelsohn's own understandings themselves require this kind of attention. A specific example derives from his discussion of the direction of African thought in which he suggests,

> The Africans have left aside all attempts to discover physical laws and to domesticate matter; instead they have tried to discover the spirit of each being and object in order to enable man to move about the world according to its inner rhythm. This concept of the relations between man and the world surrounding him has resulted in a mode of existence which is so devoid of any dynamic principle that it is very near to mere equilibrium, though it has allowed the preservation of the black race and civilization in spite of its technical weakness.[4]

Mendelsohn's conclusions that Africans left aside the search for physical laws, and that their efforts resulted in a mode of existence near to equilibrium do not seem quite accurate. African thought and African life suggest that they were fully aware of the operation of physical laws and were also concerned with what Mendelsohn has called the "inner rhythms of the world." I suspect that what is difficult for us (of the West) to understand is that some of the African concepts are elegant to the point that they encompass in their operation both the spiritual (man) and the physical (not-man). The concept of "Nommo" so well described by Janheinz Jahn[5] and Chief Fela Sowande[6] seems to involve notions of physical energy (in the sense that physics defines it as the capacity for doing work or overcoming resistance) and the nature of man's spiritual ascendancy. In short, it seems to express the relationship between man and the forces of the universe in both theoretical and practical terms. At the same time it is possible that Mendelsohn's characterization of African cultural life as "mere equilibrium" is a misunderstanding that result from imposing western standards on African belief systems. It is obvious from Janheinz Jahn's discussion of the African notion of Kuntu[7] and Fela Sowande's rendition of *IFA*,[8] that the African notion of life, is anything but static. The dynamic quality of African life is expressed spiritually whereas we of the West perceive dynamism as a function of changes in the material features of the world. The continued creation of both spiritual and physical life (the birth and naming of babies) and its counterpart in the spirit world (the creation of gods) expresses the dynamic quality of African life.

Now, I cite my disagreements with Jack Mendelsohn to point out the need for extensive research that is based on the forms of African understanding and at the same time capable of translation into western terms. In effect my disagreements are hypotheses that can be tested through research structures such as that described above.

I must hasten to add that there is need for extensive research into the experience of black folks in the New World. It would be important to determine the degree to which New World blacks (Afro-Americans) still retain remnants of their African past in their conceptions of the universe and man's place in it. Conceptions of morality, beauty, goodness among other things also seem to be open to this kind of research effort. No doubt such remnants have been extensively influenced by European forms but it is possible that they have retained their essential African quality. I am prepared to suggest, according to my best judgments, that E. Franklin Frazier was wrong in concluding that the African social and cultural heritage of American blacks was utterly devastated and replaced by European forms.[9] I submit that there is still a lot of African in most black Americans despite an incredible campaign of de-Africanization by both blacks and whites. One can hypothesize that such remnants can be observed in religious worship, food preparation, speech, walking and lounging behavior, social taboos, sexual taboos, family forms and functioning, child rearing and a variety of non-verbal cultural forms, such as listening behavior and the use of space, among other things.[10] It is likely that these "Africanisms" with various modifications were passed on from generation to generation at an imperceptible level of cultural transmission, that is to say, over time, elders who passed them on to youngsters became unconscious of the fact they were passing on "Africanisms." They probably, say, their teaching as simply functional within the context of the life of blacks in an extremely hostile environment. It is critically important to begin to confront some of these issues in a serious and systematic way. There are, of course, innumerable other questions that beg answering. The Center for Research in the Black Experience can provide a resource through which a good many of the issues can be investigated.

The Center must also have its applied side. That is, its research should not be restricted solely to the scholarly undertakings of the "pure researcher." There are myriad problems that have immediate relevance to the way black folks live or fail to live their lives right now. The Center should have the capacity to meaningfully and successfully define and resolve certain of these problems. Moreover, the focus of the efforts of the Center should be directed toward problem that are articulated by lay people of the black community. That is to say, that the interests pursued should be for the most part a function of the expressed concerns of the people of the community. It is conceivable that the Center could investigate problems as diverse as whether foods such as milk and pork are in fact harmful to blacks and whether items sold in supermarkets in black neighborhoods are more expensive than the same items sold in white neighborhoods. This component of the Center should provide a meaningful service to the black community.

The Center should over time develop a capacity for educational efforts in its own right. From the outset, however, it should involve the staff and students of the department of African and Afro-American Studies and the School of Ethnic Studies in its operation. It could provide a base and resources from which the students of these structures can carry out their research activities. The applied researchers should be full-time paid professionals, preferably individuals who have served a scholarly apprenticeship in the Center on their way to acquiring their professional competence. I suggest this because I believe it takes a good deal more than "being black" to teach in and service the black community. It requires competence and in most cases that competence will be unrelated to color.

It should be noted that what has been suggested here as an academic vehicle for African and Afro-American Studies and the research Center can be seen as appropriate for carrying out scholarly teaching and research on any ethnic group. Moreover, it is important for university and college personnel to realize this and respond appropriately. It is the absence of the legitimation of ethnicity in America (because of the "melting pot" nonsense) that lurks behind the complex responses of whites to the efforts of blacks to achieve a more equitable position in the society. Indeed, the absence of socially legitimate mechanisms for preserving ethnicity, and the insistence that all ethnic distinctiveness be left in the melting pot may prove to be an important element in racism. Ethnic research and study must become a more important area for scholarly concern.

Some Gains to be Accrued from Black Studies

It is obvious that black studies will spin-off a variety of beneficial results apart from those noted above. I would like to discuss briefly several of these possible outcomes—obvious benefits that will accrue to blacks. Important among these will be an increased psychological and emotional liberation of black people. It is necessary at this point in the growth of black awareness for blacks to begin to establish evaluative standards against which, for example, the self-worth of blacks can be appropriately measured. Most of the existing standards are appropriate for white people but when applied to blacks can only yield self-denigrating assessments. I suspect that what results from the application of "white standards" to black behavior patterns and characteristics is what social scientists have identified as indicators of the self-hate that blacks supposedly have. Seen in another way, however, what blacks have been forced to do is to accommodate to the operation of cultural standards of, for example, beauty, content of which could only result in assessments that found them non-beautiful. These standards of beauty have been articulated around the physical characteristics of whites, thus the lack of such physical attributes by blacks leads to a negative valuation of the physical attributes of blacks by both blacks and whites. In response to this many blacks attempted to take on the attributes of whites by using skin lighteners, hair straighteners, etc. It was in effect an attempt to "live up" to the content of the white standard of beautiful, in this case. It is obvious that any standard of beauty appropriate for blacks would have to be strongly influenced by the quality of their own racial attributes.

A good example of this kind of accommodation and the painful results it yields is illustrated in the following. All cultures have norms that apply, to individual physical appearance. These norms identify certain physical qualities as desirable and others as undesirable e.g. beautiful and ugly. In an effort to fulfill the requirements of this norm the technical element of the culture produces instrumentalities (artifacts and techniques) for making oneself beautiful, or non-ugly. Now consider the need for grooming the hair (norm) and the comb (instrumentalities and the process of combing (technique) as a normative complex. Consider also that an operational definition of the verb "to comb" presupposes the presence of reasonably straight and flowing hair. Apply the normative complex to the grooming of kinky hair and the yield is an experience that can result in a negative evaluation of kinky hair. Blacks have over time accommodated in a number of ways to this normative bundle with what I consider negative yield. In Africa, specifically in Yorubaland, the same imperative for grooming the hair exists and the appropriate instrument is an *oya*. The requisite process is let's say *oyaing*. Now both this instrument and this technique is as appropriate to kinky hair as the comb is to straight hair. The absence of the *oya* in America and the corollary possibility of *oyaing* the kinky hair of blacks led to a definition among blacks of kinky hair as *"bad hair"* and straight hair as *"good hair."* Hair is still often classified in this fashion. The opposite would have been the case—the kinkier the hair the "gooder" the hair and straighter the hair the "badder" the hair—if the standards for judging hair quality had been appropriate to the attributes of black folks. It is for reasons such as these that these standards must be re-articulated in a fashion appropriate to blacks.

Black studies will also contribute to the development of a body of knowledge about blacks and their history that has been for the most part denied, ignored or deprecated. Along with this denial and deprecation went a denial and deprecation of blacks by whites and self-deprecation by blacks. Study of the black experience will yield a proper perspective of the world black experience in historical and contemporary affairs of the world. With this more accurate perspective will come a new sense of the importance of the non-white experience. Although this will be of especial significance for blacks, it will be greatly important for whites also. Whites need the knowledge of the black experience to temper their unearned sense of superiority. Moreover, such a contribution will place both the black, and white experience in proper historical perspective and contribute to the correction of a good many historical untruths.

In another way the black studies efforts will force the conventional disciplines out of their present provincial mold. The theories of the present social science disciplines are narrowly cast and based on the experience of the western world. They tend to reflect the provincialism of European scholars who ethnocentrically order and interpret phenomena of the world from the disadvantage of their western-most evolutionary perch. It is not surprising that looking at the black experience "through the glass whitely," as it were, they concluded that Africans were primitive and savage. They were afflicted by an enormous case of cultural myopia and self-inflicted at that. Cultural myopia, the scientific method notwithstanding, has continued to afflict the western social scientists, both black and white. It is necessary for these myopic disciplines and their practitioners to discover the experience of the non-white world. This experience, to be truly understood, must be confronted in its own right and not through the screen of western evaluation. When this happens the theoretical formulations of these disciplines will be shown to be incapable in their present form of handling the data that derive from the black experience. It will also be necessary to recast these theories so as to make them applicable to the majority of the world experiences (the non-white elements of the world). Then and only then will these disciplines be prepared to become disciplines whose theories and bodies of knowledge are truly reflective of the entire world.

Finally, black studies, as I have outlined it here, will truly constitute what Matthew Holden has referred to as "education for black power." In Dr. Holden's formulation both black students and black professors need this type education. He suggests:

> Moreover, the new mission will be to avoid the speciousness of developing students into mere verbalists, sophists, and rhetoricians. If there is a single obvious difficulty with current students . . . it is their addiction to a language of social action, without an honest and sustained attention to the facts underlying that reality or the logic involved in any proposal to change that reality. If mature black intellectuals have failed in any significant way, it is that they have become intimidated by student militancy . . .[11]

Holden goes on to suggest a strategy for education for the wielding of black power:

> The business of the black intellectual, in forwarding the development of other black intellectuals (his students) is to tell the truth (or as much as he can discover) and to aid in imaginative searches for ways to male the truthful situation most productive. This is what we must mean—and must insist upon—in "the regimen of fact and logic."
>
> This is a vital part of our understanding of the liberal education—the education appropriate to a man who will be a man of power. To be a man of power means that one must acquire a strategic position such that one can survive, grow, and develop—even in adverse circumstances.
>
> . . . the objective in black education, is, therefore to provide those forms for training which will most greatly enhance black men's capacities to penetrate the strategic points of influence and decision.[12]

I believe Dr. Holden's position to be entirely consistent with the notions of black studies as put forth here. I remind you again that these efforts hold potentially salutary outcomes not only for the university and our society but for the world. It is imperative that these activities be understood and undertaken by universities, colleges and other educational structures of our society.

Endnotes

1. C.F. Janheinz Jahn's discussion of Nommo in his book *MUNTU* (Grove Press, 1962), Chapter 5, "Nommo: The Magic Power of the Word," pp. 121-155.

2. This calls to mind Levy-Bruell's characterization of the Nuer as "prelogical."

3. Mendelsohn, Jack, *God, Allah and Ju Ju* (Boston: Beacon Press, 1963), p. 84.

4. *Ibid.*, p. 85.

5. Jahn, *op. cit.*

6. Sowande, Fela, *IFA* (Sowande: Institute of African Studies, University of lbadan, Nigeria). Chief Sowande, in his discussions of traditional Yoruba religious beliefs, describes a bat-

tle between factions of Irunmoles (angel-like beings). He reports these factions as being "armed to the teeth with *words* of terrible and awesome destructive power."

7. Jahn, *op. cit.* See Chapter 6, "KUNTU: Immutability of Style."

8. Sowande, *op. cit.*

9. Frazier, E. Franklin, *The Negro Church in America* (New York: Schocken Books, Inc., 1963).

10. Edward T. Hall, among others, has written extensively about these areas, c.f. *The Hidden Dimension* (Garden City: Doubleday and Company, Inc., 1966).

11. Matthew Holden, "Education for Black Power" (Wayne State University mimeo, 1967), p. 13.

12. *Ibid.*, p. 14.

11.

African-American Studies
and the State of the Art

Russell L. Adams

Introduction

The field of Afro-American Studies is relatively new as an institutional feature of higher education in America. The focus of this field is on the (1) experiences, (2) problems, and (3) prospects of individuals and groups whose heritage, wherever they may be, is African. The experience dimension of the field examines the historical record of black people in Africa and the Western Hemisphere. In the problem areas of African-American Studies, the sociological conditions confronting African-Americans and Africans (both seen as independent and interacting groups) are stressed. The prospects aspect of this new field deals with theoretical questions of several kinds: (a) conceptual theory for thinking about how best to approach the black experience, (b) analytical theory or sets of ideas and concepts to study the black experience, and (c) strategical or social change theories. As in any field, the experience, problems, and prospects components in Afro-American Studies frequently overlap it being impossible in practice to completely isolate them from one another. Although the study of the black experience is old, institutional support for it at the level of course concentrations is relatively new. The youthfulness of the field is indicated by the fact that programs and departments are known by a variety of names: "Afro-American Studies," "African-American Studies," "American Studies," "Afro-American and African Studies," "Black Studies, and Pan-African Studies." As a generic label, the term "Afro-American Studies" will be used in the following discussion.[1]

Major terms and concepts: Afrocentrism, analytical perspectives, black experience, intellectual perspectives, core/boundary, curriculum, Eurocentrism, epistemology, legitimacy, multi-disciplinary, inter-disciplinary, traditional disciplines field, Afrocentricity.

Foundations and Structure

Until recent years, Afro-American Studies has been a community-based endeavor, sparked by the work of the Association for the Study of Afro-American Life and History, the legacy of Carter G. Woodson, the "Father of Black History." Although a few schools, such as Howard and Fisk universities, had course concentrations within traditional fields and disciplines, Afro-American Studies won institutional visibility in the late 1960s as a consequence of black student demand.

Today, more than sixty departments of Afro-American Studies are to be found throughout the nation, primarily in predominantly white colleges and universities. Most of them offer the bachelor of arts degree; nearly a dozen of them offer master's degrees; and one offers both the master's degree and the doctorate.

As an organized, institutional approach to the black experience, Afro-American Studies takes a variety of forms. The most common is that of the program rather than department. A program enables students to complete either required or elective courses while doing most of their studies within a traditional field. This arrangement permits them to do work in single discipline departments and in the multi-disciplinary Afro-American Studies program. Programs are usually managed by a coordinator who may or may not be full-time. Faculty for a program may be anchored in a traditional department but teach a course in the program. Persons teaching full-time in programs, however, usually are not on a "tenure track." Tenure usually is a departmental matter, a situation suggesting the importance of a department. It is generally understood that programs have a shorter lifespan than departments, being mainly dependent on enrollments for their institutional survival. On the other hand, the program format allows for greater ease in team-teaching and multi-interdisciplinary collaboration, a feature used by this particular configuration of instruction. What has some institutions to been said about programs applies also to institutes of Afro-American Studies. (Incidentally, it may be noted that the often reported decline in the Afro-American Studies has to do with the decline in programs rather than departments. Of the full-fledged departments organized since 1969, less than a half dozen have been abolished or merged. Thus, the most durable Afro-American Studies unit is the department.

The typical Afro-American Studies Department is found in predominantly white institutions. The departmental format also means that a college or university, at least in theory, has accepted the idea of Afro-American Studies as a significant area of academic instruction, which was the original intent of the pioneers in the Afro-American Studies movement. A regular departmental structure implies that (a) funding is from general departmental budgets, (b) the college or university tenure rules cover departmental faculty, (c) the unit can offer a minor or a major leading to the bachelor of arts degree, and (d) it can have a full-time support staff. It must be pointed out, however, that most institutions have supported the Afro-American Studies' presence on a campus for reasons other than academic. Some have supported departments as a "political settlement" with their proponents; some have funded programs as "Insurance" against further demands. Still others have established such units as a handy way of increasing faculty diversity, without having this diversity appear in the traditional departments. In any case, a Department of Afro-American Studies is seen as the strongest possible vehicle for assuring the continued presence of this field on a campus.

The impact of the student demand for institutional support for the coverage of the black experience went beyond the setting up of institutes, programs, and departments. Virtually all of the traditional social science and humanities departments and programs in many universities have revised relevant syllabi or offered courses giving greater attention to some aspects of black life. Such coverage has not been automatic, as shown by the Stanford University controversy over making its "civilization" courses more inclusive of non-European peoples. The different Afro-American Studies units, however, make possible in-depth treatment of topics about blacks, whereas there is a tendency for the black experience to disappear in a multi-ethnic, multi-cultural curriculum. Typical majors in a department of Afro-American Studies are required to take thirty or more hours of undiluted instruction on various topics and as-pects of the black experience and perhaps eighteen to twenty hours in a traditional discipline. Departments frequently require some fieldwork in conjunction with on-campus academic activity. Critics of Afro-American Studies curricula often do not re-alize that, beyond the department, majors and minors in this field also must fulfill a given institution's general education and courses or hour distribution requirements for graduation. Students completing work in a program or institute usually receive graduation credit or some official recognition of involvement.

At present, Afro-American Studies departments vary significantly in curriculum content. From the very, beginning of the monument, proposals were made recom-mending the contents of the "ideal" department. John Blassingame (in *New Per-spectives on Black Studies*) summarizes the 1971 conclusions of a group of scholars on the objectives of "A Model Afro-American Studies Program":

— "to give students a clear conception of the complexity of American life,"

— "to acquaint students with the problems, successes, and failures of America's largest minority group,"

— "to enable students to lead fruitful lives in a multi-racial society"

— "to help students to understand the nature of contemporary racial and social turmoil and to guide them into constructive modes of thought about current issues," and

— "to enable students to see the black experience in a world setting."

In 1969, Harvard University set up a Committee on African and Afro-American Studies which determined that "what the black student wants is an opportunity to study the black experience and to employ the resources of Harvard University in seeking so-lutions to the problems of the black community." This report accurately identified the desires and interests of black students in many other institutions during this period. Dur-ing the late 1960s, many people were persuaded that major institutions had a direct re-sponsibility to improve the conditions of the inner cities. Knowledge was to be socially relevant and, in the words of a much-quoted slogan of the time, Afro-American Studies departments were to be embodiments of "academic excellence and social responsibil-ity." Nor was this view limited to departments in predominantly white institutions. The Howard University Afro-American Studies departmental catalog of 1975, for example, announced that its departmental goals were to provide "a fundamental under standing of those economic, social and political forces which have shaped the Afro-American ex-perience in the Western Hemisphere" and to provide students with a "basic under-standing of the special problems of Afro-Americans in contemporary American life."

The Afro-American Studies movement has been as interested in developing new curricula as in criticizing existing ones. Afro-American Studies specialists carry out frequent surveys of departments seeking data on enrollment, funding, and curricula. In 1981, the National Council for Black Studies published Black-Studies Core Cur-riculum in an attempt to provide a model for the standardization of African Ameri-can Studies curricula around the country. The Council suggested that the ideal core curriculum be constructed along the following lines: Three broad areas of instruction and research should form the structural array of courses. These areas were cited as (1) Social Behavioral Studies, (2) History Course Area, and (3) Cultural Studies Course Area. Each of these areas would have introductory courses, followed by four levels of treatment for the focus of the respective area subject matter.

The National Council model is as much a summation of existing curricula arrangements as a recommendation for the same. Typically, departments of Afro-

American Studies have course arrays which are historical, sociological, and cultural, with a given department stressing one array more than others. Some departments direct their attention to black literature as an introduction to the black experience, as in the case of the University of Iowa program under the late literary scholar Darwin T. Turner. Some departments divide their course offerings between Africa as a continent and the black urban experience in North America, the Black Studies Department of Ohio State University being perhaps the leading example of this configuration. For nearly two decades, under the leadership of James Turner, the Cornell University African Studies Department has split its course content between Africa and the Americas, as did the Department of Afro-American and African Studies at the State University of New York at Albany and the University of North Carolina at Charlotte. Occasionally, a program or department will use an area/theme approach to its basic subject, the example being Professor Richard Long's extended conduct of basically a Caribbean Studies program at Atlanta University. The Afro-American Studies programs at Harvard and Yale universities are organized around historical and cultural topics. Temple University has the only operational African-American Studies Ph.D.-granting program in the country. This graduate program, which includes the master's, is composed of two major "tracks": the "Cultural/Aesthetic" and the "Social/Behavioral." The former is subdivided into "Religion and Philosophy" and "Art and Literature," and the latter into "Society and Communication" and "History and Political Economy." Taught with a full-time faculty of ten and an "associated" faculty of eight, these subdivisions cover a total of sixty-six courses.

Whatever the make-up of announced curricula, the largest proportion of students enrolled in programs and departments take Afro-American social science courses. In 1976, a major study of Afro-American Studies operations among 178 institutions revealed that 65 percent of them offered a social science and humanities curriculum. Some programs stress mainly cultural matters, the one at the University of California at Santa Barbara being an example of this type. On the other hand, few have curricula like the Afro-American Studies program at the University of Maryland, College Park, where students concentrate on urban policy analysis courses requiring the use of quantitative skills. For the past fifteen years, Professor Abdul Alkatimat and some of the leading African-Americanists have been trying to solve the problems of (a) conceptual theory, (b) analytical perspective and (c) time segmentation through a series of extended workshops for the production of *Introduction to Afro-American Studies: A People's College Primer*. "*Intro*, as it is called, is essentially a sociological outline of the black experience at different historical eras. This work has an internal dialectic of change and evolution and employs ideology, nationality, class and race to examine levels of social cohesion and disruption during the pre-colonial traditional African period, the slavery era, the emancipation epoch, the time of the "rural" experience, the great migration, and the final urbanization stages. More than half of the departments of Afro-American Studies use "*Intro*" to give students its overview of the field, even as other approaches are being developed. It is significant that its organizational scheme is labeled "Toward a Paradigm of Unity in Afro-American Studies." To date, this has been one of the most intensive and prolonged effort to lay the perceptual foundations for Afro-American Studies, although there continue to be periodic conferences on Afro-American Studies and curriculum building in general. As yet, no nationally observed curriculum model is to be found. Each institution adjusts to its particular set of circumstances involving Afro-American Studies.

In this new field, the construction of curricula often is a matter of faculty availability. Due to a variety of reasons, African-American Studies specialists are relatively few in number. Until the 1960s, most black professors were forced to seek careers in the predominantly black teaching colleges, primarily live in the South. In the days of legally enforced segregation, the attainment of the doctorate was the crowning achievement of the black professor. Teaching was the main activity expected and supported by these institutions, their academic reputations being a function of the extent to which they simply reproduced what they were taught. To be sure, with courage and enormous persistence, a few from this first wave of black professors did make contributions to their disciplines: Charles S. Johnson and E. Franklin Frazier in sociology, Charles H. Wesley and John Hope Franklin in history, Albert Whiting and Kenneth Clark in psychology, Charles H. Thompson and Allison Davis in education. However, when predominantly white institutions opened their rosters to African-Americans, they faced a shortage of black faculty. In many cases, the curriculum arrived with whomever was available as faculty. Frequently, a director was hired and given wide authority to create a curriculum. It is probably no accident that the strongest departments are in locations near populous urban black communities. The list of strong departments includes Temple University in Philadelphia, Harvard near Boston, Rutgers and Princeton near New York City, University of California-Berkeley, near San Francisco, and Ohio State University, in Columbus. Cornell, UCLA, Temple, SUNY at Albany, Berkeley, Ohio State, and Wisconsin offer the M.A. degree in Afro-American Studies, while Temple offers the Ph.D. in the field, and Berkeley a Ph.D. in Ethnic Studies, with an African-American Studies component. A few notable programs are found in areas with small black populations, the program at the University of Wisconsin at Madison being an example.

Curriculum development also has been hampered by the multi-disciplinary character of programs and departments. In various curriculum conferences, theories and multi- and inter-disciplinary models are praised. In actual operation, however, the faculties implement a multidisciplinary curriculum. Individuals in these units tend to cling to the ideas and canons of their disciplines, hesitating to venture into new ones. Often, departments have two or more individuals trained in the same traditional discipline, a situation which contributes to unnecessary tensions and reluctant cooperation in an inter-disciplinary direction. With one doctoral program in operation and at least two additional ones in the discussion stage, the field may soon have persons whose training has been intensively multidisciplinary. Most fields require a long time to evolve from a field to discipline, not to mention a specialty within a discipline. Two decades have passed and, for all practical purposes, Afro-American specialists in predominantly white institutions are in a sense repeating the patterns of their forebears in historically black colleges: they are primarily involved in teaching undergraduates, with de facto counseling and committee representation. This situation reduces the amount of time available for research and publication and thus puts some departments at a competitive disadvantage in faculty recruiting. The University of North Carolina at Charlotte, for example, has grappled with this problem by adding a strong Educational Support Service component to academic advising (and counseling) to free the faculty in every department including the Afro-American and African Studies which maintains a specific faculty member who serves as a liaison between the department and that unit.

Most of the research work done in Afro-American Studies is archival, this being less time-consuming mind expensive than survey and field investigations. Whatever the problems of curriculum building, undergraduates earning the bachelor of arts degree tend to continue their education, at least to the level of the master's, in one of the traditional disciplines such as history and sociology. A few go on to earn the doctorate. The Temple University graduate level department, of course, represents an opportunity for instructional continuity in this field. Graduates also enter the fields of law, social work, and education while the Afro-American Studies major and the traditional minor give students the benefits of both.

What does an Afro-American Studies major or minor learn that cannot be done in traditional departments? One could study black political life in the twentieth century in a department of political science, or African-American family organization in a department of sociology. Excellent instruction In economics is able in some departments of the same name. An English department with qualified instructors doubtless could do a good job with the Harlem Renaissance. A department of philosophy with outstanding individuals, such as black philosophers Cornel West of Princeton and Lucius Outlaw of Haverford College, could match any Afro-American Studies philosophy offerings. The same could be said of certain departments of psychology.

From the perspective of the professional Afro-Americanist, however, two things by the combining of a number of disciplines into a single department. The justification first has to do with the ideological character of traditional disciplines. Afro-American Studies emerged as a field in reaction to the failure of established disciplines to cover adequately and fairly the black experience. In the field of history, for example, down until the mid-1930s, majority group scholars produced works implicitly justifying racist treatment of African-Americans. Even as late as the 1950s, as eminent and as widely read a white historian as Henry Steele Commager could casually call black male slaves "Sambo" and declare that "Sambo" was happy in bondage. Kenneth Stampp, another and more recent white historian, in 1956, wrote that blacks were whites with black skins and so should be treated equally. A generation earlier, historians William A. Dunning and John W. Burgess, at Columbia University, produced squads of shamelessly pro-Southern and anti-black historians of Reconstruction politics. This group of historians helped to shape elite opinion about African-Americans, some of whose works echoed Burgess's dictum that "a black skin means membership in a race of men which has never of itself succeeded in subjecting passion to reason, has never, therefore, created an civilization of any kind."[2]

Seeing Southern black poverty, sociologists wrote of an imputed genetic incapacity preventing blacks from living white middle-class life-styles. As a result, the black presence in American culture was interpreted as a "problem" in basic group remediation and acculturation, to be solved via racial "uplift" operations. Instead of identifying the black presence as a research challenge, establishment academics chose to ignore it, except as an insoluble "problem." These historical and sociological perspectives regarding blacks began to change in the 1930s, with the great W.E.B. DuBois reversing the anti-black accounts of the post-emancipation years via his exhaustive work, *Black Reconstruction in America*. The publication, in 1944, of Gunnar Myrdal's *An American Dilemma* also represented a change in perceptions of the causes of the plight of African Americans. This pivotal book was written from materials complied by highly talented black and white scholars possessing sound empirical knowledge of their subject manner and with fairly objective views about race and power. Myrdal, the Swedish-born synthesizer of their research labors, concluded that the condition of African-Americans was a function of an immoral split between America's egalitarian professions and its Caucasian color mania and not some inherited genetic deficiency among African-Americans.[3]

Before the educational establishment had fully absorbed this new perspective, a judicial revolution from above and a social revolution from below brought about the Civil Rights movement of the 1960s. This failure to see the black experience as essential material for curriculum use outraged the new cadres of black students attending historically white institutions. Since the black presence had either been ignored or denigrated by the traditional disciplines, African-American students

demanded that this experience be treated in separate instructional formats with professors fully committed to Afro-american Studies units. In many cases, students also
insisted that these units be given full autonomy to determine curriculum. They argued that many historically white institutions had over a hundred years to recognize
the black presence. Having failed to do so, professors representing traditional disciplines could not be considered suddenly competent enough to take part in setting up
curricula in this new field. Institutional responses ranged from that of Denison University which funded *student* travel to gather information about curriculum efforts in
other places to that of Harvard University with a once controversial committee on
Afro-American Studies chaired by a Dean. Most departments developed their own
curricula, subject to technical approval by college-wide curriculum groups. A curriculum alone, however, is merely a collection of prescribed courses, and does not
constitute a discipline. As a general rule, teaching and research together contribute to
the development of a discipline, with the emphasis being on how both shape the theoretical and practical visions of what a discipline should be. This is more the case in
the social sciences than in the natural sciences, for a given phenomenon in nature
suggests the most effective approach to it. When matured, a discipline is assumed to
have worked out an *empirical* definition of what often is called a "core" or defining
center of attention as well as its "boundary" or the maximum limits of work perceived as legitimate for and to a field. For example, the "core" of the field of political science is the phenomenon of authoritative power, its management and distribution. When the limits of authority phenomena are passed by political science
practitioners, when an economist cannot be discerned as working on some feature of
the goods and services exchange process, then he or she is no longer regarded as
doing economics. In short, a specified segment of collective life is identified as distinct
enough to have its own technical and academic followers or disciples, hence the term
"discipline." All disciples are expected to use the tools and follow the rules governing their "order" or academic category.

In addition to institutional resistance, Afro-Americanists thus faced the problems
of defining the core and boundary of their chosen field. They were confronted with
complex tasks of (a) developing intellectual perspectives free of the exclusionary Eurocentric views of things African, (b) criticizing existing perceptual models of analysis in order to do so, and (c) creating curricula and research agenda supportive of an
alternative version of the black experience that met the varied service, cognitive, and
affective needs of students. Under the circumstances, it was not possible to do well
all of these things in a few years. Black scholars pointed out that the established disciplines were still redefining themselves after many, many years, and thus it was unfair to evaluate an African-American Studies still at the field stage of academic evolution. African-Americanists also saw that a new cultural perspective on the black
experience was imperative. In order to do this, they had to show how cultural and social positions and orientations shape perception of research problems. White historians, for example, have just begun writing history "from below" rather than from
"the top." The so-called "worm's-eye-view" of power in political science has joined
the "bird's-eye-view" of the state as the essential and proper object of study for political "scientists." Economists now write of "micro-economics."

The second argument for creating multi-disciplinary Afro-American Studies departments recognizes that the interwoven nature of the black experience calls for
holistic coverage. At this stage, no one discipline can do the job. Students and teachers in the early days of institutional Afro-American Studies were intuitively aware of
the connecting character of this experience, especially in terms of its outer connections with continental and overseas European societies. They knew that Europeans

had fought one another over Africans and Africa itself and that the world's greatest civil war had been fought about Africans in North America. They were aware of inequalities of power and status in black-white relations. Yet, they also realized that, from elementary school through college, formal education curricula had barely touched on the presence of black people in the world. The institutional study of the black experience in its fullness was just beginning and the subject had to be thought of as a field rather than a discipline. Afro-American Studies specialists could take advantage of the enforced commonalities among black people by using the multi-disciplinary approach as the preferred method of study. Thus, the emphasis would be on the subject matter rather than disciplinary "purity." The traditional disciplines would be seen for what they truly are, instruments for learning about something other than themselves.

Disciplinary traditionalists did not accept this picture of the field of Afro-American Studies. They held that the field was academically unorganized, as had identified a field, but its cultivation had on in indeed it was. Afro-American entity just begun. Opponents of institutional support for Afro-American Studies unfamiliar argued that, if it could not meet prevailing standards for disciplines, it should not be granted academic legitimacy. The argument, of course, ignored the many societal, regional, and area studies programs receiving institutional support, as a result of political and economic power. In other words, if this new field had been suggested by establishment academics, neither their premature expectations nor the legitimacy issue would have been as controversial. The insistence by African-Americans on the value of including the black experience angered many academics who were often puzzled by the vigor and zeal they brought to this issue. Because of the controversial position of many, African-American Studies programs and departments and the fact that most of their enrollment was African-American, white students have had the Perception that the programs were remedial and just for black students when in reality, although they have a special mission to the black students, they are supposed to serve the entire university. To understand the deeper sources of confusion and conflict about Afro-American Studies it is helpful to go to the field of epistemology and related issues.

Epistemology, Afrocentricity and Ideology

Epistemology is defined by *Webster's Unabridged Dictionary* as "the theory or science of the *methods and grounds* of knowledge, esp. with reference to its limits and validity" (emphasis added). Epistemology involves the understanding of how groups of people come to hold the ideas and viewpoints characteristic of them and their cultural heritage. Afro-American Studies specialists claim that, since the traditional disciplines were shaped without awareness of the nature of the subjective, internal communities of persons of African descent, their vaunted "objectivity" is compromised by their practitioners (a) social distance from blacks, (b) basically tourist/anthropologist methods of research on blacks, (c) lack of intimate familiarity with the real effects of the actions of the larger societies on black social formations and psyche, and (d) deliberate distortion of the African American and African social record, past and present. The rising black research groups reject the intrinsic elitism and cultural ethnocentrism of establishment academics as flawed at best and degradingly unfair at worst.

This rejection of establishment academic perceptions has deep roots in the black intellectual experience. Carter G. Woodson, the best-known exponent of this view (and founder of the Black History Week, now Month, in 1926), saw his work as a corrective endeavor. Over the three-quarters of a century since the establishment of the Association for the Study of Afro-American Life and History by Woodson (a Harvard Ph.D.), in 1915, critical black thought has moved from accepting the "myths of the Negro past" through a rejection of epistemological viewpoints of blacks as deviations from the stock of humankind and from the standards of "host" societies to an assertiveness which recently has sprung forth as Afrocentrism. For the first time, the concern of professional Afro-Americanists have spilled over into the popular media and public discussion. For this reason, attention here will be given to this new concern.

The purest form of Afrocentrism places Africa at its center as the source of the world's peoples and its most fundamental ideas and inventions. As a term, however, it also refers to African and African-American culture, education, ideologies, and social interests. Perhaps it is not surprising that the foremost exponents of a proactive epistemological stance toward the assumptions of Afro-American Studies have emerged most fully in historically white institutions and in conjunction with the search of predominantly black urban school systems for answers to problems of student self-concept, motivation and performance. Nor is it surprising that the leading exponent of Afrocentrism, Molefe Asante, is developer and star of Temple University's African-American Studies Department, the most advanced in the nation. Through his many writings, Asante, with the assistance of black professors at other historically white institutions, has made "Afrocentrism" a buzz word. The collection of supporting scholars around Professor Asante often are identified as "Nile Valley" Afrocentrists.

Adherents to this school of thought assert the primacy of Egyptian Africa as the creative locus of the major ideas and practices which undergird the foundations of humanity. They declare that not only did humankind split off from the simian or ape world in East Africa, but assert that this African segment of humankind generated a still-living stock of ideas produced by its long history alongside the Nile. In one of his recent works, Asante said of the Nile that "it played a vital role in the creation of Kemetic (black) philosophy, agriculture, technology, and religion." Consequently, black people in particular, and the rest of the world, in general, should acknowledge their debt to black Egypt (Kemet) and revive those ideas which contributed to black achievement in many areas of life during antiquity. This school asserts that recovery of ancient Egyptian knowledge would fill the spiritual void and raise the self-esteem of those peoples with clearly African legacies and that curricula based on Nile Valley philosophy and values are most appropriate for Egypt's African-American descendants and are of great use to others.

Continental Afrocentrists assert that the entire African continent is the true cultural source of black trans-Atlantic communities. Adherents of this school celebrate their version of authentic black cultural values and practices in the Diaspora and declare that they are prerequisites for the revitalization of African American communities. They also hold that a common Afrocentric world view can be synthesized out of the complex of traditional African life and history through careful study of existing artifacts and print materials. *It is a conviction of this group that African social values are more humanistic than those derived from Europe.*

Afrocentric Infusionists assert, instead, the positive value of infusion or blending historical data into the curricula. This Africa-based ideas, concepts, values, and historical school holds that all Americans can profitably share positive African viewpoints, experiences and practices. While such blending would have the effect of reducing stereotypes and enhancing conceptions of others about blacks, sharing would enable people to discern the common humanity of European and African societies. *This group seeks close collaboration with public school curriculum specialists.* Afrocentric infusionists see black people as Americans of African descent with a rich and valuable heritage, which has been ignored and under-used. Professor Asa Hilliard of Georgia State University is perhaps the leading advocate of infusionism, even though he also is partial to the Nile Valley school.

Social Afrocentrists, on the other hand, place greater stress on the *use of knowledge and resources in protecting and promoting the best interests of black people as interacting members of the societies where they live.* They do not use the African background as much as the other Afrocentrists. They agree that the heritage of America's black population is insufficiently appreciated, but hold that it is not possible nor desirable to try to reproduce ancient Africa in a world headed toward the twenty-first century. Adherents of this school take an interest group approach to the topic of Afrocentrism and hold that intellectual fads come and go but group interests are permanent. Thus, *social Afrocentrists do not see the black experience as so specialized that only blacks may be involved in exploring it.* This version of Afrocentrism is "less hard line" about who can participate in the work of using education to promote the concerns of African-Americans. It recognizes the complexity of human experience and the difficulties in identifying the "culturally African" from the non-African elements which societies absorb over time. Africa per se is more of a target of interest than of inspiration. *In a sense, this conception of Afrocentrism is but a continuation of the position taken by the first wave of individual black scholars in the era of forced segregation.*

The types of Afrocentrism cited above represent the *thinking* about how to avoid the negative aspects and consequences of traditional curricula and attitudes toward people of color. The very concept of Afrocentrism has stimulated a great deal of debate about the role of different perspectives in guiding instruction and research in the field of Afro-American Studies. At the level of practice, Afro-American Studies departments are (1) endeavoring to create an independent world view free of the defects of misleading claims of Eurocentric "universality" and "objectivity," (2) still trying to develop and present once-omitted factual material to their students, (3) hoping to evolve from multi-disciplinary to interdisciplinary instruction, (4) responding more effectively to issues of curriculum balance in the area of academic skills, and (5) enhancing their institutional foundations. Although only a quarter-century old, the institutional field of Afro-American Studies has already made a major contribution to education by raising anew questions about the nature, content, and direction of American education in this era of ethnic and cultural diversity. The debate over Afrocentricity is generally an epistemological and a pedagogical one. The differences in ideology within the black studies programs and among black intellectuals, however, have generated a more heated debate, sometimes used by the establishment as well as by students to indict the programs as venues of "Indoctrination" rather than of intellectual exposure to facts, theories, and opinions which might assist young men and women, both black and white, in determining, for themselves, the best course of action in their lives and relationships with their fellow citizens. The controversy heightens tensions because these ideologies are action-oriented thought systems or philosophies, advanced as solutions to the problems of the African-American community in a predominantly white, Anglo-Saxon, and male-dominated society, which, throughout the centuries, has shown little concern for the plight of minorities, blacks in particular.

Following is a brief summary of the most popular ideologies of which students of Africa and African-America ought to be aware. One of the most concise discussions of the issue appears in the volume edited by James Turner, *The Next Decade: Theoretical and Research Issues in African Studies* (1984), in an article authored by Tilden LeMelle of Hunter College titled "The Status of Black Studies in the Second Decade: The Ideological Imperative."

LeMelle classifies black ideologies into two broad categories: the assimilationist and the self-determinationist (the latter also known as the nationalist ideology). While the first category comprises the accommodationist, the reconciliationist, the liberal idealist, and the Marxist-Leninist, the second category encompasses the psychological and the separatist nationalist ideologies.

The accommodationist, exemplified by the philosophy of Booker T. Washington, who advocated economic self-help taken to a higher level through vocational mandatory and appeasing toward the white majority, does not dare to challenge the status quo, and is geared toward accommodating and accepting the white set parameters within which blacks can advance. The followers of this course of action are often dubbed as "Uncle Tom's." Of course, the defenders of this philosophical strategy hold the view that Washington was a realist, a pragmatist, who lived in a terrifying, black lynching, southern white environment, which under no circumstances would tolerate the political empowerment of black people. The reconciliationist ideology, in Lemelle's analysis, exemplified by W.E.B. DuBois's thinking, differs from the accommodationist in that it does not avoid conflict; it challenges but seeks compromise within "the rules of the game" established by society's white majority. It is assimilationist (it accepts and emulates mainstream culture), and holds that blacks can achieve their goals only if they have a group of highly educated and qualified leaders — *the talented tenth* — who will speak for them and lead them in the crucible of daily confrontation for access to political, social, and economic opportunities.

The black liberal idealists, instead, essentially believe in the goodness of man and the ultimate triumph of good over evil and cherish the democratic and liberal ideals of American society. This type of assimilationist (integrationist) philosophy, identified with Martin Luther King, Jr.'s crusade — the Civil Rights movement of the mid-fifties through the mid-sixties — relies on the good will and the guilty conscience of (white) liberals, who, allied with blacks, in a "rainbow coalition," to use a contemporary phraseology, will peacefully transform America from a racist society to one of brotherhood.

The Marxist-Leninists, clothed in the aura of scientism, adopt and impose a European model on the black community, analyzing its problems on the basis of class (incomes, living standards, and ownership of the means of production) while giving little weight to the race issue which they think will disappear once classes have been eliminated. They focus their hopes on the actions of the workers (the *lumpen proletariat*), both black and white, united, and intent on overthrowing the middle-class or the bourgeoisie.

The problem with this approach, the critics say, is that, as with the liberal idealists, it counts on the goodness of white workers and their solidarity with their black counterparts, ignoring the fact that, historically, rarely did the two see eye to eye their mutual needs and that, in times of economic crisis, black workers often become the target of white workers, whom they accuse of "stealing their jobs," accepting lower wages, and acting as strike-breakers. Forgetting the perennial reality of race and racial discrimination and the fact that the black middle-class is more of a consuming than a producing and owning society make the Marxist-Leninist position utopian and therefore untenable. LeMelle believes that the Marxist-Leninists constitute one of the most subtle but more dangerous ideologues. Of course, now that communism has lost its grip over important world societies and regimes, the validity of Marxism-Leninism is in serious question as a strategy designed to replace capitalism.

LeMelle defines black nationalism, which emerged out of frustration with American policies and the insignificant gains of the Civil Rights movement, as the "identification with the interests and as of Black people wherever they may be, regardless of state boundaries." As an earlier manifestation of this general category, he includes the slave revolts, the Harlem Renaissance, the Garvey movement, and the philosophy of Carter G. Woodson. Separatist nationalism, often mislabeled as "anti-white," attempts to actually separate black people physically and socially from the majority society and create an independent environment such as a state in which blacks can implement their survival strategies. It appears that the Nation of Islam would fall under this category, if one sees it as "non anti-white," but "pro-black," to use LeMelle's terminology.

Finally, the psychological black nationalist is "satisfied with his or her own worth and posits self-directed interests and goals," while remaining a part of established society. This approach is exemplified, according to LeMelle, by the attitude of the black students of the 1960s who demanded the establishment of black studies programs across the nation, insisting that they combine relevant and inclusive education with social action to benefit the masses of the black people.

Unfortunately, the tendency of most ideologues is to expect or force everyone to embrace one of these ideologies, and, in specific, theirs, to deserve respect within the black community and the (black) academy. They overlook the fact that most people never consciously formulate or follow a specific philosophy to guide every moment of their lives. In most cases, people may combine one or two or more of these ideologies to face a reality which is not, as they say, all "black or white." The debate on ideological behavior has of late brought about the controversy over "political correctness" mainly on predominantly white campuses and in the political arena across the nation.

Socio-Scientific Trends

While Afrocentricity and ideologies have emerged as debates regarding the proper philosophy and perspective African-American scholars *should* take toward their work and the best action-oriented strategies they should propose to the African-American community, it is helpful to understand what *has been* the nature of the themes and theories guiding their previous efforts, especially in the context of their treatment of the concept of community. The term "African-American (or Black) Community" has been used to mean (a) the collectivity of Americans of African ancestry, and (b) blacks as a cohesive sociopolitical group. The idea of an African-American or black community has been used most explicitly in the fields of history, sociology and psychology. These disciplines respectively deal with: (1) the historical dimensions of the black experience, (2) the sociological dilemmas of racial stratification and subordination in a democracy, and (3) the impact of the community's historical legacy and its contemporary effects on the mentality of black people.

The philosophies of African-American scholars in these fields appear to have been the result of their own socialization, their individual attitudes toward the canons of their disciplines, the major political and intellectual currents of their eras, and the particular topics, problems, or questions addressed by them. By and large, their ideologies must be inferred from their works. If all of them are unified by any single ideology, it is the ideology of freedom. The individuals and books mentioned below are to be understood as exemplars and examples of the themes and theories of the intellectual cutting edges of their times.

Black scholarly production in the United States originated in the field of history. It began as an effort to have Africa descended people seen as human subjects among humankind and not as inanimate commodities in the economic systems of non-Africans. Consequently, the central theme and objective of black historiography has been the elimination of four centuries of silence, ignorance, and error regarding the human experiences, conditions, and achievements of countless millions once denied voice of standing Western culture. In the words of historian Earl E. Thorpe, "the central theme of Black History is the quest of Black Americans for freedom, equality and manhood (sic)." The dean of African-American historians, John Hope Franklin, has noted several distinct thematic phases in the evolution of black history.

From the publication of George Washington Williams's *History of the Negro Race in America* in 1882 to about 1915, writes Franklin, "the common objective of the writers of this period was to define and describe the role of Afro-Americans in the life of the nation." The few black historians of the era tried to counteract this by writing amateur histories and biographies as correctives to the growing belief that Africans anywhere were incapable of making history. To combat this, African-American intellectuals established the American Negro Academy in 1897 with the idea of enhancing, as Alexander Crummell notes, "the civilization of the Negro race in the United States by the scientific processes of literature, art and philosophy through the agency of the cultured men of this same Negro." To this end, its members put out nearly two dozen scholarly publications on the black experience.

The next phase began in 1915 with the founding, by Carter G. Woodson, of the Association for the Study of Negro Life and History. Woodson declared, as noted by Franklin, that the objective of his new national organization was "to save and publish the records of the Negro, that the race may not become a minor factor in the thought of the world"—hence, the establishment of *Journal of Negro History* in 1916 and the *Negro History Bulletin* a decade later. The practical intention of contributionism was the bolstering of community pride and confidence in an era of official racism.

Overlapping the second, the third phase covers the years between 1935 and 1960, a period which saw the rise and fall of Nazism, the urbanization of the black community, and the beginning of the Civil Rights revolution. In 1933, Woodson wrote *The Mis-Education of the Negro* which opened the next stage of black historiography, that of epistemology, or the study of ideological foundations of knowledge itself. In this work, he urged blacks, the lettered and unlettered alike not to depend on the majority group for the definition of itself and of social reality. Two years later, the multi-disciplinary DuBois made a declaration of black intellectual independence with a fresh and provocative interpretation of the immediate post-civil war years in *Black Reconstruction*, a magisterial study that placed the African-American community at its center. With this work, black historians quickly evolved from historical narration to historical explanation. The idea of the black community was revised to fit an interactionist interpretation of history. Black history also became overtly critical of the larger social order. This made it possible for historians to use sociology and vice-versa. An excellent example of this is *The Negro in the United States* (1949), a work of sociological history of the African-American community by the eminent sociologist, E. Franklin Frazier.

The fourth and current phase is one in which no level of historical analysis is omitted. Black historiography now includes work from Thomas Holt's *Black Over*

White: Negro Political Leadership in South Carolina during Reconstruction (1977) to the global sweep of St. Clair Drake's *Black Folk Here and There* (1990). Moreover very large numbers of scholars of both races are employing a variety of methods to study and reconstruct the history of the black community from a host of analytical perspective.

Just as African-American historians moved from narrative to analysis, so did black scholars in the field of sociology. Even before emancipation, free blacks were producing narrative reports on the condition within their communities. In 1897, with his *The Philadelphia Negro*, W.E.B. DuBois did for African-American sociology what Carter G. Woodson did for history: he used it to explain, in scientific terms, the black community to itself and to others. He and other sociologists such as Charles S. Johnson and E. Franklin Frazier used an evolutionary approach to the study of the black community. Many of these early works measured the development of the black community in terms of rates of growth in income, health, education, and occupational diversity. As a consequence, African-American scholars produced sociological studies with pronounced historical content, Frazier's *The Negro in the United States* being the most notable of them. At the same time, other sociologist stressed the role of contemporary forces in determining the shape and life style of the black community. St. Clair Drake and Horace Cayton produced a classic of this genre in *Black Metropolis* (1945).

By the 1940s, as black historians strove to promote racial and community pride via the contributionist approach, African-American sociologists sought to understand the contemporary status of the race though a number of theories; acculturation, deprivation, segregation, discrimination. Whatever the emphasis, each of the theories presented stressed comparisons between the white and black national communities. By conceptualizing the social conditions within the white community as the norm, inequalities were seen as negatives. The implications of intrinsic human equality espoused by black historians and the sociological observations of group inequalities sparked the search for theories to explain the latter. Thus began the *pathological* theory of the black community. The hypothesis was that the African- American community was "ill," and the white community was not. Sociologists then sought internal and external causes for the "illness" of the community. Some sociologists pointed to the "legacy" of slavery and hypothesized a culture of black dependency it fostered. Others saw the difference in "inappropriate" African cultural "survivals" which had the effect of slowing down the evolution of the race toward a technologically oriented culture. Sociologists who assumed the existence of external sources of the black community's problems called for a return to an interactionist approach as the best way to understand the black community. This meant, again, stressing the conflictive relations and power disparities between the two communities of color. Thus *deprivation* theories were used to guide sociological research on the African American community. The deprivation argument held that persistent racism and discrimination by white America had deprived black communities of opportunities to evolve at the same rate as white immigrant communities. In the 1960s, some scholars defined the black community as an internal *colony*, existing to be exploited by a callous "mother country." Some scholars also saw the black community as a "nation" within a nation and several brands of "black nationalism" gained prominence among the more radical black intellectuals.

The internal and external causation theories were blended in the "systems theory" approach which mainstream sociologists applied to the total social order, an approach which at bottom justifies the status quo on a law-and-order basis. In reaction to the inherent conservatism of this conception of the social order, a group of critical sociologists contributed to *The Death of White Sociology*, edited by Joyce Ladner, calling for a new sociology which would supersede black community pathology theories and escape the ideological trap of the systems theory. They sought a black sociology powerful enough to do this. A major volume aimed in this direction is *The Truly Disadvantaged*, written in 1987 by William J. Wilson, the most prominent African-American sociologist in the 1990s. This work places the black community in the vortex of national social forces, but recognizes the role of conscious decision making by government as a major factor influencing the quality of life in black America.

The theories of the African-American community espoused by black psychologists embody the concatenated effects of its historical past and sociological present. Some psychologists (and social psychologists) have argued that polarities of racial status and dualities of black-white interactions have created a cultural schizophrenia resulting in a schizoid mentality for African-Americans, the kind of "two-ness" of identity mentioned by W.E.B. DuBois at the beginning of the century. The functional stress of this "two-ness" or double consciousness, of being full of but not fully in American society, has created pathological problems for the black community, among them an enervating sense of collective inadequacy and individual impotence. For at least two generations, this was the common theme of both black and white psychologists using "reference group" theory, which asserts that the basic template of personal identity is the group of which individual is a socialized member, whatever the social status of the group.

The unquestioned low status of the African-American community in the society thus forced self-concept and self-esteem among blacks to be correspondingly low. Beginning in the 1930s, the black psychologists Kenneth and Mamie Clark built national careers featuring this particular theme of the psychological reactions of African-Americans to racial subordination. The white preference responses of children to color-graded dolls and the apparent adoption of Caucasian models by black adults In defining "good features," "good hair," and a "good life," together were seen as creating a psychological dilemma for African-Americans whom neither nature nor society would permit to be what they wished to be. In the 1950-1960 period, themes and theories of deprivation and deficiency undergirded arguments aimed at shaping public and legal policy, particularly in the field of education.

During the 1960s heyday of the Civil Rights movement, however, the thematic emphases of black psychologists began to shift. Black was "beautiful," psychological responses included, succeeding the prideful contributionism of the historians of the 1930s and rejecting the pathos of the pathogenic sociological themes of the 1940s and early 1950s, black academics began promoting what Maulana Karenga called the "adaptive vitality" model of black sociology and psychology. In his *Introduction to Black Studies* (1982), Karenga declares "the adaptive vitality school contends that adaptation by Blacks to socioeconomic pressures and limitations must not be seen as pathologies, but as strength." This was the Andrew Billingsley's highly influential *Black Families in White America* (1968) and Charles W. Thomas in *Boys No More: Black Psychologists Views of Community* (1971). Adelbert Jenkins in *The Psychology of Afro-Americans: A Humanistic Approach* (1992) suggested a revised model of normality based on proven psychological findings and employing a humanistic perspective to promote positive self-concept and esteem among African-Americans. In 1991, William E. Cross in *Shades of Black: Diversity in African American Identity* produced a masterly critique of previous psychological studies and a stimulating African-American-oriented model, an ambitious attempt to create a model of the structures and dynamics determining the nature of black identity in contemporary life.

The overview of the issue addressed by black psychologists suggests that the following tasks are of major interest and importance:

— defining and developing a concept of "normality" which is scientifically sound and socially positive;

— creating "treatment" protocols for the African-American community strong enough to cover the human diversity among its members; and

— generating implementation strategies powerful enough to neutralize the normal human reactions to the impact of community subordination and socialization in a theoretically egalitarian social order.

Whatever the ideological future of Afrocentrism as currently debated, this overview of the themes and theories permeating the work of African-American historians, sociologists, and psychologists indicates that perspectives arise from the nature of the work done as much as they do from the work anticipated. Regardless of their individual ideological "isms," black academics are deeply interested in having their labors make a positive impact in the battle to liberate the African-American community. By ties of affection and circumstance, black intellectuals are bound to the primary community through which they, as human beings, entered this world. Its struggle is inescapably their own.

Summary

Originating out of the concerns of black students newly present on the campuses is of predominantly white institutions in the late 1960s, Afro-American Studies a new field of instruction and research in higher education in America. In the context of that socially expansive and innovative time proponents of Afro-American Black Studies were keenly disappointed to discover that the black experience was of minor concern to adherents of the traditional academic disciplines. More than 60 colleges and universities responded to African-American Studies by establishing full-fledged departments. Several times this number set up Black Studies programs and institutes. Of the various institutional arrangements for this new field, the department became the most durable type of unit, closely followed by the program configuration.

Reluctantly accepted by the academic establishment, professional Afro-Americanists confronted problems of (a) recruiting faculty, (b) field and disciplinary definition, (c) curriculum construction, and (d) legitimating a counter-perspective on the nature of the black experience in the world. Since traditional academics had failed formally to explore the black experience, the small pool of qualified black academics was the source of Afro-American Studies faculty. Defining the field and creating curricula within it have been especially difficult, for many Afro-American Studies departments have tried to squeeze into small units a reverse mirror image of the entire range of received historical and social reality. These heroic efforts have been made with insufficient resources and time.

Thus far, curricula redefinition in this field have evolved around the social sciences and humanities. Most Afro-American Studies units offer the bachelor of arts degree, although a half dozen offer the master of arts and one the doctorate. When leading professional Afro-Americanists attempted to share their curricula perspectives with inner city public schools, the theoretical and practical problems of legitimizing Afro-American Studies beyond the college campus attracted much attention among hitherto indifferent segments of both black and white communities. The popular media saw Afrocentrism as "news," one of the rare times an intellectual concept from the black academic community has gone "national."

African-American scholars have been concerned about the epistemological, political, and pedagogical consequences of their endeavors. A review of the most influential works by African-American scholars in history, sociology, and psychology suggests that social and situational circumstances stimulate the evolution of a variety of approaches to the academic treatment of the experience of communities containing persons of African descent. This evolution spans at least a century and is characterized by the contributions of a small group of especially influential individuals such as W.E.B. DuBois, Carter G. Woodson, E. Franklin Frazier, and Kenneth and Mamie Clark, to name but a few. These scholars were lonely warriors during days of official racial segregation and uncontested white control of public school curricula throughout the nation. In the last two or three decades, a second and larger group of African-American intellectual leaders appeared, examples being John Blassingame in history, Andrew Billingsley in sociology, and William Cross in psychology. The black intellectual community not only has grown larger in numbers and stronger in resources, but also has produced several notable academic generalists, among them Molefe Asante, Maulana Karenga, and Cornel West.

Afrocentricism, then, is an evolving movement, carrying with it the momentum of previous African-American scholarship and concern with epistemological perspectives through which people perceive and evaluate human experience. Afrocentrism as ideology arrives on the American educational scene at the precise moment the traditional mono-cultural perspective is being challenged by a nascent and tepid multi-culturalism. Afrocentrism appears to be far more disturbing because it challenges the very foundations of the traditional perceptual order. In contrast, multi-culturalism is at the contributionist appreciation stage of historical and social analysis, a stage black scholars passed through a quarter-century earlier.

Afrocentrism has also been nurtured by the persistent, and perhaps atavistic racism within the larger society, and by, community separatism in daily life. In reaction to this historically enforced racial separatism, Afrocentrists represent a continuation of the academic and social struggle of African-Americans to locate an authentic perspective which reflects the deeper truths about themselves and the society they are seeking to liberate from racial paranoia and color irrationality. Thus, from its inception to the present, as an institution, and as instruction and ideology, the Afro-American Studies movement has stimulated discussion and debate about the nature and direction of American education.

The debate among African-American scholars has not been limited to epistemology and scientific methodology, however. It has also extended itself to action oriented approaches or ideologies as strategies to guarantee the survival of the black community in a predominantly racist white society. As succinctly summarized by Tilden LeMelle, the ideologies have ranged from the assimilationist accommodationist, reconciliationist, liberal idealist, and Marxist-Leninist) to the self-determinalist (psychological and separatist nationalist), and have generated a healthy debate which demonstrates the heterogeneity and creativity of the black leadership and African-American scholarship.

References

Russell L. Adams. "Intellectual Questions and Imperatives in the Development of Afro-American Studies." *Journal of Negro Education*, vol. 53, 3 (Summer 1984): 201-225.

"Africa Dreams." *Newsweek*, September 23, 1991, pp. 42-50.

Abdul Alkalimat et al. *Introduction to Afro-American Studies: A People's College Primer*. Chicago, IL: Peoples College Press, 1986.

Molefe Asante. *Kemet, Afrocentricity, and Knowledge*. Trenton, NJ: Africa World Press, 1990.

John Blassingame. New Perspectives on Black Studies. Urbana, IL: University of Illinois Press, 1971.

John Bracey, August Meier, and Elliott Rudwick (eds.). *The Black Sociologists: The First Half Century*. Belmont, CA: The Wadsworth Publishing Co., 1971.

John Bracey, August Meier, and Elliott Rudwick (eds.). *The Rise of the Ghetto*. Belmont, CA: The Wadsworth Publishing Co., 1971.

William E. Cross, Jr. *Shades of Black: Diversity in African-American Identity*. Philadelphia, PA: Temple University Press, 1991.

Alexander Crummell. "Civilization: The Primal Need of the Race," in Herbert Aptheker. *A Documentary History of the Negro People in the United States*. New York: The Citadel Press, 1951.

Philip T.K. Daniel et al. *The National Council for Black Studies—Northern Illinois Black Studies, Four-Year College and University Survey*. DeKalb, IL: Afro-American Studies Program, 1983.

Department of Afro-American Studies Curriculum Committee. The Department of Afro-American Studies. Washington, DC, 1974.

St. Clair Drake and Horace R. Clayton. *Black Metropolis*. New York: Harcourt, Brace, 1945.

W.E.B. DuBois. *Black Reconstruction in America: 1860-1880*. New York: The World Publishing Company, 1964.

———. *The Philadelphia Negro*. Philadelphia: The University of Pennsylvania Press, 1899.

Walter Fisher. *Ideas for Black Studies: The Morgan State College Program*. Baltimore, MD: The Morgan State College Press, 1971.

John Hope Franklin. "On the Evolution of Scholarship in Afro-American History," in Darlene Clark Hine (ed.). *The State of Afro-American History*. Baton Rouge, LA: Louisiana State University Press, 1986.

E. Franklin Frazier. *The Negro in the United States*. New York: The Macmillan Co., 1949.

Maulana Karenga. *Introduction to Black Studies*. Los Angeles: Kawaida Publications.

Joyce A. Ladner (ed.). *The Death of White Sociology*. New York: Vintage Books, 1973.

Tilden LeMelle. "The Status of Black Studies in the Second Decade: The Ideological Imperative," in James E. Turner (ed.). *The Next Decade: Theoretical and Research Issues in Africana Studies*. Ithaca, NY: Cornell University Africana Studies Center, 1984.

Gunnar Myrdal. *An American Dilemma: The Negro Problem and Modern Democracy*. 2 vols. New York: Harper & Row, 1944.

National Council for Black Studies, Inc. *Black Studies Core Curriculum*. Bloomington, IN: 1971.

Phil Petrie, "Afrocentrism in a Multi-cultural Democracy." *American Visions: the Magazine of Afro-American Culture*, vol. 6, 4 (August 1991): 20-26.

David W. Southern. *Gunnar Myrdal and Black-White Relations: The Use and Abuse of An American Dilemma: 1944-1969*. Baton Rouge, LA: Louisiana State University Press, 1986.

Daniel C. Thompson. *Sociology of the Black Experience*. Westport, CT: Greenwood Press, 1974.

Earl E. Thorpe. *The Central Theme of Black History*. Westport, CT: Greenwood Press, 1969.

Louis N. Williams. *Black Psychology: Compelling Issues and Views*. Washington, DC: University Press of America, 1978.

William J. Wilson. *The Truly Disadvantaged*. Chicago: University of Chicago Press, 1990.

Endnotes

1. "Afro-American" is used interchangeably with "African-American or African American."

2. W.E.B. DuBois, *Black Reconstruction in America: 1860-1880* (New York: The World Publishing Company, 1964), pp. 718-719.

3. For a startlingly vivid example of how ideological revision projects can e managed, see David W. Southern, *Gunnar Myrdal and Black-White Relations: The Use and Abuse of An American Dilemma: 1944-1969* (Baton Rouge, LA: Louisiana State University Press, 1986), *passim*.

II

Section II

African American Women's Studies

Key Concepts and Major Terms

- Gender
- Womanist
- Feminist
- Sexual Oppression
- Women of Color
- Misogynist
- White Feminist
- Black Nationalist
- Afrocentric Feminist
  Epistemology

- Black Feminism
- Women Studies
- Black Feminist Thought
- Black Women's Studies
- Black Lesbianism
- Racism
- Sexual Orientation
- Third World Women
- Eurocentric Masculinist
  Epistemology

- Feminist Studies
- Black Feminist Politics
- Combahee River
  Collective Statement
- Sexism
- Africana Women
- Marxist-Leninist

Introduction

The intersecting socio-political variables of race, gender, class and sexual orientation provide the foundation for the development of African American Women's Studies. Womanist and feminist movements challenged the existing focus and paradigms of African American Studies, suggesting that the role of women in the history and struggle of African people had been underemphasized and insufficiently recognized within the discipline. African American women scholars such as bell hooks, Vivian Gordon, Darlene Clark Hine, Rosalyn Terborg-Penn, Beverly Guy-Sheftall, Paula Giddings, Patricia Hill-Collins, Angela Davis, Barbara Christian, Joyce Ladner, Delores P. Aldridge, Carlene Young, Barbara Smith, Gloria Hull, Patricia Bell-Scott, Miramba Ani, Gloria I. Joseph, Bertha Maxwell, Toni Morrison and Michele Wallace helped create an area of study centrally focusing on African American women. Yet just as questions were raised about what constitutes African American Studies, similar questions have been asked about the proper focus of African Women's Studies. Practitioners have discussed the content and structure of African American Women's Studies and its philosophical, theoretical and political paradigms, considering whether issues pertinent to African American Studies differ in black women's studies and what its role and function is in particular.

African American Women's Studies is the focus of this section, and it discusses the dual emphases of African American and Women's Studies to determine the concepts and purposes which underlie and link both areas. The selections reflect the politics, problems and progress existing in this field. The first selection in this section, by Charles Henry and Frances Foster, poses the question of the relation between African American Studies and African American Women's Studies. Beverly Guy-Sheftall's article explores intersections between race, sex and class in the scholarship produced by women and its connection to African American Studies. The seminal, often-cited article by Gloria Hull and Barbara Smith asserts the political significance of African American Women's Studies. Delores P. Aldridge argues for the continued involvement of Africana women's perspectives in Africana Studies. And the last selection in this section, by Barbara Christian, poses the important question of the place of African American Women's Studies in the academy.

Charles P. Henry and Frances Smith Foster, in "Black Women's Studies: Threat or Challenge?," argue that "Black women's studies has also suffered because few of the courses on black women have been innovative.... Most courses are constructed according to the presuppositions that black women's studies must be either a threat or challenge and that black women's studies is essentially synonymous with black feminism.... Black women's studies can only grow in cooperation with women's studies and Black Studies and the sharing of different perspectives."

In "The Politics of Black Women's Studies," Gloria T. Hull and Barbara Smith suggest: "The politics of Black women's studies are totally connected to the politics of black women's lives in this country.... The very fact that black women's studies describes something that is really happening, a burgeoning field of study, indicates that there are political changes afoot.... To examine the politics of black women's studies means to consider not only what it is, but why it is and what it can be."

According to Beverly Guy-Sheftall, in "Women's Studies and Black Studies": "Though theoretical problems are inherent in Black Women's Studies, scholars in this field are in a unique position because of their ability to explore the intersection of race, sex, and class as experienced by black women in ways that are impossible for other segments of the population. They are also in a position...to challenge accepted scholarship."

In her seminal article "The Social Construction of Black Feminist Thought," Patricia Hill-Collins posits that black feminist thought specializes in formulating and rearticulating the distinctive, self-defined standpoint of African American women. One approach to learning more about a black woman's standpoint, according to Hill-Collins, is to construct standard scholarly sources for the ideas of specialists on black women's experiences. But investigating a black woman's standpoint and black feminist thought is much more difficult and requires more ingenuity than that required for examining the standpoints and thought of white males since one can not use the same techniques to study the knowledge of the dominated as those used to study the knowledge of the powerful.

Perhaps most important in regard to the relationship between African American Studies and Women's Studies, Delores P. Aldridge states: "Integrating Africana women into Africana Studies should not need to be a topic for dialogue. This is particularly true if those in the field share a fundamental womanist perspective... (there should be) continued involvement of Africana women with womanist perspectives in leadership positions in the professional bodies for Africana Studies so that programs and policies reflect their perspectives."

In her essay, "But Who Do You Really Belong To—Black Studies or Women's Studies," Barbara Christian posits that "...the study of women of color is itself a critique of Afro-American Studies and Women's Studies, yet these groups are hardly powerful institutions in the university and their validity is still in question...it depends on the number and quality of young women scholars of color who will be inclined to pursue this perspective and who will be hired in Afro-American Studies and Women's Studies Programs."

The essays in Section II were selected because they deal with the defining (interrelated) issues which make Black Women's Studies distinct and separate from Women's Studies along with the various points of contention it raises in regard to African American Studies. The authors address topics that have often been neglected in both Women's and African American Studies such as racism within Women's Studies, the role of Gay and Lesbian scholars and activists in the black community, and rampant sexism within African American Studies, etc.

12.

Black Women's Studies: Threat or Challenge?

Charles P. Henry and Frances Smith Foster

In August 1970, The New American Library published *The Black Woman: An Anthology*, "a collection," they asserted, "that for the first time truly lets her bare her soul and speak her mind." The editor, Toni Cade, had recognized that the struggle for Black liberation of the 60s necessitated that Black women first "find out what liberation for ourselves means, what work it entails, what benefits it will yield." When Cade turned to "various fields of studies to extract material, data necessary to define that term in respect to ourselves," however, she discovered that there was little relevant material—and that the experts, whether Black or white, tended to be male. Their work on females was scanty and inaccurate. The emerging bibliography by feminists was European centered; that which directly applied to the experiences and concerns of Black women wouldn't fill a page." Cade was heartened, however, by information that research was beginning and that soon "there will be appearing books dealing exclusively with the relationships between Black men and women, with the revolutionary Black women of the current period, with the Black abolitionists, with the whole question of Black schools." *The Black Woman*, then, was a beginning. And since then, it is true that information on, for, and by Black women has proliferated. The New American Library had recognized, as did other media vendors, that the current combination of the Black liberation movement and the emerging women's liberation movement would surely spawn a market for materials on Black women.

Also during this period popular magazines such as *Ebony* and scholarly journals such as *The Black Scholar* came forth with special issues on Black women; so, too, television shows and other magazines began to cater to "today's Black woman." The universities, high schools, and adult schools got into the act—tentatively—by offering a course or two, on Black male/female relationships, the Black family, and, in a few noted instances, on "the Black Woman." Conferences and workshops began to schedule sessions an Black women's concerns. Black professional organizations developed women's caucuses and predominantly white organizations tolerated Black — or more often, third world—women's caucuses. The federal government got a piece of the action, funding small projects here and there designed to stimulate research in Black Women as Contributors to America, or to assemble directories of Black women in specific professions. In short, there has been over the last ten years a flurry of activity which would seem to indicate the existence of a thriving area of scholarship and interest in Black women—a discipline, perhaps, called Black women's studies.

It would certainly seem logical. Black women, after all, are past of the two movements which have achieved high visibility and a notable impact upon American rhetoric, if not contemporary American institutions. These movements are the civil rights movement, which inspired and gave strength to the existence of Black studies, and the feminist movement, many of whose leaders were products of the civil rights movement and most of whose tactics and articulated philosophies for the creation of women's studies programs are adapted from the civil rights and Black studies movements. One would think that an overlapping of interests would form and nurture something that would be, if not an essential link, at least a bridge between the two, allowing a coalition of strength against common enemies and for their common stated goals of inclusive education, something which could be called Black women's studies.

However, this is not true. *Who's Who and Where in Women's Studies* states that between 1970 and 1973, courses which concerned minority women or which considered race and class in addition to gender comprised only 4 percent of women's studies courses. Three years later, within the 15 "mature" women's studies programs, only 11 percent of the courses were devoted to considerations of race and class, or to minority women's experiences. Within that number, there were some courses that specifically addressed the experiences of Black women; some of these were, in fact, jointly sponsored by Black studies and women's studies programs. Proportionately, however, they still "wouldn't fill a page." Even more interesting are the facts that (1) Black Studies programs have been particularly reluctant to distinguish the Black women's experiences from those of Black males; (2) The few textbooks on Black Studies confine their discussion of Black women to traditional African society or combine it with an examination of the Black family (Peoples College 1978); (3) None of the major examinations of the development of Black Studies discusses such differences nor offers comparative data on the status of females vis à vis males in the discipline (Ford 1973; Robinson 1969); (4) A 1978 report on Black Studies programs in western land-grant colleges indicates that none offered an independent course on Black women; and (5) It is only recently that course syllabi in Black Studies have begun to include Black female authors.

Given the great publicity concerning Ntozake Shange's phenomenal choreopoem, *For Colored Girls Who Have Considered Suicide*, and Michelle Wallace's *Black Macho and the Myth of the Superwoman*, one would perhaps think that critical attention had at last begun to fulfill the promise of the early 70s; however, one sees that the discussion of these works focuses upon male/female relationships, that in spite of all the flurry, the debate continues around the traditional question of Black female sexuality: "Is she an Eve or a Madonna?"; "Is she a ball-buster or a battered woman?"

Black women's studies has also suffered because few of the courses on Black women have been innovative. Some have been casually created by selecting any available work that is by, about, or for Black women. Most courses are constructed according to the presuppositions that Black women's studies must be either a threat or a challenge and that Black women's studies is essentially synonymous with Black feminism. Such perceptions assume that "Black feminism," as the essence of Black women's studies, must be decoded, that women's studies and feminism must in some way modify one another, and that until the nature of the relationship is clear, Black women's studies must be held in abeyance. Such an interpretation has generated a conflict that, when considered with the debilitating myths which still surround Black studies and women's studies themselves, makes Black women's studies a radical upstart, an invader whose sudden appearance can only be viewed with suspicion.

Much of the criticism of Black women's studies has been similar to that confronting Black feminism historically: those operating from a class orientation have tended to view it as a secondary issue having economic roots, while Black nationalists and white feminists have tended to denounce it as an obstacle to unity. This paper will briefly examine each of these orientations.

The White Feminist Position

The absence of substantial numbers of Black women in the women's liberation movement has led many to conclude that Black women are either nor aware of sexual oppression or are unwilling to act to eliminate it. However, such a conclusion ignores a long history of activism on the part of Black women. It also denies Black women the role models provided by leaders like Harriet Tubman, Sojourner Truth, Frances Harper, Josephine St. Pierre Ruffin, Mary Church Terrell, Ida B. Wells-Barnett, and Mary McCloud Bethune.

In addition, such a conclusion denies the activism of the Afro-American woman to confront racial discrimination even within the women's rights movement. In delineating the discrimination against Black women in the women's movement from 1830 to 1920, Rosalyn Terborg-Penn states that

> although white feminists Susan B. Anthony, Lucy Stone, and some others encouraged Black women to join the struggle against sexism during the nineteenth century, antebellum reformers who were involved with women's abolitionist groups as well as women's rights organizations actively discriminated against Blacks. The late-nineteenth century woman's club movement and the woman suffrage movement of the early twentieth century were also characterized by discriminatory policies and contained individuals who discriminated against Black women (Terborg-Penn, p. 17).

Sarah Douglass, in writing to fellow Quaker and feminist Sarah Grimke in 1837, reports that even the liberal Quakers reserved a special bench for Black members of the congregation. Degree of skin color was also used in determining the acceptability of some Blacks in white female groups (Terborg-Penn, p. 19).

Among leaders of the national suffrage movement, fear of offending white southern women was the excuse used to segregate Black women. Of course this same racial rationale was being used by white males in the American labor movement and in the Republican Party against Black males. Despite white resistance, Black female and male leaders continued to support woman's suffrage in the hope that the franchise would give Blacks increased influence. However, the record of their struggle is not to be found in the history of the white organizations. By way of contrast, the roots of the modern feminist movement lie in the organization of a Black-led movement.

Sara Evans has traced the development of the modern women's liberation movement to the civil rights movement. Specifically, the Mississippi Summer Project of 1964 coordinated by the Student Non-Violent Coordinating Committee (SNCC) brought several hundred white female college students to the South. When these students returned to their northern homes or campuses, it was with a heightened consciousness of their own deprivations. This consciousness stemmed from the limited role that was assigned to women in the "new student left" whose white male leadership, in part, had roots in the civil rights movement.

The white females working in the civil rights movement found role models in Black female activists such as Ella Baker, Diane Nash, Ruby Doris Smith Robinson, Fannie Lou Hammer and in white females like Jane Stembridge. Yet as SNCC moved towards "Black Power," they also witnessed the initial split between white and Black female activists. As Evans states, "the start of violence in a community was often tied to white women." Not long after the summer of 1964, Black women in SNCC began to challenge their subordinate role in the organization. Ruby Doris Smith Robinson led a protest in the SNCC offices concerning the relegation of women to clerical and secretarial duties. A paper written by Robinson (an early leader of the Black nationalist faction) on the position of women in SNCC is often cited as the earliest example of "women's consciousness" within the new left. In the fall of 1965, two white female SNCC workers, Mary King and Casey Hayden, drafted a document in which they contrasted the movement's egalitarian ideas with the replication of sex roles within it. It was addressed chiefly to Black women and called for some reconciliation or at least dialogue between Black and white women in the movement (Evans 1979, pp. 17-18).

The unwillingness of many Black women to respond to the challenge of modern white feminists like King and Hayden is a function of both internal an external factors. Few Afro-American women (as well as Americans in general) are aware of the historic role of Black female activists. Until very recently, the best-known Black supporters of feminist issues were Black men such as Frederick Douglass. Thus, many Black women face artificial identity problems that question whether they could be both feminists and Blacks.

Contemporary Black women leaders Toni Morrison and Angela Davis raised several external reasons for the rejection of feminism by Black women. Among them were that feminism was a concern of the upper-middle class only, that Black women had already achieved a degree of self-sufficiency, that Black women feared Black male-white female relationships, that Black women were too involved in a daily struggle for survival that left no time for feminist politics, and that the reference group for Black women centered on Black men rather than white men.

The result in terms of Black women's studies was predictable. Women's studies courses, usually taught in major universities, focused almost exclusively upon the lives of white women, according to Barbara Smith. Black female literary figures ranging from Phyllis Wheatley through Zora Neale Hurston and Margaret Walker to today's Black female authors were ignored.

The Black Nationalist Position

The rise of Black Studies has been clearly traced to the Black power movement and the increasingly militant attitude of the growing numbers of Black students entering college in the late sixties and early seventies. In a sense, Black studies reflected the heightened nationalist consciousness of the Black community during this period. Such organizations as the Republic of New Africa, the Nation of Islam, the Congress of African People, and Ron Karenga's US received a great deal of attention both inside and outside the Black community. However, this nationalist sentiment offered few if any incentives for Black female advancement. In fact, the Black woman's position seemed more rigidly defined than ever. The nationalist position as reflected on a much circulated poster of the time stated:

Black Gold

I am the Black woman, mother of civilization
queen of the universe, through me the Black
man produces his nation
If he does not protect his woman he will not
produce a good nation

It is my duty to teach and train the young,
who are the future of the nation.
I teach my children the language, history,
and culture when they are very young.
I teach them to love and respect their father,
who works hard so that they may have
adequate food, clothing, and shelter.
I care and make our home comfortable
for my husband.
I reflect his love to the children as the
moon reflects the light from the sun
to the earth.
I sit and talk with my husband to
work out the daily problems and necessities
of running a stable and peaceful household.
The best that I can give my nation is
strong, healthy, intelligent children who
will grow to be the leaders of tomorrow.
I'm always aware that the true worth of a
nation is reflected through the respect and
protection of the women, so I carry myself
in a civilized manner at all times, and teach my
children to do the same.
I am the Black Woman.

(Firestone 1970, p. 119)

While there is a commendable emphasis on protecting Black women from whites, the Black woman is forced to contribute to a better world through her husband and her children. Black leaders like Stokely Carmichael, Imarnu Baraka, and Malcolm X saw the role of the Black woman as a supportive one. In a sense, she is raised to the pedestal of the white woman—the happy homemaker who produces and educates the children. The assumption of dominance on the part of the Black mate was viewed as a favor to the Black woman who was now *theoretically* relieved of the responsibility as a breadwinner. Moreover, it was assumed that she should assist her man in attaining his newly found manhood, even at the expense of her own rights. Ironically, these Black nationalists ignore a long tradition of relative equality of the sexes among many African tribes, and accept the Western notion of the male-dominated society.

Black historians John G. Jackson, Chancellor Williams, and Cheikh Diop have clearly demonstrated the relative egalitarianism of traditional African societies. Communalism and the extended family are the distinguishing characteristics of such societies. It was not until the arrival of the Europeans carrying the twin ideologies of capitalism and Christianity that African women were relegated to a secondary status in most African tribal groups.

In promoting sexism, modern Black nationalists also ignored two towering figures in Black history in this country. It was Martin Delany, the father of Black nationalism, who proposed that females be invited to participate in the deliberations of the National Convention of Colored Freemen held in Cleveland in 1848. Frederick Douglass offered an acceptable compromise moving that the word "person" be understood to include "women" as delegates. The militant Delany, however, was able to confront the issue directly at the 1854 National Emigration Convention in Cleveland. For the first time at a national convention, 29 fully accredited Black female delegates, including Delany's wife, Catherine, were able to participate equally with Black men (Terborg-Penn, p. 34).

Amy Jacques Garvey, the wife of Marcus Garvey, was among the first to recognize the racism in the suffrage movement among white women. Through her writing in the *Negro World*, the UNIA newspaper, she addressed the topics of social justice, "third world" liberation, feminist struggles, modernization, and the contribution of Black women to the Black movement. She saw the concept of the male-dominated polity as no longer valid and encouraged Afro-American women to follow the lead of women in Egypt, China, and India who were challenging role stereotypes (Matthews, pp. 4-6). In many ways, then, the UNIA was more progressive than its recent counterparts.

The Marxist-Leninist Position

Perhaps the bridge between the women's liberation movement and the Black nationalist movement could have been the Black Panther Party. On 15 August 1970, Huey Newton issued a call for "a working coalition with the gay liberation and women's liberation groups." At the plenary session of the Panther-sponsored Revolutionary Constitutional Convention in Philadelphia on 5 September 1970, both groups were represented in large numbers, and there were workshops dealing with self-determination for women and sexual self-determination in which the participants themselves were given responsibility for drafting specific items for a new United States constitution (Pinkney 1976, p. 121).

In his widely read *Soul on Ice*, the then Black Panther leader Eldridge Cleaver attempts to link class status to particular sexual images coinciding with its class-function in society. This leads Cleaver to define white males as Omnipotent Administrators, Black males as Supermasculine Menials, white females as Ultrafeminines, and Black females as Amazons. The weaknesses of each group lead it to seek its psychic Other. Since the Black male does not have sovereignty over himself or the Black female, he is seen as half a man, Cleaver can thus explain his attraction to white women as seeking something forbidden to him by the white male and also seeking the femininity not found in the Black woman.

Cleaver's attraction to white females parallels that of another "revolutionary" of the era, Franz Fanon. In *Black Skins, White Masks*, Fanon states:

> Out of the blackest part of my soul, across the zebra striping of my mind, surges this desire to be white. I wish to be acknowledged not as a black man but as white. Now—and this is a form of recognition that Hegel had not envisionaged—who but a white woman can do this for me? By loving me she proves that I am worthy of white love. I am loved like a white man. I am a white man. Her love takes me onto the noble road that leads to total realization. I marry white culture, white beauty, white whiteness. When my restless hands caress those white breasts, they grasp white civilization and dignity, and make them mine (Fanon, p. 63).

Yet neither Fanon nor Cleaver falls into the trap of viewing sexism as merely a psychological problem of the white male.

Black scholars as far back as Oliver Cox criticize the naivete of social scientists such as Gunnar Myrdal who rank intermarriage and sexual intercourse involving white women as the highest in motives for discrimination. According to Cox, "both the Negroes and their white exploiters know that economic opportunity comes first and that the white woman comes second; indeed, she is merely a significant instrument in limiting the first" (Cox 1948, pp. 526-527). Cox's viewpoint is echoed in several of the responses to Michelle Wallace's work *Black Macho and the Myth of the Superwoman* contained in *The Black Scholar* (see Karenga; Anderson and Mealy; Toure; Fabio). Staples himself notes each author's similar middle-class background and its effect on their frames of reference, claiming that "they were raised away from the realities of the Black experience and tend to see it all as pathological in the same way that whites view us" (Staples 1979, p. 32; one is reminded of Harold Cruse's attack on Lorraine Hansberry in *The Crisis of the Negro Intellectual*). Despite Staples' statement, a recent class study of Black and white families pointed out that although both white and Black marriages become more stable with a rise in class position, Black marriages' disruption rates are uniformly far higher than white marriages at all class levels. The conclusion is that "one must number among the burdens that Black marriages bear not only class factors but also the legacy of slavery" (Rossides 1978, p. 189).

Class and sexual behavior have often been linked in scholarly and popular studies. However, it was the Black lower classes that were particularly singled out for political attack during the Jim Crow era. That is, the imputed sexual immorality of the ex-slaves was used as a prime example of their "uncivilized" nature and "unpreparedness" for full citizenship rights (Gutman 1976, pp. 531-544). Furthermore, Herbert Gutman's massive study of the Black family suggests that class consciousness was often inhibited by kin and enlarged quasi-kin obligation (Gutman, pp. 223-224).

Karen Sacks has identified class as the key element distinguishing the social ideologies and strategies of Black and white working-class women from white middle-class women as far back as the 1830s. The pre-Civil War struggles were more social and thus collective among working-class women, and more equatable with self-help among middle-class women. For example, the economic demands of women factory workers involved collective action directed against both mill owners and legislators, while efforts to improve the education of middle-class women were more self-help ventures that did not identify enemies. After the Civil War, Black women's clubs were organized for the purpose of providing a particular social service and were often composed of workers, tenant farmers, or poor women; at the same time, white women's clubs were middle-class and professional (Sacks 1973).

Many would argue that Wallace's book is not typical of the Black feminist movement. The Combahee River Collective (a group of Black feminists) has stated that their experience and disillusionment within the various liberation movements including the Black Panthers, as well as their experience on the periphery of the white male left, led to their need to develop a politics that was antiracist, unlike those of white women, and antisexist, unlike those of Black and white men. Moreover, they advocate the destruction of the political-economic systems of capitalism and imperialism as well as patriarchy (Eisenstein 1978, p. 363 and 366).

Conclusion

In the actions of groups like the Combahee River Collective, one begins to see a synthesis of class, racial, and sexual politics. The motivation is obvious when it is realized that 38 percent of all Black families are headed by women, that 44 percent of all Black children live in female-headed families, and that the median income of Black female-headed families is $5,900, or $800 per year below the poverty line (*Black Enterprise*, Oct. 1979). The tragedy of this growing trend is not that the families are female-headed (Moynihan's position), but that the Black women heading these families are usually locked into positions that limit their life chances as well as those of their children. Both Toni Cade and Robert Staples have suggested that Blacks should return to the degree of non-competitive companionship and collective responsibility for children characteristic of traditional Africa and early Afro-America.

Black women's studies can only grow in cooperation with women studies and Black Studies and the sharing of differing perspectives. It is in facing these perceptions in an honest and open manner that one builds an egalitarian, democratic, morally consistent, and ideologically secure mechanism for Black liberation. Little is to be gained by asking who is oppressed most. But when the focus becomes the identification of varying forms of oppression used to oppress, Black women in contrast to Black men, one will have taken the first step toward the resolution of the problem.

In summary, the current debate over Black feminism in general and Black women's studies in particular suffers from at least three misconceptions: (1) that Black female activists have not played a significant role in American history since the Eighteenth Century; (2) that the initial developmental efforts of Black women's studies is the beginning of Black feminism; and (3) that the three ideological positions outlined above are socially or politically acceptable. To eradicate these misconceptions, both Black studies and women's studies must make more than a token effort to pursue Black women's studies. By making only token efforts, they are repeating the reactionary responses of those academics who opposed the development of women's studies and Black studies, citing questions of the economic value of such majors, demanding mature definitions of an emerging discipline, and generally obstructing the natural development of academic pursuits for entirely unacademic reasons.

References

1979. "The Black sexism debate," *The Black Scholar*: 14-67.

Cade, Toni (ed.), 1970. *The Black Woman*. New York: New American Library.

Child, Lydia Maria (ed.). 1861. *Linda Brent, Incident in the Life of a Slave Girl*. Boston:

Cleaver, Eldridge. 1968. *Soul on Ice*. New York: McGraw-Hill.

Cox, Oliver. 1948. *Caste, Class, and Race*. New York: Doubleday.

Cruse, Harold. 1967. *The Crisis of the Negro Intellectual*. New York: Morrow.

Diop, Cheikh Anta. 1974. *The African Origin of Civilization*. New York: Lawrence Hill & Co.

———. 1959. *The Cultural Unity of Black Africa*. Chicago: Third World Press.

Eisenstein, Zillah R. (ed.). 1978. "The Combahee River Collective," in *Capitalist Patriarchy and the Case for Socialist Feminism*. New York: Monthly Review Press.

Evans, Sara. 1979. *Personal Politics: The Roots of the Women's Liberation Movement in the Civil Rights Movement and the New Left*. New York: Knopf.

Fanon, Franz. 1967. *Black Skins, White Masks*. New York: Grove Press.

Ford, Nick Aaron. 1973. *Black Studies: Threat or Challenge?* Port Washington, N.Y.: Kennikat.

Freeman, Jo. 1975. *The Politics of Women's Liberation*. New York: McKay.

Gutman, Herbert G. 1976. *The Black Family in Slavery and Freedom, 1750-1925*. New York: Pantheon.

Harley, Sharon, and Rosalyn Terborg-Penn (eds.). 1978. *The Afro-American Woman*. Port Washington, N.Y.: Kennikat.

Hernton, Calvin. *Sex and Race in America*.

Jackson, John G. 1970. *Introduction to African Civilization*. New York: University Books.

Jordan, June. 1976. "Notes of a Barnard dropout," The Women's Center Reid Lectureship. New York: Barnard College.

Killens, John O. 1965. *Black Man's Burden*. New York: Trident.

Lerner, Gerda (ed.). 1972. *Black Women in White America*, New York: Vintage.

Matthews, Mark D. 1979. "'Our women and what they think,' Amy Jacques Garvey and the *Negro World*," *The Black Scholar*, 2-13.

Peoples College. 1978. *Introduction to Afro-American Studies*. Chicago: Peoples College Press.

Pickney, Arnold. 1979. *Red, Black, and Green*. New York: Cambridge University Press.

Rich, Adrienne. "Toward a woman-centered university."

Robinson, Armstead et al. (eds.). 1969. *Black Studies in the University*. New Haven: Yale University Press.

Rossell, Daniel L. *The American Class System*. Boston: Houghton Mifflin.

Russell, Michele. 1977. "An open letter to the academy," *Quest* 3(4): 70-79.

Shange, Ntosake. 1976. *For Colored Girls Who Have Considered Suicidal When the Rainbow is Enuf*. New York: Macmillan.

Simmons, Judy. 1979. "The Black woman's burden," *Black Enterprise*: 57-60.

Smith, Barbara. In press. *The Politics of Black Women's Studies*. Old Westbury, N.Y.: Feminist Press.

Smith, Beverly. "Some thoughts on racism," *Aegis: Magazine on Ending Violence against Women*.

Staples, Robert. 1972. *The Black Family*. Belmont, Ca.: Wadsworth.

Williams, Chancellor. 1974. *The Destruction of Black Civilization*. Chicago: Third World Press.

13.

Black Women's Studies:
The Interface of Women's
Studies and Black Studies

Beverly Guy-Sheftall

The most significant reforms in American higher education over the part two decades have come as a result of the Black Studies and Women's Studies[1] movements. Less well known but also important has been the development within the past several years of a new field of study—Black Women's Studies—which emerged in part because of the failure of Black and Women's Studies to address adequately the unique experiences of black women in America and throughout the world. In the first publication on this newly emerging discipline called *Black Women's Studies*, the editors, all three of whom were solid Black Studies scholars, attempt to define the new concept, trace its development, and provide a rationale for its existence:

> Women's studies courses... focused almost exclusively upon the lives of white women. Black studies, which was much too often male-dominated, also ignored Black women.... Because of white women's racism and Black men's sexism, there was no room in either area for a serious consideration of the lives of Black women. And even when they considered Black women, white women usually have not had the capacity to analyze racial politics and Black culture, and Black men have remained blind or resistant to the implications of sexual politics in Black women's lives.[2]

It is important to understand the context out of which this first interdisciplinary anthology in Black Women's Studies emerged and without which it could not have been produced. The most noteworthy developments in Black Women's Studies (though this designation was not in use) came from a relatively small but ever expanding group of women scholars who had been teaching and doing research on black women for at least twenty years. Many probably would have considered themselves Black Studies scholars. The pioneering work of educator Anna J. Cooper, who wrote *The Voice of the South By A Black Woman of the South* in 1892, has the distinction of being the first scholarly publication which now we would call Black Women's Studies. The publication of Toni Cade's *The Black Woman* in 1970, the first anthology of writings by and about black women, was significant because of the value it attached to bearing the distinct voices of black women themselves as they analyzed a number of contemporary issues. Two years later, Gerda Lerner's documentary history *Black Women in White America* (1972) underscored the importance of treating the experiences of Afro-American women as distinct from those of white women and black men.[3]

Several other pioneers in the newly emerging field of Black Women's Studies were historians Rosalyn Terborg-Penn and Sharon Harley, whose anthology (also a first)

The Afro-American Woman: Struggles and Images (1978) contains original essays which treat black women's experiences from a historical perspective. Terborg-Penn's bibliographic essay "Teaching the History of Black Women" contains an exhaustive listing of the secondary sources available in black women's history.[4] Similarly, the work of La Frances Rodgers-Rose and Filomina Chioma Steady, both of whom edited the first social science anthologies on black women, has been critical as far as sociological and anthropological approaches to the study of black women are concerned.[5]

Attempts to celebrate the existence of a distinct black female literary tradition in America, which can be traced further back in time, also fall under the rubric of Black Women's Studies because they acknowledge the politics of sex as well as the politics of race in the texts of black women writers. This celebration has taken place in two phases. The first phase is characterized by efforts to document that such a tradition exists. Frances Collier Durden's master's thesis, "Negro Women in Poetry from Phyllis Wheatley to Margaret Walker" (Atlanta University, 1947), is probably the first work that falls into this category. One of the earliest doctoral dissertations to analyze the black female literary tradition (which is different from examinations of images of black women in literature) is Beatrice Horn Royster's "The Ironic Vision of Four Black Women Novelists: A Study of the Novels of Jessie Fauset, Nella Larsen, Zora Neale Hurston and Ann Petry" (Emory University, 1975). Sharyn Skeeter's "Black Women Writers: Levels of Identity" (*Essence*, May 1973) is better known and reached a broader audience.

The second phase was ushered in by the publication of Mary Helen Washington's scholarly article "Black Women Image Makers" (*Black World*, August 1974). Moving beyond the descriptive approach of Skeeter, she argued that black women writers are a distinct group not only because of their long history but because unique themes recur in their works. The introduction to her pioneering anthology *Black-Eyed Susans: Classic Stories By and About Black Women* (1975) contains a more detailed analysis of these major themes. Alice Walker's essay "In Search of Our Mother's Gardens: The Creativity of Black Women in the South" (*Ms.*, May 1974) is perhaps the most eloquent and poignant account of the black woman artist ever written. It should be mentioned also that Walker designed the first course on black women writers, which she taught in 1977 at Wellesley College. Another publication in the second phase was *Sturdy Black Bridges: Visions of Black Women in Literature*, edited by Roseann Bell, Bettye Parker, and Beverly Guy-Sheftall (1979), which was credited with being the "first book-length critical work devoted to a 'minority' literature."[6]

The second phase is distinguished also by the emergence of black feminist literary criticism, notably Barbara Smith's and Deborah McDowell's groundbreaking work[7] and Barbara Christians's *Black Women Novelists: The Development of a Tradition 1892-1976 (1981)*, the first full-length study of the novels of black women. The publication of Gloria Wade-Gayle's *No Crystal Stair, Visions of Race and Sex in Black Women's Fiction* (New York, 1984) links her to a small but productive body of black feminist critics who "analyze the works of Black female writers from a feminist or political perspective."[8] Wade-Gayle's outstanding contribution to Black Women's Studies is that she provides a coherent conceptual framework for understanding what it has meant to be black and female as this experience is portrayed in the literature of black women of the mid-twentieth century. Her use of two central metaphors — the narrow space and the dark enclosure — to illuminate the double burden of race and sex, which is unique to black women, is stunningly perceptive. She describes three circles, asserting boldly:

In one circle white people, mainly males, experience influence and power. Far removed from it is the second circle, a narrow space in which black people, regardless of sex, experience uncertainty and powerlessness. And in this narrow space, often hidden but no less present and real, is a small Clark enclosure for black women only. It is in this enclosure that black woman experience the unique marks of black womanhood.[9]

The most valuable theoretical work in Black Women's Studies is Bell Hooks' controversial monograph, *Ain't I A Woman: Black Women and Feminism* (Boston, 1981), which is a long overdue examination of the complexity of black womanhood from the perspectives of black women themselves. The major strengths of the book are its delineation of the impact of sexism on the lives of black women; its analysis of the devaluation of black womanhood, both historically and contemporaneously; its discussion of the persistent racism of the women's movement, and its careful treatment of the involvement of black women in struggles to achieve equality for women even when they were discouraged from doing so by various segments of the white and black communities. Hooks' major contribution both to Black Studies and Women's Studies, however, is the theoretical framework she provides for analyzing what it has meant to be a black woman in America. In her chapter on "Sexism and the Black Female Experience," for example, she advances the thesis that slavery, a reflection of a patriarchal and racist social order, not only oppressed black men, but it defeminized slave women as well. Though scholars have emphasized the impact of slavery on black men, which focuses in large part on the theory of the emasculation of the slave male, Hooks and other black feminist scholars argue that it is imperative that historians and other researchers begin to pay more attention to the impact of sexual exploitation on slave women. Furthermore, it is important to point out that black women were not permitted to conform to the dominant culture's model of True Womanhood in the nineteenth century, just as the black male was unable to act out the majority culture's definition of "true manhood." Hooks' more recent book *From Margin to Center: Feminist Theory* (Boston, 1984) is a brilliant critique of contemporary feminist theory from the perspective of a black feminist and illustrates in a provocative manner how a Black Studies and Women's Studies perspective can provide profound insights about the nature of female experience.

Until the emergence of Black Women's Studies, most of the research on black women, excluding the work on black women writers, focused on their roles within the black family, especially the role of the black matriarch, a persistent theme in Black Studies scholarship.[10] A second area of research has focused on the public lives of notable black women such as Sojourner Truth, Harriet Tubman, Mary Church Terrell, and Mary McLeod Bethune. Part of the motivation for this "great black women" in history approach which characterizes much of the Black studies work on black women is simply to record the fact that black women were indeed present in history. In her analysis of research priorities in Black Women's Studies, Patricia Bell Scott has argued that there should be "more examinations of the black and female experience that are sensitive to the ways in which racism and sexism bear upon black women."[11] While such approaches to the study of black women are appropriate, a major problem that continues to confront the Black Women's Studies scholar, whose primary challenge remains exploring the intersection of race, gender, and class, is the difficulty of arriving at theoretical frameworks which will enable one to understand the complexity and diversity of the black female experience throughout the world.

According to Gerda Lerner, the major conceptual framework for studying American women has been provided by feminist scholars who, using the women as minority group model (the minority group model has been frequently used by Black Studies Scholars as well),[12] see women mainly in terms of their oppression and their struggles to overcome it. The shortcomings of this widely used minority group model to explain the history of American women have been analyzed by historian William Chafe, who has written both black and women's history, and others. His major points concerning the problematic nature of the analogy between race and sex are that the collective oppression of blacks, especially the physical abuse they have suffered, is substantially greater than that of white women; that there is physical distance between whites and blacks, whereas white women live in close contact with white men, which gives them greater access to the sources of power than is the case with black women; and that white women as a group are not as conscious of their oppression as are blacks.[13] The major weakness in this analogy between women and blacks, which Chafe also argues, is that it obscures the critical differences between black and white women, the major one being that black women suffer the double burden of racism and sexism, which makes them a unique group in American society. Moreover, black women have not had the so-called benefits of being female; they have not been sheltered, protected, or idealized by their men to the extent that was possible for white women. More importantly, because of the thoroughly entrenched and therefore persistent racial caste system which defined relations between blacks and whites (and relegates blacks to a subordinate position), the oppression of black women links them to black men rather than to white women. Finally the economic realities of the black community have forced black women to participate in the labor force to a greater extent than white women.

This brief summary of the weaknesses of the blacks/women parallel, which Chafe and others have discussed, points to a major problem that confronts the Black Women's Studies scholar which is not as thorny an issue for Black Studies and Women's Studies scholars. If women do form a distinct social group, as some feminist scholars argue, how does one formulate a conceptual framework that takes into consideration race and its interaction with gender (and class) in the case of black women's experience. A number of conceptual issues arise when one considers the race/gender nexus in this context. Is it possible, given the rigidity of the racial caste system, to perceive American women as a distinct social group? Since black women belong to a minority group, can one reject completely the minority group model when conceptualizing them as a group? What happens to the minority group model when one considers that, despite their subordination to whites, including women, black men are in a position to exercise power over black women because of the benefits that accrue to them because of their gender? Are the bonds of womanhood sufficiently strong to counteract the racial barriers which separate black and white women, or does race override gender in most interactions between these two groups?

Though theoretical problems are inherent in Black Women's Studies, scholars in this field are in a unique position because of their ability to explore the intersection of race, sex, and class as experienced by black women in ways that are impossible for other segments of the population. They are also in a position, as Black Studies scholars always have been, to challenge accepted scholarship. The study of black women, for example, renders invalid many of the generalizations that abound in the historiography of American women and are considered "universal." An example from the introduction to *Root of Bitterness,* a documentary social history of American women, will illustrate this point. Here Nancy Cott states that most of the late nineteenth-century women who initiated significant social welfare activities in cities did their work while unmarried or widowed, and one thinks immediately of Jane Addams and nods in agreement. Cott then speculates that these educated women were unable to reconcile the demands of the nuclear family with their newly defined roles so they evaded the problem by remaining single. When one recalls the history of black women during this same period (as one familiar with Black Studies would), one thinks of Lugenia Burns Hope, Ida Wells Barnett, and other middle-class, educated married black women who performed pioneering social welfare activities when racial uplift preoccupied the black elite. A critical question for the Black Women's Studies scholar (which might not be raised by the conventional Black Studies scholar) is why these black women were better able to juggle the roles of wife, mother, and career than their white female counterparts. For example, Ida Wells Barnett, determined not to give up her public life, carried her baby Charles (and nurse) along with her to women's conventions and political campaigns. He became such a fixture at the National Association of Colored Women's meetings that on one occasion he was elected Baby of the Association.[14] In order to explain why black women's lives diverged from white women's lives in this respect, it would be helpful to consider the special historical experiences of blacks, the particulars of the women's lives, and the sociology of sex roles.

Another generalization in women's history is that women can be compared to other minority groups because their physical characteristics make them easily identifiable and therefore they can be "singled out from the others in the society in which they live for differential and unequal treatment."[15] The case of Lucy Parsons renders invalid even this seemingly indisputable fact. Lucy is the relatively obscure "invisible" black woman who was married to Albert Parsons, one of the anarchists accused of the Haymarket bombing in 1886 and later executed.[16] Because Lucy refused to acknowledge her racial identity (she pretended she was of mixed ancestry, mainly Indian) after her marriage, she becomes "invisible" as a black person. That is, her name is mentioned on numerous occasions in histories of working women (because of her life-long struggle to alleviate their plight) and in histories of radical movements, but her race is ignored, as Lucy would have preferred. She therefore is missing from black history. She is missing from "general" histories because of her sex, for it is presumed that her only significance was that she was the wife of Albert Parsons. She is missing frequently even from women's histories because her anarchist activity was out of the mainstream of nineteenth-century women's activities such as suffrage, settlement, and club work, which have attracted more of the historians' attention.

Thus, despite Lucy Parsons' persistent and dedicated struggle to improve the lives of the working class (before and after her husband's untimely death), which can be documented because of her many publications and because her activities were followed in newspapers throughout the country, she mainly appeared in footnotes before the publication of Carolyn Ashbaugh's study, which rarely appears on Black Studies reading lists. That very little about her life prior to her marriage (except that she was an ex-slave born in Texas) was uncovered by her biographer is indicative of the "invisibility" of blacks during slavery, one of the most difficult periods of study for the Black Women's Studies scholar. Though Lucy is certainly easily identifiable as a woman, she avoids the "differential and unequal treatment" which she would have experienced as a black by passing and denying her minority group status. She, therefore, escapes the indignities which members of her own race suffer even though she is female because, in effect, she becomes white. As a member of the dominant race, despite her gender, she does not suffer the differential and unequal treatment that proponents of the race/sex analogy argue is universal among blacks and women.

There is exciting and challenging work yet to be done in Black Women's Studies. Much more is needed in the area of reconceptualizing Black Studies and Women's Studies so that the history, experiences, and cultures of black women will be more effectively taught and studied, thereby enabling both disciplines to reflect more accurately the diversity and complexity of experiences of blacks and women throughout the world. *But Some of Us Are Brave* provided a needed shot in the arm for the expansion of Black Women's Studies on college campuses throughout the nation. The birth of *Sage: A Scholarly Journal on Black Women* in 1984, which is edited by Patricia Bell Scott, Beverly Guy-Sheftall, Jacqueline Jones Royster, and Janet Sims Wood, and is housed at Spelman College's Women's Research and Resource Center, is a concrete manifestation of the "coming of age" of Black Women's Studies. Numerous periodicals and journals are continuing to produce special issues on black women. Approximately fifty dissertations on black women with a variety of subjects are listed with University Microfilms since 1970 compared with less than ten prior to that time. The ultimate challenge, however, is for Women's Studies and Black Studies scholars to recognize that black women's history is, in fact, women's history and black history. Such a perspective would render Black Women's Studies unnecessary or at the very least redundant over the long run.

Endnotes

1. For a comprehensive examination of women's studies generally see Marilyn J. Boxer, "For and About Women: The Theory and Practice of Women's Studies in the United States," *Signs*, 7 (Spring 1982): 660-95.

2. Gloria T. Hull, Patricia Bell Scott, and Barbara Smith, eds., *All the Women Are White, All the Blacks Are Men, But Some of Us Are Brave: Black Women's Studies* (Old Westbury, New York, 1982), pp. xx-xxi. Subsequent references will refer to this source as *But Some of Us Are Brave*.

3. Recent publications in black women's history are Dorothy Sterling, ed., *We Are Your Sisters: Black Women in the Nineteenth Century* (New York, 1984); Paula Giddings, *When and Where I Enter. The Impact of Black Women on Race and Sex in America* (New York, 1984); Jacqueline Jones, *Labor of Love, Labor of Sorrow: Black Women, Work, and the Family from Slavery to the Present* (New York, 1986); Bettina Aptheker, *Woman's Legacy: Essays on Race, Sex and Class in American History* (Amherst, 1982); Angela Y. Davis, *Women, Race, and Class* (New York, 1981), and Deborah Gray White, *Ar'n't I A Women? Female Slaves in the Plantation South* (New York, 1985).

4. *The History Teacher*, 13 (February 1980): 245-50.

5. See La Frances Rodgers Rose, *The Black Women* (Beverly Hills, California, 1980) and Filomina C. Steady, ed, *The Black Woman Cross-Culturally* (Cambridge, Mass., 1981).

6. Cheri Register, "Literary Criticism," *Signs*, 6 (Winter 1980): 270.

7. See Barbara Smith, "Toward A Black Feminist Criticism," *Conditions: Two* (October 1977): 27-28 and Deborah McDowell, "New Directions for Black Feminist Criticism," *Black American Literature Forum*, 14 (October 1980): 153.

8. McDowell, "New Directions," p. 156.

9. *No Crystal Stair*, pp. 3-4.

10. See W.E.B. DuBois' *The Negro American Family* (Atlanta, 1908); E. Franklin Frazier's *The Negro Family in the United States* (Chicago, 1939); and Daniel Moynihan's *The Negro Family: A Case for National Action* (Washington, D.C., 1965) for a discussion of the black matriarch theory. Critics of this theory include Robert Staples, "The Myth of the Black Matriarchy," *The Black Scholar*, 1 (January/February 1970): 8-16, and Andrew Billingsley, *Black Families in White America* (Englewood Cliffs, N.J., 1969).

11. *But Some Of Us Are Brave*, p. 89.

12. The women as minority group analogy was developed in 1961 by Helen Hacker. See her "Women as a Minority Group," *Social Forces*, 30 (October 1951): 60-9.

13. William Chafe, *Women and Equality* (New York, 1977): pp. 45-8.

14. Dorothy Sterling, *Black Foremothers* (Westbury, N.Y. 1979): pp. 97-8.

15. Louis Wirth, "The Problems of Minority Groups," in *Man in the World Crisis*, ed., Ralph Linton (New York, 1945), quoted by William Chafe, *Women and Equality*, p. 4.

16. See Carolyn Ashbaugh's *Lucy Parsons: American Revolutionary* (Chicago, 1976), for the most comprehensive account of Parsons life.

14.

The Politics of Black Women's Studies

Gloria T. Hull and Barbara Smith

Merely to use the term "Black women's studies" is an act charged with political significance. At the very least, the combining of these words to name a discipline means taking the stance that Black women exist—and exist positively—a stance that is in direct opposition to most of what passes for culture and thought on the North American continent. To use the term and to act on it in a white-male world is an act of political courage.

Like any politically disenfranchised group, Black women could not exist consciously until we began to name ourselves. The growth of Black women's studies is an essential aspect of that process of naming. The very fact that Black women's studies describes something that is really happening, a burgeoning field of study, indicates that there are political changes afoot which have made possible that growth. To examine the politics of Black women's studies means to consider not only what it is, but why it is and what it can be. Politics is used here in its widest sense to mean any situation/relationship of differential power between groups or individuals.

Four issues seem important for a consideration of the politics of Black women's studies: (1) the general political situation of Afro-American women and the bearing this has had upon the implementation of Black women's studies; (2) the relationship of Black women's studies to Black feminist politics and the Black feminist movement; (3) the necessity for Black women's studies to be feminist, radical, and analytical; and (4) the need for teachers of Black women's studies to be aware of our problematic political positions in the academy and of the potentially antagonistic conditions under which we must work.

The Political position of Black women in America has been, in a single word, embattled. The extremity of our oppression has been determined by our very biological identity. The horrors we have faced historically and continue to face as Black women in a white-male-dominated society have implications for every aspect of our lives, including what white men have termed "the life of the mind." That our oppression as Black women can take forms specifically aimed at discrediting our intellectual power is best illustrated through the words of a "classic" American writer.

In 1932 William Faulkner saw fit to include this sentence in a description of a painted sign in his novel *Light in August*. He wrote:

Bill now and then a negro nursemaid with her white charges would loiter there and spell them [the letters on the sign] aloud with *that vacuous idiocy of her idle and illiterate kind.*[1] [Italics ours.]

Faulkner's white-male assessment of Black female intellect and character, stated as a mere aside, has fundamental and painful implications for a consideration of the whole question of Black women's studies and the politics that shape its existence.

Not only does his remark typify the extremely negative wags in which Afro-American women have been portrayed in literature, scholarship, and the popular media, but it also points to the destructive white-male habit of categorizing all who are not like themselves as their intellectual and moral inferiors. The fact that the works in which such oppressive images appear are nevertheless considered American "masterpieces" indicates the cultural-political value system in which Afro-American women have been forced to operate and which, when possible, they have actively opposed.

The politics of Black women's studies are totally connected to the politics of Black women's lives in this country. The opportunities for Black women to carry out autonomously defined investigations of self in a society which through racial, sexual, and class oppression systematically denies our existence have been by definition limited.

As a major result of the historical realities which brought us enslaved to this continent, we have kept separated in every way possible from recognized intellectual work. Our legacy as chattel, as sexual slaves as well as forced laborers, would adequately explain why most Black women are, to this day, far away from the centers of academic power and why Black women's studies has just begun to surface in the latter part of the 1970s. What our multilayered oppression does not explain are the ways in which we have created and maintained our own intellectual traditions as Black women, without either the recognition or the support of white-male society.

The entry entitled "A Slave Woman Runs a Midnight School" in Gerda Lerner's *Black Women in White America: A Documentary History* embodies this creative, intellectual spirit, coupled with a practical ability to make something out of nothing.

> [In Natchez, Louisiana, there were] two schools taught by colored teachers. One of these was a slave woman who had taught a midnight school for a year. It was opened at eleven or twelve o'clock at night, and closed at two o'clock a.m.... Milla Granson, the teacher, learned to read and write from the children of her indulgent master in her old Kentucky home. Her number of scholars was twelve at a time and when she had taught these to read and write she dismissed them, and again took her apostolic number and brought them up to the extent of her ability, until she had graduated hundreds. A number of them wrote their own passes and started for Canada....
>
> At length her night-school project leaked out, and was for a time suspended; but it was not known that seven of the twelve years subsequent to leaving Kentucky had been spent in this work. Much excitement over her night-school was produced. The subject was discussed in their legislature, and a bill was passed, that it should not be held illegal for a slave to teach a slave.... She not only [re]opened her night-school, but a Sabbath-school.... Milla Granson used as good language as any of the white people.[2]

This document illuminates much about Black women educators and thinkers in America. Milla Granson learned to read and write through the exceptional indulgence of her white masters. She used her skills not to advance her own status, but to help her fellow slaves, and this under the most difficult circumstances. The act of a Black person teaching and sharing knowledge was viewed as naturally threatening to the power structure. The knowledge she conveyed had a politically and materially transforming function, that is, it empowered people to gain freedom.

Milla Granson and her pupils, like Black people throughout our history here, made the greatest sacrifices for the sake of learning. As opposed to "lowering" educational standards, we have had to create our own. In a totally antagonistic setting we have tried to keep our own visions clear and have passed on the most essential kind of knowledge, that which enabled us to survive. As Alice Walker writes of our artist-thinker foremothers:

> They dreamed dreams that no one knew — not even themselves, in any coherent fashion — and saw visions no one could understand.... They waited for a day when the unknown thing that was in them would be made known; but guessed, somehow in their darkness, that on the day of their revelation they would be long dead.[3]

The birth of Black women's studies is perhaps the day of revelation these women wished for. Again, this beginning is not unconnected to political events in the world outside university walls.

The inception of Black women's studies can be directly traced to three significant political movements of the twentieth century. These are the struggles for Black liberation and women's liberation, which themselves fostered the growth of Black and women's studies, and the more recent Black feminist movement, which is just beginning to show its strength. Black feminism has made a space for Black women's studies to exist and, through its commitment to all Black women, will provide the basis for its survival.

The history of all of these movements is unique, yet interconnected. The Black movements of the 1950s, '60s, and '70s brought about unprecedented social and political change, not only in the lives of Black people, but for all Americans. The early women's movement gained inspiration from the Black movement as well as an impetus to organize autonomously both as a result of the demands for all-Black organizations and in response to sexual hierarchies in Black- and white-male political groupings. Black women were a part of that early women's movement, as were working-class women of all races. However, for many reasons — including the increasing involvement of single, middle-class white women (who often had the most time to devote to political work), the divisive campaigns of the white-male media, and the movement's serious inability to deal with racism — the women's movement became largely and apparently white.

The effect that this had upon the nascent field of women's studies was predictably disastrous. Women's studies courses, usually taught in universities, which could be considered elite institutions just by virtue of the populations they served, focused almost exclusively upon the lives of white women. Black studies, that was much too often male-dominated, also ignored Black women. Here is what a Black woman wrote about her independent efforts to study Black women writers in the early 1970s:

> ...At this point I am doing a lot of reading on my own of Black women writers ever since I discovered Zora Neale Hurston. *I've had two Black Lit courses and in neither were any women writers discussed.* So now I'm doing a lot of independent research since the Schomburg Collection is so close.[4] [Italics ours.]

Because of white women's racism and Black men's sexism, there was no room in either area for a serious consideration of the lives of Black women. And even when they have considered Black women, white women usually have not had the capacity to analyze racial politics and Black culture, and Black men have remained blind or resistant to the implications of sexual politics in Black women's lives.

Only a Black and feminist analysis can sufficiently comprehend the materials of Black women's studies; and only a creative Black feminist perspective will enable the field to expand. A viable Black feminist movement will also lend its political strength to the development of Black women's studies courses, programs, and research, and to the funding they require. Black feminism's total commitment to the liberation of Black women and its recognition of Black women as valuable and complex human beings will provide the analysis and spirit for the most incisive work on Black women. Only a feminist, pro-woman perspective that acknowledges the reality of sexual oppression in the lives of Black women, as well as the oppression of race and class, will make Black women's studies the transformer of consciousness it needs to be.

Women's studies began as a radical response to feminists' realization that knowledge of ourselves has been deliberately kept from us by institutions of patriarchal "learning." Unfortunately, as women's studies has become both more institutionalized and at the same time more precarious within traditional academic structures, the radical life-changing vision of what women's studies can accomplish has constantly been diminished in exchange for acceptance, respectability, and the career advancement of individuals. This trend in women's studies is a trap that Black women's studies cannot afford to fall into. Because we are so oppressed as Black women, every aspect of our fight for freedom, including teaching and writing about ourselves, must in some way further our liberation. Because of the particular history of Black feminism in relation to Black women's studies, especially the fact that the two movements are still new and have evolved nearly simultaneously, much of the current teaching, research, and writing about Black women is not feminist, is not radical, and unfortunately is not always even analytical. Naming and describing our experience are important initial steps, but not alone sufficient to get us where we need to go. A descriptive approach to the lives of Black women, a "great Black women" in history or literature approach, or any traditional male-identified approach will not result in intellectually ground-breaking or politically transforming work. We cannot change our lives by teaching solely about "exceptions" to the ravages of white-male oppression. Only through exploring the experience of supposedly "ordinary" Black women whose "unexceptional" actions enabled us and the race to survive, will we be able to begin to develop an overview and an analytical framework for understanding the lives of Afro-American women.

Courses that focus on issues which concretely and materially affect Black women are ideally what Black women's studies/feminist studies should be about. Courses should examine such topics as the sexual violence we suffer in our own communities; the development of Black feminist economic analysis that will reveal for the first time Black women's relationship to American capitalism; the situation of Black women in prison and the connection between their incarceration and our own; the social history of Black women's domestic work; and the investigation of Black women's mental and physical health in a society whose "final solution" for us and our children is death.

It is important to consider also that although much research about these issues needs to be done, much insight about them can be arrived at through studying the literary and historical documents that already exist. Anyone familiar with Black literature and Black women writers who is not intimidated by what their reading reveals should be able to develop a course on rape, battering, and incest as viewed by Black female and male authors. Analysis of these patriarchal crimes could be obtained from the substantial body of women's movement literature on the subject of violence against women, some of which would need be criticized for its conscious and unconscious racism.

In addition, speakers from a local rape crisis center and a refuge for battered women could provide essential firsthand information. The class and instructor could work together to synthesize the materials and to develop a much-needed Black feminist analysis of violence against Black women. Developing such a course illustrates what politically based, analytic Black feminist studies can achieve. It would lead us to look at familiar materials in new and perhaps initially frightening ways, but ways that will reveal truths that will change the lives of living Black women, including our own. Black feminist issues — the real life issues of Black women — should be integral to our conceptions of subject matter, themes, and topics for research.

That politics has much to do with the practice of Black women's studies is perhaps most clearly illustrated by the lack of positive investigations of Black lesbianism in any area of current Black scholarship. The fact that a course in Black lesbian studies has, to our knowledge, yet to be taught has absolutely nothing to do with the "nonexistence" of Black lesbian experience and everything to do with fear and refusal to acknowledge that this experience does in fact exist.[5] Black woman-identified-women have existed in our communities throughout our history, both in Africa and in America. That the subject of Black lesbianism and male homosexuality is greeted with fearful silence or verbalized homophobia results, of course, from the politics of institutionalized heterosexuality under patriarchy, that is, the politics of male domination.

A letter written in 1957 by Black playwright and political activist Lorraine Hansberry to *The Ladder*, a pioneering lesbian periodical, makes clear this connection between homophobia and the sexual oppression of all women. She wrote:

> I think it is about time that equipped women began to take on some of the ethical questions which a male-dominated culture has produced and *dissect and analyze them quite to pieces in a serious fashion*. It is time that 'half the human race' had something to say about the nature of its existence. Otherwise — without revised basic thinking — the woman intellectual is likely to find herself trying to draw conclusions — *moral conclusions* — based on acceptance of a social moral superstructure which has never admitted to the equality of women and is therefore immoral itself. As per marriage, as per sexual practices, as per the rearing of children, etc. *In this kind of work there may be women to emerge who will be able to formulate a new and possible concept that homosexual persecution and condemnation has at its root not only social ignorance, but a philosophically active anti-feminist dogma*. But that is but a kernel of it speculative embryonic idea improperly introduced here.[6] [Italics ours.]

Hansberry's statement is an amazingly prescient anticipation of current accomplishments of lesbian-feminist political analysis. It is also amazing because it indicates Hansberry's feminist and lesbian commitments, which have previously been ignored and which will best be investigated through a Black feminist analysis of Black women's studies. Most amazing of all is that Hansberry was speaking, without knowing it, directly to us.

An accountable Black women's studies would value all Black women's experiences. Yet for a Black woman to teach a course on Black lesbians would probably, in most universities, spell career suicide, not to mention the personal and emotional repercussions she would inevitably face. Even to teach Black women's studies from a principled Black feminist perspective might endanger many Black women scholars' situations in their schools and departments. Given the difficulty and risks involved in teaching information and ideas which the white-male academy does not recognize or approve, it is important for Black women teaching in the white-male academy always to realize the inherently contradictory and antagonistic nature of the conditions under which we do our work. These working conditions exist in a structure not only elitist and racist, but deeply misogynist. Often our position as Black women is dishearteningly tenuous within university walls: we are literally the last hired and the first fired. Despite popular myths about the advantages of being "double-tokens," our salaries, promotions, tenure, and general level of acceptance in the white-male "community of scholars" are all quite grim. The current backlash against affirmative action is also disastrous for all Black women workers, including college teachers.

As Black women we belong to two groups that have been defined as congenitally inferior in intellect, that is, Black people and women. The paradox of Black women's position is well illustrated by the fact that white-male academics, like Schockley and Jensen — in the very same academy — are trying to prove "scientifically" our racial and sexual inferiority. Their overt or tacit question is, "How could a being who combines two mentally deficient biological identities do anything with her intellect, her nonexistent powers of mind?" Or, to put it more bluntly, "How can someone who looks like my maid (or my fantasy of my maid) teach me anything?" As Lorraine Bethel succinctly states this dilemma:

> The codification of Blackness and femaleness by whites and males is seen in the terms "thinking like a woman" and "acting like a nigger" which are based on the premise that there are typically Black and female ways of acting and thinking. Therefore, the most pejorative concept in the white/male world view would be that of thinking and acting like a "nigger woman."[7]

Our credibility as autonomous beings and thinkers in the white-male-run intellectual establishment is constantly in question and rises and falls in direct proportion to the degree to which we continue to act and think like our Black female slaves, rejecting the modes of bankrupt white-male Western thought. Intellectual "passing" is a dangerously limiting solution for Black women, a non-solution that makes us invisible women. It will also not give us the emotional and psychological clarity we need to do the feminist research in Black women's studies that will transform our own and our sisters' lives.

Black women scholars must maintain a constantly militant and critical stance toward the places where we must do our work. We must also begin to devise ways to break down our terrible isolation in the white-male academy and to form the kinds of support networks Black women have always formed to help each other survive. We need to find ways to create our own places — conferences, institutes, journals, and institutions — where we can be the Black women we are and gain respect for the amazing depth of perception that our identity brings.

To do the work involved in creating Black women's studies requires not only intellectual intensity, but the deepest courage. Ideally, this is passionate and committed research, writing, and teaching whose purpose is to question everything. Coldly "objective" scholarship that changes nothing is not what we strive for. "Objectivity" is itself an example of the reification of white-male thought. What could be less objective than the totally white-male studies which are still considered "knowledge"? Everything that human beings participate in is ultimately subjective and biased, and there is nothing inherently wrong with that. The bias of Black women's studies must consider as primary the knowledge that will save Black women's lives.

Black Women's Studies as
an Academic Area

Higher education for Black women has always been of serious concern to the Black community.[8] Recognition that education was a key mechanism for challenging racial and economic oppression created an ethic that defined education for women as important as education for men. Nearly 140 Black women attended Oberlin College between 1835 and 1865, prior to Emancipation, and Mary Jane Patterson, the first Afro-American woman to receive a B.A., graduated from Oberlin in 1862. The only two Black women's colleges still in existence, Spelman in Atlanta, Georgia, founded in 1881, and Bennett in Greensboro, North Carolina, founded in 1873, played a significant role in the education of Black women, as did those Black colleges founded as co-educational institutions at a time when most private white colleges were still single-sex schools.

Although Black women have long been involved in this educational work and also in creating self-conscious representations of ourselves using a variety of artistic forms, Black women's studies as an autonomous discipline only began to emerge in the late 1970s. At the moment, it is impossible to gauge definitely how much activity is going on in the field. There have been few statistical studies that have mapped the growth of women's studies generally, and there have been no surveys or reports to establish the breadth and depth of research and teaching on Black women.

One of the few sources providing some documentation of the progress of Black women's studies is *Who's Who and Where in Women's Studies*, published in 1974 by The Feminist Press. This book lists a total of 4,658 women's studies courses taught by 2,964 teachers. Approximately forty-five (or less than one percent) of the courses listed focus on Black women. About sixteen of these are survey courses, ten are literature courses, four are history courses, and the rest are in various disciplines. The largest number of courses taught on Black women was in Afro-American and Black Studies departments (approximately nineteen) and only about three courses on Black women were being taught for women's studies departments. Approximately nine Black colleges were offering women's studies courses at that time. None of the forty-five courses used the words "feminist" or "Black feminist" in the title.

More recent relevant comment can be found in Florence Howe's *Seven Years Later: Women's Studies Programs in 1976*.[9] She states:

> ...Like the social movement in which it is rooted, women's studies has tended to be predominantly white and middle-class, in terms of both faculty and curriculum, and there is a perceived need for a corrective.... The major strategy developed thus far is the inclusion of separate courses on Black Women, Chicanos, Third World Women, etc. Such courses, taught by minority women, have appeared on most campuses with the cooperation and cross-listing of various ethnic studies programs. For the most part, it is women's studies that has taken the initiative for this development.

However, as Howe proceeds to point out, more seriously committed and fundamental strategies are needed to achieve a truly multiracial approach.

Clearly, then, if one looks for "hard data" concerning curriculum relating to Black women in the existing studies of academic institutions, we are seemingly nonexistent. And yet impressionistically and experientially it is obvious that more and more study is being done about Black women and, even more importantly, it is being done with an increasing consciousness of the impact of sexual-racial politics on

Black women's lives. One thinks, for instance, of Alice Walker's groundbreaking course on Black women writers at Wellesley College in 1972, and how work of all sorts by and about Black women writers has since blossomed into a visible Black female literary "renaissance."

It seems that after survey courses (with titles like "The Black Woman in America") which provide an overview, most courses on Black women concentrate on literature, followed by social sciences and history as the next most popular areas. An early type of course that was taught focused upon "famous" individual Black women. Partly because at the beginning it is necessary to answer the basic question of exactly who there is to talk about, this is the way that materials on oppressed people have often been approached initially. Printed information written about or by successful individuals is also much more readily available, and analytical overviews of the field do not yet exist. Nevertheless, such focusing on exceptional figures is a direct outgrowth of centuries of concerted suppression and invisibility. When the various kinds of pedagogical resources that should exist eventually come into being, teachers will be able to move beyond (his ultimately class-biased strategy.

The core of courses on Black women at colleges and universities has grown slowly but steadily during the 1970s. And increasing interest in Black feminism and recognition of Black women's experiences point to the '80s as the time when Black women's studies will come into its own. Perhaps this may be seen less in teaching than in the plethora of other activity in Black women's scholarship. Some essential books have begun to appear: the Zora Neale Hurston reader, *I Love Myself When I Am Laughing...* (Old Westbury, N.Y.: The Feminist Press, 1979); and Sharon Harley and Rosalyn Terborg-Penn's *The Afro-American Woman: Struggles and Images* (Port Washington, N.Y.: Kennikat, 1978), to name only two. Special issues of feminist magazines—like *Conditions and Heresies*—are being devoted to Black/Third World women. Workshop sessions and entire conferences on Black women (e.g., The Third World Lesbian Writers Conference in New York City and the National Council of Negro Women's national research conference on Black women held in Washington, D.C.—both in 1979) have been organized.

Other indications that Black/Third World women are talking to each other and carving out ways of thinking, researching, writing, and teaching include the founding of *Sojourner: A Third World Women's Research Newsletter*, in 1977, and the founding, in 1978, of the Association of Black Women Historians, which publishes the newsletter *Truth*. Finally, research and dissertations by young Black female scholars for whom the developments of the past few years have opened the option of studying Black women have begun to produce the knowledge that Black women's studies will continue to need. These scholars—many of them activists—are working on a wide range of subjects—including revising the Black woman's role in slavery, recovering Black female oral and popular culture, and revamping the reputations of earlier Black women authors.

At this point, we are on the threshold—still in our "Phase One," as it were. There are still far too few courses and far too few Black women employed in institutions where they might have the opportunity to teach them. Although people involved in women's studies are becoming increasingly aware of issues of race, the majority of white women teachers and administrators have barely begun the process of self-examination which must precede productive action to change this situation. The confronting of sexism in Black studies and in the Black community in general is a mostly unfought battle, although it is evident from recent Black publications—e.g., *Black Scholar's* Black Sexism Debate issue—that the opposing anti-Black-feminist and pro-Black-feminist forces are beginning to align.

Ideally, Black women's studies will not be dependent on women's studies, Black studies, or "straight" disciplinary departments for its existence, but will be an autonomous academic entity making coalitions with all three. Realistically, however, institutional support will have to come from these already established units. This will be possible only in proportion to the elimination of racism, sexism, and elitism.

Black Women's Studies: The Book Itself

Assembling this volume was a challenging task. It appears at an appropriate historical moment when Black women are consciously manifesting themselves culturally, spiritually, and politically as well as intellectually. The book illuminates and provides examples of recent research and teaching about Black women. We hope, too, that in true harbinger fashion, it will be a catalyst for even greater gains in the future.

The publication of this book, *But Some of Us Are Brave*, fulfills a long-term need for a reference text and pedagogical tool. Those visionary women who pioneered in teaching courses on Black women can attest to the interest generated among other colleagues, friends, and even far-flung strangers—as shown by numerous requests for syllabi, reading lists, and other helpful information. Heretofore, those desiring access to such learning and teaching aids have had to rely largely on growing informal networks and the lucky acquisition of a syllabus here or there. Given this kind of hunger and wealth of materials already existing to satisfy it, it seems particularly important to facilitate the necessary sharing. This becomes imperative when one further considers that Black women's studies is at a crucial initial stage of development where the first flurry of excited discovery must be sustained and deepened if not to become just another short-lived enthusiasm or thwarted possibility.

This book is, in essence, the embodiment of "things hoped for, yet unseen." Beyond this, it owes its existence to the dedicated labor of many individuals and a fortuitous confluence of circumstances. When Barbara Smith became the first Black member of the Modern Language Association Commission on the Status of Women in the Profession, she suggested a book on Black women's studies as a publication idea. Gloria Hull, who was later appointed to the Commission, assumed primary responsibility for it as a CSW project. During the first half of 1977, a prospectus was drawn up and a call for contributions issued. That same spring, with the assistance of Florence Howe, Pat Scott became a third editor, thus adding some clearly needed expertise in the social sciences. Responses and contributions continued to trickle in, augmented by specific solicitations. The Feminist Press, having always expressed a commitment to the volume, formally accepted it for publication in the winter of 1977-78, and Black Women's Studies was given near-final shape in an editorial meeting in May 1978.

Pulling the book together was a struggle—for reasons which are not unrelated to the politics of our lives as Black women/scholars. Why did our call for papers not yield at least one essay on teaching about Black women? Why don't more Black women write up their research and critical insights? Why do contributors and possible contributors fail to meet deadlines? Why are people reluctant to send so innocuous a piece as a syllabus for inclusion in the book? Why was it nearly impossible to arrange "one simple little" editorial meeting?

The answers appear in many forms. One woman admitted that the death of feminist energy in her essay was caused by her having been recently traumatized by a well-known Black male critic who consistently made misogynistic statements both about Black women writers and about the women in the seminar of which she was a part. Another young woman, isolated at a Big Ten university where she had newly accepted an appointment, wrote:

> ...There's not much I can say to compensate for the inexcusable lateness of this response, but I have really had my hands full just staying above water. You might say that I haven't adjusted to my new environment very well. All of my writing—including my essay and the dissertation—are at a virtual standstill. No poetry coming forth either. It's cold as hell out here—and as lonely.

> ...Perhaps I'll get myself together and write, but I just haven't been able to do anything. Seems like some kind of crazy block—some indication, perhaps, of the intense isolation I feel. And there is nothing romantic about it either.

And then, too, one wonders about the accumulated generations of psychic damage which the descendants of Faulkner's nursemaid must heal before being able to put pen to paper, thinking, acting, (and writing) like the wonderful Black women we are. Finally, for a Black woman/feminist intellectual who is trying to live the various aspects of her identity and be a whole person amidst the contradictions and negations of this society, nothing is ever simple.

As a finished product, Black Women's Studies does not reveal these myriad complications. What it does openly reflect is the "state of the art" at the present time. The book's two opening sections provide materials essential to establishing the framework in which Black women's studies can most successfully be taught, that is, from a pro-Black-feminist and anti-racist perspective. Materials on Black feminism have only recently begun to be available, and Pat Bell Scott's annotated bibliography is a particularly useful resource for encouraging readers in this area. The section on racism contributes to an ongoing and essential dialogue between/about Black and white women. It is significant that several of the contributors to this section are not academics, but feminist activists. The deplorable increase in neo-racist backlash in the country as a whole makes this dialogue among women not only timely, but critical.

In the social sciences, reevaluations are needed—new definitions, conceptions, and methodologies which encompass the reality of Black women's experiences. The three essays of this section have all have such "debunking" recasting as their primary motivation. Stetson's article also illustrates how an interdisciplinary approach encourages new uses and interpretations of already-existing materials on Black women.

The book's fourth section offers often-inspiring examples of the various strategies Black women have used to survive. In particular, the articles concerning Black women's health, Black women's music, and Black women in religion are characterized by a sense of Black women's remarkable spiritual vision as well as providing concrete information about struggle and achievements.

The fifth section indicates that much of this beginning work originates in literature and literary study, as was the case with women's studies in general. Even though this in itself is not surprising, one *is* struck by the variety of people's interests and hence their submissions. They range from broad, descriptive investigations of genres and issues to treatments of more specialized subjects and approaches. The literature section that results may not look like anyone's *a priori* dream, but it is representative, useful, and even provocative.

The variety of multidisciplinary bibliographies are meant to encourage integrated work and lively classroom teaching and are a uniquely useful gathering of resources on Black women. The course syllabi (perhaps the most valuable part of the book for many readers) should begin to suggest some possibilities.

We regret that there is no essay here which scrutinizes Black women from the perspective of the pure, or hard sciences; which investigates questions like: What impact do the basic concepts of science such as objectivity and the scientific method have on researching Black women? Are there certain proscribed areas of the science profession that Black women are allowed to operate in? What are research priorities as Black women would establish and pursue them? Unfortunately, we were also unable to include essays on Black women written from an historical perspective, although stimulating research is being done is this area. Other disciplines that we would have liked to give more coverage, such as art, had to be limited because of space, money, and other difficulties.

Originally, we had thought to make this book, not "Black Women's Studies," but "Third World Women's Studies." It became apparent almost immediately that we were not equipped to do so. We hope that this one volume on Black women helps to create a climate where succeeding works on American Indian, Asian American, and Latino women can more swiftly come into being.

Not all of those who research Black women are themselves Black women (in this book, Joan Sherman and Jean Yellin, who contributed bibliographies, are both white). Similarly, we expect that many different types of individuals will do research and teach about Black women. Our only hope is that we have provided materials that everyone can use and, moreover, materials that will help to prepare the least prepared as well as enlarge the understanding of even the most well-suited or ideally qualified persons. Some of the inclusions—for example, the "Combahee River Collective Statement"—are so generally applicable that they might be used in any course, at any level. Others—such as the bibliographies on nineteenth-century Black women—could easily lend themselves to upper-division research projects.

Whatever the uses and results of this anthology, they will be satisfactory as long as the combined acts of faith and courage represented in it do indeed help to save Black women's lives and make Black women's studies a greater educational reality.

Visions and Recommendations

Our visions and recommendations for the future of Black women's studies are myriad. Countless projects and areas of research concerning Black women have not even been conceptualized. The following are merely examples:

Many of our visions require financial and institutional support. We would like to encourage:

- Funding of individual research by Black women scholars.
- Funding of teaching projects and curricular materials.
- Funding of summer seminars for college teachers, like those sponsored by the National Endowment for the Humanities.
- Funding of a directory of who's who and where in Black women's studies.
- Funding of a Black women's research institute at an institution with significant holdings on Black women.
- Funding of a national interdisciplinary Third World women's studies conference.

- Funding to allow the creation of our own publications, including both academic and Black feminist movement journals.

Already existing institutions can/must respond to the following needs and recommendations:

- That university departments provide a climate open and supportive to the teaching of materials on Black women.

- That universities and individual departments make hiring, promotion, and tenure of Black women faculty a priority and fulfill affirmative action directives.

- That universities implement more programs for "reentry" women, with particular outreach to Third World and working-class communities.

- That Black women's studies programs be made accessible to all Black women, not only those who are in universities.

- That Black women's studies programs be implemented on the elementary and secondary levels.

- That journals make a serious (effort to identify and publish the work of Black women scholars, particularly their research on Black women.

- Accreditation of women's studies programs on the basis of their approach/ inclusion of Third World women's studies.

- Accreditation of Black and Third World studies programs on the basis of their approach/inclusion of Third World women.

All of our visions require fundamental social, political, and personal change. For Black women's studies to flourish, we call for:

- The eradication of racism in the white women's movement through a serious examination of their own racism and recognition of Black history and culture.

- The eradication of antifeminism and homophobia in the Black community, and particularly among Black women academics.

- A strong Black feminist movement supported both by white feminists and by the Black community.

Endnotes

1. William Faulkner, *Light in August* (New York: Modern Library, 1932), p. 53.

2. Laura S. Haviland, *A Woman's Life-Work, Labors and Experiences* (Chicago: Publishing Association of Friends, 1889; copyright 1881), pp. 300-301; reprinted in Gerda Lerner, ed., *Black Women in White America: A Documentary History* (New York: Vintage, 1973), pp. 32-33.

3. Alice Walker, "In Search of Our Mother's Gardens," *Ms.* (May 1974): 64-70, 105.

4. Bernette Golden, Personal letter, April 1, 1974.

5. J.R. Roberts, *Black Lesbians: An Annotated Bibliography* (Tallahassee, FL: Naiad, 1981) contains over three hundred entries of books, periodicals, and articles by and about Black lesbians and provides ample material for developing a variety of courses.

6. Quoted in Jonathan Katz, *Gay American History: Lesbians and Gay Men in the U.S.A.* (New York: T.Y. Crowell, 1976), p. 425.

7. Lorraine Bethel, "'This Infinity of Conscious Pain': Zora Neale Hurston and the Black Female Literary Tradition."

8. Most of the material in these first two paragraphs about Black women in higher education was gleaned from an unpublished paper by Patricia Bell Scott, "Issues and Questions in the Higher Education of Black Women: Taking a Brief Look Backwards."

9. This is a report of the National Advisory Council on Women's Educational Programs published in June 1977. Another study sponsored by the National Institute of Education, "Involvement of Minority Women in Women's Studies," promises additional data.

15.

Womanist Issues in Black Studies: Towards Integrating Africana Womanism into Africana Studies*

Delores P. Aldridge

Two of the most significant reforms in American higher education over the past two decades have emerged from the Africana (Black Studies) and Women's Studies movements.[1] Black or Africana Studies began as a field of study in the 1960s in the wake of the civil rights movement and in the midst of pervasive campus unrest. From the outset it had both an academic and social mission. Though contemporary Black Studies as an interdisciplinary enterprise is a product of the sixties, it draws much of its academic content from earlier times.

Students of the sixties were confronted with an absence or distortion of the Black Experience in the higher education curriculum and a sense of cultural alienation generated by the predominantly white colleges and universities they entered. First they demanded black recognition in any form, such as black faculty and staff, black programs, more black students, necessary financial aid, and black history courses. But, it quickly became clear that black history was simply a beginning and that a broader demand would and did emerge for a comprehensive interdisciplinary curriculum with history at its center.

Women's Studies sought to introduce the study of women as a means of providing her story and to eradicate many of the myths and distortions surrounding the lives of women. The Women's Liberation movement following on the heels of the civil rights movement served as a catalyst for conscious-raising on women's issues. And, though much controversy has surrounded the movement with the opposition from both men and women, whites and nonwhites, its effects have pervaded the society at all levels, including the university, where women faculty and staff have led attempts to bring equity to gender issues. For the most part, white women benefiting from and modeling after the efforts of the civil rights and Black Studies movements have fostered an explosion of new approaches and content in the academy. Their increasing numbers and continuity have played heavily into their institutionalization in American higher education. Whereas Africana students, who are transient but in larger numbers than Africana faculty, have been a mainstay in pecking away at institutional barriers to the incorporation and perpetuation of African Studies, Women's

* *A revised version of the earlier work which appeared in* The Afrocentric Scholar, vol. 1, no. 1 (May 1992).

The author appreciates the discussion of the original draft of this work with LaFrances Rodgers-Rose who provided valuable insights.

Studies has enjoyed the growing critical mass of women faculty and staff with real access to structural change.

While both movements addressed some very real inadequacies such as paucity of faculty, absence and distortion of curriculum content and programmatic resources in the academy, neither has been particularly sensitive to the unique experiences of women of African descent in America, on the continent or through the Diaspora.

Some Africana women intellectuals have viewed the struggles of women of African descent in America as part of a wider struggle for human dignity and empowerment. As early as 1893, Anna Julia Cooper, in a speech to women, provided this perspective:

> We take our stand on the solidarity of humanity, the oneness of life, and the unnaturalness and injustice of all special favoritisms, whether of sex, race, country, or condition.... The colored woman feels that woman's cause is one and universal; and that... not till race, color, sex, and condition are seen as accidents, and not the substance of life; not till the universal title of humanity to life, liberty, and the pursuit of happiness is conceded to be inalienable to all; not till then is woman's lesson taught and woman's cause won—not the white woman's nor the black woman's, not the red woman's but the cause of every man and of every woman who has writhed silently under a mighty wrong.[2]

This humanist vision led Alice Walker to identify with the term womanist, of which she says "womanist is to feminist as purple is to lavender," addressing the notion of the solidarity of humanity. She defines "womanist" in *In Search of Our Mother's Gardens: Womanist Prose*. For Walker, a "womanist" is one who is "committed to the survival and wholeness of an entire people." Clinora Hudson-Weems (1993) enlarges upon this notion grounding us in Africana Womanism. The term "Africana" refers not only to continental Africans but also to people of African descent worldwide. In *Africana Womanism: Reclaiming Ourselves*, Hudson-Weems explores the dynamics of the conflict between the mainstream feminist, the black feminist, and the Africana womanist. In the book, she names and defines traits that characterize an Africana woman. According to Hudson-Weems, Africana Womanism is neither an outgrowth nor an addendum to mainstream feminism but rather a concept grounded in the culture and focuses on the experiences, needs and desires of Africana women. Africana womanists and feminists have separate agendas. Feminism is female centered; Africana Womanism is family centered. Feminism is concerned primarily with riding society of sexism; Africana Womanism is concerned with ridding society of racism first, then classism and sexism. Many feminists say their number one enemy is the male; Africana womanists welcome and encourage male participation in their struggle. Feminism, Hudson-Weems says, is incompatible with African women, as it was designed to meet the needs of white women. In fact, the history of feminism reveals a blatant, racist background. For example, in reaction to the ratification of the 15th Amendment to the Constitution in 1870, which granted Africana men voting rights, suffragist leader Carrie Chapman Catt asserted that middle-class white men recognize "the usefulness of woman suffrage as a counter-balance to the foreign vote, and as a means of legally preserving white supremacy in the South." And, so it is from the perspective of Africana Womanism that this discourse is developed.

The civil rights movement, which stressed liberation in the late sixties, marked the first time African people engaged in a struggle to resist racism, whereby distinct boundaries were established which separated the role of women and men. African male activists publicly acknowledged expectations that women involved in the movement conform to a subservient role pattern. This sexist expectation was expressed as women were admonished to manage household needs and breed warriors for the revolution. Toni Cade (1970) elaborated on the issue of roles that prevailed in black organizations during the sixties:

> It would seem that every organization you can name has had to struggle at one time or another with seemingly mutinous cadres of women getting salty about having to man the telephones or fix the coffee while the men wrote the position papers and decided on policy. Some groups condescendingly allotted two or three slots in the executive order to women. Others encouraged the sisters to form a separate caucus and work out something that wouldn't split the organization. Others got nasty and forced the women to storm out to organize separate workshops. Over the years, things have sort of been cooled out. But I have yet to hear a coolheaded analysis of just what any particular group's stand is on the question. Invariably, I hear from some dude that Black women must be supportive and patient so that Black men can regain their manhood. The notion of womanhood, they argue—and only if pressed to address themselves to the notion do they think of it or argue—is dependent on his defining his manhood. So the shit goes on.[3]

Though many black women activists did not succumb to the attempts of black men to reduce them to a secondary role in the movement, many did. Bell Hooks writes:

> Black women questioning and/or rejecting a patriarchal black movement found little solace in the contemporary women's movement. For while it drew attention to the victimization of black women by racist and sexist oppression, white feminists tended to romanticize the black female experience rather than discuss the negative impact of oppression. When feminists acknowledge in one breath that black women are victimized and in the same breath emphasize their strength, they imply that though black women are oppressed they manage to circumvent that damaging impact of oppression by being strong and that is simply not the case. Usually when people talk about the "strength" of black women they are referring to the way in which they perceive black women coping with oppression, that endurance is not to be confused with transformation.[4]

Thus, to be an activist in the liberation of black people or women did not necessarily mean there was sensitivity for Africana women.

In *All the Women Are White, All the Blacks Are Men, But Some of Us Are Brave*, three Africana women scholars wrote:

> Women's Studies...focused almost exclusively upon the lives of white women. Black Studies, which was much too often male-dominated, also ignored Black women.... Because of white women's racism and Black men's sexism, there was no room in either area for a serious consideration of the lives of Black women. And even when they have considered black women, white women usually have not had the capacity to analyze racial politics and Black culture, and Black men have remained blind or resistant to the implications of sexual politics in Black women's lives.[5]

The above characterization has seemingly been acknowledged, for within the last several years there has been increasing advocacy for recognition and correction of this failure to deal equitably with African women in scholarship and the academy.

Throughout the country, Africana men and women speak to the existence of racism in Women's Studies and sexism in Africana Studies in courses on campuses, in associations, and in scholarly publications. It would seem to follow, then, that there are a number of critical areas for attention: Africana women and scholarship, Africana women and the academy, and Africana women and professional organizations.

Scholarship, Africana Studies Africana Women

The increased number of Africana women scholars in the academy has yielded an increase in scholarly research about them. Prior to their significant presence, Africana men and others had largely written from their own interests and perspectives — excluding, minimizing or distorting the reality of Africana women. This, then, has been a major factor in the absence of African women in Africana Studies curriculum — the lack of a critical mass of Africana women scholars equipped to write about Africana women. Even with a growing number of Africana women scholars, it has been difficult for them to publish. Though it has not been easy to publish the works of Africana women scholars in general, Africana women have seen the doors closed more often on their publishing interests. But in spite of obstacles pertaining to the relevance and seriousness of African women's issues, there has been considerable scholarship over the last two or three decades. The seventies and eighties — which witnessed the rise and institutionalization of both Africana and Women's Studies — have surfaced much previous work and added to the continued productivity. There were various pioneering works in the seventies and eighties that included Toni Cade's *The Black Woman* (1970), the first anthology of its kind on African women in America with the focus on the voices of Africana women themselves who analyzed contemporary issues.

In 1972 Gerda Lerner provided *Black Women in White America: A Documentary History* demonstrating the importance of examining the experiences of women of African descent as distinct from those of non-Africana women and African men. Following on the heels of these two works was the first anthology by two Africana historians, Rosalyn Terborg-Penn and Sharon Harley. Their work, *The Afro-American Woman: Struggles and Images* (1978), is a collection of original essays from a historical perspective. A single-authored historical volume by Deborah Gray White, entitled *Ar'n't I a Woman?* (1985), provided some new insights into the lives of slave women. And, at the beginning of the decade of the eighties, two social science anthologies were developed by LaFrances Rodgers-Rose and Filomina Chioma Steady entitled respectively, *The Black Woman and The Black Woman Crossculturally*. The former work was and remains the first edited, definitive volume of original research by African American women social scientists on African American women. The latter volume was an outstanding accomplishment in arraying a wide range of work focusing on women of color throughout the world.

A single-authored volume of significance in the 1980s was by Lena Wright Myers, entitled *Black Women: Do They Cope Better?* This sociological work provided a new framework for understanding how women of African descent in America viewed themselves positively in spite of a racist, sexist, classist society. Another sociological work which has not received the exposure it deserves, *Black Women,*

Feminism, and Black Liberation: Which Way? was published by Vivian Gordon (1985). This work places in perspective the critical issues facing Africana women and African Studies if the field of African Studies is to fully realize its potential. A trail-blazing work of the nineties was authored by the writer. It attempted for the first time to theoretically conceptualize black male-female relationships in America. Aldridge (1991) in *Focusing: Black Male-Female Relationships* provided a foundation for understanding relationships with strategies for developing healthy ones. Earlier in 1989, she had laid the groundwork with *Black Male-Female Relationships: A Resource Book of Selected Materials* which was an edited volume comprising the most comprehensive collection of scholarly work available written by social scientists. Another work of significance for the nineties was authored by sociologist Patricia Collins, *Black Feminist Thought: Knowledge, Consciousness, and the Politics of Empowerment.* It encompasses most of the relevant work on Africana women and will probably serve as a point of departure for research for many on the subject in the future, notwithstanding the even more revolutionary work on Africana Womanism by Clinora Hudson-Weems. Hudson's work has no parallel as a new way of understanding Africana women.

Dozens of books and articles in the literary humanist tradition were authored over the last two decades. And, perhaps the most visible work to emerge in the nineties is the huge encyclopedia volumes on black women edited by Darlene Clark Hine. Other earlier works included: Mary Helen Washington's *Black-Eyed Susans: Classic Stories by and about Black Women* (1975) and *Sturdy Black Bridges: Visions of Black Women in Literature* edited by Roseann Bell, Betty Parker, and Beverly Guy-Sheftall (1979). In the decade of the eighties, a number of valuable works were set forth on feminist literary criticism for Africana women. Among these notable works were Barbara Christian's *Black Women Novelists: The Development of a Tradition 1892-1976* (1981) and Gloria Wade-Gayle's *No Crystal Stair, Visions of Race and Sex in Women's Fiction* (1984). A controversial, but valuable, piece for illuminating the complexity of Africana womanhood is the interdisciplinary work of Bell Hooks' *Ain't I a Woman: Black Women and Feminism* (1981).

This growing scholarship is necessary to move toward integrating African women into Africana Studies in the academy. If there continues to be this flowering of scholarly products, the future in encouraging for the institutionalization of Africana women throughout curriculum, programming and academic appointments at all levels.

The Academy, Africana Studies and Africana Women

Presently, entrenchment in the academy in terms of formal courses has been far less observable than the scholarship developed over the last two decades. Significantly, the *Core Curriculum Guide* developed by the National Council for Black Studies (1981) did not address the issue of inclusion of women as a distinct focus for study. And, Colon's particularly crucial work, "Critical Issues in Black Studies: A Selective Analysis," (1984) failed to devote attention to the lack of inclusion of women in curriculum in any significant way as an area of concern. These omissions were addressed a decade later in the revised *Core Curriculum Guide of the Council for Black*

Studies and the subsequent works by visible male Africana Studies scholars as well as female Africana Studies scholars.

A cursory examination of curricula in Africana Studies or Women's Studies units reflects very few, if any, courses that treat Africana women in their own right. And, when they do, most often the courses are in literature and occasionally tied to a family course. There are some exceptions, usually where courses are jointly listed in Africana and Women's Studies with titles such as "The Black Woman in America" or "The Black Woman in History." Notably where proactive Africana Women's scholars are located, there are generally one or two courses in the course listings.

The above tenuous assessment is based on an examination of a limited sample of schools with both Africana and Women's Studies academic units. It should also be noted that institutions that have white women scholars who are sensitive to Africana women's issues and are politically astute enough to recognize the fertile terrain for research are more likely to have courses that give attention to issues of importance for Africana women. But, it is necessary to bear in mind the struggle which exists to control curricula on Africana women as well as to gain and maintain loyalty and commitment to Africana Studies by Africana women on campuses where strong Women's Studies programs exist. In *But Some of Us Are Brave*, there are course descriptions of African American Women's Studies. Some of these courses may prove to be useful as a point of departure for developing courses on Africana women in programs where they are nonexistent.

Beyond the courses on campuses, the campus cultural arena must be examined to determine the extent to which it fosters educational enlightenment on issues of relevance to Africana women. How many lectures by and about Africana women occur during the academic year? What kinds of audiences turn out for these occasions? What accounts appear in campus media on Africana women: Who or what units are the promoters of Africana women on campuses? Data has to be systematically gathered to respond to these kinds of questions to get a handle on the extent to which Africana women are being incorporated into Africana Studies, specifically, and on campus in general. Again, the data from the dozen or so campuses are not very impressive. The list of women as speakers is much more limited than men in numbers as well as in the subfields of Africana Studies.

Very few women emerge as "famous people" to bring to campus outside of the political activists, entertainers or the popular novelists such as Maya Angelou, Alice Walker, Toni Morrison, etc. Virtually no Africana women theoreticians among the social and behavioral science scholars, or, for that matter, humanists such as historians surface immediately for student groups or faculty to bring to campus except when brochures from speakers bureaus are consulted. The point is that we have virtually no highly visible "giants" among Africana women who are committed to and who are doing significant work on Africana women within the field of Africana Studies.

Most of those who are visible view themselves as part of a traditional discipline or as part of a newly emerging discipline of Black Women's Studies and as such are not an integral part of the promotion and development of African Studies as a discipline. They seek to emphasize issues of women while minimizing the experiences of people of African decent as a totality. The overriding issue today is: do we need an African Women's Studies movement separate from the general movement or will African Studies be able to incorporate the experiences of black women?

It must be borne in mind that, until recently, an overwhelming majority of African Studies units were administered by Africana males who controlled curriculum development and cultural programming activities and were guilty, even if unintentionally, of treating Africana women as whites had treated both men and women of African descent in the academy—distorting or dismissing them and their experiences. And, where women were administrators their faculties were usually still heavily male—probably sensitive but unequipped to teach courses. This suggests the dual need for sensitivity and necessary resources. The decade of the nineties is witnessing positive changes in both of the aforementioned.

There are growing numbers of scholars with interest in women's issues as well as an increasing number of Africana administrators, both male and female, who are sensitive to women's issues, realizing the need to incorporate significantly curriculum and experiences of students both male and female. For example, the Emory University African American and African Studies program, under its founding Africana woman director, inaugurated an endowed lecture series in the name of an African American woman and subsequently created a distinguished chair in the name of an Africana woman with an African American woman as the first individual to hold the chair. Both incidents were firsts at a major institution in this country. But significantly there has never been a strong presence of African women in the curriculum in this institution for a variety of reasons, including most importantly the lack of continuity of faculty equipped to teach these courses.

Professional Organizations, Africana Studies and Africana Women

Just as scholarship and the academy have been largely void of a significant Africana women's presence and skill in "directing traffic," such has been the case for Africana Studies professional organizations until the late eighties and nineties. It is in these very organizations that Africana women have begun to have their presence felt—not simply by being the leaders or presidents but through drawing more women into all levels of the organizations.

Organizations must have infrastructures which develop their character and form.

The National Council for Black Studies (NCBS), The African Heritage Studies Association (AHSA), and the African American Life and History Association (ASALH) have contributed to professionalizing the field of African American Studies. They have taken steps to move towards parity among women and men with respect to key positions throughout the organizations; integration of women's issues and experience in the annual conference programs; recognition of women with awards; and special projects devoted to them.

Much of this movement came about due to efforts of women as they have gained in numbers but also because some men have come to see the injustice and the waste of talent in not fully actualizing the wealth of resources which abound when men and women come together in enlightening the world. But, it probably has been easier to integrate women in the professional organizations than in the curriculum because of the nature of political machinery in organizations, as opposed to garnering resources for faculty positions to staff courses on African women. All too often, these courses are seen as frills rather than staples, not only, and perhaps, not even as much by Africana scholars as by central administrators who control budgets.

Toward Integrating Africana Women into Africana Studies

Integrating Africana women into Africana Studies should not need to be a topic for dialogue. For the incorporation of Africana women should be as natural to the field as breathing is to living. This is particularly true if those in the field share a fundamental womanist perspective as mentioned earlier in this chapter and which more recently has been summarized by Gordon (1985) and Hudson-Weems (1993). In *Black Women, Feminism and Black Liberation: Which Way?* Gordon contends black liberation represents freedom from racism and sexism, and as such black women should not have to compartmentalize themselves into segments of race versus gender. Both black men's and black women's central goal is to be liberated, and it can happen only if both are fairly treated.[6] Hudson-Weems points out specifically what encompasses a liberated people as she details the characteristics of the Africana woman. She lists 18 features: (1) a self-namer, (2) a self-definer, (3) family-centered, (4) genuine in sisterhood, (5) strong, (6) in concert with male in struggle, (7) whole, (8) authentic, (9) a flexible role player, (10) respected, (11) recognized, (12) spiritual, (13) male compatible, (14) respectful of elders, (15) adaptable, (16) ambitious, (17) mothering and (18) nurturing.[7]

Guided by an African Womanist perspective, then, and by way of summary and emphasis, the following points are offered for consideration as challenges or opportunities for integrating Africana women into Africana Studies:

1. Continued development of scholarship by and about Africana women, particularly with increased focus in the social and behavioral sciences, the natural sciences, professions and policy studies.

2. Increased contributions by women to conceptualization of theoretical and empirical issues of the field in general. Women are invisible for the most part in framing central issues of the discipline of Africana Studies. Two notable exceptions are Young (1984) and Aldridge (1988), who guest edited special issues of the *Journal of Negro Education and Phylon: Review of Race and Culture*. Earlier in 1972, Young had edited the significant and widely used *Black Experience: Analysis and Synthesis*. More recently, Marimba Ani (1994) has emerged with what may were be the major theoretical piece for Africana Studies produced by male or female in this century.

3. Continued involvement of Africana women with womanist perspectives in leadership positions in the professional bodies for Africana Studies so that programs and policies reflect their perspectives.

4. Increased attention to developing new and restructuring old curricula to reflect a balance that is inclusive of Africana women.

5. Increased balancing of speakers and cultural activities on campuses that draw upon both men and women not only from the literary tradition but other orientations. Much more effort will have to be exerted to draw upon talent among the less famous but no less substantive than some of the famous.

6. Concentrated efforts to search out and quote the work of both Africana women and men in the field as scholars of other fields do.

While by no means exhaustive, the aforementioned points are offered as challenges or opportunities for integrating Africana women into Africana Studies. Thus, Integration would foreclose on any needs for African Women scholars to abandon the disciplines—a discipline which can only grow stronger and richer with the full treatment of both its men and women.

References

Aldridge, Delores P., ed. "New Perspectives on Black Studies," Special issue, *Phylon: Review of Race and Culture* 49, 1 (Spring 1988).

———. *Black Male-Female Relationships: A Resource Book*. Dubuque, Iowa: Kendall-Hunt, 1989.

———. *Focusing: Institutional and interpersonal Perspectives on Black Male-Female Relations*. Chicago: Third World Press, 1991.

Ani, Marimba. *Yurugu: An African-Centered Critique of European Cultural Thought and Behavior*. Trenton, NJ: Africa World Press, 1994.

Bell, Roseann P., Bettye J. Parker and Beverly Guy-Sheftall, eds., *Sturdy Black Bridges: Visions of Black Women in Literature*. New York: Anchor Books, 1979.

Boxer, Marilyn J., "For and About Women: The Theory and Practice of Women's Studies in the United States," *Signs* 7 (1981): 660-695.

Cade, Toni, ed. *The Black Woman: An Anthology*. New York. New American Library, 1970.

Christian, Barbara. *Black Women Novelists: The Development of a Tradition 1892-1976*. Westport, CN: Greenwood Press, 1981.

Collins, Patricia H. *Black Feminist Thought: Knowledge, Consciousness, and the Politics of Empowerment*. London: Harper Collins Academic, 1990.

Colon, Alan K. "Critical Issues in Black Studies: A Selective Analysis," *The Journal of Negro Education* 53 (1984): 268-277.

Gordon, Vivian V. *Black Women, Feminism, Black Liberation: Which Way?* Chicago: Third World Press, 1991.

Harley, Sharon, and Terborg-Penn, Rosalyn, eds. *The Afro-American Woman: Struggles and Images*. Port Washington, NY: Kennikat Press, 1978.

hooks, bell. *Ain't I a Woman: Black Women and Feminism*. Boston: South End Press, 1981.

Hudson-Weems, Clinora. *Africana Womanism: Reclaiming Ourselves*. Detroit: Dunlap Press, 1993.

Hull, Gloria T., Scott, Patricia Bell, and Smith, Barbara, eds., *All the Women Are White, All the Men Are Black, But Some of Us Are Brave: Black Women's Studies*. Old Westbury, NY: Feminist Press, 1982.

Ladner, Joyce. *Tomorrow's Tomorrow*. Garden City, NY: Doubleday, 1971.

Lerner, Gerda, ed. *Black Women in White America: A Documentary History.* New York: Pantheon Books, 1972.

Loewenberg, Bert J., and Bogin, Ruth, eds. *Black Women in Nineteenth Century American Life*. University Park. Pennsylvania State Press, 1976.

Myers, Lena Wright. *Black Women: Do They Cope Better?* New York: Prentice-Hall, 1980.

National Council for Black Studies. *Black Studies Core Curriculum*. Bloomington, IN: National Council for Black Studies, 1981.

Rodgers-Rose, LaFrances. *The Black Woman*. Beverly Hills, CA: Sage Publications, 1980.

Steady, Filomina, ed. *The Black Woman Cross-Culturally*. Cambridge, MA: Schenkman, 1981.

Turner, James E., ed. *The Next Decade: Theoretical and Research Issues*. Ithaca, NY: Africana Studies and Research Center, Cornell University, 1984.

Wade-Gayles, Gloria. *No Crystal Stair, Visions of Race and Sex in Women's Fiction*. New York: Pilgrim Press, 1984.

Walker, Alice. *The Color Purple*. New York: Washington Square Press, 1982.

———. *In Search of Our Mother's Gardens: Womanist Prose*. New York: Harcourt Brace Jovanovich, 1983.

Washington, Mary Helen. *Black-Eyed Susans: Classic Stories by and about Black Woman*. Garden City, NY: Doubleday, 1975.

White, Deborah Gray. *Ain't I a Woman? Female Slaves in the Plantation South*. New York: W.W. Norton, 1985.

Young, Carlene. "An Assessment of Black Studies Programs in American Higher Education," special issue of *The Journal of Negro Education* 53 (1984).

———. *Black Experience: Analysis and Synthesis*. San Rafael, CA: Leswing Press, 1972.

Note

For a comprehensive examination of women's studies generally, see Marilyn J. Boxer, "For and About Women: The Theory and Practice of Women's Studies in the United States," *SIGNS*, 7 (1982): 660-95. For an overview of Africana Studies refer to James E. Turner (ed.), *The Next Decade: Theoretical and Research Issues*. Ithaca, NY: Cornell University, 1984.

Endnotes

1. Bert J. Loewenberg and Ruth Bogin, eds., *Black Women in Nineteenth-Century American Life*. University Park: Pennsylvania State University Press, 1976.

2. Bell Hooks, *Ain't I a Woman: Black Women and Feminism*. Boston: South End Press, 1981, p. 6.

3. Toni Cade, ed., *The Black Woman: An Anthology*. New York: New American Library, 1970, pp. 107-108.

4. Bell Hooks, *op cit.*, p. 6.

5. Gloria T. Hull, Patricia Bell Scott, and Barbara Smith, eds., *All the Women Are White, All the Blacks Are Men, But Some of Us Are Brave*. Black Women's Studies. Old Westbury, N.Y.: Feminist Press, 1981, pp. xx-xxi.

6. Vivian V. Gordon, *Black Women, Feminism, Black Liberation: Which Way?* Chicago: Third World Press, 1985, pp. 68-69.

7. Clinora Hudson-Weems, *Africana Womanism: Reclaiming Ourselves*. Troy, Mich.: Bedford Publishers, 1993, p. 179.

16.

The Social Construction
of Black Feminist Thought

Patricia Hill-Collins

Sojourner Truth, Anna Julia Cooper, Ida Wells-Barnett, and Fannie Lou Hamer are but a few names from a growing list of distinguished African American women activists. Although their sustained resistance to black women's victimization within interlocking systems of race, gender, and class oppression is well known, these women did not act alone.[1] Their actions were nurtured by the support of countless, ordinary African American women who, through strategies of everyday resistance created a powerful foundation for this more visible black feminist activist tradition.[2] Such support has been essential to the shape and goals of black feminist thought.

The long-term and widely shared resistance among African American women can only have been sustained by an enduring and shared standpoint among black women about the meaning of oppression and the actions that black women can and should take to resist it. Efforts to identify the central concepts of this black women's standpoint figure prominently in the works of contemporary black feminist intellectuals.[3] Moreover, political and epistemological issues influence the social construction of black feminist thought. Like other subordinate groups, African American women not only have developed distinctive interpretations of black women's oppression, but have done so by using alternative ways of producing and validating knowledge itself.

A Black Women's Standpoint

The Foundation of Black Feminist Thought

Black women's everyday acts of resistance challenge two prevailing approaches to studying the consciousness of oppressed groups.[4] One approach claims that subordinate groups identify with the powerful and have no valid independent interpretation of their own oppression.[5] The second approach assumes that the oppressed are less human than their rulers and, therefore, are less capable of articulating their own standpoint.[6] Both approaches see any independent consciousness expressed by an oppressed group as being not of the group's own making and/or inferior to the perspective of the dominant group.[7] More important, both interpretations suggest that oppressed groups lack the motivation for political activism because of their flawed consciousness of their own subordination.

Yet African American women have been neither passive victims of nor willing accomplices to their own domination. As a result, emerging work in black women's studies contends that black women have a self-defined standpoint on their own oppression.[8] Two interlocking components characterize this standpoint. First, black women's political and economic status provide them with a distinctive set of experiences that offers a different view of material reality than that available to other groups. The unpaid and paid work that black women perform, the types of communities in which they live, and the kinds of relationships they have with others suggest that African American women, as a group, experience a different world than those who are not black and female.[9] Second, these experiences stimulate a distinctive black feminist consciousness concerning that material reality.[10] In brief, a subordinate group not only experiences a different reality than a group that rules, but a subordinate group may interpret that reality differently than a dominant group.

Many ordinary African American women have grasped this connection between what one does and how one thinks. Hannah Nelson, an elderly black domestic worker, discusses how work shapes the standpoints of African American and white women: "Since I have to work, I don't really have to worry about most of the things that most of the white women I have worked for are worrying about. And if these women did their own work, they would think just like I do—about this, anyway."[11] Ruth Shays, a black inner city resident, points out how variations in men's and women's experiences lead to differences in perspective: "The mind of the man and the mind of the woman is the same. But this business of living makes women use their minds in ways that men don't even have to think about."[12] Finally, elderly domestic worker Rosa Wakefield assesses how the standpoints of the powerful and those who serve them diverge: "If you eats these dinners and don't cook 'em, if you wears these clothes and don't buy or iron them, then you might start thinking that the good fairy or some spirit did all that.... Black folks don't have no time to be thinking like that.... But when you don't have anything else to do, you can think like that. It's bad for your mind, though."[13]

While African American women may occupy material positions that stimulate a unique standpoint, expressing an independent black feminist consciousness is problematic precisely because more powerful groups have a vested interest in suppressing such thought. As Hannah Nelson notes, "I have grown to womanhood in a world whore the saner you are, the madder you are made to appear."[14] Nelson realizes that those who control the schools, the media, and other cultural institutions are generally skilled in establishing their view of reality as superior to alternative interpretations. While an oppressed group's experiences may put them in a position to see things differently, their lack of control over the apparatuses of society that sustain ideological hegemony makes the articulation of their self-defined standpoint difficult. Groups unequal in power are correspondingly unequal in their access to the resources necessary to implement their perspectives outside their particular group.

One key reason that standpoints of oppressed groups are discredited and suppressed by the more powerful is that self-defined standpoints can stimulate oppressed groups to resist their domination. For instance, Annie Adams, a southern black woman, describes how she became involved in civil rights activities.

> When I first went into the mill we had segregated water fountains.... Same thing about the toilets. I had to clean the toilets for the inspection room and then, when I got ready to go to the bathroom, I had to go all the way to the bottom of the stairs to the cellar. So I asked my bas man, "What's the difference? If I can go in there and clean them toilets, why can't I use them?" Finally, I started to use that toilet. I decided I wasn't going to walk a mile to go to the bathroom.[15]

In this case, Adams found the standpoint of the "boss man" inadequate, developed one of her own, and acted upon it. In doing so, her actions exemplify the connections between experiencing oppression, developing a self-defined standpoint on that experience, and resistance.

The Significance of Black Feminist Thought

The existence of a distinctive black women's standpoint does not mean that it has been adequately articulated in black feminist thought. Peter Berger and Thomas Luckmann provide a useful approach to clarifying the relationship between a black women's standpoint and black feminist thought with the contention that knowledge exists on two levels.[16] The first level includes the everyday, taken-for-granted knowledge shared by members of a given group, such as the ideas expressed by Ruth Shays and Annie Adams. Black feminist thought, by extension, represents a second level of knowledge, the more specialized knowledge furnished by experts who are part of a group and who express the group's standpoint. The two levels of knowledge are interdependent; while black feminist thought articulates the taken-for-granted knowledge of African American women, it also encourages all black women to create new self-definitions that validate a black women's standpoint.

Black feminist thought's potential significance goes far beyond demonstrating that black women can produce independent, specialized knowledge. Such thought can encourage collective identity by offering black women a different view of themselves and their world than that offered by the established social order. This different view encourages African American women to value their own subjective knowledge base.[17] By taking elements and themes of black women's culture and traditions and infusing them with new meaning, black feminist thought rearticulates a consciousness that already exists.[18] More important, this rearticulated consciousness gives African American women another tool of resistance to all forms of their subordinations.[19]

Black feminist thought, then, specializes in formulating and rearticulating the distinctive, self-defined standpoint of African American women. One approach to learning more about a black women's standpoint is to consult standard scholarly sources for the ideas of specialists on black women's experiences.[20] But investigating a black women's standpoint and black feminist thought requires more ingenuity than that required in examining the standpoints and thought of white males. Rearticulating the standpoint of African American women through black feminist thought is much more difficult since one cannot use the same techniques to study the knowledge of the dominated as one uses to study the knowledge of the powerful. This is precisely because subordinate groups have long had to use alternative ways to create an inept consciousness and to rearticulate it through specialists validated by the oppressed themselves.

The Eurocentric Masculinist
Knowledge-Validation Process[21]

All social thought, including white masculinist and black feminist, reflects the interests and standpoint of its creators. As Karl Mannheim notes, "If one were to trace in detail...the origin and...diffusion of a certain thought-model, one would discover the affinity it has to the social position of given groups and their manner of interpreting the world."[22] Scholars, publishers, and other experts represent specific interests and credentialing processes and their knowledge claims must satisfy the epistemological and political criteria of the contexts in which they reside.[23]

Two political criteria influence the knowledge-validation process. First, knowledge claims must be evaluated by a community of experts whose members represent the standpoints of the groups from which they originate. Second, each community of experts must maintain its credibility as defined by the larger group in which it is situated and from which it draws its basic, taken-for-granted knowledge.

When white males control the knowledge-validation process, both political criteria can work to suppress black feminist thought. Since the general culture shaping the taken-for-granted knowledge of the community of experts is one permeated by widespread notions of black and female inferiority,[24] new knowledge claims that seem to violate these fundamental assumptions are likely to be viewed as anomalies.[25] Moreover, specialized thought challenging notions of black and female inferiority its unlikely to be generated from within a white-male-controlled academic community because both the kinds of questions that could be asked and the explanations that would be found satisfying would necessarily reflect a basic lack of familiarity with black women's reality?[26]

The experiences of African American women scholars illustrate how individuals who wish to rearticulate a black women's standpoint through black feminist thought can be suppressed by a white-male-controlled knowledge-validation process. Exclusion from basic literacy, quality educational experiences, and faculty and administrative positions has limited black women's access to influential academic positions?[27] Thus, while black women can produce knowledge claims that contest those advanced by the white male community, this community does not grant that black women scholars have competing knowledge claims based in another knowledge validation process. As a consequence, any credentials controlled by white male academicians can be denied to black women producing black feminist thought on the grounds that it is not credible research.

Those black women with academic credentials who seek to exert the authority that their status grants them to propose new knowledge claims about African American women face pressures to use their authority to help legitimate a system that devalues and excludes the majority of black women?[28] One way of excluding the majority of black women from the knowledge-validation process is to permit a few black women to acquire positions of authority in institutions that legitimate knowledge and to encourage them to work within the taken-for-granted assumptions of black female inferiority shared by the scholarly community and the culture at large. Those black women who accept these assumptions are likely to be rewarded by their institutions, often at significant personal cost. Those challenging the assumptions run the risk of being ostracized.

African American women academicians who persist in trying to rearticulate a black women's standpoint also face potential rejection of their knowledge claims on epistemological grounds. Just as the material realities of the powerful and the dominated produce separate standpoints, each group may also have distinctive epistemologies or theories of knowledge. It is my contention that black female scholars may know that something is true but be unwilling or unable to legitimate their claims using Eurocentric masculinist criteria for consistency with substantiated knowledge and Eurocentric masculinist criteria for methodological adequacy.

For any particular interpretive context, new knowledge claims must be consistent with an existing body of knowledge that the group controlling the interpretive context accepts as true. The methods used to validate knowledge claims must also be acceptable to the group controlling the knowledge-validation process.

The criteria for the methodological adequacy of positivism illustrate the epistemological standards that black women scholars would have to satisfy in legitimating alternative knowledge claims?[29] Positivist approaches aim to create scientific descriptions of reality by producing objective generalizations. Since researchers have widely differing values, experiences, and emotions, genuine science is thought to be unattainable unless all human characteristics except rationality are eliminated from the research process. By following strict methodological rules, scientists aim to distance themselves from the values, vested interests, and emotions generated by their class, race, sex, or unique situation and in so doing become detached observers and manipulators of nature.[30]

Several requirements typify positivist methodological approaches. First, research methods generally require a distancing of the researcher from her/his "object" of study by defining the researcher as a "subject" with full human subjectivity and objectifying the "object" of study.[31] A second requirement is the absence of emotions from the research process.[32] Third, ethic and values are deemed inappropriate in the research process, either as the reason for scientific inquiry or as part of the research process itself.[33] Finally, adversarial debates, whether written or oral, become the preferred method of ascertaining truth—the arguments that can withstand the greatest assault and survive intact become the strongest truths.[34]

Such criteria ask African American women to objectify themselves, devalue their emotional life, displace their motivations for furthering knowledge about black women, and confront, in an adversarial relationship, those who have more social, economic, and professional power than they. It seems unlikely, therefore, that black women would use a positivist epistemological stance in rearticulating a black women's standpoint. Black women are more likely to choose an alternative epistemology for assessing knowledge claims, one using standards that are consistent with black women's criteria for substantiated knowledge and with black women's criteria for methodological adequacy. If such an epistemology exists, what are its contours? Moreover, what is its role in the production of black feminist thought?

The Contours of an Afrocentric Feminist Epistemology

Africanist analyses of the black experience generally agree on the fundamental elements of an Afrocentric standpoint. In spite of varying histories, black societies reflect elements of a core African value system that existed prior to and independently of racial oppression.[35] Moreover, as a result of colonialism, imperialism, slavery, apartheid, and other systems of racial domination, blacks share a common experience of oppression. These similarities in material conditions have fostered shared Afrocentric values that permeate the family structure, religious institutions, culture, and community life of blacks in varying parts of Africa, the Caribbean, South America, and North America.[36] This Afrocentric consciousness permeates the shared history of people of African descent through the framework of a distinctive Afrocentric epistemology.[37]

Feminist scholars advance a similar argument. They assert that women share a history of patriarchal oppression through the political economy of the material conditions of sexuality and reproduction.[38] These shared material conditions are thought to transcend divisions among women created by race, social class, religion, sexual orientation, and ethnicity and to form the basis of a women's standpoint with its corresponding feminist consciousness and epistemology.[39]

Since black women have access to both the Afrocentric and the feminist standpoints, an alternative epistemology used to rearticulate a black women's standpoint reflects elements of both traditions.[40] The search for the distinguishing features of an alternative epistemology used by African American women reveals that values and ideas that Africanist scholars identify as being characteristically "black" often bear remarkable resemblance to similar ideas claimed by feminist scholars as being characteristically "female."[41] This similarity suggests that the material conditions of oppression can vary dramatically and yet generate some uniformity in the epistemologies of subordinate groups. Thus, the significance of an Afrocentric feminist epistemology may lie in its enrichment of our understanding of how subordinate groups create knowledge that enables them to resist oppression.

The parallels between the two conceptual schemes raise a question: Is the worldview of women of African descent more intensely infused with the overlapping feminine/Afrocentric standpoints than is the case for either African American men or white women?[42] While an Afrocentric feminist epistemology, reflects elements of epistemologies used by blacks as a group and women as a group, it also paradoxically demonstrates features that may be unique to black women. On certain dimensions, black women may more closely resemble black men, on others, white women, and on still others, black women may stand apart from both groups. Black feminist sociologist Deborah K. King describes this phenomenon as a "both/or" orientation, the act of being simultaneously a member of a group and yet standing apart from it. She suggests that multiple realities among black women yield a "multiple consciousness in black women's politics" and that this state of belonging yet not belonging forms an integral part of black women's oppositional consciousness.[43] Bonnie Thornton Dill's analysis of how black women live with contradictions, a situation she labels the "dialectics of black womanhood," parallels King's assertions that this "both/or" orientation is central to an Afrocentric feminist consciousness.[44] Rather than emphasizing how a black women's standpoint and its accompanying epistemology are different from those in Afrocentric and feminist analyses, I use black women's experiences as a point of contact between the two.

Viewing an Afrocentric feminist epistemology in this way challenges analyses claiming that black women have a more accurate view of oppression than do other groups. Such approaches suggest that oppression can be quantified and compared and that adding layers of oppression produces a potentially clearer standpoint. While it is tempting to claim that black women are more oppressed than everyone else and therefore hour the best standpoint from which to understand the mechanisms, processes, and effects of oppression, this simply may not be the case.[45]

African American women do not uniformly share an Afrocentric feminist epistemology since social class introduces variations among black women in seeing, valuing, and using Afrocentric feminist perspectives. While a black women's standpoint and its accompanying epistemology stem from black women's consciousness of race and gender oppression, they are not simply the result of combining Afrocentric and female values—standpoints are rooted in real material conditions structured by social class.[46]

Concrete Experience as a Criterion of Meaning

Carolyn Chase, a thirty-one-year-old inner city black woman, notes, "My aunt used to say, 'A heap see, but a few know.'"[47] This saying depicts two types of knowing, knowledge and wisdom, and taps the first dimension of an Afrocentric feminist epistemology. Living life as black women requires wisdom since knowledge about the dynamics of race, gender, and class subordination has been essential to black women's survival. African American women give such wisdom high credence in assessing knowledge.

Allusions to these two types of knowing pervade the words of a range of African American women. In explaining the tenacity of racism, Zilpha Elaw, a preacher of the mid-1800s, noted: "The pride of a white skin is a bauble of great value with many in some parts of the United States, who readily sacrifice their intelligence to their prejudices, and possess more knowledge than wisdom."[48] In describing differences separating African American and white women, Nancy White invokes a similar rule: "When you come right down to it, white women just think they are free. Black women *know* they ain't free.[49] Geneva Smitherman, a college professor specializing in African American linguistics, suggests that "from a black perspective, written documents are limited in what they can teach about life and survival in the world. Blacks are quick to ridicule 'educated fools,'...they have 'book learning,' but no 'mother wit,' knowledge, but not wisdom."[50] Mabel Lincoln eloquently summarizes the distinction between knowledge and wisdom: "To black people like me, a fool is funny—you know, people who love to break bad, people you can't tell anything to, folks that would take a shotgun to a roach."[51]

Black women need wisdom to know how to deal with the "educated fools" who would "take a shotgun to a roach." As members of a subordinate group, black women cannot afford to be fools of any type, for their devalued status denies them the protections that white skin, maleness, and wealth confer. This distinction between knowledge and wisdom, and the use of experience as the cutting edge dividing them, has been key to black women's survival. In the context of race, gender, and class oppression, the distinction is essential since knowledge without wisdom is adequate for the powerful, but wisdom is essential to the survival of the subordinate.

For ordinary African American women, those individuals who have lived through the experiences about which they claim to be experts are more believable and credible than those who have merely read or thought about such experiences. Thus, concrete experience as a criterion for credibility frequently is invoked by black women when making knowledge claims. For instance, Hannah Nelson describes the importance that personal experience has for her: "Our speech is most directly personal, and every black person assumes that every other black person has a right to a personal opinion. In speaking of grave matters, your personal experience is considered very good evidence. With us, distant statistics are certainly not as important as the actual experience of a sober person."[52] Similarly, Ruth Shays uses her concrete experiences to challenge the idea that formal education is the only route to knowledge: "I am the kind of person who doesn't have a lot of education, but both my mother and my father had good common sense. Now, I think that's all you need. I might not know how to use thirty-four words where three would do, but that does not mean that I don't know what I'm talking about...I know what I'm talking about because I'm talking about myself. I'm talking about what I have lived."[53] Implicit in Shays's self-assessment is a critique of the type of knowledge that obscures the truth, the "thirty-four words" that cover up a truth that can be expressed in three.

Even after substantial mastery of white masculinist epistemologies, many black women scholars invoke their own concrete experiences and those of other black women in selecting topics for investigation and methodologies used. For example, Elsa Barkley Brown subtitles her essay on black women's history, "how my mother taught me to be a historian in spite of my academic training."[54] Similarly, Joyce Ladner maintains that growing up as a black woman in the South gave her special insights in conducting her study of black adolescent women.[55]

Henry Mitchell and Nicholas Lewter claim that experience as a criterion of meaning with practical images as its symbolic vehicles is a fundamental epistemological tenet in African American thought-systems.[56] Stories, narratives, and Bible principles are selected for their applicability to the lived experiences of African Americans and become symbolic representations of a whole wealth of experience. For example, Bible tales are told for their value to common life, so their interpretation involves no need for scientific historical verification. The narrative method requires that the story be "told, not torn apart in analysis, and trusted as core belief, not admired as science."[57] Any biblical story contains more than characters and a plot—it presents key ethical issues salient in African American life.

June Jordan's essay about her mother's suicide, exemplifies the multiple levels of meaning that can occur when concrete experiences are used as a criterion of meaning. Jordan describes her mother, a woman who literally died trying to stand up, and the effect that her mother's death had on her own work:

> I think all of this is really about women and work. Certainly this is all about me as a woman and my life work. I mean I am not sure my mother's suicide was something extraordinary. Perhaps most women must deal with a similar inheritance, the legacy of a woman whose death you cannot possibly pinpoint because she died so many, many times and because, even before she became your mother, the life of that woman was taken.... I came too late to help my mother to her feet. By way of everlasting thanks to all of the women who have helped me to stay alive, I am working never to be late again.[58]

While Jordan has knowledge about the concrete act of her mother's death, she also strives for wisdom concerning the meaning of that death.

Some feminist scholars offer a similar claim that women, as a group, are more likely than men to use concrete knowledge in assessing knowledge claims. For example, a substantial number of the 135 women in a study of women's cognitive development were "connected knowers" and were drawn to the sort of knowledge that emerges from firsthand observation. Such women felt that since knowledge comes from experience, the best way of understanding another person's ideas was to try to share the experiences that led the person to form those ideas. At the heart of the procedures used by connected knowers is the capacity for empathy.[59]

In valuing the concrete, African American women may be invoking not only an Afrocentric tradition, but a women's tradition as well. Some feminist theorists suggest that women are socialized in complex relational nexuses where contextual rules take priority over abstract principles in governing behavior. This socialization process is thought to stimulate characteristic ways of knowing.[60] For example, Canadian sociologist Dorothy Smith maintains that two modes of knowing exist, one located in the body and the space it occupies and the other passing beyond it. She asserts that women, through their child-rearing and nurturing activities, mediate these two modes and use the concrete experiences of their daily lives to assess more abstract knowledge claims.[61]

Amanda King, a young black mother, describes how she used the concrete to assess the abstract and points out how difficult mediating these two modes of knowing can be:

> The leaders of the ROC [a labor union] lost their jobs too, but it just seemed like they were used to losing their jobs.... This was like a lifelong thing for them, to get

out there and protest. They were like, what do you call them intellectuals.... You got the ones that go to the university that are supposed to make all the speeches, they're the ones that are supposed to lead, you know, put this little revolution together, and then you got the little ones...that go to the factory everyday, they be the ones that have to fight. I had a child, and I thought I don't have the time to be running around with these people.... I mean I understand some of that stuff they were talking about, like the bourgeoisie, the rich and the poor and all that, but I had surviving on my mind for me and my kid.[62]

For King, abstract ideals of class solidarity were mediated by the concrete experience of motherhood and the connectedness it involved.

In traditional African American communities, black women find considerable institutional support for valuing concrete experience Black extended families and black churches are two key institutions where black women experts with concrete knowledge of what it takes to be self-defined black women share their knowledge with their younger, less experienced sisters. This relationship of sisterhood among black women can be seen as a model for a whole series of relationships that African American women have with each other, whether it is networks among women in extended families, among women in the black church, or among women in the African American community at large.[63]

Since the black church and the black family are both woman-centered and Afrocentric institutions, African American women traditionally have found considerable institutional support for this dimension of an Afrocentric feminist epistemology in ways that are unique to them. While white women may value the concrete, it is questionable whether white families, particularly middle-class nuclear ones, and white community institutions provide comparable types of support. Similarly, while black men are supported by Afrocentric institutions, they cannot participate in black women's sisterhood. In terms of black women's relationships with one another then, African American women may indeed find it easier than others to recognize connectedness as a primary way of knowing, simply because they are encouraged to do so by black women's tradition of sisterhood.

Epistemology and Black Feminist Thought

Living life as an African American woman is a necessary prerequisite for producing black feminist thought because within black women's communities thought is validated and produced with reference to a particular set of historical, material, and epistemological conditions.[64] African American women who adhere to the idea that claims about black women must be substantiated by black women's sense of their own experiences, and who anchor their knowledge claims in an Afrocentric feminist epistemology, have produced a rich tradition of black feminist thought.

Traditionally, such women were blues singers, poets, autobiographers, storytellers, and orators validated by the larger community of black women as experts on a black women's standpoint. Only a few unusual African American feminist scholars have been able to defy Eurocentric masculinist epistemologies and explicitly embrace an Afrocentric feminist epistemology. Consider Alice Walker's description of Zora Neale Hurston: "In my mind, Zora Neale Hurston, Billie Holiday, and Bessie Smith form a sort of unholy trinity. Zora belongs in the tradition of black women singers, rather than among 'the literati.'... Like Billie and Bessie she followed her own road, believed in her own gods, pursued her own dreams, and refused to separate herself from 'common' people.

Zora Neale Hurston is an exception for, prior to 1950, few black women earned advanced degrees, and most of those who did complied with Eurocentric masculinist epistemologies. While these women worked on behalf of black women, they did so within the confines of pervasive race and gender oppression. Black women scholars were in a position to see the exclusion of black women from scholarly discourse, and the thematic content of their work oft reflected their interest in examining a black women's standpoint. However, their tenuous status in academic institutions led them to adhere to Eurocentric masculinist epistemologies so that their work would be accepted as scholarly. As a result, while they produced black feminist thought, those black women most likely to gain academic credentials were often least likely to produce black feminist thought that used an Afrocentric feminist epistemology.

As more black women earn advanced degrees, the range of black feminist scholarship is expanding. Increasing numbers of African American women scholars are explicitly choosing to ground their work in black women's experiences, and, by doing so, many implicitly adhere to an Afrocentric feminist epistemology. Rather than being restrained by their "both/and" status of marginality, these women make curative use of their outsider-within status and produce innovative black feminist thought. The difficulties these women face lie less in demonstrating the technical components of white male epistemologies than in resisting the hegemonic nature of these patterns of thought in order to see, value, and use existing alternative Afrocentric feminist ways of knowing.

In establishing the legitimacy of their knowledge claims, black women scholars who want to develop black feminist thought may encounter the often conflicting standards of three key groups. First, black feminist thought must be validated by ordinary African American women who grow to womanhood "in a world where the saner you are, the madder you are made to appear."[66] To be credible in the eyes of this group, scholars must be personal advocates for their material, be accountable for the consequences of their work, have lived or experienced their material in some fashion, and be willing to engage in dialogues about their findings with ordinary, everyday people. Second, if it is to establish its legitimacy, black feminist thought also must be accepted by the community of black women scholars. These scholars place varying amounts of importance on rearticulating a black women's standpoint using an Afrocentric feminist epistemology. Third, black feminist thought within academia must be prepared to confront Eurocentric masculinist political and epistemological requirements.

The dilemma facing black women scholars engaged in creating black feminist thought is that a knowledge claim that meets the criteria of adequacy for one group and thus is judged to be an acceptable knowledge claim may not be translatable into the terms of a different group. Using the example of Black English, June Jordan illustrates the difficulty of moving among epistemologies: "You cannot 'translate' instances of Standard English preoccupied with abstraction or with nothing/nobody evidently alive into Black English. That would warp the language into uses antithetical to the guiding perspective of its community of users. Rather you must first change those Standard English sentences themselves into ideas consistent with the person-centered assumptions of Black English."[67] While both worldviews share a common vocabulary, the ideas themselves defy direct translation.

Once black feminist scholars face the notion that, on certain dimensions of a black women's standpoint, it may be fruitless to try to translate ideas from an Afrocentric feminist epistemology into a Eurocentric masculinist epistemology, then the choices become clearer. Rather than trying to uncover universal knowledge claims that can withstand the translation from one epistemology to another, time might be better spent rearticulating a black women's standpoint in order to give African American women the tools to resist their own subordination. The goal here is not one of integrating black female "folk culture" into the substantiated body of academic knowledge, for that substantiated knowledge is, in many ways, antithetical to the best interests of black women. Rather, the process is one of rearticulating a preexisting black women's standpoint and recentering the language of existing academic discourse to accommodate these knowledge claims. For those black women scholars engaged in this rearticulation process, the social construction of black feminist thought requires the skill and sophistication to decide which knowledge claims can be validated using the epistemological assumptions of one but not both frameworks, which claims can be generated its one framework and only partially accommodated by the other, and which claims can be made in both frameworks without violating the basic political and epistemological assumptions of either.

Black feminist scholars offering knowledge claims that cannot be accommodated by both frameworks face the choice between accepting the taken for-granted assumptions that permeate white-male-controlled academic institutions or leaving academia. Those black women who choose to remain in academia must accept the possibility that their knowledge claims will be limited to their claims about black women that are consistent with a white male worldview. And yet those African American women who leave academia may find their work is inaccessible to scholarly communities.

Black feminist scholars offering knowledge claims that can be partially accommodated by both epistemologies can create a body of thought that stands outside of either. Rather than trying to synthesize competing worldviews that, at this point in time, defy reconciliation, their task is to point out common themes and concerns. By making creative use of their status as mediators, their thought becomes an entity unto itself that is rooted in two distinct political and epistemological contexts.[68]

Those black feminists who develop knowledge claims that both epistemologies ran accommodate may have found a route to the elusive goal of generating so-called objective generalizations that can stand as universal truths. Those ideas that are validated as true by African American women, African American men, white men, white women, and other groups with distinctive standpoints, with each group using the epistemological approaches growing from its unique standpoint, thus become the most objective truths.[69]

Alternative knowledge claims, in and of themselves, are rarely threatening to conventional knowledge. Such claims are routinely ignored, discredited, or simply absorbed and marginalized in existing paradigms. Much more threatening is the challenge that alternative epistemologies offer to the basic process used by the powerful to legitimate their knowledge claims. If the epistemology used to validate knowledge comes into question, then all prior knowledge claims validated under the dominant model become suspect. An alternative epistemology challenges all certified knowledge and opens up the question of whether what has been taken to be true can stand the test of alternative ways of validating truth. The existence of an independent black women's standpoint using an Afrocentric feminist epistemology calls into question the content of what currently passes as truth and simultaneously challenges the process of arriving at that truth.

Endnotes

1. For analyses of how interlocking systems of oppression affect black women, see Frances Beale, "Double Jeopardy: To Be Black and Female," in *The Black Woman*, ed. Toni Cade (New

York: Signet, 1970); Angela Y. Davis, *Women, Race, and Class* (New York: Random House, 1981); Bonnie Thornton Dill, Race, Class, and Gender: Prospects for an All-Inclusive Sister-hood," *Feminist Studies* 9, no. 1 (1983): 131-50; bell hooks, *Ain't I a Woman? Black Women and Feminism* (Boston: South End Press, 1981); Diane Lewis, "A Response to Inequality: Black Women, Racism, and Sexism," *Signs: Journal of Women in Culture and Society* 3, no. 2 (Winter 1977): 339-61; Pauli Murray, "The Liberation of Black Women," in *Voices of the New Femi-nism*, ed. Mary Lou Thompson (Boston: Beacon Press, 1970), 87-102; and the introduction in Filomina Chioma Steady, *The Black Woman Cross-Culturally* (Cambridge, MA: Schenkman, 1980, 7-41.

2. See the introduction in Steady for an overview of black women's strengths. This strength-resiliency perspective has greatly influx empirical work on African American women. See, eg., Joyce Ladner's study of low-income black adolescent girls, *Tomorrow's Tomorrow* (New York: Doubleday, 1971); and Lena Wright Myers's work on black women's self-concept, *Black Women: Do They Cope Better?* (Englewood Cliffs, NJ: Prentice-Hall, 1980). For discussions of black women's resistance, see Elizabeth Fox-Genovese, "Strategies and Forms of Resistance: Focus on Slave Women in the United Starts," in *In Resistance: Studies in African, Caribbean and Afro-American History*, ed. Gary Y. Okihiro (Amherst: University of Massachusetts Press, 1986), 143-65; and Rosalyn Terborg-Penn, "Black Women in Resistance: A Cross-Cultural Perspective," in Okihiro, *In Resistance*, 188-209. For a comprehensive discussion of everyday resistance, see James C. Scott, *Weapons of the Weak: Everyday Forms of Peasant Resistance* (New Haven, CT: Yale University Press, 1985).

3. See Patricia Hill-Collins's analysis of the substantive content of black feminist thought in "Learning from the Outsider Within: The Sociological Significance of Black Feminist Thought," *Social Problems* 33, no. 6 (1986): 14-32.

4. Scott describes consciousness as the meaning that people give to their acts through the symbols, norms, and ideological forms they create.

5. This thesis is found in scholarship of varying theoretical perspectives. For example, Marx-ist analyses of working-class consciousness claim that "false consciousness" makes the working class unable to penetrate the hegemony of ruling-class ideologies. See Scott's critique of this liter-ature.

6. For example, in Western societies, African Americans have been judged as being less ca-pable of intellectual excellence, more suited to manual labor, and therefore less human than whites. Similarly, white women have lien assigned roles as emotional, irrational creatures ruled by passions and biological urges. They too have been stigmatized as being less than fully human, as being objects. For a discussion of the importance that objectification and dehumanization play in maintaining systems of domination, see Arthur Brittan and Mary Maynard, *Sexism, Racism and Oppression* (New York: Basil Blackwell, 1984).

7. The tendency for Western scholarship process to assess black culture as pathological and deviant illustrates this process. See Rhett S. Jones, "Proving Blacks Inferior: The Sociology of Knowledge," in *The Death of White Sociology*, ed. Joyce Ladner (New York: Vintage, 1973), 114-35.

8. The presence of an independent standpoint does not mean that it uniformly shared by all black women or even that black women fully recognize its contours. By using the concept of stand-point, I do not mean to minimize the rich diversity existing among African American women. I use the phrase "black women's standpoint" to emphasize the plurality of experiences within the over-arching term "standpoint." For discussions of the concept of standpoint, see Nancy M. Hartsock, "The Feminist Standpoint: Developing the Ground for a Specifically Feminist Historical Material-ism," in *Discovering Reality*, ed. Sandra Harding and Merrill Hintikka (Boston: D. Reidel, 1983), 283-310; *Money, Sex, and Power* (Boston: Northeastern University Press, 1983); and Alison M. Jaggar, *Feminist Politics and Human Nature* (Totowa, NJ: Rowman & Allanheld, 1983), 377-89. My use of the standpoint epistemologies as an organizing concept in this essay does not mean that the concept is problem-free. For a helpful critique of standpoint epistemologies, see Sandra Hard-ing, *The Science Question in Feminism* (Ithaca, NY: Cornell University Press, 1986).

9. One contribution of contemporary black women's studies is its documentation of how race, class, and gender have structured these differences. For representative works surveying African American women's experiences, see Paula Giddings, *When and When I Enter: The Im-*

pact of Black Women on Race and Sex in America (New York: William Morrow, 1984); and Jacqueline Jones, *Labor of Love, Labor of Sorrow: Black Women, Work, and the Family from Slavery to the Present* (New York: Basic Books, 1985).

10. For example, Judith Rollins, *Between Women: Domestics and Their Employers* (Philadelphia: Temple University Press, 1985); and Bonnie Thornton Dill, "'The Means to Put My Children Through': Child-Rearing Goals and Strategies among Black Female Domestic Servants," in *The Black Woman*, ed. LaFrances Rodgers-Rose (Beverly Hills, CA: Sage Publications, 1980), 107-23, report that black domestic workers do not see themselves as being the devalued workers that their employers perceive and construct their own interpretations of the meaning of their work. For additional discussions of how black women's consciousness is shaped by the material conditions they encounter, see Ladner, *Tomorrow's Tomorrow*; Myers, *Black Women*; and Cheryl Townsend Gilkes, "'Together and in Harness': Women's Traditions in the Sanctified Church," *Signs* 10, no. 4 (Summer 1985): 678-99. See also Marcia Westkott's discussion of consciousness as a sphere of freedom for women in "Feminist Criticism of the Social Sciences," *Harvard Educational Review* 49, no. 4 (1979): 422-30.

11. John Langston Gwaltney, *Drylongso: A Self-Portrait of Black America* (New York: Vintage, 1980), 4.

12. *Ibid.*, 33.

13. *Ibid.*, 88.

14. *Ibid.*, 7.

15. Victoria Byerly, *Hard Times Cotton Mill Girls: Personal Histories of Womanhood and Poverty in the South* (New York: ILR Press, 1986), 134.

16. See Peter L. Berger and Thomas Luckmann, *The Social Construction of Reality* (New York: Doubleday, 1966), for a discussion of everyday thought and the role of experts in articulating specialized thought.

17. See Michael Omi and Howard Winant, *Racial Formation in the United States* (New York: Routledge & Kegan Paul, 1986), especially 93.

18. In discussing standpoint epistemologies, Hartsock, in *Money, Sex, and Power*, notes that a standpoint is achieved rather than obvious, a mediated rather than immediate understanding" (132).

19. See Scott, *Weapons of the Weak*; and Hartsock, *Money, Sex, and Power*.

20. Some readers may question how one determines whether the ideas of any given African American woman are "feminist" and "Afrocentric." I offer the following working definitions. I agree with the general definition of feminist consciousness provided by black feminist sociologist Deborah K. King: "Any purposes, goals, and activities that seek to enhance the potential of women, to ensure their liberty, afford them equal opportunities, and to permit and encourage their self-determination represent a feminist consciousness, even if they occur within a racial community (in "Race, Class and Gender Salience in Black Women's Womanist Consciousness [typescript, Dartmouth College, Department of Sociology, Hanover, NH, 1987], 22). To be black or Afrocentric, such thought must not only reflect a similar concern for the self-determination of African American people, but must in some way draw upon key elements of an Afrocentric tradition as well.

21. The Eurocentric masculinist process is defined heir as the institutions, paradigms, and any elements of the knowledge-validation procedure controlled by white males and whose purpose is to represent a white male standpoint. While this process represents the interests of powerful white males, various dimensions of the process are not necessarily managed by white males themselves.

22. Karl Mannheim, *Ideology and Utopia: An Introduction to the Sociology of Knowledge* (1936; reprint, New York: Harcourt, Brace & Co., 1954), 276.

23. The knowledge-validation model used in this essay is taken from Michael Mulkay, *Science and the Sociology of Knowledge* (Boston: Allen & Unwin, 1979). For a general discussion of the structure of knowledge, see Thomas Kuhn, *The Structure of Scientific Revolutions* (Chicago: University of Chicago Press, 1962).

24. For analyses of the content and functions of images of black female inferiority, see Mae King, "The Politics of Sexual Stereotypes," *Black Scholar* 4, nos. 6-7 (1973): 12-23; Cheryl Townsend Gilkes, "From Slavery to Social Welfare: Racism and the Control of Black Women," in *Class, Race, and Sex: The Dynamics of Control*, ed. Amy Smerdlow and Helen Lessinger

(Boston: G. K. Hall, 1981), 288-300; and Elizabeth Higginbotham, "Two Representative Issues in Contemporary Sociological Work on Black Women," in *All the Women Are White, All the Blacks Are Men, But Some of Us Are Brave*, ed. Gloria T. Hull, Patricia Bell Scott, and Barbara Smith (Old Westbury, NY: Feminist Press, 1982).

25. Kun, *The Structure*.

26. Evelyn Fox Keller, *Reflections on Gender and Science* (New Haven, CT: Yale University Press, 1985), 167.

27. Maxine Baca Zinn, Lynn Weber Cannon, Elizabeth Higginbotham, and Bonnie Thornton Dill, "The Cost of Exclusionary Practices in Women's Studies," *Signs* II, no. 2 (Winter 1986): 200-303.

28. Berger and Luckmann (in *The Social Construction of Reality*) note that if an outsider group, in this case African American women, recognizes that the insider group, namely, white men, requires special privileges from the larger society, a special problem arises of keeping the outsiders out and at the same time having them acknowledge the legitimacy of this procedure. Accepting a few "safe outsiders is one way of addressing this legitimation problem. Collins's discussion (in "Learning from the Outsider Within") of black women as "outsiders within addresses this issue. Other relevant works include Frantz Fanon's analysis of the role of the national middle class in maintaining colonial systems, *The Wretched of the Earth* (New York: Grove, 1963); and William Tabb's discussion of the use of "bright natives" in controlling African American communities, *The Political Economy of the Black Ghetto* (New York: W. W. Norton, 1970).

29. While I have been describing Eurocentric masculinist approaches as a single process, there are many schools of thought or paradigms subsumed under this one process. Positivism represents one such paradigm. See Harding, *The Science Question*, for an overview and critique of this literature. The following discussion depends heavily on Jaggar, *Feminist Politics*, 355-58.

30. Jaggar, *Feminist Politics*, 356.

31. See Keller, *Reflections on Gender*, 67-126, especially her analysis of static autonomy and its relation to objectivity.

32. Ironically, researchers must "objectify" themselves to achieve this lack of bias. See Arlie Russell Hochschild, "The Sociology of Feeling and Emotion: Selected Possibilities," in *Another Voice: Feminist Perspectives on Social Life and Social Science*, ed. Marcia Millman and Rosabeth Kanter (Garden City, NY: Anchor, 1975), 280-307. Also, see Jaggar, *Feminist Politics*.

33. See Norma Hann, Robert Bellah, Paul Rabinow, and William Sullivan, eds., *Social Science as Moral Inquiry* (New York: Columbia University Press, 1983), especially Michelle Rosaldo's "Moral/Analytic Dilemmas Posed by the Intersection of Feminism and Social Science," 76-96; and Robert Bellah's "The Ethical Aims of Social Inquiry," 360-81.

34. Janice Moulton, "A Paradigm of Philosophy: The Adversary Method," in Harding and Hintikka, *Discovering Reality*, 149-64.

35. For detailed discussions of the Afrocentric worldview, see John S. Mbiti, *African Religions and Philosophy* (London: Heinemann, 1969); Dominique Zahan, *The Religion, Spirituality, and Thought of Traditional Africa* (Chicago: University of Chicago Press, 1979); and Mechal Sobel, *Trabelin' On: The Slave Journey to an Afro-Baptist Faith* (Westport, CT: Greenwood Press, 1979), 1-76.

36. For representative works applying these concepts to African American culture, see Niara Sudarkasa, "Interpreting the African Heritage in Afro-American Family Organization," in *Black Families*, ed. Harriette Pipes McAdoo (Beverly Hills, CA: Sage Publications, 1981); Henry H. Mitchell and Nicholas Cooper Lewter, *Soul Theology: The Heart of American Black Culture* (San Francisco: Harper & Row, 1986); Robert Farris Thompson, *Flash of the Spirit: African and Afro-American Art and Philosophy* (New York: Vintage, 1983); and Ortiz M. Walton, "Comparative Analysis of the African and the Western Aesthetics," in *The Black Aesthetic*, ed. Addison Gayle (Garden City, NY: Doubleday, 1971), 154-64.

37. One of the best discussions of an Afrocentric epistemology is offered by James E. Turner, "Foreword: Africans Studies and Epistemology; a Discourse in the Sociology of Knowledge," in *The Next Decade: Theoretical and Research Issues in African Studies*, ed. James E. Turner (Ithaca, NY: Cornell University African Studies and Research Center, 1984), v-xxv. See also Vernon Dixon, "World Views and Research Methodology," summarized in Harding, *The Science Question*, 170.

38. See Hester Eisenstein, *Contemporary Feminist Thought* (Boston: G. K. Hall, 1983). Nancy Hartsock's *Money, Sex, and Power*, 145-209, offers a particularly insightful analysis of women's oppression.

39. For discussions of feminist consciousness, see Dorothy Smith, "A Sociology for Women," in *The Prism of Sex: Essays in the Sociology of Knowledge*, ed. Julia A. Sherman and Evelyn T. Beck (Madison: University of Wisconsin Press, 1979); and Michelle Z. Rosaldo, "Women, Culture, and Society: A Theoretical Overview," in *Women, Culture, and Society*, ed. Michelle Z. Rosaldo and Louise Lamphere (Stanford, CA: Stanford University Press, 1974), 17-42. Feminist epistemologies are surveyed by Jaggar, *Feminist Politics*.

40. One significant difference between Afrocentric and feminist standpoints is that much of what is termed women culture is, unlike African American culture, treated in the context of and produced by oppression. Those who argue for a women's culture are electing to value, rather than denigrate, those traits associated with females in white patriarchal societies. While this choice is important, it is not the same as identifying an independent, historical culture associated with a society. I am indebted to Deborah K. King for this point.

41. Critiques of the Eurocentric masculinist knowledge-validation process by both Africanist and feminist scholars illustrate this point. What one group labels "white" and "Eurocentric," the other describes as "male-dominated" and "masculinist." Although he does not emphasize its patriarchal and racist features, Morris Berman's *The Reenchantment of the World* (New York: Bantam Books, 1981) provides a historical discussion of Western thought. Afrocentric analyses of this same process can be found in Molefi Kete Asante, "International/Intercultural Relations," in *Contemporary Black Thought*, ed. Molefi Kete Asante and Abdulai S. Vandi (Beverly Hills, CA: Sage Publications, 1980), 43-58; and Dona Richards, "European Mythology: The Ideology of 'Progress,'" in Asante and Vandi, *Contemporary Black Thought*, 59-79. For feminist analyses, see Hartsock, *Money, Sex, and Power*. Harding also discusses this similarity (see Chap. 7, "Other 'Others' and Fractured Identities: Issues for Epistemologists," 63-96).

42. Harding, *The Science Question*, 166.

43. D. King, "Race, Class and Gender Salience."

44. Bonnie Thornton Dill, "The Dialectics of Black Womanhood," *Signs* 4, no. 3 (Spring 1979: 543-55.

45. One implication of standpoint approaches is that the more subordinate the group, the purer the vision of the oppressed group. This is an outcome of the origins of standpoint approaches in Marxist social theory, itself a dualistic analysis of social structure. Because such approaches rely on quantifying and ranking human oppressions—familiar tenets of positivist approaches—they are rejected by blacks and feminists alike. See Harding, *The Science Question*, for a discussion of this point. See also Elizabeth V. Spelman's discussion of the fallacy of additive oppression in "Theories of Race and Gender: The Erasure of Black Women," *Quest* 5, no. 4 (1982): 36-62.

46. Class differences among black women may be marked. For example, see Paula Giddings's analysis (in *When and Where I Enter*) of the role of social class in shaping black women's activism; or Elizabeth Higginbotham's study of the effects of social class to black women's college attendance in "Race and Class Barriers to Black Women's College Attendance," *Journal of Ethnic Studies* 13, no. I (1985): 89-107. Those African American women who have experienced the greatest degree of convergence of race, class, and gender oppression may be in a better position to recognize and use an alternative epistemology.

47. Gwaltney, *Drylongso*, 83.

48. William L. Andrews, *Sisters of the Spirit: Three Black Women's Autobiographies of the Nineteenth Century* (Bloomington: Indiana University Press, 1986), 85.

49. Gwaltney, *Drylongso*, 147.

50. Geneva Smitherman, *Talkin and Testifyin: The Language of Black America* (Detroit: Wayne State University Press, 1986), 76.

51. Gwaltney, *Drylongso*, 68.

52. *Ibid.*, 7.

53. *Ibid.*, 27, 33.

54. Elsa Barkley Brown, "Hearing Our Mothers' Lives" (paper presented at the Fifteenth Anniversary Faculty Lecture Series, African American and African Studies, Emory University, Atlanta, 1986.

55. Ladner, *Tomorrow's Tomorrow.*

56. Mitchell and Lewter, *Soul Theology.* The use of the narrative approach in African American theology exemplifies an inductive system of logic alternately called "folk wisdom" or a survival-based, need-oriented method of assessing knowledge claims

57. *Ibid.*, 8.

58. June Jordan, *On Call: Political Essays* (Boston: South End Press, 1985), 26.

59. Mary Belenky, Blythe Clinchy, Nancy Goldberger, and Jill Tarule, *Women's Ways of Knowing* (New York: Basic Books, 1986), 113.

60. Hartsock, *Money, Sex, and Power*, 237; and Nancy Chodorow, *The Reproduction of Mothering* (Berkeley and Los Angeles: University of California Press, 1978).

61. Dorothy Smith, *The Everyday World as Problematic* (Boston: Northeastern University Press, 1987).

62. Byerly, *Hard Times Cotton Mill Girls*, 198.

63. For black women's centrality in the family, see Steady, *The Black Woman*; Ladner, *Tomorrow's Tomorrow*; Brown, "Hearing Our Mothers' Lives"; and McAdoo, *Black Families.* See Gilkes, "'Together and in Harness,'" for black women in the church; and chapter 4 of Deborah Gray White, *Ar'n't I a Woman? Female Slaves in the Plantation South* (New York: W. W. Norton, 1985). See also Gloria Joseph, "Black Mothers and Daughters: Their Roles and Functions in American Society," in *Common Differences: Conflicts in Black and White Feminist Perspectives*, ed. Gloria Joseph and Jill Lewis (Garden City, NY: Anchor, 1981), 75-126. Even though black women play essential roles in black families and black churches, these institutions are not free from sexism.

64. Black men, white women, and members of other race, class, add gender groups should be encouraged to interpret, teach, and critique the black feminist thought produced by African American women.

65. Walker, *In Search of Our Mothers' Gardens* (New York: Harcourt Brace Jovanovich, 1974), 91.

66. Gwaltney, *Drylongso.*

67. Jordan, *On Call*, 130.

68. Collins, "Learning from the Outsider Within."

69. This point addresses the question of relativity in the sociology of knowledge and offers a way of regulating competing knowledge claims.

17.

But Who Do You Really Belong To — Black Studies or Women's Studies?

Barbara Christian

I entitled my paper, "But Who Do You Really Belong To—Black Studies or Women's Studies?" because in the last decade I, and many of my sisters, have been asked that question, not so often in words as in the social gestures and roles demanded of us in Black Studies and Women's Studies, both marginal institutions in the universities. When we black women scholars who came out of the sixties see each other, we inevitably discuss that question and even though we know the correct answer is "Both Black Studies and Women's Studies," the realities of a university process belie such a pat response.

There is another reason for my title. Not so long ago, one of the graduate women of color on my campus came to me in tears because she'd been directly asked that question. Her rage, her frustration at her integrity being questioned, her awareness that she was being characterized as marginal to these already marginalized university programs caused her to doubt whether she could endure being a feminist scholar of color. Fragmentation, dilution, the need continually to defend one's existence, she thought, would be her fate.

Her outburst was not the first I've heard (nor do I expect it to be the last) from younger women who I'd hoped would continue the work we'd begun. Inevitably I am left with a quickening sense of my own rage and a question about whether our point of view can be articulated in the halls of academe. But this piece is not about the sexism and racism that exist in the university and are kept in place to some extent by the very structures within which we attempt to critique the university, I am sure we all know that I know we've also heard many times that Third World Women often fall between the cracks, between the two categories, minorities and women. This brief paper is focused more on *how* we fall between the cracks what conflicts of choice we have and what possibilities for action are open to us. My analysis is rooted not only in my own personal history and experience but also in the experiences of some of my peers with whom I have discussed this issue. And my aim is to raise these issues in the woman's community in general, and in Afro-American Studies and literary circles in particular, in order to enlarge our understanding of the experience of trying to be a feminist scholar of color in America.

As many of you know, I've spent much of my adult life studying the literature of black women. Yes—there was a particular moment in time when I asked myself the question—Where am I in the literature? The first time I asked, Where am I in British and American literature? Where was the black, the colonized, the racially oppressed woman? What have we said? The second time, some years later, I looked for my place in Afro-American literatures. Where am I?—the girl, the woman, the sexual female, the abused woman. What have we said?

I doubt I would have asked these "obvious" questions when I did, if the social context had not provided me with a psychologically exciting though not necessarily safe space within which to ask them. The words, gestures, music of the fifties and sixties, the Black movement and the seventies' women's movements suggested the power and the richness of those previously neglected literatures. Not only were my personal moments significant, but that they were *two* different moments rather than *one* is an indication of the complexity of the American social context. The first moment did not cancel out the need for the second. Yet there seemed to be a conflict of choice and possibility that feminist scholars sometimes experience, for Afro-American Studies, Ethnic Studies, and Women Studies, the institutions which grew out of political movements of the sixties and seventies, are themselves sometimes in conflict.

So the specific ways in which these two institutions evolved on specific campuses, the sequence in which they developed, the extent to which one was more successful than the other in maneuvering campus bureaucracy, and the faculty of each institution—all these factors affect the choices black feminist scholars make about their home and their proper alliance. We, or more precisely the *singular one* that we usually are, often become a kind of bride between Afro-American Studies, Women Studies, and even traditional disciplines. There is often a black feminist scholar on one university campus who is one-third in Afro-American Studies, one-third in Women Studies, and one-third in English, let's say, or who is situated in one of these departments with the understanding that she is the liaison person between the three. The one that we are is usually the only *woman* in Black Studies, the *only person of color* in Women Studies, or in one's traditional department. It is not that we fall between the cracks but that we are the filler for too many cracks. What that kind of fragmentation can do to one's time is obvious. Not always so obvious is the possible effects such fragmentation or "bridging" (depending on your point of view) might have on one's scholarly foci and intentions.

Many of us chose to be black feminist scholars because we believed ideas could help to effect social change and that the university, though imperfect, *was* a place where ideas are important. Many of us entered academe not only because we liked doing research and teaching but because we believed the study of black and Third World Women would necessarily involve a critique of existing structures. We reasoned that since black and Third World Women occupied that vortex at which race, sex, and class interact and since we had been excluded from academic life for so long, the university had itself lost out. It had lost a source of energy from the world it purported to contemplate. We thought our presence in academia would be a galvanizing one. However, many of us were not prepared for the exclusive ways in which the categories of race, class, and gender are studied, the way the very definitions of these concepts imply that women of color do not exist.

The scholar who explores questions of race within the context of different disciplines often sees gender as a wrinkle on the group fabric, as if people do not always come in two sexes. The woman scholar often sees race or class questions as somehow diluting rather than strengthening a feminist approach, as if men and women do not usually belong to a particular ethnic group and do not belong to or aspire to belong to a particular class. Each sees the other's subject as "deviant" in his or her field. Race, of course, usually refers to non-white; gender, of course, to non-male—the "nots" and "nos" indicate deviations from a pure field. That black feminist scholars bridge two, sometimes three, fields immediately suggests the inaccuracy of viewing these categories as pure and exclusive. Such abstractions negatively affect our work because they limit our possible perspective. For example, I have seen studies of Toni Morrison from an exclusively Afro-American perspective, from an exclusively "woman's" perspective, and from an exclusively "literary" perspective. So exclusive are these treatments that someone who did not know that Morrison was a black, female, writer would not know that these papers were all about the same writer's work. How to satisfy the "pure" demands of any of these three areas, or, what is more common, how not to be perceived as merely marginal to any of these three areas, as mere icing on the real cake, can be devastating for the black feminist scholar and can result in paralysis, in a sense of alienation, in the feeling that one is in a position of always validating oneself, that one must subscribe to reigning concerns of others. As one black feminist scholar said to me recently, instead of having to deal with the term "universal," we now have to contend with "theory" and with the pure categories of Gender, Race, and Class upon which it relies.

Increasingly, the term "theory" has come to represent to some of us the co-optation of these marginal points of view by academic language. By theory, let me hasten to add, I mean the tendency towards gross generalizations about culture, language, literature, and gender; theory also suggests the tendency towards philosophical and abstract logic in which some American academic circles have been engaging for the last few years. Activism has been reduced to that moment when one produces a theory that can be understood by only a few others in the world. As was the case in the sixties, standards of excellence are again the reason for exclusivity—thus the irrelevance of people who are not in one's very specific field—for there is no reason why any others should understand the ideas that might affect their lives. Scholarly focus and intentions have shifted even for marginal groups like Afro-American Studies and Women Studies from the need for social transformation that implies some responsibility to constituencies outside academe to the scholar's need for validation within academic situations.

There are scholars, I hear, who produce feminist theory and there are those of us, I guess, who practice feminist theory. Among the latter are usually listed women of color. Theory, in other words, occupies a different space from the study of the intersection of class/race/gender that the study of American women of color implies. It is so much easier, though, to make general statements about WOMEN in the abstract or BLACKS in the abstract than it is to make general statements about, let's say, poor black women who may be from the North, South, East or West, from an extended or nuclear family, which is why the concrete theorizing one finds in narratives is so appealing to me. Theory is precisely the problem upon which a black feminist scholar stumbles. Having been excluded so many times from so many camps, we are, I think, particularly attuned to the dangers of the abstract generalization. It may be why the concrete theorizing we find in our literature is so appealing even to those of us in the social sciences. And, frankly, I find the narrative theorizing of say a Toni Morrison or an Alice Walker to be far more dynamic, significant, and useful than the majority of lit crit theory being published today. Most of us barely know our own literature exists, yet we often feel compelled to create "smart" categories within which to contain it, as if it were a completed object, we are contemplating rather than engaging in a live intellectual process.

Another area of concern for women scholars of color is a tension between cultural style and ideological position. Most Ethnic Studies and Afro-American Studies programs, for example, either avoid issues about lesbianism or are downright hostile to them. That is an ideological conflict that feminist scholars often face in an Ethnic Studies or Afro-American Studies frame of reference. Women scholars of color often experience discomfort with the cultural style of Women's Studies, with its language, its modes of maneuvering, its assumptions about goals. *We must*, for example, be concerned about the men of our cultural groups, and that concern affects our understanding and articulation of feminist issues. For example, it is important to me that black men in America have been just as fetishized as sex objects, as women have been. And that realization affects my critique of gender issues. Yet I and most of my sisters who are concerned about the relationship between men and women in our group would not replace the word "feminist" with "gender" as so many Women Studies institutions are doing today so that men will feel more comfortable about the research on women.

One of my colleagues pointed out:

> I've work with black men all my life, sometimes in rage, sometimes in harmony. I understand that terrain. But it is only recently that I've begun working with white women, who after all until recently were conceptualized as part of the problem rather than part of any solution. I'm still learning to read their style which often spells "white" to me rather than "women."

Trust, then, is another issue that affects the choices we make. Who can we trust if we are to help ourselves? Lately, as both Ethnic Studies and Women Studies programs purge themselves, in order to fit into the more conservative scheme of the eighties, I have heard many a young feminist scholar of color speak more confidently of the traditional department as the place where one might be safest. What such a tendency will mean for the development of a Third World feminist approach is not hard to predict.

Our problem is that we do not have "home really fitted to our needs," for the study of women of color is itself a critique of Afro-American Studies and Women Studies, yet these groups are hardly powerful institutions in the university and their validity is still in question. Consequently, even though we are often perceived as "asides" in these groups, we are in the unenviable position of having to protect them, since they are usually the only groups that even acknowledge our existence.

Barbara Smith has proposed a solution to the homelessness we experience — Black Women Studies Institutes. Frankly I do not see this solution as a viable one, given the political tone of the country and the way in which the few women scholars of color who are secure enough to engage in such an experiment are scattered all over the country. But more importantly, such units would bypass the central issue — the inappropriateness of studying gender, race, and class as pure categories.

It is this challenge that I see as one exciting possibility for women scholars of color, a possibility that has developed out of the conflict of choices we face. It is, I think, the great contribution we can make to scholarship, despite the fragmented situations with which we must contend. How strong and well-wrought our critique will be depends, I think, on the number and quality of young women scholars of color who will be inclined to pursue this perspective and who will be hired in Afro-American Studies and Women Studies and Women Studies Programs. It is why I think this issue must receive as much discussion and analysis as we can give it so that a student such as the one I mentioned at the beginning of the paper will see that she is central to a great intellectual challenge. Her work may help substantially to change the way we study ourselves. Rather than being marginal to the concerns of Afro-American Studies and Women Studies, the women scholar of color must work toward redefinition of traditional categories.

III

Section III

Historical Perspectives

Key Concepts and Major Terms

- Historical Foundations
- Contemporary Academia
- Transdisciplinary
- Negro History
- Social Inquiry
- American Negro Studies
- Talented Tenth
- Black Curriculum
- Professionalization

- Pan-African
- Extracurricular Activities
- Diaspora
- Africana
- Afro-Caribbean Studies
- Separatism
- Intellectual Validity
- Black Studies
- The New Discipline

- African Heritage
- Afrocentric
- Traditionalist
- Feminist
- Slavery
- White Social Science
- Black Social Science
- Institutionalization

Introduction

Although the study of African American life, culture and history was included in the course offerings of most historically black colleges/universities and some predominantly white institutions, it was not until the 1960s that courses in African American Studies were developed and offered widely in institutions of higher education. Prior to this period, however, there were a variety of attempts to institute African American Studies in one form or another (on and off college campuses) by numerous individuals, groups, and organizations, and these efforts provide the historical foundation of the discipline.

For example, Alexander Crummell worked to establish the American Negro Academy (1897), a forum which would recognize and present the scholarly work of African Americans while simultaneously protecting "...the race from vicious assaults, in all lines of learning and truth"; W.E.B. DuBois instituted a pioneer series at Atlanta University to study African American families, churches, schools, and other socio-political institutions within the community; the Negro Women's club movement had an impact on prospectives about the relationship between education and a social, moral responsibility to the race; Arthur A. Schomburg, in a 1913 speech, informed black teachers at Cheyney University that he wished to "fire [their] racial patriotism by the study of... Negro books," and proceeded to provide a virtual sanctuary, the Schomburg Center for Research in Black Culture, where they could "amend [the curriculum to] include the practical history of the Negro race... " using his extensive collection of historical information on the African world; and finally, the "Father of Black History," Carter G. Woodson, organized the Association for the Study of Negro Life and History in 1915, the Journal of Negro History in 1916, Negro History Week in 1926, and finally, the Negro History Bulletin in 1933, through which he wanted to make African American history available to all, irrespective of age, education, class, or color.

In this section, then, each of the articles focuses on the history of the development of African American Studies and the study of African American culture more broadly. The first selection by Lawrence Crouchett offers evidence of early African American Studies practiced by white and black advocates, looking closely at nineteenth century efforts to produce and disseminate scholarship about African people. John Bunzel provides a detailed description of the creation of the first African American Studies department at San Francisco State University, considering the role of black students and the president in hiring Dr. Nathan Hare along with the subsequent conflict and bitterness (they) created among the white faculty.

The next three articles describe the historical background of the discipline. Ronald Bailey articulates concern about the critical and interpretative history of the black intellectual tradition, suggesting that the full significance of this scholarship in contemporary academia can be grasped only by reading it in its historical context. The selection by St. Clair Drake treats conflicts that have developed within African American Studies in the existing educational system regarding its initial purpose in the discipline. The next selection reviews the extent to which three groups of scholars respond to past and present social, economic, political and educational conditions of African Americans. The last selection in this section argues that African American Studies will be compelled to strengthen its transdisciplinary and global thrusts.

In "Early Black Studies Movements," Lawrence Crouchett reports: "Prior to the eighteenth century, the first known and white-approved organized advocacy of what might be termed 'black studies' came from the Quaker educators.... A second attempt to organize a black historical unit came in Philadelphia, in 1892, where a group of blacks incorporated the American Negro Historical Society... at the turn of the century, a black studies 'curriculum' was simply a course in 'Negro history,' designed to give blacks dignity in the face of growing daily insults from white Southern Americans and... of increased published assertions of Negro inferiority by white-Northern and Southern scholars."

In "Black Studies in Historical Perspective," Ronald Bailey contends: "If Black Studies is to become a workable area of endeavor, what is perhaps most needed is some explication of the notion of social inquiry... the context in which black social inquiry is embedded and argues for the development of the Pan-African frame as the most relevant one for black intellectual activity.... Conspicuous by its absence in contemporary academia is a critical and interpretative history of black intellectual traditions. Such a history seems essential if we are to properly understand current attempts to develop a newer framework for black social inquiry."

Vivian V. Gordon, in "The Coming of Age of Black Studies," makes the observation that black studies may be defined as analysis of the factors and conditions which have affected the economic, psychological, legal, and moral status of the African in America as well as the African in the Diaspora. Not only is Black Studies concerned with the culture of the ethnic Afro-American, as historically and socio-logically defined by the traditional literature, it is also concerned with the development of new approaches to study of the Black experience and with the development of social policies which will impact positively upon the lives of Black people.

In the article, "The Struggle and Dream of Black Studies," Carlene Young explains that Afro-American Studies, Black Studies, Pan-African, Africana, and Afro-Caribbean Studies are but different names for programs of study that focus on the systematic investigation of people of African descent in their contacts with Europeans, their dispersal throughout the Diaspora, and the subsequent institutionalization of racism and oppression as means of economic, political, and social subordination. The systematic study of the Afro-American experience from its African heritage to contemporary society and beyond is nowhere else pursued in the Academy than in Black Studies programs and departments.

In "The Black Studies Movement: Afrocentric-Traditionalist-Feminist Paradigm's for the Next Stage," Darlene Clark Hine argues that: "The tortured birth of Black Studies has long affected how this newest of the academic disciplines has been perceived and evaluated. But this is not the only difficulty impeding a judicious assessment of its institutional and intellectual evolution. Race remains a substantial barrier that blocks and distorts our views."

In a study commissioned by the Ford Foundation in 1984, Nathan Huggins concluded that: "It seems to me that the movement to make academically legitimate the study of a wide range of issues and questions having to do with its black experience in America has been the most valuable outcome of the [Black] struggle during the last decade. Afro-American Studies will achieve greater impact and influence the more it is permitted to resonate in the conventional disciplines."

Finally, in "What Happened to Black Studies," St. Clair Drake recalls that: "The primary goal of the black studies movement during its early stages was to utilize the classroom as well as extracurricular activities for raising the consciousness and heightening the group pride of black students so that they would be transformed from 'Negroes,' anxious to be integrated into 'blacks,' convinced that 'black is beautiful' and ready to struggle for Black Power."

The essays which comprise Section III all focus on the central importance on the relationship between African American history and the evolution of African American Studies. Students need to be made more aware of the various struggles African American Studies has experienced both in and outside the university. At the same time, it is essential for readers to know that the questions (i.e. relevance, validity, content, focus, and direction) surrounding African American studies in its beginnings, and especially since its emergence and evolution on predominantly white campuses continue to resonate in the twenty-first century.

18.

Early Black Studies Movements

Lawrence P. Crouchett

The ways the first Afro-Americans—slaves and free blacks—acquired and transmitted their knowledge of their history and culture are very significant. Some picked up the knowledge in a piecemeal fashion, others through a formal educational process, such as the Sabbath schools and true bands. Often the more literate blacks secretly communicated to their fellow men what they knew of Africa, African heritage, and the ways blacks were being exploited and oppressed in America. Shrewdly, these early black "teachers" and "preachers" gave private lessons in black history and culture unbeknown to whites. Their secret classrooms were the fields, work groups, restricted social gatherings, and black churches. Their textbooks were the Scriptures and "Ethiopianism," which they acquired from Greek and Roman literature.

Prior to the eighteenth century, the first known and white-approved organized advocacy of what might be termed "black studies" came from the Quaker educators. Though only a minor part of their total "educational" program for blacks, these Quaker efforts still served to inspire the developing interest in African and Afro-American history and culture. The Hicksite Quakers, having organized the earliest, most permanent, and best developed schools devoted to the education of blacks, endeavored to teach them "to be capable of discharging the duties of equal and total citizenship" (Drake, 1950: 43-44).

A well-defined movement to disseminate information about black history, culture, and contributions appeared as early as 1713, when the Pennsylvania Quakers devised a definite program for educating and training free blacks to serve as missionaries on the African continent (Woodson, 1919: 54). They saw a need for a "special" type of education for such blacks and taught them about the culture, history, and geography of black Africa. This was in line with Quaker educational philosophy of providing the individual with a chance to correct his "narrow individualism" in the light of the experiences of the group. George Fox, a great Quaker teacher of the time, urged an education that included "everything civil and useful." Quaker education passing through this transitory stage—from a "guarded" to a more fearless, broad and expansive curriculum—could easily feel the teaching about Africa was morally right.

In 1741, for example, Bishop Secker, a Quaker "colonizationist," suggested "special" education for blacks who could return to Africa to teach their countrymen about Christianity, including "stories" about Africa and its people (Woodson, 1919: 40). In fact Quakers, despite their alleged interruption of the religious uniformity of the colony, showed such determination and zeal in this new effort that the Virginia colonial legislature enacted a law excluding Quakers from the teaching profession (Drake, 1950: 18-169).

These Quaker colonizationists, who sought to resettle freed slaves in Africa, often urged the teaching of "black history" to the free blacks with the hope that this would cause them to see more clearly their humiliation and would make them so discontented with America that they could welcome emigration to Africa.

Between 1799 and 1826, knowledgeable blacks were reciting the exploits of Toussaint L'Overture, the black Haitian revolutionary, to fellow blacks. Black refugees from Haiti— settling in Baltimore, Norfolk, Charleston, and New Orleans—often gave firsthand accounts of how particular West Indian blacks had defeated whites— French, Spanish, and English—to right the wrongs against island blacks. These accounts served as examples that both enslaved and free black men later emulated in their many insurrections against oppression. Afro-Americans who could not read learned of Toussaint's feats from others in their Sabbath schools and by word-of-mouth (Russwurm, 1826). Blacks now had before them the daring deeds of Toussaint and his cohorts, the bold attempt of Gabriel Prosser in 1800, and, later, the far-reaching plans of Denmark Vesey in 1822; and there were the autobiographical "slave narratives" to counter any disparagement of their bravery and willingness to escape from slavery.

In 1806, a French statesman, Gregoire (1967) wrote a book to answer charges made by Thomas Jefferson (1964: 135-143), who questioned the mental capacity of blacks. Gregoire prepared a list of distinguished black men who had reached eminence and distinction in all lines of endeavor throughout history. In dedicating the book to Jefferson, he urged the President to read and familiarize himself with the history and accomplishments of blacks. During his second term of office, Jefferson (n.d.: 429) responded to M. Gregoire:

> My doubts were the result of personal observation on the limited sphere of my own state, when the opportunities for the development of their genius were not favorable, and those exercising it still less so. I expressed them, therefore, with great hesitation; but whatever be their degree of talent, it is no measure of their rights.... I pray you, therefore, to accept my thanks for the many instances you have enabled me to observe of respectable intelligence in that race of men, which cannot fail to have effect in hastening the day of their relief.

Outstanding black individuals, such as David Walker (1965: 19) who pointed to the "greatness of Africa" in his 1829 *Appeals*, the former slave Frederick Douglass, and David Ruggles and Charlotte Forten, both free blacks, in the 1850s, all spoke of the need for black and white understanding of the cultural and historical contributions of black Americans. Even Northern teachers in the Freedmen's schools during Reconstruction (1865-1868) often inserted "black contributions" in their lessons, using "slaves narratives" and tattered copies of James W. C. Pennington's 1841 *Text Book* as teaching aids. Laura Towne, a New Englander teaching in the Port Royal Freedmen's school in 1865 describes a geography exercise used there which included a unit extolling the "wisest country of all times being Egypt in 'Africa'" (Rose, 1957: 372).

Library societies founded in Philadelphia (1832) and New York (1833) before the Civil War were representative of black Americans' early interest in history and culture (Aptheker, 1963: 138). Their emphasis on Africa and the military role of black Americans in the Revolution and the War of 1812 paralleled typical American interests of the time. Though limited by laws which prohibited the teaching of reading and writing to black slaves and freemen, these societies did supplement their lending libraries with forensic societies, where Afro-Americans' oral history and contributions were popular topics (Porter, 1936: 562-563, 568, 570). In a few black and white educational institutions, teachers and students learned lessons about "blackness" in geography class.

Interest in Afro-American history and culture gained fresh vigor following the Reconstruction Era. "Negro history" became the thread that was to carry all aspects of the past black Americans. Many historical works by black authors appeared during this period. The first to attract the attention of scholars was George W. Williams' two-volume *History of the Negro Race in America* in 1882, followed by E.A. Johnson's *School History of the Negro Race* in 1893.

The widespread interest aroused by these books led to attempts to form Negro historical societies. The first such movement came in 1873 when a resolution was introduced at the National Equal Rights Convention "to create a national historical and statistical association for the purpose...[of gathering] all such facts, historical and statistical, in relation to the Negro race in America, for the reference of all who desire to know the true history" (Wesley, 1952). This effort was preceded only by the German-American historical societies that had been organized as early as 1868. Several other ethnic historical societies were born during this period: the Huguenot Society of America, which also had a religious basis, in 1883; the Holland Society of New York, in 1885 — (the Jewish Publication Society of America was publishing historical works that same year) — and the integrated Scotch-Irish Society of America in 1889.

A second attempt to organize a black historical unit came in Philadelphia, in 1892, where a group of blacks incorporated the American Negro Historical Society. Local in scope, it confined its collection about the blacks in Philadelphia. This same year saw the founding of the American Jewish Historical Society.

Two more societies organized in 1897 both noted the need to rectify wrongs committed by historians of that period: the American Irish Historical Society and the American Negro Academy. The latter ceased operation in 1915.

Though black Americans made many efforts to begin their own historical society during this "age of historical societies," permanent success did not come until September 9, 1916 when the Association for the Study of Negro Life and History was organized in Chicago under the leadership of Edward Bruce, Arthur A. Schomburg, and Dr. Carter G. Woodson. Earlier Bruce and Schomburg had founded the Negro Society of Historical Research at the turn of the century which published a work by Schomburg calling for the teaching of Negro history in schools and colleges (Schomburg, 1906).

In arguing for first-class citizenship, black leaders as early as 1896 had expressed the hope that "black children be taught something about their African past and the role their people played in the development of this country" (Terrell, 1896). And in 1898, the Cleveland Gazette (a black newspaper) insisted that "Every Afro-American school ought for obvious reasons to compel its students to study Williams' *History of the Negro Race.*"

As the lines of racial hatred hardened during the 1890s, collective efforts among Afro-Americans to enhance self respect and a new self-image in their people increased. While white America passively watched the lynching of black Americans grow to a rate of one every 54 hours (NAACP, 1919), these black advocates sought to use "Negro history" to foster racial pride and solidarity and, at the same time, serve as an antidote to prejudice and discrimination against Afro-Americans.

Some credit for the general interest in the African past and black Americans' contributions can be assigned to the dominance of Booker T. Washington's educational philosophy in the 1890s. The study of "Negro history" augmented Washington's goal of renewing black self-pride and the desire for self-help through vocational rather than classical education. However, greater credit must be reserved for the efforts of Dr. W.E.B. DuBois. DuBois initiated and taught the first formal "black curriculum" at Atlanta University in 1897. Here he taught sociology and inaugurated the first scientific study of the conditions of black people covering all important aspects of black life.

The felt needs for a "black studies" thrust in the early 1900s can be found in the rhetoric of contemporary protest Lawrence Reddick's (1937: 17) words can still be heard, loudly and clearly: "Negro History is quite different from the study of the Negro. Frankly, the former differs from the latter in that Negro History has a purpose which is built upon a faith." Obviously, then and now, black studies served to provide compensatory and ideological purposes. To repeat, at the turn of the century, a black studies curriculum" was simply a course in "Negro history," designed to give blacks dignity in the face of growing daily insults from white Southern Americans and to provide arguments for equality in the face of increased published assertions of Negro inferiority by white—Northern and Southern—scholars (Newby, 1968: 22). This "black history" sought to focus on black Americans' historical roles (for example by revealing the deeds of Negroes in American wars) and cultural traditions (including study of early black poets, writers, and inventors). The curriculum tried to locate the "basic cause of their [Negro] problems within the realm of segregation" (Bullock, 1967: 203)—which was the common pattern of race relations in this period. It also attempted to reveal any Negro ancestry in prominent figures such as Dumas, Pushkin, and Alexander Hamilton. To paraphrase Myrdal (1964), black studies always served the same purpose as general education: to make [black] students functional participants in this democratic society—except, perhaps, that black studies includes special strategies for meeting and resolving Afro-Americans'—individual and collective—problems in the United States.

Advocates of black studies in the first two decades of the twentieth century concentrated on "sanitizing" their black brothers, whom they accused of displaying shame of their ancestry by not wishing to belong to Negro churches, live in Negro neighborhoods, send their children to Negro schools, or patronize Negro business and professional men. Negro children, these advocates said, "should be taught about the 'glorious deeds' of Negro men and women" before they learned of the deed of other [white] Americans. They hoped this exposure would stimulate and foster race pride "and furnish an atmosphere of mutual cooperation and helpfulness that will change the winter of our discontent into the glorious summer of racial solidarity, that magic alembic in which most of our racial difficulties will disappear" (Roman, 1911: 30).

This era saw a renewed interest among black intellectuals in African history. Questing for a larger identification, they began to write and encourage "lay" interest in African culture. This gave rise to a renewed pride in American Negro folk culture, especially the "spirituals." Black colleges and high schools soon organized choral groups around these "plantation songs" introduced to a national audience by the famous Fisk Jubilee Singers during Reconstruction. Ironically, a group of Howard University students revolted against singing the melodies to visitors, preferring to sing them only among Negroes (New York Age, 1890).

Black Americans' use of "history" as a tool to rectify wrongs committed by white writers is best understood in the context of the pre-World War I generation, when Americans were probably more historically minded than in any other period. Thus the blacks, in choosing this device, did not differ from white Southerners who were still waving the "bloody shirt" of Reconstruction.

By World War I, a diffusion of knowledge, through pamphlets, newspaper articles, books, and propaganda from black scholars caused a few colleges to initiate a "black studies" curriculum—usually one course such as "Negro Problems," "Race Relations," or "Negro History."

The Association for the Study of Negro Life and History deserve much credit for stimulating this movement. Under the direction of Dr. Carter G. Woodson, the organization sought to collect "sociological and historical documents and promote studies bearing on the Negro." Again, black scholars and teachers joined in the effort, by writing scholarly articles and transposing the black "perspective" into their classrooms in the Negro colleges. Later, a few white scholars found the association a good medium for publication of their works.

The first report on black studies courses offered in a Northern college was made by Woodson in 1919, when he also reported that no Southern institution of higher learning included a course bearing on Negro life and history. He reported the following black studies offerings:

(1) Ohio State University—Slavery Struggles in the United States

(2) Nebraska University—The Negro Problem Under Slavery and Freedom

(3) Stanford University—Immigration and the Race Problem

(4) University of Oklahoma—Modern Race Problems

(5) University of Missouri—The Negro in America

(6) University of Chicago—The Negro in America

(7) University of Minnesota—The American Negro

(8) Harvard University—American Population Problems: Immigration and the Negro.

Woodson (1919: 278) concluded:

This study of the race problem has in many cases been unproductive of desirable results for the reason that instead of trying to arrive at some understanding as to how the Negro may be improved, the work [in courses] has often degenerated into a discussion of the race as a menace and the justification of preventive measures inaugurated by the whites.

He also reported that a few Negro colleges were offering courses in sociology and history "bearing on the Negro." Though handicapped by the lack of trained teachers, Tuskeegee, Atlanta University, Fisk, Wilberforce, and Howard offered such courses, even at the risk of their becoming expressions of opinions "without data to support them."

Marcus Garvey and his black nationalist movement of the 1920s gave further impetus to Woodson's crusade for Black Studies courses. Public schools, especially high schools, in New York and Philadelphia, allowed free time for courses in black history. Garvey's emotional speeches on the "grandeur of Africa" and "the racial superiority of blacks" sent interested scholars and teachers back to library shelves in search of materials on Afro-Americans.

Isolated progress in the development of black studies is reported in the *Journal of Negro History* each year until 1926, when the first celebration of "Negro History Week" was held. Woodson (1929: 238) reported the state departments of education in Delaware, North Carolina, and West Virginia, and city school systems in Baltimore, had appealed to their teachers to cooperate in the celebration of Negro History Week. Available records of that decade (the 1920s) show educational institutions, particularly in the Southern states, laggard in developing or instituting black studies courses. Their most significant participation was in the annual volunteer Negro History Week, with its emphasis on Negro life and culture.

Federal programs during the Depression such as WPA and NRA brought renewed interest in the Negro's past. Writers were put to work researching Negro life. Though preceded by the Harlem Renaissance of the 1920s, this was the most productive period for writers of black history and literature.

In the mid-thirties, black studies curricula gained a place in many Southern Negro schools, which now began to make provisions for teaching black history and culture in particular courses. Woodson in his annual report to the association, reported that Delaware had taken the lead by offering Negro history in black junior high schools. Texas, Georgia, and Oklahoma permitted and made provisions for a black history course in senior high schools (J. of Negro History, 1936: 105).

Black educators and leaders seem to have abandoned the advocacy of black studies between 1940 and 1960, though there were always isolated cases of public schools and colleges offering courses in Negro history and literature. The only recognizable organized efforts were those of the association and of black and white orators during Negro History Week (held annually during the week of Abraham Lincoln's birthday).

With the rise of the contemporary Black Muslim movement and their emphasis on race pride and self-help, we find a rebirth of this advocacy — but with a renewed vigor, now, not only coming from lower-income blacks — as in Garvey's days — but also from middle-class and black intellectuals. Coming at the tail end of the sit-ins and school integration drives of the 1950s, the call for black studies courses was echoed by black nationalists, white liberals, and the black bourgeoisie. The movement spread from the North to the South; from colleges to secondary schools, and finally to the elementary grades.

The chief advocate of black studies today, the Black Students Union, owes its birth and influence to the black studies movement. The group's main platform and cause celebre was founded on the need for "blackness" and black studies on predominantly white-controlled secondary school and college campuses. As on most campuses, the BSU has played a major role in the pleading for the writing and implementation of black studies programs.

Presently, many Northern, Southern and Western colleges and universities have initiated black studies programs and departments. Most of these institutions are awarding majors, minors, and undergraduate degrees in the programs. Yale, Harvard, Brown, Boston University, Duke, San Jose State College, UCLA, UC-Berkeley, and San Francisco State College are just a few institutions offering graduate degrees.

Because of the rapid growth of this movement in California secondary schools, the California State Board of Education, in June 1968, recently authorized the issuance of a two-year college provisional teaching credential. Oakland's Merrit College, a pioneer in black studies, recommended the first recipients of the provisional credential. Beyond these schools, scores have programs in black studies; the discipline long in blossoming may be near a period of steady growth.

References

Aptheker, H. (1963) *A Documentary History of the Negro People in the United States.* New York: Citadel.

Bullock, H.A. (1967) *A History of Negro Education in the South from 1619 to the Present*. Cambridge, Mass.: Harvard University Press. Cleveland Gazette (1898) November 12.

Drake, T.E. (1950) *Quakers and Slavery in America*. New Haven: Yale University Press.

Gregoire, H. (1967) *An Enquiry Concerning the Intellectual and Moral Faculties and Literature of Negroes*. College Park, MD: McGrath.

Jefferson, T. (1964) *Notes on the State of Virginia*. New York: Harper & Row.

———. (n.d.) *The Writings of Thomas Jefferson*.

Journal of Negro History (1936) "Negro history week: the eleventh year." 21 (April).

Meek, D.A. (1968) "Black power and the instructional council: the development of an Afro-American studies curriculum." *Junior College Journal*.

Myrdal, G. (1964) *An American Dilemma*. New York: McGraw-Hill.

NAACP, National Association for the Advancement of Colored People (1919) Thirty Years of Lynching in the United States, 1889-1918. New York: National Office.

New York Age (1890) March 8. (Hampton University)

Newby, I.A. (1968) *The Development of Segregationist Thought*. Homewood, IL: Dorsey Press.

Pennington, J.W.C. (1841) *Textbook of the Origin and History of the Colored People*. Hartford.

Porter, D.B. (1936) "The organized educational activities of Negro literary societies, 1828-1846." *Journal of Negro Education* 5 (October).

Reddick, L. (1937) "A new interpretation for Negro history." *Journal of Negro History* 22 (January).

Roman, C.V. (1911) *A Knowledge of History Is Conducive to Racial Solidarity*. Nashville.

Rose, W.L. (1957) *Rehearsal for Reconstruction: The Port Royal Experiment*. New York: Random House.

Russwurm, J.B. (1826) Commencement speech, Bowdoin College.

Schomburg, A.A. (1906) "Racial integrity: a plea for the establishment of a chair of Negro history in our schools and college." Negro Society for Historical Research Occasional Paper 3.

Terrell, R.H. (1896) Letter to E.J. Bruce, March 29.

Walker, D. (1965) In C.M. Wiltse (ed.) *David Walker's Appeal*. New York: Hilt & Wang.

Wesley, C. (1952) "Racial historical societies and the American heritage." *Journal of Negro History* 37 (January).

Woodson, C.G. (1929) "Negro history week." *Journal of Negro History* 11 (April).

———. (1919) "Negro life and history in our schools." *Journal of Negro History* 4 (July).

19.

Black Studies at San Francisco State

John H. Bunzel

On college campuses across the country today, black nationalism, still only in its earliest stages but emerging with considerable force and purpose comes in many different sizes, shapes, and even colors. (It is no accident that in many quarters negro is "out" and Black is "in," or that the NAACP is sometimes referred to as the National Association for the Advancement of Certain People.) Yet one thing is clear: just as one finds black artists in the existing theater calling on one another to stop assimilating and imitating white standards, and instead to begin building cultural centers "where we can enjoy being free, open and black, where," as actress and director Barbara Ann Teer put it, "we can literally 'blow our minds' with blackness," so one also finds black students in our existing academic institutions demanding a program of Black Studies—one that will not only lead to the affirmation of their own identity ad self-esteem, but will recognize the new needs of the black community and thereby help to define the concept of "black consciousness": Black Power, black nationalism, a black society—whatever meaning these terms will come to have for the whole of American society in the years ahead, the curricular idea of Black studies will become the principal vehicle by which blacks students will press their claim for a black "educational renaissance" in colleges and universities throughout the nation.

Although it is still too early to tell how the demand for Black Studies will ultimately be incorporated into different undergraduate instructional programs, it is already evident that the idea itself represents a formidable problem for American educators. For one thing, the concept of Black Studies, at least on many campuses, is as much a political consideration as an educational one. At San Francisco State College, the demand for inclusion of black courses in the curriculum has capitalized on an atmosphere of student militancy, black and white, real and potential. Privately, it is acknowledged that one of the reasons the blacks did not participate in the sit-in demonstrations organized last May by the Mexican-American students (and supported in full force by the Students for a Democratic Society) was that the president of the college had already appointed a man—chosen by the Black Students' Union—to develop and coordinate a Black Studies curriculum, a job for which he had been specifically recruited and on which he was hard at work. It is also worth noting that the appointment of a Black Studies Coordinator was made by the president alone—that is to say, without the knowledge of, or consultation with, the Vice President for Academic Affairs, the Council of Academic Deans, or the faculty. The president, characteristically, was candid about what he had done: this college is going to explode wide open, he said, if the blacks do not get what they want soon. (In the fall semester, he had suspended four members of the Black Students' Union after they had pushed their way into the office of the campus newspaper and physically attacked the editor.) Yes, the man he had asked to be the Coordinator of Black Studies had recently been fired from Howard University for what the *Negro Digest* called "his militant pro-black activities"; but, said the President, he had a Ph.D. in sociology from the University of Chicago and was anxious to come to San Francisco State. No, he had not spoken with any one in the sociology department about the appointment, because he felt he had to move quickly "if we are going to keep the lid on this place."

The point is that the President had reacted to what he felt to be a critical situation. His response was a political one, in the most practical and urgent sense of that term. He may very well have been right; no one will ever know. However, in terms of the acutely difficult academic problems involved in developing a curriculum of Black Studies and its implications for the educational program as a whole, his interest and concern was something less than visible. In point of fact, the President was soon to resign and leave the college.

Yale, Harvard and Elsewhere

Many of the major universities in the United States have already taken steps toward developing their own form of Black Studies. At Yale, a faculty-student committee has proposed the creation of an undergraduate major in Afro-American studies that, according to Robert A. Dahl, professor of political science, will involve "an interdisciplinary approach to studying the experience and conditions of people of African ancestry in Africa and the New World." Students would be provided a broad view of the African experience, but would be required to concentrate on one of the relevant disciplines by way of enlightening their understanding and knowledge of the cultural, economic, political, social, artistic, and historical experiences of Africans and Afro-Americans. Beginning this September, Harvard will offer a new full-year course in "The Afro-American Experience," and is considering a degree-granting program in Afro-American studies for the not-too-distant future. The new course will begin with the African background and the Negro experience in American history through 1945 and, in the second semester, will consider issues of race relations, psychology, civil rights, housing, employment, and education from 1945 to the present. A faculty group of four will be headed by Frank Freidel, professor of American history and biographer of Franklin D. Roosevelt. He will be joined by another historian with a professional interest in poverty studies, a political scientist who specializes in African and American Negro studies, and an expert on American and Latin American history. As a social science offering, it is comparable to the Introduction to Western Civilization and will be limited, at least initially, to 200 students. Parallel to this course, Harvard's Institute of Politics of the John F. Kennedy School of Government will offer a series of lectures on the Afro-American experience by visiting scholars, required of students taking the course and open to others. In addition, the Association of African and Afro-American Students will offer a series of films and television tapes.[1]

Other colleges and universities around the country are similarly engaged in considering the direction their program of Black Studies will take. The problems to be resolved are as difficult as they are numerous, but they are significantly different depending on the institution involved. An Ivy League university, for example, will be very much concerned with the academic substance and soundness of any proposed Black Studies curriculum. Given its educational tradition and philosophy, the heavy research emphasis of its faculty, and the particular undergraduate constituency it attracts and admits (virtually no "underclass minorities" of the slums), a Yale or a Harvard can insist on and expect a considerable measure of intellectual discipline in all of its academic programs. Or consider a university such as Stanford. Comfortably located in the white suburban area of Palo Alto, it has little or no sustained involvement with the poverty environment in general (San Francisco-Oakland) or the core-city minorities in particular, and therefore has not had to deal with the problem of large numbers of militant blacks renouncing, not only the normal curricular offerings, but their whole college experience for being totally irrelevant to their own perceived needs and the needs of the larger black community.

Understandably, the way a college or university approaches the problems of its minority students will depend In part on the view it holds of its mission as an academic institution. Thus, a Black Studies program that is geared primarily to the needs of black students will follow one set of tracks if it is designed primarily to develop future academicians, but will move in a very different direction and at a very different pace if its major purpose is to equip and train its students to present "the black perspective" when they return to the black community to help transform it.

San Francisco State College, a microcosm of the diverse and polyglot urban and suburban society of the Bay Area, has seen more and more of its energy in the past few years converge on the needs and demands of its black students. It may be illuminating therefore, to consider the recent proposal for a Department of Black Studies in what has generously been designated "this tumultuous educational scene."

The Black Students' Union at SFS

The academic year 1965-1966 has been called the year of the student revolution at San Francisco State, for it was during this year that changes in the attitudes of a small but influential number of students were consolidated and expressed in new functions of student government and new forms of faculty involvement. The most important of the Associated Students' programs were channeled into three major activities: (1) the Experimental College, which offered a diversity of courses never before seen in a college bulletin; (2) the Community Involvement Program, which placed students in neighborhoods throughout the city to help support them in their efforts to work in the communities, principally the ghettos and slums; and (3) the Tutorial Program, which concentrated on helping Children learn to read, to do arithmetic, and to want to stay in school. The programs were regarded as successful, and in the words of a later report, "The experience was earned, the price was paid, and our point was made, the point being that students on this campus wanted forms of education that the institution was not providing." It was the same point that would be made over and over again, reflecting the growing disaffection among black and other minorities on the campus.

In the summer of 1966, the Black Students' Union emerged and almost immediately became a major force in the student government.[2] During the following year, it turned its attention to the educational problem of black and other minority students on the campus, which they saw in its broadest terms as the problem of relevance, estrangement, and identity. The high drop-out rate, low grades, and general lack of motivation among large numbers of these students was due, they said, not only to a general feeling of separateness, but to the more compelling fact that education from kindergarten through college under the authority of the white community fails to focus on subject matter that is germane to the life experiences of the people in the minority community. Specifically, the charge was repeatedly made that black and other minority students have little opportunity to place themselves in an identifiable historical and personal context in the traditional curriculum. Disregarding the question of its intellectual worth and value, some of the perceptions and feelings of a leader of the Black Students' Union on why the present college curriculum is inadequate are revealing:

> One Black student told us of sitting in an Anthropology class for an entire semester and being interested in the class on only two occasions—once when the instructor offered a lecture on the Negro in America, and again when there was a lecture on Africa.

> Few Black students are really interested in the western, "classical" music which characterized entire departments of music. Black students have no fundamental cultural understanding of western music. And since a part of many beginning music classes is spent instructing students that the only legitimate music is that of Beethoven, Mozart, Stravinsky, etc., this is seen as a denial of Black students themselves. For example, a Black student interested in music theory spent his first semester arguing with his instructor for the legitimacy of Black musicians, Charles Parker and John Coltrane. He lost the argument by receiving a "D" grade and is now out of college.

> Black people are not western; they are "westernized," made to be western. So basically their psychology is not Freudian, Adlerian, or Jungian, only so far as they have accepted westernization. Students find themselves enchanted by the schools of psychology, but as they probe deeper they find less and less in an association with their lives. Other Black students pretend they can relate to western psychology by "becoming" Freudian. They psyche themselves out as we say, by trying to describe manifestations of every desire by description directly from the psychology textbook.

> When Black students begin to describe themselves in real situations, they are at times put down. A Black woman student wrote a paper on Marxism and alienation in which she said that she could not be alienated from a society of which she had never been a part. She had recently joined the Black Students' Union. The instructor attacked the student's basis of thought and gave her a low grade. She soon afterwards had a nervous collapse and has been out of the school for more than a year.

As perceived by the Black Students' Union, their educational problem at San Francisco State is clear and unambiguous: they read *white* literature, study *white* families, analyze *white* music, survey *white* civilizations, examine *white* cultures, probe *white* psychologies. In a word, the college curriculum is white-culture-bound.

An Improvised Black Curriculum

To remedy the situation, which in concrete terms meant attracting the interest and enthusiasm of the black student, the Black Students' Union quickly set its sights on the development of a black curriculum. The Black Arts and Culture Series was instituted in the fall semester (1960) as a part of the Experimental College. The purpose was to introduce a positive focus on the life experiences of black people In

America. Classes covered the areas of history, law, psychology, humanities, social science, and dance. One year later the first Black Studies was enacted, with a total of eleven classes for which thirty-three units of college credit were given. Several hundred students, black and white, enrolled in the courses, which were taught on a voluntary or part-time basis either by members of the faculty or graduate students sympathetic to the program. Among the classes listed in the Black Studies Program for the spring semester (1968) were the following:

Anthropology: *Historical Development of Afro-American Studies (3)*

Dramatic Arts: *Improvisations in Blackness*

Education: *Miseducation of the Negro*

English: *Modern African Thought and Literature*

History: *Ancient Black History*

Psychology: *Workshop in the Psychology of, by, and for Black People*

Sociology: *Sociology of Black Oppression*

The improvisation of a black curriculum during the past two years at San Francisco State has reflected a growing feeling among members of the faculty and student body that educational innovation starting at the college level be given a chance to remedy the perceived ills of the past and create a model for other levels of education as well. By the end of the 1967-1968 academic year, it was taken for granted that there would be a Black Studies program. The question was no longer whether it would happen, but what direction it would take and how the administration, faculty and students would choose to react.

Nathan Hare's Proposal

Meanwhile, the newly appointed Special Coordinator of Black Studies, Nathan Hare, has circulated a proposal for a degree-granting Department of Black Studies that deserves careful study. The document is his and his alone, and for this reason his particular angle of vision, indeed his basic assumptions and attitudes, are especially pertinent. He has been described as "a man seething with anger about the path of Negro leadership, the duplicity of whites, and the fallibility of many Negroes who 'follow' both!" A sample of his remarks made in a public speech at Stanford University does not belie the description:

> I had expected to speak to a black audience. You can build a wall a mile high, but white people will always climb up and peer over at what you're doing. [He added that he was glad white students were interested in black culture and history, in spite of the environment of the "white brainwashing factory," the university.]

> The bourgeois nationalists (among pre-Civil War Black Power groups) were more interested in personal gain and mobility within their group than freeing the slaves. The main difference between them and the revolutionaries was in their outlook on the world in which they lived. The revolutionaries had lost faith in the routine means of righting wrong. They were crippled, though, by a feeling of powerlessness against the white power structure. It's like today. They say we are too few to fight. We should vote. But I can kill 20

(white) men. I can cut one's throat, shook another, drop a hand grenade in the middle of a whole bunch. I get only a single vote, and that's between the lesser of two evils.

On white historians: It is anachronistic for white men to teach black history to black militant students. The white man is unqualified to teach black history because he does not understand it.

On black historians: Black people must declare void what the white slave masters have written and must begin to write their own history and direct their destiny. Black historians, presenting other than the white viewpoint, are forced into copious footnoting and must accept the conventions of the white academic overlords in order to make our history valid and get it published in white journals.

On the draft: I was asked if I am an American first or a Negro first. I said I'm a black man first and not an American at all. Since most Americans do not consider me an American, I see no reason to fight for them. I said that before it was fashionable. I did serve six months, in the Army, but that was in peacetime. And I said I couldn't fight for them, and if I did I would shoot as much as possible at the whites around me.

I don't believe in absolutes, so I do not categorically reject all white men, only 99 and 44/100ths of them.

The importance of Hare's pronouncements is not that they are angry or bitterly anti-white. This, after all, is part and parcel of the militant black rhetoric today that derives its own satisfaction in constantly putting down "whitey," including those who have a "hunger for humiliation." What is important is that they provide a backdrop against which his "conceptual proposal" for a Department of Black Studies can be more clearly understood and evaluated in terms of its basic rationale and philosophy.

Hare acknowledges at the outset that the whole idea of Black Studies is "more far-reaching than appears on the surface." His conversations with academicians across the country on the education of black Americans leave no doubt in his mind that even those who have accepted the idea of Black Studies do not fully understand its need. "They see the goal as the mere blackening of white courses, in varying number and degree," he writes. "They omit in their program the key component of community involvement and collective stimulation." Their program is individualistic, aimed at "rehabilitating" individual students by means of pride in culture, racial contributions generally, and regenerated dignity and self-esteem. "They fail to see that the springboard for all of this is an animated communalism aimed at a Black educational renaissance." Thus many well-intentioned efforts, Hare says, are doomed to inevitable failure. "They comprise piecemeal programs that, being imported, are based on an external perspective." Put simply, they are white, not black.

Nor will Hare accept any form of "tokenism." He cites the example of "an eminent Negro professor" who proposed increasing drastically the ratio of Black — "by which he meant 'Negro,'" Hare adds — students and professors. "The students for the most part would be admitted with the expectation that, excepting those salvaged by tutorial efforts presently in vogue, they would eventually flunk out, the merrier for having acquired 'at least some college.'" This approach, flare says, is not the answer to the problem. Although he is willing to "endorse the professor's suggestion in fact though not in theory insofar as to do otherwise would appear to condone current tokenism," he dismisses the approach on the grounds that it may be used "to appease the black community while avoiding genuine solutions."

When a representative from a foundation proposed giving full financial assistance to the "talented tenth" and hiring black persons to recruit such students and inform them of the availability of such aid, Hare responded by saying that this is only slightly better than providing no aid at all. "A talented-tenth approach is largely superfluous to the educational needs of the black race as a whole," Hare writes. "Talented-tenth students, for whatever reason, have escaped the programmed educational maladjustment of the Black race, just as some trees survive the flames of a forest fire." Such a program, "though noble on the surface, offers super-tokenism at best, but neglects the important ingredient of motivation growing out of collective community involvement. It is individualistic in its orientation and only indirectly, therefore, of collective consequence."

"Separatism?"

Of concern to many members of the faculty and student body at San Francisco State is the question of "separatism" — specifically, will a Department of Black Studies result in "a college within a college?" Hare's comments on this point deserve to be quoted in full:

> Even if it be so that Black Studies would ring more separatist in tone than Latin American Studies, Oriental Studies, and the like, this is not the issue. The question of separatism is, like integrationism, in this regard essentially irrelevant. The goal is the elevation of a people by means of one important escalator — education. Separatism and integrationism are possible approaches to that end; they lose their effectiveness when, swayed by dogmatic absolutism, they become ends in themselves. It will be an irony of recorded history that "integration" was used in the second half of this century to hold the Black race down just as segregation was so instituted in the first half. Integration, particularly in the token way in which it has been practiced up to now and the neo-tokenist manner now emerging, elevates individual members of a group, but paradoxically, in plucking many of the most promising members from a group while failing to alter the lot of the group as a whole, weakens the collective thrust which the group might otherwise muster.

A related question is whether or not white students would be admitted into the program. The answer, Hare says, "must be ambivalent inasmuch as the program has to be aimed primarily at the Black student, particularly in its motivational activities involving the Black community." Hare is concerned that white students will flood Black Studies courses.

> One way to draw white students off (or/and care for the surplus) is for existing departments to increase their offerings in blackness as they are doing now under the guise of "dark" (or, as sociologists say, "color-compatible") courses. This would probably result in greater benefit to the white students' needs anyway and most certainly would offset the apparent sense of threat in the minds of conventional departments.

Hare then makes an important admission:

It may be necessary eventually to distinguish Black education for Blacks and Black education for whites. There is no insurmountable incompatibility or mutual exclusiveness between Black Studies and ethnic group courses in other departments. Indeed they are easily reinforcing and could make a major contribution to better "race relations" or, as politicians are fond of saying now, "the effort to save the nation" in decades ahead.

The principle of inclusion

In a section of the proposal called "Redefinition of Standards," Hare offers some singular observations. He begins by saying that current standards evolved in large part from a need to restrict the overflow of recruits—what he calls "the principle of exclusion"—into existing professional niches.

This gave rise to occasionally ludicrous requirements. The late social theorist, Thorstein Veblen, author of *Theory of the Leisure Class*, might hold that the liberal arts approach grew out of the leisure class mentality, where it was prestigious to be non-productive and to waste time and effort in useless endeavor. Hence footnoting minutiae and the like. When middle class aspirants began to emulate these codes, the principle of exclusion evolved. However, now we are faced with the educational enticement of a group conditioned by way of the cake of time and custom to being excluded. How do we transform them into an included people, For example, a law school graduate with high honors might fail the "bar" exam (pun intended) because of political views, or fail the oral exam for teacher certification because of an unpopular approach to teaching.... Or pass everything required except the "language" exam. It is widely known that languages studied for graduate degrees are quickly almost totally forgotten and are rarely of any use after graduation. Much of the motivation for the retention of this and even more useless requirements apparently stems from the "leisure class" origin of the liberal arts" approach where, as Thorstein Veblen explained, prestige was attributed to "non-productive" or wasteful useless endeavor.

What Hare is saying is that requirements were devised "to serve the functions of exclusivity rather than recruitment" and that now "we are facing the necessity for collective recruitment from a group victimized as a group in the past by racist policies of exclusion from the educational escalator." While the two most "salient 'qualifications'" for professorial rank today are a Ph.D. "and a string of 'scholarly' publications," Hare wants the freedom "to depart from those criteria without risking the suspicion of 'lowering standards.' That the Ph.D. is not necessarily synonymous with teaching effectiveness," he adds, "is accepted by most persons confronted with the question." Less understood is the question of publication.

Consider two candidates for a position in history, one qualified a la conventional standards, the other not. Never mind the fact that articles outside the liberal-moderate perspective have slim chances of seeing the light of day in "objective" scholarly journals. More ludicrous is the fact that the Black historian, in adhering to the tradition of "footnoting," is placed in the unenviable position of having to footnote white slave master historians or historians published by a slaveholding society in order to document his work on the slavery era.

When it comes to recruiting a faculty, Hare believes that a Black Studies program would want to redefine the notion of a "qualified" professor "by honoring teaching effectiveness and enthusiasm more than qualities determined by degrees held and other quantifiable 'credentials.'" Is there to be a role for the white professor? "Their participation," Hare states, "at least during the early, experimental stages of the program, must be cautious and minimal." He admits, however, that the impracticality of recruiting a sufficient number of black professors may force a relaxation of this principle. But on one point there is no compromising: "Any white professors involved in the program would have to be Black in spirit in order to last. The same is true for 'Negro' professors."

Central to Hare's whole proposal for a Department of Black Studies is the component of community involvement. To bring about this development it is necessary "to inspire and sustain a sense of collective destiny as a people and a consciousness of the value of education in a technological society. A cultural base, acting as a leverage for other aspects of Black ego development and academic unit, must accordingly be spawned and secured." Students and other interested parties "will be organized into Black Cultural Councils which will sponsor cultural affairs (art, dance, drama, etc.) in the Black community and establish Black holidays, festivities and celebrations." For example, a Black Winter Break could begin on February 21, the day they shot Malcolm X, run past George Washington's birthday and end with February 23, the birthday of the late Black Scholar, W.E.B. DuBois. "This," Hare says, "could approximate the Jewish Yom Kippur." There are many other suggestions: Black Information Centers to increase communication, interpersonal contact, knowledge and sociopolitical awareness"; a Black Community Press, put together by "members of Black Current Events clubs and students taking courses in Black journalism"; a Bureau of Black Education "to provide Black scholars mutual aid and stimulation, and to organize Black textbook and syllabi writing corps."

The New Curriculum

Finally, Hare outlines his plan for the Black Studies curriculum. The initiation of the program is to be accomplished in two stages: (1) Phase 1, involving the pulling together of some of the currently experimental courses into a new department; and (2) Phase II, the inauguration of a major "consisting of an integrated body of black courses revolving around core courses such as Black history, Black psychology, Black arts, and the social sciences." (See Table 1.) In addition, as part of the course requirements, there will be student field work in the black community, involving an effort to transform the community while educating and training the student. (This, observes Hare, is the key ingredient which "Yale's program omits.") Although the Black Studies Program "would not preclude electives outside the Black curriculum, even for majors, it would seek to care for a wide range of academic training in the humanities, the social and behavioral sciences." Although most persons enrolled in Black Studies courses would not be majors,

> those graduating as such could become probation officers, case workers, poverty workers, or enter graduate or professional schools in preparation for careers as lawyers, social workers, teachers, scholars, professors, research scientists, businessmen, administrators, and so on. They would, other things being equal—we feel certain—quickly emerge and predominate in the upper echelons of the Black community.

The specific content of the curriculum as proposed by Hare follows below. "Although much of it is expressive" (geared to ego-identity building, etc.), concludes Hare, "the utilitarian function has by no means been omitted.... The Black race

Table 1
Tentative Black Studies Major for Fall, 1969

Core Courses	Units
Black History	4
Black Psychology	4
Survey of Sciences: Method & History	4
Black Arts and Humanities	4
	16 units

Black Arts Concentration	
The Literature of Blackness	4
Black Writers Workshop	4
Black Intellectuals	4
Black Fiction	4
Black Poetry	4
Black Drama	4
The Painting of Blackness	4
The Music of Blackness	4
Sculpture of Blackness	4
	36 units

Behavioral and Social Sciences Concentration	
Black Politics	4
Sociology of Blackness	4
Economics of the Black Community	4
The Geography of Blackness	4
Social Organization of Blackness	4
Development of Black Leadership	4
Demography of Blackness	4
Black Counseling	4
Black Consciousness and the International Community	4
	32 units

woefully needs concrete skills…both for individual mobility and community development."

Some Problems

The proposal outlined above will get a full hearing this coming year before an academic program of Black Studies is recommended for adoption at San Francisco State and sent to the State College Board of, Trustees for its final approval. The range of opinion and reaction will be wide, from those who see no reason to make special curricular provisions for black students to those who believe that whites are not competent to pass judgment on an educational program for blacks. Some members of the faculty will rush to support whatever the most militant black students want simply to show that they are not up tight about militant black students. (These faculty members are never up tight, except about being up tight.) Others will oppose Black Studies with the question: why not a Department of Jewish (or Indian or Chinese or Mexican-American) Studies? Still others will propose alternate plans—for example, that existing academic departments increase the number of minorities on their teaching staffs and develop course offerings that will meet the different ethnic needs on the campus. Predictably, however, the great majority of the faculty, the "silent middle," will choose to be uninterested and uninvolved. They will have nothing to say.

Any proposed program of Black Studies will inevitably produce a flood of questions. The trouble is that dispassionate answers are difficult to come by. Perhaps the most that can be done, in keeping with the commitment of the academic community to the use of reason in the resolution of problems, is to suggest a number of issues that deserve consideration and analysis.

1. It was not too long ago that the battle was fought to dissuade college admissions offices from requiring a candidate to submit a photograph or to state his race or religion. In many colleges and universities the specific target was the so-called "quota system," which had a special application to Jews. Today the "new-liberal" position is that Negroes must not only be identified but admitted to college by special quotas. Race and color are no longer to be ignored. (When Nathan Hare was asked if he believed the admissions office at San Francisco State should require a photograph with each student application, he replied, "Of course. How else are we going to identify the blacks?") At a number of universities, militant students have demanded the admission of specific numbers of Negroes, which increasingly is being translated into quotas roughly equal to the proportion of Negroes in the total population of the locality or of the nation.

Daniel P. Moynihan, speaking for many who subscribe to the "old-liberal" position, has warned that quotas for one group inevitably turn into formulas against another. "Let me be blunt. If ethnic quotas are to be imposed on American universities. ..Jews will be almost driven out. They are not 3 per cent of the population." (This, said Professor Moynihan, would be a misfortune for Jews, but a disaster to the nation.) According to a report in *The New York Times*, undergraduates at Harvard enthusiastically endorsed ethnic representation, if not exactly quotas, on the faculty, but had misgivings about applying the same principle to student enrollment. As Professor Moynihan pointed out, if such quotas were to be applied, seven out of eight Jewish undergraduates would have to leave, and much the same exodus would be required of Japanese and Chinese Americans. "America," Professor Moynihan said, "has known enough of anti-Semitism and anti-Oriental feeling to be wary of opening that box again."

Virtually everyone is agreed that special efforts should be made to increase the enrollment of Negro students in our colleges and universities. The problem is to find a way to open the doors "without going from the assumption of color-blindness to the extreme of forcing on every institution quotas of racial and religious membership."

2. Many whites have not yet fully understood the psychological meaning and force of an issue that to many blacks, is even more critical than white racism—namely, pride and personal identification. More than any other component of the racial question, it pervades every discussion of a black curriculum. Its importance and enormous power cannot be minimized. The fact is that black students do respond directly and positively to a black instructor. The relationship is clear, personal

and effective. It is a potent consideration, and is at the heart of every argument in support of a Department of Black Studies.

On another level of analysis, however, many in the academic community are concerned about its ultimate meaning and implication. At issue, at least for some, is the matter of standards. Is the color of a professor's skin more important than the substance of the course? The Black Studies Coordinator phoned the Chairman of the Political Science Department to inquire about a course in *African Government and Politics* scheduled for the fall semester. "What color is the instructor?" was his only question. "White," he was told. He was not interested in the fact that she was writing her Ph.D. dissertation in the area of African politics and had received her training under the supervision of a leading authority in African problems at the University of California. His single concern was color. Thus a fundamental professional question is raised: Is color the test of competence? It has only been recently that colleges and universities have succeeded in removing *politics* as a test for hiring and firing. Now is it to be color?

A Department of Black Studies, it should be said, would make such questions unnecessary. All personnel in Black Studies would be black, with the sole and avowed purpose of concentrating on blackness.

"Collective Stimulation" and Academic Propriety

3. At a time when educators throughout the United States are trying to devise new ways to reach their students on a more personal, individual basis, it is significant that Hare's proposal for a Department of Black Studies is aimed at "collective stimulation" — that is, to get black students to stop thinking individualistically and to begin thinking collectively. Put another way, the black curriculum is not explicitly designed to encourage black students to develop qualities of independence, skepticism, and critical inquiry — in a word, to think for themselves — but rather to intensify the motivation and commitment of all who enroll in the program to return to the black community and translate everything to which they have been exposed into black leadership and black power. As a political program for community action it is not to be faulted. As an academic program — or, perhaps more properly, as a program in academic surroundings — it poses some different problems.

For those whose total educational philosophy and concern is contained in the penetrating nugget, "Let them do their own thing," there will, of course, be no problems at all. Others, however, will have some questions. Will those who teach in the Department of Black Studies be of the same political and ideological persuasion, or will efforts be made to recruit a black staff that purposely reflects different and opposing points of view? Would Black Studies hire a black undergraduate to teach one of its courses for credit? Will the Department of Black Studies mirror the views of the Black Students' Union, thereby reinforcing the Union's political goals and purposes on campus?

4. Nathan Hare has said that "Black people understand black problems better than anyone else. We are determined to solve our own problems and the important first step is education." Few will dispute the first half of the statement. There may be some question, however — in an academic community it could not really be other-

wise—as to what is meant by education. It is certainly not to be confused with in-doctrination, any more than tales of heroism, white or black, can pass for genuine history. It is true that for many students in this country the history of man has too often been treated as though it "started in Athens and ended in California," with the Afro-American story simply left out. The question now is whether a Department of Black Studies would substitute propaganda for omission, or, as some have said, new myths for old lies. For example, many highly respected historians view black history in the United States as a problem of deciding where and when the question of race or religion, or any particular characteristic or trait, has historical significance. Would this approach, this form of intellectual discipline, be acceptable to Black Studies? Would Black Studies look on a course in African history as an opportunity simply to venerate the great achievements of cultural forebears, or would it also lay stress on, say, the historical fact that the more advanced African peoples and energetic leaders were often the very ones who sold other Africans to slave traders, thereby helping to bring about Negro slavery in America?

Or consider Hare's own book, *The Black Anglo-Saxon*, published three years ago. Writing as a sociologist, he argues that black, would-be Anglo-Saxons are for-getting or denying their "Negroness." However, Professor Troy Duster, a social scientist at the University of California (Riverside), points out that much of E. Franklin Frazier's scholarly life was spent documenting the fact that the Negro in the United States was stripped of almost every vestige of his African culture, and that his primary substantive culture is an American one. In discussing one type of black Anglo-Saxon, Hare states that "their pathetic pursuit of white values is an effort to elude their true personal and social identities." But, asks Professor Duster, "do Negroes really have a separate set of ethical and moral precepts, or separate standards for evaluating themselves and others? If so, what is the well-spring of this distinctly Negro culture if it is not that of the whites who brought Negroes to this country in the chains of slavery?" Would this intellectual position be fully recognized and discussed in a Department of Black Studies? Would open and sharp disagreement over the nature and substance of an American Negro culture be encouraged?

Martin Luther Kilson, Jr., assistant professor of government at Harvard and advisor to Harvard's Afro-Americans, has asked some pointed questions: "What community or segment of Black peoples should be used as representative of whatever the Black Experience is or has been? Should it be the Republic of Haiti where Black Power has been oppressive of the black masses? Or black fratricide in Nigeria? Or the black experience with 200 years of white racism in the United States?" Professor Kilson does not hesitate to say that all men, black, white, yellow, and red, are capable of oppressive abuse of power, without gaining from such experience any special will or capacity to rid human affairs of oppression. "Indeed," he concludes, it is a common fallacy to believe that what is momentarily politically serviceable is ipso facto intellectually virtuous."

Endnotes

1. The Information here on Yale and Harvard is from a report by Fred M. Hechinger, *The New York Times*, June 23, 1968.

2. It should be kept in mind that out of a total college enrollment of 18,000, a good turnout for student government elections each spring is about 3,000-4,000. One other point worth mentioning, the annual budget of the Associated Students, derived from student fees, is over $300,000.

20.

The Coming of Age of Black Studies

Vivian V. Gordon

The Beginnings: Challenge and Promise

The Challenge

Afro-American studies, or Black studies, was established as an academic discipline on white university campuses in the late 1950s and early 1960s in the midst of the protest movements of that era. Most often Black studies programs began as a means of quieting the demands of a Black/white student coalition that spoke of some abstract notion called relevance in higher education. Such students were pointing to a failure of the universities to address the many pressing social problems of the day, in particular, the dominant issues of war, peace, racism, and socioeconomic inequality. These students protested what was viewed as traditional academic isolation from the world that was to be their social reality. Universities were viewed by students as "ivory towers," unconcerned with translating theory or research into policies relevant to the complexities of the lives of ordinary individuals in American society.

While sharing the concerns of white students about a need for an increased relationship between the university and the so-called real world, Black students also protested the traditional Eurocentric foci of American higher education. They spoke about the lack of relevance of their courses to the minority experience and the absence of academic attention to study and research about the experience of Blacks who have been outstanding contributors to the development of the nation. The protesting Black students emphasized that a few courses which considered Negro history, or selected categories of Black music or Black writers, were not a sufficient commitment to the study of the Black experience.

Yielding to the demands of protesting students, often after serious on-campus conflict, many universities initiated Black studies programs to which there was not a genuine academic commitment. In many instances Black studies programs were hastily developed, while it was precluded that the impetus for the program would decline once the "on guard" students' demands were abated. At such universities little attention was given to program needs for adequate long-range financial or faculty support. All too often, Black studies programs were designed to fail, or, at best, were intended or expected to have limited academic impact.

It should be understood that in many instances Black studies programs emerged only after many conference hours between students, faculty, and administrators who attempted to persuade traditional departments to expand their curricula and courses so as to give appropriate attention to study about the Afro-American. Traditional departments were most often not open to such new directions. It was only after many efforts to influence traditionalists failed that Black students and their supporters used their collective power to pressure for separate programs through which the African and the Afro-American experience might be studied as a primary topic.

Although those early undergraduate students were successful in initiating a number of Black studies programs in predominantly white institutions of higher education, they were most often not aware of the kinds of academic underpinnings necessary for a valid new discipline to be sustained and to flourish. In the long run, many of the most active and capable students became victims of the programs they initiated for they were allowed to pursue a poorly planned, often unorganized and nondirected course of study which touched upon "popular" Black concerns, but which made limited contribution to the development of those academic skills needed for critical evaluation. Consequently, many Black studies programs came to be viewed by both Black and white students and faculty as rhetorical therapy sessions rather than programs of serious academic intent.

Although this failure in academic content did not exist among all of the Black studies programs, a stereotype was easily promoted among institutions which were still smarting from the impact of many student power movements, and non-supportive faculty and administrators pointed to a selected group of poor programs as means to justify inattention to the development of quality programs. Moreover, in some instances where Black studies programs were established with serious intent with capable and concerned faculty involvement, faculty members were restrained professionally from participation by a small number of Black students who presumed that since student efforts had resulted in the initiation of Black studies, students were also to be the monitors of the faculty, the developers of the curriculum, and the evaluators of the administrators of such programs. Caught in a conflict resulting from the need for a validation of their heritage through formal study, and a suspicion of the traditional presentation of the Black experience by whites, many of the early student leaders who tried to control initial programs were overtly reflecting, the frustration resulting from the psychological consequences of being Black in a society which recognized little of the Afro-American contribution.

The problems which confronted Black studies in those earliest days were many. The point for emphasis here is that it was against overwhelming odds, often within very hostile environments, that Black studies was cast and challenged to develop and prove its intellectual validity. For Black studies this continues to be the challenge.[1]

The Promise

The young people who were in the forefront of the activities leading to the establishment of Black studies programs were students of courage and commitment. Clearly, they were students who placed an especial value upon the concept of education for freedom and service. In so doing, they reflected the historic call to Blacks in higher education for leadership—the call to be the scholar/activist. Such students were reading, discussing, and responding to the mandate which clearly emerged from works of such Black scholars as W.E.B. DuBois, E. Franklin Frazier, and Harold Cruse, to name only a few.

Thus, an important part of the promise of Black studies is the on-going resilience and resourcefulness of the Black student who has not yet experienced the full impact and the validity of the study of the Afro-American experience. These are the students who pursue Black studies today in a continuous search for information about the range of the Afro-American contribution to the development of America and western society. The inquiring minds of today's students are the catalyst that contributes to the dynamics of Black studies. These students are well in agreement with the statement that "Afro-American Studies is ripe with the essence of intellectual creativity."

The New Discipline:
Emergence and Definition

The Emergence

Emphasis has been given to the conditions of protest from which programs of Black studies emerged on the campuses of most white colleges and universities. It is, therefore, appropriate that it also be emphasized that this struggle for emergence and recognition is a process with many historical precedents. First, all new disciplines have had to face a lengthy and difficult adolescent period in which they detached themselves from an academic parent reluctant not only to let go but also to accord legitimacy to its offspring. One may liken the emergence of other social science disciplines, such as sociology. Consider, for example, this discussion by Robert Bierstedt:

> All inquiries were once a part of philosophy, that great mother of the sciences (*mater scientiavum*), and philosophy embraced them all in an undifferentiated and amorphous fashion. One by one, however, with the growth of Western civilization, the various sciences cut the apron strings, as it were, and began to pursue separate and independent courses. Astronomy and physics were among the first to break away, and were followed thereafter by chemistry, biology, and geology. In the nineteenth century two new sciences appeared: psychology, or the science of human behavior; and sociology, or the science of human society. Thus, what had once been cosmology, a subdivision of philosophy, became astronomy; what had once been natural philosophy became the science of physics; what had once been mental philosophy, or the philosophy of mind, became the science of psychology; and what had once been social philosophy, or the philosophy of history, became the science of Sociology.[2]

It is hardly surprising, then, that Black studies has had to share with disciplines that gained autonomy and recognition earlier the charges that Black studies is a fad, merely trendy, or even pseudointellectual.

Second, one cannot fully understand the emergence of the field of Black studies without taking into consideration the study and research on the Black experience undertaken over many years by predominantly Black institutions. Such schools have, historically, given extensive attention to the works of Black scholars, many of whom were among their own distinguished faculty. Most graduates of southern Black institutions are familiar with the works of such scholars as W.E.B. DuBois, Charles S. Johnson, Carter G. Woodson, Luther P. Jackson, James Hugo Johnson, E. Franklin Frazier, James Weldon Johnson, Sterling Brown, J. Saunders Redding, John Hope Franklin, Horace Cayton, Horace Mann Bond, and St. Clair Drake, to name only a few such persons. These scholars, who persisted in their research on the Black people in a time when such research went unheralded, developed the body of information upon which contemporary Black studies programs are founded.

The tradition established by these and other Black scholars, provides today's Black studies scholars with a mandate to continue to report and record the cultural experience, and to develop new paradigms or models for the analysis of the Afro-American experience as opposed to continued attempts to fit the interactions of culturally different Blacks into models or paradigms designed for Euro-Americans. By expressing this concern as one of importance to the Black studies scholar, the discipline is not to be viewed as rejecting the value of established methodologies and perspectives, but rather to call for an expansion and enrichment of analysis which often challenge conventional concepts.

A Definition

Black studies may be defined as an analysis of the factors and conditions which have affected the economic, psychological, legal, and moral status of the African in America as well as the African in diaspora. Not only is Black studies concerned with the culture of the Afro-American ethnic, as historically and sociologically defined by the traditional literature, it is also concerned with the development of new approaches to the study of the Black experience and with the development of social policies which will impact positively upon the lives of Black people.

Although a definition of Black studies has been proposed, it is imprecise and will remain so in the foreseeable future. The boundaries of the discipline are subject to dispute, just as they are in other disciplines in terms of both theoretical and methodological approaches. Such variation in approaches to discipline are found throughout higher education.

When one examines most university structures one finds that departments, vis à vis disciplines, develop around one of two foci: (1) subject matter, or (2) a methodology. By way of illustration, consider language departments that could include English, French, German, and so forth, because of a generally consistent methodological approach. Languages, on the other hand, are usually taught within the structure of departments which define their subject areas as disciplines—that is, the French department, the English department, the German department. Obviously, with respect to languages, the definition of the "discipline" has emerged from a definition of subject matter. Even that definition, however, is subject to question, for there are specialists in comparative literature and such persons cut across the various language studies.

Consider also the social science disciplines. In economics, for example, one speaks of various "schools of thought": the Keynesian school, the neo-Marxist school, and the neo-classical economics of Milton Friedman. Similarly, there are those who consider social psychology to be misplaced if taught in sociology programs, while others would consider the subject matter misplaced if taught in psychology programs. Psychologically oriented social psychologists have long traditions which follow the personal perspective or the behavioral perspective. Sociologically oriented social psychologists increasingly pursue the perspective called symbolic interactionism. Fortunately, American higher education has tolerated such diversity within most of its disciplines. The same courtesy must be extended to Black studies, which continues to be burdened by demands for exact definitions.

Perhaps it is not totally negative that the guardians of American higher education demand that new studies meet certain academic rigors and are not "fads," or "trendy," or "pseudointellectual." However, the requirements of a rigorous course of study — academic validity and quality — should not be confused with questions about the legitimacy of the subject content when that legitimacy is evaluated from an ethnocentric perspective. Moreover, rigorous, inflexible requirements that the discipline be precisely defined in terms of subject, method, and philosophical perspective reflect an intolerance contrary to American higher education, as previously mentioned.

Attention must be given to the nature of Black studies in the quest for academic excellence. Speaking to the unique nature of Black studies and its emergence as a discipline, Harold Cruse writes:

> Now you must understand chat in a period of seven to eight years you can't develop a new discipline to perfection. It will take many generations of students and teachers to develop Afro-American Studies to the level of a traditional discipline. Afro-American Studies is going to demand high order of intellectual creativity. It cannot fit into the functional educational mold of all.
>
> ...Afro-American Studies deserves a creative approach. It is one of the few disciplines in the academic world that is so conducive to innovation and creativity.[3]

In a similar vein, Russell L. Adams writes:

> The professional academic field of Afro-American studies is relatively new, despite the individual work of scholars and others on topics related to the Black experience in the modern world. As an emergent field, Afro-American studies bears the mark of its early status. Unlike the established disciplines, this area of interest has nor had time to evolve through all of the stages characteristic of traditional and relatively settled disciplines.... The contents of Afro-American studies as a movement and an intellectual concern constitutes an inter-disciplinary enlargement of interest and perception which implicitly and often explicitly go to the roots of value, social structure, and societal dynamics.[4]

Black Students and Black Studies in the 1980s

Inevitably, the question arises about the "value" of Black studies. As is so often the case in a society which increasingly adjusts its higher education focus to the demands of military/industrial employment, persons question how one will "use" a degree in Black studies, as if one is able to "use" other specific liberal arts degrees for some specific, predestined employment position. The question of the value of Black studies or how one would "use" such studies emerges from those who have lost the vision of the aims of higher education in America.

Typically, persons raising such questions are themselves engaged in the education of students in as equally broad-based disciplines as Black studies. As Richard Long illustrates:

...the insistent question comes: what use is a degree in Black Studies? The question makes as much sense or nonsense if one substitutes English Literature, Philosophy or Sociology. Few of the majors in these well-known specialized disciplines "use" their training in any vocational sense. Is it then all a mistake? Some would say yes; others would say no, because it makes them "understand." By the same token, a broad-spectrum took at any portion of the human race leads to understanding, which is certainly in international short supply.

Seen within the framework of the role and rituals of American higher education, Black Studies may be viewed as a not unnatural, but vastly overdue, development in the programs of institutions devoted, in at least one dimension, to the exploration of the world around them. The extravagant expectations, the journalistic monitoring, the academic backbiting, the public breast-beating—led at one point by the now fallen Spiro Agnew—were all inevitable by-products, not of the movement itself but of America's paranoia at the contemplation of its Black minority.[5]

Given the present economic conditions of the nation, and of Black Americans in particular, as an increased number of Black college students prepare to enter the job market and the "American mainstream," such persons may anticipate problems when they hold credentials reflecting specialized study in so-called soft science areas," sociology, history, English, philosophy, psychology, and so forth. Moreover, an increasingly technological society demands an increasingly more educated employee. The B.A. becomes only the first of a required list of credentials. Clearly, the current employment outlook mandates that an increased number of Black college students plan either for graduate or professional study, and the areas for concentration appear to be those of the exact sciences and the professions of law, medicine, and dentistry.

The curriculum of Black studies must help the student develop his or her skills in the use of the tools which are important to both a critical analysis of interaction of the past and present, and to the student's future participation in the analysis of factors which affect the life of Black people in America. Such a curriculum will prepare the student, as does a solid broad-based liberal arts curriculum, for graduate study and post-college employment in a range of areas. The curriculum structure should also allow for specialized courses which will focus upon topics of concern to students with specific applied and preprofessional courses of study, Black studies curriculum include a range of such courses as: "Health Care Delivery," "Black Aging," "Black Americans and The Law," "Black Enterprise and American Capitalism," and so forth.

Equally obvious is the need for core courses which focus upon the introductory course unit topics and which place a particular emphasis upon research and the historical record from the Black perspective and definition of the social reality. The curriculum diagram which follows illustrates the flow relationship between the introductory course and the various subject area concentrations. This curriculum model was presented by the National Council for Black Studies Curriculum Committee and was adopted for inclusion in the Council's accreditation recommendation.

The exception to the model is the exclusion of a unit of research which the writer has added because of the extent to which Black students need to develop a mastery of basic research skills—a serious omission in education in these times of complex analysis and computer language. Obviously, where possible not only should the fundamentals of the various research methodologies be taught, but, also, students should be directed in the reading of the best examples of research utilizing such methodologies.

Too often the Afro-American ethnic is viewed as homogeneous. Perhaps this view prevails because of the common historic experience of oppression. Black studies is founded upon a recognition of the diversity of the Afro-American and the diversity of the experience of the subcultures within the ethnic. Therefore, a well-developed Black studies curriculum will meet the range of needs for information and skills that are vital to today's Black student, regardless of that student's post-college aspirations. As the previous discussion and diagram illustrate, the Black studies curriculum recognizes the diversity of the Black community and the right of the individual to choose the place and the manner for participation in the Black struggle.

Cruse has called attention to the need to maintain the spectrum of diversity within the Black community that allows for progress in a multi-faceted manner. Pointing to the need for the philosopher as well as the physician, for the individual to understand his or her own cultural underpinnings as a first point of departure before attempting to either serve others or participate in reform, Cruse writes:

> Black students in Afro-American Studies programs are no longer children of the sixties. They did not participate in the initial stages of Afro-American Studies and are, therefore, not motivated by the same needs and drives that created Afro-American Studies... radically creative academic endeavors have given way to career concerns,... many Black students no longer relate to academic studies unless these studies are essentially geared toward career goals... they are questioning the values of the intellectual approach to academic studies; they want the more functional approach... Afro-American Studies cannot thrive in such an atmosphere. It can only thrive where there is intellectual curiosity about society at large.
>
> ...Many people—and this includes students—have taken a dim view of what constitutes an intellectual, because they have been induced to think that an intellectual is someone who resides in an ivory tower and does nothing but contemplate abstractions. But that is not my interpretation of an intellectual;... An intellectual,...is someone who works with his or her brain on whatever level that may entail. There are people who work with their hands and brain; and some with their brain alone. All of these kinds of labor are necessary in a developing society...when it comes to social progress, what is demanded of as is the concept of this necessary division of labor harnessed for the pursuit of unified goals in society.[6]

This statement by Cruse places the contemporary Black student dilemma in perspective. Regardless of the student's educational intent, whether it be for a predominantly vocational program, a broad-based liberal arts program or some combination of these, the importance of Black studies as a part of the course agenda remains. As Holly M. Carter writes:

> The discussion of the functional significance of higher education has focused on whether Black Americans should approach education with a professional/vocational emphasis, or with an intellectual approach; the latter encompasses both the idealism of education for education's sake, and the individual's accumulation of academic credentials. The rationale for the professional/vocational emphasis, proffered that Black college students must be prepared for a specific vocational career as a means to social advancement. The Washington/DuBois debate.

Proposed Core Curriculum for a
Model Black Studies Program

```
┌─────────────────────────────────────────────┐
│         Introduction to Black Studies         │
└─────────────────────────────────────────────┘
```

Social/Behavioral Study Courses	History Course Area	Cultural Studies Course Area

| **Level Two** Basic Literature Review or Survey (race relations, social movements, etc.) | **Level Two** African Pre-History through Reconstruction | **Level Two** Basic Literature Review or Survey (music, aesthetic, etc.) |

| **Level Three** Current Research & Emerging Issues (demographics, social problems, etc.) | **Level Three** Post-reconstruction Current & Emerging Issues in Historical Interpretation & Evaluation | **Level Three** Current Research & Emerging Issues (contemporary cultural expression & transformation, etc.) |

```
                                    ┌────────────────────┐
                                    │  Research Methods   │
                                    └────────────────────┘
```

```
┌──────────────────────────────────────────────────────────┐
│ Level Four                                                 │
│ Senior Seminar Course Area,                                │
│ Synthesis & Application of Insights or  Previous Study     │
└──────────────────────────────────────────────────────────┘
```

Research   Job Market   Graduate Study

... It should be clear, then, that neither of these alternatives, the acquisition of credentials, nor the quest for careers, is adequate on its own... The Black student must strive to combine both of these quests, and he/she, unlike the white student counterpart, must add something else to this program of pursuits: concern, and a sense of purpose. The Black student must not think only in terms of his/her personal success, academically and professionally, but also of the community from which he/she came, and its needs. Black students... must both sacrifice their identity in order to succeed in the white-dominated United States.

...Blacks must make a serious effort, especially if they are to comprehend the past and present realities of the Black experience adequately to take
their legitimate place not only in higher education, but in a white dominated
society which has stereotyped the Black personality for too long.[7]

Education in the 1980s:
Black Studies for All Students

Students representing all the divergent backgrounds in higher education should
be encouraged to participate in Black studies programs. The support of these programs should not fall entirely upon the shoulders of Black students and faculty alone.
In particular, the importance of the study of the Black experience should be recognized by all who propose to provide quality and thoughtful service in a nation where
there is an increased emphasis upon a united but culturally diversified people.

Endnotes

1. For a discussion of the impact of the sixties upon faculty teaching Black studies and race
relations, see Wilson Record, "Response of Sociologists to Black Studies," in *Black Sociologists:
Historical and Contemporary Perspectives*, edited by James E. Blackwell and Morris Janowitz
(Chicago, IL: University of Chicago Press, 1974), pp. 368-402 and 253-366.

2. Robert Bierstedt, *The Social Order* (New York: McGraw-Hill, 1974), p. 4.

3. Harold Cruse, "The Academic Side of the Movement and the Movement Side of the Academic," in *Lectures: Black Scholars on Black Issues*, edited by Vivian V. Gordon (Washington,
DC: University Press of America, 1979).

4. Russell L. Adams, "Evaluating Professionalism in the Context of Afro-American Studies,"
The Western Journal of Black Studies, 4, no. 2 (Summer 1980), pp. 140-141.

5. Richard A. Long, "Black Studies Fall Into Place," *The Nation*, Vol. 218 (July 6, 1974),
pp. 19-20.

6. Harold Cruse, *op. cit.*

7. Holly M. Carter, "The Functional Significance of Higher Education for Black Students,"
The Western Journal of Black Studies, 4, no. 2 (Summer 1980), p. 114.

21.

The Struggle and Dream of Black Studies

Carlene Young

Afro-American Studies, Black Studies, Pan-African, Africana, and Afro-Caribbean Studies are but different names for programs of study that focus on the systematic investigation of people of African descent in their contacts with Europeans, their dispersal throughout the diaspora, and the subsequent institutionalization of racism and oppression as means of economic, political, and social subordination. The departments and programs vary in size, format, emphasis, and resources, but there is common understanding of the human predicament that resulted in the transformation of black people from African to slave.

It is now fifteen years since the Black Studies movement forced the American society to be aware that black people were no longer willing to accept their subordinate and subservient positions without challenging the system that continued to oppress them. The truism, oppression breeds rebellion, is as relevant today as it was centuries ago, even decades ago, and continues to be demonstrated on the world scene.

This article briefly highlights the background and circumstances that led to the development of Black Studies as an area of specialization, its subsequent institutionalization, and the role and function it serves for present and future generations.

Background

For Afro-Americans, the civil rights movement of the 1950s and rebellions of the 1960s provided the historical moment when a statement had to be made. That statement was, in fact, a declaration that white America could no longer feel comfortable with its assertions of superiority and expectations of acquiescence by blacks, regardless of the power of an oppressive system. The people, in their collectivity, responded very much as one who, pushed to the limits of endurance, responds to attempts to drive him/her mad by striking out at the symbols of abuse and the pathology of the experience.

Generations of Afro-Americans had experienced such wrongs as the violence and savagery of white lynch mobs; organized intimidation of the Ku Klux Klan and like-minded groups; injustice from legal and political systems theoretically committed to the principles of democracy and fair play; politicians and law-makers spouting ideals of freedom, equal opportunity, and justice while benefitting at all levels from the exploitation and oppression of persons of African ancestry; and, exclusion from participation in white institutions. Further, the mores of society had developed institutions and ways of life dependent on beliefs in the inherent superiority of Euro-Americans and the genetic inferiority of African Americans. The desire to maintain a dependent, powerless, and exploitable pool of cheap labor colored every aspect of American life and permitted excesses that continue to characterize the social fabric of its contemporary society.

The realization that persons of African ancestry — although more than a hundred years out of slavery — were freed but not free to explore their potential or the opportunities available to the white citizenry, became part of the collective consciousness and sparked a movement. The movement, although dominated by Black consciousness and identification with African heritage and values, included pragmatic demands for general changes in the system and specific changes in institutions relative to Afro-Americans. The demand for representation at all levels of government, guarantees of civil rights, access to educational institutions, economic opportunity, and social equality were the clarion calls of the day. Armed battles, loss of life, imprisonment, economic intimidation and reprisals were the price paid by countless Afro-Americans to bring about some basic restructuring in the society. The system, taken aback at this revolution of behavior and thought, was forced to respond.

The introduction of Black Studies programs into institutions of higher education was a direct response to this mandate for change. These institutions, both literally and figuratively, were understandably reluctant to incorporate Black Studies programs into their curricula — there was indeed a direct correlation between community activism and program implementation. The size, quality, resources, and effectiveness of the Black Studies programs varied with the skill, expertise, commitment, and community support of the implementer of each program.

The systematic study of the Afro-American experience from its African heritage to contemporary society and beyond is nowhere else pursued in the Academy than in Black Studies programs. Although the body of knowledge, for the most part, which forms the basis for the subject matter and content area of Black Studies has been available to scholars for several generations, it was not until the Black consciousness movement of the 1960s forced the issue that Afro-Americans began to be accorded their rightful place in the annals of the history and development of American society. The security of that progress depends on the existence of Black Studies programs.

Institutionalization

The future of Afro-American/Black Studies as a discipline is grounded in present day programs, personnel, and progressive philosophical orientations. The framework for continuity and perpetuity demands rigorous definition and support. Admittance to the "halls of ivy" was grudgingly given to these "newcomers" to academe. The tenuousness of acceptability has remained the same over the past fifteen years since their introduction. Arguments for the denial, abridgment, or withdrawal of Black Studies programs extend along a continuum of objections. There are those rationales based solely on beliefs of inferiority about any matter directly related to or directed by Afro-Americans. The other extreme is the "liberal" position that purportedly supports Black Studies concepts but equivocates on championing the programs because ideally there should be no need for such separate approaches. Neither argument is persuasive in view of the fact that there is continuing omission and distortion of the Afro-American experience from traditional course content, and limited numbers of Afro-American faculty and administrators in the university. These conditions contribute to the small number of Afro-Americans who graduate from predominantly white institutions.

In general, one may conclude that there has been little evidence of largesse or acceptance of this new discipline. Afro-American/Black Studies holds the potential to expand the dimensions of knowledge, explore uncharted areas of research, attract and reach an untapped pool of students, and provide the society with trained professionals who contribute to the positive growth and development of their communities.

On the contrary, Afro-American Studies units have been forced to struggle against continual assaults on their limited resources and structural integrity while maintaining strong academic programs, highly qualified faculty, and good enrollments. There are still too many in the Academy who resent the "intrusion" and, as a consequence, agitate for the demise of Afro-American Studies. It is important to note that the mere existence of Afro-American/ Black Studies as a discipline is in itself an affront to the sensibilities of the white power structure. The Afro-American Studies program serves as a commentary on a historical reality embedded in slavery, racism, segregation, and discrimination. This unpleasant reminder of a past at odds with espoused ideals of freedom, justice, and liberty for all is part of the psychological baggage that Black Studies carries, albeit unknowingly. The ethnocentrism of Euro-Americans is also a factor, insofar as it does not recognize the value or validity of any cultures other than that of Western civilization.[1]

This form of cultural racism, or the individual and institutional expression of belief in the superiority of one race's cultural heritage over that of another, was a primary target for redress by students in the '60s and '70s. Astin states, "The almost exclusive focus on Western culture and civilization of the traditional liberal arts program was under attack. Minority students complained justifiably that not only was consideration of minority cultures and values absent from the curriculum, but support service mechanisms were unavailable to them. As a result of these pressures, ethnic studies were introduced in various forms."[2]

The formation of Black Studies programs ranged from: (1) course offerings in various departments having to do with black subjects; (2) courses offered by faculty based in traditional departments, teaching courses under the direction of a coordinator; (3) one or two full time positions assigned to the program with faculty from other departments offering courses under the aegis of Black Studies; (4) some combination of the above and/or faculty holding joint appointments in Black Studies and another discipline; (5) research institutes, centers, or programs; (6) traditional academic department with a core of full-time faculty, chairperson, degree granting status, tenured positions, and representation on university governance committees. Kamoche analyzed these configurations and grouped them into three major structural types: (a) autonomous programs; (b) interdepartmental programs; and (c) joint-appointment programs.[3] The definitions and example of each type are most instructive and are based on a survey of one hundred programs. Departmental status has proven to be the most efficacious for achieving desired goals of scholarship, faculty autonomy, institutional stability, and student support networks.

The National Council for Black Studies (NCBS), the field's primary professional organization, has taken the official position that departmental format is the preferred structure for achievement of the goals and objectives of successful, sound Black Studies programs. The policy position of NCBS is one that urges non-departmental units "to establish the long-range goal of achieving departmental status" and pledges to provide support to units that seek to achieve that goal.

Structure is but one aspect of permanence and integration into a system. There are others: the *sine qua non* curricula, the quality of faculty and staff, responsive administrators, and effective support programs.

In an effort toward providing a foundation and guideline for all Black Studies entities regardless of structure, a core curriculum was devised by the NCBS. This paradigm outlines the content areas essential to any program purporting to provide an effective and comprehensive Black Studies concentration. The core curriculum for a model Afro-American/Black Studies program includes an introductory course that constitutes the first level of studies. The second and third levels involve basic review of literature, survey courses, current research, and emerging issues. Senior seminars that synthesize the insights of previous study and relate them to advanced study or research constitute the fourth level.

The primary areas of focus for the curricula are social/behavioral, historical, and cultural studies. Key constructs or "centrally important concepts, frameworks, or perspectives that serve as organizing principles" are clearly delineated.[4]

The core curriculum is the foundation upon which accreditation rests. Guidelines for accreditation have been developed by the NCBS. The organization is in the process of making application: to the Council on Post-Secondary Accreditation for recognition as the official accrediting body for Black Studies programs throughout the nation. These attempt at standardization and the establishment of quality levels stem from a felt need, maturation in the discipline, and recognition of the importance of diversity within definable parameters. Inherent in the definition of any profession is the capability of setting standards, monitoring members, providing assistance to neophytes, and providing self-definition.

Afro-American/Black Studies programs have come of age; now they provide the criteria and expertise essential for the selection, retention, and career mobility of its personnel, as well as of designating the institutional character of its programs. Unfortunately, some highly visible programs, as well as some of lesser stature, already have been co-opted both in terms of leadership and personnel. As a result, a number of Black Studies courses are being taught by persons who are not committed to the discipline and the goals of Black Studies. They have no understanding of the valuable contribution that these programs provide to students, the university, and the society.

Role and Function

It is commonly known that historically black colleges continue to play a vital role in the training of black professionals. Their record is formidable, even with all of their limitations. Yet, "Black colleges have been traditionally less well equipped in terms of resources, equipment, highly trained faculty, and suffer from a perpetual need of adequate funding.... Competition with some of the most prestigious white institutions of higher learning for students and faculty has aggravated the situation."[5] Because two-thirds of black college students are enrolled in predominantly white institutions, Black Studies programs on predominantly white campuses must serve

Afro-American students in the same manner and to the same extent that historically black colleges have served the black community.

Black Studies programs must function as the center of support networks, and provide role models and mentors for those students who have managed to enter institutions of higher learning. "Mentoring," as Charles Willie explains, "is providing a link of trust between individual and institutions and centering both until they embrace each other.... A mentor is a source of support, a sign of security, as a symbol of service that issues forth from a trusting relationship. Mentors share the dreams of their proteges. A mentor is the first line of defense whose belief in others enables them to believe in themselves."[6] The expectation that these young people can and will succeed, given the support, encouragement, and exposure to a learning process built on that premise, is fundamental to achievement against all other odds. "Minority students, young faculty and administrators on predominantly white college campuses feel as if they are on trial. Too few people believe in them...."[7]

The problem is not simply one of black students; it also affects black personnel at all levels in predominantly white institutions. Astin states: "Minority educators feel that they face special problems as professionals. Among the most serious of these problems are lack of institutional commitment to minorities, difficulty in gaining acceptance by and respect of their colleagues, institutional ethnocentrism that ignores the perspectives and values of other cultures, and being stereotyped and exploited as 'minority experts' in ways that limit opportunities for professional advancement."[8] If Afro-American/Black Studies programs are to function in an effective manner at predominantly white institutions, meeting the academic as well as the social-psychological needs of students and staff as they attempt to cope in an environment that for many is hostile, alienating, and overtly racist, they must take on many of the characteristics of black institutions and function in their stead.

New Challenges

Afro-American/Black Studies also must be what the writer has termed a VOICE that provides (a) Visibility—in academia and community; (b) Organization—structural and intra-intergroup resources; (c) Information—research, dissemination, and effective networking; (d) Community linkages—with responsibility, interaction, and reciprocity; and, finally, but most importantly, (e) Education—scholarship and training. To further elaborate on these areas of concern, the following suggestions or information extend from resources of data available to skilled personnel and effective linkages with other professional organizations. Organization is essential for structural integrity and stability as well as professional productivity, interaction, and coalition. Visibility is important insofar as issues need to be raised relevant to needs the black community and positions of advocacy on public policy. The black community was the instrument of creation of Black Studies programs. It maintains a proprietary interest in their continuation, perpetuity, and advancement. Therefore, Black Studies programs have a responsibility to identify community needs and concerns, and provide the expertise necessary to implement programs and policy to improve the quality of life for all Afro-Americans.

Black Studies faculty must get black students involved in their ongoing teaching and research interests. One of the major concerns has to be black students enrolled at predominantly white institutions. In many instances they are psychologically abused and intimidated as they pursue professional careers in medicine, law, and other specializations. It is incumbent upon Black Studies faculty, as experienced and knowledgeable persons, to assume the responsibility for ensuring the success of these students through individual and collective efforts. Afro-American/Black Studies departments can play a key role in providing support and encouragement to these students to complete their designated career goals by identifying them on the respective campuses and establishing a direct relationship with them.

Finally, the questions that one most frequently hears in the context of the liberal arts are, "What value is the degree in Black Studies?" or "What can one do with a B.A. in Afro-American Studies?" and "What jobs are available to your graduates?" Experience has shown that Afro-American Studies graduates are as capable and adept as graduates from any of the other social sciences. All social sciences require specialization and/or professional training in order to achieve upwardly mobile career positions. Even business and industry report, generally, that graduates from the social science and the liberal arts are much more effective in the work-place than those who are more narrowly trained. In a higher specialized, technological society, narrow areas of specialization quickly become obsolete. NCBS findings indicate that Afro-American majors are employed in business as personnel managers, affirmative action officers, public relations officers, computer systems analysts and programmers, and so forth. There are a number of graduates who have pursued careers as lawyers, community college counselors, public school teachers, and educational administrators. Others are employed as probation and parole officers and corrections and recreational specialists. In other words, Afro-American Studies graduates are taught to think, question, analyze, synthesize, identify, and use sources of knowledge and information. They are equipped to apply, these critical thinking and research skills in a most effective manner in the job market.

Black Studies grew out of a people's movement. In order to prosper and thrive, those people who are committed to the goals and objectives of Afro-American Studies must make American institutions accountable and responsive to the needs of black citizens and taxpayers.

The 1970s were years in which Black progress was confronted with "new, more subtle barriers."[9] The decade was characterized as one of retrenchment[10] in which the struggle for equality entered a new stage of development. Robert Hill of the National Urban League warned that "...what once appeared to be receptivity to and support for full equality for black Americans may well have been, at best, a temporary phenomenon and, at worst, an illusion."[11] This is the general climate in which the youth of today must struggle for their just place in American society and maintain their identity and sense of self.

The year 1984 marks the point of departure for a new generation who will reach maturity in the twenty-first century. This generation of Afro-Americans carry all the potential of their forebears, none of their experiences, and a limited sense of the continuity of their people. The problems that historically have been the bane of existence for Afro-Americans confront the new generation with as much vehemence as formerly, yet the perception that the ideals of American democracy are available to them merely for the seeking is a cruel hoax.

Segregated housing and schools (most frequently lacking in human and material resources), massive unemployment, limited job opportunity, inferior public education, pervasive poverty, unequal income for similar work, limited political representation, inadequate health care, and a criminal justice system that protects the monied and influential are issues that plague this generation with as much rapaciousness as in any earlier period in history. This is not to deny that changes have occurred in some overt forms of racism and discrimination. Yet, there is overwhelming evidence that attitudes, belief systems, and institutionalized racism rooted in ideologies of white supremacy persist in the United States. The segregated cities of this country provide little opportunity for meaningful interaction between racial/ethnic groups or opportunity for exchange of ideas and development of understanding and mutual respect. In 1980, there were thirty major cities with black residents comprising at least 45 percent or more of the total population. Over one-half (56 percent) of all poor blacks and one-fourth (27 percent) of all poor whites lived in central cities of metropolitan areas; and 72 percent of poor blacks lived in metropolitan areas.[12]

Census figures indicate there is a continual decline in objective measures of progress. In 1960, black families had a median income of 55 percent that of white families. The black/white family median income peaked in 1975 when black families had a median income of 62 percent that of white families. By 1982, however, black family median income had reverted to 55 percent that of the white family.[13]

Labor force participation rates since 1960 reflect the same dismal pattern. The percentage of black males 18-64 years of age in the labor force fell from 86 percent in 1965 to 75 percent in 1983. At the same time, there was a small increase in the labor force participation rate of black females 18-64 years of age, from 52 percent in 1965 to 58 percent in 1983. The real winners in this period of growth and affirmative action technology, however, were the large numbers of white females who entered the labor force, jumping from 45 percent in 1965 to 63 percent in 1983, an increase of 18 percent compared to 6 percent for black females.[14] The increase in the number of white females in the labor force between 1960 and 1980 (20 million) represents more people than the entire black labor force (male and female) of 12.5 million persons.[15] Despite these alarming statistics, white America persists in believing that Afro-Americans have reached parity, want something for nothing, and are overbearing in their demands for justice.[16] The National Opinion Research Center (NORC), which has monitored racial attitudes for more than thirty-five years, continues to report on changing attitudes.[17] The significance of these circumstances has far-reaching implications for both educational and public policy.

The full responsibility for the development and implementation of appropriate, equitable, and just policies lies with the present generation of young adults, both black and white. Afro-Americans must ensure each new generation that existence of a sound knowledge base that informs and elucidates the history and experience of black people, and keeps them aware that their history is not yet an integral part of instructional materials and curricula offerings. This is the continuing role of Black Studies programs as they struggle to exist in an era of advanced technology, with rapidly changing social patterns and limited resources. The dream of Black Studies programs lies in the ability to provide the foundation which supports and enriches; to nourish the vision and motivation of present and future generations; and to reaffirm the continuity between past, present, and future. The fundamental changes that are taking place in the world community will not allow Afro-Americans to be complacent as a people.

Endnotes

1. See Joel Dreyfuss, "The New Racism," *Black Enterprise* (January 1978), pp. 41-44, 54.

2. Alexander Astin, *Minorities in American Higher Education* (San Francisco: Jossey-Bass, 1982), p. 194.

3. Jidlaph Kamoche, "The Interdepartmental and Autonomous Types of Afro-American Studies Program: A Comparative Perspective on Personnel Strengths and Weaknesses," in *The*

State of Black Studies in White Institutions (Conference proceedings, October 27-28, 1978, California State University, Chico).

4. National Council for Black Studies, Inc., *Black Studies Core Curriculum* (Bloomington: Indiana University, 1981).

5. Carlene Young, "Restructuring Society: Education and Afro-Americans," Western Journal *of Black Studies*, in press.

6. Charles V. Willie, "Mentoring Methodologies for Minority Students in White Institutions" (Address delivered at University of Santa Clara, September 10, 1982).

7. *Ibid.*

8. Astin, *Minorities in American Higher Education*, p. 184.

9. Allen Pifer, "Black Progress: Achievement, Failure and an Uncertain Future," (New, York: Annual Statement, Carnegie Commission, 1977).

10. See James D. McGhee, "Changing Demographics in Black America," *The State of Black America 1983* (New York: National Urban League, Inc., January 1983), p. 1.

11. Robert Hill, *The Illusion of Black Progress* (Washington, DC: National Urban League Research Department, 1978), p. 6.

12. U.S. Bureau of the Census, Advance Report, PHC 80-VI, *1980 Census of Population and Housing* (Washington, DC: U.S. Government Printing Office, 1980).

13. McGhee, "Changing Demographics," p. 7.

14. See U.S. Bureau of Labor Statistics data in Denys Vaughn-Cooke, "The Economic State of Black America — Is There a Recovery?" in *The State of Black America 1984* (New York: National Urban League, Inc., January 1984).

15. McGhee, "Changing Demographics," p. 9.

16. J.M. Ross et al., "Patterns of Support for George Wallace: Implications for Racial Chance," *Journal of Social Issues*, 32 (1976), 69-91, and, R. Farley et al., "Chocolate City, Vanilla Suburbs," *Social Science Research*, 7 (1978), 319-344.

17. D.G. Taylor et al., "Attitudes Toward Racial Integration," *Scientific American*, 238 (June 1978), 42-49.

22.

Black Studies in Historical Perspective

Ronald Bailey

This paper presents an overview of the major intellectual forces affecting black scholars in the past and an outline of what will occur in the future. The role of the white researcher is discussed in relationship to the concept of scientific objectivity, with an illustration of how the very concepts employed by researchers ("Integration" versus "liberation") channel their energies in one direction as opposed to another. Discussion of black behavior is grounded in a consideration of African behavior. Black Americans are viewed as fundamentally African, not European; the difference between these two provides the legitimate epistemological foundation for a distinctive Black Studies.

The purpose of this paper is to contribute to the development of sounder scholarship in Black Studies. This purpose can be accomplished if some of the major historical forces which have influenced and are now influencing the selection and explication of problems by black scholars are clearly understood. If effort along these lines serves to clarify at least one point of contention or presents a simple new aspect on which further development of black social inquiry can proceed, a contribution of worth will have been made.

The effort here is undertaken first by attempting to review and identify the trends in black intellectual activity. That the rise of Black Power is correlated with a new intention regarding black social inquiry is assumed; it is then necessary to deal with the development of Black Studies—what it has been, what it is, and what it is to be.

The focus then turns to the context in which black social inquiry is embedded and argues for the development of the Pan-African frame as the most relevant one for black intellectual activity. Black Studies is suggested as the formulation which best reconciles the context with our present needs. The basic theme throughout this paper is the desire not only to present the arguments for various perspectives, but to do so in a way that leads to a better understanding of what led to them; consequently, arguments which may be used to counter the points herein are anticipated and commented upon.

Black Social Inquiry: A Review

Conspicuous by its absence in contemporary academia is a critical and interpretative history of black intellectual traditions. Such a history seems essential if we are properly to understand current attempts to develop a newer framework for black social inquiry. With the recognition that such a treatment is underway, the discussion below provides only an outline of the broader themes.

It is perhaps first necessary to note the causal primacy of Euro-American racism in creating the context in which black social inquiry (and all social inquiry and thinking about blacks) has been undertaken. The impact of this racism distorts the questions selected, influences the modes of analysis adopted, and shapes the conclusions reached. Neither black nor white scholars have escaped this phenomenon. The full explication and understanding of this reality will reveal much about the true nature of the problems faced by black people—then and now. The quality of intellect demonstrated by black scholars functioning in the face of racist absurdities should serve to inspire generations to come.

To begin, we might well let W.E.B. DuBois (1898), as much a precursor of black intellectual traditions as any, pose the guiding question:

> The present period in the development of sociological study is a trying one; it is the period of observation, research and comparison—work always wearisome, often aimless, without well-settled principles and guiding lines, and subject ever to the pertinent criticism: What, after all, has been accomplished? [p. 14].

In assaying the tremendous opportunities a developing United States offered for the field of sociologists, DuBois was moved to make an observation which seems strikingly current:

> In one field, however, and a field perhaps larger than any other single domain of social phenomena, there does not seem to have awakened as yet a fitting realization of the opportunities for scientific inquiry. This is the group of social phenomena arising from the presence in this land [circa 1898] of eight million persons of African descent [p. 14].

DuBois' treatment is one which strives to place the problems of black people in the context of American society; he describes them as "not one problem, but rather a plexus of social problems...that...group themselves about those Africans whom two centuries of slave-trading brought into the land."

The prophetic vision which was to characterize much of what DuBois would say is obvious:

> So far as the Negro race its concerned, the Civil War simply left us face to face with the same sort of problems of social conditions and caste which were beginning to face the nation a century ago. It is these problems that we are to-day somewhat helplessly—not to say carelessly—facing, forgetful that they are living, growing social questions whose progeny will survive to curse the nation, unless we grapple with them manfully and intelligently [p. 17].

A recent review of the beginnings of black sociology asserts that "DuBois' plea for an objective study of American blacks and American race relations became the hallmark of the next stage in the history of the sociology of the black community—the monographs emanating from the famous Chicago school of American sociology [Bracey, 1971, p. 5]." Bracey discusses what he sees as the substantial impact of the Chicago school and Robert Park on black sociology as exemplified by such black scholars as Charles S. Johnson, E. Franklin Frazier, Bertram W. Doyle, St. Clair Drake, and Horace Cayton. Park demanded that the discipline of sociology attempt to cast off much of the racism that characterized it in his day; he emphasized a conviction that scientific knowledge could help to solve race problems, but that only detachment in research would produce scientific knowledge. His popularity with young black scholars was due perhaps in part to his liberal attitude and "objectivity," displayed in the racist climate of that period. Park also viewed detached social knowledge as essential for decisions of policymakers. His conceptual and methodological influence can be seen in the work of his students, most of whom viewed race relations in an international context. Park's advocacy of the use of techniques such as participant observation, case studies, and his conceptualization of race relations in terms of conflict, competition, and accommodation were carried on by the young black scholars of the day.

It is necessary to understand the climate in which earlier, black social scientists endeavored if we are to recognize the forces which shaped them. Much of the work of such scholars as Johnson and Frazier was in the spirit of detachment urged by Park, but significant in the sense of urgency with which it was undertaken. The classic themes that pervade much of the social research on black people were epitomized by DuBois:

> I determined to put science into sociology through a study of the condition of problems of my own group. I was going to study the facts, any and all facts, concerning the American Negro and his plight, and by measurement and comparison and research, work up to any valid generalization which I could [1940, p. 51].

It is important to note that Gunnar Myrdal's *An American Dilemma* (1944) was completed with the assistance of several of the black scholars mentioned above. According to Myrdal, "The primary purpose of studies of this character is the collection, analysis and interpretation of existing knowledge." Guided by this, he attempted no less than a "comprehensive study of the Negro in the United States, to be undertaken in a wholly objective and dispassionate way as a social phenomenon [1944, p. 36]."

The classic study of Chicago by Drake and Cayton (1945) reflected the influence of Park, to whom it is dedicated. An important commentary is found in Richard Wright's introduction to this volume:

> *Black Metropolis* is not a volume of mere facts. The basic facts are assumed. The hour is too late to argue if there is a Negro problem or not. Riots have swept the nation and more riots are pending. This book assumes that the Negro's present position in the United States results from oppression of Negroes by white people, that the Negro's conduct, his personality, his culture, his entire life flow naturally and inevitably out of the conditions imposed upon him by white America [Wright, 1945, p. xxix].

Clearly the volume is substantially different from earlier studies of "the Negro problem" in America, particularly with respect to its underlying assumptions.

The assumption guiding such research was that "racial prejudice" and "discrimination" were the causes of the predicament of black people. The implications of this assumption are succinctly noted by Alkalimat (1969):

> While the concepts prejudice and discrimination are helpful on an analytical level of theory because they are so easily operationalized and quantified, racism is the more appropriate theoretical description because it captures the qualitative nature of the oppression [p. 29].

Alkalimat notes also that the kind of empirical research associated with such concepts as prejudice and discrimination has increased our access to more incidents of social reality but only at the cost of the "falsification of our understanding."

Closely allied to the above generalization is one which seems to indicate that many of the scholars we have discussed adopted the conviction that only detached scientific research could help to solve race problems—a point repeatedly stressed by Park. This is understandable, given the scientific tenor of the times. There was also a general desire to give the nation a body of "truth" upon which it might act intelligently. Yet, black scholars have always recognized the limits of "detached scientific" research.

Regarding the state of sociological study DuBois (1940) once stated, "What, after all, has been accomplished?" His answer provides an appropriate introduction to the current critique of black intellectual traditions in social inquiry:

> To this the one positive answer which years of research and speculation have been able to return is that the phenomena of society are worth the most careful and systematic study, and whether or not this study may lead to a systematic body of knowledge deserving the name of science, it cannot fail to give the world a mass of truth worth the knowing [DuBois, 1940, p. 20].

The crux of the current critique is that while a "mass of truth" is necessary for black survival, it is no longer—indeed never has been—sufficient. Inherent in the current critique is the need to work out the imperatives of present necessities. Realizing this temporal shift, we can recognize that the works of DuBois, Frazier, Drake, Cayton, and others have laid substantial foundations on which to construct a newer framework for guiding black social inquiry. With the confidence of knowing that we have been proceeded by black intellectual giants, we can proceed successfully to meet our present duties.

Black Studies: Past and Present

It is difficult to specify the point at which the watershed in the quality of race relations in the United States occurred. Certainly the rise of Black Power, which surfaced dramatically during the summer of 1966, should be considered. The cry heard around the world from Africans domiciled in North America was no longer one for "integration," but one which signalled a determination among black people to amass the power necessary to secure their liberation—by any means necessary. It is this same context which hastened a crystallization of a newer perspective on the recording and interpretation of black experiences.

Black Power was fueled by and in turn spurred on intensification of the questioning of prevailing modes in (black) social inquiry. In areas characterized by more militant or nationalist thought (mainly the urban North), the upsurge of interest in new interpretations was most profound. Those who were very early followers of (or listeners to) the Honorable Elijah Muhammad and the late Malcolm X, for example, were exposed to such interpretations.

Interest in a newer black interpretation which had for a long time remained in the province of the mosque and headquarters of nationalist organizations soon began to spill over into other areas of the black community. The appearance of a variety of black student organizations on white campuses facilitated an organized drive for the institutionalization of this new black perspective into the college curriculum. Under pressure to provide (or allow or tolerate) an educational experience more relevant to the lives of black students, many colleges and universities took steps to grant this demand, invariably formed in terms of the need for "Black Studies" programs. Those schools that were initially reluctant in 1965-66 were sufficiently guilt-ridden after the slaying of Martin Luther King in 1968 to capitulate to student demands.

It is interesting to note that this was not the first time that turmoil had led to the creation of new mechanisms to deal with the scholarly treatment of the experiences of Africans. The successful struggles of several African countries against colonial rulers in securing their independence had much to do with the expansion of African Studies Programs in the U.S. during the 1950s.

This push for the introduction of Black Studies into traditional white curriculums, when properly chronicled, contributes much to our understanding of what may prove to be a critical factor in the struggle of African people for their liberation. Its parameters are thus very important.

The case of Yale University, one of the few where a meaningful body of published material emerged from its developmental stages (Robinson et al., 1969), is perhaps characteristic of the general movement. After several months of effort, the Black Students Alliance of Yale "discovered that little progress was being made in the struggle to convince the faculty at large of the validity and importance...[and] the urgent necessity for including the study of Afro-American societies and cultures in the curriculum of Yale College [p. vii]." The immediate solution was to convene an educational experience for professional educators designed to bring together faculty and administrative personnel from a number of schools and a group of respected and recognized black and white intellectuals who were vitally concerned with the issues raised by student demands. The conference proceedings provide some critical comments regarding issues related to Black Studies. But a careful perusal of the document reinforces the view of the young black sociologist, Abdul Alkalimat:

> I think the symposium that's being held here is very impressive, but—as many people feel—I think there are many false issues being raised. I don't know whether or not these are consciously being raised as false issues, but I think the question whether or not the black experience is relevant for intellectual inquiry is indeed beyond a question of a doubt—and everybody here, it seems that if any human experience is relevant for intellectual consideration—the black experience has to be included. And the notion that it would be questioned in such an audience is too grotesque to be amusing [Robinson et al., 1969, p. 54].

If we are not to engage in definitional acrobatics, how then are we to approach Black Studies? Let us look at some of the issues. Since these concerns are very valid ones, no attempt at refutation will be attempted. One criticism voiced was that Black Studies was nothing more than a diversionary outlet—a mere palliative offered by white college administrators as a ploy to further subvert the struggle for liberation. A quote in an article by Howard (1970) is appropriate:

> The problem which the European in South Africa must face is what to do with those Africans whose learning has given them ambitions beyond the industrial colour bar. Ambitions need outlets if their latent energies are not to be diverted by continual frustration into anti-social activities [p. 67].

Howard's comment following the quote is most instructive: "Perhaps we can begin to see the booming 'black studies business' in light of the South African experience!"

The relationship of activism and scholarship and the question of "relevance" have also been sharply raised. Drake (1969) suggests that:

> The activism of the black student movement has resulted in an anti-intellectual bias among some of the most committed students, and in a demand for

greater relevance of intellectual activity among a wider segment of the student population...there are intellectual tasks associated with the Black Revolution just as there are with any revolution; and these tasks are as important as the "street tasks [p. 4]."

The tenuous and historic relationship of many black intellectuals to the struggle of black people certainly has as much to do with the demands now being placed upon them as does the activism of students. That such pressures are likely to intensify in the future is probable, but how responsive black scholars are in making themselves accessible and relevant to the legitimate aspirations of black folk will prove to be the decisive factor in the outcome.

Despite indications to the contrary, there are some very important questions which suggest themselves in the discussion of Black Studies. A most important one has been pinpointed by Drake (1969):

> The very use of the term Black Studies is by implication an indictment of American and Western European scholarship. It makes the bold assertion that what we have heretofore called "objective" intellectual activities were actually white studies in perspective and content; and that a corrective of bias, a shift in emphasis, is needed, even if something called "truth" is set as the goal. To use a technical sociological term, the present body of knowledge has an ideological element in it, and a counter-ideology is needed. Black studies supply that counter-ideology [p. 5].

The point being made in the above quotation is at the base of most of the current discussions of the need for Black Studies. The whole process of education is seen as one that is basically geared to produce those supportive inputs for the system of which it is a part. In a Western setting, of course, this can only mean the perpetuation and embellishment of values and norms that are part and parcel of the Western tradition. As Turner (1970) notes:

> White studies is a system of intellectual legitimacy which defines the activities and experiences of white Western people as the universal yardstick of human existence. Black studies challenges this assumption and asserts that white is not now, nor has it ever been either intrinsically right or complete. However, whites have attributed universal value to their own Anglo-American particularism, and have sought to absorb and distort other cultures in their midst [p. 6].

Implied in the comments above are several ideas related to a long-standing debate in the social sciences. An anonymous lawyer who participated in the Yale symposium on Black Studies cited above put the point in excellent fashion:

> It seems to me that the question before this university is whether there is some intellectual integrity in widening further and further the range of inquiry and the range of discussion in looking at new problems and also those problems which we've never explored before...Then...we've created a viable basis for expanding the curriculum and inquiry without acquiescing in the notion that tied to such expanded inquiry has to be any particular programmatic notion of how our society should be changed [Robinson et al., 1969, p. 29].

This comment raises two issues. One of these involves the relationship between theoretical and applied research. The other — widening the range of inquiry and discussion — is related to that area of social inquiry termed the sociology of knowledge.

The position of the relativity of knowledge is dealt with rather thoroughly in the work of Karl Mannheim (1936). He suggests that much of what we "know" — and almost all of the process of arriving at this knowledge—is socially conditioned. And, further, that certain kinds of knowledge are only accessible to people who have experienced particular kinds of social reality. The discussion centering around this issue has usually been referred to as the problem of objectivity in science. The pitfalls of this argument for the treatment of the experiences of African people are becoming more clearly understood.

In an excellent argument charging that problems of epistemology (i.e., the validity of knowledge) have been neglected in favor of rampant empiricism, and that social scientists have ignored the question of the relativity of social knowledge "as though Mannheim and Marx never existed," Clark (1970) states the thrust of Black Studies as follows: (a) all forms of knowledge in the social sciences emanate from the social reality created by the organization of society; (b) to the extent that race forms the basis of American social organization, there are different domains of social reality possessed by blacks as opposed to whites; (c) there is an official version of social reality legitimized by those in control of the dominant knowledge generating apparatus in society; and (d) this official social reality forms the basis of theoretic inquiries into social problems, and to the extent that it does, such theories are racist.

Thus, Clark defines Black Studies as:

the research, practice, and teaching of a social science whose repertoire of concepts include as fundamental and essential these derived directly from the Black American cultural experience. Black Studies is a *weltanschauung*, an orientation, a way of viewing problems—particularly those problems related to the life of Black Americans. . . .

The genesis of Black Studies lies not so much in a complex of reactions to traditional disciplines, per se, as it does from a need to employ concepts which have direct empirical referents [are relevant] in the body of Black cultural experience. Traditional concepts are reacted insofar as these deny, distort, or otherwise modify the content of Black social reality [1970, p. 4].

What is indicated above, it seems, is the explication of the beginnings of a new mode for black social inquiry—a mode that is substantially different from the prevailing mode rooted in the Euro-American academic tradition which has guided what Clark refers to as "the study of Black people" (as opposed to Black Studies). In part a reaction to white social science but in larger measure providing its own internal justification, this new mode is becoming the philosophical foundation on which much of black social inquiry in years to come will be built.

It is possible, indeed necessary, to point to the growing body of writings flowing from this emerging tradition. In an excellent unpublished manuscript, "Toward a Black Social Science," Walters (1970) applauds the work of black social scientists "who have had the courage to try to criticize wrong-headed approaches whether from whites or blacks and the originality to try and create a black framework for their analysis [p. 12]."

Harold Cruse, an important commentator on the overall thrust of black social inquiry, states in a recent essay:

[The] critical assault on Black social, political, and cultural thought was premeditated. It was my conviction that black social thought of all varieties was in dire need of some ultra-radical overhauling if it was to meet the comprehensive test imposed by the sixties. Now that the sixties are history, I am still convinced—even more so—that black social thought is in need of ultra-radical overhauling. In fact, the arrival of the seventies revealed to me that I had underestimated the critical reassessing black social thought really needed [1971, p. 15].

Writing on the ideology of black social science, Alkalimat claims that:

Social science has constructed a set of terms to explain black people and their experiences and, for the most part, these terms have suffered from being based on sterile analytical theory that attempts to classify social reality and not explain its essential nature [1969, p. 31].

And, in response, he argues, "We must develop a social theory consistent with a revolutionary Black ideology so that what we know will be worth knowing." Furthermore, Alkalimat develops for social analysis in line with this need a set of concepts presenting a clear alternative to those prevalent in conventional (i.e., Euro-American) social science. A partial list of these follows:

White Social Science	*Black Social Science*
Negro	African (Black)
Segregation	Colonization
Tokenism	Neo-Colonialism
Integration	Liberation
Equality	Freedom
Assimilation	Africanization

The conceptual framework implicit in the work of Carmichael and Hamilton (1967) is an indication of this new mode in black social inquiry. They characterize the relationship between black communities and the American system as one of political, economic, and sociocultural colonization. Their use has contributed much to the clarification and use of the concept of colonization as a paradigm in analyzing such relationships. It is important to note, again, that the new modality in black social inquiry does not begin in a reaction to Euro-American social science. As Walters notes, "Black life has been distinctive enough and separate enough to constitute its own uniqueness and it is on the basis of that uniqueness that the ideology and the methodology of Black Social Science rests [1970, p. 18]."

Conclusion

If Black Studies is to become a workable area of endeavor, what is perhaps most needed is some explication of the notion of social inquiry. Much of the polemics that revolve around Black Studies can be traced to a basic misunderstanding of what is involved in this process. Consequently, reactions are usually based on stereotyped notions of what science is or should be, or what validation is, or should be, and the like. Definitional clarity of the process of social inquiry is essential. From the perspective of Black Studies, what do such words as "fact," "concept," "generalization," "hypothesis," "theory," "model," and the like suggest? What are the *facts* about the black experience? What purposes will concepts serve? With what process do we test and validate hypotheses; What is involved in the process of theorizing, and why is it at all significant? Are we in search of explanation, prediction, or something else?

These questions have been broached in a more practical sense. The colonial anal-ogy is being widely used as a model that offers an explanation of the plight of African peoples throughout the world. Perhaps "political traumatism" might serve better to explain the impact of Euro-American intrusion on African peoples than "alienation," "apathy," and the like (Bailey, 1971). The use of such terms as "oppression," "slav-ery," "pan-Africanism," "negritude," and a host of others suggests itself as worthy of consideration if we are serious about an understanding and alteration of the pre-sent conditions of black people.

The question of methodology also needs serious attention. The task ahead is to create new methodologies that flow from and do justice to the exigencies of our ex-periences as a people. How much time we have to engage in the kind of polemics that attack established disciplines is an open question. From my own experiences, debates over the quantitative/ qualitative tension in social science, the implications of the be-havioral persuasion in political science, the developmental polemic, and similar oth-ers have proven, in the words of Bennett, "abstract, false, and diversionary."

This is not to suggest that anything which is traditional is not useful for our pur-poses. As Hare (1969) suggests, our attempts at dealing with these questions anew will "in some regards... subsume and overlap existing norms of scholarly endeavor [p. 62]." The essential difference will be that our goals will be something other than the blind attachment to ideas, ideals, and norms that tend to destroy rather than clar-ify and to classify rather than explain the nature of our situation.

References

Alkalimat, A.H. The ideology of black social science. *Black Scholar*, 1969, 1 (2), 28-35.

Bailey, R. *Black business enterprise*. New York: Basic Books, 1971.

Bracey, J. *The black sociologists*. Belmont, California: Wadsworth, 1971.

Carmichael, S., & Hamilton, C. *Black power*. New York: Vintage, 1967.

Clark, C. Black studies and the study of black people. Unpublished manuscript. Stan-ford University, 1970.

Cruse, H. Black and white: Outlines of the next stage (Part I). *Black World*, January 1971.

Drake, St. C. Black studies: Toward an intellectual framework. Address delivered at Brooklyn College, September 23, 1969.

Drake, St. C., & Cayton, H. *Black metropolis*. New York: Harcourt, Brace & World, 1945.

DuBois, W.E.B. *Dusk of dawn*. New York: Harcourt, Brace, 1940.

DuBois, W.E.B. The study of the Negro problem. *Annals of the American Academy of Political and Social Science*, 1898 (January), XI.

Hare, N. The challenge of a black scholar. *Black Scholar*, 1969, 1 (2), 58-63.

Howard, J. How to end colonial domination of black America. *Negro Digest*, Janaury 1970.

Mannheim, K. *Ideology and utopia*. New York: Harcourt, 1936.

Myrdal, G. *An American dilemma*. New York: Harper & Row, 1944.

Robinson, A.L., et al. (Eds.) *Black studies in the university*. New Haven: Yale University Press, 1969.

Turner, J. Black studies and a black philosophy of education. *Blacklines*, Winter 1970, 5-9.

Walters, R.W. Toward a black social science. Unpublished manuscript, 1970.

Wright, R. Introduction to St. C. Drake & H. Cayton, *Black metropolis*. New York:Harcourt, Brace & World, 1945.

23.

The Black Studies Movement: Afrocentric-Traditionalist-Feminist Paradigms for the Next Stage

Darlene Clark Hine

In 1987 the Ford Foundation asked me to visit a select number of Black Studies programs, departments, centers, and institutes and to prepare a report that would help to determine and direct the nature and extent of foundation involvement over the next few years. After I completed the project the Foundation decided to publish in essay format the report's introduction, and summaries of similar investigations conducted by Robert L. Harris of Cornell University, and by Nellie McKay of the University of Wisconsin. The document was appropriately edited to protect the identities of those interviewed. Although the report became a basis for the subsequent distribution of over three million dollars in grant moneys not all Black Studies scholars and administrators were pleased.

Most critical of my specific involvement in the Ford Foundation examination of Black Studies was Selase W. Williams, chair of National Council for Black Studies (NCBS). Williams maintained in the fall 1990 NCBS *Newsletter*, "While Hine is a reputable historian, her minimal contact with the Black Studies Movement and lack of understanding of the real issues in this developing discipline become readily apparent to the initiated reader." He elaborated, "After reading Hine's essay, it appears that Hine does not view the mission of Black Studies as fundamentally different from that of traditional academic disciplines." It was this latter comment that started me on a course of systematic review of just about everything that I could find concerning the evolution of Black Studies over the past two decades.

Williams was correct on one score, I had assumed that as an academic endeavor the purpose or mission of Black Studies was to create and disseminate new knowledge about the social, political, cultural, and historical experiences of Black people of African descent throughout the Diaspora. Yet, his criticism struck more than a defensive chord. I wondered indeed if I had missed something, and therefore determined to discover what it was that made Black Studies, as Williams asserts "fundamentally different from that of traditional academic disciplines."

Inasmuch as sufficient time has passed since the modern incarnation of Black Studies as an intellectual movement, what are we to make of its accomplishments, contributions, and shortcomings?[1] This essay, is at heart an exercise in Black intellectual history of both the movement of Black Studies and the idea of Black Studies.

In their text, *Introduction to Afro-American Studies* Adbul Alkalimat and Associates define Black Studies by contrasting it with traditional or "mainstream" disciplines. They hold that, "In general, the mainstream disciplines have focused on the

Black experience by emphasizing race relations from the point of view of the interests of white people. They have lacked a theoretical perspective that is dynamic and
is focused on the politics of social change. The mainstream disciplines thus were unprepared to deal with both the Intellectual concerns of Black people and the political
actions of the masses of Black people."[2] It must be pointed out that many black
scholars working within mainstream disciplines have offered brilliant critiques and
have successfully transformed the work being done in key disciplines.

In 1969, the chair of the Black Studies Department at the University of Pittsburgh, Jack L. Daniel, maintained in another definition:

> Black Studies constitutes an attempt to understand the human experience
> using Black experience as both a focal point and a platform from which to
> view...Black studies is not a matter of empirical versus descriptive, histori-
> cal, and intuitive, nor is Black Studies a matter of politics and economics ver-
> sus culture and consciousness. Black Studies in this sense is not a matter of
> "versus," and at a minimum Black Studies is concerned with the integration
> of these "approaches." Similarly, Black Studies is concerned with the inte-
> gration of the objective and the subjective, the material and the spiritual, or
> the visible and the invisible.... Black Studies is for all Human beings.[3]

In 1969, Nathan Hare and Jimmy Garret at San Francisco State organized the
first Black Studies program in the country. Hare offered the following assurances as
to the purpose of Black Studies; "The main motivation of Black Studies is to entice
black students (conditioned to exclusion) to greater involvement in the educational
process. Black Studies is, above all, a pedagogical device."[4] His view was consistent
with those of the students whose demands were intended to make Black Studies a
pedagogical instrument. The twin pillars of student demands called for the teaching
of Black history and the hiring of Black faculty. Out of this oppositional Black student consciousness emerged a two-decade long critique of institutional racism in
higher education.

It is well to underscore that members of other excluded or distorted minority, or
emerging majority groups, and women took cues from the Black Studies movement
and made their own demands for curriculum revision and faculty diversification.
Thus on the heels of, or in some instances, contemporaneously with Black Studies,
Ethnic Studies and Women Studies appeared on college and university campuses.

Most Black Studies scholars agree that the field is distinguished from other academic endeavors because of the tension between theory and practice and that they
must always respond to the needs of two masters, the academy on the one hand, and
the Black community on the other. Due to the political underpinnings surrounding
the birth of the field and a persistent, though often muted and intangible academic
racism, however, some Black Studies scholars nurture an oppositional consciousness
to the very mainstream institutions that employ them, and from the more established
disciplines in which they received their graduate training. Their "outsider within"
posture arose, in part, out of the radical protests and demands of the first generation
of Black college students on predominantly white college and university campuses
during the late 1960s. As one scholar has described the impetus, "Black college students recognized the urgent necessity for Black Studies in the nation's higher education institutions as one way to make schools more understanding of diversity. These
students had marched in Mississippi, been spat upon in Alabama, survived attacks in
the inner cities of Chicago, Detroit and Newark, and they were ready to revamp
higher education and rid it of its racist policies. One way to do this was to insist on
intellectual treatment of the Black American experience."[5] Recently, Molefi Asante,

the author and architect of "Afrocentricity,"[6] has argued that there were problems with the initial formulation of Black Studies. He declared that,

The field of Black Studies or African-American Studies was not born from a clear ideological position in the 1960s. Our analyses as students were correct, but our solutions were often fragmentary, ideologically immature, and philosophically ill-defined. The absence of a comprehensive philosophical position, with attendant possibilities for a new logic, science, and rhetoric condemned us to experimentation with an Islamic base, a Marxist base, a civil service base, a reactionary nationalist base, a social service base, a systematic nationalist base, or a historical-cultural base.[7]

Asante further maintains that systematic nationalists tended to be grouped with the historical-cultural school because they, at least, understood that Black Studies implied a different perspective although they could never thoroughly articulate that perspective. Asante, however, names the Afrocentric perspective, and highlights the crucial distinction that just because a professor is Black, it does not mean that the professor is Afrocentric. Afrocentricity as that perspective becomes indispensable to our understanding of Black Studies; otherwise, we have a series of intellectual adventures in Eurocentric perspectives about Africans and African Americans. That is why the students of the sixties, in their moment of intellectual purity which remained uncaptured until now, railed against white instructors of Black Studies. As we now know the mistake was not in their intention: to have a black perspective (they did not refer to it as Afrocentricity) but it was in their misunderstanding that Afrocentricity meant black professors."[8]

The tortured birth of Black Studies has long affected how this newest of the academic disciplines has been perceived and evaluated. But this is not the only difficulty impeding a judicious assessment of its institutional and intellectual evolution. Race remains a substantial barrier that blocks and distorts our view. In one regard, Asante is on target. All African American academicians who work on subject matter pertaining to peoples of African descent regardless of individual perspective and orientation are, as a rule, lumped together and categorized as Black Studies scholars. It would appear that their racial identity outweighs other differences. The past few months I have experimented with ways of ordering and distinguishing difference between Black Studies scholars, and analyzing the Afrocentric impulse. Risking oversimplification, and the ire of those mentioned and unnamed, I have devised a model of ideal types within the Black Studies community of scholars, writers, and thinkers. It is important to emphasize that these are ideal types and that there is considerable movement between them.

The three groups of scholarly practitioners fueling the Black Studies mission of creating and disseminating new knowledge that illuminates the past and present social, economic, political and educational conditions of African Americans and of all peoples of African descent throughout the diaspora can be separated into "Traditionalists," "Authentists" and/or "Afrocentrists," and Black Feminists.

When I prepared the Ford Foundation report I essentially focused on the scholarship produced by the "Traditionalists," consisting of both Black and White academicians in sociology, history, and in literary theory. Based upon an assessment of their work, I concluded that Black Studies was alive and well and indeed flourishing at institutions fortunate enough to boast a critical representation of academically respected, highly visible scholars. It was easy for me to "roll call" the names and titles of the books authored by James D. Anderson, John Blassingame, Clayborne Carson, Barbara Fields, Thomas Holt, Earl Lewis, Nell Irvin Painter, Leslie Owens, Albert Raboteau, Joe Trotter, and the late Nathan I. Huggins, to name only a few historians. Among the scholars of African American Literature the stellar roster included

Michael Awkward, Houston Baker, Hazel Carby, Barbara Christian, Henry Louis Gates, Jr., Deborah McDowell, Nellie McKay, Arnold Rampersad, Valerie Smith, and Mary Helen Washington. Similarly, among the acknowledged Black sociologists are Walter Allen, Elijah Anderson, Bart Landry, Aldon D. Morris, and William Julius Wilson. Neither time nor space permit the listing of all the traditional scholars of African descent who have enriched intellectual discourse and through their works have challenged old paradigms that diminished, distorted, and dismissed the meaning and essence of Black thought, culture, and history. Virtually every established social science and humanities discipline, including art history, music, psychology, political science, and economics has had to contend with the fresh interpretations and perspectives, innovative methodologies, new sources, and probing questions that characterize the best of traditional Black Studies scholarship.

The scholarly monographs collectively gave notice to and unveiled the myriad accomplishments and experiences of Black men and women from every strata, segment, and territory in the African World. The previously muted voices and actions of slaves, agricultural workers, urban migrants, industrial laborers, writers, artists, musicians, reformers, accommodationists, and nationalists demonstrate a relentless critical reflection on the fundamental principles, and the as yet largely unrealized ideals, that undergird our total society.

Let's take the history of slavery as a case in point. The pioneering generation of Black Studies scholars who entered the academy in the post civil rights movement era amassed clearly impressive records. We now know a great deal more about slavery as an institution and about the inner lives of slaves. The innovative and imaginative scholarship on slave communities, slave religion, slave resistance, slave health, and slave families not only provided more factual data but deepened our appreciation of non-traditional sources. We know, thanks to the new social history methodologies and to reclamation Black history, that even the most oppressed and downtrodden people who did not leave manuscript collections, write diaries, or build monuments, nevertheless created and sustained significant institutions and fashioned a remarkably resilient and progressive culture reflected in song, folktales, dance, and in quilts. Their essential humanistic values and belief in the sanctity of life and black world views grounded largely upon a theology of hope ensured the survival of African Americans in slavery and in freedom.

In spite of the dazzling achievements of slavery historians, a sober assessment revealed a special lacuna. The voice and experiences of Black women remained mute, unexamined. In most of the studies both the slaves and the masters were male. Beginning in the late 1970s an emergent group of Black Feminist scholars raised disturbing and challenging questions about the androcentric bias in Black history. Were not Black women captured and enslaved on the coasts of Africa? Did not Black women suffer the middle passage and participate in the often future rebellions on board the slave ships? Did not Black women bear the responsibility of reproducing the entire slave labor force after the 1808 close of the African slave trade? To be sure, Angela Davis, writing from prison in the early 1970s suggested that Black women had a unique slavery experience worth exploring on its own merits, but few heeded her call.[9]

The appearance of Deborah Gray Whites study of slave women in the plantation South significantly altered our understanding of the "peculiar institution" and its gender relations."[10] Her critique of the stereotypes of Black women as Jezebels, mammies, and Sapphires revealed the myriad ways in which our society attempted to devalue and to dehumanize Black women. Raped with impunity both in and out of slavery, exploited as producers and reproducers, Black women developed a culture of dissemblance and self-reliance in order to survive.[11] They had no choice but to become creative agents for change and to embark upon the heroic task of re-imaging themselves and their sex. Moreover, the study of women's experiences under slavery revealed the layered depth of white women's complicity in the exploitation and oppression of Black women and the extent to which white women were privileged on the backs of Black bondwoman in slavery and on Black domestic servants in freedom. When Black women occupy the center of the intersection, then slavery studies and all labor studies of the late 19th and 20th centuries will examine new, more complex questions of gender as well as of racial power relations.

I am much encouraged by the number of scholarly works that have appeared in the past decade chronicling the historical and literary experiences and contributions of Black women. The monographs by historians Cynthia Neverdon-Morton, Jacqueline Rouse, Adrienne Lash Jones and Marilyn Richardson to name only a few have legitimized the study of Black women's history. The textbook history written by Paula Giddings, the collected essays of Angela Davis, the important anthologies edited by Rosalyn Terborg-Penn, Sharon Harley, and Filomina Chioma Steady attest to the vibrancy of this field. Of course, the numerous works in progress including Gwendolyn Keita Robinson's study of the Black cosmetic industry, and Elsa Barkley Brown's examination of Maggie Lena Walker and the Order of the St. Lukes, plus Evelyn Brooks Higginbotham's research on Black women and the Black Baptist church, along with Wilma King's, Brenda Stevenson's and Stephanie Shaw's work on Black women and children in slavery bode well for a provocative future in Black women's history.

Armed with impressive scholarship in Black women studies, we are able to speak with greater confidence and accuracy about the external and inner lives of Black women in the United States. We now know that Black women played essential roles in ensuring survival and progress of families, institutions, and communities. We know that even oppressed Black women were able to develop, as in the case of Maria Stewart, a political agenda for Black liberation that pivoted on the emancipation of Black women. We now know that Black women's angle of vision enabled them collectively and individually to fashion an autonomous world view and opposition consciousness.

Black feminist scholars have been especially critical in the development of theories of intersectional analyses of race, class, and gender. In describing the existence of sexism among Black men, and by documenting "the ways in which racism empowers white women to act as exploiters and oppressors" Black Feminists have opened a Pandora's box. In short, as bell hooks declares, "By calling attention to interlocking systems of domination—sex, race, and class—Black women and many other groups of women acknowledge the diversity and complexity of female experience, or our relationship to power and domination."[12] Patricia Hill Collins writing along the same line in her book, *Black Feminist Thought*, argues that race, class, and gender may not be the most fundamental or important systems of oppression, but they have most profoundly affected African American women. She adds that one significant dimension of Black feminist thought is its potential to reveal insights about the social relations of domination organized along other axes such as religion, ethnicity, sexual orientation, and age. Collins and hooks agree that "investigating Black women's particular experiences thus promises to reveal much about the more universal process of domination."[13] Clearly "Black Feminists" are working within the prescribed definition of Black Studies scholarship while at the same time challenging androcentric biases. Arguably, it may well be the case that the "Traditionalists" and "Black Feminists" make up one camp in the Black Studies debate. Both groups critically interrogate reigning intellectual systems, but with the positive intention of somehow reforming the academic, or making it live up to its potential.

The "Authentic" Black studies scholars and writers have likewise engaged in and produced important intellectual work. Most prominent among this group are Wade Nobles, Maulana Karenga, James Turner, Molefi Asante, Nathan and Julia Hare, Robert Staples, Ronald Bailey, Cedric Robinson, Haki Madhubuti, James Stewart, Asa Hilliard, Na'im Akbar, and a host of others too numerous to mention. Among Black women "authentists," I would include the following: Vivian Gordon, Kariana Welsh-Asante, Carol Barnes, Roszlind Jeffries, and Frances Cress Welsing.

Although I list these names together I am not unmindful or unaware of the critical perspectival and ideological differences among these scholars and thinkers. Some "Authentists" are cultural nationalists, pan-Africanists, Afrocentrists, and Marxists. Their works are either descriptive, prescriptive, or proscriptive. At the outset, I must underscore that I do not wish to suggest that the scientific merit of the work of the "Traditionalists" is more important than that of the "Authentists." Nevertheless, the acceptance accorded the work of the "Traditionalists" if the larger academy suggests what white and some Black academic gatekeepers deem meritorious. Suffice it to say that there are many leading edges and many streams in multidimensional academic intellectual space.

The theme unifying the work of "Authentists" is an intellectual and often overt political commitment to Black liberation from European, or more crassly white, categories of thought and analysis. "Authentists" are determined to create a new African methodology that allows Africans to control knowledge about themselves. Their rejection of European categories often means a rejection of "Traditionalist" and even "Black Feminists" approaches which remain rooted in "European" tenets of research, evidence and argument, even as they transform those tenets in use.

Of the earlier generation of Black Studies scholars and liberation activists who most inform the work of contemporary "Authentists" are Carter G. Woodson, W.E.B. DuBois, E. Franklin Frazier, Booker T.Washington, Marcus Garvey, Elijah Muhammad, Malcolm X, Langston Hughes, C.L.R. James, Franz Fanon, Kwame Nkrumah, Cheikh Anta Diop, and Eric Williams.

Until quite recently neither the writings nor the identities of the "Authentic" Black studies academicians penetrated mainstream awareness. Recent magazine and newspaper articles have effectively captured the excitement, controversy, and tension surrounding the concept of Afrocentricity and the growing prominence of a contingent of speakers, writers, adjunct or retired professors variously referred to as Nile Valley scholars, Egyptologists, or African World scholars. I refer to this important subset of "Authentists" as "Originists." The most prominent "Originists" are Yosef ben-Jochannan, John Henrik Clarke, John Jackson, Drusilla Dunjee Houston, St. Clair Drake, Ivan Van Sertima, and Cheikh Anta Diop. Originists, as the titles of their many books attests, argue that Africa is the cradle, or origin, of civilization (High Culture) and that most significantly Egyptians were African. In sum, the "Originists" provide African Americans with their own origin stories that lay claim to the credit for much of the knowledge that allegedly has been erroneously attributed to Greeks and Romans. Asante defines Afrocentricity as "the belief in the centrality of Africans in post modern history. It is our history, our mythology, our creative motif, and our ethos exemplifying our collective will."[14]

Although "Originists" have been teaching, writing, and privately publishing their own books and pamphlets for decades, they went into eclipse for a period of years, but they are experiencing a resurgence. The degree to which this resurgence is related to the problems growing out of modern manifestations of racism is unclear.

A brief survey of the arguments and titles of some of "Originists" books is suggestive. Martin Bernal, author of the controversial *Black Athena*, declared that "the political purpose...is, of course, to lessen European cultural arrogance."[15]

John G. Jackson in his *Introduction to African Civilizations* declares on the dedication page, "This book is dedicated to everybody with an African ancestry — the whole human race!" Jackson's main point is that "Civilization did not start in European countries, and the rest of the world did not wait in darkness for the Europeans to bring the light. "Then there is the trilogy of Yosef ben-Jochannan, *African Origins of the Major Western Religions* (1970), *Black Man of the Nile and His Family* (1978), and *Africa: Mother of Western Civilization* (1978)."[16] ben-Jochannan declares that the purpose of his *Black Man of the Nile*, is to help African peoples' "Re-identification with their great ancestral heritage. For the Black Peoples have maintained that: If the European Jews can fight for an arid piece of desert; the Irish for a small emerald island; the British for a barren island of misery; protestant Anglo-Saxon American for their stolen "Indian" empire; why should the Black man (the African, African-Caribbean, and African-American) not fight for the richest piece of real estate on the planet earth—His original homeland—Mother Africa."[17] Linking the African past to the discovery of the New World, Ivan Van Sertima declared in 1976 in *They Came Before Columbus: The African Presence in Ancient America* that by design and by accident, "in several historical periods long before the coming of Columbus, Africans traveled to America."[18] Van Sertima writes, "We now know, without a shadow of a doubt, through the most modern methods of dating, that some of the Negroid stone heads found among the Olmecs and in other parts of Mexico and Central America are from as early as 800 to 700 B.C."[19]

The father of the scholarly project to reclaim and reconstruct the African basis of Western civilization, beginning with a reidentification of Egypt as African was Cheikh Anta Diop, author of *The African Origin of Civilization: Myth or Reality*. Diop espoused the theory of the cultural unity between Egypt and Africa in order that a revision of the curriculum of African history would teach the young their own history "rather than that of the colonizer."[20] The most recent additions to this literature are the two volumes of St. Clair Drake, *Black Folk Here and There* (1987).

Traditional Black Studies scholars have generally remained aloof from the passion engulfing Nile Valley Civilization scholarship, and Afrocentricity. But as these topics capture the imagination of students, it becomes important to take a closer look, not to dismiss but to explain what is happening. All groups and societies need origin stories. Taken collectively the works of Diop, Jackson, ben-Jochannan provide a sense of beginning and belonging. The late Nathan Huggins observed that, "Tradition is a legitimizing phenomenon. All peoples and all nations want to tie themselves to an ancient past (ideally, preliterate and mythic)." He continued, "The Founding Fathers were conscious that the actual history could not be the rationale on which their new nation could rest. They wanted to found their roots in a classical and honored past, while they were deliberately severing themselves from the one tradition that gave them place and reason." But then Huggins departs sharply from "Originist" claims of how African Americans came to be. He declared, "Afro-Americans, too, are new, a new people brought into being as a consequence of American history, a new people for whom after several generations in America, it was impossible to trace back to any tradition beyond the American experience itself. This newness of people and nation has caused in both a problematic relationship with tradition."[21]

As may be imagined, assertions or descriptions of African Americans as new people is guaranteed to raise the ire of any "Originist." The important question remains unresolved. Is there a problem or intrinsic threat to the intellectual integrity of Black Studies, and the larger field of historical studies, from the thought-control implicit in the writings of "Originists" and "Authentist?"

In other words, the development and dissemination of origin stories must not comprise the final objective of Black Studies. The battlefield remains the minds of students and the goal is control or liberation, depending on one's perspective, through the development of an oppositional consciousness. A recent issue of *Black Issues in Higher Education* featured the current debate over Egypt's and Africa's place in the ancient world. As the article pointed out, the real challenge was how to move school systems towards Afrocentric education.[22] John Henrik Clark in an article excerpted from his book, *The Afrikan World at the Crossroads: Notes for an Afrikan World Revolution* (1991) summed it up boldly. He announced:

> "What I've been pointing to is that if there's going to he a world revolution among African people we have to locate African people and connect with African people. No matter what we call ourselves and what island we came front or what part of Georgia or Alabama, we can still identify, with these regions. But the overall identification is with Africa and with Afrikan people wherever they are on the face of this Earth."[23]

Black Studies is heterogeneous and complex. No single category of analysis should be allowed immunity from criticism. In order that the intellectual domain remain healthy each group of Black Studies scholars must engage in continuous critique, not in a quest for academic dominance, but to keep the ongoing movement free from dogma or absolutes. We must continually ask questions in order to keep the discipline vital. For example, is the Nile Valley view a fundamental acceptance of the old-racist-imperialist European view that nothing of note was accomplished in sub-Saharan Africa, and certainly not after, say 1000 B.C.? Or, is it that true "civilizations" are literate (versus oral), political, economically and socially centralized (versus decentralized), and architecturally monumental; and that all less complex cultures are "backward" and unimportant?

Black Studies in now poised at the most propitious moment in its evolution. I suspect that the long-range consequences of the contemporary phase of the struggle pivots on the theoretical coherence of the field, the extent to which Afrocentrism wins converts and gains currency, and how the entire Black Studies movement responds to the Black Feminist call for gendering. In conclusion, we must remember that there is much Black Studies work that remains to be done. There is room for innumerable contributions. Above all, dignity across categories must be maintained.

*The author wishes to thank for their generous and thoughtful comments Joseph Scholten and Victor Jew of Michigan State University; Aldon D. Morris of Northwestern University; James D. Anderson of University of Illinois at Urbana; and Robert L. Harris of Cornell University. I also appreciate the thoughtful comments of Earnestine Jenkins, Ph.D. candidate in African History at Michigan State University.

Endnotes

1. Robert L. Harris, Jr. "The Intellectual and Institutional Development of African Studies," in *Three Essays: Black Studies in the United States* by Robert L. Harris, Jr., Darlene Clark Hine, and Nellie McKay (New York: Ford Foundation, 1990), 7-14.

2. Abdul Alkalimat, *Introduction to Afro-American Studies: A Peoples College Primer*, (Chicago: Twenty-First Century Books and Publications, 1986), 14-15.

3. Jack Daniel quoted in, Charles A. Frye, *The Impact of Black Studies on the Curricula of Three Universities* (Washington, DC: University Press of America, 1976), 12-13.

4. Nathan Hare quote in William E. Sims, *Black Studies: Pitfalls and Potential* (Washington, DC: University Press of America, 1978), 9.

5. Sims, *Black Studies: Pitfalls and Potential*, p. 4.

6. Molefi Asante, *The Afrocentric Idea* (Philadelphia: Temple University Press, 1987).

7. Asante, *Afrocentricity* (Trenton, New Jersey: Africa World Press, 1987, revised edition), 58.

8. *Ibid.*

9. Angela Davis, "Reflections on the Black Woman's Role in the Community of Slaves," *The Black Scholar* (December 1971): 3-15.

10. Deborah Gray White, *Ar'n't I A Woman? Female Slaves in the Plantation South* (New York: W.W. Norton, 1985).

11. Darlene Clark Hine, "Rape and the Inner Lives of Black Women in the Middle West: Preliminary Thoughts on the Culture of Dissemblance," in *Unequal Sisters* edited by Ellen Carol DuBois and Vicki L. Ruiz (NY and London: Routledge, 1990). Patricia Morton, *Disfigured Images: The Historical Assault on Afro-American Women* (New York: Praeger Publishers, 1991).

12. bell hooks, "Feminism: A Transformational Politic" in Deborah L. Rhodes, editor, *Theoretical Perspectives on Sexual Difference* (New Haven, CN: Yale University, 1990), 187.

13. Patricia Hills Collins, *Black Feminist Thought: Knowledge, Consciousness and the Politics of Empowerment* (Boston: Unwin Hyman, 1990).

14. Asante, *Afrocentricity*, p. 6.

15. Martin Bernal, *Black Athena: The Afroasiastic Root of Classical Civilization, Vol. I, The Fabrication of Ancient Greece 1785-1985* (New Brunswick: Rutgers University Press, 1987), 73.

16. John G. Jackson, *Introduction to African Civilizations* (Secaucus, NJ: The Citadel Press, 1970), 3. Yosef ben-Jochannan, *African Origins of the Major Western Religions* (New York: Alkebu-Lan Books, 1970). *Black Man of the Nile and His Family* (Baltimore: Black Classics Press, 1978). *Africa: Mother of Western Civilization* (New York: Alkebu-Lan Books, 1971). Drusilla Dunjee Houston, *Wonderful Ethiopians of the Ancient Cushite Empire* (Baltimore, MD: Black Classic Press, 1985, 1st pub. 1926).

17. Yosef ben-Jochannan, *Black Man of the Nile and His Family* (Baltimore: Black Classics Press, 1978), xiii.

18. Quoted James D. Anderson, "Secondary School History Textbooks and the Treatment of Black History," in *The State of Afro-America: Past, Present, and Future* (Baton Rouge: Louisiana State University Press, 1986), 262.

19. Ivan Van Sertima, *They Came Before Columbus: The African Presence in Ancient America* (New York: Random House, 1976), 24.

20. Cheikh Anta Diop, *The African Origin of Civilization: Myth or Reality*, edited and translated by Mercer Cook (New York: Lawrence Hill and Company, 1956), 258. Also see St. Clair Duke, *Black Folk Here and There* (Los Angeles: University of California at Los Angeles Press, 1987).

21. Nathan I. Huggins, "Integrating History," in *The State of Afro-American History: Past, Present, Future* (Baton Rouge: Louisiana State University Press, 1986), 160-161.

22. *Black Issues in Higher Education* (February 28, 1991): 1.

23. John Henrik Clarke, *The Black Collegian* (January/February, 1991): 165.

24.

Afro-American Studies

Nathan I. Huggins

This essay—on the present state and future prospects of Afro-American studies—addresses what twenty years ago would have been considered two separate spheres of social concern: first, the growth and change taking place at American colleges and universities and, second, the struggle of blacks for social justice. During the late sixties these two spheres became interrelated; to some, indeed, inseparable. To understand Afro-American studies, a product of that period and of the interaction of those spheres, it is thus necessary to consider both American higher education and the American civil rights movement.

It is hard to know how much blacks students wanted Afro-American studies as a field for possible academic concentration. Doubtless much of their demand arose from their desire to shake the complacency of their institutions. In that sense, black studies was symbolic; its presence was more important than its substance. But it was also a field of legitimate scholarly inquiry, as black scholars have been saying for more than a century. Black studies, as fact and symbol, would continue to create tension among black scholars and student reformers because some black scholars wanted their scholarship to be taken seriously and were as likely to be put off by anti-intellectualism and hostility to academic work as were their white peers. We should consider more closely of the reasons advanced for the establishment of these programs.

Assumptions of Reform

In most institutions, black studies was part of a larger package of reforms insisted on by black students and their supporters among the reform-minded faculty and students. The demands for reform began with a general malaise among all students and particularly among blacks; I would suggest that the remedies they seized on were "in the air" rather than derived from specific needs in particular circumstances. I am persuaded in this by the near-uniformity of the demands nationally and by the adamantly collective character of the protest; there was little if any individual refinement or qualification. It is therefore hard to judge the significance of black studies to any particular campus. As we will see, there were many different expectations as to what black studies should be. It is worth reviewing some of the assumptions behind the demands. For the sake of clarity, I will discuss three distinct expectations, although they were generally confounded.

"To Have Something That Is Ours"

In striking contrast to the reported experience of black undergraduates in pre-dominantly white schools in the fifties, blacks in colleges in the sixties felt racially alienated and isolated. It might seem that, because the earlier group was so small in number, its members should have felt isolated, but generally they reported fitting in. They differed also in that their admission to college was untainted by suspicions that it was attributable to special standards or compensatory policy. They were highly motivated to succeed in mainstream, middle-class America. They were likely to see their presence, success, and achievement in a white college as a sign of racial progress and thus uplifting. If they had a sense of alienation from whites or from the black community, they did not make their feelings public.[1]

Ironically, as the numbers of black students increased in the late sixties, the students increasingly reported that they were alienated and isolated from the rest of the campus. That, undoubtedly, had to do with a number of factors: (1) a large number of students were drawn from socioeconomic circumstances where the conventional academic expectations and values were weak or lacking; (2) the lowering of admissions standards to increase the number of black, inner-city youth enrolled was publicly acknowledged, encouraging those so admitted to regard themselves—and to be regarded—as second-class enrollees; (3) many black students were, in fact, poorly prepared for college, lacking adequate academic preparation, discipline, study habits, or all three; (4) many found college work not only difficult but uninteresting and irrelevant to their lives as black people; (5) many felt that the ultimate end of success in college would be adaptation to the values of conventional white America, and thus a placing of distance between themselves and other black people; (6) their larger numbers, rather than making them feel more at home, gave them a collective sense of malaise and made it easy to divide the world into black and white; (7) greater numbers also meant peer-group pressure on those who otherwise might have adapted easily to join in the general malaise; (8) the institution in all it's aspects—courses, student activities, facilities—could easily be divided into "theirs" and "ours."

Black students could call little of what normally existed at predominantly while institutions "ours." Much of the emotional energy of black student protest was aimed at forcing faculties and administrations (generally liberal and integrationist in values) to accept race differences in ways that guaranteed blacks a sense of "turf" while refraining from any racial distinctions suggestive of racism. While the student demands might have begun as requests for programs and activities "relevant to black people," with no implication of being exclusionary, they almost always evolved into de facto black dormitories, cultural centers, programs, etc. The few curious whites who ventured in were soon made to feel hostility against them and their alienation. Demands for black "turf" generally resulted in separatism. Students at San Francisco State (1968), U.C. Berkeley (1968), Cornell (1968-1969), Wesleyan (1970), and Barnard (1970) were, in fact, explicit in their demand for racially separate programs or facilities.

Little wonder that in such an atmosphere demands were heard for "courses relevant to us as black people." The standard curriculum's indifference to the special problems, concerns, and basic humanity of Afro-Americans and other non-Europeans seemed glaring. Socrates, Plato, Aquinas, Goethe, Kant, Hegel, Milton, Shakespeare, Donne, Eliot, Dylan Thomas, were all *theirs*, and *they* celebrated them. "Who are we?" black students asked. "What is ours?"

It was generally assumed that those questions could best be answered by courses on the African and Afro-American experience: on black history, literature, music, and "culture." For some, the informational content of such courses was paramount. For others, course content was less important than the mere presence of such courses in the catalog. Students in the former group were likely to be more concerned with the quality of instruction than with the color of the instructors. Students in the latter group were likely to insist that only blacks were qualified to teach such courses; some even demanded all black classes or sections.[2] Carrying such thinking to its logical end, some demanded complete academic autonomy": a separate college (as was called for at Berkeley, San Francisco State, and Cornell) or a separate department (as was called for at Harvard). The indifference to course content and preoccupation with symbolism rather than substance of those in the latter group caused many black studies programs to be ridiculed and eventually abandoned by black students as well as white.[3]

Quest for Identity

Many black students on white campuses regarded the college experience as a threat to their sense of ethnic identity, and thus to their sense of personal identity.[4] Ironically, it was the very liberalization taking place in society—residential desegregation, greater prospects of upward mobility—that created the problem. In the past, blacks had all been pretty much in the same boat regardless of class and education. Now, black prospects included admission to a good college, a position—if only "token"—in corporate America, entry into the mainstream middle class, a move "out of the ghetto" and into the suburbs, and acceptance by conventional white America. Such "upward mobility," though attractive to many black students and increasingly common, was repugnant to others, who claimed that it cut black people off from the vast majority of their brothers and sisters and from their ethnic and cultural roots. The best way to guarantee one's personal identity, it seemed to many blacks, was to assert one's ethnic identity. The university could be transformed from a potential threat to identity into an instrumentality through which to find a new wholeness—an instrumentality potentially more effective than church, family, and community.

For those black students, references in reading assignments or lectures that tended to enhance blacks' sense of identity and self-worth seemed few and far between. In the liberal arts, blacks (and practically all other nonwhites) scarcely existed. In American history, blacks were viewed as slaves or as problems, rarely as contributing anything of value, or even as being central, to the American experience. Black authors were seldom included in courses in American literature; such black characters as occurred in "white" fiction, like Twain's Nigger Jim and Faulkner's Dilsey, often raised difficult questions about black identity. Social science, with its pose of objectivity, was perhaps most painful of all to Black students, who complained that blacks were viewed by most sociologists, economists, and political scientists as deviants from a norm arbitrarily defined by white social scientists.

The solution, as many blacks saw it, was courses in African history and civilization, Afro-American history, Afro-American literature, Afro-American "culture," or Afro-American contributions to American "culture." But most white faculty members knew next to nothing about those topics, and were inclined, not surprisingly, to regard what they did not know about—what none of their colleagues ever talked or wrote about—as being of little or no importance. Few scholars were sympathetic, most were condescending, and some were actively hostile to the suggestion that the black experience in any of its manifestations was worthy of study. Many were heard to comment that the very idea of black economics, black sociology, or black literature was ludicrous. All of which is to say that the problem is implicit in the student complaint—the blind ethnocentrism of American higher education—was for the most part ignored.

A major obstacle for those who wanted courses for identity building was that this was not what most scholars understood their function to be. Courses in history explicitly intended to identify and venerate heroes and heroines, to celebrate a people's "contribution," to make students feel good about themselves did not command the respect of good scholars. History had a different—a critical and analytical—role to play. Of what good was a literature course taught and attended by people so in awe of the mere existence of certain works that there was little room for criticism and textual analysis? Most teachers were likely to say "You can read anytime; courses are to make you think in a disciplined way." The onus was on Afro-American studies to prove that it did just that.

Students in search of their ethnic and personal identity did not automatically seek separatist solutions, although the hostility or indifference of faculty members tended to move them in that direction. These students generally believed that there was no intrinsic reason to deny Afro-American studies recognition as a bona fide academic discipline. They felt that the major obstacle to Afro-American studies was faculty members who did not take it seriously. The real problem, however, was the students' uncritical acceptance of courses that celebrated the Afro-American past and their hostility to faculty (black more so than white) who insisted on a critical analysis that showed heroes and heroines to be merely human.[5]

A Field of Study

Apart from the need to define an academic turf in a sea of Eurocentric whiteness, and beyond the psychological rationale arguing that courses in history and literature and culture would lead to a healthy discovery of "self," there was the claim that the African/Afro-American experience and culture provided subject matter of legitimate academic study in its own right. The African diaspora, the black presence in the Western Hemisphere and particularly in the United States, provided, it was argued, a historical reality worthy of study for its own sake as well as for its value in understanding conventional history. Afro-American writers had left a literature, there was an Afro-American musical heritage, and there was folklore, none of which had received adequate academic attention. Courses should be offered in Afro-American studies to fill a gap in scholarship and to spur scholarly interest in a neglected field.

By the sixties, actual scholarship in what was to be called Afro-American studies had a considerable history. The names of W.E.B. DuBois, Carter G. Woodson, and Arthur Schomburg, whose works date back to the first decade of the twentieth century, are well enough known to illustrate this point. There were others like them whose names are not so well known. Aside from their personal scholarship, they joined with others in support of such scholarly organizations as the American Negro Academy (1897-1915) and Woodson's Association for the Study of Negro Life and History, which was established in 1916 and which is now called the Association for the Study of Afro-American Life and History.

This early generation established a tradition of careful and conventional scholarship. Their work, however, was largely unacknowledged by professional historians. Except for a small group of blacks (academics in southern schools and amateurs) and a smaller number of whites, there was little interest in Afro-American life and history. By the fifties one might have identified a subfield of American history called "Negro history," but that was something taught almost exclusively in black schools. Less could be said for Afro-American literature. Articles on Negro history could not be found in the two major historical journals— *The American Historical Review* and the *Mississippi Valley Historical Review*— unless they could pass as "southern history." As a consequence, the *Journal of Negro History* (Carter Woodson's creation) had its pick of the very best scholarly work being done.

The white scholarly establishment was not hospitable. There was a predisposition among historians, for instance, to believe that blacks could not be objective about their history, especially since their interpretations were likely to run counter to conventional wisdom.[6] The onus was on the black scholar to prove himself or herself unbiased; ideally such scholars would produce scholarship that disguised the fact that the authors were black. Only whites could be presumed unbiased. In the effort to gain professional respectability, black scholars were likely to try to make themselves color-blind in their work.

Despite efforts at conformity, such scholars as DuBois, Woodson, Rayford Logan, and Benjamin Quarles were aware of the entrenched racism in their profession. They were of a "progressive" generation, however, and imagined that reason and demonstrated quality would in time be recognized. Meanwhile, something should be done to educate Afro-American young people to understand and appreciate their past, to see themselves not only through the eyes of white American scholars whose interpretations of slavery, Reconstruction, and the historical oppression of blacks were by no means disinterested. That was much of the reason behind the establishment of the American Negro Academy and the Association for the Study of Negro Life and History, that is, the creation and dissemination of a useable past for black Americans. Carter Woodson railed against what he called "the mis-education of the Negro," arguing that conventional schooling in America (the North as well as the South) brainwashed blacks into a belief in the superiority of whites and in blacks' lack of history or culture. To correct that, one needed scholarship. DuBois, too, came to argue the special responsibility of southern black colleges to support such scholarship for the purpose of teaching black youth who, otherwise, would be mis-educated.[7] All of these men, however, called for the soundest scholarship.

In the sixties, the few black Ph.D.'s were likely to echo these beliefs. They were prepared to support Afro-American history courses, willing to advocate their scholarly importance, but insistent on professional standards of scholarship. In the last regard they differed with student advocates of such programs. This older generation of scholars tended also to be distrustful of (or ambivalent about) the students' efforts to politicize the program, to make an academic program the instrument of ideology. They preferred to see such courses taught within conventional departments, for two reasons: (1) the department would give a legitimacy and stability to something new to the institution; and (2) such courses would be a foothold, a beginning, in the reform of the scholarly profession. As we will see, these expectations ran counter to what students and some of their faculty allies wanted.

I have written here mainly of historians, in part because they were asked to play a major role in Afro-American studies. (To the extent that there was a field, it depended on them.) Sociology, perhaps, had the largest number of black scholars interested in the Afro-American. Race relations had, from the 1890s, been a recognized academic field, one in which both white and black scholars had built reputations. Beginning with the work of Robert Park, the University of Chicago had been a center of this study, supporting such scholars as Eric Reuter, E. Franklin Frazier, Horace Cayton, and St. Clair Drake. Black sociologists like Charles S. Johnson, Ira De A. Reid, Frazier, Cayton, and Drake had built national reputations. But sociology as a field was not ready to supply leadership to Afro-American studies.

In the first place, most of the old scholarship (whether by blacks or whites) seemed to view its black subjects pathologically, with whites as the exemplary norm. Furthermore, the field of sociology was beginning to splinter. The newer, positivistic, quantifying scholarship was becoming predominant in the field (as it was in other social sciences), and such qualitative and relatively subjective topics as race relations were receiving less respect. The profession began to split over methodology and, as the sixties advanced, it split racially as well. Black sociologists created separate caucuses to establish an independent direction and to criticize what they began to refer to as "white sociology."[8] The deep racial and ideological divisions within sociology were perhaps best illustrated by the rancor and division generated by the so-called Moynihan Report.

It is important to observe that the black sociologists who took the lead as advocates of Afro-American studies were likely to be at the radical edge in this split. Both Nathan Hare and Harry Edwards were deeply cynical about, and distrustful of institutions and traditional academic fields. Their tendency was to be anti-intellectual and anti-"Establishment." Edwards saw the black student movement as providing the "impetus for violent and irreversible revolution in America." And he saw the object of black leadership and black studies as being to "fight the mainstream to establish black authenticity and to achieve full equality or be overwhelmed in the attempt."[9] It should be said, however, that St. Clair Drake, a senior and respected scholar, early took on the direction of Afro-American studies at Stanford and made it one of the best programs in the country.

The humanities (excluding history) were always the most Eurocentric of American scholarly field. English literature, philosophy, art history, and music were, in the sixties, the fields least touched by subject matter having to do with black Americans. Of these fields, literature, music, and the fine arts had the least excuse; American literature was a field where blacks had played a role. It was a rare college course in a northern school that taught any black author—until Ralph Ellison and James Baldwin became fashionable. There were, however, a number of senior black scholars in American literature: J. Saunders Redding, Blyden Jackson, Charles Davis, George Kent, to name a few. Most taught in southern black colleges. Professionally, the modern languages are so factionalized that it was almost natural for scholars of black literature to become merely another faction within the professional ranks. As activity in the subject developed, room was made for them, as it would be made, for example, for chicano literature. Very little room would be made, however, in the canon of American literature or in the mainstream curriculum.

Those who wanted Afro-American studies to be recognized as an academic discipline generally held that it should emphasize three existing academic fields: history, literature, and sociology—especially history.[10] Once one confronted the problem of getting scholars to take Afro-American studies seriously, one also had the task of explaining how such disparate fields could be brought together in it. Those who took the matter most seriously were the most uncomfortable with the character of student demands. As scholar-teachers, they saw their object as being the development of a teaching field that would remain academically respectable to their peers, and they saw as the primary object of any course the giving of an academic competence to students. Those aims could be hostile to demands for a program as a quest for power or personal (racial) identity. These conflicts would plague the supporters of Afro-American studies throughout the seventies.

Three basic concerns lay behind the demand for Afro-American studies — the political need for turf and place, the psychological need for identity, and the academic need for recognition. While they might be discussed as separate questions for the sake of convenience, they were really inseparable. Individuals could be driven by more than one of these needs. As long as matters remained at the reform stage, implicit differences could be ignored. When it came time to build and define programs, compatibility among the various agents of reform became strained. Scholars who once found the "student constituent" useful in establishing the urgency of the program might well find that student views of an academic program did not comport well with their own. Students who had hoped to find psychological and emotional support in new courses might find them both academically difficult and emotionally troubling. Once the programs were in place — the need for "turf" having been achieved — black students might not even take the courses, or might act as though taking them were a political statement rather than an academic choice. Furthermore, there came in the mid-seventies a generation of students — both black and white — who were highly career-oriented. Courses that existed largely to make rhetorical and political statements had little appeal to students whose main concern was admission to a professional school. By 1975, the decade of ideology was over.

Typical Models

The models on which Afro-American studies programs were built were influenced by ideology and conditions on individual campuses. Naturally, each particular form had intrinsic strengths and weaknesses.

The Program

From an academic point of view, the "program" approach has been the most successful. It acknowledges the interdisciplinary character of Afro-American studies by using faculty from established departments. It relies on the president and the dean to guarantee the program through budget allocations to the departments involved. While a faculty member's appointment may be principally to offer courses and service to Afro-American studies, his or her membership remains within the department of discipline. By definition, all senior faculty in a program are jointly appointed to a department and to the program. Because of this structure, it is relatively easy for the program to exploit the curricula of other departments; it is not necessary for the program to provide all of the courses its students are expected to take.

Most Afro-American studies offerings in the country follow the program model. A good example is the Yale program. Its success had much to do with the willingness of student advocates to accept this plan rather than insist on "autonomy." It has been noted for the broad range of faculty involvement. Names like Sidney Mintz, Charles Davis, Robert Thompson, and John Blassingame have been associated with it. Davis, until his recent death, served as director; his place has been taken by Blassingame. Young scholars of remarkably high quality have been in the program—especially in literature. Names like Robert Stepto, Henry Gates, and Houston Baker come to mind. Apparently from the beginning, association with the program has been judged with approval in academic circles. The Yale program is one of the few in the country offering a graduate program leading to a master's degree.

The strengths of this model are obvious, but principally they reside in its capacity to engage a wide range of departments and faculty in the service of Afro-American studies. This, of course, would not have been a strength to those of markedly separatist persuasion. Its major weakness, as those who argued for autonomy predicted, is its dependence for survival on the continued support and good will of others in the university: the president, dean, and the heads of cooperating departments, among others. Yale's program has not been troubled in this regard, but other programs have, especially when enrollments drop or when there is disagreement about standards or goals.

Programs like Yale's are designed to offer undergraduates a major (or field of concentration) for their degree. Not all programs do. Some merely offer a few courses with a focus on subject matter having to do with Afro-American life. Such courses may be accepted for credit by the student's major department (for example, economics) or may serve merely as an elective. Wesleyan, for instance, until recently had a complicated system in which an Afro-American studies major was possible but in which students found it difficult to put the necessary courses together; they thus majored elsewhere and took the one or two Afro-American studies courses as electives. (The Wesleyan program has undergone changes designed to strengthen and improve it.) The program at the University of Rhode Island is also of interest in this regard. It offers special courses: one, for example, on free-enterprise zones, and another on human resources. Such courses are designed to serve students interested in working in the community or in Third World countries. These courses do not lead to a degree in Afro-American studies, but they serve students in special programs such as a master's program in international development.

The College

The most radical kind of Afro-American studies program was that of the independent college—sometimes a all-black college—within the university. That was the demand at San Francisco State and at Cornell. The ethnic studies department at Berkeley, existing outside the College of Arts and Sciences, had for a while something of a de facto college status. Afro-American studies, however, defected and became a standing department in Arts and Sciences in 1974. No other major university came close to acceding to this extreme demand.

Local community colleges sometimes became de facto all-black colleges. That was surely the case with Malcolm X College in Chicago. It is a community college, supported by public funds, but located in an area almost wholly black. Former Crane Junior College, it became Malcolm X in 1968 when it moved to its present location. Its student population is about 80 percent black, 8 percent Hispanic, and 12 percent other. While it offers a range of black-oriented courses, it specializes in computer sciences and health services. Whether or not it was planned to be so, circumstance permits it to be the kind of college the separatists demanded. It is difficult to know how many other such community colleges there are.

The Department

The more practical model for those who insisted on autonomy was the department. A department had its own budget, could appoint and dismiss its own faculty and staff, design its own curriculum, and service its student concentrators without any control or oversight by others. It was also assumed to be a more permanent structure than a program. Some institutions established Afro-American studies departments without much ado. In others, like Harvard, departmental status remained a bone of contention years after it was established. The more it was resisted, of course, the more it appeared to be worth fighting for and defending.

The argument against it was mainly that a department normally represented a discipline. Afro-American studies, being interdisciplinary in character, should, critics said, be organized into a program made up of faculty from the various departments serving it. Its defenders most often claimed it was a discipline defined by its particular perspective on a topic none of the other departments offered. In these terms the argument was tendentious. As defined by the nineteenth-century German university, departments were identical with academic disciplines. By 1969, however, that had ceased to be true of American university departments. Interdisciplinary departments had developed within the sciences, and occasionally area studies were departmentally organized. On the other hand, a perspective, which was what Afro-American studies offered, could hardly be thought of as a discipline. Whatever it once was, a department is now largely an administrative convenience. Afro-American studies departments have worked reasonably well in some institutions, Berkeley and the University of Indiana being examples. It did not work well at Harvard, and its problems illuminate some of the weaknesses of the model.

Departmental autonomy, it turns out, is not as absolute as some believed. Such autonomy as exists carries problems. Under a program, the president and dean can, in effect, direct departments to make searches and appoint competent faculty approved by the program's committee. The department has the power and budget to make recommendations for appointment, but, lacking other arrangements, it must find scholars willing to take positions in Afro-American studies alone. In practice, most senior scholars with major reputations insist on joint appointments with the departments of their discipline. So, most often, an Afro-American studies department's appointment is contingent on another department's approval of its candidate. Such arrangements presuppose good will and respect among the departments involved. In such ways, autonomy can work against the department's efforts. Furthermore, even when university budgets were more ample, it was impossible for an Afro-American studies department to provide faculty in all of the disciplines thought useful to it. As a result, they are forced to depend on a very limited program (history and literature) or rely on other departments offerings.

Whatever the expectation of those who struggled to create departments rather than programs, joint appointments are the general rule throughout the country. Sometimes this resulted from administrative fiat, sometimes out of necessity. Ewart Guinier, the first chairman of Harvard's department, had no joint appointment himself and attempted to make the question of departmental autonomy and integrity rest on the power to promote a junior person to tenure from within. The president and the dean, responding to university-wide criticism of the department's program and standards, in 1974 made promotion from within the Afro-American studies department conditional upon joint appointment. Guinier failed in his effort to force this issue in his favor. This case illustrates another important limit to departmental autonomy. Appointment and tenure matters must be concurred in by university-wide and ad hoc committees (in Harvard's case these committees are made up of outside scholars appointed by the dean), and, finally, only the president makes appointments.

The practice of joint appointments is a good thing when it works well. It dispels suspicion about the quality of a department's faculty, especially necessary in a new field in which standards and reputation are in question. Furthermore, it gives Afro-American studies a voice and an advocate within the conventional departments, which is quite useful for communication and good will. In this regard, the practice achieves some of the good features of programs. Whether imposed by the administration or adopted as a matter of convenience, however, joint appointments may be the cause of problems and friction. A candidate may fail to win tenure in the second department, its faculty claiming a failure to meet their standards. Since questions of standards are seldom easy to resolve, these decisions are likely to cause antagonism and ill will. Joint appointments also raise questions of service, loyalty, and commitment of faculty to Afro-American studies. Once appointed, a faculty member may find it more congenial working in the field of his discipline; if he is tenured, little can be done. From the faculty member's point of view, moreover, joint appointments can pose problems. It is time-consuming to be a good citizen in two departments. Junior faculty, particularly, are likely to feel themselves to be serving two masters, each having its own expectations.

Graduate Programs

Few black studies departments or programs offer work toward a graduate degree. Yale, as has been noted, offers an M.A. in Afro-American studies, which seems to attract student teachers and those who expect to be able to use knowledge thus acquired in community or public service work. The University of Rhode island offers courses that supplement other master's programs in, for example, human resources and international development. UCLA has a graduate and postdoctoral program and provides no formal undergraduate offering.

The small number of graduate programs is not difficult to understand. Graduate programs in the humanities and social sciences have been shrinking everywhere; some have ceased to exist. Student interest has shifted from academic careers to law, medicine, and business. Furthermore, those who wish to follow scholarly careers are better off working in conventional departments; in universities where they exist, such study could be directed by scholars of Afro-American life. One advantage of this arrangement is that it can help to stimulate scholarship about Afro-Americans in conventional disciplines. In general, however, Afro-American studies faculty lack the advantages that come from having graduate students.

The Undergraduate Center

Sometimes, when there is neither a department nor a program of Afro-American studies, there will be a center, as, for example, the Center for Afro-American Studies at Wesleyan. Such centers have little or no academic program. Mainly, they provide such services to undergraduates as counseling and career guidance. (As at Wesleyan, those services are also available elsewhere in the institution for all students, blacks included.) These centers sponsor programs of interest to black students, are a focal point for extracurricular activities, and are, in effect, black student unions. The existence of such centers reflects the continued sense of exclusion among some black students from such general student activities as campus newspaper, dramatics, and literary magazines, the sense that the typical campus lecture or program has little to say to them and that they must maintain "turf" that is clearly theirs. In places where student-community programs exist, these centers often serve to coordinate them. If Wesleyan is the rule, the existence of such centers is likely to result in a weak academic program and student indifference to that weakness."[11]

The Research Center or Institute

Institutes have long been a means to encourage and support advanced scholarship in the social sciences and, to a lesser degree, in the humanities. While some are unattached to a university, most major universities have been eager to house such centers because they are a source of prestige and serve as inducements to the best and most productive scholars, who, by means of the institute, can pursue advanced studies among colleagues of kindred interests and talents while sheltered to some extent from teaching obligations. Since examples of successful institutes abound, it is little wonder that persons interested in Afro-American studies would attempt their own. The results have been mixed, at best.[12]

Columbia University, with funds from the Ford Foundation, established the Urban Center in 1968-69. Because none of the funds were invested as endowment, and because the university interpreted the terms of the grant as permitting their use for related projects and programs, the Urban Center had either to seek other funding or to expire when the Ford money ran out. Its first director, Franklin Williams, served only a short time before taking a position at the Phelps-Stokes Fund. The bulk of the original grant went for staff salaries and university overhead. Except for some community-related programs that were federally funded, the Urban Center did very little. Nothing of an academic or scholarly character was developed in the center, and few of the university's faculty were involved. The funds ran out in 1977, and the center was allowed to expire.

The Institute of the Black World (IBW) was established in Atlanta in 1969. It was originally intended to be part of the Martin Luther King, Jr., Memorial Center and to work in cooperation with the Atlanta University Graduate Center, but in the summer of 1970, for ideological and other reasons, IBW split with the King Center and Atlanta University. The King Center came to focus almost entirely on King's literary and ideological legacy, and its leadership was far more integrationist in its approach than the leadership of the IBW.

From the beginning the IBW attracted many of the most capable among those who followed the "black power" mode. Vincent Harding, William Strickland, Howard Dodson, Lerone Bennett, St. Clair Drake, and Sylvia Wynter were among its original board of directors. Claiming to be a "gathering of black scholar/activists," it remained consistently intellectual and serious in scholarly intent.[13]

IBW's funding came from a variety of sources. In 1969-70, perhaps its most promising year, it received grants from Wesleyan University, the Ford Foundation, the Cummins Engine Foundation, and the Southern Education Foundation. The level of funding was far lower over the next decade, yet the institute managed to generate position papers from scholars and others that were generally of good quality and provocative. In 1983, with its staff much reduced and its principal office now in Washington, D.C., IBW, it is fair to say, has ceased to function as a center for scholarly research. It is now seeking funds for a major film that will provide a black perspective on American history.

The W.E.B. DuBois Institute for Afro-American Studies was established at Harvard in 1975 by President Derek Bok. Seen perhaps as a corrective to Harvard's highly political, radical, and contentious Afro-American studies department, the DuBois Institute was designed for advanced study of Afro-American life, history, and culture. During its first five years, led by a series of "acting directors," the institute supported lectures and other programs, but mainly offered predoctoral fellowships to four or five advanced graduate students a year. The object of the predoctoral program was to identify promising graduate students and to support them through the successful completion of their dissertations. Funding for that program (from the Henry R. Luce Foundation) ran out in 1981. Funds for the balance of the institute's program were provided by the university.

In the past three years, the institute has sponsored major art exhibits, lectures, and concerts. With funds from the Ford Foundation, it has inaugurated an annual lecture series and, since 1983-84, it has supported in residence two senior scholars a year. It has appointed four postdoctoral research fellows each year since 1980-81. Proposals are now being designed for multiyear research projects on criminal justice, economics and public policy, public health, and education. The intention is that the DuBois Institute will generate major research projects on questions and problems related to Afro-American life and experience, sustaining a broad range of scholarship.

The Carter G. Woodson Institute for Afro-American and African Studies was established by the University of Virginia in 1981 with a mandate to encourage research and teaching in all the geographic components of the black experience: the African, Afro-Latin, Afro-Caribbean, and Afro-American. Funded by the Ford Foundation, the institute supervises the university's undergraduate Afro-American and African Studies Program; sponsors colloquia, lectures, and conferences; and others both pre- and postdoctoral fellowships in the humanities and social sciences for research and writing in black studies.

At UCLA, the Afro-American Studies Program is a quasi-institute in form. It supports research by graduate students and postdoctoral scholars. This program offers no instructional courses.

The research institute seems the most attractive and useful instrument to develop serious scholarship in this field. So far, none have succeeded in establishing themselves. There are several reasons: (1) there are too few high-quality scholars in the field to support several competing centers; (2) ideology has tended to dominate some, weakening their appeal to some of the best scholars; (3) lack of capital funding has forced them all to rely on funds generated year by year and on the generosity of a host institution. Furthermore, most university-based institutions can rely on university faculty to generate their own funds, which then can be funneled through the appropriate institute. Scholarship on Afro-American topics is in no university general enough to offer much help in this way. Afro-American institutes' directors and program officers must both generate their own programs and discover the scholars to do the work.

Varieties of Curriculum

A continuing debate rages as to whether Afro-American studies is a legitimate discipline. Many in the black studies movement have taken this question very seriously and have attempted to define the discipline in a core curriculum. The National Council for Black Studies, in a 1981 report, defined the purpose and rationale of such a program: (1) to provide skills; (2) to provide a standard and purposefully direct student choice; (3) to achieve "liberation of the black community"; (4) to enhance self-awareness and esteem. Black studies, the report says, "inaugurates an unflinching attack on institutional oppression/racism." It also aims to question "the adequacy, objectivity and universal scope of other schools of thought; it assumes a critical posture."[14]

The National Council apparently understood discipline to mean doctrine, for it goes on to outline in detail a course of study that would cover the four undergraduate years. It would begin in the African past and end in the American present, touching on the nonblack world only to show racism and its oppressive consequences. If students following this program were to take courses in the sciences, or acquire any of the specific analytical skills associated with the social sciences, they would have to take them as electives. There have been other efforts to design a core curriculum in Afro-American studies, for example, at the University of Illinois-Chicago Circle. Such efforts are notable for their attempt to create an undergraduate curriculum totally independent of other departments and offerings.

Limited budgets and the interdisciplinary nature of most Afro-American studies programs make it impossible to staff such a program as the National Council recommends. For the most part, existing programs stress Afro-American history and culture. That stands to reason, because the great teaching opportunities have been in this area. Afro-American history and literature are fairly well-developed fields, and there has been a notable black production in music and the arts. It has been harder to create good courses in the social sciences (or to appoint good scholars, for that matter). That is because, except for sociology, none of the social sciences have taken subject matter and problems related to black Americans to be of such importance in their disciplines as to constitute a specialization. Few economists or political scientists are willing to define themselves as specialists on Afro-American questions.

The recent shift in student interests to business and law, and the universal interest (especially among funding sources) in public policy is pushing Afro-American studies programs to emphasize the social sciences more than they have. I suspect, also, that the growing preoccupation among social scientist with public policy will push them into more questions having to do with blacks, and they may find it to their advantage to be associated with an Afro-American studies department. Courses on the economics of discrimination, urban politics, social mobility,and the like are logical offerings in an Afro-American studies department.

A word should be said about typical courses in the humanities. Except for those in literature, the tendency of Afro-American programs is to offer courses in the performing arts rather than their scholarly counterparts. Art courses are seldom art history; music is taught rather than musicology and music history; and there are courses in dance. This is important to note because it varies from the traditional liberal arts relegation of performing arts to extracurricular activities.

Afro-American studies programs remain tailored to available talent and other institutional resources. For the most part, they are based on some combination of history and literature with enough additional courses to fill out an undergraduate major. Many closely resemble such interdisciplinary programs as American studies. In practice, however, few students choose to major in Afro-American studies, preferring to select Afro-American studies courses as electives or, when possible, as course credit toward a conventional major in, for example, history. At the University of Illinois at Urbana/Champaign, for instance, the majority of course offerings in Afro-American subjects are in other departments, Afro-American studies acting as a service department. Harvard has attempted in the past four years to design an undergraduate concentration similar to other interdisciplinary programs in the college, namely history and literature and social studies. Beginning with a base in Afro-american history and literature, the student is directed through tutorials and selected courses toward achieving an academic competence in more than one discipline. Harvard also permits joint concentrations in the college, so it becomes possible for students to link Afro-American studies with one of the other departments. This has become a popular option. At Harvard, as elsewhere, the current preprofessional emphasis among undergraduates makes many wary of a major which they think might jeopardize admission to a professional school.[15]

After the initial demand for Afro-American studies courses, there followed a rather sharp decline in interest. The peak years were 1968 through 1970. By 1974, there was general concern that these programs would become extinct for lack of enrollment. The reasons for the decline in student interest were many: (1) students, both black and white, increasingly turned from political to career concerns; (2) the atmosphere in many courses was hostile and antagonistic to white students; (3) many of the courses lacked substance and academic rigor; and (4) campus communities had been exhausted by the rhetoric, bombast, and revolutionary ideology that still permeated many of these courses and programs. The white guilt many black activists had relied on had been spent.[16] Born, as these programs were, out of campus crises, in an era of highly charged rhetoric, unconditional demands, and cries for revolution, it was difficult for them to shake that style and reputation.

Conclusion

American higher education has changed dramatically in recent years. A college education is now available to a much broader portion of the socioeconomic spectrum than in years past. The university's role in producing useful knowledge and useful people and in preparing the way for social reform is now universally acknowledged. The fragmentation of scholarly fields into narrower specialties has accelerated, undermining the assumed coherence of broadly conceptual fields like the humanities. The rationale and efficacy of the traditional liberal arts core in undergraduate education have been called increasingly into question. This transformation—now of nearly four decades' duration—continues, and Afro-American studies will necessarily be affected as the American university continues to adapt to changing social, political, economic, and academic conditions and circumstances.

The postwar assumption that the university is an agent of democratic change and an instrument of social reform is now well established and is not likely to be reversed. Demographic changes—specifically those resulting from the ebbing of the tide of applicants produced by the coming-of-age of the postwar "baby boom" generation— are already having effects on college admissions policies, which will in turn have significant consequences on the social mix of future college classes. Many private colleges, competing for their share of shrinking numbers of applicants, are beginning to question (and to modify) the principle of "need-based" financial aid. High tuitions and other college costs have made the greatest impact on middle-class parents and students, and some college administrators have been tempted to shift scholarship funds to merit-based criteria so as to attract the most gifted student applicants. This shift has not been entirely unwelcome to black students and their parents. The great majority of black students now attending private institutions are considered "middle-class," but often only because both parents work full-time to make ends meet. Need-based financial aid formulas place a heavy burden on many parents and force students into considerable debt for their college education. Some among them would benefit from scholarships based on achievement rather than on need.

In any case, rising college costs, reduced federal and state assistance, and smaller numbers of students will make a difference in the number of black students in college, in the socioeconomic background of those who attend, and in the attitude of those students toward their education and the institutions they choose. In the next decade, many black students who might once have attended private colleges will choose state and city institutions instead; many will settle for community or other two-year colleges; many others will be unable to go to college at all. The result is already being felt in all colleges and universities: the return of de facto middle-class higher education. For many scholars and administrators, especially those with unpleasant memories of the tumultuous sixties and seventies, this will be a welcome development.

The earlier crises have passed. Administrators, faculty, and students no longer hear or make demands comparable to those of the 1960s and 1970s. There have been costs, however, particularly to the traditional concept of the liberal arts. The extraordinarily high costs of higher education (especially in the private institutions) have provoked parental and student demands for a clear and immediate payoff. As a result, many colleges have written into a preprofessionalism that undermines the traditional concept of general and liberal education. Black parents and students, no less than white, now search for the most direct route to the professional schools. Students may want to study the fine arts, philosophy, music, or literature, but they are quick to give them up in favor of what they think is "good for them" professionally— economics, political science, biology, and so forth. In this sense, Afro-American studies is just one more field perceived by many undergraduates as being of marginal utility. The assumption is, in fact, faulty: most professional schools are indifferent to a student's undergraduate field of concentration; in most instances, a major in Afro-American studies has been considered an asset by admissions officers. But combined parental pressure, personal ambivalence, and overly cautious academic advising tend to push students into the conventional and well-worn paths.

There will, of course, be those students who see their professional careers (in law, government, business, or medicine) as being enriched by a knowledge about blacks in America, and there will be those who follow their tastes and intellectual interests despite the trends. With the political motive no longer compelling, it will be from among this minority of black and white undergraduates that Afro-American studies will draw its students and its future scholars. And programs and departments of Afro-American studies will become more attractive as they bring the most sophisticated methodologies of the social sciences to bear on contemporary black issues and as they enliven discourse in the humanities by the broadening of perspective.

In small Afro-American studies departments and programs, high quality of faculty and teaching will be even more essential to success than it is in larger departments and programs. Great care must be given—more than in conventional and larger departments—to faculty appointments and questions of promotion and tenure. Needless to say, even one tenured professor who is mediocre or worse can seriously damage or even kill a program. But even poor choices of junior (untenured) faculty may have woeful consequences. Great patience, sustained attention to scholarship and teaching, and a willingness to dismiss marginal faculty even in the face of emotional and political opposition are thus called for. Black and white faculty and administrators must also resist the temptation to make Afro-American studies appointments a substitute for meeting affirmative action goals.

After an increase in the sixties and seventies in the number of blacks entering graduate schools, there has been a sharp drop in the eighties. The increased numbers of blacks pursuing academic careers was an anomaly of the past decade. Earlier, the chances of a black scholar being appointed to the faculty of a northern university were extremely slight—so much so that very few blacks chose to pursue scholarly careers. Projections of the academic job market for the next fifteen or twenty years are not promising for most fields in the humanities and social sciences. High costs and relatively lengthy periods of training for the Ph.D. (seven years on average as opposed to three years for law and two years for business) will push many of the best and brightest black undergraduates into nonacademic fields. The number of blacks enrolled in doctoral programs has been declining and very few blacks are coming forth to fill faculty vacancies. If this trend continues, affirmative action in faculty hiring will be moot as far as blacks are concerned.

Of course, the field of Afro-American studies need not depend on black scholars alone, nor should it. It is desirable, furthermore, that blacks, like other academics, should choose their fields of study on the basis of personal interest and intellectual commitment, not of race. It is nevertheless natural to assume that consequential gains in our knowledge of Afro-American life, history, and culture depend in large part on the presence of significant numbers of black scholars in the humanities and social sciences. The prospect of declining numbers of black scholars thus portends more serious problems for the field than small class enrollments do.

Given the still uncertain status of Afro-American studies departments and programs throughout the country, probably the best institutional support for the development and extension of the field of study will come from one or two centers or institutes of advanced study devoted to the subject. It seems to me that the movement to make academically legitimate the study of a wide range of issues and questions having to do with the black experience in America has been the most valuable outcome of the struggles during the last decade. Afro-American studies will achieve greater impact and influence the more it is permitted to resonate in the conventional disciplines. Standard offerings in history, American literature, economics, political science, and so on should be informed and enriched by scholarship in Afro-American studies.

Endnotes

1. Clarke and Plotkin, op. cit., pp. 28-39. This study does reveal, however, that the small number of dropouts in this survey voiced complaints anticipating (mildly and without political intent) black student complaints of the sixties. This may suggest that objective conditions were the same but expectations differed.

2. M.L. Dillon, "White Faces in Black Studies," *Commonweal* XCI (January 30, 1970): pp. 476-479.

3. John Blassingame, ed., *New Perspectives on Black Studies* (Champaign, IL: University of Illinois Press, 1971).

4. This crisis of identity is by no means unique to black people; witness the upsurge of "ethnicity" in the sixties and seventies.

5. This became a general criticism raised by black and white scholars; for instance, by John Blassingame, op. cit., pp. 75-168; by C. Vann Woodward, in "Flight from History," *Nation* CCI (September 20, 1969): pp. 142-146 and by Benjamin Quarles.

6. Consider, for instance, the general treatment of W.E.B. DuBois's *Black Reconstruction*, a work that eventually brought about a general revision of the history of that period.

7. Carter G. Woodson, *The Mis-Education of the Negro*, Washington, D.C.: AMS Press, 1933; W.E.B. DuBois, "The Field and Function of the Negro College," in Herbert Aptheker, ed., *The Education of Black People: Ten Critiques 1906-1960* (Amherst, MA: University of Massachusetts Press, 1973), pp. 83-92.

8. Wilson Record, "Can Black Studies and Sociology Find Common Ground?" *Journal of Negro Education* CLIV (Winter 1975): pp. 63-81; Morris Janowitz and James Blackwell, eds., *The Black Sociologists* (Chicago, IL: Chicago Center for Afro-American Studies and Research, 1973); Joyce A. Ladner, ed., *The Death of White Sociology* (New York: Random House, 1973); other divisions are in psychology, political science, and African studies.

9. Harry Edwards, *Black Students* (New York: Free Press, 1970). The quotes are from the dust jacket, which contains proposed curricula for black studies. See also Nathan Hare, "The Sociological Study of Racial Conflict," *Phylon* XXXIII (Spring 1972): pp. 27-31.

10. The strengths in history had to do with the fact that Afro-American history was a lively and developing area in American history. Black scholars, of course, and many whites — Leon Litwack, Winthrop Jordan, Eugene Genovese, Herbert Gutman, August Meier, Lawrence Levine, etc. — were building reputations in the field.

11. Wesleyan appointed a new chairman/director in 1981: Robert O'Meally, a fine scholar with strong academic interests. He plans to establish a strong program with interdepartmental cooperation. The center remains quasi-independent, however, and it has withstood, because of student loyalty, past attempts at reform.

12. The Afro-American Studies program at UCLA, for instance, is a quasi-institute. It offers no instructional courses but provides means for research for graduate students and postdoctoral scholars.

13. My information about IBW comes from the pamphlet "About the Institute of the Black World" and from manuscript reports, copies of which are in my possession.

14. National Council for Black Studies, *Black Studies Core Curriculum* (Bloomington, IN: National Council for Black Studies, 1982), pp. 4-7.

15. Undergraduates also report considerable parental pressure to follow courses of study with a "payoff." Black students, often able to attend college only as a result of great sacrifice by their parents, are especially susceptible to parental pressure to make their education "practical."

16. Blassingame, op. cit., "Black Studies, an Intellectual Crisis," pp. 149-168. See also his "Model of an Afro-American Studies Program," ibid., pp. 229-239.

Editor's Note: This selection is excerpted from Nathan I. Huggin's (1985) *Afro-American Studies: A Report to the Ford Foundation.*

25.

What Happened to Black Studies?

St. Clair Drake

As the black studies movement became depoliticized and adjusted to the existing educational system, the universities accepted the concept of a multiethnic constituency and permitted ethnicity some form of institutional expression. That was the trade-off.

During the sixties, Afro-American student leaders, like some of their white counterparts, were seeking a "more relevant" education. By 1967 they were involved in negotiations here and there with college and university administrators for the acceptance of what they had begun to call "black studies." After the murder of Dr. Martin Luther King, Jr., in 1968 requests became demands, and campus confrontations were prevalent throughout 1969. Black Studies programs, departments, centers, and institutes at predominantly white institutions trace their origin to that time a decade ago.[1]

Beginnings

The primary goal of the black studies movement during its early stages was to utilize the classroom as well as extra-curricular activities for raising the consciousness and heightening the group pride of black students so that they would be transformed from "Negroes," anxious to be integrated, into "blacks," convinced that "black is beautiful" and ready to struggle for Black Power.[2] The need for self-definition was considered urgent at predominantly white universities and colleges because there were so few black role models functioning as administrators, professors, or counselors, and white middle-class values were dominant.

Black studies would foster an alternative value-system expressed succinctly and ritualistically in the seven principles of black solidarity that had been popularized by author Leroi Jones and student organizer Ron Karenga as Swahili slogans: KU-JICHA-GULIA (self-determination); NIA (purpose); IMANI (faith); UMOJA (Unity); KUUMBA (creativity); UJIMA (collective work and responsibility); and UJAMAA (cooperative economics). Black studies were to provide the much-needed "supplementary education" that would help black students steel themselves against the seductive pull of integration and develop attitudes, knowledge, and skills needed to build institutions for serving poor and neglected black communities in Africa and the Caribbean as well as in the U.S.A.

The still-active Institute of the Black World, founded in Atlanta in 1969 by historian Vincent Harding, was one of several agencies that formally expressed a sharp distinction between Negro studies and black studies. Negro studies accepted white norms and values as correct and desirable. Black studies would approach history and the social sciences from a black perspective, from the viewpoint of what Frantz Fanon called a "colonized people" in the process of liberating themselves. Black studies sought, too, to develop a black aesthetic and a philosophy—*negritude*—grounded in what were assumed to be sound African values that neither slavery in the New World nor colonial imperialism in Africa had erased. The Institute fellows pleaded for more than a reluctant acceptance of the fate of being born black, urging a positive affirmation, a "celebration of blackness," which would involve participation in black music, dance, drama, and religion, and appreciation of black literature. They also emphasized disciplined scholarly work.[3]

Simultaneously, some black historians, including Professor John Henrik Clarke of Hunter College, who founded the African Heritage Studies Association, emphasized "reclaiming" African and Afro-American history. Dr. Harding called for "exposure, disclosure, or reinterpretation of the American past" from a critical, black point of view, while historian Lerone Bennett, an Institute fellow, presented African appreciation of communal concern as a value worthy of adoption by Afro-Americans.[4]

To create a focus for black students on a predominantly white campus, the student leaders considered it imperative to lay claim to a special niche. Thus their demand for autonomous departments, centers, or institutes offering courses designed by students working together with black faculty members. The militant student leaders refused to accept the view that only those with traditional academic credentials should teach in black studies programs, believing that rich experience could outweigh formal training. They wanted all faculty and administrators in the programs to be black and some of the courses to be for black students only. They asked that black students have a dominant voice in faculty recruitment, evaluation, promotion, and retention. They insisted, too, that a satisfactory educational experience should provide some contact with off-campus black people; students were to serve as interns in black institutions, as tutors and aides in ghetto schools, or in other socially useful community roles.[5]

All of this went against the grain for those, black or white, who believed strongly in integration or in academic traditions. Few white professors and administrators questioned the need for curriculum enrichment by incorporating more material on the black experience into existing courses in the humanities and social sciences, but the introduction of new courses was another matter entirely, even when they were not taught from a militant black perspective. In addition to budgetary considerations, black student insistence that only blacks were qualified to teach "black" courses was seen as a reinforcement of tendencies toward separatism that had appeared in other black student demands. Fears that academic standards would be lowered by unqualified teachers and easy grading were also frequently expressed.[6]

For administrators already under pressure to allow white students a greater role in governance and to liberalize admission procedures, distribution requirements, and grading practices, concessions to the black student movement meant setting dangerous precedents. Nevertheless, some concessions were made throughout 1968 and 1969 as confrontations continued. When the autumn term began in 1969, at least seventy institutions, half of them in the northeast, had black studies programs in operation.[7]

Most black studies programs were interdepartmental with all tenure-track appointments being made within an existing department but with a special chairman, director, or coordinator reporting to a faculty-student committee as well as to a university official. Some were autonomous departments having their own faculties. A few were centers or institutes devoted to research or to community-oriented action. The names varied—Black Studies, Afro-American Studies, Pan-African Studies,

African and Afro-American Studies, or Africana Studies — but virtually all of them made black history the basic subject in the curriculum.

Where departments instead of interdepartmental programs were established, they offered their own courses in literature, history, and the social sciences from a black perspective but usually allowed for the expression of a wide range of ideological tendencies. There were far fewer of what were contemptuously called "soul courses" than opponents of black studies charged, and within a few years these disappeared.[8]

That the quest for black studies was taken seriously from the start was apparent when Yale University moved in May, 1968, to open discussion of the new program with a symposium to which black and white professors were invited along with black students. The collected papers were published soon after by the Yale University Press as Black Studies in the University. The Ford Foundation, the Danforth Foundation, and the National Endowment for the Humanities supported a number of conferences and workshops between 1968 and 1971 for the discussion of problems facing the new programs and for encouraging high academic standards and the utilization of interracial teaching personnel.[9]

Institutionalization

Black studies grew steadily and became entrenched in the next five years, though there were some erroneous reports in newspapers and magazines during 1974 that such programs were in decline. In fact, in 1974 there were at least 250 departments, centers, institutes, and programs in existence, and in that year alone 392 A.B. degrees were granted as well as 19 master's degrees and 3 doctorates. Between 1970 and 1975 over 1,500 bachelor's degrees were awarded as well as 99 master's degrees and 4 Ph.D.'s. Harvard, Yale, Stanford, Cornell, and the University of California at Berkeley were among the group that granted the undergraduate degrees. Other institutions refrained from offering the major but encouraged students to take black studies as electives and to participate in community-oriented projects or performing arts. Some did not have the faculty and library facilities for degree work. Yet it was clear by 1974 that black studies were here to stay at an impressive number of institutions, although perhaps barely surviving at some.[10]

However, what black studies were turning out to be was neither what their most youthful, dedicated supporters had envisioned nor what white faculties and administrators had wanted them to accept. The black studies movement was becoming institutionalized in the sense that it had moved from the conflict phase into adjustment to the existing educational system, with some of its values being accepted by that system.[11] One of these was the concept that an ideal university community would be multi-ethnic, with ethnicity permitted some institutional expression, and with black studies being one of the sanctioned forms. A trade-off was involved. Black studies became depoliticized and deradicalized.

The rate of institutionalization accelerated after 1974 because most of the students who had led the confrontations and the negotiating teams during the late sixties and the early seventies had either been graduated, dropped out, or been dropped. Also, some militant black groups had moderated their positions, while others did not feel that black studies programs were where the action was anymore. Entering freshmen, who had been only twelve or thirteen years old when King was killed and the last large-scale ghetto rebellion occurred, were less alienated and less in need of what sociologist Nathan Hare had described in 1969 as the "therapeutic aspect" of black studies.[12]

Increasing numbers of graduate students with serious scholarly interests began to serve as teaching assistants and lecturers in black studies programs and became role models for some of the majors. The theses and doctoral dissertations of students working on problems in the humanities and social sciences from a black perspective became subjects for seminar discussions and a stimulus for black undergraduates to give peer approval to academic achievement instead of rhetoric and "rapping."[13] Students who had chosen undergraduate black studies majors wanted their degrees to "mean something." The quieting-down that resulted was often erroneously interpreted as apathy. But it was, in fact, a change in style of expressing "blackness."

Stabilization of personnel occurred as the earlier rapid turnover in chairmen and directors ceased and more black studies professors on the tenure track were employed. Those from the original group who remained and the new faculty members tended to have a strong academic orientation in addition to their commitment to the idea of "blackness" as something all Afro-Americans should cultivate. They wanted the respect of their peers as well as realistic prospects of promotion.

However, with the process of institutionalization black studies did not revert to Negro studies. The theoreticians had invoked the mainstream social science concept of "the sociology of knowledge" to lend legitimacy to the idea that the position of black people in the social structure not only gives them insights others might not have, but also that their partial perspectives need to be known by others seeking the "truth," and that all knowledge is value-laden.[14] Black studies profited, too, from the increasingly widespread acceptance among social scientists of the idea that much of what professes to be "objective" in university teaching and research is explicitly policy-related, and much more of it has an implicit action potential. It is a victory for the students who initiated the black studies movement that the intellectuals who administered and taught in the programs after they became institutionalized did not have to profess a spurious objectivity or deny their commitment to the struggle against racism and for black self-determination in order to retain the respect of their peers in other departments. Repudiation of "blackness" was not demanded as the price for survival.

Professionalization

By 1975 at least 200 black college teachers were giving their primary allegiance to black studies rather than to the disciplines in which they had received their graduate training. They did not share identical political positions or levels of zeal, but a universe of discourse existed that had been built up during a half-decade of conferences and symposia sponsored by individual black studies programs. Also, the Institute of the Black World and the African Heritage Studies Association as well as black studies centers and institutes at Atlanta University, Jackson State College, New York University, several units of the State University of New York (SUNY) and City University of New York (CUNY), and the Black Economic Research Center supplied continuity of intellectual leadership through specialized publications, seminars, and conferences.

Several journals were regularly publishing critical essays, reviews of books and monographs, professional notices, and the results of research relevant to the black experience. Of four journals that began publication in 1970, three still exist: *The Black Scholar* (founded by Nathan Hare in northern California); *Journal of Black*

Studies (established at UCLA and now published at SUNY-Buffalo); and *Black Lines* (University of Pittsburgh). *Afro-American Studies* (Graduate Center, CUNY) ceased publication in 1976. Two new ones were established in 1977: *Western Journal of Black Studies* (Washington State University-Pullman) and *Studia Africana* (University of Cincinnati). In 1978, the former literary magazine *Umoja* (University of Colorado-Boulder) was transformed into *A Scholarly Journal of Black Studies*.

During the first five years of the movement, teachers and administrators in black studies programs were also meeting locally and regionally to discuss their common struggle for adequate funding and the problem of securing faculty promotions at predominantly white institutions, where reappointment and tenure committees sometimes refused to consider any black studies publications as well-refereed or research from a black perspective as legitimate. Also, the heavy demands imposed on faculty by the nature of innovative programs and extra counseling activities for minority students lessened their chances of success in the competition for recognition through publication. A feeling emerged of need for organizations that could present the problems of black studies faculties and administrators to public and private funding agencies and to university administrators.

In 1975, informal faculty networks in New York and North Carolina were transformed into professional organizations and state conferences were convened.[15] One of the leaders of the North Carolina group, Dr. Bertha Maxwell, suggested the formation of a national association at a meeting in Atlanta that same year. Dean Herman Hudson and Dr. J.J. Russell of Indiana University, who had been publishing on organizational problems in black studies, offered to provide a home for such an association.[16] The result was the National Council for Black Studies, which defined as its primary task "to insure the survival, expansion, and continued acceptance of black studies at a time of declining enrollments, fiscal stringency, and emergent policies of benign neglect towards minorities in institutions of higher education."[17]

There was little danger of wholesale elimination of programs, but most were funded at a level that permitted only bare survival. As the leaders of the National Council pointed out, many programs were caught in a "bind." Funds for additional tenured positions and normal growth depended upon maintenance of high academic standards, continuous faculty research and publication, and efficient administration. And all of this required larger budgets. They recommended the autonomous department as the most desirable structure, with an Office of Afro-American Affairs to relieve the black studies program of personal counseling functions and to serve as an advocate in budget negotiations. Double majors for students were recommended to link them to other departments as well as to black studies. Large annual conventions in 1977 and 1978 discussed evaluation procedures and the desirability and feasibility of a standardized curriculum, or at least a standardized introductory course.

Wider Impact

After a funded, systematic on-site study in 1972 and 1973 of the impact of the black studies movement on fifty campuses throughout the country, sociologist Wilson Record noted that the standardized university procedures for curricular innovation and faculty recruitment had been either challenged directly or effectively circumvented, and he suggested that colleges and universities would never be quite the same again. Although he approved of some of the changes, Record saw dangers in continuing black student opposition to types of research they considered irrelevant and to white professors studying the black experience. There was the possibility, too, of entrenching substandard black studies departments. He suggested that one of the most challenging pieces of research that might be undertaken would be the exploration of the actual enduring impact of the black studies movement on the institutions' structure, functions, and values.[18]

No such comprehensive assessment has been made of the more-lasting impact of black studies on the academy; nor have any major studies of the programs themselves been undertaken since Nick Aaron Ford's survey published in 1973 and the less extensive one by Elias Blake and Henry Cobb published in 1976. That the impact on university life has not been studied may be because the sense of urgency diminished as the institutionalization process accelerated. Or it might be because of a policy of "let well enough alone" after the stormy early years. Research of the type suggested by Record might have been inhibited, too, by the virtual impossibility of separating the influence of the general black student movement from the black studies aspect of it. Nor can the impact of both of these be disentangled from that of other student movements.

In the absence of significant recent research on the influence of black studies on affirmative action, university governance, campus ethnic and racial relations, and on off-campus perception of the black experience, I made an attempt in 1977 and 1978 to gather some data by mail on the opinions and attitudes of college administrators and directors of black studies programs. These data supplement information secured through interviews and participant observation. The summary that follows uses all these sources and constitutes a basis for developing hypotheses that might be examined by carefully designed research.[19]

The direct role of the black studies movement in black faculty recruitment has been minimal in recent years, although at one time the programs exerted pressure for general recruitment as well as for their own staffing needs.[20] They often brought the first black faculty members to the campus. The initial appointments of black studies faculty on white campuses had generated discussion among whites about the ethics and mechanics of recruiting blacks to teach, the competence of black professors, and the special problems that blacks must deal with in a racist society. Today, the quality of individual faculty members in black studies programs is no longer questioned, and the number of black faculty members outside of black studies has increased dramatically in response to a variety of pressures and emergent new values during the past decade: Still, in some situations, only the continued existence of black studies will maintain a black faculty presence.

During the sixties, the black studies movement, like the white student movement, demanded a decisive voice in college and university governance. Wilson Record wrote in 1973: "It is difficult to identify prior situations in which students were given so much control over curriculum and faculty as the black militants were during the last three or four years."[21] White students, too, increased their participation in governance, but it turned out to be largely token.[22] It seems probable that black students have retained a larger measure of influence in black studies than students have achieved in other departments and programs. This fact does not affect the broader institutional structure, however, despite hopes often expressed in the early days of the movement that it would.

In 1972, Professor Roscoe C. Brown, Jr., speaking as director of the Institute of Afro-American Affairs at New York University, sized up one area of influence accurately when he said: "A major impact of the black studies movement has been to provide insight into the black experience for literally hundreds of thousands of students, both black and white, who had not previously had the opportunity to study some aspect of that black experience in depth."[23] The prevalence of programs with an interdepartmental structure has continued to bring hundreds of white students annually into contact with courses about the black experience, especially in history and literature, although where black studies departments exist there is still sometimes subtle pressure on the part of black students to make black studies "a black thing." With the institutionalization of black studies, however, has come a striking decrease in such opposition to white participation.

In proportion to the total number of white students on college campuses, the number who take any courses dealing with the black experience is always small. But black studies have had indirect effects that operate outside of black studies classes. With their courses listed regularly, their public events advertised in official publications, and their textbooks and collateral readings displayed in campus bookstores, black studies programs have brought about a highly visible superficial "blackening" of academia. The black presence has become inescapable and legitimized. But of even greater import, professors in the social sciences and the humanities generally cannot avoid exposing their students to the published results of a decade of research, creative work, and sheer propaganda that has been stimulated by black studies. They must react to the black perspective, even if with disapproval, and that, in itself, precipitates student reflection and dialogue in their classes. Even institutions without black studies programs have become involved in this manner.

When black studies began, fears were expressed that a kind of "separatism" was being accepted that would be detrimental to good race relations on campus and that might set up a pattern of some classes being attended by blacks only, which in turn might lead to a deterioration of academic standards. In most contemporary situations some types of courses do tend to have a predominantly black clientele, but the administrator respondents to my 1977-78 questionnaire agreed overwhelmingly that black studies had neither created enclaves of academic inferiority nor resulted in the establishment of patterns of separatism in the classroom. Nor did they believe that black studies were presently increasing the level of racial antagonism on campus. Indeed, some educators, white and black, feel that black studies programs have a potential for use in on-campus inter-ethnic education made necessary by disquieting expressions of resurgent racism that are appearing at some institutions in the wake of the Baake decision and in the face of increasing economic retrenchment in the field of higher education.[24]

One outcome of the black studies movement has had repercussions off campus as well as on. Scores of books on Afro-Americans from the earlier Negro history movement[25] were reprinted with the word Negro replaced by black, and occasionally they were revised to effect a change in orientation. More timely introductions have been written for some older books, and thousands of new titles dealing with the black experience have appeared, Alex Haley's *Roots* being the most conspicuous recent example. Book reviewers now discuss the implication of "blackness" in the poetry and fiction of black writers routinely. The black studies movement has thus had a profound influence through the publishing industry.

Current Status

At least 250 programs devoted to the study of the black experience in the United States exist today.[26] Half of these have been operating since 1970, and of the 64 that were granting degrees in 1971, all except four have survived. All give some attention to the implications of an African origin for black people in the New World, and increasingly a "diaspora" frame of reference focuses some attention upon the Caribbean and Latin America for comparison with the United States. A few programs that carry the name Africana Studies—like the outstanding program at Cornell—or Pan-African Studies are distinctive in their emphasis upon Black Nationalism. Programs differ in emphasis and a study of the curricula, not the names, will reveal orientations that range from preparation for graduate work in the humanities and performing arts to training in community organization skills. For most, however, "supplementary education" for black undergraduate liberal arts students remains the goal. Some of the most vigorous programs are in community colleges.

There are significant regional differences in black studies programs, and variations within regions are related to size and prestige of institutions, to whether they are publicly supported or private, as well as to the most crucial variable, the proportion of black students to white.[27] During the early 1970s, the centers of most rapid growth in black studies were New York, New England, and California. Black colleges in the South established some of the first black studies programs. Howard, Morehouse, Morgan, and a few others still have programs. But most now have the philosophy and practice of "blackening" the whole curriculum instead of offering special programs. The development of black studies in southern white institutions has been less impressive than in other regions, the University of Texas at Austin being the highly significant exception. However, as compliance with recent federal orders brings more blacks to white campuses and more whites to the traditional Negro colleges, black studies programs are likely to increase in number, some through revival of those in decline. Some may assume new functions related to what southern liberalism calls "interracial cooperation." At previously all-black southern institutions, however, an upsurge of Black Nationalism in some form is likely to occur during the integration process.

Administrators of California universities, as well as in some of the southwestern states, have favored the organization of ethnic studies divisions with Black, Chicano, Asian, and Native American subdivisions. The more militant proponents of black studies in California have opposed this format, which seems to them to be an attempt to prevent the formation of autonomous black studies programs. They also claim that it encourages inter-ethnic antagonism in struggles for funds. Moderate black educators have been divided in their opinions, some seeing security in this structure during periods of financial stringency.

Black studies at some large midwestern state institutions have attained an impressive degree of stability and growth that have made their programs a base for the strong current drive toward professionalization. They, along with Harvard and Yale, Five Colleges, Inc. (University of Massachusetts, Amherst, Smith, Amherst, Mt. Holyoke, and Hampshire), and some SUNY and CUNY units, have announced plans for the expansion of graduate work and research. Some programs plan to stress inner-city problems and to encourage increased enrollment of white graduate students in the hope that the social workers, teachers, and civil servants of the future will have a better understanding of the problems of the minority people with whose affairs they will be concerned. Programs at the larger private institutions do not report apprehension about future financing, but those at publicly supported institutions have already experienced some retrenchment and express concern about prospects for realizing their plans for the second decade of black studies.

But no matter how receptive their programs are to larger non-black enrollments, black studies faculties and administrators feel that the primary raison d'être for black studies must still be to serve the needs of black students, for they still have the problem of defining themselves for themselves, although in other dimensions than in the past.[28]

The predominantly white campus is a simulation model of contemporary American society, where absence of discrimination in the public life of work and politics is gradually becoming the norm, but where neither the white majority nor non-white ethnic minorities are sure about what degree of integration they wish to sanction in churches and voluntary associations, friendship groups, dating relationships, marriage, and family interactions. Some form of ethnic pluralism is replacing caste, but its structure has not yet crystallized. Yet, within northern college communities, as in the surrounding society, the first generation of black students is being educated, some of whose members have the option of living a predominantly integrated style of life as opposed to a predominantly black one, or the opportunity to decide how much of an interracial mix is desired. Black students and faculty, in their informal conversations and occasional publications, reveal an attitude of anxious questioning about how to live "integrated" without becoming deracinated, and how to occupy positions of influence that bring honor and high material rewards in business, government, or the educational system in such a way as to serve broad multi-racial constituencies without neglecting the problems of black people. Educators in black studies programs feel that one of their major responsibilities should be to assist students in coping with the problems related to this concern. One approach is through providing opportunities for discussion and debate among themselves and with a variety of role models. Another is through the serious study of biographies and autobiographies of black Americans.

Most black studies programs, in addition to their work in the humanities, try to focus attention upon the problems of the black masses trapped in rural and urban ghettos. An opportunity is provided for discussing and analyzing their problems in classes in economics, sociology, and political science as well as through special and extracurricular events. These concerns are reflected, for instance, in Yale's courses on "Urban Ghetto Economic Development" and "Education and Low-Status Populations." One midwestern city university includes among fifty-nine black studies courses in 1977-78 "Sociology of the Black Community," "The Law and Black People," and "The Black Perspective in Practice." A small West Coast city college has a required introductory course in its black studies degree program described as "A brief survey... of black experience in America... with primary emphasis on the problems of poverty, racism, and violence." Some program directors in interviews with me have expressed the wish that every black student should be required to take such a course prior to graduation, though recognizing that this is impossible, except at a few all-black institutions where it actually occurs.

A moderate amount of student interest in registering for black studies courses is reported by program directors, with somewhat less interest in majoring. Black studies faculties now actively encourage students to develop minor sequences or to make purposive choices of electives to supplement their career-oriented major concentrations or devotion to a traditional discipline. But the widest student impact comes through sponsoring occasional lectures by eminent black visitors and organizing regular annual observances of Black History Week and the birthdays of Martin Luther King, Jr., and Malcolm X. Remedial work, personal counseling, and financial-aid problems are generally left to other campus agencies with which the black studies program maintains close liaison.

While academic goals are central, program directors, generally, judge success not by the number of majors and degrees granted, but by the number of individuals who take the courses offered and who participate in the program's extracurricular activities. In the future, at some of the institutions, scholarly production by staff and graduate students will become an increasingly important criterion.

Black studies began with the utopian vision of a constant stream of young black people from the colleges and the universities helping ghetto dwellers to achieve Black Power and to transform their neighborhoods. Zeal, on campus and off, has cooled, and the temper of the times has so changed that suggestions are even being made occasionally that black studies programs should consider training personnel for governmental service in Africa and the Caribbean and for assisting multi-national corporations to carry out their overseas work more effectively.[29] While a large proportion of the black population still remains consigned to low economic status in deteriorating inner-city areas and rural slums, the rapid expansion of the American black middle class due to access to occupations formerly not open to them, federal aid to minority businesses, and vastly increased political power, excited realistic expectations of "success" among the constantly growing group of black college students. Utopian dreams and revolutionary rhetoric lost the appeal they had for college students a decade ago. A "supplementary education" for upwardly-mobile black students that assists them to cope with their own personal problems as well as satisfying their intellectual and aesthetic needs, but without forgetting "those left behind," has become the goal of most black studies programs.

The value of all utopian visions lies not in the possibility of their realization but in the inspiration they give to people to move to new levels of experience and social relationships, to achieve higher plateaus rather than to scale peaks. This happened to black studies.

Endnotes

1. Harry Edwards, *The Black Student* (New York Free Press, 1970); Robert Chrisman, "Student Strikes: 1968-69," *Black Scholar* 1, 3-4 (January-February 1970): 65-75; Special Issue on Black Studies, *Black Scholar* 2, 1 (September 1970).

2. W.E. Cross, Jr., "The Negro-to-Black Conversion Experience," in *The Death of White Sociology*, ed. Joyce A. Ladner (New York: Random House, 1973), pp. 267-80.

3. Black Studies Directors' Seminar: Panel Presentations, November 7-9, 1969 (Atlanta: Institute of the Black World, 1970).

4. See V. Harding, *Beyond Chaos: Black History and the Search for the New Land*, Black Paper No. 2 (Atlanta: Institute of the Black World, 1970); L. Bennett, *The Challenge of Blackness*, Black Paper No. 1 (Atlanta: Institute of the Black World, 1970). J.H. Clarke, "The African Heritage Studies Association." *Issue: A Quarterly Journal of African Opinion* 6 (Summer-Fall 1976): 5-11.

5. R.A. Fischer, "Ghetto and Gown: The Birth of Black Studies," in *New Perspectives on Black Studies*, ed. John W. Blassingame (Urbana University of Illinois Press, 1973), pp. 16-27; Stephen Lythcott, "Black Studies at Antioch," ibid., pp. 123-32.

6. For a sampling of opinions expressed during 1969 see Blassingame, *New Perspectives*. See also Bayard Rustin, ed., *Black Studies: Myths and Realities* (New York: A. Philip Randolph Educational Fund, 1969). Among the articles by black academics interpreting the movement to the fearful and the skeptical were I.S. Reid, "An Analysis of Black Studies Programs," *Afro-American Studies* 1 (1970): 11-21; J.A. Moss, "In Defense of Black Studies," *Afro-American Studies* 1 (1971): 217-22; T.J. Le Melle, "Black Studies for What?" *Black Prism: Perspectives on the Black Experience* (Brooklyn College) 2 (Winter 1972): 5-10.

7. The figures cited and the kinds of programs mentioned in the following paragraph were derived from an annotated list of black studies programs prepared by Armstead L. Robinson for the Ford Foundation Seminar on Black Studies. Aspen, CO, Summer 1970.

8. Nick Aaron Ford, *Black Studies: Threat or Challenge?* (Port Gibson, NY: Kennikatt, 1973), pp. 105-35.

9. A.L. Robinson, G.C. Fosler, and D.H. Ogilvie, eds., *Black Studies in the University* (New Haven: Yale University Press, 1970); L. Bornholdt, "Black Studies: Perspective 1970," *Danforth News and Notes 5* (March 1970): 1, 5-6; N.A. Ford, *Black Studies*, pp. 136-43. See also *Widening the Mainstream of American Culture: A Ford Foundation Report on Ethnic Studies* (New York Ford Foundation, 1978), pp. 2-4.

10. Elias Blake, Jr., and Henry Cobb, *Black Studies: Issues in Their Institutional Survival* (a survey of Afro-American studies programs carried out during 1974) (Washington, DC: U.S. Government Printing Office, 1976); Curtis O. Baker and Agnes O. Wells, *Earned Degrees Conferred 1972-73, 1973-74, and 1974-75* (Washington, DC: National Center for Educational Statistics, 1976 and 1977); J. Albert, R.L. Goldstein, and T.F. Slaughter, Jr., "The Status of Black Studies Programs at American Colleges and Universities," in *The Black Studies Debate*, ed. J.U. Gordon and J.M. Rosser (Lawrence: University of Kansas, 1974).

11. J.V. Baldridge, *Sociology A Critical Approach to Power, Conflict and Change* (New York: Wiley 1975), pp. 296-335: Le Roi R. Ray, Jr., "Black Studies, a Discussion of Evaluation," *Negro Education* 45 (1976): 383-96.

12. Nathan Hare, "What Should Be the Role of Afro-American Education in the Undergraduate Curriculum?" in Blassingame, *New Perspectives*, pp. 3-15.

13. J.B. Peebles, *Black Studies: A Dissertation Bibliography* (Ann Arbor: University Microfilms, 1978).

14. Karl Mannheim, *Ideology and Utopia* (New York: Harcourt, 1936); Ronald Bailey, "Black Studies in Historical Perspective," *Social Issues* 29 (1973): 97-108.

15. W.D. Smith, "Black Studies: Recommendations for Organization and National Consideration," *Negro Education* 44 (Spring 1975): 170-76; J.J. Russell, "Strides Toward Organization," in *The National Council of Black Studies: 1976—A Year of Decision*, ed. Herman Hudson (Bloomington, IN: National Council for Black Studies, 1977), pp. 16-20; *Conference Reporter*, Newsletter of New York State Conference on Black Studies in Higher Education, 1976.

16. Herman Hudson, "The Black Studies Program: Strategy and Structure," *Negro Education* 41 (Fall 1972): 294-98, J.J. Russell, "Afro-American Studies From Chaos to Consolidation," *Negro Education Review* 26 (October 1975): 185-89.

17. Quoted from an announcement of the Second Annual Convention of the National Council of Black Studies in *Black Studies: A Journal of Afro-American Studies* 1 (1977): 2.

18. Wilson Record, "Some Implications of the Black Studies Movement for Higher Education in the 1970s," *Higher Education* 44, 3 (1973): 191-92, 214.

19. The generalizations in the sections on Wider Impact and Current Status are based primarily on data I gathered as a participant-observer at several conferences dealing with black studies and during campus visits in 1977 and 1978, as well as through interviews, correspondence, and telephone conversations with university administrators of Harvard, Yale, Cornell, Stanford, Northwestern, Indiana University, the University of Virginia, Jackson State, Tulane, Dillard University, the University of Massachusetts at Amherst, California State University at San Jose, and the University of California at Santa Barbara, Berkeley, and Los Angeles. Responses to a mailed checklist soliciting facts and opinions have also been analyzed for 67 institutions distributed regionally, varying in size, some public and some private. All of the major black studies programs are represented in either the interview sample or the mailed checklist sample. Several program self-surveys and official reports have been available as well as responses from 28 program directors to a mailed checklist, which supplies a black perspective.

20. See Jane C. Record and Wilson Record, "Ethnic Studies and Affirmative Action: Ideological Roots and Implications for the Quality of American Life," *Social Science Quarterly*, (September 1974): 508.

21. W. Record, "Some Implications," p. 194

22. G.L. Riley, S.H. Schlesinger, J. Victor Baldridge, "Is Student Power Dead," *New York University Education Quarterly* 9, 3 (Spring 1978): 9-15.

23. R.C. Brown, Jr., "Future Directions in Black Studies," *Black Prism* 2 (Winter 1972) 35-41.

24. L. Middleton and W. A. Sievert, "The Uneasy Undercurrent," *Chronicle of Higher Education* (May 15, 1978).

25. R. Adams, "Black Studies Perspectives," *Negro Education* 46, 2 (1977): 99-117.

26. This is a conservative estimate arrived at by adding to the surviving programs from N.A. Ford's 1973 *Black Studies*, pp. 191-95 and the Earned Degrees list for 1970 and 1971 of the National Center for Educational Statistics, additional programs mentioned in various journals, publications of the National Council of Black Studies, and catalogs of four-year and community colleges. The Ford Foundation survey of 1978 reported "some 300 Afro-American studies programs, about 125 of which grant B.A. or M A. degrees." The estimate is apparently based upon data supplied by the National Council for Black Studies.

27. *Ethnic Studies Curricula and Related Institutional Entitles at Southwestern Colleges and Universities, a special issue of Bulletin of the Cross Cultural Southwest Ethnic Study Center* (University of Texas-El Paso), October 1975 (ERIC ED 120 088); Frank G. Pogue, *The Status of African/Afro-American Studies in the State University of New York*, a special issue of Habari (SUNY-Albany), Autumn 1977; *A Report on the Status of Black Studies Programs in Midwestern Colleges and Universities* (DeKalb, IL: Center for Minority Studies, Northern Illinois University, 1977).

28. Philip Carey, Black Studies: Expectation and Impact on Self-Esteem," *Social Science Quarterly* 57 (1977): 811-20; R. Bailey and G. McWorter, compilers, *Introduction to Afro-American Studies* (Chicago People's College, 1977): W.J. Lyda, "Black Studies and the Black Revolution: A Longitudinal Case History," *Contemporary Education* 48 (Winter 1977): 73-75.

29. W.B Johnson and T. Nichols, "Black Studies: A Key to the Future," *Negro Education* 46 (1977): 118-23.

IV

Section IV

Philosophical Perspectives

Key Concepts and Major Terms

- Bodies of Knowledge
- Epistemologies
- Philosophical Foundations
- Values
- Spirituality
- Traditionalist
- Inclusionist
- Black Epistemic
- Black Assimilationist
- Black Accomodationism
- Black Reconciliationism
- Paradigm
- African Worldview

- Self-Determinist
- Nationalist
- Marxist-Leninist
- Afrocentricity
- Intellectual Imperatives
- Praxis
- Aesthetics Issue
- Axiological Issue
- Epistemology Issue
- Cosmological Issue
- Optimal Theory
- Black Liberal Idealism
- Humanity

- Social Thought
- Africology
- Normative Theory
- Ideological Imperatives
- Moral Concepts
- Moral Reasoning
- Disciplinary Matrix
- Nommo
- Popular Afrocentrism
- Metaphysical Component
- Grand Theory
- Ethical Discourse
- Classical Civilization

Introduction

Within the general context of American society and academia, African American Studies has not only contributed to existing bodies of knowledge and schools of thought, but it has also generated new and challenging epistemologies, perspectives and approaches for examining the historical and contemporary experiences of people of African descent. At the crux of African American Studies' philosophical foundation lies an attempt to create a viable system of knowledge capable of raising levels of consciousness and rescuing and (re)constructing identities. In the name of the mental and physical liberation of people of African descent as well as the rest of humanity, it seeks to provide answers to basic questions about nature, knowledge, values, spirituality, art and other areas of human existence and expression.

279

Simultaneously however, some of the most frequently reoccurring discussions and debates over the past thirty years have focused around central philosophical questions about the approach, utility, and function of knowledge (and all of its subject areas) within the field. Historically, there have been five major philosophical tendencies in African American Studies: traditionalist/inclusionist; self-determinist/nationalist; Marxist-Leninist; and most recently Afrocentricity and Black Feminist Thought.

This section emphasizes the philosophical interpretation of the discipline and speculates about possible relationships between ideological and intellectual imperatives in the development and maintenance of African American Studies. Engaging the challenges raised above, some of the most articulated philosophical interpretations of African American Studies are provided in the articles here.

Maulana Karenga writes in "Black Studies and the Problematic of Paradigm: The Philosophical Dimension": "One of the most critical challenges facing Black Studies today is the need to rescue and exercise its right to self-definition and self-determination with scholarship and vision and to reassess with rigor its original paradigm in both theory and practice... Black Studies in one sense, then, follows the paradigm process for Black Studies perceptibly different and more difficult. These are (1) the interdisciplinary nature of Black Studies, (2) its dual character and thrust of scholarship and praxis, and (3) the tendency to assume its origins as a discipline in the 1960s and deny its longer history as an intellectual enterprise."

Linda J. Myers' "Optimal Theory and the Philosophical and Academic Origins of Black Studies" introduces the concept of optimal theory and argues that this perspective is necessary for constructing the content and structure of African American Studies. She suggests that the optimal frame of reference responds to the Afrocentric principle of the greatest good for developing everlasting peace and happiness.

In "Intellectual Questions and Imperatives in the Development of Afro-American Studies," Russell L. Adams states, "If professionals in the field of Afro-American/Black Studies are to increase the intellectual depth and academic significance of their work, they must manifest a profound understanding of the present epistemological context of American social thought and the formal institutions through which this thought is mediated. They must look hard at the 'traditional disciplines.' They must understand how these disciplines came to be and to what extent their epistemological foundations complicate the creation of an alternative and perhaps more accurate epistemic for approaching the black experience."

In his article "The Intellectual and Institutional Development of Africana Studies," Robert L. Harris, Jr. lists four stages in the development of Africana Studies as an area of inquiry. According to Harris, the first stage began in the 1890s and lasted until the second world war; the second stage began with the study of black America by Gunnar Myrdal in the mid 1940s; the third stage was from about the mid 1960s to the mid 1980s; and the fourth stage of theoretical refinement and more sophisticated analysis and interpretation is currently in process.

In "The Status of Black Studies in the Second Decade: The Ideological Imperative," Tilden LeMelle warns that, "The Black self-determinationist ideologies are... self-assertive and purport to base their self-assertion on an evaluation of the realities of the Black world... despite their role in reorienting blacks to a positive sense of self-identity and providing a realistic rationale for Black Studies, the self-determinationist ideologies can all too easily be corrupted. The danger increases as Black Studies staff and students lose sight of the functional role of ideology and make ideology an end in itself."

Molefi K. Asante, in "African American Studies: The Future of the Discipline," posits that "Africology is defined as the Afrocentric study of phenomena, events, ideas, and personalities related to Africa.... The future of Africology will depend upon those who are committed to the principles of academic excellence and social responsibility. Those principles must be interpreted within the framework of an Afrocentric vision in order to maintain a space and location for Africology within the academy."

Finally, in "Reaching for Higher Ground: Toward an Understanding of Black/Africana Studies," James B. Stewart delineates the directions for the developments of Black/Africana Studies disciplinary matrix: "... seven developmental thrusts can contribute significantly to the project: (1) generation of a theory of history, (2) articulation of a theory of knowledge and social change, (3) delineation of a theory of race and culture, (4) expansion of the scope of inquiry encompassed by the disciplinary matrix, (5) expanded examination of the historical precedents to modern Black/Africana Studies, (6) increased emphasis on applications of theoretical work, and (7) strengthened linkages to interests outside academe to minimize misappropriation of a knowledge and improve information dissemination."

The selections in Section IV were chosen to illustrate that African American Studies has a deep and rich philosophical framework and to examine the various positions regarding epistemological, ideological, and paradigmatic dimensions within the field. Each article focuses on a different concept and raises questions about the nature of knowledge, along with its role and function in relation to African American Studies.

26.

Black Studies and the Problematic of Paradigm: The Philosophical Dimension

Maulana Karenga

In spite of its ideals and continuing promise, it was clear from its inception that Black Studies would encounter a series of internal and external challenges to its realization as a legitimate and effective discipline. And it was equally clear that how it responded to those challenges would determine its course, content, and ultimate future (Hare, 1972). At the heart of these challenges is the problematic of paradigm that, although it was posed and pursued at the inception of Black Studies, was never definitively resolved. This, in turn, has led to an ongoing and crisis-oriented struggle to define, develop, and defend the discipline and at the same time defend Black Studies scholars' preeminent right to internal definition and development of the discipline. For given its academic and political vulnerability as a relatively young discipline, there is a continuing thrust—politically and philosophically—to define and/or disestablish it from external sources. Hare (1975:46), a founding father of the discipline, has recognized this vulnerability and its possible consequences. He observed that although "Black Studies remains relevant indeed...we are slowly letting the discipline slip from our political grip." For "it is being increasingly shaped and defined for us rather than by us."

Nowhere is this attempt to define the discipline from outside the discipline clearer than in the recent report to the Ford Foundation by Nathan Huggins (1985). Huggins's (1985:1) claim that it is an "essay on the present state and future prospects of Afro-American Studies" is clearly unfounded. In fact, his piece, for all its pretensions and in spite of Ford Foundation's prefatory assurance of his previous scholarship, is little more than European hagiography masquerading as history, and an unscholarly melange of personal preferences posing as meaningful analysis. The melange begins with and is pervaded by a paean to American universities and colleges and includes, among other items of varying merit and meaning, an undeclared and problematic "psychohistory" of Black students who continually suffer from and are motivated by "malaise," an unsubstantiated attempt to rank Black Studies programs and departments, and ad hominem attacks on some Black Studies scholars. Given this and other equally deficient attempts to define Black Studies externally and Eurocentrically it becomes even clearer that one of the most critical challenges facing Black Studies today is the need to rescue and exercise its right to scholarship and vision and to reassess with rigor its original paradigm in both theory and practice.

Internal Dialogue

The problem of developing and establishing a paradigm, however, has confronted, perhaps even plagued, all disciplines in varying degrees and at various stages of their development. Moreover, as Gutting's (1980) collection of essays on the question demonstrates, the project poses not only intellectual problems, but practical and political ones also, and thus is not easily accomplished. This has certainly been the experience of Black Studies, whose historical and ongoing concern and struggle around the development and establishment of a paradigm are well documented (Hare, 1969; Turner, 1984b). Black Studies in one sense, then, follow paradigm process for Black Studies perceptibly different and more difficult. These are (1) the interdisciplinary nature of Black Studies, (2) its dual character and thrust of scholarship and praxis, and (3) the tendency to assume its origins as a discipline in the 1960s and deny its longer history as an intellectual enterprise, thus restricting "the data base from which exemplars can be drawn."

Stewart's observations and concerns are correctly focused and well founded. The problem of producing a paradigm for interdisciplinary and/or multidisciplinary studies has challenged academia for some time without effective resolution (Charlesworth, 1972; MacRae, 1976). Whether one talks about organic or theoretical integration of disciplines or of various subject areas into one discipline, fundamental problems are posed by the need for specialization of labor and the analytic decomposition of reality resorted to in the process of rigorous research. Experience tends to reveal that scholars seldom achieve sufficient grounding in more than one discipline or subject area and thus often reject the holistic approach for a more manageable specialized area of concentration. What one does, then, is work on discipline boundaries, crossing them tentatively and temporarily without ever intermeshing them.

However, Black Studies, since its inception, has sought to develop an interdisciplinary paradigm. In fact, by conception and definition, it was compelled to attempt a holistic approach to the study of Black life. As I have argued, "The scope of Black Studies is expressed in its definition and by the parameters it has set for itself as an interdisciplinary discipline" (Karenga, 1982:33), for Black Studies is essentially "the scientific (or systematic) study of the multidimensional aspects of Black thought and practice in their current and historical unfolding." The category of totality here is key to the self-conception and definition of Black Studies. It stresses not only the totality of social life—that is, the multidimensional aspects of Black thought and practice—but also the totality of time, that is, "their current and historical unfolding," which envisions and expresses an ongoing process.

Again, then, the inclusive focus of Black Studies compels it to be interdisciplinary and integrate various subject areas into a coherent discipline rather than submit to the vitiating compartmentalization of knowledge established by white studies. After all, even if one decomposes reality at first to achieve a more intimate understanding of it, this does not preclude or obviate the need to include in that understanding the relations of each part to the other as well as to the whole. This is what Turner (1984a:x-xi) means when he states that "the intellectual task (for Black Studies scholars) is not then simply to pick or choose among the conceptual and methodological togs of traditional disciplines, but to reconceptualize the social fabric and rename the world in a way that obliterates the voids that have inevitably occurred as a result of artificial disciplinary demarcations."

Stewart's second assertion concerning the difficulties posed by Black Studies' dual nature and stress of scholarship and praxis is of equal importance. It is a measure of his insightfulness and commitment to the development of the paradigm that he concedes the difficulties without submitting to them. From its very beginning, Black Studies has had both an academic and social thrust and mission. Rooted in the social theory and struggles of the 1960s, it sheltered the assumption that the Black experience clearly represented a truth worth knowing, but also one worth living and offering as a paradigm for human liberation and a higher level of human life. Conceiving of intellectual emancipation as a prerequisite and parallel support of political emancipation, Black Studies advocates posed their discipline as a synthesized and synthesizing enterprise that links thought and practice into a paradigm of active self-knowledge. At its best, such a paradigm represented a quest for self-realization that expresses itself as both self-knowledge and self-production, that is, a people's critical grasping of its inherent possibilities and its self-consciously bringing them into being both as a distinct people and as a fundamental part of society.

Stewart's third concern, though well grounded, would benefit from a bit more conceptual preciseness. Certainly, Stewart (1984:297 is correct to argue that one of the central problem paradigm construction determination of the historical origin of Black Studies as a discipline. He disagrees with my contention that "Black Studies, as an *academic discipline*" began in the 1960s (Karenga, 1982:17; emphasis added). Stewart argues that "if this view is valid, it severely restricts the data base from which exemplars (fundamental achievements) can be drawn since there is no long history of continuously intellectual development to trace." However, he continues, "there are historical Black Studies analysts/activists whose primary efforts included the clear delineation of a research program or paradigm linked to specific implementation strategies that can provide guidance for contemporary development efforts."

Responding to Stewart must begin with an eager admission that the study of Black people and society by Blacks goes back far beyond the 1960s. In fact, Egypt as the preeminent classical African civilization offers a wealth of written data in this regard (Diop, 1981). Similarly, in more recent times, W.E.B. DuBois, Leo Hansberry, Carter G. Woodson, Anna J. Cooper, Mary M. Bethune, and others have contributed tremendously to our understanding of African Americans and their thought and practice in the social and historical process. However, one must also restate that as an academic discipline, as opposed to the general study of Blacks from the aspect of one or more other disciplines, Black Studies did begin in the 1960s. A discipline is by definition a self-conscious, organized system of research and communication in a defined area of inquiry and knowledge, not simply a literature,series of courses in schools and universities, or research focus in a given area.

Stewart's use of the category "coherent intellectual enterprise" to define what he means by Black Studies offers a necessary definitional element, but it is not in itself sufficient. The elements of self-consciousness, organization, and demarcation of the intellectual enterprise are too glaringly absent to provide the conceptual inclusiveness and preciseness required to define the discipline adequately. Nevertheless, we are still left with the legitimacy and cogency of Stewart's concern that we not mistakenly limit our data base and be dismissive of the valuable works of our precursors who laid foundations on which we can and must build our intellectual and practical project. This we would indeed do, as he suggests, if we artificially abbreviate the history of Black Studies, limiting its relevant intellectual and practical activity to the 1960s.

Perhaps the solution to this problem lies in first accepting Stewart's contention that Black Studies has a history beyond the 1960s. Second, wherever we begin its history, it should be divided into two fundamental periods—prediscipline and actual discipline history. The prediscipline period would include the scholars who often worked alone and outside a formal structured program or department, but with a clear purpose of rescuing and reconstructing African history and humanity. The discipline period will be marked by self-consciousness, organization, demarcation, and institutionalization. Third, one must concede that use of a data base produced by Black scholars does not historically or currently compel us to claim them or their works as part of the discipline. In fact, the distinction between discipline-specific work and contributions used by the discipline is not only key to the solution of the above problem, but also fundamental to discouraging Black Studies scholars from using general works by Black scholars outside the discipline as a substitute for intellectual production within the discipline. By discipline-specific intellectual production, I essentially mean work done within and for the discipline by Black Studies scholars who identify themselves primarily as such. Such discipline-specific work is indispensable, for, in the final analysis, it is the community of scholars within the discipline that are primarily and ultimately responsible for its definition, defense, and development. And their failure to realize and respond creatively to this can only ensure the discipline's deformation and underdevelopment and, eventually, its dissolution.

This, of course, returns us to the need for a paradigm within which such critical work can be designed and accomplished. Although there are other critical areas fundamental to the development and establishment of the Black Studies paradigm, that is, curriculum development, collegial collaboration, and social praxis, I will treat in this article only the philosophical problematic. For it is the foundation on which all the other basic compositional elements are raised, the prerequisite that makes possible and facilitates the success of all other efforts.

The efforts of theoretical construction must begin with the essential, even indispensable definition, the definition of paradigm. The category has been used in Black Studies literature in various ways, that is, to denote a grand theory, a text based on or offering a grand theory, a model curriculum, a process of analysis, a methodology of research, and so on. Eckberg and Hill (1980) have identified three fundamental meanings of paradigm thought to be implicitly or explicitly posed in Kuhn's (1970) fundamental work on the question. These are (1) metaphysical structure of unquestioned presuppositions; (2) a disciplinary matrix of shared commitments, beliefs, and values; and (3) exemplars, that is, concrete achievements used as temporary or ongoing models. For the purposes of this article, I will use paradigm in both a cognitive and practical sense as essentially a generally recognized achievement—whether of theory, principles process, or practice—used as a model by the community of scholars within the discipline to conceive, execute, and substantiate their work.

This essentially agrees with and incorporates Stewart's emphasis on exemplars—theoretical and practical—as the definitive element and foundation of paradigms. It is also in correspondence with Turner's (1984a:xviii) assertion that "Black Studies is a conceptual paradigm that principally tells us, like other academic discourse, what counts as facts and what problems of explanations exists." Moreover, I will of necessity concentrate in this article on exploring the possibilities and suggesting guidelines for a theoretical exemplar in the form of a grand theory, that is, a philosophy of Black Studies that would offer an analytic, empirical, and ethical framework for studying, understanding, and explicating African American life in its historical and current unfolding.

The importance of theoretical construction to the development of a philosophy of Black Studies is well recognized in the discipline. In fact, Weber (1984:71) contends that "the first challenge of [the discipline] is to develop a sound philosophy of operation." Recognizing the profound historical resistance to a definitive philosophy that sets basic guidelines and parameters of research and relevance, Weber asserts that while a philosophy "does restrict, it also gives direction and purpose to the program." Stewart (1984:311), so clear and cogent on other issues, is correctly concerned that "one of the current barriers to paradigm development is the absence of a synthesis of Nationalist and Marxist approaches to Black Studies." And LeMelle (1984:60) reasons that "success or failure of Black Studies programs and departments will depend to a large degree on the resolution of ideological struggles within Black Studies."

It is important, however, to note here that although there is *undeclared* and *declared* sentiment in Black Studies for a grand theory or philosophy that would offer a framework for scholarship and the resolution of needless ideological struggles, there are serious problems that hinder its production and acceptance. The first of these problems is general academic and internal discipline distaste for and opposition to grand theories resulting from fashionable rejection of the value and groundedness of normative theories of human nature and conduct and the rise of the positivistic fetish for quantification, puzzle solving, and the search for lawful regularity. However, as Skinner (1985) demonstrates, the return to grand theory in the human sciences has already begun by such theorists as Gadamer, Foucault, Kuhn, Habermas, and Rawls et al. Such a return, as he in part suggests, had been occasioned by widespread reaction against the assumption that natural science offers a relevant or adequate paradigm for the human sciences; the moral objection to positivistic attempts to establish a nonethical science of society and the interest in returning to the question of the requirements of a just society and world order.

Second, there is the problem of priority in the competition for paradigmatic achievement. As King (1980:102-103) points out, the recognition of a paradigmatic achievement is not easily accorded given the fact that to accept a paradigmatic achievement is not merely to recognize owed esteem, but is also to concede that the achiever has earned "the right to be heard on questions concerningly [the paradigms] future." Third, in terms of production, the paradigm requires a developmental process that although emerging in Black Studies, has not proven as supportive as it could be in terms of collegial collaboration and creative challenge that are always essential, for it is in such a context of collegiality and creative challenge and collaboration that intellectual initiative and creativity is cultivated and achieved. A final problem in the production and acceptance of the grand theory is misconceptions concerning its theoretical and compositional requirements. Given the various definitions of paradigm, what one usually finds in the marketplace of propositions and offerings are simply theoretical elements of a possible paradigm rather than an inclusive cognitive framework that contains and imposes coherence on the essential elements. Williams's (1986) contribution to the paradigm discourse is a case in point. He has produced a valuable piece and has cogently argued it, but it represents a contribution to the establishment of central elements in a paradigm, that is, its Afrocentric character and focus, rather than a grand theory or model itself.

Afrocentric Conceptualization

A Black Studies philosophy must begin self-consciously and self-definitionally as an Afrocentric enterprise. As Asante (1986:1-2) contends in his critique of Huggins's (1986) impoverished report on Black Studies discussed above, "Black Studies is not merely the study of Black people." It involves and necessitates the study of Blacks from a definite perspective. In fact, he contends, "an Afrocentric perspective constitutes the critical difference between African American Studies and other fields." Asante is referring here to a fundamental building bloc in the conceptual edifice of the Black Studies paradigm, that is, its Afrocentricity. Although Asante's treatment of Afrocentricity is more descriptive than definitional, more connotative than denotative, in both this piece and his book titled *AfroCentricity: The Theory of Social Change* (1980), his contribution to the appreciation of its essentiality in and to the discipline is recognized and respected. And it is clear from both works as well as from general Black Studies discourse that when Asante and other Black Studies scholars use the term, they are employing it to suggest a certain African quality that a given perspective or approach possesses.

Synthesizing the various yet similar ways in which the concept is used, *Afrocentricity is essentially a quality of perspective or approach rooted in the cultural image and human interests of African people.* To say an approach or perspective is in the African cultural image is to say it is rooted in an African value system and worldview, especially in the *historical* and *classical sense.* And to say that an approach or perspective is in the human interests of African people is to say it is supportive of the just claims African people have and share with other humans in terms of freedom from want, toil, and domination, and freedom to realize oneself in one's human fullness, that is, to know and produce oneself through meaningful work, uncoerced and non-manipulative leisure time, and effective and enjoyable encounters with other humans and nature without coercion or repressive limitation.

It is important that the specific *cultural* and general *human* character of Afrocentricity never be conceived of or employed as a reaction to or an African version of Eurocentricity with its racist and structured denial and deformation of the history and humanity of Third World peoples. Afrocentricity at its best is a quest for and an expression of *historical* and *cultural anchor*, a critical reconstruction that dares to restore missing and hidden parts of our historical self-formation and pose the African experience as a significant paradigm for human liberation and a higher level of human life. To be no more than "an obscene caricature of Europe"—to use Fanon's phrase—is to violate historical memory and vitiate historical possibilities inherent in the special truth Africans can and must speak to the world given their ancient, rich, and varied experience.

Having established the *essentiality*, even indispensability of the Afrocentric worldview and approach, one is still left with questions of grounding, further compositional elaboration, and application. Thus the Afrocentric approach and worldview produces a need to address several related and attendant problems or intellectual challenges that must be resolved in the successful construction of a paradigmatic philosophy.

A primary challenge, of course, is the need to specify clearly the priority and centrality of the African American experience in the discipline of Black Studies. As I have argued, the priority focus on the Afro-American experience is both necessary and correct for several reasons (Karenga, 1982:367-368).

First, such a priority focus is a due recognition and respect for the history of the discipline as an intellectual enterprise conceived and established by African Americans, first and foremost, for their own intellectual and political emancipation. Obviously and unavoidably, this project was linked to the liberation project of all African people and even to the Third World, but the priority was given to African Americans. It was a project informed by the assumption that the rescue and reconstruction of one's history and humanity was the prerequisite for one's ability to assist, effectively exchange, and join with others in a similar and common project.

Second, the priority focus on African Americans in Black Studies gives a necessary rootedness and point of departure from which the systematic study of the Black world can proceed and expand. As Turner (1984a:viii) states, "The *Black World* is perceived as patterns within a trilateral relationship between Africa, the African Caribbean and the African Americans with, understandably, primary concentration on African America." Moreover, Aldridge's (1984:365) stress on the internationalization of the Black Studies curriculum fits within this model, for she is concerned that Black Studies is holistic in its approach to social and human reality.

It is at this point that Turner's (1984a) and Clarke's (1984) argument for the category "Africana Studies" instead of Black Studies is best understood. As Clarke (1984:31) states, Africana "relates . . . to land, history, culture" and thus gives greater grounding than color, for color simply "tells you how you look without telling you who you are." Turner (1984a:viii), stressing the fact and function of *linkage*, observes that "the concept *Africana* is derived from the 'African continuum and African consociation' which posits fundamental interconnections in the global Black experience." These are points well taken, but the duality of the African American experience, even synthesized and correctly delineated, must always be critically studied and understood. Given this need, it is not a violation of conceptual etiquette if one uses African American Studies — even Black Studies — interchangeably with Africana Studies.

Finally, the priority focus on African Americans makes the praxis dimension of Africana Studies immediate, readily recognizable, and easier to implement. The original call by Hare to "bring the campus to the community and the community to the campus" finds its practical expression in the African American community. Both the campus and the community, then, become contested areas, centers of conflict and resolution in the ongoing project of intellectual and political emancipation.

Rationale and Mission

A second challenge for a paradigmatic Black Studies philosophy is to provide a definitive rationale and mission for Black Studies. As I (1982:371-372) have stated, the development of Black Studies has already contributed to the evolution in broad terms of a rationale that is at the same time a suggestion of mission. Moreover, as I have also contended, whatever its final form the rationale-mission should contain six basic contentions of relevance. Since I have explained these in detail in the first chapter of *Introduction to Black Studies*, I will simply state and treat them briefly. A seventh contribution Black Studies must also make, given the seriousness of the problem it seeks to solve, will be discussed below.

These first six contributions that Black Studies makes and that provide it with its fundamental rationale and mission are its contributions (1) to humanity's understanding of itself, using the African experience as a paradigmatic human struggle and achievement; (2) to the university's realizing its claim of universality, comprehensiveness, and objectivity by demanding and facilitating a holistic approach to the study of truth and the class, race, and sexual contradictions that constrain and distort it; (3) to U.S. society's understanding itself by critically measuring its claims against its performance and its variance with a paradigmatic just society; (4) to the rescue and reconstruction of Black history and humanity from alien hands, and the restoration of African classical culture on and through which we can build a new body of human sciences and humanities; (5) to the creation of a new social science, more critical, corrective, holistic, and ethical; and (6) to the creation of a body of conscious, capable, and committed Black intellectuals who self-consciously choose to use their knowledge and skills in the service of the Black community and, by consequence and extension, in the interest of a new and better society and world.

The seventh contribution that Black Studies can and must make to reinforce its relevance and expand the scope and content of its mission is the contribution to the critique, resistance, and reversal of the progressive Westernization of human consciousness, which is one of the major problems of our times. By the Westernization, or more precisely the Europeanization of human consciousness, I mean the systematic invasion and effective transformation of the cultural consciousness of the various peoples of the world by Europeans through technology, education, and the media so that at least three things occur: (1) the progressive loss of, historical memories of these people; (2) the progressive disappreciation of themselves and their culture; and (3) the progressive adoption of a Eurocentric mode of assessment of self, society, and the world that induces cognitive distortion and deprivation, and the destruction of human richness in diversity. The need, then, is for Black Studies scholars to critique, resist, and attempt to reverse this by joining with other Third World scholars in exposing its antihuman character and consequences and by posing an alternative paradigm for discourse among those whose quest is the same or similar.

Even Stewart's concern with a creative synthesis of nationalism and Marxism is hampered by this problem of Eurocentricism and the intellectual imperialism this imposes. Without an honest recognition of this cultural and epistemological limitation by Black Marxists and an attempt to creatively deal with and diminish it, a synthesis is neither possible nor desirable for Black Studies. Certainly, Robinson (1983) is to be commended for his honest a critical appraisal of this problem in a well-thought-out and impressive volume on Black Marxism. It is obviously a model for other Black Marxists in its ability to give credit to Marxism for its class perceptions, yet recognizes, as Robinson (1983:2) states, that is still fair to say that at its base...its epistemological substructure, Marxism is a Western construction" and that this produces as tendency for Marxists to perceive and pose their project as "identical with world historical development." And, of course, there always the problem of their reductive translation of race and culture that must be resolved if any meaningful creative synthesis to take place.

Ethical Discourse

Another fundamental compositional element of the Black Studies paradigmatic philosophy is ethical discourse. The historical rootedness of the Black Studies concern for ethical discourse goes back to the ancient African interest in the just society. This interest is expressed in the ancient Egyptian text, *The Book Khun-Anup*

(Karenga, 1984:31ff.; Lichtheim, 1975:169ff.), which is the oldest text on social justice, appearing in the Middle Kingdom (2040-1640 BCE). In addition, African Americans' greatest contribution to social change in this country has been its ethical criticism—both theoretical and practical—of the anti-human constraints and contradictions of U.S. society. Whether one talks of Henry M. Turner, Anna J. Cooper, Malcolm X, Mary M. Bethune, Frederick Douglass, or Martin Luther King, one talking about an Afro-American tradition and legacy of setting the moral and progressive agenda for U.S. society. And Black Studies is obligated to raise up, honor, and critically elucidate that tradition and legacy.

Moreover, from its inception—in both its prediscipline and discipline stages—Black Studies has stressed the ethical dimension of its mission. It was begun, as W.E.B. DuBois (1971:64) note as "primarily scientific—a careful search for truth conducted as thoroughly, broadly and honestly" as possible. However, its more expansive dimension was "not only to make the truth clear, but to present it in such shape as will encourage and help social reform." In a word, the Black Studies paradigm, even in its prediscipline stage, posed the possibility of an intellectual paradigm that combined valuative discourse with factual discourse without doing damage to either.

Furthermore, we live at a critical juncture in U.S. and world history in which ethical discourse has become one of the major critiques of the social and human condition. In fact, it could be argued that even the Marxist critique demonstrates its greatest strength, especially among Third World peoples, not in its scientific claims, but its ethical discourse concerning the social and human condition. This seems clearly to be the case of liberation theology that has absorbed the Marxist stress on praxis and translates it as reflective ethical action (West, 1982; Cone, 1975).

Moreover, one need only survey the literature in the field to see ethics as a central discipline and discourse in the fundamental areas of human and social concern, that is, nuclear ethics, biomedical ethics, judicial and legal ethics, feminist ethics, and, of course, liberation ethics. Given this centrality of ethics in our tradition and the current world, a Black Studies philosophy must exhibit and stress an effective grounding in ethical discourse that provides indispensable tools for grasping the place and value of ethics in society and critical competence in identifying and analyzing the ethical issues of our times as they relate not only to social policy questions, but to the enduring questions of the nature, function, and dimensions of a just society and world order.

Critique and Corrective

The paradigmatic grand theory of Black Studies must also be self-consciously a holistic enterprise of critique and corrective. It must be a fundamental contribution to the development of an analytic, empirical, and ethical framework in which every aspect and element of African American life can be investigated, understood, and explained. It must begin as critique and culminate corrective on both the theoretical and practical level. For as I (1982:32) have argued elsewhere, Black Studies is both an investigative and applied discipline and requires this dual thrust contemplation and intervention, and observation that inspires informs social action.

By *critique*, I mean the systematic unrelenting battle again both *ignorance* and *illusion*, the struggle against the poverty knowledge as well as the perversion of truth. In being holistic, will be of necessity *cultural* in the broadest most inclusive sense of the word. By *culture*, I mean the totality of thought and practice by which a people creates itself, defines and celebrates itself, and introduces itself to history and humanity. Culture becomes a key concept then not only for the critique of society, but for the critique and corrective for the Black Studies paradigm that must erect its conceptual, curricular, and practical project out of its understanding of its culture — historically and currently.

It is in its critique of domination as well as the underdevelopment that it has produced in the African world culture that the Black Studies critique-corrective becomes a central contribution to human consciousness and liberation. The interpretative task to break through the wall of social distortions and obstacles that damage vision, corrupt human values, and justify the social order at the expense of social justice. Such a critical theory will place even scientific "facts" in a given context and show that they already propose and project a theory in which they are grounded. It will at its best demonstrate that history without interpretation is empty and self-deceptive, that facts without context is illusory, and that empirical observation without analysis is useless and, at one stage impossible.

The Paradigmatic Classical Civilization

The final compositional element of a paradigmatic Black Studies philosophy is the identification and restoration of a paradigmatic classical African civilization. This would give grounding to the claims of Afrocentricity by producing a paradigm for a truly African social thought and practice. It would also then give a cultural basis on which to build a new body of human sciences and humanities, and enable Black Studies to stand on the firmest of grounds in its cultural, historical, and epistemological claims. The delineation and development of an African worldview, then, presupposes and necessitates a definitive historical paradigm that involves both models of historical practice and historical possibility, and the restoration and effective utilization of a classical African civilization yields the framework for this.

Carruthers (1984:16) has made a cogent call for an African worldview, focusing on the relevance of Egypt as a classical source of the African worldview. He states that "the formulation of an African worldview is the essential beginning point for all research which is based upon the interests of African people." In fact, he goes on to say, "there can be no African history, no African social science without an African worldview." Carruthers (1984), Diop (1981), this author, and others (Karenga and Carruthers, 1986) argue that this worldview must evolve from the rescue and reconstruction of the classical African legacy of Egypt. Diop (1981:12) writes that "for us, the return to Egypt in all fields is the necessary condition to build a body of modern human sciences, and renew African culture." That is why it is necessary to state that "far from being a diversion in the past, a look toward ancient Egypt is the best way of conceiving and building our cultural future." In fact, "Egypt will play, in a rethought and renewed African culture, the same role that the ancient Greco-Latin civilizations play in Western culture" (translation mine).

The importance of Egypt to constructing an African worldview and indeed to the building of an authentic and effective Black paradigm rests on several factors: (1) its antiquity, (2) authenticity, (3) level of achievement, (4) document availability, (5) relevance to other Africans including us, and (6) its relevance to world history and culture (Glanville, 1957; Karenga and Carruthers, 1986; James, 1976).

The production of the "Negro," as Robinson (1983:4) argued effectively savaged our history and created historical amnesia in Europe and among Africans concerning the contribution of Africans to the forward flow of human history. It "substantially eradicated in Western historical consciousness the necessity of remembering the significance of Nubia for Egypt's formation of Egypt in the development of Greek civilization, of Africa for Imperial Rome, and more pointedly of Islam's influence on Europe's economic, political and intellectual history" to which Africans also contributed significantly. Having produced this artificiality, "from such a creature not even a suspicion of tradition needed to be entertained.... In its stead, there was the Black slave a consequence masqueraded as an anthropology and a history."

It is the obligation, then, of Black Studies to rescue and reconstruct this rich, complex, and varied legacy that introduced the basic disciplines of human knowledge, produced the oldest sacred texts on which a significant part of Judeo-Christian ethics an theology are based, contributed the calendar among other critic things, and was a school for the Greeks to whom other European pay so much homage (James, 1976).

Conclusion

The needed thrust, then, for Black Studies in its solving the problematic of paradigm is what Gouldner (1985:204) has called "creative rupture" as opposed to "routine competence." Such creativity comes, he tells us, from "paradigm-distancing, i.e., the ability to adopt a position apart from, outside or in critique of the established paradigms of normal science or scholarship." Strickland (1975:7), reminding Black scholars of their continuing historical project, has reaffirmed the Black Studies mission and the philosophical paradigm that frames and fosters it. The demands of history and social conditions pose "a most precise challenge to Black intellectuals in America," he states. And "that is nothing more, but also nothing less, than the challenge to create a new intellectual tradition — and practice — in these United States." It is in the context and practice of Black Studies, as a self-conscious interdisciplinary discipline, that this new intellectual tradition and practice will be both posed and realized. For in this framework, Black Studies scholars will rescue and restore the lost and hidden experimental dimension of African history and find in it a paradigm of human emancipation and possibility. The essential need, then, is that we do our work so well that even when other scholars are emotionally or culturally unable to accept our conclusions, they are still compelled to concede the rigor of our research and the groundedness of our theory. It is upon such critical work that both the continuing legitimacy and academic life of Black Studies depend.

References

Aldridge, D.P. (1984) "Toward a new role and function of Black Studies in white and historically black institutions." *Journal of Negro Education* (Summer): 359-367.

Asante, M.K. (1980) *Afro-Centricity: The Theory of Social Change.* Buffalo, NY: Amulefi.

—— (1986) "A note on Nathan Huggins: report to the Ford Foundation on African American studies." Temple University (unpublished).

Carruthers, J.H. (1984) *Essays in Ancient Egyptian Studies*. Los Angeles: University of Sankore Press.

Charlesworth, J.C. [ed.] (1972) Integration of the Social Sciences Through Policy Analysis. Philadelphia: American Academy of Political and Social Science.

Clarke, J.H. (1984) "Africana Studies: a decade of change, challenge and conflict," pp. 31-45 in J.E. Turner (ed.) *The Next Decade: Theoretical and Research Issues in Africana Studies*. Ithaca, NY: Cornell University Press.

Cone, J. (1975) *God of the Oppressed*. New York: Seabury.

Diop, C.A. (1981) *Civilisation ou Barbarie*. Paris: Presence Africaine.

DuBois, W.E.B. (1971) *Dusk of Dawn*. New York: Schoken.

Eckberg, D. and L. Hill, Jr. (1980) "The paradigm concept and sociology," pp. 117-136 in G. Gutting (ed.) *Paradigms and Revolutions*. Notre Dame: University of Notre Dame.

Glanville, S.R.K. (1957) *The Legacy of Egypt*. London: Oxford University Press.

Gouldner, A. (1985) *Against Fragmentation*. New York: Oxford University Press.

Gutting, G. (1980) *Paradigms and Revolutions*. Notre Dame: University of Notre Dame Press.

Hare, N. (1969) "What should be the role of Afro-American education in the undergraduate curriculum?" *Liberal Education* 55 (March): 42-50.

—— (1972) "The battle of Black Studies." *Black Scholar* 3 (May): 32-37.

—— (1975) "A black paper: the relevance of Black Studies." *Black Collegian* 6 (September/October): 46-50.

Huggins, N. (1985) Afro-American Studies: A Report to the Ford Foundation. New York: Ford Foundation.

James, G. (1976) *Stolen Legacy*. San Francisco: Julian Richardson.

Karenga, M. (1982) *Introduction to Black Studies*. Los Angeles: University of Sankore Press.

—— (1984) *Selections from the Husia: Sacred Wisdom of Ancient Egypt*. Los Angeles: University of Sankore Press.

Karenga, M. and J.H. Carruthers [eds.] (1986) *Kemet and the African Worldview*. Los Angeles: University of Sankore Press.

King, M.D. (1980) "Reason, tradition and the progressiveness of science," pp. 97-116 in G. Gutting (ed.) *Paradigms and Revolutions*. Notre Dame: University of Notre Dame Press.

Kuhn, T. (1970) *The Structure of Scientific Revolutions*. Chicago: University of Chicago Press.

Lemelle, T. (1984) "The status of Black Studies in the second decade: the ideological imperative," pp. 47-61 in J.E. Turner (ed.) *The Next Decade: Theoretical and Research Issues in Africana Studies*. Ithaca, NY: Cornell University Press.

Lichtheim, M. (1975) *Ancient Egyptian Literature*. Berkeley: University of California Press.

MacRae, D. (1976) *The Social Function of Social Science*. New Haven, CT: Yale University Press.

Robinson, C.J. (1983) *Black Marxism: The Making of the Black Radical Tradition.* London: Zed.

Skinner, Q. [ed.] (1985) *The Return of Grand Theory in the Human Sciences.* New York: Cambridge University Press.

Stewart, J.B. (1984) "The legacy of W.E.B. DuBois for contemporary Black Studies." *Journal of Negro Education* (Summer): 296-311.

Strickland, B. (1975) "Black intellectuals and American social science." *Black World* 25 (November): 4-10.

Turner, J.E. (1984a) "Foreword: Africana Studies and epistemology: a discourse in the sociology of knowledge," pp. v-xxv in J.E. Turner (ed.) *The Next Decade: Theoretical and Research Issues in Africana Studies.* Ithaca, NY: Cornell University Press.

Turner, J.E. [ed.] (1984b) *The Next Decade: Theoretical and Research Issues in Africana Studies.* Ithaca, NY: Cornell University Press.

Weber, S. (1984) "Intellectual imperative and necessity for black education," in J.E. Turner (ed.) *The Next Decade: Theoretical and Research Issues in Africana Studies.* Ithaca, NY: Cornell University Press.

West, C. (1982) *Prophesy Deliverance! An Afro-American Revolutionary Christianity.* Philadelphia: Westminster.

Williams, W. (1986) "Unified theory in Black Studies: insights from the Creole language model." Presented at the joint annual NCBS and AHSA Conference, Boston (March 13-16).

27.

Optimal Theory and the Philosophical and Academic Origins of Black Studies

Linda James Myers

Abstract

Using the methodology of optimal theory, the events of the sixties can be seen as simply the resurgence of the higher self in the evolutionary cycle of humankind toward greater self knowledge, such can be discerned from the philosophical origins of Black Studies. The higher self refers to that aspect of all of ourselves that responds to the Afrocentric principle of the greatest good, summmum bonum. It is termed higher only in the context of a strong value for development toward everlasting peace and happiness, and that it requires going beyond seeming opposites for comprehension, or diunital reasoning. This paper will highlight the nature o this evolutionary process and its implications for reassessing and understanding the history of African people for immediate survival and future preparedness.

According to Manley Palmer Hall (1949), philosophy is that branch of learning devoted to the understanding and application of knowledge. It has as its first work the elevation of the human intellect to a realization of the divine plan. It has as its final consummation the elevation of humankind to absolute union with universal wisdom. Wisdom is described as thinking with God and nature. Black Studies emerges from this kind of philosophical tradition, which dates back to the beginnings of human culture and civilization before a more segmented Cartesian view of humanity and knowledge came into being and began to characterize Western thought. The purpose of this paper is to further explore the philosophical and academic origins of the discipline of Black Studies based on the Afrocentric perspective of optimal theory (Myers, 1988) with the intent of highlighting necessary evaluative criteria for the discipline, presenting a tool to measure from whence we have come, where we are, and where we must go in the future. Optimal theory creates a framework for examining several important issues relative to the development of the discipline. One issue, that of perspective, this paper will address, following a point of view through history to illustrate and substantiate the prophetic nature of the discipline's origins and its usefulness in interpreting past and present-day realities for future preparedness.

In discussing the philosophical and academic origins of Black Studies the question of perspective is critical. Frye (1980) notes that the philosophy of the ancients had seven overlapping layers, divided for convenience but not as academic territorial preserves. The layers, representing a synthesis of all learning, were metaphysics, logic, ethics, psychology, epistemology, aesthetics, and theurgy. These layers encompassed explorations of the nature of being and knowledge, rules governing reason, the science of morality, individual responsibility, character, and the soul, the urge to beauty and harmony, and the living of wisdom. Utilizing the perspective of optimal theory lifted from the philosophical orientation of ancient classical African civilization, Black Studies emerges as more than just the study of Black people or the nature of human existence as static and ahistorical. Black Studies seeks to appropriately and accurately reflect the evolution of humanity in the process of becoming "more better." [Nobles (1991, p. 10)]. This perspective on examining humankind and its environment based on and informed by an Afrocentric philosophical base may not be readily understood by those utilizing a more fragmented perspective, however the resurgence of Black Studies in the sixties illustrates the principle being identified.

Some suggest that the academic discipline of Black Studies grew out of the political demands made primarily by Black Students in the 60's [Brisbane (1974); Karenga (1982); McEvoy and Miller (1969)]. While this is true at one level, it is also true when observed from a more holistic perspective that the sixties experience was but one phase in a long process of the evolution of human consciousness toward the greater good. A time of much social unrest, the struggle against the structure and functioning of racism and oppression (wrong doing) in this society began off campus. However, such a struggle has to address the institution whose historical role has been to maintain and perpetuate the established social order, the formal education system, higher education in particular. Thus, Black Studies resurged to combat that key institution in the larger system of coercive institutions designed to foster and develop the exclusion of Blacks, and other Third World and poor people from knowledge, wealth, and power [Karenga (1982)].

In many ways the ultimate aim of the demands of students in the 60's was for a means to correct the wrong doing and gain freedom from the conceptual incarceration imposed by the hegemonous Eurocentric world view which had for so long dominated and oppressed the minds of people acknowledging African descent through an insidious intellectual imperialism and scientific colonialism. That aim, now being realized, has necessitated breaking the bonds of the conceptual incarceration created by the dominant world view. Through examination and reconceptualization, Black Studies as a discipline can now offer a viable alternative for the development of humankind. From the philosophical orientation of an authentic Afrocentric world view which optimal theory provides [Myers (1988); Myers, et al. (1991)], human consciousness has been and is being advanced by Black Studies, but not without struggle.

Black Studies in contemporary times has been forced to develop its competing paradigm within the context and confines of the world view dominant in the Western academy. The segmented or fragmented nature of that world view [Capra (1975); Myers (1988)] predisposed the structure of academic disciplines to synchronic approach. A major issue which Black Studies has had to address is that of trying to fit round pegs into square holes, or facing the challenge of attempting to create new room for itself in a closed system.

Black Studies and Disciplinarity

Williams (1982) described a discipline as a field of study that has established a precise and orderly framework for examining humankind and its environment, and whose primary objective is to organize knowledge, which is acquired during learning through application of scientific processes. The framework of Black Studies as a discipline from the Afrocentric world view of optimal theory is not only precise and orderly, but also inclusive enough to be traced to the early beginnings of human culture and civilization. This framework for examining humankind and its environment, meets the need identified by Kahn (1969) in observing the problems of traditional disciplinary fields, to change the nature of intellectual inquiry itself.

A potential advantage to a synchronic approach is that it may allow scholars to gain considerable knowledge about specific aspects of a subject or individual. The disadvantage is that it often does so at the expense of reducing the ability of scholars to understand the totality of human experience [Kahn (1969)]. The basic relationship between world view and the orientation toward synchronicity compounds the problem contributing to a fragmented system of knowledge not based on any ethical standard that would lead to cohesion, harmony, and order. The synchronic approach to intellectual inquiry regarding the human experience splits it into three general academic specialties, the natural and social sciences, and the humanities, with numerous more specific disciplines within each area.

One primary difficulty in the establishment of Black Studies as a discipline in the Western academy centers around the necessity of diachronic study that attempts to deal with phenomena as it changes over time. Such study has a broad focus that often appears interdisciplinary or multi-disciplinary in nature. This dilemma is to be predicted for a discipline emerging for and from an alternative cultural frame of reference, whose roots and world view are much more holistic and integrated than that of the West. The philosophical origins and basis of the discipline of Black Studies predate the emergence of the more segmented world view and can even now offer a great deal towards understanding the totality of human experience. Providing a unifying lens for synthesis of knowledge across many "disciplines," such a vantage point could be used to help shape their field of study. Fit within the context of the artificial disciplinarity of the Western academy, the development of this role for Black Studies is underway. Tracing of the evolution of the field of inquiry cuts across many disciplines as the perspective is not fragmented, and has historically never been.

According to Frye (1980) this perspective on examining humankind and its environment based on and informed by an Afrocentric philosophical orientation, included the seven layers of metaphysics, logic, ethics, psychology, epistemology, aesthetics, and theory, and warrants the label Black. Black symbolizes the absorption of all of the colors of the spectrum, all of the energies into harmony as one. It is also the term used to describe people acknowledging African descent (although all people are), and classified as members of the Negroid race. This kind of Black Studies perspective is fully inclusive and acknowledges that all of humankind can trace their personal ancestry, if they chose to be truly holistic in their approach to themselves relative to the totality human history, to these roots.

Within the fragmenting context of the Western academy the only layer to emerge as a discipline in its own right is that of psychology. The others exist in part under the general rubric of philosophy, or not at all. Consistent with the framing principles, optimal theory most readily fits and evolves within the field of inquiry known as psychology, although it carries all the philosophical layers conceived in ancient times with it. As such, as we look at the Afrocentric theory of optimal psychology [Myers (1988)] within Black Studies, origins dating back to the earliest records of human history can be interpreted and understood with consistency through to contemporary times. The oldest book in the world, according to Hilliard, Williams, and Damali

(1987), *The Teaching of Ptahhotep*, provides the first historical record of the shaping and movement of human will toward a higher consciousness as framed by optimal theory and allows the articulation of a human behavioral code for the achievement of the ideal.

Optimal Theory, Ethical Behavior and Black Studies

As early as 2,500 B.C., and perhaps earlier, a human behavioral code had been identified and articulated in the 37 teachings or *Instructions of Ptahhotep* [Hilliard, Williams, and Damali (1987)]. Ptahhotep, literally translated, means, God of Peace. The teachings themselves articulate a code of conduct quite consistent with that taught in the building of good character across the ages. In terms of good character, the instructions caution against arrogance, taking advantage of the weak, violence, scheming and manipulation of others, boasting, disrespecting women, greed, repeating slander, and so on.

Self control, honesty, fairness, generosity, respect, responsibility, building trust, gentleness of speech, humbleness, being circumspect in matters of sexual relations, and wisdom are among the behaviors strongly encouraged. Emphasis is placed on not allowing the shortcomings of others disturb your peace, maintaining control of your own thoughts and feelings (many principles characteristic of modem psychotherapies, such as rational-emotive and cognitive-behavioral therapies), silence, and supporting the principles of Maat (truth, justice, and righteousness). Thus we see in this example that from the perspective of optimal theory, Black Studies appropriately provides a framework for beginning the examination of humankind and its environment in its evolution toward the achievement of fuller realization of itself and its potential, since the most ancient of days. This growth and evolution takes place on multiple levels from the intraindividual and interindividual to that of cultural and global collectives.

Humanity needs the kind of examination that includes and reflects an understanding of the processes of life, growth, and change (diachronic). Growth is a dialectical process, according to optimal theory, in which movement is toward unifying, containing, and transcending opposites. The opposition serves the purpose of providing the opportunity for increased learning and development. The principles of polarity, cause and effect, and gender are replicated at all levels from the individual to the societal, as are others passed down to us as the seven hermetic principles or keys, that can be found at the root of the most profound teachings among all people [Frye (1980)]. Hermetic principles are important because as Keita (1977) observes, the bulk of what may be considered genuine African classical thought, can be found in the writings known as the Hermetica, representing the core of ancient Egypt philosophical theories.

In earlier works I have identified the philosophical parameters of the Afrocentric world view on which optimal theory is based in terms of ontology, epistemology, axiology, logic, and process [Myers (1988)]. Further elaboration of the philosophical roots and origin of Black Studies is made possible and contemporarily relevant by examining the relationship between these assumptions and the seven hermetic principles put forward by Frye (1980) and espoused in the livingness of the situations ancients encountered. For example, the ontological position that reality is a spiritual/material unity, all is spirit (that which is known in an extra-sensory fashion) manifest, is seen in the first principle of mind, all is mind and the universe is mental. Other principles are easily interwoven and have been mentioned — polarity, cause and effect, and gender.

To the extent African people have adopted this world view founded on these principles, they were able to not only survive 400 years of the most vicious and brutal form of slavery ever known in the history of humankind, but also emerge thriving with the ability to analyze the experience and push humankind to a new level of consciousness and accountability. Facilitating this endeavor has been the charge of the Black intelligentsia and can be traced through Black Studies.

The epistemological position that self knowledge is the basis of all knowledge lays the foundation and framework for diachronic study, and makes the most sense in the context of the principle of correspondence, as above, so below; as below, so above. Such informs not only the focus, but also the order of the process of evolution. While self at the higher levels of development and in this instance is perceived as multidimensional, including venerated ancestors, the yet unborn, nature, and community, the system of organization is identical to that depicted in the decorative mats woven by some American Natives. At the center or core of the circle is the creative force or spirit, the outer rim or edges of the mat represent the forms of self within which all else is contained. Full realization of self is reached through the implicit order of productive movement, the fourth principle of vibration, which says nothing rests. Movement is from the most inward to the most outward, the third principle of rhythm.

As the consciousness of individuals is developed and elevated, corresponding changes can be noted in the behavior and interactions of the greater humanity. Greatest good is maximized through an axiology consistent with spirituality, communalism, and oneness with nature, which require the manifestation of qualities such as love, peace, and harmony. Optimal theory posits the interrelatedness and interdependence of all things as an essential feature of reality, another example of the principle of cause and effect. Emphasis is placed on the central role of the spiritual (i.e., extra-sensory as in thought/feeling and consciousness) in the evolution of humankind. This framework creates an implicit standard of ethics, which is missing in a more fragmented world view, but allows for the articulation of a human behavioral code for the achievement of the ideals in the foundation of the philosophy.

If we rely on optimal theory to guide us, the philosophical and academic origins of Black Studies provide an excellent tool to measure from whence we have come, where we are, and where we must go in the future. Our roots are pure, grounded in the highest ideals for human potential. The nature of the life/growth/change process is built on oppositions with movement toward the unification, containment, and transcension. To the extent we can understand, recapture, and utilize the philosophical legacy left us by our ancestors, we are equipped to interpret our history, assess our current situation, and prepare to meet a better future.

Cornel West (1977) describes the major function of Afro-American philosophy as being the reshaping of the contours of Afro-American history and providing a new self-understanding of the Afro-American experience which suggests desirable guidelines for action in the present. The philosophical origins of Black Studies do just that when interpreted based on optimal theory. Our heritage emphasizes the building of character, and positive human interactions and relationships. Optimal theory provides the method and procedures requisite for their realization, the specific mindset and process that must be experienced. We have much to offer the world as it seeks to overcome the desolation created by the fragmented orientation so long dominant in the world. Not the least of which is a framework for developing ethical behavior.

Relevance of the Discipline as Evaluative Criteria

The reality of Black Studies is noted in the apparent resurgence of its root philosophical orientation and principles. The on-going movement culminating today out of the Black thrust into the Western academy in the '60s has always been concerned with the concept of relevance. Karenga (1982) points out that relevance, as a fundamental category, was inevitably defined in contemporary times as emanating from educational contributions to liberation and a higher level of life for Black (and thus from an optimal point of view, all people). Heretofore, the Western academy had only included "white studies," which were seen as incorrect and incomplete, propaganda for the established hegemony, totally resistant to growth and change (Karenga, 1982). Karenga identifies six areas in which a broad, fundamental, and undeniable relevance of Black Studies has been established, which clearly define its academic and social contributions and purpose. Let us consider these in the context of optimal theory and our previous discussion as criteria for the continued evaluation of the discipline.

Karenga (1982) raises the question, does Black Studies make a definitive contribution in the following six areas? In each area the answer continues to be a resounding affirmative from the perspective of optimal theory.

1) Humanity's understanding of itself is enhanced by bringing to fore a holistic integration of our historical record of how it was in the beginning, how the growth process unfolds, and what we can anticipate in the future, depending on the choices we make now.

2) U.S. society's understanding of itself is deepened by exploring the role it has played in the devolution of human culture as well as part of the evolution.

3) The university's realization of its claim and challenge to teach the whole truth or something as close to it as humanly possible is greatly promoted by confronting the competing paradigm and being forced to openly display its decision to remain exclusive or become inclusive.

4) The rescue and reconstruction of Black history and humanity can now be placed on more positive footing with the constructive, reasonable reassessment of what has happened and why.

5) A new social science emerges that is not based on methodologies flowing from Cartesian philosophy, but rather that consistent with the discoveries in modern physics.

6) With this propensity toward revelation a Black intelligentsia and professional stratum whose knowledge, social competence, and commitment translate as a vital contribution to the liberation and development of the Black community, and thus society as a whole, can emerge clearly and consciously free from the conceptual bondage imposed by miseducation.

Conclusion

The relevance criteria identified by Karenga (1982) over a decade ago demonstrate the consistency with which the philosophical and academic origins of Black Studies are realized in contemporary times, when viewed through the lens of optimal theory. Black Studies in the beginning, as now, is concerned with improving the capacity to realize humanity's fullest potential. As it resurged in the sixties among those of us whose name symbolizes the union of opposites, African-Americans (representing the oldest of civilizations and the newest), another level of consciousness emerges that brings to a fuller, more conscious awareness the nature and necessity of ethical and moral behavior. Such is required to be in harmony with the universe, harmony is the direction toward which the universe is moving.

Within the optimal frame of reference we can account for the current seeming chaos and disorder reflected in the inordinate proportion of immortal and unethical behaviors manifest in the dominant culture. This negativity and wrong-doing is necessary to the process of becoming "better." It provides the opportunity and impetus for learning, for further growth and development (evolution). Black Studies comes to fore as a necessary force at the vanguard of change, bringing enlightenment to a fallen humanity. The understanding Black Studies contributes to the Western academy may not be easily accepted, but it has the potential to lead humanity to a renewed and conscious health and wholeness. Optimal theory predicts this is the age of either coming in line with the truth or old or being destroyed.

References

Brisbane (1974). *Black activism.* Valley Forge, PA: Judson Press.

Frye, C.A. (1980). The role of philosophy in Black Studies. In C.A. Frye (ed.) *Level three: A Black philosophy reader.* Lanham, MD: University Press of America.

Hale, Manley Palmer (1949). *First principles of philosophy.* Los Angeles: Philosophical Society.

Hillard, A., Williams, and Damali (1987). *The teachings of Ptahhotep.* The oldest book in the world. Atlanta: Blackwood Press.

Kahn, T.C. (1969). *An introduction to hominology.* Springfield, IL: Charles C. Thomas Publisher.

Karenga, M. (1982). *Introduction to Black studies.* Inglewood, CA: Kawaida Publications.

Keita, L. (1977). African philosophical systems: A rational reconstruction. *The Philosophy Forum,* 9 (2-3), 169-189.

McEvoy and Miller (1969). *Black power and student rebellion.* Belmont, CA: Wodsworth Publishing, Co.

Myers, L.J. (1988). *Understanding an Afrocentric world view: Introduction to an optimal psychology.* Dubuque, IA: Kendall/Hunt Publishers.

Myers, L.J., Speight, S., Highlen, P., Cox, C., Reynolds, A., Adams, C., and Hanley, P. (1991). Identity development and worldview: Toward an optimal conceptualization, *Journal of Counseling and Development,* 70, 54-63.

Nobles, W. (1991). Essences from African psychology: The responsibility to reclaim the African character. *Psych Discourse* 23 (1), 8-11.

West, C. (1977). Philosophy and the Afro-American experience, *The Philosophy Forum* 9 (2-3), 116-147.

Williams, S.W. (1982). The African intellectual revolution: The devolution: The defining, developing, and defending of Black Studies as discipline. Paper presented at National Council for Black Studies Conference, University of California, Berkeley, California, 1982.

28.

Intellectual Questions and Imperatives in the Development of Afro-American Studies

Russell L. Adams

The primary purpose of Afro-American/Black Studies consists of the research and instruction designed to help change the way people perceive the social world, particularly the aspects of race and the black experience. If professionals in the field of Afro-American/ Black Studies are to increase the intellectual depth and academic significance of their work, they must manifest a profound understanding of the present epistemological context of American social thought and the formal institutions through which this thought is mediated. They must look hard at the "traditional disciplines." They must understand how these disciplines came to be and to what extent their epistemological foundations complicate the creation of an alternative and perhaps more accurate epistemic for approaching the black experience.

To date, the orienting paradigms of Afro-American Studies appear to be political ideologies bearing the impress of the founding years of the field. Concepts such as "cultural nationalism," "structural separatism," "optimistic integrationism," "revolutionary socialism," and so forth, are perhaps quite useful in a purely political situation, but black academicians are not politicians.[1] They have no major influence on the political processes of this society, nor even on the political actors within the black religious, commercial and economic communities. They are first and foremost critics of society and among their responsibilities is that of attempting to if change perspectives and habits of thought. The ideological "isms" which require so much energy are, in a sense, premature. Consequently, as scholars, Black Studies professionals should direct their energies and talents toward re-shaping the epistemic or perceptual foundations of social thought in America.[2] This approach requires that attention be given to what here will be called the pre-political context of the problems of influencing change, inside black America and the wider society as well.

To be sure, the organizational work of Afro-American/Black Studies professionals over the past fifteen or so years has been of tremendous significance. This was political activity within the realm of the educational establishment. As a movement, Black Studies was created by the political explosion of intellectual outrage over the omission and distortion of the black experience in the curricula of most institutions of higher education. The drive to give the black experience some institutional legitimacy was absolutely necessary. The struggles of this period consumed the intellectual and social energies of a large number of young black academicians, leaving them relatively little time to work on the larger tasks which they claimed to be their institutional *raison d'être*.[3]

Institutional staffing and curriculum building have been the main activity of professional Afro-Americanists. Staffing has been plagued by problems of (a) source, (b) authority, and (c) quality. Black holders of the doctorate make up less than three percent of persons fully trained for university work, including those serving the historically black colleges.[4] Competition for black scholars by traditional departments further complicated the staffing situation. Because of the way the field originated — through student protest and on the premise that blacks know blacks best — the issue of authority in final decision-making regarding staff raised serious questions. For example, should central administration have the *de facto* final word or should the department possess the last say on staffing?[5] Available black academicians often had questions about the quality of the proposed Black Studies departments in terms of their handling of subject matter and, thus, the quality of persons applying for the task of delivering this subject matter. To date, then, the Afro-American/ Black Studies movement has concentrated on standardization of staff requirements and questions of field boundaries and curriculum content.

Most persons now active in the movement have not been trained to teach Afro-American/Black Studies as a field. Rather, they have transferred to its curricula their previous training, occasionally augmented by self-training in the areas where they are expected to teach. A typical member of an Afro-American Studies department has taken his final degree in one of the traditional social science disciplines under the direction of white academics steeped in the prevailing epistemology. A sociologist in an Afro-American Studies/ Black Studies department, for example, may be expected to teach one course in sociology and two or more courses in fields for which he was not trained. This raises questions of quality and depth. As yet there exist no advanced training programs for professionals in the field of Afro-American Studies. Concentrated attempts to expose a small number of professionals to the basic questions of field definition and curriculum development were conducted by the Institute of the Black World in Atlanta and the Afro-American Studies program at the University of Illinois, Champaign-Urbana, in 1982 -1983. But, for the most part, professional Afro-Americanists must retrain themselves to meet the demands of the curriculum of a given program or department.

There exists no institutional basis for evaluating and accrediting the level of expertise of the professional Afro-Americanist. This means that Afro-American/Black Studies teachers are faced with a series of professional and intellectual problems. They are confronted with the task of re-shaping perspectives while having an intuitive and perhaps partial perspective via their own training. They must learn something of the epistemological background of their graduate fields. They must also gain enough control over their curriculum assignments to rise above intellectual dilettantism. They must be able to critique the work of professionals in traditional fields while simultaneously suggesting alternative ways to approach and perceive the black experience in the world, especially in the Western world. While faced with all of these tasks, they must cope with the campus politics of survival, professionally and institutionally, and at the same time do an effective job in the classroom. Whether or not a given individual actually does all of these tasks, the field collectively is confronted with them.

If Afro-American/Black Studies is to gain greater respectability and support, it must begin to demonstrate that, academically, it goes beyond mere correction of the factual record of the black experience. Professionals in the field must set for themselves the task of *revising* the perceptual foundations of the various traditional disciplines. As has been the case in many other areas, black academicians must take the inherited views regarding the social construction of reality and transform them into more accurate and useful accounts of the diasporan experience.[6]

If the major contribution of Afro-American/Black Studies is to be in the area of perspective and interpretation, then much attention must be given to grasping more firmly and in greater detail the question of epistemology — the area of intellectual inquiry that is concerned with the most basic questions of the relationship between the scholar-critic of society and the society itself in its manifold dimensions. The process of intellectual renovation has no question more fundamental than the one that follows: What is the process through which humans claim to know and how can them verify their claims to knowledge? This question is very old, reaching back in time beyond the philosophers of ancient Greece, but it is also very new in that answers to the question appear to vary with time and with social groups. The word *epistemology* dates back only to the late 1800s, when it was employed as a technical concept in the field of philosophy. In the twentieth century, however, the word is often employed to refer to what is called the sociology of knowledge.

Epistemology, The Academy, and the Black Experience

What is the relationship between awareness of epistemological problems in the Western intellectual tradition and the study of the experience of persons of African descent in the Western Hemisphere? The superficial answer to this question is the following: The established institutional arrangements are too ethnocentric to perceive with accuracy the significance of the black experience conjointly with that of Western civilization and to appraise properly the black experience as human experience possessing its own legitimacy, worth, and significance. In short, Euro-American scholars are afflicted with a built-in bias that distorts their interpretative and analytical vision when they attempt to study the black portion of humankind. A more fundamental answer requires a brief review of the Western epistemological experience from the perspective of the sociology of knowledge.

From an intellectual perspective, the outline of the history of Western epistemological problems begins with the Greeks. Both Plato and Aristotle thought that true knowledge was available mainly through the use of right reason. Plato held that reason must apprehend a real, transcendental world hidden by murky reflections in the world of raw sense. Aristotle felt the same way, except that he saw the truth not in changeless form, but in material essences characterized by potentiality and actuality.[7] The Church Fathers, notably Sts. Augustine and Thomas Aquinas, blended these classical Greek views and asserted that real knowledge of eternal truth came through the Scriptures and through revelation via the grace of God. With the beginning of the expansion of Europe, men such as René Descartes, Francis Bacon, and Isaac Newton held that true knowledge was reached primarily through the use of the senses applied to logic and mathematics. Descartes's ideas in particular laid the epistemic groundwork for today's natural and humanistic sciences. At each major stage of the evolution of the Western epistemic, learned men wrote at length about the relationship between the would-be knower and the intended object of his knowing. Indeed, subject/object relationships form the heart of the sociology of knowledge.

Afro-American/Black Studies specialists are thus engaged in epistemic renovation but appear to have given relatively little professional attention to the basic questions involved in the sociology of knowledge. To be sure, comments frequently are made about the fact that virtually all persons in the movement who hold terminal degrees were trained at predominantly white institutions and have satisfied predominantly white departments in their passage through higher education. Nonetheless, the almost inevitable differences in interpretations between white and black academicians on the fundamentals of race (especially qualitative questions) suggest the existence of a difference in epistemological content, in that individuals of different races fail to share in their pre-collegiate backgrounds and in functional social status even in graduate school. This "fault-line" in the pre-analytical aspects of white/black intellectual interpretation is too consistent to be coincidental. These differences could very well lead to a subfield, the sociology of differential social perception. We shall, however, confine our attention to a review of the question of epistemology as a basic aspect of the sociology of knowledge.

What is the scope of modern epistemological concerns? Kurt Wolff, a leading student in the field, supplies this answer when he writes that in the area of the sociology of knowledge.

> ...some of the most important areas of research and theory seem to be these: in the social sciences, in addition to general sociological findings and to more specialized findings (as in communication, public opinion, and propaganda), social psychology in a very broad sense (including child psychology, abnormal psychology, and psychiatry, psychoanalysis and related movements, psychological testing, learning theory, and the study of perception, attitudes, and social norms); cultural anthropology, particularly linguistics with its various sub-divisions, the study of culture and personality, and the study of culture itself; in the humanities, social and cultural history, literary criticism, historical linguistics, and the methodological and empirical aspects of philosophy — epistemology, semiotics, logic, metaphysics, ethics, and aesthetics,...[8]

At first glance, this passage seems to be a bewildering listing of complex areas of academic interest, but when examined closely it becomes clear that the list focuses on the topic of how the individual comes to know self and others and how social phenomena are converted into systematic reliable knowledge. The ideas embedded in these topics may be reduced to the proposition that thought does exhibit the influence of society. The task of students of the sociology of knowledge is to discern and articulate the myriad ways in which this occurs. Just as the acquisition of language is social, so is the acquisition of the initial contents of thought itself. By obtaining a better understanding of the factors involved in the knowing process, Afro-Americanist/Black Studies specialists can bring to their criticism much more than the intuitive and indubitably correct moral criticism of the failings of their erstwhile academic mentors. They can bring to bear a heightened epistemic self-consciousness, especially in the area of the social sciences where virtually all of the professional Afro-Americanists are concentrated. This is necessary, for it means that once such a review is completed, these professionals then can sort through this legacy and identify aspects that hold a special value for developing independent perspectives upon which more detailed work can be done later.

The institutional presence of Afro-American/Black Studies offers the first collective opportunity to deal with basic epistemic problems. The traditional black colleges have been engaged in transmitting the prepared knowledge of the larger educational establishment to its students and affording these students opportunities to become socialized to futures in a social system resting upon the inherited epistemic. The work of Carter G. Woodson and others, of course, was directed toward changing the contents of the epistemic legacy.[9] Individual black scholars, particularly those whose ideas still attract the attention of Afro-American/Black Studies, made significant contributions, especially in history, sociology,[10] and education. Such work was aimed essentially at correcting historical, sociological, and educational records. The need for this work still exists, and as the pages of the various Afro-American/ Black Studies journals indicate, it is being done. Less work has been done, however, on the basic questions of epistemological framework for perceiving the black experience. Both kinds of work must proceed simultaneously.

In the exploration of an alternative epistemic, black scholars do not have to think of themselves as promoting intellectual separatism. The separation is already present. As a collective presence, black scholars are new to a resistant, and ninety-seven percent, white upper-level academia. Their non-professional lives generally are spent with members of their own genetic team; their deepest roots are in the soil of Black America. The first step in epistemic retooling is incumbent upon the black newcomers to higher education.

Having suggested the scope of the sociology of knowledge problem, let us define the concert of epistemology. *Webster's Third New International Dictionary* defines the word "epistemology" as the "theory of the science of the methods and grounds of knowledge, especially with reference to its limits and validity." The same source defines the word "epistemic" as "knowledge or knowing as a type of experience, purely intellectual or cognitive." Over fifty years ago, one of the founders of the sub-field of the sociology of knowledge, Max Scheler, stated that "a society's ethos, condensed in its epistemology, determines what constitutes knowledge for a group, what a group considers worth knowing, as well as what it considers trivial...."[11] Thomas S. Kuhn, in his highly influential work, *The Structure of Scientific Revolutions*, stresses the social foundations of epistemologies.[12] He argues that formal systematized knowledge arises from the existence of a community of like-minded persons who come to share the basic beliefs about the metaphysical and empirical foundations of cognitive ideas.[13] Epistemologies, then, serve as a source of standards of discernment, reference, and evaluation of phenomena. An epistemology is a social code for mapping a group s definition of various levels of reality. It helps to decide what it is that we "see" cognitively. It functions reflexively to connect new data with pre-existing ideas and information. An epistemology serves as a guide for ranking the significance of certain areas of human activity in the context of systematic knowledge. Epistemologies themselves are distillates of ideas, values, and beliefs that arise from the experiences and desires of the prevailing elites in a social system. It was in recognition of this fact that Scheler considered a society's epistemology to be closely akin to its ethos and system of moral judgment.[14]

The particular character of the moral order affords strategic elites their rationale for determining the working epistemology of their group.[15] In the history of Western civilization, the Greek philosophers held that the moral order of the secular world was but a reflection of a higher transcendent moral order. Plato in particular promoted the idea of a metaphysical order consisting of unchanging form and content available to humankind through the use of reason. Located in the upper classes or strategic elites from the time of Christ to that of Columbus, some epistemological variant of Platonism and neo-Platonism predominated among the interpretive strategic elites of western Europe. Both Grecian and Christian epistemological thought was deductive, i.e., antecedent to the initial process of gaining knowledge.

The Greek philosophers and the Church Fathers alike were working members of what today would be called intellectual communities, that is, most of their time was spent on matters related to the moral foundations of their societies and the conduct of collective life within them. In the West, over the centuries, these contemplative communities were housed in stoa, academies, monasteries, universities, and learned societies. The premises of their respective societies and their epistemological and moral systems helped to determine, in their judgment, what was genuine knowledge and what was not. Strategic elites rise and fall over time. With the so-called era of European expansion, the Churchmen had to give way to the rising class of secular elites, to those members of the upper class who had the time, the leisure, and the social connections necessary for the support of their speculative and experimental activities.

The Newtonian Age constituted the forerunner of the high-born but secular "scientific community of intellect."[16] According to Jerome Blum et al., this was a new scientific community whose "fundamental concepts were the reasonableness of nature and the capacity of man to comprehend the rational order of nature by observation and the use of reason."[17] René Descartes had speculated that the physical world's underlying mechanisms could be disclosed through the use of mathematics, and Isaac Newton proved that certain motions of particles (in this instance, the planets) could be calculated through the application of mathematics. During the great creative period of the seventeenth century, these "natural philosophers" formed a literal community of scholars. They established learned societies and academies and read papers before one another. Many of the experiments and projects of these scholars had royal and noble support. Such support was not accidental, for the ruling classes were greatly interested in the technical and practical benefits of the discoveries of these new men of learning. During their time, men such as Newton and Descartes were called *virtuosi,* for they attempted to do many difficult things, and, remarkably, often did them extraordinarily well. The persons making up this community of intellectuals were thus more broadly based than our conception of scientists, because they "comprised a readily identifiable community of intellectuals with interests ranging over the three areas known today as the natural sciences, social sciences, and humanities.[18] Their method of discovering knowledge was inductive, with mathematics being used to sum up large quantities of discrete data.

While modern scientists have greatly refined and revised the insights of the *virtuosi* into the nature of gravitation, light, the human body, and planetary motion, they have maintained the epistemic legacy of the seventeenth century. To a lesser degree, modern intellectuals have sustained the ancient connection with the strategic elites. A half dozen years before Isaac Newton was born, Harvard College was established in Massachusetts to educate white males in the ways of Christian piety and Calvinistic virtue to rule a new society along the lines of "the proper moral order." Thomas Jefferson planned the University of Virginia to produce practical-minded men who would be indoctrinated with a prescribed vision of what America should become. Formal education in England and America down to the early part of the nineteenth century was still a prerogative of the middle classes. According to one commentator, mass public education for whites was introduced to secure their allegiance to prescribed moral and behavioral doctrines dedicated to the factory system and the production of material wealth for the upper classes.[19] Martin Carnoy writes that "well before 1900, then, the schools were organized to promote capitalist industrial development—to produce a working class with desired behavior patterns, particularly the internalization of an authoritarian work structure and loyalty to a society which was run by the bourgeoisie."[20]

Five years after Isaac Newton was born, blacks in the English colonies were defined as slaves in *durance vita* (for life). From the Charter of Liberties drawn up by the Massachusetts Colony in 1641, to the amendment of the Georgia Charter to permit the holding of slaves, blacks became objects in a trans-Atlantic society created out of the combination of technical devices invented by men of learning, the financial support of the ruling elites of the European maritime nations, and the labor demands of the overseas colonists. The long epistemic tradition excluded them as persons from its definition of humankind, and their thoughts were regarded as of no consequence. Until after the Civil War, a black scholar was actually a contradiction in terms.[21] For a century following emancipation in North America, blacks in education were mainly instructors, purveyors of the content prepared by others. Black colleges were "communities of *teachers*." A W.E.B. DuBois, or a Carter G. Woodson, or a Charles S. Johnson did not make a community of scholars. The American Negro Academy of the 1890s and the Association for the Study of Negro Life and History (presently Afro-American Life and History) were the closest organizational forms of blacks engaged in any sort of scholarly endeavor. Only within the last twenty-five years has the number of blacks engaged in teaching and research risen to a level where the phrase "community of scholars" has any practical meaning. The various social science disciplines developed for most of this century without any significant input from Afro-Americans. Consequently, the orienting epistemic character of these disciplines reflect overwhelmingly the influence of their Caucasian creators.

Establishment Social Science: All Too Human Without and Within

Perhaps the attempt to construct a new and different community of scholars should begin with a review of the established community of scholars representing the traditional disciplines. Although many black scholars who are not involved with Afro-American/Black Studies as a movement take great delight in virtuously identifying themselves with the dominant group's scholarly society, a simple review of the record indicates that this establishment not only has its own epistemic but also its political and social interests. The pursuit of these interests often does not serve science or social justice.

American social science has presented itself as socially objective, methodologically balanced, and professionally fair. Instead of its frequent announcements of a disinterested search for "truth," however, many establishment scholars have placed their talents and disciplines in the service of public policymakers in return for financial support and professional prestige. For a time, younger members of certain fields, especially political science and sociology, thought that finesse in quantitative methods would enable them to learn the truth of the black experience, especially in urban America. When black scholars attempted to share substantively in the organized life of several disciplines, and presumably to assist in defining social reality, they found not only epistemic resistance but also resistance to their participation. The following review of certain aspects of the scholarly community is intended as a reminder of the all too human nature of any scholarly community, a fact that is frequently overlooked by many conservative black scholars who idealize their roles in "established disciplines."

Assertions of intellectual autonomy and purity to the contrary, the interaction between specific disciplines and community policy issues is both complex and intimate. In America, the strategic elites of scholarship and politics engaged in a minuet, dialectically influencing each other.

American sociology, for example, actually gained institutional salience when apprehensions and "puzzles" about European immigration alarmed the non-academic leadership of this nation.[22] Psychology in American life gained respectability when World War I intelligence testing "confirmed" the popular prejudices against the various groups from whom draftees were taken for military service.[23] The Immigration Act of 1924 reflected the non-scientific prejudices of the dominant group, with immigration quotas being calibrated to favor northern European and English immigrants over those of eastern and southern Europe and the virtual exclusion of black

Africa.[24] The distribution of troops in the United States Army of World War I relied on a social science that was fully in tune with the popular prejudices regarding the proper place of blacks, Italians, lower-status white Southerners, and so forth, in the military system.[25] Sociology was further stimulated by the immigrant settlement house movement, with the practical aspects of this movement evolving into social work. The discipline of economics moved up in status as the nation sought the causes of the Depression.

World War II was an additional stimulus to the growth of the social sciences. Disciplines such as social psychology, anthropology, economics, and history were affected by the multiplicity of demands of the war, which greatly accelerated the tempo of human experience—nations rapidly and often violently changing course; groups within nations, because of "military necessity," being hauled from previous roles that fitted the prevailing assumptions to new ones on a purely functional basis (e.g., black agrarians being converted into skilled urban laborers in a matter of months); white military commanders having to deal with peoples whose cultures were often different from their own (e.g., cultures of the islands of the Pacific, Japan, North Africa); and, the need to meld the combat units of socially disparate individuals into a nuclear fighting brotherhood. With victory came the socially determined need to explore the causes of the war via historical reconstruction of events that were assumed to be causally connected with the eruption of war and also the need to understand an expanding and prospering peacetime America. Indeed, the years between 1940 and 1950 are of seminal importance for understanding the community foundations of modern social science.[26]

It was inevitable that the sheer scale of these events would bring quantification to the heart of the social sciences. To be sure, places such as the University of Chicago and Harvard were timidly experimenting with statistical analyses in sociology and political science during the interwar period.[27] But the demands of the post-war social system called for rapid employment of quantification in forecasting demands, anticipating needs, and detecting consumer preferences. Thus the social scientists had the opportunity for large-scale testing of their mathematical formulae, with heightened expectations of reducing the gap between themselves and the natural scientists. Social scientists desired to gain the ability to predict social changes in the way astronomers were able to calculate solar eclipses or the mass of electrical charges. This desire reached the proportions of a frenzy, leading one eminent sociologist, Pitirim Sorokin, to label the rush to numbers "Quantrophrenia," as social scientists constructed scales for measuring qualitative continuities and quantitative discontinuities, both seen and unseen.[28] Accelerated public and commercial funding of social research and the resultant anathematizing of certain aspects of social life led directly to a view of humankind that was given the label "behaviorism."[29] Behaviorism was as much an attitude, an epistemic stance, as it was a method of seeking knowledge of human dynamics. All of the social sciences sought to incorporate the behaviorist approach in their work, although several of them were internally sundered. Young social scientists welcomed this approach, especially if they had above-average backgrounds in mathematics. They felt that they could surpass the older social scientists in unlocking the truths of what was then called the social system, for they did not feel the need to rely on what is still called general experience of routine socialization to gain insights as a foundation for their perspectives. Journals in the social sciences began to show the impact of the behavioral "revolution," for they were festooned with mathematical treatments of social phenomena on topics that would be regarded as whimsical if not taken seriously.

A climax of sorts was reached, ironically, in the field of history. Fogel and Engerman published *Time on the Cross*, a statistical treatment of the black experience in slavery which led to the conclusion that it was a benign institution affording greater personal security and comfort than that of free white laborers in the ante-bellum urban North.[30] Another peak was reached in psychology when Arthur Jensen, in his infamous 1969 *Harvard Educational Review* article, used a smorgas-bord of statistical studies to conclude that test score disparities between white and black pupils were eighty percent explainable by genetic factors.[31] The re-emergence of sociobiology in the 1970s, celebrating the habits of the beneficiaries of the status quo, became a subgenre of sociology and was employed as a tool to cover those be-havioral outcomes in social situations that could not be covered, mathematically.[32] Here we have an instance where the analytical focus shifted from a quantification of externalities to a positing of internal qualities and functions to explain in-group similarities and out-group differences of various kinds. This curving of the epis-temic circle matches the curve from the conservatism of the pre-World War II years through the stratified liberalism of the 1960s, back to the status quo ante-conser-vatism of the present. Social scientists in effect are now of the opinion that blind human processes cannot be altered by conscious, informed intervention alone. Yet, the entire premise of earlier social science was that enough could be learned through various "scientific" methods to have an impact on human process. Scien-tific knowledge, under this view, can then be seen as "knowledge for knowledge's sake," a position that would not have convinced government funding agencies dur-ing the period when it was thought that rational and informed planning could alter the environment.

The social upheaval of the sixties brought social science to the black community, with the basic funding and formulating of research themes being done by the estab-lished (i.e., white) academicians. The epistemic framework upon which this research rested dated back to the early nineteenth century—that blacks in America were so-cial "anomalies," collectively suffering various kinds of "pathologies."[33] The Moyni-han Report echoed reports of white "charitable" associations of earlier decades.[34]

In general, in order to avoid physical danger from a healthy but angry black pop-ulace, funding became available for black social science researchers with the "proper" (i.e., accepted) epistemological background regarding the presumed im-peccable canons of the social sciences. This occurred, of course, during the period when white America could grudgingly agree that the various kinds of racism of which blacks complained were endemic to the social system.[35] This took place at a period when it was believed that positive social education and planning could reduce racism and that the data and conclusions of research by black social scientists were close-up confirmations of the then prevailing assumptions about systemic racism. Policy research in education and poverty involved both black and white social scien-tists. Blacks attached to major white and northern educational institutions received the bulk of the monies for this sort of research. The massive funding of urban stud-ies programs at Columbia, Harvard, and Massachusetts Institute of Technology, however, reached only a few black intellectuals. Consequently, the cottage industry level of research by blacks on blacks never matched the assembly line, factory style research activities of predominantly white institutions. The insights tucked away in the better projects of black social scientists thus have been overshadowed by the sheer bulk of over-hasty and negative impact studies of white social scientists. White social scientists never got to "know" the internal black America, nor fully grasp the impact of their own unexamined epistemic biases on their perception of problems and discernment of causal changes in the areas of race and racism. Those who at-tempted to do this were labelled "radical" and often penalized for partial apostasy for the shared definitions of the important and unimportant.

In the shared communities of scholars connected with various disciplines, conflicting and pre-existing differences over whether black newcomers to the community finally would be adopted into the center of academic influence and power led inevitably to the splintering of professional associations into white and black units. For example, political science experienced its Committee on the Status of Blacks after some tension over associational roles. Black economists formed their own caucus and started *The Journal of Black Political Economy*. Psychology had the same bifurcations and the Association for the Study of Afro-American Life and History reached its apogee in terms of membership and participation by black scholars.

These splits were not engendered in the belief that blacks could "take over" professional associations which had long antedated their appearance on the academic scene. The struggles were over the resources for epistemic definition. In this situation, epistemological interests translate into influence and direction of funding foci. In order to do any sort of extended research, academicians must be able to obtain research funds. Even the most conservative academic could see that social science ultimately turns out to be people and their ideas, and people are still classified on the basis of their pigmentation packages. To date, however, these different clusters of black scholars in the various black associations and caucuses have not followed up the implications behind their differences with their white disciplinary colleagues in the form of sharing their views and experiences in an organized manner.

In this context, the case can be made for attempting to seek increased interaction among black scholars who are concerned with the foundations of what here will be called the Black Epistemic. The Black Epistemic exists; otherwise, the movement of black scholars toward the center of the disciplinary associations would have proceeded without the appearance of black divisions of social science disciplines. We must assert that the lack of serious interaction between Black Studies professionals and other black scholars in the social sciences and the humanities is unnecessary and unfortunate. In general, both groups share this incipient Black Epistemic, with institutional Black Studies differing from established fields mainly in terms of seniority and of proximity to the subject matter of the black experience.

Establishment social science, during the last quarter century, has been immensely helpful in beginning the large-scale study of the black/white relationship in America. As we have seen, however, it has been reduced in effectiveness as a consequence of its own legacy and connection with the strategic elites beyond the Academy. University life and education is sociologically elitist in nature, independent of the racial groups involved.[36] This is compounded in situations where attempts are made to blend disparate social strata, i.e., upper-status whites and lower-status blacks, in efforts to understand and communicate the human meaning of their research endeavors, particularly as related to the structural dividers insisted upon by the dominant society.

Epistemic differences are further heightened when one considers that blacks have only recently become functionally urbanized whereas the white scholarly community has been essentially urban since the beginning of the university system several hundred years earlier. Black and white scholars thus find themselves looking at research problems and suggesting interpretations that inevitably reflect their immediate social positions and previous backgrounds. If black scholars are to avoid the epistemic errors of the established scholarly community, they should not only know this older community in detail but also seek a wider and different frame of reference upon which to ground their most profound grasp of social life in this hemisphere. Afro-American/Black Studies scholars can begin to escape intellectual claustrophobia and, perhaps, suggest newer contexts of analysis by looking at the structure and dynamics of the Americas considered as a single entity.

Geographic Basis for a Comprehensive Black Epistemic

In creating a comprehensive and valid epistemic, Afro-American/Black Studies scholars must construct a total outline of the black hemispheric experience. Otherwise, many crucial questions will not arise, and we may have only a partial vision of the diaspora. A much fuller vision of the continental character of the diaspora should form a backdrop for conceptualizing, refining, and researching themes and variables. Until this is done, we can assume that conclusions and generalizations made solely on the North American experience will, of necessity, remain tentative.[37]

How may the field of Afro-American/Black Studies incorporate a functional awareness of the presence and experience of perhaps thirty million blacks located elsewhere? It is imperative that thought be given to ways and means of addressing this question. What follows is but a sketch of a possible approach to this problem.

By functional awareness, one means the ability to remain mindful of the general location or status of a particular research project or academic findings in relationship to similar projects and findings in the widest possible context. This awareness should result in a sophistication that is not always present in much of the contemporary Afro-American research.

Thoughts and research aimed at enlarging the Black Epistemic should perhaps begin with considerations of the similarities, differences, and uniqueness of the structures of the hemisphere black diaspora.[38] The concept "structure" refers to those salient features of a social organization that form the framework of systems of relations and behaviors by individuals and their socio-biological groups. In the diaspora, the features of external biology, color in particular, has been the most basic classifying agent in determining group membership, for color in the Americas determines both biological and social race. A physical attribute has been converted into a classifying instrument by the dominant groups. The color question is perhaps the most significant aspect of the American epistemic, determining definitions of history, status, and social worth. Nowhere in the hemisphere is color without significance when related to what here shall be referred to as (a) realms of structure, (b) resource control, and (c) system maintenance activities.[39]

Analytically and functionally, societies are characterized by realms of structures, the most important realms are those related to governance and government, economics, social groupings, religious expression, and education. In the realm of governance—the strategic elites, first of Europe and then of their overseas surrogates—raw political power led to the establishment of the system of black/white relations throughout the hemisphere. Today, with the possible exception of the Caribbean, blacks exist on the peripheries of power. An elementary method for determining degrees of regional differences in the realm of government is that of assembling pictures of incumbents of office at various levels of government in the hemisphere.[40] Another method of determining influence is that of assessing participation rates and levels in the selection of governmental incumbents. Still another method is to assess the degrees to which both real and felt needs and desires of blacks are responded to by governments in the societies in which they live.

In the realm of economics we already know, via simple extrapolation, that persons of African descent are generally located near the nether edges of occupations, managerial and supervisory structures, and at the bottom of income systems. A functional awareness of the economic situation of blacks in other parts of the Americas must likewise include at least implicit questions about similarities, dissimilarities, exceptions, degrees, and variations. We should have some sense of the dominant groups' core values with regard to economic matters and, of course, the form these values take in the economic system of locations outside the United States. Gross economic trends and changes should be known, with some sense of the possible variables related to these trends. In terms of epistemic renovation, we should have a general awareness of the black interpretation of economic values and situations in these other places.[41]

In the social realm, our search for similarities, dissimilarities, and exceptions should continue. How is the "color line" reflected in the stratification systems of these societies? What are the degrees of color-status gradations these societies regard as important? What are the variables affecting mobility of individuals and groups on either side of the pigmentation picket line, and what are the typical subjective reactions to individuals assuming various social roles in stratification systems unconnected with ethnicity per se, e.g., the military, the church, the governmental bureaucracies? What are the types, patterns, and degrees of endogamy and exogamy, and what variables affect each of them? How do socialization styles resemble one another? How do they differ? These and many other aspects of biracial, segmented, pluralistic societies should be of general interest to Afro-American/Black Studies specialists interested in contributing to a new interpretation of the black experience.[42]

In the realm of religious expression we are vaguely aware that blacks in Protestant-dominated societies tend to be Protestant and those in Catholic-dominated societies tend to be Catholic.[43] But again questions of types, degrees, and exceptions are important. Questions of in-group stratification on the religious axis, of creolization and syncretism, of specific modalities and instruments of religious expression should form at least a background portion of the implicit new Black Epistemic. Some commentators assert that this epistemic already has a basic religious dimension representing African survivals as affected by non-African locations and that this feature should be the centerpiece of any Black Epistemic. The role of religious institutions as related to community structure and behavior in various locations is important and should be known in those locations at least in outline in much the same manner as they are known in North America. Secularization professes and trends in specific societies should be a part of our, awareness as we examine similar topics in the North American black experience.

In the realm of education much remains to be learned about the black diaspora.[44] While Afro-America/Black Studies specialists may have some vague conception of West Indian education, it is quite likely that other diasporan educational experiences are not so well known. Some of the questions are obvious. One could fist the countries and islands involved and "interview" them on the topic of education. What are the aims of education in general as well as for specific groups? How are the systems supported financially? What is the relationship between stratification systems and educational systems? How are the educational systems articulated with the economic system? the governmental systems? How are the various roles of students and teachers perceived by themselves and by various segments of the societies involved? What are the school entry and exit trends? Above all, what implicit epistemic ideas appear to be common to these non-American educational systems? Are there differences in the imputed content of these emergent epistemics as related to racial stratification?

Resource control is a major aspect of any group's existence and welfare. Resource control interpenetrates the economic and governmental systems of all societies everywhere. With the possible exception of certain of the Caribbean islands, resource control is clearly and overwhelmingly in the hands of the racially dominant group, from Canada to Brazil. Here we use the term energy as a synonym for resource—energy for moving inanimate objects and energy for moving organisms, including humans. Control of land and space is basic to the control of energy. In turn, energy is used (a) to extract elements from the land and sea, and (b) to convert, via fabrication, extractive products in goods for commerce and human consumption. It is already known that the social support for these activities rests with the dominant group: they control the permissions, the finance, the mediating equipment and services, and the delivery of the products of energy conversion. It is generally known that blacks participate as lower-level extractors and fabricators and as consumers. The awareness questions here revolve around degrees, similarities, exceptions, and trends of black involvement. An especially intriguing question is the degree that such a relationship to resource control has had on the attitudes of diasporan blacks toward the physical appurtenances of life and toward questions of scale with regard to the possession and management of objects. This particular question has an added significance when asked in the context of the fact that the right to possess was denied all members of the group as one of the basic attributes of their status as objects in the possession of others. Obviously, in societies based on the production of goods and services, possession and management of resources are directly related to the shaping of a given group's view of the world.

The concept of system maintenance activities includes not only the activities subsumed under the realms of government, social structure, religion, education, and resource control but also those activities and dynamics that must be continuous and ubiquitous if a society is to maintain itself through stasis and change. The two principal maintenance activities through which all of the other conceptualized aspects of structure are mediated are (a) communication in its diverse forms and (b) transportation of objects and persons. Symbols, signs and signals move from head-to-head and carry messages of roles, status, structure, and situation. Our concern here is with types and levels of communication media. The basic system-control media (newspaper, radio, television, messenger services) are in the hands of the dominant group as an instrument of dominance. Here we are confronted with fair questions about similarities, dissimilarities, and exceptions. We are also faced with the question of source, content, and volume of epistemic cues communicated. A practical matter facing Afro-American/Black Studies scholars, even during their quasi-political stage, is that of the scale and scope of the circulation of their ideas. The discovery, retrieval, processing, and dissemination of information varies within societies and among them. The diasporan "grapevine" is not nearly as efficient as the other media in helping to shape the epistemic consciousness of the group. Comparative questions of a wide range may be asked regarding communicative behaviors and media among blacks in this hemisphere, including the key matter of language and translation.

In order to comprehend the structure of the diaspora and the prospects for various kinds of changes, one must have an understanding of the relationship of blacks to the transportation of objects and persons. One of the ironies of history is that during the slavery period, a major activity of blacks was the physical processing and movement of objects. Today such activity Increasingly is mechanized, with the machines and supporting financial structures primarily in the hands of whites, on land, sea, and air. Throughout the hemisphere, blacks are most heavily involved in the movement of objects on the land, as they were during slavery, and are less involved on the sea and in the air.

The growth of the kinds of epistemic awareness suggested above clearly requires accelerated work by members of the Afro-American/Black Studies movement as a whole. The critical posture characterizing the attitude of black scholars toward North American group relations must be extended to cover the two continents. Inherent in the critical posture are the possibilities of the Black Epistemic. If after several decades black scholars are able to bring to their work an enlarged critical sensitivity, they would have broadened and deepened North American social science and reduced the likelihood of the American epistemic being regarded as the only way of knowing human experience.

Any field of study consists of practitioners working within its assumptions and methodologies. How may the individual Afro-American/Black Studies professional participate in the suggested expansion of an epistemic reference base? The first step may require the individual scholar to examine, in much greater detail than before, the foundations of his/her traditional discipline and particular specialty within that discipline. The central measure of the adequacy of a given traditional epistemic should be seen in the way in which it handles the central themes of the black diaspora. This writer has discerned these themes as central, based on years of reviewing materials related to instruction and research on the questions of the black presence in the world. These themes appear to be freedom, identity, community, authority, power, and justice. Another observer, of course, may see a different set of themes, but the massive movement from Africa and the containment of millions of persons of color in the Americas is perhaps the most awesome achievement of European social systems. Certainly every value associated with the definition of humankind and civilization was implicated in the creation, literally, of two worlds of color.

In practice, a scholar might select one theme and one crucial variable related to race and trace them out in the scholarly literature for a better picture of the epistemic vision which informs them. Or a scholar may take the concept of distributive justice, identify the particular type of distribution, and see how the traditional scholars have handled it. A combinatory permutation of such exercises would take one through the several themes and the resulting composite would be an even sharper image of the informing epistemic. Methodologies already exist for this sort of secondary re-analysis. A political scientist, sociologist, economist, educator, psychologist, or historian, for example, might then repeat this process, first through the relevant literature produced by black scholars over the years and then through a literature search of the same topic in works produced by persons located in the Caribbean or in South America. Emerging from this operation should be conclusions about the dominant and subordinate groups' fundamental vision and values in relation to the particular topic. In this, as in the case of identifying the structure of the diaspora, one should find similarities, differences, exceptions, trends, and degrees in what are perhaps three epistemological systems: (1) that of the North and South American white Academy; (2) that of black scholars in North America, and (3) that of black scholars in the Caribbean and South America. At the bottom, what is likely to be discovered is that the Black Epistemic is a function of the structural location of blacks in this hemispheric culture. If such an exercise by many Afro-American/Black Studies practitioners fails to uncover epistemic differences in this context, then one may be able to argue that the themes of black expression, scholarly and otherwise, are the products of false consciousness, and that the negative constraints shaping the black experience are mere illusions.

In this paper attention has been called to (1) questions of the sociology of knowledge and the social basis of intellectual thought, (2) social science methods and relations with non-academic sponsors and clients, and (3) the possibilities of using the structure of race relations in the Western Hemisphere as a means for enlarging the implicit Black Epistemic in the scholarly community. Such an enlargement would represent another step in the growth of black social thought. The earlier steps appear to have been (1) the slave narratives and protest pamphlets, (2) formal history, (3) sociology, (4) the political analysis, and (5) theological commentary. Concern with epistemology may be the next stage on the route to what here will be called black philosophy. If black scholars in the Afro-American/Black Studies movement are able to contribute further to this growth, then they will have re-ordered their priorities. Such a reordering falls within their powers and could lead to the Black Studies movement having as much influence on American scholarship and epistemological thought as black musicians have had on the music of the Western world.

Endnotes

1. Professionals in the field are individuals operating in a de facto political environment. For a discussion of this point, see Russell L. Adams, "Evaluating Professionalism in the Context of Afro-American Studies," *The Western Journal of Black Studies*, 4 (Summer 1980) 140-148. See also Robert L. Alleti, "Politics of the Attack on Black Studies," *The Black Scholar*, 6 (September 1974): 2-7. The issue also contains other relevant articles.

2. From the beginning of the movement, a significant volume of prescriptive literature accompanied the call for Black Studies, but since then comparatively little descriptive epistemological literature has been produced. For a good list of prescriptive articles see, Center for Black Studies-Santa Barbara, *Selected Working Bibliography in Black Studies* (Santa Barbara: University of California, 1977), pp. 1-28. Charles A. Frye's, *Towards a Philosophy of Black Studies* (San Francisco: R and E Associates, Inc., 1975) is an interesting work that suggests how the very foundations of African or Black epistemological styles differ from those of Euro-American styles; see pp. 14-45 *passim*. Frye is noted for his efforts to take the concept of black philosophy beyond epistemology to ontology.

See also Clovis E. Semmes, "Black Studies and the Symbolic Structure of Domination," *The Western Journal of Black Studies*, 6 (Summer 1972): 116-122; and *idem*, "Foundations of Afrocentric Social Science: Implications for Curriculum Building, Theory and Research in Black Studies," *Journal of Black Studies*, 12 (September 1981): 3-17.

3. See Adams, "Evaluating Professionalism."

4. In order to view black academics in the context of the larger scholarly community, see Everett C. Ladd, Jr. and Seymour Martin Lipset, *The Divided Academy: Professors and Politics* (New York: McGraw Hill Book Co., 1975), pp. 11-112, 149-167, 324-339.

5. Those early administrators of Afro-America/Black Studies departments who called for full autonomy and approval in the area of staffing collided with the settled norm of the central administration having the last word over such matters, even if this word was a rubber stamp. The standard department-central administrative tension continues to arise over the number of "slots," with the central administration having the final word while the department generally has the de facto last word on the choice of persons for the "slot." See Peter M. Blau, *The Organization of Academic Work* (New York: John Wiley and Sons, 1973), pp. 158-188.

6. On the concept of "social construction of reality," see Peter L. Berger and Thomas Luckmann, *The Social Construction of Reality* (Garden City, NY: Doubleday and Company, Inc., 1966). See also Max Scheler, *Problems of a Sociology of Knowledge* (London: Routledge and Kegan Paul, 1980), pp. 33-80; and, Zymunt Bauman, *Hermeneutics and Social Science* (New York: Columbia University Press, 1978), pp. 23-47, 194-246.

7. A good treatment of the definitional problems confronting the ancients (and us) is found in William O. Martin, *The Order and Integration of Knowledge* (Ann Arbor: The University of Michigan Press, 1957), pp. 3-58, 98-123, 212-255. The now classic work on how the social process affects epistemic vision is Thomas S. Kuhn, *The Structure of Scientific Resolutions*, 2nd ed., enlarged (Chicago: University of Chicago Press, 1970), passim, but especially "Postscript." A blend of the concerns of Martin and Kuhn may be found in Stanley Rosen, *The Limits of Analysis* (New York: Basic Books, 1980), pp. 149-260.

8. Kurt H. Wolff, *Trying Sociology* (New York: John Wiley and Sons, 1974), p. 512. Section VI of this volume is rich in ideas about the nature of the sociology of knowledge.

9. The organizational work of Carter G. Woodson was the culmination of a long drive to systematize the struggle to revise the reigning epistemic through historical research, especially his founding of the Association for the Study of Negro Life and History in 1915. A precursor to this was the American Negro Academy, founded in 1897.

A good summary treatment of earlier thinking on the means of social change and the nature of the black experience is found in William Toll, *The Resurgence of Race: Black Social Theory from Reconstruction to the Pan-African Conferences* (Philadelphia: Temple University Press, 1979), passim.

10. The general outlines of major themes via the works of individual black scholars are found in S. P. Fullinwider, *The Mind and Mood of Black America: 20th Century Thought* (Homewood, IL: The Dorsey Press, 1969), passim.

11. Scheler, *Problems of a Sociology of Knowledge*, p. 26.

12. Kuhn, *The Structure of Scientific Revolutions*, pp. 35-51.

13. *Ibid.*, pp. 183-194.

14. Scheler, *Problems of a Sociology of Knowledge*, pp. 20-22.

15. The term "strategic elites" is used in Suzanne Keller, *Beyond the Ruling Class: Strategic Elites in Modern Society* (New York: Random House, 1963). In this work, see "Introduction" and pp. 88-106. See also Joseph Ben-David, *The Scientist's Role in Society* (Englewood Cliffs, NJ: Prentice-Hall, 1971), pp. 139-168; and Martin E. Marty, "Knowledge Elite and Counter-elites," *Daedalus* (Fall 1974): 104-109.

16. For a handy account of the contextual background of the secularization of basic thought, see Jerome Blum, Rondo Cameron and Thomas G. Barnes, *The European World: A History* (Boston, MA: Little, Brown and Co., 1966), pp. 574-600; and for an overview of the process of shifting from religious to secular explanations of knowledge, see B.A. Gerrish, "The Reformation and the Rise of Modem Science," in *The Impact of the Church Upon Its Culture: Reappraisals of the History of Christianity*, ed. Jerald C. Brauer (Chicago: University of Chicago Press, 1968), pp. 231-265.

17. Blum et al., *The European World*, p. 384.

18. *Ibid.*

19. Martin Carnoy, *Education as Cultural Imperialism* (New York: Longman, Inc., 1974), pp. 233-269.

20. *Ibid.*, pp. 244-245.

21. Scholars such as William Wells Brown, Martin Delany and James W. C. Pennington constituted exceptions to the rule. On this point, see Michael R. Winston, "Through the Back Door: Academic Racism and the Negro Scholar in Historical Perspective," *Daedalus* (Summer 1971): 678-719.

22. European peasant and ghetto migration coincided with black rural plantation migration to the Middle Atlantic States and the Midwest in the decades on either side of the turn of the century. Thus, it was not an accident that American sociologists of both races were interested in exploring the adjustment of former rural dwellers in urban settings. On this point see Dan S. Green and Edwin D. Driver, "W.E.B. DuBois: A Case in the Sociology of Sociological Negation," *Phylon*, 37 (December 1976): 308-334; and John Bracey et al., "The Black Sociologists: The First Half Century," in *The Death of White Sociology*, ed. Joyce A. Ladner (New York: Vintage Books, 1973), pp. 4-22.

23. See Allan Chase, *The Legacy of Malthus: The Social Costs of the New Scientific Pacism* (Urbana: University of Illinois Press, 1980), pp. 111-175, and Thomas F. Gossett, *Race: The History of an Idea in America* (Dallas: Southern Methodist University Press, 1963), pp. 367-369.

24. Chase, *The Legacy of Malthus*, pp. 274-322.

25. *Ibid.*, pp. 254-273.

26. Outstanding among the various journals on the social sciences is the *Journal of the History of the Behavioral Sciences*, a quarterly publication of Psychology Press, Inc. of Brandon, Ver-

mont, since 1965. It contains scattered articles specifically treating the stages of the growth of sociology, psychology, economics, etc. Covering the social sciences today are two excellent works, *The Social Sciences Today*, ed. Paul Barker (London: Edward Arnold Publisher, 1975), and *The New Social Science*, ed. Baidya Nath Varma (Westport, Conn.: Greenwood Press, 1976).

27. Political science and its epistemological dilemmas are covered in Thomas A. Spragens, Jr., *The Dilemma of Contemporary Political Theory: Toward a Post Behavioral Science of Politics* (New York: Dunellen Publishing Co., 1973); sociology is given an intensive scrutiny in Alvin W. Gouldner, *The Coming Crisis in Western Sociology* (New York: Basic Books, Inc., 1970), *passim*. An older treatment of the stresses facing academics is found in Paul F. Lazarfeld and Wagner Thielens, Jr., *The Academic Mind: Social Scientists in a Time of Crisis* (Glencoe, IL: The Free Press, 1958), pp. 35-71, 92-112, 192-217. The work of Everrett C. Ladd and Seymour M. Lipset (see note 4 above) is an update of this earlier treatment of the topic.

28. See Pitirim A. Sorokin, *Fads and Foibles in Modern Sociology and Related Sciences* (Chicago: Henry Regnery Co., 1956), p. 103. He argues that the naive application of mathematical models to many areas of research had resulted in the "age of *quantrophrenia and numerology*." Quantitative methods are, of course, most useful when employed with a full comprehension of the context of analysis. W.E.B. DuBois was a pioneer in the use of quantitative methods as a supplement to insight and theory. On DuBois, as a much neglected giant in the field of sociology, see Dan S. Green and Edwin D. Driver, "W.E.B. DuBois: A Case in the Sociology of Sociological Negation," *Phylon*, 37 (December 1976): 308-334.

29. Many critiques of behaviorism exist but see especially Charles A. McCoy and John Playford, *Apolitical Politics: A Critique of Behaviorism* (New York: Thomas Y. Crowell, 1967), passim; and Hugh Mehan, *The Reality of Ethnomethodology* (New York: John Wiley and Sons, 1975), pp. 62-65.

30. Robert W. Fogel and Stanley L. Engerman, *Time on the Cross: The Economics of American Negro Slavery*, 2 vols. (Boston: Little, Brown and Co., 1974), with Volume 11 being exclusively on methodology that commits virtually every error Sorokin had warned against twenty years earlier in his *Fads and Foibles*. See also Herbert L. Gutman, *Slavery and the Numbers Game* (Urbana: University of Illinois Press, 1975), passim, who attempted to correct Fogel and Engerman.

31. Arthur R. Jensen, "How Much Can We Boost IQ and Scholastic Achievement?" *Harvard Educational Review*, 29 (Winter 1969): 1-123.

32. See Philip Green, *The Pursuit of Inequality* (New York: Pantheon Books, 1981), Part 1; Edward O. Wilson, *On Human Nature* (Cambridge, MA: Harvard University Press, 1978) was a book summing up a trend toward "innate" differences and explanations of circumstantial variability. For a good account of the changing "mood" of the strategic elites in the area of opinion formation, see Faustine Childress Jones, *The Changing Mood in America: Eroding Commitment?* (Washington, DC: Howard University Press, 1977), especially pp. 21-80; and for the concrete impact of this on black education, see Kenneth S. Tollett, *The Right to Education: Reaganism, Reaganomics, or Human Capital* (Washington, DC: Institute for the Study of Educational Policy, 1983), pp. 13-37.

33. Gossett, *Race*, and Chase, *The Legacy of Malthus*, pp. 253-286; pp. 85-111.

34. Lee Rainwater and William L. Yancey, *The Moynihan Report and the Politics of Controversy* (Cambridge, MA: The M.I.T. Press, 1967). This volume contains the full text of Daniel Patrick Moynihan, "The Negro Family: The Case for National Action," pp. 39-124 and the various reactions of black and white strategic elites, passim. The Moynihan Report was quite typical of the kind of failure to understand the dynamics of the larger society as reflected in the conditions of the black community. This failure to understand led to a "blaming the victim" conclusion.

See Rainwater and Yancey, *The Moynihan Report*, for a good overview of the types of statements that admit the existence of racism in the social system, especially then President Lyndon B. Johnson's Howard University Address, "To Fulfill These Rights," June 4, 1965), pp. 125-128. Also see, Jerome H. Skolnick, *The Politics of Protest* (New York: Simon and Schuster, 1969), pp. 179-326.

35. As indicated above, see note 15, this is in line with the history of institutional learning in the West.

36. On the ambivalence of the professoriate, see Robert Engler, "Social Science and Social Consciousness: The Shame of the Universities," in Theodore Roszak, *The Dissenting Academy* (New York: Pantheon Books, 1968), pp. 182-207.

37. In re-tooling and enlarging his/her perceptual background, an Afro-American/Black Studies specialist could review with profit Philip Mason, *Patterns of Dominance* (New York: Oxford University Press, 1970), a general introduction to the question of the processes through which European dominance was extended to non-European locations. And for an introduction to the topic, see V. G. Kiernan, *The Lords of Human Kind: Black Man, Yellow Man and White Man in an Age of Empire* (Boston: Little, Brown and Company, 1969); H. Hoetink, *Slavery and Race Relations in the Americas* (New York: Harper and Row Publishers, 1973), especially pp. 97-160; Anya Peterson Royce, *Ethnic Identity: Strategies of Diversity* (Bloomington: University of Indiana Press, 1982), Parts 2-3; and, John Hope Franklin, ed., *Color and Race* (Boston: Houghton Mifflin Company, Inc., 1968). A basic introductory volume for studying the black presence in Spanish America is Leslie B. Rout, Jr., *The African Experience in Spanish America: 1502 to the Present Day* (New York: Cambridge University Press, 1976).

38. A model for the study of the details of specific locations of persons in the diaspora is George E. Simpson and J. Milton Yinger, *Racial and Cultural Minorities: An Analysis of Prejudice and Discrimination*, 4th ed. (New York: Harper and Row Publishers, Inc., 1972). In this volume the authors deal with history, sociology, social structure, economics, and personality as related to the two variables of prejudice and discrimination.

39. Franklin, *Color and Race*, passim. Also see, on social structure, Peter M. Blau, *Inequality and Heterogeneity: A Primitive Theory of Social Structures* (New York: The Free Press, 1977), pp. 1-18; and Richard Frucht, ed., *Black Society in the New World* (New York: Random House, 1971).

40. Ceremonial pictures of the formal governing bodies, presidents, cabinets, legislatures, military high commands, bureaucratic top leadership and judicial systems in the Americas would make an impressive statement of the differences in formal power between groups of European descent and groups of African descent.

42. The work of Ali Mazuri, *A World Federation of Cultures: An African Perspective* (New York: The Free Press, 1976) is suggestive of comparative possibilities, as is John Hope Franklin's *Color and Race* (see note 37 above).

43. Two works done by persons outside the field illustrating the variety of religious expressions in the Diaspora are George E. Simpson, *Black Religions in the New World* (New York: Columbia University Press, 1978) and John Lovell, *Black Song: The Forge and the Flame* (New York: Macmillan Co., 1972). These two books should be required reading in the field.

44. A modest start on the study of comparative educational experiences is John U. Ogbu, *Minority Education and Caste: The American System in Cross-Cultural Perspective* (New York: Academic Press, 1978). Ogbu examines the topic of occupational expectations and minority student performance in several widely located regions of the Diaspora.

29.

The Intellectual and Institutional Development of African Studies

Robert L. Harris, Jr.

Africana studies is the multidisciplinary analysis of the lives and thought of people of African ancestry on the African continent and throughout the world. It embraces Africa, Afro-America, and the Caribbean, but does not confine itself to those three geographical areas. Africana studies examines people of African ancestry wherever they may be found — for example, in Central and South America, Asia, and the Pacific Islands. Its primary means of organization are racial and cultural. Many of the themes of Africana studies are derived from the historical position of African peoples in relation to Western societies and in the dynamics of slavery, oppression, colonization, imperialism, emancipation, self-determination, liberation, and socioeconomic and political development.

There have been four stages in the intellectual and institutional development of Africana studies as an area of scholarly inquiry. The first stage began in the 1890s and lasted until the Second World War. During this first stage, numerous organizations emerged to document, record, and analyze the history, culture, and status of African peoples. For example, the Bethel Literary and Historical Association of Washington, D.C., formed in 1881, sponsored lectures on numerous topics, such as the Egyptians, the Zulus, and various aspects of African culture, in addition to contemporary issues affecting African Americans. Other organizations functioned in a similar manner — for example, Philadelphia's American Negro Historical Society, established in 1897; Washington, D.C.'s American Negro Academy, also started in 1897; and New York's Negro Society for Historical Research, organized in 1911.

These early black literary and historical associations sought to preserve and to publicize the legacy of African peoples. They were superseded in 1915, when Carter G. Woodson formed the Association for the Study of Afro-American (formerly Negro) Life and History (ASALH), which still survives today. Woodson laid the groundwork for systematic study of African peoples through the association's annual meetings; the *Journal of Negro History*, launched in 1916; the national observance of Negro History Week (now Black History Month), started in 1926, publication of the *Negro History Bulletin*, begun in 1933; and the formation of Associated Publishers to print books on the black experience in America and throughout the world. ASALH has been the premier organization in promoting historical consciousness and in generating greater understanding of African heritage in the United States.

In 1897 W.E.B. DuBois initiated an ambitious program at Atlanta University to examine various categories of African-American life in ten-year cycles. He proposed that such studies be continued for at least 100 years to provide knowledge and understanding of the black family, church, social organizations, education, and economic development in the United States. From 1898 to 1914, the Atlanta University studies produced sixteen monographs, which consisted of more than 2,100 pages of research. DuBois, Woodson, Lorenzo J. Greene, Charles H. Wesley, E. Franklin Frazier, Ralph J. Bunche, Charles S. Johnson, Abram Harris, Sterling Brown, and other pioneering black scholars produced an impressive body of scholarship to correct the errors, omissions, and distortions of black life and history that prevailed among white academics and the American public.

The second stage for Africana studies began with the study of black America by Gunnar Myrdal. This stage was in some respects a setback. Myrdal, who began his project for the Carnegie Corporation in 1939, confined his analysis to the American social, political, and economic order. There was growing concern about the role and place of the black population during the Second World War, as a majority of African Americans became urban. Black migration northward, which had begun in large numbers during the 1890s, had accelerated during World War I, and had slowed during the Depression of the 1930s, mushroomed during World War II, making the black presence in America more a national than a regional or primarily southern concern. Believing that black people in the United States were fundamentally Americans who had no significant African cultural background or identity, Myrdal accepted the formulation Or the University of Chicago School of Sociology that ethnic and racial contact led not only to conflict but also to inevitable assimilation and absorption into the dominant society. His two-volume study, *An American Dilemma: The Negro Problem and Modem Democracy*, published in 1944, had an important influence on scholarship, especially the work of white academics during this second stage.

White scholars, by and large, had ignored black people. The Columbia University historian John W. Burgess had boldly stated: "[A] black skin means membership in a race of men which has never itself succeeded in subjecting passion to reason; has never, therefore, created any civilization of any kind." After World War II, as the black population in the United States became predominantly urban and as scholar ship in general shed notions of inherent racial inferiority and superiority with the Nazi debacle, white scholars devoted increasing attention to African Americans' status in the United States. They sought environmental rather than biogenetic explanations for African Americans' inferior status.

In *Mark of Oppression* (1951), Abram Kardiner and Lionel Ovesey hypothesized that African Americans emerged from slavery without a culture, with "no intrapsychic defenses — no pride, no group solidarity, no tradition." They argued: "The marks of his previous status were still upon him — socially, psychologically, and emotionally, and from these he has never since freed himself." Stanley Elkins in his book *Slavery* (1959) concluded that African Americans were not genetically inferior but were made inferior by the process of enslavement, which they internalized and passed on to succeeding generations. In *Beyond the Melting Pot: The Negroes, Puerto Ricans, Jews, Italians, and Irish of New York City* (1963), Nathan Glazer and Daniel B. Moynihan attributed African-American status to the absence of middle-class values and norms among the black population in general. Two years later, in *The Negro Family: The Case for National Action*, Moynihan wrote: "Three centuries of injustice have brought about deep-seated structural distortions in the life of the Negro American." He concluded that "the present tangle of pathology is capable of perpetuating itself without assistance from the white world."

Whereas Burgess had implied that Africans had never created anything of worth and therefore African Americans were descended from an inferior people, post-World War II white scholars, in the main, identified African-American status not with an inglorious African past but with deficiencies occasioned by slavery, segregation, and discrimination. It is important to note that these scholars believed that the end of racial oppression would not immediately produce racial equality, not because of lack of social opportunity but because of the accumulated pathological behavior of black people. In other words, black people were not divinely created inferior but were made inferior over time. The sum of racial oppression and its alleged internalization by black people dramatically affected their lives across generations.

Another significant post-World War II development was the creation of African studies programs that had no real link to black people in the New World. Although Melville Herskovits, a white anthropologist and proponent of African studies, tried to join the study of Africa with the lives of black people in the New World, African studies became wedded to a modernization theory that measured African societies by Western standards. African history, culture, and politics were explored more within the context of the colonial powers than with any attention to African cultural continuities in the Western hemisphere. This compartmentalization of knowledge regarding black people departed significantly from the scholarship of individuals such as DuBois and Woodson during the first stage in the development of Africana studies.

The civil rights revolution, the black power drive, and the black consciousness movement initiated a third stage of Africana studies. During this era, larger numbers of black students entered predominantly white colleges and universities. Most of these students were the first generation of their families to attend college. They encountered faculties that were almost entirely white and a curriculum that was primarily Eurocentric in perspective. The "melting pot" thesis prevailed as the paradigm of American society in which all groups, regardless of background, assimilated to an ideal that was primarily white, Anglo-Saxon, and Protestant. Ironically, at a time when African nations were achieving independence from colonial rule, Africa seemed unrelated to black people in the United States. If Africa was discussed in classes, it was generally as an adjunct to European imperialism. In large measure, black people were seen as pawns rather than as actors, as victims more than as victors.

Together with many black scholars from the first stage of Africana studies, black college students challenged the prevailing orthodoxies on predominantly white campuses. They demanded the employment of black professors and the establishment of Africana studies departments and programs. They pressed for the inclusion of African studies in the newly formed Africana studies programs. The inclusion of African studies was important for several reasons. First, African Americans have historically linked their destiny with the future of Africa. Second, the image of Africa has had significant consequences for the status of African Americans. Third, African ancestry has informed the cultural heritage of African Americans as much as their presence in the United States. Fourth, the history, politics, and culture of Africa could stand as a counterweight to the dominance of Western culture in American education.

The Eurocentric focus of the college curriculum basically excluded people of African ancestry or studied them through a European filter. Eurocentrist scholars ignored the growth of civilization in Africa, especially in Egypt, or coopted Egyptian civilization as part of a European rather than an African continuum. They also ignored the African heritage of African Americans, characterizing them as having begun their existence in North America as tabulae rasae—blank slates to be imprinted with Euro-American culture.

Although some colleges and universities were willing to establish Africana studies programs, they were less willing to organize Africana studies departments. Faculty within the traditional departments were reluctant to give up their prerogative of determining what constituted a course in history, literature, or government; who would take such courses; and how the professors teaching them would be evaluated for employment, promotion, and tenure. Advocates of Africana studies departments questioned how members of traditional departments that had not offered courses on the black experience or hired black faculty could sit in judgment on the nature and quality of work being done in this newly emerging field of study.

The third stage of Africana studies, from about the mid-1960s to the mid-1980s, was a period of legitimization and institutionalization. Few scholars were prepared to teach Africana studies courses. The shift in perspective from Eurocentrism to Afrocentrism required the recovery, organization, and accessibility of research materials that made black people, their lives, and their thoughts the center of analysis and interpretation. Many white scholars in particular had assumed that there was not sufficient documentation on which to base sound judgments about the personal and collective experiences of black people in the United States. However, with the new interest in black life and culture, federal, state, and local archivists combed their collections for materials on the African-American experience and published several useful guides. Major projects began assembling and publishing the papers of black leaders, writers, and organizations. It is now clear that there are abundant materials (print, visual, and sound) to reconstruct and to interpret the African-American past.

The prodigious research of black and white scholars has dramatically changed the manner in which we now view African Americans. Most scholars today acknowledge the persistence of African culture in the United States. They no longer accept the idea that African Americans passively acquiesced to oppression, recognizing that, on the contrary, they actively resisted oppression in a variety of ways. In large measure, scholars have come to accept the United States as a pluralistic society with multiple viable cultures, rather than as a "melting pot." We think more of acculturation, with give-and-take, than of assimilation—particularly in the form of total absorption into the dominant culture, which itself is now being redefined.

Africana studies has achieved legitimacy and has become institutionalized within higher education. It now has moved into a fourth stage of theoretical refinement and more sophisticated analysis and interpretation. The fundamental research tools have been developed, although there will certainly be a need to update and to supplement them as new materials become available. In general, the field is in fairly good condition, but there are some problems, or perhaps opportunities to improve it.

Because the formats for multidisciplinary programs vary from campus to campus, there will probably not be a single method of organization for Africana studies. The ideal format is the department structure, which allows for selection of faculty and development of curriculum. Programs with faculty in traditional departments can also be successful, provided that they have some control of faculty lines. The program, however, becomes a more complex arrangement, especially in decisions for hiring, promotion, and tenure. Joint appointments carry similar problems, especially for junior faculty. They are less burdensome for senior faculty, whose tenure has already been established. Cross-listing of courses is one means by which departments and programs can take greater advantage of faculty resources on their campuses. However, before such cross-listing can be effective, there must first be a strong core faculty within the department or program. Otherwise, the Africana studies curriculum becomes too dependent on the priorities of other departments.

One goal for the fourth stage of Africana studies should be to broaden and deepen the field of inquiry. This prospect becomes somewhat difficult for those departments and programs with limited numbers of faculty. Small faculties are stretched thin when they attempt to offer a major and to cover Africa, Afro-America, and the Caribbean. Offering a comprehensive program in Africana studies has meant that some departments and programs play primarily service roles in providing introductory courses that are used to fulfill one or more distribution requirements for graduation. These efforts have little opportunity to supply depth in the field of study. Faculty become very much occupied with servicing large introductory courses and have little time for research and writing in an area of specialization. There is a tendency for faculty to become generalists familiar with a broad range of knowledge rather than specialists who advance the frontiers of specific areas of knowledge.

As Africana studies moves into its fourth stage, as well as its third decade on predominantly white campuses, there is a need to re-examine the curriculum on many campuses. Some departments and programs offer a hodgepodge of courses that have evolved over time in response to student interest and faculty availability. Many departments and programs, particularly those with small faculties, need to deter mine what they can do best with their resources. Some have specific strengths upon which to build; others need to reconsider where they want to concentrate their resources. Unless they have the faculty and the administrative support, many departments and programs cannot offer successful comprehensive Africana studies courses. In a 1986 report on the "Status of Afro-American Studies in the State University of New York," Dr. Kenneth Hall showed that the preponderance of students are attracted by courses on Afro-American history, the civil rights movement, film, music, and contemporary Africa. Courses on history and culture (literature, music, film, drama, and dance) seem to appeal most to a cross section of students (black and white), with politics close behind.

In many respects, Africana studies faculty need to return to the basic question: Africana studies for what? There was much discussion and debate on this question during the early days of organizing, when the focus was on the quest for legitimacy and institutionalization. On many campuses, Africana studies was to provide the black presence, to supply role models for students, to have an active advising and counseling function, to organize film series, lectures, and symposia, and to influence traditional departments in the composition of their faculty and curriculum. This was a tall order that exhausted many Africana studies faculty. Having expended their energy on getting the new field off the ground, many faculty had not devoted sufficient time to research and publication and thus were caught short when evaluated for promotion and tenure.

Today, there is some debate about whether Africana studies faculty should play their former roles of counselors and mentors or give more time to research. Some of this tension would be eased if administrators supported campus-life specialists who would organize cultural activities for black students in particular and for all students in general. Faculty development is an important element within the university, and it is especially important for Africana studies faculty, many of whom need to reorient themselves toward greater scholarship.

Public colleges that are clustered in metropolitan areas have a unique opportunity to foster scholarship in Africana studies by establishing master's degree programs and research institutes. Such projects might encourage Africana studies departments and programs to develop strengths in specific areas. These strengths could be drawn upon for graduate programs and research institutes to promote greater scholarship by identifying areas of investigation and by bringing together scholars with similar interests. Research institutes might also be a means to influence more students to pursue advanced degrees and expand the number of minority scholars.

Answers to the question of "Africana studies for what?" will have a significant effect on the shape and content of the curriculum. To address these issues, the National Council for Black Studies has already embarked on a program of summer institutes for college teachers. Such responses will also influence the role of Africana studies on different campuses. Africana studies will continue to vary from college to college. Ultimately, however, there is a need for greater clarification and understanding through more dialogue about its specific function on various campuses.

30.

The Status of Black Studies in the Second Decade: The Ideological Imperative

Tilden LeMelle

In its second decade the status of Black Studies will be a function largely of the kinds of answers its faculty and students give to two as yet unresolved questions that confronted Black Studies in the first decade. Indeed, though the answers may change according to the changing realities that the Black world must address, the questions will always remain the same:

1. Why Black Studies? What are the historical and academic imperatives for Black Studies?

2. Black Studies for what? What is the educational mission of Black Studies?

The answer to the first question has been, is, and will remain the same for a long time to come. The historical imperative for Black Studies is now a matter of record, and the academic imperative will remain until the socialization function of Black Studies has transformed the psyche of the United States—Black and non-Black—to the point that the legitimacy of Blackness is as fully institutionalized as the legitimacy of whiteness is today. That point lies beyond the lifetime of every member of this conference.

The historical and academic imperatives of Black Studies are founded in the following historical logic:

1. Traditional education afforded Black Americans in the United States has been largely dysfunctional. It has been designed and has served primarily to meet the needs of a white dominant, racially stratified society. Thus, it has not only neglected and disregarded the needs and interests of the Black American but has aimed to socialize the Black man to anti-Black values and has aimed to tool the Black man only to the degree it was necessary for the Black man to serve the needs and interests of the dominant white community. In a word, education has served to maintain and secure the dominant/subordinate relationships between white and Black in the United States.

2. This dysfunctionalism is largely a product of the almost total and systematic exclusion from the various academic disciplines—especially the humanities and social sciences—of the Black experience as a legitimate subject matter.

3. When the Black experience has been included as part of the academic curriculum, it has been studied from the dominant white point of view.

327

4. Since the Black experience is an inherent and integral part of the total American experience, it must be included as an integral and essential part of the total educational process.

5. Finally, since Blacks cannot now entrust whites with what whites failed to do or did poorly in the past, the establishment and development of the Black curriculum must be in the hands of and under the control of Blacks.

To most participants in this conference, this statement of the historical and academic imperatives of Black Studies may seem a statement of the obvious, but it has not always been perceived as such. Moreover, there remain many for whom these historical and academic imperatives are not obvious or for whom they must be ignored or subsumed under some ideological prerogatives. These latter are the ideologues — the political religionists — who view ideology as an end in itself rather than as a means to an end. Blinded by this teleological approach, they fail to recognize that in a white dominant, racially stratified society such as the United States, Black Studies is per se political and, accordingly, constitutes its own justification. Consequently, they look for an ideological justification that imposes a priori directions and limitations on matters of curriculum and methodological development.

The danger that the continuing irresolution of the first question poses for Black Studies in the next decade is the same that has plagued traditional education for American Blacks for the last century and that currently plagues education for Blacks in the newly independent African states on the continent and in the Caribbean. That danger is the development of countervailing ideologies and philosophies of education that will make Black Studies a mere servant of their ends — a situation that would ultimately render Black Studies irrelevant to the educational needs and interests of Blacks. It was, of course, the irrelevancy of much of traditional education that contributed, at least in part, to the demand for Black Studies in the first place. The reduction of Black Studies to irrelevancy would be a travesty of the highest order.

The countervailing ideologies that have traditionally plagued education for American Blacks and that now pose a threat to Black Studies as well can be reduced to two categories: Black assimilationist ideologies and Black self-determinationist ideologies.

The Black assimilationist ideologies are those that historically have informed the traditional education of American Blacks at both the Black and the predominantly white colleges. These ideologies are born of the ambivalence that white America has had about American Blacks and that those Blacks have had about themselves — ambivalence about the Black man's place in the United States, ambivalence about the educatability of Black people, and, therefore, ambivalence about the realistic function of education for Blacks and their relationship to U.S. society in general and to the Black community in particular.

This environment of uncertainty has naturally had an impact on the educational process in all aspects of Black education: Could the American Black be educated? Was he to be educated for total participation in American life or only for participation in the Black community? What kind of education should he have? These were some of the questions that those concerned with education for Blacks had to answer. A philosophy of education depended on the answers and an ideology for educational development demanded precise answers.

Whether the American Black was educable was answered by the fact that, when given the opportunity, Blacks successfully completed the best curricula U.S. education had to offer. Despite their achievement, however, and notwithstanding the fact that they were considered inferior in all other respects, Black educational achievers were looked upon either as the exceptions that proved the rule or as people who owed their success to the "white" blood of their slavemaster progenitors or to their associations with "superior" whites.

Lest some of us think that the foregoing are the racist assumptions of a bygone era, we should be reminded that the Jensens and the Shockleys are of our own day and are bent on "proving scientifically" that Blacks are less capable of educational achievement than whites. Moreover, since the *Brown v. Board of Education* decision of 1954, the basic premise of school desegregation has been that Blacks can achieve quality education only through "integration" with whites. Not only do racist whites accept this premise and fight it through antibusing tactics, but such Black organizations as the NAACP also believe it and support it through their insistence that school "integration" is the only means for achieving quality education for Blacks, regardless of whether such integration achieves this end or not. Furthermore, the attitude, often expressed by many inner city Black youth, that Blacks who achieve in school are trying "to be white" is a further, unconscious expression of the belief in the superior educability of whites. The doubters, Black and white, persist today despite all evidence to the contrary.

American Blacks have not yet resolved the questions about the academic rationale of education for Blacks philosophically and ideologically, but factually and historically these questions were resolved by the reality of the American Blacks' dual existence in a racially stratified American society. Education for Black citizens has reflected the irresolution and ambiguity of the Black/white conflict, and answers to the question about the content of education for Black citizens have reflected the same duality. As a result, education for American Blacks has not developed its potential in relation either to white dominant American or to subordinate Black America. The old ambivalence remains the millstone it has always been and the rhetoric goes on, now threatening even Black Studies. Such ambivalence derives from the utter futility of assimilationist rationalizations in a fundamentally anti-Black society.

Black Assimilationist
Ideologies and Black Studies

The Black assimilationist ideologies are Black Accommodationism, Black Reconciliationism, Black Liberal Idealism, and Black Marxism-Leninism. These ideologies are essentially "other" oriented and, accordingly, they are anti-Black. In a racially stratified society (racist) such as the United States, where there is only one legitimate point of reference in terms of race (i.e., white), any Black who is "other" oriented is fundamentally anti-self—anti-Black.[2]

The "other"-orientation of these Black ideologies is manifested in:

1. The expressed need to be accepted by the "other," as illustrated by:

    (a) Positing change in the relationships with the "other" by making accommodations to the will of the "other" (Accommodationism).

    (b) Positing change in the relationships with the "other" by appealing to the *good will and in oral sense* of the "other" (Liberal Idealism).

2. The need to be associated with the "other," as illustrated by:

(a) Positing the reconciliation of differences in Black/white relationships solely in accordance with the rules established by the "other"
(Reconciliationism).

(b) Positing change in the relationships with the "other" through the
formation of coalitions with some members of the "other" on the
basis of a misconceived notion of class which disregards "race" as if
it did not exist (Marxism-Leninism).

Each of the Black assimilationist ideologies gives rise to a philosophy of education which defines its goals primarily from a non-Black context.

The Ideology of Black Accommodationism

Among American Blacks, the best-known exponent of Black Accommodationism was Booker T. Washington, who clearly enunciated that ideology in his Atlanta
Exposition Speech:[3]

> The Negro in the South has it within his power if he *properly* utilizes the forces
> at hand, to make of himself such a valuable factor in the life of the South that
> he will not have to seek privileges, they will be freely *conferred* upon him.[4]

In other words, Washington advised the Black man to serve his white betters in
a way that would demonstrate his ability to achieve the levels of responsibility and
respectability deemed acceptable by the white community, in return for which he
would be deemed worthy of the rights and privileges enjoyed by the responsible and
respectable white man. In pursuit of his policy of conciliation and accommodation,
Washington formulated an educational program that called for the vocational training of Black men—in essence an attempt to fulfill the basic role inherited from slavery and assigned to the Black American by the post-slavery white community. More
important, the black education that Washington envisaged nurtured attitudes of res-
ignation to and compliance with the Black man's status in a racist society. It tended
to legitimize only those aspirations which did not disturb the status quo and, in limiting what he *ought* to achieve, in reality imposed arbitrary limits on what the Black
man *could* achieve. Contrary to the stated goals of Black self-development, this program tailored Black education to the needs and aspirations of the white community,
thereby thwarting meaningful development, in the Black community. Fortunately for
Black education and the Black community as a whole, Washington's philosophy did
not prevail. It was countervailed by the ideology of reconciliationism.

The Ideology of Black Reconciliationism

The ideology of Black Reconciliationism, which unlike accommodationism does
not avoid conflict, seeks compromise through confrontation—confrontation within
the established rules of the game. This ideology was best articulated by W.E.B.
DuBois in his dissertation, *Talented Tenth*. Here DuBois writes that

> the Negro race, like all races, is going to be saved by its exceptional men.
> The problem of education, then, among Negroes must first deal with the Tal-
> ented Tenth; it is the problem of developing the Best of this race that they
> may guide the Mass away from the contamination and death of the Worst,
> in their own and other races.[5]

It is interesting to note DuBois' allusion to the type of leader Black education should produce—a leader like the *Best* in other races. He continues:

> Indeed the demand for college-bred men by a school like Tuskegee, ought to make Mr. Booker T. Washington the firmest friend of higher training. Here he has as helpers the son of a Negro senator, trained in Greek and the humanities, and graduated at Harvard; the son of a Negro congressman and lawyer, trained in Latin and mathematics, and graduated at Oberlin; he has as his wife a woman who read Virgil and Homer in the same classroom with me; he has a college chaplain, a classical graduate of Atlanta University; as teacher of science, a graduate of Fisk; as teacher of history, a graduate of Smith....[6]

This passage clearly expresses the type of Black leadership to be produced by this kind of Black education: the select Harvard and Smith graduate of the day, easily quoting from the Latin Virgil and the Greek Homer, fashionable and proper, using the correct fork at banquets and quoting the latest witticism from Europe. These were the people who would *speak* to the plantation Black and to the domestic worker—undoubtedly in the idiom of Virgil and Homer.

Aside from his unrealistically elitist orientation, the assimilationist reconciliationist assumes that the culture—the values—of the "other" are superior and, hence, he shapes Black education to produce Blacks who define the "good" in terms of those values and define their goals in terms of the interests of the assumedly superior "other." Clearly, in a racially stratified (racist) society, to pursue the goals of the "other" is to act in a way that is inherently anti-self.

The Ideology of Black Liberal Idealism

Black Liberal Idealism has been best espoused in recent times by Martin Luther King, Jr. It is the philosophy of the "last true believers" in the values and ideals of the normative theory of American liberal democracy. It is the expression of an undying faith both in the assumption of man's basic goodness and in the conviction that goodness will eventually triumph over the evils of American society.

The political and economic realities of U.S. society force liberal idealism to remain an ideal as an ideology for Black educational development. The vested interest in the present brokerage and group orientation of U.S. politics and the quid pro quo of the economic marketplace preclude the concrete realization of liberal idealism in any U.S. social institutions, thus making it impossible to conceive of this ideology as the basis for the renewal of education for U.S. Blacks. As expressed in the dictum "Education for Democracy," this ideology has even been rejected by many young whites.

The real danger in Black liberal idealism is that despite its irrelevancy to progressive change and development in U.S. Black/white relations, both groups may accept it because it is emotionally and psychologically satisfying. It holds out to Blacks the traditional assimilationist hope of "Black and white together," whereas it provides whites with a cathartic assuagement of conscience which allows them to think of themselves as "nice guys." The disengagement of white liberals from the Civil Rights Movement once they were confronted with Black self-assertion is evidence of the futility of liberal idealism as an ideology for Black educational development.

Like Black Accommodationism and Reconciliationism, Black Liberal Idealism channels Blacks toward dependency on the "other" as the guarantor of their rights and the legitimizer of their interests and aspirations. That "other" is the same liberal who screamed racism-in-reverse and condemned Black self-assertion as Black separatism, and for whose anti-Black behavior the term "white backlash" was created.

The Ideology of Black Marxism-Leninism

Black Marxism-Leninism deludes itself in disregarding the racial factor and instead defining its plans for Black education solely on a misconceived class basis. At the same time, its exponents erroneously equate class with income level, defining middle and upper income Blacks as a "Black middle and upper class" — a definition fully consonant with the self-delusions of many such Blacks. These Black Marxist-Leninists view low-income whites as "working class," and, in an attempt to actualize the rhetoric of "working classes of the world unite," they seek coalitions with the white working class — precisely the group that has perennially been the overseer keeping U.S. Blacks in their place. That American Blacks neither individually nor collectively control the regulation of society (political power) or the production and distribution of wealth (economic power) escapes the Black Marxist-Leninists. That the pension funds and collective wealth of white labor vie with and join with white corporate and financial institutions to control political and economic decisions in the United States also escapes them. Moreover, they seem unaware that middle and upper incomes for Blacks indicate only an ability to consume (often conspicuously) and that this consumption in turn strengthens the hands of those who regulate society and control the production and distribution of its wealth. Accordingly, the Black Marxist-Leninist — often in the middle and upper income brackets and a conspicuous consumer — spurns fellow Blacks in his pursuit of an alien ideology that tells him to make coalitions and alliances with the "other."

These same ideologues label African communalism "primitive" and "unscientific," deriding it as a source of socialist inspiration. Their, "scientific" rhetoric blinds them to the fact that race and class are coterminous in a white dominant, racially stratified society, and that the race/class controversy is therefore irrelevant. The Black Marxist-Leninist believes that education for Blacks should develop values that transcend race, incorporating the values and interests of those members of the "other" who are most often the immediate instruments of the oppression of Blacks. Noble though those seemingly nonracial ideals are, they are as unrealistic as the assumptions that provided a rationale for Washington's accommodationism and as racist as the assumptions that underlay the paternalism of the French *colons* and the white liberalism of the 1960s.

The Ideologies of Black Self-Determination

At best, Black assimilationist ideologies lead to activities that provide an opportunity to change only the *conditions* of American Black existence while retaining their *position* as the underclass. In a reaction to that realization and to the futility of the assimilationist ideologies of the Civil Rights Movement, the ideologies of Black Self-Determination came to fruition in the mid-1960s. These were the ideologies that led Black students and faculty on predominantly white college campuses to demand the establishment of Black Studies programs.

The Black self-determinationist ideologies can be categorized under the more general heading of Black Nationalism. Like the assimilationist ideologies, Black Nationalism in the U.S. was not a phenomenon unique to the 1960s. Black slave revolts, the Garvey Movement, some aspects of the Harlem Renaissance, Carter G. Woodson's Black History Movement, and so on, are all manifestations of a Black Nationalism in the United States. Furthermore, it should be noted that the confusion that often surrounds the false dichotomy between Black Nationalism and Pan-Africanism derives from the attempt to make a real distinction between the domestic and the international focus of Black Nationalism. Borrowing the limited European definition of nationalism as a phenomenon of the modern nation-state, some of us impose that definition on Black realities, thereby distorting our perception of them. If Black Nationalism means anything, it means identification with the interests and aspirations of Black people wherever they may be, regardless of state boundaries.

In analyzing the history of Black Nationalism in the United States, we can draw a useful distinction between Psychological Nationalism and Separatist Nationalism. The former distinguishes clearly between the self and the other and identifies self-interest as *distinct* though not necessarily always separate from the interest of the other. Thus, it does not inherently seek physical separation or social distance from the other, but rests satisfied with its own worth and posits self directed interests and goals. Separatist Nationalism, on the contrary, while positing self-directed interests and goals, seeks physical separation and social distance from the other. Psychological Black Nationalism is the ideology that informed the demands and efforts leading to the creation of Black Studies programs and departments on predominantly white college campuses, whereas Black Separatist Nationalism is best reflected in the establishment of the independent Black institutions of the early 1970s.

The Ideological Threats to Black Studies

Outside Black Studies programs and curricula, the Black Nationalist ideology has had little impact on education for U.S. Blacks. Traditional education for Blacks has generally continued in the assimilationist mode, the persistence of which is one of the threats to Black Studies in the next decade.

The Assimilationist Ideologies

All the assimilationist Black ideologies pose threats to Black Studies, but that from the Black Marxist-Leninists is less easily perceived and therefore the most serious.

First of all, Black Marxism-Leninism, like Black Liberal Idealism, is Black only in the sense that ideologues socially defined as Black subscribe to it. As pointed out earlier, this ideology is fundamentally "other" oriented. Its "other" orientation lies not so much in the alien nature of its source as in its attempt to define Black reality solely in terms of the "other." By equating the status of Blacks with that of an undefined white working class, the Black Marxist blithely dismisses the role of race in a society that he simultaneously and facilely, labels as racist — a society that has defined itself as racists through its history, laws, traditions, and institutions. The Black in Marxist-Leninists further ignore the historical fact that their would-be ally — the white "working class" — has been just as discriminatory toward the Black working class as toward the so-called Black bourgeoisie. How then does one analyze the relationship of American-Blacks to the American labor movement? How does one account for the cycles of displacement of Black labor by, European immigrants? For the recent *Webber* case? How can we explain the South African-type wage differential until recently existed between Black and white worker in the United States? Or the expulsion of the Black Knights of Labor by the all-white AFL in an attempt to reserve employment for European immigrants? Are these realities to be explained by, a "scientific" class analysis just because Karl Marx says so? Are our students to be so naive as to look forward to the embrace of the white working class or the white proletariat because Marx says so?

A second danger of Black Marxism-Leninism is the seductiveness of its militant anticapitalist rhetoric, which can engender an easy identification on the part of Blacks. Because the white capitalist has in fact been the oppressor of Blacks, such identification is understandable. It is, however, based on a very superficial analysis. Leftist hostility to white capitalism is easily misconstrued as a pro-Black sentiment. The illogic of this misunderstanding, however, is no different from that which for generations led Blacks in the American South to misconstrue the conflict between the industrial North and the agrarian South as a sign that they should seek refuge in the de facto segregated North. That illogic, coupled with the fact that the white working class whom the Black Marxist-Leninists identify as the natural ally of American Blacks is in fact a partner in capitalism, defies the class analysis. One cannot, at the same time, be both capitalist and noncapitalist; the terms are mutually exclusive. How does Black Studies reconcile this contradiction? Do Blacks have no alternative but to choose between "good" capitalists and "bad" capitalists?

The emotionally satisfying militant rhetoric and the unquestioning acceptance of the political religion of Black Marxism-Leninism are, indeed, serious problems for Black Studies in the decade ahead. The danger is a subtle one that, unless addressed head on, can transform Black Studies into a platform for the dissemination of an alien ideology that contradicts the realities of the Black experience. Black Studies has no need to develop a separate class analysis. In racially stratified systems such as the United States and the current international system, race and class are coterminous—one and the same thing. In contrast to the situation for whites, there is no Black middle class, for class, or a group's position in society, is a function of its political and economic power. A group's political position is a function of its ability to control the decisions that regulate the society. Its economic position is a function of its ability to control decisions governing the production, distribution, and consumption of the society's wealth. Income, which is often used as the indicator of class, is only an indicator of the ability to consume. In the United States, a white dominant, racially stratified system, the mobility factor is governed by race, and white incomes are therefore usually also an indicator of the ability both to control directly the decisions that regulate society as well as those that direct the production, distribution, and consumption of wealth. The mobility factor prevents middle- and upper-income Blacks from gaining access to the levers of political and economic power. As such, Black incomes are indexes of the ability to consume, not to control, except as expressed in a negative sense when Blacks have the will to withhold their consumption—the selective boycotting by the Civil Rights Movement being one example. When Blacks do exercise their ability to consume, they thereby *increase* the ability of the decision makers to control the production and distribution of wealth. Based on government-defined levels of income, there are Blacks who indeed can be categorized as middle and upper income. Since these definitions are based on levels of white income, however, those same Blacks can be defined out of a particular income level, as the white level changes. Black middle income cannot be equated with middle class.

The Marxist-Leninist analysis may have some validity when applied to the Black community itself. Given the declining importance of color among Blacks, that community is indeed stratified primarily along class lines. But those class lines cannot be defined by government-established income levels, nor do they reflect any real political and economic power on the part of Blacks within the Black community. Instead they are based more on differences among Blacks in terms of their ability to consume. Some Blacks have interpreted this ability to consume at a level higher than other Blacks as a real class difference, whereas it is more a reflection of the house servant's condescension to the field hand than an indication of any real political and economic power. It represents a change in the *condition* in which the higher consuming Black exists and not a change in his *position* or *class* in the society. Since any differences having a common denominator can be classified, one might talk about classes of consumers, but this is a notion quite different from the concept of class as defined by Marx and purportedly applied by the Black Marxist-Leninists.

The Self-Determinationist Ideologies

The Black self-determinationist ideologies are also something of a threat to Black Studies in the next decade. They are self-assertive and purport to base their self-assertion on an evaluation of the realities of the Black world, but there is a thin line between being pro-Black and anti-white. The understandable anger and frustration of Blacks as a racially subordinate group both in the United States and throughout the international system makes it easy to confuse anti-white with pro-Black sentiments — but it is an unnecessary and dangerous confusion.

To set out to be anti-white in a white dominant, racially stratified system is unnecessary because in such a system to espouse any group except the whites (or to favor anything other than what they define as legitimate) is in effect to be anti-white. That is, since white is the only legitimate point of reference — all the protestations about racial pluralism notwithstanding — the very existence of Black Studies is a statement that the dominant group perceives as hostile — as anti-white. This was the reason that Black Studies Programs were often labeled as racist-in-reverse, separatist, un-American, and so on, by both whites and assimilationist Blacks. To be pro-Black, however, is not the same as defining Black as the only legitimate point of reference. To label a pro-Black stance "racism-in-reverse" is the epitome of racism, for such a label implies the legitimacy of white exclusivity. Racism is based on the assumption of the a priori exclusivity of one race. Accordingly, an anti-white stance is irrelevant and unnecessary to the mission of Black Studies, and Black Studies faculty should be ever vigilant that curricula and students do not confuse the program's proper subject matter.

In addition to being unnecessary, anti-white posturing is essentially "other" oriented. In contrast to a pro-Black position, an anti-white posture retains a white point of reference, negative though that reference may be. It is a further indication of the task that still awaits Black Studies — the task of breaking the emanative ties that have bound Blacks psychologically to the dominant group.

Thus, despite their role in reorienting Blacks to a positive sense of self-identity and providing a realistic rationale for Black Studies, the self-determinationist ideologies can all too easily be corrupted. The danger increases as Black Studies staff and students lose sight of the functional role of ideology and make ideology an end in itself.

Many tasks await Black Studies. For some relatively well-established programs, the revisionist or reconstructive critique of the past is an important part of their curricula. For them there is an opportunity to begin moving toward the development of what we might call the constructive curriculum. That is, there is a need to construct new concepts and theories about human behavior, social institutions, and social systems. One can argue that the revisionist critique by Black Studies shows not only the need for the development of a new social science and a new humanities, but also demonstrates that Black Studies is the only hope for such a development. Even white scholars are conceding that Euro-American "conventional schooling has failed to prepare people for the complexity of global issues and is thereby contributing to further deterioration of the human condition."[7]

Yet, there are some Black Studies programs that are still grappling with the problems of survival — problems created in some instances by the struggle over countervailing ideologies. These programs play into the hands of those who would encourage them to destroy Black Studies, and thus make the task of those who oppose Black Studies easier.

For all Black Studies programs, success or failure in developing curricula, recruiting competent and dedicated staff, and attracting studious and inquiring students — that is, in developing programs that realistically answer our second question, "Black Studies for what?" — will depend to a large degree on the resolution of the ideological struggles within Black Studies. A successful philosophy of education depends on a unified base of ideological support. Without the clear resolution of the ideological problem, the African proverb will become a reality: If a person does not know where he is going, any road can take him there!

Endnotes

1. Tilden J. LeMelle, "Black Studies for What?" *Black Prism*, vol. 2 (Winter 1972): pp. 5-6.

2. For a detailed analysis of Black ideologies affecting education for American Blacks, see Tilden J. LeMelle and Wilbert J. LeMelle, *The Black College*, chap. 3, ("An Ideology for Black Educational Development") (New York: Praeger, 1969), pp. 38-53.

3. The Cotton States and International Exposition in Atlanta, Georgia, September 1895.

4. Booker T. Washington, *The Future of the American Negro* (Boston: Small, Maynard and Co., 1899), pp. 201-244 (italics in original).

5. W.E.B. DuBois, "The Talented Tenth," in Booker T. Washington et al., *The Negro Problem: A Series of Articles by Representative Negroes Today* (New York: James Pott & Company, 1963), pp. 33-75 *passim*.

6. *Ibid.*

7. "Colleges Still Living in Yesteryear, Futurists Charge," *The Chronicle of Higher Education*, 28 (July 1980): p. 3.

31.

African American Studies: The Future of the Discipline

Molefi Kete Asante

To the Ancestors in whose path I walk and the Elders whose son I am I give thanks for being invited to participate in this historic conference.

It is my intention to discuss the maintenance and future of African American Studies within the context of contemporary intellectual ideas. I will begin, of course, where I always begin, with a discussion of Afrocentricity as a theoretical instrument for the examination of phenomena. Afrocentricity is a simple idea. The reason that I know it is simple is because I have yet to meet a person on the streets of North Philadelphia who could not understand it. I also know it is simple because I have met a lot of Africans and Europeans in the Academy who deliberately misunderstand it. At its base it is concerned with African people being subjects of historical and social experiences rather than objects in the margins in European experiences. I recall seeing the book by Charles Wesley and Carter Woodson entitled *The Negro In Our History* and feeling that they were truly speaking from and to a Eurocentric perspective if they felt that such a title captured the essence of our experience. These were two of the most successful African American historians and yet they could not totally disengage their critical thinking from the traditional views held by whites. Viewing phenomena from the perspective of Africans as central rather than peripheral means that you secure a better vantage point on the facts. It also means that you have a better handle on your own theoretical and philosophical bases.

It is not a biological issue, anybody can see if they have the right vantage point. There are two aspects to Afrocentricity, the theory and the practice. One could master the theory and not be involved in the practice or vice versa. In my case, I have tried to merge the two aspects in my intellectual work and lifestyle. Of course, if one is not culturally African, that is, if one does not possess the historical and social memories that constitute Africanity, and practices Afrocentricity as a life style it would be strange although it is possible, just as weird and possible as Africans who have adopted Eurocentric styles.

Dislocation, location and *relocation* are the principal calling cards of the Afrocentric theoretical position. My attempt is always to locate a situation, an event, an author. I have identified through historical and literary analysis two fallacies of position: the *locational* fallacy and the *linguistic* fallacy. The first occurs when a person is de-centered, misoriented, or disoriented and cannot possibly be looking from the proper angle. This is the problem Malcolm X recognized when he spoke of some enslaved Africans thinking they had come to America on the Mayflower or when he told us that there some who took the slavemaster's perspective when it came to the plantation. Such people are not only dislocated but disoriented. The second fallacy occurs when a person is located in the proper place but does not have the experience or the ability to explain or to describe what is being seen. The second fallacy leads to a sort of naive nationalism because the viewer has only a vantage point but no adequate discipline or skill for analysis. Both types of persons bound in the academy.

The Nature of Criticism

The critics of Afrocentricity fall into two classes, those who are simply opposed to any African self determination and those who favor African self-determination within the framework of European experiences. Africans and Europeans occupy places in each category of those who have attacked the theoretical position staked out by a growing number of Afrocentric theorists. There are Marxists, liberals, reactionaries and various apologists for white racism in both groups. Recently Anne Wortham, the "colored" sociologist as she referred to herself at a symposium "Education and Afrocentrism" organized by the Heritage Foundation, went so far as to say that Afrocentricity was much like Nazism because it articulated a cultural viewpoint. I could not tell from listening to her on C-SPAN whether she actually believed that Afrocentricity was like Nazism or was doing as the late Louis Lomax once said some blacks do, "fooling white people." She could have received nothing from my works, which she attempted to discuss, to lead her to such a silly conclusion. There is nothing in the form or substance of Afrocentricity that is like Nazism.

In an opposing lecture from the left, Harold Cruse, in a major address on Afrocentricity at Temple University, said it was like Marxism in its transformative potential. Cruse saw the meta-theoretical possibilities of the idea extending to the psychological, cultural, and economic recovery of African people for ourselves. His criticism of the idea was essentially around the abstract nature of the metatheory. He kept asking, where is the practice? This is a legitimate question to ask of any Africalogical theory. The answer in African American Studies at Temple is the doctoral program itself, a product of Afrocentric theory and practice. Of course, Diane Ravitch, William Raspberry, Henry Gates, Manning Marable, Michele Wallace, Orlando Patterson, Arthur Schlesinger, Glenn Loury, George Wills, and other less well known lights have had something to say about Afrocentricity. Much of what many of them have had to say is a result not of reading or quoting my works but of responding to a popular cachet. Let me add that these are not all individuals of the same quality or insight.

I shall attempt to clarify several points with reference to Afrocentricity and the future of African American Studies or Africology. Let me start with a rather broad statement that, in a white supremacist environment, you are either for white supremacy or against it. There is no middle ground for the intellectual in an oppressive society. White supremacy is not just a sociological or political theory or ideology, it is also a literary project in the sense of the Great Books of the Western World as described by Mortimer J. Adler and William Buckley. One hundred and thirty authors and not one African American is included, not even an African who sees herself or himself on the margins of the European experience. To an Afrocentrist, of course, some things are predictable within the context of a white supremacist society. Let me state a less broad proposition, the institutions of a society will most often reflect the dominant political hegemony of the society. A racist political structure will give you racist institutions; a Marxist political structure will give you Marxist institutions, and so forth.

The Lack of Clarity

To object to Afrocentricity, a fundamental stepping stone to any multicultural project as an effort to marginalize African Americans is to criticize amiss. The aim, that is, the purpose, of centered positions that contribute to the multicultural discussion is to bring about harmony within society. Otherwise what one gets is an off-white contribution to the pale white stream. A better option is always to contribute the richness of the African American, the Latino, the Asian, the Native American, and the European to the common purpose. But there is no mainstream; this is a misnomer. Those who speak of the mainstream are often speaking about a white stream with African eddies bubbling on the side. Whatever the word "mainstream" means it has rarely included Africans. And those who use the term do not think of African American poetry or people as being mainstream. Those who speak of "mainstreams" and "universals" are most often speaking of whites. And therefore when someone says "universal man" it is not simply a rejection of women but of the Mandinka, the Zulu, the Hmong, the Yaqui, the African American. Yet there really are only tributaries and our cultural flow is a part of the grand delta of ideas.

The opposition to racism is not abstract, it is concrete. In our present social, economic, and intellectual condition the resistance to white supremacy is not black supremacy but pluralism without hierarchy, a frightening idea in the context of the long white domination of ideas. Manning Marable has developed a similar thesis in his book *How Capitalism Underdeveloped Black America*. Afrocentricity is not a black version of Eurocentricity, which is an arrogant imposition of a particular view as if it is a universal view. Such a position is ethnocentric and leads to racism when it is enforced by custom, law, or physical force. It degrades other views and valorizes the European viewpoint.

The African American Studies Idea

My thesis is simply stated. During the past twenty or so years since the establishment of African American Studies, two major changes have occurred in the American Academy in reference to African American Studies which have altered the academic landscape for years to come. The first was the institutionalization of African American Studies, Africology, as a discipline alongside other disciplines within the Academy. The second was the creation and mounting of the first doctoral program in African American Studies in the nation at Temple University. The first transformed the student movement of the 1960s into a concrete reality in academic units as well as in theories and methods. The second transcended the parochial and provincial role that had been assigned to the field by keepers of the Academy. What were the characteristics that manifested themselves in this flowering of a new intellectual reality?

I am a child of the Black Studies Movement, having been born to it in the late night and early morning labors of love and emotion that saw young men and women at UCLA, members of the Harambee Club, and later SNCC-UCLA of which I was chair, totally absorbed in the creation of the new, the novel, the radical. The processes by which the curricula documents were produced by African American students in the late 1960s and early 70s were unknown in, the history of the creation of academic fields and very few of us at that time had any real idea what the future would bring. We knew that curricula were to universities what oxygen is to the lungs. Curricula were inseparable from the concept of the university, just as lungs and breathing could not he separated from the inhaling and exhaling of oxygen. With the curricula changes there would have to he fundamental changes in the institution. We knew this, it now seems, instinctively because the few African American professors who were on those campuses often had not been there long or could not give us advice. As the first permanent director of the UCLA Center for Afro American Studies I wrote the interdisciplinary M.A. program and in 1969 started, along with Robert Singleton, who had been an interim director at the Center, the *Journal of Black Studies*. We knew then, as most of you knew, that Black Studies was not the mere aggregation of courses about our experiences but had to be courses taught from what we called at the time "the black perspective." In our rush to establish the perspective, we even demanded that only black teachers teach in the programs until we discovered that perspective is not a biological issue. Some of the black professors taught from a white perspective. It is from this reality that I shall attempt to answer the question posed above regarding the nature of disciplinary transformations, their characteristics, and future.

The Context of Discipline Development

African American Studies is a discrete discipline with certain critical perspectives, theories, and methods which are necessary for its role in discovery and understanding. Inherent in this statement is the radical idea that African Americans are largely responsible for producing the only new discipline in the social sciences and humanities in the last fifty years. The attendant propositions suggest creativity, innovation, genius, and authority in disciplines. Assaults on Africology as a discipline, as we shall see, are nothing more than attacks based upon the idea that African Americans can neither create theories nor disciplines, and are ultimately the same tune played in previous discussions of African intelligence. A number of books, such as George Mosse's *A History of Racism in Europe*, Michael Bradley's *The Ice Man Inheritance*, and Stephen J. Gould's *The Mismeasure of Man*, exist on this subject. When this tune is played by Africans themselves it is often the result of dislocation, that is, the assumption of the place where Africans have been pushed by white racial hegemony in the Academy. In such situations the African feels that he or she must act in ways much more correct (in the white sense) than even whites themselves. There is a felt pressure to be hard, as it were, on any African who raises the possibility of escape from the mental plantation. What I am saying is that it becomes necessary to suspend judgment or to kill one's traditional sensibilities so to speak in order to understand the language of the new reality, that is, Africans as subjects instead of objects in the European project. This is difficult to discern from the same tired portals of traditions which are rooted in the conquest of Africans by Europeans. Africology becomes a discipline whose mission is, *inter alia*, the critique of domination. Of course, there are implications for institutional and organizational issues in the disciplinary question. That is, whether or not departments are more valuable in the maintenance of the discipline than programs in which faculty members share joint appointments. There is also the issue of the symbolic meaning, as well as the political implication, of joint appointments. At Temple University it was to our advantage to share the same paradigm of power and structure as the other organized academic units. Thus, the department is the basic unit and all of our faculty have full appointments in the department.

To examine these issues I will discuss the principal areas of inquiry, the shape of the discipline, classificatory aspects of the discipline, and heuristics for methods.

Issues in Inquiry

I am not sure whether it is necessary any longer to debate the question of perspective in terms of the Africalogical discipline as had been the case during the past twenty years; at least, in the circle of scholars with whom I am associated it is pretty well agreed that the fundamental basis for Africology as a separate discipline is its unique perspective. Nevertheless, the ground is clearly established in the works of Linda James Myers, C. Tsehloane Keto, Maulana Karenga, Dona Richards, and Wade Nobles. Their arguments are expertly placed within the ongoing creative project of African liberation, now more than ever, an intellectual liberation.

The Afrocentric enterprise is framed by cosmological, epistemological, axiological, and aesthetic issues. In this regard the Afrocentric method pursues a world voice distinctly Africa-centered in relationship to external phenomena. I did not say distinctly African, which is another issue, but Africa-centered, a theoretical perspective.

Cosmological Issue

The place of African culture in the philosophy, myths, legends, literatures and oratures of African people constitutes, at the mythological level, the cosmological issue within the Afrocentric enterprise, which is an enterprise entirely consistent with the Africalogical discipline. What role does the African culture play in the Africans interface with the cosmos? The debate over "African cultures or culture" is answered definitionally within the context of the Afrocentric perspective so I will not discuss it at this juncture, no more than to say that it has been dealt with in the writings of Afrocentric scholars. For a discussion of this issue, one might see *African Culture: The Rhythms of Unity* edited by Asante and Asante.

Among the questions that might he dealt with under the cosmological umbrella is, What dramas of life and death, in the African tradition, are reflected in metaphysical metaphors? How are those dramas translated by lunar, solar, or stellar figures? The fundamental assumptions of Africalogical inquiry are based on the African orientation to the cosmos. By "African" I clearly mean a "composite African" not a specific discrete African ethnicity, which would rather mean African American, Yoruba, Ibo, Fulani, Zulu, Mandingo, Kikongo, etc. C. T. Keto has taken this up in his book *Afrocentricity and History* by writing that "African American thinkers were among the first to feel the need to create the concept 'composite' African and, in so doing their reference was the whole of the African continent which included, historically, ancient Kemet." (Keto, 1991 p. 5). He continues that "denied a precise ethnic linkage, they created a holistic African vision that . . . influenced Africans on the continent." (Keto, 1991, p. 5)

There are several concerns which might he considered cosmological in that they are fundamental frames for research initiatives in this discipline. I shall only make reference to them here and refer you to my recent book *Kemet, Afrocentricity, and Knowledge*, for greater commentary. The concerns are: Racial Formulation, Culture, Gender, and Class. Race as a social factor remains prevalent in heterogeneous but hegemonically Eurocentric societies. In the United States, the most developed example of such a society, the question of race is the most dominant aspect of intersocial relations. Cultural questions are usefully viewed in the context of shared perceptions, attitudes, and predispositions that allow communities of people to organize responses in similar ways. Gender also must he seen as a substantial research area in questions of social, political, economic, and cultural dimensions. Since the liberation of women is not an act of charity but a basic premise of the Afrocentric project, the researcher must he cognizant of sexist language, terminology, and perspectives. Class becomes for the Afrocentrist aware of our history, much more complicated than capitalists and workers, or bourgeoisie and proletariat. Finding the relevant class positions and places in given situations will assist the Africalogical scholar with analysis. Indeed, Eurocentrism with all of its potential for asserting its particular self as universal becomes the repository for race, class, and gender conflict. Rather than an isolated or isolatable discussion of race, or class, or gender one begins to view the dominant Eurocentric mythos as containing all of these elements.

Epistemological Issue

What constitutes the search for truth in the Afrocentric enterprise? In Africology, language, myth, ancestral memory, dance-music-art, and science provide the sources of knowledge, the canons of proof and the structure of truth.

Discussions of language from an Afrocentric perspective or research into African language, diasporan or continental, may lead to understanding about the nature of truth. Ebonics, the African American language, serves as the archetype of African American language in the United States. A variety of languages in Brazil, Ecuador, Colombia, Panama, and Belize serve this function in other American communities. One of our students, for example, is centering her research on the Garifuna people of Belize. However, while her work will include much that is historical and linguistic, she is principally concerned with an epistemological question rooted in the inquiry on methods of retention as expressed in the declarative, as opposed to the cognitive culture, of the people.

The strong, expressive, inescapable myth of the African presence in America, indeed, in the world has value for the discovery of truth in many dimensions of human life. Thus, behind and in front of our banquet of possibilities are the refracting elements of myths which appropriately mediate our relationships. Knowing these myths, making a habit of investigating them in a serious manner, allows the researcher to form new metaphors about our experiences. In dance-music-art, performing and representational art forms are central to interpretation of cultural and social reality. Our analysis is informed by the way dance is seen in African culture, even in the way we view the Africanization of the walkman.

Axiological Issue

The question of value is at the core of the Afrocentric quest for truth because ethical issues have always been connected to the advancement of the discipline. One cannot speak of Africology apart from its origin in the drive to humanize education, to democratize the curriculum, to advance the understanding of humanity. This is the birth-right of the discipline more than any other discipline in the social sciences or humanities. What constitutes the good is a matter of historical conditions and cultural developments within a particular society. A common expression among us relates to the good and beautiful in this way, "beauty is as beauty does!" We are also sure that a person "is beautiful because he or she is good." When a sister says, "that's a beautiful brother," she is usually meaning something more than his physical looks. Doing good is equivalent to being beautiful. The Afrocentric method isolates conduct and action in social or literary analysis. The aim is to see what conduct has been sanctioned, and if sanctioned, carried out.

Aesthetic Issue

Kariamu Welsh Asante has identified seven aspects of the African aesthetic which she calls "senses." Based upon her field research into Zimbabwe dance she isolated *polyrhythm, polycentrism, dimensionality, repetition, curvilinearity, epic memory,* and *wholism* as investigative categories for African aesthetics. Each aspect might be examined from the disciplinary perspective by any researcher using the idea of African centrality. Particularly useful in the context of drama, dance, the plastic arts, and literature, the aesthetic senses represent an Afrocentric approach to the subject of African art.

The Shape of the Discipline

The groundedness of observations and behaviors in the historical experiences of Africans becomes the main base for operation in the field of Africans becomes the main base for operation in the field of African American Studies. Centrism, the operation of the African as subject (or the Latino as subject or the European as subject, and so forth), allows Africology to take its place alongside other disciplines without hierarchy and without hegemony. As a discipline, Africology is sustained by a commitment to centering the study of African phenomena, events, and persons in the particular cultural voice of the composite African people. But it does not promote such a view as universal. Furthermore, it opens the door for interpretations of reality based upon evidence and data secured by reference to that world voice.

The anteriority of the classical African civilizations must be entertained by any Africalogical inquiry, simply because without that perspective, our work hangs in the air, detached, and isolated or becomes nothing more than a sub-set of the Eurocentric disciplines. As I have often said, without Afrocentricity in this way, our research becomes disconnected, without historical continuity, incidental, and nonorganic.

The Eurocentric dogma creates an intellectual structure that locks the African in a conceptual prison. One key to this dogma is that philosophy is the highest discipline and that philosophy is Greek. Thus, Greece becomes the model for the structure of knowledge in the West. According to this dogma, everything starts with the Greeks: philosophy, politics, art, drama, literature, and mathematics. There is no philosophy in Africa, Asia, or the Americas, only the Europeans have philosophy. However, since the first Greek philosophers, Thales and Socrates, studied philosophy in

Kemet (Ancient Egypt), philosophy could not have started with the Greeks. Cheikh Anta Diop, perhaps the greatest African intellect of the 20th century, argued that there could be no understanding of things Africans without linkage to ancient Kemet. Thus, Egypt is to the rest of the African world as Greece is to the rest of the European world. Europe constitutes itself around several principles including its connection, however mythical or distant, to ancient Greece, to certain ideas that are traced to the Greeks and to the Romans, and to Christianity as a unifying theme from the 10th century A.D.

Subject Fields

To say that Africology is a discipline does not mean that it is without subject fields or interest areas. There are seven general subject fields which I have identified following the work of Maulana Karanga in *Introduction to Black Studies*: communicative, social, historical, cultural, political, economic, and psychological. Most of the people who are working in the fields are approaching their work from one of the above subject fields. A student of Africology chooses a research issue that fails within one or more of these subject fields. In any endeavor to uncover, analyze, criticize, or anticipate an issue, the Africalogist works to use the appropriate methods for the subject. To examine cultural nationalism, for example, within the historical or political subject field would require a consonant method for research.

There are three paradigmatic approaches to research in Africology: *functional*, *categoral*, and *etymological*. The first represents needs, policy, and action orientations. Categoral refers to schemes, gender, class, and themes. The etymological paradigm deals with language, literatures, and oratures. Studies of either sort might be conducted in the context of African society, either on the continent or in the Americas. The aim is to provide research results that are ultimately verifiable in human experience.

A student of Africology might choose to study in the general field of history but use the functional paradigm. Or choose psychology and use the etymological paradigm. Of course, many combinations are possible and the student is limited only by her or his ability to properly conceptualize the topic for study in an Afrocentric manner. Since Africology is not history, political science, communication, literary analysis, or sociology, the student must be well-grounded in the assumptions of the Afrocentric approach to human knowledge.

Scholars in our field have often been handicapped in their quest for clear and authoritative statements by a lack of methodological direction for collection and analyzing data, choosing and interpreting research themes, approaching and appreciating cultural artifacts, and isolating and evaluating facts. This has been the case, although works by Larry Neal and Paul Carter Harrison in the literary theory field introduced us to the possibilities inherent in our own centered positions as early as the Sixties. However, as an increasingly self-conscious field African American Studies, Africology, has begun to produce a variety of philosophical approaches to Afrocentric inquiry. These studies have served to underscore the need for solid methodological studies at the level of basic premises of the field and have become, in effect, pioneer works in a new perspective on phenomena.

Afrocentric psychologists have led in the reconceptualization of the field of African personality theories. Among the leaders in this field have been people like

Daudi Azibo of Temple, Wade Nobles of San Francisco State, Joseph Baldwin of Florida A and M, Linda James Myers of Ohio State, and Na'im Akbar of Florida State University. They have explored areas of human psychology which impinge on the African experience. Political Scientists qua political scientists such as Ronald Walters, Leonard Jeffries, Mack Jones, Manning Marable and James Turner have argued positions that may be called Afrocentric. Maulana Karenga, Patrick Bellegarde-Smith, and Jacob Carruthers, from their original base in political science, have become Afrocentrists. The work of Houston Baker in the area of vernacular theory might be considered Afrocentric inasmuch as the source of his images are culturally centered. In addition, the works of several writers, such as Henry Louis Gates, Abu Abarry, Joyce Joyce, and Eleanor Traylor have elements of centered locations. The field of sociology, since the early days of the first departments in 1882 and 1884 at Chicago and Columbia respectively, has remained bogged down in social problems and paradigms that do not permit adequate assessment of African cultural data. A number of African American sociologists are attempting to break out of those quagmires. Robert Staples had been an early pioneer in this field and now the work of Bruce Hare at Syracuse is significant in this respect. Vivian Gordon has long been a major force in the Africana Womanist project in which sex and race are joined rather than separated as in the work of the Afrofemcentrists or the Black Feminists. Indeed, Gordon's work is joined with that of Clenora Hudson Weems and Brenda Verner to make the most Afrocentric statement on the woman question we have seen in Africology. They have found their models, like Dona Marimba Richards, in the ancient models of Auset-Ausar and Mawu-Lisa. In design and architecture, scholars such as Bill Harris at the University of Virginia are exploring Afrocentric designs in housing. What would we have done without the porch as a day-care platform?

Africology is defined as the Afrocentric study of phenomena, events, ideas, and personalities related to Africa. The mere study of African phenomena is not Africology but some other intellectual enterprise. I make no judgment on those enterprises, I simply say that they are not Africalogical. Like other disciplines, more or less severe, our discipline is based upon certain assumptions, objectives and constructions of language. Thus, the Temple Circle of Afrocentric scholars have tried to exorcise terms such as sub-Saharan, Hottentot, Bushmen, pygmy, and minority. Such a massive project of redressing and de-centering of Africans will surely take us deep into the 21st century. The scholar who generates research questions based upon the centrality of Africa is engaged in a very different research questions based upon the centrality of Africa is engaged in a very different research inquiry than the one who imposes Western criteria on the phenomena. Afrocentric is the most important word in the definition, otherwise one might think that any study of African phenomena or people constitutes Africology. It is the commitment to perspective and method that distinguishes the discipline from others.

Geographical Scope

The geographical scope of the African world, and hence, the Africalogical enterprise, includes Africa, the Americas, the Caribbean, various regions of Asia and the Pacific. Wherever people declare themselves as African, despite the distance from the continent or the recency of their out-migration, they are accepted as part of the African world. Thus, the indigenous people of Australia and New Guinea are considered African and in a larger context subjects for Africalogists who maintain a full analytical and theoretical discussion of African phenomena.

Although the major regions of the African culture are Africa, the Caribbean and the Americas, even within those regions there are varying degrees of cultural and technological affinity to an African world voice. Africology is concerned with Africans in any particular as well as all regions. Thus, Abdias do Nascimento, our visiting professor from Brazil at Temple this year, can remind us that Brazil is significant for understanding the African presence in the Americas. In Brazil, Zumbi, the greatest king of the Palmares Republic, Luisa Mahin, and Luiz Gama are principal figures in the making of history; in the Dominican Republic, Diego de Campo and Lemba provide the same historical and intellectual energy one finds in Venezuela with Oyocta, King Miguel, and King Bayano; and in Columbia there is Benkos Bioho; and Mexico the Great African American, Yanga.

Africology rejects the Africanist idea of the separation of African people on the continent from African people in the Diaspora as being intellectually short-sighted, analytically vapid, and philosophically unsound. One cannot study Africans in the United States or Brazil or Jamaica without some appreciation for the historical and cultural significance of Africa as source and origin. The reactionary position that sees African American Studies as African Slave Studies, that is the making and the un-making of the slave, is categorically rejected. Thus, if one studies Africans in a Northeast city in the United States, one must do it with the idea that one is studying African people, not Made-in-America Negroes without historical depth. This has a direct bearing on data gathered for any analysis or study of African people. The researcher must examine everything possible to be able to make an adequate case. Actually the gathering of data must proceed on the basis that everything that can be used must be used. Therefore, it is impossible for a person to become an Africalogist simply by using the historical method, or the critical method, or the experimental method, and so forth. In order to become the best type of Africalogist one must use all the elements of data gathering, in any particular area, for an adequate assessment. This means that I might have to use literary analysis and historical analysis in examining one theme or issue. Video records and oral records are as important as written records and must be seen as a part of the portfolio of documentation that is available to the Africalogist.

The Temple Project

A final statement ought to he made about the classificatory aspects of Africology. These ideas are given within the framework of the creation of the doctoral program at Temple. Two fields, cultural aesthetics and social behavioral, exist in our department. They are the results of debate, discussion, consensus within the faculty. With twelve faculty members we have established a reputation for intellectual debate and dialogue that opens the discourse on discipline questions. Africology is a severe discipline. It became necessary for us to commit traditional discipline suicide in order to advance Africology within the structure of the university. The students we are training will not have that particular problem. They will start out being Africalogists who have read everything in their concentrations, as well as the theoretical works in the discipline. Already we have seen our students expand the discourse in almost every field. Thus, we have proposed the following two areas of research and responsibility.

Creative, inventive, artistic, literary:
epistemic issues, ethics, politics, psychology, and modes of behavior;
scientific issues, history, linguistics, economics, and methods of investigation;
artistic issues, icon, art, motifs, symbols, and types of presentation

Social, behavioral, action, historical:
relationships, the living, the dead, the unborn;
cosmos, culture, race, class, gender; mythoforms,
origins, struggles, victories; and
recognitions, conduct, designs, signs

These principal areas, cultural/aesthetic and social/behavioral, constitute the grounds upon which we must stand as we continue to build this discipline. I am certain that the scholars who will replace us will advance the relocating process in theory and practice as the generalship of the field improves in the give-and-take of critical debate. As it has been necessary in every aspect of the African's existence for the past five hundred years, it is also necessary in the area of human knowledge for us to struggle to enhance our perspective, recovering it from the distorted junk heap of Eurocentric hegemony. And, as in the past, there will be those scholars of whatever cultural and racial background who will understand our abiding interest in free and full inquiry from our own centered perspective and who will become the new Melville Herskovitz and Robert Farris Thompsons. A field of study must be open to all who share its perspective and methodology; ours is no different.

The future of Africology will depend upon those who are committed to the principles of academic excellence and social responsibility. Those principles must be interpreted within the framework of an Afrocentric vision in order to maintain a space and location for Africalogy within the Academy. I have no doubt that this will be done by the scholars and students who are coming after us. They will find in their own time and energy and will to carry out their intellectual mission as we are trying to carry out ours in order to create new spaces for human discussion.

References

Asante, Molefi K. *Afrocentricity.* Trenton: Africa World Press, 1987.

———. *Kemet, Afrocentricity, and Knowledge.* Trenton: Africa World Press, 1990.

———. *The Afrocentric Idea.* Philadelphia: Temple University Press, 1987.

Asante, Molefi K. and K.W. Asante. *African Culture: The Rhythms of Unity.* Trenton: Africa World Press, 1988.

Bellegarde-Smith, Patrick. *Haiti: The Breached Citadel.* Boulder: Westview Press, 1990.

Bradley, Michael. *The Ice Man Inheritance.* Toronto: Dorset, 1980.

Diop, C.A. *The African Origin of Civilization.* New York: Lawrence Hill, 1974.

———. *Civilization of Barbarism.* New York: Lawrence Hill, 1991.

———. *The Cultural Unity of Black Africa.* Chicago: Third World Books, 1976.

Gould, Stephen J. *The Mismeasure of Man.* New York: Norton, 1981.

Karenga, M. *Introduction to Black Studies.* Los Angeles: University of Sankore Press, 1987.

Keto, C.T. *The Africa-Centered Perspective of History*. Blackwood, N.J.: K & A Publishers.

Marable, Manning. *How Capitalism Underdeveloped Black America*. Boston: South End Press, 1983.

Mosse, George. *A History of Racism in Europe: Toward the Final Solution*. Madison: University of Wisconsin Press, 1985.

Nascimento, Elisa. *Pan Africanism and Sough America*. Buffalo: Afrodiaspora, 1979.

Obenga, Theophile. *The African Origin of Philosophy*. Paris: Presence Africaine, 1990.

Richards, Dona. *Let the Circle Be Unbroken*. Trenton: Africa World Press, 1991.

Rodney, Walter. *How Europe Underdeveloped Africa*. Washington: Howard University Press, 1980.

32.

Reaching for Higher Ground: Toward an Understanding of Black/Africana Studies

James B. Stewart

Introduction

This chapter explores two issues that are central to assessing the current developmental trajectory of Black/Africana Studies. The issues of particular concern are (a) the nature of the linkage between traditional disciplines/approaches to inquiry and Africana Studies, and (b) the concept of Afrocentricity and its impact on the current status and future development of the field.

The first issue has been discussed and debated extensively over the last two decades. The debate has intensified recently, in part due to the visibility afforded to writings by literary critics and historians who, although they identify primarily with traditional disciplines, assert connections to Black Studies (Baker, 1984; Gates, 1988; Harris, Hine, and McKay, 1990; Huggins, 1985). This turf battle has re-energized discussions about the nature of Black Studies, i.e., is it a self-contained and distinct body of knowledge or simply an adjunct to traditional disciplines?

The second issue is of more recent origin. The work of Asante (1980, 1987, 1990) and other prominent figures who employ complementary approaches, e.g., Maulana Karenga (1982, 1988, 1990), have popularized the concept of Afrocentricity both within and outside academe. Their contributions and those of an older generation of "scholarly/community griots" (John Henrik Clarke and Josef Ben-Jochannon) have spurred commentators outside of academe to develop popularized "Afrocentric" analyses. These popular treatments have been integrated into various media, including music and film. Unfortunately, the analytical precision of the academic conceptions is typically lacking, with accuracy sometimes sacrificed for the sake of art.

"Popular Afrocentrism" is being confused increasingly with systematic intellectual approaches in the field. This confusion has contributed to a distorted view of the state of the field and is fueling uneasiness in some circles about the intellectual credibility of Black/Africana Studies.

The context outlined above grounds the present discussion. First, an overview of evolving conceptions of the field over the last two decades and the rationales used to support those conceptions is presented. That discussion serves to explicate why the disjunction persists between discipline-linked and stand-alone models. It also attempts to establish the general limitations of traditional disciplines to inform modern Black/Africana Studies. The focus is on the general linkage between traditional disciplines in the aggregate and Black/Africana Studies. The third section examines the field's specific linkages to the subject areas of history, literature/literary criticism, and psychology.

The significance of the concept of Afrocentricity for Black/Africana Studies is explored in the fourth section. The concept is first defined and critiqued. Its use in three systems of thought identified with the field is then examined.

The final section suggests possible directions for future development that can address the problems identified in the preceding sections. A synthesis of elements of the field's three major systems of thought is proposed as a foundation for future efforts.

In Search of a Philosophical Base

Conceptions of Black/Africana Studies. The general academic and non-academic conceptions of the field are first discussed. Attention is then focused specifically on academic conceptions of Africana Studies. Five distinct rationales used to support various academic conceptions of the field are explored.

Allen (1974) provides a useful classification of modern conceptions of Black Studies that emerged during the formative stage of the late 1960s and early 1970s. Three conceptions were identified: (1) an *academic conception* that treats the mission of Black Studies as researching black history and illuminating the contributions of blacks; (2) an *ideological conception* that identifies Black Studies as an instrument of cultural nationalism; and (3) an *instrumental conception* whereby the role of Black Studies is to serve as a vehicle for social change within black communities.

Allen's scheme is a useful reminder that discussion of the relationship between Black/Africana Studies and traditional disciplines cannot ignore the historical symbiotic relationship between academic and political conceptions of Black Studies. However, throughout the formative period and subsequently there have been efforts to de-emphasize the linkage between scholarship and social activism. As a consequence, care must be taken in discussing the relationship between Black/Africana Studies and traditional disciplines to avoid misrepresentation of the multifaceted character of the enterprise.

These concepts require modifications to accommodate both the Marxist school of thought and the emergent Africana Women's Studies movement. The Marxist approach rejects cultural nationalism as the appropriate ideological orientation and simultaneously denies the usefulness of traditional disciplinary demarcations. This approach is consistent with the view of Karl Marx (1971, p. 44) who wrote, "we know only of a single science, the science of history." Marxist scholars, of course, have advocated aggressively for strong linkages between academic inquiry and political struggle. They are, in fact, responsible for institutionalizing this value by coining the slogan, "Academic Excellence and Social Responsibility." This phrase has been adopted as the official motto of the National Council for Black Studies.

The Africana Women's Studies movement is challenging traditional patterns of male chauvinism in the field. Two intellectual tendencies exist within this movement. One school of thought embraces the field's long standing cultural nationalist ideology. It urges the forging of a new partnership between Africana men and women in pursuit of previously articulated intellectual and political objectives (*see* Henry and Foster, 1982). The second school of thought elevates feminism to a higher ideological status than cultural nationalism (*see* Hull, Scott, and Smith, 1982). Advocates of the second approach tend to be more directly connected to traditional academic disciplines than are their counterparts and, more specifically, they are clustered in the areas of literary criticism and creative writing. The specific disciplinary linkages and the visibility afforded those advocating priority to feminist perspectives have reinforced the misperception that the principal bases of activity in Black/Africana Studies are in the humanities or outside academe.

Although the historical precedents of the field were clearly forged outside of academe, the locus of development during the modern era has been and remains solidly inside the academy. Moreover, as emphasized in the next section, within the academic arena the social sciences, rather than the arts and humanities, have come to provide the major models that have shaped conceptions of the field.

Disentangling Academic Conceptions. The extreme version of Allen's academic conception is exemplified by the comments of Blassingame (1969), who argued that Black Studies programs were inappropriate vehicles for promoting development in black communities. Ford (1974, p. 224) defines the field almost exclusively as an academic venture: "The term Black Studies refers to educational courses concerned with the study of research in various aspects of the experience, attitudes, and cultural artifacts of peoples of African origin.... Black Studies is concerned primarily with the history, literature, art, music, religion, cultural patterns and lifestyles developed in America by a race of people cut off completely from all contact with the land of their origin." Russell (1975, p. 185) takes a similar approach arguing that Black Studies "....has a respectable body of knowledge and researchable content with the Black humanities and social sciences comprising its core curriculum..."

General descriptions of this type spawned five more specific approaches to justifying the existence of a distinct body of knowledge: (1) the value-added rationale, (2) rationale by negation, (3) multidisciplinary rationales, (4) rationales based on applications of Western philosophies of science, and (5) rationales based on historical precedent.

Value-Added Rationales: The language used by Allen in describing the academic conception of Black Studies and the specifications of Ford and Russell are useful for establishing a baseline position regarding the linkages between Black/Africana Studies and traditional disciplines. All three statements ascribe a special status to the humanities and the social and behavioral sciences. In addition, all three implicitly employ what can be described as a "value added" rationale for the existence of the field. In other words, Black Studies has a legitimate role in academe because it extends the explanatory power of traditional disciplines. Significantly, the issue of whether the theories and methods utilized in traditional disciplines are directly applicable without modification to the study of the experiences of peoples of African descent is not addressed. As a consequence, this line of argument can support either a model of "black studies" as a subset of the knowledge base of traditional disciplines or a model identifying "Black Studies" as a self-contained and distinct body of knowledge.

In recognition of this problem, another strategy used to differentiate between Black/Africana Studies and traditional disciplines is rationale by negation.

Rationale by Negation: This approach both critiques the limitations of traditional theories and methods and defines the distinct nature of Black/Africana Studies analyses. This unique aspect of the field is said to emanate from the synthesis of either the academic and ideological or the academic and instrumental sub-missions. To illustrate, Alkalimat (1973, pp. 187-188) argues that "the conceptual approach of white social science is only useful on the analytical level of classification since for each term the social content must be specified. The concepts presented for a Black social science clearly suggest a specific socio-political content to be understood as the race problem." In a complementary vein, McClendon (1974, p. 18) asserts that "Black Studies will insist that students examine and comprehend a multitude of theories and teachings. The relevance of each body of knowledge to black liberation can be determined only through obtaining an understanding of the substantive content."

Jackson (1970, p. 132) claims that Black Studies scholarship should be geared toward improving life in the black community, an approach that would be accomplished by creating a closer symbiosis "between pure and applied roles of science with a greater stress on application of knowledge."

These approaches to synthesis do not introduce any particular conceptual difficulty in linking social-scientific and humanistic approaches in a self-contained model of Black/Africana Studies. This is true, in part, because the concept of a "black aesthetic" provides a parallel in the humanities and the arts to the idea of a unique "black" value orientation and observational language in the social sciences of the type suggested by Alkalimat (1973) and McClendon (1974). Potential problems do arise, however, in reconciling an "arts for arts' sake" philosophy with the notion of instrumental knowledge. In addition, the disjunction between social scientific and humanistic approaches has contributed to a gradual decline in the frequency of formal statements about the role of humanistic scholarship and the creative arts as integral components of Black/Africana Studies.

The social sciences increasingly have become the senior partner in the social science/humanities/creative arts nexus of Black/Africana Studies. It is from that vantage point that Karenga (1982, p. 32) asserts that "Black Studies, as both an investigative and applied social science, poses the paradigm of theory and practice merging into active self-knowledge which leads to positive social change. In a word, it is a discipline dedicated not only to understanding self, society and the world but also to them in a positive developmental way in the interest of human history and advancement."

If, as Karenga argues, Black Studies is a discipline, then how does it relate to other disciplines? One approach to answering this question involves attempts to define the field as a combination of existing disciplines, i.e., articulation of a *multidisciplinary rationale*.

Multidisciplinary Rationales: Distinctions can be drawn between weak and strong multidisciplinary rationales. *Weak multi/interdisciplinary rationales* take the existing disciplinary structure as given but argue that Black/Africana Studies provides unique added value because it develops knowledge that represents disciplinary syntheses. Most advocates of this position simply assume that because Black/Africana Studies examines aspects of life experience that cut across traditional disciplinary boundaries, the resultant analyses are by definition interdisciplinary. However, virtually no attention is devoted to the examination of the underlying theoretical constructs necessary for "interdisciplinarity" or "multidisciplinary" to be manifested.

The weak multidisciplinary rationale can be contrasted to what can be described as the *strong multidisciplinary rationale*. The principal distinctions between the two are (a) the efforts of advocates of the strong rationale to ground their arguments in the philosophy of science, and (b) the emphasis on subject areas rather than disciplines as the unit analysis. One important statement of this position is found in

Karenga (1982, pp. 35-36): "Black Studies...as an interdisciplinary discipline has seven basic subject areas. These intradisciplinary foci which at first seem to be disciplines themselves are, in fact, separate disciplines when they are outside the discipline of Black Studies, but inside, they become and are essentially subject areas which contribute to a holistic picture and approach to the Black Experience. Moreover, the qualifier Black, attached to each area in an explicit or implicit way, suggests a more specialized and delimited focus, which of necessity transforms a broad discipline into a particular subject area. The seven basic subject areas of Black Studies then are: Black History; Black Religion; Black Social Organization; Black Politics; Black Economics; Black Creative Production (Black Art, Music and Literature); and Black Psychology."

In particular, several critical questions can be raised regarding Karenga's assertions, including (1) does the transformation from discipline to subject area involve the transformation of the underlying disciplinary constructs, (2) how can affixing the prefix "black" produce the hypothesized transformation, and (3) if Black/Africana Studies is a social science how exactly are the subject areas of black history, black religion, and black creative production integrated into the enterprise?

Questions of the type proposed above are typically within the province of the philosophy of science. And, in fact, some proponents have turned to this field to generate a fourth approach to establishing the case for the intellectual legitimacy of Black/Africana Studies.

Western Philosophy of Science-Based Rationales: Various scholars including Karenga (1988); Stewart (1979, 1982a, 1982b); and Turner (1984) have used this approach to clarify the intellectual project of Black/Africana Studies. The most popular framework used is that of Kuhn (1970), although selected analyses draw upon the writings of other philosophers including, Lehrer (1975) and Toulmin (1972) (see Stewart, 1982a). Even members of the Marxist school of thought have adapted Kuhn's basic constructs to explicate their approach to the field (see Alkalimat, 1990).

In contrast to the use of Western philosophies of science as a means to generate analogies, Asante (1987) has used the work of critical theorists as a foil to differentiate their project from that which he ascribes to "Africalogy." This thrust is understandable given the neo-Marxist overlay associated with the constructs of most critical theorists. Asante's commitment to cultural nationalism thus engenders an approach to critical theory that is a variant of the rationale of negation.

In general, the use of Western philosophies of science to define Black/Africana Studies has further removed the humanities and the arts from center stage. Philosophies of science are just that—philosophies designed to examine intellectual processes in scientific disciplines, not intellectual processes associated with other areas of inquiry. In fact, even the range of applicability across different scientific fields is restricted. Generally, philosophy of science models have been fashioned to examine intellectual processes in the physical and natural sciences. Thus, even the extension of the models to the social and behavioral sciences requires relaxation of some critical assumptions. The role of the humanities and the arts in Black/Africana Studies further complicates matters. Moreover, as described in Stewart (1982a), there remains the problem of how to handle the activist mission of Black/Africana Studies within a philosophy of science framework.

Toulmin's (1972) specification of the necessary conditions for disciplinary status highlights the nature of the problem. For Toulmin (1972, p. 133) an area of inquiry develops into a scientific discipline when it has "one and only one set of well-defined goals at a time (that is explanation of phenomena falling within the scope of the disciplinary inquiry), and one set of selection-criteria." Reconciling this notion of discipline with Karenga's specification of Black Studies as a discipline presented previously is a major intellectual task.

While acknowledging these caveats regarding the applicability of philosophy of science models to describe Black/Africana Studies, experimentation with such models has added substantial precision to the discussion of many important topics. As a means of illustration, Kuhn (1970) introduces the use of the term "research paradigm" to characterize the specific application of the scientific method within an area of inquiry. The term "disciplinary matrix" was later offered as an alternative to "paradigm." Disciplinary matrices are said to be comprised of four components: (a) a metaphysical component; (b) values shared by practitioners; (c) symbolic generalizations, observational language, and research methods, and (d) exemplars (concrete examples of the application of the theoretical and empirical framework).

The metaphysical component of disciplinary matrices consists, in part, of beliefs about the explanatory power of particular models.

One metaphysical component that could be used to differentiate Black/ Africana Studies analyses from other investigations is the model of peoples of African descent as actors continuously striving to achieve sufficient power to maintain their cultural identity and define their collective destiny. This model contrasts with alternative "metaphysical" orientations that either treat blacks as perpetual victims or as a population of individuals in the process of assimilating Euro-American culture. Other beliefs that differentiate Black/Africana Studies from competing orientations include the preference for collectives rather than individuals as the unit of analysis and the emphasis on modeling social processes as cyclical rather than linear phenomena.

In Kuhn's model, the second component of the disciplinary matrix values actually has two sub-categories: macro- and micro-order values. Kuhn (1970) uses the example of beliefs in whether or not "science should or need not be socially useful" as an example of a macro-order value, and indicates that scientists in a field may disagree about this issue. This observation has clear relevance for the earlier discussion of the disagreement between those committed to a more detached academic conception of Black/Africana Studies and those advocating for a more applied research focus. The operative point is that Kuhn's framework provides a means for incorporating such discussions in a way that reaffirms the "scientific" character of Black/Africana Studies. Micro-order values are beliefs about the nature of the scientific enterprise that guide the behaviors and judgments of practitioners. For example, some micro- order values specify how the relative merit of competing theories is to be judged. Again, the relevance to the earlier discussions about differences among the academic conceptions of Black/Africana Studies Occasional Papers are obvious. Black/Africana Studies analyst/activists who support a stand alone conception of the field place more weight on the applicability of knowledge to guide social change than on esoteric explanatory power, measured, for example, by statistical robustness. In addition, there are potential tradeoffs among judging criteria. In Black/Africana Studies, theories and applied analyses are judged on the bases of "beauty," "functionality," "rhythm," and "compatibility with folk wisdom," in addition to "precision." Consequently, precision could be self-consciously sacrificed to achieve other objectives in some cases.

Micro-order values also address how information generated by practitioners in the discipline is to be disseminated. In traditional disciplines, there is typically a stated preference between articles in referred journals and monographs. In the case of Black/Africana Studies, the multiple missions have led to emphasis on monographs and on another mode of dissemination, i.e., public speeches. The controversy surrounding a speech given by Leonard Jeffries in July 1991 is instructive regarding the strengths and weaknesses associated with this medium.

Rationale by Exemplar: The generation of a body of exemplars to support the documentation of an intellectual history of Black/Africana Studies is consistent with the metaphysical belief in cyclical social processes. Intellectual production is also a social process. This means that historical theory and praxis can serve as a means of gauging the degree of compatibility between contemporary scholarship/activism and long term cultural trends in these arenas.

Since many traditional disciplines are largely products of the twentieth century, Black/Africana Studies predecessors were not saddled with the ideological baggage associated with twentieth century disciplines. In addition, prior to the affirmation of the social values of disciplinary specialization and detachment of academics from the public sphere, it was much more likely that scholars would be engaged in a wide range of activities in addition to intellectual inquiry.

The multiple missions of Black/Africana Studies necessitate the generation of a much wider variety of exemplars than envisioned by Kuhn. In particular, the expectation that practitioners win not be simply scholars but scholar/activists suggests the importance of examples of historical figures who combined scholarly activity and social activism in ways comparable to that advocated for contemporary Black/Africana Studies scholar/activists. Thus, there is a need for a collection of biographies of figures whose value orientation mirrors that of the contemporary Black/Africana Studies community. Strengthening the instrumental and nationalist dimensions of the field will require examples of how quasi-autonomous African and African American societies organized social relations. Conversely, examples of failed attempts would facilitate identification of ineffective strategies that should not be replicated.

In the cases of both individual "intellectual/activist autobiographies" and "community development models," "pure" cases of unambiguous correspondence to contemporary values win not be found. The reality of the historical experiences of peoples of African descent and the pattern of domination of the intellectual landscape by traditional disciplines will cause most case studies to exhibit significant ambiguity. Consequently, the most useful exemplars are likely to be composites of several examples rather than distinct individual cases.

In some cases, the generation of exemplars involves the wresting of "heroes" and "heroines" from the clutches of other fields. To illustrate, Stewart (1984) has provided an interpretation of the life, career, and writings of W.E.B. DuBois that clearly defines him as a predecessor of modern Black/Africana Studies. Earlier interpretations either linked DuBois' writings to specific disciplines or subject areas, or examined his political movements in isolation from his scholarly activity. These approaches necessitated the use of edited volumes in an attempt to capture the complexity of his life and writings (see, for example, Clarke, Jackson, Kaiser, and O'Dell, eds., 1970). This "shotgun" approach mirrors the attempt through individual traditional disciplines to capture the complexity of the experiences of peoples of African descent.

From this vantage point, Stewart's Black/Africana Studies interpretation of DuBois eliminates the clumsiness and fragmentation of discipline-oriented interpretations. It can serve, then, as an exemplar for a general approach that could be usefully applied to examine a variety of historical figures, including Maria Stewart, Martin Delany, Edward Blyden, Alain Locke, and Zora Neale Hurston. In the case of Locke and Hurston, efforts to graft simplistic discipline oriented interpretations or topical treatments have been undertaken by scholars outside of Black/Africana Studies, comparable to those applied to DuBois (*see* Linneman, 1982 and Wallace, 1990).

There are a number of African American societies that would be appropriate subjects for the type of historical community studies advocated above. These include the various maroon societies-communities founded as a result of the Exoduster movement: Mound Bayou, Mississippi; Durham, North Carolina; and Promiseland, South Carolina (*see* Painter, 1977; Bethel, 1981; Herman, 1981; and DuBois, 1912).

Unfortunately, only limited attention is currently directed at developing the types of exemplars described above. Current attention is focused disproportionately on classical African civilizations, and in particular on ancient Egypt or Kemet. The thrust of interest in this area in general has been to identify the African origins of Egyptian civilization and, more specifically, to document the extensive presence and impact of peoples of sub-Saharan African origin in various dynasties. This research is necessary and important for several reasons. It provides the ammunition to mount a direct attack on traditional interpretations of ancient Egyptian society as a pseudo-European civilization. The Europeanization of Egypt has facilitated the efforts of historians of Western thought to project the notion of a continuous intellectual history of strictly European lineage. Current research that debunks this interpretation can provide a foundation for reconstructing a continuous intellectual history of African thought that can connect to modern Black/Africana Studies.

The examination of value systems in classical African civilizations prior to the emergence of Western political domination can provide exemplars that can clarify the metaphysical and values components of the Black/Africana Studies disciplinary matrix. In such societies, peoples of African descent were rulers rather than subjects. As a consequence, their world views were not shaped by the history of domination that has conditioned much of the thought of peoples of African descent who were kidnapped and transplanted to the West. Studies of classical civilizations have also identified individual figures who can serve as exemplars for contemporary Black/Africana Studies scholar/ activists, e.g., Imhotep.

Despite the potential benefits associated with the study of classical African civilizations, there are drawbacks to such an emphasis. Unfortunately, the vast majority of the scholarship to date is contributionist in orientation, rather than undertaking systematic investigation of the degree of applicability of classical ideas and social formations for the present and future. Most of these studies have embodied a "rationale by negation," with the goal of disputing traditional claims that ancient Egyptian civilization bore little connection to sub-Saharan Africa. Little effort has been made to shape these studies in ways that contribute to the generation of the continuous intellectual history advocated previously. Finally, the focus on Kemetic studies needs to be balanced with comparable levels of scrutiny of other classical African civilizations and societies/communities in the Western Hemisphere.

Summary: In this section five general approaches to establishing the intellectual credibility of Black/Africana Studies have been explored. The discussion has examined the relationship between the field and traditional disciplines. Although no effort was made to establish a temporal progression in the development of the various rationales, the different approaches could be loosely grouped into "early" and "contemporary" rationales. The first category would encompass the value added, negation, and multidisciplinary rationales, while the philosophy of science and exemplar rationales constitute more contemporary approaches. The intellectual ground established by the contemporary approaches is generally more solid than that associated with the earlier lines of argumentation.

Recognition of the evolutionary path of academic justifications used in promoting the field is helpful in approaching the examination of the confluence of specific disciplines or areas of inquiry with contemporary Black/Africana Studies.

Afrocentricity and the Ontology
of Black/Africana Studies

The principal thrust in this section is to explicate how the concept of Afrocentricity is affecting efforts to refine the Black/Africana Studies disciplinary matrix. That discussion first requires critical examination of the concept of Afrocentricity. Some definitions or specifications of Afrocentricity have created the perception that the concept reflects a closed and homogeneous ideology. However, as emphasized in the introduction to this chapter, there are critical distinctions between academic and popular conceptions. Further, there are also subtle but important differences among various academic conceptions.

Afrocentricity. Two distinct claims are generally identified with the concept of Afrocentricity. What will be termed the "strong claim" is the assertion that the liberation of peoples of African descent requires a psychological reorientation that focuses on reconstructing selected aspects of traditional African psychology, values and behaviors in the present. The "weak claim" entails the position that liberation requires that top priority be assigned to the interests of peoples of African descent in social and political intercourse with other collectives.

Most of the criticisms directed at Afrocentricity have relevance only with respect to the strong claim. Three specific criticisms will be considered for clarification. One criticism suggests that predetermined models of society and individual behavior are attached to the concept that adherents seek to impose on all peoples of African descent. A related criticism alleges that the models of society and individual behavior celebrated by Afrocentrists are drawn from epochs long past and are largely irrelevant to the modern world. A third criticism suggests that the concept encourages racial chauvinism and inter-group conflict by asserting the superiority of peoples of African descent relative to other populations.

There is no question that the most "radical" formulations of Afrocentricity are vulnerable to the criticisms cited above. However, as implied above, these radical formulations are grounded in the strong rather than the weak claim. Some formulations, for example, reject the possibility that non-Africans can generate authentically Afrocentric analyses through application of some type of biological notion of race and culture. One line of reasoning identifies the chemical melanin as the source of unique powers inherent in African peoples. Another position makes the case for racial/cultural distinctiveness among groups using evolutionary models. As an example, Nichols (1990) uses a quasigeographical/ biological evolutionary model to argue that different survival imperatives in diverse climates generated systematic and continuing variation in the world views, axiologies, epistemologies, and logics employed by different groups.

This latter approach establishes a foundation for the existence of multiple and parallel centrisms. However, some Afrocentrists who acknowledge plural centrisms generally also aggressively attempt to distinguish Afrocentricism from Eurocentrism. Advocates of this view argue that Eurocentrism is plagued by an inherent predisposition toward control and domination that produces attempts to create hierarchical rather than cooperative relationships with other peoples. It is argued that this predisposition is absent in other centrisms.

There are obviously a number of critical issues that require further discussion in respect of the nature of, and relationship among, centrisms. Space does not permit such a discussion. For present purposes, however, the most critical question is the extent to which specific groups have maintained culturally conditioned or biologically determined privileged access to certain types of knowledge or ways of knowing over time. This question is problematic because, as noted previously, the treatment of the phenomenon of "race consciousness" among African Americans in the historical scholarship focuses on the problem of "psychic duality" or "double consciousness." This concept invokes imagery of the bifurcation of the African American psyche. The general conclusion reached by historical writers is that the optimal solution to this dichotomy is achieving a balance between the two components of the psyche with the African/African American component providing the core structure. In contrast, as discussed earlier, the radical school of African American psychologists generally argues that it is necessary to eradicate totally au non-African constructs from the psyche for Africans and African Americans to attain mental health and pursue liberation effectively.

One of the implications of psychic duality is that it will (a) generally increase the degree of disjunction between expressed ideology and observed behavior, and (b) reduce self-efficacy. To illustrate, DuBois (1979) argued that "incessant self-questioning and the hesitation that arises from it...is making the present period a time of vacillation and contradiction for the American Negro; combined race action is stifled, race responsibility is shirked, race enterprises languish, and the best blood, the best talent, the energy of the Negro people cannot be marshalled to do the bidding of the race."

Further clarification can result from examining a specific form of the strong claim that reflects the type of psychological dynamics implied above. For the sake of argument, let Afrocentricity refer to the degree of overlap between an idealized model of thought and behavior generated from an interpretation of traditional African thought and practice and an individual's actual thought and behavior. The process of becoming, Afrocentric, then, can be disaggregated into three components: (a) increasing the causal connection between an individual's expressed ideology and observed behavior; (b) increasing the degree of overlap between an individual's impressed ideology and observed behavior and the modal thought and behavior of African Americans (or Africans depending on the selected reference group); and (c) increasing the degree of overlap between an individual's current expressed ideology and behavior and the ideology and behavioral patterns advocated by "strong claim" Afrocentrists.

The foregoing suggests that systematic intervention strategies will be required to facilitate the Afrocentric transformation of individuals. But this is a project that is more compatible with the mission of those trained in psychology than that of Black/Africana Studies grand theorists. The normal inquiry of the field's generalists is not likely to affect individual psyches directly.

Asante (1987, p. 6) suggests that Afrocentricity entails "placing African ideals at the center of any analysis that involves African culture and behavior." Karenga (1990, p. 1) suggests that Afrocentricity entails thought and practice "in the cultural image and human interests of African Americans." Within the context of these "weak claim" specifications, two general guidelines can be offered regarding the praxis of Black/Africana Studies scholar/ activists. First, the field's disciplinary matrix must incorporate provisions for a collective process to determine "the cultural image and human interests of African Americans" rather than allowing special interests to dominate dialogue and impose a set of artificial strictures. Second, the intellectual leaders in the field must advocate simultaneously for the necessity of "placing African ideals at the center of analyses involving African culture and behavior" and the right of individuals and collectives to determine the course of their own intellectual production and personal development.

These suggested guidelines are designed to recognize that individual and collective psychology are both developmental and cyclical in character. They seek to minimize unproductive labeling and conflicts over ascriptive status rather than intellectual coherency. Although these definitions allow for cultural exchange, they do not specifically define the boundaries of race and culture as they relate to scholarly inquiry. To illustrate, Asante (1990, p. 40) suggests that as a theory, Afrocentricity "is not, nor can it be, based on biological determinism. Anyone willing to submit to the discipline of learning the concepts and methods may acquire the knowledge necessary for analysis." The specifics of the linkage between Afrocentricity and selected stand-alone paradigms are examined in more detail below.

Afrocentricity and the Black/Africana Studies Disciplinary Matrix. The focus of this discussion is how the concept of Afrocentricity is linked to the disciplinary matrix of Black/Africana Studies. A comparison of the use of the concept in different systems of thought is undertaken. The frameworks examined are those of Asante, Karenga, and a collective of Marxist-oriented scholars (see Alkalimat and Associates, 1986).

Figure 1 presents a classification scheme that clarifies the conceptions of the field discussed to this point. The contributions of Asante and Karenga are identified with a conception of the field as a "Disciplinary Matrix Driven Enterprise." The Marxist collective's "Paradigm of Unity" is identified with a view of the field as an "Adjunct to Traditional Metatheories." Figure 1 characterizes various other conceptions including syntheses of traditional disciplinary perspectives, adjuncts to traditional disciplines, and selective Afrocentric foci. These other conceptions are peripheral to efforts to generate a fully developed disciplinary matrix.

Specific components of the systems of thought developed by Asante, Karenga, and the Marxist collective are compared in Figure 2.

Focusing first on the function concept of Afrocentricity, per se, it is critical to note that in Karenga's system, the concept is derived from a model of culture based on the Nguzo Saba. From this vantage point, the term "Afrocentricity" simply renames a focus that was inherent in the values expressed by the Nguzo Saba. These values constitute a synthesis of various African traditions rather than being culled from the examination of classical African civilizations per se, although the usefulness of the value framework has been reinforced by Karenga's research examining classical African civilizations (see, for example, Karenga, 1990).

Asante's contribution is a theory of inquiry for the discipline of Africalogy built upon the concept of Afrocentricity. Africalogy is defined as "the Afrocentric study of African concepts, issues, and behaviors" (Asante, 1987, p. 16). Asante (1990, p. 141) asserts, in the spirit of Karenga (1982), that "Africalogy is a separate and distinct field of study from the composite sum of its initial founding disciplines," i.e., seven subject fields comparable to those specified by Karenga (Asante, 1990, p. 12). In addition, the geographical locus of the field is defined as the African world, i.e. "Wherever people declare themselves as African, despite the distance from the continent or the recentness of their outmigration" a concept that "includes Africa, the Americas, the Caribbean, various regions of Asia and the Pacific" (Asante, 1990, p. 15).

Asante's concept of Afrocentricity is generated from the general concept of centrism. According to Asante (1990, p. 12) "Centrism, the groundedness of observa-

---

Figure 1

**Categorization of Alternative Conceptions
of Black/Africana Studies**

1. Black/Africana Studies as a Disciplinary Matrix Driven Enterprise
       Kawaida Theory (Karenga)
       Africalogy (Asante)
2. Black/Africana Studies as a Discipline constituting syntheses of
   Traditional Disciplines
       Multidisciplinists
       Non-disciplinists
3. Black/Africana Studies as an adjunct to Eurocentric Metatheories
       Marxism—Paradigm of Unity (Alkalimat and Associates)
       Feminism
4. Black/Africana Studies as a sub-component of Individual Disciplines
       History
       Literature
       Sociology
5. Black/Africana Studies as a Component of Non-Disciplinary
   Aggregates
       African Studies
       American Studies
       Ethnic Studies
       Multi-Cultural Studies
6. Black/Africana Studies as expressions of selective emphases
       Kemetologists
       Melanists
       Generalized Folk Approaches

---

tion and behavior in one's own historical experiences, shapes the concepts, paradigms, theories, and methods of Africalogy." Africalogy is said to incorporate three paradigmatic approaches: functional, categorical, and etymological (Asante, 1990, pp. 12-13). According to Asante (1990, p. 6) "The Afrocentrist seeks to uncover and use codes, paradigms, symbols, motifs, myths, and circles of discussion that reinforce the centrality of African ideals and values as a valid frame of reference for acquiring and examining data."

Although Asante's definitional grounding appears at first glance to be holistic and comprehensive, more detailed scrutiny reveals the continuing influence of his earlier training in the field of communication. He asserts that the effort is to "bring the consciousness of rhetorical structure to the study of African communication" and "set a conceptual field for exploring the Afrocentric perspective on discourse where *nommo* as word-force is a central concept (Asante, 1987, p. 17). This focus on language undergirds a notion of social dynamics whereby "social or political change is nothing more than the transmitting of information as an act of power" (Asante, 1987, p. 35). It is from this value framework that Asante (1987, p. 16) defines Africalogy as "systematic exploration of relationships, social codes, cultural and commercial customs, and oral traditions and proverbs, although interpretation of communicative behaviors, as expressed in discourse, spoken or written, and techniques found in jazz studies and urban street-vernacular signifying, is also included."

Figure 2

Comparison of Systems of Thought
Associated with Black/Africana Studies

Comparative Criteria	Kawaida Theory	Systematic Africology	Paradigm of Unity
Concept of	"In the cultural image and human interest of African Americans"	"placing African ideals at the center of any analysis that in volves African culture and behavior"	Unspecified
Treatment of Gender	In the context of male/female relationships	Unspecified	As a biological category
Theoretical Focus	Theory of Culture	Theory of Inquiry	Theory of Social Change
Theoretical Emphasis	Social Organization Cultural Authenticity	Authenticity of Knowledge and Culture	Socal Dynamics Class Relations
Key Constructs	Nguzo Saba	Afrocentricity Nommo	Social Cohesion Social Disruption
Treatment of Race	Cultural (Emphasis on Consciousness	Cultural (Emphasis on Language and Symbols)	Biological
Observational Language (Degree of Transformation	Partial	Complete	Standard Marxist
Subject Areas	History, Religion, Social Organization, Economic Organization, Political Organization, Creative Production, Ethos	Society, Communication, Historical, Culture, Politics, Economics, Psychology	Consciousness, Society, Economy, Biology
Periodization Scheme	Unspecified	Unspecified	Two-state cycle
African Emphasis	Classical Civilization	Classical Civilization	Traditional Pre-slave trade
General Methodology for Assessing Research	Determine if a study can be incorporated into a theoretical	Locate study in an Africalogi-Grid synthesis	Locate study in a Temporal/Structural Grid
Special Data Sources	Classical Texts	Oral and Visual Data	Collections of Primary Source Materials
Central Crises Threatening Africana Peoples	Cultural Amnesia Eurocentrism	Dislocation Eurocentrism	Capitalism Racism
Resistance Strategies	Creation of a National Culture	Centering	Class Consciousness

One of the interesting characteristics of Asante's formulations is that it overlaps significantly with the perspective advanced by Gates (1988) discussed previously. Specifically, both scholars focus on communication and language as the foundational frame of reference. For Gates, "signifying" becomes the dominant mode of discourse because it reflects cultural powers in conflict. This notion is similar to the imagery invoked by Asante in discussing the concept of "Nommo." The point is that Asante's concepts are very much discipline-tied and area specific and that in many respects he and Gates stand on the same ground. The question is whether the field can reach higher ground by synthesizing multiple foci. As noted previously, the contributions of Karenga and the Marxist collective provide alternative foci.

Focusing again on Figure 2, it is critical to understand that the extent to which a system of thought is Afrocentric is only one of many criteria that are relevant for judging the overall usefulness of a conceptual framework. A comparative examination can facilitate refinement of the field's composite disciplinary matrix by identifying the collective strengths and weaknesses of its major systems of thought. As an example, none of the frameworks address the issue of gender adequately and the collective treatment of history is weak.

Ameliorating the collective weaknesses in the self-contained systems of thought under discussion is a strategy that can guide efforts to refine the collective disciplinary matrix in a manner that can help Black/Africana Studies scholar/activists to reach higher ground. This requires a foundation in the form of a synthesis that reflects the strengths of each system of thought, i.e., a theory of history (Marxists), a theory of society (Karenga), and a theory of inquiry (Asante). The beginnings of such a synthesis are outlined below.

Reaching for Higher Ground

Several directions for the continuing development of the Black/Africana Studies disciplinary matrix can be gleaned from the preceding discussions. In particular, seven developmental thrusts can contribute significantly to the project: (1) generation of a theory of history, (2) articulation of a theory of knowledge and social change, (3) delineation of a theory of race and culture, (4) expansion of the scope of inquiry encompassed by the disciplinary matrix, (5) expanded examination of the historical precedents to modern Black/Africana Studies, (6) increased emphasis on applications of theoretical work, and (7) strengthened linkages to interests outside academe to minimize misappropriation of knowledge and improve information dissemination. Space does not permit a detailed discussion of each point, but an effort is made below to suggest possible directions in each area.

DuBois (1953) warned that "there is...on the part of the overwhelming majority of the people in the world, a feeling that the Anglo-Saxon type of cultural organization has failed and that new cultural patterns should be tried, and that for the trial of these new cultural patterns there is demand for cultural democracy and intercultural tolerance. That without this, civilization in its present form is doomed." In this spirit, the refinement of the Black/Africana disciplinary matrix is critical for the salvation of human civilization and for ushering in the multicultural world that DuBois envisioned. This chapter has attempted to establish the ground upon which Black/Africana Studies scholar/activists can stand to meet this challenge.

References

Airhihenbuwa, C. Race and Health Care in America," *The Western Journal of Black Studies* 9, 4 (1985): 204-211.

Alkalimat, A. "The Ideology of Black Social Science," in J. Ladner, ed., *The Death of White Sociology*. New York: Random House, 1973.

Alkalimat, A., and Associates. *Introduction to Afro-American Studies: A Peoples College Primer*. Chicago: Twenty-First Century Books and Publications, 1986.

Alkalimat, A., ed. *Paradigms in Black Studies*. Chicago: Twenty-First Century Books and Publications, 1990.

Allen, R. "Politics of the Attack on Black Studies," *The Black Scholar* 6, 1 (September 1974): 2-7.

Asante, M. *The Afrocentric Idea*. Philadelphia: Temple University Press, 1987.

———. *Afrocentricity: The Theory of Social Change*. Buffalo: Amulefi Publishing Co., 1990.

———. *Kemet, Afrocentricity and Knowledge*. Trenton, NJ: Africa World Press, 1990.

Baker, H. *Blues, Ideology and African-American Literature*. Chicago: University of Chicago Press, 1984.

Baldwin, J. "The Psychology of Oppression," in M. Asante and A. Vandi, eds., *Contemporary Black Thought*, pp. 95-100. Beverly Hills, CA: Sage Publications, 1980.

Bethel, E. *Promiseland; A Century of Life in a Negro Community*. Philadelphia: Temple University Press, 1981.

Blassingame, J. "Black Studies: An Intellectual Crisis," *The American Scholar* (1969): 38.

Boyi, H. "From the Sixties to the Nineties: The Problematics of Canon Formation in Afro-American Literature" (June 1991). Paper prepared for the NCBS Summer Faculty Institute, Ohio State University.

Brossard, C. "Classifying Black Studies Programs," *The Journal of Negro Education* 53 (1984): 278-295.

Bullard, R. *Dumping in Dixie: Race, Class, and Environmental Quality*. Boulder, CO: Westview Press, 1990.

Cheatham, H., and Stewart, J., eds. *Black Families, Interdisciplinary Perspectives*. New Brunswick, NJ: Transaction Publishers.

Clarke, J. H., Jackson, E., Kaiser, E., and O'Dell, J. H., eds. *Black Titan: W.E.B. DuBois*. Boston: Beacon Press, 1970.

Coulburn, Rushton, and DuBois, W.E.B. "Mr. Sorokin's Systems," *Journal of Modern History* 14 (1942): 500-521.

Cross, W. "The Negro-to-Black Conversion Experience." *Black World* (July 1971): 13-27.

———. "The Thomas and Cross Models on Psychological Nigrescence: A Literature Review," *Journal of Black Psychology* 4 (1978): 13.

———. *Shades of Black Diversity in African-American Identity*. Philadelphia: Temple University Press, 1991.

Diop, C.A. *African Origins of Civilization, Myth or Reality*. M. Cook, ed. & trans. Westport, CT: Lawrence Hill, 1974.

———. *The Cultural Unity of Black Africa*. Chicago: Third World Press 1990.

DuBois, W.E.B. "The Beginnings of Slavery," *Voice of the Negro* 2 (1905): 104-106.

———. "The Evolution of the Race Problem," *Proceedings of the National Negro Conference* (1970): 142-158.

———. "The Upbuilding of Black Durham," *World's Work* 13 (1912): 334-338.

———. [Review of *History of the Negro Church*]. *The Freeman* 6 (1922).

———. "The Social Origins of Negro Art," *Modern Quarterly* 3 (1925).

———. "Negroes and the Crisis of Capitalism," *Monthly Review* 12, 4 (1953): 478-485.

———. "Race Relations: 1917-1947," *Phylon* 9 (1948): 245-249.

———. "The Field and Function of the Negro College" (Alumni Reunion Address, Fisk University, 1933). Reprinted in H. Aptheker, 2 ed., *W.E.B. DuBois: The Education of Black People, Ten Critiques 1900-1960*. Amherst: University of Massachusetts Press, 1973.

———. "Postscript," *The Ordeal of Mansart*. Millwood, NY: Kraus Thomson, 1976. Reprinted from Mainstream Publishers, 1957.

———. "The Conservation of Races," in P. Foner, ed., *W.E.B. DuBois Speaks: Speeches and Addresses 1890-1919*. New York: Pathfinder Press, 1979. (Originally published as Occasional Paper No. 2, American Academy Occasional Papers, 1897.)

Ford, N. "Black Studies Programs," *Current History* (November 1974).

Gayle, Addison, ed. *Black Aesthetic*. Garden City, NJ: Doubleday, 1971.

Gates, H. *The Signifying Monkey: A Theory of Afro-American Literary Criticism*. New York: Oxford University Press, 1988.

Hanson, A., and Martin, R. "The Problem of Other Cultures," *Philosophy of the Social Sciences* 3 (1973): 191-208.

Herman, J. *The Pursuit of a Dream*. New York: Oxford University Press, 1981.

Harris, R., Hine, D., and McKay, N. *Three Essays, Black Studies in the United States*. New York: Ford Foundation, 1990.

Hendrix, M., Bracey, J., Davis, J., and Herron, M. "Computers and Black Studies: Toward the Cognitive Revolution," *The Journal of Negro Education* 53 (1984): 341-350.

Henry, C., and Foster, F. "Black Women's Studies: Threat or Challenge?" *The Western Journal of Black Studies* 6, 1 (1982): 15-2 1.

Huggins, N. *Report to the Ford Foundation on Afro-American Studies*. New York: Ford Foundation, 1985.

Hull, G., Scott, P.B. and Smith, B. *All the Women Are White, All the Blacks Are Men, But Some of Us Are Brave: Black Women's Studies*. Old Westbury, NY: Feminist Press, 1982.

Jackson, M. "Towards a Sociology of Black Studies," *Journal of Black Studies* 1, 2 (December 1970): 131-140.

Jaynes, G. and Williams, R., eds. *A Common Destiny: Blacks and American Society*. Washington, DC: National Academy Press, 1989.

Karenga, M. *Kawaida Theory: An Introductory Outline.* Inglewood, CA: Kawaida Publications, 1980.

———. *Introduction to Black Studies.* Los Angeles: University of Sankore Press, 1982.

———. "Black Studies and the Problematic of Paradigm," *Journal of Black Studies* 18, 4 (1988): 395-414.

———. "The Challenge of Culture: A Kawaida Analysis." An Outline of a presentation delivered as part of the Summer Faculty Institute organized by the National Council for Black Studies, Ohio State University, Columbus, Ohio (June 1990).

———. "Towards a Sociology of Maatian Ethics: Literature and Context," in *Reconstructing Kemetic Culture*, pp. 66-96. 1989.

Kuhn, T. *The Structure of Scientific Revolutions*, 2nd ed. Chicago: University of Chicago Press, 1970.

Lehrer, K. "Social Consensus and Rational Agniology," *Synthese* (1975): 23.

Linnemann, R., ed. *Alain Locke, Reflections on a Modern Renaissance Man.* Baton Rouge: Louisiana State University Press, 1982.

Marable, M. "The Modern Miseducation of the Negro: Critiques of Black History Curricula," in *Institute of the Black World, Black Studies Curriculum Development Course Evaluations*, pp. C1-C28. Conference I. Atlanta: Institute of the Black World, 1981.

Marx, K. Reprinted in A. Schmidt, *The Concept of Nature in Marx.* London: NLB, 1971. (Originally printed in *Marx-Engels Gesamtsausgabe, V, Part I* Berlin: 1932.)

McClendon, W. "Black Studies: Education for Liberation," *The Black Scholar*, (September 1974).

Nobles, W. "African Philosophy: Foundations for Black Psychology," in R. Jones, ed., *Black Psychology*, pp. 23-36. New York: Harper & Row, 1980.

Painter, N. *Exodusters: Black Migration to Kansas After Reconstruction.* New York: Knopf, 1977.

Russell, J. "Afro-American Studies: From Chaos to Consolidation," *The Negro Education Review* (1975): 25.

Sorokin, P. *Social and Cultural Dynamics*, vols. 1-4. New York: Bedminster Press, 1937-41.

Stewart, J. "Black Studies and Black People in the Future," *Black Books Bulletin* 4 (1976): 21-25.

———. Introducing Black Studies: A Critical Examination of Some Textual Materials," *UMOJA* 3 (1979): 5-18.

———. "Alternative Models of Black Studies," *UMOJA* 8 (1982): 17-39.

———. *Toward Operationalization of an Expansive Model of.* An analysis prepared for the Black Studies Curriculum Development Project, Institute of the Black World, Atlanta, Georgia, 1982.

———. "Factors Affecting Variation in Published Black Studies Articles Across Institutions," *The New England Journal of Black Studies* 4 (1983): 72-83.

———. "Psychic Duality of Afro-Americans in the Novels of W.E.B. DuBois," *Phylon* 44 (June 2, 1983): 93-108.

————. [Review of *An Introduction to Black Studies*]. *The Western Journal of Black Studies* 7 (1983): 113-117.

————. "The Legacy of W.E.B. DuBois for Contemporary Black Studies," *The Journal of Negro Education* 53 (1984): 296-311.

————. "Kondratieff Cycles and the Political-Economic Status of Blacks in the United States" (1985 mimeo).

————. "Toward a Black Studies — S-STS Interface." An analysis prepared for the project "Improving the quality of secondary science and technology instruction for urban and minority students through science/technology/society," STS Urban Education Project, U.S. Department of Education, 1987-88. Leonard Waks, Principal Investigator.

Toulmin, S. *Human Understanding*, vol. 1. Princeton, NJ: Princeton University Press, 1972.

Turner, J. "Africana Studies and Epistemology, A Discourse in the Sociology of Knowledge," in J. Turner, ed., *The Next Decade: Theoretical and Research Issues in Africana Studies*, pp. 23-36. Ithaca, NY: Africana Studies and Research Center, 1984.

———— and McGann, C.S. "Black Studies as an Integral Tradition in African-American Intellectual History," *Issue* (1976): 73-78.

Upton, J. "Applied Black Studies: Adult Education in the Black Community — A Case Study," *The Journal of Negro Education* 53 (1984): 322-333.

Wallace, Michele. "Who Owns Zora Neale Hurston? Critics Carve Up the Legend," *Invisibility Blues*. London: Vengo, 1990.

Willie, C., Garibaldi, A., and Reed, W. *The Education of African-Americans*, New York: Auburn House, 1991.

Woodson, C. *The History of the Negro Church*. Washington, DC: Associated Publishers, 1922.

Wright, R., ed. *African Philosophy: An Introduction*, 3rd ed. Lanham, MD: University Press of America, 1984.

Young, C., and Martin, G. "The Paradox of Separate and Unequal: African Studies and Afro-American Studies," *The Journal of Negro Education* 53 (1984): 257-267.

V

Section V

Theoretical Foundations

Key Concepts and Major Terms

- Theoretical Foundations
- Theory
- Conceptual Models
- Theoretical Models
- Frameworks
- Empirical Generalizations
- Qualitative Method
- Anti-Foundationalism
- Decursive Field
- Afrocentric Metatheory
- Location
- Double-Consciousness
- Ideological and Philosophical Concepts

- Disciplinary Modifications
- Classical Africa
- African-Centered
- Afrocentric Paradigm
- Traditionalist Paradigm
- Feminist Paradigm
- Radical Movement
- Paradigm of Unity
- Normative Theory
- Policy Making
- Institutionalization
- Reconstruction Approach
- Methodological Approaches

- Professional Standards
- African Worldview
- Africentrism
- Theoretical Coherence
- Disciplinary Matrix
- Theory of Knowledge
- Theory of Race & Culture
- Subjectivity
- Conflict Theory
- Experimentation
- Objectivity

Introduction

In any academic discipline, there exist varying, oftentimes even conflicting, conceptual and theoretical models, methods and paradigms. Theory incorporates new and alternative models and frameworks that are designed to give meaning and provide clarity to existing information, as well as to provide the building blocks for the foundation and construction of new knowledge. The essential functions of theory in African American Studies are to provide a general orientation to the important concepts central to the discipline; establish parameters regarding form and content, formulate empirical generalizations by fusing qualitative and quantitative methods; utilize different paradigms and disciplinary modifications in the interplay of theory and practice (see the introduction to Section I).

Given its unique history in higher education, African American Studies has also experienced numerous ideological shifts throughout its evolution. Ideological shifts over the course of the first ten years (1968-1978), following the institutionalization of the field, revolved around various notions of inclusion. For example, practitioners considered whether it should be interdisciplinary or multidisciplinary. They asked what academic form African American Studies should take: department, program, institute or center? Did African American Studies constitute a separate, autonomous academic discipline or was it merely a field of study or an area of inquiry? Would there be degrees conferred or certificates in concentration awarded? Were whites capable or qualified to teach African American Studies?

The second decade (1978-1988) was marked by a rise in interpretative challenges which sought to approach historical and intellectual information from a classical African or African-centered perspective, popularly known as "afrocentricity." No other theoretical perspective in African American Studies has generated the caliber of debate among scholars within and without the academy than that of Molefi Asante. Among his propositions was the contention that African American Studies must begin with and center around the life experiences and principles of Africans the world over (namely, ancient Egypt).

From 1968 to the present, African American Studies has mainly been seeking solutions to the myriad of challenges it has confronted questions posed from its inception. Such matters are discussed in this section.

Philip T.K. Daniel, in "Theory Building and Black Studies," posits that "Many of the problems in Black Studies are directly related to the affirmation that little systematic theoretical work has been done in the field. The lack of theoretical linkages in Black Studies is one thing, but far more disturbing is the attempt by some individuals to subsume theory building in Black Studies under other academic disciplines.... The whole emphasis on objectivity and empirical theory as opposed to normative theory is out of place in Black Studies and the arguments concerning it should be dropped."

In "Black Studies: Overview and Theoretical Perspectives," Talmadge Anderson illustrates the fact that "Academically, a discipline refers to a specific body of teachable knowledge with its own set of interrelated facts, concepts, standardized techniques and skills. Black Studies emanates from an African or African American ethos and background. Thus, Black Studies may be defined as an interdisciplinary field of study or discipline that systematically treats the past and present culture, characteristics, achievements, issues, and problems of the black race and in a context that interacts relevantly with other peoples of the world."

In "Toward A Paradigm of Unity in Black Studies," Abdul Alkalimat notes that: "Afro-American Studies is designed to meet people's need to understand the Black experience. Before considering the specific content of that experience, one should have some grasp of the broad field of Afro-American Studies. We [must] discuss Afro-American intellectual history, Afro-American scholarship within the traditional academic disciplines, and the radical movement for Black Studies in the 1960s and 1970s. The institutionalization of the field is the current stage of Afro-American Studies, one likely to carry into the 21st century. This involves the issues of curriculum, program, professional standards, and theoretical coherence to the field."

Molefi K. Asante, in "The Afrocentric Metatheory and Disciplinary Implications," defines: Afrocentricity [as] a metatheoretical framework, a philosophical position... Africology, as an area of inquiry, aspires to reach mature disciplinary status.

As such, it must address a portion of what it does to the generating of conceptual focus... Africology is defined as the Afrocentric study of phenomena, events, ideas, and personalities related to Africa. The mere study of African phenomena is not Africology but some other intellectual enterprise."

In "Articulating the Distinction Between Black Studies and the Study of Blacks: The Fundamental Role of Culture and the African-Centered World View," Daudi Ajani ya Azibo posits that: "In order to develop a matured apprehension of the concept of Afri- or Afro-centricity (or any terminological variant like Africentrism, African-centered, Africentric, African-centric, and so on) it is imperative to understand that fundamentally what is being referred to is (and can only be) no more or less than the very foundational thought-base upon which rests the conceptual ideation that has proved to be characteristic of African people's civilizations.... The African worldview is the answer. When Africans do not embrace it, our wretchedness ensues; when Africans cleave to it, sustention and great achievement are attained."

Philosopher Lucius Outlaw, in "Africology: Normative Theory," posits that "... [Africology] can be taken to mean theoretical discourse about norms in general—what they are, their basis, etc.—but discourse steered by partisan foreconceptions about 'Africans.' On the other [hand], it can be understood as referring to (or calling for) the specification of particular norms for Africology as a disciplinary complex. The third possibility is the notion that Africology should conceptualize (theorize) and prescribe norms by which peoples of African descent ought to live a 'way of life.' In each of these cases, the concern is with the specification of rules to guide action—whether in the context of a research enterprise (i.e. rules to govern production, producers, the quality and distribution of the products) or the social, historical, worlds of peoples of African descent."

33.

Theory Building in Black Studies

Philip T.K. Daniel

Many of the problems in Black Studies are directly related to the affirmation that little systematic theoretical work has been done in the field.[1] Moreover, I want to argue that many of the approaches to theory building in Black Studies which have heretofore been suggested are unsatisfactory. That is, they represent attempts that have had little direction or ones that have erroneously sought to subsume the field of Black Studies under another academic discipline. Following this analysis, this essay will present some suggestions for an unambitious, but perhaps more satisfactory, effort toward theory building in the multidiscipline. Much of the latter discussion will be geared toward the creation of fundamental postulates that this author believes all or most ventures into Black Studies must abide by.

When we look for constructs or postulates in Black Studies we find a collection of unordered attempts at theory building. Theories in Black Studies are like ships steaming ahead toward one destination, but at different longitudes. This obviously means that if they all keep their present course, only one, or perhaps none will reach the docking point. Thus, they will be in a perpetual circular motion until they run out of fuel.

At the top of the longitudinal scale there are numerous speculative ideas about cultural patterns rooted in an African or eastern philosophy, or social theories immersed more in reality with the goal of fundamental change of the social order. For example, Charles Frye, in his work "Black Studies: Definition and Administrative Model" posits the idea that Black Studies is essentially an eastern philosophy with "Black cultural patterns...characterized by a feeling-intuitive-subjective-internal-figurative-wholistic-communal...approach to life and living. Turner and Perkins, on the other hand, dismiss such attempts toward spiritualism by indicating that the goal of Black Studies should be to direct the social, economic, and political forces which oppress and exploit the black studies should be to "disect the social, economic, and political forces which oppress and exploit the black masses."[3]

At a slightly lower longitude we discover scholars who advocate theories which are consistent with Robert Allen's three conceptual categories in Black Studies: (1) those that emphasize the creation of a knowledge base, (2) those concerned with the establishment of a discipline and (3) those which purport to be rooted in the black community.[4] Nick Aaron Ford's *Black Studies: Threat or Challenge* helped to define the area of study and added to our knowledge of the kinds of programs in existence.[5] Articles by Nathan Hare,[6] Charles Hamilton[7] and Ronald Bailey[8] all provided initial steps in the establishment of Black Studies as a representative and permanent field of study. Robinson, et al., and their *Black Studies in the University*[9] helped us to realize that of all the disciplines, Black Studies sought to immerse itself in the black community and in black problem solving techniques.

There are, of course, numerous other important works that sought to add theoretical knowledge to the field. But no matter how much this review of research is padded, this exercise will still come to the same set of conclusions. *First*, progress in the field of Black Studies must attempt to link and build upon all of these ideas. In other words, they must all be put on a collision course, resulting in their meeting at the same place at the same time. *Second*, a realistic and viable set of postulates, which may encompass all or most of these ideas, must be delineated so that efforts in the field, intellectual or practical, can be scrutinized and criticized for the good or ill they do for the black community.

If you desire more support for this thesis, I am not alone in my assessment of the state of affairs in Black Studies. James Stewart, of the Pennsylvania State University, espouses a similar point of view when he says that "no school of thought within the Black Studies movement has developed a basic framework for analysis."[10] In addition Turner and Perkins of Cornell University comment that Black Studies theorists have done little in the way of espousing new theoretical concepts or constructs.[11]

Black Studies and Other Disciplines

The lack of theoretical linkages in Black Studies is one thing, but far more disturbing is the attempt by some individuals to subsume theory building in Black Studies under other academic disciplines. This has been attempted by several authors. Three will be examined in this essay.

One scholar thinks of Black Studies and its theoretical components as being embodied in the methodology of sociology. He defines Black Studies as "the systematic study of Black people" in social rather than racial terms.[12] All paradigms in this area must therefore be based on the "social" qualifier.

Another author views Black Studies as a component of the field of economics. He therefore proposes that blacks should be studied in the field under two approaches: (1) men of ideas, inventors and innovators, and (2) the successes and failures of blacks in their entrepreneurial history.[13] The qualifier in his analysis is that although blacks may be innovators and men of ideas, they may not perform the coordinating function of bringing together the "factors of production."

Still another researcher writes that the best approach to theory building in Black Studies is through an assortment of established disciplines "like economics, anthropology, sociology, psychology and so on."[14]

Unfortunately for these scholars, but fortunately for Black Studies theorists, classifying Black Studies under one academic discipline is an impossible task. In sociology, seeing the black experience in only social and not racial terms is ludicrous. One need look no further than the criticisms of William J. Wilson's study, *The Declining Significance of Race* to understand that.[15] In economics, the fact that blacks are not seen as important actors in the field of production smacks of ethnocentrism and the pinnacle of Anglo-Saxon, racist belief. And to suggest that Black Studies cannot exist without the covariant presence of several other disciplines represents the worst kind of conjectural puerilism, for it sees the black experience as the recipient of an alien academic process rather than one which can produce theoretical constructs of its own. Most other disciplines have something to offer Black Studies, but a Bohemian bazaar does not make for theory building.

We have engaged in a demolition operation of sorts. Nevertheless, the need for theory building and theoretical linkages remains for the remainder of this presentation. I would like to offer some suggestions for a more satisfactory way of proceeding toward theory. There must be a set of fundamental postulates that are missing at present. Without these postulates, we will have to take whatever other disciplines consent to throw to Black Studies. With a set of constructs we will help ourselves more selectively.

I am under no illusions about my ability to delineate my ideas or those of others, particularly within the limits of the current research. Nonetheless, some statements are attempted. In setting these forward, I do not mean to imply that they incorporate the final form of the subject. Indeed, I have adopted an attitude about Black Studies which is similar to that of V.F. Lenzen, who supports the notion of a "successive definition."[16] He notes that only through successions," i.e., allowing a discipline to constantly replenish itself, can we as Black Studies theorists hope to achieve success in forming a permanent body of knowledge. However, the current forms in the field are far from adequate and the next few years must bring the development of more imaginative classifications.

Knowledge and Change

In 1892 W.S. Jevans remarked that "almost every classification which is proposed in the early stages of a...[discipline]...will be found to break down as the deeper similarities of its objects come to be detected."[17] In other words, every paradigm, every taxonomy and every model proposed represents something which is provisional. As our, knowledge grows, so do our concepts and generations; and as our concepts and generalizations grow, so does our subject matter. As our subject matter grows, we learn more and our colleagues and proteges learn more. But as all this takes place in the beginnings of a multidiscipline, we must always see this theory building as provisional. It is this philosophy that I have internalized in talking about theory building in Black Studies.

Currently, the two principal pillars which support theory building in Black Studies are the concepts of: (1) knowledge development or consciousness raising and (2) the liberation of black people, translated as a change in the social, political and economic order. These concepts provide the link between the rhetoric that seeks to understand or manipulate the black experience and the actions which result. They also serve as the center pieces from which radiate the spokes of spiritualism, liberation, curriculum building, community autonomy, social and political reform and all the rest. They set Black Studies as an autonomous sphere of knowledge, understanding and action apart from other academic entities.

These building blocks are important to note, because they establish Black Studies as a vehicle for looking at the black experience, either past, present or future. When we look, for example, at the activities of Nat Turner, Denmark Vessey, Fred Hampton or Mark Clark or the writings of W.E.B. DuBois or Paulo Freire, we see elements of consciousness raising and/or attempts at the liberation of black people. At the same time when we look at Thomas Jefferson's *Declaration of Independence* or Bartolome de Las Casas' *The Relationship of Brevissima to the Destruction of the Indians* we see just the opposite. Using the development of consciousness and the change in the social order as theoretical backdrops, we are permitted to retrace, relive and predict the steps an individual or group has taken or will take vis-a-vis the black condition. We look at treatises individuals write; we examine the treatises written about their actions; and we always compare these to how they affect or have affected the black community.

Both intellectually and practically, the Black Studies theorist or analyst maintains the autonomy of Black Studies in the same way that members of other disciplines maintain theirs. He or she sees consciousness raising and change in the political, economic and social order as the fundamental concepts of Black Studies in the way same as an artist sees beauty, the educator sees knowledge or the anthropologist sees culture as fundamental concepts in their disciplines.

This essay has no quarrel with the Stewartian hypothesis that "a discipline implies only one set of selection criteria to determine what information qualifies as a component of its knowledge set."[18] Indeed, in another publication I have contended that the field of Black Studies is not a discipline but a multidiscipline."[19] We do take issue, however, with the contention that the development of black consciousness and black liberation are temporary conditions devoid of logical or conceptual systems.[20] Indeed, it is my contention that if ever that elusive condition of black liberation were achieved, theories on black consciousness would abound and be sustained in order to maintain the positive condition of the race.

The Black Studies theorist, also has no conflict with other disciplinary studies on the black experience. Doubtlessly, those in Black Studies are very much aware of the existence and relevance of some decent treatises in other disciplines on their domain. As separate entities they accomplish tasks for which no other disciplines are a substitute. However, a Black Studies analyst can only subordinate these standards or components to those theoretical building blocks already mentioned. And he certainly divorces himself from other disciplines when they impose standards of thought and deed and hence do injustice to his multidisciplinary sphere. In other words, when all is said and done, research and analysis in another field of study is no substitute for a job that should be done in Black Studies.

The concept of consciousness raising and a change in society impose a kind of framework for operating upon the black studies analyst and infuses a rational order in the information he must collect and digest. This makes understanding of actions past, present, and future, toward the black community possible. Without such concepts, theories in Black Studies, whether one examines the African continent, the Americas, a small segment of the black community or any other piece of real estate within its domain, would be altogether impossible.

Policy Making

The goal of Black Studies is not merely to seek knowledge for its own sake, but knowledge for the purpose of pragmatic manipulation. This is an instrumentalist view of theory building in Black Studies. That is, the significance of research and the uprooting of information lies in the actions they guide. Just as important is the conduct of research in Black Studies guided by momentous events and actions. The revolutions of the 1960s, the Black Studies analyst dedication to local, national and international causes, the interest that the scholar has in the betterment of the community, and our ever important task of advising policy makers about how to make substantive changes in our condition, must be the purpose of our substantive research.

It is important for the "policy" component of our multidiscipline to radiate directly to our theoretical center. In this sense a Black Studies analyst is simultaneously a theorist, a reformer and a pragmatic manipulator. His or her job is not only to provide studies in heritage and consciousness raising, but to also attempt to improve the lot of the black masses. A Black Studies analyst is well trained in a multitude of subjects, but his interests in these areas must be further distinguished by his or her total commitment to the betterment of the black community. In effect the Black Studies practitioner must be an "interested" scientist within the DuBoisian realm as opposed to a "disinterested" scientist in the Einstein realm.

The Black Studies analyst, therefore, parts company with other schools of thought when he/she deals with the important question of reform. He or she is persuaded that transformation of society can only occur through a look at all resources and forces that have shaped the past and will shape the future. The Black Studies analyst cannot be persuaded that change can be brought about by conformity to any current theory of practice that is rooted in "the obsolete ideological baggage"[21] of traditional non-sensitive disciplines.

Community as Core

When one attempts to comprehend a field of study, there is no better method than to draw questions and concepts from the action source. This action source in this instance is the black community, locally, nationally, and internationally. Black Studies, like all multidisciplines which involve themselves heavily in the social sciences, study and interact with people, not dispassionate and disinterested forces. It is people and groups of people, their successes and disappointments, their mores and values, their thoughts and actions, their institutions and their environment which affect progress in Black Studies. Therefore, the consideration of what happens to, in and around the black community is indispensable in Black Studies.

The Black Studies theorists must also be aware of all of the forces, black and non-black which impact on the black community. However, the basic stuff of theory building and analysis in Black Studies must have as its core the black community. DuBois in his analysis of the black college perhaps said it best... "the American (black) college cannot begin with history and lead to (black) history. It cannot start with sociology and lead to (black) sociology."[22] A Black Studies analyst must check his research and his activities against the movement in the black community, past, present and future, and not against inanimate objects or abstract theoretical constructs which make up the substance of other disciplines.

To reiterate, examination of what happens to, in or around the black community by Black Studies theorists is not enough. We must approach political, economic and social reality in society with the idea of seeing ourselves in the position of black leaders, or just plain ordinary black people, and we design strategies which serve to give better decisions, which give answers for bettering our condition. This means that the Black Studies analyst is "always intuitively testing the knowledge base of Black Studies via his daily interactions."[23]

Objectivity vs. Subjectivity

Theoretical constructs, whenever they are proposed, are usually attended by warnings about objectivity and the use of empirical rather than normative research methods. This paper will not abandon this procedure. However, the explanation given for judging objectivity and theories of some other disciplines will not conform to past practices.

Many Black Studies theorists, or perhaps those who are mistaken for Black Studies theorists, often act as if subjectivity in the field were some sort of researcher's separate and distinct personality to be locked away in the recesses of the mind. The contention is that objectivity, in a multidiscipline, represents the only way which we can create and establish true modes of thought and action. This means that the whole of the Black Studies experience must be compartmentalized in order to understand it and to insure that value judgements are not made about some particular form of behavior. The analytical models used to date, therefore expect members of the black family to be understood in terms of adjustment or maladjustment to their surroundings.

The philosopher Emmanuel Kant wrote that "judgement is indispensable because, even where we have rules for its exercise, judgement is required to apply the right rules to particular cases."[24] Theories in any discipline are not validated because they are accepted. Practitioners in the discipline accept theories because they believe them to be validated. The validation of theory is not the act of granting its existence, but the act of acting upon it. Said actions in Black Studies, although at tended by objective inquiry, are still actions and thus inherently subjective.

The whole emphasis on objectivity and empirical theory as opposed to normative theory is out of place in Black Studies and the arguments concerning it should be dropped. We scrutinize and act as we live. Analysis in Black Studies is a purposeful activity and the conditions of the black community involve questions of, right and wrong. To emphasize only objective behavior or to resort only to investigations that involve the scientific method is like trying to equate human nature to the movements of a puppet. The appendages only move when they are manipulated by some outside force.

This is no argument against scientific objectivity. However, we must move away from the kind of objectivity which tends to emphasize empty verbalization which is characteristic of many of the present day social sciences. They steer us into abstractions rather than practical problems. We are told that a practical problem may bias an investigation if it is carried out to provide justification for a policy. But the determination to exclude from an investigation the data and hypotheses pertaining to practical conditions may be just as much an expression of bias. Black Studies "is no better protected against biases by the entirely negative device of refusing to arrange its results for practical or political utilization."[25]

No Universal Altruism

The subject of ethics or altruistic principles is another corollary to theory building. I maintain that universal altruism cannot be applied to the theoretical constructs and subsequent actions that concern the black community. First of all there is no such thing as a universal philosophy that has no cultural base. Too often, other ethnic philosophies, disguised in the garb of a saint, have imposed themselves on the black populace with the result that we practice other people's ways of doing things better than they do. Altruistic principles cannot be applied to the actions of the black community in the absolute sense. They must be filtered through a process which looks at the condition of the community in existence at the time. There can be no universal altruistic principles without consideration of their consequences under black cultural circumstances.

Malcolm X in the book, *By Any Means Necessary*, said it best. When asked about the Gandhian Christian principle of non-violence, he said, "I've never heard of a revolution that was brought about by turning the other cheek, and so I believe that it is a crime for anyone to teach a person who is being brutalized to continue to accept that brutality without doing something to defend himself. If this is what the Gandhian philosophy teaches then it is criminal—a criminal philosophy."[26] The good of the black community, therefore, is the supreme virtue for all Black Studies theorists and analysts. Altruism in the abstract judges action by conformity to an equally abstract universal law. Black Studies analysts judge actions as either indifferent, for, or against the black community.

Conclusion

The foregoing analysis has attempted to contribute something, and I hope in the right direction, toward establishing a theoretical base in Black Studies. None of the postulates put forward is seen as the only way of looking at an action or deed that concerns the black community. In every multidiscipline, and quite obviously in Black Studies, the facts we gather are too numerous, too unstructured, and too open to interpretation to fit into one analysis. This treatise has tried to remedy some of that.

Nonetheless, I am positive that my attempt will not meet unanimous approval. I have accepted the fact that no proposed thought and no proposed theory can be made in isolation. These ideas need support and they desperately need discussion by scholars in the field of Black Studies. I hope they represent a step forward away from "the tyranny of tightly knit, gracelessly presented"[27] principles in other disciplines which only serve to deface and level criticisms on the black community.

Acknowledgements

I wish to acknowledge the research contributions and constructive criticism given by Dr. Admasu Zike. Without his help the scope of this paper would have been much more limited.

Endnotes

1. This statement has been explored by Daniel, Philip T.K., "Black Studies: Discipline or Field of Study?" *The Western Journal of Black Studies* Vol. 4, No. 3 (1980): 195-200.

2. Frye, Charles A., *Towards A Philosophy of Black Studies* (San Francisco: R and E Research Associates, 1978), p. 37.

3. Turner, James and Perkins, W. Eric, "Towards a Critique of Social Science," *The Black Scholar* Vol. 7, No. 7 (1976): 8.

4. Aflen, Robert, "Politics of the Attack on Black Studies," *The Black Scholar* Vol. 6, No. 1 (1974): 3.

5. Ford, Nick Aaron, *Black Studies: Threat or Challenge* (New York: Kennikat Press, 1973).

6. Hare, Nathan, "What Should Be the Role of Afro-American Education in the Undergraduate Curriculum?" *Liberal Education* Vol. 40, No. 1 (1969): 42-50.

7. Hamilton, Charles, "The Question of Black Studies," *Phi Delta Kappan* Vol. 57, No. 7 (1970): 362-363.

8. Bailey, Ronald, "Why Black Studies?" *The Education Digest* Vol. 35, No. 9 (1970): 41-47.

9. Robinson, et al., *Black Studies in the University* (New York: Bantam Books, 1969).

10. Stewart, James B., "Introducing Black Studies: A Critical Examination of Some Textual Materials," *Umoja* Vol. 3, No. 1 (1979): 8.

11. Turner and Perkins, *op. cit.*, p. 7.

12. Jackson, Maurice, "Toward A Sociology of Black Studies," *Journal of Black Studies* Vol. 1, No. 2 (1970): 132.

13. Ijere, Martin, "Whether Economics in A Black Studies Program?" *Journal of Black Studies* Vol. 3, No. 2 (1972): 151.

14. Kilson, Martin, "Reflections on Structure and Content in Black Studies," *Journal of Black Studies* Vol. 1, No. 3 (1973): 303.

15. Washington, Joseph R., ed., *The Declining Significance of Race: A Dialogue Among Black and White Social Scientists* (published proceedings of a symposium held at the University of Pennsylvania, March, 1979).

16. Lenzen, V.F., "Procedures of Empirical Science," *International Encyclopedia of Unified Science* Vol. 1 (Chicago, 1938), p. 19.

17. Jevons, W.S., *The Principles of Science* (London: MacMillan and Co., 1877), p. 58.

18. Stewart, James, "The Legacy of W.E.B. DuBois for Contemporary Black Studies," a paper presented at the 65th Annual Convention of the Association for the Study of Afro-American Life and History. This treatise is part of a larger work (soon to be book) and was funded by a grant from the National Endowment for the Humanities, p. 10.

19. For a complete definition of the term "multidiscipline" used in the Black Studies context see Daniel, Philip T.K., "Black Studies: Discipline or Field of Study?" *The Western Journal of Black Studies* Vol. 4, No. 4 (1980): 195-200.

20. Stewart, *op. cit.*, p. 10.

21. Turner and Perkins, *op. cit.*, p. 7.

22. DuBois, W. E. B., "The Field and Function of a Negro College," (Alumni Reunion Address, Fisk University, 1933) as quoted in Stewart, James, "Introducing Black Studies: A Critical Examination of Some Textual Materials," *Umoja* Vol. 3, No. 1 (1979): 15.

23. Stewart, "The Legacy of W.E.B. DuBois... *op. cit.*, p. 11.

24. Kant, Emmanuel, as quoted in Kaplan, Abraham, *The Conduct of Inquiry* (San Francisco: Chandler Publishing Company, 1965), p. 312.

25. Myrdal, Gunnar, *An American Dilemma* (New York: Harper Press, 1944), p. 1041.

26. Breitman, George, ed., *By Any Means Necessary* (New York: Pathfinder Press, 1970), p. 9.

27. Colodny, Robert G., ed., *The Nature and Function of Scientific Theories* (Pittsburgh: University of Pittsburgh Press, 1970), p. 301.

34.

Black Studies: Overview and Theoretical Perspectives

Talmadge Anderson

Historical Overview

The dramatic emergence and institution of Black Studies as an academic field at colleges and universities have few if any parallels in the history of American education. As a branch of knowledge, Black Studies in the United States does not attribute its origin to any European scientific theorist or philosopher of the seventeenth and eighteenth centuries as in the cases of the "traditional" disciplines. Moreover, formal curricula or programs did not begin initially as a result of America's acknowledgment of their omission nor voluntarily by enlightened faculty and academic administrators, especially at predominantly white institutions of higher education. However, Black Studies was founded formally as the result of petition, protest and demand by informed Black intellectuals and students for social, cultural, political and economic relevance in their education (Hare 1976; Karenga 1982). The movement by Black students and Black intellectuals for educational institutions, at all levels to integrate the study of African Americans into textbooks and curricula was often joined by white students who understood their own need to learn of the Black American's experience.

The development of Black Studies towards a legitimate and respected field of study evolved from a controversial process. At first, there was no agreement among scholars, faculty, administrators or students relative to definition, program structure, staffing and curricula design. Consequently, the field was accepted before it was totally defined.[1]

The demands for the initiation of Black Studies in American education was buttressed and aided by the Civil Rights Movement of the 1960s. Societal pressures for Black Studies began to build slightly with the assassination of Malcolm X, accelerated after the Black Power March of 1966, and escalated anew with the assassination of the civil rights leader Martin Luther King, Jr. in 1968. Prior to 1968 a small number of colleges began "experimenting" with "Negro" history and literature courses (Hare 1976). However, it was not until the end of 1968, after procrastination by the board of trustees, a flare up of campus riots, and Black community involvement that San Francisco State College became the first institution to establish a "formal" Black Studies program and department on the direction of Dr. Nathan Hare (Karenga 1984).

There were both white and Black proponents and opponents to establishing Black Studies as a separate field of study at colleges and universities. Whites questioned the "profundity" and "legitimacy" of courses treating solely the Black experience. Black opponents were concerned that separate and autonomous curricula in Black Studies would induce the voluntary segregation of Blacks and impede the progress achieved by integration towards the elimination of racism. Controversy relative to the acceptance of Black Studies as a legitimate academic field of study continued until in 1969 when Harvard University created an Afro-American Studies Department. Because Harvard is the archetypical institution of higher education in the United States, almost all other major colleges and universities followed its example by initiating various forms and structures of Black Studies courses, programs or departments.

The need and the demand for African American Studies emanated from the virtual systematic exclusion of the history, culture and experience of Black people from most academic and educational curricula. However, the exclusion of the Black experience from the American traditional academic curricula does not mean that scholarly research studies, books, various other literature and courses did not exist prior to the 1960s. For as Alex Poinsetts (1973) states:

> Despite this cultural deprivation in white academia, Black Studies—the multidisciplinary analogies of the experience of African peoples throughout the world—was born more than [60] years ago at some Black colleges under the tutelage of such distinguished Black scholars as W.E.B. DuBois, Carter G. Woodson, Charles S. Johnson, E. Franklin Frazier, Benjamin G. Brawley and Alain Locke. Both DuBois and Woodson stressed the importance of a "special" education for Black students to counteract the cultural bias built into white studies and to embrace broader areas of human endeavor. But these notions did not begin to gain a hearing in white colleges and universities until the 1960s....

Moreover, there is virtually no field, subject or disciplinary area relating to Black peoples of ancient Africa or African Americans in the New World that had not received major scholarly treatment between the late nineteenth century and the end of World War II, 1946. Both white and Black scholars contributed to the study of Black peoples during this period. The few eminent white scholars and forerunners in the study of African and African American peoples were Robert Park, the co-founder of the University of Chicago School of Sociology; Thomas Woofter, an economist who spent his professional life studying the socioeconomic status of Black Americans; and Melville Herskovits, an anthropologist who spent a lifetime studying Black societies throughout the world (Kilson 1973).

Definition, Relevance, and Rationale

Changes in the socioeconomic and political experiences of Blacks in America have, concomitantly, affected Black ideological perspectives relative to preferred terms of racial identification (Wright 1981). Since the Civil Rights Movement of the 1960s, Americans of African descent have repudiated "Negro" and "Colored" as labels of racial identity and "Black" has become the generally accepted term. More recently a prominent Black political figure urged the adoption of the ethnic description "African American." However, the description of "African American" is limiting and restrictive in concept. While "Black" connotes the universality of African peoples or the diaspora of Blacks, "African American" may refer technically and academically to only persons of African descent who are natives or citizens of the United States or

Latin America. Abdul Alkalimat (1986) considers "Afro-American Studies" to cover the entire American hemisphere, including North, Central, and South America, the Caribbean, and northern countries such as Newfoundland and Greenland. The concept of "Black Studies" is more comprehensive and universally accepted in the study of peoples of African descent.

Academically, a discipline refers to a specific body of teachable knowledge with its own set of interrelated facts, concepts, standardized techniques and skills. However, Black Studies draws upon and interacts significantly with the traditional disciplines of the arts, humanities, and the social and behavioral sciences. Clearly, then, Black Studies has developed as an interdisciplinary study or learning experience. Since knowledge and learning within a discipline flows out of the culture in which it is set, Black Studies emanates from an African or Afrocentric ethos and background. Thus, Black Studies may be defined as an interdisciplinary field of study or discipline that systematically treats the past and present culture, characteristics, achievements,, issues and problems of the Black race and in a context that interacts relevantly with other peoples of the world.

Gordon's (1981) concept of Black Studies is indicative and descriptive of the scope of African (Afro)-American Studies:

> Black studies may be defined as an analysis of the factors and conditions which have affected the economic, psychological, legal and moral status of the African in America as well as the African in diaspora. Not only is Black studies concerned with the culture of the Afro-American ethnic, as historically and sociologically defined by the traditional literature, it is also concerned with the development of new approaches to the study of the Black experience and with the development of social policies which will impact positively upon the lives of Black people.

It is difficult to conceive that the culture and experience of Blacks have been virtually excluded from treatment in the textbooks and curricula of the educational system, especially since people of African descent are an integral part of the history and development of America. The omission has been and continues to be interpreted by African Americans as a conscious policy reflecting the ethnocentric proclivity of white people. The cursory and peripheral mention of the African's contribution towards the development of the United States has produced generations of mis-educated white and Black students. Even today, there is little in the textbooks and literature of the typical school or college curriculum that treats Black history and culture as an integral, integrated and "legitimate" part of American society. Consequently, Black or African American Studies programs often function as auxiliary academic units for the sole purpose of servicing or complementing the traditional disciplines relative to the African experience. While some educators and social integrationists might view the establishing of Black Studies as a distinct and separate discipline as less than ideal, the question is-to what extent would the African's contribution and experience be taught and learned if Black Studies did not exist?

Indeed, Black Studies was founded as a result of the American education system's failure to fulfill its purpose and commitment to all citizens. Johnson (1969) submits that schools and colleges are committed to: (1) preserve traditions and heritage; (2) universality of education; (3) equality of opportunity; and (4) liberation, i.e. seek to satisfy normative and psychological needs. Although the educational system substantially meets its commitment towards white students, it is, at the same time, significantly, deficient in providing the same benefits for Blacks and other ethnic-racial minorities.

For example, within the multi-ethnic context of American society, does education serve to preserve the traditions and heritage of all its citizens or is it committed to the preservation of only white European or Eurocentric cultures and heritage? The concepts of universal education and equal opportunity are fulfilled basically at the primary and secondary levels. It is debatable whether or not *genuine* educational access and opportunity exist for Blacks in the post secondary, professional and graduate fields.[2] Universality of education further implies equality and respect for all races and cultures of the world. Neither Africa, Africans nor peoples of African descent are treated in educational curricula on a par with Europe and Europeans. Thus, by denying or ignoring the African experience and ethos, traditional disciplines fail to satisfy the normative and psychological needs of Blacks. The systematic subordination of Blacks to white people in the curricula negatively affects the psyche and personality of African Americans (Wright 1985).

Traditional American education fails to treat the Black or African American experience as an integral part of the broader society. The educational system through its textbooks. testing methods and design maximizes the values and interests of the dominant white majority to the social and psychological disadvantage of Blacks and non-White minority groups. The effect has been that of consciously and unconsciously politicizing and socializing both Blacks and whites into accepting the myths of white supremacy and the inferiority of persons of African descent. If American education is ever to be a unifying and harmonizing force for its multicultural-racial population, the traditional disciplines will have to modify their current structures and integrate or synthesize the African American experience into the academic curricula. Until this ideal becomes a reality, separate and distinct American cultural and racial studies, programs and departments will continue to exist or will be demanded by those population groups whose experience, values and interests have been excluded.

Consequently, the role of Black Studies as a field of study is to provide education that is consistent with the reality and truth of the Black experience and to study, research and present those ideological values that might achieve the cultural, political and economic betterment of Black people. Black Studies must also expose to the dominant white society in the United States the gulf between the ideals of the Constitution and the actual practice of human equality and social justice. More important than all of these is the task of evaluation, synthesizing and elucidating a Black ideology in relation to other prevailing ideologies of the world.

Ideological and Philosophical Concepts

It is not sufficient to propose that culture per se is the basis for the academic differentiation of Black Studies without further elucidation. Black Studies is significantly ideologically and philosophically distinct from European social scientific theory — simply and logically because Africa is the genesis and foundation for any knowledge or study related to Black peoples. Although eminent Black scholars such as W.E.B. DuBois, Carter G. Woodson, Chieikh Anta Diop and numerous others have asserted the dissimilarity, the school of thought is being advanced currently by a new school of African American scholars (DuBois 1961; Woodson 1933; Diop 1978; Williams 1974).

Baldwin's (1985) work treats almost exclusively the fundamental differences in social realities between African Americans and European Americans. By social reality, he refers to the distinct historical, cultural, philosophical and ideological conditions that exist between Blacks and European Americans. These differences constitute distinct orientations or "worldviews" of how each race perceives nature or the universe reflective of their dissimilar approaches to conceptualizing, organizing and experiencing reality. In fact, during the initial and formative stages of formal Black Studies programs in the United States, Lerone Bennett (1968) spoke of the need for proponents to develop a new frame of reference that transcends the limits of white concepts of Black people. Bennett further states that, "By and large, reality has been conceptualized in terms of the narrow point of view of the small minority of white men who live in Europe and North America. We must abandon the partial frame of reference of our oppressors and create new concepts which will release our reality...."

While the African ethos has always been preferred by Black Americans, Asante (1980) conceptualizes or defines this social reality as "Afrocentricity." Asante's pronouncement and interpretation of Afrocentricity was revealed nationally in the *Chronicle of Higher Education* (CHE) upon the release of a new book on the subject. The CHE article states that as scholars today understand the term, Afrocentricity is essentially a way of interpreting the history, culture, and behavior of Blacks universally from an African or Black perspective (Coughlin 1987).

Some may argue that Afrocentricity is basically a reaction to what scholars refer to as the "Eurocentric" perspective of Western scholarship. However, differences in African and European ideologies and philosophies are reflected in their social and economic development and, indeed, their respective definitions and interpretations of "development."

The implications of how a race of people's culture and worldview affects even what type of technology they develop and the applied use of that technology are evident. Asante's (1980) classic work on Afrocentricity, presents general descriptions of the worldviews or cultural realities of the three major races of the world. Although the descriptions or comparisons may be oversimplified, the differentiation characteristics are especially salient. They differ to the extent of their cognitive value and relationship to the material versus the spiritual. The Afrocentric worldview holds that there can be no separation between the material and the spiritual, the bonding of and continuity from material to spiritual being the reality of the Afrocentric worldview. The Asiocentric worldview holds that the material is an illusion and that the real only comes from the spiritual. Asante suggests that the Asian cultural reality is enamored with spirit-over-matter notions. In contrast, he asserts that the Eurocentric perspective of reality holds that the material and the experiential are the only phenomena that are real and that the spiritual is an illusion. In essence, everything that is not scientific and that the senses cannot experience is nonsense.[3]

From an assumption of these descriptive and distinct worldviews, the inference is that the Eurocentric cultural reality ascribes to technology, science and materialism a deific or divine-like status which are pursued as the ultimate objectives and purposes of mankind. Thus, as Richards (1985) writes:

> A people's worldview affects and determines behavior. A universe understood totally in materialistic or rationalistic terms will discourage spirituality. An ethos characterized by a will to power, by the need to control, will derive pleasure from a technical order....

Early opponents of Black Studies postulated that the nature of the emerging discipline was too ideologically and politically oriented. However, Black Studies is no more ideological or philosophical than European, Slavic, Asian, or American Studies. The ideological, political and philosophical values of each race or ethnic group are reflected in their specific ethos and culture. An ideology is a set of values derived from the historical experience of a given people exposed to or having experienced the same general social, political and economic realities. One can not logically deny that the social realities and ideologies of African and European peoples have been and continue to be quite dissimilar.

Theoretical and Methodological Approaches to Black Studies

Nathan Hare (1973), who many acknowledge as the father of contemporary Black Studies, proposed from the beginning that Black scholars must develop new norms and values grounded in a new (African) ideology and from such ideology new methodologies might evolve. He conceded, however, that the new approaches and methods in Black Studies may subsume and overlap existing norms of scholarly endeavors. Skepticism of much of the previous study and research on Blacks was based on the fact that prior to the 1960s, a preponderance of the study and research on African Americans represented white studies from "without" rather than Black self-knowledge from "within." Black skepticism was not an indictment of all white scholars. However, too much of the literature was based upon distorted assessments, reckless assumptions and vested Eurocentric interests that were not conducive to the enhancement of peoples of African descent. Consequently, the entire academic ideology of Black Studies involves the reassessment of methodology, reinterpretation of fundamental assumptions of knowledge, and review of subsequent conclusions from Black perspectives.

One of the major conflicts relating to approaches and methodologies in Black Studies arose between white and Black social and behavioral scientists on the issue of "objectivity" and the scientific ideal." Although European sociologists had begun to disclaim the notion of objectivity" and admit that the study of society requires a different theoretical method than those of the natural sciences, the American stress on objectivity in the rigid empiricist tradition was unrelenting (Forsythe 1973).

Richards (1979) writes that many Black social theorists have no use for the myth of objectivity which has served the interest of Western European political objectives relative to African peoples. Contrary to the propaganda of academe, she asserts, white social theory does not represent the only valid and "objective" body of thought, nor is it a *neutral* tool to be used for the purpose of understanding all human experiences.

Since its inception as a formal field of study, a school of Black scholars in history, sociology, anthropology, psychology, political science and economics have challenged the traditional theoretical and methodological constructs for the study of African people. The challenge or contention is based upon the divergent concepts related to an acknowledgement of the existence and distinctiveness of Black culture or its "deviancy" from middle-class white or Eurocentric cultural standards. Blacks allege that white social and behavioral scientists deny any special significance to the meaning of Blackness and, consequently, their research and studies on African American sociocultural values are distorted from their Eurocentric perspectives. Furthermore. Black social and cultural traditions that do not conform to white norms are often viewed as pathological or deviant. Thus, the most heated discord between many Black and white scholars relative to theoretical and methodological constructs has been in the areas of history, sociology, and psychology-not excluding interpretative approaches to Black aesthetic and creative arts.

In relation to history, theoretical and methodological errors have occurred when attempts have been made to interpret the Black experience through the analysis of the white experience. Under such a premise, it is assumed that the Afrocentric experience can be understood by analysis of Eurocentric oriented external determinants of which the African experience is judged to be a function. Blacks during the Civil Rights Movement of the 1960s satirically alluded to traditional textbook history of African Americans and Africans as "his-story." Justifiably, they felt that they had the right to describe their own history and experiences. They were cognizant of the fact that prior to the 1960s most historical studies on Blacks were done by white Euro-pean, Western and Jewish scholars. Consequently, distortions, stereotypical conclu-sions, omissions and falsifications in much of the traditional presentation of African American and African history served the ends of oppression and its perpetuation. A people must write their own history and portray the primary role in the formation of their own intelligentsia. A Black historian at Cornell University succinctly states that "history can no longer be written without taking into account the thoughts as well as the actions of Black Americans-we have gone beyond the point where the Black ex-perience can *only* be interpreted by others."[4]

Beyond the earlier debates of Black-white interpretation of African American and African history is the continuous omission of the Black experience from history textbooks of the educational systems. Furthermore, there is the tendency of *denying* either through omissions or implications that African peoples have contributed pro-foundly and immeasurably to the history of humanity. Thus, the inherent fallacy in the theoretical and methodological approaches to Black history are evident by the obvious neglect of the African experience and perspective. By this omission the Eu-rocentric scientific ideal and claim of a standard of value-free or objective scholarship is invalidated.

Traditional sociology offers two major paradigms toward the theoretical assess-ment or study of human conduct-the equilibrium and the conflict models. The equi-librium theory argues that a social system must maintain a condition of checks and balances among the interdependent parts. Any phenomenon that causes disequilib-rium is perceived as being problematic and must be resolved in order that the system may be restored to its static existence. On the other hand, conflict theorists see human world society in terms of conflict and power-competition between groups for scarce social and economic privileges and resources (Babbie 1977, Taylor 1987). A growing number of Black social theorists consider both of these traditional para-digms as insufficient towards the analysis of Black-white relationships in the United States. They argue that erroneous assumptions are made relative to the Black com-munity and Black life in general based upon equilibrium and conflict paradigms.

It is obvious that the equilibrium model proposes that African Americans must become adapted, adjusted and socialized to fit into the normative social order that is defined and subscribed to by the dominant white society. Disequilibrium exists within the society because of the cultural, economic and educational deprivation of Blacks, yet, race or racism is not submitted as the major destabilizing factor. The fal-lacy inherent in the equilibrium theory is that whites tend to discount the notion that values, cultural norms. social goals and strategies exist in the Black community inde-pendent of white society. Thus, the problem may be less that of Black social pathology or deviancy, but more that of racism and ethnocentrism on the part of white society.

Although the conflict theory is not completely adequate in its approach towards the study of African Americans, certain aspects are valid. Karl Marx saw conflict in human society as based upon economic inequities and class struggles. Other traditional social theorists argue that conflict is inevitable as long as individual ethnic groups or races maintain opposing positions and have different opinions and worldviews within a society. Afrocentricity by definition is in many ways opposite in cultural and ideological orientation to Western European thought or Eurocentricity. Moreover, Cruse (1977) and Karenga (1984) also posit that the Black community is not only disparate but simply an internal domestic colony controlled and dominated by the external white population.

Yet in spite of Asante's (1988), Baldwin's (1985), and Richard's (1985) thesis of Afrocentricity. African Americans are bicultural and share in varying degrees some of the same values, attitudes, beliefs, social goals and characteristics as white Americans. Thus, it may be difficult to disprove Chimizie's (1985) assertion that Blacks in America have both Afrocentric and Eurocentric elements of culture. The inner conflict of culture compounded with the unquantifiable effects of racism produce modified characteristics of the Afrocentric personality. W.E.B. DuBois (1969) describes the socio-psychological ambivalence of African Americans as:

> ...this double-consciousness, this sense of always looking at one's self through the eyes of others, of measuring one's soul by the tape of a world that looks on in amused contempt and pity. One ever feels his twoness—an American, a [Black], two souls, two thoughts, two unreconciled strivings two warring ideals in one dark body, whose dogged strength alone keeps it from being torn asunder.

The "double-consciousness" theory introduced by W.E.B. DuBois has spurred contemporary Black psychologists to examine and question the applicability of traditional psychological models and approaches in relation to African Americans and African peoples. Black behavioral scientists (Semaj 1981; Wright 1984; Akbar 1984; Azibo 1988; Baldwin and Bell 1985) submit that racism and oppression cause many Blacks to live psychologically disordered lives, and that their adoption of or adaptation to Eurocentric materialistic goals and values contribute towards an alien Afrocentric self. The systematic frustration caused by racism. discrimination and oppression results in Black Americans developing anti-self and self-destructive life styles causing organic disorders including many psychophysical malfunctions. Thus, existing psychological models may provide inappropriate foundations for the development of a psychology of liberation for Black people. Important in psychology as well as sociology, models for the study of Black people or the Black personality in order to possess validity must be based upon African culture and the theoretical constructs of Afrocentricty (Asante 1987).

The equilibrium and conflict paradigms in sociology as well as the comparative or crosscultural frameworks of psychology raise complex problems and questions relative to their reliability in the research and study of Blacks. Consequently, the new social and behavioral theorists may be justified in mandating that new models, methodologies and isntruments be constructed based on the unique status and experience of Blacks in American society.

The aesthetic and creative aspects of African American and African experiences require different theoretical approaches for interpretation, analysis, and evaluation in the same relative measures as in the social and behavioral sciences. Black music, visual arts and performing arts are the products of an Acrocentric ethos. Attempts by critics and analysts to interpret or evaluate Black music and art based upon Euro-centric rhythmic or aesthetic cultural art standards may lead to erroneous theoretical assumptions and distorted conclusions. Tyler (1972) writes that the uniqueness of African American music is determined by a musico-cultural criteria which reveals an African and not a European continuum in America. Afro-American music is African and racial in origin, nature and kind.

African American music is derived from and reflects the spirit of struggle and re-sistance. Spiritual-gospel, blues and jazz are the music of Black Americans crated within the Black community under conditions of social, economic and political op-pression. Thus, the foundations of Afro-American and European American music are different in context, time, rhythm and form. Each worldview of culture represents its own unique values, experiences, attitudes and behaviors.

Traditional Black paintings, sculpture, theater, dance, poetry and literature are value laden and subjective reflecting the social consciousness, politico-economic sta-tus and aspirations of people of African descent. African American and African art are conceived by Blacks as functional in terms of social and political perspectives. They differ fundamentally and intrinsically from the Eurocentric elitist tradition of *art-for-art's sake*.

Summary

For clarification and contrast it was necessary to point out in the initial discus-sion of this paper the significance of the socio-political and ideological factor which contributed to the unique emergence of Black Studies as a formal field of study in the United States. One must be aware of the history and complex nature of African peo-ple's experience to fully understand the "anomalous" and auxiliary status Black Studies hold in American education. Unlike European immigrants, Blacks came to America on slave ships and were enslaved for over 200 years. The nature of their subjugation, repression and treatment at the hands of white European Americans represents a form of "racism" based on color never practiced anywhere in the world. Even after the era of overt slavery and basically until the 1960s, Blacks were barred from access to the mainstream of American life. Black Studies virtually ex-ploded into existence in defiance of repression and resulted in the self-realization of African Americans that had been denied since slavery. Blacks Studies continues to develop and to become institutionalized in American education because it reflects and responds to the *continuing* attitudes and practice of racial discrimination against Black people to only in the American society, but also within the Euro-West-ern world.

Charges of academic illegitimacy, in substantiality, politicization; and problems of definition, structure and professional personnel became issues which were high-lighted simply because Black Studies became a phenomenon during the national Civil Rights Movement and Social Revolution of the 1960s. Essentially, there was a "war" between the races—the oppressed versus the oppressors. *Healthy* dialectical discus-sion and controversy were evident in and during the founding of what is now termed the "traditional" disciplines. However, these fields of study were developed within the aura of academe and outside of a socially hostile and politically revolutionary era and environment.

Neither Adam Smith, John Stuart Mill, Karl Marx or John Maynard Keynes of economics, or Auguste Comte, Max Weber, George Mead, Emile Durkheim of sociology advocated identical theoretical and ideological perspectives relative to their respective disciplines. Black social theorists also are not necessarily monolithic in their theoretical and ideological approaches to Black Studies. W.E.B. DuBois, E. Franklin Frazier, Nathan Hare. Martin L. Kilson, Maulana Karenga or Molefi K. Asante do not share exactly the same ideology of Black Studies or philosophical thought in terms of the liberation, survival and destiny of African Americans. However, these African American scholars and others have a common heritage of slavery, oppression or/and racial discrimination under European American domination. This commonality per se should lend credence to the belief expressed by a growing number of Black social theorists that new paradigms, theories and methodologies must be initiated in Black Studies because of the unique dual nature of the African American experience.

The redeeming reality of human and race relationships is that theoretical, ideological and philosophical positions are not static. As world and universal conditions change new paradigms and theoretical constructs are founded and put forth in response to new orders of social, political and economic phenomena and events. Black Studies is an academic result of inevitable changes in the American order.

References

Akbar, Na'im. 1984. *Chains and Images of Psychological Slavery.* Jersey City: New Mind Productions.

Asante, Molefi Kete. 1980. *Afrocentricity: The Theory of Social Change.* Buffalo: Amulefi Publishing Company.

———. 1987. *The Afrocentric Idea.* Philadelphia: Temple University Press.

Azibo, Daudi Ajani Ya. 1988. "Personality, Clinical, and Social Psychological Research on Blacks: Appropriate and Inappropriate Research Frameworks," *The Western Journal of Black Studies.*

Babbie, Earl R. 1977. *Sociology: An Introduction.* Belmont, CA: Wadsworth Publishing Company.

Baldwin, Joseph A. and Yvonne R. Bell. 1985. "The African Self-Consciousness Scale: An Afrocentric Personality Questionnaire," *The Western Journal of Black Studies,* Vol. 9, No. 2.

———. 1985. "Psychological Aspects of European Cosmology in American Society," *The Western Journal of Black Studies,* Vol. 9, No. 4.

Bennett, Lerone, Jr. 1968. *The Challenge of Blackness.* Chicago: Johnson Publishing Company, Inc.

Chimezie, Amuzie. 1985. "Black Bi-Culturality," *The Western Journal of Black Studies,* Vol. 9, No. 4.

Coughlin, Ellen K. 1987. "...of the Life and History of Black Americans," *The Chronicle of Higher Education,* October 28.

Cruse, Harold. 1967. *The Crisis of the Negro Intellectual.* New York: William Morrow & Company.

Diop, Cheikh Anta. 1978. *The Cultural Unity of Black Africa.* Chicago: Third World Press.

DuBois, W.E.B. 1961. *The Souls of Black Folk*. New York: Fawcett Publications, Inc.

Forsythe, Dennis. 1973. "Radical Sociology and Blacks," in *The Death of White Sociology*, edited by Joyce A. Ladner, pp. 214-215. New York: Vintage Books.

Gordon, Vivian. 1981. "The Coming of Age of Black Studies," *The Western Journal of Black Studies*, Vol. 5, No. 3, pp. 231.

Hare, Nathan. 1973. "The Challenge of a Black Scholar," in *The Death of White Sociology*, edited by Joyce A. Ladner, p. 76. New York: Vintage Books.

———. 1976. "A Black Paper: The Relevance of Black Studies," *The Black Collegian*, September, pp. 46-50.

Johnson, J.A., et al. 1969. *Introduction to the Foundations of American Education*, pp. 12-13. Boston: Allyn and Bacon.

Karenga, Maulana. 1984. *Introduction to Black Studies*. Los Angeles: Kawaida Publications.

Kilson, Martin. 1973. "Reflections on Structure and Content in Black Studies," *Journal of Black Studies*, March.

Poinsett, Alex. 1973. "The Plight of Black Studies," *Ebony*, December.

Richards, Dona. 1979. "The Ideology of European Dominance," *The Western Journal of Black Studies*, Vol. 3. No. 4.

Richards, Dona. 1985. "The Implications of African-American Spirituality," in Molefi K. Asante and Kariamu W. Asante (ed.) *African Culture: The Rhythms of Unity*. Westport: Greenwood Press.

Semaj, L.T. 1981. "The Black Self, Identity, and Models for a Psychology of Black Liberation," *The Western Journal of Black Studies*, Vol. 5, No. 3.

Taylor, Ronald L. 1987. "The Study of Black People; A Survey of Empirical and Theoretical Models," *Urban Research Review*, Vol. 11, No. 2.

Tyler, Robert. 1972. "The Musical Culture of Afro-America," *The Black Scholar*, Summer 1972.

Woodson, Carter G. 1933. *Mis-Education of the Negro*. Washington, DC: Associated Publishers, Inc.

Wright, Beverly H. 1981. "Ideological Changes and Black Identity during Civil Rights Movements," *The Western Journal of Black Studies*, Vol. 5, No. 3, pp. 186.

Wright, Bobby E. 1985. *The Psychopathic Racial Personality*. Chicago: Third World Press.

Endnotes

1. Danforth Foundation, "Black Studies Perspectives 1970," *Danforth News and Notes* Vol. 5, No. 2 (March 1970).

2. See James L. Miller, Jr. and Arland F. Christ-James in *The Expanded Campus*, edited by Dyckman W. Vermilye (San Francisco: Jossey-Bass Inc., 1972).

3. Asante's description of the different worldviews cited in Carlton W. and Barbera J. Molette, *Black Theater: Premise and Presentation* (Wyndham Hall Press, 1986), pp. 8.

4. A quote by Robert L. Harris taken from a *New York Times* article (January 13, 1983).

35.

Toward a Paradigm of Unity in Black Studies

Abdul Alkalimat and Associates

> You have to be careful, very careful, introducing the truth to the Black man who has never previously heard the truth about himself, his own kind, and the white man.... The Black brother is so brainwashed that he may even be repelled when he first bears the truth.
>
> Malcolm X, *The Autobiography of Malcolm X*, 1965

Afro-American Studies is an academic field that combines general intellectual history, academic scholarship in the social sciences and the humanities, and a radical movement for fundamental educational reform.

Afro-American Studies: Who, What, Why, for Whom

Afro-American Studies covers the entire American hemisphere, including North, Central, and South America, the Caribbean, and northern countries like Newfoundland and Greenland. Our main focus will be on the United States, but it should always be kept in mind that there are nearly 103 million Black people of African descent throughout the Americas.

There is a great deal of diversity in this Black population spread throughout the hemisphere, but there is one general point of unity. All of these Black populations derive from an African origin. Black people come from Africa as compared to white people who come from Europe.

In the world experience of Africans, subjugation by hostile people and migration have led to great crises. First, as a result of their subjugation, their past has been distorted or simply omitted from the libraries and curricula. Second, the living descendants of Africans who live outside Africa are faced with an identity crisis because they have been stripped of their cultural heritage and forced to use languages which are not conducive to maintaining links with Africa.

In the United States today, there is also a crisis of identity in terms of what name to use for African descendants. It can be thought of as a naming crisis. We list eight names that have been used since the 18th century: African, colored, Negro, nonwhite, minority, Afro-American, African-American, and Black. Many have been omitted, especially the derogatory names like "nigger," "jig-a-boo," "spade," "coon," darky," "spook," "swartzes," "blackie," etc. These types of negative names can be found for all nationalities in the United States.

Rationales exist for these diverse names, although each must be viewed within its historical context. For example, the term "African" was used during the 18th century because slaves were still being brought from Africa itself. This was a direct form of naming. After the mid-twentieth century victorious struggles that liberated most African countries, some Black people in western countries chose to call themselves "Africans" to identify with both their origins and the contemporary politics of African liberation. It is the same term, but each historical context and the material condition of the people generated its own meaning.

The critical issue is the power to define. Some focus more on the practical character of names, the difficulty of making a change, and status recognition based on existing societal norms. A different focus makes naming a matter of political control, a critical principle of self-determination. The difference can be demonstrated with the name "Negro." DuBois, argued in the 1920s that the name "Negro" was acceptable as long as it was capitalized. Richard Moore, in his book *The Name Negro: Its Origin and Evil Use* (1960), condemns the name and argues that a preferred name is "Afro-American" (although he disagrees with the hyphen). His point is that Black people must name themselves, because "dogs and slaves are named by their masters; free men name themselves!"

In the 1960s, the issue of naming was one of the important struggles reflecting a cultural identity crisis. Faced with white racism, the Civil Rights Movement was an expression of "Negroes" fighting to integrate themselves into white society. By 1966, this struggle was transformed into a liberation movement for Black people. The Nation of Islam, mainly represented by Malcolm X, carried out widespread publicity to convince the "so called Negro" to become "Black." Black became popular, a positive affirmation of self. This was a symbolic victory for the masses of people, since for historical reasons the Black middle class was brown or tan in skin color. Black was a replacement for subordination to white that was reflected in the terms *non-white* and *minority*.

"Afro-American" and "African American" were more historically specific terms to describe a synthesis of Africa with America and to replace "Negro" and of course "colored." ("Colored" is really a misnomer since if you were not colored you'd be colorless and that means invisible. The issue has always been what color!) This field of study thus is called Afro-American Studies. In the early campus struggle against white racism to set up programs, it was named Black Studies, and many programs retain their original name. Also in use are Africana Studies and Pan African Studies.

In addition to the general issue of who is being studied and what they are to be called, the issue of who is the constituency for an Afro-American Studies program should be considered. This is linked to the special purposes Afro-American Studies serves in the general academic curriculum. In general, Afro-American Studies has two main objectives: (1) to rewrite American history and reconceptualize the essential features of American society; and (2) to establish the intellectual and academic space for Black people to tell their own story. Afro-American Studies is also important because of its impact on affirmative action. Blacks constitute only 4.3% of faculty and only 8.8% of students in U.S. higher education. The presence of an Afro-American Studies program encourages Black employment and attendance. On virtually every campus, the activities of Black faculty members are related to Afro-American Studies and Black students are likely to enroll in at least one course before they graduate. Black students need to be tied into scholarship on the basis of an anti-racist affirmation of their own experience as part of the overall human condition. Further, their study must be the basis for reinterpreting the overall American experience, especially correcting the centuries of racist distortions and omissions. White students, believing liberal generalities at best and racist stereotypes at worst, are the most ignorant of the Black experience. Their gain from Afro-American Studies is essential if recurring crises of racial ignorance and conflict are to be avoided.

Apart from students, there are many others who would benefit from Afro-American Studies. For instance, everyone who desires to work in government—whether it is making or implementing policy—should have knowledge of the Black experience. All future legislators, administrators, and most mayors should be required to take Afro-American Studies because much of their legislative and policy-implementing activities deal with Black people. Similarly, people in business or labor should take Afro-American Studies. Blacks constitute a growing market for business, and they are an essential component of the trade union movement (Blacks are even more unionized than whites when you compare them industry by industry).

This general text in Afro-American Studies is designed to meet people's need to understand the Black experience. Before considering the specific content of that experience, one should have some grasp of the broad field of Afro-American Studies. We thus turn to a discussion of Afro-American intellectual history, Afro-American scholarship within the traditional academic disciplines, and the radical movement for Black Studies in the 1960s and 1970s. We will then discuss the conceptual framework that is used in this text to analyze the Black experience. The conceptual framework is both a model for unity in Afro-American Studies and the basic structure of the chapters the follow.

Intellectual History

Afro-American intellectual history in the U.S.A. is being written for the first time, and even now is only partially being given the academic attention that it deserves. It is the history of Black men and women fighting to establish professional careers as scholars, journalists, writers, etc. They had to fight against racism and discrimination. For these reasons this is a history that mainstream white scholarship has not included.

The institutional concentration of a Black intellectual tradition took place in graduate education and dissertation research. This was supplemented by newspapers, magazines and journals, and specialized organizations. Blacks who got higher degrees have been overwhelmingly in the social sciences, education, and the humanities. Further, most of their research has been on the Black experience. Harry Greene, in *Holders of Doctorates Among American Negroes* (1946), lists all Black doctorates between 1876 and 1943. Of 77 dissertations in the social sciences, 56% were on the Black experience; 67% out of 71 in education; 21% out of 43 in language and literature; and 15% out 26 in psychology and philosophy. This graduate research has been a point of tension between intellectual currents within the Black community and the academic mainstream. It is therefore one of the most intense and dynamic indicators of how important and deeply rooted is the desire of Black people to study the Black experience.

The overall written record of Black intellectual history is perhaps most easily traced in journals that specialize in some aspect of Afro-American Studies. This began with the *Journal of Negro History*, founded by Carter G. Woodson in 1916, and includes *Phylon*, founded by W.E.B. DuBois in 1940. The number of journals has expanded greatly since the 1960s, even though aspects of the Black experience have been increasingly integrated into mainstream journals. The growth of these journals is proof of a continuing commitment to the field. Afro-American Studies is a field anchored in a professional journal literature, just as are all other recognized fields in the contemporary academic swing.

There are also a number of published bibliographies that give a codified view of the entire field. These range from *A Bibliography of the Negro in Africa and America* by Monroe Work (1928, 700 pages) to *Blacks in America: Bibliographical Essays* by James McPherson, et al. (1971, 430 pages). The most recent reference tool is *Black Access: A Bibliography of Afro-American Bibliographies* by Richard Newman.

We will highlight the contours of this intellectual history by briefly discussing four key individuals: W.E.B. DuBois, Carter G. Woodson, E. Franklin Frazier, and Langston Hughes. DuBois and Woodson, both trained in history, were mainly broad generalists who focused on the role of race in history, especially for Black people in the United States. Hughes and Frazier, of a later generation, made outstanding intellectual contributions. Hughes was trained in the humanities and Frazier was in the social sciences. One of the critical similarities among these intellectuals is that they all produced a paradigmatic text of the Black experience. A paradigmatic text is a coherent survey of the main aspects of the Black experience throughout the dynamic historical stages, from Africa to the Afro-American present. It constitutes an overall treatment of the Black Experience.

William Edward Burghart DuBois (1868-1963)

W.E.B. DuBois was a first-class intellectual of the late 19th and first half of the 20th century, and clearly the most dominant Black intellectual of all time. He was educated at Fisk University and Harvard University, the best Black and white institutions of higher education. One example of the racism he faced was that Harvard admitted him as a college junior, only giving him two years credit for his four years of study at Fisk. After two years of study at the University of Berlin, he went on to be the first Black Ph.D. in the social sciences in the U.S.A.

His work is best exemplified by two sets of conferences that made a great impact in terms of both understanding the Black experience and changing the world for Black people. DuBois was a leading force in the five major Pan-African Congresses held to develop a world-wide movement for African liberation. He was also the leading figure in the Atlanta University Conferences held between 1898 and 1930 to summarize research and public policy regarding the conditions of life for Black people in the U.S.A. during the early decades of the 20th century. The proceedings of each Atlanta University Conference were published, and together they constitute the beginning of modern applied research on the Black experience. This work was the early origin of Black Studies.

DuBois lived 95 years, and he published during 80 of those years. His contribution can be seen in the breadth of his research concerning the Black experience.[1] He had hoped to culminate all of his research in a major encyclopedia. He proposed an *Encyclopedia Africana* in 1909, but he could not secure funding. He planned an *Encyclopedia of Colored People* in 1934, but was only able to publish a preparatory volume by 1944. In 1959, he was invited by Kwame Nkrumah, President of Ghana (West Africa), to work on the *Encyclopedia Africana*. He was working on the project when he died in 1963. His entire dramatic story, nearly a century long, was recorded in two autobiographical volumes, *Dusk of Dawn* (1940) and *The Autobiography of W.E.B. DuBois* (1968).

Perhaps the most important contribution made by DuBois was his relentless search for truth and his untiring devotion to the cause of clarifying the meaning of his people's experience. In 1903, he published a major collection of essays, *The Souls of Black Folk*. From then on he was a critical interpreter of the Black experience. He went on to write several works of fiction, including a trilogy of novels called *The Black Flame* (1957, 1959, 1961).

DuBois led the life of an intellectual and an activist. He founded *Crisis*, the journal of the NAACP, and was its editor from November 1910 to July 1934. In 1940, he founded the academic journal *Phylon* (Greek for race) at Atlanta University and edited it from 1940 to 1944. His life epitomized academic excellence and political activism.

Carter Godwin Woodson (1875-1950)

Carter G. Woodson is known as the father of Black history. He not only made major contributions through his scholarly research, but he also was the key organizer in building a Black history movement. He was educated at Berea College, the University of Chicago, Harvard, and the Sorbonne (University of Paris), getting the Ph.D. from Harvard University in 1912. His parents were ex-slaves, and he didn't enter high school until he was twenty years old.

Woodson made great contributions to research about Blacks, both by creating new data sets and by analyzing existing data.[2] He wrote the first general history that became a standard reference, *The Negro in Our History* (1922). Woodson published nineteen editions of this work. He also published an extensive study guide, *The African Background Outlined* (1936), which included a focus on Africa as well as the Black experience in the United States. At the time of his death, he was writing a projected six-volume, comprehensive historical study of the Black race. He maintained a stubborn allegiance to the facts, to rigorous historical methods, and to a desire to expose racist lies and distortions in the scholarly study of the Black experience.

No one person has created an intellectual movement comparable to the Black history movement organized by Carter G. Woodson. In 1915, he organized the Association for the Study of Negro Life and History. The following year, he began to publish a scholarly journal, *The Journal of Negro History*. He went on to found a publishing company, Associated Publishers, and by so doing completed the task of organizing professional resources for Black history. There was an organization, with a newsletter and an annual meeting; a professional journal scholarly articles; and a publishing company for books.

He also took Black history out of the classroom into the Black community by founding Negro History Week, now Black History Month and Black Liberation Month. This was the major project that helped to spread an appreciation for Black history among the broad Black population, especially since the activity was based in schools and churches. Woodson combined academic scholarship with a broad commitment to community education. He fought against racism and for the development of a healthy Black consciousness rooted in a firm grasp of the historical record.

Edward Franklin Frazier (1894-1962)

E. Franklin Frazier was the most renowned Black social scientist of the 20th century. Further, he was elected president of the American Sociological Association (1948), indicating his white colleagues held him in the highest regard as well. He was educated at Howard University, Clark University, University of Copenhagen, and the University of Chicago where he earned a Ph.D. in sociology in 1931. Utilizing the most advanced research techniques of his time, he was a preeminent analyst of the changing patterns of race relations in both the United States and the world.

His books made strong contributions to many aspects of the Afro-American experience.[3] His major research was on the family. Frazier shared the puritanical values of his generation, and so his research is conditioned by a Black middle-class bias concerning proper behavior. While his work remains quite controversial, his analysis is comprehensive, historical, and based on the documentary testimony of Black people themselves.

The entire scholarly literature concerning Black people was summarized by Frazier in his major work, *The Negro in the United States* (1949). With the keen perception of a research social scientist, he brought together widely diverse information and organized a coherent pattern of structural change and institutional development, from the slave experience to the urban, experience.

Langston Hughes (1902-1967)

Langston Hughes could justifiably be called the Afro-American poet laureate of the 20th century. He not only won critical acclaim for his writing in virtually every genre, but he also wrote a newspaper column that had great popular appeal among the masses of Black people.[4] Moreover, he translated other Black writers into English from Haitian French, Cuban Spanish, and Creole from New Orleans. Langston Hughes is known all over the world.

Langston Hughes was both a poet and a political voice in the Black community. His orientation is clear from this 1934 essay entitled "Cowards from the Colleges," in which he commented on the political weakness of the Negro college and how change must come from students:

> More recently, I see in our papers where Fisk University, that great (?) center of Negro education and of Jubilee fame has expelled Ishmael Flory, a graduate student from California on a special honor scholarship, because he dared organize a protest against the University singers appearing in a Nashville Jim-crow theatre where colored people must go up a back alley to sit in the gallery. Probably also the University resented his organizing, through the Denmark Vesey Forum, a silent protest parade denouncing the lynching of Cordie Cheek who was abducted almost at the very gates of the University.

Hughes then made a prediction that was to come true nearly thirty years later in the southern students' sit-in movement:

> Frankly, I see no hope for a new spirit today in the majority of the Negro schools of the South unless the students themselves put it there...the younger teachers, knowing well the existing evils, are as yet too afraid of their jobs to speak out, or to dare attempt to reform campus conditions.

But Langston was also deeply mindful of the deep historical heritage that could serve as the basis for a strong Black consciousness. This was true even in the very first poem that he published, which was in the *Crisis* edited by DuBois:

The Negro Speaks of Rivers (1921)

I've known rivers:
I've known rivers ancient as the world and older than the flow of
    human blood in human veins.

My soul has grown deep like the rivers.

I bathed in the Euphrates when dawns were young.
I built my hut near the Congo and it lulled me to sleep.
I looked upon the Nile and raised the pyramids above it.
I heard the singing of the Mississippi when Abe Lincoln went down
    to New Orleans, and I've seen its muddy bosom turn all
    golden in the sunset.

I've known rivers:
Ancient, dusky rivers.

My soul has grown deep like the rivers.

Langston Hughes wrote this poem when he was only nineteen years old. He went on to capture the essence of the hopes and dreams, as well as the trial and tribulations, of Black people.

The Movement

The current phase of Afro-American Studies has been nurtured by a radical social movement in opposition to institutional racism in U.S. higher education. But many people had called for it earlier. Arthur Schomburg, a collector of Black books after whom the famous collection of Black materials in New York is named, put it this way in 1913:

> We have chairs of almost everything, and believe we lack nothing, but we sadly need a chair of Negro history. The white institutions have their chair of history; it is the history of their people and whenever the Negro is mentioned in the text books it dwindles down to a foot note....
>
> Where is our historian to give us, our side view and our chair of Negro History to teach our people our own history. We are at the mercy of the "flotsam and jetsam" of the white writers....
>
> We need in the coming dawn the man, who will give us the background for our future, it matters not whether he comes from the cloisters of the university or from the rank and file of the fields. We await his coming....

By 1915, Carter G. Woodson had his activities going. And by the mid-1960s, a movement rising to meet this challenge was raging in the United States. Students had played a strong role in the Civil Rights Movement, and young activists were the main basis for the Black-consciousness developments. (See Edwards, 1970; Gurin and Epps, 1975; Orum, 1972; and Tripp, 1982.)[5]

Emerging from this context, the Black studies movement has gone through four main stages of development:

Innovation—The origin of the movement came through social protest and disruption of the university. Blacks sought to attack and to change the policies and practices of institutional racism.

Experimentation—The initial actors in the protests for Black studies sought to bring the general rhetorical orientation of the national movement within local campus administrative and cultural style. Many different types of academic structures and programs were developed on a trial and error basis.

Crisis—When the post-1960s fiscal and demographical shift hit higher education (less money and fewer students) Afro-American studies was challenged for immediate results. It was faced with the prospects of diminished status and decreased resources (as was becoming common for all academic structures in the social sciences and the humanities).

Institutionalization—The strategic orientation for Afro-American Studies was developed in 1977 as "Academic Excellence and Social Responsibility." Under this banner, a set of professional standards began to put the field on a permanent academic foundation.

Innovation

Several case studies have been done that helps to shed light on the innovation phase of the movement. Orrick (1969) describes the context of the first Black Studies program at San Francisco State University.[6] Baraka (1984) sums this up:

Nathan Hare was...at San Francisco State during that period and he and Jimmy Garrett helped put together the first Black Studies program in the country. Humanitarian California? No, some niggers with guns had just walked into the California legislature.

He is referring to the emergence of the Black Panther Party, which had a tremendous influence on the militancy of the Black student movement and its drive to create Black Studies on the campus. In this same context, Walton (1969)[7] presents a documentary case study of the emergence of Black Studies at Merritt College in Oakland, California.

The case of Cornell University is described by Donald (1970) and Edwards (1980).[8] Edwards titles the chapter "Black Power and War Come to Cornell," because Black students were attacked by a cross-burning, Ku Klux Klan reign of terror and responded with an armed take-over of a campus building. This was the subject of a *Newsweek* cover story, which depicted armed Black students defending themselves against racist attacks and demanding Black Studies. This was not in a working-class community college; this was in the ivy league schools! Not the 1860s but the 1960s.

At the Black colleges, the situation was somewhat different because the Afro-American intellectual tradition had been based there. Here the contradiction expressed itself in generational terms and in challenging what was called the "predominantly Negro college" to become a Black university. Mays (1971)[9] tells his version of the struggle at Atlanta University. The essence of that struggle was contained in a statement the Trustees of Morehouse, Spelman, and Atlanta University signed after being held captive by a group of students and faculty for nearly thirty hours:

> We, the undersigned, resign from the Board of Trustees of the schools within the Atlanta University Center. Our purpose in resigning is to enable the black community to control their own education and toward this end an entirely new process of control must be established. We recognize and support the necessity of Black Power in education, and so we step aside. This act will release us from all responsibility and leaves the schools in the hands of an interim committee of alumni, faculty and students to be elected from those respective groups.

This phase of the Black Studies movement was summed up in two collections of articles. The *Negro Digest* (March 1967, March 1968, and March 1969) published three special issues under the guest editorship of Gerald McWorter. The articles in these issues presented a critique of institutional racism and a vision of what a Black university that would be in a position of providing an alternative might be like. The proceedings of a conference at Yale University, Robinson (1969),[10] was nationally significant because the Ford Foundation joined Yale in pulling together the leading activists of Black Studies with a leading group of white mainstream scholars. This conference resulted in greater mainstream legitimacy for Black Studies. It provided a useful critique of the mainstream and several examples of the types of scholarship to be developed in the field, and it led to a substantial investment in the field by the Ford Foundation.

Experimentation

The experimentation stage of Black Studies was marked by both its origins and the diversity of the academic mainstream. Most of the colleges and universities developed programs as a function of three things: (1) a demographical imperative (large Black student population or Black community that provided a demand); (2) a curriculum void (no courses being taught that dealt substantially with the Black experience); and (3) a protest movement (specific agitation to mobilize students to fight for Black courses). It follows that the nature of these three things, in conjunction with the overall local conditions, would produce a diversity of activity.

In general, Afro-American Studies includes the following variety of administrative structures: (1) Department: full academic units with academic majors, and a secure budget; (2) Institute/Center: a permanent, research-oriented special program with minimum financial support; (3) Program: formally organized program of activities with no permanent status; (4) Committee: informally organized program with no permanent security. Each of these types of structures must be evaluated in terms of how it meets the needs of the local campus. In general, however, the critical question is the extent to which there is some multi-year commitment so that Afro-American Studies is secure from immediate political pressures and can be focused mainly on the academic performance of its faculty and students.

Three key works summed up this experimentation stage of Black Studies: Ford (1973), Blassingame (1971), and Cortada (1974).[11] These works were reactions to the diversity and apparent loss of academic quality that many attached to Black Studies because of its political origins. Each attempts to define a program that would be acceptable to the mainstream. At the same time, new forms of organization were developing to further develop the movement into something new, something that might help to transform all of higher education in the United States. An example of this is the Institute of the Black World, led by Vincent Harding. Black Studies scholars also were beginning to develop a professional literature discussing the character and future of the field (e.g., Frye (1976), Butler (1981), and Sims (1978).[12]

Institutionalization

The institutionalization of the field is the current stage of Afro-American Studies, one likely to carry into the 21st century. This involves the issues of curriculum, program, professional standards, and theoretical coherence to the field.

Curriculum—A core curriculum model has been widely adopted as the academic foundation of the field (see Figure A).

This curriculum model is designed to provide a coherent framework for major and minor programs of study. As a field it covers the social sciences, historical analysis, and the humanities. There are several levels: an introductory course, survey and advanced courses in the substantive areas, and an integrative senior seminar in which the many aspects of Afro-American studies are pulled together in a review of the current research in the field.

Figure A

Core Curriculum for Black Studies
(Adopted at 4th annual Conference by National Council
for Black Studies March 26-29, 1980)

Level 1	INTRODUCTION TO BLACK STUDIES		
	Social/Behavioral Studies Course Area	History Course Area	Cultural Studies Course Area
Level 2	A. Basic Literature Review or Survey	A. Survey of Black History	A. Basic Literature Review or Survey
Level 3	B. Current Research & Emerging Issues	B. Current & Emerging Issues in Historical Interpretation & Evaluation	B. Current Research & Emerging Issues
Level 4	Senior Seminar Course Area Synthesis & Application of Previous Study		

Program — Many activities have developed as regular features of Afro- American Studies at most, colleges. One of the most important ones is the expansion of Negro History Week into Black Liberation Month. Carter G. Woodson founded Negro History Week in 1926 in the context of a virtually total racist denial of the contributions of Black people to world history. As a result of the 1960s, the issue was popularized and Negro History Week was turned into Black History Month. This was carried even further by the national television production of "Roots" by Alex Haley watched by millions of people. The question became history for what? This led to the origin of Black Liberation Month. Here is the explanation developed by Peoples College:

> Black Liberation Month is our attempt to unite with the founders and supporters of Negro History Week, and join their emphasis on study with our emphasis on struggle. Moreover, the concept of Black Liberation Month more accurately reflects the needs of our movement, particularly the need to build on the massive participation of people in the upsurge of struggle during the 1960's.

> Carter G. Woodson, noted Afro-American nationalist historian, founded Negro History Week in 1926. In addition to the newspaper column of J. A. Rodgers, this was the major source of information that Black people had about their history. Every year in schools, churches, civic and political organizations, Negro History Week has been a time for historical reading and discussion.

> We believe that Negro History Week has made a great contribution to awareness of Black History. Moreover, the recognition of Negro History Week has caught on, and has become an intellectual tradition in the 20th century Afro-American experience. However, times have changed considerably since 1926. In political and cultural terms, the time has come to transform our orientation: from Negro to *BLACK*, from History to *LIBERATION*, from Week to *MONTH*.

> The revolutionary upsurge of the 1960's is our most recent historical experience of massive militant protest. It continues to be a rich source of lessons for current and future struggles. *BLACK LIBERATION MONTH* unites with Woodson's effort, but does so by raising it to a higher level based on the lessons of the 1960s.

> In sum, our study of history must be linked with the revolutionary history of the Black liberation movement. Our goal is not simply to symbolically institutionalize a change in our yearly calendar of events, but to use this month as one more way to raise the consciousness of the masses of people about the historical nature of exploitation and oppression, to unite people around a correct political line, and to mobilize people to actively take up the struggle for Black liberation.

Professionalism — The development of Black Studies has been mainly a reaction to the racism and conflict Blacks have experienced in other disciplines and areas of the university. So it is particularly important to indicate the affirmative action taken by Black scholars to impose high quality professional standards on Black Studies. Professional achievement is a function mainly of research and publication, acceptance and approval of one's work in professional organizations that decide future developments, and productive organization of graduate level programs of study. In short, Black Studies is consolidating around professional journals, professional organizations, and graduate programs. Achievement is being judged on the basis of a shared value-orientation in the field. This is clearly spelled out in a 1981 study by McWorter, "The Professionalization of Achievement: Ranking of Black Studies Programs."

Theory — Another aspect of the development of Black Studies is the theoretical coherence of the field. Alternative theoretical models that serve to organize ideas and guide research have been clarified. George (1984)[13] deals with four models of race relations theory, including the ethnic group model, the caste model, the colonial model, and the Marxist model.

Different theories are most clearly found in the alternative texts that have developed in the field. Each text is an expression of a basic position in Afro-American Studies. There are three fundamental points of unity: the central theme of Black Studies is "ACADEMIC EXCELLENCE AND SOCIAL RESPONSIBILITY"; Afro-American intellectual history is the foundation of the field; and Africa remains an important reference for the historical origin of the Afro-American experience and for comparative analysis as well. But some differences do exist.

Karenga (1982)[14] provided a text based on his nationalist theory of Kawaida:

The seven basic subject areas of Black Studies then are: Black History; Black Religion; Black Social Organization; Black Politics; Black Economics; Black Creative Production (Black Art, Music and Literature) and Black Psychology...this conceptual framework is taken from *Kawaida* theory, a theory of cultural and social change.

Asante (1980) put forward a theory called "Afrocentricity," which consciously attempts to build on Kawaida.[15] Munford (1978) presented a Marxist analysis.[16] He focuses on making historical analysis of class and class struggle the basis for understanding the Black experience. His analysis especially concentrates on slavery, the lumpenproletariat, racism, and Africa.

Our text is based on a paradigm of unity for Black Studies, a framework in which all points of view can have the most useful coexistence. While maintaining a dynamic process of debate, everyone involved can remain united and committed to the field. This includes Marxists, nationalists, pan-Africanists, and old-fashioned civil rights integrationists as well. Further, our specific orientation is anti-racist, anti-sexist, and anti-capitalist. We are basing our analysis on most of our Black intellectual tradition and that leads us, as it did Langston Hughes, Paul Robeson, and W.E.B. DuBois, to a progressive socialist position. This text, therefore, has a definite point of view, but it presents the basis for clarity, understanding, and dialogue between different schools of thought and different disciplines.

The Text

This section is designed to introduce you to the specific conceptual framework of this text. A conceptual framework involves the clarification of theoretical ideas on the basis of which one proceeds to do an analysis. In a text that introduces the entire field of Afro-American Studies, it is necessary to have a conceptual framework that is inclusive of the entire subject matter. The conceptual framework focuses on two questions: What is the Black experience? How does it change?

Table 1	
Basic Aspects of the Black Experience	
Level of Human Reality	Key Black Studies Concept
BIOLOGY	RACE
POLITICAL ECONOMY	CLASS
SOCIETY	NATIONALITY
CONSCIOUSNESS	IDEOLOGY

The Black experience is the sum total of the content of Black peoples lives. There are four main levels of this experience, as can be seen in Table 1.

Biology and Race

On the biological level, the overall key variables are race, age, and gender. All biological traits are controlled by a genetic code found in every cell of a person's body. This genetic code is inherited from one's biological parents. A race or gender group is defined as a human population sharing specific physical traits (e.g., sexual organs for gender and skin color for race). A great controversy continues to rage in scientific circles regarding the relative importance of the view that human behavior is biologically determined versus the view that people become who they are as a result of socio-historical forces. This is known as the "nature versus nurture" debate.

There is little convincing evidence that biological differences between races make a social or historical difference. Racial differences almost always are put forward to explain inequality, where one racial group has a lower standard of living and less power. An argument of biological inferiority rationalizes the group's being on the bottom. The logic is that they are inferior, and they therefore belong on the bottom. This is not a scientific discussion of race, but RACISM, which is an ideology of racial inferiority. White racism is the overall position that Blacks are inferior and whites are superior. An example of how silly this is can be seen in South Africa, the most racist country in the world. The South African government restricts the freedom of everyone who isn't white. However, when the Japanese became economically powerful (as they are now in the automobile, steel, electronics, and computer fields), the racist white South Africans reconsidered. They wanted excellent trade relations with Japan so they decided to make the Japanese honorary white people!

Political Economy and Class

On the level of political economy, the central concept is class. Economic activities involve the production, distribution, and consumption of scarce material things needed for human survival and that otherwise serve human wants. Class is a historical relationship between groups of people. It is a relationship of power that determines who works, what they get from it, and what impact they can have on the society at large. There is a ruling class in every society, although different types of societies are not organized in the same way. In feudal Europe royal families made up the ruling class. In traditional African society, this was often the case as well. This is class rule based on heredity. In a capitalist society, heredity is much less important. Some mobility in and out of the ruling class occurs despite the status of one's family by birth.

The overwhelming majority of adults in the U.S.A. get up every morning and go to work. They have to do this because only by doing so will they earn an income necessary for their families' survival. Therefore, political economy is a universal feature of the human experience and a necessary aspect of Afro-American Studies

Society and Nationality

There are two major aspects of society: culture and social institutions. Culture refers to values and life style, whereas social institutions refer to roles and collective forms of social interaction. These are not temporary phenomena, but are permanent features of a society that are reproduced and transmitted across generations. Nationality (sometimes called ethnicity) is the particular identity of a group based on its culture and social institutions. Historically, such identity is correlated with economic interdependence and a common language. The issue of nationality is one of the key issues of the Afro-American experience in the U.S.A.

Ideology and Consciousness

How each of these three aspects of the human experience is known, thought about, and discussed is the focus of consciousness. This is the experience of the abstract, mental images that enable one to make choices and realize human freedom regarding the physical and social worlds. While the "brain" is a physical reality, it works as a "mind" full of ideas, conceptions, imagination, opinions, beliefs, etc. There can be no "mind" without a "brain," although it is possible to have a damaged brain or be mentally ill and to be, what people call "out of your mind."

The most formal organization of one's consciousness is the realm of ideology. Ideology is a set of beliefs that serve to define physical, social, mental, and spiritual reality. Everyone in society has an ideological orientation, but only trained and disciplined thinkers have a comprehensive and coherent ideological orientation.

The Black experience is the complex sum total of all aspects of the human experience as lived by Black people. The Afro-American experience has a beginning and a definite logic of change, as can be seen in Figure B.

Historical change in the Afro-American experience has alternatively represented social cohesion and social disruption. Social cohesion is an established and relatively stable pattern of social life that is transmitted across generations. This is not social life without conflict, but rather social life that can be taught to the next generation. Social disruption occurs when these patterns are broken and people have to adjust to a new environment, to a new set of relations, to a new way of life. Of course, out of

Figure B
Historical Change and the Black Experience

SOCIAL COHESION	SOCIAL DISRUPTION
Traditional Africa	Slave Trade
Slavery	Emancipation
Rural Life	Migration
Urban Life	Crisis

every experience of disruption emerges a new form of social cohesion. This dynamic pattern of change, historical periodization, is universal for all Black people in the U.S.A. Every person and family can locate their own experience within this pattern.

The overall framework constitutes a paradigm of unity in Afro-American Studies. This chart defines a logical space for the entire field of Afro-American Studies. The columns are historical stages marked with letters, and the rows are aspects of the Black experience marked with numbers. Each box (e.g., A-1 or G-4) is a logical connection of experience within a specific historical context. With this analytical tool, it is possible to have a conception of the entire field and begin to identify boxes and sets of boxes to codify and sum up existing research, as well as to chart the path for additional new research.

The field of Afro-American Studies is an exciting Intellectual Adventure, an experience that will open new worlds of knowledge to both Blacks and whites.

Toward a Paradigm of Unity in Afro-American Studies

Logic of Change	*Social Cohesion*	Traditional Africa	—	Slavery	—	Rural Life	—	Urban Life
	Social Disruption	—	Slave Trade	—	Emancipation	—	Migrations	—
Units of Analysis	Ideology	A1	B1	C1	D1	E1	F1	G1
	Nationality	A2	B2	C2	D2	E2	F2	G2
	Class	A3	B3	C3	D3	E3	F3	G3
	Race	A4	B4	C4	D4	E4	F4	G4

Endnotes

1. Selected Works by DuBois: on Africa, *The World and Africa* (1947); on slavery, *The Suppression of the African Slave Trade to the United States of America, 1638-1870* (1896), *John Brown* (1909), *Black Reconstruction In America* (1935); on the rural experience, *The Negroes of Farmville, Virginia* (1898), *The Negro Landholder of Georgia* (1901), *The Negro Farmer* (1906); on the urban experience, *The Philadelphia Negro* (1899).

2. Selected Works by Woodson: on Africa, *African Heroes and Heroines* (1939); on slavery, *Free Negro Owners of Slaves* (1924), *Free Negro Heads of Families* (1925), *The Mind of the Negro As Reflected in Letters Written During The Crisis 1800-1860* (1926), *The Education of the Negro Prior to 1861* (1915); on the rural experience, *The Rural Negro* (1930); on the urban experience, *A Century of Negro Migration* (1918), *The Negro as a Businessman* (1929), *The Negro Wage Earner* (1930) with Lorenzo Greene, *The Negro Professional Man and the Community* (1934); on institutions, *The History of the Negro Church* (1921), and *The Miseducation of the Negro* (1923).

3. Selected Works by Frazier: on Africa *Race and Culture Contacts in the Modern World* (1957); on slavery, *The Free Negro Family* (1932); on the urban experience, *The Negro Family in Chicago* (1932), *Negro Youth at the Crossways* (1940), *Black Bourgeoisie* (1955); on institutions, *The Negro Family in the United States* (1939), and *The Negro Church in America* (1964).

4. Selected Works by Hughes: autobiographical works, *I Wonder As I Wander* (1956), *The Big Sea* (1940); general work, *The Book of Negro Folklore* (1958) with Arna Bontemps, *A Pictorial History of the Negro in America* (1956) with Milton Meltzer, *The Poetry of the Negro 1746-1949* (1949) with Arna Bontemps; poetry, *The Weary Blues* (1926), *Shakespeare in Harlem* (1942), *Montage of a Dream Deferred* (1951), *The Panther and the Lash* (1967); plays, *Mulatto* (1935), *Tambourines to Glory* (1963); novels, *Not Without Laughter* (1930), *Simple Speaks His Mind* (1950), *Simple's Uncle Sam* (1965); short stories, *The Ways of White Folks* (1934), *Something in Common and Other Stories* (1963).

5. Patricia Gurin and Edgar Epps, *Black Consciousness, Identity, and Achievement: A Study of Students in Historically Black Colleges* (New York: Wiley, 1975); Harry Edwards, *The Struggle that Must Be: An Autobiography* (New York: Macmillan, 1980); Luke Tripp *Black Students, Ideology, and Class* (Urbana: Afro Scholar Working Papers, no. 9, University of Illinois, 1982).

6. William Orrick, "Shut it Down! A College in Crisis: San Francisco State College, October 1968-April 1969" *A report to the National Commission on the Causes and Prevention of Violence* (Washington, DC: U.S. Government Printing Office, 1969).

7. Sidney F. Walton, Jr., *The Black Curriculum: Developing a Program in Afro-American Studies* (East Palo Alto: Black Liberation Publishers, 1969).

8. Cleveland Donald, Jr., "Cornell: Confrontation in Black and White" in *Divided We Stand: Reflections on the Crisis at Cornell*, ed. Cushing Strout and David I. Grossvogel (Garden City: Doubleday, 1970); Edwards, *The Struggle that Must Be*.

9. Benjamin E. Mays, *Born to Rebel: An Autobiography* (New York: Charles Scribner's Sons, 1971).

10. Armstead Robinson et al., eds. *Black Studies in the University: A Symposium* (New Haven: Yale University Press, 1969).

11. John W. Blassingame, ed., *New Perspectives on Black Studies* (Urbana: University of Illinois Press, 1971); Rafael L. Cortada, *Black Studies: An Urban and Comparative Curriculum* (Lexington, MA: Xerox College Publishing, 1974); Nick Aaron Ford, *Black Studies: Threat-or-Challenge* (Port Washington: Kennikat Press, 1973).

12. Charles A. Frye, *The Impact of Black Studies on the Curricula of Three Universities* (Washington, DC: University Press of America, 1976); William E. Sims, *Black Studies: Pitfalls and Potential* (Washington, D.C.: University Press of America, 1978).

13. Hermon George, Jr., *American Race Relations Theory: A Review of Four Models* (New York: University Press of America, 1984).

14. Maulana Karenga, *Introduction to Black Studies* (Inglewood, CA: Kawaida Publications, 1982).

15. Molefi Kete Asante, *Afrocentricity: The Theory of Social Change* (Buffalo: Amulefi, 1980).

16. Clarence J. Munford, *Production Relations, Class and Black Liberation: A Marxist Perspective in Afro-American Studies* (Amsterdam: B.R. Brüner, 1978).

36.

The Afrocentric Metatheory and Disciplinary Implications

Molefi Kete Asante

It is my intention to discuss the Afrocentric metatheory, research methodologies and the Africological discipline with an eye toward the development of an ongoing discourse about the future of this relatively new field of inquiry. As we know, methods refer to processes and procedures which govern how we approach a subject. Methodology, on the other hand, is the study or methods or the science of methods. A discipline manifests itself in its attachment to certain theoretical directions, philosophical assumptions, and methods of engaging phenomena.

In examining these topics I will begin, of course, with a discussion of Afrocentricity as a theoretical instrument for the examination of phenomena. Afrocentricity is a simple idea. At its base, it is concerned with African people being the subjects of historical and social experiences rather than objects in the margins of European experiences. I recall seeing the book by Charles Wesley and Carter Woodson entitled *The Negro In Our History* and feeling that they were truly speaking from and to a Eurocentric perspective if they felt that such a title captured the essence of our experience. These were two of the most successful African American historians and yet they could not totally disengage their critical thinking from the traditional framework of Eurocentric scholarship. Viewing phenomena from the perspective of Africans as central, rather than peripheral, means that you secure a better vantage point on the facts.

Afrocentricity is a metatheoretical framework, a philosophical position. Therefore, one cannot speak logically of several types of Afrocentricity, since it is, as I have explained in my own works, a metatheory. There may be various theories within the metatheory but the metatheory itself is decided, it is not debated. One either operates from an Afrocentric perspective or one does not. Of course, one can take the *khephra* position and push the ball in many directions; you can be Afrocentric on some things and not on others. The definition of what constitutes an Afrocentric perspective has been expounded in several places, again, including my own articles and books on the subject. There should not be or there does not have to be any confusion about the meaning of Afrocentricity.

This does not means that a *cartouche* of position is impossible; it simply means that you must choose your positions carefully. Neither is this an attempt to concentrate solely on the question of identity, though in most cases, for the scholar of African descent especially, it is useful; the past few hundred years of domination have often dislocated us. However, what is more important is to say that such concentration on making something alien does not necessarily make them or you hostile. E.T. was definitely portrayed as an alien, but not unfriendly: To concentrate on my family and find the origin of my own roots may make others strangers, but not hostile strangers.

Dislocation, location and *relocation* are the principal calling cards of the Afrocentric theoretical position. My attempt is always to locate a situation, an event, an author. Location tells you where someone is, that is, where they are standing. It may not tell you where they are headed, but you do know where they are given certain markers of identity. Thus, the person who uses terms like minority, third world, primitives, natives, mainstream is definitely in a particular intellectual space. As I would know a political conservative, a Marxist, a deconstructionist, or a racist by language and behavior, I can also know a Eurocentrist. Of course, one can frequently use language to signify, that is, as an instrument to conceal or point to a direction away from representation. Sometimes that space may not be of the person's choosing; one could be pushed into a space by circumstances. Of course, in such instances we will say that the person is a servant of forces beyond his or her immediate control. Not controlling one's space seems to reflect more of the slave than a human agent acting with authority. More will be said on this throughout the presentation.

I have identified through historical and literary analysis two fallacies of position: the *locational* fallacy and the *linguistic* fallacy. The first occurs when a person is de-centered, misoriented, or disoriented and cannot possibly be looking from the proper angle. This is a problem Malcolm X recognized when he spoke of some enslaved Africans thinking they had come to America with the Mayflower or when he told us that there were some who took the slavemaster's perspective when it came to the plantation. Such people are not only dislocated but disoriented. The second fallacy occurs when a person is located in the proper place but does not have the experience or the ability to explain or describe what is being seen. The second fallacy leads to a sort of naive nationalism because the viewer has only a vantage point but no adequate discipline or skill for analysis. Both types of persons abound in the academy.

Theory and Research

Research which is most instrumental to the development of Africology as a discipline will have to be conducted within the context of theory development. I have recently read Perry A. Hall's "Historical Transformation in African American Musical Culture" published in the Spring 1991 issue of *Word: A Black Culture Journal*. The work is an example of good scholarship about African people that is neither Afrocentric nor Africological. That is, it does not deal with a particular vantage point or perspective on the facts and phenomena which places it uniquely within the discipline of Africology. I have no intention of saying that Hall's research is not useful or should not have been done. My point is that such work adds little to the development of the discipline. Anyone from psychology could have taken Erving Goffman's work and done the same kind of "Goffmanian" analysis. Yet the author had available to him a number of Africological instruments that would have assisted him in his research if he had been interested. The question most scholars ask is, what are the elements of theory and method most useful in the advancement of our intellectual discipline?

I believe that a high priority should be assigned to research in Africology that makes a contribution to theory for several reasons. In the first place, any field of study prospers or languishes according to the power of its theory. Secondly, theory sets the tone for the research methods, allows the scholars to find ways to discover new truths. Theory, for me, does not refer only to formal propositions that characterize the hard sciences, but more generally to a coherent set of concepts that serve as a central focus of a field of study. We have begun to develop such concepts, gaining some of them from traditional fields, and adding others that have emerged out of our own research. Africology, as an area of inquiry, aspires to reach mature disciplinary status. As such, it must address a portion of what it does to the generating of conceptual focus. This is the most valuable contribution scholars can now make to the future bank of Africology. Unlike the field of physics, the Africologist is not seeking to find verification or prediction but explanation and clarification. Our research should help us to clarify theory by subjecting our key concepts, e.g., location, dislocation, Africa-centeredness, etc., to intense critical tests. With regard to this point it should be noted that conceptual clarification and consequent development of theory will probably add a bias in favor of the social/behavioral area rather than the more humanities oriented cultural/aesthetic area. This will happen simply because observation rather than textual or historical analyses are the central elements of empiricism. This does not mean that we must throw away concepts that are irrelevant to observations but rather that we must be aware of the dual possibilities of our particular discipline.

Specification of Relations

The problem of specification of relations is tied to methods because it deals with how symbols and signs, concepts and values, contexts and contents are related to each other. From a methodological point of view one must ask questions about relationships of concepts and contents in order to understand the material or physical interaction in any given case of Africological research. I have worked with my students on developing an approach to what has been called ethnography, a term I abhor because it is a Eurocentric word that sees us as objects. We have developed the concept of introspection, which means what you as the researcher feel about the topic before you undertake to study it. Thus, in any ethnography we ask the scholar to put down his or her introspection first. We are working on these issues because theory is intimately related to research method, and theory is the principal power behind the creation of disciplinary maturity. Theory-oriented research should be encouraged in all departments with the aim of clarification and explanation.

The Lack of Clarity

To object to Afrocentricity, a fundamental stepping stone to any multicultural project, as an effort to marginalize African Americans, is to criticize amiss. The aim, that is, the purpose of centered positions which contribute to the multicultural discussion is to bring about harmony within society. Otherwise what one gets is an off-white contribution to the pale white stream. A better option is always to contribute the richness of the African American, the Latino, the Asian, the Native American, and the European to the common purpose. But there is no mainstream; this is a misnomer. Those who speak of a mainstream are often speaking about a white stream with African eddies bubbling on the side. Whatever the word "mainstream" means it has rarely included Africans. And those who use the term do not think of African American poetry or people as being mainstream. Those who speak of "mainstreams" and "universals" are most often speaking of whites. And therefore when someone says "universal man" it is not simply a reflection of women but of the Mandinka, the Zulu, the Hmong, the Yaqui, the African American. Yet there really are only tributaries and our cultural flow is a part of the grand delta of ideas.

The opposition to racism is not abstract, it is concrete. In our present social, economic, and intellectual condition the resistance to white supremacy is not black supremacy but pluralism without hierarchy, a frightening concept in the context of prolonged white domination of ideas. Manning Marable has developed a similar thesis in his book, *How Capitalism Underdeveloped Black America*. Afrocentricity is not a black version of Eurocentricity, which is an arrogant imposition of a particular view as if it is a universal view. Such a position is ethnocentric and leads to racism when it is enforced by custom, law, or physical force. It degrades other views and valorizes the European viewpoint.

The African American Studies Idea

My thesis is simply stated. During the past twenty or so years since the establishment of African American Studies, two major changes have occurred in the American Academy which have altered the academic landscape for years to come. The first was the institutionalization of African American Studies, Africology, as a discipline alongside other disciplines within the Academy. The second was the creation and mounting of the first doctoral program in African American Studies in the nation at Temple University. The first transformed the student movement of the 60s into a concrete reality in academic units as well as in theories and methods. The second transcended the parochial and provincial role which had been assigned to the field by keepers of the Academy. What were the characteristics that manifested themselves in this flowering of new intellectual activity?

The processes by which the curricula documents were produced by African American students in the late 1960s and early 70s were unknown in the history of the creation of academic fields and very few of us at that time had any real idea what the future would bring. Curricula were inseparable from the concept of the university, just as lungs and breathing could not be separated from the inhaling and exhaling of oxygen. With the curricula changes there would have to be fundamental changes in the institution. We knew this, it now seems, instinctively because the few African American professors who were on those campuses often had not been there long or could not give us advice. As the first permanent director of the UCLA Center for Afro American Studies I wrote the interdisciplinary M.A. program and in 1968 started, along with Robert Singleton, who had been an interim director at the Center, the *Journal of Black Studies*. We knew then, as most of you knew, that Black Studies was not the mere aggregation of courses about our experiences but had to be courses taught from what we called at the time "the black perspective." In our rush to establish the perspective, we even demanded that only black teachers teach the programs until we discovered that perspective is not a biological issue. Some of the black professors taught from a white perspective. It is from this reality that I shall attempt to answer the question posed above regarding the nature of disciplinary transformations, their characteristics, and future.

The Context of Methods

African American Studies is a discrete discipline with certain critical perspectives, theories, and methods which are necessary for its role in discovery and understanding. The attendant propositions suggest creativity, innovation, genius, and authority in disciplines. Assaults on Africology as a discipline, as we shall see, are nothing more than attacks on the idea that African Americans can neither create theories nor disciplines, and is ultimately the same tune played in previous discussions of African intelligence. A number of books, such as George Mosse's *A History of Racism in Europe*, Michael Bradley's *The Ice Man Inheritance*, and Stephen J. Gould's *The Mismeasure of Man*, exist on this subject. When this tune is played by Africans themselves it is often the result of dislocation, that is, the assumption of the place where Africans have been pushed by white racial hegemony within the Academy. In such situations the African feels that he or she must act much more "correct" in the white sense than the whites themselves. There is a felt pressure to be hard, as it were, on any African who raises the possibility of escape from the mental plantation. What I am saying is that it becomes necessary to suspend judgement or to kill one's traditional sensibilities so to speak in order to understand the language of the new reality, that is, Africans as subjects instead of objects in the European project. This is difficult to discern from the same tired portals of traditions which are rooted in the conquest of Africans by Europeans. Africology becomes a discipline whose mission is, *inter alia*, the critique of domination.

Issues in Inquiry

I am not sure whether it is necessary any longer to debate the question of perspective in terms of the Africological discipline, as has been the case during the past twenty years; at least, in the circle of scholars with whom I am associated it is fairly well agreed that the fundamental basis for Africology as a separate discipline is a unique perspective. Nevertheless, the ground is clearly established in the works of several scholars with whom you are familiar. Their arguments are expertly placed within the on-going creative project of African liberation, now more than ever, an intellectual liberation.

Let me digress a bit here and discuss the issue of Kemet, that is, the primacy of Kemet in the thinking of Afrocentrists. First of all, it is not a desire to go back to Africa because African Americans are African, just as white Australians are Europeans. Moreover, it is not a desire for gloriana, for self esteem, any more than factual historical information in any context about any culture is gloriana. Furthermore, it is not an attempt to replace the European information we have learned with African information. Rather, for the discipline of Africology, it is the endeavor to see in the most monumental civilization of antiquity patterns, concepts, connections, and relationships which will assist us in the process of explanation and clarification. Cheikh Anta Diop said it, "Egypt is to Africa and African people everywhere as Greece is to Europe and European people." What he meant was that until we were able to examine the classical Nile Valley civilizations we would not know how to handle our contemporary cultural manifestations, either on the continent or in the Diaspora. I do not believe, as E. Franklin Frazier believed, that Africa disappeared in the African American during the Enslavement.

Therefore, the Afrocentric enterprise is framed by cosmological, epistemological, axiological, and aesthetic issues. In this regard the Afrocentric method pursues a world voice distinctly Africa-centered in relationship to external phenomena. I did not say distinctly African, which is another issue, but Africa-centered, a theoretical perspective. The work of Robert Farris Thompson, Basil Davidson, and Sidney Wilhelm should be cited in connection with their research that has shown Africans as subjects rather than objects.

Cosmological Issue

The place of African culture in the philosophy, myths and legends, literatures, and oratories of African people constitutes, at the mythological level, the cosmological issue within the Afrocentric enterprise, which is an enterprise entirely within the Africalogical discipline. What role does the African culture play in the African's interface with the cosmos? The debate over "African cultures or culture" is answered definitionally within the context of the Afrocentric perspective so I will not discuss it at this juncture, no more than to say that it has been dealt with in the writings of Afrocentric scholars. One might see particularly the book of *African Culture: The Rhythms of Unity* edited by Kariamu Asante and myself for a discussion of the issue.

Among the questions that might be dealt with under the cosmological umbrella are: What dramas of life and death, in the African tradition, are reflected in the metaphysical metaphors? How are those dramas translated by lunar, solar, or stellar figures? The fundamental assumptions of Africological inquiry are based on the African orientation of the cosmos. By "African" I clearly mean a "composite African," not a specific, discrete African ethnicity, which would rather mean, African American, Yoruba, Ibo, Fulani, Zulu, Mandingo, Kikongo, etc. C.T. Keto has taken this up in his book *Afrocentricity and History* by writing that "African American thinkers were among the first to feel the need to create the concept 'composite' African and, in so doing, their reference was the whole of the African continent which included, historically, ancient Kemet" (Keto, 1991, p. 5). He continues that "denied a precise ethnic linkage, they created a holistic African vision that...influenced Africans on the continent."

There are several concerns which might be considered cosmological in that they are fundamental frames for research initiatives in this discipline. I shall only make reference to them here and refer you to my recent book, *Kemet, Afrocentricity, and Knowledge,* for additional commentary. The concerns are: Racial Formation, Culture, Gender, and Class. Race as a social factor remains prevalent in heterogeneous, but hegemonically Eurocentric, societies. In the United States, the most developed example of such a society, the question of race is the most dominant aspect of intersocial relations. Cultural questions are usefully viewed in the context of shared perceptions, attitudes, and predispositions that allow communities of people to organize responses in similar ways. Gender also must be seen as a substantial research area in questions of social, political, economic, and cultural dimensions. Since the liberation of women is not an act of charity but a basic premise of the Afrocentric project, the researcher must be cognizant of sexist language, terminology, and perspectives. Class becomes, for the Afrocentrist aware of our history, much more complicated than capitalists and workers, or bourgeoisie and proletariat. Finding the relevant class positions and places in given situations will assist the Africalogical scholar with analysis. Indeed, Eurocentrism with all its potential for asserting its particular self as universal becomes the repository for race, class, and gender conflict. Rather than an isolated or isolatable discussion of race, or class, or gender one begins to view the dominant Eurocentric mythos as containing all of these elements.

Epistemological Issue

What constitutes the search for truth in the Afrocentric enterprise? In Africology, language, myth, ancestral memory, dance-music-art, and science provide the sources of knowledge, the canons of proof, and the structure of truth.

Discussions of language from an Afrocentric perspective or research into African language, diasporan or continental, may lead to understanding about the nature of truth. Ebonics, the African American language, serves as the archetype of African American language in the United States. A variety of languages in Brazil, Ecuador, Colombia, Panama and Belize. One of our students, for example, is centering her research on the Garifuna people of Belize. However, while her work will include much that is historical and linguistic, she is principally concerned with an epistemological question rooted in the inquiry on methods of retention as expressed in the declarative culture, as opposed to the cognitive, of the people.

The strong, expressive, and inescapable myth of the African presence in America, indeed in the world, has value for the discovery of truth in many dimensions of human life. Thus, behind and in front of our banquet of possibilities are the refracting elements of myths that appropriately mediate our relationships. Knowing these myths, making a habit of investigating them in a serious manner, allows the researcher to form new metaphors about our experiences. In dance-music-art, performing and representational art forms are central to interpretation of cultural and social reality. Our analysis is informed by the way dance is seen in the African culture, even in the way we view the Africanization of the walkman.

Axiological Issue

The question of value is at the core of the Afrocentric quest for truth because ethical issues have always been connected to the advancement of the discipline. One cannot speak of Africology apart from its origin in the drive to humanize education, to democratize the curriculum, to advance the understanding of humanity. This is the birthright of the discipline more than any other disciplines in the social sciences or the humanities. What constitutes the good is a matter of historical conditions and cultural developments within a particular society. A common expression among us relates to the good and beautiful in this way, "Beauty is what beauty does." We are also sure that a person "is beautiful because he or she is good." When a sister says, "that's a beautiful brother," she is usually meaning something more than his physical looks. Doing good is equivalent to being beautiful. The Afrocentric method isolates conduct and action in social or literary analysis. The aim is to see what conduct has been sanctioned, and if sanctioned, carried out.

Aesthetic Issue

Kariamu Welsh Asante has identified seven aspects of the African aesthetic which she calls "senses." Based upon her field research into Zimbabwe dance she isolated *polyrhythm, polycentrism, dimensionality, repetition, curvilinearity, epic memory,* and *wholism* as investigative categories for African aesthetics. Each aspect might be examined from the disciplinary perspective by any researcher using the idea of African centrality. Particularly useful in the context of drama, dance, the plastic arts, and literature, the aesthetic senses represent an Afrocentric approach to the subject of African art.

Our motifs should be reflective of our historical experiences and where we have found them, the people have responded. The best of our music, the best of our art, and the best of our literature use the motifs of the people's path. This is culture. What is it to be a cultured person if you are an African American? Does this mean that you master only the European historical experiences? Are those the ones that we have been reinforced in and therefore believe are superior to our own? How should a scholar study the person who seeks to write or paint as an African? Does it not depend upon what the person claims to be doing?

The Shape of the Discipline

The groundedness of observations and behavior in the historical experiences of Africans becomes the main base for operation in the field of African American Studies. Centrism, the operation of the African as subject or the Latino as subject, or the European as subject, and so forth, allows Africology to take its place alongside other disciplines without hierarchy and without hegemony. As a discipline, Africology is sustained by a commitment to centering the study of African phenomena, events, and persons in the particular cultural voice of the composite African people. But it does not promote such a view as universal. Furthermore, it opens the door for interpretations of reality based upon evidence and data secured by reference to that world voice.

The anteriority of the classical African civilizations must be entertained by any Africological inquiry, simply because without that perspective, our work hangs in the air, detached, and isolated or becomes nothing more than a sub-set of the Eurocentric disciplines. As I have often said, without employing Afrocentricity in this manner, our research becomes disconnected, lacks historical continuity, and is incidental and nonorganic.

The Eurocentric dogma creates an intellectual structure that locks the African in a conceptual prison. One key to this dogma is that philosophy is the highest discipline, and that philosophy is Greek. Thus, Greece becomes the model for the structure of knowledge in the West. According to this dogma, everything starts with the Greeks: philosophy, politics, art, drama, literature, and mathematics. There is no philosophy in Africa, Asia, or the Americas, only the Europeans have philosophy. However, since the first Greek philosophers, Thales and Isocrates, studied philosophy in Kemet (Ancient Egypt), philosophy could not have started with the Greeks. Cheikh Anta Diop, perhaps the greatest African intellect of the 20th century, argued that there could be no understanding of things African without linkage to ancient Kemet. Thus, Egypt is to the rest of the African world as Greece is to the rest of the European world. Europe constitutes itself around several principals including its connection, however mythical or distant, to ancient Greece, to certain ideas that are traced to the Greeks and to the Romans, and to Christianity as a unifying theme from the 10th Century A.D. onward.

Subject Fields

To say that Africology is a discipline does not mean that it is without subject fields or interest areas. There are seven general subject fields which I have identified following the work of Maulana Karenga in *Introduction to Black Studies*: communicative, social, historical, cultural, political, economic, and psychological. Most of the people who are working in the field are approaching their work from one of the above subject fields. A student of Africology chooses a research issue which falls within one or more of those subject fields. In any endeavor to uncover, analyze, criticize, or anticipate an issue, the Africologist works to use the appropriate methods for the subject. To examine cultural nationalism, for example, within the historical or political subject field would require a constant method for research.

There are three paradigmatic approaches to research in Africology: *functional, categorical* and *etymological*. The first represents needs, policy, and action orientations. Categorical refers to schemes, gender, class, and themes. The etymological paradigm deals with language, literatures, and oratories. Studies of either sort might be conducted in the context of African society, either on the continent or in the Americas. The aim is to provide research results that are ultimately verifiable in human experience.

A student of Africology might choose to study in the general field of history but use the functional paradigm. Of course, many combinations are possible and the student is limited only by her or his ability to properly conceptualize the topic for study in an Afrocentric manner. Since Africology is not history, political science, communication, literary analysis, or sociology, the student must be well-grounded in the assumptions of the Afrocentric approach to human knowledge. Scholars in our field have often been handicapped in their quest for clear and authoritative statements by a lack of methodological direction for collection and analyzing data, choosing and interpreting research themes, approaching and appreciating cultural artifacts, and isolating and evaluating facts. This has been the case although works by Larry Neal and Paul Carter Harrison in the literary theory field introduced us to the possibilities inherent in our own centered positions as early as the Sixties. However, as an increasingly self-conscious field, African American Studies, Africology, has begun to produce a variety of philosophical approaches to Afrocentric inquiry. These studies have served to underscore the need for a solid, methodological approach at the level of basic premises of the field and have become, in effect, pioneer works in a new perspective on phenomena.

The Afrocentric psychologists have led the reconceptualization of the field or African personality theories. Certainly, I count the work of Daudi Azibo, Joseph Baldwin, Linda Myers, and Wade Nobles in this vein. They have explored areas of human psychology which impinge on the African experience. Political Scientists qua political scientists such as Ronald Walter, Leonard Jeffries, Mack Jones, Manning Marable, and James Turner have argued positions that may be called Afrocentric. Maulana Karenga, Patrick Bellegarde-Smith, and Jacob Carruthers, from their original base in political science, have become Afrocentrists. The work of Houston Baker in the area of vernacular theory might be considered Afrocentric inasmuch as the source of his images are culturally centered. In addition, the works of several writers, such as Henry Louis Gates, Abu Abarry, Joyce Joyce, and Eleanor Taylor have elements of centered locations. The field of sociology, since the early days of the first departments in 1882 and 1884 at Chicago and Columbia respectively, has remained bogged down in social problems and paradigms that do not permit adequate assessment of African cultural data. A number of African American sociologists are attempting to break out of those quagmires. Robert Staples had been an early pioneer in this field and now the work of Bruce Hare at Syracuse is significant in this respect. Vivian Gordon has long been a major force in the Africana Womanist project in which sex and race are joined rather than separated as in the work of the Afrofemcentrists of the Black Feminists. Indeed, Gordon's work is joined with that of Clenora Hudson Weems and Brenda Vemer to make the most Afrocentric statement on the women question we have seen in Africology. They have found their models, like Donna Marimba Richards, in the ancient models of Auset-Ausar and Mawu-Lisa. In design and architecture, scholars such as Bill Harris at the University of Virginia are exploring Afrocentric designs in housing. What would we have done without the African porch as a daycare platform?

Africology is defined as the Afrocentric study of phenomena, events, ideas, and personalities related to Africa. The mere study of African phenomena is not Africology but some other intellectual enterprise. I make no judgment on those enterprises, I simply say that they are not Africalogical. Like other disciplines, more or less severe, our discipline is based on certain assumptions, objectives, and constructions of language. Thus, the Temple Circle of Afrocentric scholars has tried to exorcise terms such as sub-Saharan, Hottentot, Bushmen, pygmy, and minority. Such a massive project of redressing the decentering of Africans will surely take us well into the 21st century. The scholar who generates research questions based upon the centrality of Africa is engaged in a very different research inquiry than the one who imposes Western criteria on the phenomena. "Afrocentric" is the most important word in the definition, otherwise one might think that any study of African phenomena or peoples constitutes Africology. It is the commitment to perspective and method that distinguishes the discipline from others.

Geographical Scope

The geographical scope of the African world, and hence, the Africological enterprise, includes Africa, the Americas, the Caribbean, various regions in Asia, and the Pacific. Wherever people declare themselves as African, despite the distance from the continent or the recency of their out-migration, they are accepted as part of the African world. Thus, the indigenous people of Australia and New Guinea are considered African and in a larger context subject for Africalogists who maintain a full analytical and theoretical discussion of African phenomena.

Although the major regions of African culture are Africa, the Caribbean, and the Americas, even within those regions there are varying degrees of cultural and technological affinity to an African world voice. Africology is concerned with Africans in any particular as well as all regions. Thus, Abdias do Nascimento, our visiting professor from Brazil at Temple this year, can remind us that Brazil is significant for understanding the African presence in the Americas. In Brazil, Zumbi (the greatest king of the Palmares Republic), Luisa Mahin, and Luiz Gama are principal figures in the making of history; in the Dominican Republic, Diego de Campo and Lemba provide the same historical and intellectual energy one finds in Venezuela with Oyocta, King Miguel, and King Bayano; in Columbia there is Benkos Bioho; and in Mexico, the great African American, Yanga.

Africology rejects the Africanist idea of the separation of African people on the continent from African people in the Diaspora as being intellectually short-sighted, analytically vapid, and philosophically unsound. One cannot study Africans in the United States or Brazil or Jamaica without some appreciation for the historical and cultural significance of Africa as source and origin. The reactionary position which sees African American Studies as African Slave Studies, or a branch of European Studies of the Slave (that is, the making and the unmaking of the slave) is categorically rejected. Thus, if one studies Africans in a Northeast city of the United States, one must do it with the idea that one is studying African people, not made-in-America Negroes without historical depth. By being conscious of this history one does not have to record it every time, only understand its connection to the project at hand. This has a direct bearing on data gathered for any analysis or study of African people. The researcher must examine everything possible to be able to make an adequate case. Actually, the gathering of data must proceed on the basis that everything that can be used must be used. Therefore, it is impossible for a person to become an Africalogist simply by using the historical method, or the critical method, or the experimental method, and so forth.

In order to become the best type of Africalogist one must use all the elements of data gathering, in any particular area, for an adequate assessment. This means that I might have to use literary analysis and historical analysis in examining one theme or issue. Video records and oral records are as important as written records and must be seen as part of the portfolio of documentation available to the Africologist.

The Temple Project

A final statement ought to be made about the classificatory aspects of Africology. These ideas are given within the framework of the creation of the doctoral program at Temple. Two fields, cultural aesthetics and social behavioral, exist in our department. They are the results of debate, discussion, and consensus within the faculty. With twelve faculty members, we have established a reputation for intellectual debate and dialogue that opens the discourse on discipline questions. Africology is a severe discipline. It became necessary for us to commit traditional discipline suicide in order to advance Africology within the structure of the university. The students we are training will not have that particular problem. They will start out being Africalogists who have read everything in their concentration, as well as the theoretical works in the discipline. Already we have seen our students expand the discourse in almost every field. Thus, we have proposed the following two areas of research and responsibility:

Creative, inventive, artistic, and literary:

Epistemic issues, ethics, politics, psychology, and *modes of behavior*;
Scientific issues, history, linguistics, economics, and *methods of investigation*;
Artistic issues, iconography, art, motifs, symbols, and *types of presentation*.

Social, behavioral, action, and historical:

Relationships, the living, the dead, the unborn;
Cosmos, culture, race, class, gender;
Mythoforms, origins, struggles, victories; and
Recognitions, conduct, designs, and signs.

These principal areas, cultural/aesthetic and socio/behavioral, constitute the grounds upon which we must stand as we continue to build this discipline. I am certain that scholars who replace us will advance the relocating process in theory and practice the generalship of the field improved in the give-and-take of critical debate. As it has been necessary in every aspect of the African's existence for the past five hundred years, it is also necessary in the area of human knowledge for us to struggle to enhance an Afrocentric perspective, recovering from it the distorted junk heap of European hegemony. As in the past, there will be those scholars of whatever cultural and racial and academic background who will understand our abiding interest in free and full inquiry from our own centered perspective and who will become the new Melville Herskovits and Robert Farris Thompsons. A field of study must be open to all who share its perspective and methodology; ours is no different.

The future of Africology will depend upon those who are committed to the principles of academic excellence and social responsibility and who, through their research methods, demonstrate the vision of harmony. Those principles must be interpreted within the framework of an Afrocentric vision in order to maintain a space and location for Africology within the Academy. I have no doubt that this will be done by the scholars and students who are coming after us. They will find in their own time the energy and will to carry out their intellectual mission, as we are trying to carry out ours, in order to create new spaces for human discussion.

References

Asante, Molefi K. *Afrocentricity*. Trenton: Africa World Press, 1987.

———. *Kemet, Afrocentricity and Knowledge*. Trenton: Africa World Press, 1990.

———. *The Afrocentric Idea*. Philadelphia: Temple University Press, 1987.

Asante, Molefi K. and K.W. Asante. *African Culture: The Rhythms or Unity*. Trenton: Africa World Press, 1988.

Bellegarde-Smith, Patrick. *Haiti: The Breached Citadel*. Boulder: Westview Press, 1990.

Bradley, Michael. *The Ice Man Inheritance*. Toronto: Dorset, 1980.

Diop, C.A. *The African Origin of Civilization*. New York: Lawrence Hill, 1991.

———. *The Cultural Unity or Black Africa*. Chicago: Third World Books, 1976.

Gould, Stephen J. *The Mismeasure of Man*. New York: Norton, 1981.

Karenga, M. *Introduction to Black Studies*. Los Angeles: University of Sankore Press, 1987, (edition).

Keto, C.T. *The Africa-centered Perspective of History*. Blackwood, NJ: K & A Publishers, 1988.

Marable, Manning. *How Capitalism Underdeveloped Black America*. Boston: South End Press, 1983.

Mosse, George. *A History of Racism in Europe: Toward the Final Solution*. Madison: University of Wisconsin Press, 1985.

Nascimento, Elisa. *Pan Africanism and South America*. Buffalo: Afrodiaspora, 1979.

Obenga, Theophile. *The African Origin of Philosophy*. Paris: Presence Africaine, 1990.

Richards, Dona. *Let the Circle Be Unbroken*. Trenton: Africa World Press, 1991.

Rodney, Walter. *How Europe Underdeveloped Africa*. Washington: Howard University Press, 1980.

Thompson, Robert Farris. *The Flash of the Spirit*. Berkeley: University of California, 1986.

37.

Articulating the Distinction Between Black Studies and the Study of Blacks: The Fundamental Role of Culture and the African-Centered Worldview

Daudi Ajani ya Azibo *

Introduction

In whole and in parts, "the field and function of Black Studies," to use James Stewart's (1991) terminology, has been thoroughly examined from various points of view and for a variety of purposes (e.g., Aldridge, 1984, 1991; Alkalimat, et al., 1988; Anderson, 1990; ben-Jochannan, 1972; Black Studies Core Curriculum, 1981; Gordon, 1981; Karenga, 1982, 1988; Kershaw, 1990; King, 1982; Semmes, 1981, 1982; Stewart, 1981, 1991; Swindell, 1988, 1991; Turner, 1984b). Much of this work has steered a steady course for Black Studies toward an authentic articulation of current and historic Black thought and practice.

Because the forces of institutionalized white supremacy (Fuller, 1984) recognize the potential of "Africana Studies...to overcome the system [white supremacy] that oppresses it" (Swindell, 1991, 5), it is imperative for them to control Black Studies at the gateway, which is the Academy. An effective strategy to this end has been for concerns with interests that are inimicable to Black Studies in the image and interests of Africans to attempt to effect the direction of Black Studies away from authenticity and toward the pedagogical and scholarly currents of the Eurostream (as opposed to mainstream) American Academy. The promulgation of two specific kinds of scholarship by these concerns, one an ignoble "Negro" scholarship (a contradiction in terms if ever there was one) and the other an apparently genuine, but nonetheless ill- and/or misinformed incorrect scholarship, has proved to be an effective method. My use of the concepts "Negro scholarship" and "Negro" in this paper refers exactly to that

* Asante sana to my wife, Muthy Fatama, for being so patient while I completed this work and to Nadia Kravchenko for her expert typing. A great debt is owed to Drs. Joseph Baldwin, Terry Kershaw, Warren Swindell, and the reviews for their commentary on an earlier version. This work is dedicated to my colleagues in the African Psychology Institute and our major benefactor, psychologist Lou Ramey. It was from them, most especially Joseph Baldwin, Wade Nobles, Gerald Jackson, and Na'im Akbar, that I learned and gleaned the fundamentality of the African Worldview to authentic African scholarship and pedagogy.

kind of work and personality identified and condemned by Chancellor Williams (1976,40) as "'Negro teachers...limiting) themselves to the viewpoints of the white masters who trained them...see[ing] the world through the blue eyes of the Saxons. .. [locating themselves] in the camps of the 'enemy'" and by ben-Jochannan (1974, xix) as "derogatory...a Black person whose orientation is conditioned white [or Arab]."

The Ford Foundation has been notorious of late in supporting Negro (e.g., Huggins, 1985) and ill-informed scholarship (e.g., Ford Foundation, 1990) in what many regard as an all too transparent effort to effect the direction of Black Studies.[1] The work of Huggins (1985) is simultaneously a shameless and classic example of Negro scholarship. It has been roundly and soundly condemned (e.g., Asante, 1986; Karenga, 1988] and aptly placed as "European hagiography...and an unscholarly melange of personal preferences posing as meaningful analysis...pervaded by a paean to American universities and colleges...[all the while attempting to define black Studies externally and Eurocentrically" (Karenga, 1988, 396). As a result of its dispersal throughout the Academy, Huggins' report indeed was a setback to the nascent, emerging, evolving "'expansive' model of Black Studies" as discussed by Stewart (1981) and Aldridge's (1984) visionary model that extends Black Studies beyond the U.S. Diaspora. The National Council for Black Studies (NCBS) is most aligned with these two models, as indicated by its statement of purpose (see Leonard and Little, 1988, 3).

Thus, Huggins' Negro scholarship succeeded in doing what Negro scholarship is supposed to do: stymie and thwart production and institutions that are in the image and interests of Africans and provide an avenue for external penetration. Our field could only be shaken to its roots and have its fundamental character seriously imperiled by such Negro scholarship, and the ill-informed scholarship sponsored by the Ford Foundation (see S. Williams, 1990), regardless of support from inimicable and anti-African interests, because of our failure (so far) to coalesce around and to meaningfully imbue our scholarship and our Black Studies curriculum with an irrefragable conceptual foundation.

The African Worldview: The Irrefragable, Enduring, and Original Conceptual Foundation for Black Studies

The Key Question

Syed Khatib (a.k.a. Cedric X [Clark]) has made major contributions to Black Studies in general and Black psychology in particular, especially in the late 1960s and the 1970s. He (Clark, 1972) posed a question that is key for understanding the conceptual foundation of our field: "Black Studies or the Study of Black People?" The purpose of the query was to force the field to address what constitutes the "Black" in Black Studies. For Khatib, among others, the defining characteristic of Black Studies had to be more than the studying of Black people as opposed to white people.

Most of the analyses of the field and function of Black Studies cited above (as well as the many more uncited) have either left this question unaddressed or nondefinitively dealt with it. Consequently, "the problematic of paradigm" (Karenga,

1988) has proliferated over the years, thereby continuing the vulnerability of Black Studies to external influence.

The Answer

The position taken here is that what makes Black Studies "Black" is the usage of the conceptual universe afforded by the African worldview (see below) in studying any and all manner of phenomena and African worldview of which I speak is the universal and timeless worldview characteristic of African people throughout space and time, as discussed by Carruthers (1980, 1984). Contemporary, nascent Black Studies is by and by reforming to or *re*-centering itself on this worldview window to the conceptualization of phenomena. The very contemporaneity of the present-day movement to *re*-center should not mask or obscure the fact that by becoming explicitly Africentric Black Studies is *re*turning to a pre-existing conceptual base that was employed in a systematic fashion in the study of phenomena, prior to the contribution by Asante (1980), (see section on Africentricity below). Baldwin (in press) presented the Africentric paradigm in a way that captures its contemporaneity while maintaining the integrity of historical continuity:

> the Africentric paradigm...as it has evolved over the past 20 years...consists of four basic characteristics: (a) It generates the construction of African social reality from the framework of the history, culture and philosophy of African civilization; (b) It recognizes and articulates the basic continuity of the African worldview throughout the diverse African populations... (c) It recognizes and articulates the basic distinctness and independence of the African worldview... (d) It projects the African survival thrust as the center of African social reality.

By re-centering on the African worldview source, contemporary Black Studies will rediscover its irrefragable, enduring, and original conceptual foundation.

The African Worldview as Centric or Centered Thought

In order to develop a matured apprehension of the concept of Afri-or Afro-centricity (or any terminological variant like Africentrisn African-centered, Africentric, African-centric, and so on) it is imperative to understand that fundamentally what is being referred to is (and can only be) no more or less than the very foundational thought-base upon which rests the conceptual ideation that has proved to be characteristic of African people's civilizations. Literally, logically, and historically the concept of Africentricity means an employing of the centric thought or conceptual universe of the African, as articulated in the traditional African worldview ("African cosmology" and "African philosophy" are terms used interchangeably with "African worldview" in the literature).

> Perforce, at the heart of Africentric analysis of any phenomena lies the African worldview [which]...comprises the natural indigenous/authentic conceptual framework of African people growing out of their history, culture and philosophy. Thus, foremost to our generating an understanding of [Black Studies]...is an articulation of the nature of the National African worldview. (Baldwin, 1991, 14)

Articulating the African Worldview

The position is taken here that there is one singular African worldview as opposed to a multiplicity of "African worldviews." Diop's work on African cultural *unity* (see Carruthers, 1984; Diop, 1978a, 1978b) undergirds the position. Further, the observation of the African worldview throughout space and time (e.g., Baldwin, 1980, 1985; Baldwin and Hopkins, 1990; ben-Jochannan, 1980b; Carruthers, 1980, 1984; Richards, 1989) is testimony to its universality. Articulating just what the African worldview is essential because to have "good 'science' and 'knowing'... [scholars] must be forthright in their declaration and honest in their evaluation of the conceptual system used in their work" (Myers, 1991, 25).

Culture according to Wade Nobles. As pointed to above, the African worldview is a product of the African's history, culture, and philosophy. It is safe to say, then, that the centricity of African thought derives from the African cultural perspective. Culture has been defined in Kawaida Theory as the totality of a people's thought and practice by which they celebrate themselves, themselves, and introduce themselves to history and humanity (Karenga 1982, 1983). In defining culture as a scientific construct, Wade Nobles gets to the heart of what it is and in effect fleshes out the skeletal definition provided by Kawaida theory: culture is "the process which gives a people a general design for living and patterns for interpreting reality" (Nobles, 1982, 43-44; Nobles et al., 1985, 5-8). The process is explained in a three-level model in which the "primary" level unfolds into and influences the "secondary or intermediary" level which, in turn, unfolds into and influences the "surface" level. The model has a cybernetic character to it.

A people's "patterns for interpreting reality" are generated in the primary and secondary levels, which taken together comprise the deep structure of culture. A people's "general design for living" is the upshot of their patterns for interpreting reality. It is expressed overtly in the vast array of manifest behaviors, values, customs, ideas, beliefs, symbols, language, and so on that are characteristic of that people's experiences and practice. This is the third or surface level and comprises the surface structure of culture (often erroneously construed to represent a culture in toto).

The "deep structure of culture" is a popular term used imprecisely (with various meanings) in Black Studies circles. Nobles' model of culture affords a more precise definition and explication, due to its development as a scientific construct. The primary level of culture consists of the "cultural factors," which are cosmology,[2] ontology, and axiology. The secondary or intermediate level of culture consists of the "cultural aspects," which are worldview,[3] ideology, and ethos. Again, the primary and secondary levels together make up the cultural deep structure. Therefore, based on Nobles' model, *a people's cultural deep structure is seen to be their conceptual universe as it emerged in response to, or in answer to, the notions of the three cultural factors and the three cultural aspects.* This, then, represents a people's centric thought base. Table 1 provides a skeletal summary of the cultural deep structure for African and European people. Indispensable for fleshing out them two cultural deep structures are Nobles (1982), Nobles, Goddard, and Cavil (1985), Baldwin (1980, 1985), Carruthers (1984), Dixon (1976), and Azibo (in press c, Ch. 5).

Nobles' model of culture substantiates the assertion made above that the centricity of African (or any group X's) thought derives from the African (or group X's) cultural perspective. By advancing "a conceptualization of culture which places its varied features in functional order... [Nobles reveals how] cultures function in de-

Table 1

The African (Black) and European (White) Answers to the Cultural Factors and Cultural Aspects[a-b]

CULTURAL FACTORS

Cosmology:	The structure and origins of the universe
African Answer	An interconnected and interdependent edifice, all things in the universe are interconnected and independent; origination by the Divine (Supreme Being, etc.)
European Answer	Independence and separation of entities constituting the universe; human exists apart from/ outside of nature
Ontology:	The nature of being or existence
African Answer	"Spirit" or "force" endows all things, the Divine provides a spirit essence to all creation; world is inherent in being
European Answer	Materiality; worth only in utility for exploration
Axiology:	The defining/governing character of universal relations
African Answer	Rhythmic and harmonious interchange of syntheses (connections) and contradictions (antagonisms)
European Answer	Conflict of opposing forces; one force must conquer the opposers

CULTURAL ASPECTS

Worldview:	The most comprehensive ideas about order
African Answer	Divine law, as revealed in the laws of nature (interpreted Afrocentrically), governing an active, alive universe; order is inherent
European Answer	Order is imposed by the stronger force; overcome chaos and impose or reorder order (to fit one's own interests)
Ethos:	Set of guiding principles for determining human conduct
African Answer	Life is primary; the oneness of all things; "one with/harmony with" nature
European Answer	Control and mastery of nature and all life
Ideology:	How a people should see their reality; how things should be
African Answer	Oneness of things and the primacy of life reflecting a Divine nature; group maintenance, collectiveness, sharing
European Answer	Survival of the fittest; drive for mastery and control of nature; accumulation of possessions

CULTURAL MANIFESTATIONS[c]

Note:	The philosophical and sometimes mystical elaboration relevant to these notions is beyond the scope of this article, but nonetheless must be achieved (e.g., Memphite Theology, Dogon Cosmgony, Akan Philosophy, etc.).

---

a. The deep structure of culture for Africans and Europeans, the African and European centric thought bases.

b. Based on the work of Dr. Wade W. Nobles (Nobles, 1982; Nobles, et al., 1985) and Dr. Joseph Baldwin (1985) primarily and Others (e.g., Azibo, in press c, ch. 5; Dixon, 1976; Myers, 1988).

c. The surface structure of culture, consisting of behavior, language, mores, customs, values, symbols, ideas, beliefs, and so on, which mark a people's experiences and practice. Baldwin's work is essential here (Baldwin, 1985; Baldwin and Hopkins, 1990).

termining the 'centrality' of a people's conceptual universe" (Nobles, 1982, 44) or their characteristic, traditional centric thought base.

The Importance of the African worldview. Cheikh Anta Diop (1991, 324) concluded that "African philosophy cannot develop except on the original terrain of... African thought. Otherwise, there is the risk that it will never be." If we substitute Black Studies for African philosophy, the statement remains valid. However, we add to the last sentence the assertion that "it [Black Studies) will never be" authentic, but will only be the alien-centered, externally influenced (non-African) study of Blacks. Understanding African thought (e.g., Akbar, 1985; Carruthers, 1984; Diop, 1991, Ch. 17; Karenga and Carruthers, 1986; Nobles, 1986, Chs. 3, 4), will be paramount in the building of a body of African human sciences as envisioned by Diop (see Moore, 1986) and others (e.g., Semaj, in press; Speight, 1977).

The essence of the pedagogy and curriculum of Black Studies must certainly consist of this Afrocentric body of human sciences (sciences broadly defined), not unlike that in the ancient days of the Mystery System (e.g., ben-Jochannan, 1980a; Gilbert, 1980; James, 1976). Indeed, on this point, the reader is queried what conceptual system:

(a) substantiates the knowledge that made Kemet "The Light of the World?"

(b) did Imhotep, Ptahotep and the authors of the Memphite Theology employ in their work?

(c) substantiates the political, military, and cultural successes of Pharaoh-Queen Hatshepsut? and

(d) substantiates authentic Black theology and its scripture (e.g., Barashango, 1982; ben-Jochannan, 1974; Karenga, 1984)?

The African worldview is the answer. When Africans do not embrace it, our wretchedness ensues; when Africans cleave to it, sustentation and great achievement are attained (e.g., Azibo, in review; Carruthers, 1980). "That is why, if we are to return to the source culturally, it [the worldview window on Kemetic/classical African civilization knowledge] must be at the foundation of our humanities [and sciences, i.e., our Black Studies]. We must teach it systematically," opined C. A. Diop (Finch, 1986, 237).

We close and embellish this point drawing on the redoubtable Chancellor Williams' (1976, 94-100) observations on Kemetic pedagogy represented in the great educational centers at Wa'rit and Wa'set [Thebes for the Greeks, Luxor for the Arabs (see ben-Jochannan, 1986)]. Dr. Williams pointed out that the themes and specific accomplishments that are associated with education centered at Wa'rit and Wa'set are a direct function of the strong spiritual-religious orientation of the African (e.g., Osei, 1970), which at once is seen as deriving from the African cultural deep structure as just articulated (see Table 1). Some of the documentable themes were "the highest standards of excellence," inspiration for "bigness" and grandness, and "the idea of permanence." Of necessity, this "called for reflective thinking, invention and discovery," which gave rise to the specific accomplishments of "science and learning, art, engineering, architecture, [which are] *the resources for a nation political control*" (my emphasis). The reader should note how Warren Swindle's point stated earlier that "Africana Studies [has the potential] to overcome the system that oppresses [African people]" (1991, 5) is echoed in this historic observation. Some other accomplishments, Williams pointed out, were history, writing, music, the healing art, the song and the dance. Additionally, all of this "did not just happen... every forward step made by these early Blacks was made... by the imperatives of what had to be done to survive." With a little reflection, we see here that what James Stewart (1981) called the expansive model of Black Studies (i.e., manifest involvement and outreach for Black community maintenance and transformation) was part and parcel to this early, original "Black Studies." A final point to extract from Williams' observation of the pedagogical atmosphere of Wa'rit and Wa'set is that nowhere is it apparent that whatever contemporary Black Studies is to gain from this period of antiquity — and it affords a great deal, as we have pointed out, including its relevance for paradigm formation — should have a priority focus" on the Africans in the U.S. diaspora. Karenga (1988) has suggested that Black Studies focus on the U.S. diaspora. However, the applicability of and the imperative to apply all that which contemporary, nascent Black Studies can gain from the terrain of African thought and practice to the entire African world (and the non-African world where possible) appear discernable from Williams observations. This supports Delores Aldridge's (1984) point that Black Studies would do well to focus beyond the U.S. diaspora.

Implications of the African Worldview Base for the Discipline of Black Studies

Having articulated the distinction between Black Studies and the Study of Blacks as dependent on the African worldview and discussed this worldview's importance, it will be invaluable to at least address implications of our analysis for certain issues with which the discipline is grappling. Handling forthrightly such issues as the notion of discipline, the origin, essence, and destiny of the field, graduate training, Black Women's Studies, and a matured understanding of Africentricity (its meaning, the ramifications for meaning of its application as social theory vs. epistemology, and its history) should contribute to the forward march of Black Studies.

The Notion of Discipline

What makes Black Studies a singular discipline at the most *fundamental level* is its African worldview conceptual basis, i.e., its *Africentricity*. What makes White Studies a singular discipline is its European worldview conceptual basis, the artificial boundaries that separate its so-called disciplines (psychology, religion, sociology, etc.) notwithstanding. That Black Studies must avoid the artificial boundary distinction that characterizes White Studies has been pointed out by many writers (e.g., Karenga, 1988; Stewart, 1984). Semaj (in press) has understood this in articulating the "cultural science" concept: the African worldview base makes our work culturally centered. That is, applying the African patterns for interpreting reality (cultural deep structure, see Table 1) as the conceptual starting point for our work perforce *locates* what we do in the African worldview and thereby provides the unifying disciplinary basis. This an actual point of fact, not just a logical derivation. For example, consider the position that there is no distinction between African (Black) psychology and Black religion (Nobles, 1991), because each owes its existence and unfolding to the dictates of the African worldview (Azibo, in press c, Ch. 3).

In a personal communication Warren Swindell (1992) pointed out that at a more *micro level* disciplines can be distinguished: "history becomes history because historians do specific things, and manipulate variables in agreed upon ways, hence, a discipline. Likewise, Black Studies becomes a discipline because of the manner in which the content is approached [and] ... because of how we manipulate phenomena." Swindell listed 6 ways that characterize the approach to content in Black Studies:

(1) we look at contemporary phenomena in terms of past antecedents, (2) we factor in the impact of White Supremacy on human activity, (3) we analyze relationships which on the surface do not appear to be related, for example the rise of white women and the inevitable corresponding decline of African males...the rise of capitalism and the decline of Africa...and on and on, (4) the practical application of knowledge to the social needs of our people as contrasted with the Eurocentric construct of 'knowledge for the sake of knowledge', (5) inclusion of the masses in the discourse rather than exclusion and (6) stress on liberation above all.

Within these contexts of "fundamental" and "micro" levels as just discussed, it is inescapable that Black Studies is both an interdisciplinary field and a singular discipline. The African worldview base of Black Studies eliminates any seeming contradiction on this point. It renders moot the unidiscipline vs. multidiscipline vs. interdiscipline issue that some writers pursue.

Disciplinary caucuses. The development of "disciplinary caucuses" under the auspices of NCBS (Leonard and Little, 1988) is encouraged, from the point of view of the present analysis. Such caucuses *operating from the African worldview base* can facilitate two important trends: (a) the advancement of different areas of specialization within the Black Studies discipline context and (b) the organization of cadres of African scholars tackling issues requiring expertise in many areas, as Diop and others (e.g., Semaj, in press) have called for.

Name of the discipline. The present analysis suggests that the discipline can be properly called by any nomenclature that does not vitiate, deny, or preclude all or any part of what is connoted by the African worldview, especially its cross-national/ethnic/geopolitical character and its applicability to all manner of phenomena (not just African phenomena). Several terms are seen to be acceptable, including Afrocentric, Black, and Africana Studies. Perhaps the better term is the obvious one: African Worldview Studies. Terms that are more restrictive in scope and meaning, like African- and Afro-American Studies and Afrology and Africology, appear at once to be inadequate. A profoundly ironic point to bear in mind is that the term "Africa" (and any of its variants) is not, if you will, an "African" term and will soon have to be displaced! (Definition of the discipline and related political issues are addressed below in the essence and destiny subsections.)

Origin, Essence, and Destiny of the Discipline

The destiny of a thing depends on how great or lame its essence is. The character of a thing's essence is determined in its origins. The perspective on a thing afforded by an origin-essence-destiny analysis usually proves out to be invaluably revealing, typically requiring significant reconceptualization. For example, this has been shown regarding the field of African (Black) psychology where we find (a) that it did not begin with Dr. Francis Cecil Sumner in 1920 or with the formation of the National Association of Black Psychologists in 1968; but (b) the "constructionist" approach is original and was in operation in ancient Kemet (Azibo, in press a). When applied to the African (Black) personality construct, the origin-essence-destiny analysis reveals the necessity to incorporate spiritual biogenetic constructs (e.g., Akbar, 1979). Additionally, the prevailing view of collective white psychological functioning vis-à-vis Africans is radically altered when Diop's environmental (Wobogo, 1976) and Welsing's (1991) genetic theses inform our understanding of their origin and essence and Wright's (1985, Ch. 1) clinical diagnosis as "psychopathic" is seen as a consequent (and manifested) destiny. At this point, we apply this type of analysis to Black Studies, albeit abbreviatedly.

Origin. The present analysis compels us to take the position that *Black Studies began as a discipline at the time when the Nile Valley Africans coalesced the manifold dictates of the African worldview into a systematic epistemological base and applied it in an extant pedagogy.* A return to the Nile Valley source indicates indisputably that the pedagogy of which I speak was in place (e.g., Hilliard, 1985, 1986, 1988). Perhaps an actual pinpointing of the discipline's origin will be advanced in the future.

The idea of Black Studies originating in the 1960s (Karenga, 1982) and encompassing a pre-discipline aspect (Karenga, 1988) is reconceptualized here as the nascent, towards the post Eurocentric era of Black Studies. This phase of Black Studies has, out of sheer necessity, emphasized the reactive deconstruction of White Studies and miseducation while all the while moving toward a proactive return to or recentering in the African worldview. The staunch stand in Africentricity by the NCBS represents the culmination of the recentering. It also signals the attendant death knell for White Studies' hegemony over Black Studies (e.g., Semmes, 1982), which has occurred directly and indirectly through Negro and ill-informed scholarship.

The notions of Black Studies beginning formally in the 1960s and having a "pre-discipline" aspect should be reconceptualized as *historical markers* in the history of Black Studies, which as just contended is a longstanding one. To construe the 1960s and "pre-discipline" phases otherwise disrupts and distorts historical continuity. It also creates, unnecessarily, the following problematic: when the Africans of Fiji, India, New Guinea, Brazil, Columbia, Britain, Arabia, South Africa, and so on formally establish the study of Black thought and practice in its current and historical unfolding (Black Studies as defined by Karenga, 1982), perforce there is the origin of a new Black Studies for each geopolitical/ ethnic African population. This is absurd, but inescapable of the 1960s and pre-discipline phases are conceptualized as more than historical markers. There has been a tendency to distort the history of African Psychology in this very manner and I have argued against it (Azibo, in press a).

Essence. The essence questions concern definition, scope and content, purpose, and character of Black Studies. Regarding the latter two, the themes and specific accomplishments associated with the pedagogical atmosphere characteristic of ancient Wa'rit and Wa'set, as gleaned from our earlier discussion of Chancellor Williams, are illustrative of Black Studies' defining characteristics. Far from the picture painted by the vulgar careerists, opportunists, and failed White Studies personages (addressed so well by Karenga, 1982) whose production or lack of same undermines Black Studies, the present analysis reveals the worldview induced commitments to excellence, grandness, and permanence, all within the context of purpose to maintain and transform one's group, epitomize the expectations for Black Studies scholars.

Regarding scope and content, Karenga's (1982) analysis is seen to be adequate, with a few caveats however. Generally, anything that would undermine the African worldview base and associated ramifications would be objectionable from the viewpoint of the present analysis. Specifically, the priority focus on the U.S. diaspora

(Karenga, 1988) or the continental Africa-U.S.-Caribbean trilateral Black world configuration (Turner, 1984a) is not supported by our analysis. Recall Joseph Baldwin's (in press) astute observation that "the Africentric paradigm . . . recognizes and articulates the basic continuity of the African worldview throughout the diverse African populations." Perforce the scope and content of Black Studies must do likewise. For example, Hawaii (e.g., Clegg, 1980, 1981), Fiji, New Guinea, Oceania (e.g., ben-Jochannan, 1980b), India (e.g., Rajshekar, 1987), Asia in general (e.g., Houston, 1985; Means, 1980; Parker, 1981; Van Sertima, 1985), ad infinitum are just as critical to Black Studies as the trilateral world.

Also, our present analysis reveals the position that Black Studies is limited to African phenomena (Asante, 1988, 58) is myopic. The African worldview is a window for viewing *all* phenomena, not just Black. This includes the physical and medical sciences (e.g., Finch, 1983; Speight, 1977), not as is generally presumed just the humanities and social sciences (e.g., Semmes, 1981). And, most assuredly, this includes the Africentric study of non-African people, or "Black Studies about non-Blacks" (Association of African Historians, 1973, 2), repercussions notwithstanding.

Melanin studies (e.g., King, 1990; Welsing, 1975, 1988), one example of a physical science enterprise, must be recognized as legitimate for Black Studies and incorporated into the field formally and respectfully. Akbar's (1989) point should be heeded: "this thing of melanin is extremely important . . . we [must] understand what is the purview of our study [of melanin]." According to King (1990) the Kamites were vigorously pursuing melanin studies. In African (Black) psychology melanin studies is entrenched as a critical area (e.g., Cedric X, et al., 1975; McGhee, 1976; Nobles, 1976; Pasteur and Toldson, 1982; N. Stewart, in press). Indeed, the theories of African (Black) personality that qualify as "advanced" rely on melanin to explain large parts of African psychological functioning (see Azibo, 1990). And, the very articulation of spirituality as a scientific construct in African personality theory depends on the functions of melanin (Azibo, 1991) or what Nobles (1975) labeled the "essential melanic system." In White Studies, the melanin literature is voluminous (e.g., King, 1977, 1979; N. Stewart, in press).

The Black Studies scholar who is skeptical about melanin is advised to hold in abeyance her or his position until more definitive and soundly conducted studies are produced. Suffice it to say, for now, that all indications, inclusive of the voluminous hard evidence extant and the more popularized soft boasts, point to gifts in the blackness (e.g., Akbar, 1989; Barnes, 1988; N. Stewart, in press; Welsing, 1988). And, this area of study is deserving of our best scholarship, not our ignorant, out of hand, and deferential to white sensibilities derision.

Regarding definition, Karenga's (1982, 33) is adequate: the "study of the multidimensional aspects of Black thought and practice in their current and historical unfolding." However, in expounding on this (or a similar) definition, care must be taken not to violate or diminish that which is connoted by Black Studies' African worldview base. The three most frequent violations found across the gamut of writers seem to be the myopic focusing on (a) the Western hemisphere diaspora, (b) Africans as the only subjects, and (c) humanities and social sciences while bypassing the physical and medical sciences.

Destiny. That Black Studies has survived the continuing backlash of white America (return to the right), and has an Africentric authoritative body overseeing it (NCBS), bodes well for the discipline. The African worldview base of the discipline ensures a nonexhaustive and self-perpetuating subject content. The Africentrically located Black Studies scholar will pursue this content proactively, reproducing her/himself in perpetuity through student progeny in the process. Indeed, if all of the enemies of the African were purged this minute, we would still conduct Black Studies because our pursuit is independent of alien-centered oppression. The African worldview base affords this. The field is not reactive in origin, notwithstanding the anti-oppression impetus for the field's reemergence in the 1960s, rather it began as an Africentric cultural construction in ancient African civilizations. Having such an origin, the destiny of Black Studies is unlimited, in principle, since cultural construction is an insulated, self-reproductive activity.

Adverse political intervention, however, is an ever-present possibility in the Studies and neo-colonialized Academies. The litany of impediments imposed on Black Studies under White Studies hegemony is well known (e.g., Aldridge, 1991; Karenga, 1982; Swindell, 1991). The point to be taken regarding destiny is that as we struggle with the perennial practical problems we make the uppermost commitment not to capitulate and surrender aspects of our discipline. Admittedly, the White Studies Academies will continue to limit us here, but at our respective institutions we must go to the wall kicking and screaming, so to speak, and never be comfortable or satisfied with having programs and departments. The African worldview base of Black Studies requires nothing less than a School or College within a White Studies post secondary institution to adequately handle its content. The multifaceted curriculum of the Mystery System (Gilbert, 1980; James, 1976) and the varied and vast activities at the Wa'rit and Wa'set educational centers discussed earlier (Williams, 1976) support this point.

Additionally, it bears explicit mentioning that the African worldview base of Black Studies also compels the infusion in the curriculum of the *cultural intent* of African self- maintenance, African excellence, and the attainment of transformation to perfectibility (Nobles, 1990, 1991). The Council of Independent Black Institutions (1990) has recognized this. This too is witnessed by the educational activities of the ancient Nile Valley. African cultural content alone is inadequate.

Clearly, neither the White Studies Academy nor the neocolonial Academies are about to accommodate the destiny of Black Studies as discussed here. It appears that independent postsecondary Black Studies education must be forthcoming. Perhaps this is the ultimate destiny of Black Studies. Certainly the African worldview base provides the NCBS with its ultimate challenge (to date): to establish by the year 2000 a freestanding postsecondary and professional African worldview based university or professional school of Black Studies!

Graduate Training

At once, it is undeniable, given the analysis herein, that a formalized grounding in the African worldview is an indispensable imperative for Black Studies graduate students. A *formally required course* on the African worldview must occupy a central position in any graduate curriculum. Not only does this logically follow our analysis, but it is a practical necessity as well because only it will the chances "of providing a cadre of [Afrocentrically located] scholars to replace those of us who have committed our lives to the development of the field as a legitimate intellectual one" (Aldridge, 1991, 21). Such a formal requirement as this must be juxtaposed with and distinguished from the mere, meager, meanderous offerings on "worldview" or "deep structure" of this or that professor in this or that seminar, if s/he branches the topic at all. The teaching of the African worldview must not be handled in this slip-shod manner.

In closing this section on graduate training, a final point is that the expansive model idea (see Stewart, 1981), i.e., the overturning, transformation, and sustentation of community, must be made experientially real in the curricula. This can be accomplished through practical course instruction on activism, or both. Activism can range from tutoring and lecturing where needed to full blown political endeavors. At no time should activism supplant intellectual production. The ivory tower notion of scholarly activity should be balanced or augmented with activism. Indeed, student activism of the radical, grass roots, "take Afrocentricity to the community and make it work" sort is to be encouraged.

Black Women's Studies

Standing steep in the African worldview, as it were, Dr. Iva Carruthers has provided an utterance that essentially conveys what the African worldview base of Black Studies implies for a proper conceptualization of Black Women's Studies:

> unapologetically refuse to separate the discussion [study] of the African woman from African man, community and universal order. (I. Carruthers, 1980, 15)

This position is compelled by the deep structure of African culture, the cultural factors and cultural aspects, which projects interconnectedness, interdependency, appositional harmony, oneness, and the primacy of life (procreation an imperative). The African creation myths[4] reveal the principles upon which the *inseparableness* of Black Women's Studies from the rest of Black Studies is based:

> [In] African creation stories... [the hue]man into the picture as husband and wife, male and female [simultaneously].... The first accomplishment of the African woman, in partnership with the man, was the creation of a functioning family unit. (I. Carruthers, 1980, 15-16)

The principles are (a) the simultaneity of the creation of the male and female "hue-man": innate equality of value, worth; (b) their emergence as husband and wife: appositional harmony, interconnection, interdependence, etc.; (c) their first, and hence priority, accomplishment being the construction of fancily life: primacy of life, procreation, oneness, self-extension, group maintenance. Surely, "this philosophy deems it impossible to describe [study] the nature of the... African woman or man except in the context of marriage, procreation, and the family" (Harper-Bolton, 1982, 34).

Where and when Black Women's Studies exits. Based on our analysis, any disciplinary conceptualization of Black Women's Studies that runs counter to the set principles is flawed. Such could never be Black Women's Studies; rather it would be an alien-centered study of Black women, even if conducted by Black women. Immediately, any such conceptualization exits as a contender for defining Black Women's Studies.

When and Where Black Studies Enters. Black Women's Studies entered at the origin of Black Studies in the ancient Nile Valley civilizations (see earlier discussion). This is not just a logical derivation from our African worldview base, but also a practical point of fact. For example, the highly sophisticated institutions of "HRW (Divine Kingship) and (Divine Motherhood)" (I. Carruthers, 1980) required systematic study of the nature and functioning of the African (Black) woman and man. As a result of these Africentric Black Women's Studies—fully integrated with Black Studies, we underscore—the lot of the African woman was characterized by an independent, nonoppressive status, sitting on tribunals, witnessing documents, inheriting and selling property, independent income, equal rewards for labor, and access to education, courts, and occupations without regard to gender [notwithstanding that certain specific male and female occupations existed; see I. Carruthers, 1980, 17; Jogunosimi, 1986; and Wimby, 1984).

Basing Black Studies in the African worldview reveals that *Black Women's Studies enters as female gender foci under the auspice of Black Studies.* This is both a pedagogical and historical truth. Black Women's Studies does not, and indeed cannot possibly enter as a discipline. There is simply no disciplinary base for it. Black Women's Studies can no more be a discipline than can "Black Men's Studies," "Black Children's Studies," or "Black Family Studies," which themselves can only be distinct foci under Black Studies' auspice. It should be apparent that Black Women's Studies has absolutely no relationship, save female gender foci, with "Women's Studies" as configured in the western Academy. Therefore, Black Women's Studies is not to be housed in "Women's Studies."

The legacy of African patriarchy has generated a void of knowledge about, and a disparagement and curtailing of the production by, the African woman. We need to rescue Black Studies from this state, which undermines and contradicts its African worldview base, is critically urgent. Redress on this point is to be regarded as compulsory. However, that Black Women's Studies does not enter as a reaction to the fallout caused by patriarchy and sexism is a point not to be missed.

Toward a Matured Understanding of Africentricity

Africentricity as a term and concept has come into vogue. Vague, however, is the understanding of its meaning and knowledge of its history. Clarity on these points is critical for NCBS, an avowedly Africentric organization.

The meaning of Afrocentricity. A matured apprehension of the concept of Afrocentricity reveals its meaning to be no more or less than construing, interpreting, negotiating, and otherwise acting on the world using the system of conceptual thought generated from the African cultural deep structure, also known as the African worldview. The cultural factors and cultural aspects as developed by the African (see Table 1) thus parametrize Africentricity. When an African actually employs this conceptual universe, she or he is *located* Afrocentrically.

It bears pointing out again that the African worldview is imbued with the self-extension maintenance, i.e., group/race maintenance imperative (e.g., Azibo, in press d). Many Africans incline toward extended-self maintenance (desire to do that which helps of the African) without being located. Such persons may be said to be *oriented* Afrocentrically.

Location is paramount because it provides the cultural anchoring, indeed the centering, in some thought. Thence derives the idea of centric thought—Afrocentric, Eurocentric, and so on. Distortion in the meaning of Afrocentricity often arises when considering the production of an African who is oriented Afrocentrically but not located. The production here may well be "pro-Black," entering proactively or reactively, but is not Afrocentric. For example, the using of this or that Eurocentric psychological system (Freud's, Rychlak's, Maslow's, etc.) by an African psychologist to enhance African life is not Afrocentric, even though the psychologist may be oriented (Azibo, in press a). Similarly, although Reverend Stallings' Imani Temple (Randolph, 1989) may be oriented, it is not Afrocentric because its doctrine (which remains Roman Catholic) is not located in the African conceptual universe (Azibo, in press c, Ch. 3).

The orientation vs. location distinction as articulated here clearly and rigidly relegates as non-Afrocentric that work which does not use concepts, variables, and formulations deriving from the African cultural factors and cultural aspects. By this standard, much, if not most, of what Black Studies scholars produce today would appear to be not Afrocentric. Objections, I am sure, might abound. What would make such admittedly oriented work Afrocentric is not to be found in its mere conduction or in carrying it out; rather, it is only when ensuing interpretations and recommendations are in arguably derived from, traceable to, or congruous with the African worldview that such work qualifies as Afrocentric. The catch-22 here is that if the concepts, variables, and formulations used in the conduct of the work are incongruous with the African worldview to begin with, and this is the likely case, achieving Afrocentric interpretations and recommendations will be difficult (perhaps impossible). The dreadful specter of alien-centered thought fully ensconced in mainstream Black Studies scholarship via the backdoor is a looming, nightmarish possibility. Much alien-centered thought—especially Eurocentric and Arab-centric—is incompatible and diametrically opposed to African-centered thought (Azibo, in press c, in review; Baldwin, 1985; Baldwin & Hopkins, 1991). Devastation of Africans has resulted when we adopted or adapted to alien-centered thought and practice that was incongruous with the African worldview. Although African-centered thought does not have a monopoly on useful ideas, for alien-centered thought to be useful it must not be incongruous with the African worldview.

The solution for the Black Studies scholar using non-African concepts, variables, formulations, etc. would be to deconstruct them. The *deconstruction approach* renders void theses and formulations that are anti-African or alien. Undermining and destroying the edifice of anti-African and alien scholarship though deconstruction qualifies as Afrocentric work on two counts: (a) when the interpretations and recommendations derive from or are congruous with the African worldview (this is repeated here to ward off the tendency to debunk one alien way, say Eurocentrism, and replace it with another alien way, say Arabcentrism) and (b) because it embodies the extended-self maintenance dictate that is innate in the African worldview.

The *reconstruction approach* revises, revamps, and otherwise alters alien-centered formulations to better fit or jibe with African reality. This approach must be used with caution because it is prone to mistakes of meaning: the alien-centeredness of the formulation may persist though the recasting into a "Blackenized" version. This type of work may qualify as Afrocentric because the African worldview is open to other-centered formulations that are not at variance with it. The *constructionist approach* proceeds with formulations and concepts derived from the African cultural deep structure. It is the approach used at the origin of Black Studies in the ancient Nile Valley civilizations. It is the approach that puts the Black in Black Studies. Ideally, the deconstruction and reconstruction approaches should bridge to the constructionist approach. Azibo (in press a) and Nobles (1986) discuss these approaches in the context of African psychology, which Gerald Jackson (1982) pointed out is an avenue to the study of African people generally.

Afrocentricity: social theory vs. epistemology. Because the concept of Afrocentricity is frequently used in reference to social theory as well as epistemology, some confusion in its meaning has resulted. According to Dr. Bobby Wright a social theory establishes a people's "guidelines of life ... [defining] their relationship with other living things ... [including] how enemies are to be dealt with" (Carruthers, 1985, vi-xii; Wright, 1979). It is here as a social theory only that it is acceptable to say that Afrocentricity is a simple idea that means doing what is good for or in the interest of African people. All such statements must be construed as contemporary expressions of the African worldview's inherent, extended-self maintenance dictate (i.e., Race maintenance). Otherwise it becomes mere mouthing. This Race maintenance dictate has received confirmatory support in an empirical investigation of the African personality construct (Azibo, in press b).

Epistemologically speaking, however, from the African worldview base it is apparent that the meaning of Afrocentricity is not simplistic. It is not a simple idea capable of being captured in cute phraseology like "Afrocentricity is a simple idea, all it means is doing what is good for Black People."[5] Location is not necessitated here, only orientation. Oversimplification like this diminishes the meaning of Afrocentricity indistinguishable from pro-Black. Consequently, if one assumes the requisite orientation, then the production of Crispus Attucks, Colin Powell, and Clarence Thomas could be argued to be as Afrocentric as that of Piankhy and Dessalines!

From the standpoint of epistemology, Afrocentricity becomes a superfluous, watered-down concept when divorced from the a priori African worldview base. At the same time, however, watering the concept down in this manner opens the door for an unscrupulous writer to attempt to pass off his or her production vis-à-vis the concept as initiatory, authoritative, and definitive. The history of the concept of Afrocentricity, like the history of anything, will set the record straight.

Afrocentricity: a history of the concept. It is no secret that the term Afrocentricity or a variant of it has been used here and there by scholars and activists for more than two centuries. The critical issue is when did the African scholar use the term and concept systematically in the epistemological, pedagogical, and social theory senses that today are in vogue. This issue is really about contemporary developments in Black Studies, even though we can (and did) argue that our ancient scholars proceeded Afrocentrically. Inasmuch as Afrocentricity is a function of the African worldview, African-centric thought, this argument is understandable. Still, what it the history in contemporary times?

Molefi Asante has done much to popularize the term Afrocentricity. Equally his work popularizes and promotes his version of this concept which is not anchored in the African worldview as elucidated in this paper. His exposure has been so great that many, especially those Johnnies-come-lately to the concept might believe that he is responsible for initiating the term, the concept, and its systematic theoretical development. Any such perception, however, is contradicted by well known facts.

As early as 1973, Dr. Jacob Carruthers and the Association of African Historians (AAH) published a journal entitled *The Afrocentric World Review*. The AAH's objective for their journal was to develop an "ethnic awareness and racial consciousness ... that pointed the way to ... A World Wide African Community." They defined the concept and the approach of Afrocentricity: "Putting Black interests first, [is] the view of Afrocentricity ... Afrocentrism strives for ... a collective identity [and is] founded on Black ideas, rather than the ideas of non-Blacks...the best place to begin this endeavor is with our collective experience, rather than the preconceived theories of aliens" (Association of African Historians, 1973, 1).

Lorenzo Martin (1973, 43-44, 46) pointed out how as early as 1971 Chancellor Williams had "written [history) from an Afrocentric point of view. He [Williams] states that he 'has shifted the main focus from the history of Arabs and Europeans in Africa to the Africans themselves.... They will be coming back—center stage—into their own history at last.'" This reflects a profound systematic approach by Chancellor Williams that Martin, in 1973, correctly interpreted as applied Afrocentricity: "what Professor Williams is calling for is a re-examination of African history, using Africa as the center and starting point.... His [is a systematic] Afrocentric approach to the study of Black history."

We have just seen the concept of Afrocentricity defined, employed, and in print before Asante's (1980) major work on the topic. Additionally, Wade Nobles laid out an Afrocentric approach in the systematic, theory development sense prior to Asante's Afrocentricity. Nobles articulated an African worldview conceptual base from which to inquire. Then, he called for and initiated systematic study using this base, all under the nomenclature of "An Afro-Centric Analysis of the Black Family" (Nobles, 1978, 686). I encourage all Afrocentrists to pay attention to theory, build on theory, and give credit to the theoretical development."

It is dubitable whether Molefi Asante would be unaware of these systematic usages of the *Afrocentricity* concept that entered prior to his Afrocentricity. In any event, because his version of the concept is not anchored in the African worldview, Asante's idea of Afrocentrism can only culminate in ruminatively following the opinions and observations that he offers. Fortunately, the concept of Afrocentricity as developed by the Association of African Historians and Wade Nobles, and as yoked to the African worldview as articulated in this paper, is not so limited. To this author that basing Black Studies in the African worldview would preclude this. Students could then become Aldridgeists, Akbarists, Karengaists, Noblesists, Stewartists, and so forth—all under the African worldview umbrella. Again, the lesson for forthcoming doctoral programs in Black Studies is self-evident.

Concluding Recommendations and Remarks

The author hopes to have overcome any impercipience of the fundamentality of the African worldview for Black Studies on the part of the reader. As we have seen, the African worldview basis of Black Studies generates far-reaching implications. Several of these we have pointed out with recommendations being apparent. Three concluding recommendations warrant explicit stating. Given the centrality of the African worldview in Black Studies, it is recommended that the NCBS hire Drs. Wade Nobles, Joseph Baldwin, Donna Richards, and Jacob Carruthers[6] as consultants to develop an African Worldview course syllabus for adoption by and dissemination to all Black Studies units. A graduate course syllabus is imperative; an upper-level undergraduate course syllabus might also be desirable.

The second recommendation is that the NCBS take the position officially that every graduate program in Black Studies have a required course on the African worldview. At a minimum, the content covered in this course would be that found in the syllabus produced by the consultants just recommended.

Third, the NCBS should seriously consider creating its own professional school of African Worldview Studies (Black Studies). This school should be launched in the decade of the 1990s. This would obviate many of the problems associated with the White Studies institutions. Perhaps this is the ultimate challenge, to date, to our kujichagulia (self-determination) imperative.

Having firmly, and hopefully irrefragably, established that the American worldview is the basis of Black Studies the necessity that the Black Studies scholar steep himself or herself in it is obvious. Only by doing this can we meaningfully carry on in the work started by our ancestors and overcome, that which oppresses us. By standing in the African worldview, we become Afrocentric. The resulting conceptualization is the pathway for the founding and furtherance of African liberation (Azibo, in press c, in review).

References

Akbar, N. (1979). African Roots of Black Personality. In W. Smith, K. Burlew, M. Mosley, and W. Whitney (Eds.), *Reflections on Black Psychology*. Washington, DC: University Press of America, 1979.

Akbar, N. (1985). Nile Valley origins of the science of the mind. In Van Sertima (Ed.), *Nile Valley Civilization*. New Brunswick, NJ: Transaction Books.

Akbar, N. (April 1989). Psychosocial and spiritual implications of a virgin acceptance of Blackness (audiotape). Lecture at the 3rd annual Melanin Conference, Howard University, Washington, DC.

Aldridge, D. (1984). Toward a new role and function of Black Studies in white and historically Black institutions. *Journal of Negro Education* (summer), 359-367.

———. (1991). 20 years as an Africana Studies Administrator. *Word: A Black Culture Journal*, I (1), 19-28.

Alkalimat, Abdul and Associates. (1988). *Introduction to Afro-American Studies: A People College Primer*. Chicago: Twenty-first Century Books and Publications.

Anderson, T. (1990). *Black Studies: Theory, method, and cultural perspectives*. Pullman, Washington: Washington State University Press.

Asante, M.K. (1980). Afrocentricity: The Theory of Social Change. Buffalo: Amulefi. (Republished in 1988 by Africa World Press, Trenton, NJ).

———. (1986). A Note on Nathan Huggins Report to the Ford Foundation on African-American Studies. *Journal of Black Studies*, 17 (2).

Association of African Historians. (1973). Prefatory remarks to our readers. *The Afrocentric World Review*, I (1), 1-2.

Azibo, D. (1990). Advances in Black/African personality theory. *Imhotep: An Afrocentric Review*, 2 (1).

———. (1991). Towards a metatheory of the African personality. *Journal of Black Psychology*, 17 (2), 37-45.

———. (In press a). African psychology in historical perspective and related commentary. In D. Azibo (Ed.), *African psychology in historical perspective and related commentary*. Trenton: African World Press.

————. (In press b). An empirical test of a fundamental postulate of an African personality metatheory. *Western Journal of Black Studies.*

————. (In press c). *Liberation psychology.* Trenton: Africa World Press.

————. (In press d). Mental health defined Africentrically. In D. Azibo (Ed.), *African psychology in historical perspective and related commentary.* Trenton: Africa World Press.

————. (In review). A pathway for the founding and furtherance of liberation: Africentric conceptualizing. Manuscript submitted for publication.

Baldwin, J.A. (1980). The psychology of oppression. In M.K. Asante & A. Vandi (Eds.). *Contemporary Black Thought.* Beverly: Sage Publications.

————. (1985). Psychological aspects of European cosmology in American society. *The Western Journal of Black Studies,* 9 (4), 216-223.

————. (1991). An Afrocentric perspective on health and social behavior of African American males. Unpublished manuscript.

————. (In press). The Africentric paradigm and African-American psychological liberation. In D. Azibo (Ed.), *African psychology in historical perspective and related commentary.* Trenton, NJ: Africa World Press.

————, and Hopkins, R. (1990). African-American and European-American cultural differences as assessed by the worldviews paradigm: An empirical analysis. *Western Journal of Black Studies,* 14 (1), 38-52.

Banks, W.C. (1982). Deconstructive falsification: Foundations of a method in black psychology. E. Jones & S. Korchin (Eds.), *Minority mental health.* New York: Praeger Press.

Barashango, I. (1982). *God, the Bible and the Black Man's Destiny.* Washington, DC: IV Dynasty Publishing Co.

Barnes, C. (1988). Melanin: the chemical key to Black greatness (vol. 1). The author.

ben-Jochannan, Y. (1972). *Cultural genocide in the Black and African Studies curriculum.* New York: Alkebu-lan Books Associates.

————. (1974). *Black man's religion and comments and extracts from the Holy Black Bible.* New York. Alkebu-lan Books Associates.

————. (1980a). *In pursuit of George G. M. James' study of African origins in "Western Civilization."* New York: Alkebu-lan Books Associates.

————. (1980b). *They All Look Alike!* (Vols. I & II). New York: Alkebu-lan Books.

————. (1986). *Abu Simbel-Ghizeh: Guide book manual.* New York City: Alkebu-lan Books.

Black Studies Core Curriculum. (1981). Published by the National Council for Black Studies (NCBS, Ohio State University, 190 Ovall Mall, Columbus, Ohio 43210-1358).

Carruthers, I. E. (1980). Africanity and the Black Woman. *Black Books Bulletin,* 6, 14-20:71.

Carruthers, J. (1980). Reflections on the history of the Afrocentric worldview. *Black Books Bulletin,* 7 (1), 4-7, 13, 25.

————. (1984). *Essays in ancient studies.* Los Angeles: University of Sankore Press.

————. (1985). *The irritated genie: An essay on the Haitian Revolution.* Chicago: The Kemetic Institute.

Cedric X (Clark, now S.M. Khatib), McGhee, D.P., Nobles, W.W., and Luther X (Na'im Akbar). (1975). Voodoo or IQ: An introduction to African Psychology. *Journal of Black Psychology*, 1, 9-29.

Clark, C. (1972). Black Studies or the Study of Black People? In R. Jones (Ed.), *Black Psychology* (1st ed.) New York: Harper and Row.

Clegg, L. (1980). Black royalty in the Pacific. *Uraeus: The Journal of Unconscious Life*, 2 (1), 35-38.

————. (May 1981). Hawaii: The untold story. *Sepia*, 16-18, 20.

Council of Independent Black Institutions. (1990). *Positive Afrikan Images for Children*. Trenton, NJ: Red Sea Press.

Diop, C.A. (1991). *Civilization or barbarism: An authentic anthropology*. New York: Lawrence Hill Books.

Dixon, V.J. (1976). World views and research methodology. In L.M. King et al. (Eds.) *African philosophy: Assumptions and paradigms for on Black persons*. Los Angeles: Fanon R & D Center.

Finch, C. (1983). The African background of medical science. In I. Van Sertima (Ed.), *Blacks in science: ancient and modern*. New Brunswick, NJ: Transaction Books.

————. (1986). Further conversations with the Pharaoh. In I. Van Sertima (Ed.), *Great African thinkers*. New Brunswick, NJ: Transaction Books.

Ford Foundation. (1990). *Three essays: Black Studies in the United States*. New York: The Ford Foundation.

Fuller, Jr., N. (1984). *United Independent Compensatory Code/System/Concept Revised Edition*. Washington, DC: The Author.

Gilbert, G. (1980). Journey into the secret fife. *Black Books Bulletin*, 7 (1), 9-12, 25.

Gordon, V. (1981). The coming of age of Black Studies. *Western Journal of Black Studies*, 5 (3), 231-236.

Harper-Bolton, C. (Winter 1982). A reconceptualization of the Black Woman. *Black Male/Female Relationships*, 32-42.

Hilliard, A.G. (1985). Kemetic concepts in education. In Van Sertima (Ed.), *Nile Valley civilization*. New Brunswick, NJ: Transaction Books.

————. (1986). Pedagogy in ancient Kemet. In Karenga & Carruthers (Eds.), *Kemet and the African worldview*. Los Angeles: University of Sankore.

————. (1988). Free your mind, Return to the source: African origins (The Transcript). East Point, Georgia: Waset Educational Productions (P.O. Box 91123, 30364).

Houston, D.D. (I 985). Wonderful Ethiopians of the Ancient Cushite Empire. Baltimore, MD: Black Classic Press.

Huggins, N.I. (1985). Afro-American Studies: A Report to the Ford Foundation. New York: Ford Foundation.

Jackson, G. (1982). Black Psychology: An avenue to the study of Afro-Americans. *Journal of Black Studies*, 12 (3), 241-260.

James, G.G.M. (1976). *Stolen Legacy*. San Francisco: Julian Richardson Associates.

Jogunosimi, I. (1986). The role of royal women in ancient Kemet. In M. Karenga & J. Carruthers (Eds.), *Kemet and the African worldview*. Los Angeles: University of Sankore Press.

Karenga, M. (1982). *Introduction to Black Studies*. Inglewood, CA: Kawaida Publications.

———. (1983). Towards a national Black value system (videotape). Keynote address at the Black Family Conference. University of Louisville, Louisville, Kentucky.

———. (1984). *Selections from the Husia*. Los Angeles: Kawaida Publications.

———, Carruthers, J. (1986). *Kemet and the African worldview*. Los Angeles: University of Sankore Press.

Kershaw, T. (1990). The emerging paradigm in Black Studies. In T. Anderson (Ed.), *Black Studies: Theory, method, and culture perspectives*. Washington: Washington State University Press.

King, G. (1982). Black Studies: An idea in crisis. *Western Journal of Black Studies*, 6 (4), 241-245.

———. (1977). *Pineal gland review*. Los Angeles: Fanon Center Publication.

———. (1979). *Melanin: Selected annotated references*. Los Angeles: Center Publication.

———. (1990). *African origin of biological psychiatry*. Germantown, TN: Seymour-Smith, Inc.

Leonard, C., and Little, W. (1988). National Council for Black Studies, Inc.: Constitution and bylaws/organizational handbook. Columbus, Ohio: National Council for Black Studies.

Martin, L. (1973). Arab imperialism. *The Afrocentric World Review*, (1), 43-46.

McGhee, D.P. (1976). Psychology: Melanin, the physiological basis for psychological oneness. In L. King, V. Dixon and W. Nobles (Eds.), *African Philosophy: Assumptions and Paradigms for Research on Black Persons*. Los Angeles: Fanon Center Publications.

Means, S. (1980). *Ethiopia and the missing link in African history*. Harrisburg, PA: The Atlantis Publishing Co.

———. (1986). Interview with Cheikh Anta Diop. In I. Van Sertima (Ed.), *Great African thinkers*. New Brunswick, NJ: Transaction Books.

Myers, L. (1988). *Understanding an Afrocentric world view: Introduction to an optimal psychology*. Dubuque, IA: Kendall/Hunt Publishing Co.

———. (1991). Expanding the psychology of knowledge optimally: The importance of world view revisited. In R. Jones (Ed.), *Black psychology* (3rd ed.). Berkeley, CA: Cobb and Henry Publs.

Nobles, W. (1976). African science: The consciousness of self. In L. King, et al. (Eds.), *African philosophy: Assumptions and paradigms for research on Black persons*. Los Angeles: Fanon Research and Development Center.

Nobles, W. (November 1978). Toward an empirical and theoretical framework for defining Black families. *Journal of Marriage and the Family*, 679-688.

———. (1982). The reclamation of and the right to reconciliation: An Afro-centric perspective on developing and implementing programs for the mentally retarded offender. In A. Harvey & T. Carr (Eds.), *The Black mentally retarded offender: A wholistic approach to prevention and habilitation*. New York City: United Church of Christ Commission for Racial Justice.

Nobles, W. (1986). *African Psychology: Toward Its Reclamation, Reascension and Revitalization*. Oakland, CA: Black Family Institute.

———. (1988). Education: Infusing African cultural content and intent (audiotape). Address given at the First World Lecture Series, Harlem, New York.

———. (1991). African psychology: The responsibility to the Africanca (videotape). Distinguished Psychologist Address at the annual Association of Black Psychologists Convention, August 15, 1991, New Orleans (contact ABP, P.O. Box 55999, Washington, DC 200-40-5999).

———, Goddard, L. and Cavil, W. III. (1985). *The KM EBIT Husia*. Oakland, CA: Institute for the Advanced Study of Black Family Life and Culture.

Osei, G.K. (1970). *The African philosophy of life*. London: African Publication Society.

Parker, G.W. (1981). *The children of the sun*. Baltimore, MD: Black Classic Press.

Pasteur, A. and Toldson, I. (1982). *Roots of Soul: The psychology of Black Expressiveness*. Garden City, NY: Anchor Press/Doubleday.

Rajshekar, V. (1987). *Dalit: The Black Untouchables of India*. Atlanta: Clarity Press.

Randolph, (November 1989). What's behind the Black rebellion in the Catholic Church? *Ebony*, 160-162, 164.

Richards, D. (1989). *Let the circle be unbroken*. New York City: The Author.

Semaj, L. (In press). Cultural science. In D. Azibo (Ed.), *African psychology in historical perspective and related commentary*. Trenton: Africa World Press.

Semmes, C. E. (1981). Foundations of an Afrocentric Social science. *Journal of Black Studies*, 12, 3-17.

———. (1982). Black studies and the symbolic structure of domination. *Western Journal of Black Studies*, 6, 116-122.

Speight, C. (1977). Towards Black science and technology. *Black Books Bulletin*, 5 (3), 6-11, 49.

Stewart, J. (1981). Alternative models of Black Studies. *Umoja: A Scholarly Journal of Black Studies*, 5 (3), 17-39.

———. (1984). The legacy of W.E.B. DuBois for contemporary Black Studies. *Journal of Negro Education* (Summer), 296-311.

———. (1991). The field and function of Black Studies. In C. Willie, A. Garibaldi, & W. Reed (Eds.), *The Education of Black Americans*. Westport, CT: Auborn House.

Stewart, N. (In press). Melanin, the melanin hypothesis, and the development and assessment of Afrikan infants. In D. Azibo (Ed.), *African psychology in historical perspective and related comments*. Trenton: Africa World Press.

Swindell, W.C. (1988). Black Studies and the community obligation. *Minority Voices*, 11 (1), 16-18.

———. (1991). On the administration of Africana Studies. *Word: A Black Culture Journal*, I (1), 1-8.

Thomas, C. (1971). *Boys no more: A Black psychologist's view of community*. Beverly Hills, CA: Glencoe Press.

Turner, J. (1984a). Foreward: Africana Studies and epistemology: a discourse in the sociology of knowledge. In J. Turner (Ed.), *The next decade: Theoretical and research issues in Africana Studies*. Ithaca, NY: Cornell University Press.

———. (1984b). *The next decade: Theoretical and research issues in Africana Studies*. Ithaca, NY: Cornell University Press.

Van Sertima, I. (1985). *African presence in early Asia*. New Brunswick, NJ: Transaction Books.

Welsing, F. (June, 1975). Blacks, hypertension, and the active skin melanocyte. Urban Health: The Journal of Health Care in the Cities.

———. (1988). The Cress Theory on melanin (videotape). Lecture given at the annual Melanin Conference, Oakland, CA.

———. (1991). *The Isis papers: The keys to the colors*. Chicago: Third World Press.

Williams, C. (1976). *The Destruction of Black Civilization*. Chicago: Third World Press.

Williams, S. (1990). The Ford Foundation Survey: More smoke than light. *The Voice of Black Studies Newsletter*, 17 (3), 1-2, 4.

Wimby, D. (1984). The female Hourses and great wives of Kemet. In I. Van Sertima (Ed.), *Black women in antiquity*. New Brunswick, NJ: Transaction Books.

Wobogo, V. (1976). Diop's two cradle theory and the origin of white racism. *Black Books Bulletin*, 4 (4), 20-29, 72.

Wright, B. (1979, September). Mentacide. Paper presented at the First Annual Conference of the Black Psychology Task Force, Atlanta, Georgia.

———. (1985). *The psychopathic racial personality and other essays*. Chicago: Third World Press.

Endnotes

1. The Ford Foundation also funded a grant to the NCBS for $300,000 in 1989. However, was the motivation to counter the adverse fallout Ford received behind the Huggins report?

2. In Nobles' model of culture the concepts "cosmology" and "worldview" have specific definitions that distinguish one from the other. The usage of few terms in reference to Nobles' model must not be confused with their commonplace, interchangeable usage (African cosmology/worldview/philosophy) in which the terms generally refer to the cultural deep structure, as in the title and subheadings of this article.

3. See the second footnote.

4. Cheikh Anta Diop's response to a query about Frances Cress Welling's melanin thesis vis-à-vis white psychological functioning is instructive here [Moore (1986, 242)]. In no substantial way does Diop support her melanin thesis. His response, however, seized upon that which they both were in agreement— "the white race...was the product of a process of depigmentation... if we try to delve deeper...in this abstract realm...of individual consciousness...caution is in order. I think what Dr. Welsing has accurately assessed is than at the origin of racism we are to find a definite defensive reflex"—in a manner that precluded any subsequent usage of his response to the detriment or disparagement of Dr. Welsing. Apparently this lesson in African adroitness and collegial courtesy in responding to an interviewer was lost on Molefi Asante who in the September 23, 1991 issue of *Newsweek* (p. 45) attempted to disassociate Afrocentrism from melanin in sending to a query about an earlier statement by Dr. Leonard Jeffries. Asante stated: "[Afrocentrism] is not wrapped up with melanin." The recklessness of the delivery and the timing of Asante's remarks enabled the anti-Black forces to use them via *Newsweek* to the detriment and disparagement of Dr. Leonard Jeffries, a righteous African who was/is being attacked by various anti-Black forces. I hope that Asante's "agemates" admonish of him on this, as he certainly needs to be reined in. Appeasing the master deferentially and headline grabbing, at the expense of Dr. Jeffries and the curriculum of inclusion movement in New York City with which he is affiliated an unconscionable and reprehensible act.

5. Note "that mythology is [a peoples] symbolic writing designed to reveal a natural law and forces governing the universe.... It should be viewed as a carefully constructed symbolic cloak for their abstract thought" (Nobles, 1986, pp. 39, 45).

6. These four, among others, have established their expertise in this subject with production over several years. Also, they are committed to the worldview and are not encumbered by allegiances or linkages with any major camp or personality in the field.

38.

Africology: Normative Theory

Lucius Outlaw

Critical Prelude: The "Africology" Project and Normative Theory

Norms and Theory in Black Studies

The structuring norms of a discipline, we have seen, are localized in *foreconceptions* constitutive of the "internal steering field" of rules, thus of the practitioners, and constitutive of the "external steering field," i.e., the wider intellectual and social milieu that the practitioners share. Norms—rules—are thus foundational to a discipline: they mark off the field of its operation, set its boundary conditions, and steer the practices executed in its name. Thus, we come to a discussion of "normative theory" in the context of "Africology" already loaded with pre-conceptual baggage—regarding norms, theory and theorizing, disciplines, "Africology," etc. We would do well to take the normative turn proffered by the criticist frame and examine some of this baggage.

We might begin with the ambiguity of the phrase "Africology: Normative Theory." On the one hand, it can be taken to mean theoretical discourse *about* norms in general—what they are, their basis, etc.—but discourse steered by partisan foreconceptions about "Africans." On the other, it can be understood as referring to (or calling for) the specification of particular norms *for* Africology as a disciplinary complex. A third possibility is the notion that Africology should *conceptualize* (theorize) and *prescribe* norms by which persons of African descent ought to live, a "way of life." In each of these cases the concern is with the specification of *rules* to guide action— whether in the context of a research enterprise (i.e., rules to govern production, producers, the quality and distribution of the products) or the social, historical worlds of peoples of African descent more generally. I understand this conceptualizing and specifying of norms to comprise, in part, the *theory* anticipated in "Africology: Normative Theory."

However, the three possibilities are neither unrelated nor mutually exclusive. If we expect Africology to set out the norms to guide African peoples' living, then we must know everything important to know about norms in general, about the normative bases and parameters of Africology, about what *ought* to be the case for black peoples, and how we *ought* to go about achieving and/or maintaining what ought to be. Thus, what at first may have seemed a simple case of ambiguity in a title is really a matter of the inherent complexities involving two aspects of the basis and practices of a research enterprise: its *structuring* norms, and the norms it might *prescribe*. In other words, what is involved are the inherently related matters of theory and practice, knowing and doing.

Insights such as these with respect to norms have served as major planks in the platform of Black Studies: "Afrocentric" research emerged as a *normative* turn vis-à-vis European- and Euro-American-centered research. It (Black Studies) is an explicitly *partisan* venture consciously and explicitly devoted to serving interests of black peoples by way of "the systematic study of black people...an examination of the deeper truths of black life...[Black Studies] will examine the valid part that black people have played in man's development in society...[and] differs from academic disciplines rooted in European tradition by relating to African history and culture."[1] Further, it is a venture that, from the outset, seeks an intimate and *necessary* connection between theory and praxis, between systematic knowledge development, and social action, "science" and "ways of life":

> Currently, the two principal pillars which support theory building in Black Studies are the concepts of (1) knowledge development or consciousness raising and (2) the liberation of black peoples, translated as a change in the social, political and economic order.... The goal of Black Studies is not merely to seek knowledge for its own sake, but knowledge for the purpose of pragmatic manipulation. This is all instrumentalist view of theory building in Black Studies. That is, the significance of research and the uprooting of information lies in the actions they guide.[2]

In short, Black Studies is about *both* "science" and "ways of life," has both "an academic and social mission, and is, therefore, both an investigative and applied social science."[3]

In such statements we get a sense of the normative commitments of Black Studies. If Africology is to be its refinement, while consciously attending to norms in its (Africology's) theorizing and direction setting for black life, then it is imperative that we review these normative principles and commitments at work in—and advanced on behalf of—Black Studies in service to its partisan agenda.

Black Studies: A Partisan Venture

Nick Aaron Ford's *Black Studies: Threat-or-Challenge?* is one of the earliest surveys and analyses of Black Studies programs conducted.[4] In it he presents seven categories of objectives for Black Studies programs (drawn from a survey of two hundred programs with approximately two hundred objectives listed):

1. concern with "the need for the educational experience *to provide for black students a feeling of personal identity, personal pride, and personal worth*";

2. the programs are "based on the assumption that a study of black history and culture will aid blacks in understanding the basis for an identity that is satisfying and fulfilling";

3. "the need to promote sympathetic interest and dedicated involvement in the improvement of the black community (local, national and world-

wide)" [Ford notes that, in the programs surveyed, more space is given to this objective than to any other];

4. *"the radical reformation of American education by attacking its basic racist assumptions and making it truly democratic and relevant to the current needs of blacks and whites"*;

5. *"to train black students in the philosophy and strategies of revolution as a prelude to black revolution"*;

6. *"preparation for career opportunities, including the professions"*;

7. *"the determination to encourage and actively develop intellectual growth and broad scholarly interests in their students."*[5]

But how are these objectives to be met? In the words of Maulana Karenga, one of the leading theorists of Black Studies, the matter of first priority is the elimination of our "ideological deficiency" by posing and answering "the fundamental question": "what ideology—coherent system of theories and value system—can give us a correct worldview and analysis of our situation, pull us together and weld us into the conscious and progressive *social force* we need to be in order to achieve in *struggle* and alliance with other oppressed and progressive people, the liberation of ourselves and all people?"[6] Such systems of theories and values, sanctioned as principles or rules to guide theoretical and social praxis, are *norms*.

In the effort to set out a "coherent system of theories and value system," one aspect has involved a revaluation of the notions of "objectivity" and of its corollary "disinterestedness." One of the stronger claims advanced by some proponents of Black Studies is that "objectivity," in the sense expressed by Nielsen, is not achievable, and any claim that it is in fact operative in conceptualizing and setting out principles for "ways of life" is at best an ideological cover for ethnocentric and/or racial—if not racist (and/or gender-based)—power moves. A less stringent—and, I think, more appropriate—view is expressed by Maurice Jackson:

> Objectivity in sociology cannot be taken for granted. Although scientific objectivity can be safeguarded, to a degree, by the scientific method, the sociology of Black Studies makes explicit the interdependence of science and society referred to by Max Weber.... [B]lack Studies follows the modern scientific view that facts do not speak for themselves, but are informed by perspectives and assumptions which are implicit if not explicit.... [B]lack Studies questions the presumed disinterestedness of much current knowledge and is explicit in its assertion that appropriate knowledge should be used for and by black people as well.[7]

The same is true, say some proponents of Black Studies, with respect to intellectual practices and their results in general: their justification, objectivity, and truth are ultimately *group* based, thus are not secured in disinterested objectivity and universality simply by their cognitive, epistemological character. Molefi Asante, for example, argues that "all analysis is culturally centered and flows from ideological commitments"; therefore—to extend his argument—analysis serves *particular* agendas of *particular* persons.[8] Thus, values *cum* norms structuring the practices of a research enterprise, and, through their deployment, the explicit attempt to structure "ways of life" are not *objective* in the sense that the grounds of their truth, objectivity, and justification are without reference to *any* group, or any person as a member of some particular group. Rather, such norms can be justified only *relative to* some group(s) or to some person as a member of a particular group; hence they do not automatically and necessarily transcend historical social life-worlds. In the words of Philip Daniel:

The whole emphasis on objectivity and empirical theory as opposed to normative theory is out of place in Black Studies and the arguments concerning it should be dropped. We scrutinize and act as we live. Analysis in Black Studies is a purposeful activity and the conditions of the black community involve questions of right and wrong.[9]

As "purposeful activity" also concerned with questions of right and wrong, Black Studies is to provide rules for answering such questions. Since it is in *lived* social worlds, in the rules structuring this living, that norms are at work, Black Studies must address such matters guided by the life-practices of the people comprising them. Norms, then, are "culturally relative":

The cultural relativist emphasizes the cultural tradition as a prime source of the individual's views and thinks that most disagreements in ethics among individuals stem from enculturation in different ethical traditions, although he need not deny that some ethical disagreements among individuals arise from differences of innate constitution or personal history between the individuals.[10]

In contemporary Black Studies this position has been termed "cultural nationalism."[11] In fact, it has been the dominant orientation in contemporary Black Studies and accounts for much of its platform. Molefi Asante and Maulana Karenga, among others, are two of its leading proponents. A brief review of (some of their arguments will be helpful not only for insight into the "ideology" of Black Studies that they offer, but also because both attempt to refine and advance the enterprise.[12]

"Afrocentricity"

Molefi Asante's contribution centers on the concept of "Afrocentricity," which, together with its corollary "Eurocentricity," have come to have a pervasive life of their own in Black Studies discourse. "Afrocentricity" is offered as the name for a perspective that is centered on "the African Cultural System" in which all African people participate "although it is modified according to specific histories and nations."[13] The core of Afrocentricity is *Njia*: "the collective expression of the Afrocentric worldview based in the historical experience of African people.... Incorporating Njia into our lives, we become essentially ruled by our own values and principles. Dispensing with alien views at our center, Njia puts us in and on our own center."[14] With Njia, we become Africa-centered, if you will, in our normative commitments and practices. Thus, "Afrocentric," "Afrocentricity."

Oriented and guided by Afrocentricity, Asante argues, a new criticism emerges. "It introduces relevant values, denounces non-Afrocentric behavior, and promotes analysis. ..the Afrocentric critical methods start with the primary measure! Does it place Africans in the center?"[15] For the present, the primary task of this new criticism is the "recapturing of our own collective consciousness.... It is reclaiming Egypt, deciphering the ancient writing of Nubia, circulating the histories and geographies of Ibn Khaidun and Ibn Battuta, and examining records of Africans in Mexico and other places in the new world."[16] On the way to this collective consciousness there are five levels of awareness:

1. *skin recognition* — "when a person recognizes that his or her skin is black and or her heritage is black but cannot grasp any further reality";

2. *environmental recognition* — seeing the environment "as indicating his or her blackness through discrimination and abuse";

3. *personality awareness* — "It occurs when a persons [sic] says 'I like music, or dance or chitterlings.'..." Even if the person speaks truthfully, this is not Afrocentricity;

4. *interest-concern* — "demonstrates interest and concern in the problems of blacks and tries to deal intelligently with the issues of the African people." This level is also not Afrocentricity since "it does not consume the life and spirit of the person";

5. *Afrocentricity* — is achieved "when the person becomes totally changed to a conscious level of involvement in the struggle for his or her own mind liberation."[17]

Further, once achieved, Afrocentricity allows one to predict the actions of whites and non-Afrocentric persons "with certainty." And, one does not refuse to "condemn mediocrity and reactionary attitudes among Africans for the sake of false unity."[18] Within an Afrocentric perspective, the "two aspects of consciousness" are operative: toward oppression, toward victory.

Specifically, what does this mean for the practices of Black Studies? It means, according to Asante, that Black Studies must become the discipline of *Afrology*. Pertinent to this discussion, the "outlines" of the normative base of the discipline are available: they are "rooted in the social, political and economic values of our people." And the discipline will be the crystallization of "the notions and methods of black-oriented social scientists and humanists" whose "basic qualities" will be *competence* ("the analytic skills with which the scholar investigates his subject"), *clarity of perspective* ("the ability to focus on the Afrocentric issues in the subject area and to interpret those issues in a way that will expose the essential factors constituting the subject"), and *understanding of the object* [sic] ("Understanding the subject means that the scholar knows something of the inter-relationship of his subject and the world context").[19]

Asante offers two "theoretical propositions" that will "set the tone" for an analysis of the emerging discipline of "Afrology" with its Afrocentric core:

> Afrology is primarily pan-Africanist in its treatment of the creative, political and geographic dimensions of our collective will to liberty.... A second proposition is that the Afrologist, by virtue of his perspective, participates in the coming to be of new concepts and directions. His perceptions of reality, political and social allow him to initiate novel approaches to problems and issues. Not being encapsulated by the Western point of view he is a person who is mentally as free as possible.... In fact, the Afrologist...is a person who is capable of participating in both the African and the Western point of view; however, as a practicing Afrologist he must act Afrocentrically. What he has learned is the value of every viewpoint.[20]

The Future of Afrology?

Since Afrology is based upon an Afrocentric interpretation and a particular conception of society, the results of our work will alter previous perceptions and set standards for future studies of African peoples. It is here that Afrology comes into its own as an organizing methodology, and a reflective philosophy, able to open the door to a more assertive, and therefore proper, consciousness of cultural and historical data. Such a proper consciousness is founded upon the genuine acceptance of our African past, without which there is no Afrological discourse or basis for peculiar analysis.[21]

Molefi Asante continues his articulation of Afrocentricity in *The Afrocentric Idea*.[22] Here Afrocentricity is further defined and deployed as "a critique that propounds a cultural theory of society by the very act of criticism" and proposes "a cultural reconstruction that incorporates the African perspective as a part of an entire human transformation." The object of critique: "Eurocentricism" that is to say "the preponderant...myths of universalism, objectivity, and classical traditions [that retain] a provincial European cast." Afrocentric analysis will "reestablish...the centrality of the ancient Kemetic (Egyptian) civilization and the Nile Valley cultural complex as points of reference for an African perspective in much the same way, as Greece and Rome serve as reference points for the European world." Afrocentricity, as the foundation of the discipline of Afrology, will "expand...the repertoire of human perspectives on knowledge."[23] The goal: "a pos-tEurocentric idea where true transcultural analyses become possible."[24]

> Sustained by new information and innovative methodologies, Afrology will transform community and social sciences, as well as arts and humanities, and assist in constructing a new, perhaps more engaging, way to analyze and synthesize reality. Perhaps what is needed is a post-Western or meta-Western metatheory to disentangle us from the consuming monopoly of a limited intellectual framework.[25]

"Afrocentricity," then, may be viewed as a covering term for *rules of construction* for the disciplinary field of Black Studies — or "Afrology" — guiding the formation of enunciative modalities (statements and ways of speaking about objects and practices in the field) and inclusive of foreconceptions that provide the field's boundary conditions and platform.

"Kawaida" Theory

Maulana Karenga has provided an even fuller articulation of what the disciplinary project of Black Studies should involve. His most complete discussion is presented in his *Introduction to Black Studies*. After setting out a number of objectives for Black Studies, he discusses, as well, a number of points of "relevance":

1. a "definitive contribution to humanity's understanding itself...Black Studies...becomes important because it is a study of a particular people which aids in the study of humanity as a whole";

2. "its contribution to U.S. society's understanding of itself";

3. as a logical consequence, "a contribution to the university's realization of its claim and challenge to teach the whole truth, or something as close to it as humanly possible";

4. "a contribution to the rescue and reconstruction of Black history and humanity";

5. "a critical contribution to a new social science which will not only benefit Blacks, but also the U.S. and the world."[26]

Both Karenga's objectives and his points of relevance are well represented in the categories of objectives, listed above, assembled by Nick Aaron Ford in his survey.

Clearly they help to set the agenda for Black Studies and thus shape part of its normative platform. Other planks are added when Karenga discusses the "scope" of Black Studies as a discipline. It is to be

> the scientific study of the multidimensional aspects of Black thought and practice in their current and historical unfolding Black Studies... is both a particular and general social science... [and]... as an interdisciplinary discipline has seven basic subject areas...: Black history; Black Religion; Black Social Organization; Black Politics; Black Economics; Black Creative Production (Black Art, Music and Literature) and Black Psychology.[27]

For Karenga, these subject areas constitute the "core" of Black Studies. However, an essential point to note is that he grounds this "conceptual framework" on a normative platform of his own articulation: *Kawaida* theory, "a theory of cultural and social change which has as one of its main propositions the contention that the solution to the problems of Black life demand critiques and correctives in the seven basic areas of culture...: mythology (religion), history, social organization, economic organization, political organization, creative motif and ethos."[28]

These normative principles, combined with the objectives, relevances, and conceptual framework of Black Studies, support what Karenga terms a set of "core integrative principles and assumptions" that are the "thematic glue" holding together the core subject areas:

1. "each subject area of Black Studies is a vital aspect and area of the Black experience and, therefore, contributive to the understanding and appreciation of its wholeness";

2. "the truth of the Black experience is whole and thus, any partial and compartmentalized approach to it can only yield a partial and incomplete image and understanding of it";

3. "effectively integrated into the pattern of the discipline as a whole, each subject area becomes a microcosm of the macrocosm, the Black experience, which not only enriches our knowledge of the Black experience, but also enhances the analytical process and products of the discipline itself";

4. "all the subject areas mesh and intersect not only at the point of their primary focus, i.e., Black people in the process of shaping reality in their own image and interest, but also in their self-conscious commitment and contribution to the definition and solution of the social and discipline problems which serve as the core challenges to Black Studies."[29]

But the challenges—the "social and discipline problems"—are serious and multi-dimensional. Karenga addresses them directly. His discussion of what he terms the "intellectual" challenge to Black Studies is pertinent.

First is the problem of definition, i.e., "the need of Black Studies to... establish in clear terms in a body of critical literature its academic and social missions." A central aspect of this problem for Karenga are the matters of focus and thrust:

> Whether Black Studies should be Afro-American centered or Pan-African. Usually, a Pan-African emphasis means a Continent centered program, but it may include Caribbean studies, the study of South American and Islander Blacks or any other Blacks as well.... Such a broadly based focus might satisfy some Pan-Africanists, but it still leaves fundamental questions unanswered. For example, which of these areas or peoples should get the most at-

tention, and if it is to be equally divided, why? If Black Studies is still to link the campus to the community, how does it now define the community given its expanded focus?[30]

Karenga proposes a less "over-ambitious" scope that "begins where it is, in the U.S., among Afro-Americans, and then as it grows stronger, expands outward."[31]

A second problem of focus has to do with the debate regarding "values," particularly whether the value focus of Black Studies should be on "survival" or "development." Karenga opts for the latter: "Development is obviously the superior value, for not only does it stress the need for new competencies, but inherent in the concept of development, itself, is the assumption and insurance of survival."[32] Other problems include: the absence of a "standard rationale" for the existence of Black Studies, and, connected with this, theoretical and administrative thrusts toward "integration"; the absence of a standard curriculum; and, finally, the challenge of developing a definitive, substantial body of literature without which the future—even the worth—of the discipline will continue to be in doubt.[33]

Karenga's proposed correctives for these problems take us to the heart of the discussion regarding the move from Black Studies to Africology as a *discipline*:

> The thrust of Black Studies toward contribution of a body of literature which will help bring into being a new social science and at the same time contribute to the rescue and reconstruction of Black history and humanity, must have at least four characteristics. It must be holistic, critical, corrective and committed.[34]

What does each of these mean? For Karenga, a *holistic* approach is a "comprehensive inquiry into the core process and practices of Black life as well as an investigation into related internal and external factors which confront and affect us as a people."[35] A *critical* approach is

> concrete, rational and incisive.... Critical intellectual production moves beyond the insubstantiality of free flows of consciousness and pitiful calls for survival, digs beneath the surface and raises that which is absent in traditional literature, i.e., the rich variousness and potential of Black life and the subversive content of our history. Its search is for possibilities as well as achievements, for contradictions as well as tendencies that will lead us beyond the established state of things.[36]

An approach that is *corrective* moves beyond criticism to *reconstruction: "the most severe and effective criticism of a society is self-conscious practice which transforms it."* Thus, "a corrective body of Black Studies literature must begin with a redefinition of the world in our own image according to our own needs."[37] Finally, Black Studies as a *partisan* enterprise

> must be unashamedly committed to a set of values contributive to its task—which in the final analysis—is both theoretical and practical. Committed intellectual work reflects the acceptance of one's role as an *unashamed partisan of one's people*. Moreover, it recognizes the fact that there is no pure research isolated and divorced from the urgencies of the day.[38]

Combining the arguments of Karenga with those of Molefi Asante (a legitimate combination in that both, in fact, are colleagues involved in some of the same organizations working to fulfill the Black Studies agenda), the following profile of Black Studies emerges. It is:

1. a multidimensional enterprise, centered on Africa and African peoples as the primary measure, with both theoretical and practical "missions"

(i.e., knowledge production in service to social change) that cover seven key aspects of life;

2. guided by a conceptual framework that maps these aspects;

3. held together by a core of thematic principles;

4. grounded on a particular set of values thought to be indigenous to the lives of black people: the *Nguzo Saba* for Karenga, *Njia* for Asante;

5. holistic, critical, corrective, and committed; and

6. practiced by persons who are competent, clear, knowledgeable; who contribute new concepts and directions; and who know the value of other viewpoints while remaining *Afrocentric*

Black Studies through the Criticist Frame

How has Black Studies in the Asante-Karenga mode fared as an enterprise devoted to the systematic development of conceptual schemes (among other things) needed for knowledge production and refinement? Apparently not sufficiently well if the implications of the call for the formation of a field and discipline of Africology are drawn out: the "discipline" is yet to be fully developed, the production of various works and the establishment of programs, departments, institutes, journals, and a national organization (The National Council for Black Studies) notwithstanding.

Others are in agreement. Again, Philip T.K. Daniel:

When we look for constructs or postulates in Black Studies we find a collection of unordered attempts at theory building. Theories in Black Studies are like ships steaming ahead toward one destination, but at different longitudes. This obviously means that if they all keep their present course, only one, or perhaps none will reach the docking point. Thus, they will be in a perpetual circular motion until they run out of fuel.[39]

James Turner addresses this matter in his "Introduction" to *The Next Decade: Theoretical and Research Issues in Africana Studies*, a collection of essays from the Cornell University Africana Studies and Research Center's Tenth Anniversary Conference (1980). For Turner, Black Studies is a discipline of "reconstruction" by way of "a synthesis of what its criticisms imply, convergence with theories reviewed, and the philosophic methods of its pedagogical emphasis."[40] Further, Black Studies provides a unique "paradigm" for critical scholarship, and is fundamentally involved in "renaming the world." Still, Turner notes, the appropriate theory and methodology for this renaming continue to be matters of serious debate, one he thinks should continue. The question, however, is whether we have sufficiently completed the tasks necessary to provide the functions he identifies as common to all disciplines, thus to Black Studies:

First, the intellectual parameters of the field must be relatively clearly established with rather apparent theoretical configuration. Second, the ideational and analytical "meanings" of the discipline—that is, what characterizes what *we* do as different, and significantly, from what is done in other disciplines—must be delineated. In sum, a fairly commonly adhered-to definition of the raison d'être of the field must emerge, for example, what is the consequence of [an] "Afro-centric" perspective for the pursuit of truth.[41]

These issues are central to questions about the normative platform of Black Studies. Certainly, Black Studies has been particularly productive in this area, at the very least in setting out the programmatic-normative agenda for what the enterprise *ought* to be about, *whose* interests *ought* to be served, against what/whom to take *critical* stands, etc. As noted earlier, these concerns — the normative agenda — have been shepherded and nurtured most forcefully and consistently within the tradition of cultural nationalism, particularly along paths forged by Karenga and Asante. (This is not to disregard or deny the importance or influence of other "schools" of thought in Black Studies: e.g., Marxism-Leninism, Nkrumahism, and "integrationist" — i.e., non-racially centered — approaches, the latter being one that seeks to have studies of peoples of African descent "integrated" into prevailing disciplines.) Since Africology is an attempt, in part, to refine and continue this agenda, an assessment of Black Studies by way of the criticist might prepare the way for a consideration of Africology's normative possibilities.

A. *The Historicity of Discursive Fields*: From the beginning, Black Studies has been radically and consistently historist. A major part of its program involves the critique of, and struggle against, institutionalizations of the articulation and deployment of disciplines a the supposed evolutionary flow of reason embodied in the history of Europe and America, subsequently in the discursive practices of persons of European descent. Black Studies emerged in the space opened by this historicist, relativizing and in its cultural-nationalist orientations remains firmly we wedded to this position.

B. *Anti-foundationalism*: From a critical, anti-foundationialist perspective, Black Studies does not fare well. A close reading of the Asante-Karenga agenda, for example, reveals that it involves a critique of, and opposition to, claims that "Eurocentric" styles of rationality[42] are, in fact, the telos of all of humankind, and that these styles — thus humankind's telos — spring from epistemologically originary foundations uncovered, as it were, in and by "European" thinkers who were said to be the originators of philosophy as the science of reason. But the move is then made to substitute an equally originary "African" foundation by way of reclaiming, rehabilitating narratives offering reassurance of our "Afrocentricity" through identification with forms of Africanness or Africanity supposedly preserved in their essence across all cultural spaces and times. The critical reconsiderations prompted by the criticist frame require that the discontinuities resulting from the spatial and temporal disruptions and from cultural and sociological differences (e.g., gendered experiences and class stratifications) be taken seriously.

Certainly we must question the veracity of our attempted reclamations and rehabilitations as "total history," given that they are executed from the platform of, and in service to, agendas constructed in the present. Further, our efforts are conditioned by anticipated, desired, or hoped-for futures the likes of which our ancestors did not live. Nor, for that matter, are the presents and anticipated futures the same in all their important particulars for *all* African peoples. The *similarities* of experiences of African peoples as a function of patterned and linked practices part and parcel of the global political economy of capitalism notwithstanding, it is also the case that, at the level of lived experience and its perpetuation as tradition, significant *differences* exist among us. Thus, we have to take much more seriously our characterization of our historiography as *reconstructive*, a project the meaningfulness and truthfulness of which are always controlled by the agenda by which it is shaped and deployed from the site of our prevailing historicity, our claims with regard to "cultural unity" notwithstanding.

We can invoke such unity among African peoples only by disregarding very important dissimilarities. But is the cost of that disregard too high for serious, self-critical scholarship that aspires to reasonableness and "truthfulness" with regard to the totalities that are involved? The unifying power "African" ("black" or "African-American" "civilization") will have to be reconsidered: "unity" can no longer be presumed to be pre-given and automatically recovered with the deployment of "African," as though the term "gathers us all together" through the unifying power of its conveying of a trans-historical, trans-geographical racial *essence*.

C. *The Discursive Field*: In light of these considerations, we are left to review Black Studies as a discursive field. *What* we speak about on the plane of this field, *who* speaks *how*, using what *concepts*, for what *purposes*— all of these are determined by the *rules of discourse* at work in the constitution of the field. And if Foucault is right, these rules do not define "the dumb existence of a reality, nor the canonical use of a vocabulary" but, instead, involve "the ordering of objects." The greater the historical distance from the "objects"[43] we order, then it is *our* rules of ordering that are in force, not those of the objects we study.

But these are items on an agenda of the *present* that is conditioned by the lived experiences of disruption and marginalization. The rules of our discourse have thus been formed in the crucible of struggle: contemporary Black Studies emerged from the context of the contemporary Civil Rights and Black Power movements. The connection between the historicity and dimensions of those struggles and our African "origins" is anything but simple continuity.

Furthermore, there are serious questions with regard to the conceptual rigor and intellectual cogency of some of the normative positions of Black Studies. For example, consider the issue of the claimed "relativism" of all cultural norms. A rather stringently drawn—though not a necessary—consequence of a cultural relativist position is the radical claim that across cultures there is, necessarily, "fundamental" disagreement about normative matters with no possibilities of resolving the differences.[44]

However, it is important that we consider closely whether—and to what extent, if at all—it is ultimately in the best interest of Africology to push the relativist position to such an extent. To the degree that Africology is intended as a *discipline*, for which the most constitutive medium and form or praxis is discourse, then it cannot be the case that *inherently* its governing norms will be available only to persons of African descent, even though the discipline emerges out of, and works to be in service to, our life-worlds. Discourse is possible, and proceeds successfully, only if participants abide by shared governing rules. And, given the committed social imperatives conditioning Black Studies/ Africology—for example, the requirement that the enterprise contribute to the rehabilitation of black folks and provide them normative guidance—the rules must be available to those to whom we, wish to speak, in whose behalf we speak: in short, the rules of discourse must be *public*.

More fundamentally, it is certainly inconsistent with intellectual praxis conducted in institutional settings and by way of disciplinary practices that are part and parcel of the modern academy with its "European" legacies. For these legacies provide much of the context within which, and the rules by which, Black Studies emerged and was shaped by efforts to make it a "discipline"—the importance and truth of the claims that it was to be a radically *different* discipline notwithstanding. Subsequently, if Africology is to involve practices of *systematic* knowledge development, acquisition, refinement, and distribution, and, as part of these efforts, is to contribute to the articulation and institutionalization of appropriate norms for peoples of African descent—if Africology is to be the disciplinary matrix that continuously constructs and is structured by the *logoi* of Africa and the African diaspora—then its structuring norms must satisfy rules that, among other things, promote such activities as critical and *self*-critical endeavors. Furthermore, since a discipline is an inherently social enterprise in which some degree of consensus is necessary, shared rules are required. Without them there can be no agreement, even among ourselves. The rules—the norms—for obtaining such agreement are not provided by melanin. And while particular rules may be "necessitated" by political demands having to do with the racial/ethnic, gender, class, and/or cultural realities of historical life-worlds, this necessity follows from particular *choices* attendant on reconstructions of histories and projections of preferred futures.

Still, the rules are not *necessarily and irrevocably* restricted to the cultural, historical life-worlds of particular racial/ethnic—or gender—groups. Norms can transcend particular groups such that they cover the intellectual and social life praxes of different groups in ways that make it possible to resolve what otherwise might seem to be fundamental disagreements. Norms, governing "ways of life" in general, systematic intellectual praxes in particular, are *strategies serving choices*, ultimately a choice about life "in general," in service to which research enterprises have their ground and being. Thus, the question whether those of us involved in the refinement of Black Studies into Africology will be concerned to shape it—at least in part—in conformity with norms whose range of universality, justifiability, objectivity, and truthfulness will extend, with consistency, beyond us to non-African peoples is a matter of choice. But it is a choice not only about our intellectual praxis, but about the world we would co-make and share with others *even as we do so with uncompromising commitment to ensuring, as best we can, "our" survival and "our" flourishing, now and in the foreseeable future.*

Thus, a crucial and complex question: How shall we shape our intellectual praxis to serve our best interests, and thereby provide us with normative guidance, while, at the same time, we preserve norms that secure truthfulness and appropriate objectivity in larger socio-historical contexts within which our praxis is situated? The answer to this question cannot be provided by "us" alone. Even if we would have that sharing based on consensus regarding the rules of disciplinary discourse—for Africology as well—a consensus arrived at through *open, free, and democratic* discussion, we might question whether "others" will abide by these same rules. Still, as an enterprise of the modern academy that seeks to speak authoritatively to black folks and to others for and about black folks, the rules of discourse for Africology will have to satisfy institutionalized rules governing scholarly practices to a significant extent, even as we continue the legacy of Black Studies and refine institutional rules for disciplines to bring them into greater harmony with the agendas of our lives and our hoped-for futures.

As evidence of this need to "play by house rules" if you will, we need only to remind ourselves of the pressures on Black Studies programs and departments to justify themselves in terms of the substance, coherence, and, of course, the persuasiveness of the arguments in behalf of the enterprise (as well as in terms of the number of matriculating students and the productivity of program or departmental faculty). While the recognition that these matters are deeply grounded in cultural politics has been foundational to contemporary Black Studies, that recognition does not free us to do as we wish. We can change—have changed—the rules of discourse in the academy; however, as long as we consent to share in such institutional settings and to participate in national and international publics—whether academic or non-academic is irrelevant—through our disciplinary practices, our discourse cannot proceed by private rules.

But the same questions have to be faced when black folks are the focus of discussion. Some persons insist that the most appropriate values and norms for orienting Black Studies are to be found in a unique cultural system, said to be shared by all African and African-descended peoples world-wide, which orders ways of life generally, worldviews and belief systems in particular. "We are all African people!" was a frequent declaration heard during the years of the Black Power movement, when efforts to initiate Black Studies programs were most intense. At the heart of such declarations is the belief that "cultural unity" among African and African-descended peoples makes for a shared "Africanity."[45]

The concern for norms to structure the formulation of Africology as a discipline may be interpreted as anticipating (if not presupposing) norms that can be *distinguished* as "African" and *traced* across historical and cultural spaces and times—efforts in historical reconstruction and description. What this might mean for Africology as a discipline that completes these tasks and, further, that *prescribes* norms can be better determined by now recalling the questions posed for me to answer and by examining them in light of all that has been discussed.

First consider the proposition that there are *"fundamental, ontological axiomatic assumptions over time among peoples of African origin."* I am deeply suspicious of this complex proposition. I do not think such assumptions exist if we take "fundamental" as qualifying "assumptions" such that we think of them as being the same for all peoples of African origin throughout history ("over time"). Nor do I regard norms, in general, as "axiomatic," unless we speak analogously. A stringent foundationalist reading of this question might suggest (presume?) that the "fundamental assumptions" are somehow emergent at "the origin" and are preserved "over time," historical ruptures (colonization) and dispersals of peoples (relocation and enslavement in the New World) notwithstanding.

Here I have invoked a complex of norms for structuring the disciplinary praxis of Africology. We might refer to these collectively as a "criticist frame" that incorporates awareness of our historicity and of historical discontinuity and is supported by rules of discourse constitutive of democratic social-political praxis.[46] And as an enterprise devoted to the most complete understandings possible of Africans and peoples or African descent—understandings that will contribute to enhanced living—I would have Africology continue the cultural-nationalist legacy of Black Studies of seeking to root itself in and devote itself to black life-worlds, but be guided by a critical appreciation of the complexities of these same life-worlds, thus of the complexity of competing normative agendas within them. I do not regard it as either appropriate or possible for Africology as a discipline to set the normative agenda for black life in general, nor for any particular African or African-descended people. What the enterprise might do—and do rather well—is offer a critical *mediation* of competing normative agendas relative to the goals and objectives of the particular people in question. Such a contribution requires the fulfillment of one of the definitive commitments of contemporary Black Studies to be in touch with and service to the communities that are the object of study; but, refined through the criticist frame, it also redefines the limits of this same commitment. The sincerity and intensity of our commitment must not degenerate into authoritarian dogmatism.

Nor into racism. As a socially and politically conditioned and conditioning intellectual enterprise of the modem academy, Africology, in its relations with non-black others, must manifest in its norms and practices the best world we would have for ourselves and our peoples that is shared with others, and on terms that, while doing so, also support critical scholarship of the highest levels of excellence possible as we have helped to define "excellence." This will require that the enterprise of Africology move beyond a restrictive cultural nationalism and be governed by refined norms for truth, objectivity, and justification that support the praxes of scholarship as, in the words of Molefi Asante, a "post-Eurocentric, transcultural" venture within which our understandings of our peoples bespeak their integrity.

It is a matter of perspective: the "frame" through which we structure and go about our work. The consequences, of course, are enormous. At stake is the safety of negotiating the mined field of life on the way to a chosen destination. Norms to govern theorizing about norms for social life are themselves part of social life, and are likewise conditioned by the choices of destination and route. No amount of theorizing can eliminate the risks involved in choosing, either in social life or in theorizing. Thus, we must not be pretentious about what is to come from an attempted refinement of Black Studies into a more mature and socially responsible "discipline" of *Africology*.

A revision of an essay prepared in response to a request to contribute to the Symposium on "Africology" sponsored by the Department of Afro-American Studies, The University of Wisconsin-Milwaukee, April 24-25, 1987.

Endnotes

1. Maurice Jackson, "Toward a Sociology of Black Studies," *Journal of Black Studies*, Vol. 1, No. 2 (December 1970, pp. 131-140), pp. 132-133.

2. Philip T.K. Daniel, "Theory Building in Black Studies" *The Black Scholar*, Vol. 12, No. 3 (May/June 1981, pp. 29-36), pp. 31-32.

3. Maulana Ron Karenga, *Introduction to Black Studies* (Los Angeles: Kawaida Publications, 1982).

4. (Port Washington, New York: Kennikat Press, 1973).

5. *Ibid.*, pp. 55-63, emphasis in original.

6. Maulana Ron Karenga, "Ideology and Struggle: Some Preliminary Notes," *The Black Scholar*, Vol. 6, No. 5 (January-February 1975, pp. 23-30), p. 23, emphasis in original.

7. Jackson, "Toward a Sociology of Black Studies," pp. 134, 135.

8. Molefi Kete Asante, "Afrocentric Theory," *Critical Social Issues*, Vol. 1, No. 1 (Spring 1987, pp. 46-56), p. 46.

9. Daniel, "Theory Building in Black Studies," p. 34.

10. Richard B. Brandt, "Ethical Relativism," *The Encyclopedia of Philosophy*, Vols. 3 & 4, p. 75.

11. There is a sizable and still growing body of literature on the various forms and history of black nationalism, cultural nationalism included. Two helpful bibliographies include Betty Jenkins and Susan Phillis, *Black Separatism: A Bibliography* (Westport, Connecticut: Greenwood Press, 1976); and William Helmreich, *Afro-Americans and Africa: Black Nationalism at the Crossroads* (Westport, Connecticut: Greenwood press, 1977). In addition, also see Rodney Carlisle, *The Roots of Black Nationalism* (Port Washington, New York: Kennikat Press, 1975); Sterling Stuckey, *The Ideological Origins of Black Nationalism* (Boston: Beacon Press, 1972); and, for a critique of black nationalism in the 1960s, see several essays by Harold Cruse ("Negro Nationalism's New Wave," "The Economics of Black Nationalism") in his *Rebellion or Revolution?* (New York: William Morrow, 1968).

12. For other discussions of Black Studies, see, for example, Armstead L. Robinson et al., ed., *Black Studies in the University: A Symposium* (New Haven: Yale University Press, 1969); John W. Blassingame, ed., *New Perspectives on Black Studies* (Urbana: University of Illinois Press, 1971); *Introduction to American Studies* (Chicago: People's College Press, 1978); and

James E. Turner, ed., *The Next Decade: Theoretical and Research Issues in Africana Studies* (Ithaca, New York: Africana Studies and Research Center, Cornell University, 1984).

13. Molefi Kete Asante, *Afrocentricity: The Theory of Social Change* (Buffalo, New York: Amulefi Publishing Co., 1980), p. 5.

14. Asante, *Afrocentricity*, p. 26.

15. Asante, *Afrocentricity*, p. 52.

16. Asante, *Afrocentricity*, p. 55.

17. Asante, *Afrocentricity*, pp. 55-56.

18. Asante, *Afrocentricity*, p. 57.

19. Asante, *Afrocentricity*, pp. 65-75.

20. Asante, *Afrocentricity*, pp. 69-71.

21. Asante, *Afrocentricity*, p. 75.

22. (Philadelphia: Temple University Press, 1987).

23. Asante, *The Afrocentric Idea*, pp. 6, 8, 9, 16.

24. Asante, *The Afrocentric Idea*, p. 8. "Most of the so-called universal concepts fail transculturally, and without transcultural validity there is not universality." *The Afrocentric Idea*, p. 56.

25. Asante, *The Afrocentric Idea*, p. 34.

26. Karenga, *Introduction to Black Studies*, pp. 28-51.

27. Karenga, *Introduction to Black Studies*, pp. 33-35.

28. Karenga, *Introduction to Black Studies*, p. 36.

29. Karenga, *Introduction to Black Studies*, pp. 37-38.

30. Karenga, *Introduction to Black Studies*, p. 361.

31. Karenga, *Introduction to Black Studies*, p. 361.

32. Karenga, *Introduction to Black Studies*, p. 362.

33. Karenga, *Introduction to Black Studies*, pp. 364-366.

34. Karenga, *Introduction to Black Studies*, p. 369.

35. Karenga, *Introduction to Black Studies*, p. 369.

36. Karenga, *Introduction to Black Studies*, pp. 369-370.

37. Karenga, *Introduction to Black Studies*, p. 370, emphasis in original.

38. Karenga, *Introduction to Black Studies*, p. 370, emphasis in original.

39. Daniel, "Theory Building in Black Studies," p. 29.

40. James E. Turner, "Africana Studies and Epistemology: A Discourse in the Sociology of Knowledge," *The Next Decade*, p. xviii.

41. Turner, "Africana Studies and Epistemology," p. xvi.

42. For a discussion of "cognitive style" see Alfred Schutz and Thomas Luckmann, *Structures of the Life-World* (Evanston, Illinois: Northwestern University Press, 1973).

43. Foucault, *The Archaeology of Knowledge*, pp. 48.

44. "To say that a disagreement is 'fundamental' means that it would not be removed even if there were perfect agreement about the properties of the thing being evaluated.... There is fundamental ethical disagreement only if ethical appraisals or valuations are incompatible, even when there is mutual agreement between the relevant parties concerning the nature of the act that is being appraised: Brandt, "Ethical Relativism," *The Encyclopedia of Philosophy*, p. 75.

45. For important discussions see Cheikh Anta Diop, *The Cultural Unity of Black Africa* (Chicago: Third World Press, 1978); and Jacques Maquet, *Africanity: The Cultural Unity of Black Africa*, translated by Joan R. Mayfield (New York: Oxford University Press, 1972).

46. See Jürgen Habermas, *The Theory of Communicative Action, Vol. I: Reason and the Rationalization of Society*, Thomas McCarthy, translator (Boston: Beacon Press, 1984).

Editor's Note: This selection is excerpted from the Chapter "Africology: Normative Theory" in Lucius Outlaw, Jr.'s— *On Race and Philosophy* (New York: Routledge, 1996): 97–134, (notes): 218–222.

VI

Section VI

Political Perspectives

Key Concepts and Major Terms

- Political Endeavor
- African Independence
- Socio-Political Struggles
- Anticolonial
- Civil Rights
- Black Power
- Politics of Academia
- Intellectual Validity
- General Systems Theory
- Third World
- African Socialism

- Ethnocentric
- Canons
- Academic Departments
- Black Radicalism
- Black Community
- Liberation
- Intellectual Offensive
- Cultural Heritage
- Marxist-Leninism
- Communist

- Political History
- Oppressors
- Global Perspectives
- Political Socialization
- Intellectual Colonialism
- Political Indoctrination
- Academic Governance
- Historically Black Institutions
- Pan-Africanism

Introduction

As a natural extension of the protracted socio-political struggles involved in African independence and anticolonial, Civil Rights/Black Power, and other student movements of late 1960s, the initiation and institutionalization of African American Studies can and should be seen as an expressly political endeavor. Moreover, the dilemmas African American Studies was confronted with almost immediately upon its arrival on predominantly white and historically black campuses were directly related to both the politics of academia and debates surrounding the direction in which African Americans should continue to pursue social, political, and economic parity with America at large.

On predominantly white campuses, faculty members, academic departments, administrators, and students questioned the intellectual validity and viability of the emerging field. "Traditional" disciplines, in particular, viewed African American Studies as a threat to the racist, ethnocentric, and sexist "canons" which they had

461

maintained and defended as the bedrock of human knowledge. Notions held that African Americans had not contributed anything in the service of the advancement of humanity, were physically and culturally inferior, had not yet produced men and women of letters, were mentally incapable of reason or logical thought were articulated by white men and women in fields such as history, anthropology, literature, and psychology. At the same time, there were also some black intellectuals skeptical of the practical applications and utility of African American Studies. In addition to holding the same disciplinary biases as many of their white counterparts, they viewed the petitions made and some of the goals sought by proponents of African American Studies regarding curricula, teacher accountability, and student life as having no place in higher education. Some viewed the minimal acquiescence university officials made to student demands as a sign of cowardice in the face of an increasingly visible and forceful black radicalism, present both on and off campus.

As the political ideology of the African American freedom movement shifted from a struggle for civil rights (primarily in the form of integrated coalitions) to one grounded in the concept(s) of Black Power and efforts toward internal autonomy within organizations and the community, it was natural for black students—who made up the core and leadership of most organizations—to bring their struggles with them once they arrived on predominantly white and historically black campuses. These young men and women, who made up the students, faculty members, and administration of the first Black Studies departments and programs felt a special obligation to ensure that the emerging discipline would take an active role in improving black communities.

The articles in this section share a concern with the nature of the political perspectives distinguishing African American Studies when the ideological relations between social, educational, historical, and political variables are at issue. In "Black Studies: A Political Perspective," Michael Thelwell argues that "The political struggle for liberation and cultural integrity must be accompanied by an intellectual offensive—and this is one of the tasks of black studies. The most obvious and pressing imperative is the reexamination and rehabilitation of our cultural heritage and political history—African and American—from the intellectual colonialism that has been imposed upon it."

J. Owens Smith's "The Political Nature of Black Studies Departments and Programs," suggests that "The greatest contribution that Black Studies Department makes to the political socialization process is its control over the curriculum. The curriculum content is the major instrument of political socialization in which many of America's basic values and beliefs are embedded... Black Studies Departments and Programs are agents within the political socialization process.

In "Toward a New Role and Function of Black Studies in White and Historically Black Institutions," Delores P. Aldridge points out that as the twentieth century comes to a fast close, "Black Studies is now at the stage of readiness to assume a leadership role on white and black campuses, in the community, and throughout the black world as a critical resource for defining the black past, present, and future. What has been unsettling is that the predominantly and historically black schools have not taken strong positions in systematically incorporating Black Studies."

Robert L. Allen, in "Politics of the Attack on Black Studies" concludes that "...The attack on Black Studies coincides with the consolidation of reaction under the Nixon regime.... In 1972 the counterattack against Black Studies started in earnest. Cutbacks in departmental budgets and students aid, especially at public institutions, forced the dismantling of many programs and student enrollments."

In "Black Studies and Global Perspectives: An Essay," St. Clair Drake contends that "The role of Black Studies programs is not to impose ideologies but to expand consciousness and to present alternatives for action. It is to help students discover for themselves where the fine line runs between being patriotic and being co-opted.... Our global perspective must involve, in the first instance, the world and all of its people, not just Africa and the black diaspora peoples."

William H. McClendon, in "Black Studies: Education for Liberation," notes: "The development of Black Studies from the very outset was accompanied by blacks being compelled to evaluate the largely racist nature of established education in America at all levels from kindergarten to doctorates...blacks in many sectors of life came to the conclusion that educators occupied only one of two positions: they were either oppressors or liberators...many blacks began to consider black education as having a special assignment to challenge and eventually replace white education because it was deficient and corrupt."

All of the essays included in Section VI address not only the inherent socio-political implications of African American Studies in the academy, but the empowerment of the larger African American community and diaspora as well. As a direct challenge to the curricula, faculty, and administration of both historically black and predominantly white institutions, African American Studies has had to face a number of attacks on many different ideological and intellectual fronts. As a direct result of its institutionalization during the past thirty years, these essays provide an introduction to the question of the socio-cultural and political role of African American Studies, which has recently resurfaced.

39.

Black Studies: A Political Perspective

Michael Thelwell

*The two things that we black folk need most
is a lot of patience and a sense of irony.*

> Junebug Jabbo Jones, Pool Hall Address,
> "Don't Let White Folks Run You Crazy,"
> Jackson, Mississippi, October 2, 1964.

Any attempt to discuss the question of what has come to be called "Black Studies," or "ethnic studies" as they say in California, that incubator of meaningless pop jargon, outside of a political perspective is futile. The demands on the part of black students and their activist mentors is a response to political realities in the black community. The considerations out of which these pressures come are clear, so clear in fact, that there should be no need for an essay of this kind were it not for the apparently limitless capacity for the debasement of language and the obscuring of issues demonstrated by the mass media of the society. It is true that in this enterprise, the media has enjoyed the cooperation, witting or otherwise, of any number of hastily discovered "spokesmen" for black studies whose "revolutionary" fervor and extravagant rhetoric is equalled only by their mysticism and anti-intellectualism.

As if this outpouring of definition from the left which serves, more often than not, to obscure more than it illuminates were not enough, there is an attendant motion on the right flank of the black community which is equally uninformed, short-sighted and dogmatic. This faction, which includes such established Negro intellectuals as Andrew Brimmer of the Federal Reserve Board, Sir Arthur Lewis, the West Indian economist presently at Princeton, Kenneth Clarke who recently resigned from the Board of Trustees of Antioch College after they had yielded to student demands for a black residence hall, Prof. Martin Kilson of Harvard, Bayard Rustin, Roy Wilkins of the NAACP (naturally), and a number of old guard Negro administrators from Southern Negro Colleges, seem to have become the cutting edge of the establishment backlash against the movement for Black Studies. The burden of their objections, which reflects very clearly a class position if not their political sentiments — they seem to have no discernible common political perspective save for an acceptance of the "one society myth" — is best reflected in Sir Arthur Lewis' comment that "black studies will not prepare a black student to be president of General Motors." Well, neither will it prepare him to be Pope, but that hardly seems to be the issue since it is not clear that anything short of civil revolution on the one hand and divine intervention on the other will accomplish either.

Equally interesting, not to say informative, in what it reveals of the attitudes of the men currently entrusted (by white society) with the education of young blacks, is the story rather gleefully reported in a recent issue of the *New York Times*. This concerns a "joke" which circulated at a meeting of The United Negro College Fund.

While most of the administrators present admitted rather sheepishly that their schools were initiating "some kind of Black Studies" programs to anticipate and forestall student militance, their attitude toward the undertaking was made graphically clear by the story reported by the *Times* as exciting great mirth among them. The essence of this story has to do with a student applying for a job and being told by a computer that his training in black studies had prepared him only to pick cotton. To quote Ralph Ellison's nameless protagonist, "Bledsoe, you ain't nothing but a greasy chittlin' eater."

That this story and the *Times'* prominent and snide presentation of it was the greatest possible indictment of these men, the process of so-called education that produced them, and the alleged institutions of learning that they preside over at the command of racist southern legislatures was perhaps lost on them. But the Bledsoes[1] of this world are distinguished less for their sense of irony than by their ill-disguised contempt for the black community and its heritage and traditions.

The most substantive objections coming from the Negro right—despite a certain intemperance of expression as when he sneers at "soul courses," a phenomenon of his own invention—comes from Rustin. His concern is that white colleges will attempt to cop out of what he sees as their responsibility to the black community by the expedient of hastily manufactured and meaningless programs designated "black studies," taught by semi-literate dashiki-clad demagogues with nothing to offer but a "militant black rap." Rustin fears that white schools will accept this as an easier and less expensive alternative than providing the massive and costly programs of remedial education which are required. To be sure, there is little in the history of these institutions that would suggest that they are not capable of such a ploy. I know of very few isolated campuses where this is happening to some degree and I suspect that there are at least some others which will not be inhibited by questions of principle, morality or their own internal standards from attempting to follow suit. But the places where this can happen are not educational institutions in any but the most superficial sense and are at present educating no one, black or white. Besides which, it is inconceivable that such programs can survive, and even to exist they require the complicity of self-seeking and socially irresponsible black charlatans and careerists. Though few in number, such a type exists and their destructive potential is great. But it is the responsibility of the students and the adult black community to resist any such development in any institution where it becomes evident. It would be pointless to pretend that this danger does not exist in some small degree, but my impression of the basic good sense of this student generation, and their serious commitment and sense of responsibility to themselves and their community reassures me that this tendency will be a short-lived one.

Whatever unity is to be found in the positions of the black establishment—figures mentioned seem to reside in a thoroughly uncritical acceptance of the methods, goals and the educational practices of white America save for its traditional exclusion of black people. They are joined in this assessment by the overwhelming majority of white academics. There are other critical positions to the left of them in the black community, ranging from a nationalism impractical at this time: "The place for black students is in black schools" (Consequently the establishment of Black Studies programs on white campuses is a delusion luring black students onto white campuses "to be co-opted and corrupted by the 'devil.'") to militant activism: "All of whitey's education is bullshit; all black people need to know is streetology. Black students should come on home to the streets and take *real* black studies in the areas of judo, karate, demolitions and assorted martial arts."

The second position speaks for itself, the first is more emotionally appealing until one checks some figures — of the 400,000 black college students in the country last year, fully one half were from the North and were in white schools, many of them as a consequence of "conscience" programs of recruitment and financial aid on the part of these white schools. Few of the black southern colleges can accommodate more students than are currently enrolled even if we ignored their chronic financial problems and the educational philosophy (political control, really) within which they are forced to operate.

At this point in history black students in increasing numbers will either have to attend white schools or no school at all. This being the case, certain problems arise: how can the almost inevitable psychological and spiritual demoralization of the small minority of blacks in an overwhelmingly white institution — which was conceived, created, structured and operated so as to service an oppressive social order — be avoided? Are the educational needs, both psychological and practical of the black student identical with the white? What elements of the society control these institutions and to what ends? What finally, when one cuts through the liberal rhetoric and the humanistic bombast, is the essential social and political function of these institutions? Is this function at all coincident with the necessities and aspirations of the black population as articulated by the growing nationalist consciousness of all elements of the community? Can anyone reasonably expect, in a situation where even the white student, the beneficiary and inheritor of the system, has begun to question its economic and political functions at home and abroad — to reject the yawning gap between its pious, self-justifying rhetoric and its viciously exploitative and murderous reality, and to question the role of the universities in this pattern — that black students who, for the most part have never been allowed the luxury of any delusions about the meaning of their relationship to this society and who are now quickening to a vision however tentative and problematic, of collective black possibility, will find it possible or desirable to make a smooth and easy adjustment to institutions with the historical record and contemporary posture of the Universities? The answer must be, in Stokely Carmichael's cryptic phrase "Hell, No."

And even if they wanted to, the attempt at emotional integration into these institutions would necessitate a process of psychological and cultural suicide. (Last spring during the "troubles" at the City College of New York an incident occurred which is significant. Black and Puerto Rican students came under attack for "vandalism" when they destroyed what was described as "a work of Art." One had to read the press reports very carefully to discover that what was destroyed was a tapestry depicting George Washington receiving the worshipful homage of a group of black slaves. A small incident, but symptomatic of a seemingly endless accumulation of gratuitous, racist affrontery.)

As the current academic year opens there is some evidence that a reaction against the concept of Black Studies is beginning to take form from another and possibly more troublesome source — the faculty and administration of the universities. The two groups need to be considered separately for their interests, although congruent, are not identical. In every case with which I am familiar, the administration has adopted a posture that can best be described as interested neutrality. That is, they take no substantive position on the *issues*, being more interested in peace-keeping operations with the parties to the action, namely the black students and their supporters and conservative elements on the faculty which see the agitation for black studies as threatening their class prerogatives and traditional jurisdictions. In every case the rhetoric coming from these pockets of resistance has been couched in terms of lofty liberal principles, and considerations of the highest academic and professional integrity, but the rhetoric barely conceals a most vulgar political and professional self-interest and occasionally an overt old-fashioned white paternalism. One canard, coming most often from the least informed members of the faculty, maintains that there is simply not sufficient material in the field to support and justify Black Studies as a major field of academic endeavor. This statement reveals more than the ignorance of its authors because were it in fact true, it would constitute the strongest possible confirmation of the covert racism and cultural chauvinism which informs the intellectual and scholarly establishment. And the patent absurdity of the "insufficient material" assertion does not really absolve the scholarly establishment because the existence of this basic research is due to the lonely and heroic efforts of past generations of black scholars and a few whites—Herbert Aptheker, Melvin J. Herskovits, Sydney Kaplan come to mind—in the face of the active opposition and indifference of the "profession." And in the case of the black scholars who had to endure the condescension, skepticism and disparagement of their efforts by white colleagues and publishers, our indebtedness is beyond expression or recompense. It is some small consolation that some of these morally courageous and dedicated pioneers, men like C.L.R. James, Sterling Brown, John H. Clarke, George Padmore, Arna Bontemps, and many more whose works are only now being "discovered" and published are present to witness the turning of the tide and the recognition and vindication of their efforts. And we have inherited from such men as W.E.B. Dubois, J.A. Rogers, E. Franklin Frazier, Alain Locke, Edward Wilmot Blyden, James Weldon Johnson, J. Carter Woodson, Kelley Miller, Leo William Hansberry both a scholarly example and the legacy of a distinguished tradition upon which to build.

Let us, for the moment, ignore this tradition and pretend, as those who make the charge of insufficient material must be doing, that these men never existed and their work had never been done. Would this in any way affect the necessity of this generation of black intellectuals to engage and demolish the racist mythology and distorted perception and interpretation of the black experience, culture and reality which constitutes the intellectual underpinnings of white racism in the society? The political struggle for liberation and cultural integrity must be accompanied by an intellectual offensive—and this is one of the tasks of black studies. The most obvious and pressing imperative is the reexamination and rehabilitation of our cultural heritage and political history— African and American—from the intellectual colonialism that has been imposed upon it. This is merely the first responsibility. The next level of responsibility accruing to black studies is related integrally to "issues" raised by its white academic opponents and has literally to do with the decolonization of education in this country. We need to examine these objections in the context of necessities and goals of the black community. There is the procedural objection to separate autonomous departments of black studies. It is important to note that these objections come most often from white academics in those disciplines most clearly affected by what we are about, which is to say history, the humanities and the social sciences. Frequently they come from the upper echelons of these departments and include the faculty mandarins, the men least involved in teaching, and whose reputations and prestige derive from their roles as advisors and resource personnel to the political, military and industrial managers of the society.

Their style is as constant as is their approach. First they trot out their liberal credentials as friends of "The Negro." Then they proceed to the startling admission that there have been errors of omission on the part of the white scholarly and educational community. Next they demonstrate how little perception they have of the mood or aspirations of the black community by presenting an analysis and a solution based on the fallacy of an integrated society and of identical interests. Certainly, they say, black literature and history should be a part of the curriculum. (Two years ago this faction was denying that the concept of black literature or history had any validity. On the question of a distinctive black culture, they still are not sure.) In fact, they say, there should be courses dealing with the black experience in every relevant discipline. But, to set up an autonomous entity—be it department, program or institute—of black studies is antithetical to everything we believe. It creates a false dichotomy, smacks of separatism, not to say black racism, creates a serious problem of standards and violates the concept of academic *objectivity*. Also, what assurances will we have that what will take place within that autonomous entity will be *education* and not indoctrination? (This is said without ironic intent.) And besides that—these black instructors that you plan to bring in—what acceptable (to us) academic credentials do they have? We would not want to short-change these black students! (That this concern for the academic wellbeing of black students is a recent development and consequently suspect can be seen by the fact that few if any of these men ever expressed any concern at their absence from that institution in the past.) How will you guarantee the ideological purity of this autonomous department? All of these questions are predicated on the assumption of a culturally homogenous society, the myth of scholarly objectivity, a rejection of history, the denial of conflicting class interests within the society, and differing perceptions of necessities by the black and white community. The consequences of these objections, if followed, would simply be the perpetuation of their control over the education of black people and the imposition of their definitions of social and political reality upon the black community. This is precisely the issue, white cultural and ideological terrorism, and the right of black people to define for themselves the meaning of their past and the possibility of their future.

In order to deal with this position it is necessary to remind ourselves of some basic history. The black experience in this country is not merely one of political and cultural oppression, economic exploitation, and the expropriation of our history. It also includes the psychological and intellectual manipulation and control of blacks by the dominant majority. The liberation of blacks requires, therefore, the redress of all of these depredations. The relationship of the white community to the black has been and continues to be that of oppressor and oppressed, colonizer and colonized. To pretend anything else is merely to prolong the social agony that the society is currently experiencing.

Scholarly objectivity is a delusion that liberals (of both races) may subscribe to. Black people and perceptive whites know better. The fact is that the intellectual establishment distinguishes itself by its slavish acceptance of the role assigned to it by the power-brokers of the society. It has always been the willing servant of wealth and power, and the research done in the physical sciences, the humanities and social sciences has been, with very few honorable exceptions, in service to established power, which has, in this country, always been antithetical to the interests of black people. The goals of the research undertaken, the questions asked, the controlling assumptions governing it, and consequently, the results obtained have always fitted comfortably into a social consensus which has been, by definition, racist.

Look at two examples affecting black people in the history of the institutions of higher learning. In 1832 a young professor named Dew, at William and Mary College, published a widely circulated and praised pamphlet that was to propel him to the presidency of that institution. The thesis of this piece of objective scholarship was "...It is in the order of nature and of God that the being of superior faculties and knowledge and therefore of superior power, should control and dispose of those who are inferior. It is as much in the order of nature that men should enslave each other, as that other animals should prey upon each other."

This example of objective scholarship and the attendant upward mobility which greeted it was not lost on a Professor named Harper at the University of South Carolina. His work published in 1838 proclaimed that "Man is born to subjection. The proclivity of natural man is to domineer or to be subservient. If there are sordid servile and laborious offices to be performed, is it not better that there should be sordid, servile and laborious beings to perform them?" Professor Harper ended his career in the office of Chancellor of his institution. Needless to say, the style as well as the issues have changed with history (witness Prof. Jensen), but has the basic dynamic of "academic objectivity?"

The "let the established departments handle it" proposal is as specious as it is fraudulent. These departments have, over the years displayed no interest in incorporating the black experience, a black perspective, or even Negro faculty-members into their operations. What should now dispose us to trust them? And even if we should, how will they, after centuries of indifference, suddenly develop the competence and sensitivity which would enable them to do an acceptable job? Will they really undertake to adjust the entire intellectual ambiance, the total perspectives from which they have operated? This is not likely, and for our purposes nothing less will do.

Such an adjustment on the part of these departments, though quite improbable, is at least conceivable. But this approach—leaving the responsibility to individual departments to proceed at their own pace and in their own unique styles will merely institutionalize and perpetuate the fragmented, incoherent approach to the subject which has been the only approach in the past. Besides which, this would deprive the black community of any effective organ within the structure of the university that would be principally directed to the educational needs in that community. It is important that we emphasize the two equally important considerations that are basic to the concept of black studies. The first requires an autonomous interdisciplinary entity, capable of coordinating its curriculum in traditional disciplines, to ensure an historical, substantive progression and organic coherence in its offerings. The second function, which is no less crucial, requires this entity be sufficiently flexible to innovate programs that involve students in field study and social action projects in black communities.

Another issue which is frequently raised is that of the "racial" and academic qualifications of the faculty for these programs. Some groups insist that the presence of white faculty contradicts everything that black studies represents, i.e., the freeing of the black community from the tyranny of white experts and their endless definition of black reality. *The fact is, however, that there are few academics, white or black, who are qualified by their training in "traditional" white-culture-bound graduate schools to undertake the aggressively radical transformation of their fields that is the purpose of these programs. In fact, almost the reverse is true: the cultural condescension and chauvinism that has dominated graduate departments, coupled with an absence of racial consciousness and cultural nationalism on the part of most traditionally-trained black academics, makes them little more qualified than their white peers.* This means that an effective black studies faculty must be recruited from the handful of academics who have a particular radical stance towards the reevaluation of the treatment of the black experience in their disciplines, and from among it ranks of active black intellectuals with experience in the political and cultural battlefronts of this country and the Third World.

There have been attempts by affluent white schools to attempt to lure the most able and committed black scholars from southern Negro schools. The faculty in black studies programs on white campuses have the responsibility not to allow themselves to be used by white institutions to recruit blacks away from predominantly Negro colleges, and the prohibition of recruitment from this source should be a stated of every such program. The same conditions hold true for schools in the Third World. The black academic community of country must not participate in expanding the brain drain from countries. Rather, what should take place is that exchange programs for students and professors should be established between Black studies programs in this country and Third World universities. Thus will the academic community lead the way in the reaching out to the black nations of the Third World and reuniting the black community in American exile with the African and West Indian nations.

These alternatives are admittedly not a permanent solution to the problem of faculty. This lies in the establishment of institutions for the training of the kind of aggressive, culturally nationalist intellectual that is needed. Given the urgency of this need, established black studies programs should invest some resources in the creation and support of these institutes, in return for the privilege of sending their best students to these centers. An excellent start in this direction has been made by Dr. Vincent Harding of Atlanta and his associates at the Institute of the Black World.[2] This is a crucial and timely development and promises to be of great importance in the creation of a national network of black educational institutions.

It is not possible to over-emphasize the historical importance of this movement to control and define the quality and terms of black education in the nation at this time. It has been clear for some time that white educational institutions are in grievous default so far as black people are concerned. What we project is nothing less than a coordinated effort to secure our just portion of the educational resources of the country and make it over in our own image. The extent to which we are able to do this will determine the form, the reality and the role of the black community for generations to come. If the black community is able to establish here — in the intellectual center of western technology — a series of institutions devoted to the training of a generation of dedicated, proud, and culturally liberated black intellectuals and technicians whose commitment and energies are dedicated to the service — in whatever way is necessary — of the international black community, then perhaps the travail of centuries, the dues paid in America by generations of our ancestors will not have been in vain. What is at issue is the cultural survival of a nation of people, a nation without borders, without land, and without government, but nevertheless a nation with a population greater than many European countries.

The present generation of black college students is perhaps the most important generation of black people ever to live in the United States. They stand poised between two cultures, their loyalties are being besieged, they must choose between a culture and a heritage they have been taught to despise and a social establishment that, having rejected and oppressed their parents, is now making a determined bid to dissolve history and obscure reality. The vision that this generation leaves college with, the commitments they espouse, the decisions that they take, will determine not only the future of the black community in America, but will affect the nature of the struggle in the motherland and other areas of the Third World. The obstacles are formidable, the opposition great, the goal, to some, perhaps quixotic, but history is full of surprises (particularly to bourgeois historians) and while the consequences of failure are dismal, it will be an unspeakable dishonor to this generation of black intellectuals if the effort is not made. We have, quite literally, nothing to lose.

Endnotes

1. From Dr. Professor Bledsoe, the autocratic yet servile college president in *Invisible Man*, who cooperates with the white managers of the society in destroying the spirit and emasculating the consciousness of his students. As used here it is a generic term for all of his too numerous tribe.

2. See Statement of Purpose and Program in Section VII.

40.

The Political Nature of Black Studies Departments and Programs

J. Owens Smith

Approximately fifteen years after their initiation, the nature of Black Studies Departments and Programs has not fully been understood by administrators at desegregated institutions, i.e., predominantly white, institutions which are sponsored by the state. Currently, many administrators are of the opinion that these units and programs were established to placate those Black Students who were demanding a "more relevant education." Now that peace and tranquillity has been restored on these campuses, many administrators are advocating the dismantling of these units or, to state it more subtly, streamlining them. The climate in which these programs came into existence lends credence to this belief.

Unlike other disciplines, Black Studies did not have the full support of deans and academic senates. It came into existence in response to the pressure placed upon administrators by Black students in their demands for a "more relevant education." In order to maintain social stability on their campuses, administrators capitulated to Black students' demands by establishing Black Studies Departments and Programs (hereafter, Black Studies) on campuses throughout the nation. Other nonwhite ethnic groups piggy-backed on Black students' demands. In the process, the purpose, scope, and the nature of Black Studies have never been adequately defined.

This paper advances the thesis that one of the primary reasons why administrators of desegregated institutions have failed to view Black Studies as a serious academic discipline has been because they have inadvertently overlooked its political nature within the educational process. Within this process, its nature is multifarious: (1) it satisfies the unique needs of Black students, (2) It is an agent of political socialization, (3) it awakens Black students to their cultural and historical experiences, i.e., making them better citizens, (4) it awakens white students to those misconceptions and stereotypical categorizations which tend to perpetuate future patterns of discrimination against Black, and (5) it creates an environment that is conducive to learning for Black students.

The Unique Needs of Black Students

When Black students started demanding a "more relevant education," they were making two broad statements to administrators.[1] Essentially, they were telling the administration that (1) it was forcing them to study in an environment that was not conducive to their learning, and (2) a meaningful discourse of their cultural and historical experiences had been excluded from the curriculum.

472

These political statements left administrators baffled because they could not fully comprehend their ramifications. Even today, administrators view Black Studies not as a serious academic discipline in awakening or fulfilling the cultural values of Black students nor as an agent of political socialization but as remedial programs or welfare handouts. This can partially be accounted for by the fact that these institutions were forced to educate a large number of first-generation nonwhite college students for the first time in their history. Consequently, they were not equipped to meet the special needs and requirements of Black students.

Until the late 1960s, the largest percentage of nonwhite students attending college were Blacks. They were educated at the traditional Black colleges in the South. These colleges had designed an educational environment that was conducive to learning for Black students. Essentially, these colleges and universities had (1) included in their curricula a meaningful discourse of the cultural and historical experiences of Blacks, and (2) employed an adequate number of mentors and positive role models in the classrooms with which Black students could identify. These factors have been overlooked by administrators of desegregated institutions.

Education: An Agent of Political Socialization

In considering Black Studies, educators too often overlook the fact that educational institutions are agents of political socialization. These agents have two major political functions: instruct students in civic education and orient them toward a specific political indoctrination.[2] As Richard E. Dawson and Kenneth Prewitt have perceptively noted, this process is carried out within the classroom by means of "formal curriculum of instruction, various ritual activities, and activities of the teacher.[3]

The Politicized Curriculum: Students of political socialization have found that the entire school curriculum in all nations is very political. It has a nationalistic orientation and serves as an agency for "transforming knowledge and values conducive to good citizenship."[4] For example, civic education places emphasis upon a citizen's participating in the political life of his community and nation.[5] It acquaints him with a political unit where the question of loyalty and patriotism is taken for granted.

The curriculum is the initiator and reinforcer of cultural values. It is at the heart of the educational system. As students have found:

Its content embraces diversed culture traits believed to be requisite for participation in the society...Many of the basic values of society are to be reinforced (if not originally transmitted to pupils) by means of the choice of materials placed before them (students) in society.[6]

Political Indoctrination: Political indoctrination, on the other hand, takes on a different character. It addresses the question of political ideology where the emphasis is placed upon rationalizing and justifying America's nationalistic values. For the average American citizen, such instruction poses few, if any, problems. Its underlying assumption is that good citizenship is a goal that every citizen should strive to achieve. For Black Americans, and other nonwhite students such indoctrination raises the following serious questions concerning citizenship: (1) Is the curriculum content designed to socialize Blacks to become good citizens? (2) Is the curriculum structured to socialize Black children in such a way to control their "antisocial" tendencies? (3) Does the curriculum include a meaningful discourse of Blacks' cultural and historical experiences?

Students of political socialization have found that courses in America's national history seem to be very selective: "those episodes that redound most of America's national glory receive emphasis; and the picture of the past is deficient in cracks and crevices."[7] The institution of slavery, for example, and the impact that it had in shaping and forming American attitudes toward Blacks is seldom mentioned in the course of instruction—except for Black Studies. The effect which the institution of slavery had upon America's nationalistic view is that it has built into the character of the nation a political socialization process which indoctrinates white students to accept the misconceptions and stereotypical categorization of Blacks as the empirical truth. Such indoctrination perpetuates patterns of discrimination that in turn significantly curtails Blacks' freedom and desire to achieve their goal of becoming good citizens. Black Studies, on the other hand, has emerged to counteract this process; that is, it further democratizes the education institutions. This is, perhaps, why the nature of Black Studies has not been fully understood.

The Awakening of Cultural and Historical Experiences: The freedom to become a good citizen is a constitutionally protected right. To realize such a right, a citizen must acquire knowledge about his or her cultural and historical experience. For whites, this knowledge is presented to them in the core curriculum. There is little, if any, contradiction between this curriculum and the American political values of freedom, justice, and equality for all. But for Black America, this same curriculum places them at a disadvantage. History has demonstrated that not only have these values been traditionally denied to Blacks as a matter of practice but also a meaningful discussion of their cultural and historical experiences has been omitted. Therefore, the content of the curriculum could be designed to educate white students with the maximum degree of efficiency and at the same time it could contain cultural relevance for Blacks.

The inclusion of Blacks' cultural and historical experience into the core curriculum would serve three functions within the political socialization process. First, it will serve as a therapeutic process for Black students which operate to strengthen their self concept.[8] With such strength, Black students are able to overcome many of their fears and uncertainties to the extent that they feel sufficiently secure to risk failure in order to succeed at desegregated institutions.

Secondly, Black Studies enables Black students to become good citizens. The relationship between good citizenship and acquiring knowledge of one's culture and history was echoed by John F. Kennedy in a foreword to the book, *The American Heritage New Illustration of the History of the United States.*[9] Here he gives one of the most succinct, and yet, political justification as to why an American citizen should acquire such knowledge:

> There is little that is more important for an American citizen to know than the history and tradition of his country. Without such knowledge, he stands uncertain and defenseless before the world, knows neither where he has come from nor where he is going with such knowledge, he is no longer alone but draws a strength far greater than his own from cumulative experience of the past and a cumulative vision of the future.
>
> History, after all, is the memory of a nation. Just as memory enables the individual to learn, to choose goals and stick to them, to avoid making the same mistake twice—in short, to grow—so history is the means by which a nation establishes its sense of identity and purpose. The future arises out of

the past, and a country's history is a statement of the values and hopes which, having forged what has gone before, will now forecast what is to come.[10]

This book was published in 1963 long before the question of Black Studies. If this rationale for studying history is true for the average American citizen who has not been a victim of past discrimination, then it is even more important to Blacks whose present day political and social status is cast into the shadow of the past. A past that has been characterized by the institution of slavery, an institution which savagely detribalized their ancestries, stripped them of their household gods, broke up their family structure, denied them the right to transform their cultural heritage; and in the process, stamped a natural feeling of inferiority into their hearts and minds.[11]

The exclusion of Black Studies from the political socialization process serves to perpetuate "ignorance of minority problems in the community...[which]...creates mistrust, alienation, and all too often hostility toward the entire process of government."[12] It also places Black students at a disadvantage because education is, as the United States Supreme Court has noted in *Brown v. Board of Education*:

> ...a principal instrument to cultural values, in preparing him (a child) for later professional training, and in helping him adjust normally to his environment. In these days, it is doubtful that any child may reasonably be expected to succeed in life of he is deprived of the opportunity of an education.[13]

Especially for the Black male child, the awakening of cultural and historical experiences is imperative for survival. Without such knowledge, he is defenseless before the world. He will be unaware that his present day status in society is cast into a shadow of the past. Any show of aggression on his part, or assertion of manhood, is subjected to be met by a system of oppression which is designed to put him back into his assigned inferior status in society. Black Studies socializes Black students to become good citizens. Beyond civic education, Black Studies exposes Black students to the contradictions in the American political indoctrination process. Here, Black students learn the politics of, what W.E.B. DuBois calls, "double-consciousness," "an American, a Negro; two souls, two thoughts, two unreconciled strings; two warring ideals In one dark body."[14] It is within this framework that Black students have to learn that they are not included in the concept of freedom, justice, and equality before the law, and that they must adjust to a double consciousness, i.e., the American contradiction. Therefore, it is the task of Black Studies to politicize Black students to make this adjustment, and at the same time, accept their responsibility to participate in their race struggle for survival; and pick up the baton of freedom from their elders and pass it on to the next generation in an uninterrupted and orderly manner. This is necessary for Blacks to become good citizens.

The Elimination of Misconceptions and Stereotypical Categorizations

Another function of Black Studies in higher education is that it operates to eliminate those misconceptions and stereotypical categorizations of Blacks which perpetuate future patterns of racial discrimination against them. White students enter college from a system of education that has ignored or played down the cultural and historical contributions that Blacks have made to society. Consequently, white students are indoctrinated to accept racial stereotypical images of Blacks which in turn affect their behavior toward Blacks in later life.

Racism in Education: The existence of discrimination in the political socialization process is no great secret. As the United States Committee on Labor and Public Welfare (hereafter Senate committee) noted in 1972, some of our most famous civil rights cases have involved discrimination in education. To continue to exclude Black Studies from the political socialization process would no doubt serve a destructive purpose to white students. For it will simply perpetuate discrimination in education. As the Senate Committee acknowledged:

> The presence of discrimination in educational institutions is particularly critical. It is difficult to imagine a more sensitive area than educational institutions, where the youths of the Nation are exposed to a multitude of ideas and impressions that will strongly influence their future development. To permit discrimination here will promote existing misconceptions and stereotypical categorizations which in turn would lead to future patterns of discrimination.[15]

The Senate Committee also noted that discrimination in education spills over into the economic and social institutions in society. Many of these institutions play a dominant role in the daily lives of the average citizen. This includes government agencies, social services, law enforcement, fire department, and even the process of government itself. Citizens in every community are in frequent contact with these large agencies. In communities where there is forced racial isolation, it is necessary to expose white students to the cultural and historical experience of nonwhite groups in order to eliminate patterns of discrimination against them.

Racism in the Textbooks: The existence of racism in education has been adequately documented by Louis Knowles and Kenneth Prewitt in their book, entitled *Institutional Racism in America* (1969). They describe how patterns of discrimination in society are perpetuated by the educational institutions. They wrote that there is an organized attempt by the establishment to miseducate white students:

> The most affluent, best-equipped schools present white children with a distorted view of black people and other races. Textbooks do not even touch on the depth and pervasiveness of racism within the white community. It is almost as though we were indoctrinating our children rather than helping them to learn for themselves what the world of people is all about. "...we are not honest about ourselves, our own fears, limitations, weakness, prejudice, motives. We present ourselves to our children as if we were gods, allknowing, all powerful, always rational, always just, always right. Such an education, rather than preparing white children to recognize, understand, and deal with the racial contradiction in our society, glosses over it as though it did not exist or was not of major importance. Children are brought up to accept America's racism and yet to "believe in" freedom, justice, and equality for all. Social studies textbooks, because they provide a common element in teaching in many classrooms of many schools, are prime contributors to the institutional racism which pervades white education.[16]

Knowles and Prewitt also found that the treatment of nonwhites in traditional textbooks had been atrocious. A survey of history textbooks written between 1949 and 1961 showed the treatment of Asian and Spanish-speaking ethnic groups had improved only slightly. But the treatment of Blacks had not changed at all.

They found that the authors of these textbooks took great pains and effort not to mention anything that might cause disagreement among whites. As late as 1964, a survey indicated that the texts played down or ignored the long history of violence directed against Blacks. These books denied the deprivation and suffering of nonwhites.

More importantly, Knowles and Prewitt found that textbooks consistently ignored or stereotyped the Black man's present position in American society as well as his historical role. One study found that three-fourths of the books mentioned Blacks somewhere, but only half referred to them in present day society. Six textbooks gave the name of some contemporary Blacks. Of these, one mentioned only a baseball player, and one limited its coverage to two prizefighters.

Either explicitly or implicitly, the survey found that most of the textbooks implied approval for the repression of Blacks or patronized them as being unqualified for life in a free society. This pattern of discrimination persisted until the administrators of desegregated institutions started capitulating to the demands of Black students for a "more relevant education," i.e., establishment of Black Studies Departments and Programs.

Black Studies Departments and Programs

Black Studies Departments and Programs are agents within the political socialization process. One of their major functions is to fill the academic voids in this process by creating an environment that is conducive to learning for Black students. Embedded in this environment are the following political socialization agents: (1) mentors and role models with which Black students can identify, (2) a formal relationship with the academic governance body, and (3) a process of political indoctrination and reeducation. These agents fill the academic voids in the political socialization process for Black students.

Academic Voids in the Political Socialization Process: Too often, administrators of desegregated institutions feel that by just providing Black students with counselors, recruiters, and placement examinations that they have fulfilled their obligation of equal education opportunity. Such a thought pattern has created academic voids in the education process. These voids can explain in part the high attrition rate found among Black students on desegregated predominantly white campuses.

The American education system is designed to educate middle class America, which consists mostly of second- and third-generation college students. On the other hand, Black students attending desegregated colleges are predominantly first generation college students. For the most part, they come out of an educational environment where social promotion is a common practice. Unlike white students, over 80 percent of Black students are first-generation of college students and come predominantly from the lower class plateau of society. Their educational experience is categorized by a process of social upward mobility. A Bachelor of Arts Degree from any college will place them on the middle class plateau psychologically, if not, economically. For white students, a college education is an obligation that they have to fulfill in order to remain on the middle class plateau.[17]

It follows then that the needs and requirements of Black students on desegregated campuses are keenly different from those of whites. There is no contradiction between the political socialization process of white students and American political orientation, i.e., the value of democracy, free enterprise, innocent until proven guilty, etc. However, American society has traditionally denied Blacks these values. Therefore, the political socialization process has to broaden its perspective to include the needs and requirements of Black students, i.e., including mentors and positive role models in this process.

Mentors and Positive Role Models: Administrators of desegregated institutions have failed to see the significant role that role models play in the political socialization process of Black students. During the turbulent days of the 1960s administrators marshalled Black faculty and administrators on campus to quell the storm of disruptive behavior by Black students. Many of these faculty members were not recruited on the basis of their academic credentials but their skills in controlling Black students.[18] Once on campus, many of them inadvertently assumed the role of mentors and role models. The role was imposed upon them by circumstances rather than by calculated efforts on the part of administrators to create an environment conducive to learning for Black students.

Many Black professors have reported that Black students are frequently referred to them by their white colleagues when they are seeking a faculty member to supervise an independent study course or direct a research project. This occurs despite the fact that the student's research interest may be in their white colleague's field of specialization. Again, Black professors constantly find themselves in a position where they are asked to interpret the unique behavior of Black students to the administration and their colleagues." This is called mentoring.

The Role of Mentors: In order to understand the role of a mentor, one must first examine the role of a teacher within the political socialization process. Students of political socialization have identified the teacher as a disseminator of political orientation. He represents to the student an authoritative spokesman of society similar to that of political authority. The student learns that

> ...the authority role and incumbent of the role are separate factors. He learns he should obey any incumbent who happens to occupy the role "teacher." Further, he discovers that rewards and punishments from authorities are affected by identifiable constraints that operate on particular person in the role. The teacher, like the policeman, president, or mayor, is part of an institutional pattern, a constitutional order.[20]

Researchers have also found that teachers are expected to propagate political views, ideologies, and moral beliefs appropriately labeled "consensus values."[21] American consensus values are those that support middle class white America. Teachers are very effective in conveying these values primarily because they are products of the same political socialization process in which they serve as agents. These consensus values do not include nonwhites, who have been locked out of mainstream America. For example, the value of the Protestant work ethic which encourages students to procrastinate present gratification for future one does not work for Blacks.[22] History has shown that Blacks have traditionally subscribed to this value only to find that there are no future gratifications because the rules of the game are constantly being changed at half-time. Changing the rules of the game at such time is a common practice in the political socialization process. This is the primary reason why mentors and positive role models are needed for Black students at desegregated institutions.

Mentors who sponsor Black students as their proteges have several roles to assume in an academic setting. First, his or her role is to interpret the institutional settings to Black students, on the one hand, and their unique behavior to the university on the other, until the two can reconcile each other. This is what white faculty are asking Black faculty to do when they refer Black students to them.

The second role of a mentor is to build a link of trust between Black students and the university so that the former can overcome their fears and uncertainties. In his research, Sociologist Charles Willie of Harvard University discovered that too many Black students are invited to come on campuses of desegregated institutions as though they are on trial. The administration too often sends them a clear message: Make yourselves loveable in order that you might be loved. This message is not calculated to building a link of trust between Black students and the university. Again, Willie found that Black students are too often judged by who they are rather than their academic performance.[23] This can be explained by the fact that these administrators came out of a political socialization process which has indoctrinated them with misconceptions and stereotypical images of Blacks.[24] Without the presence of Black role models and mentors, the political socialization process will simply perpetuate future patterns of discrimination against Blacks in present day society.

Third, a mentor's role is to intercede on behalf of Black students to ensure that the rules and regulations are being equally and fairly applied. This role was more or less imposed upon Black faculty by the political climate of the 1960s. As Black Studies became entrenched in the education system, Black faculty began to embrace the mentoring methodology and made it a part of their program. This methodology developed a level of trust and belief among Black students to the extent that many were able to risk failure in order to succeed.

The Function of Black Studies Department vs. Programs: A university's commitment to equal education for Black students can be measured by its support for a Black Studies Department over a program. This is particularly true when the surrounding Black population constitutes four percent or more of the population. A Black Studies Department is an institutional pattern within the political socialization process. It serves as the foundation on which political socialization is programmed.

The greatest contribution that Black Studies Department makes to the political socialization process is its control over the curriculum. The curriculum content is the major instrument of political socialization in which many of American basic values and beliefs are embedded. Among these beliefs are the misconceptions and stereotypical categorizations of Blacks which perpetuate patterns of discrimination against them.[25] Black Studies Departments have the constitutional order to offset these values and beliefs by means of the choice of materials placed before students.

The existence of Black Studies Departments becomes very crucial when it comes to selecting instrumental materials concerning racism. Currently, there, is a revisionist movement which attempts to show (1) that slavery was not all that bad for Blacks,[26] and (2) Blacks' present day position can be attributed more to their biological inferiority than anything white America has done to them. The primary thrust of this revisionist movement is to resist any change in the political socialization process. To this end, there are numerous books written since the beginning of the civil rights movement to justify racial oppression.

Racial material within the content of curricula is designed to indoctrinate students with myths and legends from the past as well as the policies and programs of the present, which in turn allocate values and resources on the basis of rights and privileges by law. A good example of such materials can be found in the following textbooks: *The Declining Significance of Race*,[28] *The Politics of Economic and Race*,[29] *The Time on the Cross*,[30] and the *Unheavenly Cities*[31] are widely used in classrooms on many college campuses throughout the nation.

Researchers have considered curriculum to be a major instrument of political socialization. Therefore, it is imperative that some kind of centralized control is placed on the curriculum that will insure the discussion of Blacks' cultural and historical experiences. This control must extend not only to the course offerings but also to the instructors selected to teach Black Studies. To satisfy this need, a departmental status is needed.

Advantage of Departmental Status: A departmental status offers many advantages over a program. First, it gives Black faculty a formal relationship with the governing body of the university to protect and promote Black Studies Programs. This governing body consists of the academic senate, college committees, the deans, and presidents or chancellors. In order to protect their program, Black faculty need the freedom to lobby the governing body for support. Only departmental status can give them that freedom.

Without departmental status, Black faculty members are forced to assume the role of program coordinator or director. This role significantly limits their capacity to protect their programs. Structurally, the coordinator is forced to fight for his program through another department. Consequently, Black Studies is forced to depend not on a principle of law, but on the good will of the chairperson of other departments. If the latter does not support Black studies, which is often the case, then the former has no formal means of redress. If the coordinator of Black studies were to attempt to appeal his or her case to the dean over the head of his chairperson, he would be flirting with political suicide. First, such an attempt on its face will constitute insubordination. Secondly, there always exists the possibility that the department chairperson will use this action to damage the coordinator's chances for gaining tenure or promotion.

The second advantage that a departmental status offers is that it gives the chairperson control over Black Studies course offerings and class scheduling. If, for example, the chairperson does not like the scheduling of Black Studies courses at unpopular hours, he has a formal procedure that can be initiated to protest it to the dean. It must be noted here that course scheduling is the key to survival of many programs, particularly non-traditional programs. Any non-General Education requirement courses that are scheduled at 8:00 a.m. and 2:00 p.m. normally have low enrollment. Since faculty positions are allocated on the basis of students-faculty ratio, a low enrollment will guarantee the failure of a program.

The third advantage that departmental status offers is continuity in the Black Studies curriculum. Without department status, Black Studies and other ethnic studies programs too often becomes the stepchild of the academic community. For example, California State University at Dominguez Hills leads the system in offering multicultural courses. Students are required to take six units of multicultural courses before graduation. However, the university does not have a Black Studies Department to control course offerings. Black Studies courses are offered in various departments throughout the university. The coordinator of Black Studies has very little influence in determining course offerings and scheduling. Consequently, Black Studies courses receive low priority in each department. There is no planned curriculum for Black studies majors and minors. As a result, the university ends up with a paper program and no serious commitment to the discipline of Black Studies.

The fourth advantage that departmental status offers over a program is the power to recruit and grant tenure to its faculty members. This power is the cornerstone for (1) offsetting adverse political indoctrination toward nonwhite students, and (2) creating a wholesome environment for Black students.

As students of political socialization have recognized, the teacher has considerable influence over students' political orientations. Such influence has major political consequences because the teacher can significantly affect the political development of the students in classrooms by designing a learning culture. For example, in higher education, he has the discretion to select materials and textbooks he uses in the classroom. For a white instructor who teaches the cultural and historical experience of Blacks, the political consequences are great. White instructors are products of the same political socialization process for which they serve as agents. This process expects them to be models of behavior and social values of dominant society. Dawson and Prewitt have argued that the teachers are viewed as having the following charges:

(1) The teachers as a holder of specified political values and opinions and a disseminator of such orientation; and

(2) the teacher as a creator and manipulator of a "learning culture" in the classroom, which has important indirect political consequences.[32]

These charges can augment or significantly hamper the political socialization process of educational institutions to eliminate those misconceptions and stereotypical categorizations of Blacks which tend to perpetuate patterns of discrimination. For example, a white professor, who teaches Black history in a state university, takes great pains and efforts to emphasize the point that some slave women went to bed with their slave masters willingly. When challenged in class by Black females, he attempted to present them with documentation to prove his argument. Since his students are undergraduates and predominantly freshmen, they are not endowed with the intellectual skills to question him on philosophical grounds. Philosophically, it is impossible for him to prove the truth of his statement. The institution of slavery gave the slave masters *absolute authority* over his slaves. Under such authority, the question of free will cannot be raised. The only question that can possibly be discussed is whether or not the slave women went to bed with their slave masters to seek rewards or to avoid punishment. The question of willingness (or free will) cannot logically be raised.

The fifth advantage departmental status offers over a program is the control over the recruitment process of its faculty members. The crucial issue here is to select those faculty members who are willing to serve as mentors. When given the authority, many Black Studies Departments recruited faculty members with impressive academic credentials and who had a commitment to the discipline. When the administration attempted to disestablish these departments, they found it extremely hard to justify their action.

The political significance of a tenure track position is that it confers upon the individual property interest rights, i.e., constitutionally protected rights.[33] These rights are compounded when a Black Studies Department has the power to recommend to the college committee and the dean to grant a faculty member tenure. Once these recommendations have been made, the college committee and dean are obliged to accept it or show just cause as to why not. The justifications must be legitimate and not arbitrary and capricious.

In their attempt to adjust to past discrimination, Blacks have developed the habit of acquiring social credentials that are two to three times more impressive than their white colleagues. If, for example, the emphasis is placed on publication as a condition for tenure and promotion, Black faculty tends to develop an over zealous academic publication record. Take Harry Edwards, for example at the University of California at Berkeley.[34] Although he was not in Black Studies, he embraced the university's policy of publish or perish to its fullest extent. When time came up for tenure, he had published over 40 articles in professional journals and two books. In addition, he was the most popular lecturer in the department of sociology. All of his classes had high enrollments. In short, he met all of the conventional criteria for tenure. But his department turned him down on the basis that his research interest was too Black.

If Edwards was in the Afro-American Studies Department at UC Berkeley, he would have more likely been recommended tenure with little, if any, reservation. The responsibility to deny him tenure would have been left up to the college committee or the dean. They could not use the lack of publication and research focus because the mission of Afro-American Studies Department is to study the role of Blacks in society.

After the Edwards battle for tenure at UC Berkeley, university after university started re-evaluating their ethnic studies programs throughout the state. In many instances, this in-house evaluation team picked by the dean, and president or chancellor, recommended "disestablishment" of ethnic studies. Such recommendations were often met by strong opposition from ethnic studies faculty and both nonwhite and white politicians. To avoid confrontation with politicians and a possible legal battle, administrators resorted to attempting to constrain the growth and development of ethnic studies programs or diluted them by expanding them to include all ethnic groups, and not just discussing nonwhite ethnic groups.

Departments Build a Wholesome Environment: Departments also contribute significantly to the academic performance of Black students. By having departmental status, Black Studies faculty members are able to recruit those faculty members who have impressive academic credentials and a conscious for the academic career of Black students. This calibre of faculty members function to build a link of trust among Black students and the university to the extent that they feel sufficiently secured to risk failure in order to succeed.

The recruitment of Black faculty members is a very delicate process. Just because a faculty member is Black does not automatically mean that he/she is willing to serve as mentor to Black students. There are some Black professors who seek employment in Black Studies Departments because they cannot find employment elsewhere. These individuals have little, if any, commitment to the discipline of Black Studies and often hold Black students in contempt. They do not contribute to the creation of an environment that is conducive to learning. Nor are they willing to serve the role of a mentor.

A mentor has to be more than just a member of an ethnic group. The mentor must, in the words of Sociologist Willie, believe in their proteges so that they can believe in themselves. Mentors must accept Black students before they can induce change in their behavior. Above all, a mentor must be willing to suffer the redemption of Black students so that the students can overcome their fears and uncertainties.

Endnotes

1. Nathan Hare, "What Should Be the Role of Afro-American Education in the Undergraduate Curriculum?" *Liberal Education* IV (March, 1969): pp. 42-50.

2. Richard E. Dawson and Kenneth Prewitt, *Political Socialization* (Boston: Little, Brown and Company, 1977), p. 140.

3. *Ibid.*, pp. 140.

4. *Ibid.*

5. James Coleman (ed.), *Education and Political Development* (Princeton: Princeton University Press, 1965), p. 226.

6. C. Arnold Anderson and Suellen Fisher, "The Curriculum as an Instrument for Inculcating Attitudes and Values," Comparative Education Center, University of Chicago, unpublished manuscript, 1967. Quoted from Dawson and Prewitt, p. 140.

7. V.O. Key, Jr., *Public Opinion and American Democracy* (New York: Knopf, 1961), p. 317.

8. Nick A. Ford, *Black Studies: Threat-or-Challenge* (Port Washington, NY/London, 1973), p. 10.

9. *The American Heritage New Illustrated History of the United States* (Washington: American Heritage Publishing Co., Inc., 1963).

10. *Ibid.* p. v.

11. See E. Franklin Frazier, *Black Bourgeoisie* (New York: Collier MacMillan, 1957).

12. "Legislative History of the Equal Employment Opportunity Act of 1972," Subcommittee on Labor and Public Welfare United States Senate (H.R. 1746, P.L. 92-261) (November 1972), p. 419, hereafter Senate Committee.

13. *Brown v. Board of Education of Topeka*, 347 U.S. 483; 74 S. Ct. 686; 98 L. Ed. 873 (1954).

14. W.E.B. DuBois, *The Soul of Black Folks* (Greenwich, CT: Fawcett Publications, Inc., 1961), p. 17.

15. Senate Committee, p. 421.

16. Louis L. Knowles and Kenneth Prewitt, *Institutional Racism in America* (Englewood Cliffs, NJ: Prentice-Hall, Inc., 1969), pp. 46-47.

17. See Joseph Kahl, *The American Class Structure* (New York: Holt, Rinehart and Winston, 1961), pp. 251-57.

18. See Edward J. Barnes, "The Black Community and Black Students in White Colleges and Universities," in Edgar A. Epps, *Black Students in White Schools* (Worthington: Charles A. Jones Publishing Company, 1972).

19. These comments were made by Charles Willie at the "Minority Students Retention" Conference at The University of Santa Clara, August 1981.

20. Dawson and Prewitt, p. 149.

21. *Ibid.*, p. 150.

22. Edward C. Banfield, *The Unheavenly City* (Boston: Little, Brown and Company, 1968), p. 84.

23. Willie.

24. See Prewitt (ed.), *Education and Political Values: Essays about East Africa* (Nairobi: East African Publishing House 1969).

25. U.S. Senate Committee.

26. See Robert W. Fogel and Stanley L. Engerman, *Time on the Cross* (Boston: Little, Brown and Co., 1974).

27. Thomas Sowell, *The Economics and Politics of Race* (New York: William Morrow and Company, Inc., 1983).

28. William Wilson, *The Declining Significance of Race* (Chicago: The University of Chicago Press, 1978).

29. Sowell.

30. Fogel and Engerman.

31. Edward C. Banfield.

32. Dawson and Prewitt, p. 159.

33. In *Board Regents of State College v. Roth*, 408 U.S. 564, the United States Supreme Court defined the parameter of "Property" and "liberty" interest rights.

34. Harry Edwards, *The Struggle That Must Be* (New York: MacMillan Publishing, 1980), Chapter 20.

41.

Toward a New Role and Function of Black Studies in White and Historically Black Institutions

Delores P. Aldridge

The task of researching the number of Black Studies programs existent in colleges, together with the curricular characteristics of each of these programs, yields a distribution of numbers and a variety of curricula. Both task and task outcome are of interest to the scholar of Black Studies if only to gain an understanding of what has happened since the inception of this area of study in American institutions of higher education. One would suggest, however, an equally if not more important task — that of extending the Black Studies curriculum into a wider arena of concern, one that moves from the individual to the macro-systemic level. Such a curriculum reach includes all that is now considered relevant within the various social systems of Black people within this country. But such a curriculum also involves the extending of scholarly concern toward human systems external to this country but which are affected by and are affecting the lives of Black American.

Rethinking Black Studies

Ideas for a multi-systemic theoretical perspective for Black Studies emanated from extended correspondence between the writer and a Black Studies scholar resident in a Latin American country. The scholar noted that the relationships between that country and the United States resemble, at a different level of abstraction, the relationships between Black people and those who wield power in this country. This article, therefore, presents an attempt to begin development of a general systems approach to curriculum expansion within the framework of Black Studies programs, be they located on predominantly Black or predominantly white campuses.[1]

It would be, within these few pages, counter-productive to dwell overly long upon the origins, theory, and outreach of general systems theory since the initial paper of Von Bertalanfy.[2] Berrien's volume on general and social systems[3] furnishes the interested reader with a well-written introduction to general systems theory and its applications to the social sciences. What is of principal concern within this article is the application of certain concepts of general systems theory to the possible future of Black Studies curricula. An insight is provided by the notion that human systems are composed of a variety of systems linked together by networks of communication that move from the individual to the international collection of national states.

Within each system one may detect a system and its attendant environment. Any system contains a set of components, each in transactional relationship with the other, a permeable boundary that allows for the exchange of information between the system and its environment, and an environmental system affecting and being affected by the system. Within the system, components exchange information in such a manner as to enable the system to maintain a steady state. Exchanges between the system and its environment also proceed in such a manner as to maintain a steady state. If, for example, we consider one's sense of self as a steady state, it will be seen that all that one does is an attempt to maintain internally as well as externally, one's sense of identity, i.e., a system-relevant steady state.

General Systems Theory as a Frame of Reference

But what does this have to do with Black people and with Black Studies curricula? The relevancy is contained within a recognition that Black people are not simply conscious members of their community, state, region, or nation. No, the relevancy of using a general systems frame of reference is the gradual growth in understanding that Black Americans are linked, through a variety of systems, to a worldwide community of people of color. And it is, therefore, in the vital interests of Blacks that Black Studies programs expand their curricula on predominantly white campuses in order to focus upon this particular reality. And, on predominantly black campuses that are largely void of systematically organized programs, it would be necessary to initiate and develop programs that incorporate this perspective. A concrete example should serve to make the point.

The news that a major American manufacturer of automobiles was planning to establish an automobile plant in a northeastern state of Mexico was greeted with a great deal of enthusiasm by state authorities.[4] It was pointed out that the state, heretofore heavily based in an agricultural economy, could broaden its economic base through the training and utilization of local people in the automotive industry. A second, more insightful, look by scholars at the state university raised some troubling questions. Given the economic condition of the Mexican consumer market, ninety percent of the automobiles produced at the new plant were destined for sale in the United States. It was further revealed that the lowest paid workers in Dearborn, Michigan, earn twenty-three dollars an hour; the Mexican workers in the company's Mexican plant would be paid twelve dollars per day.

Aside from the fact that a substantial part of the Mexican state's economy would rely upon what happens to the American consumer's buying power and that the wage differential between the Mexican worker and the American worker is rather wide, what lessons can be learned from this example for the Black Studies scholar? Given the closing down of some Ford assembly plants in the United States, a reality that affects many Black workers, is there not an economic linkage between the lower-paid Mexican worker and the out-of-work Black worker? And through the creation of further economic dependency of Mexico upon the American economy, is there not a relationship to be drawn between the uneven power practiced by the American private sector upon Mexico and the uneven power practiced by the American private sector upon Black Americans? In other words, each time a major American manufacturer decides to relocate in a country where lower wages can bring on higher profits, is there not an adverse effect upon that sector of the American population undergoing severe economic strain—Black Americans?

Given the example stated above, it can be seen that a variety of academic disciplines can be brought to bear upon the analysis of the combinational situation—one in which those most affected by change have the least to say about the implementation of that change. We might pause here to question whether the example, as drawn, does not stand at too great a distance from the everyday concerns of Black Americans. Such, however, is not the case. We live in a country where clothing, tools, automobiles, shoes, and food increasingly tend either to display foreign labels or are of foreign origin. Black reality, therefore, involves Black people in increasingly complex human systems that, in many cases, go far beyond the limits of one's neighborhood, city, state, region, and country. And while it may be too much to expect that the average resident in the Black community should be aware of the ways in which international events affect his life, it is not too much to expect that students and scholars involved in Black Studies refocus their energies in this direction. While such an effort may appear to be new, in actuality it is a continuation of the same academic thrust that has revealed the dynamics and outcomes of Black dependence upon majority social, cultural, and economic systems. In this same line of action there arises another academic need in the area of Black Studies, a broadening of focus to include comparative histories, current events, and future possibilities for Black people in Central America and South America. While these are acute needs in all institutions, they are even more pronounced in most of our predominantly black institutions which are for the most part without Black Studies programs or International Studies programs with focus on people of color.

Since the majority of Black Africans brought to the New World as slaves arrived in Latin America,[5] their descendants form a fertile population for cross-cultural analysis between North American Blacks and Latin American Blacks. While languages separate Latin American Blacks from North American Blacks, there appears to be no valid reason why Black Studies curricula could not contain mandatory study of Portuguese and Spanish. Given that one of the largest Black populations outside of Nigeria is in Brazil, one wonders why Black Studies curricula have not familiarized students with the Black Brazilian experience and its similarities to and differences with the Black North American experience? One plausible response is that for predominantly white institutions there has not been the commitment to extend support beyond the very basics, while at the Black institutions there has been the general assumption that a systematic study of Black people abounds throughout the curriculum by virtue of Black people teaching the courses. That is, Black faculty untrained in Black Studies automatically incorporate information on, and an analysis of, Black people in whatever they teach. This makes about as much sense as assuming that because most people have teeth and can perhaps extract a tooth, they qualify to be dentists. Another very fitting response to the question raised would be that Black Studies programs, wherever located, have been intensely circumscribed by the important need for making some sense out of the Black American experience. But, as was noted above, one needs to be intensely aware of the kinds of definitions and decisions that affect one in this country, even though they occur external to one's native land.

As can be seen from the current situation existing between the United States and Central America, a failure to understand the basic dynamics that create unstable situations in countries close to these borders makes a powerful country liable to serious errors in its attempts to bring about a situation more favorable to the U.S. One needs now, however, to turn to Central America for additional impetus toward what can be termed the comparative Black experience at the international level. Post-revolutionary Cuba appears to be a country where racism has received official disapproval and where conscious efforts are being made at every level to wipe out racism. Is there not a need for Black Studies curricula to focus some portion of their academic energies upon situations, say, in Havana and in Miami, Florida, as far as Black Cubans and Black Americans are concerned? Unless one reads widely and is, at minimum, literate in Spanish, the Cuban experience can be lost upon Black Americans.

The reader should not assume that the inclusion of Cuba in this paper automatically defines the author as necessarily sympathetic to that nation's politics. But the central thrust of scholarly activity is the dispassionate investigation of whatever phenomena fall within one's field of study. And, as is being argued here, the central business of Black Studies is the antecedent, contemporary, and possible experience of Black people no matter where they are, especially in a time when international events heavily affect Black reality in the United States.

General Systems Theory in Practice

Having, then, presented some grounds for internationalizing the Black Studies curricula on predominantly Black or predominantly white campuses, we need to return to general systems theory so as to make a better case for utilizing this body of theory as a frame of reference. The primary value, one suspects, for exercising general systems theory upon the internationalization of Black Studies rests upon the continuities of communication that can be revealed. Since all systems, from the person to the world system, are interconnected, the task of Black scholarship within the discipline of Black Studies is that of revealing the origin, extent, outcome, and possible modification of such interconnections so that Black people become managers rather than unwitting victims of these interconnections. It seems that the term that would further enlighten what we are trying to save their is "information." It is information in both its narrowest and broadest sense that uncovers the linkage among Black scholars, Black students, Black communities, and those persons who attempt to exploit Black people as well as those whose life conditions reflect that of Black people. The tools required to uncover such information rest in the linkages that tie human systems together. These linkages can be expressed as fields of studies within the university. Another example might serve to illustrate the point.

Essential hypertension, hypertension that is symptomatic as well as unknown in its causes, affects Black people in this country more than any other ethnic group in the population. Among the various causes theorized to underlie the onset of hypertension is psycho-social stress, perhaps better termed "environmental stress." There has been a major thrust over the past years at the Federal, state, and local levels to identify undetected hypertensives and move them through a health care system that enables them to bring their elevated blood pressures down to normal levels. Since, in the majority of cases, hypertension cannot be cured—only controlled—the drugs that are prescribed must be taken throughout one's life. If we recall that hypertension is an asymptomatic disease, the side effects of antihypertensive drugs, however transient, tend to make one feel worse while under medication than during the undetected phase of the disease. Nausea, mental depression, drowsiness, fatigue, diarrhea, and ejaculatory impatience are among some of the transient side effects. When it is realized that hypertension is most frequent among voting Black males, the latter side effect tends to raise serious problems in the area of patient compliance with the medication regimen.

Now, as has been noted, the attempt to control undetected hypertension is a major effort in this country. What one finds interesting, however, is the amount of research by medical scientists in the physiology of hypertension that has led to drugs being the treatment of choice. But what about environmental stress? While it is true that the obstacles that stand in the way of effective research in environmental stress are substantial, this country's scientific establishment has solved problems that, at first, seemed insurmountable. Why, then, is there a seeming lack of financial and scientific effort toward adequate research in the area of environmental stress, its contribution to hypertension—especially among Black Americans—and its ultimate reduction?

We would not pretend to answer the question in this paper. What we would suggest, however, is that a finding that environmental stress is a definitive variable in causing hypertension would have tremendous political implications. What could national leaders and diplomats say to other countries in the face of a finding that the stress of being Black and living in America puts its Black citizens at maximum risk of a deadly disease?

There is yet another issue to be raised in connection with hypertension among Black Americans. What are the comparative statistics for Blacks living in other countries insofar as rates of hypertension are concerned? Would such statistics show that Blacks in other countries are at the same level of risk, at higher levels of risk, or at lower levels of risk? And what would be the implications of any or all of these findings?

Here, again, the use of a general systems frame of reference in conjunction with the internationalization of the Black Studies curriculum enables the Black scholar to develop and implement a line of research that has life-extending implications for Black people. One would want to look at such data as is available, the sources of control for the studies that have been made, the type and degree of rigor of research designs, and the implications of the outcomes of one's research. And, most importantly, one would want to determine sources of research support as well as the level of priority such research would have.

The two examples presented above are intended to stimulate the reader toward recognizing the need to link the basically American, perhaps local, focus of Black Studies programs to a broader frame of reference. The tools for such a linkage exist in the university. Some fields of study as psychology, sociology, political science, economics, foreign language, comparative religion, policy science, history, music, public administration, health sciences, and education are among those required at the undergraduate level of Black Studies is to assume the challenge implied in these pages. But each of these disciplines needs to be informed by a particular frame of reference unified by a particular purpose. The purpose, of course, is that of revealing the various connections and interconnections that form the everyday reality of Black people here and abroad. It will be seen, therefore, that the internationalization of the Black Studies curriculum should not call for a shift of focus from local conditions. Instead, the internationalization of Black Studies curriculum combined with a general systems perspective would serve to intensify the resources that Black scholars and students have when they relate to the Black community.

We suggested that there are many disciplines existent within the university that are able to be utilized in line with the curricular directions discussed above. It would appear obvious, however, that those disciplines cannot serve a maximum purpose unless their study is viewed within the context of increasing Black consciousness concerning Black reality. This leads to the troubling issue of faculty to teach these particular disciplines from a Black Studies perspective.

It would appear that it is of maximum importance that each of the disciplines involved in the Black Studies curriculum be taught by scholars who have a high level of conscious awareness of the issues raised above. Being Black in an ethnic sense does not suffice. Perhaps it makes some sense, in the context of this paper to substitute "becoming" for "being" and argue with the nomenologists that one's every choice is a definition of one's developmental state of Blackness. Precisely what Blackness is within such a course of development cannot be discussed adequately in this brief article. What can be said, however, is that Blackness is less related to skin color than it is to a cognitive and emotional set.

However one wishes to define Blackness, what is certain is that the teaching of the various courses outlined above—and philosophy should not be excluded from the list—calls for a depth of insight, research, and continuing professional and personal development that far exceeds what is usually required of a university faculty person. Lest this seem to be a formidable challenge, it should be remembered that survival as Black people in this country is no less a formidable challenge now than it was during the days of slavery. Black Studies is now at the stage of readiness to assume a leadership role on white and black campuses, in the community, and throughout the Black world as a critical resource for defining the Black past, present, and future. What has been unsettling is that the predominantly and historically black schools have not taken strong positions in systematically incorporating Black Studies. Black Studies degree grading units are virtually non-existent in these institutions.[6] The real challenge, then, is for Black institutions to systematize approaches to Black Studies so that no matter the level of system analyzed, students will be able to relate similarities as well as differences at every level.

Conclusions and Implications

In reviewing what has been written, the direction of the thoughts presented here rests upon a firm conviction that the temper of the times calls for taking what has been learned about Black people in the United States of America and placing it in a broader context. This requires an understanding of how other peoples and other countries forced into similar roles have negotiated obstacles in their quest for social justice. Aside from the advantages cited above to such an understanding, there is yet another advantage. Minorities in this country have traditionally fought one another for low-level social benefits. Differences between minority have surfaced in various ethnic studies departments within the university. What has not been understood is that under-powered minorities and nations play precisely the same role within the world's economies that Black Americans play within the American economy. Thus, for example, rather than continue a degree of strained relationships between ethnic studies departments on the campus, there can be coordinated efforts at the upper division and graduate levels that lead to joint studies involving people of color within a systems framework. Should this goal be achieved, Black Studies could be proud of having furnished the impetus for achieving such a feat.

Endnotes

1. There have been many attempts to articulate perceptual and analytical paradigms for Black Studies. See, for example, *Black Studies Core Curriculum* (Bloomington, IN: National

Council for Black Studies, Inc. 1981); John W. Blassingame, *New Perspectives on Black Studies* (Urbana: University of Illinois Press, 1971); Armstead Robinson, et al., Black Studies in the University: A Symposium (New Haven: Yale University, Press, 1969); Bayard Rustin, *Black Studies: Myths or Realities* (New York: A. Philip Randolph Educational Fund, 1969); and Inez Smith Reid, "An Analysis of Black Studies Programs," *Afro-American Studies*, I (1970). The classic work of this period, of course, is Nick Aaron Ford, *Black Studies: Threat or Challenge* (Port Washington, NY: Kennikat Press, 1973).

2. Von Bertalanfy, "An Outline of General System Theory," *British Journal of Philosophical Science*, 1 (1950): 134-165.

3. F. Kenneth Berrien, *General and Social Systems*, (New Brunswick, NJ: Rutgers University Press, 1968).

4. Frederico Campbell, "Con la llegada de la Ford Sonora empieza a integrarse a la economia estadunidense," *Proceso,* 384 (March 12, 1984): 12-15.

5. Manuel Moreno Fraginals, "Aportes culturale y deculturación," in *África en Américan Latina* (Mexico: Siglo Veintiuno Editores, SA, 1977), p. 13.

6. *Directory of Black Studies Programs*, (Bloomington, IN: National Council of Black Studies, 1980).

42.

Politics of the Attack on Black Studies

Robert L. Allen

Black Studies, one of the newest additions to the academic curriculum, is in deep trouble. The Black Studies movement that began with such enthusiasm and optimism in the late 1960s is now fighting a rearguard battle; its very survival on campus is in doubt. Wholesale cutbacks in operating budgets and student financial aid, coupled with intellectual ambushes by academic critics, have crippled or destroyed dozens of Black Studies departments and programs around the country. In 1971 some 500 schools provided full-scale Black Studies programs; today that figure has dropped to 200.

This gloomy picture is not helped by the fact that internal uncertainties and contradictions have weakened many of the remaining programs. Indeed, internecine feuding and opportunism have alienated many former Black Studies supporters. Moreover, many serious black scholars have been dismayed by the confusion over exactly what constitutes the subject matter of Black Studies. The result: optimism and enthusiasm are being replaced by cynicism and apathy.

Of course, it must be said that exceptions abound; numerous Black Studies departments and programs have not only survived but have established reputations for excellence, and have attracted outstanding faculty and administrators and enthusiastic students. Also, the internal problems of Black Studies are not exactly unique to it. Most academic departments are rife with conflict and jurisdictional disputes with other departments, and sharply contradictory schools of thought have been a general feature in the emergence of new academic disciplines. Black Studies cannot be blamed for a condition that is endemic to university life. Yet, with these provisos noted, the general situation of Black Studies remains problematical. The battle for Black Studies is still far from finished, and certainly a post-mortem is not in order, but an examination of some of the factors and forces in this on-going struggle may clarify its nature and suggest ways in which the outcome can be affected.

The demand for Black Studies cannot be separated from the rise of the militant black student movement in the 1960s. In fact, it is no exaggeration to say that the establishment of hundreds of Black Studies curricula in colleges and universities across the land was a major achievement of the black student movement. This is not to suggest that there was no black educational thrust before 1960. On the contrary, access to higher education has always been a central concern of black activism. Almost a century and a half ago the necessity for education was debated at a series of national black conventions. Later, the founding of black colleges, although made possible by white philanthropy, represented a continuation of black interest in education, as did the turn-of-the-century debate between Booker T. Washington and W.E.B. DuBois over whether industrial training or academic education should be given priority in the black struggle for equality. Thus, the demand for Black Studies was not so much a sudden departure as it was a variation in a traditional theme within the black movement.

What was new about the 1960s was that (1) for the first time masses of black students became involved in the struggle for educational change, and (2) it was widely recognized that not only were black students and teachers largely excluded from American higher education but the totality of the black experience was not to be found in the curricula of the vast majority of colleges and universities. It was these two factors that led to the demand for Black Studies departments as vehicles for incorporating black people and the black experience into American higher education. (Black colleges did not escape the scrutiny of militant students. These schools were accused of being white colleges in blackface, and courses in black history, literature and art were demanded, along with a demand that the black colleges must "relate" to the local black community.)

The demand for Black Studies was therefore in essence democratic and even integrationist, although it took a form that was superficially separatist. It was a response to educational racism—the virtual exclusion of black people and the black experience from higher education in the United States. By demanding open admission of black students and the establishment of separate Black Studies departments the student activists and their adult supporters were in effect calling for group or collective integration into higher education rather than token integration of a few selected black individuals. This was certainly a militant demand but not revolutionary, since at its core it simply called for a widening of American democracy not the institution of a totally new educational or social order. However, by widening educational democracy Black Studies could pave the way for the introduction of new and revolutionary ideas into the curriculum, and this was correctly perceived as a threat by conservative administrators and faculty.

In the early 1960s, with the culmination of the student sit-in movement in the South, black students began turning their attention to the black college campuses which had served—reluctantly—as their bases of operations. The students' political experience in confronting the white power structure led them to question the political function of black colleges in particular, and higher education in general. They began to understand that despite all the talk about developing a critical intellect, higher education in practice served also to inculcate bourgeois cultural values and behavior patterns and to channel young people into professional slots in the economy. In short, higher education served to strengthen and conserve the prevailing social order. To the young black students, having just done battle with the racism of the downtown businessmen (guardians of the prevailing social order), this realization came as an affront to their newly awakened black consciousness. On black campuses, students and militant teachers began demanding not only curriculum changes but a restructuring and reorientation of the colleges themselves. The student activists moved to turn black college campuses into political bases for organizing the surrounding black communities. To this end they wanted classrooms and other school facilities made available for community use.

In the spring and fall of 1968, the black student rebellion spread to predominantly white campuses in the North and West. At Columbia, Cornell, San Francisco State and countless other schools a familiar scenario was repeated. Students would go on strike (sometimes occupying buildings) and present the administration with a list of demands (sometimes "non-negotiable") that usually included a demand for admission of more black students, hiring of more black faculty, and initiation of a Black Studies curriculum. The fad word of the period was "relevant" (sometimes "revelant"), and it was believed that these demands would make the university relevant to the struggle for liberation, or at least prevent it from remaining an accomplice in racial oppression.

Almost overnight these demands were taken up by other black students, Third World students and sympathetic white students on campus after campus. The outcome (after hundreds of arrests and much head-busting) was a virtual tidal wave of new courses, programs and departments. No school wanted to be the target of demonstrations and disruptive strikes, especially in the face of demands that were generally just (although many administrators were offended by the expletives that usually were not deleted). But the hastiness with which many of the new programs were patched together suggested that they were being offered as palliatives, or pacification programs to cool out the students, rather than as serious innovations in the educational process. Some schools simply took all their courses touching upon race relations and minority groups, lumped them together and called this potpourri Black Studies. Others hired one or two consultants to come and design a few courses dealing with black history and art.

The serious question of what constitutes Black Studies was all but lost in this mad scramble to come up with something—anything—that could be *called* Black Studies. Black students and scholars were themselves far from agreed on what is Black Studies. One school of thought viewed Black Studies as a purely academic field concerned with researching black history and illuminating the contributions of blacks to American society. Others, such as Harold Cruse, considered Black Studies to be an instrument of cultural nationalism specifically concerned with critiquing the "integrationist ethic" and providing a counterbalance to the dominant Anglo-Saxon culture. Still a third viewpoint, best expressed by Nathan Hare, saw Black Studies as a vehicle for social change, with a functioning relationship to the black community, to break down the "ebony tower" syndrome of alienated black intellectuals. According to Hare, Black Studies must transform the black community. "A Black Studies curriculum," he wrote, "must include race analysis, class analysis, and the study of the oppressor as well as his black victims. There must be a study of the march toward freedom of other peoples in other eras and other lands—why they succeeded, their failures, an analysis of their goals and strategy, their tactics. Not surprisingly, the advocates of this overtly revolutionary viewpoint came under severe attack. Dr. Hare found his efforts at San Francisco State College obstructed by the school's administration and finally he resigned to establish *The Black Scholar* with Robert Chrisman, another black faculty activist at San Francisco State College at that time.

While the purpose of Black Studies was being debated by black educators, the future of these programs was being decided by other—not necessarily friendly—forces. Just as Slavic Studies rose to prominence following World War II when the United States was seeking ways of opposing the communist thrust in Eastern Europe, it soon became apparent that Asian Studies, African Studies and Black Studies were to become new focal points of government and private foundation interest. By selecting certain programs for funding while denying support to others, government agencies and foundations could manipulate the political orientation of these programs and the direction of academic research. With hundreds of such programs competing for limited funds, effective control of the future of Black Studies was thereby shifted away from black scholars and students, and instead govern over to the funding agencies—college administrations, government and foundations. Departments that were thought by the establishment to be dangerously independent or radical could thus be crippled or destroyed without the necessity of resorting to violent repression. At the same time, departments that were more moderate or conservative might find themselves being used as tools for researching better ways of manipulating and controlling black communities.

These dangers did not immediately become apparent. Instead the Black Studies movement enjoyed victory after victory as intimidated college administrators scurried to piece together programs (or acquiesce to hastily drafted proposals) that they hoped would keep the black students at bay. Black Studies supporters were jubilant. Certainly, there were clashes and debates over direction, but the growing opportunities and exuberance of the moment overshadowed and minimized contradictions.

Between 1968 and 1971 the number of Black Studies courses, programs, and departments featured by white colleges increased sharply. One investigator[1] reports that at one time "close to 1,300 schools offered at least one Black Studies course." A 1970 survey[2] found that larger public colleges and universities were the most likely to have offered Black Studies curricula. (This study also confirmed that student pressure was a major factor sparking the initiation of such programs.)

However, the illusion of quick success was soon to be shattered. In 1972 the counterattack against Black Studies started in earnest. Cutbacks in department budgets and student aid, especially at public institutions, forced the dismantling of many programs and curtailed student enrollments. In 1973, for the first time in a decade, the percentage of black youth entering college decreased. (This decrease, along with repression, signalled the decline of the black student movement, which had been a chief supporter of Black Studies.)

Cutbacks were the means used to attack Black Studies but they do not explain why this attack came. For this it is necessary to look to the larger political economy of which the educational system is a part. The attack on Black Studies coincided with the consolidation of reaction under the Nixon regime. On the one hand, the domestic economy was in trouble—plagued by chronic stagnation, rampant inflation, and rising unemployment. On the other, the United States had been beaten in Vietnam and placed on the defensive internationally by the socialist countries, revolutionary struggles in the Third World, and contradictions with its capitalist allies.

Faced with these problems the Nixon Administration, as the mouthpiece of America's rulers, launched a campaign to shift the burden of economic instability onto the working population in general while singling out blacks and other potential dissidents as scapegoats for intensified repression (code name: law and order). Great efforts were made to convince any doubtful whites that (black) militants, (black) "welfare chiselers," (black) AFDC mothers, (black) "criminals," (black) student radicals, etc., were the cause of the whites' present economic and political distress. This ideological assault served to cover the malicious attack (code name; benign neglect) being made against the black community as social welfare and education programs were slashed, public funding for housing undermined, and prices and unemployment allowed to skyrocket. Academic racists were trotted out and used to justify this attack on the grounds of the "inherent inferiority" of the black race.

On campus a similar kind of scapegoating took place, and served to obscure the racism in the cutback process. It was "militant Negro students, often academically marginal," in the words of Black Studies critic Martin Kilson, who were accused of making trouble. Moreover, according to the critics, these "ill-suited Negro students" were often aided and abetted by Black Studies departments of "questionable" academic validity. From this it was an easy step for college administrations to rationalize shifting cutbacks to Black Studies programs and black student enrollment in the secure knowledge that the enemies of Black Studies would provide ample justification for the attack.

The intellectual arguments against Black Studies centered on several points:

1. Black Studies as political, not academic. Black Studies Departments have been accused of "politicizincy" black students and encouraging mili-

tancy and confrontations with the administration, while ignoring the need for "academic achievement." The university, of course, is a political institution. In this way the responsibility for racial tensions on campus is shifted from the racism of the university and instead blamed on the militancy of black students and Black Studies. Such a charge also serves to obscure the political function of the university as servant of the bourgeois order, preparing an academic and professional elite that can "manage" America in behalf of the white power-holding classes. The university therefore is not apolitical, and to call for the "depoliticization" of Black Studies only obscures and confuses the issue.

2. Black Studies as intellectually bankrupt. Black Studies has often been accused of having no proper subject matter and of being merely an attempt to boost the collective black psyche by glorifying black history. However, the critics never point out that such a charge could be leveled against any new discipline in its early formative years. Whereas many other academic disciplines have required decades to clarify their subject matter and establish a standard curriculum, Black Studies advocates are expected to come up with an instant discipline.

This is a new twist in racist logic: if blacks can't do it better and faster than whites then the black effort is deemed inferior. Actually, the current debates over subject matter in Black Studies are a sign of its health and vitality, not an indication that it is moribund.

3. Black Studies as reverse racism. This is a particularly insidious charge since it confuses voluntary self-organization with externally imposed segregation. Because of racism blacks have generally had to organize collectively to break through the barriers of discrimination in American life. The individual black person is helpless before a powerful and racist institution. Only a confused mind could equate mass action to break down discrimination with the use of state power to maintain it. While some black students may prefer an all-black experience the fact of the matter is that the overwhelming majority of Black Studies courses are open to any and all students. It is a travesty of history and logic to equate the preferences of a few black students with the oppression of the southern Jim Crow system. The two are entirely incommensurate. Nevertheless, this charge has received wide currency among the opponents of Black Studies.

Many other minor charges have been brought against Black Studies but most of them stem from or are related to those already mentioned.

The charges against Black Studies cannot simply be dismissed as irrelevant since they have helped rationalize devastating financial cutbacks. True, the cutbacks were on the agenda in any case for reasons already cited, but without this process of intellectual scapegoating it would not have been so easy to force Black Studies to bear a disproportionate share of the cuts.

The cutbacks must be opposed by a coordinated, nationwide campaign to save Black Studies, since isolated individual departments are relatively powerless. Such an organized campaign could bring pressure to bear on state legislatures, federal agencies, foundations, and educational organizations. Such an all-out campaign is imperative if the present setbacks to Black Studies are to be reversed.

Beyond this it is necessary to recognize that although the criticisms of Black Studies may be self-serving, still they are not entirely without merit. Moreover, a host of other problems is also confronting Black Studies. Thus, in addition to the problem of cutbacks, any program or campaign to save Black Studies must be cognizant of the following:

- The need to define the field, and clarify its relationship to Ethnic Studies and other disciplines. (This latter point is important since Black and Ethnic Studies are often counterposed and forced into an antagonistic relationship.)

- The need for curriculum development and standardization.

- The need for extensive faculty recruitment and staffing, including the use of quota systems to achieve proportionate representation. (Here a thorough critique of Affirmative Action hiring programs is in order since these programs often pit members of different racial minorities against each other, or pit the racial minorities against white women, to the detriment of all.)

- The need to bring pressure to bear on professional organizations (e.g., National Education Association, American Association of University Professors, American Federation of Teachers, organizations in the various disciplines) to compel full and general recognition of Black Studies and active support of the black presence in higher education.

- The need for watchdog committees in Washington and state capitals to review legislative proposals and assess their impact on Black Studies. Black elected officials could play an important part in aiding such committees.

- The need to analyze career prospects for Black Studies graduates, and to find ways by which these prospects could be enhanced.

Many other needs and problems could be listed, but this should give the reader some idea of the dimensions of the problem.

There is no crash program that can resolve these problems; they are inherent in the process of establishing a new discipline and will require patient practice and development for their resolution. And no one should be deceived into thinking that this process of development will be gentle; it will be marked by violent debates, agitation, and conflict. The academic world likes its veneer of gentility, but this only conceals furious struggles in which academics and politics are usually mixed.

In this regard the critics are right when they note that politics is a fundamental problem for the development of Black Studies. But the question is not politics or no politics; rather it is *which* politics? Whom will Black Studies serve? Will it be truly democratic in its intellectual and political vision, or will it become "apolitical" and acquiesce to a narrow, elitist and bourgeois view of education? This question lies at the heart of the present attack on Black Studies.

Endnotes

1. Martin Weston, "Black Studies: Dead or Alive?" *Essence* (August 1974): 57.

2. Rhoda Lois Goldstein and June True Albert, "The Status of Black Studies Programs on American Campuses, 1969-1971," *Journal of Social and Behavioral Sciences* (Winter 1974): 1-16.

43.

Black Studies and Global Perspectives: An Essay

St. Clair Drake

I

In 1951, six years after the end of World War II, the *Journal of Negro Education* (which, along with the *Journal of Negro History*, was required reading at the time for all well-informed Afro-Americans) published its summer yearbook issue (v. 20, no. 3) on the topic "The American Negro and Civil Rights in 1950." In his editorial note, Charles H. Thompson stated:

> Since World War II, the effort to obtain equal enjoyment of civil rights by all citizens, particularly the fight to eliminate segregation and its attendant evils from our national life, has been lifted from the isolated realm of a series of minority group struggles to a level of national and international political concern.... In the current struggle of democracy versus communism, more and more people have begun to see that the status and treatment of racial and other minorities in our borders speak much more authoritatively and convincingly abroad than does the 'Voice of America'.... The struggle for civil rights in any particular country is of world concern and...the efforts on behalf of any oppressed group anywhere are part and parcel of the fight against man's inhumanity to man everywhere (pp. 250-51).

The writer was invited to contribute an article to that yearbook. The article appeared under the title "The International Implications of Race and Race Relations" (pp. 261-278). It stressed the reinforcement that came to the civil rights movement when the United States assumed the post-World War II role of "leader of the Free World." It presented documentation of the way in which the U.S. had found itself in an untenable position concerning the existence of racial discrimination within its borders and was taking some first timid steps toward trying to see that discrimination was gradually eliminated from the national life.

Racial discrimination in the United States had international implications in 1951 because the USSR was using the race issue to embarrass the United States in the eyes of other nations, at the United Nations and elsewhere. Lifting the burden of racial discrimination from the backs of Afro-Americans was proclaimed as a patriotic duty by American public officials, and the argument *did* make sense. How could Africa and Asia be expected to trust the United States when, by custom generally and by law in some states, black people were discriminated against on the basis of their color? Could the nation be sure that its black troops would not mutiny someday or even use their arms against discriminators in certain parts of the U.S.A.? In a war against the USSR might its propaganda lead some black groups to defect? How could the U.S. propaganda agencies deal with Soviet ridicule of a "Free World" that included South Africa as well as European powers holding colonies? The United Nations provided an ideal platform for anti-racist speakers to point the finger at racism in the U.S.A., thus placing this country in an embarrassing position which Afro-American leaders used to exert pressure for change.

The Pan-African movement was in a strong position to profit from the need of Britain, the U.S.A., and France to modify colonialist-imperialist excesses in order to undercut the appeal of the international Communist movement. Kwame Nkrumah's West Indian Adviser on African Affairs, George Padmore, published *Pan-Africanism* or *Communism?* in 1955. The title of this book could be interpreted as either a query or a threat, and the book called for "a Marshall Plan for Africa." It failed to secure this or to win any support in Washington for Pan-African socialism. Padmore's book did, however, help to stimulate aid programs for the new African nations, an action deemed necessary to prevent a drift or a slide into communism. President John F. Kennedy used the "Don't let Africa fall to the Reds" appeal very effectively in spurring Congress to support grants and loans to African states between 1961 and 1964. His predecessor, President Dwight D. Eisenhower, had inaugurated a policy of offering a small amount of aid to the new African nations in the hope that it would keep them on the side of the "Free World," particularly after Egypt signed an agreement with the USSR for the building of a large dam on the Nile. Richard M. Nixon was President Eisenhower's roving ambassador in 1957, charged with sizing up the situation among newly independent African nations.

Between 1961 and 1964 the Kennedy regime ended a period of Republican "Red-baiting" that had pilloried Nkrumah and Sékou Touré as willing satellites of the Soviet Union and labelled other members of the pro-Lumumba Casablanca Group as naive puppets, Morocco and Libya. Nasser of Egypt was placed somewhere in between. Kennedy introduced a sophisticated form of anti-Communist operations that took seriously the African argument that they could develop forms of socialism that would insulate the continent against the Russians and the Chinese, while carrying out a policy of non-alignment in foreign policy and welcoming American investment if it was prepared to respect African sovereignty. Nkrumah's Ghana began to build the Volta River Dam with U.S. aid. Kennedy's assassination ended that African honeymoon period and inaugurated a long period of suspicion about U.S. motives and resentment over manipulation.

Guerrilla warfare in southern Africa was escalating at the time of Kennedy's death. Something close to urban guerrilla warfare broke out in America's cities in the years following his death. The U.S. experienced ghetto rebellions during the years 1964 through 1967, and an extremely violent outburst after the assassination of Martin Luther King, Jr., in 1968. By then, the country was deeply mired in the Vietnam War but many black youth were much more interested in how the war against Portugal was going in Mozambique, Angola, and Guinea-Bissau than in the war against the Vietnamese. *The modern Black Studies movement emerged within this international context.* Unlike African Studies that began in the fifties, the movement was not Establishment-sponsored. It was both ideological and militant, a source of weakness as well as strength for an innovation that university administrators were determined to reshape into a purely academic phenomenon.

Stopping the "Communist menace," is still the centerpiece of American foreign policy but the U.S. government no longer seriously considers black Americans to be a potential Soviet Trojan Horse or possible Communist fifth column. "Treating Negroes right" is also no longer deemed a necessary response to foreign charges of racism in America. The massive changes resulting from the success of the civil rights movement have virtually eliminated the appeal of the international Communist movement as a useful weapon to African-Americans. But between 1952, when Nkrumah became prime minister of Ghana, and 1966, when he was overthrown by a coup, "treating Negroes right" in order to woo *African* leaders to cooperate with the United States rather than with the USSR was considered an important justification for improved race relations in the U.S.A. A non-racist policy toward Africa itself also was deemed absolutely essential in Cold War maneuvering, especially since Nkrumah had proclaimed himself to be "a Marxian socialist and a non-denominational Christian."

Was Nkrumah a disguised underground Communist throwing dust in capitalist-imperialist eyes? Could black Americans who knew him during his student and teaching days in the United States become a "link" and an influence for keeping him in the American orbit? Would large-scale U.S. aid be wasted in the pursuit of such a goal? And what of other left-wing African leaders? Could contacts with Afro-Americans be useful in keeping African leaders close to the Free World? The raising of such questions in the early fifties resulted in the following: (1) the inclusion of Afro-Americans in the new programs established to encourage graduate students to specialize in African Studies through fellowship awards for study in Africa, (2) appointment of several black ambassadors, and (3) encouragement by the State Department, foundations, and trade unions of organizations founded by Afro-American intellectuals such as the American Society for African Culture and the American Negro Leadership Conference on Africa.

As the theory of "the link" worked itself out, increasing numbers of Afro-Americans found themselves adding to their Pan-African connections some contact with powerful sectors of American life. Scores of black Americans found themselves in the position of trying to interpret for white Americans the motives and actions of African acquaintances. To what extent they also tried to interpret the sometimes seemingly inexplicable actions of white Americans to African is difficult to assess.

In the attempt to keep Africa from "going Communist" during the decade between 1951 and the murder of Patrice Lumumba in 1961, there was little active involvement of black Americans in African affairs at the diplomatic level or in official advisory posts. Nor was there any organized activity by Afro-Americans—Communist or non-Communist—to give *political* content to Pan-African sentiments, although they did so at the symbolic level through clothing, hair styles, and, to some extent, name changes. There was also affirmation of identification with Africa among broad sectors of youth of high school age. Newspaper editorials and public speeches, on numerous occasions within black institutions, made clear Afro-American sympathies with new African states and nationalist movements—even those like the Mau Mau in Kenya that used insurrectionary violence. However, by 1955, the new aggressive non-violent civil disobedience movement against unjust laws in the South, not Africa, was at the forefront of Afro-American attention. This was a movement led by adult middle-aged, church-going Afro-Americans.

At this point, the civil rights movement was not a youth movement, as were the African nationalist movements. Most of the people in the civil rights movement were Africa-conscious, but they had gained this broadening of their outlook through the Christian missionary movement. (For instance, the best hospital in the capital city of

Liberia at the time was built with money contributed by black Baptists.) Afro-American adults had always been taught that education and religion lay at the center of African "uplift," just as it did at the center of their own. Their own decision to become non-violent activists now gave them some appreciation of Kwame Nkrumah's philosophy and what its outcomes could be. And Dr. Martin Luther King, Jr., was constantly telling them about Gandhi and the people of India. However, Jorno Kenyatta and the Kenya Mau Mau, not Nkrumah and his "non-violent positive action," were the heroes of the militant black youth for a decade before Black Studies programs burgeoned.

II

A new variable entered the race relations struggle in 1960, with the organization of the Student Non-Violent Coordinating Committee (SNCC). The Southern Christian Leadership movement had an ideological global orientation relevant to the Christian faith and the Gandhian philosophy of some of its leaders. Stokely Carmichael, James Forman, Courtland Cox, and other youthful leaders from the North brought to the southern movement an explicit Pan-Africanism that perceived the American desegregation struggle as the counterpart of Africa's decolonization struggle. Kwame Nkrumah, Sékou Touré, and Jommo Kenyatta were role models with whom they felt closer kinship than with Martin Luther King, but they were perceptive and realistic enough to know that the tactics and strategy of a black minority enclaved in "the belly of the beast" had to be quite different from those of Africans and West Indians struggling for the right to organize and administer-sovereign states. SNCC leaders, unlike the members of the Nation of Islam (Black Muslims) and the Republic of New Africa, were interested in generating a mass movement, not in organizing what Karl Marx and Friedrich Engels once called "duodecimo editions of the New Jerusalem." SNCC leaders found theoretical support for their views in the writings of Kwame Nkrumah and George Padmore. The ideas of those writers were superseded, however, by those of Frantz Fanon when the English translation of his book *The Wretched of the Earth* became available in the U.S. and when Malcolm X began to develop a variety of Pan-Africanism that had a "tilt" toward both the Pan-Islamic movement (including the Pan-Arab movement it contained) and some varieties of Marxism. While they organized sit-ins, the young leaders were thinking!

Fanon was especially influential among the youth because he posed the problems of the future. He showed them that when people of all class levels fought together to defeat colonialism, or to abolish segregation as in the United States and southern Africa, they eventually faced class divisions that had to be minimized before the victories were won. It is no accident that former SNCC leader Stokely Carmichael eventually became a citizen of Guinea, and under the name of Kwame Sékou, has been trying to organize an international all-African socialist party, or that Courtland Cox, Carmichael's associate during SNCC days, played the primary role in convening the Sixth Pan-African Congress that met in Tanzania in 1974, during which issues of class versus race were debated.

The black youth movement of the 1960s, like the older Southern Christian Leadership Conference, had little time or energy to expend on international affairs between 1961 and 1965. The members of SNCC and the Congress of Racial Equality (CORE) were functioning as the sharp cutting edge of the movement that intended to demolish the caste system in the South. These groups mobilized the forces that pushed President Lyndon Johnson into calling for passage of the Voter Registration Act of 1965. After that victory, the leaders left to others the job of ringing doorbells to get the voters registered and to the polls while they moved to the North where the Black Panthers and other ghetto-based groups were trying to keep alive and extend the ideas of Malcolm X, who had been assassinated in 1965. By 1967 James Forman of SNCC had become head of the International Department of Panthers for a brief period, after which he became a registered observer at the United Nations for the rapidly disintegrating SNCC. The African Liberation Support Committee (ALSC) and SNCC were defining outlines of what was to become the focus of Pan-African international attention for the future, and remains the meaningful focus for the 1980s—the completion of the African revolution by forcing South Africa to withdraw from Namibia and by assisting the South African Freedom Fighters to win the victory over *apartheid*.

When the Africans defeated the Portuguese in 1974, a wave of jubilation swept through the ranks of young people in the black world. For Afro-Americans who admired the Black Panthers this was vicarious identification with blacks who had done what the Panthers were incapable of doing. The Afro-American youth who empathized with the Angolan and Mozambique Freedom Fighters included in their ranks thousands of college students and recent graduates. The newly organized Black Studies programs contributed toward the raising of consciousness with regard to Africa between 1970 and 1974, and to the emergence of the group that had organized a very effective lobby, the ALSC.

The ALSC created widespread favorable public opinion and helped to educate the members of the Congressional Black Caucus about southern Africa. The result was the passage of legislation in Congress prohibiting the use of the Central Intelligence Agency to overthrow the victorious Marxist government in liberated Angola. After 1975, on campus and off, this intense identification with an African cause subsided. The consolidating of gains from the civil rights movement was the preeminent Afro-American concern. But the Congressional Black Caucus operated as a watchdog agency for black Americans where African interests were concerned. There was a new generation of black students who had not experienced the "revolutionary" years. These youths wanted to express their black pride through academic achievement and conventional success. This desire was reflected in Black Studies programs as elsewhere. Pan-Africanism and global concerns demanded new forms of expression.

The current executive branch of the U.S. government has staked much of its international reputation upon becoming the broker for a southern African settlement that would explicitly destroy the influence of Marxist movements and states in the area, and would curb guerrilla action. This scenario offers moderate political advances for Africans to be realized through the great economic gains expected to result from a strong South African free enterprise system heavily financed by outside investors. This is Professor Chester Crocker's formula— infinitely superior to Henry Kissinger's insulting "Tar Baby" perspective for South Africa's future, but not enough. Not all of South Africa's Bantus, Coloureds and Asians will accept this formula. Some of the dedicated Freedom Fighters, black and white, in South Africa are fighting *against* apartheid but *for* socialism. Violent conflict is inevitable even if "Crockerism" prevails in the short run. As southern African affairs approach their climax during the next five or six years, Black Studies should play the same educational role that it did for Angola and Mozambique between 1970 and 1974. But, during a period when campus zeal tends to be low, the ingenuity of those devoted to

Black Studies will be taxed to find a way to make themselves heard in international consciousness-raising.

Having taught in Liberia and Ghana during the 1950s, having assisted in the training of Peace Corps teachers for Ghana and taught again at the university there in 1965, having pondered over the wave of military coups since 1965 (and over the Biafra War, the Mau Mau rebellion, and the recent skirmishes in Angola, Mozambique, and Namibia), I can foresee dilemmas that Afro-Americans will face in trying to confront events of southern Africa in the future. A black perspective is absolutely necessary. It must begin with the constant reminder that in 1957 there were only eight independent African states; today there are over fifty. Never have so many become free so fast. These are young nations still experiencing growing pains. It is imperative that a single standard be applied when assessing the role of violence. What the Western world takes as the legitimate use of force in fighting for freedom it tends to denounce when Africans use similar means. When the cries break forth that guerrilla warfare in South Africa is reprehensible, the matter must be placed in global perspective.

The rigid belief among Americans who control foreign policy that "free enterprise" and "democracy" are causally linked and that to work for democracy in the Third World means, by definition, working for the extension of capitalism makes relations with African, Asian, and Latin American elites difficult to maintain. Most of the elites do not see any such automatic connection. On the other hand, many, perhaps most, Afro-Americans do. Most of the latter, however, are willing to admit (1) that when the chips are down in Third World areas, American foreign policy will support "free enterprise" even when democracy is trampled underfoot, and (2) that dictators devoted to socialism are excoriated. This evident fact needs critical analysis by black Americans. Many African leaders have been arguing for the right to develop mixed economies, even socialist societies, with American aid money and to develop African-style economies. Incidentally, they have had to argue with the USSR and the Chinese on this point, too!

Sékou Touré, Julius Nyerere, and Leopold Senghor, though different in many respects, all tried to draw a distinction between "African socialism" and that of Russian, Chinese, or even Cuban communism. Their efforts were viewed in Washington as either sophistry or the naive behavior of people who do not know that they are being used and manipulated by Moscow and Peking.

III

Our global perspective must involve, in the first instance, the world and all of its peoples, not just Africa and the black diaspora peoples. The prevention of the nuclear holocaust obviously is the most important issue of our age. However, it is not the function of Black studies programs to supply leadership to the anti-nuclear war forces; other structures on and off campus exist to do that. It would seem though that programs and departments should lend support by use of their names upon various occasions where endorsement of anti-nuclear war activity is solicited. Resolutions, reports of official action, and statements made by the Congressional Black Caucus, the Organization of African Unity (OAU), and various organizations of Afro-Americans, Africans, and West Indians concerning nuclear disarmament should be made available to black students. These groups emphasize what nuclear disarmament would mean in freeing up funds that could be used for development programs in the Third World, a secondary but very important aspect of trying to reduce nuclear weapons. Human survival is, of course, the primary reason for supporting progressive reduction of weapons.

The implications of policies established by the Great Powers for development within the Third World and in Africa, the West Indies, and Latin America, particularly, would seem to be an important aspect of black alternative and supplementary education. The visual and print media occasionally touch upon this issue but what is said needs continuous expansion and reinforcement. The preparation of occasional summaries and campus-wide distribution by a program would not only be campus-wide education of value, but would also give visibility to the Afro-American Black Studies program as a serious agency for research and dissemination of information. Debt payment crises and the impact of rigorous International Monetary Fund (IMF) conditions for assistance need to be kept constantly before black college students, who not only are going to face these issues as voters, but often as political and economic leaders. During the eighties the number of black public officials at local, state, and national levels will continue to increase. Black students will become some of those officials who will be responsible for the welfare of all, not just that of Afro-Americans. Education for these new responsibilities, which seemed so remote as not to be imaginable twenty-five years ago, places a great obligation upon Black Studies programs. "What would you do if...?" role playing ought to be part of the routine education of this generation of future black leaders.

Of even greater importance than Great Power policy in general is the matter of United States policy. Two elections during the eighties—1984 and 1988—will determine the general orientation of American foreign policy toward the black world, as toward global relations generally. As the world is now divided, Third World nations inevitably interpret the dominant nations as "white" oppressors of "colored" people. The revolutions are inevitable, being generated by poverty and inequitable distribution of gross national income within states. International Monetary Fund's insistence upon belt-tightening provokes further explosions. Chapter two of Frantz Fanon's *The Wretched of the Earth* should be required reading to understand why coups break out so frequently in Africa, or why black-on-black conflict occurs in places like Nigeria, Ethiopia, Jamaica, Guiana, and Grenada. Black students cannot understand their world if they are not familiar with Walter Rodney's *How Europe Underdeveloped Africa* as well as the works of Nkrumah, Padmore, Cabral; and Manley. Once an understanding of the role of class struggles within the black world is gained, some attempt should be made to share the understanding with white students and colleagues on campus and to insist upon a single standard of evaluation for "colored" and "white" nations.

If meaningful changes take place in American foreign policy during the eighties, their implications should be mastered. All Americans are reaping some profit from American foreign policy, although some more than others. This ought to be known and understood by students—black or white—even if they decide that repression is justified in order to crush the international Communist movement and they plan to adopt careers that will make them party to it. Some will oppose the current policies. Some, perhaps, will find, as Andrew Young did, that dilemmas will be faced that may end their careers as diplomats. Others will survive. Some will thrive. South Africa is going to be the testing ground for Americans who are charged with implementing U.S. policy. Until that policy changes drastically, the dilemmas for black Americans often will be painful, dividing friends and relatives as they try to relate to the African struggle.

IV

The role of Black Studies programs is not to impose ideologies but to expand consciousness and to present alternatives for action. It is not to try to foreclose options that are open to black students, but to make all options clear so that choices can be made with better understanding. It is to help students discover for themselves where the fine line runs between being patriotic and being co-opted for ends that are not in the best interests of the broadest masses of black people. Black students must have a clear view of how change takes place through a constant interaction among radicals, liberals, conservatives, and reactionaries, with individuals choosing according to temperament, ideals, and self-interest—and various combinations of these motives—where in the pattern of change they wish to play their part. Never before in America have the options been so wide for black people; and for the first time, a few college-trained black conservatives like economist Thomas Sowell have emerged and won respect for their minds and vilification for their politics. They oppose affirmative action and ask for elimination of the minimum wage for teenage workers, unpopular positions with many black people.

This is a period when Jesse Jackson is carrying on in the tradition of Martin Luther King, Jr., who used his influence to try to affect foreign policy as well as to liberate his people domestically. All members of the future black middle-income group now in training on our campuses will have to decide how to respond to the Jesse Jacksons of the future. Black Studies programs should help prepare them for that decision-making process.

Some Black Studies programs are frankly and openly Black nationalist in their orientation. A very few are openly Black Marxist. Most try to accommodate the widest variety of ideological views within a generalized Black perspective. None can avoid the responsibility for dealing with global policies during the remaining years of the eighties. Pan-Africanism has provided a distinct global focus for Black Studies since the programs became a part of the campus scene in the late sixties and early seventies.

The world situation during the eighties, however, demands that we move beyond the concept of Black Studies programs as agents that confine themselves to providing supplementary or alternative education for black students at predominantly white colleges and universities. The action-oriented mood among black students on predominantly white campuses disappeared during the late seventies and preoccupation with personal concerns related to future careers now leaves little time for or interest in the kind of activist politics and community-related voluntarism that were present during the early seventies. Black Studies has continued to perform its strictly academic services, with fewer black students majoring in the field or even taking classes related to the black experience. As measures are taken to increase interest in the purely academic concerns that many deans feel should be the exclusive concerns of the field, some attention should be given to restoration of the broader objectives of the Black Studies movement.

In 1968 and 1969, many program chairpersons and directors visualized Black Studies as having a salutary—and even revolutionary—impact on many phases of life on predominantly white campuses. To some extent they did bring about changes in values and curriculum content. They did not, however, have a strong impact in areas not directly related to teaching and research. On the issue of greatest student concern at the time, the ending of the Vietnam War, black students, as individuals or organized groups, seldom acted in concert with or as a part of white student groups. Even on an issue that, at times, stirred considerable numbers of white students to action—the issue of disinvestment in South Africa—black students often preferred to act alone, if they acted at all. The legacy of the 1965 and 1966 Black Power disengagement still existed: "Define yourself for yourself," "Get yourself together," and "Take care of business." Making coalitions with white students or educating whites were not concerns; these activities seemed to be a futile waste of the scarce resources available to Black Studies programs. Directors of programs had to be responsive to the black student consensus. After all, the students had brought the programs into existence.

There is no strongly felt need today among black students for separatism in order to protect their group boundaries; off campus, extreme Black nationalism is no longer fashionable, as witness changes within the Nation of Islam or the transformation of Amiri Baraka from a leading cultural black nationalist into an exponent of Marxist-Leninist ideology. The opportunity is now present to experiment with realizing the early objective sought by some program directors of having Black Studies programs assume the role of educating the white educators and white students, in addition to providing the supplementary education for Blacks—which is, of course, its primary *raison d'etre*. Perhaps, Black Studies programs actually have an obligation in this period to take the lead in providing campus education on three crucial issues: (a) the serious plight of perhaps one-third of all black Americans, those who have had to bear the brunt of the operations to reduce inflation by tolerating a high level of unemployment and the drastic cut-back in spending for social programs; (b) the serious difficulties facing contemporary African nations as the first thirty years of their independence from colonial rule is ending; and (c) the problem of ending racism and exploitation in the Republic of South Africa as the liberation struggle there approaches its climax.

Devising the means through symposia, forums, special speakers, films, celebration of special events to carry out campus-wide education on these issues should be given high rank in budgeting time and money. Administrators must be educated to see the need for, and legitimacy of, such campus-wide education and to include this goal in annual budgetary allocations.

To allow Africa to be vilified and ridiculed as the press is now beginning to do, charging Africans with having proved they cannot rule themselves, would be to abdicate responsibility. Complicated matters such as the role of a chronic prolonged drought, of financial disasters stemming from the 1973 fuel crisis that consumed foreign exchange needed for debt servicing, and the exploitation involved in the existence of a high debt level for Third World nations, need to be simplified and explained to the next generation of leaders now on campus.

The attempt of the incumbent U.S. administration to play the broker role in southern Africa, operating on the principle that the primary objective in the situation is to remove Soviet and Cuban influences, not to abolish apartheid, demands critical examination. The decisions of the African National Congress of Azania (i.e., South Africa) to expand its program of guerrilla warfare will polarize black Americans as well as white, who will shrink from endorsing a movement that involves considerable bloodshed. Freedom Fighters will be defined as "savage terrorists."

The ethics of national liberation struggles need open discussion, and Black Studies programs focusing on Namibia and South Africa have an obligation to stimulate such discussion from a broad black perspective. The tactics and strategies used by the black leadership in southern Africa and American responses to various groups in the region need discussion as well.

The tentative first steps have been taken to involve the black middle class as partners in suppression of any kind of revolutionary solution in southern Africa. A glow-ing picture has been painted of financial rewards to be reaped by becoming partners in extensive commercial and industrial expansion in South Africa. Ultimate decision making will lie in the hands of transnational corporations, white South Africans, and a token representation of blacks. Without exerting any pressure on students to choose one way or another, Black Studies programs need to extend the circle of awareness of what personal and national options exist in confronting the challenge presented by South Africa.

With the CIA now recruiting on college campuses, using high pressure advertising, all students need to know what they are doing if they choose to place their university education at the disposal of the CIA. What groups other than Afro-American Studies programs are in a position to provide this kind of campus education? During the sixties the American Anthropological Association thrashed out this matter and took a stand against cooperation with the CIA. Could not the National Council for Black Studies, without compromising its patriotism, take similar action?

One of the most significant recent developments in the field of Black Studies resulted from the initiative taken by Professor Joseph Harris of the Department of History at Howard University to involve African universities in teaching and research about diaspora communities. A number of African scholars attended a conference at Howard in 1979; a subsequent conference was held in Kenya in 1981. (The Howard University Press published the 1979 conference proceedings under the title *Global Dimensions of the African Diaspora*, edited by Joseph Harris, 1982.) At both conferences, not only were scholarly papers read that focused on black people in Africa and in the diaspora, but plans were discussed to introduce into African institutions courses on Afro-American and Caribbean history and contemporary life. Insofar as this Pan-African extension of Black Studies continues to develop, the preparation of syllabi, textbooks, and supplementary reading probably will involve scholars and teachers from Africa, the Caribbean, and the United States. Black Studies programs in the U.S. eventually should develop one-to-one working relations with some of their counterpart programs, or at least with individuals, devoted to diaspora studies in African institutions.

The global dimension of Black Studies that Professor Harris's project is developing in cooperation with the African scholars, has always been one facet of black intellectual history. The modern Black Studies movement simply added a more militant youthful thrust to an intellectual movement that extends back into the eighteenth century. It would benefit us all, if the National Council for Black Studies could someday make available for use in Africa, the Caribbean and the United States, a small monograph or a pamphlet describing the roots of the U.S. Black Studies movement. I think it would reveal a situation in which a global dimension has always been present.

A Bibliographic Note

Black Students by Harry Edwards (now professor of sociology at the University of California, Berkeley), although published fourteen years ago (New York: Free Press, 1970), remains the most valuable source for documenting the existence of a global dimension in the earliest Black Studies program. It presents sample curricula as well as interviews with black students and professors. The social context within which Black Studies emerged is described with a freshness and vigor that makes the book a valuable teaching tool for interpreting the 1967-1970 period to the present generation of students.

The historic concern of Afro-American intellectuals with world wide conditions as they affect colored people is evident in the writing of early nineteenth century individuals as diverse in temperament and ideology as Benjamin Banneker, who proposed an organization similar to a League of Nations; Richard Allen, who considered the A.M.E. church to be a special (and perhaps temporary) formation within the universal Christian brotherhood; and David Walker, whose Appeal displays knowledge of, and sensitivity to, the struggle of oppressed people in Europe with whom he compared enslaved blacks in the United States.

The unity of a global black perspective despite ideological differences is continued later in the century as we contrast Martin Delany and Frederick Douglass, and Alexander Crummell and E. Wilmot Blyden. Thus, continuity culminates in the international perspectives of both W.E.B. DuBois and Booker T. Washington. (See, for instance, Washington's book, *The Man Farthest Down: A Record of Observation and Study in Europe* originally published in 1910 and reprinted in 1983 by Transaction Books with a new introduction by St. Clair Drake, as compared with Chapter X, "Europe 1892-1894," in *The Autobiography of W.E.B. DuBois*, International Publishers, 1968.) The global dimension in the thought of Dr. DuBois is further documented in the first five chapters of *The Autobiography*, which focus on the period when his perspectives had become decidedly Marxist. See also excerpts from DuBois's writings, spanning sixty-six years, in a section on "The World of Color — The Third World Concept" in *A W.E.B. DuBois Reader*, edited by Andrew G. Paschal (Macmillan, 1974, pp. 261-286).

No meaningful interpretation of black history since World War I can ignore the continuous need for black intellectuals and leaders to grapple with the implications of Communist attempts to influence black political and social movements and to organize segments of the black world themselves. The first comprehensive analysis of this phenomenon is Wilson Record's *The Negro and the Communist Party*, published in 1953. The emphasis was upon attempted manipulation and dominance by American Communists who were in turn manipulated and dominated by Soviet leaders. The extent of black American collaboration with Communists is assessed and reasons are given for failure to win widespread Afro-American adherence. The book is as objective as an assessment written during that period could be. Modern black historiography is correcting and balancing the assessment of Communist influence, and among the most important books are the autobiography of Harry Haywood, an early black Communist leader, written with a grant from The Institute of the Black World, and Nell Painter's book about Hosea Hudson, an important black Communist in Alabama during the Depression years. (See Harry Haywood, *Black Bolshevik* [Chicago: Liberator Press, 1978] and Nell Irvin Painter, *The Narrative of Hosea Hudson* [Cambridge: Harvard University Press, 1979].)

The most searching criticism of the impact of the American Communist movement on the cultural life of Harlem remains Harold Cruse's *The Crisis of the Negro Intellectual*, published by William Morrow & Co. in 1967. It is written in the genre made familiar by other ex-Communists. A scholarly and temperate assessment of some individuals and of the issues was published in 1983 by the director of the Black Studies Center at the University of California, Santa Barbara — Dr. Cedric J. Robinson's *Black Marxism: The Making of the Black Radical Tradition* (1983). This author considers Caribbean as well as American intellectuals but leaves for future consideration Africans such as Nkrumah, Sékou Touré, Cabral, Machel, and younger scholars such as Magubane. The recent publication of the first two volumes of the *Marcus Garvey and UNIA Papers*, edited by Professor Robert Hill of the University of California — Los Angeles, provides important source material for understanding one important negative reaction to the Red international movement during the 1920s.

Discussion of the Communist issue can no longer be confined to a review of relations with a now unimportant Communist Party of the U.S.A. Marxism confronts black America in new forms. The debate between Amiri Baraka (Le Roi Jones) and his opponents in the January/February 1975 issue of *The Black Scholar* signalled the beginning of a transformation of the Congress of Afrikan Peoples into Baraka's present organization, The League of Revolutionary Struggle (Marxist-Leninist). Poet Haki Madhubuti (Don Lee) had accused Baraka of "selling out" to whites. The shift in orientation of an important leader in the ranks of cultural black nationalism to an interest in building what he calls "a multi-racial communist party" in the U.S.A. based upon "Marxist-Leninist-Mao-Zedong Thought" was occurring at the same time that the Black Muslim leadership was shifting toward a Pan-Islamic rather than a black nationalist orientation and becoming "integrationist." In 1976, the Johnson Publishing Company ceased to publish the important journal (*Black World*, formerly titled *Negro Digest*) devoted to the Black esthetic, edited by Hoyt Fuller. Black scholars have not yet presented a plausible comprehensive analysis of why these shifts in orientation were occurring at that specific time. Increased emphasis upon graduate work in Black Studies should provide us with a deeper understanding of the changes that occurred between 1974 and 1980. Manning Marable's *Blackwater* (a play on DuBois's *Darkwater?*) has given us an excellent succinct survey of the events during the period and the five years that followed it, but theses and dissertations are needed before a definitive account can be written.

An indispensable handbook for understanding what DuBois called "the problem of the twentieth century" as modified by class and nationality problems, can be found in the report of a conference in Copenhagen sponsored in 1965 by *Daedalus* and funded by the Ford Foundation. The report was published in 1968 as *Color and Race*, edited by Afro-American historian John Hope Franklin. Particularly relevant to Black Studies concerns for the immediate future are articles on Brazil by Professor Florestan Fernandes, on South Africa by Colin Legum, on North Africa by Leon Carl Brown, and on the West Indies by David Lowenthal. The role of blackness in these specific situations should be made explicit to students and the public.

In preparing a new generation of Black students to face the problems of an Africa stricken by drought, disturbed by repeated coups, buffeted by International Monetary Fund demands for austerity, and menaced by the increasing strength of white settler-dominated South Africa, constant contact with Trans-Africa, the lobbying organization that is successor to the American Negro Leadership Committee on Africa, should be maintained in order to receive current reports. In addition, the *Report of the NAACP Task Force on Africa: Report and Recommendations 1978* should be available on every Black Studies library shelf for reference. The literature on South Africa is voluminous, of course. Therefore bibliographies and reading lists should be compiled periodically by students and made available to the public as the situation in South Africa moves toward the inevitable crisis point.

44.

Black Studies: Education for Liberation

William H. McClendon

> *We shall never have a science of history until we have in our colleges men who regard truth as more important than the defense of the white race, and who will not deliberately encourage students to gather thesis material in order to support a prejudice or buttress a lie.*
>
> W.E.B. DuBois, *Black Reconstruction in America, 1860-1880.*

Black Studies has been around for a long time. Ample evidence of this is to be found in any perfunctory review of the monumental scholarly works of distinguished black people such as Walker, Garnet, Delaney, Douglass, Williams, Fortune, Trotter, Wells, DuBois, Woodson, Hunton, Robeson, et al. Much of what early black scholars produced remained obscured, however, until the struggles of blacks for improved and meaningful higher education were better planned and organized. The earliest efforts for black courses occurred on the campuses of black schools. The more impressive, attention gathering crusades to establish black educational offerings on white campuses me later.

Education has been viewed for some time by many observers from assorted placements as falling apart throughout the American nation. In many ways this is seen as similar to the disintegrating of American imperialism. In considering the conventional roles of American education and its institutionalized discriminations, exploitations, rejections and particularizations, black in many sectors of life came to the conclusion that educators occupied only one of two positions: they were either oppressors or liberators. The response to this by white educators and the media was to label blacks as volatile and incendiary influences. In return, many blacks began to consider black education as having a special assignment to challenge and eventually replace white education because it was deficient and corrupt. Out of this grew the realization and acknowledgement for a large number of blacks that all education is unequivocally political and black education can ill afford to be less so.

Throughout the country public school systems are also strongholds of white racism. There is abundant evidence to prove that in many places they are the early contributors to the currently existing waves of intellectual decline and academic degradation. Most urban school districts now are burdened with more than a controllable share of debilitating social ills of their own making. In all of these systems the overwhelming percentages of administrative and teaching personnel are white and if professionals of other ethnicities are slightly visible they invariably are goose-stepping to white policies, regulations and directions. Those in charge of urban public schools are glaring failures at what they promise to do which is to educate students. For their failures they are rewarded with PR build-ups which attract for them more public support. Often it seems that the greater the damages that are done to the mass of students from poor and defenseless backgrounds the more accolades these miseducators are able to arrange for themselves through contrivances with their mutual admiration cliques and professional organizations. There are indications now that some minor reprimands are to be imposed because the failures to educate are evident among the students from the upper reaches of white middle class affluence. If this condition is corrected the benefits in all probability will not be extended to the less influential.

The development of Black Studies from the very outset was accompanied by blacks being compelled to evaluate the largely racist nature of established education in America at all levels from kindergarten to doctorates. Some of the early organized Black Studies courses began by giving critical attention to those blacks who hang on tenaciously to conventional white racist dogma that in most sections of this country is largely disguised as education. A number of attempts were made to have these persons give up their masochistic admiration for the deleterious ways in which this kind of miseducation operates. It is believed by many black teachers that the seductive illusions contained in the warped rationale used by those black apologists for "white is right" serves to lead uninformed and apolitical students further astray and contributes to their acting as morons. In addition to this, a false consciousness is deepened and the students are often imbued with many doubts and fears. At about the same time in a wider context there were some whites who began to recognize that the existing systems of education needed to be transformed. Many of them were quick to learn however that they were not going to be the ones to perform the tasks required.

Most Black Studies advocates and supporters saw the need for their programs to be intellectually strong and stable but in some settings whites who were aligned with the forces opposing strong programs (or weak ones) saw every symbol of growth and achievement as threats. Unfortunately some black proponents were deluded into believing that the purpose of Black Studies was centered around the mere posing of threats rhetorically because by doing so they would have a personal radical experience. It is easily perceived that the practicing of such absurd self-deception, if it became widespread, could bring about a disastrous dissipation of the usefulness of Black Studies programs everywhere.

More often, however, politically astute black scholars went about the business of providing certain specific insights for students in how to deal with the many labels and definitions coming from white quarters which affected black life and scholarship negatively. An example is the so-called black revolution myth (highly propagandized by the white press) which was analyzed very early as a white racist attempt to deceive blacks into believing that their ego trips in manure-dipped rhetoric, plus the wearing of funky clothes, dark glasses and disarranged hair were revolutionary weapons that would intimidate less aggressive blacks and terrorize whites.

Black studies does not avoid recognizing that psychologically the white establishment and the government of this country in many situations are overcoming the need for black people. The recently concluded Presidential political administration continued to move beyond its previous practices of manipulation, containment, disregard and repression of the masses of the black population. Often blacks were forced out of the position of being able to absorb each other (humanely, politically, protectively) and this contact with themselves is the substance of the communication that gives meaning to all human existence.

Black Studies, in remaining compatible with the assorted needs of black people to obtain useful and purposeful formal education, is compelled to teach contrary to much of what has become customary and routine in a variety of disciplines. This requires a distinct determination not to permit black perspectives, humanistic values and black people to be further denigrated by eloquently stressed anti-black academic attitudes that have been developed and nurtured in the hostile quarters of the dominant society. For longer than it is worthwhile to remember, some white social scientists have made a lucrative business out of researching black people. Most of this searching has amounted to little more than institutionalized curiosity by the practitioners. Black Studies has been effective in demonstrating from the standpoint of scholarship that most of this material is nothing more than sophisticated voyeurism.

A great deal of the social searching that is done about black people by whites, even if it is glaringly faulty, is permitted to be used to serve social science as a beginning and potentially connecting movement for even more deficient social information (remember Moynihan!). Moynihan may be the criterion of what white sociologists are but to most black scholars and students he is just another of the intellectual mercenaries. Interestingly enough most of these social scientists who pride themselves on being unprejudiced never subject their root feelings and gut attitudes to thorough critical analyses by black scholars. When this does take place, as can happen accidentally sometimes, the disclosures are often shattering. Black Studies rather effectively establishes that white social scientists cannot have the black experience that America metes out to black people for the simple reason that whites are not black. But whites can have traumatic and painful ordeals such as America holds in readiness for all persons (white or otherwise) who for whatever reasons confront and challenge its basic racist policies and practices.

Many black scholars have been busily concerned with directing their research and teaching proficiencies toward developing Black Studies to be a major force to enable black people to take control over their own lives. This demands that it be shown to black people and all others that white directed and dominated education should not be lamented as having failed black people, because it never promised to do anything for them in the first place. It has only served the purpose demanded of it by the white racist system. If the educational institutions of this country had been directed towards providing adequate educations for blacks then the white racist system would have failed because blacks would undoubtedly have brought an end to their subjugation and oppression long ago. Black studies rings into sharp focus the fact that blacks are not behavior problems but they are unknown and unpredictable elements of human responses and reactions to the continued abuses offered up so abundantly by the racist institutions of white America.

Black education is also improving in some of its subject areas the techniques to end the effects of the brainwashing that causes blacks to believe they have been restricted from competing in America's proclaimed pluralistic society. This is grossly inaccurate. Blacks were programmed by white racists from the beginning to be property and the servants of whites. As a result they have never been a part of the self-determining peoples of this world. This is what the black struggle is all about! In a racist, capitalist nation only those who are racist and free can compete. All others are forced into concentrating their efforts in a continuing series of survival maneuvers. Blacks are being taught now that they cannot continue to indulge America by showing sentimental attachment for its long time social blundering.

Black Studies decisively and positively develops within students a patience and persistence to struggle and learn. Dropping out is tantamount to surrender and no dropout wins anything anywhere. Black students especially have to maintain a clear perspective about what they must do in order to prepare themselves to engage in those lifetime intellectual, social and political campaigns that will result in fundamental change. To the dismay of some, Black Studies has not turned out to be the academic trip which gives to the young brothers and sisters those grades of A or B unless they have demonstrated the studiousness and scholarship which merit such rewards. Most black teachers are impervious to color being a passport to grades of excellence. The black community does not profit if Black Studies returns to the community students who have not oriented themselves to understanding the meaning of academic excellence and a commitment to achieve this. The contagion of Black Studies has spread immensely in terms of its intellectual richness, and the culture and philosophy endemic to black life is being realized (no matter how reluctantly) as a humanistic component the world needs.

Black Studies brings under sharp scrutiny those blacks with white minds who under a variety of circumstances have been selected by white educators to be celebrated and eulogized for their performance in behalf of the status quo. A classic case in point is Booker T. Washington. He understood white racism but he chose slavery over struggle. His philosophy of survival in itself represented the disgraceful subjugation and ultimate death of his own manhood and if there had been no William Trotter, W.E.B. DuBois, Ida B. Wells, et al., the total and permanent destruction of black people could have occurred. Black people must make positive decisions about their lives. They do not need to be in a state of anxiety about this leading to their being alienated from white people. They must be constantly working to remove their alienation from other black people.

All students of Black Studies are helped to understand that critical analysis and interpretation are major facets of Black History and there will exist for some time many opposing viewpoints. Critical analysis and its abiding significance to Black Studies does not mean the exercising of calloused and unthoughtful disagreement nor does it suggest there will be an easy embracing of the varieties of appealing thought covering the range from DuBois to Soyinka. It means that Black Studies will insist that students examine and comprehend a multitude of theories and teachings. The relevance of each body of knowledge to black liberation can be determined only through obtaining an understanding of the substantive content, and not by practicing avoidance, disregard and indifference as these are the tools for turning common unawareness and simple stupidity into strongholds of colossal ignorance. There is no guarantee that a unity of thought will be found among the various scholars. This does not mean that black scholars will not continue to be able to provide scholarly direction and intellectual leadership for their students.

Black Studies comes to grips with the various social science fabrications that were/are used to delineate alleged inferiority of the blacks. There is emerging now a rather clear understanding of the dominant society's stereotypical tendency to find all other ethnic peoples as hyper-emotional, irrational, sexually irresponsible, and anti- or nonintellectual. But because of Black Studies students are now better able to evaluate from a liberating perspective the assorted materials pouring forth from all sectors of the white media treating of everything black. They are able to recognize the contrast between the black experience and the white advantage and to understand the pathology of white society as being the basic reason for black people living in harsher environments and under greater internal stresses. Also historical, political and social documentation clearly reveals the evidence as to why blacks enjoy America less and suffer from it more. Students in turn are developing more care and vigilance and are being taught more effectively to exercise discretion and prudence in using those strengths and resources that must be expended by all peoples whose aspirations are to be free.

The Black Studies impact is apparent in the new directions that are beginning to be adopted by some career professionals in furnishing special knowledge and information about the services and functions of their professions. Black people are aware of the long lamented inequities throughout the country in various professional services including law and medicine. Legal protection and medical care for blacks have been in abominable states throughout the American existence.

While there have been numerous black professionals in the past who have given aid to blacks who found themselves distressed and handicapped because of medical problems or legal difficulties, most of this assistance was provided to relieve special crises. Now the larger need of the black communities all over this land is to have professionals in every field involved in those tasks and programs that will enable increased numbers of people to understand how these professions should serve the people routinely. The expertise of more of these blacks is being shared with the people in order that they will be able to cope with and offset those kinds of difficulties that are often created by the professions themselves.

Not only white education but all other institutionalized areas of this system follow unwaveringly the guidelines of white racism. These, in addition to many other derogatory intentions, have as their purpose to assure the maximum development of all blacks into states of acceptable boyhood or girlhood. All whites are programmed to remain white and blacks are programmed to think and act as white as possible. Black Studies is, without reservation, diametrically opposed to this. This is why courses do not become Black Studies merely because a white Board of Education (higher or lower) or departmental chairmen display liberal magnanimity by ordering or allowing the word Black to be used in a course title or label.

The customary exhibitions of patriotism among whites are clearly understood by "politically black" people to be sanctimonious ways of manifesting more white racism. These displays of KKK type nationalism and religion have glorified and sustained horrendous white societal behavior patterns toward all peoples of other ethnicities in this country. These result in black people being born to the conditions that produce anger and dissatisfaction. The expressing of this anger has made it possible for some long submerged aspects of black culture to expand and strengthen. Black culture is basically rich in the noble, heroic and sacrificial struggles of blacks seeking for hundreds of years to achieve liberation. A variety of cultural treasures has been developed in the centuries-long resistance of some blacks to all forms of subjugation and oppression.

Competition is advertised as the essence of the American way of life. The damaging implications of this for black people are manifold and for those who become competitively indoctrinated certain negative social manifestations are inevitable. Competition fosters individualism and for black people individualism obstructs the development of strong group black consciousness. At the same time, this system regards black people as an undifferentiated mass, and this supports and sustains the varied rationales that are employed whenever and wherever the treatment of blacks is clearly revealed to be based upon mass presumptive inferiority. The forces that control this nation are revealed in numerous studies, articles, books and documents to be tightly organized, and in total collaboration on all matters that insure their powerful status. Students are being given the opportunities to study the possibilities of black people reversing the effects of long-standing white customs and attitudes by thinking of themselves as an undifferentiated social class in a white racist system. This is a vital step in establishing a humanistic relationship that reduces individualistic self-aggrandizement practices and at the same time serves as the foundation for a politicization of the mass of black people around legitimate black protest, reaction and resistance.

Walter Wilson, co-chairman of the DuBois Memorial Committee, stated in his syllabus for the Study of Selective Writings by W.E.B. DuBois, 1970, that "DuBois was merciless in criticizing any sign of neglect, laxity, rowdiness, or intemperance on the part of his students that might give substance to the accepted stereotypes of black behavior. At the same time, he was tireless in counseling with his students as to their work habits, personal problems, and future professional appointments. Despite some resentment of his strictness, the end result was the creation of a body of trained black sociologists, scientists and scholars, who, in retrospect, recalled his stern admonitions with gratitude and his personal friendship with affection."

Black Studies is in part, of course, a creation of DuBois, and now in this era which Wilson states is the "age of DuBois," Black Studies can be no less demanding. There has to be at all times a basic commitment of service to black communities through intellectual preparation and teaching competence of the highest order. The integrity of the learning process must be respected and teachers must have self-respect and acknowledge that there are distinct roles for students and teachers. The responsibilities of each must be explicit and filled with honor. Care is to be taken to avoid meaningless rhetoric and uncouth performances that will deprecate these standards. Carter G. Woodson discovered that almost all education offered to blacks by white America is demoralizing and crippling, therefore, Black Studies must be strong and remain in the forefront for developing and strengthening the intellectual, social and political thought necessary for human liberation.

VII

Section VII

Critical Issues and Perspectives

Key Concepts and Major Terms

- Academic Excellence
- Extra-University
- Scope
- Relevance
- Educational Aims
- Ideological Battles
- Paradigmatic Battles
- Revolutionaries
- Afro-Significationism
- Subjectivism
- Institutionalization

- Black Revolt
- Reactionaries
- Liberals
- Exclusion of Whites
- Politics of Confrontation
- Black Expert
- White Expert
- Afrosubjectivity
- Standardization
- Nomenclature
- Postindustrial-Management Society

- Afrosynthicity
- Afrosyncretism
- Social Development
- Social and Political Ethics
- Policy Studies
- Critical Social Theory
- Black Philosophical Identity
- Historical Continuity
- Americentricism
- Specialization

Introduction

From its beginnings, African American Studies has sought to maintain commitments to both academic excellence and extra-university community responsibilities. That is, all social, political, educational, economic, and cultural issues pertaining to African Americans have in some ways been associated or connected with the scope, relevance, and purpose of the discipline. Given that the roots of African American Studies lie significantly outside the realm of academia, this is not surprising. However, what quickly became (and, furthermore, remains) a cause for serious concern were the central issues which arose within the discipline as a result of this relationship.

Each of the essays in this section identifies a number of reactions and responses to the political and academic conditions reflecting both the unique structural situation of the discipline. Included are questions surrounding the nature of African

517

American Studies and the relationship to the community, shifts in the social, political, and educational aims and objectives of the field throughout the past thirty years, the part(s) white and other "non-black" students, faculty, and administrators could or should play in the discipline, the important (though lessening) role of historically black colleges and universities as centers of knowledge and training for black students, and finally, the ideological and paradigmatic battles among competing schools of thought within the field.

Alan K. Colon, in "Critical Issues in Black Studies: A Selective Analysis," writes that from its earliest beginnings, the scholarly tradition from which African American Studies stems, as well as its alternative movements for African American educational development, have been aimed at "devising and perpetuating a liberating educational process in a countervailing social/political/cultural/economic climate.

In "Critical Issues on Black Studies," Ronald Walters argues that the strongest component is that Black Studies should deal with are the "immediate realities of the everyday oppression of black people" in this country. Regardless of the structural assumptions under which Black Studies is operating is the tension between power and responsibility."

In "Black Studies: Trouble Ahead," Eugene D. Genovese offers the "prototypical" white academic "concern" about the initial objectives of African American Studies and black student demands when he warns that "If one black group is allowed to exclude other black groups or whites from participation in the programs, this will lead to campus-wide purges of 'reactionaries,' 'liberals,' and 'revolutionaries' as the power of these groups vacillates...the black studies question, like the black revolt as a whole, has raised all the fundamental problems of class power in American life, and the solutions will have to run deep into the structure of the institutions themselves."

Pat M. Ryan, in "White Experts, Black Experts, and Black Studies," contends: "The joint problem of black identity and majority establishment support of 'black studies' programs partly involves a kind of 'Afro' bias, or halo, that is not so much scholarly as therapeutic, to both black and non-black. It would be unfair to say that Kaiser (black) and Genovese (non-black) thrive on controversy. It would be more accurate to say that American scholarship thrives on the controversy that these men— 'black expert' and 'white expert'—provoke."

Ford argues further, in "The Black College as Focus for Black Studies," that the tradition of historically black colleges and universities as central sites of research in African American Studies needs to be reexamined for the future. He states: "The black college of the future has two possible directions open to it. It can become a revolutionary institution with a major emphasis on ideology and training for the overthrow of the current political and economic system of the United States or it can develop a curriculum that will devote minor attention to ideology and black philosophical identity and major attention to cultural, historical, political, and economic studies and disciplines designed to enhance the success of the black graduate in competing for and winning places of influence and power.

In the selection "White Colleges and the Future of Black Studies," Nick Aaron Ford writes: "The white college will begin or continue to make available on a permanent basis interdisciplinary programs (or independent departments) in Black Studies which will provide opportunities for black and white students who so desire to major or concentrate in the field. In addition, institutions qualified to offer the M.A. and/or the Ph.D. degree will begin or continue to encourage (or at least not to discourage) black and white graduate students to choose theses and dissertation projects in a wide variety of areas of black life and culture."

Erskine Peters' "Afrocentricity: Problems of Method and Nomenclature" addresses the most controversial aspect of African American Studies during the past fifteen years, the theory of Afrocentricity. Peters provides a cogent, critical analysis of the school of thought which took flight at Temple University beginning in 1988. He finds that, overall, "There appear to be four discernible aspects of Afrocentricity at work in written and oral discourse... Afrocentricity derives from an understanding of African cultural world view or cosmology... Afrosubjectivity places emphasis on the African person as the neglected being,... Afrosynthicity... explores Afro-America as a cultural and political entity emphasizing Afro-America's need to assert its sheer autonomous existence... Afrosyncretism... the earliest form of scholarly discourse which emphasizes the threads of African culture to have survived in the Americas."

In "Taking Stock: African American Studies at the Edge of the 21st Century," Floyd W. Hayes, III, asserts: "... African American Studies will be compelled to strengthen its transdisciplinary and global thrusts... and broaden its intellectual scope and horizons to such areas of study as policy studies and advocacy, critical social theory, critical cultural studies, women's studies, social and political ethics, futures research, organizational development, and leadership preparation."

The essays in Section VII deal with some of the most crucial, controversial, ideological and intellectual positions taken by some of the leading proponents of African American Studies since its institutionalization on predominantly white campuses in 1968. Topics include the role(s) of white teachers and students; the utility of a degree in African American Studies with regard to employment and service; the hostile reception of Afro-American Studies by faculty and students in "traditional" academic disciplines; and the increased role African American Studies has come to play on both historically black and predominantly white institutions over the past thirty years.

45.

Critical Issues in Black Studies:
A Selective Analysis

Alan K. Colón

Introduction

Black Studies is the most recent mass expression of a venerable tradition of Afrocentric scholarship among African-Americans.[1] This tradition has sought to incorporate scholarly pursuits with (1) the transmission of knowledge relevant to the individual and group achievements of African-Americans, (2) the vindication of Black people from scholastic and ideological onslaughts against them, and (3) the creation and application of means for African-American group problem-solving.

Proposed in the mid-1960s as a theoretical critique of and practical departure from the racist-elitist aspects of Euro-American scholarship and schooling, the essence of Black Studies has been to bring a critical analysis of the black experience into the educational process. This was to be done by infusing the realities of African-American life into that process, by changing the process itself through articulation of the needs of Black liberation, and, by working toward established goals. In this task, a wedding of scholarship to community development was to transpire. Black Studies was to be a bold and audacious new approach to social change through education.

Black Studies, then, refers to the attempt to create a systematic body of knowledge and experience based in the history of Black people. Black Studies theory and practice examines and enhances the survival, well-being, development, and perpetuation of people of African origin, particularly those in the United States. As such, Black Studies serves three major functions: (1) corrective—the distortions and fallacies surrounding and projected against Blacks for elitist and racial and cultural supremacist purposes are countered with factual knowledge and critical historical interpretation; (2) descriptive—the past and present events that constitute the Black experience are accurately documented; and (3) prescriptive—concepts, theories, programs, and movements toward the alleviation or resolution of group problems faced by Blacks are generated and promoted.

The historical problem confronting Black Studies—the scholarly tradition from which it stems, and, indeed, all alternative movements for African—American educational development—has been that of devising and perpetuating a liberating educational process in a countervailing social/cultural, political/economic climate. Measurements of the effectiveness of Black Studies and its impact on this central problem of alternative Africa American education have been limited. From the literature of the last fifteen years, the thrust of evaluations of Black Studies as a scholastic enterprise and of specific programs within it can be categorized into four major areas: perceptions,[2] achievement,[3] development,[4] and status.[5]

The aim of the research[6] that forms the basis for this essay was to contribute to a fuller understanding of the current condition of prominent programs in Black Studies and to project the future of the field. Data for the academic year 1978-79 was drawn from interviews with directors of Black Studies programs at ten institutions: Brown University, City College of the University of New York, Cornell University, Howard University, Indiana University, The Ohio State University, San Jose State University, State University of New York at Albany, University of Cincinnati, and Yale University. The administrators who were interviewed indicated that the difficulties faced by their respective programs were generic to the field of Black Studies. The issues identified by the program heads as having greatest bearing on the future of Black Studies are interrelated but can be grouped, for analytical purposes, into nine categories: historical continuity, definition, legitimacy, funding, faculty, pedagogy, curriculum development, research and publication, and expansion. This article examines and explores some prescriptions for the following major Black Studies problem areas: historical continuity, definition, institutionalization and legitimacy, and expansion.

Historical Continuity

Most students enter college with little or no comprehension of the Black experience in general and the evolution of contemporary Black Studies in particular. This perplexing phenomenon poses a crucial problem, for it retards the progressive development and transmission of the Black Studies knowledge base as students need to be minimally acquainted with a fundamental history that is not taught in normative educational structures and processes. In interview, James Turner, director of the Africana Studies and Research Center at Cornell University, stated that "the consciousness and world view of younger students are not informed by the early challenges and development of the field, its major thrust and the important questions which generated out of that thrust. Do these students," he asked, "come into the field for the same reasons as their predecessors? Do they see the same issues as important?" This becomes a matter of inter-generational socialization into Black Studies so that its participants will have a historical grounding in the field. Most other disciplines and fields of study have senior scholars who set for the field the theoretical arguments, tone, and pace to which others respond. Persons who occupy endowed chairs and journal editors, for instance, help young scholars to be socialized into the field. By that arrangement, Turner continued, Black Studies

> ... gets defined not by the common denominator but by its distinguished frontier who are pulling the discipline together and who help challenge the others. Now we are stressing too much of the common denominator, which is our minimal level of achievement.... We need people who are seen as significant others, who are recognized and respected for their level of achievement as well as their facility of perspective and integrity of work in the field in setting the outer range of distinction.

Due in large part to a preoccupation with consolidating the field against great odds, very few such giants in Black Studies have emerged. While "worshipping at the feet of Buddha" would surely stifle growth, having "elders" for the field brings coherence and a level of challenge to it and increases the academic facility of Black

Studies scholars to reproduce themselves. Otherwise, if the economic and political factors in American higher education remain constant Black Studies and Black scholarship itself will be faced with a serious problem. This point was echoed by Francis Botchway, chairman of the Department of Afro-American Studies at the University of Cincinnati when interviewed. He saw the necessity for building upon the work of such Black Studies pioneers as John Henrik Clarke, W.E.B. DuBois, Carter G. Woodson, and St. Clair Drake in order to advance the scholastic thrust of the field. "We have not done so, even though more opportunities have been available to us," he asserted.

Just as the history of Black Studies has not been taught in normative educational endeavors, it has not been adequately addressed in Black Studies programs either, which is a glaring contradiction. The broad transmission of a well-developed history would facilitate an orientation into the discipline across generations. This would help Black Studies to ensure its own perpetuity, as a more meaningful dialogue can be engaged in toward resolving the field's problems and charting its course into the twenty-first century. Black Studies programs at collegiate institutions could do more in introductory courses (and in courses at other levels, too) to offer the history and philosophy of the field. While the format and sequence of these courses would have to be determined by the circumstances of the individual programs, they could eventually, if not immediately, be prerequisites for Black Studies majors, minors, and concentrators. These courses could also satisfy divisional and elective requirements for other students and, in such situations, would have to be non-restrictive, remaining open to any student interested in them. Students would then benefit from basic theoretical-historical perspectives in the field and would be better equipped and motivated to pursue further study in it.

A course covering the history of Black Studies might encompass the following: (1) definition (purpose, importance and scope), (2) historical foundations (philosophical bases and socio-political background), (3) contemporary origins, (4) opposition, (5) program models, (6) research issues, (7) evaluation and literature review, and (8) projections for the future.

Definition: Standardization, Specialization and Philosophical Orientation

For more than ten years, there has been some motion in Black Studies for the nation-wide standardization of course content. This drive is rooted in the belief that there should be a core of material homogenous to and shared by all efforts in Black Studies, especially at the introductory course level. In the 1970s, some programs adopted the text *Introduction to Afro-American Studies*[7] edited by Abdul Alkalimat and Ronald Bailey of Peoples College in Chicago, as a primary vehicle in the standardization effort. This book, tested and accordingly revised in actual teaching-learning situations, lays the groundwork for building and synthesizing the Black Studies knowledge base. Movement toward meeting this objective was significantly advanced with the July, 1982, publication of Karenga's *Introduction to Black Studies*.[8] This is a single author text which establishes new standards in its approach to and instruction of Black Studies, and which offers an alternative to the Peoples College book.

Judging from outcomes of the study conducted by the writer, programs in Black Studies must also intensify the cultivation of their unique programmatic strengths.

This would engender specialization in the field, and individual programs would become distinguished for the expertise they have developed in specific areas of study and/or in their ability to carry out certain of the field's practical tasks. Here, the admonition of Brown University's Rhett Jones is instructive. He advocated the assessment of needs, problems and possibilities in institutional and community settings so that the mission of individual Black Studies programs would be realistically delineated. With each program concentrating on what it does best, a special contribution to larger Black Studies aspirations could be made. Thus, over-extension and, to a lesser degree, duplication of effort would be avoided. Also, the field itself would be provided with more substance. Finally, this approach would move Black Studies beyond the minimal level of achievement articulated by Cornell's James Turner as being a stress on consolidation around similarity to higher, broader, and more diverse points of accomplishment.

This curricular and extracurricular specialization could be monitored by the National Council for Black Studies, the eight-year-old umbrella coordinating organization for the field. The National Council for Black Studies could compile a registry with program descriptions and emphases to be disseminated to collegiate institutions, secondary schools, and community organizations. The registry would supply valuable information which prospective college and university students could use as they formulate career choices in Black Studies and prepare for scholarly pursuits.

There is a concomitant need, as yet insufficiently satisfied, for dialogue and eventual establishment and dissemination of a well-developed, coherent and comprehensive philosophy of Afro-American education to which programs in Black Studies could subscribe and serve. Such a philosophy might institute and monitor standards to which any Afro-centric educational enterprise concerned with African-American group development would adhere. In so doing, it might also answer these crucial questions: What kind of education is needed for Black (and human) liberation? What would Black persons so educated think and how would they act? Could such persons be recognized if we saw them? In what settings would this education be dispensed?

Institutionalization and Legitimacy

Nine of the ten Black Studies directors interviewed in 1978-79 indicated that their programs were incorporated as relatively secure components of the institutions in which they were housed. In these cases, the battle for institutionalization, at least at the structural level, appears to have been won. The struggle for conceptual legitimacy, which is the handmaiden of institutionalization, continues, however. It is one thing for Black Studies to be tolerated in an institutional setting; for it to be accepted on par with other programs of study is another matter. Attitudinal opposition to Black Studies, no doubt, will be generally correlative with the perception and social status of Black people in American society. Moreover, resistance to Black Studies is exacerbated as present generations of students opt for a more narrow academic-vocational pragmatism. Students select course work and academic majors that they perceive as providing the greatest probability of leading directly to a job. Relative certainty of employment is a major consideration. Black Studies, for many of them, is, at worst, a waste of time or, at best, peripheral to the educated man/woman. The ignorance of or de-emphasis on Afrocentric learning is reinforced by the closing of ranks in the education industry around a neo-conservative educational fundamentalism that extols the virtues of teaching and acquisition of minimal competencies in more "conventional" core curricula. Hence, in the American education complex, the specific study of African-Americans as a critical component of the examination of the human experience still is not seen as a valid scholastic enterprise. This seems especially so when programmatic stress is placed upon Afro-centric relevance and social change which, even more so in the context of the Black experience, is often at cross purposes with the de facto ethos of collegiate institutions.

An institution, of course, is centered on the needs and desires of some person or group of persons around whose best interests it is organized. Much attention has been concentrated on the evolution of Black Studies in American collegiate institutions, white and Black. It must not be forgotten that an integral component of the African-American tradition of Afro-centric scholarship is that which historically has been located beyond the campus in community-based organizations.

When the needs of Black education are taken into account and when it is understood that Black Studies on Black and white campuses cannot alone satisfy all of the educational demands of Black liberation, one must conclude that a more comprehensive approach to the education of African-Americans is required. As part of an earlier discussion around the concept of a Black university, James R. Lawson, former resident of Fisk University, outlined the broad objectives of a Black education. His comments are pertinent here:

> Essentially, . . . the education of black Americans must encompass at least three objectives — . . . (1) an increased awareness and knowledge of their heritage and of the contributions they have made throughout history; (2) a motivation and ability to render much-needed assistance and services, of various kinds, to the total black community; and (3) the development of knowledge and skills necessary for gainful employment and satisfactory living in the larger ever-changing society. In terms of what is necessary for sustained upward economic and social mobility of black Americans, I think it meaningless, if not dangerous, to attempt to assign priorities as between these three objectives. . . . [9]

The basis for a systematic, holistic approach to African-American education can be found in Lawson's statement. Moreover, it is one that is philosophical and practically indispensable to the eventual resolution of the central dilemma of alternative Black education, that of producing a process of education for liberation. To repeat, the content of such an education cannot — and should not — wholly emanate from and reside in the normative institutions of higher learning. A multifaceted development of Black Studies is necessary in three arenas: (1) mainstream (white) colleges and universities, (2) traditionally Black collegiate institutions, and (3) alternative institutions that are based in the outside community. It stands to reason that for the foreseeable future, the Black presence In white schools will be felt in shifting degrees and it is in these institutions where most organized programs in Black Studies exist today. These schools cannot, then, be overlooked as a locus for development. It is a well-known fact that the majority of college-educated African-Americans are graduates of historically Black universities and colleges. This situation may persist for some time, notwithstanding the process of desegregation. With a ready-made pool of students and the rudiments, at least, for a more comprehensive servicing of Black educational needs, there is potential for these institutions to become more the centers of liberation-directed learning than they have been thus far. Black Studies programs in these settings ought to serve a supportive and catalytic role in this regard.

The patterns of social change in African-American culture will determine whether or not Black Studies will set the direction for the movement for Afro-centric

African-American education. Those currents are rooted in the larger community of Black people, not on the campus. Community-based institutions (such as cultural centers; community development organizations; agencies, clubs, and museums that have an Afro-centric agenda) help to give substance, form, and expression to those realities. This was the case with the creation of modern Black Studies which was fueled in the 1960s by the broader, more visible civil-rights phase of the Black liberation movement. It would be disastrous to rely exclusively on collegiate institutions, for all of their accumulated expertise, to provide the needed prescriptions for African-American education. It bears reemphasizing that these institutions must be involved in the motion toward African-American educational liberation. But when movements become institutionalized, at least in certain contexts, their originality, potency, and relevance tend to be decimated, if not lost, despite the continuing impact of innovations associated with them. Because community-centered institutions (a) might be free of certain debilitating dependencies, (b) may present better opportunity for control, and (c) could be most capable of passing on desirable cultural continuities, they serve a vital complementary function in any systematic attempt at African-American educational development that is campus-based.

Expansion

The Black Studies directors in our sample were asked about the expansion of their programs to other academic levels. Eight of the ten sampled could point to Black Studies having curricular ties to graduate studies at their institutional home and three directors said their programs had such a relationship at other institutions. Curricular linkages of Black Studies to secondary schools through teacher-training, consulting, and other arrangements at the host institution were reported in two cases, while five of the Black Studies programs had developed curricular ties on the secondary school level beyond the home institutional structure. In four instances, programs had Black Studies curricular ties to elementary schools. The data here suggests that Black Studies programs emanating from collegiate institutions remain very much enterprises in higher education.

As contrasted with an earlier period of proliferation—the number of schools providing Black Studies programs reached a high of about five hundred in 1971[10]—the number of such programs in 1984 has shrunk, according to National Council for Black Studies estimates, to approximately two hundred twenty-five. Attempts to dismantle numerous programs which have survived continue, a reality that was not lost on the administrators interviewed. The horizontal expansion of Black Studies—for the increase in the number of quality undergraduate programs—is seen as a given need.

However, of foremost importance for the future of Black Studies is the capacity of individual programs for vertical expansion toward the offering of the doctorate. Citing the lack of trained, qualified personnel, Joseph Russell, dean of Afro-American Affairs at Indiana University and executive director of the National Council for Black Studies, stated that there are not sufficient opportunities for graduate study to meet the demands for faculty in Black Studies. James Turner put the problem in even more urgent terms when he warned, "If the field is to survive and develop and thrive with any degree of significance in American higher education, there will have to be developed, at least at some places, Ph.D. level training." The terminal degree in Black

Studies would help to produce young scholars, attract good people into the field, and provide a reward for scholarly productivity. Across the country, some schools (such as UniversIty of California, Los Angeles, Yale, Ohio State, Wisconsin, and Cornell) offer a master's degree program in Black Studies.

Conclusions

While Black Studies clearly has not transformed American education as its early advocates ambitiously envisioned, some progress in the movement for Black Studies has been made. In its fifteen years of formalized existence Black Studies has had noticeable impact on higher education in the United States. With the appearance of Black Studies, the very nature of education in relationship to the total society once again came under serious scrutiny. Just as the larger Black liberation movement catalyzed activity against various facets of oppression, Black Studies gave rise to calls by other groups—Puerto Ricans, Mexican Americans, Asian Americans, Native Americans, white ethnics, women, and homosexuals—for scholastic treatment of their experiences. Indeed, Black Studies has been, in the words of William H. McClendon, "in the forefront for developing and strengthening the intellectual, social and political thought necessary for human liberation."[11]

Still, some pressing developmental problems and evaluative concerns persist in Black Studies which were not specifically dealt with in the scope of this essay. For example, will Black Studies continue as a separate field? Further, given recent and current restrictive trends in the labor market and the devaluation of a bachelor's degree in the liberal arts, social sciences, and related areas, what can be done to expand the possibilities for Black Studies graduates for the "gainful employment and satisfactory living" advocated by Lawson? These questions and others embody lingering critical issues to which subsequent research should be directed.

Whether Black Studies as we have known it can and will realize its larger aspirations of forwarding the legacy of the scholarly tradition from which it stems to its logical conclusion remains to be seen. The difficulties associated with advancing Black Studies are surpassed by the need to do so. To be remiss in continuing that struggle would be a catastrophe that we can ill afford, with consequences that future generations should not have to bear.

Endnotes

1. The tradition can be identified first through the "lone-wolf" achievements of individual scholars. It continues through the institutionalization and professionalization of the study of the Black experience through collective accomplishments such as the Atlanta University Studies from 1897 to 1910. Other examples of group efforts include the work of the American Negro Academy from 1897 to 1928 and the Association for the Study of Negro (now Afro-American) Life and History that is celebrating its 68th anniversary of continuous operation.

2. Examples of efforts to assess how Black Studies is perceived include works such as Nathan Hare, "The Contribution of Black Sociologists to Black Studies," in *Black Sociologists: Historical and Contemporary Perspectives*, ed. James Blackwell and Morris Janowitz (Chicago: University of Chicago Press, 1974), pp. 253-266; and Wilson Record, "Response of Sociologists to Black Studies," ibid., pp. 368-401.

3. Some of the published studies that sought to measure achievement in Black Studies are: Phillip Carey and Donald Allen, "Black Studies: Expectation and Impact on Self-Esteem and

Academic Performance," *Social Science Quarterly*, 57 (March 1977): 811-820; and James Newton, *A Curriculum Evaluation of Black Studies in Relation to Student Knowledge of Afro-American History and Culture* (San Francisco: R and E Research Associates, 1976).

4. See, for example, Charles V. Hamilton, "The Challenge of Black Studies," *Social Policy*, 1 (1970): 15-16; Inez Smith Reid, "Black Studies Programs: An Analysis," in *The Black Prism: Perspectives on the Black Experience*, ed. Inez Smith Reid (Proceedings of the Summer Institute in Afro-American Studies, Brooklyn College, City University of New York, June 10-12, 1969), pp. 181-188; and, Herman Hudson, "The Black Studies Program: Strategy and Structure," *Journal of Negro Education*, 41 (Fall 1972): 294-298.

5. Some of the works on the state of the field of Black Studies or its status at various junctures in its evolution are: Rhoda L. Goldstein, June T. Albert and Thomas F. Slaughter, Jr., "The Status of Black Studies Programs at American Colleges and Universities," Paper presented at the 67th Annual Meeting of the American Sociological Association, August 29, 1972; Nick Aaron Ford, *Black Studies: Threat or Challenge?* (Port Washington, NY: Kennikat Press, 1973); Elias Blake, Jr., and Henry Cobb, *Black Studies: Issues in Their Institutional Survival* (Washington, DC: Institute for Services to Education, 1976); Center for Minority Studies, Northern Illinois University, "A Report on the Status of Black Studies Programs in Midwestern Colleges and Universities," April 1977; and, Alan K. Colón, "A Critical Review of Black Studies Programs" (Ph.D. diss., Stanford University, 1980). Also see various articles in the Summer 1970 yearbook issue of *The Journal of Negro Education*.

6. Colón, "A Critical Review of Black Studies Programs."

7. Peoples College, Introduction to Afro-American Studies (Chicago: Peoples College Press, 1977).

8. Maulana Karenga, *Introduction to Black Studies* (Inglewood, CA: Kaivaida Publications, 1982).

9. James R. Lawson, "Black University Concept: Educators' Response," *Negro Digest*, 18 (March 1969): 66-67 + (68).

10. Martin Weston, "Black Studies: Dead or Alive?" *Essence*, 5 (August 1974): 57.

11. William H. McClendon, "Black Studies: Education for Liberation," *Black Scholar*, 6 (September 1974): 20.

46.

Critical Issues on Black Studies

Ronald Walters

Cooperation implies equality of the participation in the particular task at hand. On the contrary, however, the usual way now is for the whites to work out their plans behind closed doors, have them approved by a few Negroes serving nominally on a board, and then employ a white or mixed staff to carry out their programs. This is not interracial cooperation — it is merely the ancient idea of calling upon the "inferior" to carry out the orders of the "superior." [This should stop.]

Carter G. Woodson, 1933

Now that the Black Studies Movement has established some programmed effort at many universities, there begin to appear wide differences of opinion about the basic rationale for the undertaking in the black community (whites aside). Of the various attitudes toward Black Studies there can be said to be very extreme poles of opinion within the black community — those who feel that it is an embarrassment to the race and is most certainly doomed to produce a race of useless experts on "soul."

When the Black Studies Movement began, the reactionaries, black and white, were right in the forefront of the argument against establishing programs and departments on most campuses and one would have suspected that with the development of so many efforts in so many places, they would have settled down to find ways to most efficiently utilize them. In fact, the trend seemed to be going the other way. They seem more determined than ever, spurred on by a paranoid fear born of perceived dangers of "separatism," to malign efforts of the black community to control these centers, and to see to it that control is maintained by the white intellectual establishment — that same group which is responsible for the mess which has been made of the black intellectual tradition thus far. They are vigorously at work sponsoring conferences, informing on brothers and sisters to white boards of trustees, and publishing innocuous little pamphlets which, for all the names of the learned and wise men listed in their contents, bespeak of the most naked motives involved in the desire to salvage what is left of black middle-class connections to status in the eyes of whites, intellectuals and politicians.

The conservative message is one of caution, generally in the establishment of the academic effort in black studies and insofar as caution is needed and desired, it is not difficult to accede to this concept. But there are others who have left caution to prophesy the downfall of Black Studies by imputing characteristics to it that are really not evident. After all, where is the data, where is *one* class of graduates in the field, where is there a program which has been in operation so long that it has solidified the ideological and practical ground rules for its operation, and where, then, is the evidence for the prognoses of the conservative pundits? By such premature maligning, they may well be helping to stifle whatever viability some programs can muster; even those who would accept some of the criticisms they are suggesting may be hampered by whites who read and heed the mouthings of black reactionaries.

The radical pole of ideology in Black Studies, on the other hand, is growing farther and farther in the direction of orthodox African nationalism. In the year 1 of the Black Studies Movement, there was more or less wide agreement among blacks that the end purpose of black studies was to produce manpower and to heighten the level of political awareness for the black nation *in the United States*. For that reason most of the concern was manifested in the titles of the programs—Afro-American, although a few had, very early in the game, shown another level of activity, African and Afro-American, African and Caribbean Studies, etc. Now, however, some of the brothers involved in the independent black education movement are saying that it is the mission of black education to produce for the black nation, but they are talking about the only visible black nations that there are those in Africa.

This analysis continues with the thought that it has been proven by the Panthers that black people cannot protect themselves in this country and that therefore, nationhood is impossible under these circumstances when to have a nation at least requires that meager ability. Therefore, everything we do here should be temporary in nature and should point to the development of a really viable black nation outside America.

Although Black Studies has to be able to set priorities for black people, this particular view is really getting the Movement too far out in front of the people. I will not stand in the middle between these two ideological extremes because I too believe that we are all African peoples; I believe the end result of the Black Studies Movement will be international, but I also believe that the strongest component in Black Studies in this country must deal with the immediate realities of the everyday oppression of black people. We have a duty to be realistic about the goals of black studies, but we cannot determine what those will be without some assessment of what the goals of black people in America will be. True, those goals increasingly do not exist in isolation of the world of blackness, but much needs to be done to begin to clarify the dialogue between black peoples in the world before the negritude of Senghor and the common feeling we share can be turned into a living, working relationship for the masses.

And so we must not put off the necessity to deal with our real situation here in America and, if we must, validate the concept of nationhood in this unique context. It is time for us to analyze the meaning of the black revolution for blacks here in America now that we have read Blanqui, and Marx, and Debray, and Che Guevarra, and Fanon, Nkrumah and even Harold Cruse.

Commitment

What this new stage of the Black Studies Movement requires is a new level of commitment or perhaps the same level of commitment channeled into different directions.

The Black Studies leadership must not take white institutions so seriously that they will be deluded into believing that all things can be accomplished there. The main business of the liberation of black people requires the kind of education and programming that will come about outside of the control exercised upon us by white institutions. This implies two things which may seem contradictory but which are really one in the same strategy. For the present time we must continue to work inside white institutions under whatever black framework and measure of independence we can construct because for the foreseeable future, the masses of black students will be coming to those institutions. (Clarification: There has been some recent advice to black students not to support black studies in white institutions but the alternative, until black parents have reached a certain level of political and cultural awareness, is to count on them to send their sons and daughters to these schools. In such cases, not to have some Black Studies would be to leave these brothers and sisters at the mercy of the white machine again. Clarification: by masses of blacks I mean the masses. Once one gets beyond a small fraction of the population of black college age people, all the things that characterize the life style of the average black populations coming into these colleges no matter how rich it is.) At the same time we have a duty to see to it that there is continued movement toward the establishment of independent black educational centers and systems. This will require assisting the black community to develop meaningful relationships between some of the various structures within which black education in some form now takes place.

Some of the structures are:

Black Universities

Colleges or Schools of Black Studies

Schools of Third World Studies

Schools of Ethnic Studies

Autonomous Centers for Black Studies on campus

University Centers or Institutes for Black Studies

Urban Centers or Institutes for Black Studies

Departments of Black Studies

Programs of Black Studies

Courses within Departments on Black Studies

The question arises how can these structures be utilized? What follows are some Models for Supportive Service for Black Studies (taken from my paper on "Philosophical Concepts in Black Studies") based on the perceived necessity to blend Black Studies, Liberal Arts and Humanities emphasis with some emphasis in the technical or scientific studies.

A. Development of a Black University which would be composed of Liberal Arts, Humanities and the technical sciences with a specific mission to produce manpower for the black community.

B. Development of a Black Studies University with a primary orientation in many of the supportive services.

C. Development of Cross-registration systems between technical schools and traditional schools of Liberal Arts and Humanities that have Black Studies programs.

D. Development of Black Studies (Schools, Centers, Programs, etc.) within a University which Would be open to science majors and professional students as well.

E. Development of an autonomous center/institute for Black Studies that would serve several technical and professional schools.

F. Development of Black Studies programs within technical and scientific schools.

Since it may be possible to define a concept with respect not only to its genre (i.e., science or technology), but with respect not only in which it is utilized (i.e., in the service of black people) it is possible to describe those things as "black" which become primary tools to counter the application of racism upon.the black community.

It should be clear that in any choice of strategies to fulfill this mission, preference would be for the development of special supportive services within a framework of black control educational institutions which are committed to the black community and to radically new solutions for its development. However, in those places where there are no educational systems that fit the most desired model, it is the duty of the Black Studies leadership to utilize whatever they have while at the same time moving to try and establish the most correct institutions for our liberation.

It seems to me that students should also maintain the same level of seriousness about struggle which initially led them to agitate for the development of Black Studies. It is possible now to hear brothers and sisters saying that they must abandon Black Studies to move into the arena of direct confrontation with the system which exploits black people, and so they have carried the struggle to the labor unions and into the city—and that is good. But if the sustained struggle is perceived in terms of the necessity to act out the physical confrontation and to do the intellectual homework to make it pay off, then the relationship between instant and sustained success must come from strategies developed through Black Studies.

Of course, this does not even touch on the very urgent task of Black Studies which is to reconstruct the black intellectual tradition from the standpoint of black history and culture which is in some ways just as important. If we are concerned with sensitizing the masses and raising the level of black awareness so that by the time the black student gets to college, he has read Malcolm X and is ready to find ways to put him into practice, then we are directly concerned with the institutionalization of Black Studies in the black community.

Also, there is operating what one may call the "pay-off syndrome" that is, some black students conceive of Black Studies as a pay-off for their involvement in the struggle to the extent that it should be an easy place in white institutions which they can use somewhat like they would use a prostitute. But Black Studies should indeed be a pay-off, but in the sense that it is an opportunity to do the kind of creative analysis which the black experience has needed, the kind of truth which the black experience should lend to continuing struggles, and it should be part of the hope for showing people out of the depths of slavery and colonization. When looked at in this light, Black Studies requires more respect than one would give to the intellectual colonizers and much more work and sacrifice in order to make the promise of Black Studies a living reality for all black people.

The effort to construct viable systems of black education will fail unless the black community, at the level of the average brother and sister, believes in the capacity of black people to educate their own, and in the power of the group to define itself. That same energy and creativity which it took and which it still takes for everyday survival must be harnessed to bring about a more vigorous movement toward the creation of independent black institutions. One has to be impressed by the lesson of our African brothers and sisters in Africa, who, although per capita income is not more than $500 per year in most cases, believe that it is possible for economic development to come from the pennies they save. Perhaps they are misguided, and perhaps it only means that the pace of their development will be slower, but the most important lesson is that *they believe they can do it within the limits of whatever they have.* The knowledge that black people are the richest oppressed minority in the world leads me to believe that through sacrifice some measure of economic development is also possible within this colony.

We must discover better ways to utilize our money when it is known that most black people work and pay taxes, but only 2% of the state college population is black! Reparations are fine, but can they galvanize the masses to an awareness of the nature of their oppression? Will they last forever, or even long enough to sustain the reconstruction of the black community? In fact, if it is not watched very carefully, reparations may just be another form of neo-colonialism because it still is a dependent relationship. Reparations cannot liberate us: i.e., very recently students at Fisk University demanded that the administration cease receiving reparations from the Ford Foundation. Of course the University would not do this because it had become used to the dependent status. The relationship had not been conceived as one of the Foundation paying "reparations," but what is the difference! I am not suggesting that we enter into a new phase of black chauvinism and reject money which is sorely needed, but if it stands in the way of self-determination then it is profit from the slave ship.

Developing Issues Inside Black Studies

The internal struggle regardless of the structural assumptions under which Black Studies is operating is the tension between power and responsibility.

Many people have been struggling with the problem of trying to develop criteria for determining the viability of Black Studies programs which are springing up. May I suggest that besides the yard stick of the interactions between such programs and the black community, one might look inside the structure for keys to why that relationship is or is not viable. Inside the structure the ability of the entity to define itself and to control its operations should be the criteria of its viability and hence of its potential usefulness to black people. If it is able to name itself, if it is able to mount programs of study which will be relevant to the liberation of black people, then it has power. Some of this power is a result of the fact that the structure, i.e., school, center Department, etc., gives automatic access to higher levels of power within the institution. For example, if the Director of a program has to report to Department Head who has to report to a Dean of Faculty who has to report to the Dean of Faculties or Provost or Vice President for Academic Affairs who is ultimately responsible to the President, then one can see that there may be some political problems within the institution as communication from one level to another may end tip in delay, frustration and inaction. If such a Director has direct access to the Provost or the President then the messages, at least, stand a chance of being clearly understood. In some cases, the good politician may be successful in obtaining access to the decision-making levels of power no matter what status of the Black Studies entity itself. This too is power.

Now that one has access what is there to give some assurance of the fact that access will indeed result in action in the direction of that desired by the black constituency. There are two main determinants of power if one has access, they are money and/or support in numbers of people. Some Black Studies programs have adequate budgets and no black control; in those cases the Director will always be going to whites for approval and clearance. Others have control and no money; this still leads to a situation of dependence and the cases are rare indeed that Black Studies in any institution has the necessary money and control in order to make them viable.

Perhaps the most necessary determinant of power within the context of Black Studies is the support of Black people in the immediate black community. The only reason why white institutions of higher education have given up any power at all is the threat of organized confrontation by black people. This power is what has enabled some Black Studies programs to define the substance of their curriculum without difficulty from the white power structure, and this is the power that will keep Black Studies viable with or without money. One implication here is that the Black Studies community needs to constantly keep before it the imperative for unity and the familyhood as organizing principles. Another is the only reason why so many black faculty and administrators are in their positions can be traced directly to the struggle of black students. Their responsibility, therefore, is one of serving the fundamental interest of the black community on campus.

Looking for a moment at the needs of the brothers and sisters in the immediate black community who will shoulder much of the success or failure for Black Studies, one must understand the necessity to see to it that they are in every way prepared to execute their responsibility. Responsiveness to their needs dictates an acute sensitivity to their individual abilities and desires and, therefore, the construction of systems of learning out of the traditional mode of operation which might include:

1. Construction of systems of learning with students.
2. Abolishing rigid distinctions between teacher and student and moving to the simple concept of "class leader."
3. Asking each one to teach one.
4. Posting standards of excellence that have to do with one's contribution to the community as well as knowledge of the subject.
5. Realizing that we cannot wait for graduate students and professors to do all the basic research.
6. Greater utilization of black educational resources such as Topographical centers, Community Newspapers, resource personnel from various organizations, etc.
7. Realizing the value of Home Study (field experience) in every class situation.
8. Greater utilization of the experiential variables of members of the black community in teaching and learning.
9. Conscious development of black values.
10. Validate oral tradition.

This brief, suggestive list has some implications which need exploration and which relate to the two knotty problems of evaluation and supportive assistance.

How will you evaluate students within this framework since the aim of it clearly points the way to a new type of humanity? One of the great problems here is to devise a balance between non-punitive types of educational systems and yet retain enough discipline so that the end product is worthy of the mission of Black Studies. I believe it is important that Black Studies not merely constitute itself as one more addition of the punitive instruments which operate against black students and which therefore, more often than not threaten their very survival in the institution. There is something to be said for people who survive systems of institutionalized racism; other blacks have survived them, but once out they have displayed the type of humanity toward other black people which has been characteristic of the institution itself. How do we help black students survive and develop a different type of humanity toward other black people? Is competition which is nourished in the institution perhaps the key ingredient which produces the individual-oriented person? One strategy suggests itself which has wide ramifications and that is to evaluate not only one's ability for written understanding of a subject, but one's attitude toward it. (Nothing new here is there!) One of the things this does is to put some of the onus on the class leader to perform at a high level of competence, helping to instill and develop within other class members some sense of the new humanity *and* the information for their liberation. I am suggesting a "wholistic" approach to the evaluation of class members which has to do with their intellectual and human characteristics.

What happens when you find in these evaluations a number of brothers and sisters who are not able to deal with the information or the humanity? Dealing with one man's humanity and sense of identity and commitment is difficult because there are not guidelines, one can only hope that this happens in the process of enlightenment and in the establishment of personal relationships. The question of the information, however, is a bit different and in many ways relates to concrete skills which brothers and sisters do or do not possess; the problem, therefore, becomes one of trying to make up for a life time of neglect. Let us be very clear: *brothers and sisters need to learn to deal with the information on a high level of understanding within the parameters of their existence as black people using oral and written methods.*

One aspect of supportive assistance is financial in the sense that some brothers and sisters must hold down jobs which keep them from studies. This is an especially critical issue at a time when people in high places are demeaning "open admission" (they really mean black admissions) and saying that it won't work because any extra addition of blacks means that they have to increase the amount of financial assistance to them and they don't have it. Some say they have it but are worried about their institutions being composed of rich whites and poor blacks at the expense of aid to poor whites. It should be made clear that black people have been kept out of these institutions because of racial quotas (even for the so-called qualified) so that some reparation is due black people on the same grounds — their blackness! In addition, black students do not see themselves arrayed against poor whites, but against the whole population of white people who inhabit those institutions, and that in any choice, the universities should find additional aid money to bring in extra numbers of poor whites, Chinese, Indian, Eskimo, Malayan, Turkish, and etc., if it wants to keep up its responsibility to black people. If it does not, why play games? It is not the job of the federal government, but the job of those liberal educational institutions who claim they are for "equal educational opportunity" until it comes time to pay.

Other kinds of supportive assistance is needed which will dramatically increase basic skills in reading and writing. There has been a rash of special programs aimed at these problems such as Upward Bound, Transitional Year Programs, and others. The university has a responsibility to see to it that they work and that they do not become merely revolving doors for blacks, letting us in to be flunked out a little later. One is sensitive to the attitude of black students that to partake of these special services puts them in a special caste, but in terms of their ultimate mission to be of service to their communities in some way, it is jiving to be in the institution and not to want to significantly increase one's capability to deal on an intellectual level. If they don't, what will they be able to offer besides a decent rap? We should, then, admit these deficiencies to the society which has produced them and charge them with the responsibility for acting on them in some viable way.

Outside the structure and function of the Black Studies on the campuses, there are some indications that there is indeed a movement of international and national significance to wrest the control of black education from the intellectual colonizers.

One indication of such a movement is the growth of centers of education and research such as Malcolm X College in Chicago, Center for Black Education in Washington, Malcolm X Liberation University in Durham, N.C., the Institute of the Black World in Atlanta, the Black World Foundation in San Francisco, Topographical Centers in Chicago and Boston. In one sense the growth of such new institutions should give some cause for rejoicing because the strength of the image points to the beginnings of the validation of the black experience on a wide scale with some indications of permanence.

On the other hand, the insidiousness of the white establishment is hard at work pouring a great deal of money into those other institutions which it has selected to represent its own interest in the developing field of Black Studies. Such that, in the same city one is able to find one viable black research institute being challenged for leadership by another group which has newly acquired its share of the white man's money and support. Clearly, there needs to be some emphasis coordination of resources and some mutual support for black efforts whether they are in the same city or across the country.

Another manifestation of the Movement is the attacks which have been launched upon the white professional intellectual organizations by black caucuses of political scientists, sociologists, historians, etc. They are challenging the personnel practices which have kept blacks out of University positions, they are challenging the strangle hold which whites have over the research and teaching about black people and they are challenging the value assumptions implicit in the methodologies themselves as they have operated to distort the black experience. This clearly is a Movement and whether or not it results in greater integration into these existing groups, as some would argue, one would hope that the awareness which created these confrontations on the part of black intellectuals would lead them to invest their energies into areas and organizations where they can be both black and professional with meaning.

Perhaps the most vivid indication that there is indeed a movement (aside from mere professionalism) that aims directly at the colonization of black history and culture by whites are the recent confrontations which have occurred in Birmingham and in Montreal in October of 1969.

The Association for the Study of Negro Life and History met in October at Birmingham, Alabama and was immediately confronted by younger brothers and sisters demanding that the association begin to address itself to the needs of black people by seeking positively to develop an interpretation of history and culture from which would spring the black perspective. The Association was also challenged to develop a policy that would favor black leadership in black education. It was charged that the organization had been co-opted by whites, from those who were permitted to give papers to those who controlled publishing manuscripts in the *Journal of Negro History* and in the establishment presses. The organization was challenged to live up to the precepts of its founder, Dr. Carter G. Woodson who long ago cautioned blacks, from slipping into positions of white co-optation of black history and culture:

...Negroes who think as the author does and dare express themselves are branded as opponents of interracial cooperation. As a matter of fact, Negroes are the real workers in carrying out a program of interracial effort. Cooperation implies equality of the participants in the particular task at hand. On the contrary, however, the usual way now is for the whites to work out their plans behind closed doors, have them approved by a few Negroes serving nominally on a board, and then employ a white or mixed staff to carry out their program. This is not interracial cooperation. It is merely the ancient idea of calling upon the "inferior" to carry out the orders of the "superior." ("The Mis-Education of the Negro," Carter G. Woodson, Associated Publishers, 1933, p. 29)

And also:

...if the men who are to administer them and teach in them (universities to be established for blacks in Washington, Atlanta, Nashville, and New Orleans) are to be the products of roll-top desk theorist who have never touched the life of the Negro, the money thus invested will be just as profitably spent if it is used to buy peanuts to throw at the animals in a circus. (Ibid., p. 31)

Today the men who spout the platitudes of interracial cooperation with blacks in the study of black history and culture and the theorist from the "roll-top desks" are hard at work picking and choosing over the meat of our heritage. They sit on boards of editors and decide which black manuscripts are published, they edit journals, write book reviews and generally, sit astride many of the papers and documents of famous black figures blocking their use by *black* scholars—and they are making a fortune! And all the while it is difficult to hear the criticism from our so-called responsible organizations like ASNLH, of course it is when either official or unofficial sanction is implied by cooperation—Woodson style.

The charge given this organization was to begin to speak out and disengage themselves from these practices, to open up the *Journal of Negro History* to the pens of black scholars, to assist in the development of young black scholars by giving them *preference* in the presentation of papers and research assistance, and to generally begin to be more visible in the struggle for black control of black education. *Africa Today*, October/November/ December 1969 issue; for a good treatment of the nature and origin of the confrontation, see *Pan-African Journal*, Vol. 1, No. 4, pp. 161-2.

This issue was raised to another level of confrontation a week later in Montreal, Canada, when, at the meeting of the African Studies Association, blacks again challenged the system of intellectual exploitation by effectively shutting down the conference. Details of this action are available in January 1970 editions of *Africa Report*, and in African Studies Bulletin. The *Pan-African Journal* is an example of "open door" policy to pens and preferences of Black scholars. Yet while it does maintain this policy, it lacks funding due to the fact that its aim is to promote Black creativity and scholarship and destroy "white traditional academia." It is well to note that this action had national implications because a black organization, the African Heritage Studies Association, was born and shows signs of having the potential to create a black framework for the development and reconstruction of the black intellectual tradition. It also had international ramifications in that many members of the black caucus were from Europe, Africa, Asia and the Caribbean and were sensitized to the necessity to carry this struggle with them to their home grounds.

Maybe now that there are some budding black institutions which are beginning to attempt the job of coordinating curricular planning providing research and teaching resources, giving evaluations of programs, there should be a slow-down in the number of conferences. Every month there are two or three poorly-run, poorly-attended sessions which all promise follow-through and do not deliver (basically because they are not set up to do so) and at which, consequently, there is endless duplication of time, effort and money. Maybe now we can begin to more closely coordinate our moves and begin to support the most viable efforts and generally move in the direction of some consensus on matters of philosophy, ideology and tactics which must be if we are to carry out the legacies which those who struggled so bravely in phase I of the Black Studies Movement have a right to expect fulfilled.

47.

Black Studies: Trouble Ahead

Eugene D. Genovese

No problem so agitates the campuses today as that posed by the growing pressure for black studies programs and departments. The agitation presents special dangers since it can be, and sometimes is, opportunistically manipulated by the nihilist factions of the radical white student movement. For the most part, black students have shown considerable restraint in dealing with dubious white allies and have given strong indication of being much more interested in reforming the universities than in burning them down. The black student movement, like some parts of the white radical student movement and very much unlike others, represents an authentic effort by young people to take a leading role in the liberation of an oppressed people as such, exhibits impressive seriousness and developing sophistication. The political forms that the agitation takes and the deep frustrations from which it stems nonetheless open the way to reckless elements among black, as well as white, student militants.

The universities must now choose among three courses: a principled but flexible response to legitimate black demands; a dogmatic, repressive adherence to traditional, liberal, and essentially racist policies; and a cowardly surrender to all black demands, no matter how destructive to the university as an institution of higher learning or to American and Afro-American society in general. This last option, which, has been taken in a notable number of places, ironically reflects as much racism in its assumptions and implications as the second, and it takes little skill in prophecy to realize that its conclusion will be a bloodbath in which blacks are once again the chief victims. Yet, the debate over black studies proceeds without attention to the major features of the alternatives; it proceeds, in fact, in a manner that suggests the very paternalistic white racism against which, so many blacks are today protesting.

The demand for black studies and for special black studies departments needs no elaborate explanation or defense. It rests on awareness of the unique and dual nature of the black experience in the United States. Unlike European immigrants, blacks came here involuntarily, were enslaved and excluded from access to the mainstream of American life, and as a result have had a special history with a profoundly national-cultural dimension. Unlike, say, Italo-Americans, Afro-Americans have within their history the elements of a distinct nationality at the same time that they have participated in and contributed immensely to a common American nationality. Despite the efforts of many black and some white scholars, this paradoxical experience has yet to be explored with the respect and intellectual rigor it deserves.

This essential justification for black studies, incidentally, raises serious questions about the demands by white radicals for "ethnic studies" and for special attention to people from the "third world," especially since the term "third world" is, from a Marxist and revolutionary point of view, a reactionary swindle. These demands, when sincere, have their origin in a proper concern for the fate of Mexican-Americans, Puerto Ricans, Asians, and other ethnic groups in a white-racist culture, but the study of the attendant problems does not, at least on the face of it, require anything like an approach similar to that of black studies. For the most part, the discrimination against these groups is largely a class question, requiring sober analysis of class structure in America; for the rest, much of the racism directed against these minorities can be traced directly to the by-products of the enslavement of blacks by whites and the ideology derived therefrom. In any case, the issues are clearly different, for the black question is simultaneously one of class and nationality (not merely minority ethnic status), and it is therefore a disservice to the cause of black liberation to construct a politically opportunist equation that can only blur the unique and central quality of the black experience in the United States.

The duality of the black experience haunts the present debate and leads us immediately into a consideration of the ideological and political features of the black studies programs. It is, at best, irrelevant to argue, as DeVere E. Pentony does in the April 1969 issue of the *Atlantic*, that all professors of history and social science bring a particular ideology and politics to their classroom and that a black ideological bias is no worse than any other. There is no such thing as a black ideology or a black point of view. Rather there are various black-nationalist biases, from left-wing versions such as that of the Panthers to right-wing versions such as that of Ron Karenga and other "cultural nationalists." There are also authentic sections of the black community that retain conservative, liberal, or radical, integrationist and antinationalist positions. Both integrationist and separatist tendencies can be militant or moderate, radical or conservative (in the sense generally applied to white politics in relation to social questions). The separatists are riding high today, and the integrationists are beating a retreat; but this has happened before and may be reversed tomorrow.

All these elements have a right to participate in the exploration of black historical and cultural themes. In one sense, the whole point of black studies programs in a liberal arts college or university ought to be to provide for the widest and most vigorous exchange among all these groups in an atmosphere of free discussion and mutual toleration. The demand for an exclusively black faculty and especially the reactionary demand for student control of autonomous departments must be understood as demands for the introduction of specific ideological and political criteria into the selection of faculty and the composition of programs. Far from being proposals to relate these programs to the black community, they are in fact factionally based proposals to relate them to one or another political tendency within the black community and to exclude others. The bloody, but by no means isolated, feud between black student factions on the UCLA campus ought to make that clear.

One of the new hallmarks of white racism is the notion of one black voice, one black experience, one black political community, one black ideology — of a black community without an authentic inner political life wracked by discussion and ideological struggle. In plain truth, what appears on the campuses as "what the blacks want" is almost invariably what the dominant faction in a particular black caucus wants. Like all people who fight for liberation, blacks are learning the value of organizational discipline and subordination to a firm and united line of action. Sometimes, the formulation of particular demands and actions has much less to do with their intrinsic merits or with the institution under fire than with the momentary balance in the struggle for power within the caucus itself. This discipline presents nothing unprincipled or sinister, but it does present difficult and painful problems, which must be evaluated independently by those charged with institutional and political responsibility in the white community.

The pseudo-revolutionary middle-class totalitarians who constitute one temporarily powerful wing of the left-wing student movement understand this dimension, even if few others seem to. Accordingly, they support demands for student control as an entering wedge for a general political purge of faculties, a purge they naïvely hope to dominate. These suburban putschists are most unlikely to succeed in their stated objectives of purging "reactionaries," for they are isolated, incoherent, and without adequate power. But they may very well help to reestablish the principle of the campus purge and thereby provide moral and legal basis for a new wave of McCarthyism. The disgraceful treatment of Professors Staughton Lynd and Jesse Lemisch, among many who have been recently purged from universities by both liberal and right-wing pressure, has already set a tone of renewed repression, which some fanatical and unreasoning left-wing militants are unwittingly reinforcing. If black studies departments are permitted to become political bases and cadre-training schools for one or another political movements, the door will be open for the conversion of other departments to similar roles; that door is already being forced in some places.

Those blacks who speak in harsh nationalist accents in favor of all-black faculties, departmental autonomy, and student power open themselves to grave suspicions of bad faith. The most obvious objection, raised sharply by several outstanding black educators in the South, concerns the systematic raiding of black colleges by financially stronger white ones. The shortage of competent black specialists in black history, social science, and black culture is a matter of general knowledge and concern. Hence, the successful application of the all-black principle in most universities would spell the end of hope to build one or more distinguished black universities to serve as a center for the training of a national Afro-American intelligentsia. One need not be partial to black nationalism in any of its varieties to respect the right of black people to self-determination, for this right flows directly from the duality of their unique experience in the United States. Even those who dislike or distrust black nationalism as such should be able to view the development of such centers of higher education as positive and healthy. If there is no place in the general American university for ideological homogeneity and conformity, there is a place in American society for universities based on adherence to a specific ideology, as the Catholic universities, for example, have demonstrated.

Responsible black scholars have been working hard for an end to raiding and to the scattering of the small number of black professors across the country. Among other obstacles, they face the effort of ostensibly nationalist black students who seek to justify their decision to attend predominantly white institutions, often of high prestige, by fighting for a larger black teaching staff. The outcome of these demands is the obscurantist nonsense that black studies can and should be taught by people without intellectual credentials since these credentials are "white" anyway. It is true that many black men are capable of teaching important college-level courses even though they do not have formal credentials. For example, the Afro-American tradition in music, embracing slave songs, spirituals, blues, jazz, and other forms, could probably be taught best by a considerable number of articulate and cultured, if sometimes self-taught, black musicians and free-lance critics who are largely unknown to the white community. But few good universities have ever refused to waive formalities in any field which genuine intellectual credentials of nonacademic order could be provided. What has to be resisted firmly is the insanity that claims, as in one recent instance, that experience as a SNCC field organizer should be considered more important than a Ph.D. in the hiring of a professor of Afro-American history. This assertion represents a general contempt for all learning and a particular contempt for black studies as a field of study requiring disciplined, serious intellectual effort—an attitude that reflects the influence of white racism, even when brought forth by a black man.

The demand for all-black faculties rests on the insistence that only blacks can understand the black experience. This cant is nothing new: it forms the latest version of the battle cry of every reactionary nationalism and has clear antecedent, for example, in the nineteenth-century German Romantic movement. To be perfectly blunt, it now constitutes an ideologically fascist position and must be understood as such. The general reply to it — if one is necessary — is simply that the history of every people can only be written from within and without. But there is a specific reply too. However, much the black presence has produced a unique and distinctly national Afro-American experience, it has also formed part of a broader, integrated national culture. It would be absurd to try to understand the history of, say, the South without carefully studying black history. Any Southern historian worth his salt must also be a historian of black America — and vice versa — and if so, it would be criminal to deny him an opportunity to teach his proper subject. Certainly, these remarks do not add up to an objection to a preference for black departmental directors and a numerical predominance of blacks on the faculty, if possible, for every people must write its own history and play the main role in the formation of its own intelligentsia and national culture. These measures would be justified simply on grounds of the need to establish relations of confidence with black students, for they involve no sacrifice of principle and do not compromise the integrity of the university. But preference and emphasis are one thing; monopoly and ideological exclusion are quite another.

We might mention here the problem of the alleged "psychological need" of black people to do this or that or to be this or that in order to reclaim their manhood, reestablish their ostensibly lost dignity, and God knows what else. There is a place for these questions in certain kinds of intellectual discussions and in certain political forums, but there is no place for these questions in the formation of university policy. In such a context they represent a benevolent paternalism that is neither more or less than racist. Whites in general and university professors and administrators in particular are not required to show "sympathy," "compassion," "understanding," and other manifestations of liberal guilt feelings, they are required to take black demands seriously — to take them straight, on their merits. That is, they are required to treat political demands politically and to meet their responsibility to fight white racism while also meeting their responsibility to defend the integrity and dignity of the university community as a whole.

Only if the universities have a clear attitude toward themselves will they be able to fulfill their duty to the black community. Our universities, if they are to survive — and their survival is problematical — must redefine themselves as institutions of higher learning and firmly reject the role of cadre-training schools for government, business, or community organizations of any kind. Blame for the present crisis ought to be placed on those who, especially after World War II, opened the universities to the military, to big-business recruitment, to the "fight against Communism," to the CIA, and to numerous other rightist pressures. If Dow Chemical or ROTC belongs on a college campus, so does the Communist Party, the Black Panthers, the John Birch Society, the Campfire Girls, or the Mafia for that matter. Students have a clear political right to organize on campuses as Democrats, Republicans, Communists, Panthers, or whatever, provided their activities are appropriate to campus life, but the universities have no business making special institutional arrangements with this or that faction off campus and then putting down other factions as illicit. And government and business represent political intrusions quite as much as do political parties. The same is true for the anachronistic and absurd practice of having American universities controlled by boards of trustees instead of by their faculties in consultation with the students. In short, the black studies question, like the black revolt as a whole, has raised all the fundamental problems of class power in American life, and the solutions will have to run deep into the structure of the institutions themselves.

What the universities owe to black America is what they owe to white America: an atmosphere of freedom and dissent for the pursuit of higher learning. Black people have largely been excluded in the past, for the atmosphere has been racist, the history and culture of black people have been ignored or caricatured, and access to the universities themselves has been severely circumscribed. Black studies programs, shaped in a manner consistent with such traditional university values as ideological freedom and diversity, can help to correct this injustice. So can scholarships and financial assistance to black students and special facilities for those blacks who wish to live and work with some degree of ethnic homogeneity. But no university is required to surrender its basic standards of competence in the selection of faculty or the admission of students. If not enough black students are equipped to enter college today, it is because of atrocious conditions in lower education. The universities can take a few steps to correct this injustice, but the real fight must take place elsewhere in society and must be aimed at providing black communities with the financial resources, independence, and autonomy necessary to educate their people properly from the earliest appropriate ages. There are limits to what a particular institution like a university can do, and it dare not try to solve problems that can be solved only by the political institutions of society as a whole. And above all, university need surrender its historical role and essential content in order to right the wrongs of the whole political and social system; it need only reform itself to contribute to a solution of the broader problems in a manner consistent with its character as a place of higher learning with limited functions, possibilities, and responsibilities.

Black studies programs have two legitimated tasks. First, they can, by their very nature, provide a setting within which black people can forge an intelligentsia equipped to provide leadership on various levels of political and cultural action. Black studies programs themselves can do only part of this job. For that reason many able and sophisticated sections of the Black Student Alliance organizations wisely call on their brothers and sisters to participate in these programs but also to specialize in medicine, engineering, sociology, economic analysis, or in fact any scientific or humanistic field. They know that only the emergence of a fully developed intelligentsia, with training in every field of knowledge, can ultimately meet the deepest needs of the black community. In this respect, notwithstanding strong elements of nihilism in their own organizations, their seriousness, maturity, discipline, and realism stand in striking contrast to the childish anti-intellectualism of those bourgeois whites who currently claim to speak for the radical student movement and who impose upon it their own version of generational revolt.

Second, black studies can help immeasurably to combat the racism of white students. The exclusion of whites from the faculty and student body of the black studies programs would therefore defeat half the purpose of the programs themselves. Undoubtedly, there are problems. To the extent that black students view these courses as places of refuge where they can rap with their brothers, they are certain to resent the white presence, not to mention a possible white numerical predominance among the student body. Black students who want all exclusively black setting are entitled to it—in a black university. They are not entitled to tear any institution apart to suit their present mood. The universities owe black people a chance to get a liberal or technical education, but that debt can only be paid in a way consistent with the proper role of the university in society. Beyond that, no university may safely go. If it tries, the result can only be the end of any worthwhile higher education. The inability of so many radical whites to grasp this obvious point is especially galling. It ought to be obvious that the elite schools will protect themselves from this kind of degradation, even if they continue to accept the degradation that accompanies complicity with the war machine and with big business. It is the others — the ones serving the working-class and lower-middle-class youth — that will perish or be transformed into extensions of low-grade high schools. Universities must resist the onslaught now being made against them by superficially radical bourgeois students who have exploited the struggles over black studies programs to advance their own tactical objectives. Fortunately, these elements do not speak or the radical student movement as a whole but represent only a tendency within it; the internal diversity of organizations like SDS, for example, far exceeds the level revealed in the press.

No matter how painful some of the battles are or will become, the advent of black studies programs represents a momentous step toward the establishment of relations of equality between white and black intellectuals. But, if these programs are to realize their potential in support of black liberation and in the fostering of genuinely free and critical scholarship, our universities must resolve honestly the questions of limits and legitimacy. Those who blindly ignore or cynically manipulate these questions, and the reforms they imply, corrupt the meaning of black studies and risk the destruction of institutions necessary to the preservation of freedom in American life.

48.

White Experts, Black Experts, and Black Studies*

Pat M. Ryan

"The mad scramble in recent year to include the Negro in American history has resulted in some rather ludicrous steps taken by historians and publishers."

John Hope Franklin[1]

"Didn't you know that Moby Dick was a *black* whale?"

from *The Harangues*, by Joseph A. Walker[2]

Since I am addressing a community of scholars, I have begun with two epigraphs—whose point is not the impugned excesses of either black political nationalism or black revolutionary cultural consciousness. Their relevance has to do with the distance that so-called "black studies" have come during the last five years; and they partly signify the premise, now at issue, that only a black person can *feel*, or "tell it like it is." Their point involves the adjustment problems lately encountered by both "white experts" and "black experts." But this nomenclature is not of my own coinage: some will recognize it is bad-mouthing of the man, angry talk from the pages *of Negro Digest*.[3] "White experts" is a pejorative.

It's one thing for *black* poet Don L. Lee to write something—"Don't Cry, Scream!"—which ironically notices misspelled words in the *Chicago Daily, Defender* (black); but it's a very different thing for a *non-black* professor, William Loren Katz, to write a put-down of the *Negro Heritage Library*. And the fact that he did this in the *non-black* magazine *Saturday Review* involves still another subtle difference. Katz complained that the initial volumes of the *Negro Heritage Library* (black) weren't really reference books at all—that they were not, as he had hoped, a black encyclopedia:

> One of the most serious faults of the Negro Heritage Library is its inadequate writing and editing...The attempt to oversimplify is often a failure...It is disheartening to find this first Negro encyclopedia so handsome in format and illustrations, yet so carelessly constructed intellectually.[4]

Well, I agree with him, though in doing so I realize I am expressing a predictably *non-black* point of view. And I would extend this criticism to much of the ten-volume *International Library of Negro Life and History* (predominantly black).[5] But William Loren Katz has compounded the problem—he has become part of the problem, not the solution.

---

* An expanded (and documented) version of remarks presented in a Black Studies Symposium at Canisius College, Buffalo, April 3, 1970, under auspices of the Northeast Modern Language Association.

Thanks partly to his articles in *Saturday Review*, he became "editor" of Arno Press' (*The New York Times*) multi-volume series, *The American Negro: His History and Literature*, still proliferating into the marketplace. The black editors and publishers of *Negro Heritage Library* and the *International Library of Negro Life and History*, in my view, have both produced works of restricted usefulness as reference tools. These expensive sets are largely scrapbooks, or commonplace books, miscellanies of articles and documents—often simply anthologies, without adequate indexing or bibliographical apparatus. But "white expert" Katz's performance is also disappointing, since he has given his name to an expensive reprint series—not a reference work. Arno Press even removes the original bibliographical data—place, publisher, and date—from these reprints; and until recently, when this publisher began to issue some titles in paperback, only libraries could really afford to buy the series. *Non-black* Arno Press is making money; but the job of producing a *black* encyclopedia is about where W.E.B. DuBois and Guy B. Johnson (*et al.*) left it in 1945, with their preparatory volume for an *Encyclopedia of the Negro*, sponsored by the Phelps Stokes Fund. There are of course several other reprint series, most of them costly; and *Time*, in its "Black America 1979" issue (April 6, 1970), pointedly complained that "The educational market has been fed mainly with reprints (of black books)."

Johnson Publishing Company's *Negro Handbook*[6] (*black*-edited by *Ebony*) is seriously inadequate to the present needs of developing Afro-American studies programs; and on this most black and non-black scholars tend to agree. This book, five years old, is now woefully outdated. Its major competitors, Irving J. Sloan's *The American Negro*[7] and Harry A. Ploski and Roscoe C. Brown, Jr.'s *Negro Almanac*,[8] manage only to pick up some of the slack. (For one thing, there is still urgent need for a competent and comprehensive biographical dictionary—not simply a mug-book of anyone who happens to be canvassed and sends in his photograph and bio sheet.) But John P. Davis' *American Negro Reference Book*,[9] in two volumes, ranks far below any of the three works just cited: its title is a misnomer, for it is actually a miscellaneous anthology of articles, rather than a systematic reference book. One cannot "look up" anyone in Davis' *Negro Reference Book*.

There are, happily, some excellent specialized bibliographic tools recently in print—notably Earle H. West's meticulous *Bibliography of Doctoral Research on the Negro 1933-1966*[10] and Darwin T. Turner's impressive *Goldentree Bibliography of Afro-American Writers*.[11] More good news is that Dudley Randall, of Broadside Press, is compiling a bio-bibliography of Broadside poets,[12] and that Charles Evans, editor of the compendious thirteen-volume *American Bibliography*, is currently preparing an index to black American poetry published in anthologies.

Last year, when the *International Library of Negro Life and History* was published, the *Journal of American History* (*non-black*) cited it with approval,[13] but did not then review it. The series just wasn't "scholarly" enough. *Negro Heritage Library*, on the other hand, did not even warrant mention. Yet Ernest Kaiser (*black*) reviewed this latter set favorably; and in a series of provocative review-essays in *Freedomways*[14] he has carefully covered the gradually emerging field of black reference tools. He has even written a piece on "The Negro Heritage Library and Its Critics," in which he takes Katz to task (unjustly, I think) for not having done some of his homework. What troubles me is that Kaiser, in another essay, severely puts down the work of three non-black researchers, Elizabeth Miller, Erwin A. Salk, and Erwin K. Welch[15] (who can do almost nothing right), while commending the industry of three unnamed black women responsible for *Bibliographic Survey: The Negro in Print*: "a very valuable and useful history." But *Bibliographic Survey* turns out to be fragmentary, color-blind, and hit-and-miss, at a time when authorial blackness is vitally important to black pride.[16] The truth is, I now believe, that Ernest Kaiser and *Freedomways* and its editor John Hendrik Clarke, are indulging in black revolutionary paternalism (if such a thing is possible): they are losing their editorial-scholarly cool and indulging in the game of "black experts versus white experts," by the rules set down by Hoyt W. Fuller and *Negro Digest*. What they condone in black writers they condemn in non-black ones. I find *Bibliographic Survey: The Negro in Print* mediocre at best; and neither I nor my black and non-black students have been able to rely on this, or any other black serial bibliography currently available.

The dilemma from the black side of things needs to be stated: when one is waging a revolution, and fighting to win it, he doesn't have the luxury of being polite. Nobody wants to be a polite, dead black revolutionary. It is time to realize that there *is* this revolution, even among the "harmless drudges," the bibliographers.

Ernest Kaiser does not spare black authors. He was particularly harsh with Harold Cruse's *The Crisis of the Negro Intellectual*[17] recently (an eighteen-page essay in the Winter 1969 *Freedomways*).[18] And for abrasiveness he is more than matched by Eugene D. Genovese (*non-black*), chairman of the History Department at the University of Rochester, who makes a career of baiting and infuriating black scholars and engaging them (and also liberal non-black authors) in debate. Lately, he has been squaring off against black historian John Henrik Clarke and non-black Marxist historian Herbert Aptheker in particular; and in an essay published last year in the *New York Review of Books*, he asserted:

> In the past, southern history and culture have been the special provice of white southerners; with a few important exceptions ... northern white scholars have been blinded by self-righteousness whereas blacks have largely restricted themselves to those problems which bear most directly on their own people, (thought) John Hope Franklin and a few other black historians ... have refused to limit themselves to "black" subjects.[19]

Most readers might regard this statement as objective, fair-minded, and valid. But Genovese is *non-black*; and while he implicitly badgers Aptheker (for "cause"), his own "Sambo" posture is calculated to distress both black and liberal non-black scholars alike. Genovese is a professional polarizer.[20]

It would be unfair to say that Kaiser (*black*) and Genovese (*non-black*) thrive on controversy. It would be more accurate to say that American scholarship thrives on the controversy that these men — "black expert" and "white expert" — provoke. To have read William Styron's *The Confessions of Nat Turner*[21] without also having read John Henrik Clarke[22] and Herbert Aptheker,[23] or to have read Clarke and Aptheker without Genovese's rejoinders, or to have read Cruse's book without also having noticed Kaiser's review, is to be merely playing at "black studies" — or faking it.

The trouble with Genovese's statement, just quoted, is its painful implication that neither black or non-black scholars have long enjoyed the latitude of sustained research in the black history/literature field. As most of us should be poignantly aware, "black studies" have attracted public attention and institutional support only during the past half dozen years. It is — not alone an evolving field of scholarship — now big business.

This field is not new, of course.

As early as 1896, W.E.B. DuBois (black) published *The Suppression of the African Slave-Trade to the United States of America 1638-1870*[24] (initial in the Harvard historical Series); and in 1899, he brought out *The Philadelphia Negro*,[25] a pioneer work on black culture in an urban environment (based on field work done at a time when such field work was rare). From 1896 to 1914, DuBois supervised annual conferences on black history and culture at Atlanta University, each year generating important research reports. Of DuBois' prolific writings one can generalize that they were in advance of their time—that most Americans, black and non-blacks, were unready for his level of scholarship. The list of DuBois' publications, over a period of nearly eighty years, fills ten pages (209 catalog cards) of the Schomburg Collection catalog; and a 45-page DuBois bibliography was published at Accra, Ghana, in April 1964, by the Padmore Research Library on African Affairs.[26]

In *The Souls of Black Folk* (1903), DuBois prophesied: "The problem of the Twentieth Century is the problem of the color line."[27] Roy Wilkins, commenting on this work and that statement, urged that "No serious research in the Negro field can be done without reference to this book...a timeless and vital contribution to the understanding of Negro culture and one of the great books of our time." Yet DuBois' downright honesty made him unpopular, and his overt Marxism made him a pariah— so that he spent his last years in Ghana, in voluntary exile from his homeland. In 1954, black sociologist E. Franklin Frazier was the only man with both stature and courage enough to come up to New York from Howard University to make a presentation speech when a bust of DuBois was given to the Schomburg Collection.

W.E.B. DuBois died in 1963, at the age of 95, in Ghana. His passing was not widely lamented in white America. Then, half a dozen years ago, when there was some excitement about communism on our college campuses, in the DuBois Clubs, Richard M. Nixon (the same one—Spiro Agnew's friend) publicly confused his name with the Boys Clubs of America. And last May, when somebody donated a public park in DuBois' name at his birthplace, Great Barrington, Massachusetts, the local VFW indignantly protested, claiming it would be like "putting up a statue of Adolf Hitler."

W.E.B. DuBois was a pioneer "black expert."

So was Carter G. Woodson, born of ex-slave parents, in 1875, at New Canton, Virginia. Not so controversial as DuBois, nor nearly so prolific, Woodson was educated at Berea College, the University of Chicago, Harvard University, and the Sorbonne. In 1915, he established the Association for the Study of Negro Life and History at Chicago, and in the following year, at Washington, D.C., founded the *Journal of Negro History*. From that date to the year of his death, 1950, Woodson kept this journal alive; so that today, in the good times of black scholarship, it is still flourishing. It is the only American learned journal to sprinkle its pages with enthusiastic exclamation marks (stylistic usage which editors of non-black journals tend to regard as undignified).

Wilhemena S. Robinson, in *Historical Negro Biographies*,[28] emphasizes: "By 1965, his conception that the Negro had a past worthy of study had been adopted by the leading institutions and scholars of America, and they were developing programs to fill the long neglected gap in their versions of the history of mankind. Woodson had set the pace for research in this area over half a century earlier." And he did it without government support, or foundation support, or public support. He is now venerated by black and non-black scholars (including Professor Genovese) as "the father of modern Negro historiography." Woodson established, during hard times, and sustained, during decades of pervasive neglect, the scholarly base which "black studies" enjoy today.

I might also dwell on the important work of Swedish scholar Gunnar Myrdal (*non-black*), who oversaw the initial researching and writing of *An American Dilemma* (2 volumes, 1944), sponsored by the Carnegie Corporation, during the late 1930's;[29] and I ought to say more about the abiding influence of Marxist historian Herbert Aptheker (also *non-black*), whose turbulent career has been largely devoted to black American history.[30] Alternatively, I could affirm here the distinguished scholarship of John Hope Franklin (*black*), Chairman of the History Department of the University of Chicago—whom Harvard University, moving belatedly into the Afro-American orbit last year, vainly sought to recruit.[31] Or I might enlarge on the vital activity of Alain Leroy Locke (*black*), late professor of philosophy at Howard University, from 1912 until his retirement in 1953.[32] But I mention these men, in order to contrast briefly the respective contributions to "black studies" of Melville J. Herskovits and E. Franklin Frazier.

Herskovits (*non-black*) was the first anthropologist appointed at Northwestern University, and, apart from interim assignments at Columbia University and Howard University, remained at Northwestern his entire career, or about forty years. In time, he became Director of Northwestern's African Studies program; but he was not hired to teach Afro-American anything. He was supposed to handle the usual range of conventional anthropology courses; yet from the start he insisted on offering special black, and Mexican, and Cuban, but especially African courses. He did so under a sense of compulsion, acutely conscious there was a myth abroad in the land—in America, shared by most people—that the black population of this continent had no past, that their past had been obliterated, and that this past was negligible or (it at all present) only marginal and insignificant.

Herskovits was determined not only to oppose these views, but to counter the corollary argument that America's future had to be built out of the stuff of this new continent and that, accordingly, the black man's African past was irrelevant to his future. His *Myth of the Negro Past* (1941),[33] which originated as a memorandum to Myrdal's *An American Dilemma*, challenged this myth with an insistence that black people's cultural antecedents ("Africanisms") are important, vital to the populations and civilizations of South America, the Caribbean, and the American South. Herskovits looked into the arts, literature, music, dance, and family and social structures, and appraised the distinctive cultural input of these people to the new civilizations of the New World. (There is a name for this: *ethnogenesis*—the emergence of new cultures.) And he demonstrated that new cultures in this hemisphere are different from Old World (European) antecedent cultures. The myth, of course, had denied both these propositions.

Emphatic confirmation of Herskovits' case is lately found in Yale Southern historian C. Vann Woodward's (*non-black*) April 1969 Presidential Address to the Organization of American Historians, "Clio with Soul," in which he compellingly urges: "So far as their culture is concerned, all Americans are part Negro. Some are more so than others, of course, but the essential qualification is not color or race."[34] Though Herskovits testified before Congress from time to time, his testimony was little read, and less heeded. Few paid serious attention, in the 1940s, to what Herskovits and Myrdal had to say about race relations in America. (It is paradoxical that in the early 1960s LeRoi Jones—not yet Ameer Baraka, nor yet possessing his own language and lyricism—should have read Herskovits' *Myth*, with approval and drawn heavily on it for documentation of *Blues People*).[35] Today, the American government and American people are catching up on their reading—*at least* thirty years late.

The Herskovitsian hypothesis for African backgrounds, entailing black ego-building "retentions, reinterpretations, and syncretisms," did not go unchallenged for long. Almost immediate rebuttal came from sociologist E. Franklin Frazier (*black*), who mainly disagreed about the relationship and significance of Africanisms to the black American family. Frazier argued that the circumstances of recent history, in which both black and non-black Americans are caught, have been more crucial than the ostensible "survivals." He developed his thesis in *The Negro Family in the United States* (1939) and, more aggressively, in *The Negro in the United States*

(1949), offering point-by-point refutation of *Myth* chapters and topics.[36] (The so-called *Moynihan Report* of March 1965 often resorts to "synthesis" of Frazier's work.[37]

It is said that Frazier, as a child, spat on the buildings of Johns Hopkins University, in his native Baltimore, because he knew he couldn't enroll there. In the late 1920s, possessed of a B.A. with honors from Howard, a M.A. in Sociology from Clark, and field experience in New York and Denmark, he indignantly departed Atlanta University for the University of Chicago, from an unwavering insistence (though at the time seemingly utopian) on full citizenship and full participation in American society. A man of action, who used to tell friends he was "forced" into academic life, Frazier rejected the prevailing compromise of accepting certain other things first; and Atlanta's loss proved to be scholarship's gain. He received his Ph.D. in 1931 from the University of Chicago and remained there until his migration to Howard, where he remained for the rest of his career.

In an article rarely noticed in the scholarly bibliographies, "My Most Humiliating Jim Crow Experience,"[38] Frazier recounts how white bellhops once hustled him off the public elevator of a metropolitan hotel where he was attending a professional meeting, and compelled him to ride the freight elevator. He afterwards discovered that other black scholars at this meeting, docilely accepting second-class status, had gone up "the back way" in the first place. Frazier broadly attacked this black American elite in his 1948 Presidential Address to the American Sociological Society. Speaking authoritatively, from within the situation, he charged that this class had not merely accepted, but were making certain dubious gains from a segregated system which he deplored. (And *Black Bourgeoisie*, published in French in 1955 and in English in 1957, amplifies Frazier's position regarding the black American middle class.) In 1954, before a bare handful of persons gathered to hear him present the DuBois bust to the Schomburg Collection, he paid tribute to DuBois' awareness and his emphasis, and urged the necessity for scholarly, not just journalistic notice of black contributions and black culture. Once again, he was insisting upon full participation in the best America had to offer.

Frazier died in 1962, and Herskovits died in 1963—both men leaving the scene just before the eruption of the current debate over the role of so-called "black studies" in the arena of American higher education. Both were most visible during the 1940s—they had been low-profile during the 1930s simply because of the problem of survival (a factor I feel Professor Genovese occasionally overlooks in some of his steady public utterances), the problem of maintaining the very existence of Afro-American studies. During the 1940s, because of full employment for all (the old, women, and black Americans), it was possible for patterns of debate to evolve. Herskovits and Frazier were frequent collaborators; both had worked in Brazil and in the Caribbean; and over the years they fought and disagreed in person and in print. (John V. Murra, to whom these remarks are manifestly indebted, knew both men well and has told me that their clashes were not entirely staged, or academic, but were to some extent personal.)

And the sides of their debate, their respective positions, to some extent predicted the future, the course which Afro-American studies would take after World War II. This future, of course, has now become our present. What I have hoped to emphasize in extending these remarks on Herskovits and Frazier is not that black won and non-black lost (though such now seems to be the case, notwithstanding the emotional appeal of Herskovits' *Myth* to black college undergraduates). What I mean to stress is that Herskovits and Frazier have made these tremendous contributions, achievements more important than their debate, *per se*. It is especially significant that they fought the issues in a time of general indifference.

Today, "black studies" are thriving, African studies are gaining, and the difference now is that the thrust is total, no longer an intermittent series of marginal projects by self-sacrificing black and non-black pioneers. There is growing institutional support for studying millions of New World black people. The incentive is finally present, and the question becomes: How to attract talented young people to study in this field? There is also a need for critical study of present programs (actually, for fundamental knowledge of these programs). But there is, further, need for better definition of objectives.

The joint problem of black identity and majority establishment support of "black studies" programs partly involves a kind of "Afro" bias or halo, that is not so much scholarly as therapeutic, to both black and non-black. At times, the situation is an amalgam of student pressure, the politics of confrontation, and combined guilt, reparation, and intimidation. In some instances, American academe is yielding to a kind of bribery.

Bayard Rustin, well known to black American militant youth as an "Uncle Tom" (he is a longtime associate of A. Philip Randolph, thought a militant twenty years ago, but now regarded as not-so by the Panthers and Mau-Maus), in *Ebony's* "Black Revolution" issue, last August, assailed what he called "The Myth of Black Studies" in these words:

> While Black Studies *should* mean is a thorough and objective scholastic inquiry into the history of the black man in America. This history has been scandalously distorted in the past, and, as a field of study it has been relegated to a second-class status...But...Black Studies, as it is presently conceived... will not correct these errors...but will) serve the *ideological* function of creating a mythologized history and a system of assertive ideas that will serve the *political* function of developing and educating a cadre of activists in the black community...What I find most distressing is the contempt that is shown toward black history and culture as potential academic disciplines...And finally, the *psychological* function of (improving) the self-image of young blacks.[39]

Obviously, this is redolent of the "true scholastic stink." It is, deliberately, "Uncle-Tom" talk.

We are, then, back at the "Afro" myth that Herskovits evolved to replace the previous "Sambo" or "benign plantation" myth. And so there is violent debate across the land, once more. Last June, I attended the Afro-American Seminar at Yale University and heard Armstead Robinson, an eloquent black divinity graduate, characterize American universities in general and Yale in particular as "racist"—then qualify this by saying he didn't intend "racist" as a pejorative. The non-black, over-thirty alumni in attendance were variously chastened and outraged by his black rhetoric and confrontation tactics. Robinson is an editor of *Black Studies in the University*, a report on the Black Student Alliance at Yale's spring 1968 "educational experience for professional educators."[40]

Whatever Frazier may have thought about Herskovits' theories, they do deal with the tangible phenomenon of *ethogenesis*, whose central point in this context is the important cultural contributions made by black people in South America, the Caribbean, and the United States. But through multifarious modes of institutional brainwashing, these achievements have been persistently suppressed. It is no accident that there have been and still are, in this country, vast sums of money available for studies in Southeast Asia. The U.S. government variously supports so-called "area studies"—political "area studies" of places under indirect American control, which some liberal critics have discourteously disparaged as "imperialism." (Gunnar

Myrdal long since switched over to Southeast Asia: his most notable recent books are *Asian Drama and Objectivity in Social Research*.)

In this frame of reference, then, the issue of whether or not to launch "black studies" should seem less a matter of sentiment, or palliating black pride, or massaging white guilt. We are, surely, considering a legitimate—though long neglected—field of scholarship. And there is much point to these lines from Gil Scott-Heron's poem about life in Harlem:

> A rat done bit my sister Nell.
> (with Whitey on the moon)
> Her face and arms began to swell.
> (with Whitey on the moon).[41]

Ethnogenesis doesn't always "hatch" in the universities; and this fact applies particularly to "black studies." A member of a minority culture, or ethnic group, may not know his remote cultural past, but he does know his present oppressed (and brainwashed) condition; and, in such a situation, he sometimes invents a past to explain that condition. There are, for instance, the cases of Elijah Muhammed and his most brilliant disciple, Malcolm X. Elijah Muhammed, J. Edgar Hoover's opinion of him notwithstanding, founded the Muslims—the so-called "black Muslims"—in Chicago; and this black separatist organization has rehabilitated thousands of dispirited black Americans. (Which is more than Mr. Hoover has done. And have you read Sam Greenlee's *The Spook Who Sat by the Door?*) To the scholar—black or non-black scholar, "white expert" or "black expert"—Elijah Muhammed's bizarre myth of black origins and white origins is simply a fabrication; but this myth has inspired people, and many militant young men have gone to jail because they are fanatically committed to it.

The job of "black studies" must surely be to recognize this phenomenon objectively, and to present it objectively. I am talking about sociology, not fantasy. Hitherto, I have conveniently employed Eugene D. Genovese as a kind of intermittent villain; but I am now bound, in fairness, to disclose that in February 1970, addressing faculty of the University of Rochester, he pleaded that black culture *should* be considered a serious academic discipline, because it is "a unique and paradoxical situation." And the only thing the university can do, he added, "is to guarantee that the classroom will be a place of intellectual content, and if the students take their knowledge and translate it into political ideologies you don't like or I don't like, that's just too bad."[42]

I began these remarks with epigraphs, and I will close with a statistic. There are some 13,000 professional sociologists in the United States today, and of these only 85 are black. That is less than one percent. Thus, part of the task of "black studies" in this country must be to correct that imbalance. The future—Afro-cuts, dashikis, Swahili, W.E.B., Woodson, Herskovits, Frazier, Elijah Muhammad, Minister Malcolm—is up to us.

Endnotes

1. "The Negro in History Textbooks," *The Crisis*, LXXII (August-September 1965): 427-428.

2. Produced earlier this year by the Negro Ensemble Company at St. Mark's Playhouse in New York City.

3. Hoyt W. Fuller, "Black Images and White Critics," *Negro Digest*, XIX (November 1969): 49: "The White Literary Establishment is not willing to release its stranglehold on black literature. Robert A. Bone, for one, has been floating along for years on a reputation as the leading 'authority' on black literature on the basis of his book, *The Negro Novel in America*...Other white 'experts' on black literature include Edward Margolies and Herbert Hill...These white experts

on black literature say to black writers what, in effect, whites always have said to blacks: that black people approach wholeness as human beings to the extent to which they approximate whiteness. Black literature, the white critics maintain, approaches the standards of genuine literature to the degree that it reflects the American literary mainstream'" Cf. Irving Howe, "New Black Writers," *Harper's*, CCXXXIX (December 1969): 10 ff., and (response) Ishmael Reed, "Books in Black," *Harper's*, CCXL (March 1970): 6: "A dying culture will always call up its intellectual warhorses—no matter how senile they may be—when pagans are breaking down the gates." Also cf. Julius Lester, "The Black Writer and the New Censorship," *Evergreen Review*, No. 70 (April 1970): 20: "White editors are not equipped, by education or psychology, to evaluate a manuscript by a black writer."

4. "Ignored by Historians," *Saturday Review*, XLIX (July 16, 1966): 67-68,

5. New York, Washington, London: Publishers Company, Inc., under the auspices of the Association for the Study of Negro Life and History, 1967-1969.

6. Chicago: Johnson Publishing Company, 1966.

7. Dobbs Ferry, NY: Oceana Publications, 1965; second edition 1968.

8. New York: Bellweather Publishing Co., 1968.

9. Englewood Cliffs, NJ: Prentice-Hall, 1966; Yonkers, L.I., NY: Negro Heritage, 1966 (2-volume edition).

10. (Ann Arbor, Michigan:) University Microfilms, 1969.

11. New York: Meredith Corporation (Appleton-Century-Crofts), 1970.

12. "Biographical Notes" of contributing poets are included in the anthology *For Malcolm*, ed. Dudley Randall and Margaret G. Burroughs (Detroit: Broadside Press, 1969), pp. 95-112.

13. *Journal of American History*, LVI (June 1969): 207-208: "Each volume is clear and direct rather than interpretive. A few of the essays were written by whites. Since there is still a paucity of reliable information about Negro life, despite the current outpouring of books in this field, this compendium will prove a convenient aid and directory for students. Experts in Negro culture will see in it the weaknesses which afflict most encyclopedias, but it will prove much easier to keep up to date because of its topical nature."

14. "The Literature of Negro Revolt," *Freedomways*, III (1963): 36-48; "Literature on the South," *Freedomways*, IV (1964): 149-167; "The Negro Heritage Library and Its Critics," *Freedomways*, VII (1967): 64-74; "Negro History: A Bibliographic Survey," *Freedomways*, 7 (1967): 335-348; "Recently Published Negro Reference and Research Tools," *Freedomways*, VI (1966): 358-368.

15. Elizabeth Miller, The *Negro in America: A Bibliography* (Cambridge, Mass.: Harvard University Press, 1966); Erwin A. Salk, *A Layman's Guide to Negro History* (New York: McGraw-Hill, 1967); Erwin K. Welsch, *The Negro in the United States: A Research Guide* (Bloomington: Indiana University Press, 1965).

16. Cf. Tacoma Community College Library's anomalous *Bibliography of Afro-American Print and Non-Print Resources...* (Tacoma, 1969), which classifies writers like William Kunstler, Mary White Ovington, and Henry A. Wallace (all non-black) as "Afro-American Authors: Western Hemisphere.

17. New York: William Morrow and Company, 1967.

18. "The Crisis of the Negro Intellectual," *Freedomways*, XI (1969): 24-41.

19. "Southern Exposure," *New York Review of Books*, September 11, 1969, p. 27.

20. Cf. Genovese, "The Legacy of Slavery and the Roots of Black Nationalism," *Studies on the Left*, VI (November-December 1966): 3-26, with comment by Herbert Aptheker (pp. 27-35), C. Vann Woodward (pp. 35-42), and Frank Kofsky (pp. 43-54), and rejoinder by Genovese (pp. 55-65).

21. Excerpted in *Harper's* (September 1967): 51-102, and published by Random House, October 9, 1967.

22. *William Styron's "Nat Turner": Ten Black Writers Respond* (Boston: Beacon Press, 1968).

23. "Styron-Turner and Nat Turner: Myth and Truth," *Political Affairs*, XLVI (October 1967): 40-50. But see also Nancy M. Tischler, "Negro Literature and Classic Form," *Contemporary Literature*, X (Summer 1969): 352-365.

24. New York: Longmans, Green and Co., 1896.

25. Philadelphia: University of Pennsylvania, 1899.

26. Cf. Ernest Kaiser, "A Selected Bibliography of the Published Writings of W.E.B. DuBois," *Freedomways*, V (1965): 207-213.

27. "The Forethought," *The Souls of Black Folk: Essays and Sketches* (Chicago: A.C. McClurg, 1903). Cf. Dorothy B. Porter, "The Librarian and the Scholar: A Working Partnership," *Materials by and about American Negroes* (Atlanta: Atlanta University School of Library Services, 1967), p. 76. "There have been twenty-one editions of *Souls of Black Folk* published between 1903 and 1937."

28. Second edition, revised (New York, Washington, London: Publishers Company, Inc., 1969), pp. 264-265.

29. The Gunnar Myrdal MSS., now in the Arthur A. Schomburg Collection of the New York Public Library, comprise eighty-one volumes of notes and memoranda.

30. Among Aptheker's numerous and continuous contributions to black historiography *American Negro Slave Revolts* (1943) and *A Documentary History of the Negro People in the United States* (2 vols., 1951) are perhaps best known.

31. Franklin's most notable works are *The Free Negro in North Carolina, 1790-1860* (1943), *From Slavery to Freedom* (1947), *The Militant South* (1956), *A Fool's Errand* (1961), *Reconstruction after the Civil War* (1961), and *The Emancipation Proclamation* (1963). He is also a co-author (with John W. Caughey and Ernest R. May) of the controversial eighth-grade American history textbook *Land of the Free* (1965).

32. For a comprehensive list of Locke's wide-ranging publications, see Robert E. Martin, "Bibliography of the Writings of Alain Leroy Locke," in Rayford W. Logan, *et al.*, eds., *The New Negro Thirty Years Afterward* (Washington: Howard University Press, 1955), pp. 18-25.

33. New York: Harper & Brothers, 1941; second edition, Boston: Beacon Press, 1958.

34. *Journal of American History*, LVI (June 1969): 17. Cf. p. 16: "Either black history is an essential part of American history and must be included by all American historians, or it is unessential and can be segregated and left to black historians. But Negro history is too important to be left entirely to Negro historians. To disqualify historians from writing Negro history on the grounds of race is to subscribe to an extreme brand of racism. It is to ignore not only the substantial corrective and revisionary contributions to Negro history made by white Americans but also those of foreign white scholars... Some Americans who present themselves as qualified by color to write 'black' history would mystify many Latin Americans, since by their standards such people are not black at all, and deem themselves so only by unconsciously adopting white racist myths peculiar to the United States."

35. New York: William Morrow, 1963.

36. See also "The Negro Family," in Donald Young, ed., *The American Negro* (Philadelphia: American Academy of Political and Social Sciences, 1928), pp. 44-51; *The Free Negro Family* (Nashville: Fisk University Press, 1932); *The Negro Family in Chicago* (Chicago: University of Chicago Press, 1932; "Traditions and Patterns of Negro Family Life in E.B. Reuter, ed., *Race and Culture Contacts* (New York: McGraw-Hill, 1934), pp. 191-207; "Ethnic Family Patterns: The Negro Family in the United States," *American Journal of Sociology*, LIII (May 1948): 435-438. Michael R. Winston, Writings of E. Franklin Frazier," (Program of A Lecture Series in Honor of Edward Franklin Frazier, March 13, 14, 15, 1962, Cranston Auditorium, Howard University (Washington: Howard University, 1962), pp. 9-16, lists 117 titles.

37. Office of Policy Planning and Research, United States Department of

Labor, *The Negro Family: The Case for National Action* (Washington: U.S. Government Printing Office, 1965).

38. *Negro Digest*, IV (November 1945): 8-82.

39. "The Myths of the Black Revolt," *Ebony*, XXIV (August 1969): 101.

40. *Black Studies in the University: A Symposium* (New York: Bantam Books, 1969), p. vii.

41. From *Small Talk at 125th & Lenox*, cited in *Time*, XCV (April 6, 1970): 98.

42. "Fall Black Program Urged at UR," *Rochester Democrat and Chronicle* (February 18, 1970): 5B.

49.

The Black College as Focus
for Black Studies

Nick Aaron Ford

I pointed out that Black Studies were a part of the curriculum in some black colleges more than fifty years ago. I predict that in the year 2000 the most innovative and significant developments in the field will be found in whatever black colleges still exist. By that date it is possible that more than half of the current number will have either discontinued the struggle completely or will have lost their identities in mergers with predominantly white institutions or have been transformed by a gradual takeover by white students, white faculties, and white administrators. Such a development will, of course, be catastrophic for American blacks unless by that time, which is extremely doubtful, white racism as we know it now will have disappeared.

The 1971 report of the Carnegie Commission on Higher Education entitled *New Students and New Places* contains the following commentary:

> Higher education in the United States until about 1940 was largely for the elite; from 1940 to 1970, we moved to mass higher education; and, from 1970 to 2000, we will move to universal-access higher education—opening it to more elements of society than ever before.

> We do not anticipate a further move to universal higher education in the sense of universal attendance; in fact, we consider this undesirable and believe that public and private policy should both avoid channeling all youth into higher education and create attractive alternatives to higher education.

> But we clearly are moving from mass to universal-access higher education.

> This creates problems.

> It also creates opportunities for more nearly equal treatment of all our citizens, for more nearly adequate service to all localities of our nation, for more varied response to the increasingly varied composition of the enrollments in higher education, for a more thoughtful consideration of the future role of each of the major components of our universe of higher education, for a more careful look at the essential nature of each of our institution, for a more systematic examination of the effective use of resources.[1]

This brief resume of the aims of American education in the past and the future direction in which it seems to be moving should be of some aid to black colleges as they prepare for new roles in the future. Of course, the major deterrent to the growth and expansion of black colleges is now and will continue to be the lack of adequate funds. In 1967 a Task Force on Education, appointed by President Johnson and headed by William C. Friday, president of the University of North Carolina, said in its report published for the first time in 1972, "the federal government should provide substantial aid to predominantly Negro institutions,"[2] but at the same time it urges that this aid should be extended with the understanding that the long-time goal must be the elimination of all segregated institutions of higher education. Until we know the commission's definition of "segregated institutions of higher education" we cannot have a valid conception of how this recommendation would affect current black colleges. Almost all black colleges are already integrated according to the government's definition as applied to the public schools. The Task Force admits that "At the present it is the predominantly black institutions which offer the effective opportunity for an education to Negroes," but it seems to believe that this "effective opportunity" is not truly valid unless the black college is affiliated in some manner with a "non-developing" (white) institution.

In their controversial book, *The Academic Revolution*, Christopher Jencks and David Riesman say, "We believe that substantial numbers of Negroes grossly overestimate the academic quality of Negro colleges. We think many Negro undergraduates would be better off in an integrated college—especially one that had enough other Negroes to form it partially self-contained culture.... We regret this [the publication of this opinion],.but we do not think that individuals should be sacrificed for institutions, however worthy the latter may be and however honorable their historical role."[3] They also remind the reader that in an article published earlier they had suggested that instead of being third-rate imitations of Harvard and Berkeley the Negro colleges should reconsider their role and strike out in new directions. "As far as we have been able to discover," they lament, "no Negro college president took these suggestions very seriously. Apparently it is Harvard or bust." They assert that black colleges now are living reminders of how bad most white colleges in an earlier era had been. They admit to only a few exceptions:

> Nevertheless, as we have already emphasized, Negro colleges are not all alike. At the head of the Negro academic procession stands a handful of well-known private institutions, such as Fisk, Morehouse, Spelman, Hampton, Tuskegee, and Dillard, an even smaller number of public ones such as Texas Southern and Morgan State, and that peculiar hybrid [privately controlled but largely federally financed] Howard. By most criteria, these institutions would probably fall near the middle of the national academic procession. They attract a few brilliant students, employ a few brilliant professors, and run a few very lively programs.... By almost any standard these [other] 110 colleges are academic disaster areas.[4]

These two eminent white "authorities" on Negro education would undoubtedly agree with the recommendation of the Friday Task Force that the federal government should seek to provide higher education for all minorities in integrated educational contexts, thus promoting the elimination of black colleges and universities (those with predominantly black administrators, faculties, and student bodies). Of course, the Friday report recommends covert methods for eliminating such as the government's furnishing funds to support the operation of a currently black institution with insurmountable financial problems provided that it merges with a much larger white college or university. Naturally, the administrative pattern would be on a cooperative basis similar to the one in the black anecdote of a meat processor who when questioned by FDA examiners about the ingredients in a certain suspect product he was selling declared that he used a fifty-fifty mixture of horse and rabbit meat. When pressed for a more detailed explanation, he said he meant by a fifty-fifty mixture "one horse to one rabbit." Of course, there could be no further doubt about the resultant flavor.

President King V. Cheek, Jr., of Morgan State College presents an enlightened rationale for the black college, present and future, which places its problems and opportunities in proper perspective:

There is the third demand that black colleges relate more to the black communities—that we become more social-action-oriented. This demand has some legitimacy, but we must carefully define the role. Colleges are first and foremost educational enterprises. This is all the expertise they can claim. Their contributions must be in the form of knowledge and data which appropriate agencies in society can use to make alternative judgments and decisions. Second, they must produce the intelligent and skilled manpower and effective agents of change for our society.

Indeed, if these contributions are conscientiously pursued, they will have overwhelming impacts upon problems black people face. This is the way we realize and fulfill our roles as Black Power bases within the black community. We cannot be expected to go further and involve our institutions, rather than the individuals, without sacrificing our previous neutrality as critics of society. We cannot afford as an institution to politicize ourselves to become protagonists for a specific cause. If we do, we diminish our role as hostels for persons with a variety of views and opinions.

Fourth, there is the demand that we become and remain black institutions with a commitment to serve black students. This demand grows out of the fear that integration may engulf us, destroy our identities and thus diminish our service. It is true that we live in a multi-racial and pluralistic society. Our educational institutions must reflect this reality. I for one will passionately resist the misuse of the slogan or aim of integration to eliminate or reduce our institutions. I have seen the decline of black high school administrators in the South—black principals, more qualified than their white counterparts, reduced to the demeaning status of assistant principals in charge of buses. I have seen the elimination of black schools and their absorption by the white ones with the discarding of the symbols of black pride. I have witnessed resegregation in the midst of desegregation, with accompanying humiliation and dehumanization of black children, and with the dominant culture more in complete command. I recall the black high school students in a western North Carolina city who, one morning, suddenly discovered they no longer had a school song and a trophy case—symbols of deep emotional meaning for them. This is the dilemma of integration. Promote it we must, but not at our educational and psychological detriment.

When HEW insists that many of our colleges must lose their racial identification, we must understand what this really means. I must rise to protest.

A Different Form of Racial Identification

Black colleges will lose their identities as black colleges and simply become predominantly white with a minority black enrollment. We fail to see that racial identification has not ceased to be. It has simply changed its form. What we have there are all predominantly white colleges. The racial identity is still there, except that it is white. But we are told the real concern is not the label or identity of the college, but the increasing of educational opportunity for black youth. The issue, we are told, is minority access to higher education. This is more illusory than real. The dominant and genuine concern is not so much with minority access to higher education as it is with minority success in higher education. This is where the black colleges have made their case—have proven their competency.

So long as our society is infected with any vestige of racism and disregard for human identity, there will always be a need for black colleges to answer the needs of our black student populations. We will remain symbols of pride for our people. We still belong to them. They have emotional investment and stake in our present and in our future. We cannot forsake this cause. Let us build upon the legacies of our black and beautiful past—careful never to distort the realities and never to ignore our blunders and shortcomings—forever tolerant of dissent among ourselves and keeping our strong commitment to high levels of scholarship and service. If we do, we will overcome the handicaps of our past and insure the future of our race.[5]

The Ford Foundation *Letter* for July 15, 1971 announced that it had given grants of $1,750,000 each to two black universities, Atlanta and Howard, "to sustain their efforts to become graduate centers of excellence in the social sciences." The *Letter* stated that these two are the only predominantly black universities among the estimated 250 American institutions that grant the doctorate. It was stated that Atlanta's student body is approximately eight percent white and its faculty thirty percent white, while Howard's percentages are fifteen percent and forty-eight percent respectively. In each case the administration and general image are characteristically black. It is fairly safe to predict that both institutions will still be predominantly black in the year 2000. It is also safe to predict that during the intervening years no other black institution will be accorded the right to offer a Ph.D. degree recognized by the academic establishment. It is the expressed hope of the Ford Foundation that Howard's and Atlanta's "bid for eminence in the social sciences is not only to stimulate a growing black intellectual life but to offer fresh insights for white and nonwhite students and scholars alike." It is further suggested that "perhaps a more humanistic and socially relevant study of man will emerge under black leadership as scholars at Howard and Atlanta examine traditional social science perceptions."

But in the immediate future the major effort and achievement in black-oriented education will be in the predominantly black undergraduate colleges where the majority of the administrators, faculty, and students is black. It will be in the hundred or more black colleges that Jencks and Riesman condemned as "academic disaster areas," as well as the eight they cited as meeting the current general standards for American higher education. What prediction can we make for their survival and their transformation into more racially oriented institutions than they have been? First, it is only fair to observe that the two white "authorities" whose judgments were made with such godlike omniscience and finality admit that their conclusions were based on very brief visits to a few black colleges with no general acquaintance over the years with the problems to be assessed, that their final judgments were formed on the basis of testimony of a few hostile blacks who had attended black colleges as undergraduates and had gone on to work in white universities and a few others who had merely spent a few years in white graduate schools and then became Negro college teachers. The caliber of informants they sought when they did visit black campuses was the kind that dealt in such gossipy items as incidents of "petty blackmail and fraud, ranging from such relatively subtle things as college officials' profiteering on textbooks to more egregious incidents like a president's 'borrowing' money from a new, untenured faculty member and not repaying it...of grades being used to black-mail students into mowing lawns, sweeping offices, or even providing sexual favors [they admit that this sexual thing could happen on a white campus, but on a white campus the professor pretends interest in the exploited girl for herself since the white girl is more reluctant than her black counterpart to admit her willingness to use her sexuality for extrinsic purposes]."[6]

The black college of the future has two possible directions open to it. It can become a *revolutionary* institution with major emphasis on ideology and training for the overthrow of the current political and economic system of the United States as the only means of black liberation, or it can develop a curriculum that will devote minor attention to ideology and black philosophical identity and major attention to cultural, historical, political, and economic studies and disciplines designed to enhance the success of the black graduate in competing for and winning places of influence and power in the established political and economic fabric of the nation and thus help to change the establishment into a truly democratic and egalitarian system. All signs point to the latter prospect.

Since 1968 there has been much controversial talk among blacks concerning future directions for the black college. Under the rubric "The Black University," *Negro Digest* (now *Black World*) devoted the major portion of three issues between March 1968 and March 1970 to the subject. On November 13, 1968, a conference attended by nearly 2,000 students, faculty members, and nonacademicians was convened on the campus of Howard University for the announced purpose of discussing the issues involved in the concept of a truly black college or university. The invitations contained the following statement: "The concept of a black university is revolutionary. It emerges out of the frustrations of black students, educators, activists and community leaders who recognize that the present institutions of higher learning have no relevance to the total black community and who realize the contradictions of allowing themselves to be accultured into a society which debilitates black people...our responsibility as conference participants is to define the structure and mechanics of that university."[7]

The official roster included the names of such well-known blacks as Amiri Baraka (LeRoi Jones), Ossie Davis, Stokely Carmichael, Maulana Ron Karenga, Harold Cruse, and Dr. Alvin Poussaint, but reports indicate that the major plans and crucial decision were made by the student leaders, a trend which was first established in the organization of Black Studies programs at white institutions. In fact, the conference was conceived, sponsored, and financed by the Howard University Student Association. Numerous workshops discussed the major problems that would be encountered in any attempt to establish and operate a black college or university designed as a revolutionary instrument for black liberation, but no viable guidelines were agreed upon.

The fact that no black leaders from the established black colleges appeared on the guest list of participants at the Howard University conference indicates that all currently solvent black colleges are primarily interested in the *evolutionary* rather than the *revolutionary* root to black liberation and that their future development will move in the direction of the second alternative previously mentioned. There are signs that the strongest and most progressive colleges in this category will get financial assistance from some philanthropic foundations and from the federal government as they seek to implement black-oriented academic and community programs.

The Ford Foundation announced October 9, 1971, a six-year program of $100 million for minority education. Although approximately half of the total will be awarded to blacks, Mexican-Americans, Puerto Ricans, and American Indians to attend the colleges and universities of their choice; the other half will be given to a limited number of private colleges, not more than twenty, over the next six years to be used at their discretion for student financial aid, curriculum and instructional changes, faculty salaries, professorial chairs, endowment, and special projects. The main focus will be aimed at improvements on the undergraduate level in accordance with the priorities designated by the collages themselves. McGeorge Bundy, president of the Ford Foundation, emphasized in his announcement that this heightened commitment to black colleges "should in no way be interpreted as support of segregated education," since these colleges do not bar students of any race. "The central point," he declared, "is that it is important for American society that institutions under black leadership and with a tradition of service to black students have an opportunity to thrive and share fully in our national efforts in higher education."

In his initial announcement Bundy listed the first four black colleges selected for participation in the program as Benedict College, Columbia, South Carolina, and Fisk University, Nashville, Tennessee, both liberal-arts-oriented with a strong black focus, with the latter having the largest number of courses in black life and culture. The other two selectees are Hampton Institute, Hampton, Virginia, and Tuskegee Institute, Tuskegee, Alabama, both of which have developed high-quality academic programs on earlier foundations of agricultural and technical education generally associated with the name of Booker T. Washington. A brief statement of the philosophy of the two presidents of Fisk and Benedict, both of which were always oriented towards the liberal arts and toward the white genteel conception of education, might give some hint of the future directions of black colleges associated with the Ford Foundation concept, especially since President Benjamin Payton of Benedict has taken a leave of absence from his institution to accept the task of supervising the Foundation's $100 million project.

James R. Lawson, president of Fisk, in response to a request by *Black World* to react to previous articles in the magazine concerning the concept of the black university, said:

> Essentially, then, the education of black Americans must encompass at least three objectives—i.e. (1) an increased awareness and knowledge of their heritage and of the contributions they have made throughout history; (2) a motivation and ability to render much-needed assistance and services, of various kinds, to the total black community; and (3) the development of knowledge and skills necessary for gainful employment and satisfactory living in the larger ever-changing society. In terms of what is necessary for sustained upward economic and social mobility of black Americans, I think it meaningless, if not dangerous, to attempt to assign priorities as between these three objectives. They are all necessary. Moreover, they constitute the basis for the continuing validity and relevance of predominantly or traditionally black institutions of higher education."[8]

He admits that the realization of the three objectives will require "rather basic modifications in the curricula of our colleges and universities, modifications which involve new directions, new and different courses, and innovatively different techniques and methodologies of instruction."

One indication of the thinking of Benedict's President Payton can be seen in his insistence when he assumed the presidency that a three-hour course in The Black Experience be included in the Liberal Core of 57 semester hours as a requirement for graduation. Benedict thus became the first and only accredited American college to require every student to earn as a prerequisite for graduation three semester hours in a course dealing exclusively with black life and culture. In his answer to the question concerning the concept of the Black University posed by *Black World* he expresses strong disagreement with those who maintain that the curriculum of the black college should accede priority to the humanistic disciplines such as "the social sciences, literature, art and the like." He regards such a contention as "a narrow conception of black identity which, if actually pursued, would isolate the black university even further than some of these same authors say it is today from the black community." He believes:

> A functional Black University will strive to engage in the kind of teaching and research and public service which provides people with the disciplines of thought and action by which they can mature as persons and help shape the world into a more human place of habitation. The irremediable blackness of Afro-Americans would be accepted both as a fact of life and as a positive value. But, it would not restrict the experience of black identity to the immediacies of skin-associated cultural values. The black experience is one crucible in which we work our way to a vision of and a connection with the human potential in all men.... A functional Black University will see the need for instruction in the disciplines of personal moral responsibility as well as the techniques of social action. Asserting and achieving one's humanity means that black people are not exempted from the universal idiom as well as a group style. Black people, too, need the art of transforming and transcending even the materials and patterns of black culture. In the words of the spiritual: "You got to walk this lonesome valley by yourself."⁹

It is clear that both President Lawson of Fisk and President Payton of Benedict, who are perceptive representatives of the established black colleges most likely to survive in modified forms into the twenty-first century, are acutely conscious of the need for new objectives and new emphases as they face the future. Both are committed to the enhancement of the black image in a cultural and utilitarian sense. Both are concerned that the curriculum and the application of the curriculum contribute to this enhancement. Both also reject the separatism of the advocates of the revolutionary concept of the black college by emphasizing the necessity for the black-college-trained products to compete with their white counterparts for places of preferment and power within the system. It appears that they are reconciled to the prospect of integrated faculties for the future, as well as the present. But certain troublesome questions arise at this juncture which must complicate even their liberated views of the situation: (1) In order to maintain the identity of the black college is it imperative for the majority of the faculty to be black? (2) Should there be a maximum percentage level set for white faculty members in order to maintain the black identity of the college? (3) Even with no more than twenty-five percent of the faculty white, what guarantee can there be that the non-black members will or can conscientiously support proper emphases on black values? (4) Should any one individual or any one group of individuals at a black college be permitted to choose or prescribe the values to which the college community must subscribe? (5) Should black faculty members at a black college be expected to surrender their individualities for the sake of group solidarity? (6) Should the black faculty of a black college consist of representatives of all major shades of opinion in the black community? Although these questions may be troublesome, they must be wisely answered by or for the administration, faculty, and students of every black college that expects to face the future honestly.

At present some of the most distinguished black colleges have one or more departments with more white than black teachers. In a recent survey of 37 English departments in representative black colleges I discovered that twelve, approximately 32 percent, have white majorities on their faculties, and only two have no white members. Of a total of 475 teachers in the 37 departments, 254 are black and 221 are white. These statistics indicate that if departmental policies concerning the number and nature of courses in black literature to be offered had to be determined by faculty vote there would be almost an even chance that white members would have as much decision-making power as black members. This revelation indicates that forty-six percent of the English teachers in black colleges that enroll approximately 75,000 black students are not black. However, it is significant that eighty-six percent of the black department chairmen testified that they believe, without reservation, that white teachers are "capable of teaching courses dealing with the black experience if they are willing to make reasonable preparation by study and research."

On the other hand, my survey of 120 English departments in representative white colleges and universities revealed that of 4,815 faculty members only 106 (2.2%) are black. One-half of all white departments surveyed has no black faculty members, approximately one-third has one black teacher each, and the remainder has from two to five blacks. Ninety-six percent of white chairmen believe, without reservations, that white faculty members are capable of satisfactorily teaching courses dealing with the black experience it only black students would give them a fair chance, but most indicate that they prefer black or a combination of black and white instructors for such courses. Since on the basis of these statistics it is difficult, if not completely impossible, to imagine a department in a white institution with a majority of black teachers, should black colleges accept as satisfactory departments with white majorities?

Frank A. DeCosta, dean of the Graduate School at Morgan State College, and Frank Bowles, academic vice-president of Haile Selassie I University, Addis Ababa, say in their book *Between Two Worlds*:

> After all has been said and written about changing patterns, educational needs, emerging opportunities, community development, and all other ideas and phrases that are part of the social upheaval of our time, the fact remains that the role of the historically Negro colleges will be determined by their own definition of their responsibility. They face a simple choice. Either they accept the responsibility for the planning and direction of Negro education or they do not. If they do not, no one else will.
>
> The question of whether they enroll the majority of Negro students in higher education is not relevant to this point. The point is that the historically Negro colleges were created by Negroes for the education of Negroes. They have been responsible for the formation, the development, and the present condition of education for Negroes. They are in a position to understand the problems, to make decisions, to supply leadership, and, above all, to speak for the Negro in American education. If they fail to do so, they fail in their ultimate mission.[10]

Although I highly regard the important contributions that DeCosta and Bowles have made in their book to all understanding and appreciation of the historical role of the Negro college in American education, in the foregoing quotation I think they have overstated the power black college administrators have had in determining the general direction in which Negro higher education has moved in the past and will move in the future. I am convinced that the power structure of American society, represented by individual white philanthropists, the national leadership of religious denominations, philanthropic foundations, and U.S. government agencies, has set the rules and the limits for black colleges, even those that are under the auspices of black religious denominations. In my opinion black college educators do not face a simple choice of deciding the direction in which higher education for blacks will go in the future. Their only choice is to decide whether they will make their plans within the limits the white power structure can be pressured to accept, or to surrender the outward trappings of power and retire completely from the field.

The private black college has already seen the handwriting on the wall. In the spring of 1972 several of these most progressive institutions have experienced financial crises so severe that they could not meet their monthly payrolls. In two instances fantastic cuts in teaching and nonteaching personnel were announced for the following year. Among these hard-pressed colleges were two of the four that the Ford Foundation had recently selected as the most promising of the private group with the understanding that each will be given annually more than a million dollars for the next six years. There call be no doubt that "He who pays the piper exercises the right to call the tune."

The fate of black public colleges and universities is now being decided in the state legislatures. In West Virginia and Missouri the traditionally black institutions have already lost their racial identity. In Arkansas the A. M. and N. college at Pine Bluff, the only black public institution of higher education in the state will become a branch of the University of Arkansas next fall by legislative decree. In Tennessee the white president of the new University of Tennessee at Nashville has pronounced black sixty year-old Tennessee A. and I. University a "dying institution" that must be annexed to or merged with his two-year-old fledgling in order to preserve the state's capital investment.

In North Carolina more than 500 black college students from all sections of the state met in Raleigh, November, 1971, to protest a proposed plan of white political and educational leaders to "reorganize" the state system of higher education. The law, if passed in its original form, would create a thirty-two-member Board of Regents with absolute authority over programs and budgets of all individual institutions. The students, consisting of representatives not only from the five black universities that would lose their semiautonomy but black students from practically every other black and white institution of higher education in the state, were aroused because there was general agreement among their elders, that "Such a plan would result in the phasing out of the predominantly Black institutions that are state supported, just at a time when students at these universities are developing widespread Black consciousness."[11] Although the students were well aware of the overwhelming white power arrayed against them, they felt that some faint hope could be kept alive if they could persuade the establishment to assign thirty percent of the places on the proposed state-wide governing board to black members, since blacks constitute that percentage of the population. Even if such a "generous" arrangement could result, the black minority could not be expected to have the deciding voice in charting the direction of black colleges under the board's jurisdiction.

In the light of the variety of limitations imposed on the black college because of its peculiar nature and the paucity of genuine opportunities for the control of its own destiny, what are the most promising future directions within the bounds of white toleration that might yield desirable results? One answer is in the reorganization of the entire curriculum of the college so that each course will reflect the realization of the black experience as a legitimate part of the American experience.

Such a realization will require that teachers incorporate in all social science and humanities courses unbiased information and interpretation of all significant aspects of black life and culture, as well as other ethnic minorities, which have been previously ignored by textbooks and instructional syllabi. This means that every course in literature (American and world), history (American and world), geography, anthropology, government, sociology, economics, psychology, philosophy, journalism, and so on will include the black and other ethnic dimensions, as well as the white. In mathematics and the natural sciences, materials for illustrations and experiments will be concerned with black as well as white experiences. Problems in mathematics will include ghetto situations as well as stock market manipulations.

If these kinds of emphases were enforced, there would be no need for a Black Studies department in a black college, as there is no need now for a White Studies department in a white college. Under this kind of reorganization every graduate of the black college, white as well as black (it is understood that enrollment will be open to all qualified applicants regardless of race or ethnic origins), would be thoroughly familiar with the significant aspects of black life and culture and, therefore, prepared to accept the responsibilities of living in a multi-ethnic society. Of course, there would be opportunity for "concentration" in Black Studies on all interdisciplinary basis, as is the case now in most colleges that have Black Studies programs, but, as is also the case in most colleges that have such programs, the student would be required to have a major in all established department. Some black colleges have already begun to achieve this kind of projection. Fisk University and Morgan State College are two examples.

Another answer might be found in some of the recommendations of a task force appointed in 1969 by Robert H. Finch, then Secretary of Health, Education, and Welfare, headed by Frank Newman, associate director of University relations in Stanford University. The report, which was released in March, 1971, suggests that the college could consider adapting to the student instead of trying to adapt the student to the college. Additional specific recommendations include: (a) providing a diversified faculty that includes members whose experiences range beyond that gained in the traditional departments; (b) accepting experience as a legitimate part of education; (c) organizing the curriculum around the professional skills to be learned, including work experience and learning geared to community service; (d) organizing "courses" as responses to needs developed by the students as they progress; (e) considering the academic process essentially as a means to ascertain truth as against falsity, to gain knowledge as against ignorance, and to improve intellectual excellence as against shoddiness.

Finally, since the future of the black college is greatly dependent upon social change in the larger community, the black college could profit by the experiences of white Antioch College, whose Institute for the Solution of Social Problems has been in operation since the spring of 1970. The proposal for the establishment of the institute contains the following rationale: "In any complex activity or profession, training is necessary to insure that persons involved participate, not simply on the basis of abstract ideas or intuition but with understanding and skill. This is as true for the agent of social change as it is for the research chemist. To develop and carry out strategy and tactics for social change, a person must act as a social scientist.... This means that he or she needs training in social sciences but not in an ad hoc or value-free fashion.... As part of its training of agents of social change then ISSP courses cross the bounds of the traditional academic areas.... The result is a curriculum which, for the first time at Antioch and perhaps at any established college or university in the U.S., insures that the theoretical and practical education required for the training of agents of social change call be obtained."[12]

Endnotes

1. *Chronicle of Higher Education* (October 12, 1971): 7.

2. February 7, 1972, p. 7.

3. *The Academic Revolution* (New York: Doubleday and Company, 1969), p. 478.

4. *Ibid.*, p. 433.

5. "Black Students, Black Studies, Black Colleges," *The Chronicle of Higher Education* (November 22, 1971): 8.

6. Jencks and Riesman, p. 427.

7. George Davis, "The Howard University Conference," Howard University, *Negro Digest* (March 1969): 46.

8. *Black World* (March 1969): 68.

9. *Ibid.*, pp. 97-98.

10. *Between Two World* (New York: McGraw Hill Book Company, 1971), p. 250.

11. Jim Grant and Milton R. Coleman, "Save Black Colleges in North Carolina," *Integrated Education* (March-April 1972): 36. (In the fall of 1972 the state of North Carolina began the operation of its system of higher education in accordance with the pattern condemned by the black protesters, with Dr. Harold Delaney, a black educator, as one of the six Vice Chancellors.)

12. "Proposal for the Establishment of ISSP," Antioch College, p. 1.

50.

Afrocentricity: Problems of Method and Nomenclature

Erskine Peters

Evident in contemporary American culture are numerous types of "Afrocentricities." These "Afrocentricities" have been appropriated into almost every domain along the cultural continuum from the sacred to the secular. Some rap groups distinguish themselves from other rap groups by designating themselves "Afrocentric";[1] some feminist/womanist, eco-feminist,[2] gay[3] and lesbian groups do the same. Some christian ministers[4] and churches label themselves "Afrocentric" and some erotic and pornographic videos[5] do so too. Many of these varying notions of Afrocentricity are what James Stewart alludes to in stating that "'popular afrocentricism'[6] is being confused increasingly with systematic intellectual approaches to the field."[7] The crucial issue is whether the reference to Africa in the word "Afrocentric" is a tribute designation indicating that traditional African worldviews have something supremely and expressly foundational to offer or whether the reference is a mere label of behavioral and racial differentiation, a mere way of expressing resentment for the European, instead of a profound way of relocating one's world view.

The use and coinage of so many different terms in this essay is employed only to highlight the great disparities existing under the rubric of so-called "Afrocentricity." The various terms are used to show that there is little or no consistent logic at work in much of popular as well as intellectual designations of the Afrocentric and to show that when there is consistency it is not necessarily grounded in indigenous and traditional African values.

Before moving to the focal discussion of this essay, as a point of information, a few words should be said about the key players in the post-mid-twentieth century Afrocentric movement. Four of the major theoretical figures to be considered when undertaking a formal study of Afrocentricity are John Henrik Clarke, Jacob H. Carruthers, Molefi Asante, and James B. Stewart.[8]

(1) *John Henrik Clarke*: The key founding figure of the post-mid-twentieth century Afrocentric movement is perhaps John Henrik Clarke. Based on the work of political historian Ronald Walters in *Pan Africanism in the African Diaspora*, Clarke advocated, via the Pan-Africanist oriented Black Caucus of the African Studies Association, the establishment, in 1968, of the African Heritage Association, as a reconstructive challenge to the Eurocentric scholarship and governance of the African Studies Association that had been established in 1956.[9] Speaking on behalf of the "adoption of the Pan Africanist (or Afrocentric) perspective" (Walters 1993, p. 368) at the Twelfth Annual meeting of the two-thousand member African Studies Association, Clarke explained that "this perspective defines that all black people are African people and rejects the division of African peoples by geographical locations

based on colonialist spheres of influence" (Walters, p. 368). According to Walters, the "concept of 'Afro-centrism' emerged from this political struggle as a product of expressing the need of this collection of Black scholars to articulate the ideology of Pan Africanism as applied to the study of the land of their parents" (Walters, p. 369). Walters emphasizes that "the first point made in the collectively drafted objectives of the newly formed AHSA would indicate that in the field of education, AHSA's purpose was the 'reconstruction of African history and cultural studies along *Afrocentric* lines while effecting an intellectual union among black scholars the world over" (Walters, p. 369). Articulating his Pan-Africanist/Afrocentrist challenge before the Black Caucus of the ASA, Clarke summed up the thrust of their collective thought by declaring that "[w]hen pseudo political independence was given to Africa, the one thing the European did not give up was his domination over the direction of African history" (Qtd. in Fraser 1969, p. 21). Stating that "how a man thinks about himself determines how he acts, Clarke added that "the one thing the Europeans did nor want us to do is to think that we can rule nations and institutions. And, more dangerous, that we could question his institutions. We have come to this point in our history where we must not only question old institutions, but we must make new institutions distinctly our own..." (Fraser, p. 21).[10] A direct result of the AHSA challenge, Walters's own Walters's Afrocentric emphasis, as he defines it, is in determining "what forces drive African-origin peoples to continue identifying with the source of their cultural origin and in determining how...these forces affect the quality of relationship both among Africans in the Diaspora and between Africans on the continent" (Walters, p. 14).

(2) *Jacob H. Carruthers*: Foundational Afrocentric proponent Jacob H. Carruthers, of the Kemetic Institute in Chicago and co-founder of the Association for the Study of Classical African Civilization, and author of *Essays in Ancient Egyptian Studies* (1984), sounded the Afrocentric mandate not only through argumentation but very importantly through demonstration. Having taking seriously the call for Pan-Africanist/Afrocentric studies made in the 1960s, Carruthers immersed himself so deeply in the study of ancient and traditional African cultures that by 1978 he was able to deliver a body of penetrating and sophisticated lectures stating and demonstrating, through an emphasis on Kemetic/Tawitic/Ancient Egyptian culture, the Afrocentric rationale. Carruthers's intellectual and academic justification for using Tawi (his preferred term for Ancient Egypt, meaning "The United Two Lands") as a starting point is reflected in Mongameli Mabona's statement that "to arrive at the proper estimation of the cultural values of any society, it is necessary to grasp first the philosophy or rather the metaphysical attitude which underlies these values. History and archaeology show that there has been in Africa a civilization which extended from Egypt to Angola from Timbuctu to Zimbabwe. This civilization consisted of a complex of cultures which in their structure showed a marvelous formal and thematic uniformity" to be observed in their literature and mythologies" (Qtd. in Carruthers, p. 13).

Stated in Carruthers's own terms, the Afrocentric mandate is to formulate "an African worldview" as an "essential beginning point for all research which is based upon the *interests* of African people. There can be no African history, no African social science without an African worldview." Carruthers adds that "[by] African, I do not mean merely a history or social science of Africa but a world history and a universal method of analysis designed by and for Africans" (Carruthers, p. 17).

(3) *Molefi Asante*: Molefi Asante holds the singular historical position of having spearheaded the founding of the first African-American Studies Ph.D. granting program in the United States and the world, for that matter. Particularly because of his tireless efforts at promoting the Afrocentric perspective and because of his long

record of publishing on the topic, Asante's presence as founding Chairperson of the Temple University's African-American Studies doctorate program identifies it historically with his Afrocentric theoretical efforts. Asante's prominence and popularity as the most easily identifiable proponent of Afrocentricity merits him therefore special attention in several parts of this essay.

Asante has published perhaps the most single-authored texts with "Afrocentricity" in the title. Included in these are *The Afrocentric Idea* (1987), *Afrocentricity* (1988), and *Kemet, Afrocentricity and Knowledge* (1990). What Asante attempts in *Afrocentricity* (1988), and most of his works, is to present the Afrocentric mandate. However, so busy is he in writing and re-writing the mandate that he rarely convincingly, or demonstrably, writes African culture. Consequently, it is difficult to find Afrocentricity demonstrated sufficiently in his thought even when bringing together several of his books.

No matter what spiritual and intellectual admiration one might hold for Kemet/Ancient Egypt, Asante's premise, evolving out of that of the Association for the Study of Classical African Civilization, that "the centerpiece of Afrocentric theory [is] a reconnection in our minds, of Egypt to Africa" (Asante 1988, p. ix) is troubling and problematic. This premise assumes that African Americans already relate easily to the rest of the African continent, a matter which even today is highly disputable. A major part of the problem of the premise is that it stems from the Association's adoption of the highly valorized, Euro-elitist word "classical," a word which resonates easily as meaning classical like Greece, like Rome, like all the so-called prestigious artifacts of the Europeans. In general, the book *Afrocentricity* serves its purpose as a mandate, but the problem with the rhetoric of any mandate is in its preoccupation with argumentation. The student must be careful therefore not to mistake the mandate for the cultural model, that is, for Africa itself. The reader of *Afrocentricity* is left with Afrocentric argumentation but not with enough African-based conceptual models of social, political, philosophical, and economic being. As a result, in critiquing the black Christian ministry (a truly important subject), for example, a hollowness rings through Asante's statement that "[t]hose ministers who formulate clear political and social philosophies based on the African center will completely alter the church's emphasis" (Asante 1988, p. 76). Asante's statement rings with hollowness because no specific textual references or models of African-based spiritual thought and behavior are presented. In another instance, for example, too, Asante's formulations set forth in the section title "Nijia: The Way," while composing a nice general meditation for reflection, lack the specificity of African-based categories concerning the nature of life and existence. Thus, one necessarily raises the question of how one is to make a truly Afrocentric argument with so few (and even then vague) references to models of thinking and being in Africa.

Even in the later *Kemet, Afrocentricity and Knowledge* (1991), Asante still spends more time in argument with the European, racist historical legacy than he does on presenting Kemet itself. More disturbing, however, is the fact that Asante too often is not aware of the imperialist nature of his logic. To see this, one need only reflect, for example, on the empire logic implicit in Asante's statement that "[a] fundamental position of my argument is that all African societies find Kemet a common source for intellectual and philosophical ideas" (Asante 1991, p. 92). This sounds dangerously much like the erroneous historical paradigm which argues that European culture brought civilization to the rest of the globe. For might it not have been that in order to build the Kemetic empire that the Kemites collected and synthesized all the wisdom it could find in the regions of Africa with which it had contact? For Asante to set forth such a position as "fundamental" is like espousing wholeheartedly that the big life, the imperial life is the good life and that a thatched-roof village, for example, has little to offer that is good, original, or philosophically sufficient.

The problem with Asante's work is that there is never enough elaboration upon traditional Africa, its values, social, political, and economic systems. Asante emphasizes the use of traditional African communication and language functions as a theoretical building block for creating what he calls "Africology." Yet, even his limiting himself to this very restricted theoretical model is never fully nor adequately elaborated to demonstrate how the use of his theoretical model would be operative for analyzing the complex social, philosophical, aesthetic, political, and economic layers of the cultures of African peoples. The result is that Asante promulgates a disposition more than he promulgates an adequately comprehensive theory. What is discussed in Asante's several books never engages its subject on a comprehensive enough level to cover, for example, what Shaha Mfundishi Maasi and Mfundishi J. H. Hassan K. Salim articulate in their book *Kupigani Ngumi* when they identify forty-two significant aspects of the indigenous African value systems, ranging from the African conception of time to the conception of marriage and the definition of love.[12] Maasi and Salim provide a comprehensive world view[13] into which one can place one's evolving Afrocentric self whether one agrees with all the points set forth in their book or not. However, one comes away from Asante simply not having learned very much about African culture and values. Unfortunately, as a key proponent of Afrocentricity, and perhaps now the most well-known one, Asante himself leaves the door open for all types of "Afrocentric" claims by attempting to be theoretical before he is sufficiently foundational.[14] In consequence, one might wish to ponder Paul Gilroy's critique of Asante's brand of Afrocentricism reflected in Gilroy's contention that Asante's formulation "is stubbornly focused around the reconstitution of individual consciousness rather than around the reconstruction of the black nation in exile or elsewhere" (Gilroy 1992, p. 305).[15] While this particular criticism may strike one as extreme, its implications certainly merit attention. West African-born scholar Manthia Diawara even goes so far as to accuse "Afrocentric academics" of fixing "blackness by reducing it to Egypt and *kente* cloths," adding that "Afrocentricism has become a religion, a camp movement, where one can find refuge from the material realities of being black in Washington, D.C., London, or Nairobi" (Diawara 1992, p. 289).[16] While the criticisms of Gilroy and Diawara are indeed harsh, their arguments are not wholly untenable.

(4) *James B. Stewart*: Those interested in understanding how to establish a rigorous and cogent Afrocentric methodological perspective, especially on a scholarly level, should study and refer continuously to James B. Stewart's careful analysis titled "Reaching For Higher Ground: Toward an Understanding of Black/Africana Studies" published in the inaugural issue of *The Afrocentric Scholar* (May 1992). Stewart's discussion demonstrates a mastery of the history of the evolution of all the major endeavors in the United States to articulate an Afrocentric theoretical methodology. Moreover, in the last ten pages of his article Stewart synthesizes the best elements from all of the important proponents of Afrocentric theory, thus providing serious scholars with what is perhaps the best, most comprehensive methodological formulation available. Stewart's methodological formulations are the logical complement to the type of thoroughly itemized value system set forth by Maasi and Salim. Neither can substitute for the other but for both delineation of and emphasis on the indigenous African value system is essential. In effect, Stewart suggests that "for the sake of argument let Afrocentricity refer to the degree of overlap between an idealized model of thought and behavior generated from an interpretation of traditional African thought and practice and an individual's actual thought and behavior" (Stewart 1992, p. 38). To clarify his point further, Stewart argues that "the process of becoming Afrocentric, then, can be disaggregated into three components: (a) increasing the causal connection between an individual's expressed ideology and ob-

served behavior, (b) increasing the degree of overlap between an individual's ideology and behavior and the modal thought and behavior of African Americans (or Africans) depending on the selected reference group, and (c) increasing the degree of overlap between an individual's current expressed ideology and behavior and the ideology and behavior patterns advocated by 'strong claim' Afrocentrists" (Stewart, p. 38).

In conjunction with Stewart (since Stewart's article is very terse), one might want to read, as a preface to the intellectual history of Afrocentric thought, Clovis Semmes's (a.k.a. Jabulani K. Makalani) wonderfully lucid, though scholarly, sections on "African-Centered Thought" and "Afrocentric Forms." In the span of twenty pages in *Cultural Hegemony and African- American Development*,[17] Semmes, beginning with nineteenth-century United States African-American history, provides an excellent summary for understanding the historical evolution of what has come to be popularized as Afrocentricity.

What emerges when there are major discrepancies in the evolution of the Afrocentric self as a result of placing inadequate emphasis on indigenous and traditional Africa is the main subject of the present essay. Hence in considering the notion of Afrocentricity, several fundamental issues need to be raised in order to arrive at a common understanding of the factors and concepts upon which a functional and effective idea of Afrocentricity can be predicated. As we can already see, under the rubric of Afrocentricity, there are several factors at work. Which of these factors does or even should have preeminence is arguable; nevertheless, some of these factors are composed of and determined by very problematic dimensions.

Overall, there appear to be four discernible aspects of Afrocentricity at work in written and oral discourse of Afrocentric proponents, both professors and students. First, there is a form of Afrocentricity which is derived from an understanding of African cultural world view or cosmology. Second, there is a form of Afrocentricity which, in its emphasis on the African person as the neglected being, might be called Afrosubjectivity. Here the African descendant in America is assured primacy as the subject irrespective of intellectual inconsistencies, etc.

Third, there is also at work what might be called "Afrosynthicity." In the discourse of Afrosynthicity, the interest is generalized toward the exploration of Afro-America as a cultural and political entity emphasizing Afro-America's need to assert its sheer autonomous existence. The impulse here is basically nationalistic. In Afrosynthetic discourse, Africa is utilized for whatever purpose is convenient for the subject at hand. What is often revealed in this Afrosynthetic discourse is an identity crisis that is related to matters that go beyond the initial separation from Africa and profoundly into the imbibing of the European personality (e.g. African American machismo modeled along the lines of John Wayne and his frontier antecedents). Fourth, there is, of course, what might be called Afrosyncretism. This is probably the earliest form of scholarly discourse which has emphasized the threads of African culture to have survived in the Americas. In this category, one would find, for example, the important work of Lorenzo Dow Turner, Melville Herskovits, Roger Bastide, Robert Farris Thompson, et al.

When relating to anything labeled Afrocentric, one ought at least be discriminating enough to know which mode is at work, and discriminating enough to know especially that a fundamental Afrocentricity, based on African values, is not always at work. Indeed, one author may at various times work quite appropriately in various nudes. But, again, it seems crucial that one recognize what mode is operative because under the rubric of Afrocentricity, African essences can be and have been so easily misrepresented.

In the interest of respect for Africa and esteem for the African ancestors, one might advocate that the concept of Afrocentricity have at least a generalized African cosmology as its fundamental determinant. That is to say, African values and African worldview would determine, shape, and order the various facets of the thought examined or espoused and would therefore be a determinant of the discourse. But certainly, in order to adhere to this prescription for the Afrocentric, one needs first to do the requisite homework that would allow her or him to give a reasonable articulation of African philosophic, gnostic, social, political, and economic being. In its highest sense, this form of Afrocentricity is reflected in Joseph Baldwin's statement that "the Africentric paradigm . . . as it has evolved over the past 20 years . . . consists of four basic characteristics: (a) It generates the construction of African social reality from the framework of the history, culture and philosophy of African civilization; (b) It recognizes and articulates the basic continuity of the African worldview throughout the diverse populations . . . (c) It recognizes and articulates the basic distinctness and independence of the African worldview . . . (d) It projects the African survival thrust as the center of social reality" (Azibo 1992, p. 67).[18]

Asante argues in *The Afrocentric Idea* that "Afrocentricity proposes a cultural reconstruction that incorporates the African perspective as a part of an entire human transformation. . . ."[19] In his words, an understanding of "the African foundations of human societies" would provide one with another way of seeing.[20] Thus, Asante is primarily urging that Afrocentricity be grounded foremost in cultural comprehension of Africa.

More explicitly, Asante, as a proponent of Afrocentricity, defines it as "placing African ideals at the center of an analysis that involves African culture and behavior."[21] Asante footnotes his definition by adding, "I maintain that African Americans can never achieve their full psychological potential until they find congruence between who they are and what their environment says they ought to be. To be Afrocentric is to place Africans and the interest of Africa at the center of our approach to problem solving."[22]

In Asante's total definition, however, there is, a conflation of an ideology of Afrocentrism with an ideology of ethnocentrism. The convergence of these ideologies is not very philosophically compatible. Asante's phrase "the interest of Africa" can suggest so many things. Indeed the phrase can suggest as much or more about the Europeanized worldview of African-Americans than about what is truly African or in the actual interests of continental Africans. If the former is the case, then the African-American, as a Europeanized being, may fall more under the influence of ethnocentrism than Afrocentricism.

It might further be argued that the origin of the tension within Asante's total definition of the Afrocentric, that is, that "to be Afrocentric is to place Africans and the interest of Africa at the center of our approach to problem solving,"[23] is in the fact that the ethnocentric is so often merely the *egocentric writ large*. Because the egocentric is so typically narrow- visioned, inclinations toward it are problematic. Of course, egocentrism in the case of oppressed peoples is often almost politically mandated for sheer survival. Nevertheless, the egocentric is narrow-visioned and is definitely a liability when it works in collusion with the ethnocentric.

Afrocentric ideals, at large, that is ideals based upon fundamental African values and cosmology, seem to push beyond the boundaries of ethnocentrism. This transcendent attribute is mainly due to the fact that indigenous African thought has not developed extremely rigid categorizations of humanity and nature, as has European thought. The Afrocentric, therefore, would remain more cosmic in its world view. Whereas, since the Eurocentric has developed more rigid categorizations of humanity and nature, it has by its own logic become tremendously ethnocentric, terrestrially oriented and limited as opposed to having a more cosmic orientation toward the inter-connectedness of existence as would the Afrocentric.

There may be something of a paradox in the conceptualization of African culture as being more cosmically oriented, when one remembers that so much of traditional African society is quite characteristically unit-oriented or "tribal." On the surface Africa's social and political demography is so often based on small organizational units, leading one to think with regard to localization and particularity. Nevertheless, this orientation toward the smaller units was an aspect of African social genius and seems not to have rigidified boundaries of being. For above all, African cultural orientation is indeed a cosmic orientation. This cosmic orientation is rooted in the belief lying at the heart of virtually all African cultural units that the universe is a potent conglomerate of active energies, natural and human, seen and not seen and that all units of being are reflections of these energies. Herein lies the foundation for universal interconnectedness. Everything comes from and reflects the same source.

To think about the incongruence of the Afrocentric and the ethnocentric in more specific terms, it may be useful to note the pre-occupation of many Afro-Americans with the need to pin down the ethnic-racial identity of the ancient Egyptians. The need to clarify that the ancient Egyptians were not white, by which is really meant, not Anglo-Saxon, is a significant intellectual, philosophical, and political point in light of the fraudulent history that the modern Anglo-Saxons have created about themselves by appropriating unto themselves the creation of civilization as well as all claims to culture and civilization.

As a reaction to this fraudulence, the question is often raised from the African-American audience in public lectures on Africa about the racial identity of the Egyptians. The same point is sometimes hammered upon by Afrocentric lecturers and scholars to the extent that all parties, by the logic outline! above, make a precarious slip from the Afrocentric cosmic orientation of thinking into the racio-ethnocentric, terrestrial-orientation of thinking. In slipping unwittingly into the racio-ethnocentric, terrestrial orientation, the lecturers, scholars and audience miss a true comprehension of the glory of the Egypt they wish to claim and of the Egypt with which they, because of various needs, wish to identify. That is, they often end up identifying with very specific points about Ancient Egypt to the extent that they overlook the cosmic points that really should be made via true identification with Egypt. Again that is, if one focuses too much on racial specificity, then one may disregard the spiritual lessons the Egyptian priesthood sought for millennia to pass down and to teach.

In conjunction with the foregoing point, even after careful study and great appreciation of some of the historically indispensable theoretical and methodological essays in the inaugural issue of *The Afrocentric Scholar: The Journal of the National Council For Black Studies*, one may very well still stand at issue with the use of Kmet/Ancient Egypt as the almost exclusive model for representing and valorizing African civilization. The almost singular use of Kmetic/Egyptian model may veritably and inadvertently reinforce pathologies of African Americans (derived from European hegemony) with respect, for instance, to equating physical beauty with not being "too black" and having relatively long hair; with respect to equating power and self-worth with empire. African Americans must beware of their special psychological challenge which demands a real rather than abstract association with and appreciation for the Africa of the thatched roof village as well as with imperial Africa. Otherwise one may find that one is still operating out of a European paradigm of what is valuable and what is beautiful. Thus, why not cite, for example, as often as one cites Egypt the civilizations of the Dogon via the cosmology articulated Ogo-tommeli,[24] or the cosmogony of the Zulu as is relayed through authors like Mazisi Kunene in *Anthem of the Decades*[24] and Vusamazulu Credo Mutwa in *Indaba My Children*[25] and the recent, very extraordinarily informative presentations of the Dagara worldview by Malidoma and Sobonfu Some in *Of Water and the Spirit* and *We Have No Word for Sex*.[26] This admonition about metal models is crucial most of all because the multi-layeredness of African self-hatred can create peculiar zones of self-deception, even among the most outstanding intellectuals. This admonition is also important because when speaking of *the* African worldview, the truly Africentric person ought to be able to demonstrate how the African worldview manifests itself throughout various regions of Africa.

Interest in the issue of the identity of the Ancient Egyptians is complicated by the motive of the question and by the point-of-view that determines the answer. Therefore, if the conscious or subconscious motive of the interest is in affirming one's human superiority as a race, it is doubtful whether one will arrive at a creditable answer about the fundamental essence of Ancient Egypt. To put the matter in the form of a question, can an egocentric frame of reference provide an adequate interpretation of anything that is truly African? It seems logical to say that had the Ancient Egyptians, those African folk who crystallized Ancient Egypt's being and essence, been caught in racio-ethnocentric thinking Egypt never would have occupied the grand historical space of several millennia that it did. To the contrary, it was the cosmic-centric orientation that became crystallized along the Nile by ancient Africans that allowed them to surrender their ethnocentrism to a broader world view, a world view that gave primacy to cosmic law, not social law, about humanity. It was cosmic law, not parochial, social or racial law by which talent was defined and which determined even the eligibility to hold the office of Pharaoh. It was this African cultural orientation which placed emphasis on cosmic force and cosmic law that deterred atrophy in ancient Egyptian civilization and allowed it to endure for several millennia.

It is useful to consider infantile American civilization by contrast, a civilization which has operated and still does operate from the Eurocentric, racio-ethnocentric orientation. In merely two centuries as a nation, America suffers from a critical crisis of atrophy. This condition of atrophy is possibly largely due to American reluctance to embrace the law of cosmic humanity, giving preference to the terrestrial, racio-ethnocentric orientation, thereby stifling through neglect, marginalization, and alienation, the genius of its total lot of human resources.

The pertinence of an allusion to the Egyptians will be more apparent if it is kept in mind that in his conceptualization of Afrocentricity, Asante asserts that "The Afrocentric analysis reestablishes the centrality of the ancient Kemetic (Egyptian) civilization and the Nile Valley cultural complex as points of reference in much the same way as Greece and Rome serve as reference points for the European world" (Asante 1987, p. 9). In addition to the problem just discussed, another problem is inherent in this proposition of Asante, and it is certainly a problem against which the Afrocentric student must be on guard.

The problem presently referred to is the problem of structural analogue inherent in Asante's proposition. That is, the proposition is determined to a great extent by Eurocentric thinking rather than by purported Afrocentric thinking. Thus one might raise the question again: what are the ramifications of thinking in terms of Asante's proposition, viz., that Egypt serves the Afrocentric world view "the same way Greece and Rome serve as reference points for the European world"? There are indeed many intellectual liabilities in Asante's formulation of his proposition. Are Asante's followers picking up on his intended meaning? Hence the need to be intellectually and philosophically clear on why Egypt might be central to Afrocentric thinking. Is it because Egypt was a great empire and African Americans want to identity with the idea of empire, a successful African civilization along European lines? Or is it because African Americans truly value Egypt's philosophical and gnostic essence?

To put it more simply, for what reason is it that African Americans really desire to claim the pyramids? As monuments to empire or as symbols of an adept process of being and system of knowing? While I do think it is Asante's intention to claim the latter, many African-American students, in their Eurocentric and philistine thought processes, while quoting Asante, are unwittingly claiming the former. In effect, then, one can begin to understand why Paul Gilroy, a diasporic African not from the United States, feels the need to reject the term "Afrocentric," recognizing it really as what he calls "Americentricism," that is, a form of African-oriented thought biased toward a psychology of African descendants with a United States psychology (Gilroy 1992, p. 307). Gilroy's key point is that too often the Afrocentric thought emanating from the United States "attempts to construct a sense of black particularity *outside* of a notion of national identity. Its founding problem lies in the effort to figure sameness across national boundaries and between nation-states" (Gilroy 1992, p. 306).

Gilroy's interest in the way United States African Americans define the Afrocentric is reflected in the complication of Afrocentric representation in Patricia Hill Collins's *Black Feminist Thought*,[27] when from a black feminist perspective reputed African and universal women values conflate. Although she refers to African-based emphasis on the use of dialogue as a humanizing factor for all members of the African indigenous community (Collins 1991, p. 212), still problematic in Collins's use of the Afrocentric is the inclination to view the concept more in light of United States African-American oppression instead of in light of traditional African value systems. Thus for Collies to say that "an Afrocentric feminist epistemology is rooted in the everyday experiences of African-American women" (Collins 1991, p. 207) is inadequate as Afrocentric, that is, inadequate in establishing within African-American thought systems a foundational relationship with the potency of indigenous African ways of thinking. The crucial points of emphasis in African indigenous cultures, such as emphasis on gaining fundamental understanding and mastery of the female and male cosmic/personal energies, are never discussed or mentioned. The indigenous African ways to "knowledge, consciousness, and...empowerment" (words from the subtitle of Collins's book) are never investigated as gateways to empowerment and liberation.[28]

Thus one returns to Asante's definition of Afrocentricity and asks the critical question, how shall one define those crucial words in his phrase "the interest of Africa"? A necessary word of caution would be that African Americans would do well to guard their individual and collective intellect from slipping from the Afrocentric into the more ego-determined, American ethnocentric frame of reference. There is a thin line here which can make a critical difference in the value of the intellectual model one purports to be interested in constructing and reconstructing. A present fear is that too many younger proponents of Afrocentricity, particularly college students, are not aware that their mental structures are still working in the celebration of imperialism.

The most germane Afrocentric theory trust be able to predicate itself upon the most rudimentary and most unitary form of African village culture. If this is not so, then it seems difficult to assert that Afrocentricity is really working toward the affirmation or validation of Africa. That is, must one have the great empires of Mali, Benin, and Kmet in order to determine the essential value and greatness of Africa?

Some of what is called Afrocentric is better identified as Afrosubjectivity and/or Afrosubjectivism or maybe even Afro-narcissism. It is worth keeping in mind that, as stated by Lawrence Cahoone, "Subjectivity is consciousness. That is to say, subjectivity is that feature of or activity of human individuals by which humans have awareness of appearances or phenomena, by which things show themselves or are manifest or present to us; it is the awareness of anything whatsoever, the field or totality of experiences. Subjectivity is conceived in various and sometimes ambiguous ways: as an activity, as a metaphysical substance, as the things which appear, and that which allows thorn to appear" (Cahoone 1988, p. 19). To be even more specific, Cahoone's definition of subjectivism states, "Subjectivism is the conviction that the *distinction between subjectivity and non-subjectivity is the most fundamental distinction in an inquiry*" (Cahoone, p. 20). Consequently, one must learn to be aware of the disposition of the self. Although subjectivism can take on metaphysical, ethical, or other meanings, it is to its problematic methodological and/or systemic dualism that one must be alert. Too often Afrocentrists are not aware of the intellectual necessity and importance of making this recognition. That is to say, Afrocentrists are often too unaware of their involvement with subjectivism, a very European phenomenon, historically speaking.

All of this is to say that subjectivism privileges the perceiving consciousness. But frequently, the Afrocentrist's perceiving consciousness is the European or Western aspect of her or his personality, which personality is sometimes a denied identity. African thinking is not necessarily the thinking which is privileged in some of what is labelled Afrocentric thought. From a more definite Afrocentric point of view, one should be inclined to raise the question, do human consciousness and human intellectuality mandate the privileging of the subject under any circumstance? Might not there be some possibility and some value in thinking with double-consciousness, not so much in the DuBoisean sense, but in the Ancient Egyptian sense of thinking "mdu-ntrically"[29] (hieroglyphically), thinking, that is, with regard to synthesis, thinking simultaneously in reference to or from the perspective of both subject and object? When Molefi Asante speaks about "the possibilities of a world where Africa . . . is subject and not object (and where, as a result) such a posture is necessary and rewarding for Africans and Europeans" (Asante 1987, p. 3), he is speaking, of course, from a perspective that there is value in African cosmology. One should be careful, therefore, not to confuse the idea of Africa as subject with specific problems of Western subjectivity which are reflected in the self-absorption of the individual and individualized self. To restate the problem articulated above: subjectivity in terms of self-absorption does occur, unfortunately, and too often, in sonic of our thinking, that is labelled Afrocentric.

Giving additional attention to the matter of the "subject," one may pursue the vitally related issue whether Afrocentricity lends itself to the unqualified appropriation of various aspects of U.S. African-American culture simply because those cultural phenomena are identified with the U.S. African-American subject? There is little benefit in arguing defensively, as some do, that there is nothing wrong with U.S. African-American culture. It would seem that one value of the Afrocentric would be to serve as criteria for critiquing the U.S. African-American phenomenon of culture as well as the general western phenomenon of culture. Afrocentricity ought to be able to illuminate from a long-term perspective just what things are dysfunctional within U.S. African-American culture. The generally astute Adolph Reed, for example, even takes a defensive posture regarding the possible shortcomings of Afro-American culture.[30]

A serious and influential component of Afro-American culture, Afro-American Christianity, for one, definitely needs a surgical critique. Consider, for example, the messianic aspect of Christianity that has become so integral as a determinant in the U.S. African-American cultural worldview. An Afrocentric critique of the Judeo-Christian messianic view with the generally non-messianic African cultural view might be fruitful, for example, to U.S. African-American intellectual and political as well as ontological development or reconstruction.

Can an Afrocentric concept be established simply on the basis of conceptual opposition of a Eurocentric tradition and an Afro-American phenomenon? Ought not the intellectual criteria always be rooted somewhere in Africa or, at least, validated by fundamental African values? Is the U.S. African-American subject, in all his/her European complications to be so unequivocally and mistakenly identified or equated with Afrocentricity? If so, perhaps there is a real need to argue for and make plentiful use of distinct terms which will designate that which is peculiarly related to U.S. African American life as "Afrocentric" and that which is truly related to African cultural, historical and philosophic foundations and the African diasporic continuum as "Africentric."

It would be useful to analyze some specific instances in which what is labelled Afrocentricity falls victim to what is really some form of Afrosubjectivity. In "Black Heroes and the Afrocentric Values in Theatre,"[31] for instance, Barbara Molette's argument for an Afrocentric concept of the hero is significantly undermined by the logistics of the oppositional paradigm she employs. Her oppositional mode of argument is a form of refutation that simply allows her to set herself in subjective opposition rather than intellectual opposition to the dominant and privileged European culture. Her oppositional strategy is set in motion by her very essential subjectivity, a subjectivity stimulated by the need to engage in debunking rather than by the need to engage in analysis.

The subjective emphasis, as exhibited in Barbara Molette's work, causes the presumed analyst to overlook crucial dimensions of the opposed worldview as she attempts to promote her own worldview. Thus, having been taken in by her own African-American subjectivity Molette characterizes the Eurocentric heroic tradition as requiring "the trait of aggressiveness in order to achieve the status of hero" (Molette 1985, p. 449). By contrast, asserts Molette, African culture does not require the aggressive trait as part of its criteria for hero status. "Instead," Molette contends, the African concept of the heron "might involve the use of nonaggressive athletic skill to resolve a crisis accompanied by the exhibition of bravery, courage, and wit" (Molette, p. 449). One has to raise the question here of who it is Molette assumes to be her audience and what it is that she presumes about that audience. Indeed a concept of the European hero might also "involve the use of nonaggressive athletic skill to resolve a crisis accompanied by the exhibition of bravery, courage, and wit." Even a non-reading television watcher would have difficulty complying with such an overgeneralization in Molette's definition of the Eurocentric hero. Certainly, then, one need not expect the acquiescence of an audience of readers who are even lightly versed in European history, literature, or theatre. Even more improbable is Molette's assertion that "a nonracist, nonsexist concept of magnitude is necessary in order to identify and understand Black characters who are heroic" (Molette, p. 449). If such a definition of the heroic which includes the nonsexist dimension is to hold ground, what then is any reasonably enlightened person to do with a hero like Bigger Thomas in *Native Son*, not to mention the real life ones. There are other complications in Molette's logic as well, which need not be belabored here, including, most ironically, her indiscriminate use of the comic hero and most surprisingly, her use of a virtually untranslatable French word (*panache*) to express what she feels epitomizes the Afrocentric comic hero.

Thus Molette may very well be stimulated by important Afrocentric values with regard to her interest in defining and distinguishing between the African and European conceptualizations of the hero, the comic hero in particular; however, the foundation for her definition, based a great deal in aspects of her subjectivity, i.e., her obviously primary need to debunk the European, is unreliable. Suffice it to say therefore that the oppositional paradigm, a naively subjective paradigm, generated by the less than academic need to debunk rather than to enlighten, when not handled with intellectual fullness, can become very problematic and ineffective in its attempts to establish an Afrocentric value system and Afrocentric intellectual model or strategy. By contrast, the work of Cheryl Townsend Gilkes establishes itself in many respects as intellectually Afrocentric. This is demonstrated in her article "'Mother to the Motherless, Father to the Fatherless': Power, Gender, and Community in an Afrocentric Biblical Tradition."[32] Gilkes's work exemplifies Afrocentricity by making the African cultural linkage with Afro-America demonstrable by highlighting and examining certain assumptions taken for granted in the Afro-American folk tradition, by virtue of their being rooted in the traditional African worldview. Thus, Gilkes shows how a worldview constituted of both feminine and masculine deities was carried over into the New World experience of Africans as they encountered and metamorphosed Christianity.

Gilkes demonstrates how in their embracing of the Judaeo-Christian patriarchal deity, the Africans in America have nevertheless in their syncretic spiritual culture recast the Judaeo-Christian God and attributed to it maternal as well as paternal qualities. Hence, the Judaeo-Christian deity in African-American tradition is readily referred to in prayers, sermons, and gospel songs, though not in "scripture reading," as "the mother to the motherless and father to the fatherless" (Gilkes 1989, p. 57). Because their conceptualization of deity, as both masculine and feminine complements forms and essences, was rooted in their traditional African spiritual reality and heritage, "it never occurred to black people [in America] that this combined feminine and masculine image of God could possibly be an issue" as it would have been in Europeanized Christianity, Wilkes argues (Gilkes, p. 57), adding that "the images of God in songs, sermons, prayers, and testimonies are important Afrocentric expressions in the United States" (Gilkes, p. 58).

To further clarify her point of view, Gilkes states that "Black people imaged a God of power as both male and female although they were initially presented with a patriarchal God in an androcentric text" (Gilkes, p. 58). To support her argument, Gilkes's exploration of the biblical scriptures reveals that the reference to God as "father to the fatherless" appears in Psalm 68 and only in those specific terms. The Africans broadened the gender reference in order to embrace a more African conceptualization of divinity as partaking of the masculine and the feminine.

But in the case of some of Gilkes's other Afrocentric references where does one draw the line? For when Gilkes moves into the discussion of the crucial issue of black liberation and the creation of a liberationist Christian theology, is she correct in designating this issue of black American liberation as Afrocentric since she does not demonstrate how the issue of liberation has origins in traditional African cultural determinants? The critical legitimacy of the issue of liberation is not at all to be underplayed for its ramifications for the lives of African descendants in America. Nevertheless, if the term Afrocentric is to be used to designate that which is African derived, then the question must be asked whether the situation that mandates liberation is of African origin.

More specifically is the political situation of African Americans fundamentally tied to any particular African cultural derivatives? Should one critique the political situation from an African cultural perspective, one could very easily validate what is being done as Afrocentric. But is the issue of our political situation necessarily Afrocentric simply because one is focusing on matters related to African descendants? To probe further in to the matter demarcation, could an African-American who is sold, for example, on Marxism but whose focus is exclusively the situation of black people be appropriately called Afrocentric? One notices often that in the Afrocentricity of intellectual and popular culture, it is African American issues rather than African values that are foregrounded. This is not to say, though, that the issues themselves do not have value implications.

The area most fraught with problems is the realm of more abstract thinking where one is required to do more extrapolation and transferring of the African-based value systems and worldview. Nevertheless the transmissibility of an African-based worldview is what Linda James-Myers achieves in the articulation of her patent theory of optimal psychology set forth in her various articles and her book *Understanding An Afrocentric World View: Introduction To An Optimal Psychology* (1988).[33] Very exemplary, too, of African-based interpretation is Paul Carter Harrison's *The Drama of Nommo* (1972)[34] and the work of Kariamu Welsh Asante related to African-American dance and her development of the Umfundalai dance technique.[35]

A sub-category of Afrosubjectivism might be marked off as Afro-significationism. The root term, "signifying," is thought of here as the dominant form of sarcasm in Afro-American verbal culture. In this context, signifying is defined as a verbal or gestural strategy employing rhetorical indirectness or directness and is used for the purpose of ridicule. The tone of the sarcasm may run the gamut from mild to caustic.

In effect, Afro-significationism is defined in this discussion as a mode of intellectualism in which intellectual engagement is overridden by signifying itself; that is, intellectual analysis is overridden, laced with, or determined by the motive of counterhegemonic discursive retaliation. This is the mode of discursive engagement with European critical theory, which, at least in one respect, characterizes some of the recent and prolific work of Houston A. Baker, Jr., and virtually all of the work of Henry Louis Gates, Jr.[36] The extent of Baker's and Gates's awareness, their intellectualism, partly determined by this psychology, is unclear but suffice it to say that a crucial aspect of their discursive representation is structured implicitly, and perhaps even very unconsciously, around their signifying in the extreme about intellectual merit and achievement and intellectual discourse in the Western philosophic tradition, especially as this tradition began increasingly; within the past two decades to be courted and imitated by literary critics.

Perhaps owing to this type of involvement, graduate students in particular will frequently undertake to cite the work of Baker and Gates as examples of Afrocentric literary criticism. When placed in historical and critical perspective, the work of Baker and Gates over the past decade has more value as an implicitly signifying mode, a mode of mimetic productivity, than as lucid and compelling Afrocentric literary and cultural interpretation. Much of the writing of Baker and Gates, in consequence of their emphases on demonstrating and reflecting the adaptability and suitability of African-American culture for European critical theory, signifies indeed about the nature of current critical discursive productivity in the academy. Unfortunately, though, too often their excessive enthusiasm to be like the post-modernist, neo-hegemonic authorities gives to their literary and cultural enterprise a detractive and negative value. Hence the language of European history theory so dominates the discourse of Baker in his discussion of the blues that the blues itself has to struggle with the discourse to retain any kind of prominence as subject. And with Gates's almost exploitative use of Elegba figure and others aspects of West African mythology in *The Signifying Monkey*, in the conscious or unconscious service of European theory, the result is even more devastating. The outcome of the work of both critics is the further compromising of African culture to validate itself.

Some of Baker and Gates's productions might be likened to the troubled and dubious achievements of celebrated cinematographer Spike Lee. One need only remember that Lee's mode of presentation and emphasis is heavily determined by sense that to market to African Americans successfully the subject must be one of African-American controversy. The suitability of the comparison of Baker and Gates with Lee would become even clearer if one were to be reminded that in Spike Lee's posture as a satirist, the troublesome aspects of Lee's problematic achievements stem very much from his deficiencies in the areas of both dramaturgical irony and verbal irony. That is, as with Baker and Gates who often appear so mesmerized by the magical power of the language of European discourse, Lee too seems more captivated by the mandate to produce the black controversial subject than he is conscious of the need to exert over his production the ultimate in African-based verbal and dramaturgical control. Nevertheless, Spike Lee, too, is often labeled Afrocentric.

This point of view regarding Gates is corroborated by Boyi[37] who agrees that Gates arrives at his "Afrocentric" point, after his romance with validation of African culture through European theory, and that his efforts to set interpretative examples do not reach far enough into rich realm of indigenous African cultural paradigms (Qtd. in Stewart, pp. 30-31). The fixations of Baker and Gates also lead, of course, to consideration of questions about audience constituency and to fundamental questions of who (not with regard to race, but intellectual integrity) is perceived as the most valued audience constituent. This problem of audience value brings us back to the essential issue, the trap of subjectivity, the matter of self-consciousness and the determinants of self-consciousness.

In attempting to define the maturing African-American literary imagination as Afrocentric, Carol Blackshire-Belay[38] sets forth several good points in proposing that this "maturing imagination" can be defined by seeing "first and foremost [that] the writer uses language that reflects the culture. Second, [that] the writer understands the universality of African peoples' experience, that is, the emotions and attitudes are universal to the African audience. Third, [that] the writer transcends the local or fixed boundary of imagination in style, imagery, and form. [And] lastly, the writer shows a quest for justice, harmony, and peace" (Blackshire-Belay 1992, p. 6). Not overlooked by Blackshire-Belay in her proposal, however, are the myriad complications for arriving at a mature Afrocentric disposition. In dealing with the literary arts, for example, she allows therefore for factoring in and accounting for such crucial and problematic matters as the writer's voice and audience even with respect to the most favored African-American writers. Blackshire-Belay questions, for instance, "whether the voices of Hurston and Ellison and Wright were meant for a [black] or for white audience," whether blacks were only "a sideshow in their discourse," whether the object "was to explain [blacks] to whites," and whether [blacks] were for these writers and others "the aesthetic material for a larger social point than the narrative discourse?" (Blackshire-Belay 1992, p. 7).

The truly complicating factors of these issues notwithstanding, true immersion into indigenous African philosophical systems ought to offer one more spiritual intellectual potency for resolving and managing these and a range of other issues that complicate diasporic African existence. Unfortunately, though, diasporic Africans are so westernized in their thinking processes that like their colonizers and enslavers, they, too, are easily prone to dismiss the value of anything seen as very old or ancient or African.

This Afrosubjectivism is not unlike the Cartesian rationalist dictum, *Cogito ergo sum*— "I think therefore I am" from which Afrosubjectivism definitively stems. And as with the classical European tradition of thinking, too often in so-called Afrocentric thinking, too, existence itself becomes vulnerable to being defined as the privilege of the human in the West. Specifically, existence remains the singular privilege of rational perception.

In an effort to ascertain his own existence, Rene Descartes, in the *Meditations*, arrived at the position that such a verification of existence could be made only via the possession of consciousness. The Cartesian postulate, in its most popular facet, that to *think* was to be, was conceived in and eventually embraced by a world which postulated an hierarchical ordering of racial humanity.[19] The European eventually identified the Cartesian "I" primarily with himself and therefore attributed the primacy of thinking and reasoning unto himself, the European human, subsequently attempting to appropriate all of the great thinking ever done unto himself, and even further, subsequently becoming massively engaged in the material production and distribution of thought (the European self) and things (things, too, are manifestations of thought) through the printed word and book selling. This engagement with the reproduction of his own thinking self was to serve for the European as tangible justification for claiming for himself the primary status in the order of being.

A true Africanist philosopher might formulate her/his conceptualization of existence in other terms. Hence K.K.B. FU-KIAU maintains in his discussion of the African concept of being, "African society in general, and Bantu in particular, perceive a human being as a power, a phenomenon of perpetual veneration from conception to death—a perpetual reality that cannot be denied..." (FU-KIAU 1991, p. 8). Thus, the Africanist philosopher might say, for example, "I be; therefore I am." This conceptualization would therefore not appropriate existence as the singular engagement of the human. It would not encourage a bifurcation of the human and the natural in the way that bifurcation happened in the evolution of the European worldview under the Cartesian incentive coupled with the rationalist emphasis, a line of emphasis which had its historical descent through the groundwork of Aristotle and the cultivation of medieval Christian scholastic philosophy, coming later to be combined with the rationalist emphasis found in the evolution of Protestant theology and its privileging of the individual self.

The question that remains for the true Afrocentrist is, does he or she really wish to become entwined in the snares of subjectivism? And, will African Americans expend their energy attempting to become latter-day modernists, self-absorbed, appropriationist individualists? Such may be precisely what they may indeed become if they are not critical of the intellectual categories by which they operate.

If Afrocentrists are about the business of improving upon the past and present Columbian New World, it would be well for advocates and practitioners to keep in mind that the Afrocentrist is very much a product of the West and is therefore very susceptible to the Western pitfalls, particularly the pitfall of subjectivism and narcissism. Admonitions for the European and European American are, therefore, also applicable to the African American. Fred Dallmayr, author of *The Twilight of Subjectivity*, reminds us that, as Ortega y Gasset reflected on the Cartesian legacy of the "thinking substance" or the "thinking subject," he raised the following very pertinent proposition: "Suppose," said Ortega y Gasset, "that this idea of subjectivity which is the root of modernity should be superseded, suppose it should be invalidated in whole or in part by another idea, deeper and firmer. This would mean that a new climate, a new era, was beginning."[40] What role is the Afrocentric worldview playing in this invalidation of the Cartesian legacy of subjectivity—a legacy which aided in the reification and institutionalization of chattel slavery and subsequent racist oppression? Is Afrocentricity in its current modes playing a role of simple replacement, thereby perpetuating the negative phenomenological structures of that legacy, or is it playing a more radically phenomenological role of structural displacement? Hopefully, postmodern humankind (society, culture) will be able to triumph over the phenomenological dilemma to which Martin Heidegger contends it is fated in declaring that "Whatever and however we may try to think, we think within the sphere of tradition."[41]

In conclusion and to re-state the problem: Is Afrocentricity the focus on the condition of the African-American racial self and its manifold predicaments (economic, psychological, sociological, etc.) as a result of American slavery and Euro-American racism, or is Afrocentricity the affirmation of ancient and traditional African values? Both are essential areas of intellectual inquiry and are not mutually exclusive intellectual dimensions.

Perhaps for our pronouncements and inquiries more than one term is necessary: "Afrocentric," "Afracentric," and "Africentric." The first term, "Afrocentric" might be used to designate matters peculiar to the enslaved Africans and their descendants in the Americas, issues peculiar to the African-American racial self and its manifold predicaments. The second term, "Afracentric," could refer to matters relating to women, in particular. This second term might need its own subcategories, however, since there are some issues more peculiar to women of African descent in America which are not necessarily of significance to continental African women. This effort at distinction and discrimination in the nomenclature is crucial because there are dimensions of the African-American worldview that certainly ought not always carry the presumption of being essentially African. That is, African-American issues and characteristics are not universally African. Many aspects of African-American ontology are American determined, not African determined, such aspects of being which derive, for example, from basic bourgeois, the individualistic worldview of Americans rather than of Africans. The third term, "Africentric," could be the more foundational designation, bearing definite and precise grounding in indigenous African thought and customs. "Africentric" would refer specifically to African cultural attributes, ontologies, epistemologies, and axiologies with respect to their purposeful, illuminative, and regenerative agency for Africa and the African diaspora.

But again, perhaps only one term is really necessary and that is the most fundamentally reflective and comprehensive one which advocated here to be "Africentricity," resonating with Azibo's definition of "Africentricity" that states: "A matured apprehension of the concept of Africentricity reveals its meaning to be no more or less than construing, interpreting, negotiating, and otherwise acting on the world using the system of conceptual thought generated from the African deep structure, also known as the African worldview. The cultural factors and cultural aspects as developed by the African...thus paramatrize Africentricity. When an African actually employs this conceptual universe, she or he is *located* Africentrically.... Distortion in the meaning of Africentricity often arises" when one is Africentrically oriented but not Africentrically located (Azibo, p. 84), that is, when the theory is not reflected in the behavior.

References

Asante, Molefi Kete. *The Afrocentric Idea*. Philadelphia: Temple University Press, 1987.
———. *Afrocentricity*. Trenton: Africa World Press, Inc., 1988.

————. *Kemet, Afrocentricity and Knowledge*. Trenton: Africa World Press, Inc., 1990.

Azibo, Daudi Ajani ya. "Articulating the Distinction between Black Studies and the Study of Blacks: The Fundamental Role of Culture and the African-Centered Worldview." *The Afrocentric Scholar*. Volume 1, Number 1 (May 1992): 64-97.

Blackshire-Belay, Carol Aisha, ed. *Language and Literature in the African American Imagination*. Greenwood Press, 1992.

Cahoone, Lawrence E. *The Dilemma of Modernity: Philosophy Culture, and Anti-Culture*. Albany: State University of New York Press, 1988.

Carruthers, Jacob, H. *Essays in Ancient Egyptian Studies*. Los Angeles: University of Sankore Press, 1984.

Caton, Hiram. *The Origin of Subjectivity*. New Haven: Yale University Press, 1973.

Collins, Patricia Hill. *Black Feminist Thought: Knowledge, Consciousness, and the Politics of Empowerment*. New York: Routledge, Chapman and Hall, Inc., 1991.

Dallmayr, Fred. *The Twilight of Subjectivity: Contributions to a Post-Individualistic Theory of Politics*. Amherst: University of Massachusetts Press, 1981.

Diawara, Manthia. "Afro-Kitsch," in *Black, Popular Culture*. Seattle: Bay Press, 1992: 285-91.

Fraser, C. Gerald. "Black Caucus Deliberations at Montreal: Who Should Control African Studies and for What Ends?" *Africa Report* (December 1969): 20-21.

FU-KIAU, Kimbwandende Kia Bunseki. *Self-Healing, Power and Therapy: Old teachings From Africa*. New York: Vantage Press, Inc., 1991.

Gilkes, Cheryl Townsend. "'Mother to the Motherless, Father to the Fatherless': Power, Gender, and Community in an Afrocentric Biblical tradition." *SEMEIA: An Experimental Journal For Biblical Criticism*. Volume 47 (1989): 57-85.

Gilroy, Paul. "It's a Family Affair," in *Black Popular Culture*, pp. 303-16. Ed. Gina Dent. Seattle: Bay Press, 1992.

Judovitz, Dalia. *Subjectivity and Representation in Descartes*. New York: Cambridge University Press, 1988.

Maasi, Shaha Mfundishi, et al. *Kupigana Ngumi: Root Symbols of the Ntchru and Ancient Kmt*, Volume 1. Plainfield, NJ: The Pan-Afrakan Kupigana Press and Black Gold Press, 1992.

Molette, Barbara. "Black Heroes and the Afrocentric Values in Theatre." *Journal of Black Studies*, Volume 15, Number 4 (June 1985): 447-462.

Peters, Erskine. *African Americans in the New Millennium*. Oakland: Regent Press, 1991.

————. African Openings to the Tree of Life. Oakland: Regent Press, 1983.

Reed, Adolph Jr. "Steel Trap." *The Nation* (March 4, 1991): 274-79.

Riley, Shamara Shantu. "Ecology Is a Sistah's Issue Too: The Politics of Emergent Afrocentric Ecowomanism," in *Ecofeminism and the Sacred*, pp. 191-204. Ed. Carol J. Adams. New York: Continuum Publishing Company, 1993.

Roberts, Robin. "'Ladies First': Queen Latifah's Afrocentric Feminist Music Video." *African American Review*, Volume 28, Number 2 (1994): 245-247.

Semmes, Clovis E. (aka Jabulani K. Makalani). *Cultural Hegemony in African American Development*. Westport: Praeger Publishers, 1992.

Stewart, James B. "Reaching For Higher Ground: Toward an Understanding of Black/Africana Studies." *The Afrocentric Scholar*, Volume 1, Number 1 (May 1992): 1-63.

Walters, Ronald W. *Pan-Africanism in the African Diaspora: An Analysis of Modern Afrocentric Political Movements*. Detroit: Wayne State University Press, 1993.

Endnotes

1. See, for example, H.E.A.I. [Human Education Against Lies], KRS 1, "Family Got to Get Busy," *Civilization Against Technology*, Elektra/Asylum Records, 1991. See also Robin Roberts, "'Ladies First': Queen Latifah's Afrocentric Feminist Music Video." *African American Review*, Vol. 28, No. 2: 245-257. See especially page 246 where Queen Latifah is quoted as saying, "To Me Afrocentricity is a way of living.... It's about being into yourself and being proud of your origins."

2. See, for example, Shamara Shantu Riley, "Ecology Is a Sistah's Issue Too: The Politics of Emergent Afrocentric Ecowomanism," in Carol J. Adams, ed., *Ecofeminism and the Sacred* (Continuum Publishing Company, 1993), pp. 191-204.

3. There is, for example, the magazine *SBC*, published in Los Angeles, CA, whose subtitle reads "For the Afrocentric Homosexual Man."

4. For a discussion of my thoughts about some of the major problems with the African-American christian ministry, see Erskine Peters, *African Americans in the New Millennium*, pp. 16-25.

5. See, for example, an erotic series called "in Loving Color," a Sean Michaels and Video Team Production, labelled "An Afrocentric Production."

6. The best intellectual valorization of popular Afrocentrism is set forth by Ronald Walters when he writes that "there are some indications that the concept of Afrocentricity has taken hold at the grass-roots level within African-American communities in the 1990s. This has happened largely as an antithesis to and as a result of the three-decade movement for racial integration within the schools and other institutions dominated by whites that control the socialization of Black youth. The current dysfunctional condition of urban Black Educational institutions and the connection between this condition and the rise of serious youthful crime, drug involvement and other antisocial behavior, have called for a response by Black people themselves. And Blacks have embarked upon an indigenous reinvention of aspects of their life encompassing such cultural artifacts as Rap music, break dancing, inventive language, and now the movement for the 'infusion' of African and African-American studies in the schools" (Ronald W. Walters, *Pan Africanism in the African Diaspora: An Analysis of Modern Afrocentric Political Movements* (Wayne State University Press, 1993), p. 372).

7. See James B. Stewart, "Reaching For Higher Ground: Toward An Understanding of Black/Africana Studies." *The Afrocentric Scholar*, Vol. 1, No. 1 (May 1992): 2. Careful study of Stewart's article is critical for anyone attempting or interested in becoming a serious Afrocentric scholar.

8. Numerous other proponents of Afrocentricity like Maulana Karenga, Yosef A.A. bin-Jochannan, etc., are discussed in Stewart (1992), Semmes (1992), and Azibo (1992).

9. Ronald W. Walters, *Pan Africanism in the African Diaspora: An Analysis of Modern Afrocentric Political Movements* (Wayne State University Press, 1993), pp. 366-67.

10. C. Gerald Fraser, "Black Caucus Deliberations at Montreal: Who Should Control African Studies and For What Ends?" *Africa Report* 1 (December 1969): 20-21.

11. One very important aspect of the work of early Egyptologist Wallace Budge is that in translating and interpreting *The Book of the Dead* (which some have made us aware ought to be translated as "The Book of Coming Forth By Day," and which I propose ought probably be translated as "A Book For the Dead," the "Dead" bring all of us the so-called living!), Budge con-

sistently worked to relate the Kemetic/Ancient Egyptian spiritual system and its symbols to the spiritual systems and symbols of the other regions of Africa, thus working always to illustrate African cultural continuity.

12. See Shaba Mfundishi Maasi and Mfundishi J.H. Hassan K. Salim, *Kupigana Ngumi: Root Symbols of The Ntchru and Ancient Kmt, Volume I* (The Pan-African Kupigana Ngumi Press and Black Gold Press, 1992), pp. 189-95.

13. A similar effort is made from a philosophical and proverbial perspective in Erskine Peters, *African Openings to the Tree of Life* (Regent Press, 1983).

14. The reader should study Stewart's discussion of Asante's theoretical limitations (Stewart 1992, pp. 44-46). Stewart also discusses how Asante's formulations coincide with the limitations of Henry Louis Gates, Jr., whose theoretical posture I address later in this discussion.

15. Paul Gilroy, "It's a Family Affair," in *Black Popular Culture*, a project of Michelle Wallace edited by Gina Dent (Bay Press, 1992), pp. 303-316.

16. See Manthia Diawara, "Afro-Kitsch," in *Black Popular Culture*, a project of Michelle Wallace edited by Gina Dent (Bay Press, 1992), pp. 285-91.

17. Clovis Semmes, *Cultural Hegemony and African American Development* (Praeger Publishers, 1992).

18. Quoted in Daudi Ajani ya Azibo, "Articulating the Distinction Between Black Studies and the Study of Blacks: The Fundamental Role of Culture and the African-Centered Worldview." *The Afrocentric Scholar: The Journal of the National Council For Black Studies*, Vol. 1, No. 1 (May 1992): 64-97.

19. Molefi K. Asante, *The Afrocentric Idea* (Philadelphia: Temple University Press, 1987), p. 5.

20. *Ibid.*, pp. 4-5.

21. *Ibid.*, p. 6.

22. See *The Afrocentric Idea*, note #3, pp. 197-198.

23. *Ibid.*

24. See Marcel Griaule, *Conversations With Ogotemmeli: Introduction to Dogon Religious Ideas* (New York: Oxford University Press, 1965).

25. See Mazisi Kunene, *Anthem of the Decades* (Portsmouth: Heineman Educational Books, Inc., 1981).

25. See Vusamazulu Credo Mutwa, *Indaba, My Children: African Tribal History, Legends, Customs, and Religious Beliefs* (London: Kahn and Averill, 1966).

26. See Malidoma Patrice Some, *Of Water and the Spirit: Ritual, Magic and Initiation in the Life of An African Shaman* (G.P. Putnam's Sons, 1994); and Malidoma and Sohonfu Some, *We Have No Word For Sex: An Indigenous View of Intimacy* (an audiotape). Oral Tradition Archives, Box 51155, Pacific Grove, CA 93950.

27. Patricia Hill Collins, *Black Feminist Thought: Knowledge, Consciousness, and the Politics of Empowerment* (Routledge, Chatman, and Hall, Inc., 1991).

28. The student wishing to have an African-based understanding of consciousness, knowledge, And empowerment may wish to begin by studying the following: (1) Ra Un Nefer Amen, *Metu Neter*, Volumes 1 & 2 (Khamit Corporation, 1990, 1994); (2) Maya Deren, *Divine Horsemen: The Voodoo Gods of Haiti* (Dell, 1970); Henry and Margaret Drewal, *Gelede: Art and Female Power Among the Yoruba* (Indiana University Press, 1983); Erskine Peters, *African Openings to the Tree of Life* (Regent Press, 1983); and the works of Malidoma and Sohonfu Some, including *Of Water and the Spirit* (G.P. Putnam's Sons, 1994) and *We Have No Word For Sex* (audio tape from Oral Tradition Archives, Pacific Grove, California 1994).

29. "Mdu ntr" means divine words in Kmetic language and is a more appropriate term than the word "hieroglyphics."

30. Adolf Reed Jr., "Steel Trap," *The Nation* (March 4, 1991): 274ff.

31. See Barbara Molette, "Black Heroes and the Afrocentric Values in Theatre," *Journal of Black Studies*, Vol. 15, No. 4 (June 1985): 447-462.

32. See Cheryl Townsend Gilkes, "'Mother to the Motherless, Father to the Fatherless': Power, Gender, and Community in an Afrocentric Biblical Tradition," *Semeia: An Experimental Journal for Biblical Criticism*, Vol. 47 (1989): 57-85.

33. See the following by Linda James-Myers: (1) *Understanding An Afrocentric Worldview: Introduction to an Optimal Psychology* (Dubuque, IA: Kendall/Hunt Publishers, 1988); (2) "Traditional African Medicine and Optimal Theory." *The Journal of Black Psychology*, Vol. 19, No. 1: 25-47.

34. See Paul Carter Harrison, *The Drama of Nommo* (New York: Grove Press, Inc., 1972).

35. See, for example Kariamu Welsh-Asante, *African Dance: An Artistic, Historical, and Philosophical Inquiry*. Trenton: Africa World Press, 1994; (2) "Images of Women in African Dance: Sexuality and Sensuality as Dual Unity." *Sage*, Vol. 8, No. 2 (Fall 1994): 16ff.; (3) "African-American Dance in Curricula-Modes of Inclusion." *Journal of Physical Education, Recreation and Dance*, Vol. 64, No. 2 (February 1998): 48-51; and (4) "Philosophy and Dance in Africa: The Views of Cabral and Fanon." *The Journal of Black Studies*, Vol. 21, No. 2 (December 1990): 224-32.

36. As illustrations of works by Houston A. Backer, Jr., and Henry Louis Gates, Jr., I cite Houston A. Baker, Jr., "To Move Without Moving: An Analysis of Creativity and Commerce in Ralph Ellison's Trueblood Episode," *PMLA: Publications of the Modern Language Association of America*, Vol. 98, No. 5 (October, 1983): 828-845 and Baker's *Blues, Ideology, and Afro-American Literature: A Vernacular Theory*. University of Chicago Press, 1984. Regarding Gates, I cite especially *The Signifying Monkey: A Theory of Afro-American Literary Criticism* (Oxford University Press, 1988).

37. Boyi is quoted in Stewart (1992): 30-31.

38. Carol Aisha Blackshire-Belay, ed., *Language and Literature in the African American Imagination* (Greenwood Press, 1992).

39. It is important to remember, though, that the popular facet of Cartesian metaphysics, as represented in Descartes's *Meditations*, "underscore[s] the contingency of thinking by the argument that the ego, as a dependent and imperfect thing, has no power to sustain its existence, and therefore depends every moment on the power of God," according to Hiram Caton in *The Origin of Subjectivity* (New Haven: Yale University Press, 1973), p. 150.

40. Fred Dallmayr, *The Twilight of Subjectivity: Contributions to a Post-Individualistic Theory of Politics* (Amherst: University of Massachusetts Press, 1981), p. 1.

41. Quoted in Dalia Judovitz, *Subjectivity and Representation in Descartes* (New York: Cambridge University Press, 1988), p. vi.

51.

White Colleges and the Future of Black Studies

Nick Aaron Ford

I agree with those who believe that Black Studies are here to stay, although the survival will assume different or somewhat modified objectives, methods, and results from most of those now in vogue. In this chapter we shall be concerned with examining the prospects for the survival of Black Studies on the white college or university campus, the possible conditions of such survival, and the effects of the survival on the white institution and the black and white students.

To begin, let us clearly understand that although the term Black Studies is usually taken to mean an organized program, in reality it rightfully means a collection of courses dealing primarily with black life and culture, individually administered or organized into a special program. Thus an institution which offers one or more courses in Afro-American literature or Afro-American history without being a part of an organized program leading to a major or concentration is offering courses in Black Studies. Since the number of students who actually major or concentrate in Black Studies is seldom more than ten percent of the black student enrollment whereas an average of fifty percent of these students as well as a considerable number of their white classmates register for one or two such courses, the college or university with such offerings is playing an active role in promoting the cause of Black Studies.

(1) In the light of this explanation one call confidently predict that Black Studies are here to stay and that although some organized programs with chairmen or directors will be discontinued for many reasons, the trend will be to increase the number and variety of individual courses by more and more institutions until all accredited colleges and universities will be represented. Reliable evidence indicates that at least fifty percent of all accredited institutions of higher learning now offer one or more such courses. I predict, therefore, that in the future one role of the white college will be to increase the number of its courses in Black Studies until there will be at least one such course in every significant area of black life and culture.

(2) The white college must accelerate its efforts to incorporate educational materials of black life and culture into every course in the curriculum that can appropriately absorb them. Naturally all courses in the humanities and the social sciences are capable of reflecting aspects of the black experience, whereas mathematics and most of the natural sciences cannot. The acceptance of this role means that every course in American literature, American history, music, and the fine arts will include objective information and evaluation of the activities and/or contributions of distinguished blacks. Already trends of this kind have begun in representative institutions. Recently I was invited to serve as consultant to the English Department of one of the largest public junior colleges in the South to assist in the incorporation of the most

significant writings of black poets, dramatists, fiction writers, and essayists into regular courses offered by the department.

(3) The white college will begin or continue to make available on a permanent basis interdisciplinary programs (or independent departments) in Black Studies which will provide opportunities for black and white students who so desire to major or concentrate in the field. In addition, institutions qualified to offer the M.A. and/or the Ph.D. degree will begin or continue to encourage (or at least not discourage) black and white graduate students to choose theses and dissertation projects in a wide variety of areas of black life and culture. Harvard University was the first American institution of higher learning to acknowledge this role when in 1896 it accepted W.E.B. DuBois' study, *Suppression of the African Slave Trade to the United States of America, 1638-1870*, as fulfillment of the dissertation requirement for the Ph.D. degree.[1] Since 1896 other universities have occasionally accepted dissertations in the field of black history, sociology, and education, but rarely have literature and the arts been included. When dissertations have been approved in the latter two disciplines, the students involved have for the most part been white.

The phenomenon of discouraging blacks and encouraging whites to undertake dissertations in the area of black literature has resulted from the refusal of the white professors of English to admit that a black scholar is capable of an objective or valid act of literary criticism. Only recently have white journal editors and book publishers been willing to consider for publication an article or a book of literary criticism by a black scholar. In the too recent past, whenever such an article or book on literary criticism was submitted, even though it concerned black literature, the editor or publisher would send the manuscript for evaluation to a white literary scholar who admittedly knew almost nothing about black writers or their writings. The white consultant would suggest certain changes that must be made in the black critic's judgments in order to conform to the white consultant's stereotyped notions. If the black critic rejected the consultant's ill-conceived advice, as was almost always the case, the article or book was never published. Some white colleges have now begun to repudiate this blatant racism, and the number will slowly accelerate in the future.

(4) The white college which now has an organized Black Studies program with a chairman or director will be forced to face up to the problem of granting it equal status with all other programs of a similar nature, or to discontinue it. Of course, it is easier to hold on to an inferior program, make excuses for lack of adequate support, and accept the responsibility for crippling black students who have the misfortune of being affiliated with it. It is easier to offer a self-serving or misguided director a meagre, inadequate budget and give him the privilege of setting his own standards for all aspects of the program regardless of the failure to approximate the superior quality of general college standards. Such abdication of responsibility by a college or university is reprehensible and will lead to the discrediting of the legitimate concept of Black Studies in general. Such an abdication of educational responsibility by an accredited college is legitimate grounds for a protest of that accreditation. It adds strength to the assertion of Thomas Sowell, black professor at U.C.L.A., who complains, "Even where the intellectually oriented black student makes his way into and through college without being directly harmed by all this, he cannot be unaffected by the double standard which makes his degree look cheap in the market and his grades suspect to those concerned with academic standards. Worst of all, he cannot even have the full confidence within himself that he really earned them." A college which does not guard against the cheapening of its degree, whether by students in a substandard Black Studies program or athletes on a top-rated football or basketball team, deserves the condemnation and scorn of the academic profession.

(5) The white college in the future will be expected to acknowledge Black Studies as the forerunner of interest in various other kinds of ethnic studies, and to recognize the differences among them. Since the insistent demand for Black Studies began in 1967, other ethic groups have sought similar treatment. Of course, it is a well-known fact that Jewish Studies have been recognized in American education for many years. The Hebrew Bible, which embodies many historical and cultural aspects of Jewish life, is better known by the majority of Americans than the basic facts of American history. Furthermore, in the past three or four decades some of the most distinguished authors and critics studied in American literature have been Jews. Consequently, Jews are not demanding equal educational time and resources as that allotted to blacks because they know they already have enjoyed the limelight to a much greater extent than blacks. But other ethnics such as American Indians, Mexican-Americans, Asian-Americans, and Puerto Ricans are rightly seeking fair treatment for their life and culture in school and college curriculums. Furthermore, the "forgotten American," as described by President Nixon, which means the white lower-middle class worker, is often considered "ethnic" because he is usually the first, second, or third generation of central, east, or South European stock. He is also generally angry, troubled, and alienated for reasons similar to those of nonwhite minorities.

The Ford Foundation *Letter*, December 1, 1970, contains the following significant article concerning ethnic studies:

> Conspicuous absentees from the college and university curriculum include not only the black experience in America but the history and culture of other ethnic minorities as well. The melting pot ideology muted their role, but scholars and teachers have started to make up for past neglect. The aim is not a chauvinistic carving of the pie. Rather, it is to examine ethnic phenomena in order to understand the complex past and the troubled present and to illuminate the varied strands of America's social and cultural fabric.

> To facilitate such research, the Foundation has established a program of Dissertation Fellowships for Ph.D. candidates writing on the experience of black Americans, American Indians, Mexican-Americans, Asian Americans, and Puerto Ricans. Eligibility does not depend on the candidate's own race or ethnic status. Eighty-seven candidates were awarded fellowships totaling $288,052 for the 1970-71 academic year, and the program will be conducted for a second year.

> This series evolved from Foundations assistance for the development of interdisciplinary Afro-American studies at the undergraduate level, for which a total of $2.8 million was granted to twenty-eight colleges and other agencies. Also assisted in this field have been the preparation of college teachers and the collection and cataloguing of historic documents and other materials.

> In the initial round of the new series, slightly more than half of the doctoral dissertation topics for which awards were made deal with black Americans. Of the rest thirteen deal with American Indians (e.g., "The Federal Indian Policies in the Pacific Northwest, 1940-1960"); eight with Spanish-speaking Americans (e.g., "Pachuco: A Social Dialect"); four with Asian Americans (e.g., "Consequences of the Relocation of Japanese Americans on California Agriculture") and thirteen with multi-ethnic matters (e.g., "The Politicization of Ethnicity: Indians, Appalachians, and Blacks in Chicago"). The recipients are working at fifty-four universities in all regions of the country. They were nominated by their graduate schools and selected

by a multi-ethnic and multi-disciplinary committee of scholars headed by Professor J. Saunders Redding of Cornell University.

Harlan Cleveland, president of the University of Hawaii, made the following comment about ethnic studies in 1970: "At the University of Hawaii, we are moving toward an ethnic Studies program that includes black studies along with Hawaiian, Japanese, Chinese, and Filipino Studies. I would hope that both oriental and white Americans would find their way into the black studies classrooms, and I am sure that some of the black students will interest themselves in Hawaiian and other cultures of the Pacific—that is, indeed, why some of them come to college so far from home."[2]

Black Studies differ from all other ethnic varieties in that the black American was forcibly separated from the African culture of his ancestors almost three hundred years before any scholarly systematic attempt was made to study that culture and to transmit and interpret consciously its meaning to the involuntarily alienated descendants, and that during that interval the leaders of American society were deliberately attempting to suppress and/or distort its true value and meaning for predatory reasons.

(6) The white college in the future will be pressured from within and without to recognize its obligation to the black as well as the white community to which it is bound by the physical environment. The Cox Commission Report on the violent confrontation between Columbia University and the neighboring Harlem community in the spring of 1968 declared, "Columbia cannot flourish in upper Manhattan until it establishes a new and sounder relation with its present neighbors." Since that controversy, Columbia has sought in part at least to acknowledge some degree of responsibility for helping to alleviate certain community problems by the use of university personnel and resources. Reports have been published indicating that more than fifty projects have been initiated requiring close cooperation between black community groups and faculty and students from Columbia's schools of medicine, law, education, and architecture.

Almost all organized Black Studies programs have in their objectives some reference to community service and campus relations. A common objective is often worded thus: "To do research in and provide services to the black community and its organizations by jointly identifying and analyzing its problems, offering consultation, and establishing service channels into the community from the diverse resources of the college or university." In a commencement address at Southwestern College at Memphis, June, 1970, F. Champion Ward, vice president of the Education and Research Division of the Ford Foundation, explained the need for and cited all example of the kind of community service that call be rendered by a college that recognizes such all obligation:

> But some promising starts have been made recently, designed to reconcile action and direct experience with theoretical studies... The first difficulty is in finding the right "mix" of theory and practice within the curriculum; the second is in determining the appropriate contribution of a liberal arts college to the solution of national problems. There is now a widespread effort to develop courses of study that have substantial intellectual content and yet force both faculty and students to lay out a plan of possible action to cope with particular problems of the hour.... Take, for example, a group of courses that students and faculty at Stanford University developed around some complex questions of social policy in California. I recently read the product of one of the Stanford seminars, a report entitled "Logging in Urban Counties," produced by a group of eleven students under the supervision of Stanford geophysicist Allan Cox, who reported:

"We all learned a great deal. The students discovered that it isn't enough to write essays—lawmakers and supervisors require hard facts if they're going to act.

This is what we had to go after—with field trips, in talks with county officials and people in the logging industry, and by reading published research, the students got extremely interested—it really turned them on." What is impressive about the Stanford seminar is the way older and younger minds combined established knowledge, reasoned analysis, and fact-getting to move from contrary cliches concerning a controversial social question to air agreed-upon, workable solution. State and county legislators in California are now making use of the group's report.[3]

(7) Already the white college is finding it necessary to modify its admissions policies to accommodate a larger percentage of blacks and other ethnic minorities than is now possible. It will finally understand, as some institutions of recognized quality have begun to understand and as many black colleges have known for a long time, that the quality of education is measured by the finished product rather than by the initial input. College administrators will learn by forced experience that the combination of native intelligence and motivation, which cannot be accurately measured by culture-bound entrance tests, is a greater guarantee of genuine academic success than any measuring instruments currently in use. Unless some type of open admissions is adopted by all institutions of higher learning, the guarantee of equality of opportunity by the U.S. Constitution will remain an empty mockery. This reasoning does not suggest that a student whose performance indicates, after a sufficient trial period with necessary remedial aid and counseling, that he cannot succeed at that particular college should be permitted to remain. But it does suggest that every high school graduate who so desires should be guaranteed the right of admission to a public institution of higher learning within the city or state of his residence, at least until he has proved by his performance fairly evaluated that he is incapable of pursuing such a course. Naturally, unless black students are fairly considered for college admission, talk of Black Studies is but idle chatter.

Another aspect of black student recruitment and admissions that the white college must thoughtfully consider in the future is a concern for social balance in recruitment policies. Professor Thomas Sowell suggests that it is the present practice of white colleges and universities to devote their major efforts in admissions. financial aid, and counseling to the academically deprived black student because it is believed the good black student outside the ghetto will "make it anyway." He insists that many directors of special programs for black students do not seek to fill whatever number of places exist with the best recruits available. Some officials, he observes, will openly state this; others will be evasive before admitting it, and still others will continue to deny it after the evidence has piled up. Sowell charges: "What constitutes the 'right' kind of black person has varied greatly with the emotional needs of white people, but the great tragic fact of the black man's history in the United States is that his own ability has always been far less important than his satisfaction of white emotional needs. These emotional needs now include the discharge of guilt feelings, and special care for the incompetent and the abusive black student obviously discharges more guilt than the normal application of academic standards to competent and thoughtful black students."[4] White institutions in the immediate future must make certain that their policies do not produce the kind of unfair results of which Sowell complains.

(8) The white college or university must modify its academic and ethnic qualifications for faculty appointments if it intends to provide for its students, black and

white, the most knowledgeable and practical guides to the new and relevant education necessary for successful urban living. A particular type of educator is needed to prepare the student of today to cope with the problems of urban life and the problems associated with the vast technological changes; there are not nearly enough Ph.D. holders or candidates with the theoretical and pragmatic competence to fill even half the college and university positions now open or soon to become available.

Benjamin Thompson, associate professor of education at Antioch College advises, "As individuals, we need to evidence risk-taking behavior and to acknowledge the fact that only the quick will not become the dead, and this applies to the institutionalizing of new forms and programs as well as to individuals. We must give more concern and freedom to styles of teaching as well as learning in the educational establishment, which demands a faculty that knows the world as well as a particular discipline."[5] Black Students have led the way in evaluating teachers on their abilities to understand the world and its current problems, rather than on outworn theories that are no longer relevant to living and working in the modern world.

Robert Beller, president of the student body of the University of Iowa, recently reminded the administration and faculty of his university: "The purpose of the University must be to provide the students with access to the latest informational sources and, more importantly, access to the problems themselves for first-hand observation. From this point, the university staff—no longer simply lecturers and researchers but workers and practitioners—must open broad channels for the testing and revision of new knowledge and skills. In effect, the ghetto, smog, and government become laboratories. The explosive growth of knowledge and other problems have resulted in the rapid obsolescence of traditional tools of education. The university has to offer more than second-hand experience drawn from a text if the student is to place himself usefully in the mainstream of society in any role broader than that of breadwinner and if he is to have leverage for combatting environmental, social, and political shortcoming."[6]

Although Beller is white, his warning recognizes the necessity for the white college to broaden the ethnic base of its faculty as well as its curriculum. It is true that there are not now enough qualified black professors to satisfy the minimum need of white colleges and universities who are seriously seeking such additions to their faculties. Consequently, administrators must devise new methods for fulfilling this need other than on a full-time basis. Black teachers at black colleges who qualify academically as well as pragmatically could be persuaded to serve as visiting professors or lecturers for one or two semesters with options to return to the black institution or to remain longer it there is mutual agreement. Some white institutions have sought mutual exchanges of faculty members with black institutions for one or two semesters but such arrangements are seldom possible because every black college in the nation already has a larger supply of white teachers than it needs (since integration is supposed to be a two-way process) and, therefore, does not choose to exchange one of its most effective black teachers for a second-rate white teacher who would need a year or two of training and experience to perform even on the lowest acceptable level at the black college. Naturally, the average black teacher has almost no problem in adjusting to faculty service in a white institution, since in most cases his advanced degrees were earned at a white university.

Another possibility of bringing black teachers to the white campus for effective service could be the hiring of a black teacher from a nearby black college to teach an evening course once or twice a week. I have observed some satisfactory arrangements on this basis. Still another possibility is the establishment of Black Studies courses that would be coordinated by a white faculty member with a series of distinguished black professors to serve as lecturers.

In addition to the effort to secure black faculty to teach Black Studies, every white college or university should seek to recruit trained and experienced white teachers who are prepared academically and emotionally to teach such courses. On another occasion in answer to the question, "Who should teaches courses in Black Studies? I express the following conclusions:

> This is a crucial question in any discussion of the inclusion of the black experience in school and college curriculums. Black militants have demanded and won in some colleges the right to select teachers they want for these courses regardless of academic training or experience. In many instances students have decided that blackness, publication of some kind dealing with the black experience regardless of its nature and quality, loud and uncompromising allegiance to the black revolution as they understand it, and willingness to serve exclusively the needs of the black student population are the basic qualifications. These students insist that no white person is qualified to teach any subject dealing with the black experience. They believe any black teacher with the four qualifications listed above will be a more effective teacher of a course in Black Studies than any non-black with the highest academic degree and a most distinguished reaching record.

> Naturally, any reasonable, fair-minded person will sympathize with the above point of view, but in the name of reason and reality must reject it. It is true that there are many highly trained, efficient white teachers who are not qualified by temperament, social sensitivity, and lack of unconscious racial prejudice to teach Black Studies. But some white teachers do qualify in all three of these non-academic essentials. No white teacher should be permitted to teach a course unless he does meet the academic as well as the non-academic requirements. However, having lived through the black experience for twenty, thirty, or fifty years is no guarantee that a black person is qualified to teach in a satisfactory or meaningful manner and understanding or appreciation of that experience. To permit unqualified black teachers to teach a course in, say, Black Poetry or The Black Writer as Novelist for academic credit is to either admit that the course dealing with the black experience is not as important as other courses in the college curriculum or to admit that the requirements for college teaching are not valid. It is becoming more and more evident that the latter assumption may be true, but, if so, it is the duty of the college or university in which such aberrations occur to forthrightly announce its rejection of the validity of current teacher qualifications for its faculty and the basis for the formulation of its new requirements. It must be clearly understood, however, that these objections to the exceptional treatment of teachers of Black Studies are not directed at the normal practice of making exceptions to all rules in cases that involve *truly* exceptional persons of any race. Neither are these criticisms applicable to poets-in-residence or consultants in special programs not involving academic credit.

But beyond logical and emotional considerations, a recognition of the reality of the current situation demands that white teachers who are qualified academically, emotionally, and sympathetically (lack of conscious or unconscious racial prejudice) to teach courses in Black Studies must be encouraged and even urged to accept such assignments. For regardless of arguments to the contrary, it is clear that the black experience must be included in all school and college general education courses in this nation if it is to survive as *one* nation. *And never in the foreseeable future will there be enough black teachers to perform this task.* It is, therefore, necessary for all qualified colleges and universities to inaugurate a crash program, with ample provisions for scholarship aid, for the preparation of prospective teachers, black and white, for this tremendous task ahead.[7]

Endnotes

1. See page 31.

2. G. Kerry Smith (ed.), *The Troubled Campus* (San Francisco: Jossey-Bass, 1970), p. 43.

3. Ford Foundation, Office of Reports, 320 E. 43rd Street, New York.

4. "A Black Professor Says," *The New York Times Magazine* (December 13, 1970): 46, 49.

5. Smith, p. 98.

6. "What Is a University For?" *Spectator* (October 1970): 1.

7. Nick Aaron Ford, *Instructor's Manual for Black Insights* (Lexington, Massachusetts: Ginn and Company/Xerox College Publishing, 1971), pp. 10-11.

52.

Taking Stock: African American Studies at the Edge of the 21st Century

Floyd W. Hayes, III

African American Studies made its appearance with the promise of solving some of the educational problems of African Americans and of challenging the American academy's de facto racial exclusivity. Not only had individuals of African descent been excluded from university faculty and student bodies, the curricula of many disciplines had ignored African and African American achievements and points of view.

The newly recognized field emerged in the 1960s as part of a larger and turbulent social movement, which was itself a product of a transformation of American society. That transformation—and the field of African American Studies—is more than thirty years old. And now we are facing another transformation, a quiet, progressive one that has profound implications for all Americans: the shift from an industrial-manufacturing to a postindustrial-managerial society. This quiet, all-encompassing change requires us to reconsider the role and place of African American Studies not only within the academy but also in American society.

The intent of this essay is to attempt such a reconsideration. To do this, the writer examines the field's major intellectual tendencies—past and present, complementary and contradictory. The concern is to locate the logic and follow the trajectory of this evolving field. In the discussion that follows, the writer does not purport to provide an exhaustive genealogy of African American Studies; rather, the intention is to examine some of the representative intellectual trends and developments characterizing the field so far. After this examination, the possible future challenges to African American Studies and Black educational advancement posed by the current transformation of America from an industrial manufacturing society to a postindustrial-managerial society will be addressed. Although the intellectual roots of African American Studies can be traced back to a much earlier period (as shown in several of the readings included here), the scope of this analysis will be limited to the intellectual and social forces that have contributed to the field's development from the 1960s to the present.

A note on naming: In the early years, African Americanists called the field Black Studies. Later, the terms Afro-American Studies, Pan African Studies, African American Studies, and Africana Studies also came to be used. Although there might exist some distinctions or variations among these names—particularly regarding the extent of an inclusion of African Studies and Caribbean Studies—for the purposes of this discussion, these titles are interchangeable.

The Turbulent Emergence
of Black Studies

In the late 1950s and the 1960s, after the momentous Brown v. Board of Education ruling that, in effect, outlawed racial and ethnic segregation in schools, public schools systems across the nation tried to find ways to evade the law and continue segregation. In response to such practices by local school boards, a powerful coalition of civil rights leaders, educational experts, and public policy makers was created, and the coalition determined to use all means available, and especially the courts, to make school systems comply with the desegregation orders. Many school systems, Black as well as White, were caught in the middle of the war.

Scarce resources—intellectual as well as financial—were allocated to the policy battles and to moving children in buses instead of being allocated to education. Many Black community leaders and organizations tried to point this out. They challenged the schools to implement policies and programs that would promote quality education, no matter what a school's racial makeup. But the movement for school integration had gathered such momentum that it could not be stopped by rational argument or even by evidence of blatant failure. As the coalition grew more and more powerful, imposing on urban communities racial integration at any cost, the quality of classroom teaching declined. Parents increasingly were intimidated by and excluded from an urban bureaucracy in which the policymaking process was dominated by a nonlocal elite with its own agenda—an agenda based solely on civil rights, ignoring students' rights to quality education.

As the civil rights movement began to wind down in the mid-1960s, many African American high school and college students looked for an alternative. They found it in the more militant social movements of the late 1960s, particularly the Black Power movement. These powerful, and in some ways anarchic, tendencies served as the crucible for the turbulent appearance of African American Studies.

As an organized academic enterprise, African American Studies emerged at historically White universities and colleges during the late 1960s in the context of complex social change that affected virtually every sector of American society. The African American Studies movement converged with mass movements of protest against the brutalizing effects of social injustice, socioeconomic inequality, racial antagonism, the Vietnam War, and university paternalism. Militant students challenged the hegemony of traditional modes of thinking and social practice, inaugurating an assault on what they perceived as the hypocrisy and immorality of many of the nation's social institutions. Institutions of higher education became primary targets of criticism as students challenged them to address the burning questions and urgent social problems of the day. Students attacked the university's conventional disregard of their everyday life experiences and demanded, increasingly, that the content of their university education be relevant to the solution of complex social problems.

While agreeing with the general student demand for a growing interaction between the academy and the world outside of its walls, African American students also audaciously called into question the American academy's dominant Eurocentric perspective—the unchallenged assumption that Western European culture is superior, neutral, and normative. Labeling this orientation ethnocentric, African American students charged that Western education, wittingly and otherwise, diminished, distorted, and, in many instances, obliterated the contributions of African peoples to world development generally and the contributions of African Americans to America's development specifically. Therefore, African American students demanded that the university establish courses of study that provided a systematic examination of African and African-descended peoples' experiences.

Responding to the powerful challenge of these student activists, many institutions of higher learning across the nation hurriedly implemented African American or Black Studies programs as appeasement measures. Under these circumstances, little long-range planning (academic or financial) took place, since many university officials considered the issue an aberration or fad and hoped that it would shortly disappear. Significantly, many universities decided to isolate Black Studies enterprises rather than to force traditional academic departments to transform their curricula to include the study of the Black experience. In many instances, early African American Studies units drew on any African American faculty member already at the university—even if the person had no intellectual interest or academic preparation in the area—or any White faculty member who might be interested in race-related issues. More commonly, as African American students demanded that courses on the Black experience be taught by Black people, universities quickly sought to hire more Black faculty members. In that highly charged period, some new faculty possessed Ph.D.s in their fields, but many did not; some well-established Black scholars decided not to affiliate with Black Studies; and some well-prepared Black intellectuals were overlooked. Consequently, the view emerged in this early period that many African American Studies enterprises were designed to fail.

The eruption of what generally was called Black Studies in the late 1960s can best be understood as an institutional representation of the contemporary African American struggle for collective survival, socioeconomic advancement, and human rights. After having seen the white South's terroristic reaction to civil rights activists' peaceful protests, African Americans found it difficult to believe that the American social order would soon end the cultural domination, racial oppression, and economic subordination of African Americans.

Citing the limitations of the integrationist civil rights philosophy and social practice for bettering the circumstances of Black Americans, the Nation of Islam and its chief spokesman, Malcolm X, urged urban African American masses across the nation to unite on the basis of Black nationalist ideology and to expand their struggle beyond the narrow confines of the civil rights agenda to the global issue of human rights. Calling on African Americans to take their cause to the United Nations, Malcolm viewed human rights as an overall framework that included a struggle for the following: (1) personal worth and human dignity, (2) family stability and community solidarity, (3) literacy and quality education, (4) economic self-sufficiency and collective web-being, and (5) democratic political rights and self-determination. Malcolm X urged African Americans to take pride in themselves and their African heritage. He argued that Black communities should control and support their own political and economic institutions. He admonished Black Americans to respect their women and to clean up themselves and their communities by removing the socially destructive evils of family disintegration, alcoholism, drug abuse, and crime. In short, Malcolm challenged African Americans to improve the overall moral character and social stability of their communities.

The rhetoric of civil rights leaders and the decade of actual advances in legal rights had meanwhile fostered hopes in Black communities for quick changes in economic and social conditions. Such changes, of course, were not forthcoming, and the dashed hopes for social and political self-determination produced violent revolts in Harlem, Watts, Detroit, Cleveland, Newark, and other cities outside of the American south. These powerful and defiant protests shook the nation and, in the summer of

1966, ushered in a new era, signaled by the discourse of "Black Power" (Forman, 1972; Stone, 1968).

On May 29, 1966, Congressman Adam Clayton Powell, Jr., Chairman of the U.S. House of Representatives' Committee on Education and Labor and one of America's few progressive African American politicians, articulated the need for "black power" in his baccalaureate address at Howard University. He asserted: "Human rights are God-given. Civil rights are man-made. . . . To demand these God-given rights is to seek black power the power to build black institutions of splendid achievement" (Stone, 1968, p. 189). A week later, during the James Meredith protest march in Mississippi, Student Non-Violent Coordinating Committee activists Willie Ricks and Stokely Carmichael led the chant, "We want black power, we want black power" (Carson, 1981; Forman, 1972; Stone, 1968).

As with any political slogan, interpretations of Black Power differed. Although many civil rights leaders criticized the term, others appropriated it for their own agendas by articulating a variety of meanings, including group solidarity, cultural pride, political power, economic power, defensive violence, anti-integrationism, community control, black nationalism, and human rights. In 1967, leader of the Student Non-Violent Coordinating Committee Carmichael and Roosevelt University political scientist Charles Hamilton sought to define and clarify this new political vision when they wrote that Black Power

> is a call for black people in this country to unite, to recognize their heritage, to build a sense of community. It is a call for black people to begin to define their own goals, to lead their own organizations and to support those organizations. It is a call to reject the racist institutions and values of this society (1967, p. 44).

This conception of Black Power set forth the vivid necessity for African-descended Americans to center their political outlook and social practice on their own collective concerns. The concentrated focus on Black Power — its accentuation of African American collective interests characterized the ideological milieu within which African American Studies emerged.

The establishment of African American Studies was insurrectionary and emancipatory in at least two ways. First, as case studies of events at San Francisco State University (Chrisman, 1969; McEvoy and Miller, 1969), Merritt College (Walton, 1969), and Cornell University (Edwards, 1970 and 1980) disclose, African American Studies erupted in the context of university protest. African American students and their supporters sought to challenge and transform the policies and practices of institutional racism.

Second, African American Studies represented a bold movement that undertook to unmask the power/knowledge configuration of Eurocentrisin and the White cultural domination characteristic of the American academy. The new field of study sought to resist the rigid barriers between traditional academic disciplines by emphasizing an innovative multidisciplinary approach to teaching and learning. Additionally, African American Studies challenged the ideological basis of the Eurocentric paradigm, which assumes that the Western European structure of knowledge is true, objective, and politically neutral, applicable equally to all peoples and circumstances. Yet, this organization of knowledge resulted in a representation of civilization that idealizes Western culture and thought and devalues all others. From the standpoint of the Eurocentric knowledge structure, Western European views and values are and should be the human norm; hence, other cultures can be discounted insofar as they deviate from the norm.

Since Eurocentrism lay at the base of most discourse within the American academy, many African American Studies theorists and practitioners saw their task as contesting and transforming the received ideas, entrenched institutions, and questionable values of the Eurocentric tradition. But, there was no consensus on what Black Studies programs should attempt. There were differing intellectual and ideological tendencies corresponding largely to the ambiguous interpretations of Black Power. Therefore, during its first decade, Black Studies was characterized by a variety of orientations even while improvising upon and challenging the academy's Eurocentric tradition.

The advocacy of a critical approach grounded in Black cultural nationalism was a major intellectual tendency during the establishment of African American Studies enterprises. Perhaps Harold Cruse, author of the widely read and debated book, *The Crisis of the Negro Intellectual* (1967), was one of the strongest proponents of this view. At the 1968 Yale University symposium of Black Studies, Cruse attacked the integrationist ethic of American scholarship, arguing that it had precluded the development of a viable Black social theory on which to ground Black Studies. For him, any intellectually valid Black Studies curriculum had to rest on the ideology of Black cultural nationalism and had to employ a critical historical approach.

Cruse suggested that Black Studies should focus its attention on Black institutional development on all levels—cultural, political, economic, and social. While he called for a self-critical analysis—that is, investigation of the impact of the Protestant Ethic on African American social development; of W.E.B. DuBois' talented tenth thesis and the historical origins of the Black intellectual class; and of the clash between radical-revolutionary and reformist-gradualist tendencies within the Black movement—Cruse cautioned that Black Studies should not be too narrowly conceived. Rather, he argued for a critical investigation of the larger American cultural dynamic.

For Cruse, then, Black Studies needed to employ a historical approach, grounded in Black cultural nationalism, that critically examined both developments and contradictions within the African American population as well as the manifestations of the larger American cultural apparatus and its effects on Black consciousness.

Another intellectual tendency during the formative stage of Black Studies was to define the new enterprise as almost solely an examination of the Black experience because the White academy had omitted it. Although advocates of this program also sought to break the interpretive domination of the conventional Eurocentric paradigm, the effect ultimately would have been to replace White particularism with the Black particularism against which Harold Cruse earlier had cautioned. In a 1970 article, entitled "Toward a Sociology of Black Studies," Maurice Jackson advocated this point of view when he defined the meaning and scope of Black Studies as the systematic study of Black people—the deeper meaning of Black life. For Jackson, the new field needed to focus on the role Black people have played in the development of human history, concentrating on both their uniqueness and their commonality with other people.

From this standpoint, moreover, African Americans possess a rich and complex heritage of survival and achievement under oppressive circumstances—slavery, segregation, and racism. By studying African American achievements, Jackson maintained that Black Studies could foster a sense of Black pride among African Americans. In the examination of the African American experience, however, Jackson rejected the race-relations and ethnic minority approaches of conventional sociological analysis. Noting that these approaches assumed that Black people could or should be studied only in relation to White people, Jackson argued that Black people should be studied on their own terms. Because of different life experiences and values, White scholars lacked the necessary sensibility to gather and assess adequately information about the African American experience, in Jackson's view. Therefore, according to Jackson, Black scholars were more appropriate for examining the African American experience past and present. They would be the best interpreters of that experience.

This intellectual tendency within Black Studies also questions the notion of the political or value neutrality of received knowledge. Jackson pointed out that "cultural values play a dominant part in the selection of problems for study and the application of formulated knowledge" (1970, p. 134). A similar view is expressed by James Turner (1974), of Cornell University's Africana Studies and Research Center, who criticized the view that scholars have little control over the application of knowledge and the idea that education is value-free. Rather, Turner argues that education for Black people must be liberational; it must dismantle forms of "false consciousness" by uncovering the dynamics of domination.

Although the focus on the "Black experience" generally referred to the African American experience, another intellectual tendency defined African American Studies in more global terms. According to this view, the Eurocentric knowledge system is a particularism that is at best fragmented and partial knowledge; at worst, it is fictionalized data that is widely accepted. This more global intellectual perspective sees African American Studies as an expansion of the frontiers of knowledge beyond the singular and limited discourse of Eurocentrism. The original statement of objectives of the University of Maryland Baltimore County's African American Studies Program exemplified this orientation (see UMBC, 1973-1974, p. 78).

Finally, African American Studies, from its inception, sought to challenge and change the Eurocentric paradigm's rigid barriers between traditional academic disciplines by emphasizing multidisciplinary and interdisciplinary studies. Not only were African American Studies programs to incorporate courses from many conventional disciplines (multidisciplinary), but faculty and courses would seek to trespass and criss-cross traditional academic disciplinary boundaries (see Henderson, 1971).

Clearly, a number of differing ideological positions found expression in the implementation of early Black Studies enterprises. In addition, depending on local institutional arrangements and circumstances, a variety of organizational designs (programs, centers, departments) characterized the emerging field's formation. The highly charged times of the late 1960s and early 1970s did not promote ideological and organizational uniformity. In light of Black Studies' turbulent implementation process—the often nonnegotiable demands of strident student advocates for Black Studies and the differing definitions of the field by its theorists and practitioners—it was largely inevitable that problems would emerge and that criticisms would arise. The next section addresses these matters.

Black Studies: Contradictions and Dilemmas

By the late 1970s, Black Studies began to suffer growing pains resulting from the 1974-1975 economic recession and the repression of Black student and other insurgent movements (see Donner, 1980; 1990; O'Reilly, 1989). Many Black Studies operations, implemented hastily and often without much thought and planning in the late 1960s and early 1970s, closed down. The financial crisis sweeping the nation caused many universities to experience severe financial setbacks. Many universities had to reduce the budget and resource allocations of academic programs. Perhaps hit hardest were disciplines within the humanities; students reflected the uncertainties of economic crisis by choosing courses of study more immediately job related. Because Black Studies units still were in their infancy, resource and budgetary reductions especially hurt them.

It also was during the mid-1970s and early 1980s that criticism of Black Studies gained increasing professional and public attention. Some critics charged that Black Studies was reverse racism. Others noted that many Black Studies programs suffered because of internal conflicts and poor leadership. Still others maintained that Black Studies was intellectually bankrupt. Additionally, there were critics who both pointed out some weaknesses of Black Studies programs and blamed universities for not adequately supporting Black Studies enterprises (Allen, 1974; Colt, 1981; Malveaux, 1980; Poinsett, 1973; U.S. News and World Report, 1973). What follows is a brief attempt to capture some aspects of the critical environment surrounding Black Studies at its beginning and later during the 1980s.

At the 1968 Yale University symposium on Black Studies, Harvard political scientist Martin Kilson declared a profound skepticism regarding the establishment of Black Studies as an organized academic unit. Kilson, like many Black scholars, chose not to affiliate with Black Studies but to remain in the traditional academic department. He was particularly concerned about what the impact of a "black racialist outlook" would be on the interpretation of the Black experience. He argued that Black nationalists would be selective in marshalling evidence and historical data in order to fashion an analysis of the Black experience that would ipso facto castigate Whites and thus endow Black people with a special aura of righteousness. Pointing to the African entrepreneurial involvement in the Atlantic slave trade, Kilson contended that oppression has been practiced not only by Whites but by human beings everywhere. Therefore, he maintained, "The black experience is little more than an offshoot of the human experience—no better and no worse" (1968, p. 15). Kilson then rejected "the viewpoint that the black man's experience with white oppression has endowed black men with a special insight into oppression and thus a special capacity to rid human affairs of oppression" (1968, pp. 15-16).

Five years later, in a Journal of Black Studies article (1973), Kilson renewed his concern for the future development of Black Studies. He discussed four issues. First, he maintained that because of the interdisciplinary complexity of Black Studies, its faculty should originate from the traditional academic disciplines and that students should receive a sound background in a conventional discipline in addition to coursework in Black Studies.

Second, in discussing who should major in Black Studies, Kilson soundly criticized the tendency among some militant Black students to discourage White students from participating in Black Studies. He condemned this separatist tendency in Black Studies, arguing that in fact most Black students should major in the scientific and technical fields. This is the kind of educational preparation required to transform the subordinate economic and political status of the Black community. In Kilson's view, majors in Black Studies should be "those special students, black or white, who have a serious appreciation of and good aptitude for the social sciences and the humanities" (1973, p. 310).

Finally, Kilson called for the depoliticization of Black Studies in order to insure that the education of students in this field would rest on an academically and technically sound foundation. He charged that White university administrators and faculty members contributed to the academic weakness of Black Studies by yielding to militant student demands and by ignoring usual academic standards and procedures in the organization of Black Studies units and the appointment of Black faculty. In concluding, Kilson declared that if Black Studies failed to go beyond its militant style, large proportions of its faculty and students would be "relegated to the backwaters or the trash-heap of American academic and intellectual life (1973, p. 313).

Kilson made his case in the early and heady days of Black Studies. As university campuses quieted down after the turbulent 1960s, a seeming (and probably inevitable) backlash occurred in the late 1970s and 1980s in the form of mounting complaints about the academic and intellectual integrity, viability, and adequacy of the Black Studies enterprise. The youthful field of inquiry and social practice was under attack.]

Duke University English professor Kenny Williams is representative of this backlash. Writing in a 1981 issue of Change magazine, she leveled a harsh critique at the field. Williams contended that the image of Black Studies had come to be confused, wittingly or otherwise, with the relaxation of academic and professional standards. Echoing Kilson's previous concerns, Williams charged that students, faculty, and administrators perceived Black Studies as a collection of easy courses that was intellectually empty and simply gratified political and emotional demands. Examining trends in the development of Black Studies, Williams blamed many universities for yielding to strident Black student demands and hastily installing Black Studies curricula taught by newly hired faculty who often lacked conventional academic credentials and preparation.

According to Williams, many Black Studies enterprises remained unstable because institutions of higher learning employed a revolving door policy in regard to faculty hiring. This instability may have been inevitable, given the impact of the economic challenges and retrenchment of the times and the growth of the other "new studies": Women's Studies, Latino Studies, Asian American Studies, and native American Studies. Nevertheless, because universities consistently applied the law of publish or perish many Black Studies faculty were refused tenure and left the department. Black faculty members who could marshal enough protest support from Black students and White sympathizers were able to win tenure by way of political bargaining. The outcome of all this was that many Black Studies programs were viewed as temporary while their faculty remained virtually outsiders or invisible within the university community.

Williams leveled a series of additional charges. She attacked university officials for employing budgetary management strategies to constrain Black Studies operations. She criticized Black students' contradictory behavior and attitudes with respect to Black Studies. Some of these students, Williams observed, advocated Black Studies but refused to take these courses, not wanting Black Studies courses to appear on their transcripts. Some students enrolled in Black Studies courses seeking racial pride, while others expected African American professors to pass them automatically because of their common racial heritage. Finally, she cynically charged as racist the academy's rejection of Black Studies as an intellectually sound enterprise but its willing acceptance of the field as academically marginal.

With contradictions and dilemmas confronting Black Studies, an awareness emerged about the need to address critics' charges (see Davidson and Weaver, 1985; Farrell and Bridges, 1987). Leading Black Studies professionals and theorists put forward proposals to improve the status and image of the field. Perhaps the major strategies for renewal were efforts to stabilize, standardize, and (re)conceptualize African American Studies' curriculum and philosophical foundation.

From Black Studies to African American Studies: Toward Institutionalization

Over the past decade, a major goal of African American Studies practitioners has been to institutionalize the field—to build a permanent foundation within the academy. Although some tensions remain between the university and African American Studies, there has been a gradual shift from strictly reactive strategies by both parties that characterized the turbulent 1960s to forms of mutual adjustment. This and the desire for a more uniform name of the field might explain why many newer enterprises, developing in the late 1970s and after, called themselves African American Studies.

In its current and still evolving phase, a major strategy to institutionalize African American Studies has been the endeavor to standardize the curriculum. In 1980, the National Council for Black Studies, the field's professional organization, adopted a core curriculum for Black Studies (see Alkalimat and Associates, 1986; and Gordon, 1981). The purpose was to establish a model curriculum that would provide a coherent framework for standardizing African American Studies as a consistent field of study. The model core curriculum includes three broad course areas—social/behavioral studies, historical studies, and cultural studies—with four levels of courses. The first level is an introduction to the three broad course areas. The second level contains courses that review and survey basic literature on the Black experience within the categories of social/behavioral studies, historical studies, and cultural studies. The third level includes advanced courses that explore current research methods and research and analysis on emerging issues within the three broad categories. The fourth level consists of senior seminars that integrate, synthesize, and apply knowledge acquired in previous courses with the goal of reconsidering and reassessing current issues in the field. At this level, students prepare for further research, graduate study, or the work world.

An ongoing effort in the attempts at institutionalization is the search for a philosophical or theoretical grounding for the field of African American Studies. There area a number of competing theoretical, philosophical, and ideological viewpoints in the evolving field. The well-known scholar Maulana Karenga, chair of the Pan-African Studies Department at California State University at Long Beach, sets forth a conceptualization of the field in his widely-used textbook, *Introduction to Black Studies* (1982). Karenga's contribution is grounded in his longstanding Black cultural nationalist theory of Kawaida, which seeks to encompass all aspects of the Black experience—past and present. For him, Black Studies is a coherent field of study and social change that incorporates seven interconnected and interdependent core subject areas: (1) Black History; (2) Black Religion; (3) Black Social Organization; (4) Black Politics; (5) Black Economics; (6) Black Creative Production (Black Art, Black Music and Black Literature); and (7) Black Psychology.

Molefi K. Asante, editor of the *Journal of Black Studies* and chair of the Department of African American Studies at Temple University, is another leading African American Studies scholar and distinctly recognized theorist of Afrocentricity or Africalogy (Asante, 1980; 1987; 1990; Asante and Asante, 1990). Afrocentricity, as Asante informs us, is an interpretive strategy and theoretical framework that is directed at the examination of all human phenomena from an African-centered worldview. This worldview comes out of an exhaustive investigation of African and African American cultural history.

According to Asante, the African-centered standpoint can offer an alternative to the dominant Eurocentric paradigm and reveal its shortcomings by exposing its particularity, ethnocentrism, and subjectivity. While maintaining that the Eurocentric tradition is valid within its own context, Asante asserts that this tradition becomes imperialistic when it is presumed to be objective and equally applicable to all people and circumstances. Hence, Afrocentric criticism emphatically rejects Eurocentrism's representation of its view as universal and absolute. Asante does not arrogantly assert that Afrocentricity is the only interpretation of the world. Afrocentric critical practice is an interpretation of the world, according to Asante, from a particular philosophical and ideological standpoint. For example, Asante suggests that one of Afrocentricity's crucial elements is the notion of harmony and complementarity — the idea that entities can be different and yet complement each other.

Asante points out how much the concept of harmony differs from the conception of oppositional dichotomies so fundamental to Eurocentric consciousness. He notes that dichotomization pervades the Eurocentric structure of knowledge; people and things are generally grouped on the basis of their opposition to each other — for example, European/ African, male/female, mind/body, reason/ emotion, or science/nature. Moreover, the opposing categories are hierarchically related within the Eurocentric dualist conception of the world. That is, one of the dichotomous elements is superior to and therefore should dominate, silence. erase, or negate the other: European over African, male over female, mind over body, reason over emotion, or science over nature. Clearly, Asante intends a fundamental disruption of the Eurocentric paradigm's intellectual imperialism. Calling for a decolonization of the mind, Asante vigorously demands that Afrocentricity should become the theoretical and critical framework of African American Studies (1986).

Another effort to conceptualize and institutionalize African American Studies is found in sociologist Abdul Alkalimat and associates' textbook, *Introduction to Afro-American Studies* (1986). The underlying interpretive approach of the text is Marxist. Employing a historical materialist model, the authors indicate that their aim is to provide a unifying theoretical framework that can incorporate competing ideological tendencies in African American Studies: Marxists, nationalists, pan-Africanists, and old-fashioned civil rights integrationists as well. In addition, the formulators of this approach to African American Studies articulate a specific social outlook and practice that is anti-racist, anti-sexist, and anti-capitalist (for a similar view, see also Marable, 1992).

Besides the competing viewpoints just discussed, there are differences in programs, the organization and curricula of African American Studies according to their institutional environments. So the outcome of current efforts to standardize the curricula and to develop a critical theoretical practice of African American Studies is uncertain. Moreover, it is not clear that the National Council for Black Studies can ensure that African American Studies enterprises across the nation will conform to a model core curriculum. In fact, one must ask whether there should be conformity to a model curriculum and a single theoretical or ideological orientation in African American Studies. Most fields of study do not display this kind of uniformity. Perhaps an alternative is to allow a more flexible and innovative atmosphere in which African American Studies can continue to grow and develop.

Clearly, one future challenge for African American Studies is to move beyond its marginal image and status within the academy. An equally if not more important future challenge is to deal with the intellectual and social implications of the changing character of American society, as the declining industrial-capitalist order gives way to a rising postindustrial-managerial order.

Conclusion: African American Studies in the Emerging Postindustrial-Managerial Age

The postindustrial-managerial transformation of American society is characterized by the transition from a capital-intensive economy based on physical resources, which dominated the first half of this century, to a knowledge-intensive economy based on human resources, which characterizes the last half of this century. The principal resource in America's declining capital-intensive economy has been finance capital, invested in industrial plants, machinery, and technologies to increase the muscle power of human labor. In the emerging knowledge-intensive economy, the decisive resource is cultural capital: the nation's investment in and management of education, knowledge, computers, and other technologies that enhance the mental capacity of workers (Botkin, Dimancescu, and Stata, 1984; Drucker, 1969, 1993; Lyotard, 1984; Reich, 1991; Toffler, 1990). Important now are specialized knowledge, communication skills, the capacity to process and utilize collections of information in strategic decision-making processes, and an increasingly professionalized/ bureaucratic approach to managing people. With this expanding role for formal or specialized knowledge, professionals and experts—intellectuals and the technical intelligentsia—are becoming a "new class" in the public and private spheres, particularly with regard to policy making (see Bazelon, 1971; Derber, Schwartz, Magrass, 1990; Ehrenreich and Ehrenreich, 1979; Freidson, 1970; Galbraith, 1971; Gouldner, 1979; Nachmias and Rosenbloom, 1980; Perkin, 1989).

Mental capacity and managerial skills are supplanting the sole power of money and manufacturing. Learning, therefore, becomes an indispensable investment for social development, and educational credentials are more and more the key to a person's role in society (Collins, 1977). In view of these trends, many parents are becoming preoccupied with the educational advantages they can confer on their children, and many university students are realizing the importance of advanced education.

In the emerging post-capitalist society, members of a rising professional-managerial class are located in government, elite universities, philanthropic foundations, the mass media, elite law firms, political action committees, high finance conglomerates, transnational corporations, and major policy research institutions (see Benveniste, 1972; Burnham, 1960; Fischer, 1990; Keane, 1984; Lebedoff, 1981; Smith, 1991). Their influence comes from the capacity to conceptualize the character of social issues and to design strategies for handling them; they also produce and manage ideas and images that direct the cultural, intellectual, and ideological development of society. For example, the current debate about the "urban underclass" and social welfare policy reform includes professional experts and policy intellectuals of various ideological persuasions (see Jencks and Peterson, 1991; Jones, 1992; Mead, 1992; Murray, 1984; Wilson, 1987). Living by argumentation, persuasion, and critical discourse, the new ruling elite is not only a socioeconomic class, but it is also a cultural class (see Darity, 1986; Fischer, 1990; Gouldner, 1979; Luke, 1989; Majone, 1989; Perkin, 1989).

This new elite does not rise to dominance by itself. To be effective, members of the professional-managerial class must be allied to a political, legal, or organizational base. Their power comes from their access to and their ability to influence policy makers in government and private organizations. They operate at many levels to influence the intellectual direction, content, and contours of public decision making. They may be policy specialists within the offices of political executives, intellectual activists who appear at local school board hearings, renowned university professors who consult with government officials on important policy matters, or social scientists whose research findings contribute to major court rulings.

What role will African American Studies intellectuals and scholars play in the evolving postindustrial-managerial society? The need is to respond with innovation and a critical consciousness in regard to curriculum development and strategies for social development. African American scholars will be required to pursue new knowledge that can prove useful for handling complex social problems — for example, the progressive impoverishment of and resultant hopelessness in urban Black communities. Moreover, in the evolving global political economy that is anchored in knowledge production, distribution, and consumption (see Drucker, 1993; Reich, 1991; Toffler, 1990), African American Studies will be compelled to strengthen its transdisciplinary and global thrusts — the 1993 National Council for Black Studies annual meeting in Ghana was an initial international gathering that needs to be continued — by designing curricula that transgress upon the conventional academic disciplinary boundaries between the humanities and the social, behavioral, biological, and physical sciences. African American Studies needs to destroy old stereotypes, break new ground (conceptually and empirically), and broaden its intellectual scope and horizons to include attention to such areas of study as policy studies and advocacy, critical social theory, critical cultural studies, women's studies, social and political ethics, futures research, organizational development, and leadership preparation.

In the process, African American Studies theorists, practitioners, and students need to remain skeptical of received knowledge and must continue to disturb the and White American chauvinism within the academy. This is not to suggest an end to the study of Western culture. However, because the Eurocentric perspective and White American chauvinism continue to set the terms of intellectual discourse and dictate the academy's accepted structure of knowledge, this writer advocates a more careful and critical investigation of Western European culture and its American legacy — but with a different and even irreverent interpretive lens refracted by African American Studies and the other "new studies" (for example, see Ani, 1994; Hayes, 1989). Western civilization and its cultural heritage need to be seen and understood not as superior to others but as part of a democratic community of world civilizations and cultures. There is no normative civilization and culture.

Importantly, African American Studies scholars and intellectuals must be determined to grapple with the implications of the emerging postindustrial-managerial estate for African Americans and other historically oppressed peoples. How will this new social order affect such real human concerns as individual dignity and human worth; family stability and community solidarity; literacy and quality education; economic well-being and self-sufficiency; and democratic political rights and self-determination? African American Studies cannot ignore the examination of the consequences of a progressively changing world.

African American Studies, as a critically conscious intellectual endeavor, needs to hammer out a concept of social justice and morality that encompasses the growing multicultural and multiracial nature of America's evolving society. Moreover, in a social order where professional experts are gaining increasing power to design governmental policies and to direct cultural development, African American Studies critical theorists and practitioners must not only question all aspects of received truth. They must strengthen the field's interdisciplinary approach by bringing together fragments of knowledge and partial views that contest the growing hegemony of the politics of expertise. Thus, intellectual work is not apolitical, and African American Studies oppositional theorists and practitioners need to consider themselves involved in a struggle for identity and community beyond the domination of manipulative images and exploitative policies. This battle resides in cultural, political, and economic systems and can only culminate in dynamic systems that are not more exclusive but more inclusive.

In the final analysis, African American Studies needs to continue to contest the dominant modes of thinking and knowledge of the academy's intellectual and managerial elites, engage in new thinking, and refashion an independent critical social theory and practice that will promote the expansion of the frontiers of new knowledge (for example, see Collins, 1990; Wynter, 1984a; 1984b; 1984c; 1987) and give direction to the struggle against all forms of cultural domination. These critical and uncertain times demand, therefore, that African American Studies give leadership in the academic and non-academic world by developing new strategies and tactics that could save humanity and thereby save the world African community. As we approach the twenty-first century, African American Studies will continue to develop to the extent that it remains innovative, critical, self-reflective, and emancipatory.

References

Alkalimat, Abdul and Associates. 1986. *Introduction to Afro-American Studies: A Peoples College Primer*. Chicago: Twenty-First Century Books & Publications.

Allen, Robert L. September 1974. "Politics of the Attack on Black Studies," *The Black Scholar* 6 (l): 2-7.

Ani, Marimba. 1994. Yurugu: An African-Centered Critique of European Cultural Thought and Behavior. Trenton: Africa World Press, Inc.

Asante, Molefi K. 1980. *Afrocentricity. The Theory of Social Change*. Buffalo: Amulefi Publishing Co.

———. December 1986. "A Note on Nathan Huggins' Report to the Ford Foundation on African American Studies," *Journal of Black Studies* 17 (2): 255-262.

———. 1987. *The Afrocentric Idea*. Philadelphia, Temple University Press.

———. 1990. *Kemet, Afrocentricity and Knowledge*. Trenton: Africa World Press, Inc.

Asante, Molefi K. and Kariamu W. Asante, eds. 1990. *African Culture: The Rhythms of Unity*. Trenton Africa World Press, Inc.

Bazelon, David T. 1971. *Power in America: The Politics of the New Class*. New York: The New American Library.

"Black Studies Run Into Trouble on U.S. College Campuses." January 29, 1973. *U.S. News and World Report*.

Benveniste, Guy. 1972. *The Politics of Expertise*. Berkeley: The Glendessary Press.

Botkin, James, Dan Diamancescu, and Ray Stata. 1984. *The Innovators: Rediscovering Americas Creative Energy*. New York: Harper & Row Publishers, Inc.

Burnham, James. 1960. *The Managerial Revolution*. Bloomington: Indiana University Press.

Carmichael, Stokely and Charles V. Hamilton. 1967. *Black Power: The Politics of Liberation in America*. New York: Random House.

Carson, Clayborne. 1981. *In Struggle: SNCC a the Black Awakening the 1960s*. Cambridge: Harvard University Press.

Chrisman, Robert. "Observations on Race and Class at San Francisco State." In James McEvoy and Abraham Miller, eds., *Black Power and Student Rebellion*, pp. 222-223. Belmont: Wadsworth Publishing Company, Inc.

Collins, Patricia Hill. 1990. *Black Feminist Thought: Knowledge, Consciousness, and the Politics of Empowerment*. New York: Routledge.

Collins, Randall. 1979. *The Credential Society: An Historical Sociology of Education and Stratification*. New York: Academic Press, Inc.

Colt, George H. 1981. "Will the Huggins Approach Save Afro-American Studies?" *Harvard Magazine* (September-October): 38-46, 62, 70.

Cruse, Harold. 1967. *The Crisis of the Negro Intellectual*. New York: William Morrow and Company, Inc.

———. 1969. "The Integrationist Ethic as a Basis for Scholarly Endeavors." In Armstead L. Robinson, Craig C. Foster, and Donald H. Ogilvie, eds., *Black Studies in the University: A Symposium*, pp. 4-12. New Haven: Yale University Press.

Darity, William A., Jr. Spring 1986. "The Managerial Class and Industrial Policy," *Industrial Relations* 25: 217-227.

Davidson, Douglas V. and Frederick S. Weaver. March 1985. "Black Studies, White Studies, and Institutional Politics," *Journal of Black Studies* 15 (3): 339-347.

Derber, Charles, William A. Schwartz, and Yale Magrass. 1990. *Power in the Highest Degree: Professionals and the Rise of a New Mandarin Order*. New York: Oxford University Press.

Donner, Frank J. 1980. *The Age of Surveillance: The Aims and Methods of America's Political Intelligence System*. New York: Alfred A. Knopf.

———. 1990. *Protectors of Privilege: Red Squads and Police Repression in Urban America*. Berkeley: University of California Press.

Drucker, Peter F. 1993. *Post-Capitalist Society*. New York: Harper-Collins Publishers, Inc.

———. 1968. *The Age of Discontinuity: Guidelines to Our Changing Society*. New York: Harper and Row, Publishers.

Edwards, Harry. 1970. *Black Students*. New York: The Free Press.

———. 1980. *The Struggle That Must Be: An Autobiography*. New York: Macmillan Publishing Co., Inc.

Ehrenreich, Barbara and John. 1979. "The Professional-Managerial Class." In Pat Walker, ed., *Between Labor and Capital*, pp. 5-45. Boston: South End Press.

Farrell, Walter C., Jr. and Edgar F. Bridges. September 1987. "Black Studies at the Crossroads," *Thought & Action: The NEA Higher Education Journal* 3: 103-112.

Fischer, Frank. 1990. *Technocracy and the Politics of Expertise*. Newbury Park: Sage Publications.

Forman, James. 1972. *The Making of Black Revolutionaries*. New York: The Macmillan Company.

Galbraith, John K. 1971. *The New Industrial State*. Boston: Houghton Mifflin Company.

Gordon, Vivian V. Fall 1981. "The Coming of Age of Black Studies," *The Western Journal of Black Studies* 5 (3): 231-236.

Gouldner, Alvin W. 1979. *The Future of Intellectuals and the Rise of the New Class*. New York: Seabury Press.

Hare, Nathan. 1974. "The Contribution of Black Sociologists to Black Studies." In James E. Blackwell and Morris Janowitz, eds., *Black Sociologists: Historical and Contemporary Perspectives*, pp. 253-266. Chicago: The University of Chicago Press.

Hayes, Floyd W. III. Summer 1989. "Politics and Education in America's Multicultural Society: An African-American Studies' Response to Allan Bloom," *The Journal of Ethnic Studies* 17 (2): 71-88.

Henderson, Donald. 1971. "What Direction Black Studies?" In Henry J. Richards, ed., *Topics in Afro-American Studies*. Buffalo: Black Academy Press.

Jackson, Maurice. December 1970. "Toward a Sociology of Black Studies," *Journal of Black Studies* 1 (2): 131-140.

Jencks, Christopher, and Paul E. Peterson, eds. 1991. *The Urban Underclass*. Washington, DC: The Brookings Institution.

Jones, Jacqueline. 1992. *The Dispossessed: America's Underclasses from the Civil War to the Present*. New York: Basic Books.

Karenga, Maulana. 1982. *Introduction to Black Studies*. Inglewood: Kawaida Publications.

Keane, John. 1984. *Public Life and Late Capitalism: Toward a Socialist Theory of Democracy*. New York: Cambridge University Press.

Kilson, Martin, Jr. 1969. "The Intellectual Validity of Studying the Black Experience." In Armstead L. Robinson, Craig C. Foster, and Donald H. Ogilvie, eds., *Black Studies in the University: A Symposium*, pp. 13-16. New Haven: Yale University Press.

————. March 1973. "Reflections on Structure and Content in Black Studies," *Journal of Black Studies* 3 (3): 297-313.

Lebedoff, David. 1981. *The New Elite: The Death of Democracy*. New York: Franklin Watts.

Luke, Timothy W. 1989. *Screens of Power Ideology, Dominance, and Resistance in Informational Society*. Urbana: University of Illinois Press.

Lyotard, Jean-Francois. 1984. *The Postmodern Condition: A Report on Knowledge*. Trans. Geoff Bennington and Brian Massumi. Minneapolis: University of Minnesota Press.

McEvoy, James and Abraham Miller. 1969. "San Francisco State 'On Strike...Shut It Down.'" In McEvoy and Miller, eds., *Black Power and Student Rebellion: Conflict on the American Campus*, pp. 12-31. Belmont: Wadsworth Publishing Company, Inc.

Majone, Giandomenico. 1989. *Evidence, Argument, and Persuasion in the Policy Process*. New Haven: Yale University Press.

Malveaux, Julianne. 1980. "Black Studies: An Assessment," *Essence* (August): 78-79, 95, 98, 103-104.

Makable, Manning. Summer 1992. "Blueprint for Black Studies and Multicultural-ism," *Black Scholar* 22 (3): 30-35.

Mead, Lawrence M. 1992. *The New Politics of Poverty: The Nonworking Poor in America*. New York: Basic Books.

Murray, Charles. 1984. *Losing Ground: American Social Policy, 1950-1980*. New York: Basic Books.

Nachmias, David, and David H. Rosenbloom. 1980. *Bureaucratic Government USA*. New York: St. Martin's Press.

Perkin, Harold. 1989. *The Rise of Professional Society: England Since 1880*. New York: Routledge.

Poinsett, Alex. December 1973. "The Plight of Black Studies," *Ebony* 29 (2): 128-134.

Reich, Robert B. 1991. *The Work of Nations: Preparing Ourselves for 21st-Century Capitalism*. New York: Alfred A. Knopf.

Smith, James A. 1991. *The Idea Brokers: Think Tanks and the Rise of the New Policy Elite*. New York: The Free Press.

Stone, Chuck. 1968. *Black Power in America*. Indianapolis: The Bobbs-Merrill Company.

————. 1968. "The National Conference on Black Power." In Floyd B. Barbour, ed., *The Black Power Revolt: A Collection of Essays*, pp. 189-198. Boston: Extending Horizons Books.

Toffler, Alvin. 1990. *Powershift: Knowledge, Wealth, and Violence at the Edge of the 21st Century*. New York: Bantam Books.

UMBC Catalog 1973-1974. 1973. Baltimore: University of Maryland Baltimore County.

Walton, Sidney F. 1969. *The Black Curriculum: Developing a Program in Afro-American Studies*. East Palo Alto: Black Liberation Publishers.

Williams, Kenny J. 1981. "The Black Studies Syndrome: Down by One is Still Losing," *Change* (October): 30-37.

Wilson, William J. 1987. *The Truly Disadvantaged: The Inner City, the Underclass, and Public Policy*. Chicago: The University of Chicago Press.

Wynter, Sylvia. May 1984. "New Seville and the Conversion Experience of Bartolome de Las Casas," Part One. *Jamaica Journal* 17 (2): 25-32.

————. August 1984. "New Seville and the Conversion Experience of Bartolome de Las Casas," Part Two. *Jamaica Journal* 17 (3): 46-55.

————. Spring/Fall 1984. "The Ceremony Must Be Found: After Humanism," *Boundary 2* XII (1): 19-70.

————. 1987. "On Disenchanting Discourse: 'Minority' Literary Criticism and Beyond," *Cultural Critique* 7 (Fall): 207-244.

VIII

Section VIII

Curriculum Development and Program Models

Key Concepts and Major Terms

- Curriculum
- Content of Discipline
- Core Curriculum
- Social/Behavioral Studies
- Cultural Studies
- Research Areas
- Research Areas
- Course Development
- Curricula Development
- Cognitive Revolution
- Holistic Curriculum Model

- Pedagogical
- Curricula Models
- Curricula Design
- Interdisciplinary Concepts
- Consortium
- Science and Technology Policy
- Computer Technology
- Administrative Structure
- Value Inquire Model

- Unidisciplinary Aspects
- Levels of Meaning
- Financial Resources
- Administrators
- Academic & Social Needs
- Multifaceted Culture
- Social/Cultural Dynamics of the African World
- Disciplinary Model
- Multidisciplinary Curriculum Model

Introduction

Although the call for African American Studies at San Francisco State by black students is the most publicized and perhaps best known moment in the history of the field, there were a number of other pioneering efforts to establish programs and courses which would deal with the historical and contemporary experiences of people of African descent in a fair and accurate manner.

For example, in the spring of 1968, the Black Student Alliance at Yale University organized a symposium which sought to bring together key intellectuals and administrators to search for answers to the initial questions the prospect of African American Studies posed. Published as *Black Studies in the University: A Symposium*, the proceedings offer a key example of just how contentious and challenging the field would prove to be over the course of the next thirty years. Sidney Walton, of Merrit

611

College, proposed in *The Black Curriculum: Developing A Program in African American Studies*, one of the earliest comprehensive plans for establishing, developing, and evaluating the course curricula, content, materials, teachers, and administration of African American Studies Programs and Departments. And since 1980, the National Council for Black Studies (established in 1976) has proposed the development of a standardized core curriculum model for African American Studies. In its 1981 Hall Report, the Council suggested an ideal core curriculum for African American Studies to be constructed along the lines of three research areas: Social/Behavioral Studies, History Course Area and Cultural Studies Course Area.

Despite the work of the Council, there still remains a great deal of controversy surrounding the issues of curricula and course development. The existence of various programs and departments with apparently no common ideological, pedagogical, methodological contents or structures has perpetuated the question of exactly what constitutes African American Studies as a discipline. Thus, the essays in this section examine the process of becoming a discipline from the perspective of curricula design, curricula models, interdisciplinary concepts, teaching for social change, necessary research, and directions for the 21st century.

Gerald A. McWorter (Abdul Alkalimat) and Ronald Bailey state in "Black Studies Curriculum Development in the 1980s: Its Patterns and History" that "the current stage of Black Studies is focused on the consolidation of Black Studies as a concrete and definite set of activities. Black Studies has organized a substantial body of intellectual thought, has organized its trends, issues, and insights into formal curricula, and finally, has organized its practitioners (i.e. its instructors, theoreticians, writers) into institutional and professional association on a nationwide basis."

In "Black Studies Models and Curricula," William D. Smith observes "Colleges and universities have initiated various types of Black Studies models in attempt to provide their institutions with information pertaining to the black experience in America.... The structure that is adopted at various institutions will also be determined to some degree by financial resources, orientations of the directors or heads of Black Studies, the administrators, the black students, and the like. Each institution should adopt the structure that best meets the predetermined objectives."

In "Black Studies Consortia: A Proposal," Gloria I. Joseph holds that "The basic premise upon which the consortium model is developed is that individual Black Studies or Afro-American Studies programs should be eliminated from predominantly white campuses.... The consortium location must be adjacent to a black community."

Karla J. Spurlock points out in "Toward the Evolution of a Unitary Discipline: Maximizing the Interdisciplinary Concept in African/Afro-American Studies" that "One of the most vital benefits of the interdisciplinary mode is the stimulus it offers.... The interdisciplinary mode places the student/scholar in a virtual intellectual crossfire. As ideas arising out of different and potentially conflicting disciplinary methods bang against one another, the opportunity for creative synthesis—of new understandings and shared levels of meaning within African and Afro-American Studies—emerges."

A major concern as the twenty-first century approaches is the relationship between Black Studies and emergent forms of science and technology. William M. King, in "The Importance of Black Studies for Science and Technology Policy," asserts that "Science and technology policy is concerned with the care and feeding of the social institutions/processes of science and technology. Science and technology policymaking is guided by values and expectations that cannot be divorced from the policy process. And it is in the examination of those values and expectations that Black Studies can play a most important role."

An article by Melvin K. Hendrix et al., "Computers and Black Studies: Toward the Cognitive Revolution," identifies several ways that computer technology can be employed within Black Studies to enhance faculty, student, and staff skills; improve curriculum and program standards; to provide a communications linkage with research facilities, community groups, and other academic institutions and individuals, while also promoting increased scholarly productivity in the areas of publishing and research. Black Studies offers another oppotunity to strengthen the unidisciplinary aspects of our international approach to knowledge, as well as improve the academic standing of Black Studies units in the Academy."

In the statement of purpose of the Institute of the Black World, the organizers described the institute as "a gathering of Black intellectuals who are convinced that the gifts of their minds are meant to be fully used in the service of the black community. It is, therefore, an experiment with scholarship in the context of struggle. Among our basic concerns and commitments is the determination to set our skills to a new understanding of the past, and future condition of the peoples of African descent, wherever they may be found, with an initial emphasis on the American experience."

James A. Banks, in "Teaching Black Studies for Social Change," holds that "Teachers should help students to develop a *method* (or process) of deriving and clarifying their values rather than teach them a set of predetermined values.... Perhaps no more serious value questions and problems are raised in the classroom than during the study of the Black experience. Black students have important questions about the value of blackness, their identity and about effective strategies to use in releasing themselves from institutionalized racism and colonization."

The NCBS Curriculum Research Project's "Black Studies and Africana Studies Curriculum Model[s] in the United States," written by William A. Little, Carolyn M. Leonard, and Edward Crosby, concludes that the current academic disciplinary social construct was not designed to answer critical questions relevant to the social and cultural dimensions and dynamics of the African world. The Black Studies/Africana Studies curriculum was designed to examine the complexity of a multifaceted culture as well as to implement a program that would meet the academic and social needs of faculty, students and universities. A consensus determination of the function, scope and goals of Black Studies must precede the development of a Core Curriculum.

With the rapidly expanding role of technology in education, along with radical changes in curriculum which have taken place over the last fifteen years, Section VIII may very well be the most important of the text. Each essay directs its attention to providing comprehensive plans for establishing course curricula, content, and specifications for the research, planning, and teaching of Afro-American Studies. Issues such as the interrelationship between ideology, pedagogy, and methodology in the development of undergraduate and graduate programs, institutes and consortiums, the creation of effective strategies to promote cooperate relations between the campus and community for the express purpose of impacting a positive, lasting social change as well the expanding role of science and computer technology within the field are specifically addressed.

53.

Black Studies Curriculum Development in the 1980s: Its Patterns and History

Gerald A. McWorter and Ronald Bailey

Black Studies is in its second stage, in a Renaissance, a rebirth of energy, a focus on intellectual productivity, professional unity, and scholarly research as the basis for ideological and political progress of the Black Liberation Movement.[1] Though the last 15 years (1967-1982) have been period of great social change, it is important to recognize that this social change has taken two roads: change that reflects innovation(the creation of new things), and destruction (the liquidation of things).Much of Black people struggle, in virtually every sector of social, is focused on protecting society, is focused on protecting social innovations from the 60s and very early 70s, and providing resistance to the destructive change characteristic of the current period. It is this dialectical tension between innovative construction and destruction that providing the framework for understanding the development and current state of resistance in Black Studies.

And as the Black Studies Movement moved into its first substantial stage, it bore the birthmarks of its turbulent origins. What was universally true, is that there were few Black faculty, and even fewer Black faculty prepared to teach what knowledge did exist then about the Black experience. The white campus was by and large divorced or separated from Black intellectual tradition. Black students were involved in the current popular tendencies (rhetorical style, fashion, etc.) of the Black Liberation Movement with little grasp of the theoretical basis for differences (and similarities) between the tendencies. Beyond these things, of course, there was a great deal of diversity.

Black Studies Unity Counters Economic Despair

Within the current economic crisis there has been a resurgence of racism, implicating both the institutional and societal level.[2] Further, there is a technical and vocational attack being made against liberal arts education in which the value of the "soft" areas is being questioned by the hard mathematically-oriented sciences. And, of course, this not only impacts upon policymakers in the University, there is a vocational-oriented pragmatism now dominating student values, so that in some places the utility of Black Studies has been seriously called into question. In other words, most students want to know, "Can the course you want me to take in Black Studies *help me get a job?*"

But as the crisis of unemployment deepens, it has become fairly obvious that the United States, indeed, all western capitalist countries, are in a deep depression in which jobs are simply hard to come by. This is having an interesting impact upon the vocational-orientation of students which might very well lead to a new interest in non-vocationally-related areas, especially the liberal arts, because people are forced to *figure out the meaning of life outside of a job context.*

The current stage of Black Studies is focused on the consolidation of Black Studies as a concrete and definite set of activities. No longer is Black Studies simply a movement of ad hoc ambiguously interrelated individuals, programs, and practices, but now must be organized as a coherent and stable community of people, organizations, and activities.

The organization of Black Studies practitioners has followed the general historical development of Black Studies as a whole. The way the Black Studies movement started and developed initially, through social disruption and a period of experimentation, is nowhere better represented than in the history of the *African Heritage Study Association.*[3] This organization played the leading role in the early stages of the Black Studies movement, and more than any other organization reflects the early experiences.

AHSA was created by Blacks rejecting the white racist and imperialist collaboration of the African Studies Association, because it was felt that the ASA represented U.S. imperialism's interest in subordinating Africa, while Black intellectuals, scholars, and activists were interested in using their scholarly abilities to further the cause of African liberation. This conflict resulted in Blacks disrupting a meeting of the ASA in Canada and forming an independent Black organization, the African Heritage Studies Association. During the early days this organization captured the imagination and the energy of the Black Studies movement, and held very large and successful national conferences.

It was also this organization that reflected the dominant political trends and paralleled the development of organizations in the Black Liberation Movement, notably the African Liberation Support Committee. Key intellectual activists participated in both organizations and both organizations shared very important plenary at an AHSA conference in 1974 in which the dialogue between intellectuals and activists was intensified.[4]

During the current phase of the Black Studies movement, a major organization that has emerged is the *National Council for Black Studies.*[5] This organization emerged in response to the crisis on the campus that threatened the existence of existing Black Studies programs in the middle 1970s. It is in the context of an organization like NCBS that the experimentation in Black Studies can be best examined for alternative models, as the Black Studies movement takes on a more permanent and long lasting character. It is important that there be a national organization in Black Studies, including a network of affiliates on regional and state levels. This development would enable Black Studies practitioners to interact with colleagues, share experiences, and develop an organizational capacity to serve as advocates to support and protect and develop Black Studies.

At present, some level of institutional affiliation covers approximately 30 percent of the primary Black Studies practitioners. It is also important to note that Black Studies practitioners cover the entire spectrum of ideological and political positions in the Black Liberation movement. To some extent this represents the maturation of a generation, a group of people who have emerged out of the 60s and 70s with a long term commitment to struggle for unity and clarity of differences through collective scholarly research and dialogue rather than through emotional and episodic polemics.

Another critical way in which Black Studies is developing unity has to do with the professional journal literature that constitutes its primary intellectual productivity.[6] There are essentially 26 basic journals that make up the core of Black Studies journal literature. These journals are run by Black Studies activists and reflect scholarly trends. It is also an index to a much broader literature of journals and books that constitutes a much larger body of related materials, mainly material that focuses in some way on the Black experience though not necessarily in a Black Studies context. All of this journal literature reflects the professional marketplace of ideas in which Black Studies practitioners collectively engage in the search for truth and ideas that can be applied to the situation facing Black people such that they can struggle to make their lives better. It is the standard, methods, and values brought to the production of this literature and the evaluation of this literature that constitutes the intellectual character and the scholarly qualities of Black Studies. It is important that every major or trend in scholarly research is being evaluated in this context of Black Studies, but also the extent to which Black Studies is connected to mainstream scholarship in the world today.

A fourth area of institutional unity in Black Studies is the extent to which certain key institutional practices are being standardized. The two key activities currently being standardized have to do with the curriculum, the important codification of the journal literature into the classroom, and the national conference for professional organizations, the main activity by which NCBS facilitates the national dialogue of Black Studies practitioners.

National conferences of Black Studies organizations have long been important activities. Throughout the history of Black intellectuals, and certainly this has been true in the most recent decade, national conferences constitute high points, focal points, not only for the dialogue between Black Studies practitioners but as a reflection of broad intellectual shifts from one ideological or political position to another. It is significant that NCBS is having a national dialogue on a national conference handbook developed out of the most recent successful experience of the 6th Annual Conference held in Chicago. This handbook specifies methods for the development of a conference plate, a mobilization of the national constituency of Black Studies practitioners, and the organizational and programmatic logistics necessary for a successful national conference.

The Development of Core Curricula

The second aspect of standardization, and the one most relevant to the day to day work in Black Studies, has to do with the standardization of a core curriculum. NCBS took the lead in 1980 with the adoption of the report of the Curriculum Standards Committee chaired by Dr. Perry Hall of Wayne State University. This report makes the singular contribution of codifying the basic parameters of a core curriculum in such a way that the diversity of ideological and academic trends in Black Studies will be able to coexist and develop within the same standardize framework. The general framework of the NCBS model is widespread, but the content of each course varies from

Table 1
NCBS Core Curriculum for Afro-American Studies

(Adopted at 4th Annual Conference by National
Council for Black Studies, March 26-29, 1980)

Level 1	Introduction to Afro-American Studies		
	Social/Behavioral Studies	Historical Studies	Cultural Studies
Level 2	A. Basic Literature Review or Survey	A. African Pre-History through Reconstruction	A. Basic Literature Review or Survey (music, aesthetics, etc.)
Level 3	B. Current Research & Emerging Issues	B. Post-Reconstruction Current & Emerging Issues in Historical Interpretation & Evaluation	B. Current Research & Emerging Issues (contemporary cultural expression & transformation, etc.)
Level 4	Senior Seminar Course Area Synthesis and Application of Insights or Previous Study		

campus to campus. The current state of course content in Black Studies reflects trends in the Black Liberation movement, as well as trends in academic circles more generally. The main thing is that there have been two sources for curriculum development, library literature that deals with the Black experience and practical experience from the society, theory and practice. The test of how adequate our framework is must be based on the criteria of comprehensives and universality, covering all topics and being useful for all people. For this, we have developed a list of alternative foci in Black Studies courses. The purpose of Table 1 is to identify key areas that have been central to the development of Black Studies and represent necessary aspects of a curriculum, course by course. Its main point is to identify trends and clearly point to areas of strength and weakness in Black Studies so we're in a better position to improve things. But, what were the intellectual precursors of Black Studies?

Historical Review of Theoretical Literature

In his insightful article called "The Failure of Negro Intellectuals," the sociologist E. Franklin Frazier stated that Black scholar "have failed to study the problems of the Negro life in America in a manner which would place the fate of the Negro in the broad framework of man's experience in the world."[7]

Similarly, Earl Thorpe in *The Black Historians*, one of the few critical summations of Black intellectual history, suggests that "the Black historian has not joined in the twentieth century search for historical laws which has been characteristic of the majority group."[8] Harold Cruse echoed these sentiments when he stated that "the Black American as part of an ethnic group has no definite social theory relative to his status, presence, or impact on American society...."[9]

The positing of an alternative theoretical understanding of the Black experience—its meanings and its implications—was the main underlying intellectual challenge of Black Studies as a new field of study. There are three sources of *theory* which were central to Black Studies in its early years which remain critically relevant in the 1980s, and should be covered in any Black Studies course: (1) mainstream scholarship, (2) radical critiques, and (3) Black intellectual history.

Critique of Mainstream Work

In an unpublished essay, St. Clair Drake summed up the relationship of the rise of Black Studies to mainstream scholarship:[10]

> The very use of the term Black Studies is by implication an indictment of American and Western European scholarship. It makes the bold assertion that what we have heretofore called 'objective' intellectual activities were actually white studies in perspective and content; and that corrective bias, a shift in emphasis, is needed, even if something called "truth" is set as a goal. To use a technical sociological term, the present body of knowledge has an ideological element in it, and a counter-ideology is needed. Black Studies supply that counter-ideology.

Thus, a critical approach to mainstream work on Black people was at the core of Black Studies.

Johnnetta Cole, Hunter College, New York, in her review of anthropology syllabi, makes this point in her opening paragraph, as does IBW in its charge to its reviewers.[11]

> When the champions of Black Studies confronted mainstream scholarship in the 1960s, no discipline escaped criticism. In summary form, the fundamental charge of Black Studies was that the mainstream disciplines of western bourgeoisie science, arts and humanities, were pregnant with racism, as reflected in who the overwhelming majority of the disciplinarians are, where they come from, and to whom they are accountable. Many scholars and activists of Black Studies also charged that western scholarship suffered from a gender and class bias—a point that was tangential to the main charge of racism for some, but a point of equal centrality for others... Now, in the 1980s as I work in university administration, cooperating with faculty, staff and students in the revision of our undergraduate curriculum and the strengthening of that part which constitutes general education, I am no less convinced than I was in the 1960s that Black Studies can be an essential corrective scholarship for certain biases in mainstream academics... As we turn now to a consideration of the components which I suggest should be present in a Black Studies course in anthropology, it should be noted that we are in fact addressing the criticism which Black Studies scholarship has leveled against mainstream anthropology.

Lucius Outlaw (Haverford College) makes a similar claim in his review of Philosophy syllabi:[12]

> Among all of the modes of intellectual praxis which have been institutionalized in Western academies, philosophy remains one of the most elite and ethnocentric, the Black Studies movement and the independence of African countries notwithstanding... The significance of this situation is understood when we take note of a basic feature and commitment of philosophical praxis: the

articulation of a person's or peoples' understanding of themselves, or others, of the world and history, and of their place in them both, in the most fundamental sense. Western philosophy, along with religion and theology, continues to be the principal keeper of the self-image in Its most reflective, articulate form. More than that, in its dominant tendencies and driving orientations, it seeks to define and stand guard over what it means to be "a human being"' as well. The fact that the histories of peoples of Africa continue to challenge the Western self-image, and especially, to challenge the image of ourselves the European hegemonists would enforce on us, increases the urgency of sharing in the deconstruction of philosophy as the embodiment of a deficient European American self-image as *the* model for human self-knowledge. At the same time, we must control the construction of knowledge of and ideals for ourselves and the world's peoples that are more in keeping with the struggle to achieve a democratically just and liberated world. In doing so, we would, as scholars and intellectuals, have the appropriate grounding for our work.

In his essay reviewing syllabi called "The Modern Miseducation of the Negro," Manning Marable (Colgate University) makes a similar point:[13]

> The demand for Black Studies was also a call toward the systematic reconstruction of American learning. Its most advanced advocates understood that the study of the African Diaspora and its people could not simply be "added" into the standard curricula merged within the mainstream of white thought. Rather, the social science, literary and creative contributions of Blacks to the whole of human knowledge charted new and different directions of critical inquiry. First, Black Studies demanded a pedagogical approach toward learning that de-emphasized the "banking" concept of teaching and advanced mixed methodological techniques, such as discussion, informal lecturing, debate and community studies. Black Studies theoreticians declared that interdisciplinary approaches toward learning were superior to narrow, selective teaching methods which concentrated on one single subject (e.g., history) at the exclusion of other related disciplines (sociology, political theory, political economy). Students were urged to devote some of their research activities towards the transformation and liberation of their own communities. Thus, there was a basic relationship between theory and practice in the learning process that was missing from white education. Students were urged to become active participants in their own education. For these theoretical and pedagogical reasons, therefore, Black Studies represented a basic and provocative challenge to the *raison d'être* of white universities.

Tom Shick (Wisconsin), writing from the perspective of an historian states:[14] "The Black Studies movement raised fundamental issues related to the methodology and assumptions of scholarship that purported to address the experience of African people whether on the continent or in the Diaspora."

Finally, Lloyd Hogan (Amherst College) observed a similar dynamic operative in the field of political economy:[15]

> White scholars who dominate the social sciences have only been peripherally interested in problems of Black people. To them there are many and much more important problems of solution. At the same time we have the anomalous situation in which most Back scholars received their graduate tutelage from the white institutions of higher learning. Black social scientists have been subjected to a perception of their disciplines which is devoid of a significant Black component. Such a perception expunges from the collective intellectual

memory the major pathology of the American political economy as if it never existed. And the consequence has been failure of ordinary social science disciplines to clarify the issues which embody the essential description and explanation of how the system of capitalist political economy works itself out in the real world. A complex system of myths, lies, distortions, and trivia has been built up to rationalize the ways in which the system operates. And social scientists—Black and white—learn how to competently spew out these vicious concoctions in the form of weighty of scientific contributions to the disciplines.

The great strength of the mainstream social science practiced in the U.S. today is the collection of empirical data and in the operationalization and measurement of concepts and relationships. It is out of this tradition that Black Studies should gain insights and models modifying them before taking them on as such—for empirical data analysis (collection and measurement).[16]

It should be clear, therefore, that a Black Studies course should make an effort to convey what the mainstream scholarship has to say by critically examining the strengths and weaknesses of its substance and methodology. It is only in this way that the particular contribution that Black Studies scholarship might make can be clarified.

Radical Thought and the Rise of Black Studies

The surge for Black Studies was accompanied by a general surge of interest in the theory and practice of radical politics: the mass struggles for civil rights and against the Vietnam War in the U.S.; and in the international arena, China's Great Proletarian Cultural Revolution and the student-worker uprising in France, Germany, and other European countries. A "new left" (as contrasted with the pro-Soviet "old left") emerged.[17]

Black Studies has reflected the same themes, perhaps in an intensified manner, over the last fifteen years. Coming as it did as a response to perceived racism in U.S. society and in the wake of King's assassination, Black Studies was aimed at institutionalizing an academic experience with "education for liberation" as a central goal. This explicit statement of its political posture was a direct challenge to the "apolitical" claims of institutions of higher education. Students questioned war-related research and the involvement of college professors with the C.I.A., and as consultants for multi-national corporations with questionable activities abroad and at home. To them, it was proof that the university was not "neutral," but only a politically oriented institution with the image of being "value free."[18]

The plight of the Black community during this period was widely popularized by the Watts rebellions and other outbursts, and then by the National Advisory Commission on Civil Disorders (the Kerner Commission named after the former Illinois governor who was later convicted of a felony), whose pronouncements came on March 1, 1968, just one month prior to the assassination of King:[19]

This is our basic conclusion: Our nation is moving toward two societies, one black, one white—separate and unequal.... Segregation and poverty have created in the racial ghetto a destructive environment totally unknown to most white Americans. What white Americans have never fully understood—but what the Negro can never forget—is that white society is deeply implicated in the ghetto. White institutions created it, white institutions maintain it, and white society condones it.

It was precisely within this context that la new generation of Black scholars emerged and sought to shape Black Studies so that it took up "the liberation tasks," to quote Dr. Drake, that were so much on both the national and Black community agenda of that period.

Almost simultaneously, there emerged in higher education *radical movements* in almost all social disciplines. The Union of Radical Sociologists, the Union of Radical Political Economists, the Union of Marxist Social Scientists are representative of the trend. New radical journals also appeared: *The Insurgent Sociologist, Radical America, The Review of Radical America, The Review of Radical Political Economy, Radical Criminology, Antipode* (in geography), and *Radical Anthropology.*[20]

Thus, the Black Studies movement has historically been close allies with a developing radical tradition in U.S. scholarship. By radical here, we mean a critique of U.S. society which focuses on the unequal distribution of economic, political, and social power, and the resulting patterns of exploitation and oppression.

In most instances, radicals took up the study of Marxism, and introduced Marxist categories to the study of U.S. society: class and class struggle, capitalism and imperialism, revolution (versus reform) and socialism as an avenue of fundamental social change as a step in solving Such problems as racism, poverty, exploitation and male supremacy. Radicals encouraged an activist orientation and recognized, in the words of Alkalimat, that "science is inevitably a hand servant to ideology, a tool to shape, it not create, reality."[21]

This brief description is illustrated in the summations of how a radical tradition emerged in established disciplines. The editors of *Radical Sociology* make the following points:[22]

Political and racial assassination, the adoption of genocide to implement foreign policy, the federal government's abandonment of the civil rights movement, military in Latin America and Asia, a program of domestic pacification via the War on Poverty, the destruction of communities for commercial purposes in the name of urban renewal—these were the events which helped to destroy the illusion that the Kennedy Administration/New Frontier would address...the more fundamental question of the allocation of power and resources in American society...Long neglected terms racism, monopoly, capitalism, and imperialism—began to re-enter the language of political debate. Many argued that these terms were ill-suited to dispassionate analysis and measured discussion. For those who sought to understand what America had become and where it was headed, 'rhetorical' terms such as exploitation and oppression, when elaborated and concretized, served well as basic organizing concepts, and provided new perspectives for the emerging radical analysis and practice.

Perhaps the best statement of the radical critique among the reviewers is found in Lloyd Hogan's "The Political Economy of Black Americans." He states:[23]

I shall argue in what follows that Black social scientists must break away from the existing traditions in their fields. The problem at hand which needs sound scientific treatment is the problem of Black people in the U.S. Such a treatment must be guided by a comprehension of the historical forces which generated the conditions under which Black people now find themselves.... Of signal importance one must study the essential role of the state and all the other social institutions as controlling mechanisms for buttressing the systems under which Black labor has been exploited in the past. But these studies cannot be completed without attention being focused on the final outcome of these people and the new social order which they must inevitably create as they struggle for liberation from economic exploitation. This will be the final chapter of an all encompassing black political economy.

A similar thrust is shared by Cole in her review of Anthropology syllabi:[24]

Black Studies courses in Anthropology should describe the History of Anthropology, with special attention to its association with the rise of imperialism and colonialism. In an article published in 1968, Kathleen Gough described anthropology as the "Child of Imperialism," a point which has been developed and expanded in the works of such Black anthropologists as Diane Lewis, William Willis, and Anselme Remy.

Although the discipline of anthropology was born in the 18th century, it came of age in the 19th century, precisely during the period of imperialist penetration of the cultures of people of color in Africa, Asia and the Americas. This was no mere coincidence, for anthropology served the needs of certain European and U.S. powers to know more about the people they subjugated... the better to rule them. Those who teach anthropology from a Black Studies perspective the responsibility to present students with such information, thereby documenting, for example, how British social anthropology in Africa was tied to Britain's colonial interests; how the concentration of U.S. anthropologists among native American peoples of the U.S. directly find indirectly assisted U.S. government forces; and the extent to which sometimes knowingly, and often unknowingly, anthropologists have supplied information on the traditional cultures of Third World societies which has been used as the basis of policies which are not in the interest of these peoples.

Black Studies often had the result of encouraging mainstream scholarship to critique itself. Similarly, there is a more pronounced impact that Black Studies and the Black experience have had on developing radical critiques. For example, many young white scholars, active in the Civil Rights and later the anti-war movements, went on to develop significant radical interpretations of U.S. history that have been acknowledged by the mainstream.[25]

American historians interested in tracing the rise of liberty, democracy, and the common man have been challenged in the past two decades by other historians, interested in tracing the history of oppression, exploitation and racism. The challenge has been salutary, because it has made us examine more directly than historians have hitherto been willing to do, the role of slavery in our early history. Colonial historians, in particular, when writing about the origin and development of American institutions have found it possible until recently to deal with slavery as an exception to everything they had to say. I am speaking about myself but also about most of my generation. We owe a debt of gratitude to those who have insisted that slavery was something more than an exception, that one fifth of the American population at the time of the Revolution is too many people to be treated as an exception.

In a 1967 speech before the American Psychological Association, Martin Luther King provides a glimpse of how the civil rights movement posed questions about the Black condition to social scientists. The pursuit of answers to these questions led many scholars toward radical alternatives outside the bounds of conventional solutions, many never to return. After summing up the importance of urban riots, the Vietnam War, high unemployment and civil disobedience, King cites "political action" as one key area that could benefit from social science inquiry:[26]

> In the past two decades, Negroes have expended more effort in quest of the franchise than they have in all other campaigns combined. Demonstrations, sit-ins and marches, though more spectacular, are dwarfed by the enormous number of man-hours expended to register millions, particularly in the South... A recent major work by social scientists Matthews and Prothro (*Negroes and the New Southern Politics*) concludes that "the concrete benefits to be derived from the franchise—under conditions that prevail in the South—have often been exaggerated"... that voting is not the key that will unlock the door to racial equality because "the concrete measurable payoffs from Negro voting in the South will not be revolutionary."
>
> James Q. Wilson supports this view, arguing, "Because of the structure of American politics as well as the nature of the Negro community, Negro politics will accomplish only limited objectives."
>
> If their conclusion can be supported, then the major effort Negroes have invested in the past twenty years has been in the wrong direction and the major effort of their hope is a pillar of sand.

Ralph Bunche once observed: "The study of the political status of the Negro is, in itself, a partial record of the shortcomings of American democracy. I think that we should at least raise some questions concerning the seeming inability of American democracy to 'democ' and the essential reason for this failure."[27] Almost a response to Dr. King's concern, it was in studying the persistence of exploitation and racist oppression which characterized the Black experience that led many social scientists to develop this radical critique, and makes this body of theoretical work a key component to cover in Black Studies courses.

The radical tradition of social science in its recent and older manifestation has its strength in exposing the political essence of current and prevailing trends. It points one's analysis toward class forces, anchors all analysis in the very structure of the capitalist system of imperialism. It serves to politically re-orient scholarship and provide a working class basis for a partisan social science. Black Studies approaches these matters on a moral and expressive basis; the radical tradition can help it develop a set of concepts that is in synchronization with universal tools of a progressive social science and focused on the particularity of the Black experience.

Black Intellectual History Has Been Rich

The issue of Black intellectual history and the intellectual heritage of Black Studies is key. Prior to the 1960s, only a handful of Black scholars taught at predominantly white institutions of higher education.[28] Because Black Studies was mainly a movement on these campuses, often lacking was a thorough appreciation of the outstanding work that had been done by Black scholars, who were most often based at predominantly Black institutions. This lack of knowledge created a situation where a substantial number of younger scholars developed without a thorough grounding in these important works of these pioneering generations of Black scholars. We often ended up polemicizing against what we considered biased, racist treatments of the Black experience, but without the ability to stand on the shoulders of our intellectual and academic forerunners, seeing the terrain they had traveled, and being able to chart more care more carefully an agenda for further intellectual work.

This is unfortunate since it is precisely in the work of older Black scholars that we find the clearest expressions of the themes and issues which Black Studies was attempting to introduce.[29] For example, Black scholars have historically, adopted the "scholar-activist" stance central to Black Studies. DuBois launched the Atlanta University studies "not only to make the truth known but to present it in such shape as will encourage reform."[30] Woodson endeavored to turn his historical training to the best racial account."[31]

In reviewing the life and work of Allison Davis, St. Clair Drake suggests that Davis saw the role of the Black scholar on three levels:[32]

(1) make some contribution to the general theoretical work in his discipline;

(2) decide upon some aspect of the social structure in which to become expert at the empirical level, and

(3) select a problem that contributed to "racial advancement, as we used to call it. Today we call it Black Liberation."

Even John Hope Franklin echoed similar sentiments in a 1963 essay called "The Dilemma of the American Negro Scholar."[33]

I now assert that the proper choice for the American Negro scholar is to use his knowledge and ingenuity, his resources and his talents to combat the forces that isolate him and his people, and like the true patriot that he is, to contribute to the solution of the problems that Americans face in common.

Our point here is that Black intellectual history gives us the intellectual foundation for the Black Studies enterprise, but it has not been given proper attention in Black Studies courses.

It is precisely this contradiction between the importance of the work and the contributions of Black scholars to the legacy of intellectual tradition of Afro-American Studies and to all of higher education, and the negative reception that this work received in higher education that goes to the very heart of why Black Studies emerged as turbulently as it did in the late 1960s and early 1970s. While this has changed somewhat, there is still a need for Black Studies as a field of study to "return to the classics," to develop a systematic summary and critique of the contours of Black intellectual history and the foundation of Black Studies.

It was this recognition that we were encouraging when we attempted to describe "the classical tradition" of Afro-American scholarship in developing the third edition of *Introduction to Afro-American Studies* (1975).[34]

A work of Black social analysis is considered a classic when it: (A) definitively, summarizes the existing knowledge of a major Black experience; (B) represents a model of methodology and technique that serves to direct future investigation; (C) draws from the analysis theoretical concepts and oppositions that contribute to our general theoretical grasp of the socio-economic and political history of the USA and Afro-American people; (D) stands the test of time by not being proven incorrect or inadequate and replaced by a superior work an (E) guides one to take an active role in struggle to liberate Black people and fundamentally change the nature of American society.

Our point here is that there is a rich body of work done by Black scholars and this work represents an indispensable component of Black Studies courses. This recognition is shared by several of the reviewers of syllabi in the IBW project.

Policy and Contemporary Issues

Black Studies was deeply concerned about helping to resolve social problems that existed for Black people and the entire society. There was a great sense of immediacy because as a new field of study, it sought to help change the world, not just to understand it. There was an explicit policy thrust to Black Studies in its initial stages. Several universities made air explicit recognition of their policy orientation and demand for immediacy relevance that was a part of the thrust for Black Studies.

Few topics are of greater importance or more dramatic relevance than those, that concern the forces that are driving our society to a recognition of the situation and the of Black people in the United States, past and present. And few needs are more compelling than the need of providing for the future leaders of Black America the most comprehensive relevant, and disciplined education possible ... It is instinctive that a program of Black Studies was developed by purposive and intelligent Black studies, who laid it before us for our consideration. That very process can itself be exemplary, students faculty, and administration alike.... Black Studies have provided a highly appropriate example of how a curriculum can be made relevant to social needs. Northwestern University lies near and in a great city, which may one day be governed by Black leaders. The University is already committed to a study of the City and to and investigation of the total environment of urban man.... What the Black students late proposed represents an important development, which is fully consistent with the intellectual purpose of the institution.

Although the problems of Black people are receding priorities on the national agenda, we would argue that these problems are as urgent as they ever were. There is a real increase, not a decrease, in the significance of racism in the recent period. Even the justice Department has issued a special report highlighting increases in racist attacks.

A "new illiteracy" is threatening with the rapid computerization of many functions in today's society, and the increased emphasis on quantitative skills.[36]

The recent report of the U.S. Army and the Educational Testing service regarding lower scores for Blacks on standardized tests is a recent expression of racism, perhaps more subtle, especially in light of the proven cultural/class bias of standardized tests. The Black community and social institutions continue to be torn apart by various "gentrification" or urban revival schemes. Finally, in the economic arena, there is a widening of the income, gap between Blacks and Whites and within the Black community as over twenty percent of Blacks and fifty percent of Black youth are "officially" reported as unemployed.

Thus, it is the continuing responsibility of every field within Black Studies to understand the contemporary situation of Black people and to explore the policy implications of the knowledge produced in the field of study. This is nowhere more relevant than right now when there is a major policy shift in the country that is having a big impact on Black people. We have to understand the relationships between the shifts in public policy as political changes, and also changes in the very structure and functions of the capitalist system.

Black Liberation Movement

The brochure from the 1982 Sixth Annual Conference of NCBS contained this statement:[37]

The main contradiction in the work of intellectuals is between the scientific character of research and the political context for scholarship. Black Studies must be concerned with truth (about society and nature) *and* power. Matters of truth must be left to science, but changing the world is a matter for the Black Liberation Movement. BLACK STUDIES deals with both.

It is this dual character that was reflected in the conference theme: Academic Excellence and Social Responsibility: Science and Politics in Black Studies."[38]

The oppressive and exploitative conditions of Black peoples — racism, poverty, discrimination — have had an impact on Black intellectuals. Because of this, there is a consistent emphasis and effort to contribute to the understanding of the solution of these problems among Black scholars.

James Turner makes this point in his essay reviewing syllabi of Black Sociology courses, quoting a work which is useful in summing up the Black intellectual tradition in this field:[39]

In examination of the intellectual attraction of sociology to Black scholars, James Blackwell and Morris Janowitz report in their book, *Black Sociologist*: "From the earliest years of the discipline in the United States, Black sociologists were not only scholars, they engaged in social and political protest against the treatment of Blacks. The pattern of scholarly endeavors on the one hand, and civic presence in the larger society on the other, was set by W. E. B. DuBois and carried forward by Charles S. Johnson and E. Franklin Frazier. To be a Black sociologist also entailed civic activity." ... They saw in sociology the intellectual tools for redefinition of race relations and in turn a positive element for social change. It is from this tradition that Black Studies intellectuals inherit the legacy of activist scholarship in the present period.

The reverse is also true, that intellectual activity in the context of the Black liberation movement, by "scholars" and "non-scholars," has produced some of the most insightful and provocative analyses of the Black experience to date. For example, the current discussion of race and class as concepts basic to understanding the Black experience did not originate with the debate over Wilson's *Declining Significance of Race* as the *New York Times* would have us believe. The sharpest and most productive recent exchanges took place as polemics inside the African Liberation Support Committee, the leading organization in the Black liberation movement in the 1970s.[40]

Earl Thorpe in *Black History* argues that the role of the scholar-activist, often denigrated as an intrusion on scholarly activity and productivity, can have just the opposite effect:

It is questionable whether historians produce better works in the calm atmosphere of dispassionate observation, or when fired by a zealous cause or, crusade.... It may, be that before American Negro historgraphy can again produce men of the stature of DuBois and Woodson, it will have to get caught up in another crusade.

There is one last vantage point for us to argue that Black Studies courses, especially but not exclusive of those in the social sciences, should include a study of the

Black liberation movement. And this is the fact that the *object* of the Black liberation movement — that which it aims to transform — is also the *object* of Black social analysis — that which it aims to explain. Turner also makes this point in his essay.

> Sociology in Black Studies must look critically at the system of contemporary American capitalism and its historical root: and ask the salient questions about the nature of the systemic subjugation and exploitation about the nature of the systemic subjugation and exploitation of Black people. We need to understand the structural roots of large-scale and relatively permanent unemployment in the Black community, and the consequences for the quality of human life and social network in urban ghetto areas. What are the causes of persistent disproportionate poverty of Black families, and relegation of Black workers to secondary categories in the industrial labor market? Black social scientists in Black Studies are challenged to develop theoretical clarity about what, the American social experience has at times meant that freedom, success and prosperity for some depends upon the enslavement/oppression, failure, and impoverishment of others. Social injustices are usually embedded in the institutionalized patterns of relations and the infrastructure of society: "Social justice itself is a structural question." What this means is that before sociologists can proffer a remedy to redress a given social ill there must be explanation of the structural context in which these wrongs are generated. This will require more integrated study of the economic structures and political structures and cultural structures of society and the institutional alliances between various structures. Such an analysis will enable us to perceive, and therefore conceive, more clearly the racial, sexual age class and the ethnic division of society.

In Conclusion

We have demonstrated here that Black Studies has, over the previous fifteen years, organized a substantial body of intellectual thought, has organized its trends, issues and insights into formal curricula, and, finally, has organized its practitioners (i.e., its instructors, theoreticians, writers) into institutional and professional association on a nationwide basis.

A great debt has been acknowledged to the intellectual forerunners of formal Black Studies in academe, and their legacy is dignified by the current standard-bearers in this discipline.

An Addendum to Black Studies Curriculum Development in the 1980s: Its Patterns and History

Because of space limitations, the article "Black Studies Curriculum Development in the 1980s: Its Patterns and History" by Gerald McWorter and Ronald Bailey appearing in the March-April 1984 issue of *The Black Scholar* was edited by *The Black Scholar*. Important information not included appears below:

(1) The article was excerpted from a 58-page report prepared for The Black Studies Curriculum Project of the Institute of the Black World. The report was a critique of reviews by Black Studies specialists of course outlines focused on the Black experience from scholars throughout the U.S. It was circulated for comments as Afro-Scholar Working Paper No. 17 by the Afro-American Studies and Research Program at the University of Illinois at Urbana.

The authors identified six alternative intellectual foci which they felt should be included in all Black Studies courses, establishing a framework with which they analyzed and rated how 28 Black Studies syllabi covered these six areas.

Alternative Intellectual Foci in Black Studies Courses

1. Theoretical Review of Literature

    A. Critique of mainstream work

    B. Review of Radical thought

    C. Black intellectual history

2. Summation of Practical Experience

    A. Empirical data analysis (section deleted from article)

    B. Policy and contemporary issues

    C. Black liberation movement

(2) A substantial concluding section entitled "Developing a Paradigm for The Study of The Black Experience" was deleted. Drawing on the work of Thomas Kuhn in *The Structure of Scientific Revolutions*, this section suggested:

"The development of a theory of the Black experience—grand theory to use the language of Robert Merton has a high priority in the field. It is absolutely critical if Black Studies is to consolidate and claim a more permanent and productive place in higher education, one that can impact and cross-fertilize all other fields of study as well, that intellectual coherence be established.

"Concretely, this goal of contributing to a theory of the Black experience is currently taking the form of a *paradigm* for Black Studies as a field of study. Somewhat differently stated, our aim is to encourage a more conscious formulation and exploration of alternative theories within a paradigmatic framework which can guide the systematic search and ordering of knowledge abut the Black experience.

It is also reviewed recent research by Black Studies scholars and suggested two components of a broad paradigm (a) *historical periodization*: that the Black Experience has developed in four model periods of social cohesion—Africa, slavery, rural-agricultural and urban-industrial, with each separated by periods of transition or social disruption—the slave trade, Emancipation, and the migrations; (b) *conceptual tools*: four major tools for the holistic analysis of the Black Experience were suggested: *race* (biology), *class* (economy), *nationality* (social institutions/organization and culture), and *consciousness*. When combined, these two components produce the following schemes as a first step toward a more comprehensive treatment of the Black Experience.

(3) The essential thrust of the article is embodied in a new revised edition of *The Peoples College Introduction to Afro-American Studies* (1984). The text is a ten-year collaborative effort that has been widely used throughout the U.S. and abroad.

Endnotes

1. This is our assumption. Further, we think there is more evidence for optimism than the annual doom and gloom found in summary articles in the popular media. In general the activities of the current Black Studies movement is best reflected in newsletters. The key newsletter is the *Afro-Scholar Newsletter* (available from Afro-American Studies and Research Program, University of Illinois, Urbana, Illinois 61801) and it contains a listing of others. For treatments of the history of Black Studies, consult the following: Armstead Robinson, ed., *Black Studies in the University: A Symposium* (1969); John Blassingame, ed., *New Perspectives in Black Studies* (1971); and Nick Aaron Ford, *Black Studies: Threat on Challenge* (1973); Ronald Bailey, "Black Studies in Historical Perspective," *Journal of Social Issues* Vol. 29, No. 1 (1973).

2. Racism call be understood as being individual, institutional, and societal. Each of these types follows a logic of development and must be dealt with it in its specific focus. The key level is society, because to the extent that the society is racist is the extent to which racism on the institution and individual levels are considered legitimate. See Thomas F. Pettigrew, ed., *The Sociology of Race Relations: Reflection and Reform* (1980).

3. There are two articles that discuss the origin of A.H.S.A.: John Henrik Clarke, "The African Heritage Studies Association: Some Notes on the Conflict with the African Studies Association and the Fight to Reclaim African History," *Issue: A Quarterly Journal of Africanist Opinion* Volume VI, Number 2/3 (Summer/Fall 1976): 5-12; and Cyprian Lamar Rowe, "Crisis in African Studies: The Birth of the African Heritage Studies Association," *Black Academy Review* Volume 1, Number 3 (Fall 1970): 1-8.

4. The symposium was called "Imperialism and Black People." The Chairperson was Abdul Alkalimat, and the two speakers were Dawolu Gene Locke (ALSC) and James Turner (AHSA). The panelists included Owusu Sadamkai, Imanu Amiri Baraka, Ron Walters, and Leonard Jefferies.

5. The National Council for Black Studies, Inc., Memorial Hall East 129, Indiana University, Bloomington, Indiana 47405.

6. This journal literature is described in Gerald A. McWorter, ed., *Guide to Scholarly Journals in Black Studies* (1981).

7. G. Franklin Edwards, ed., *E. Franklin Frazier on Race Relations* (1968), pp. 267-282.

8. Earl E. Thorpe, *Black Historians: A Critique* (1958).

9. Harold Cruse, as quoted in Abdul Alkalimat, "Ideology of A Black Social Science," *The Black Scholar* (December 1969).

[In the original article, the text for endnotes 10-26 is missing.—ed.]

27. Ralph Bunche, *The Political Status of the Negro in the Age of FDR* (1940-1973).

28. See Lorenzo Morris, *Elusive Equality, the Status of Black Americans in Higher Education* (ISEP, 1979).

29. Some of this is suggested by the themes of graduate thesis and dissertation work. See Harry Green, *Holders of Doctorates Among American Negroes* (1946).

30. W.E.B. DuBois, *Dusk of Dawn* (1968), p. 64.

31. Carter G. Woodson is quoted from Kelly Miller's biographical introduction to Woodson's The *Negro in Our History* and cited in Thorpe's *Black Historians*, p. 109.

32. St. Clair Drake, "In the Mirror of Black Scholarship: Allison Davis's Deep South," *Harvard Education Review* (Summer 1967).

33. John Hope Franklin, "The Dilemma of the American Negro Scholar," in Herbert Hill, ed., *Soon, One Morning: New Writings by American Negroes*, 1940-1962 (Knopt, 1963), p. 76.

34. This early addition is still available from the authors of this paper. This publication is in its fourth experimental edition and will be available in a fifth edition in August 1984. All additions are available from Peoples College Press (P.O. Box 7696, Chicago, Illinois 60650).

35. Quoted in *A Community of Scholars*, a report of a Faculty Planning Committee at Northwestern University in 1968.

36. An accessible source for reviewing the impact of computers on education are recent and current issues of *The Chronicle of Higher Education.*

37. All of the preparatory material on this conference can be obtained from the Afro-American Studies and Research Program, University of Illinois. See also National Institute of Education, *Computers in Education: Realizing the Potential*—Report of a Conference (1983) and Office of Technology Assessment, U.S. Congress, Informational Technology and Its Impact on American Education (1982).

38. The theme "Academic Excellence and Social Responsibility" was first used in a conference on Black Studies in 1977 at the University of California at Santa Barbara. The general acceptance of this strategic orientation is reflected by its being adopted by the Executive Board of the NCBS (Princeton, 1983) as the permanent conference theme.

39. James Turner, "Sociology in Black Studies," *Black Studies Curriculum Development Course Evaluations, Conference II: Culture and Social Analysis* (Institute of Black World, 1982).

40. The key document in this struggle was Abdul Alkalimat and Nelson Johnson, Toward the Ideological Unity of ALSC (1974).

41. Earl E. Thorpe, *Black Historians*, p. 200.

42. James Turner, *op. cit.*

54.

Black Studies: A Survey of Models and Curricula

William D. Smith

In the late 1960s we witnessed incessant nationwide campus unrest sparked by the demands of black students that universities and colleges provide them with a curriculum that is more "relevant." Namely, a curriculum that includes "Black Studies." There were different reactions by the universities and colleges to these demands. Some schools immediately attempted to establish formal programs in Black Studies. Other schools, while not establishing formal programs in Black Studies, provided their students with a few courses. Still another group of schools did not offer their students any formal programs or any courses pertaining to Black Studies. The excuses for not establishing programs in Black Studies were varied and inconclusive.

Some "common excuses" were and still are (1) lack of finance to support such programs; (2) lack of qualified staff, (3) lack of adequate space to house such programs; (4) lack of student interest in degree programs; and (5) limited vocational opportunities for persons with degrees in Black Studies (see *Personnel and Guidance Journal*, 1970).

It was against a background of exploitation, demonstrations, confrontations, rationalization, irrelevant education, and apprehension that Black Studies emerged.

Definition

Black Studies? What is Black Studies? Black Studies is not wearing Dashikis; eating "soul food" or wearing long hair; the blackening of white courses; offering one or two courses in black history; designing imperialistic approaches based on opportunism, or white paternalism; or a means for black students to escape reality.

What, then, is Black Studies? Since Black Studies is an evolving dynamic discipline, any attempt to define Black Studies must be viewed as inconclusive and subject to the influence of contemporary thought Black Studies is a way of viewing things; it is concerned with negritude, awareness, relevancy; past, present, and future achievements and problems of black people; Africa and its relationship to black Americans; learning needs and vocational applications of Black Studies to the black community; it is concerned with power struggles, political, social, psychological, and economic independence for all black people; it is concerned with liberation, black pride, reeducating the white society with respect to racism and black myths; with attitudes, welfare, history, and the heritage of black people; and it is concerned with black representation through community participation leading to maturation.

631

Table 1[a]		
Schools Asked to Submit Data	Schools Complying with Request	Percentage of Schools Complying with Request
233	140	60%

a. Table 1 may be read as follows: Academic structures or models to establishing Black Studies curricula from two hundred thirty-three (233) colleges and universities were requested. One hundred forty (140) schools complied with the request. The total percentage of schools responding to the request was 60%.

Dr. Stephen J. Wright (1970), former Fisk University President, defines Black Studies as:

Involving that body of knowledge that records and describes the past of the black man in Africa and the other sections of the world in which he is concentrated, with very special reference to the United States, that records, defines and delineates his contemporary social, political, economic, education and cultural status and problems.

Preston Wilcox (1970) asserts that "Black Studies is that body of experience and knowledge that blacks have had to summon in order to learn how to survive within a society that is stacked against them."

In the process of proposing a structure for Black Studies at the University of Cincinnati, a nationwide survey of colleges and universities from all sections of the United States was conducted. The study included data from schools that: were privately and publicly supported, had large and small enrollments, were attended by predominantly black and predominantly white pupils, were coeducational as well as all male and all female, and were religiously oriented and non-religiously-oriented. The institutions of higher education employed in this investigation were randomly selected and were accredited by the Federation of Regional Accrediting Commissions of Higher Education.

Table 1 presents the number of schools requested to submit data, and the number and percentages of schools complying with the request.

Colleges and universities have initiated various types of Black Studies models in an attempt to provide their institutions with information pertaining to the black experience in America.

Responses to the Survey

Table 2 illustrates the number of colleges and universities responding with their different types of academic structure or models to establishing Black Studies, and the percentage of the various structure or models.

An assessment of the data in Table 2 shows that five models or trends to initiating Black Studies in colleges and universities emerged. One group of schools (5%) has initiated interdisciplinary programs. Another group of schools (6%) has initiated institutes. A third group of schools (7%) has decided on the center for Black Studies approach. A fourth group of schools (13%) has established a Department of Black

Table 2		
Schools Categorized According to Report Models	Type of Academic Structure or Models	Percentage of Academic Structures or Models
7	Interdisciplinary programs	5%
8	Institutes	6%
10	Centers	7%
18	Departments	13%
70	Afro-American courses only	50%
27	No Afro-American courses	19%
Total 140		Total 100%

Studies. A fifth group of schools and the largest category (50%) indicated that it had no formal program and offered courses only. The sixth and last group of schools reporting (19%) indicated that it had nothing to offer students interested in Black Studies.

Thus, it can be concluded that of the 140 schools complying with the request, 70 (or 50%) are offering courses to meet the current concerns about Black Studies. This category of schools does not offer a degree in Black Studies.

The second largest number of schools (27 or 19%) that submitted the requested data offers no courses at all that pertain to the black experience in America. These schools were located in the western and southern parts of the United States. Most of these schools indicated that they were not anticipating offering any courses in Black Studies in the near future.

The third largest number of schools (18 or 13%) complying with the request indicated that they have established Departments of Black Studies. They also indicated that they offer majors in Black Studies leading to bachelor's degrees. Some schools are anticipating graduate degree programs in the future.

The fourth largest number of schools (10 or 7%) that forwarded the requested information have established centers for Black Studies. Most of the centers are non-degree-granting and offer certificates of attendance; however, two centers offer bachelor's degrees.

The fifth largest number of schools (8 or 6%) that responded to the request stated that they had initiated institutes of Black Studies. Presently, these institutes do not grant degrees.

The last category of schools (7 or 5%) that submitted the requested data has established interdisciplinary programs in Black Studies. These universities indicated that they offer majors and minors leading to bachelor's degrees in Black Studies.

Objectives

Of these approaches, which one is best to make educational experiences more relevant to black Americans? At this writing a definitive answer to that question is unavailable. However, a definitive response should emerge shortly which will be based on research, practical applications, black scholarly beliefs, innovations, and so forth. The structure that is adopted at various institutions will also be determined to some degree by financial resources, orientation of the directors or heads of Black Studies, the administrators, the black students, and the like. Each institution should adopt the structure that best meets the predetermined objectives. The results of this investigation showed that although there are different structures for Black Studies in the various institutions of higher learning me objectives are similar. Generally, the objectives of the Black Studies programs received are:

(1)   to provide Americans, particularly black Americans, with a "refreshing view" of the major contributions of black people to the world and describe the historical and contemporary roles of black Americans;

(2)   to enhance the self concept of black Americans;

(3)   to provide a relevant education for black Americans whose specific interests are to educate and develop the black community;

(4)   to better understand and define the role of black people in the political, social, psychological, educational, and economic systems in America;

(5)   to render vocational preparations for today's world;

(6)   to study the relationships of black Americans and other black people of the world;

(7)   to combat racism and eliminate myths about black Americans;

(8)   to understand the role of black religion before and after black people arrived in America;

(9)   to provide a more accurate view of the black heritage and culture;

(10) to comprehend and appreciate the role of black music to black people since 1619;

(11) to provide a better understanding of the relationship between Africa and black Americans.

Since a consciousness of Black Studies emerged on the American college scene many people have charged that there were no courses available. Now that various colleges and universities have developed such courses, there is a new cry: "What courses should be required of those who seek bachelor's degrees in 'Black Studies?'" It is very difficult, if not impossible, to recommend all the courses that should be required of a Black Studies major; however, certain courses are desirable.

Generally, students seeking degrees in Black Studies should be required to select courses from the area of black history, black sociology, black political science, Africa, black arts and humanities, urban studies, selected general black subjects, black music, black psychology and other selected general black subjects including those involving the black community.

Specifically, degree-seeking students should concentrate on those subjects which are germane to their individual interests and goals—i.e., students interested in future employment in the black community would have their major enrollment in those courses which were centered on black community life. What kind of curricula in Black Studies are offered by the various institutions?

Curricula

The curricula from the responding institutions were developed into composite form, thus no single institution has this entire curriculum, while all institutions offer some of the courses referred to below. Many of the subjects that will be classified under one heading could have been classified under other headings also.

Schools which are currently developing models in Black Studies should include some of the courses indicated below into their curricula. Institutions of higher learning should also develop innovative courses that may well be germane to their own institutions but not necessarily applicable to other institutions.

Many of the graduates of Black Studies will be employed in the field of teaching; it is interesting to note, however, that not one institution reported a course in the methodology of teaching Black Studies. The vocational application of the Black Studies graduates dictates that such a course be developed in the immediate future.

The Composite Curriculum

AFRICA

(1)   Modern Africa: Interdisciplinary Approaches to its Study and to Field Work

(2)   Seminar on Water Development in Africa

(3)   Peoples and Culture of Africa

(4)   West and Central Africa

(5)   Politics of African Nations

(6)   East and South Africa

(7)   Economic History of Africa

(8)   Government and Politics of Africa

(9)   The Ethnology of West Africa

(10)   Islam and Africa

(11)   Survey of African History

(12)   Nationalism in North Africa

(13)   Introduction to African Art

ARTS AND HUMANITIES

(1)   The Afro-American Literary Tradition

(2)   Seminar in African Verbal Art

(3)   Medieval and Early Renaissance Art

(4)   Black Messianism in Afro-American Literature

(5)   Afro-American Art

(6)   Negritude and the Black Writer

(7)   Images of the Black Woman in Literature

(8)   Afro-American Drama

(9)   Afro-American Writers

(10) Black Sculpture

(11) The Black Image in the White American Writing

(12) Black Writers in America: From the Beginning to the Present

(13) Contemporary Black Poetry

(14) Black Writers Workshop

(15) The Painting of Blackness

(16) Black Journalism

(17) Black Classics

CIVIL RIGHTS

(1)   Civil Rights and Self-Respect

(2)   History of Civil Rights

ECONOMICS

(1)   Afro-American Money and Banking

(2)   The Influences of the Economic Sector on the Afro-American

(3)   Economics of the Black Community

(4)   Black Economic Workshop

EDUCATION

(1)   White Racism and Higher Education

(2)   Educating Blacks in America

(3)   Coeducational Physical Education—Primitive Dance

ENGLISH

(1)   Ghetto Speech as it Relates to Standard Speech

(2)   English as a Foreign Language

GENERAL

(1)   Negritude and Pan-Africanism

(2)   Negro Leadership

(3)   Individual Rights in an Industrial Society

(4)   Afro-American Cultural Institutions

(5)   Black Utopias

(6)   The American Muslims

(7)   Propaganda and the Black Nation

(8)   Field Work in the Black Community

(9)   The Black American Child

(10) Black Community Health

(11) The Afro-American in a Changing American Context

(12) Black Figures in the Americas

(13) Interethnic Contacts

(14) Contemporary Issues in the Black Community

(15) Geography of Blackness

(16) Black Nationalism and the International Community

GOVERNMENT

(1) The Negro and the Constitution

HISTORY

(1) Introduction to Afro-American Studies

(2) Legal Foundation of American Slavery

(3) American Slavery

(4) The Harlem Renaissance

(5) Black Women — A Historical Survey

INDEPENDENT STUDY

(1) Seminar in Afro-American Studies

(2) Independent Study

(3) Special Problems in Black Community Studies

LANGUAGE

(1) Introduction to African Languages

(2) Zulu I

(3) Amharic I

(4) Swahili I and Swahili II

(5) Twi I

(6) Twi 11

(7) Hausa I and 11

(8) Seminar in Ethiopian Languages

(9) Afro-American Dialect

(10) Bantu Linguistics

(11) Igbo

LAW

(1) Law and the Black Community

MATHEMATICS AND STATISTICS

(1) Black Statistics — Survey and Method

(2) Black Mathematics

MUSIC

(1) Sources, Evolution and Influences of Afro-American Music
(2) Spirituals and Black Religious Music
(3) The History of Jazz
(4) Musical Traditions of the Afro-American
(5) Jazz: Its Evolution and Essence
(6) African Music—Historical Review

ORAL HISTORY

(1) Afro-American Oral Tradition

OTHER CULTURES

(1) Prehistory: The Other Worlds
(2) Comparison of Culture
(3) People of the Caribbean
(4) The Igbo Culture

PHILOSOPHY

(1) Black Philosophical Thought—1619-1900
(2) Contemporary Afro-American Thought
(3) Reason and Revolution
(4) Recurring Philosophical Themes in Afro-American Literature
(5) Black Revolutionaries

POLITICAL SCIENCE

(1) Decision-Making in the City
(2) Urban Welfare Politics
(3) The Negro and the Constitution
(4) Politics of Black Power
(5) The Political Ideology of White Supremacy
(6) The Political Ideology of Blackness
(7) Black Politics
(8) Black Political Workshop

PSYCHOLOGY

(1) Minority Group Relations
(2) The Psychology of Prejudice
(3) The Psychology of Blackness
(4) Afro-American Personality: Development and Function
(5) Encounter: Group Experience
(6) The Crisis of the Negro Intellectual: Race, Class, Politics, Culture

RADIO AND TV

(1)   Black Radio, Television, Film

RELIGION

(1)   Christianity and the Racial Question

(2)   Religion in the Black Community

(3)   The Black Churches of America

SCIENCE

(1)   Black Involvement in Scientific Developments

(2)   Ethnic Science

SOCIOLOGY

(1)   Sociology of Afro-American Studies

(2)   The Development and Organization of Black Family Life in America

(3)   Black Sociology

(4)   Race Relations

(5)   Black Social Thought

(6)   Black Social Structure

(7)   Social Change

(8)   Social Organization of Black Institutions

SPEECH

(1)Black Speech

URBAN

(1)   The Black Ghettos and Urban Spatial Form

(2)   Urban Dynamics

(3)   Urban and Regional Economics

(4)   Urban Economic Problems

Summary and Conclusions

The purpose of this investigation was to examine various models or approaches to establishing programs of Black Studies in institutions of higher education.

The results of this investigation showed that of the 140 institutions responding, 113 (81%) offered something pertaining to Black Studies. Twenty-seven, or 19% of the responding institutions do not offer any courses in Black Studies and do not plan to offer any such courses in the immediate future.

Fifty percent of the reporting institutions indicated that they offered only courses in Black Studies. These institutions asserted that they are not currently granting degrees in Black Studies.

Departments of Black Studies were the models reported by thirteen percent of the responding schools. Degrees in Black Studies were granted by these institutions. Degrees were also granted by those schools that have developed interdisciplinary programs in Black Studies.

Generally those schools which have initiated the center model or the institute model in Black Studies did not award degrees.

Though the established models in Black Studies in the various institutions are different, the objectives are similar for all institutions.

Courses in Black Studies have been developed in numerous disciplines.

The courses that should be required of persons seeking degrees in Black studies should and must be selected on the bases of the goals of the individuals.

Colleges and universities, as a whole, have moved from the position of offering relatively few courses in Black Studies prior to the last two years to offering well over a hundred courses which related to black people.

Based on the results of this study, colleges and universities are responding somewhat to the current concerns pertaining to Black Studies. However, there are still too few formalized programs in Black Studies. Schools that are currently offering only a few courses in Black Studies could and should establish formal programs in Black Studies. Second, those colleges and universities located in the southern and the western parts of the United States should make every effort to establish programs in Black Studies rather than waiting for students to demand that such programs be initiated.

References

Personnel and Guidance Journal (1970) "The black studies graduate in the 'real world.'" (May).

Wilcox, P. (1970) *Negro Digest* (March).

Wright, S.J. (1970) *Phi Delta Kappan* 51 (March).

55.

Black Studies Consortia: A Proposal

Gloria I. Joseph

Abstract — It is suggested that a number of colleges or universities in the United States organize and develop a series of Black Studies Consortia around the country. The author describes the faculty and administration, student enrollment, courses and equipment, and the long range roles of such consortia.

During the past several years much has been written and said about Black Studies programs. There are numerous articles, several of excellence, that extol the why's and wherefore's of Black Studies programs.[1] Black Studies have been analyzed, criticized, defined and defended extensively since its brief existence. In this paper my comments shall be devoted to a description and rationale for "Black Studies Consortia — A Model Proposal."

The basic premise upon which the Consortium model is developed is that individual Black Studies or Afro-American Studies programs should be eliminated from predominantly white campuses. Colleges and universities throughout the country are putting together "flotsam and jetsam of Black courses" masquerading under the title of Black Studies programs. Black and White faculty with mild to medium to enthusiastic interest are all too often participants in what is frequently a fiasco or sham rather than a credible Black Studies program. Even those white campuses which sponsor the most advanced and well-developed Black Studies programs have serious short-comings. To mention a few: faculty shortages; financial problems; lack of a sustained Black ideology; lack of consistency in the presentation of subject matter from a Black perspective brought about by students taking some courses in the Black Studies program and other related courses in the regular university division; and, serious deficiencies in library, laboratory resources and equipment.

As an alternative to the individual Black Studies program, I propose Black Studies Consortia. An operational definition of a Black Studies Consortium would be as follows:

A number of colleges or universities would be jointly responsible for the development, maintenance and operation of one Black Studies College or Department. Factors that determine the participating institutions would be either geographical location or a tradition of association, such as the Seven Sisters, and the Finger Lakes Colleges. A major criteria that must be met by any and every consortium is borrowed from a criteria that has been spelled out by Dr. Vincent Harding of the Institute of the Black World, in Atlanta: The consortium location must be adjacent to a Black community.

A presentation of how consortia would function can best be described by using a specific group of colleges as the model. We shall refer to the model consortium as the Eastern Seaboard Black Studies Consortium, hereafter referred to as E.S.B.S.C.

Location of Black Studies Consortia

The ESBS College would be representative of six colleges located with a 75-100 mile radius. The physical plant would be either in one of the participating colleges or a new college constructed at as central a point as possible. If none of the existing colleges in the ESBSC are near a Black Community then a new building would have to be erected to meet that criteria.

In a similar manner other groups of institutions would form consortia; e.g., the Ivy League and Seven Sisters could form one consortium or have two separate ones; the colleges in the Finger Lake region, Hobart, Wells, Ithaca, Keuka, etc., and the five institutions in the Massachusetts complex—Smith College, Mt. Holyoke, Amherst, University of Massachusetts, and Hampshire College—could support a Black Studies department. The mid-west would provide their section of the country with a dozen or more consortia; California would have any number necessary.

Faculty and Administration

Personnel from the Black Studies department of each of the Eastern Seaboard schools would compose the initial Black Studies Consortium faculty and administration. This would hopefully create a substantial number of black faculty in each discipline. Students who wish to major, for example, in sociology and psychology, would then be able to take a number of courses of considerable depth. As it now stands in most colleges there are only one or two professors in each subject area of the Black Studies program. This limits a student who majors in a particular subject, in choice of faculty and course offerings. If a faculty member teaches a course in education, and he is the sole education professor, he cannot adequately teach elementary and advanced courses of sufficient variety and depth that would satisfy the needs of students and requirements for a major.

The argument is frequently used by many schools who are pressured for Black Studies programs that there are not enough qualified black professors. Of course there are sufficient numbers of qualified black teachers, but many do not meet the ersatz criteria set up by the colleges. The consortium would set its own criteria for hiring faculty members in addition to those already employed in the number of colleges of the Eastern Seaboard area.

The director of the ESBS consortium would be selected by the black professors and administrators who are currently employed in the individual E.S. colleges. If desired, an outside person could be selected. (Student input in the selection of personnel is a desirable component that would be instituted whenever feasible. Student involvement in the selection of a director should occur.)

Student Enrollment

Students would enroll in the E.S. college of his choice. During his freshman year a student would take those courses at the E.S. school that are essential for his academic development and are not offered at the consortium. If he wanted to major in political science at the Afro-American institute he would attend the E.S. Afro-American Consortium for two or three years. The final year could be completed either at the E.S. school or Consortium, or doing field work in the Black community in America,

Africa or the Caribbean. This would be determined by the individual, and his faculty advisors from the Consortium and E.S. nuclear college. By attending the consortium for two or three years the student would be able to complete a substantial number of courses in his major field. Upon graduation the student would have obtained an excellent background in Black Studies and would be well prepared in his particular subject area. He would graduate from a specific E.S. College with a major in Black Studies from the E.S. Consortium.

Courses and Equipment

Courses in a Black Studies Consortium would include several required core courses, plus mandatory field work in Black Communities. The courses would be concerned with the development of ideologies, philosophies, and concepts pertaining to Black perspectives and Pan-Africanism. Each department such as economics, food and nutrition, would determine the course offerings and major and minor requirements. The idea of nation building will be a primary consideration in the development of all major subjects.

The required field work would provide the opportunity for travel and exposure to different cultures as well as providing the students with an opportunity to serve other Blacks.

The traditional majors such as sociology, anthropology, psychology, writing and literature, home economics, engineering and political science, would be offered. However, the perspective and emphasis will be on Blackness, and the direction will be toward improving the present living conditions and the future lives of all Black people. For example, in the broad field of human ecology, majors in food and nutrition would be vitally concerned with the improvements of the health of the Black babies in Africa, the Caribbean and the United States. Sociology and psychology majors would *not* spend time learning more ways and better techniques to show that Blacks learn slower run faster. Instead, the social science majors would be concerned with the prevention of and treatment for the millions of black youngsters and adults who are spending their lives in mental institutions and schools for the mentally retarded. The degree in medicine would not be the signal for a large extravagant home, three cars, swimming pool and gala parties. Rather, it would mean volunteering some time to working in clinics or serving in destitute areas where the ratio of doctors to patients is one to 2000 or more. Majors in city planning might be developing communal type residence and schools similar to kibbutzim. It is this type of attitude, mentality and direction that the Black Studies consortia would develop and promulgate in the students.

In addition to the traditional courses offered in the consortium, departments would also include: library schools; communication arts; veterinary medicine; agriculture; nursing; education; art (sculpture, painting, carving); dance; musicology; theatre; city planning; languages; civil engineering and computer sciences; and technological skills which would prepare students to enter the trade unions (e.g., plumbing, electricity, masonry, carpentry).

The individual colleges and universities who are currently trying to sponsor Black Studies programs are generally ill-equipped in terms of the physical plant and the necessary resources. The Consortia would allow for the purchase and maintenance of superior equipment, which is essential for the effective functioning of any institution. For example, it is questionable as to whether any individual college in the United States has a totally substantial and efficient library for Black Studies needs. Majors in library school could play instrumental roles in the development and maintenance of such a department. Books by blacks that are out of print, books from Africa and the Caribbean that seldom reach the shelves of libraries in America, unpublished manuscripts of value could be obtained to become available at the consortium library. The cataloguing and reprinting of the books alone would cost more than any one school is willing to support. Jointly, the E.S. colleges could support an excellent library.

In the field of education lab schools would be maintained, and in the area of communication arts, fully-equipped television labs, offset printing machines, etc., would be standard equipment. (I recall entering a room in the human ecology department at Cornell University and seeing six television cameras positioned along the walls, and all I could think of was the struggle and hardship that black student-members of a cooperative went through in order to obtain *one* television.) The computer science department would have data processing and keypunch machines, as standard equipment. The physical grounds for each consortium should include acreage for agriculture majors and barns and stables for veterinary majors.[2]

Long Range Role of Black Studies Consortia

I see Black Studies Consortia as an interim measure, because in the final analysis I believe Black students, at this time in America, can only receive education in Black studies with an unadulterated Black perspective from a Black college or university. Since there are not a sufficient number of these (I consider Malcolm X to be the leading forerunner in this area), and since thousands of Black students are interested in Black Studies, we cannot afford to allow them to be adrift in makeshift curd bowls advertised as Black Studies programs. Something is needed and necessary, and certainly the Consortium model can meet the demands of a Black Studies program in a better fashion than any individual college.

Institutions such as Malcolm X University, as admirable as they are, in a sense operate unrealistically. The tentacles of white oppression do not stop at the walls of a radical, effective Black institution. The avaricious claws of corporations and capitalism disregard Black revolutionary boundaries. Institutions like Malcolm X University cannot in actuality exist untouched by white oppression or white influence. Every institution in America reacts to the ever-pervasive racism. The insularity and isolationism itself on such institutions as Malcolm X can have the deleterious effect of too much inbreeding.

On the other hand, Black students and Black Studies on white campuses find the problems created by white administrations and the white community excruciatingly frustrating. This frustration leads to and creates ingroup fighting among the blacks. There is not *enough* isolation and insulation from the oppressors. The consortia would provide an alternative. They would be physically away from the whites, yet they would be in a position to invite whites whom they feel are desirable and can make a positive contribution to the consortia.

The Black Studies Consortia could conceivably become obsolete in the field of education. If America could rid itself of racism and if the educational system could effortlessly include a valid and accurate Black perspective, then Black Studies Consortia would not be necessary. Since both of these criteria are a long time off, the Consortia could be operating indefinitely. If America continues on its polarized course, more Black universities and colleges, similar to Malcolm X University and the Center for Black Education in Washington, D.C., will develop. If this happens, the Consortia should continue to operate as part of the multiversity.

White Inclusion

The question: "Should whites be included in a Black Studies program" has been raised time and time again. The simple, sensible response is "yes." But, there are many qualifications! In my opinion, the most salient reason for the "yes" response is based on the fact that whites will be teaching both black and white youngsters for years to come. If education is to be a media for bringing about changes in racial attitudes and opinions, then it is necessary that the teachers be prepared, trained and capable of presenting a correct image of the Black man. Teachers must present materials from a Black perspective. And, if they are to remove the myths about Blacks, they must get accurate knowledge from the Blacks. The Black Studies Consortia will represent the most scholarly, accurate, and thorough resource centers for Black historical and current information and knowledge. After an initial year or two of a purely Black consortium, white educators should definitely attend. The reason for the initial year or two of purely Black consortium is to enable the faculty and students to develop Black perspectives and leadership, unchallenged and unclouded by white perspectives. White students should also be able to major in Black studies. Permission should be worked out between the student and the Consortia administration. As far as whites teaching, this too is possible, but they must be willing, for several years, if necessary, to play secondary roles. For example, a full professor from Harvard, with tenure, should not feel degraded when he serves as an assistant to a young Black sociology professor for a while. I can foresee a white professor teaching courses to Blacks after sufficient training. Training would not need be purely in subject matter, but in perspective and approach. However, Blacks would determine the inclusion of white professors.

The top administrator should be Black. Whether classes should be all Black or White should be worked out between the professor and the students and the decision would depend on the subject matter and the opinions of the professor and students.

Financing

Plans for financing the consortia are relatively simple. If people are sincerely interested in improving the quality of education in general and in providing Blacks and Whites with an opportunity to bring about substantive changes in the academic milieu in America, financing Black Studies Consortia would be a minor task. My plan is as follows: The total initial budget should be projected for three years. The federal government should provide one-half or more of this amount. This is a decisive step the Federal Government can take to improve the quality of education for Black students that would not impinge upon so-called State Rights. Aid to the study centers would not be aid to private schools but would be allocated directly to the Black Studies Consortia.

The remainder of the budget would be met by the co-operating participating schools in the Consortia, and/or private endowment. As I said initially, if the government and educators through the country are really concerned about education for and about Blacks, the money could be obtained with the stroke of a pen.

But, in more realistic terms — that is to say, since the government's interest has always been questionable, individual colleges should be prepared to contribute the necessary finances. And they, too, can do so without financial strain. It is largely a question of priorities.

Black Unity

At present there exist unnecessary infighting among Black students, administrators and faculty. A strong Black Studies department could offset this to a large extent. A well-developed consortium could supply the strength and leadership that is necessary to command the respect of the Black students. Mutual respect among all blacks engaged in a consortium is vital. Faculty and administrators could offer one another needed support and an interchange of ideas. The large numbers of faculty would enhance the growth of confidence and courage necessary for participants in an innovative organization. The elimination of financial stresses and adequate resources and equipment would diminish much of the digruntledness that now exists because of such inadequacies. The core courses would help the students and faculty develop ideologies and that would strengthen unity and diminish infighting among Blacks.

The location of the consortium adjacent to a Black community would afford the opportunity for the development of relevant constructive projects as a part of the Black Studies curriculum. The cooperation between the Black community and the consortium would be a two-way learning process that should be beneficial to all.

Concluding Comments

The model proposal that I have presented was by no means intended to be a panacea for Black Studies programs. It is offered as a proposal and like all proposals will be improved by suggestions, and constructive criticism from interested, serious-minded readers.

Additional details could have been included for all the areas. There are many unanswered questions, such as: what about students who do not attend a Consortium school but wish to major in Black Studies? What about scholarships? Who provides faculty salaries for new teachers? Why not regional consortium rather than prestigious college groupings? And why not have the Consortia financially supported by Blacks? I consider all such questions valid and people can readily come up with diverse answers. I have projected what I consider to be a realistic proposal. Blacks can speak of Blacks supporting their own institutions, but we don't. Black students speak of wanting to attend all Black colleges, not Negro Colleges, yet thousands of them still fight to get into a prestigious white or Black college or university. We must deal with the cards that we hold! The Consortia model is designed to produce Blacks who will be emotionally and spiritually prepared to carry out the ideals of Black Nationalism and Black Liberation.

Endnotes

1. (1) An Analysis of Black Studies Programs — "Afro-American Studies," Inez Smith Reid 1970, Vol. 1, pp. 11-21; (2) In Defense of Black Studies — A paper prepared for presentation at James A. Moss the University of Calif. L.A., March 21, 1970; (3) Black Nationalism: Black Studies and Black Liberator, James Turner — a reprint from the Milwaukee Courier, June, 1969; (4) Black Studies: A Concept and a Plan, Director James Turner a reprint from the Cornell Chronicle, Vol. 1, No. 2, Oct. 2, 1969.

2. At this time, I am not intending to list all the possible areas for majors, nor all the needed equipment. My intention is to present samples of courses and equipment.

56.

Toward the Evolution of a Unitary Discipline: Maximizing the Interdisciplinary Concept in African/Afro-American Studies

Karla J. Spurlock

The programs in Afro-American Studies which emerged in the late 1960s, though differing in administrative structure, ideology, course content, and degree of community involvement, seemed to have shared at least one feature in common. Almost without exception, each was avowedly committed to exploring the experience of peoples of African descent through the kaleidoscopic lens of an interdisciplinary course of study.

Black Studies came in a number of different administrative packages. At one end of the spectrum were programs whose sole offerings consisted of two courses given in sequence, joined together by a title like "Survey of the Black Experience." At the other end of the continuum were Black Studies programs organized in whole college units, either within a larger university framework like Oakes College (College 7) at the University of California, Santa Cruz, or as physically separate units like Medgar Evers Community College in Bedford Stuyvesant, Brooklyn. In between these two poles one could find the overwhelming majority of programs being established as (a) special programs, which loosely coordinated a series of closely related courses offered in different conventional departments; (b) independent institutes with power of faculty and curriculum selection, though generally funded experimentally through private sources or through temporary institutional channels; or (c) regular departments with conventional powers over faculty, course selection, and curriculum design, and with funding through conventional university channels.[1]

While it is true that, for the majority, the last option seemed by far the most realistic and viable alternative for fulfilling and sustaining the goals of the newly devised curricula, either the "department model" or the "program model" seemed infinitely preferable to a structure allowing traditional disciplines to establish Black-related courses (to fit) within the conservative bastions of conventional academic departments.

Mike Thelwell, chairman of Black Studies at the University of Massachusetts during the critical gestation period of the late 1960s, wrote: "(The approach of) leaving the responsibility to individual departments to proceed at their own pace and in their own unique styles will merely institutionalize and perpetuate the fragmented, incoherent approach to the subject which has been the only approach in the past." He continues that the concept of Black Studies requires "an autonomous interdisciplinary entity, capable of coordinating its curriculum in traditional disciplines to ensure an historical, substantive progression and organic coherence in its offerings."[2]

647

The benefits of the interdisciplinary approach whether through coordination of traditional departmental offerings or through courses devised in independent Black Studies units—even at the very inception of the Black Studies movement, held an unstated appeal. What were and are the benefits of interdisciplinary?

First, the world forces with which Black people must grapple in order to survive operate on us as an interconnected whole—not as a fragmented series of arbitrary sets of experience which neatly correspond to the established academic disciplines. Traditional, compartmentalized, academic fields are too often inadequate to deal with the holistic nature of human experience. When confronted with the challenge, such departments are immediately exposed as incapable of providing insight, either descriptively or analytically.

The Yale Afro-American Studies curriculum devised in the late 1960s, speaks as eloquently as any other to the particular strengths of Black interdisciplinary studies:

> Afro-American Studies introduces students to a great variety of approaches to human problems. Students whose interests are broader than the usual major within a specific department can learn about some of the key issues in the humanities and the social sciences and discover ways to adapt their specific knowledge to some of the most vital needs of society in Afro-American Studies.... Afro-American Studies prepares students for graduate study in a variety of careers by developing special competence through systematic training in methods, materials, tools, and interpretations of several disciplines as they relate to the Black experience in the United States, Latin America, Africa, and Europe. Afro-American Studies trains students to view contemporary issues from the perspective of several disciplines in relationship to many cultures....[3]

One of the most vital benefits of the interdisciplinary mode is the stimulus it offers to creative thinking. The student/scholar, exposed to a variety of research tools and logical systems of ordering relevant data, feels no compulsion to follow accepted, calcified versions of reality defined by any single traditional approach. With options for ordering data, the student or scholar can more readily offer an objective critique on one or another approach to research questions. Ideally, Black Studies offers an arena for disciplinary encounter.[4] The interdisciplinary mode places the student/scholar in a virtual intellectual crossfire. As ideas arising out of different and potentially conflicting disciplinary methods bang against one another, the opportunity for creative synthesis—of new understandings and shared levels of meaning within African and Afro-American Studies—emerges.

Clearly, then, the ideal of Afro-American Studies as an interdisciplinary experience is pregnant with potentialities for growth in the individual and in the academy. Unfortunately, however, one of the preeminent problems facing Black Studies programs today is their failure to maximize fully the possibilities of a truly interdisciplinary structure. Many programs have never realized the meaning of interdisciplinarity, strictly defined. According to very useful definitions coining out of an international seminar on interdisciplinarity in universities, sponsored by the Center for Educational Research and Innovation of the Organization for Economic Cooperation, "discipline" refers to a specific body of teachable knowledge with its own background of education, training, procedures, methods, and content areas. The Center then defines multidisciplinary" as an adjective to describe the juxtaposition of various disciplines assumed to be more or less related. We might usefully contrast this definition of "multidisciplinary" with that of "interdisciplinary," which is described as an adjective suggesting interaction among two or more disciplines. Interaction may range from simple communication of ideas to the mutual integration of orga-

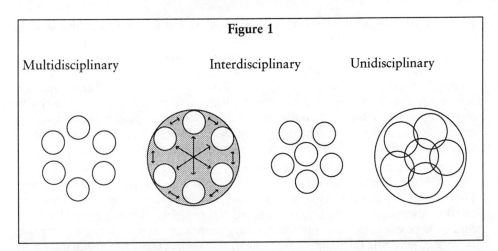

Figure 1

Multidisciplinary   Interdisciplinary   Unidisciplinary

nizing concepts, methodology, procedures, terminology, data, and organization of research and education in a fairly large field. Interdisciplinary groups, then, consist of persons trained in different fields of knowledge with different concepts, methods, data, and terms, organized into a common effort on a common problem with continuous intercommunication among the participants from the different disciplines.[5]

The schema presented in Figure 1 clearly suggests the logical potential for Black Studies to become an effective interdisciplinary unit and, ultimately, a unified disciplinary unit. But the necessity of fostering interaction among constituent disciplines is absolutely a prerequisite of progressive movement toward consolidation. It becomes obvious that the benefits of interdisciplinary exchange do not necessarily follow the declaration that several courses with "Black" in their titles are linked together in an academically discrete unit. Even the creation of an entire curriculum of Black-related courses drawn from traditional disciplinary programs does not imply a working interdisciplinary process unless meaningful interaction among these courses is encouraged.

In the absence of countervailing efforts, the tradition in Afro-American Studies of separate treatments by separate academic enclaves serves to impair communication and the development of independent, unifying core concepts—concepts which might act as a centrifugal force in the interdisciplinary orbit. Another problem arises from the fact that, of necessity, most faculty are recruited from traditional fields. Though often specialists in their areas, such faculty are often ill equipped or unwilling to grapple with the activities of colleagues of different training. Sometimes it is difficult to generate enthusiasm among faculty for any program different from the model established by their own prior training. Specialized graduate work frequently locks faculty into fixed molds, despite their subsequent employment in avowed interdisciplinary programs.

The common problem of stimulating exchange among specialists within a common traditional discipline is multiplied tenfold in the effort to bring historians, sociologists, economists, political scientists, anthropologists, and humanists into a common network of discussion. But it is not out of such discussion *alone* that an organizing framework can be realized, within which different approaches may be systematically evaluated and caught to achieve a holistic vision, fused from multiple disciplinary perspectives. This coalescence of approach is the *sine qua non* of survival and autonomy for Afro-American Studies in the coming decade.

How might Black Studies move toward a practical realization of its interdisciplinary and, ultimately, its unidisciplinary potential? First, there are a number of curricula remedies to the problem. One obvious solution is to maximize the interdisciplinary mix in the structuring and teaching of individual courses. In the Department of African and Afro-American Studies at the State University of New York at Albany, for example, such courses as "Dynamics of Racism," "Problems in the Black Community," "Black Women in America," and "Seminar on Community Development" offer a natural opportunity for the interfertilization of traditional disciplinary concepts and methods. But even courses that indicate a tie to a specific traditional discipline—for instance, "The History of the Black Man in Latin America and the Caribbean"—can be infused with the interdisciplinary spirit.

James Banks, in his important article, "Teaching Black Studies for Social Change," details how courses such as history can be made truly interdisciplinary. Though Western history has largely been the history of formal political events, history has always claimed to concern itself with the totality of man's past. History so conceived nearly fits into an interdisciplinary framework and, as such, is potentially capable of reflecting the unique conceptual frameworks carved out by separate disciplines to view human behavior. Funneling analytical concepts from each discipline into a historical vessel, Banks devises a schema for realizing an interdisciplinary perspective. In his example, history would ask more of the past than which great generals led which battles. Rather, stimulated by a concern for values and norms (borrowed from sociology), power (borrowed from political science), culture (from anthropology), personality (from psychology), regional and spatial relations (from geography), and goods, services, and production (from economics),[6] new and more meaningful questions would arise to demand an interdisciplinary reply.

The second logical solution to the problem of maximizing interdisciplinarity is through a planned, coordinated curriculum with structural inducements to interdisciplinary exchange. The State University of New York at Albany has moved toward an answer by revising the curriculum to address more adequately the challenge of interdisciplinary coordination.

Twelve major disciplines were isolated that were considered minimally essential to the task of equipping students with the knowledge and skills necessary to understand and grapple with the interplay of the myriad forces (economic, sociocultural, political, psychological, and historical) which affect the lives of peoples of African descent. Areas of study and the courses devised under each include: Anthropology: "Peoples of Africa South of the Sahara," and "African Peoples in the Americas"; Economics: "Economic Structure of the Black Community," and "Economics of Developing Black Nations"; Education: "Education and the Black Child," "Education and the Black Community," and "Teaching through the Black Experience: Methods and Materials"; Environmental Studies: "Environment and the Peoples of the Black Diaspora"; History: "Introduction to African and African-American History, A and B," "History of Black Protest in the Americas," "Black Women in America," "Black Urban History," "History of Africa South of the Sahara, A and B," "History of the Black Man in Latin America and the Caribbean," and "Selected Topics in African and African-American History"; Language: "Elementary Swahili," and "Intermediate Swahili"; Literature: "Literature of the Black Pluriverse," "The Black Novel," "The Black Essay," "The Black Short Story," "Black Theatre," "Black Writer's Workshop," and "Studies in Black Literature"; Music and Art: "The Black Musical Tradition, A and B," "African and African-American Dance," and "African and African-American Art, A and B"; Philosophy: "Third World Philosophies," and "Seminar in Third World Thought"; Political Science: "Contemporary World African Politics," "Nationalism and Pan Africanism in the Black Diaspora, A and B," "Blacks and the American Political System,"

"Black Political Thought in the Americas," and "Contemporary African-American Politics"; Psychology: "Dynamics of Racism," and "Psychology of the African and African-American Experience"; Sociology: "Social Dynamics of the Black Community," "Law and the Black Community," "African and African-American Family," "Seminar on Community Development," "The Urban Dimension," "Mass Media and the Black Community," "The African-American Church," and "African Religion"; Independent Work: "Independent Study in African and African-American Studies."

To circumvent the multidisciplinary fate predicted earlier, tremendous emphasis is placed on two courses committed to forging a truly interdisciplinary mastery of the curriculum:

1. "Colloquium in African and African-American Studies," a two-and-one-half hour per week interdisciplinary course. The requirement of participation by the entire faculty is important. The course, an exploration of key issues, is team-taught, and it serves as an interdisciplinary introduction to key issues in African and African-American Studies; and

2. "Research Tools for African and African-American Studies," an introductory exposure to the various modes of gathering and ordering data that aims toward the integration, or at least the coordination, of techniques.

These seminars are intended to have a highly integrative impact. It is hoped that students and professors brought together in this way may achieve new insights, perceive previously unnoted relationships, and arrive at different and more coherent organizations of the common store of knowledge. The integrative seminar is designed to encourage both independence and interdependence and to promote breadth, depth, and synthesis.

But there are other, extracurricular, strategies for maximizing interdisciplinarity in Black Studies. For instance, departments might encourage team teaching on a wide scale. Or they might establish a regular speaker's forum that would consider topics of general concern. The department or program should support interdisciplinary journals and conferences both locally and nationally. This support, of course, would help consolidate a separate identity and concretize a common language of scholarly interchange. Very important also is the need to define and name ourselves as a separate entity. Perhaps we might call ourselves "Africologists" or "Pan-Africologists" — the label itself being, of course, less important than the assertion of ourselves as conceptually separate from our constituent disciplinary identities. But perhaps most important of all, we should push Black Studies down the academic scale to the elementary and secondary schools and up the scale to the Ph.D., our own terminal degree. This expansion would serve to legitimize the field as a unitary discipline, providing both separate, unitary professional training and a guaranteed market for the skills of our trained scholars and educators.

There are, in sum, innumerable strategies, both curricular and noncurricular, which we may employ to maximize interaction and interdisciplinary cooperation within Black Studies. As we move toward interdisciplinarity, we assuredly move along a continuum toward the end-point of a unified perspective, toward trans- or unidisciplinarity. Enhanced interdisciplinary functioning eventually must lead to a close mesh and a blending of disciplines into a new discipline. Disciplines are, after all, nothing more than categories for ordering data. There is nothing fixed or pre-ordained about them. Traditional disciplines such as political science, economics, and sociology broke away and established themselves as distinct categories for ordering relevant information in just that way at the beginning of the twentieth century. The criteria for the emergence of new disciplines vary with time and circumstances. At one time, "method" may determine the distinction; at another time, the field of observable phenomenon; and, at another, a unique theoretical framework.

At this juncture in its history, Black Studies may very well rest its future on an aggressive claim to autonomous status, grounded in the capacity to articulate a coherent theme or set of principles unifying the tributary disciplines. There are, of course, dangers in moving toward a unitary discipline. While attaining the permanence, security, and autonomy enjoyed by established disciplines, we must take care to incorporate the positive aspects of the interdisciplinary mode — the innovation, the eclecticism, the creative spark. Nevertheless, the gains of becoming unidisciplinary far outweigh the possible risks of slipping back into more multidisciplinary coexistence.

Endnotes

1. Nick Aaron Ford, *Black Studies: Threat or Challenge*, Ch. 6 (Port Washington, NY: National University Publications, Kennikat Press, 1973). See also John Blassingame, "The Black Presence in American Higher Education," in *What Black Educators are Saying*, ed. Nathan Wright, Jr. (New York: Hawthorn Books, 1970), pp. 146-149.

2. Mike Thelwell, "Black Studies: A Political Perspective," *Massachusetts Review*, Vol. X (Autumn 1969): 710.

3. Ford, *Black Studies*, p. 129.

4. See Karla J. Spurlock, "The Value of a Major in African/Afro-American Studies," *Habari Newsletter of the Department of African/Afro-American Studies*, State University of New York/Albany, Vol. III, No. 2 (January 27, 1977).

5. *Center for Educational Research and Innovation, Interdisciplinarity: Problems of Teaching and Research in Universities* (Paris: OECD Publications 1972), p. 25.

6. James Banks, "Teaching Black Studies for Social Change," in *Black Scholars in Higher Education in the 1970's*, ed. Roosevelt Johnson (Columbus, OH: ECCA Publications, 1974).

57.

The Importance of Black Studies for Science and Technology Policy*

William M. King

In the synopsis section of my course syllabus, "Science, Technology and Public Policy," I make the statement that science and technology are artifacts of the mind. As such, they are influenced by the values, attitudes, beliefs, ideologies and behavior of their creators, and by the cultures in which they are created, developed and deployed. That is, they are fundamentally human endeavors and we lose much in an examination of the products of those endeavors whenever we separate them from the people who made them.

Moreover, science and technology are seldom without purpose (implicit in their design and construction) and/either goal, vectors conditioned by the sociopolitical and psychocultural milieux within which they are learned and practiced. That is, contrary to the conventional wisdom, they are not done for their own sake alone. Thus the untenability of believing in their objectivity (a social construct) or value neutrality, terms employed to mask their fundamentally political character.[1]

Accordingly, it is both right and proper to talk about their regulation as social products since, as devices for focusing power (a basic force of/in the universe), they have consequences for the societies which support them and employ their products in a variety of ways. Thus, science and technology policy—where policy-making is understood as a proposed course of action addressed to some specific concern executed by an actor or set of actors legitimized by some social authority to do so—concerns itself with making choices about what kinds of science and technology are encouraged and supported, and bow they will be used, managed, evaluated and regulated as they do not exist in a social vacuum however much science education is structured to foster that particular myth.

The policy-making process is comprised of what I prefer to regard as emphases rather than a series of discretely identifiable steps. This allows me to keep the entire process in view even though I may be focused on only one aspect of that process at any one time. Following James E. Anderson,[2] these emphases are: (1) problem definition; (2) policy formulation; (3) policy adoption; (4) policy implementation; and (5) policy evaluation. Each aspect of the process is subtended by a number of questions whose clarity is of far greater importance than the character of any analytic procedure brought to an examination of whatever policy happens to be the object of our affection. For, when we do not have our questions clear, then we do not know what answers we seek, nor are we in a position to assess the consequences of the policies we have formulated. As a specific case in point, consider how crucial it is for us to re-

---

* An earlier version of this paper was given as an invited lecture at Northern Illinois University, October 17, 1995.

member that definition is the enabling legislation of subsequent treatment. Naming, therefore, is a rite of power, and we must be concerned with who is doing the defining, the reasons for constructing any specific definition, the expected accomplishment of the policy in question and the interplay, in a Millsian sense, of the relation between private troubles and public issues as one kind of motivation for the promulgation of policy.[3]

With respect to policy formulation, which, unfortunately, we teach as a rational process, the chief concern is with the excludes. That is, as we define, we confine. Thus, we need to become aware of what we have left out in constructing a specific policy and the consequences that arise when we generalize from a series of partial truths. Any solution to any problem creates problems of its own. If we cannot know these problems because we have left out of the formulative process people or things that increase our sensitivity to these problems, it readily becomes apparent that we have not done the job we set out to do—indeed we may even have exacerbated the problem, as the policies generated by the War on Poverty have made clear. Necessarily, then, it makes a difference when only certain persons are allowed to participate in the formulation of policy for whatever reason, for policy is an instrument of power. Similarly, the principal issue in the matter of policy adoption is what requirements must be met by whom before a piece of policy can be prepared for actualization, the step before implementation. This aspect of the process is where the real character of policy as a political process is revealed. For we cannot talk about implementation without talking about compliance as it is a specific goal of any policy to influence behavior, which is an exercise of power, namely, the ability to act, to get something done irrespective of the resistance that shaping of reality produces. And finally, there is the matter of evaluation. Did the proposed, implemented policy do what it was intended to do; what were consequences of its implementation; who decides; who evaluates; in accord with those criteria; requiring what changes? This last item is most important in that any policy, whatever the object of its affection, is an attempt to impose certainty on an uncertain world. Too, in that policies have a sensual, seductive character, we are reluctant to move away from them even when it is clear that they are doing more harm than good, however those value-laden terms are defined. By design, all policies have built-in limitations, some more readily discernible than others. They exist to protect, preserve and serve the vested interests of those who sire them. Because of their importance and the increasing importance of science and technology in the world, they require examination. The task of this paper, then, is to lay out the value of Black Studies, whose essence I define as the application of an Afrocentric perspective to human affairs, for a "systematic investigation of scientific and technological activities and their function within society. In particular...policy-making in [and about] scientific and technological fields, and...the interrelationship between policy making, cultural values and societal goals.[4]

My purpose here is one of exploring several facets of science and technology from an Afrocentric perspective whose world view, normative assumptions, and frames of reference grow out of the experiences and folk wisdom of black people. This point of view is synthetic and transdisciplinary. Wrote Allison Davis in 1927, no "black scholar can afford the luxury of remaining in the discipline in which he was trained." The current status of black people, somewhere between the periphery and core of United States society, requires the construction of new strategies of movement for the information age now aborning. And, given that information is a facility of construction, I contend that the time is now for black people to become involved in the shaping of science and technology policy that addresses specifically the context/content issues taken for granted and left unexamined. In short, to alter the position and conditions of our existence, we must use our disciplines, which now constrain our perspectives, to free ourselves; by learning the biographies of the crafts we practice, we can learn the uses to which our endeavors have been put and, perhaps decide, that that use or pattern of uses so offends the ethic, do not unto others what you would not want done unto you, that recognition might catalyze change.

As an expositor of this perspective, it is clear to me that since Africa is the birthplace of *Homo sapiens*, a cultured animal, Africa is also the birthplace of a planetary civilization whose characters have been most eloquently expressed by their creators, not with the most sanguine of consequences however. I feel a need to say this because there is a tendency in explicating the origins of culture to overlook the inconsistency of starting man in Africa and starting civilization in the lighter-skinned Middle East. It is really a minor point for some, I suppose; but, as is often the case, minor points contain great truths about the relativity of Truth.

The object of this exercise is a new context for a new conceptualization of science and technology as social processes. This context proceeds from the premise that "everything is dual; everything has poles; everything has its pair of opposites; like and unlike are the same; opposites are identical in nature, but different in degrees; all truths are but half truths; all paradoxes may be reconciled."[5] For without doubt, existence is relational. Where there is no relation, there is no existence. What we see is what we see and that is not the same for everyone, everywhere, all the time. Second, content is, in some wise, determined by the social values of the context. Not recognizing this truth has allowed us to believe "a whole lotta things that ain't necessarily so." Indeed, what is it that keeps us from seeing Western science as the servant of Western religion—the false distinction that one is called sacred and the other is called secular—or the apparent power struggle that has existed between them since the time of Sir Francis Bacon.[6] I find it most interesting that the new thrust be gives to the mission statement of science comes at a time in European history when the heady momentum of empire building is well advanced. For according to Chinese folklore, which I find harmonious with African traditional religion, "The World is full of illusions, created for many purposes."[7] Their existence prompts the question, who benefits from these illusions and how do they benefit.

One of the most profound of those illusions, an illusion that characterizes the underside of Western civilization in its less proud moments, is the Myth of Control, whose goal is most cogently expressed in Chapter I, Verse 26 of Genesis as a moral prime directive:

> And God said, Let us make man in our image, after our likeness: and let them have dominion over the fish of the sea, and over the fowl of the air, and over the cattle, and over all the earth, and over every creeping thing that creepeth upon the earth.

And as it is that the orientation of "Western" culture is more Judeo-Christian than Greco-Roman in heritage, a correct interpretation of its biography must center about the pursuit of power to effect control: an attempt to prevent the present from becoming the past; to resist change as a natural process. For indeed, it is this very penchant for control, expressed in Genesis and the teleology of Western science and technology, for dominion, for linear conceptualizations of progress that accord with the values of the social system doing the defining, that is a source of blindness, and a source of many of our social difficulties whether we are black, white, Jewish, Islamic, or just plain-old, down-home, Sunday-go-to-meeting Baptist. We all want our own way for as long as possible, and we will sometimes go to some extraordinary lengths to realize our vision of reality. This constitutes, in my view, a reluctance to understand that the pursuit of control in a living world is a chimera that grows out of insecurity about the value of one's own worth. Necessarily, we must confront the constructs of our consciousness and the bidden agendas they contain. Yes, they are useful as explanatory paradigms. However, as with all such devices, once formulated, their focus shifts from the problem that called the paradigm into existence to the puzzles within the boundary of the paradigm—a maintenance activity—manifest in the socially sanctioned behavior of the official knowers, and custodians of the paradigm. The danger of conceptual incarceration is obvious, and I invite my readers to raise questions where they feel required to do so.

As I conceive it, a first assumption of Afrocentricity is that the purpose of life is expression. This is most clearly seen, I believe, in the wide diversity of life forms. This diversity mandates interdependence, however, since at this level of specialization, survival has no meaning.

A second assumption is that there is only one "Law of Nature." This is that everything must change; nothing stays the same. All other laws of nature are man-made and nature is not obligated to obey their command of control. The very diversity that is, is the engine of change. Thus, an important area of investigation for me addresses the ways in which we seek to resist change as a natural phenomenon, believing that we can exercise control through our constructs and/either actions. Paradoxically, the more control we cede, the more control we have. In particular, that over the meanings we make of our experiences.

A third assumption of the Afrocentric perspective as I understand it is that people are ordinary; experience is not. That is, perception is reality, making reality different for each and every one of us. There is, Wade W. Nobles[8] has argued, a mythic consciousness and an historical consciousness, both of which are required to create common sense. Our mythic consciousness is cultural, expectational; it provides a set of general guidelines for interpreting and making meaning of our experiences; it is contained in the languages we learn as a consequence of our various socializations, familial to occupational, et al. Our historical consciousness is particular, personal and experiential; it serves as the data-gathering arm for understanding the various situations we transit. These consciousnesses complement each other and are assisted in their work by the six senses: sight, bearing, taste, touch, smell and feelings. They are programmable in keeping with whatever search strategies we construct to find out what we want to know. Unfortunately, we all too often question the validity of our experience as baseline. We allow cultural expectations that do not operate in our behalf to cloud over vision. In short, we erode our own power to act and become captives of our conceptualizations. Thus,

> we have to decide whether we are going to make a commitment to the quality
> of our experience in life or make a commitment to the way the Culture believes things are supposed to look.[9]

For consensus, which is a negotiated settlement, obscures difference. Thus, there is a necessity for developing a critical perspective that begins with what happened, before we can ask what it means.

A fourth assumption is that knowledge is a social product, not an objective ideal that can be possessed, owned or brought in from the outside as if it had an independent existence. That is, knowledge is information that has been organized for some specific purpose whose intent is implicit in the organizational design. It is not so much that we discover the truth, as it is that we manufacture the truth in keeping with our own interests and agenda. To postulate an objective ideal of knowledge suggests that the scholar in some way is separate and distinct from the phenomena being investigated. This is of course patent nonsense that all too often is used to evade responsibility for the consequences of our actions. Our descriptions of reality are not independent of the realities they purport to describe.[10]

Finally, all definitions are situational definitions. As a scholar working within an Afrocentric perspective, I see one of my obligations as that of heightening my sensitivity to the limitations of such definitions: to recognize them for the freeze-framing that they are and not necessarily representative of anything other than themselves. For me, it is the experience and the meaning I make of it that provides a sense of order. I see what I do as a repetitive process of asking what I term the fundamental four questions of existence: origin, location, purpose, destiny. The approaches I employ focus more on problems than on theory building per se. I have chosen to do this because scientific theories have a tendency to become political ideologies; and also, because when one's orientation is toward theory building, there is a tendency to take for granted certain background and domain assumptions that when not challenged restrict perception, which is after all the essence of reality. With this description of my orientation to social research, let me turn now to an exploration of science and technology and the shaping of a context for policy from an Afrocentric perspective.

Science, for me, is a way of organizing information to produce meaning and beauty, where beauty is expressed in the ways we make meaning of the things we do. As such, science is an extension of a people's common sense[11] guided and bound by the background and domain assumptions of the culture in which it is. What this means, of course, is that, for me, all science is ethnoscience[12] — there is not, nor can there be a universal science, the current popular culture conceptualization of science notwithstanding.

Technology I see as information organized to realize some specific purpose. It is also a lens that is used to focus power in the form of expertise where power is a basic force of/in the universe. Necessarily, science, in the way I use the term here, is a technology, a technology of the intellect, a construct of the consciousness that has become a process structure in that it is both a way of doing something and a social institution since all technologies require a social support system for their care and feeding.

Science and technology policy is concerned with the care and feeding of the social institutions/processes of science and technology. Ultimately concerned with the allocation of resources, the direction of research and development, and the realization of desired goals whether they be in agriculture, commerce, the military, basic science, whatever, science and technology policymaking is guided by values and expectations that cannot be divorced from the policy process. And it is in the examination of those values and expectations that Black Studies can play a most important role. Simply subscribing to the shibboleths of the past regarding scientific work, arguing a position of value neutrality which we know not to be true, locks us into a technocratic mindset that more often than not exacerbates the problems of society, irrespective of the area in which they appear. This is the problem of the technological fix. Its commitment to the myth of rationalism inhibits the incorporation of whimsy into its design. Bringing rationalism to bear on the investigation of a rational phenomena creates problems of its own. Let me be more specific.

In a 1974 editorial in *Black Scholar Magazine*,[13] the point is made that the selection of problems for investigation, the methods employed to investigate those problems, the uses of the results of those studies, even the very character of training in the sciences and technology are colored by ideology. Whatever we have to say about the so-called scientific method, whose statement by Francis Bacon effected a union between science and religion, we must say that it, like the law, another species of ratio-nalism applied to arational phenomena, is not brought into play until after the concerns to be addressed are identified, defined, and detailed in keeping with the underlying assumptions that govern both processes.

This can be seen, I believe, in a careful examination of the place of science and technology in society—its sociophysical location—the purposes for which techno-scientific activities are mounted, and the theology of existence and destiny proffered to make meaning of those activities.

As a specific case in point, consider the Tuskegee Syphilis Study[14] which evolved out of late nineteenth century biological determinism and racial medicine. Initially begun in 1929 by the Rockefeller Foundation as an attempt to eradicate a pressing social problem—syphilis—when it came under the jurisdiction of the Public Health Service, it was gradually subverted into an investigation of the course of a specific, untreated venereal disease in black males because of the widely held belief—in both popular and scientific circles—that black people were biologically different from white people. Nor is this the only example of science and technology in the service of politics. For contrary to the conventional wisdom of our exercises in science education, it is our social values that determine the content of the scientific enterprise. In part, this arises from our tendency to see difference as deviance; as something that must be contained lest it disrupt our agreed upon perception of the world as we know it. And, in part, it derives from our desire to reduce the uncertainty that surrounds us. Yet, the question remains: "Have we gone too far?" Have we, in Langdon Winner's words, unleashed an autonomous technology[15] searching for its creator so that it might be told what to do. Have we allowed technique to transcend value to the point that our procedures inhibit examination of ourselves and our works; indeed, what are the questions that are worth asking about the construction of science and technology policy?

Now, I would not have you go away from this reading believing that I am antiscience, or that, as a consequence of my remarks, you must stay away from the sciences and technology as if they are some special, mystical pursuit that requires enormous intelligence for their pursuit. They are, after all, requisite for social and economic development. Rather, what I would ask you to attend to is an examination of the guiding ideology behind science, technology, and policy, and the fact that ideologies are not carved in stone: they can be changed and made to work for a large segment of the worlds they affect by changing the priorities that govern their conduct. In this case, I believe the time has come to reexamine the message of Genesis.

Endnotes

1. See, for example, Daniel J. Boorstin, *The Discoverers*, (New York, 1983); and Walter A. McDougall, ... *the Heavens and the Earth* (New York, 1985). Also see, Frank Rose, *Into The Heart of The Mind* (New York, 1984), whose interesting subtitle "An American Quest for Artificial Intelligence," forces the recognition that "who pays the piper calls the tune" is just as true in the financing of technology as it is in music.

2. James E. Anderson, *Public Policy-Making* (New York, 1975), p. 26.

3. Troubles "occur within the character of the individual and within the range of his immediate relation with others, they have to do with his self and with those limited areas of social life of which he is directly and personally aware." Issues "have to do with matters that transcend these local environments of the individual and the range of his inner life. They have to do with the organization of many much milieux into the institutions of an historic society as a whole,

with the ways in which various milieux overlap and interpenetrate to form the larger structure of social and historical life." See, C. Wright Mills, *The Sociological Imagination* (New York, 1959), pp. 8-9.

4. Quoted in Diane Crane, "Science Policy Studies," in Paul T. Durbin. ed., *A Guide to the Culture of Science, Technology and Medicine* (New York, 1980), p. 584.

5. Charles A. Frye, "The Role of Philosophy in Black Studies," *Contributions in Black Studies*, 4 (1980-81): 70.

6. Sixteenth Century English philosopher whose appearance at the transition point between Medieval and Modern Eurocentric thought profoundly affected the perception and conceptualization of Science. With the addition of the experimental methods of Galileo, the pattern for contemporary science was laid down and remained pretty much in place until the relativistic ideas of the present began to permeate the corpus of scientific understanding shortly after the publication of Einstein's paper on special relativity in 1905.

7. I use the word *Folklore* here in the same sense as does Fela Sowande in "Black Folklore," *BlackLines*, 2.1 (Fall 1971): 6-21. That is, folklore is the "lore of the folk"; the symbolic expression of a people's culture irrespective of the particular manifestation that expression takes.

8. Discussed at a seminar given at the University of Colorado, April 1984.

9. Quoted in Stewart Emery, *The Owner's Manual for Your Life* (Garden City, 1985), p. 85.

10. See Robert Horton, "African Traditional Thought and Western Science," *Africa*, 37, 1 (January 1967): 50-71; 37, 2 (April 1967): 155-87.

11. See Wade W. Nobles, "Toward an Empirical and Theoretical Framework for Defining Black Families," *Journal of Marriage and the Family*, 40, 4 (November 1978): 680-82.

12. For an exploration of this idea, see Judith Ann Bemington, "An Epistemological Study of Navajo Divination and European Science" (Unpublished Ph.D. dissertation, Northwestern University, 1982).

13. 6, 4 (March 1974): 8.

14. One history of this study, is James Jones, *Bad Blood* (New York, 1973).

15. *Autonomous Technology* (Cambridge, MA, 1977).

58.

Computers and Black Studies: Toward the Cognitive Revolution

Melvin K. Hendrix, James H. Bracy,
John A. Davis, and Waddell M. Herron

Introduction

Over the past five years the explosion in computer technology has created a revolution in processing information, one that rivals the significance of the Industrial Revolution of the nineteenth century. This rapid development in computer technology is often called the Cognitive Revolution, but unfortunately it has concentrated primarily on the medium of strict technological development rather than on the message or audience. As a result, many people have acquired and have failed to explore an effective understanding of how these new devices can be exploited. A corollary problem is that because computers usually are associated with mathematics and science disciplines too few application software programs have been developed for students and scholars in the humanities and social sciences to enhance pedagogy and research.

The Cognitive Revolution is simultaneously overwhelming and subtle. It is overwhelming in the sense that the technology is changing far faster than our knowledge and abilities to master it. This situation is unlikely to change soon. For example, according to a recent report by the Department of Electrical Engineering and Computer Science at the Massachusetts Institute of Technology, electronic and computer engineers are unable to keep abreast of this technological revolution, and engineering schools have been advised to counsel students to prepare for a lifelong process of continuous study in order to remain competent.[1] If engineers are unable to stay apace with changes in computer technology, it is unlikely that the general public can do so. All of us should be preparing for an extraordinary process of lifelong learning in relation to these developments, including career shifts or realignments.

On the other hand, the Cognitive Revolution is extremely subtle in that the widespread availability of microcomputers increases the opportunity to use this powerful information medium to enhance personal productivity as well as to advance personal and collective goals. Yet, the key element remains the mind behind the machine. It is the human mind that brings to computer technology the vision and passion to create. The fact that machine intelligence is called "artificial" is not a misnomer, for while computers are a powerful medium, they merely assist us in manipulating data, albeit at considerable speed.

For Black Studies professionals and students, computer technology offers another opportunity to strengthen the *unidisciplinary* aspects of our intellectual approach to knowledge, as well as improve the academic standing of Black Studies units in the Academy. To be successful, we must address some pertinent questions. First, will learning in a computer-based environment differ in form or content/context from earlier forms? Current data suggests that it will, but not immediately. Scholars in the Academy are still very much constrained by hegemonic concerns of individual disciplines in subject areas that directly affect Black Studies. These disciplines have traditionally inhibited the growth of Black Studies, fearing the intrusion of "alien" knowledge, methodology, and perspectives vis-à-vis the "pure" disciplines.

Charles Frye, one of the principal scholars focusing on the development of Black Studies intellection within the Academy, suggests that Black Studies offers,

> a conceptual framework for a truly unidisciplinary approach to education. A unidisciplinary approach does not mean the combining of diverse disciplines to treat a single question, as occurs in multi- or interdisciplinary approaches currently being explored by all segments of the Academy. On the contrary, the unidisciplinary approach simply denies the validity of separate disciplines by reaffirming the unity of human knowledge.[2]

For perhaps the first time in history, the development of computer technology creates the potential for a unidisciplinary approach within the social sciences. Certainly, it provides the possibility for analyzing tremendous volumes of information by the simultaneous manipulation of diverse variables with the speed and accuracy unavailable to social scientists fifteen years ago. Full utilization of computer technology requires a unidisciplinary approach. As a consequence, there probably will be increasing pressure on academicians to involve themselves in more intensive collaborative teaching and research, while curricula probably will function to meet specific needs and interests of individual students. The latter can be addressed using *computer-assisted instructional* facilities. At present, we are only at the frontiers of the debate.

A second question is, How does this development directly relate to the goals and objectives of Black Studies? The answer to this question lies in the ability of Black Studies professionals to exploit the potential created by developments in computer technology. The capacity to meet this opportunity will be determined ultimately by factors such as intellectual, behavioral, cultural and aesthetic orientations, and political and economic exigencies, factors that Johnnella Butler has grouped under the singular concept of "sensibilities." She argues that the efforts made by black scholars to affirm the identity of Black Studies in the Academy, and by extension affirm the collective identity of all African-Americans, can be successful only to the extent that we come to grips with the African-American duality postulated by W.E.B. DuBois at the turn of the century, or that aspect of our African-ness that mediates our consciousness in Euro-American dominated America.[3] In short, the creative capacity to transform the reality of computer-assisted learning and scholarship, based upon our African-American sensibilities, will determine whether of not computer technology will serve Black Studies and black peoples demonstrably in the future.

We believe that it will be the challenge of the 1980s for black scholars to seize the creative initiative to master this technology in order that we may better serve students, the community, the Academy, and, of course, ourselves. A beginning exploration for the role of the computer in this effort will be our focus in the main body of this article. To ward this end, we will look at five areas where the use of computer technology could greatly enhance the effectiveness of Black Studies course offerings and program content. These areas are curriculum, retention, network, research and publication, and externships and applied knowledge.

Computers in the Curriculum

Computer-assisted instruction is being increasingly emphasized by liberal arts constituencies throughout the Academy. This development is one effort to combat declining enrollments in liberal arts subjects. It is clear that students today are acutely concerned with the question of post-baccalaureate employment. As a result, they also question the practical utility of a liberal arts major in today's growing high technology-oriented job market. Consequently, most colleges and universities are experiencing a dramatic increase in enrollment in business and computer science. Traditional disciplines such as sociology, history, philosophy, and the rest of the humanities are, therefore, apprehensive.

Recent data show that most businesses hire and promote liberal arts majors as fast as business majors. Indeed, the data reveal that liberal arts majors are better prepared for business because they have superior communication skills.[4] Therefore, Black Studies units should emphasize that these skills are better developed within liberal arts curricula in general, and within Black Studies in particular. The important point is that Black Studies can, and does, prepare students for post-baccalaureate employment opportunities as well as any other discipline in the liberal arts curriculum.

A second factor that we must understand is that many students currently in college have a general anxiety about computers, a residual aspect of the general anxiety associated with mathematics. We, in Black Studies, can combat this anxiety with black students by providing innovative approaches to the teaching of computer literacy. For example, computers can be used to develop educational modules with a specific African-American content. Graphics can be used to illuminate African-American realities, such as social stratification, population density in Harlem, residential segregation, or rank and status in the military. Historical sites, maps, and personalities can also be rendered graphically. Specialized procedures and situations, as well as key concepts and ideas, can be simulated in order to make difficult concepts more concrete and tractable for students. Further, educational games can be devised to create accurate renditions of the human condition as it relates to the African-American experience. In manipulating data for games and simulation, students can learn elementary programming, either for the first time or for reinforcing skills they already know.

Further, Black Studies units can also assist post-secondary students, as well as secondary students where this is possible, to prepare for standardized tests, such as the Scholastic Aptitude Test, Graduate Record Examination, National Teachers Examination, Medical College Aptitude Test, and the Law School Aptitude Test. For this purpose, there are a number of software packages on the market designed specifically for use on microcomputers. These resources can be used to advance the temporal developmental learning potential of black students, increase their reading comprehension, and reduce test anxiety by familiarizing them with the types of questions they should expect. Most important, black students will be assisted to be more competitive, particularly in those cases where students cannot afford to take tutorial courses from private agencies.

Finally, Black Studies can further promote its desirability by indicating the value and the relationship of this new technology not only to pedagogy but also to the liberation from the oppression that continues to dominate ideas in the Academy, which is often reflected in the number of black faculty and students in predominantly white post-secondary institutions, as well as the meager budgetary resources available to Black Studies units in these institutions. In short, in addition to greater access to the key information technology of the future, an emphasis on African-American sensibilities, and an applied curriculum, Black Studies students will be trained to compete successfully in both the marketplace of jobs and the marketplace of ideas.

Retention

Retention is a major problem for most universities, one that is not likely to disappear in the near future. The loss of students has negative financial consequences that affect academic programs. Most black professors are in a unique, though ambivalent, position to function as role models for black students. Black Studies units certainly have a responsibility to use this position to encourage black students to succeed and to counsel them in both academic and personal matters where appropriate. Quite often, academic difficulty is but a manifestation of personal and economic problems. Most universities have learning resource centers or other tutorial programs designed for academic intervention. Some institutions might also have developed peer tutoring or group tutoring/study sessions as well as a variety of other supportive services.

Nonetheless, what is often lacking in these programs is the integration of information with a sophisticated tracking system. This could be the ideal role for some Black Studies faculty, since generally they have better relations with black students, often provide both formal and informal counseling for them, and more often have a deeper commitment to them. Consequently, where manpower permits, there could be coordinated approaches to retention that are designed to decrease dramatically the attrition of black students. These approaches might serve as a model for retention programs in general.

Black Studies involvement in this activity is self-serving. First, it gets black students, faculty, and staff directly integrated within the institution, thus making the structure stronger. Second, it can buttress demands by Black Studies units for a more equitable distribution of staff and budgetary resources, which in public educational institutions is a legal rather than merely a moral position. The use of microcomputer technology would permit us to rapidly coordinate information, profile student problems more effectively, and establish student profiles for anticipated problems in some areas such as English, mathematics, and science. The profile would permit us to devise strategies for early intervention before critical problems arise. While such a program is not suited for every Black Studies unit, it could have unlimited potential for some.

Networks

One of the greatest potential benefits from the utilization of computer technology in Black Studies is the possibility of developing a professional network among scholars. The concept of a computer network is an impressive one. By definition, a network is a multiple-user, multiple-function communications system of interconnected computers or terminals. Within it, an individual user is not limited by his own data resources or computing power, but can access data and information processed by the entire system. Types of network interaction could include scholar-to-scholar(s); department-to-department(s); scholars-to-research facilities; scholars-to-community organizations, public sector agencies, and so on.

There are several reasons why scholars would want to be involved in a network. First, information can be quickly shared, amplified, or amended. For example, a pool of data on black professionals and students seeking teaching and research positions, special degree or professional enhancement programs, lecture opportunities, or collaboration could be developed to aid programs seeking human resources to meet critical academic and administrative needs. A similar database could be developed for curriculum as provided by various Black Studies units for the purposes of developing a standardized bachelor's or master's degree program, or identify areas of duplication or scarcity, and, where feasible, develop complementary and/or shared curriculum and instruction.

Another important value of using a network is that of coordination of academic and cultural programming between Black Studies units. For example, national and local electronic newsletters can be created, together with electronic bulletin boards, that share information on research interests, pending publications, upcoming social and cultural events, methodology and pedagogy, as well as the testing of ideas, theories, or verification of facts. This type of information would help to reduce duplication of efforts in research, averting scheduling conflicts between institutions within geographical proximity or between national organizations serving relative similar constituencies. Moreover, electronic mail could serve as a "hotline" to rally support for particular causes or give assistance to besieged Black Studies scholars and units.

A third value of a network for scholars is the concept of teleconferencing. Teleconferencing permits two or more interconnected computer units to "talk" with one another through the use of a telephone communications device called a *modem*. This concept enables scholars who might otherwise find it difficult to get together to discuss ideas or transact other business. It can also promote critical thinking and professional collaboration between scholars who are geographically separated by distance and/or time far quicker and more decisively than the mails, since decisions can be made or taken immediately. Furthermore, community organizations could be tied into the system, thus permitting direct interface between "gown and town." Such groups could have direct access to research, academic, and program data. The Black Studies unit, on the other hand, could be directly involved in applied research in cooperation with community groups or provide technical assistance or training to these organizations to improve their overall organizational development, including computer literacy.

A final value that can be derived from the use of a network is the concept of shared resources. Network users can share resources, whether these resources are human (i.e., consultants, technicians, or educators) or technical (expensive printers, mainframes, hard disks, or software). Moreover, at this stage of the Cognitive Revolution, the sharing of computing ability is also very important, and through networks diverse resources and support to enhance individual skills can be provided.

Research and Publications

Black Studies faculty face the same concerns as their counterparts in other disciplines, including the need to conduct research *and* publish, together with the ongoing need to improve teaching skills in order to obtain tenure and promotion. The microcomputer serves as an excellent research tool in its ability to access automated library catalogue files and subject area databases and to manipulate packaged software. The data can be stored on *floppy disks*, in an institutional *mainframe*, on *hard disks* for later access, or output on *word processors*.

Microcomputers can also be taken to the field. Portable computers are capable of full computing functions, of utilizing *peripherals*, though small enough to be closed up in one package and taken any place that electrical power is available. Some models are designed to use portable power packs. Thus, these units make perfect companions in field research for those projects where a sea of data must be managed on a daily basis. Examples include research in population studies, health and medical research, collective biographies, migration and refugee movements, and oral historiographies.

Another extremely important research area for Black Studies scholars to apply microcomputer technology is in the reconstruction of state and local histories. A growing number of African-American museums and black historical societies have been established since the 1960s. Many of these institutions still need some assistance in managing and cataloging their resources for use by researchers. High level academic expertise coupled with the microcomputer can greatly facilitate the filing and publication of these state and local history resources. Concomitantly, the computer can also assist in quickly tracing family histories. The *Genealogical Computing* newsletter can provide information on genealogy software programs.[5]

With respect to writing, word processing can permit the amount of output generated from faculty members and research staff to increase tremendously. Manuscript preparation and grants construction time can be reduced from months to weeks with the data storage and rapid editing features common to these machines. Black Studies units acquiring such technology (or at least promoting its use in other campus facilities) can increase their research and publication capabilities as well as improve their efficiency and effectiveness in completing administrative duties.

In addition to preparing publications for national scholarly journals and books, Black Studies units will have the potential for publishing their own works locally. Microcomputers, coupled with word processing software and telephone modems, can cut typesetting costs by transmitting material directly to the typesetter. This method reduces input costs and *turnaround time* substantially while providing the benefits of professional typesetting and printing. Thus, Black Studies units can produce occasional papers, books, manuals, reference works, and brochures in-house.

Externships and Applied Knowledge

The National Standardized Black Studies Curriculum developed by the National Council for Black Studies[6] in early 1980 proposed that a series of externships be created for college students in the latter stages of their undergraduate career. Externships, or cooperative education, would provide students with practical experiences in the "world of work" so that they might gain exposure and insight into the labor market before leaving college. This excellent idea should be further developed by more Black Studies units. Some practical questions come to mind, however. Where are these placements? If they do not exist, who will develop them and how? What kinds of skills should be stressed to student applicants? How many students can be administered and at what cost? Are there alumni employed within identifiable organizations who can assist in creating such opportunities? Answers to these and other questions could be stored in the computer and be readily available for students and faculty. Further, the list of placements could be constantly updated or revised. Moreover, externship information could be shared with other Black Studies units within a limited geographic area, expanding resources, referrals, and, most important, student options.

Conclusion

The primary purpose of this article was to identify the several ways that computer technology can be employed within Black Studies. We have suggested that computers and word processors can enhance faculty, student, and staff skills; improve curriculum and program standards; monitor program effectiveness; and, at the same time, provide a communications linkage with research facilities, community groups, and other academic institutions and individuals, while also promoting increased scholarly productivity in the areas of publishing and research.

The challenge for each of us is to recognize the differences between the technology of information processing and a technology of communications. As one critic of communications in the computer industry suggests, technicians are more concerned with moving data at high speed than with human communication. While this may be good for information processing, good communications has *meaning* to the user. The determination of meaning is dependent upon a number of psychological, linguistic, and cultural factors not yet fully incorporated into the new technology.[7] The challenge for the Black Studies professional is to learn to blend the technology of information processing with the technology of human communication as this is reflected in African-American sensibilities.

Such a view has been anticipated by Charles Frye who argues that Black Studies can form a bridge between the ideational and the operational modes of being to temper both technology and humanism.[8] This role can only be achieved if we learn to use the new technology to our maximum benefit. Our inability to master it will only serve to weaken our struggle in an ever-increasing technological condition in the Western world. It is, or should be, evident to those of us in the academic community that this new technology could mean the establishment of a new basis for the delegation of social power, wealth, and authority. This is certainly an area in which Black Studies should be actively involved. As Neal Margolis succinctly observes: "Unfortunately, you can't choose not to relate to the products of technology. You have little choice in this matter. Your choice concerns how you will approach the task of learning. You can be the victim, at the mercy of the technicians who haven't the time to speak your language; or you can be responsible for your own learning."[9]

We have only begun to explore the questions and the role that computer technology can play in furthering Black Studies; or conversely, what role Black Studies will play in promoting computer technology. However, it is imperative that we seize the initiative in highlighting the strengths of Black Studies, and that we not perceive advanced technology as a monstrous threat to our expertise. Computers are merely tools, and we must creatively adapt them to our needs.

Endnotes

1. Massachusetts Institute of Technology, Department of Electrical Engineering and Computer Science, *Lifelong Cooperative Education* (Cambridge, MA: MIT, October 2, 1982. Report of the Centennial Study Committee).

2. Charles A. Frye, *Towards a Philosophy of Black Studies* (San Francisco: R & E Research Associates, 1978), p. 59.

3. Johnnella Butler, *Black Studies: Pedagogy and Revolution* (Washington, DC: University Press of America, 1981), passim.

4. *New York Times* (May 4, 1983).

5. *Genealogical Computing* newsletter (Data Transfer Associates, Inc., 5102 Pommeroy Drive, Fairfax, VA 22032).

6. National Council for Black Studies, *Report of the Curriculum Standards Committee* (Bloomington, IN: NCBS, March 1980).

7. Neal Margolis, "The Users' Manual Manual: What To Do When All Else Fails— Call for Help," *InfoWorld*, 5/6 (April 25, 1983): 23.

8. Charles A. Frye, "Higher Education in the New Age: The Role of Interdisciplinary Studies, *The American Theosophist* (March 1977): 61-64.

9. Neal Margolis, "The Users' Manual Manual," p. 23.

59.

The Institute of the Black World, Martin Luther King, Jr. Memorial Center, Atlanta, Georgia

Vincent Harding, Jr.

Statement of Purpose and Program, Fall 1969

Introduction

The Institute of the Black World is a community of black scholars, artists, teachers and organizers who are coming together in Atlanta under the aegis of the Martin Luther King, Jr. Memorial Center. (It is also a group of several dozen "Associates of The Institute" who are located in various parts of the hemisphere.)

The Institute of the Black World is a gathering of black intellectuals who are convinced that the gifts of their minds are meant to be fully used in the service of the black community. It is therefore an experiment with scholarship in the context of struggle.

Among our basic concerns and commitments is the determination to set our skills to a new understanding of the past, present and future condition of the peoples of African descent, wherever they may be found, with an initial emphasis on the American experience. This seems the least that history, or the present — to say nothing of our children — would demand of those persons who have lived the black experience and have developed certain gifts of analysis, creativity and communication.

Program of Work

In cooperating with several institutions of higher education, the Institute of the Black World has set itself to the following specific tasks in the years ahead:

1. *The definition and refining of the field now loosely called "Black Studies."* After having taken the lead in calling for a new encounter the staff of the Institute has now begun a long-range, careful analysis of the content and direction of Black Studies programs across the nation. A recently-ended summer workshop and a series of

seminars with Black Studies directors over the next academic year (1969-70) will eventually produce a set of documents which will analyze existing programs, review and respond to the major criticisms of Black Studies, put forth a set of ideological positions concerning the field and offer certain suggestions about its future directions.

2. *The development of a new Consortium for Black Education.* This consortium will involve the Institute and a group of colleges and universities drawn primarily from the historically black institutions of higher education. During the 1969-70 academic year the Institute of the Black World will definitely share its staff, personnel and Associates with Fisk, Howard, Shaw and Wesleyan Universities and probably with Tuskegee Institute and several of the Atlanta University Center schools. IBW staff and Associates will lecture, offer seminars, engage in workshops and generally consult with students, faculty and administrators on these campuses. Students from at least one of these schools will work in Atlanta with Institute personnel in seminars and individual research.

In the course of this year our staff will also be developing new, black-saturated curriculum and course models in several areas of the Humanities and the Social Sciences. The Consortium schools will experiment with and evaluate these materials over a period of several years, beginning with the 1970-71 academic year.

3. The encouragement of basic academic research in the experiences of the peoples of African descent. All of the research staff will be engaged in individual projects, such as "Education and Decolonization"; "The Poetry of the Blues"; "The Self-Concepts of Black Women"; "Black American Attitudes Towards Africa in the 19th Century"; "Black Radicalism and Black Religion." Each senior staff person will offer at the Institute one seminar per semester related to his research area. (See the attached list of research staff persons.) In addition, several persons will be encouraged to relate to the Institute on a part-time basis so that their research can add to our mutual strengthening.

4. *The encouragement of black artists, especially those who are searching for an aesthetic which will contribute to the struggle for the minds and hearts of our people.* Such artists will be invited to enter the dialogue and search of the Institute, to create out of their own vision and materials, and to share their creativity with the black community off campus.

5. *The development of new materials and methods for the teaching of black children.* Several members of the Institute staff are responsible for our work with two independent, black community schools in Atlanta, the H. Rapp Brown Community School and the Martin Luther King, Jr. Community School. These institutions will serve as laboratories for new content and approaches, especially related to the black experience. (Some relationships to the Atlanta Public School system are also being developed.) In turn, the results of this experimentation will be fed back into the teacher training programs of the colleges and universities associated with the Institute, through workshops, seminars and new curriculum.

6. *The development of a Black Policy Studies Center.* An attempt will be made to develop solid tools of social analysis focussed on the contemporary situation of the black community in America and committed totally to the struggle of that community for self-determination. Persons and organizations representing the full spectrum of ideological thought in the black community will be brought together periodically for unpublicized encounters outside of the polemical arena. It is expected that this Center will make it possible for persons who need it to find a place of creative withdrawal from the day-to-day activity of the struggle and to enter into significant dialogue with a committed community of black artists, scholars and organizers from

other parts of the nation and the world. A variety of policy papers and guidelines will likely develop out of this section of the IBW. Eventually, the Institute will move to the training of community organizers whose work flows out of a rigorous and non-romantic analysis of the situation of the black community (which includes, of course, a realistic assessment of the state of the white community and its leaders). We are certain that no significant movement for justice and self-determination can continue without this level of analysis and organization.

7. *The establishment of creative links with our counterparts in other areas of the Black World.* In Latin America, the Caribbean, Africa and elsewhere black scholars, artists, educators and organizers are grappling with many issues very similar to those which engage us in North America. The Institute will continue its attempt to carry on significant dialogue and mutually agreed upon work with such persons, through individual visits, seminars, conferences and many types of exchanges.

8. *The preparation of a new cadre of men and women who are at once precisely trained in the scholarship of the black experience and fully committed to the struggles of the black world.* Through affiliation with graduate and undergraduate schools, the Institute expects eventually to be of service to persons who wish both to relate to its work and to seek degrees. (However, the IBW has no immediate plans of its own for becoming a degree-granting institution. It prefers to serve those institutions which already have this capacity.) At the same time, the Institute will experiment with new ways to prepare non-degree educators for their role in the instruction of the black community.

9. *The sponsoring of short-term seminars and of vacation and summer workshops and conferences, both independently and in concert with one or more of the cooperating institutions.* In each of the areas of concern mentioned above, the Institute will be seeking to share its findings and to expand its own competence by meeting regularly with others who are engaged in similar concerns and commitments. Among the first of these will be a seminar for selected Black Studies Directors (November 7-9) and a Conference on "Black Studies and the Future of Negro Colleges" (December 27-29 or January 2-4).

10. *The development of a publishing program.* Such a program will make available to a broader audience much of the work and concern of the Institute and other groups and individuals working at the same tasks. Its output would include basic academic research on the black experience, policy study papers, curriculum materials and the creative productions of black artists. A newsletter of Black Studies will be one of its first periodicals. A Dictionary of Black American Biography is a long-range task.

Staff

The work outlined above is clearly the task of a lifetime for any group of persons. We do not expect to finish it in a year or a decade, but we shall begin. With this in mind an initial research staff (limited in number only by funds) has been gathered to begin our work. A list of that staff appears below. With adequate funding, the group will likely grow by at least fifty per cent in the 1970-71 academic year, with several persons from outside the North American black community anticipated. A full-time support staff of another seven to twelve persons will also be rounded out by the end of the next academic year. In addition to the full-time persons on the staff, the Institute of the Black World has regular access to the services of several dozen "Associates of the Institute" who are teachers, artists and consultants in a variety of fields. They augment the staff in its own in-house tasks and in its work with schools, organizations and individuals.

Governing Board

The immediate governing board of the Institute is called The Advisory Council and is made up of a group of black scholars, artists, community leaders and others. They are Walter F. Anderson, Margaret Walker Alexander, Lerone Bennett, Horace Mann Bond, Robert Browne, John Henrik Clarke, Dorothy Cotton, Ossie Davis, St. Clair Drake, Katherine Dunham, Vivian Henderson, Tobe Johnson, Julius Lester, Frances Lucas, Jesse Noel, Rene Piquion, Eleo Pomare, Pearl Primus, Benjamin Quarles, Bernice Reagon, William Strickland, Council Taylor, E.U. Essien-Udom, C.T. Vivian, Charles White, and Hosea Williams.

Present Research Staff and Fall Seminars, 1969

1. Lerone Bennett, Senior Editor, *Ebony*: Visiting Professor History, Northwestern (Black Protest Movements, Reconstruction). Fall Seminar: *Black Reconstruction in America*

2. Christine Coleman, Mississippi High School Teacher, Southern Education Foundation Intern

3. Chester Davis, Assistant Professor Education, Sir George Williams University, Montreal (Black Studies and the Building of Public School Curriculum; Black Studies and the Training of Teachers). Fall Seminar: *Building Black Curriculum in the Public Schools*

4. Lonetta Gaines, New Haven, Connecticut, Teacher, Southern Education Foundation Intern

5. Vincent Harding, Chairman, History Department Spelman College, Director, Martin Luther King Library-Documentation Project (Black Radicalism and Black Religion)

6. Stephen Henderson, Chairman, English Department, Morehouse College (The Poetry of the Blues; Modern Black Writers), Fall Seminar: *Blues, Soul and Black Identity*

7. Joyce Ladner, Assistant Professor Sociology, University of Southern Illinois (Black Women and the Ghetto; Black Student Protest; The Black Family), Fall Seminar: *The Socialization of the Black Child*

8. Daulton Lewis, B.A. Degree Sociology, Wesleyan University, Southern Education Foundation Intern

9. William Strickland, Consultant, CBS; Lecturer, Department of History, Columbia University (Political History of Racism; Politics and the Black Urban Community), Fall Seminar: *Racism and American Social Analysis*

10. Sterling Stuckey, Ph.D. Candidate, Assistant Professor, Northwestern University. (The Slave Experience; Black Americans and Africa)

60.

Teaching Black Studies for Social Change*

James A. Banks

The argument is advanced that effective Black studies programs must be based on a sound and clearly articulated rationale in order to result in effective student learning. It is suggested that the main goal of Black studies should be to aid students in developing their abilities to engage in reflective decision-making in order that personal and social problems can be solved. Furthermore such decision-making can also prepare the student for participation in the process of public police, construction. In order for effective student development, vital changes in instructional techniques and curricula are proposed.

With the emergence of the Black revolt of the sixties, Black people began to shape and perpetuate a new identity. "Black Power" and "Black is Beautiful" were rallying cries of this identity search. Blacks rejected many of the components of the dominant white culture, and searched for elements out of which a new identity could be formed. Such elements include intensified racial pride and cohesiveness, a search for power, and an attempt to identify cultural roots in Africa. African dashikis, tikis, Afro hair styles, and Swahilian phrases emerged as new cultural components.

Written history is an important part of a people's heritage. As the Black revolt gained momentum, demands were made to include the roles blacks played in shaping American destiny. Organized interest groups pressured school districts into banning predominantly white history books from the schools. When the pressure on school districts mounted, publishers were encouraged to include more Blacks in schoolbooks.

In response to demands for Black history and Black studies, educational institutions at all levels have made attempts to institute Black studies programs.

Despite these attempts, few have been sound because the coals of Black studies remain confused, ambiguous, and conflicting. Many Black studies programs have been structured without careful planning and clear rationales and this is understandable when we realize that goals for Black studies programs are often voiced by experts of many different persuasions and ideologies. Larry Cuban, a leader in ethnic education, argues that "the only legitimate goals for ethnic content [in the public schools]...must emphasize a *balanced* view of the American past and present..." (emphasis added). Nathan Hare, another innovator in ethnic studies, believes that Black studies should be taught from a *Black perspective* and emphasize the struggles

---

* Portions of this paper were presented at the First Congress of Blacks in Higher Education, University of Texas at Austin, April 5-7, 1972.

Parts of this paper are based on the author's, "Teaching Black History With A Focus on Decision-Making," *Social Education*, Vol. 35 (November 1971): 740-745, ff. 820-21. Reprinted with permission of the National Council for the Social Studies and James A. Banks.

and aspirations of Black people. On the other hand, many Black activists feel that the main goal of Black studies should be to equip Black students with an ideology, which is imperative for their liberation. Some Blacks who belong to the over-thirty generation, such as Martin Kilson and Bayard Rustin, feel that education designed to develop a commitment to a fixed ideology is antithetical to sound scholarship and has no place in public institutions. Writes Kilson, "...I don't believe it is the proper or most useful function of a [school] to train ideological or political organizers of whatever persuasion. A [school's] primary function is to impart skills, techniques, and special habits of learning, to its students. The student must be free to decide himself on the ideological application of his training."

As should be expected, classroom teachers are puzzled about the Black studies and have serious questions about *who* can teach Black studies because of the disagreement over goals among curriculum experts and social scientists. Needless to say, effective teaching strategies and sound criteria for judging materials cannot be formulated until goals are identified and explicitly stated. Unless a sound rationale for Black studies programs can be stated and new approaches to their instruction implemented, these programs are quite likely to fail.

Without *both* new goals and novel strategies, Black studies may become just another fleeting fad. Isolated facts about Crispus Attucks stimulate the intellect about as much as isolated facts about Abraham Lincoln. In this paper, a rationale is offered for Black studies programs as well as an illustration of how Black studies can be taught as an *integral* part of a modern social studies curriculum. The illustration is spiral, conceptual, and interdisciplinary, and emphasizes decision-making, and social action skills.

The Purpose of Black History Instruction

The goal of Black history should be to help students develop *the ability to make reflective decisions so that they can resolve personal problems and, through social action, influence public policy and develop a sense of political efficacy.* If Black Americans are to be liberated from physical and psychological captivity, they must attain effective decision-making and social action skills that can be used to solve personal problems and simultaneously influence public policy. Thus, the ultimate goal of social studies for Black students should be effective *political activation. While social action skills are* needed by *all* students, they are especially needed by Black students because many are physically and psychologically victimized by institutional racism. Only when an individual develops the ability to make reflective decisions, can he act effectively to free himself from oppression and colonialism. Poverty, political powerlessness, low self-esteem, consumer exploitation, institutional racism, and political alienation are the kinds of problems which social studies can aid Blacks in realizing through effective political action.

Assumptions

A general assumption underlying the aforementioned goal of the Black studies program is based on the assumption that man will always face personal and social problems, and that all citizens should participate in public policy decision-making. The focus for the Black studies programs recommended here is not only grounded in a cultural pluralistic ideology, but also maximum participation of all citizens in the construction of public policy. The assumption advocates cultural diversity, rather than assimilation. It rejects elitism and suggests that academic specialists should facilitate the realization of goals and values shaped by all groups within a society.

An idea also implicit in this presentation is that individuals are not born with the ability to make *reflective* decisions, but that decision-making, consists of a set of skills which can be systematical taught. Finally, a guiding principle used as a point of departure is that man can identify and clarify his *values*, and that he can be trained to reflect upon problems before attempting to solve them.

Since it has been suggested that students should develop the ability to make reflective decisions, it is necessary to distinguish between a *reflective* and a *non-reflective* decision. This distinction should become explicit in the next section of this paper.

The careful reader may raise several legitimate questions about the idea expressed thus far and wonder about the consequences for a society in much individuals are free to make uncoerced decisions which may, for example, isolate norms essential for the survival of the group. In principle, a *social actor* who arrives at some decision using this *process* may decide to murder all of his perceived enemies. Such a possibility encourages the administration of other underlying principles not previously identified. For instance, social actors involved in decision-making using the *process* advocated will act in ways that will perpetuate the cultural identity and integrity of the group, and the creation of a humane and just society. Furthermore it is suggested that most persons who habitually violate humane values do so primarily because they are the victims of a society, which perpetuates myths about the inferiority and superiority of different groups. These persons have confused values, and tend to act before rationally reflecting upon the possible consequences of their actions. Thus such actions are impetuous, impulsive, and non-reflective.

Social change is an implicit characteristic of reflective decision-making since goals and values which become obsolete and dysfunctional, will be altered through massive and effective social action.

The social studies curriculum advocated could possibly prevent chaos and destructive instability within a society, while simultaneously providing, means and methods whereby oppressed groups and new generations can shape their own destinies, use those aspects of traditional society which are consistent with their needs, and if necessary, create new, legitimate life-styles and values. *What is legitimate, normative and valued is subject to reconstruction in each new generation.* Each generation, however, can use those aspects of the past which are functional for current needs and purposes. Thus, the approach presented is characterized by stability and change.

Essential Components of Decision-Making

Knowledge is one essential component of the decision-making process. There are many kinds and ways of attaining knowledge. Reflective decision-making involves the use of the scientific method in attaining knowledge. Knowledge used to make reflective decisions must also be *powerful and widely applicable in order to insure accurate predictions*. There are several categories of knowledge which vary in predictive capacity and the ability to help us to organize our observations, and thus to make decisions.

Factual knowledge, which consists of specific empirical statements about limited phenomena, is the lowest level of knowledge, and has the least predictive capacity. *Concepts* are words or phrases which enable us to categorize or classify a large class of observations, and thus to reduce the complexity of our social environment. Because of their structure and function, concepts in and of themselves do not possess predictive value. However, *generalizations*, which state the relationship between concepts or variables, enable us to predict behavior; the predictive capacity of generalizations vary directly with their degree of applicability and amount of empirical support. Generalizations which describe a large class of behavior and which have been widely verified are the most useful for making predictions and thus decisions. *Theory* is the highest form of knowledge, *and is the most useful for making predictions*. A theory consists of a deductive system of logically interrelated generalizations. Although no grand or all inclusive theories exist in the social sciences as in the physical sciences, numerous partial or middle range social science theories exist, such as Durkheim's theory of suicide and Allport's theory of prejudice.

Reflective decision-making involves the use of the *scientific method* in order to derive higher level generalizations and theories. The most predictive generalizations and theories are those which are related to the key or *organizing* concepts in the social sciences. The identification of *key* concepts within the social sciences enables the decision-maker to generate the most powerful generalizations in the behavioral sciences, and those that can make the greatest contribution to the resolution of personal and social problems.

Students must not only master higher levels of knowledge in order to make reflective decisions, they must also learn to view human behavior from the perspectives of all of the social and behavioral sciences. A social studies curriculum that focuses on decision-making and the Black experience must be *interdisciplinary*; it should incorporate *key* (or organizing) concepts from all of the social sciences. Knowledge from any one discipline is insufficient for decision-making involving, complex issues such as poverty, institutionalized racism and oppression. To take effective social action on a social issue such as poverty, students must view it from the perspectives of geography, history, sociology, economics, political science, psychology, and anthropology.

While higher level, interdisciplinary knowledge is necessary for sound decision-making it is not sufficient. Students must also be able to identify, clarify, and analyze their own values. *Value inquiry* and *clarification* are essential components of a sound social studies curriculum that incorporates the Black experience. Students should be taught how to relate the concepts and generalizations which they derive to their values, and thus to make decisions. Decision-making consists essentially of affirming a course of action after synthesizing knowledge and clarifying values. Students should also be provided opportunities whereby they can *act* on some of the decisions that they make. "Under no circumstances should the school, deliberately or by default, continue to maintain the barriers between itself and the other elements of society." Social action and participation activities are necessary components of a conceptually-oriented, decision-making, social studies curriculum which incorporates the Black experience.

The Structure of History

We must identify the key concepts within the disciplines and their related generalizations to plan a curriculum which focuses on decision-making and incorporates

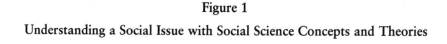

Figure 1

Understanding a Social Issue with Social Science Concepts and Theories

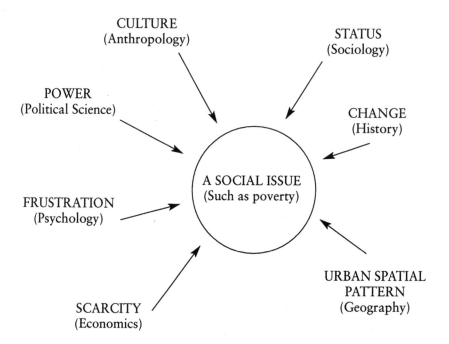

This figure illustrates how a social issue such as poverty can be sufficiently understood and therefore reflectively acted upon only after the social actor has viewed it with the concepts and theories from a number of social science disciplines. Any one discipline gives only a partial understanding of a social problem or issue. Thus, the social studies programs must be interdisciplinary.

the Black experience. Identifying the key concepts within history poses special problems. While the behavioral sciences use unique conceptual frameworks in viewing, human behavior, the uniqueness of history stems from the fact that it views behavior which has taken place in the *past*, and stresses the *totality* of man's past, and uses a modified mode of scientific inquiry. While the sociologist and the political scientist are primarily interested in human interaction and *power* respectively, the historian may be, and sometimes is, interested in how each of these concepts is exemplified in man's past behavior. History, then, is an interdisciplinary field since historians, in principle, are interested in all aspects of man's past. It is difficult to speak about unique historical concepts. Every discipline makes use of the *historical perspective*, and has historical components. When a sociologist studies *norms* and *sanctions* during the period of slavery, and the economist describes how the slaves produced *goods* and *services*, they are both studying, history.

While history, in principle, is concerned with the totality of man's past, in practice history is largely *political* because most of the concepts which it uses, such as *rev-*

Figure 2

Studying the Black Experience from an Interdisciplinary
Perspective with an Historical Framework

Discipline	Analytical Concepts	Key Questions
Sociology	*Values, Norms*	What unique value and norms have emerged within the Blackcommunity?
Political Science	*Power*	What power relationships have existed within the Black community?
Anthropology	*Acculturation*	What kind of culture exchange has taken place between Blacks and whites in the United States?
Psychology	*Self-Concept*	How has the Blackexperience affected the Black man's feelings andperceptions of himself?
Geography	*Region*	Where have Blacks usually lived within our cities and why?
Economics	*Goods, Services, Production*	What goods and services have been produced in the Black community? Why?
History	*Change*	How has the Black community changed in recent years?

olution, government, war, and *nationalism* belong to political science. History as it is usually written focuses on great political events and leaders, and largely ignores the experiences of the common man, non-Western man, ethnic groups, and key concepts from most of the other social sciences, geography. *However, since history, in principle, is concerned with the totality of man's past, it is potentially the most interdisciplinary of all of the social disciplines and for that reason can serve as an excellent framework for incorporating the Black experience into the curriculum from an interdisciplinary perspective.*

Although historians have largely ignored concepts from most of the behavioral sciences, and the struggles and aspirations of the common and Third World Man, a modern program in historical studies can and should incorporate these knowledge components. In recent years, historians have become aware of how limited and parochial written history is, and have taken steps, but still inadequate ones, to include both the contributions and struggles of ethnic groups in their accounts and to use more concepts from the behavioral sciences. Stanley M. Elkins, in his classic study of slavery, uses a number of psychological concepts and theories to explain the behavior of the slave and master. The "trend toward more highly interdisciplinary history will undoubtedly continue as historians become more familiar with behavioral science concepts.

Incorporating the Black Experience into a Conceptual Curriculum

To illustrate how a program in historical studies can be *interdisciplinary and incorporate* the experiences of Black Americans, seven key concepts have been identified. These concepts can be taught key concepts have been identified. These concepts can be taught within a historical framework, and related to the organization of generalizations, and sub-generalizations related to Black History. When the sub-generalizations in our example relate exclusively to the Black experience, a sound social studies program should include content samples that are related to man's total past, including the experiences of Native Americans, Puerto Rican Americans, Chicanos, Asian-Americans and white Americans.

Key Concept:

CONFLICT (History)

Organizing Generalization: Throughout history, conflict has developed between various racial and ethnic groups.

Sub-Generalizations:

1. Violence and conflict occurred on the slave ships.
2. Several Black leaders led slave revolts during slavery in which Blacks and whites were killed.
3. When Blacks began their migration to Northern cities near the turn of the century, violent racial confrontations occurred in major urban areas.
4. During the Black Revolt of the 1960's, racial rebellions took place in a number of United States cities which resulted in the murder of many Black citizens.

Key Concept:

CULTURE (Anthropology)

Organizing Generalization: Many different racial and ethnic groups have contributed to and enriched American culture.

Sub-Generalizations:

1. Skilled Black slaves helped to construct and decorate the Southern Mansions.
2. The slave songs made a significant impact on American music.
3. The blues and jazz forms of music created by Black Americans constitute America's most unique musical heritage.

4. The literature written by Black Americans during the Harlem Renaissance contributed greatly to American culture.

5. Black American art expresses the poignant experiences of Black people in highly creative ways.

Key Concept:

RACISM (Sociology)

Organizing Generalization: All Non-white groups have been the victims of racism and discrimination in America.

Sub-Generalizations:

1. During slavery, Blacks were not permitted to learn to read, to form groups without a white being, present, or to testify in court against a white person.

2. The "Black Codes" that were established after the Emancipation Proclamation was issued, created in many ways, a new kind of "slavery" in the South.

3. For many years, legal segregation in the South forced Blacks to attend inferior schools, denied them the ballot, and sanctioned segregation in public accommodation and transportation facilities.

4. Blacks still experience discrimination in all phases of American life, including education, the administration of justice and employment.

Key Concept:

CAPITALISM (Economics)

Organizing Generalization: In a capitalistic society, powerless groups are unable to compete equally for jobs and rewards.

Sub-Generalizations:

1. During slavery, Blacks were forced to work without wages so that whites could make large profits from Southern crops.

2. After the Emancipation Proclamation was issued, "freed" Blacks were forced to work in a sharecropping system which cheated and exploited them.

3. When Blacks migrated to Northern and Western cities, they were the last hired and the first fired.

4. Today, many Blacks are unable to find steady and meaningful employment because they control few production industries.

Key Concept:

POWER (Political Science)

Organizing Generalization: Individuals are more likely to influence public policy and to bring about social change when working in groups than when working alone.

Sub-Generalizations:

1. During slavery, Blacks, by working cooperatively, were able to help many slaves escape with a system known as the "Underground Railroad."

2. By gaining group support, civil rights organizations such as the NAACP and CORE were able to end lynchings, and to reduce legal discrimination in such areas as employment, education and transportation.

3. The Black Revolt of the 1960's was able to reduce legal discrimination in such areas as employment, law, education, and transportation.

The Nation of Islam has been able to provide educational and job opportunities for many Blacks.

Key Concept:

SELF-CONCEPT (Psychology)

Organizing Generalization: Self-Concept highly influences an individual's perceptions of the world and affects his behavior.

Sub-Generalizations:

1. The slave masters were able to convince many Blacks that they were less than human; the success of the slave masters in this task helped to reduce Black resistance to slavery.

2. Many slaves never accepted the views of themselves which were perpetuated by the slave masters and ran away of participated in slave revolts.

3. The movement led by Marcus Garvey in the 1920's enabled many Blacks to think more highly of their race and to develop group pride.

4. The Black Revolt of the 1960's caused many Blacks to feel more positively toward their race and to protest vigorous for their rights.

Key Concept:

REGION (Geography)

Organizing Generalization: Every region is unique in its own way.

Sub-Generalizations:

1. The central area of the city where most Blacks live is usually characterized by substandard housing, higher prices, and public officials who are largely unaccountable to their constituents.

2. Prices for goods and services are usually higher in the central area of the city where most live, than in outlying areas.

3. Police protection, city services, and public schools are usually inferior in the areas of a city where Black populations are concentrated.

4. Culture elements that are unique to the Black community can usually be found within a designated area of a city; often these culture elements do not diffuse outward to other metropolitan regions.

Once a teacher or curriculum committee has identified the key concepts and generalizations "which can serve as a framework for a social studies curriculum or unit, and stated sub-generalizations that relate to the Black experience, he (or the committee) can then identify the materials and teaching strategies which are necessary to help the students derive the concepts and their related generalizations. The seven key concepts and generalizations stated above can be taught at every level within a spiral conceptual curriculum and developed at increasing levels of complexity with different content samples. A conceptual curriculum should constitute the social studies program from kindergarten to grade 12.

To assure that every sub-generalization identify in the initial stages of planning is adequately developed within a unit, the teacher can divide a sheet of paper in half and list the concepts and sub-generalizations on one side of it and the strategies and materials needed to teach the ideas on the other half.

Teaching the Historical Method
(History as Process)

Because the historian's method is much more unique than substantive concepts and generalizations, it is important to teach students the historical method (process), as well as concepts related to historical conclusions (products). History is a *process* as well as a body of knowledge. A historian's view of the past is influenced by the availability of evidence, his personal biases, purposes for writing, and the society and times in which he lives and writes. Although history reflects the biases of the writer, it is often taught in school as a body of truth not to be questioned, criticized, or modified. Such a parochial approach to the teaching of history stems largely from classroom teachers' confusion about the nature of history, and the widely held belief that history contributes to the development of patriotism.

Much confusion about the nature of history would be eliminated if teachers distinguished *historical statements from past events*. The historical statement, often referred to as the historical fact, is quite different from the actual event. The event itself has disappeared, never to occur again. An infinite number of statements can be made about any past event. Historical data related to the Black experience constitute a goldmine of information which can be used to teach students about the nature and writing of history. This kind of knowledge will not only help students to become more adept decision-makers, but more intelligent consumers of history. Conflicting accounts of slavery, the Civil War, and the rebellions which took place in our cities in the sixties can be used to teach the concept of *historical bias*. To help students see the regional influences on written history, the teacher can have them compare the treatment of slavery in different textbooks as illustrated in the two accounts following, one of which is from a state history of Mississippi and the other from a junior high school Black history text:

Account 1

Slave Treatment. While there were some incidents involving the abusing of slaves, public opinion and state law generally assured the slaves of good treatment. Plantation owners usually cautioned their overseers against using brutal practices. Naturally, there were some abuses on large plantations... Most people, however, favored kind treatment of slaves...

Account 2

Under the slave codes, blacks were not allowed to own property or weapons. They could not form groups without a white person present. They could not buy or sell goods, or leave the plantation without permission of their master. In towns and cities, blacks were required to be off the streets by a specified hour each night. A slave could not testify in court against a white person. A slave who was charged with a

Figure 3

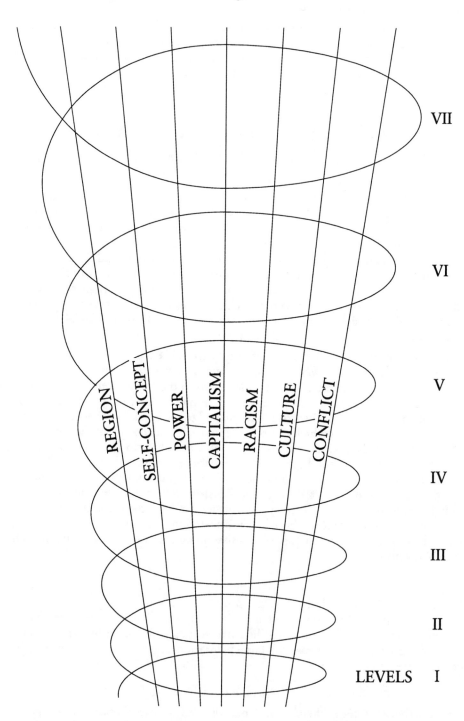

This diagram illustrates how information related to the Black experience can be organized around key concepts and taught at successive levels at an increasing degree of complexity.

Figure 4

Key Ideas and Teaching Strategies

Key Ideas	Activities
Racism Key Generalization: All non-white groups have been the victims of institutionalized racism in America. Sub-Generalization: Blacks have experienced discrimination in all phases of American life, including education, the administration of justice, and employment.	1. Reading selections from *South Town, North Town* and *Whose Town?* by Lorenz Graham. 2. Discussing the discrimination that the Williams family experienced in this story and how they coped with it. 3. Discussing the discrimination that David Williams experienced in school and how he reacted to it. 4. Viewing a filmstrip on Black slavery, and listing ways in which it was a form of discrimination. 5. Finding copies of such documents as the *Slave Codes* and the *Grandfather Clause* and role-playing how they affected the lives of Blacks. 6. Compiling statistics on the number of Blacks who were lynched during the early years of the 1900s. 7. Reading and discussing accounts of the *discrimination* which Blacks experienced in employment, education, and in the administration of justice today.

crime against a white person was therefore unable to defend himself. Any slave who violated the laws was likely to be severely punished, perhaps by death.

Questions

1. How are these two accounts alike?

2. How are they different?

3. Why do you think that they are different?

4. Who do you think wrote the first account? The second account? Why?

5. Which account do you think is more accurate? Why?

6. Which author supports his statements with facts? Give specific examples.

Figure 5
Key Ideas and Teaching Strategies

Key Ideas	Activities
Racism Key Generalization: Many different racial and ethnic groups have contributed to and enriched American culture. Sub-Generalization: The literature written by Black Americans during the Harlem Renaissance contributed greatly to American culture.	1. Reading "Montage of a Dream Deferred" by Langston Hughes. 2. Discussing what the author means by "deferred dream." 3. Discussing the dreams of Black people which have been deferred and why. 4. Reading, "If We Must Die" by Claude McKay. 5. Discussing the racial rebellions which took place near the turn of the century and the ways in which the two poems are social commentaries about racial conflict. 6. Reading "Incident" by Countee Cullen. Discussing how the child felt when he first came to Baltimore and why. 7. Discussing why and how his feelings changed. 8. Discussing ways in which the Harlem Renaissance poets expressed their feelings, emotions, and aspirations in their writings, and how they contributed to American literature and culture.

7. Read other accounts on the treatment of slaves and write in your own words about how the slaves were treated. How do your conclusions compare with the accounts written by the two authors above?

The Value Component of Decision-Making

While higher level, scientific knowledge is necessary for reflective decision-making, it is not sufficient. To make reflective decision, the social actor must also identify and clarify his *values*, and relate them to the knowledge that he has derived through inquiry.

Because of the immense racial problems within our society that are rooted in value confusion, the school should play a significant role in helping students to identify and clarify their values, and in making value choices intelligently. While the school has a tremendous responsibility to help students make moral choices reflectively, there is abundant evidence that educators have largely failed to help students deal with moral issues intelligently.

Some teachers treat value problems like the invisible man; i.e., they deny their existence. They assume that if students get all of the "facts" straight, they can resolve racial problems. Such teachers may be said to practice the cult of false objectivity. Other teachers use an evasion strategy; when value problems arise in the classroom, they try to change the subject to a safer topic. Probably the most frequently used approach to value education in the elementary and high school is the inculcation of values which are considered "right" by adults, or the indoctrination of these values. Teachers who use this method assume that adults know what the "correct" values are for all times and for children from all cultural groups. Such values as justice, truth, freedom, honesty, equality and love are taught with legendary heroes, stories, rituals and patriot songs. This approach to value education is unsound for several reasons. It assumes that most value conflicts and problems result because children are unable to distinguish "good" from "bad" values. However, this is not the case. Children can rather easily distinguish the good from the bad. Most value problems result because students often must choose between two goods. When teachers use didactic methods to teach children contradictory but equally "good" values, their conflicts are intensified when they must choose between two goods.

Teachers should help students to develop a *method* (or process) of deriving and clarifying their values rather than teach them a set of predetermined values. *This is the only approach to value education which is consistent with a cultural pluralistic ideology and that is educationally sound.* Perhaps no more serious value questions and problems are raised in the classroom than during a study of the Black experience. Black students have important questions about the value of Blackness, their identity, and about effective strategies to use in releasing themselves from institutionalized racism and colonization. Below, part of a value inquiry model is developed which present in detail, a plan to be used in teaching the Black experience in a manner which will enable students to *identify, clarify and to reflectively derive their values.*

Value Inquiry Model

- a. Recognizing Value Problems
- b. Describing Value Relevant Behavior
- c. Naming Values Exemplified by Behavior
- d. Determining Value Conflicts
- e. Hypothesizing About Sources of Values
- f. Naming, Value Alternatives
- g. Hypothesizing About the Consequences of Values
- h. Choosing (Declaring Value Preferences)
- i. Stating Reasons, Sources and Consequences of Personal Value Choice(s)

For value inquiry lessons, the teacher may use case studies clipped from the daily newspaper, such as incidents involving police attacks on the Black Panthers, or cases related to the current "bussing" controversy. Children's literature, photographs, role-playing activities, and open-ended stories related to these kinds of incidents can also be effectively used. In using a case study related to the Black Revolt of the sixties, for example, the teacher can ask the students these kinds of questions:

1. What was the problem in this case?
2. What does the behavior of the persons involved tell us about what was important to them?
3. How do you think that the values of the demonstrators differed from those who were in power?
4. What are other values that the persons in the case could have endorsed?
5. What were the possible consequences of the values held by the demonstrators?
6. What would you have done if your life experience had been similar to the experiences of the persons who protested?
7. What might have been the consequences of your beliefs?
8. Could you have lived with those consequences?

During value inquiry lessons, the teacher should be careful not to condemn values which are inconsistent with his beliefs. This is not to suggest that the teacher should remain neutral on value issues, but rather that he should not declare a value preference until the students have expressed their value choices. Unless the teacher creates a classroom atmosphere that will allow and encourage students to express their true beliefs, value inquiry will simply become a game in which students will try to guess what responses the teacher wants them to make. Even the bigoted white student or the psychologically captivated Black student should be able to express his beliefs freely and openly in the classroom. Beliefs that are unexpressed cannot be rationally examined. While we must eliminate racism in America in order to survive the challenges of the twenty-first century, students must be able to reflectively analyze racism and its effects before they can develop a commitment to its eradication. It should be stressed that this commitment must come from the student; *it cannot be imposed by the teacher.*

Providing Opportunities for Social Action

People throughout the United States are victims of colonialism, institutional racism, poverty and political powerlessness. *When the teacher identifies concepts and generalizations from the social sciences, he should select those that will aid Students in making decisions and taking actions to help eliminate these problems.* This is absolutely imperative if the social studies curriculum is going to help to liberate Black people and other oppressed groups. After they have mastered higher level knowledge related to these problems, and analyzed and clarified their values, the teacher can ask students to list possible actions which can be taken to eradicate problems in their school and community, and to predict the possible consequences of each alternative course of action. Alternatives and consequences that the students state should be realistic and based on knowledge that they have mastered during the earlier phase of the unit. They should be intelligent predictive statements and not ignorant guesses or wishful thinking.

Racism, drug abuse, forced bussing, the closing of Black schools, class stratification, theft and arson are the kinds of problems which schools have on which students can take concerted action. Other social action projects, especially for more mature students, can take place in the wider community. Social action may take the form of observation, participation or leadership. The school can work with civil rights groups and political organizations to involve students in meaningful and purposeful social action activities. The levels of involvement in such activities can be diverse. *The primary purpose of such activities should be to provide students with opportunities to develop a sense of political efficacy and not necessarily to provide community services*, although both goals can be attained in the most effective types of projects.

Student participation in social action activities within our society is not without precedence. However, the most dramatic and effective social action by American students has usually been undertaken by black and white college students. During the Black Revolt of the 1960s, students comprised one of the most cogent and effective components. The Black Revolt of the 1960s was signaled when four Black college students sat down at an "all white" lunch counteracts at a Woolworth's store in Greensboro, North Carolina on February 1, 1960. Throughout the Black Revolt of the 1960's, students remained active and influential. They helped to desegregate restaurants, interstate transportation, schools and swimming pools with such tactics as sit-ins, freedom-rides, and swim-ins. Student effectiveness in the Black Revolt of the sixties is one of the most dramatic indications of the potential of student power in America. Protests by students in the sixties also resulted in enlightened curriculum reform in public schools and colleges.

In discussing ways in which students have participated in social action and protest, we do not mean to suggest that all or even most of their actions were maximumly effective and undertaken after reflective thought. However, we must stress the fact that students in the past have become involved in important social issues in the community and nation whether or not the school facilitated that involvement. Schools did little, if anything, to facilitate the involvement of students in the actions which are reviewed here. *The involvement of students in social action must become institutionalized within the social studies curriculum so that their actions can become both more effective and thoughtfully directed.* Some of the student action that occurred on our college campuses was irresponsible and irrational. A social action focused social studies curriculum *may* have made such actions more effective and significant. In a new publication, the National Council for the Social Studies stresses the need for educators to involve students in social action projects:

> Extensive involvement by students of all ages in the activities of their community is...essential. Many of these activities may be in problem areas held, at least by some, to be controversial; many will not be. The involvement may take the form of observation or information seeking, such as field trips, attending meetings, and interviews. It may take the form of political campaigning, community service or improvement, or even responsible demonstration. The school should not only provide channels for such activities, but build them into the design of its social studies program, kindergarten through grade twelve.

Training Teachers for a
Social Action Curriculum

The most important variable for the successful implementation of the kind of Black studies program proposed in this essay is the classroom teacher. For teachers to help Black students to develop proficiency in decision-making and social action skills, some significant chances must be made in teacher education. Teachers must be prepared to understand the nature of social knowledge and the structures of the various social science disciplines. Teachers who are unfamiliar with the limitations and assumptions of social knowledge cannot intelligently teach students reflective decision-making skills. Because many teachers are unacquainted with the sociology of knowledge, they teach historical "facts" as absolutes and tentative anthropological findings as conclusive theories. Teachers often elevate social knowledge to a status far beyond that which is warranted, and therefore must be instructed about the *tentative, limited and culturally biased state of social knowledge.*

The meaning of *objectivity* and how it is derived must be an important component in the education of social studies teachers. Statements in history are especially defined as objective if white established historians can agree on them. Many myths, such as "Columbus discovered America," and "Corrupted Northern whites and ignorant Blacks *ruled* the South during reconstruction," have been perpetuated by white "scholarly" historians. In recent years, historians have been challenged by Blacks and other ethnic minority groups to write different versions of history which are based on new assumptions about Third World peoples and their contributions to American life.

Teachers must learn how social science reflects the norms, values and goals of the ruling and powerful groups in society, and how it validates those belief systems which are functional for groups in power and dysfunctional for oppressed and powerless groups. Research which is antithetical to the interests of ruling and powerful groups is generally ignored by the scientific community and the society which supports it. The fact explains why L.S.B. Leakey's seminal findings about man's African origins have never been popular among established anthropologists and within the larger society. On the other hand, for generations historians elevated Ulrich B. Phillips' racist descriptions of the nature of slavery to the status of conclusive truth.

Today, many myths about Blacks which are invented by white social scientists are perpetuated and institutionalized. Moynihan's disastrous study of the Black family. Jensen's work on Black-White intelligence, and Banfield's distorted and myotic interpretations of the Black experience are legitimized and given a wide hearing in prestigious white journals in respected universities. Myths and distortions such as those invented by Phillips, Jensen, Moynihan and Banfield were institutionalized in America because they are consistent with the value systems and self-interests of powerful and ruling groups. Jensen would have probably been ridiculed if he had argued that Blacks were intellectually superior to whites (the evidence for either argument is highly inconclusive). However, it appears that his research was widely publicized and defended by scholars because it validated the ideas and stereotypes which a large number of whites have of the Black man and his culture.

Teachers must be acutely aware of the ways in which social science has been twisted and distorted to serve the self-interests of ruling and dominant groups if they are to become effective teachers of Blacks and other suppressed groups within our society. Many teachers perpetuate the historical and social science myths that they have learned in school and that are pervasive in textbooks because they are unaware of the racist assumptions on which social science research is often based. Much information in textbooks is designed to support the status quo and to keep powerless ethnic groups at the lower rungs of the social ladder.

Teachers often tell students that Columbus "discovered" America, yet the Native Americans were here centuries before Columbus. The Columbus myth in one sense denies the Native American child his past and thus his identity. Many teachers believe that Lincoln was the great emancipator of Black people; yet he supported a move to deport Blacks to Africa and issued the Emancipation Proclamation, in his own words, "as a military necessity" to weaken the Confederacy. Primary grade teachers often try to convince the lack child that the policeman is his friends. Many ethnic minority students know from experience that some policemen are their enemies. Only when teachers get a truly liberal education about the nature of science and American society will they be able to correct such myths and distortions and make the school experience more realistic and meaningful for *all* students.

To become effective teachers of political and social action, teachers must be provided opportunities whereby they can sue social science concepts and theories which they have mastered to resolve social issues in ways which are consistent with their values. Teachers should also be provided opportunities of social action in which they can implement some of the decisions which they make. It would be unrealistic to expect teachers to fully appreciate the importance of social and political action projects if during their training program they are not given opportunities to participate in such activities themselves. Action projects involving teachers can be provided in professional methods courses. Professor Robert L. Green has written about the necessity to involve education students in social action projects.

The first two years of teacher training might parallel the VISTA or Peace Corps experience of many youngsters. Students should spend less time in the classroom and more time in field projects with racial minorities and the poor. Internships with such individuals as Cesar Chavez and the Rev. Jesse Jackson, with groups like the Black poor in Green County, Alabama, and with institutions such as the Martin Luther King, Jr. Memorial Center and the Institute of the Black World should be structured for students early in their training programs. Two years of academic coursework in the classroom could well be enough. Students should spend more time learning about people from diverse backgrounds and becoming more humanistic by actually participating in work projects with urban and rural residents from all walks of life and from diverse racial backgrounds.

The social studies methods course must take students out into the community not only to *study* problems but to actively participate in their resolution. Such action will not only equip teachers with the skills which they need to help children become effective change agents, but it can result in social changes that will make this a more humane and just society.

References

Banks, James A. (1969) "A Content Analysis of the Black American in Textbooks," *Social Education*, Vol. 33 (December): 954-957, ff. 963.

Banks, James A. (1972) "Imperatives in Ethnic Minority Education," *Phi Delta Kappan*, Vol. 53 (January): 269.

Banks, James A. (1970) Teaching the Black Experience: Methods and Materials (Belmont, California: Fearon Publishers).

Banks, James A., with contributions by Ambrose A. Clegg, Jr. (1970) *March Toward Freedom: A History of Black Americans* (Belmont, CA: Fearon Publishers), p. 16

————, with contributions by Ambrose A. Clegg, Jr. (1973) *Teaching Strategies for the Social Studies: Inquiry, Valuing and Decision-Making* (Reading, MA: Addison-Wesley Publishing Company, in press 1973), Chapter 12, "Valuing Inquiry Modes and Strategies."

Bettersworth, John K. (1964) *Mississippi Yesterday and Today* (Austin, TX: Steck-Vaughn), p. 143. This book is currently used in the state of Mississippi.

Cuban, Larry. (1971) "Black History, Negro History, and White Folk," *Teaching Social Studies to Culturally Different Children* (Reading, MA: Addison-Wesley Publishing Company), p. 318.

Elkins, Stanley M. (1963) *Slavery: A Problem in American Institutional and Intellectual Life* (New York: Grosset and Dunlap).

Green, Robert L. (1972) "Racism in American Education," *Phi Delta Kappan*, Vol. 53 (January): 276.

Hare, Nathan. (1969) "The Teaching of Black History and Culture in the Secondary Schools," *Social Education*, Vol. 33 (April): 388.

Hunt, Maurice P. and Lawrence E. Metcalf. (1968) *Teaching High School Social Studies: Second Edition* (New York: Harper and Row), Chapter 6.

Kilson, Martin. (1969) "Black Studies: A Plea for Perspective," *The Crisis* (October): 30.

NCSS Task Force (Gary Manson, Gerald Marker, Anna Ochoa, and Jan Tucker) "Guidelines for Social Studies Curriculums," (Washington, DC: National Council for the Social Studies, unpublished second draft), p. 17.

NCSS Task Force on Curriculum Guidelines (Garry Manson, Anna Ochoa, Gerald Marker, and Jan Tucker) (1971) *Social Studies Curriculum Guidelines* (Washington, DC: National Council for the Social Studies), p. 15.

Raths, Louis E., Merrill Harmin and Sidney B. Simon. (1966) *Values and Teaching: Working With Values in the Classroom* (Columbus, OH: Charles E. Merrill Publishing Company), p. 28.

Scriven, Michael. (1971) "The Social Studies in the 21st Century: What is Needed?" A paper presented at the 50th Annual Meeting of the National Council for the Social Studies, New York, New York, November 24.

Sizemore, Barbara A. (1972) "Social Science and Education For a Black Identity," *Black Self-Concept: Implications for Education and Social Science* (New York: McGraw-Hill), pp. 141-170.

61.

Black Studies and Africana Studies Curriculum Model in the United States

William A. Little, Carolyn M. Leonard,
and Edward Crosby

Introduction

The field of Black Studies/Africana Studies across the United States has culminated into a multifaceted discipline. The Black Studies/Africana Studies Curriculum was developed: (1) to ensure that students were guaranteed a certain body of knowledge; (2) to provide a vision and intellectual foundation for further growth and development in the area of Black Studies/Africana Studies; and (3) to identify intellectual stages of progression toward a structural organized course of study. The authors of this article examined the historical development of Black Studies/Africana Studies, and other scholars contributed to and assisted in fine tuning the curriculum model.* Additionally, the authors present the development of an interdisciplinary discipline model. First, an overview of the many obstacles impeding the establishment of Black Studies/Africana Studies programs and departments on university campuses nationwide is provided along with the functions of many Black Studies/Africana Studies Scholars. Secondly, academic discipline as a field of study, along with various approaches (both traditional and non-traditional) for developing fields of study are examined as a means to establishing the foundation upon which the rationale for the Black Studies/Africana Studies Holistic curriculum was structured. Thirdly, the nature of the debate surrounding the establishment of a theoretical and philosophical framework for a Black Studies/Africana Studies program is provided, detailing various scholarly views. Next, the field of Black Studies/Africana Studies as a discipline is presented. The framework from which it was designed and developed along with the Black Studies/Africana Studies curriculum model that have evolved over the years are provided. Finally, the Black Studies/Africana Studies Holistic curriculum model is presented along with a thorough description of each of its subfields.

* The NCBS Curriculum Research project was funded in part by the Ford Foundation.

Historical Overview

Black Studies/Africana Studies emerged as a new academic field of study at the height of the social unrest that occurred in the United States during the 1960s. In response to students' demands for curricula that would address the African-American experience, a number of colleges and universities created Black Studies courses, programs, and in some instances, departments. Black Studies/Africana Studies represented a direct response to the omissions and distortions of the African and African university curricula.

Working in a discipline that was born out of political and social conflict, scholars in the field of Black Studies/Africana Studies faced numerous and unusual challenges. They were required to focus energy on developing relevant programs designed to meet the needs of students, the African-American community, and the university while maintaining university standards and adhering to university policy regarding new program development. Moreover, scholars developed and taught an array of courses on the African world experience, ranging from African history to African-American culture.

Scholars faced many barriers that were associated with the development and maintenance of Black Studies/Africana Studies programs and departments.

[1] The university and college administrative process for seeking approval for new programs was tedious.

[2] The acceptance of courses for credit towards a degree, tenure issues regarding faculty, and control over the number and the kinds of courses offered was made difficult.

[3] Many (or perhaps most) scholars who entered the field of Black Studies had little substantive knowledge about the African world experience. Their primary academic training was in one of the traditional disciplinary fields (i.e., Political Science, History, Education, Psychology, Philosophy, Sociology, Economics, etc.). An observed weakness is that individuals trained in a specific discipline become wedded to particular theories and approaches. Thus, they perceive some frameworks and approaches as superior to others, and are unable to appreciate the limitations of those ideals.

[4] An additional problem was the fact that academic disciplinary fields are social organizations that compete for scarce resources and academic territory. Therefore, existing disciplines openly opposed the formation of Black Studies/Africana Studies programs.

[5] Most scholars in Black Studies/Africana Studies are self-taught or are mentored by one or two master Black Studies/Africana scholar. For quite a few scholars, Black Studies/Africana Studies was (and in some cases still is) a secondary interest. Often these scholars bring an anti-Black Studies or anti-African attitude to the field, thus contributing to social and political instability within the Black Studies/Africana Studies discipline.

Due to these barriers, Black Studies scholars had to develop various strategies to cope with the day-to-day hostilities from non-Black Studies academic colleagues and university administrators. Since the establishment of Black Studies/Africana Studies as an academic program, scholars in the field have been preoccupied with ensuring their individual survival.

Black Studies/Africans scholars have devoted considerable time and energy to establishing Black Studies/Africans Studies programs in higher education. These scholars' primary concern was addressing the social and political conditions of the African-American community. Many scholars considered themselves to be leaders in the African-American community, seeing themselves as modern day missionaries who concentrated their efforts on changing American society. This dual role as an African-American scholar and a leader has created a general conflict between Black Studies scholars and the broader university community which views the university as being detached from the surrounding community.

All things considered, Black Studies scholars have gained great knowledge and understanding about the study of the African world experience. Scholars in the field have gone through the rites of passage within the academy. If those scholars are to continue to make positive contributions to the development of human knowledge, and are to command full recognition in the academy, it is imperative that the holistic study of the African world experience be acknowledged as a discipline.

Part A
Academic Disciplinary Fields

Selase W. Williams has defined an academic discipline as a field of study that has established a precise and orderly framework for examining humankind and its environment. The primary objective of an academic discipline is to organize knowledge. Academic knowledge is acquired through the application of scientific processes. Generally, disciplines have five basic components: (1) a rationale; (2) a body of literature; (3) a curriculum based on the major areas of the field; (4) an overall theoretical framework within which the various hypotheses can be constructed and; (5) methodologies by which the various hypotheses can be tested.[2]

The current structure of academic disciplines was developed over the past century, partially in response to scientific advances made in the natural and physical sciences.[3] Theodore C. Kahn in *An Introduction to Hominology* observed:

> The development of the synchronic approach made it possible for scholars to gain considerable knowledge about specific aspects of the individual, groups and society. However, it did so at the expense of reducing the ability of scholars to understand the totality of the human experience.[4]

The synchronic approach has been limited by the fact that it assumes a static nature of human existence. This approach to intellectual inquiry is historical, capturing a specific human action in a particular time and place. The synchronic approach allows intellectual inquiry regarding the human experience to be divided among several academic specialties: (a) the Natural Sciences; (b) the Social Sciences; and (c) the Humanities. Using the synchronic approach, each area is concerned with a particular aspect of the human experience.

Thirty years ago universities and colleges began developing interdisciplinary programs in response to the limited focus of traditional disciplines, attempting to expand the scope and depth of our knowledge. An assumption was made that, by uniting scholars from different disciplinary fields under a particular rubric, an environment and conducive to cross-disciplinary fertilization would be created. This, assumably, would lead to the development of a comprehensive understanding that would produce new knowledge.

The interdisciplinary approach was used quite successfully by the scholars in the natural sciences. However, this intellectual approach has not proven to be as successful in the Social Sciences or Humanities. The interdisciplinary approach does not alter the perspective of the existing disciplinary fields dramatically, but offers a slightly broader and fragmented picture of human existence. A critical problems that confronts scholars who use the interdisciplinary approach is determining which disciplinary bridgehead should be used for studying specific phenomenon.[5]

From the beginning, scholars in traditional disciplines have viewed interdisciplinary fields as inferior and have argued that the interdisciplinary focus and perspective can easily be added or integrated into the traditional fields. An additional problem encountered by scholars to interdisciplinary fields has been their inability to develop new methods for examining the human experience. As Theodore Kahn observed, "The problem with traditional disciplinary fields cannot be simply remedied by restructuring alone, but must focus on changing the nature of the intellectual inquiry itself."[6]

The long history of the traditional disciplinary fields has given scholars circumscribed territory which they jealously guard against any encroachment by new academic fields. Scholars in the established disciplines have used their circumscribed status and power to relegate scholars in the new interdisciplinary fields to the periphery of the academic community. Thus, scholars in those interdisciplinary fields have had to invest an inordinate amount of time and energy in acquiring professional acceptance and academic creditability. As has been mentioned, academic disciplines are social organizations and do not exist in social and political vacuums. They are influenced by the social and political conditions that produce them.

Black Studies/Africana Studies has been an intricate part of the interdisciplinary movement. The historical foundation of Black Studies/Africana Studies dated to the latter part of the nineteenth century when African-American scholars began to undertake studies examining certain aspects of the African-North American life and culture.[7] W.E.B. DuBois was the first scholar to advocate the introspective study of the African world experience from their history and cultural roots during the first decade of the Twentieth Century. By hosting annual conferences from 1897 to 1910 at Atlanta University, he initiated the first organized effort to systemically study the African-North American experience.

In the first decade of the Twentieth Century, Euro-American scholars in the Social Sciences and Humanities fields began to seriously study the African-Diaspora experience, primarily in North America. The majority of research on African-North American experience was directed toward studying the issues of slavery, race and race relations, history, and poverty in the United States. In 1908, Professor Robert Park, a leading sociologist from the University of Chicago, posited the notion that:

> Slavery had so destroyed African-American society that it could only be accounted for entirely by post-slavery which was truly and passively new world. Therefore, African-American cultural processes could only be understood as unsuccessful attempts at adopting European cultural patterns.[8]

Park's thesis became the primary frame of reference for most scholarly examinations of many aspects of the African-North American experience. This thesis provided social scientists with an intellectual justification for viewing the African-American experience from a racial perspective rather than a cultural perspective. Scholars in the natural sciences have since discredited the concept of race as a measure of humanity.

Scholars in the Social Sciences also operate under the premise that race is an inappropriate unit of analysis.

The propensity of scholars to use race as their primary unit of analysis has restricted the systematic study of the African experience with a global context. The conceptualization of race as a social construct has become an integral aspect of western intellectual consciousness. Human reality is viewed in terms of race and/or color as opposed to one of the many, more appropriate cultural units of analysis (e.g., language, ethnicity, geography, religion, philosophy and expressive arts). The Curriculum Project consultants believe some units of analysis (i.e., race) significantly distort the social and political reality of academe.

Scholars in the Social Sciences often have equated the African-American experience with only those of African descent who reside within the borders of the United States. By failing to include other African-Diaspora populations and societies, much of the research has resulted in a narrow and inaccurate perspective of African culture and life. In the absence of the African world perspective, important knowledge is lost. Much of the research conducted on African people in the United States has little or no relationship with the broader African and African Diaspora experience. This is where the Black Studies/Africana Studies perspective is essential because it attempts to address the total African world experience.

Black Studies/Africana Studies Epistemology

There is an ongoing debate within the Black Studies/Africana Studies field regarding what constitutes the proper boundaries of the field. Black Studies/Africana Studies scholars have not had the time or the opportunity to define the field's philosophical foundation and intellectual boundaries. The academic debate within the university over the question of whether or not Black Studies is a discipline has severely hampered and limited the development of an epistemology for the field.

The term epistemology refers to knowledge or knowing. It also answers the question of what we know and how we claim to know something, serving as a guide for ranking the significance of certain areas of human activity in the context of systematic knowledge. Epistemologies are distillates of ideas, values and beliefs that arise from the experiences and desires of the prevailing elites in the social system.[9] Moreover, an epistemology is the basis upon which knowledge within the various disciplines rests. Each Geo-cultural group (i.e., Africans, Asians, Europeans, Indians) has a particular epistemology which has evolved from its culture over time. Professor Dona Marimba Richards suggests that:

> Culture is ordered behavior. It is not created individually. All groups of people who have been historically related over long periods of time share a way of viewing the world and the realities with which it presents them.[10]

In sum, culture can be seen as the collective heritage of a people handed down from generation to generation. It includes artifacts, laws, religion, philosophy, values, myths, and special ways individuals and societies view the world. Clifford Geertz observed:

> That cultural values and beliefs of a society are the basis in which an individual or society evaluates itself and others. Human behavior is attached to cul-

ture with some exactness, because it is thought the flow of behavior or, more precisely, social action that cultural forms find articulation.[11]

He has identified two components of culture—the ethos and world-view. "Ethos is the moral and aesthetic components of a cultural group...to their collective emotional self." The ethos is the basis through which individuals make value judgements regarding what is and is not acceptable. World-view refers to the existential and cognitive; the way in which a people make sense of their world; make sense out of life and of the universe.[12] A world-view presents us with a systematic set of ideas about ourselves and nature, and the structure of the universe. It speaks to our "Metaphysics."

While in reality there are several epistemologies (e.g, African, Asian, European and the First American), the European epistemology has been used as the linchpin that undergirds the various disciplinary fields in modern academe. Professor James Turner, a Cornell University professor, has pointed out that:

> The current theories and concepts used to explain human socio-cultural behavior patterns are rooted in the Western epistemology. Most of the major arguments in History, Social Science, Anthropology, Arts, Literature and the Humanities derive from European epistemology. This has been held as universal and reflects a dialectic historicism imperative in modern Western theoretical development.[13]

The European epistemology represents the cultural values and attitudes of mostly Western European countries (values, appearances, styles and form) which have been utilized to make generalizations about the essence of all human reality. The Eurocentric[14] epistemology has been useful in studying European peoples and societies. However, when it is used an overlay in the study of other peoples and societies, it causes a considerable distortion of the analysis. In this respect the study of non-European experience has been filtered through the "lenses" of European cultural "glasses." The Eurocentric epistemology has restricted the development of new scholarly knowledge. This is largely due to the fact that the Eurocentric epistemology is not valid for examining the social economic and political dynamics of all human populations. Sterling Stuckey has suggested that a hegemonic, European-centered intellectual perspective has been at the forefront of the political and social oppression of African peoples throughout the world during the last four centuries.

Many Africanists have commented that the current philosophy regarding the study of the African world experience relies too heavily on a European world view. A number of Black Studies/Africana Studies scholars have posited the Afrocentric epistemology as an alternative to the Eurocentric epistemology.[15] C. Tsehloane Keto argues that:

> The Africa-centered perspective of history rests on the premise that it is valid to posit Africa as a geographical and cultural starting base of the study of people of African descent. This perspective makes it easier to trace and understand the social patterns of their existence; the institutional patterns of their actions and the intellectual pattern of their thoughts within the changing context of time.[16]

Winston Van Horne, University of Wisconsin Africologist,[17] noted that the life experiences of African people in the Diaspora must be viewed both trans-millenially and universally.[18] The African-centered, or Afrocentric epistemology is rooted in African history and culture.

The African world-view or cosmology consists of the natural world and supernatural world, the living and the dead, the human and spirit world living side by side. There is a unity of the sacred and the profane, the natural and supernatural, both existing along a space continuum within the African world-view of human experience. Man is not at liberty to act out his individual fate independent of the group or the gods.[19] For this reason the group or the society is the primary reason for being. William Amoaku noted:

> That the universe in the African cosmology is an indivisible unit. It is impossible to fathom the social dynamic of African world societies without a thorough knowledge of the African world view?[20]

According to this perspective, the universe is organically interrelated and interdependent. The universe, as Donna Richards noted, is a unified "spiritual totality" where people hold within themselves both the world of spirit and nature. Perhaps the most basic concept in the African world experience has been the persistence of communalism or the notion of unity as the philosophical underpinning of African societies, whether they are on the African continent or part of the Diaspora.[21] Chancellor Williams commented that African societies have historically exhibited a high level of democracy in their political decision-making process. The ruler in African society was responsible for serving the society, not controlling it.

The Afrocentric epistemology must be the first step in the development of Multicentric epistemologies. Keto warns us about the pitfalls of intellectual hegemonic tendencies when we claim that all intellectual interpretation concerning the African world experience cannot be explained in terms of Africa alone, but must utilize other people's experiences that have helped shape the African world reality. Africana Studies scholars must combat anti-African intellectual hegemony if there is to be an intellectual movement toward multi-centric analysis.[22]

Black Studies/Africana Studies as a Discipline

Selase William has taken the position that Black Studies is a Human Science discipline.[23] His view of Human Science is a reconstructed academic discipline that combines Humanities, Natural Sciences and Social Sciences, rearranging them in a way that allows scholars to better understand African reality. Human Science allows scholars to study various human experiences from the perspective of people experiences. By approaching the study of the African experience from thematic and historical perspective. Black Studies/Africana Studies allows for both a thematic and historical analysis. The discipline of Black Studies/Africana Studies is primarily concerned with the study and examination of the African world experience from the perspective of the past, present and current historical unfolding. This process provides a broader picture of African reality, within a multidimensional reality. The discipline, brings together all aspects of other sciences that contribute to the framework for integrating material from many academic fields, the perspective and structure for analyzing this material rests solely with Black Studies/Africana Studies. The discipline begins with the study of the African experience in antiquity and journeys onward to the dispersion of Africans to the four corners of the globe.

The discipline of Black Studies/Africana Studies provides an African-centered framework for viewing the African world experience. The Black Studies/Africana Studies paradigm provides methods and approaches of the discipline that are not restricted in their application, thus providing a general framework for examining all human populations and societies within an African world context. The aim of Black

Studies/Africana Studies differs markedly from other academic disciplines in that its focus is on African peoples and societies. In terms of knowledge, appreciation, and problem solving (both Continental and Diasporic), the African human experience is deserving of study in its own right. The multi-faceted nature of the African world experience requires students in the discipline to be able to handle materials which cross several disciplinary boundaries. It must be understood that human relationships involve cultural changes. Thus human processes are naturally dynamic, mutually affecting and constantly changing, regardless of the visibility of these changes. Black Studies/Africana Studies as a discipline provides a framework that can be utilized to enhance scholars' understanding of the total human experience. Usually, scholars in the traditional disciplines are trapped in the dichotomous analysis—examining the African world experience from the perspective of similarities or dissimilarities to those of Euro-World.

Academic Core Curriculum

It is important to identify the context in which the concept "Core Curriculum" has historically surfaced, the purpose it has been designed to realize, and to make its presuppositions explicit.

A. Historical Perspective

1. A Core Curriculum has emerged as part of the legitimation process by which a new and fledgling discipline seeks to demonstrate that it incorporates a body of material (x) that is discrete, distinct and not reducible to anything more fundamental. Central to this understanding is the conclusion that each discipline has a unique structure. Even though a particular discipline is unique, part of it may include components that are also part of the structure of other disciplines.

2. A Core Curricula have emerged as part of a synthesizing activity that aims at the reformation of a discipline by providing an organic unity and centering where the discipline is regarded as chaotic.

3. This synthesizing activity is also evident in efforts to establish an authorized certification/accreditation apparatus. In this sense, a Core Curriculum seeks to formulate the sine quanon for a given discipline that articulates the minimal skills, intellectual training, etc., as these relate to proficiency and/or advancement in the field. If we allow for the distinction between what is "essential," "desirable" and "enriching," as items of descending rank order, then the Core Curriculum gives content to the category of the "essential." In this sense, the Core Curriculum seeks to identify what skills are essential for participation in the field or what constitutes adequate preparation for the discipline in question.

B. General Presupposition

Logically, a consensus determination of function, scope and goals of Black Studies/Africana Studies must precede the development of a Core Curriculum. This fol-

Table 1

Disciplinary Curriculum Model

Black Studies/Africana Studies Administrative Unit

Introductory Course(s)

History Courses

This process includes classes from only ONE discipline. The focus is in a solitary traditional area.

lows from the fact that a Core Curriculum is advanced as indispensable for the attainment of some goal acquisition of skills, inculcation of appropriate effective and cognitive data required for competency in a given field, transmission of a cultural tradition, etc. Based on this understanding, the rationale for a Core Curriculum reduces to the demonstration that (x) is the most effective means to a given end. The content and validation of the Core Curriculum is determined by reference to the coal or purpose to which it is engaged. A Core Curriculum:

(a) Affirms that the sub-units of which it is comprised exhibit an inner coherence and organizational connectedness which permit their modular linkage and sequencing.

(b) Builds synthetic structures into the sub-units of the curriculum itself rather than allowing the student to produce the synthesis personally through his or her selective and subjective choice.

(c) Seeks to provide a standard model which operates as the yardstick from which progress towards attaining the goal of acquiring knowledge may be measured.

Black Studies/Africana Studies Curricula Models

The Authors of this study examined over 400 Black Studies/Africana Studies Programs around the country to determine the types of curriculum models implemented at various colleges and universities. The data gathered indicated that there are approximately 215 Black Studies/Africana Studies units utilizing one of three general models: (1) the disciplinary model; (2) interdisciplinary model; and (3) the multidisciplinary model (See Table 1). A description of each model is provided in the following section.

Table 2

Interdisciplinary Curriculum Model (Hall Model)

Introduction to Black Studies

Level One

Social and Behavioral Studies Course Area	History Course Area	Cultural Studies Course Area

Level Two

Basic Literature Review or Survey race relations, social movements, etc.	African Pre-History Through Reconstruction	Basic Literature Review or Survey music, aesthetics, etc.)

Level Three

Current Research & Emerging Issues (demographics, social problems, etc.)	Post-Reconstruction Current & Emerging Issues in Historical Interpretation & Evaluation	Current Research & Emerging Issues (contemporary cultural expression & transformation, etc.

Level Four

Senior and Graduate Seminar Course Area
Synthesis and Application of Knowledge or insights of previous study

Research	Job Market	Graduate School

A. Disciplinary Model

The Disciplinary Model utilizes an existing discipline or field as a basis for examining the African World Experience. This model includes examination of the political system of the African populations and is linked to a traditional discipline or field. The model offers few options that can be tailored to individual needs. This model fails to make a commitment to an intellectual concern for a wide range of issues and concepts pertaining to the realities of the African World Experience. Normally this model utilizes one disciplinary framework in addressing the issues. The focus is limited and narrow. The Disciplinary Model selects one of three areas: (1) history; (2) sociology; or (3) literature. The examination tends not to focus on an African-centered framework but uses the traditional academic paradigm.

B. Interdisciplinary Model

The Interdisciplinary Black Studies/Africans Studies Curriculum Model draws upon the traditional disciplines for their primary course offerings (See Table 2). The interdisciplinary model assumes that the traditional academic fields can provide a comprehensive examination of the African world experience by coordinating the course offerings between the various departments. However, most of the courses offered in this model tend to be directed toward the curriculum needs of the traditional department rather than the Black Studies Department curriculum. The foci of the courses are designed to facilitate the philosophical and theoretical intellectual objectives of the traditional disciplines. While the course offerings might be useful for specialists interested in understanding disciplinary questions, they do not address fundamental questions that are at the center of the Black Studies/Africana Studies field. Most of the curricula in the traditional disciplines focus on correcting the historical record of the African-Diaspora (See Table 2).

C. Multidisciplinary Curriculum Model

The multidisciplinary curriculum model requires autonomous academic units. The department faculty defines the nature and content of the course offerings. The majority of the multidisciplinary program curricula reviewed indicate that most of the curricula are structured in four ways:

(1) Social Sciences and Humanities courses with a Social Sciences specialization and Humanities specialization;

(2) Social Sciences and Humanities courses with only a Social Science specialization;

(3) Social Sciences and Humanities courses with only a Humanities specialization;

(4) Social Sciences courses with only a specialization in one of the professional fields.

The course offerings in these programs reflect the same problems that the interdisciplinary model presents in that the curriculum does not offer a coherent or comprehensive body of knowledge within any specific area of content. Very seldom is there a philosophical or theoretical concept that underpins the design or structure of the curriculum. Further, the multidisciplinary model does not address the fundamental questions that are at the center of the Black Studies/Africana Studies field. Programs that utilize the multidisciplinary model are shaped and formed by the traditional disciplinary intellectual thrust (See Table 3).

Administrative Structure

Colleges and universities have utilized four types of administrative models for Black Studies/Africana Studies units: (a) department model, (b) program model, (c) institute model, and (4) center model. The preferred administrative model used by colleges and universities has been the program model. Across the country the administrative program model had a ratio of 2 to 1 over the departmental model (See Table 4). In addition there are 185 colleges and universities that offer courses either on the African experience or the African Diaspora experience, within the traditional academic disciplinary fields. The majority of the courses offered are listed under history, literature, music, and dance categories.

The majority of the Black Studies/Africana Studies Programs are clustered in eight state (See Table 5). The largest number of the Black Studies/Africana Studies academic units are located in the Northeast and Midwest. However, California and New York

Table 3
Multidisciplinary Curricula Model
Black Studies/Africana Studies Administrative Unit

Introductory Course(s)

Social Sciences: Classes offered in Psychology, Sociology; Anthropology, Social Work and other disciplines to explicate the depth of the African world social experience.

Humanities: Classes offered in Music, Art, Literature, Religion, Philosophy, History detailing the broad scope of the African world cultural Experience.

Policy Studies: Classes offered on various topics within the field, focusing on the African world experience.

Upper-class courses would be offered in each area for students seeking B.A. degrees or beyond. A focus on research and writing is derived from the higher-level classes to prepare students for work experiences.

Administrative Structure

Table 4
Black Studies/Africana Program by Administrative Structure

Unit	Progs.	Institutes	Centers	Depts.	Total
#	140	4	12	59	215

Table 5
Black Studies Programs by States with More Than Ten

STATES	CA	NY	OH	MA	NJ	IN	IL	MI	TOTAL
#	27	25	16	16	12	11	10	10	127

Table 6
Black Studies Graduate Programs

Type of Grad. Program	MA/MS	MA/MS	Ph.D.	Ph.D
	Concentration	Degree	Concentration	Degree
#	14	10	12	1

lead the nation in Black Studies/Africana Studies Programs with 27 and 25 respectively. The greatest concentration of Black Studies/Africana Studies Programs is normally located in states with large urban centers. We attribute the clustering of Black Studies programs in the regions identified to the large numbers of African-American people in the region. The data indicates that universities and colleges tend to offer comprehensive Black Studies/Africana Studies only when there is a sizable African-American presence in the state, and the state is urban and industrial.

Temple University is the only university in the United States that offers a Ph.D. degree in Black Studies. However, there are several universities offering Black Studies concentrations within their Ph.D. degree programs in the traditional disciplinary fields (See Table 6).

Black Studies/Africana Studies Holistic Curriculum Model

The Holistic Curriculum Model presented here is designed to allow programs and departments to select their own areas of curriculum concentrations. This curriculum model provides an outline of the contents that all units should include in their curricula. However, while we are not arguing strict observance of specific course content as recommended under each of the eight concentration areas, we have attempted to define the concentration areas from the perspective of disciplinary requirements. We have developed nomenclature that defines our disciplinary approach more accurately and allows scholars to avoid resorting to a use of nomenclature that may suggest our discipline's dependency on other, so-called traditional, academic disciplines. We might use history as an aspect of our discipline's analytical framework, but we do not teach history *per se*. Just as the Political Scientist uses Sociology, History, Geography, and other disciplines to explicate his or her interpretation of political reality, we can use the knowledge offered by Political Science, Sociology, and History to explicate African world reality. In this manner, we maintain the methodological integrity of our discipline's efforts to correct old knowledge and to create new ways to interpret the African world experience. The field of Africana Studies adds to the existing curriculum substantively different courses that describe and analyze the experiences of peoples of African descent, in their diversity and in relation to Europeans and European Americans.

Introduction to Black Studies/Africana Studies Holistic Curriculum

The Introduction to Black Studies/Africana Studies provides an overview of the philosophical underpinnings of the discipline, the evolution of the field of Africana Studies, its theoretical and practical applications, and the holistic method of studying African peoples and their social organizations. This course introduced students to the eight content areas/subfields of the discipline with emphasizes on the basic thrusts of the discipline: the philosophical, the theoretical, the practical, the analytical, and the axiology (values formulation) (See Figures 1 and 2). An essential aspect of the introductory course is informing students about the work of major scholars in the field through the instruction of its historical development and to provide students with the basic concepts and terminologies used by Black Studies scholars. An overarching objective of this course, therefore, is to establish the intellectual attitude requisite for meaningful passage through the curriculum add for the development of future generations of scholars. In addition, the students are introduced to academic holism from an Afrocentric perspective of view.

Figure 1

The National Council for Black Studies
Black Studies/Africana Studies Holistic Curriculum Model*

Level I

Introduction to Black Studies/Africana Studies

Level II

Foundations of Black Studies/Africana Studies

A. Methods and Approaches To Black Studies/Africana Studies
B. African World Civilization I: Antiquity-15th Century
C. African World Civilization II: 15th Century-19th Century
D. African World Civilization III: 19th Century-the Present

Level III

Geo-Cultural Regions

A. African-Diaspora [People of African descent who reside outside Africa.]
B. African-Continent [People of African descent who reside in Africa]
C. Comparative African World [A comparative examination of people of African descent and their societies around the world)

Level IV

Suggested Subfields

A. Organizational and Political Dynamics
B. Language, Literature and Communication Systems
C. Religions, Philosophy and World Views
D. Economic and Social Development
E. Individual, Family, and Community Dynamics
F. Arts and Aesthetics
G. History and Historical Development
H. Science and Technological Development

Level V

Pro-Seminar in Research Methods and Tools

Level VI

Practical Research and Fieldwork

Level VII

Capstone Course/Senior Seminar

* This Holistic Curriculum Model is a guideline for Black Studies/Africana Studies programs throughout the United Staten and Africa. The subfields described in thin model are only suggested areas. Individual programs may design or develop other content areas/subfields as their curriculum programs may require.

Figure 2

The National Council for Black Studies
Black Studies/Africana Studies Program Requirements

		B.A.	Certificate	Minor
I.	Introduction to Black Studies/Africana Studies	3	3	3
II.	Foundations of Black Studies/Africana Studies [All students are required to take the Foundation of Black Studies/Africana Studies course.]			
	(Lower Division Courses)			
	A. Methods and Approaches to Africana Studies/Black Studies	3	3	3
	B. African World Civilization I: Antiquity-15th Century	3	3	3
	C. African world Civilization 1I: 15th Century-18th Century	3	3	3
	D. African World Civilization III: 19th Century-Present	3	3	3
	Total Lower Division Credits Needed	15	15	15

III. Geo-Cultural Regions

All students are required to concentrate in one of the Geo-Cultural Regions. The Geo-Cultural Regions are:

(1) African-Diaspora; (2) African-Continent; (3) Comparative African World.

IV. Subfields of Black Studies/Africana Studies

   A. Students majoring in Black Studies/Africana Studies are required to complete 12 hours in one content area/subfield and 9 hours in another content area/subfield.

   B. Students in Black Studies/Africana Studies Certificate are required to complete 9 hours in one content area/subfield

   C. Students with a minor in Black Studies/Africana Studies are required to complete 6 hours in a content area/subfield.

      1. Organizational and Political Dynamic

      2. Language, Literature and Communication Systems

      3. Religions, Philosophy and World Views

4. Economic and Social Development			
5. Individual, Family, and Community Dynamics			
6. Arty and Aesthetics			
7. History and Historical Development			
8. Science and Technological Development			
Total Hours for Content Areas/Subfields	21	9	6
V. Pro-Seminar in Research Methods and Tool	3	–	–
VI. Practical Research and Field Work	3	–	–
VII. Capstone Course/Senior Seminar	3	3	3
Total Upper Division Credits Needed	30	15	6
Total Credits Required for Graduation	45	30	24

Foundation of Black Studies/Africana Studies

The foundation of Black Studies/Africana Studies is composed of four course of-ferings. Three of the courses are a part of a sequence that provides an overview of the Africana world experience from antiquity to the present. These courses ground the students in a historical perspective of the evolution and unfolding of African travel through time. It also provides students with an understanding of key historical events and a basis for examining the African world with greater specificity. Also, it provides students with an understanding of Afrocentric methods and theories. The basic premise of Black Studies/Africana Studies, as Selase Williams noted, is that intellec-tual inquiry and creativity are heavily influenced, if not determined, by culture. The answer to any given question is conditioned by both cultural and physical conditions. Therefore, it is imperative that methods and approaches of Black Studies/ Africana Studies be the lynchpin for examining African world phenomena. This does not sug-gest that other cultural influences have not impacted African world realities.

Geo-Cultural Regions

Geo-Cultural regions refer to geographical areas of the world which reflect a unique cultural milieu that may be discerned either by language, religion, philosophy, world views, or other cultural artifacts. There are four major geographic regions where African people reside and are identified by continental differentials, such as Europe, Asia, America and Africa.

Subfields

The field of Black Studies/Africana Studies is comprised of the following eight academic subfields.

1. Art and Aesthetics

This subfield examines and analyzes Arts and Aesthetics within the African world. This area also identifies the theories and philosophies that underpin African arts and aesthetics. Arts and Aesthetics within the African world are interconnected. It further explores the traditional African concept of arts and aesthetics and its influence on other cultures, and other cultural and societal influences on African world art and aesthetics. For example dance, drama and music is one indivisible art form within African art and aesthetics.

2. Economics and Social Development

This subfield examines and analyzes the economic structure, and social dynamics of the African world. It investigates land, tenure patterns, and kinship arrangements as they relate to social obligations. It further examines African economics as it underpins African world societies. Its primary focus is on three levels of analysis: (1) Macro analysis, (2) micro analysis, and (3) the global economic structure, and its impact on traditional structures.

3. Religions, Philosophy and World Views

This subfield examines the religions, and philosophical beliefs of African people. It further examines the ways in which African people view the world and how they interpret and perceive the universe.

4. Organizational and Political Dynamics

This subfield examines and analyzes organizations and political dynamics within the African world. The field further examines the theoretical and philosophical foundations that underpin African views of organizational and political behavior. These encompass the following: the role of government, political leaders, traditional leaders, organizational behaviors, clientale politics, ethnic politics, ethnic kinships, politics of land, African legal theories, European legal theories and others.

5. Science and Technological Development

This subfield examines and analyzes the development of mathematics, metallurgy and mineralogy, architecture, agronomy, etc. This are also examines the relationship of science and technology and the application of technology in various African societies (e.g., medicine, agriculture, architecture, education and nutrition.

6. Individual Group and Community Dynamics

This subfield examines the social intercourse and actions among individual African people as well as groups and their communities. This area is primarily concerned with the examination and analysis of the individual's and group's adaptation to political, psychological, social, and cultural influences that have evolved out of various experiences of African people. The secondary concern is how these influences impact the development of African people, communities and societies.

7. Language, Literature and Communication System

This subfield examines the development of social, artistic and spiritual forms of communication. This area further examines language as a product of the African culture and the means by which individuals and groups communicate to each other, and the world.

8. History and Historical Development

This subfield examines African people throughout the African world. It begins with antiquity and continues to the present. African people originated and continued throughout the African diaspora. This area also includes an investigation of the historical development of African people, civilizations, societies, kingdoms, nations and states.

Research or Field Work

Students will engage in either research or field work to demonstrate acquisition of the prescribed academic and research goals of the Black Studies Holistic Curriculum. Students will be provided the opportunity to apply academic theory to practice. In addition, students will design and implement research projects, OR participate in field work that will reflect the student's understanding of the meaning and purpose of Afrocentric research, and competence in using Africana Studies research methodologies specific to the discipline.

Capstone

Finally, all Black Studies/Africana Studies majors will be required to participate in a seminar during his/her senior year that has as its major components structured research and a public colloquium. Both the seminar and the colloquium are designed to help the student synthesize his/her learning and knowledge acquisition in Black Studies/Africana Studies and all knowledge acquired at the University. The Capstone course thus provides students with a structured process for synthesizing learned theoretical information and investigating how this information can and should be applied in the real world context.

Conclusion

It is our position that the current academic disciplinary social construct was not designed to answer critical questions relevant to the social and cultural dimensions and dynamics of African world. Therefore, the Black Studies/Africana Studies curriculum was designed to examine the complexity of a multifaceted culture as well as to implement a program that met the academic and social needs of faculty, students and universities. Also, it was designed to examine various aspects of African world dynamics and experiences that have evolved and continues to evolve within the world context.

Currently, a number of different rubrics exist that relate to the study of African world people. They are: Afro-American Studies, African Studies, African-American Studies, Black Studies, Pan-African Studies, Afro-Latin Studies, Afro-Cuban Studies, Afro-Brazilian Studies, and Afro-Caribbean Studies. The study of African people is based upon ethnic, geographical, religious, and other constructs and has been treated as a totally distinct area of intellectual investigation. We believe that all of the areas within the African world must be grouped together under the rubric of either Africanology, Africalogy, or Africology. There is no justification for the artificial compartmentalization of the African world experience. We suggest that the National Council for Black Studies (NCBS) adopt a policy to accept the term African Studies as an intermediary descriptor for the holistic study of the African world experience. Failure to accept a universal term for the study of African world people, may result in continued usage of multiple descriptors; may lead to confusion; and may limit intellectual growth and development. We recommend that one of the three terms used by various scholars be selected. We further challenge scholars in the field to (1) set and maintain standards in the field of Black Studies/Africana Studies; and (2) impact or provide students with information, knowledge, and skills that will impact all aspects of the university and community life.

References

Aldridge, Delores, "Toward A New Role and Function of Black Studies in Historically Black Institutions," *The Journal of Negro Education*, Vol. 53 (1984): 359-367.

Banks, James A., "Teaching Black Studies for Social Change," in Roosevelt Johnson (ed.), *Trends in Afro-American Studies*. Washington: ECCA Publications, 1975.

Blassingame, John, "Black Studies: An Intellectual Crisis," *The American Scholar*, Vol. XXXVIII (1969).

Brossard, Carlos. "Classifying Black Studies Programs," *The Journal of Negro Education*. Vol. 53 (1984): 278-295.

Colon, Alan K. "Critical Issues in Black Studies: A Selective Analysis," *The Journal of Negro Education*, Vol. 53 (1984): 268-277.

Cross, William E., "The Thomas and Cross Models on Psychological Nigrescence: A Literature Review," *Journal of Black Psychology*, Vol. 4 (1978): 13-31.

Cross, William E., "Black Family and Black Identity: A Literature Review," *The Western Journal of Black Studies*, Vol. 2 (1978): 111-124.

Daniel, T.K., "A Survey of Black Studies in Midwestern Colleges and Universities," *The Western Journal of Black Studies*, Vol. 2 (1978): 296-303.

Daniel, T.K., "Theory Building in Black Studies," *The Black Scholar*, Vol. 12 (1981): 29-36.

Diop, Cheik Anta, *African Origins of Civilization, Myth or Reality*, ed. and trans. from French by Mercer Cook. Westport: Lawrence Hill and Company, 1974.

Ford, Nick Aaron, "Black Studies Programs," *Current History* (November 1974).

Frye, Charles, *Towards A Philosophy of Black Studies*, San Francisco: R & F Research Associates, 1978.

Hall, Perry, et al., "Hall Report: Black Studies Core Curriculum." Bloomington, IN: National Council for Black Studies, 1981.

Harley, Sharon and Rosalyn, Tarborg-Penn (eds.), "The Afro-American Woman Struggles and Images." Port West, New York: National University, 1978.

Harris, William M. and Darrell Millner (eds.), "Perspectives on Black Studies." Washington: University Press of America, 1977.

Harvey, William B., "Computer Instruction and Black Student Performance," *Issues in Higher Education*, Vol. 9 (1983).

Hendrix, Melvin K., James H. Bracy, John A. Davis, and Waddell M. Herron, "Computers and Black Studies: Toward the Cognitive Revolution," *The Journal of Negro Education*, Vol. 53 (1984): 341-350.

Huggins, Nathan, "Report to the Ford Foundation on Afro-American Studies." New York: Ford Foundation, 1985.

Hull, Gloria et al., "All the Women are White. All the Blacks are Men. But Some of Us Are Brave," *Black Women's Studies* (1982).

Jackson, John, *Introduction to African Civilizations*. Secaucus, NJ: Citadel Press, 1980.

Jackson, Maurice, "Toward A Sociology of Black Studies," *Journal of Black Studies*, Vol. 1 (1970).

Karenga, Maulana, *Introduction to Afro-American Studies*. Los Angeles: Kawaida Publications, 1982.

Mbiti, John S., *African Religions and Philosophy*. Garden City, New York: Doubleday-Anchor Books 1970.

Russell, Joseph J., "Afro-American Studies: From Chaos to Consolidation," *The Negro Education Review*, Vol. XXVI (1975).

Senaj, Leaheim Tufani, "The Black Self, Identity and Models for a Psychology of Black Liberation," *The Western Journal of Black Studies*, Vol. 5 (1981): 158-171.

Stewart, James B., "Factors Affecting Variation in Published Black Studies Articles Across Institutions," *The New England Journal of Black Studies* (1983).

Stewart, James B., "The Legacy of W.E.B. DuBois for Contemporary Black Studies," *The Journal of Negro Education*, Vol. 53 (1984): 296-311.

Turner, James E. (ed.), *The Next Decade: Theoretical and Research Issues in Africans Studies*. Ithaca, NY: Africana Studies and Research Center, 1984.

Turner, James E., "Africana Studies and Epistemology, A Discourse in the Sociology of Knowledge," in James E. Turner (ed.), *The Next Decade: Theoretical and Research Issues in Africana Studies*, pp. v-xxv. Ithaca, NY: Africana Studies and Research Center, 1984.

Upton, James N., "Applied Black Studies: Adult Education in the Black Community — A Case Study," *The Journal of Negro Education*, Vol. 53 (1984): 332-333.

Walker, S. Jay, "Black Studies Phase Two," *The American Scholar* (1973).

Wilcox, Preston, "Black Studies as an Academic Discipline," *Negro Digest* (March 1970).

Endnotes

1. Delores P. Aldridge, Carolyn Cambell, Elizabeth A. Dooley, Norm Harris, Robert Maxon, Linda James-Meyers, James Stewart, Selase W. Williams and Carlene Young reviewed and commented on various aspects of the Holistic Curriculum Model.

2. Selase W. Williams, "The African Intellectual Revolution: The Defining, Developing, and Defending of Black Studies as a Discipline," Paper presented at National Council For Black Studies Conference, University of California, Berkeley, 1982.

3. Eric Wolfe, *Europe and the People Without History* (Berkeley: University of California Press, 1982), 7.

4. Theodore C. Kahn, *An Introduction To Hominology* (Springfield, IL: Charles C. Thomas Publisher, 1969), 10-11.

5. *Ibid.*, 11.

6. *Ibid.*, 12.

7. Martin Delany (1812-1883), Edward Wilmot Blyden (1832-1912), Frederick Douglass (1817-1895), W.E.B. DuBois, and George Washington Williams (1891-1949) undertook a number of specific studies on the African-American experience. W.E.B. DuBois was the first African-American scholar to conduct the significant scientific research on the subject.

8. Richard Long, "Some Backgrounds for African Continuity Studies," *Journal of African Studies*, Vol. 2 (Winter 1975-76): 561-562.

9. Russell L. Adams, "Intellectual Questions and Imperatives in the Development of Afro-American Studies," *Journal of Negro Education*, Vol. 53, No. 3 (Summer 1984): 208-209.

10. Dona Marimba Richards, "Let the Circle Be Unbroken," *Presence, Africaine*, No. 117 and 118 (1981): 4.

11. Clifford Geertz, *The Interpretation of Culture* (New York: Harper Torchbooks, 1973), 7.

12. *Ibid.*, p. 127.

13. James E. Turner, *The Next Decade: Theoretical and Research Issues in Africana Studies* (Ithaca: Cornell University press, 1984), 17.

14. Eurocentric refers to the European centered focus of Western intellectual thought. The belief that the European ideas and beliefs are universal in their application. The notion that all knowledge can be understood through examining the world from a European perspective.

15. John Henrik Clarke 1979, James Turner 1979, Maulana Karenga 1982, Molefi Kete Asante 1985, and Selase Williams 1986, have posited the Afrocentric view us an alternative to the Eurocentric epistemology for studying African-Diaspora populations.

16. Tsehloane C. Keto, *The Africa Centered Perspective of History* (New Jersey: KA Publications, 1989).

17. The term "Africalogist" refers to scholars who specialize in the study and examination of African culture and people of African descent. This includes the study of the history of all African people and their societies from antiquity to the present. This definition does not include those scholars who study one or two aspects of the African-American experience. They are considered to be traditional disciplinary scholars who happen to study certain aspects of African-American experience.

18. Winston, A. Van Horne, "Africology: The Renaming of Afro-American Studies," A Proposal to NCBS, 1988.

19. John S. Mbiti, *African Religions and Philosophy* (Garden City, NY: Doubleday-Anchor Books, 1970), 3-5.

20. William Amoaku, *African and African-American Musical Traditions* (Portland, OR: Portland Public Schools, 1986), 1.

21. Christen Potholm, *The Theory and Practice of African Politics* (Englewood Cliffs, NJ: Prentice-Hall, Inc., 1979), 25.

22. Keto, 18.

23. William A. Little first posited the position that Black Studies was a cultural science in a paper, "Toward a Theory of Black Studies," presented at the National Council for Black Studies' Eleventh Annual Conference at Cornell University, 1985; also Donna Richards posited the same position in a paper, "Afrocentricity in Black Studies," presented at the National Council for Black Studies' Twelfth Annual Conference, Philadelphia, 1988.

Selected Bibliography

Adams, Russell L. (1984) "Intellectual Questions and Imperatives in the Development of Afro-American Studies," *Journal of Negro Education*, 53, 3: 201-225.

Akbar, Na'im. (1984) "Africentric Social Sciences for Human Liberation," *Journal of Black Studies*, 14, 4 (June): 395-414.

Aldridge, Delores. (1991) *Challenges for and one Response to the Development of the Field of Black Studies*. National Council of Black Studies Summer Institute, Ohio State University, June 11.

———. (1988) *New Perspectives on Black Studies*, Special Issue, *Phylon*, 49, 1 (Spring).

———. (1984) "Toward A New Role and Function of Black Studies in White Historically Black Institutions," *The Journal of Negro Education*, 53: 359-367.

———. (1992) "Womanist Issues in Black Studies: Towards Integrating Africana Women into Africana Studies," *Journal of the National Council for Black Studies*, 1, 1 (May): 167-182.

Allen, Robert L. (1974) "Politics of the Attack on Black Studies," *The Black Scholar*, 6, 1 (September): 2-7.

Anderson, Talmadge. (1990) *Black Studies, Theory, Method and Cultural Perspectives*. Pullman, WA: Washington State University Press.

Aptheker, Herbert. (1971) "Black Studies and United States History," *Negro History Bulletin*, 34, 8 (December): 174-175.

Asante, Molefi. (1987) *The Afrocentric Idea*. Philadelphia: Temple University Press.

———. (1992) "The Afrocentric Metatheory and Disciplinary Implications," *The Afrocentric Scholar*, 1, 1 (May): 98-117.

———. (1980) *Afrocentricity: The Theory of Social Change*. Buffalo: Amulefi Publishing Co.

———. (1990) *Kemet, Afrocentricity and Knowledge*. Trenton, NJ: African World Press Inc.

Bailey, Ronald. (1970) "Why Black Studies?" *The Education Digest*, 35, 9 (May): 46-48.

ben-Jochannon, Yosef A.A. (1971) *Africa: Mother of "Western Civilization"*. New York: Alkebu-lan Books Associates.

———. (1970) *African Origins of the Major "Western Religions"*. New York: Alkebu-lan Books Associates.

ben-Jochannan, Yosef. (1989) *Cultural Genocide In the Black & African Studies Curriculum*. New York: ECA Printing.

Bennett, Lerone. (1972) *The Challenge of Blackness*. Chicago, IL: Johnson Publishing Company Incorporated.

Bernal, Martin. (1987) *Black Athena: The Afro-Asiatic Roots of Classical Civilization Volume 1.* New Brunswick, NJ: Rutgers University Press.

Bethune, Mary McLeod. (1939) "The Adaptation of the History of the Negro to the Capacity of the Child," *Journal of Negro History,* 24: 9-13.

Blackwell, James, Janowitz, Morris, eds. (1974) *Black Sociologists.* Chicago, IL: The University of Chicago Press.

Blassingame, John. (1973) *New Perspectives on Black Studies.* Chicago: University of Illinois Press.

———. (1970) "'Soul' or Scholarship: Choices Ahead for Black Studies," *Smithsonian* 1 (April): 58-65.

Brimmer, Andrew. (1969) "The Black Revolution and the Economic Future of Negroes in the United States," *American Scholar* XXXVIII (Autumn): 629-43.

Brisbane, Robert. (1974) *Black Activism.* Valley Forge, NY: Judson Press.

Bunzell, John H. (1968) "Black Studies at San Francisco State." *Public Interest* (Fall): 22-38.

Butler, Johnnella E. (1981) *Black Studies: Pedagogy and Revolution.* Lanham, MD: University Press of America.

Cade, (Bambara) Toni, ed. (1970) *The Black Woman.* New York: New American Library.

Carruthers, Jacob H. (1984) *Essays in Ancient Egyptian Studies.* Los Angeles: University of Sankore Press.

Carson, Claybourne. (1981) *In Struggle: SNCC and the Black Awakening of the 60's.* Cambridge: Harvard University Press.

Chew, Peter. (1969) "Black History, or Black Mythology?" *American Heritage* XX (August): 4-9.

Clarke, Austin C. (1970) "Cultural-Political Origins of Black Student Anti-Intellectualism," *Studies in Black Literature* I (Spring): 69-82.

Clarke, John Henrik. (1976) "AHSA: A History," *Issue: A Quarterly Journal of Africanist Opinion,* 6, 1/3 (Summer/Fall).

Clarke, John Henrik, ed. (1991) *New Dimensions in African History.* Trenton, NJ: Africa World Press.

Cleaver, Eldridge. (1969) "Education and Revolution," *Black Scholar* I (November): 44-52.

Cleveland, B. (1969) "Black Studies and Higher Education," *Phi Delta Kappan* LI (September): 44-46.

Coles, Flournoy. (1969) "Black Studies in the College Curriculum," *Negro Educational Review* XX (October): 106-13.

Colon, Alan K. (1980) "A Critical Review of Black Studies Programs." Unpublished Doctoral Dissertation, Stanford University, 206 pp.

Colon, Alan K. (1984) "Critical Issues in Black Studies: A Selective Analysis," *Journal of Negro Education,* 53, 3: 268-277.

Cooper, Anna Julia. (1892) *A Voice from the South: By a Black Woman of the South.* Xenia, OH: Aldine Printing House.

Cooper, Jean. (1971) "Women's Liberation and the Black Woman," *Journal of Home Economics,* 63, (October) 521-523.

Cortada, Rafael. (1974) *Black Studies in Urban and Comparative Curriculum*. Lexington, MA: Xerox College Publishing.

Crouchett, L. (1971) "Early Black Studies Movements," *Journal of Black Studies*, 2: 189-200.

Cruse, Harold. (1967) *Crisis of the Negro Intellectual*. New York: William Morrow Publishers.

————. (1969) *Rebellion or Revolution?* New York: William Morrow Publishers.

Cummings, Robert. (1979) "African and Afro-American Studies Centers: Toward a Cooperative Relationship," *Journal of Black Studies*, 9, 3 (March): 291-310.

Curl, Charles H. (1969) "Black Studies: Form and Content," *CLA Journal* XIII (September): 1-9.

Daniels, Phillip T.K. (1980) "Black Studies: Discipline or Field of Study?" *The Western Journal of Black Studies*, 4, 3 (Fall): 195-199.

————. (1981) "Theory Building in Black Studies," *The Black Scholar*, 12, 3 (May/June): 29-36.

Davidson, Douglas V. (1985) "Black Studies, White Studies, and Institutional Politics," *Journal of Black Studies*, 15, 3 (March): 339-347.

Dillon, Merton L. (1970) "White Faces and Black Studies," *Commonweal* XCI (January 30): 476-79.

Diop, Cheikh Anta. (1974) *The African Origin of Civilization: Myth or Reality*. Westport, CT: Lawrence Hill & Co.

————. (1991) *Civilization or Barbarism: An Authentic Anthology*. New York: Lawrence Hill Books.

Drake, St. Clair. (1987) *Black Folk Here and There, Volume 1*. Los Angeles: Center for Afro-American Studies, University of California at Los Angeles.

————. (1984) "Black Studies and Global Perspectives: An Essay," *Journal of Negro Education*, 53, 3: 226-242.

Drimmer, Melvin. (1970) "Teaching Black History in America: What Are the Problems?" *Negro History Bulletin* XXXIII (February): 32-34.

DuBois, W.E.B. (1975) *The Education of Black Folks: Ten Critiques, 1906-1960*. New York: Monthly Review Press.

————. (1961) *The Souls of Black Folk*. New York: Fawcett Publications.

————. (1969) "The Talented Tenth," in Ulysses Lee (ed.), *The Negro Problem*. New York: Arno Press and the New York Times.

Dunbar, Ernest. (1969) "Cornell: The Black Studies Thing," *New York Times Magazine* (April): 25.

Durley, G.L. (1969) "Center for Black Students on University Campuses," *Journal of Higher Education* XL (June): 473-76.

Easum, Donald B. (1969) "The Call for Black Studies," *Africa Report* XIV (May-June): 16-22.

Edwards, Harry. (1970) *Black Students*. New York: Free Press.

Fanon, Frantz. (1968) *The Wretched of the Earth*. New York: Grove Press.

Ford, Nick Aaron. (1974) "Black Studies Programs," *Current History* (November): 224-233.

———. (1973) *Black Studies: Threat or Challenge*. Port Washington, NY: Kennikat Press.

Forman, James. (1972) *The Making of Black Revolutionaries*. New York: MacMillan.

Franklin, John Hope. (1980) *From Slavery to Freedom: A History of Negro-Americans*, 5th edition. New York: Alfred A. Knopf.

Frazier, E. Franklin. (1970) *Black Bourgeoisie*. New York: Macmillan.

———. (1973) "The Failure of the Negro Intellectual," in Joyce A. Ladner (ed.), *The Death of White Sociology*, pp. 52-66. New York: Vintage Books.

Frye, Charles A. (1978) *Towards a Philosophy of Black Studies*. San Francisco: R & E Research Associates.

Giddings, Paula. (1984) *When and Where I Enter: The Impact of Black Women on Race and Sex in America*. New York: William Morrow and Co.

Gordon, Vivian. (1987) Black Women, Feminism and Black Liberation: Which Way? New York: William Morrow.

———. (1979) *Lectures: Black Scholars on Black Issues*. Washington, DC: University Press of America.

Gyekye, Kwame. (1987) *An Essay on African Philosophical Thought. The Akan Conceptual Scheme*, New York: Cambridge University Press.

Hall, Perry A. (1992) "Beyond Afrocentrism: Alternatives for Afro-American Studies," *Western Journal of Black Studies*, 15, 4 (Winter): 207-212.

Hall, Perry et al. (1980) "Hall Report: Black Studies Core Curriculum." Bloomington, IN: National Council of Black Studies.

Hamilton, Charles. (1970) "The Question of Black Studies," *Phi Delta*, 57, 7 (March): 362-364.

Harding, Vincent. "Beyond Chaos: Black History and the Search for the New Land," *Amistad* I: 267-92.

———. (1969) "Black Students and the 'Impossible' Revolution," *Ebony* XXIV (August): 141-49.

———. (1981) *There Is A River*. New York: Vintage Books.

Hare, Nathan. (1972) "The Battle of Black Studies," *The Black Scholar*, 3, 9 (May): 32-37.

———. (1978) "War on Black Colleges," *The Black Scholar*, 9, 8 (May/June): 12-19.

———. (1969) "What Should be the Role of Afro-American Education in the Undergraduate Curriculum?" *Liberal Education*, 55, 1 (March): 42-50.

Hare, Nathan and Julia Hare. (1970) "Black Women 1970," *Transaction*, 8 (November- December): 68, 90.

Harris, Robert. (1990) "The Intellectual and Institutional Development of Africana Studies," in Robert Harris, Darlene Clark Hine and Nellie McKay (eds.), *Three Essays: Black Studies in the United States*. New York: The Ford Foundation.

Harris, Robert, Darlene Clark Hine and Nellie McKay (eds.). (1990) *Three Essays: Black Studies in the United States*. New York: The Ford Foundation.

Hatch, John. (1969) "Black Studies: The Real Issue," *Nation* CCVIII (June 16): 755-58.

Hendrix, M. et al. (1984) "Computers and Black Studies: Toward the Cognitive Revolution," *Journal of Negro Education* 53: 341-350.

Henry, Charles P. (1990) *Culture and African American Politics*. Bloomington: Indiana University Press.

Henshel, A.M., and Henshel, R.L. (1969) "Black Studies Programs: Promise and Pitfalls," *Journal of Negro Education* XXXVIII (Fall): 423-29.

Hill-Collins, Patricia. (1991) *Black Feminist Thought*. New York: Routledge.

Hilliard, Asa G., Payton-Stewart, Lucretia, Obadele Williams, Larry, eds. (1990) *Infusion of African and African American Content in the School Curriculum*. Morristown, NJ: Aaron Press.

Hine, Darlene Clark. (1990) "Black Studies: An Overview," in Robert Harris, Darlene Clark Hine and Nellie McKay (eds.), *Three Essays: Black Studies in the United States*. New York: The Ford Foundation.

———, ed. (1986) *The State of Afro-American History: Past, Present and Future*. Baton Rouge: Louisiana State University Press.

Holloway, Joseph E., ed. (1990) *Africanisms in American Culture*. Bloomington: Indiana University Press.

hooks, bell. (1981) *Ain't I A Woman: black women and feminism*. Boston: South End Press.

———. (1989) *Talking Back: Thinking Feminist, Thinking Black*. Boston: South End Press.

Huggins, Nathan. (1985) *A Report to the Ford Foundation on Afro-American Studies*. New York, New York: The Ford Foundation.

Huggins, Nathan L., Kilson, Martin, Fox, Daniel M., eds. (1971) *Key Issues in the Afro-American Experience*. New York/Chicago/San Francisco/Atlanta: Harcourt Brace Jovanich, Inc.

Hull, Gloria, Patricia Bell Scott and Barbara Smith, eds. (1982) *All the Women are White, All the Blacks are Men, but Some of Us are Brave*. Old Westbury, NY: Feminist Press.

Ijere, Martin. (1972) "Whether Economics in a Black Studies Program?" *Journal of Black Studies*, 3, 2 (December): 149-165.

Jackson, John. (1980) *Introduction to African Civilizations*. Secaucus, NJ: Citadel Press.

Jackson, Maurice. (1970) "Towards a Sociology of Black Studies," *Journal of Black Studies*, 1, 2 (December): 131-140.

James, George. (1976) *Stolen Legacy*. San Francisco: Julian Richardson Associates.

Johnson, Robert C. and Melvin K. Hendrix. "The Use of Computers in Black Studies, Technologies and Implications." *The New England Journal of Black Studies*, 4: 63-71.

Karenga, Maulana. (1988) "Black Studies and the Problematic of Paradigm: The Philosophical Dimension." *Journal of Black Studies*, vol. 18, no. 4 (June), 395-414.

———. (1983) *Introduction to Black Studies*. Los Angeles, CA: Kawaida Publications.

Keto, C. Tsehloane. (1989) *The Africa Centered Perspective of History*. Blackwood, NJ: K.A. Publications.

Khatib, S.M. (1980) "Black Studies and the Study of Black People: Reflections on the Distinctive Characteristics of Black Psychology," in Reginald Jones (ed.), *Black Psychology*. New York: Harper & Row Publishers.

Kilson, Martin. (1973) "Reflections on Structure and Content in Black Studies," *Journal of Black Studies*, 1, 3 (March): 297-314.

Kilson, Martin, Woodward, C. Vann, Kenneth B. Clark, Thomas Sowell, Roy Wilkins, Andrew F. Brimmer, Norman Hill, and Bayard Rustin. (1969) *Black Studies Myths & Realities*. New York: A Phillip Randolph Educational Fund.

Ladner, Joyce A., ed. (1973) *The Death of White Sociology*. New York: Vintage Books.

LaRue, Linda J.M. (1970) "Black Liberation and Women's Lib," *Transaction*, 8 (November-December): 59-64.

LeMelle, Tilden. (1984) "The Status of Black Studies in the Second Decade: The Ideological Imperative," in James Turner (ed.), *The Next Decade: Theoretical and Research Issues in Africana Studies*, pp. 47-61. Ithaca, NY: Africana Studies and Research Center, Cornell University Press.

Lincoln, C. Eric. (1978) "Black Studies and Cultural Continuity," *Black Scholar*, 10, 2 (October): 12-17.

Little, William, Crosby, Edward, Leonard, Carolyn M., eds. (1981) National Council of Black Studies: Proposed Afrocentric Core Curriculum. Prepared by the National Council of Black Studies, Inc.

Martin, Guy, and Young, Carlene. (1984) "The Paradox of Separate and Unequal: African Studies and Afro-American Studies," *Journal of Negro Education*, 53, 3: 257-265.

McClendon, William H. (1974) "Black Studies: Education for Liberation," *The Black Scholar*, 6, 1 (September): 15-20.

McEvoy, James and Abraham Miller. (1969) *Black Power and Student Rebellion*. Belmont, CA: Wadsworth Publishing.

McKay, Nellie. (1990) "Black Studies in the Midwest," in Robert Harris, Darlene Clark Hine and Nellie McKay (eds.), *Three Essays: Black Studies in the United States*. New York: The Ford Foundation.

McWorter, Gerald and Bailey, Ronald. (1984) "Black Studies Curriculum Development in the 1980's: Its Patterns and History," *The Black Scholar* (March-April).

Miller, Howard J. (1987) "MCD Process Model: A Systematic Approach to Curriculum Development in Black Studies," *Western Journal of Black Studies*, 110, 1: 19-27.

Morgan, Gordon J. (1991) "Afrocentricity in Social Science," *Western Journal of Black Studies*, 15, 4 (Winter): 197-206.

Myers, Linda James. (1988) *Understanding an Afrocentric World View: Introduction to an Optimal Psychology*. Dubuque, IA: Kendall/Hunt Publishing Company.

Nelson, William E. (1989) *Africology: From Social Movement to Academic Discipline*. Columbus, OH: Center for Research and Public Policy of the Ohio State University Black Studies Extension Center.

Newton, James E. (1976) *A Curriculum Evaluation of Black Studies in Relation to Student Knowledge of Afro-American History and Culture*. San Francisco, CA: R & E Research Associates.

Nobles, Wade. (1986) *African Psychology*. Oakland, CA: A Black Family Institute Publication.

Obenga, Théophile. (1992) *Ancient Egypt and Black Africa*. London: Karnak House.

Oyabede, Bayo. (1990) "African Studies and The Afrocentric Paradigm: A Critique," *Journal of Black Studies*, 21, 2: 233-238.

Pinkney, Alphonso. (1976) *Red, Black and Green: Black Nationalism in the United States*. Cambridge: Cambridge University Press.

Poinsett, A. (1970) "Think Tank for Black Scholars," *Ebony* XXV (February): 46-48.

Quarles, Benjamin. (1984) *The Negro in the Making of America*, 3rd edition. New York: Collier Books.

———. (1988) Black Mosaic: Essays in Afro-American History and Historiography. Amherst, MA: University of Massachusetts Press.

Redding, Saunders. (1969) "The Black Youth Movement," *American Scholar* XXVIII (Autumn): 584-87.

Roberts, S.V. (1970) "Black Studies: More Than Soul Courses," *Commonweal* XCI (January 30): 478-79.

Robinson, Armstead L., Foster, Craig C., and Ogilvie, Donald H., eds. (1969) *Black Studies in the University*. New Haven.

Rodgers-Rose, La Frances, ed. (1980) *The Black Woman*. Beverly Hills: Sage Publication.

Rosovsky, H. (1969) "Black Studies at Harvard: Personal Reflections Concerning Recent Events," *American Scholar* XXXVIII (Autumn): 562-72.

Rustin, Bayard, ed. (1969) *Black Studies: Myths and Realities*. New York.

Semmes, Clovis E. (1981) "Foundations of An Afrocentric Social Science: Implications for Curriculum Building, Theory, and Research in Black Studies," *Journal of Black Studies*, 12, 1 (September): 317.

Simms, Margaret C. and Julianne Malveaux, eds. (1986) *Slipping Through the Cracks: The Status of Black Women*. New Brunswick, NJ: Transaction.

Smith, William D. (1971) "Black Studies: A Survey of Models and Curricula," *Journal of Black Studies*, 10, 3 (March): 269-277.

Smith, William D. and Albert C. Yates. (1980) "Editorial in Black Studies," *Journal of Black Studies*, 10, 3 (March): 269-277.

Staples, Robert. (1976) *Introduction to Black Sociology*. New York: McGraw Hill Book Company.

Stewart, James. (1991) *Comments on Afrocentricity*. National Council of Black Studies Summer Institute, Ohio State University.

———. (1987) *The Field and Function of Black Studies*. A Paper prepared for the William Monroe Trotter Institute for the Study of Black Culture at the University of Massachusetts for a Project Studying "The Assessment of the Status of Black Americans," July.

Stewart, James B. (1979) "Introducing Black Studies: A Critical Examination of Some Textual Materials," *Umoja*, 3, 1 (Spring): 5-17.

———. (1984) "The Legacy of W.E.B. DuBois for Contemporary Black Studies," *Journal of Negro Education*, 53, 3: 292-311.

———. (1992) "Reaching for Higher Ground: Toward an Understanding of Black/Africana Studies," *The Afrocentric Scholar*, 1, 1 (May): 1-63.

"Student Strikes: 1968-69." (1970) *Black Scholar* I (January-February): 65-75.

Upton, James N. (1984) "Applied Black Studies: Adult Education in the Black Community—A Case Study," *Journal of Negro Education*, 53, 3: 322-333.

Turner, James, ed. (1984) *The Next Decade: Theoretical and Research Issues in Africana Studies*. Ithaca, NY: Africana Studies and Research Center, Cornell University.

Turner, J. and C.S. McGann. (1980) "Black Studies as an Integral Tradition in African American Intellectual History," *Journal of Negro Education*, 49, 52-59.

Van Sertima, Ivan. (1985) "Nile Valley Civilizations," *Journal of African Civilizations*.

Vontress, Clemmont E. (1970) "Black Studies—Boon or Bane?" *Journal of Negro Education* XXXIX (Summer): 192-201.

Walton, Sidney F. (1974) "Black Studies and Affirmative Action," *The Black Scholar*, 6, 1 (September): 21-31.

Warr, J. (1969) "Black History and Culture," *NCEA Bulletin* LXV (May): 51-55.

Weber, Shirley. (1984) "Intellectual Imperatives and Necessity for Black Education," in James Turner (ed.), *The Next Decade: Theoretical and Research Issues in Africana Studies*, pp. 63-75. Ithaca, NY: Africana Studies and Research Center, Cornell University.

Williams, John A., Charles F. Harris, eds. (1970) *Amistad 1*. New York: Vintage Books.

Williams, Juan. (1987) *Eyes on the Prize*. New York: Viking Penguin.

Wilson, C.E. (1969) "Case for Black Studies," *Educational Leadership* XXVII (December): 218-21.

Woodson, Carter G. (1969) *The Miseducation of the Negro*. Washington, DC: Associated Publishers Inc.

Woodyard, Jeffrey L. (1991) "Evolution of a Discipline: Intellectual Antecedents of African American Studies," *Journal of Black Studies* 22, 2 (December): 239-251.

Wright, Stephen J. (1970) "Black Studies and Sound Scholarship," *Phi Delta Kappan* LI (March): 365-68.

Yee, A.H. and Fruth, M.J. (1973) "Do Black Studies Make a Difference in Ghetto Children's Achievement and Attitudes?" *Journal of Negro Education*, 42 (Winter): 33-38.

Young, Carlene. (1984) "An Assessment of Black Studies Programs in American Higher Education," *Journal of Negro Education*, 53.

Glossary of Biographies

Adams, Russell L. (b. 1930)

Chairman, Department of Afro-American Studies at Howard University. Received Ph.D. from the University of Chicago in Political Science. He has written extensively on the influence of social status and ethnic background especially in the field of African American Studies. See *Great Negroes Past and Present, 1963-1969* (1972) and *Leading American Negroes* (1965).

Aldridge, Delores P. (b. 1941)

One of the founding directors and chairpersons of the African American Studies Program at Emory University (1971-1980), Aldridge argues for the development of new curricula and restructuring of old curricula to reflect a balance that is inclusive of African and African American women. She has published in the areas of sociology, African American Studies, and Africana Women's Studies. See Delores P. Aldridge, *Focusing: Black Male-Female Relationships* (1991).

Asante, Molefi K. (b. 1942)

Professor and former chair of the first doctoral program in African American Studies at Temple University. He is the leading proponent of the intellectual theory of Afrocentricity, and the editor of the *Journal of Black Studies*. His books include *Afrocentricity: The Theory of Social Change* (1980); the *Afrocentric Idea* (1987) *Kemet, Afrocentricity and Knowledge* (1990); a high school history textbook, *African American History: A Journey of Liberation* (1995), *Classical* Africa (1995); *African American Names* (1998); and co-edited a sourcebook in African American Studies with Dr. Abu Abarry, *African Intellectual Heritage: A Book of Sources* (1996), and *A Historical and Cultural Atlas of African Americans* (1999); plus 30 other books and numerous articles. Dr. Asante is recognized as being one of the most distinguished scholars in both African and American Studies.

Baldwin, James (1924-1987)

Novelist, essayist, playwright, and expatriate. During the sixties he provided the clearest and angriest voice on racial problems in America. Baldwin was a leading literary voice of the Civil Rights Movement and was outspoken on behalf of the Gay Rights Movement. He accused Richard M. Nixon's administration, with the FBI's J. Edgar Hoover of plotting the genocide of all people of color in the United States and the African Diaspora. His works include *Go Tell It On the Mountain* (1952); *Notes of a Native Son* (1955); *Giovanni's Room* (1965); *Another Country* (1961); *Nobody Knows My Name* (1961); *The Fire Next Time* (1963); *Blues For Mr. Charlie* (1964); *If Beale Street Could Talk* (1974); and *Just Above My Head* (1979); *The Price of the Ticket: Collected Nonfiction, 1948-1985* (1985). See also James Campbell's, *Talking at the Gates: A Life of James Baldwin* (1991); Horace A. Porter's *Stealing the Fire: The Art and Protest of James Baldwin* (1989); Quincy Troupe's *James Baldwin: The Legacy (1989)*; and David L. Leeming *James Baldwin: A Biography* (1994).

Bambara, Toni Cade (1939-1997)

Social worker and teacher of English at City College of New York. Editor of the first anthology of writings which focused on Black women (*The Black Woman: An Anthology*, 1970), Bambara voiced criticism of sexism and the servile roles of Black women in the Black liberation movement during the 1960s. She questioned the position of Black women in relationship to the community and, the overwhelming tendency to subordinate gender issues to racial issues, and the apparent insensitivity to Black women's suffering. Her books include *Gorilla, My Love* (1972); *The Sea Birds Are Still* Alive (1977); *The Salt Eaters*, her major novel, won an American Book Award in 1981; *If Blessing Comes* (1987); and a collection of her social and critical essays, *Deep Sightings and Rescue Missions: Fiction, Essays, and Conversations* (1995).

Banks, James A. (b. 1941)

Educator/professor who writes on ethnic and multicultural education and curriculum. See *Teaching the Black Experience* (1970); *Teaching Strategies for Social Studies* (1973); and *March Towards Freedom: A History of Black Americans* (1978); *Multicultural Education in Western Societies* (1986); *Teaching Strategies for Ethnic Studies* (1987); *Multiethnic Education Theory and Practice* (1988); *Multicultural Education: Issues and Perspectives* (1989).

Baraka, Amiri (b. 1934)

Long-time leader in the Black Arts and Black Studies movement, playwright, poet, political activist, and essayist. Baraka, along with Larry Neal, defined the philosophy and purpose of artists and their role in the Black community in *Black Fire* (1968). Baraka also founded the Black Arts Repertory Theater in Harlem. In 1966, he moved from New York to Newark and became a leading spokesman for Black Nationalism and an exponent of African and Islamic culture. See Amiri Baraka, *The Autobiography of LeRoi Jones* (1984), *Blues People: Negro Music and White America* (1963); *The Dead Lecturer* (1964); *Home* (1966); and LeRoi Jones, *The Dutchman/The Slave* (1964); *The Systems of Dante's Hell* (1965); *Daggers and Javelins: Essays, 1974-1979* (1984). See also, Werner Sollers *Amiri Baraka/LeRoi Jones: The Quest for a "Popular Modernism"* (1978) and James B. Gwynne's *Amiri Baraka: The Kaleidoscopic Torch* (1985).

Bell-Scott, Patricia (b. 1950)

Argues for gender issues to be part of the central focus of criticism and discussion about race, women's studies, and Black Women's Studies. See Patricia Bell Scott, *Life Notes: Personal Writings by Contemporary Black Women* (1994), and Patricia Bell Scott and Juanita Johnson-Bailey (Eds.), *Flat-Footed Truths: Telling Black Women's Lives* (1998).

ben-Jochannan, Yosef (b. 1918)

Former adjunct professor of history and African Studies at Cornell University and one of the most acclaimed "historians without portfolio" in the late twentieth century. ben-Jochannan contends that the importance of Africans in history has been purposely overlooked in the classroom, which instead credits Europeans with providing the essential contributions to the history of the world. See *African Origins of the Major "Western" Religions* (1970), *Africa: Mother of Western Civilization* (1971), *We the Black Jews: Witness to the "White Jewish Race" Myth* (1983), *From Afrikan Captives to Insane Slaves: The Need for Afrikan History in Solving the "Black" Mental Health Crisis in "America,"* (1992), and *Cultural Genocide in the Black and African Studies Curriculum* (1989).

Bennett, Lerone Jr. (b.1928)

Former senior editor of *Ebony* magazine and founding member of the Institute of the Black World, Bennett is the author of perhaps the most popular book on African American History *Before the Mayflower: A History of the Negro In America, 1619-1962* (1962). Bennett was a visiting professor at Northwestern University in 1969 and became the chair of its African American Studies Program in 1972. See Lerone Bennett, Jr., *What Manner of Man: A Biography of Martin Luther King Jr.* (1964); *Confrontation: Blacks and* Whites (1965); *Black Power USA: The Human Side of Reconstruction, 1867-1877* (1968); *Challenge of Blackness* (1972); *Wade In the Water* (1979); *Forced Into Glory: Abraham Lincoln and the White Dream* (2000).

Blassingame, John W. (1940-2000)

Historian and educator. A key participant in some of the earliest debates and dialogues about the establishment of African American Studies programs and departments, Blassingame emphasized concern that the majority were ill conceived as a result of universities' reactionary responses to Black students demands. In the 1970s, he joined the faculty of Yale University, serving as chair of African American Studies and Professor of History, specializing in the area of slavery historiography. See John W. Blassingame, *New Perspectives on Black Studies* (1971); coedited *Booker T. Washington Papers, Volume I* (1972); *Black New Orleans, 1860-1880* (1973); *The Slave Community: Plantation Life in the Antebellum South* (1972); *Slave Testimony: Letters, Speeches, Interviews, and Autobiographies, 1736-1938* (1977); *The Frederick Douglass Papers: Series I* (1979-1992); *Antislavery Newspapers and Periodicals, Volumes 1-4* (1980-1984); with Mary Frances Berry, *Long Memory: The Black Experience in America* (1982).

Blyden, Edward Wilmot (1832-1912)

Liberian Nationalist, Black Nationalist, Pan-Africanist educator, Blyden argued that the African race had indeed made significant contributions to human civilization and urged the emigration to Africa of educated blacks. His views are expressed in *Hope for Africa* (1862); *Christianity, Islam, and the Negro* (1887); *Race and African Life and Customs* (1908); See also Hollis R. Lynch, *Edward Wilmot Blyden, Pan-African Patriot, 1839-1912,* (1967) and *Selected Letters of Edward Wilmot Blyden* (NY 1978).

Bunche, Ralph Johnson (1904-1971)

Scholar, diplomat, international peacemaker, political scientist, Nobel Peace Prize winner (1950). Received first Ph.D. granted to an African American in political science by an American university. On the civil rights issue, he believed black people's principal concerns were economic and that race, though significant was secondary; founded with others The National Negro Congress in 1936. He wrote *A Worldview of Race* (1937); *An African American in South Africa* (1992) and two pamphlets "A View of Race" (1936) and "The Negro in the Age of F.D.R." (1973). See Peggy Mann *Ralph Bunche, U.N. Peacemaker* (1975) and Benjamin Rivlin (ed.) *Ralph Bunche: The Man In His Times* (1988); Brian Urquhart *Ralph Bunche: An American Life* (1993); Charles P. Henry *Ralph J. Bunche: Selected Speeches and Writings by Ralph J. Bunche* (1995).

Carruthers, Jacob H. (b. 1930)

Professor at Northeastern Illinois University and the director of the Kemetic Institute in Chicago. He is a founding member of the Association for the Study of Classical African Civilizations. Among his major works are *Essays in Ancient Egyptian Studies* (1984); *Mdw Ntr: Divine Speech—A Historiographical Reflection on African Deep Thought from the Time of the Pharaohs to the Present* (1995); and *Intellectual Warfare* (1999).

Christian, Barbara (1943-2000)

The first African American woman to receive tenure and to become full professor in the Afro-American Studies Department at the University of California, Berkeley. She was a leading Black literary feminist critic, and author of the important text *Black Women Novelists: The Development of a Tradition, 1892-1976* (1980); and *Black Feminist Criticism: Perspectives On Black Women Writers* (1985).

Clark, Kenneth (b. 1914)

Psychologist and educator. Shortly after Antioch College established an exclusive, separate Black Studies program, Clark resigned from its Board of Directors, charging that the college was adopting the position of segregationists by its "primitive exclusion" of white students from its [Black Studies] program and was participating in "a shoddy evasion of the moral and educational responsibility" of an educational institution. His best known work was a seminal study of the effects of poor schools on African American children in cities, *Desegregation: An Appraisal of the Evidence* (1953); *Youth in the Ghetto* (1964); *Prejudice and your Child* (1965); *Dark Ghetto: Dilemmas of Social Power* (1965); *Pathos of Power* (1974); See also Kenneth B. Clark, "A Charade of Power: Black Students at White Colleges," *Antioch Review* 29:2, (Summer 1969) and *Crisis In Urban Education* (1971).

Clarke, John Henrik (1915-1998)

Self taught, "historian without portfolio," educator. One of the foremost scholars and advocates of Pan-African history and the interrelatedness of African peoples in the twentieth century, he was the first licensed teacher of African and African American History in the state of New York. A prolific writer and thorough researcher of literary and historical works by African Americans, he was best known for challenging myths and stereotypes created and perpetuated by European and American scholars. In 1968, shortly after a confrontation in Montreal at the annual African Studies Association meeting, where he and other African/American scholars protested the continued misrepresentation of African world history, he led in founding the African Heritage Studies Association. Clarke was also a founding member of the Black Academy of Arts and Letters. See John Henrik Clarke, *A New Approach to African History* (1967); *Marcus Garvey and the Vision of Africa* (1974); *Africans At The Crossroads: Notes for an African World Revolution* (1992) *My Life In Search of Africa* (1999), and Barbara E. Adams, *John Henrik Clarke: The Early Years* (1992).

Collins, Patricia Hill (b. 1948)

Chair of African American Studies and professor of sociology at the University of Cincinnati, she contends that the primary guiding principle of black feminism is a recurring humanist vision and that the reconstruction of womanhood should be linked with the challenge of discussing male/female relationships. See Patricia Hill Collins, *Black Feminist Thought: Knowledge, Consciousness, and the Politics of Empowerment* (2000) which has become one of the most widely used texts in Women's Studies curricula.

Cooper, Anna Julia (1858-1964)

Authored one of the earliest and most important texts of what would later develop into black womanist and feminist discourse, *A Voice from the South: By a Black Woman of the South* (1892) in which she asserted that African American women were a political and social force that could speak for their race and for women. Cooper also wrote papers on various topics affecting black people during the late nineteenth century (i.e. "The Negro Problem in America," and "The Status of Women in America.") She believed that race and sex were inseparable and that both racism and sexism affected the social status of Black women. See Louise Daniel Hutchinson *Anna Julia Cooper, A Voice From the South* (1982).

Cox, Oliver Crummell (1901-1974)

Sociologist, economist, and teacher. Best known for his attack of caste, class, race, which discussed the political and economic basis of American race relations, Cox insisted that racism was a product of class conflicts. His major works include *Caste, Class, and Race* (1948); *Foundations of Capitalism* (1959); *Capitalism as a System* (1964).

Crummell, Alexander (1819-1898)

Pan-Africanist, nationalist, minister, abolitionist, missionary, and writer. Crummell believed that God works actively in history and that the good are punished and the evil rewarded in this life. He was instrumental in the founding of The American Negro Academy, in 1897, which was dedicated to the pursuit of the higher culture and civilization for Blacks. He authored several books and many essays and sermons, including: *The Future of Africa: Addresses and Discourses* (1862); *The Greatness of Christ and Other Sermons* (1882); *Africa and America* (1891); "The Relations and Duties of Free Colored Men in America to Africa"; "The Destined Superiority of the Negro" and "The Black Woman of the South, Her Neglects and Her Needs". See also William Henry Ferris *Alexander Crummell: An Apostle of Negro Culture* (1969); Gregory U. Rigsby *Alexander Crummell: Pioneer In Nineteenth Century Pan-African Thought* (1987); William J. Moses *Alexander Crummell: A Study of Civilization and Discontent* (1989); John Oldfield, *Alexander Crummell and The Creation of an African-American Church in Liberia* (1990).

Cruse, Harold (b. 1916)

Professor emeritus of history and cofounder of the Center for Afro-American and African Studies at the University of Michigan in 1969. Cruse wrote what some consider to be the seminal text on African American intellectual activity throughout the twentieth century, *The Crisis of the Negro Intellectual* (1967), in which his major contention revolved around what he perceived as a lack of sound economic and ideological basis in most African American movements and organizations. He criticized black leaders and intellectuals for their failure to give expression to nationalist consciousness. He also authored one of the most timely (and timeless) essays on the emergence and evolution of African American Studies ("Black Studies: Interpretation, Methodology, and the Relationship to Social Movement"). See Harold Cruse, *The Crisis of the Negro Intellectual: A Historical Analysis of the Failure of Black Leadership* (1984) and *Plural but Equal: A Cultural Study of Blacks and Minorities and America's Plural Society* (1989).

Davis, Angela (b. 1944)

Law professor at the University of California, Santa Cruz, known mostly for her political and social activism, Davis is highly critical of the history of sexism and abuse of black women by both black and white men. She has consistently challenged the attempts of white female scholars to impose a definition upon black female/male relationships and, especially, strives to correct the stereotypes of black women created during the period of enslavement. See Angela Y. Davis, *If They Come in the Morning: Voices of Resistance* (1971); her seminal work, *Women, Race, and Class* (1983) and and *Women, Culture and Politics* (1989); *Angela Davis: With My Mind on Freedom, An Autobiography* (1990). See also Joy James' *The Angela Y. Davis Reader* (1998).

Delany, Martin Robison (1812-1885)

Medical doctor, abolitionist, the first African American major in the U.S. Army, and nationalist. Delany published first book-length analysis of the economic and political situation of Blacks in the United States. *The Condition, Elevation, Emigration, and Destiny of the Colored People of the United States, Politically Considered* (1852) *Political Destiny of the Colored Race* (1854); *Blake, or the Huts of America* (1861-2); *Principia of Ethnology: The Origins of Races and Color* (1879). See also Victor Ullman *Martin R. Delany: The Beginning of Black Nationalism* (1971); Victor Ullman and Cyril E. Griffith *The African Dream; Martin R. Delany and The Emergence of Pan-African Thought* (1975).

Diop, Cheikh Anta (1923-1986)

Linguist, anthropologist, physicist, historian, political scientist and activist, Diop is viewed by most African-centered and Afrocentric scholars as the founder of the African-centered school of thought. He pioneered research and scholarship that focused on Ancient Egypt as a Classical African Civilization, and sought the removal of the "falsification of history" in regard to Africa and Africans. According to Diop, Ancient Egypt was to Africa what Ancient Greece and Rome were to Europe. See *The African Origin of Civilization: Myth or Reality* (1974); *The Cultural Unity of Black Africa* (1978); *Pre-Colonial Black Africa* (1987); *Civilization or Barbarism: An Authentic Anthropology* (1991).

Drake, St. Clair (1911-1987)

Anthropologist and co-author of one of the first and finest ethnographic studies of African American communities with Horace Cayton: *Black Metropolis: A Study of Negro Life in a Northern City* (1945)—Drake was considered by many to be the dean of African American social sciences. Although most well-known for his posthumous two-volume study, *Black Folk Here and There: An Essay in History and Anthropology, Volumes 1-2* (1987, 1990), Drake was highly critical of the ramifications of the institutionalization of African American Studies and the lack of attention paid to the international aspects of the field. See St. Clair Drake *The Redemption of Africa and Black* Religion (1970); Black *Diaspora* (1972)

DuBois, W.E.B. (1868-1963)

Author, educator, and the first black man to receive a Ph.D. in history from Harvard. DuBois has been referred to as the greatest intellectual the African world has produced in the twentieth century. An historian by training, DuBois played an integral part in the founding and expansion of both sociology and anthropology and organized the first full-length study of "Negro Life" in an eleven volume study during his tenure at Atlanta University. A founding member of the Niagara Movement (1905-9), National Association for the Advancement of Colored People (1910) and its national organ *The Crisis* (1911), DuBois is most famous for his prophecy that the "problem" of the twentieth century would be that of the color line. See W.E.B. DuBois *The Suppression of the African Slave Trade to the United States of America, 1638-1870* (1896); *The Philadelphia Negro* (1899); *The Souls of Black Folk* (1901); *The Negro* (1915); *Black Reconstruction: An Essay Toward the History which Black Folk Played in the Attempt to Reconstruct Democracy in America, 1860-1880* (1935); W.E.B. DuBois, *Dusk of Dawn: Autobiography of a Race Concept* (1988) and W.E.B. DuBois, *The Autobiography of W.E.B. DuBois: A Soliloquy on Viewing My Life from the Last Decade of its First Century,* (1968); *The World and Africa: An Inquiry into the part which Africa has played in World History* (1990). See also Rayford W. Logan, ed., *W.E.B. DuBois: A Profile* (1971); James B. Stewart, "The Legacy of W.E.B. DuBois for Contemporary Black Studies," *Journal of Negro Education* (Vol. 53, No. 3, 1984); Manning Marable *W.E.B. DuBois: Black Radical Democrat* (1986); and David Levering Lewis, *W.E.B. DuBois: Biography of a Race, 1868-1919* (1995).

Ford, Nick Aaron (1904-1982)

Author and educator Ford viewed Black Studies as an exclusively academic venture that should be concerned with the study and research of all aspects of the African American Experience. He also viewed Black Studies as a simultaneous threat and challenge to the biases and prejudices that had existed in the most prestigious institutions of higher education. See Nick Aaron Ford *The Contemporary Negro Novel: A Study in Race Relations* (1936); the seminal essay "A Blueprint for Negro Authors" (1950) and *Black Studies: Threat or Challenge* (1973).

Franklin, John Hope (b. 1915)

One of the most distinguished and often-cited African American historians and historiographers of the latter half of the twentieth century, Franklin is the author of one of the most widely used African American historical texts, *From Slavery to Freedom: A History of African Americans* (1947). He has spent the larger part of his career arguing for the presence and perspectives of African American historians in the field of Southern history. His first book, *The Free Negro In North Carolina, 1790-1860*, was published in 1943. See John Hope Franklin *Reconstruction after the Civil War* (1961); *The Emancipation Proclamation* (1963); *The Militant South, 1800-1860* (1970); *Race and History: Selected Essays, 1938-1988* (Baton Rouge: Louisiana State University Press, 1989); *The Color Line: Legacy of the Twenty-First Century* (1993); and with Loren Schweninger *Runaway Slaves: Rebels on the Plantation* (1999).

Frazier, E. Franklin (1894-1962)

One of the earliest African American sociologists and the first Black president of the American Sociological Society (1948), initially argued that Blacks in the United States had not managed to retain any significant African cultural habits or traits as a direct result of enslavement, but he reversed this position towards the end of his life. A prolific writer and author of See E. Franklin Frazier, *The Negro Family in Chicago* (1932); *The Negro Family in the United States* (1939); *Traditions and Patterns of Negro Family Life* (1934); *The Negro Church in America* (1974); and his most widely read and most controversial seminal work, *Black Bourgeoisie: The Rise of a New Middle Class* (1957).

Fuller, Hoyt P. (1927-1981)

Longtime editor of *Negro Digest/Black World*, Fuller provided a cosmopolitan forum for commentary and discussion on Black politics, culture, literature, history, etc. which remains one of the most significant publications on the African American experience to date. Fuller was the founder of the Organization of Black American Culture in Chicago. See Hoyt P. Fuller, "Toward a Black Aesthetic;" *Journey to Africa* (1971).

Garnet, Henry Highland (1815-1882)

Abolitionist, minister, diplomat and one of the most formidable African American leaders of the mid-19th century, he searched for ways to liberate African Americans from the bonds of slavery and color prejudice; Served as president of the African Civilization Society (ACS) which was designed to develop an "African Nationality" through emigration to Niger Valley incipient Pan Africaners. See Joel Schor *Henry Highland Garnet: A Voice of Radicalism in the Nineteenth Century* (1971); and Earl Ofari *Let Your Motto Be Resistance: The Life and Thought of Henry Highland Garnet* (1972).

Garrett, James P. (b. 1944)

Lawyer, activist, writer was involved with the Student Non-Violent Coordinating Committee fieldwork operations, along with being one of the student leaders responsible for the initial call for Black Studies at San Francisco State University in 1968. See James P. Garrett, "Black/Africana/Pan-African Studies: From Radical to Reaction to Reform? — Its Role and Relevance in the Era of Global Capitalism in the New Millennium" *Journal of Pan-African Studies* 1:1 (Fall-Winter, 1998-1999).

Garvey, Marcus M. (1887-1940)

Orator, Pan-Africanist, nationalist, organizer who emigrated to the United States from Jamaica in 1915 after being influenced by BookerT. Washington's autobiography, *Up From Slavery* (1901). He organized the Universal Negro Improvement Association/African Communities League (UNIA/ACL) in 1914 and one of the most widely read black newspapers *Negro World* in 1918, and in 1919 launched the Black Star Steamship Line to demonstrate that black people could create their own economic opportunities. He encouraged Blacks to leave America to return to Africa, their homeland. See Amy Jacques Garvey *Philosophy and Opinions of Marcus Garvey* (1923 and 1926); Robert A. Hill (ed.) *The Marcus Garvey and Universal Improvement Association Papers* (7 vols., 1983-1991); E. David Cronon's *Black Moses* (1955); and Tony Martin's *New Marcus Garvey Library* series.

Gates, Henry Louis, Jr. (b. 1950)

Literary critic, intellectual entrepreneur, distinguished professor and Chair of the W.E.B. DuBois Institute of Afro-American Research at Harvard University. Gates has written on race, gender and literary theory. His works include *The Signifying Monkey: A Theory of African American Literary Criticism* (1988); *Black Literature and Literary Theory* (1984); *The Classic Slave Narratives* (1987); *Figures In Black: Words, Signs and the "Racial" Self* (1987); *Reading Black, Reading Feminist: A Critical Anthology* (1990); *Loose Canons: Notes on the Culture Wars* (1992); with Cornel West, *The Future of the Race* (1996); *The Norton Anthology of African American Literature* (1996); co-creator with K. Anthony Appiah of *Encarta Africana* (1998), the world's first multimedia encyclopedia of African American history and culture, and general editor of *The Schomburg Library of Nineteenth-Century Black Women Writers*.

Gayle, Addison Jr. (1932-1991)

Editor, teacher, author, and aesthete, Gayle was a major theoretician of the Black Arts Movement and was instrumental in the development of the Black Aesthetic. See *The Black Situation* (1970), *The Black Aesthetic* (1971), *Bondage, Freedom, and Beyond: The Prose of Black Americans* (1971), *Oak and Ivy: A Biography of Paul Laurence Dunbar* (1972), *The Way of the New World: The Black Novel in America* (1975).

Genovese, Eugene (b. 1930)

Historian who warned that the exclusion of one black group or white students from participation in [Black Studies] programs would lead to campus-wide purges of "reactionaries," "liberals," and "revolutionaries" as the power of these groups vacillated. See Eugene Genovese, "Black Studies: Trouble Ahead," *The Atlantic Monthly* (June 1969), 37-41 and *Roll, Jordan, Roll: The World the Slaves Made* (1972); *In Red and Black: Marxian Explorations in Southern and Afro-American History* (1972); *From Rebellion to Revolution: Afro-American Slave Revolts in the Making of the New World* (1974).

Giddings, Paula J. (b. 1947)

Historian and chair of Women's Studies at Rutgers University from 1989 to 1991, Giddings wrote the first contemporary feminist history of African American Women: *When and Where I Enter: The Impact of Black Women on Race and Sex in America* (1984); *In Search of Sisterhood: Delta Sigma Theta and the Challenge of the Black Sorority Movement* (1988) She has had a lifelong commitment to writing black women's history.

Gordon, Vivian (1934-1997)

A specialist in sociology, Gordon argued that much of the literature in Black Women's Studies has followed white feminism too closely, without recognizing and/or defining the distinctiveness of Black feminist thought. See Vivian Gordon *Lectures: Black Scholars on Black Issues* (1979); *Black Women, Feminism, and Black Liberation: Which Way?* (1987).

Guy-Sheftall, Beverly (b. 1946)

Professor of Women's Studies and English at Spelman College, Sheftall has been a major contributor to the production of Black Women's Studies literature. Founding and co-editor of *SAGE: A Journal of Black Women*. See Beverly Guy-Sheftall *Sturdy Black Bridges: Visions of Black Women in Literature* (1979); *Daughters of Sorrow: Attitudes Toward Black Women, 1880-1920* (1991); *Double Stitch: Black Women Write About Mothers and Daughters* (1992); *Words of Fire: An Anthology of African American Feminist Thought* (1995);

Hamilton, Charles V. (b. 1929)

Political scientist and educator. Best known for co-authoring the seminal study on the socio-political ideology of Black Power (*Black Power: The Politics of Liberation*) with Kwame Ture/Stokely Carmichael in 1967. He was also involved in establishing several Black Studies programs and departments (i.e., Columbia University and City College of New York). See Charles V. Hamilton *The Bench and the Ballot* (1973); *The Black Experience in American Politics* (1973); *Adam Clayton Powell Jr.: The Political Biography of an American Dilemma* (1991); "The Question of Black Studies," *Phi Delta Kappan* 57:7 (1970).

Harding, Vincent Jr. (b. 1931)

Historian, co-founded the first African American think tank, the Institute of the Black World (1969-84), one of the four components of the Martin Luther King, Jr. Memorial Center, which served as a gathering of teachers, artists, organizers who would fully utilize their talents in the service of the Black community. The research institute-Black Policy Studies Center emphasized self determination, self understanding and the role of education in the African American movement for social change. See Vincent Harding *Must Walls Divide* (1965); *The Other American Revolution* (1980); *There Is A River: The Black Struggle for Freedom in America* (1981); *Hope and History: Why We Must Share the Story of the Movement* (1990); "The Vocation of the Black Scholar," in *The Institute for the Black World* (Eds.), and Education and Black Struggle: Notes from the Colonized World, *Harvard Monograph Series* 2 (1974): 3-29.

Hare, Nathan (b. 1934)

As well as being the first chair of a Black Studies department in the United States (San Francisco State University, 1968), Hare was a founding editor of *Black Scholar* (1969), a journal which positioned itself as an alternative organ for the dissemination of the research and opinions of African American intellectuals and social activists. A trained sociologist and psychologist, he argues that the mission of African American Studies and scholars is to eschew European methods and values with insights drawn from the historical and contemporary experiences of Black life. See *The Black Anglo Saxons* (1965), *Pan-Africanism* (1974), *The Hare Plan to Overhaul the Public Schools and Educate Every Black Man, Woman, and Child* (1991).

Higginbotham, Elizabeth (b.)

Professor of history at Harvard University. She has published widely on race, class, and gender. She has been active in designing faculty development workshops on incorporating women of color into the college curriculum. See her essay "Designing an Inclusive Curriculum: Bringing All Women Into the Core," *Women's Studies Quarterly* 18 (Spring/Summer 1990).

Hine, Darlene Clark (b. 1947)

The John A. Hannah Professor of American History at Michigan State University. She argues that studying black women provided "greater illumination of the power relations that operate along the interlocking grid of race, sex, and class in America. Her scholarly work includes the sixteen volume series *Black Victory: The Rise and Fall of the White Primary in Texas* (1979); *The State of Afro-American History* (1986); *Hine Sight: Black Women and the Re-Construction of American History* (1994); *Speak Truth to Power: Black Professional Class in United States History* (1996).

hooks, bell (nee Gloria Watkins) (b. 1952)

Black feminist and cultural critic, argues for gaining insights into the quality black female/male relationships and suggests that there are problems which require serious analysis of sexism and racism. See bell hooks, *Ain't I A Woman: Black Women and Feminism* (1981); *Feminist Theory: From Margin to Center* (1987); *Talking Back: Thinking Feminist, Thinking Black* (1989); *Outlaw Culture: Resisting Representations* (1994); *Teaching to Transgress: Education as the Practice of Freedom* (1994).

Huggins, Nathan I. (1927-1990)

Scholar and historian, authored the controversial 1985 Ford Foundation Study, *Afro-American Studies: A Report to the Ford Foundation*, which fostered debate in regard to the structure, content, and direction of African American Studies. Former chair of Harvard University's W.E.B. Institute of Afro-American Studies, his works include: *Harlem Renaissance* (1971), *Black Odyssey: The Afro-American Ordeal in Slavery* (1977), and *Voices from the Harlem Renaissance* (1976); *Slave and Citizen: The Life of Frederick Douglass* (1980).

Hull, Gloria (b. 1944)

Co-editor of the seminal text in Black Women's Studies (*All the Women Are White, All the Blacks Are Men, But Some of Us Are Brave: Black Women's Studies*), Hull supports the accreditation of all Women's Studies programs and suggests that Black Women's Studies be made accessible to all Black women, not only those in universities. See Gloria T. Hull, Patricia Bell-Scott, and Barbara Smith (eds.), *All the Women Are White, All the Blacks Are Men, But Some of Us Are Brave: Black Women's Studies* (1982).

Hurston, Zora Neale (1891-1960)

Anthropolgist, folk historian, novelist, dramatist, viewed as the "literary godmother" and "spiritual ancestor" by many contemporary African American women writers. Her works include *Their Eyes Were Watching God* (1939); *Jonah's Gourd Vine* (1934); *Mose, Man of the Mountain* (1939); *Dust Tracks on a Road* (1942); *Seraph on the Swanee* (1948); as well as a collection of previously unpublished social essays edited by Alice Walker, *I Love Myself When I Am Laughing and Then Again When I Am Looking Mean and Impressive: A Zora Neale Hurston Reader* (1981).

James, Cyril Lionel Richard (CLR) (1901-1989)

Writer, historian, Marxist activist, social and cultural critic. James was a major influence in the intellectual movement for the West Indian and African independence movements. He helped develop the theoretical principles for the socio-political theory of Pan-Africanism with George Padmore. See *Beyond a Boundary* (1963), an autobigoraphy, *The Life of Captain Cipriani: An Account of the British Government in the West Indies* (1933), which called for Caribbean independence, *The Black Ja-*

cobins: Toussaint L'Overture and the San Domingo Revolution (1938). His collected works appear in *The Future in the Present* (1979), *Spheres of Existence* (1980), *At The Rendezvous of Victory* (1984), *American Civilization* (199-), and *The CLR James Reader* (1994).

Johnson, Charles S. (1893-1956)

The first Black president of Fisk University, co-founder of *Opportunity*, the official organ of the Urban League, Johnson's writings and research focused on the condition of Black people and class structure in the Black community and reveal Black people; considered to be the founder of Black sociology. See *The Negro in Chicago* (1922), *The Negro in American Civilization* (1930), *Economic Status of the Negro* (1933), *Shadow of the Plantation* (1934), *Collapse of the Cotton Tenancy* (1935), and *Growing Up in the Black Belt* (1941).

Jordan, June (b. 1936)

Although perhaps most well known for her poetry, Jordan is also one of the most prolific social essayists of the past thirty years. Presently Professor of Black Studies and Women's Studies at the University of California, Berkeley, Jordan continues to write and speak about issues of race, class, and gender. See June Jordan, *Voices of Children* (1970); *His Own Where* (1971)-written in Black English; *Things That I Do In The Dark* (1977); *Civil Wars* (Boston: Beacon Press, 1981); *Technical Difficulties* (1992), and *Affirmative Acts: Political Essays* (1998).

Joseph, Gloria T. (b.)

Writer, activist and a critic of the academy and the experience of black women within the Black community. She has written several pioneering essays in which she argues that Marxists and feminists do a poor job of analyzing the experiences of black women. See Gloria T. Joseph "The Incompatible Menage A Trois: Marxism, Feminism and Racism and Black Feminist Pedagogy and Schooling in Capitalist White America" (1981).

Karenga, Ron (Maulana) (b. 1940)

Activist, scholar, educator and founder of the African American celebration of Kwaanza, co-founder of the cultural theory of Kawaida, and head of the organization US (1966), Karenga is the author many articles on African American Studies and the foremost text utilized in African American Studies courses — *Introduction to Black Studies* (1982) — in which he suggests that African American Studies must be an interdisciplinary field concerned with the coherence and unity of its subject areas and that, of necessity, Black Studies has core integrative principles and assumptions. See also *The Quotable Karenga* (1967) *Reconstructing Kemetic Culture* (1980); *The Book of Coming Forth by Day: The Ethics of the Declarations of Innocence* (1990) and *Kemet, the African World View: Research and Restoration* (1986).

Kilson, Martin (b. 1931)

Considered conservative by most in the field of African American Studies, Kilson has nonetheless contributed a great deal to the formation and evolution of the field through his insistence on intellectual rigor. His numerous exchanges with Blassingame, et al., created a meaningful dialogue regarding the purpose, content, and responsibilities of Black Studies. See Martin Kilson, "Realism in African American Studies" (1969); "Anatomy of the Black Studies Movement" (1969); "The Intellectual Validity of Studying the Black Experience" (1969); "Paradoxes of Blackness: Notes on the Crisis of Black Intellectuals," *Dissent* 73 (1988).

King, Martin Luther, Jr. (1929-1968)

Minister, civil rights leader, Nobel Peace Prize winner, formed the Southern Christian Leadership Conference (SCLC). A believer of non-violence to achieve racial justice in America for African Americans, opposed the war in Viet Nam, and fought for social and economic equality for all. He published *Stride Toward Freedom* (1958); *Why We Can't Wait* (1964); and *Where Do We Go From Here? Chaos or Community* (1967). See also L.D. Reddick *Crusader Without Violence: A Biography of Martin Luther King Jr.* (1959); Clayborne Carson's *The Papers of Martin Luther King Jr.* (1992); Taylor Branch's *Parting the Waters: American in the King Years, 1954-63* (1989); David L. Lewis's *King: A Critical Biography* (1970); and David J. Garrow's *Bearing the Cross: Martin Luther King Jr. and the Southern Christian Leadership Conference, 1955-1968* (1986)

Locke, Alain Leroy (1885-1954)

First black Rhodes scholar, professor and chair of the Philosophy department at Howard University, and the leading spokesman for African American humanist values during Harlem Renaissance, Locke wanted to create the image of a new Negro of social values and cultural imperatives and racialism. In the 1930s, he helped to initiate a series of "Bronze Booklets" by leading black scholars in order to make black culture and history available to everyone. Edited what has become the hallmark text of the "New Negro" Movement/Harlem Renaissance, *The New Negro: Voices of the Harlem Rennaisance* (1925). Published *The Negro and His Music* (1936); *Negro Art: Past and Present* (1936); *The Negro in Art: A Pictorial Record of Negro Artists and the Negro Theme in Art* (1946). See also Russell J. Linnemann *Alain Locke: Reflections on a Modern Reanaissance Man* (1982); Leonard Harris *The Philosophy of Alain Locke: Harlem Renaissance Beyond* (1989).

Lorde, Audre Geraldine (1934-1992)

Poet, novelist, teacher—considered to be one of the first, and perhaps most influential, Black lesbian feminist writers, Lorde was instrumental in bringing issues of gender and sexual orientation to the forefront of the Black women's movement. See Audre Lorde *The Black Unicorn* (1978), *The First Cities* (1968); *Cables to Rage* (1970); *From a Land Where Other People Live* (1973); her autobiography *The Cancer Journals* (1980); *Zami: A New Spelling of my Name* (1982); Sister *Outsider: Essays and Speeches* (1984); Barbara Christian, "Dynamics of Difference" *Women's Review of Books* 1:11 (August 1984).

Madhabuti, Haki R. (nee Don L. Lee) (b. 1942)

Activist, poet, and author, Madhabuti was a major contributor to the Black Arts Movement through his writing and poetry, which incorporates elements of African American language and dialect. Founded Third World Press (1971) to publish and showcase the works of Black authors. See Haki Madhabuti *For Black People (And Negroes Too)* (1968); *Don't Cry, Scream* (1969), *Enemies: A Clash of Races* (1978), *We Walk the Way of the New World* (1970); *Black Men: Obsolete, Single, and Dangerous?* (1994).

Malcolm X (El-Hajj Malik El-Shabazz) (1925-1965)

Perhaps one of the most dynamic and brilliant political speakers in late twentieth century America, as national spokesman for the Nation of Islam, Malcolm X stressed the importance and necessity for the study of African American history as a primary tool of revolution. An ardent advocated of self-defense, he did not discount violence as a means of liberating Black people from racism and injustice in America. See Malcolm X *The Autobiography of Malcolm X* (1965); *Malcolm X Speaks* (1965); *By Any Means Necessary* (1970); *The End of White World Supremacy* (1983). See also George Brietman *The Last Year of Malcolm X* (1967); Peter L. Goldman's *The Death and Life of Malcolm X* (1979); and John Henrik Clarke (ed.) *Malcolm X: The Man and His Times* (1992).

Neal, Larry (1937-1981)

Activist, anthropologist, editor, critic, and teacher at City College of New York. One of the most prominent figures of the Black Arts movement of the 1960s, Neal argued the need for separate cultural forms as necessary to develop conscious and responsible Black artists. He was also the education director for the New York chapter Black Panther Party for Self Defense. See Larry Neal "The Black Arts Movement" *Drama Review* 12 (Summer 1968); "The Negro in the Theatre" *Drama Critique* 7 (Spring 1964); *Black Fire* co-edited with Amiri Baraka (1968); *Hoodoo Hollerin' Bebop Ghosts* (1971); *Analytical Study of Afro-American Culture* (1972); *Visions of a Liberated Future: Black Arts Movement Writings* (1989).

Newton, Huey P. (1942-1989)

Political philosopher and activist, co-founder of the Black Panther Party for Self Defense in 1966 with Bobby Seale, Newton was one of the most dynamic political figures of the Black Power Movement, calling for armed self-defense and revolution in the Black community against hostile, external aggression (especially the police). See *To Die for the People: The Writings of Huey P. Newton* (1972), *Revolutionary Suicide* (1995), and the semi-biographical *Shadow of the Panther: Huey P. Newton and the Price of Black Power in America* (1994).

Rogers, Joel Augustus (1883-1965)

Self-taught "historian without portfolio," and one of the most famous of Harlem's "street corner/soapbox orators," he pioneered the research and teaching of African, Caribbean, and African American history. See *One Hundred Amazing Facts About the Negro* (1934); *Sex and Race: Negro-Caucasian Mixing in All Ages and All Lands, Volumes 1-3* (1952); a comprehensive work on the history of miscegenation in the world; *World's Great Men of Color, Volumes 1-2* (1946); *Your History, From the Beginnings of Time to the Present* (1940); *Africa's Gift to America* (1959); and *From Superman to Man* (1956).

Rustin, Bayard (1910-1987)

Union activist and civil rights leader. Rustin joined and assisted in both the planning and organization of the attempted March on Washington in 1941 and the March on Washington in 1963. He also organized the New York branch of CORE (Congress of Racial Equality) in 1941 and led the boycott of New York City schools in 1964. See Bayard Rustin (and Martin Kilson) *Black Studies: Myths and Realities* (1969); *Down the Line: The Collected Writings of Bayard Rustin* (1971). See also

Jervis Anderson, *Bayard Rustin: Troubles I've Seen* (1998); James Haskins *Bayard Rustin and the Civil Rights Movement* (1999).

Sanchez, Sonia (b. 1934)

A founding member of the Black Arts Movement (1966), poet and activist Sanchez was instrumental in the founding of the first Black Studies Department at San Francisco State. Her work deals with such issues as drug abuse, race relations, and sexism. Along with Amiri Baraka, Larry Neal, and Addison Gayle, she also helped shape the definition of what has come to be known as Black Aesthetics. Her books of poetry include *Homecoming* (1969); *We a Badd.DDD People* (1970); and *Homegirls and Handgrenades* (1984); *Wounded in the House of a Friend* (1995); *Does Your House Have Lions* (1997); and *Like the Singing Coming Off the Drums* (1998).

Schlesinger, Arthur Jr. (b. 1917)

The son of historian, Arthur Schlesinger has always been adamantly opposed to any variation from the "normative" writing of American history. A strong advocate of the "Melting Pot" theory, in his eyes it is the attempted emphases on different groups' historical experiences which perpetuates conflict. Along with Diane Ravitch, Shelby Steele, Stanley Crouch, and Linda Chavez, remains one of the most ardent foes of African American Studies. See Arthur Schlesinger, Jr., *The Disuniting of America: Reflections on a Multicultural Society* (1992).

Schomburg, Arthur A. (1874-1938)

Historian, bibliophile, educator, and activist, long Schomburg emigrated to the United States from Puerto Rico. In 1911, along with John Edward Bruce, he founded the Negro Society for Historical Research, one of the first organization dedicated to studying the history and culture of people of African descent. He contributed numerous articles on the Negro to *Crisis*, *Opportunity*, *Negro World* and other periodicals. Schomburg was president of the American Negro Academy from 1922 to 1926, and throughout his lifetime he amassed the single largest and most comprehensive repository of information written by or about African American history and culture in the United States. This private collection became the basis for the world-renowned Schomburg Center for African American History and Culture, located in Harlem. See Elinor Des Verney Sinnette, *Arthur Alfonso Schomburg: Black Bibliophile and Collector, A Biography* (1989) and *Arthur A. Schomburg, Racial Integrity: A Plea for the Establishment of A Chair of Negro History in Our Schools and Colleges* (1999).

Smith, Barbara (b. 1946)

Co-founder with Audre Lorde, of the first publishing collective by women of color (Kitchen Table: Women of Color Press), Smith was also co-editor, with Hull and Bell Scott, of *All the Women Are White, All the Men Are Black, But Some of Us are Brave* (1982). She has published on a range of Black women's issues, most notably violence against Black women and racism in the women's movement. See "Towards a Black Feminist Criticism" (Conditions 1971) in which she dealt with black feminism and black sexuality as they relate to the study of African American literature. She holds that the academic segments of Black and women's movements of the 1960s and 1970s failed to include African American women's perspectives. See Barbara Smith *Conditions Five: The Black Women's Issues* (1979); *Homegirls: A Black Feminist Anthology* (1983); *The Reader's Companion to United States Women's His-*

tory (1998); *The Truth that Never Hurts: Writing on Race, Gender, and Freedom, 1968-1998* (1998).

Stewart, James B. (b. 1947)

Vice provost and associate professor at Pennsylvania State University and was a former director of the Black Studies Program (1984-1996). He also served as the editor of *The Review of Black Political Economy* (1987-1995). The current president of the National Council of Black Studies, he has written several pioneering essays on Black Studies. See James B. Stewart *Black Families: Interdisciplinary Perspectives* (1990); and *The Housing Status of African Americans* (1992).

Stewart, Maria Miller (1803-1879)

Cited as the first American-born woman to lecture publicly on political and religious themes. During our country's tumultuous pre-Civil War years, Stewart advocated abolition, self-published anti-slavery and women's rights pamphlets, spoke out against the colonization movement (an effort to expatriate Blacks to West Africa) and became a school teacher. Her dynamic essays and poignant speeches have been collected and edited by Marilyn Richardson in *Maria Stewart: America's First Black Woman Political Writer* (1987).

Terrell, Mary Church (1863-1954)

Prominent club woman, race woman, women's rights, and teacher. In 1892, she became president of the Colored Women's League in Washington, DC and was founding president of the National Association of Colored Women. Major themes she spoke on and wrote about included black female empowerment, lynching, woman suffrage and the contributions of black history. See Mary Church Terrell *A Colored Woman in a White World* (1940). See also Gladys B. Shepperd *Mary Church Terrell-Respectable Person* (1959); Patricia McKissack and Frederick McKissack *Mary Church Terrell: Leader for Equality* (1991).

Turner, Henry McNeal (1834-1915)

Theologian, first black president of Morris Brown College, advocate of African colonization, forerunner of the Black theology movement and considered to be one of the first and most influential Black nationalists of his time. He believed in building separate Black institutions to defend the cultural and political independence of African Americans. See Edwin Redkey *Black Exodus: Black Nationalist and Back-To Africa Movements 1890-1910* (1969) and *Respect Black: The Writings and Speeches of Henry McNeal Turner* (1971).

Turner, James (b. 1940)

Associate professor of Africana Studies in the Center for Africana Studies and Research at Cornell University. He is editor of one of the seminal texts in African American Studies , *The Next Decade: Theoretical and Research Issues in Africana Studies* (1984).

Van Sertima, Ivan (b. 1935)

Literary critic, linguist, anthropologist, and professor of Africana Studies at Rutgers University. He authored the prize winning and groundbreaking thesis which was revolutionary in the re-examination of Columbus, the role of Western Europe in world history, and the significance of the African presence in ancient history. See Ivan

Van Sertima *They Came Before Columbus: The African Presence in Ancient America* (1978); *Blacks in Science: Ancient and Modern* (1983); *Black Women in Antiquity* (1984); *Egypt Revisited* (1985); *African Presence in Early Europe* (1985); *African Presence in Early America* (1985); *The Golden Age of the Moors* (1992); *Egypt: Child of Africa* (1994).

Walker, Alice (b. 1944)

Novelist, poet,—coined the term "womanist" to emphasize/view racism and sexism as intersecting forms of oppression. Her novels, books of poetry and important essays on women's issues include *The Third Life of Grange Copeland* (1970); *Revolutionary Petunias and Other Poems* (1973); *Meridian* (1976) and *The Color Purple* (1982); *In Search of Our Mother's Gardens: Womanist Prose* (1983); *The Temple of my* Familiar (1989); *Possessing the Secret of Joy* (1992); *By the Light of my Father's Smile* (1999).

Wallace, Michele (b. 1952)

A founding member of the National Black Feminist Organization (1974), Wallace is currently on the faculty at the City College of New York where she teaches African American Literature, Women's Studies, and Film Studies. She is best known for the controversial Black feminist polemic *Black Macho and the Myth of the Superwoman* (1978) which is a critique of the male dominated Civil Rights and Black Power movements and sexual politics within the Black community..See Michele Wallace *Invisibility Blues: From Pop to Theory* (1990); *Black Popular Culture: A Conference* (1992).

Walton, Sidney (b. 1934)

Teacher, curriculum developer, involved in developing some of the first college curricula and courses which dealt specifically with African American Studies and provided the first comprehensive plan and agenda for developing and assessing Black Studies courses and departments. See *The Black Curriculum: Developing an Afro-American Studies Program* (1969); "Black Studies and Affirmative Action" (1974).

Washington, Booker Taliaferro (1856-1915)

Educator, political leader, "accommodationist," founder and first president of Tuskegee Institute in Alabama that stressed industrial education. Washington was a prominent race leader of the late nineteenth century, who urged African Americans to accommodate to the segregation and discrimination. He advocated advancement of the race through hard work, economic improvement, and self help. Considered the most powerful and influential Black man of his time, his position was vehemently opposed by DuBois, Monroe Trotter, and others who urged African Americans to fight for equality. He also founded the National Negro Business League and controlled the National Afro-American Council, the leading Civil Rights group of the early 1900s. His most famous work is *Up From Slavery: An Autobiography* (1901); See Louis R. Harlan, *Booker T. Washington: The Making of a Black Leader, 1856-1901* (1972); *Booker T. Washington: The Wizard of Tuskegee, 1901-1915* (1983) and Harlan and Raymond W. Smock (eds.) *The Booker T. Washington Papers, 14 Volumes* (1972-1989).

Wells-Barnett, Ida (1862-1931)

Legendary anti-lynching crusader, journalist, owner and editor of the *Memphis Free Speech* and a prominent club woman. Wells-Barnett founded the first black woman suffrage organization, the Alpha Suffrage Club in Chicago in 1893 and was also affiliated with Garvey's Universal Negro Improvement Association (UNIA). She is most famous for beginning the drive for federal anti-lynching legislation. See Ida Wells-Barnett *A Red Record: Tabulated Statistics and Alleged Causes of Lynching in the United States* (1895) and "The Reason Why the Colored American is Not In The World's Exposition" (1893). See also Alfreda Duster (ed.) *Crusade for Justice: The Autobiography of Ida B. Wells* (1970); Trudier Harris and Henry Louis Gates, Jr. *Selected Works of Ida B. Wells-Barnett* (1991).

Williams, George Washington (1849-1891)

The first major African American historian and author of the first comprehensive text on the history of African Americans (*The History of the Negro Race in America, 1619-1880* (1883)), which influenced the writing of history books during the late 19th and early 20th century. See George Washington Williams *A History of Negro Troops in the War of Rebellion* (1968). See also John Hope Franklin, and "George Washington Williams, Historian" *Journal of Negro History*, 31 (January 1946); *George Washington Williams: A Biography* (1998).

Woodson, Carter G. (1875-1950)

Often referred to as the "Father of Black History," founded the Association for the Study of Negro Life and History in 1915, through which he sought to create an ideological base for Black scholars and activists. He published the first volume of the national organ of the association, *The Journal of Negro History* in 1916, in 1926 he inaugurated Negro History Week, which later became Black History Month (1976). Woodson's major works include *The Education of the Negro Prior to 1861* (1915); *The History of the Negro Church* (1921); *The Negro in Our History* (1922); *Negro Makers of History* (1928); *African Myths* (1928); *The Mis-Education of the Negro* (1933); *The Story of the Negro Retold* (1935); *The African Background Outlined* (1936); *African Heroes and Heroines* (1939). For further information, see Jacqueline Goggins, *Carter G. Woodson: A Life in Black History* (1997), and Lorenzo J. Greene, *Selling Black History for Carter G. Woodson: A Diary, 1930-1933* (1996).

Index